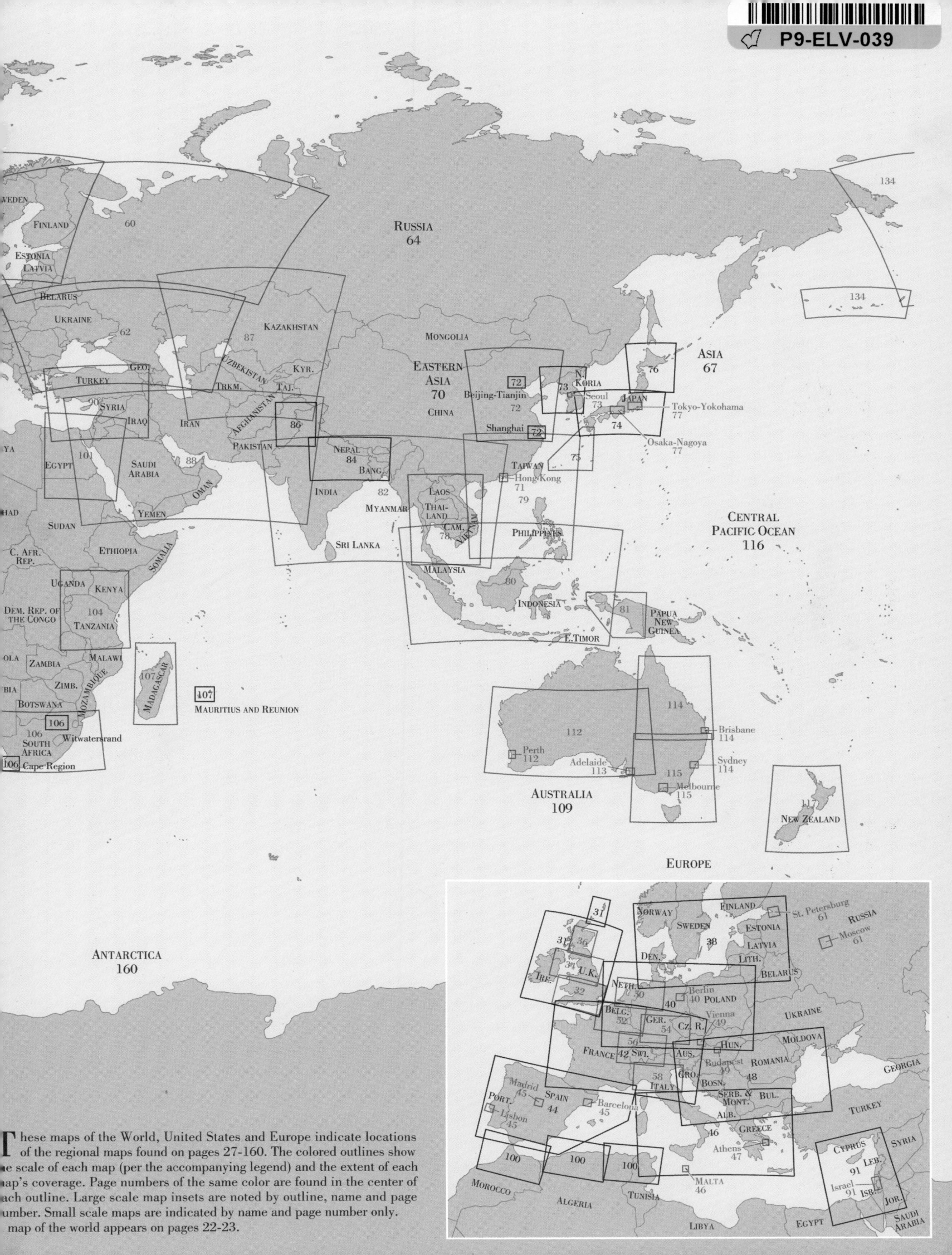

P9-ELV-039

WEDEN
FINLAND
60
ESTONIA
LATVIA
BELARUS
UKRAINE
62
GEO.
TURKEY
90
SYRIA
IRAQ
YA
EGYPT
101
SAUDI
ARABIA
88
OMAN
CHAD
SUDAN
YEMEN
C. AFR.
REP.
ETHIOPIA
SOMALIA
UGANDA
KENYA
DEM. REP. OF
THE CONGO
104
TANZANIA
OLA
ZAMBIA
MALAWI
BIA
ZIMB.
MOZAMBIQUE
107
MADAGASCAR
107
MAURITIUS AND REUNION
BOTSWANA
106
106
SOUTH
AFRICA
106 Cape Region
Witwatersrand

RUSSIA
64

KAZAKHSTAN
87

UZBEKISTAN
KYR.
TRKM.
TAJ.
IRAN
AFGHANISTAN
86
PAKISTAN

MONGOLIA

EASTERN
ASIA
70
CHINA

Beijing-Tianjin
72
72

Shanghai
72

NEPAL
84
BANG.
INDIA
82
MYANMAR

LAOS
THAI-
LAND
CAM.
78
VIETNAM

SRI LANKA

MALAYSIA

INDONESIA
80

ASIA
67

N.
KORIA
73
Seoul
73
JAPAN
76

Tokyo-Yokohama
77

74

Osaka-Nagoya
77

75

TAIWAN

Hong Kong
71
79

PHILIPPINES

CENTRAL
PACIFIC OCEAN
116

81
PAPUA
NEW
GUINEA
E. TIMOR

ANTARCTICA
160

AUSTRALIA
109

114

112

Perth
112

Adelaide
113

Brisbane
114

Sydney
114

115

Melbourne
115

NEW ZEALAND

EUROPE

EUROPE

31

NORWAY
FINLAND
St. Petersburg
61
RUSSIA
Moscow
61

31
36

SWEDEN
ESTONIA
LATVIA
LITH.

38

31
U.K.

DEN.

BELARUS

IRE.

32

NETH.
30

Berlin
40
POLAND
40

UKRAINE

BELG.
52

GER.
54

Vienna
49

Budapest
49

MOLDOVA

FRANCE
42
SWI.

CZ. R.

HUN.

ROMANIA
48

GEORGIA

AUS.

Madrid
45
SPAIN
44

58
ITALY

CRO.

BOSN.

SERB. &
MONT.

BUL.

TURKEY

PORT.
Lisbon
45

Barcelona
45

56

ALB.

GREECE
46

CYPRUS
91
LEB.
SYRIA

Athens
47

Israel
91
ISR.

100

100

100

MALTA
46

JOR.

MOROCCO

ALGERIA

TUNISIA

LIBYA

EGYPT

SAUDI
ARABIA

These maps of the World, United States and Europe indicate locations of the regional maps found on pages 27-160. The colored outlines show the scale of each map (per the accompanying legend) and the extent of each map's coverage. Page numbers of the same color are found in the center of each outline. Large scale map insets are noted by outline, name and page number. Small scale maps are indicated by name and page number only. map of the world appears on pages 22-23.

THE WORLD ALMANAC®

WORLD ATLAS

HAMMOND

HAMMOND

The World Almanac® World Atlas

© COPYRIGHT 2004 BY
HAMMOND WORLD ATLAS CORPORATION

Data in The World Almanac® sections on pages 9 to 20 and 235 to 291 are used under license from The World Almanac® and Book of Facts © 2004 by World Almanac Education Group, Inc. All rights reserved. The World Almanac® and Book of Facts is a registered trademark of World Almanac Education Group, Inc.

Printed in Canada.

Library of Congress
Cataloging-in-publication Data
    Hammond World Atlas Corporation.
    The World Almanac world atlas.
        p.   cm.
    Includes index.
    ISBN 0-8437-1924-9 (hardcover : alk. paper)
    1. Atlases.
    I. Title: World atlas.
    II. Title.
G1021. H597 2 0 0 3
912--dc22   2003056695

THE WORLD ALMANAC

WORLD ATLAS

World Almanac Facts Join Maps for Deeper Understanding

First Edition

Contents

INTERPRETING MAPS

Designed to enhance your knowledge and enjoyment of maps, these pages explain such cartographic principles as scale, projection and symbology. This section also includes a brief explanation of the boundary and name policies followed in this atlas.

Endsheet   World Time Zones
6-7   Using This Atlas
8   Map Projections

FINDING THE FACTS

9-20   **World Facts and Figures**

For individual subjects in this section, and for Nation Facts and Figues, please see the complete World Almanac Section contents on the opposite page.

WORLD/CONTINENTS/REGIONS

This collection of regional maps is completely generated from a computer database structured by latitude and longitude. The realistic topography is achieved by combining the political map data with digital bathymetric and hypsometric relief data, and shaded relief. The maps are arranged by continent, and a stunning satellite image and political map of that continent introduce each section. Continent thematic maps are also included in each section, providing for special geographical comparisons. Over 70 inset maps highlight metropolitan and other areas of special interest.

Note: Numbers following each entry indicate map scale (M=million, K=thousand).

22-23   World - Political Map 1:80.5M
24-25   World - Physical Map 1:80.5M

Europe and Northern Asia

27   Europe 1:20.7M
28   Geographical Comparisons: Temperature, Climate, Vegetation
29   Geographical Comparisons: Rainfall, Population, Land Use, Minerals
30   Metropolitan London, Metropolitan Paris 1:570K
31   United Kingdom, Ireland 1:3.45M
32-33   Southern England and Wales 1:1.15M
34-35   Northeastern Ireland, Northern England and Wales 1:1.15M
36   Central Scotland 1:1.15M
37   Scandinavia and Finland 1:6.9M Iceland 1:6.9M
38-39   Baltic Region 1:3.45M
40-41   North Central Europe 1:3.45M Berlin 1:1.15M
42-43   West Central Europe 1:3.45M
44-45   Spain, Portugal 1:3.45M Barcelona, Madrid, Lisbon 1:1.15M Azores, Canary Islands, Madeira 1:6.9M
46-47   Southern Italy, Albania, Greece 1:3.45M Athens, Malta 1:1.15M
48-49   Hungary, Northern Balkan States 1:3.45M Vienna, Budapest 1:1.15M
50-51   Netherlands, Northwestern Germany 1:1.15M
52-53   Belgium, Northern France, Western Germany 1:1.15M
54-55   Southern Germany, Czech Republic, Upper Austria 1:1.15M
56-57   Central Alps Region 1:1.15M
58-59   Northern Italy 1:1.15M Monaco 1:115K
60-61   Northeastern Europe 1:6.9M St. Petersburg, Moscow 1:1.15M
62-63   Southeastern Europe 1:6.9M
64-65   Russia and Neighboring Countries 1:20.7M

Asia

67   Asia 1:48.3M
68   Geographical Comparisons: Temperature, Climate, Vegetation
69   Geographical Comparisons: Rainfall, Population, Land Use, Minerals
70-71   Eastern Asia 1:13.8M Hong Kong 1:1.15M
72   Northeastern China 1:6.9M Beijing-Tianjin, Shanghai 1:3.45M
73   Korea 1:3.45M Seoul 1:1.15M
74-75   Central and Southern Japan 1:3.45M Ryukyu Islands 1:6.9M
76   Northern Japan 1:3.45M
77   Tokyo-Yokohama, Osaka-Nagoya 1:1.15M
78   Indochina 1:6.9M
79   Southeastern China, Taiwan, Philippines 1:10.3M
80-81   Indonesia, Malaysia 1:10.3M
82-83   Southern Asia 1:10.3M
84-85   Ganges Plain 1:3.45M
86   Punjab Plain 1:10.3M
87   Central Asia 1:3.45M
88-89   Southwestern Asia 1:10.3M
90   Northern Middle East 1:6.9M
91   Eastern Mediterranean Region 1:3.45M Central Israel 1:1.15M

Africa

93   Africa 1:34.5M Cape Verde 1:6.9M
94   Geographical Comparisons: Temperature, Climate, Vegetation
95   Geographical Comparisons: Rainfall, Population, Land Use, Minerals
96-97   Northern Africa 1:17.2M
98-99   Northern West Africa 1:6.9M
100   Northern Morocco, Algeria, Tunisia 1:3.45M
101   Northeastern Africa 1:6.9M
102-103   Southern West Africa 1:6.9M
104   East Africa 1:6.9M
105   Southern Africa 1:17.2M
106-107   South Africa 1:6.9M Cape Town, Johannesburg, Mauritius and Réunion 1:3.45M Madagascar 1:6.9M

Australia, New Zealand and Pacific

109   Australia, New Zealand 1:19.1M

110   Geographical Comparisons: Temperature, Climate, Vegetation

111   Geographical Comparisons: Rainfall, Population, Land Use, Minerals

112-113   Western and Central Australia 1:6.9M Perth, Adelaide 1:1.15M

114   Northeastern Australia 1:6.9M Brisbane, Sydney 1:1.15M

115   Southeastern Australia 1:6.9M Melbourne 1:1.15M

116-117   Central Pacific Ocean 1:31M New Zealand 1:10.3M

North America

119   North America 1:34.5M

120   Geographical Comparisons: Temperature, Climate, Vegetation

121   Geographical Comparisons: Rainfall, Population, Land Use, Minerals

122-123   Canada 1:13.8M

124-125   United States 1:13.8M Hawaii 1:3.45M Oahu 1:1.15M

128-129   Southwestern United States 1:6.9M

130-131   Southeastern Canada, Northeastern United States 1:6.9M Montreal, Toronto-Buffalo 1:1.15M

132-133   Southeastern United States 1:6.9M

134   Alaska 1:10.3M

135   Seattle-Tacoma, Sacramento-San Francisco-San Jose, Detroit, Chicago-Milwaukee 1:1.15M

136   Los Angeles-San Diego 1:1.15M Metropolitan Los Angeles 1:570K

137   Denver, Kansas City, New Orleans, Oklahoma City, Phoenix, San Antonio, Salt Lake City, St. Louis 1:1.15M

138-139   New York-Philadelphia-Washington 1:1.15M Metropolitan New York 1:570K

140-141   Middle America 1:10.3M Puerto Rico, Lesser Antilles 1:6.9M

142-143   Northern and Central Mexico 1:6.9M Distrito Federal-Veracruz 1:3.45M Distrito Federal 1:1.15M

144-145   Southern Mexico, Central America, Western Caribbean 1:6.9M

South America and Polar Regions

147   South America 1:27.6M

148   Geographical Comparisons: Temperature, Climate, Vegetation

149   Geographical Comparisons: Rainfall, Population, Land Use, Minerals

150-151   Northern South America 1:14.9M

152-153   Colombia, Venezuela, Ecuador 1:6.9M

154   Northeastern Brazil 1:6.9M

155   Southeastern Brazil 1:6.9M Rio de Janeiro-São Paulo 1:3.45M

156   Peru 1:6.9M Galápagos Islands 1:6.9M

157   Southern South America 1:14.9M

158-159   Southern Chile and Argentina 1:6.9M Santiago-Valparaíso, Buenos Aires 1:3.45M

160   Arctic Regions 1:34.5M Antarctica 1:57.5M

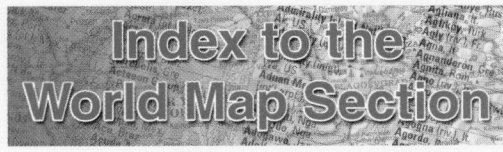

Index to the World Map Section

LOOKING IT UP

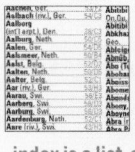

The Master Index at the end of the map section lists 60,000 places and other features appearing in this atlas, complete with page numbers and easy-to-use alpha-numeric references. Preceding the index is a list of abbreviations used in the index.

162   Index Abbreviations

163-234   Index

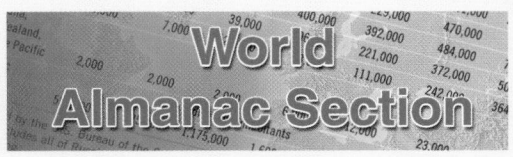

World Almanac Section

FINDING THE FACTS

These 69 pages – a 12-page section of World Facts and Figures, and a 57-page section of Nation Facts and Figures – provide a wide variety of compelling information selected from The World Almanac® and Book of Facts. The world section (pages 9-20) provides information on the world as a whole; the nations section (pages 235-291) on each individual nation. Nations are arranged by continent and in alphabetical order, and are referenced to the map section for quick access to complementary information.

World: Facts and Figures

10-11   About the World Almanac Sections; Nation Locator Guide

12   Rankings by Population and Area

13   Ocean Areas, Ocean Depths and Islands

14   Rivers and Waterfalls

15   Continental Altitudes and Lakes

16   Reservoirs and Dams

17   Global Temperatures

18   Precipitation and Deserts

19   Languages, Population, and Oil and Gas Reserves

20   Energy Charts

Nations: Facts and Figures

235-291   Nations A-Z within each Continent or Region

292   Acknowledgements

Using This Atlas

Offering a broad range of features and functions, The World Almanac® World Atlas is more than a geographical reference work of superior quality and a guide for virtual global exploration. It also includes a compendium of compelling facts and figures from The World Almanac® and Book of Facts that will enhance your understanding of the connections in the world around you. The information provided below will help you to get the most enjoyment and benefit from its use.

World Map Section

The detailed maps of all regions of the Earth are arranged by continent. The chapters for each of the continents are introduced with a stunning satellite image and a political continent map, followed by two pages of thematic maps. Eight thematic subjects range from Climate and Land Use to Population Distribution. The detailed regional maps employ a variety of different symbols: Line patterns, surface colors, and textures highlight distinctive features such as mountains, national parks, urban areas, forests, and deserts. These maps also provide a wealth of information on roadways and canals, geographic features, and political divisions. All of the geographic maps and the complex information they contain are the product of modern computer-assisted map development and compilation techniques.

Map Frames

The map frames contain a number of graphic features that make the atlas easy to use. A locator map at the top of the map page shows the position of the individual map section within a larger geographic area. The blue triangles along the four edges of each map refer by page number to the adjacent map sections, and thus make it easy to find neighboring areas quickly in the atlas. The letters and numerals positioned along the outside of the map, in the green map frame, are search coordinates used to locate places and objects listed in the map index. In addition, integrated legends provide basic information about the region covered by each map.

Map Scales

A map's scale describes the relationship of any length on the map to a corresponding length on the Earth's surface. A scale of 1:3,000,000 means that one cm on the map represents 3,000,000 cm (30 km) in nature. Thus a scale of 1:1,000,000 is larger than 1:3,000,000, just as 1/1 is larger than 1/3. The most densely populated areas are shown at a scale of 1:1 M, while selected metropolitan areas are covered at either 1: 500,000 or 1:1 M. Other populous areas are presented at 1:3 M and 1:6 M, allowing you to accurately compare areas and distances of similar regions. Remaining regions, including the continent maps, are presented at 1:9 M and smaller scales.

Boundary and Name Policies

The atlas shows the internationally recognized national boundaries. Boundary disputes, armistice lines, and de facto boundaries are indicated by special symbols where appropriate. Generally, the names of places and geographic objects appear in the language of the respective country. Accepted conventional names are used for certain major foreign places names. Name usage also tends to vary depending upon cultural factors, however, and is subject to change over time, not least of all for political reasons. In several cases where, for example, a new name has not gained universal acceptance or the use of a traditional name persists, a second name has been entered in parentheses. Thus, the selection of names is not entirely systematic and reflects important aspects of common usage.

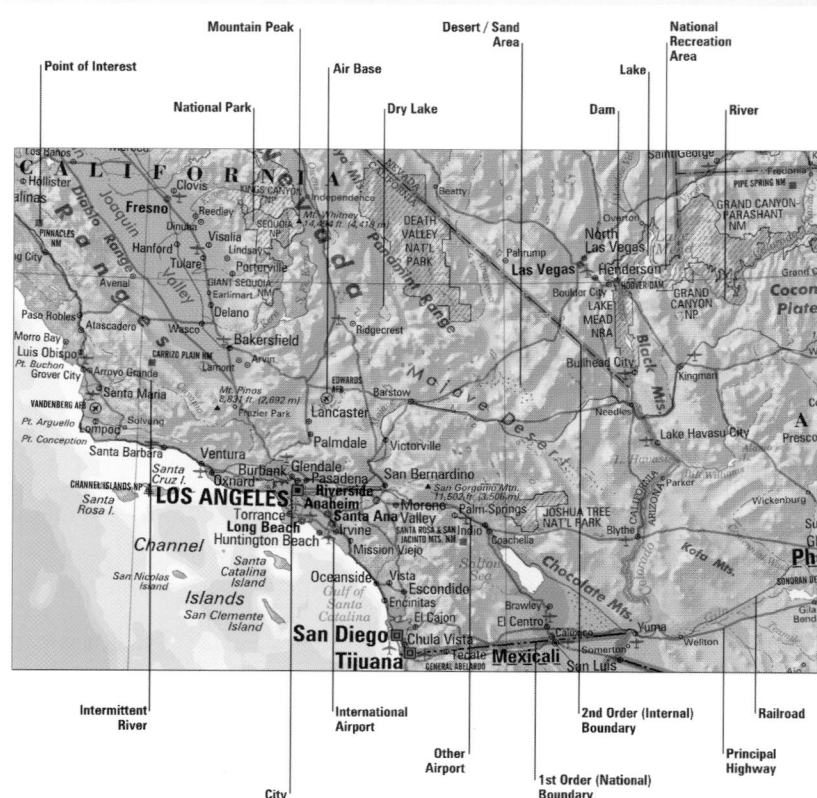

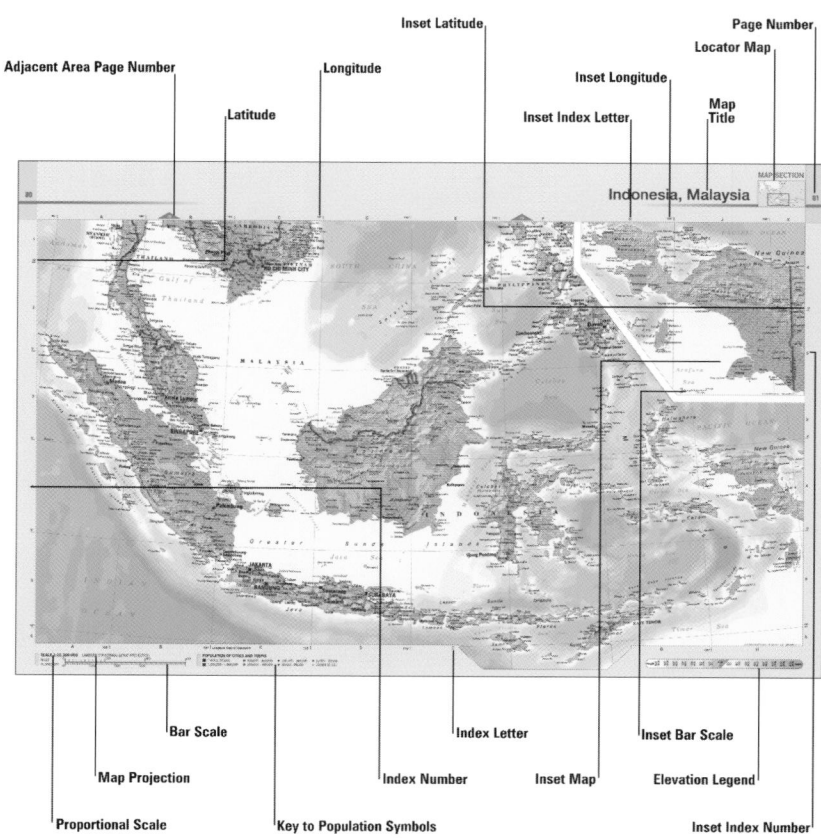

World Locator Map

A simplified world map overlaid with the outlines of all maps in the Map Section is located on the front end sheet. The World Locator Map shows at a glance which maps cover a given area. The page numbers for each map make it easy to locate specific regions quickly.

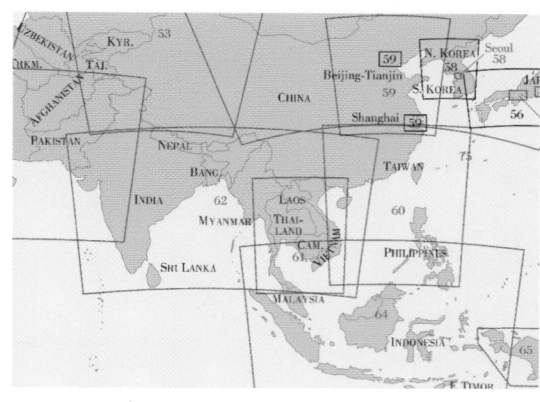

Symbols used on World Maps

FIRST ORDER (NATIONAL) BOUNDARY

Land Boundary		Armistice Boundary	
Water Boundary		De Facto Boundary	
Disputed Boundary		Undefined	

SECOND ORDER (INTERNAL) BOUNDARY

Land Boundary		Water Boundary	

THIRD ORDER (INTERNAL) BOUNDARY

Land Boundary		Water Boundary	

CITIES AND TOWNS

Stockholm First Order (National) Capital

Salt Lake City Second Order (Internal) Capital

Manchester Third Order (Internal) Capital

Towns

□ Neighborhood

City and Urban Area Limits

TRANSPORTATION

✈ International Airport — Railroads

✈ Other Airport — Ferries

— Highways/Roads — — Tunnels (Road, Railroad)

DRAINAGE FEATURES

Shoreline, River — Intermittent Lake

Intermittent River — Dry Lake

Canal — Salt Pan

Lake, Reservoir — Swamp/Marsh

OTHER PHYSICAL FEATURES

▲ Elevation

≍ Pass

● Falls

✳ Rapids

Desert/Sand Area

Lava Flow

Glacier/Ice Shelf

ELEVATION LEGEND

Height	
6000	19700
4000	13000
2000	6500
1500	5000
1000	3300
500	1600
200	700
0	m. ft.
200	700
500	1600
1000	3300
2000	6500
3000	9800
4000	13000
5000	16400
6000	19700
Depth	

The color tints in this bar represent both elevation of land areas and depth of the oceans. The changes between colors are labeled in feet and meters.

CULTURAL FEATURES

∴ Ruins

● Dam

♠ Park

✗ Wildlife Area

■ Point of Interest

⌣ Well

⊗ Air Base

⊘ Naval Base

— International Date Line

⌐⌐⌐⌐ Ancient Walls

Native Reservation/Reserve

Military/Government Reservation

State Park/Recreation Area

National Park/Forest/ Recreation/Wildlife Area

Abbreviations used on the maps

Abor. Rsv.	Aboriginal Reserve	Fk.	Fork
Admin.	Administration	For.	Forest
AFB	Air Force Base	Ft.	Fort
Amm. Dep.	Ammunition Depot	G.	Gulf
Arch.	Archipelago	Govt.	Government
Aut.	Autonomous	Gd.	Grand
B.	Bay	Gt.	Great
Bfld.	Battlefield	Har.	Harbor
Bk.	Brook	Hist.	Historic(al)
Br.	Branch	Hts.	Heights
C.	Cape	I., Is.	Island(s)
Can.	Canal	Ind. Res.	Indian Reservation
Cap.	Capital	Int'l	International
C.G.	Coast Guard	IR	Indian Reservation
Chan.	Channel	Isth.	Isthmus
Co.	County	Jct.	Junction
Consv.	Conservation	L.	Lake
Cord.	Cordillera	Lag.	Lagoon
Cr.	Creek	Mem.	Memorial
b	Center	Mil.	Military
Dep.	Depot	Mon.	Monument
Depr.	Depression	Mt.	Mount
Des.	Desert	Mtn.	Mountain
Dist.	District	Mts.	Mountains
DMZ	Demilitarized Zone	Nat.	Natural
Est.	Estuary	Nat'l	National
Fed.	Federal	Nav.	Naval

NB	National Battlefield	PN	Park National
NBP	National Battlefield Park	Prom.	Promontory
NCA	National Conservation Area	Prsv.	Preserve
NHP	National Historical Park	Pt.	Point
NHS	National Historic Site	R.	River
NL	National Lakeshore	Rec.	Recreation(al)
NM	National Monument	Ref.	Refuge
NMEM	National Memorial	Reg.	Region
NMILP	National Military Park	Rep.	Republic
No.	Northern	Res.	Reservoir, Reservation
NP	National Park	Sa.	Sierra
NPP	National Park and Preserve	Sd.	Sound
NPRSV	National Preserve	So.	Southern
NRA	National Recreation Area	SP	State Park
NRIV	National River	Spr., Sprgs.	Spring, Springs
NRSV	National Reserve	St.	State
NS	National Seashore	Sta.	Station
NWR	National Wildlife Refuge	Stm.	Stream
Obl.	Oblast	Str.	Strait
Occ.	Occupied	Terr.	Territory
Okr.	Okrug	Tun.	Tunnel
Passg.	Passage	Twp.	Township
Pen.	Peninsula	UNDOF	United Nations Disengagement Observer Force
Pk.	Peak	Val.	Valley
Plat.	Plateau	Vill.	Village

Index to the World Map Section

Aa (riv.), Ger.	50/D5
Aach (riv.), Ger.	57/F2
Aach, Ger.	57/E2
Aachen, Ger.	53/F2
Aalbach (riv.), Ger.	54/C3
Aalborg (int'l arpt.), Den.	38/C3
Aalburg, Neth.	50/C5
Aalen, Ger.	54/D5
Aalsmeer, Neth.	50/B4
Aalst, Belg.	52/D2
Aalten, Neth.	50/D5
Aalter, Belg.	52/C1
Aar (riv.), Ger.	53/H3
Aarau, Swi.	56/E3
Aarberg, Swi.	56/D3

The index facilitates the search for a specific place in the atlas. It contains an alphabetical list of place names and geographic objects shown in the maps. Each index entry gives the page and coordinate grid location of the desired place or object. A list of the abbreviations used in the index is found on the first index page.

Map type faces

The use of different type faces helps the reader distinguish between categories of map content.

Major Political Arenas

LUXEMBOURG

Internal Political Divisions

SAXONY-ANHALT

Historical Regions

Polabská Nížina

Cities and Towns

Norfolk Sumter Smyrna

Neighborhoods

BIGGIN HILL

Points of Interest

MISSION SAN BUENAVENTURA

Water Features

L. Elsinore

Capes, Points, Peaks, Passes

Cape Horn...Pt. La Jolla

Mt. Rainier

Islands, Peninsulas

Cape Breton I.

Mountain Ranges, Plateaus, Hills

Serra do Norte

Deserts, Plains, Valleys

San Fernando Valley

Spelling of names

The spelling of geographic names conforms to the rules of the respective official language of each country. Where the official language is written in Latin characters, local spellings, including diacritical marks and modified letters, have been used. For countries with languages written in non-Latin characters, such as China, Russia or the Arabic-speaking countries, an international standard form is used, which may deviate in some cases from conventional American usage.

Rankings by Populat

POPULATION AND LAND AREA OF T

Population Rank as of 2003	Continent or Region	Population (estimated, in thousands)				
		1650	1750	1850	1900	1950
1.	Asia	335,000	476,000	754,000	932,000	1,411,000
2.	Africa	100,000	95,000	95,000	118,000	229,000
3.	Europe	100,000	140,000	265,000	400,000	392,000
4.	North America	5,000	5,000	39,000	106,000	221,000
5.	South America	8,000	7,000	20,000	38,000	111,000
6.	Australia, New Zealand, and the Pacific	2,000	2,000	2,000	6,000	12,000
7.	Antarctic	No indigenous inhabitants				
	WORLD	550,000	725,000	1,175,000	1,600,000	2,556,000

Note: Areas are as defined by the U.S. Bureau of the Census and strictly apply only to 1950 a Bureau area for Europe includes all of Russia (approximately 6,600,000 sq mi [17,100,000 o totals because of rounding.

LARGEST POPULATIONS

Rank	Country	Population	Persons per sq mi	Persons per sq km	Rank
1.	China²	1,286,975,000	357	138	1.
2.	India	1,065,462,000	928	358	2.
3.	United States	288,369,000	81	31	3.
4.	Indonesia	219,883,000	312	120	4.
5.	Brazil	178,470,000	55	21	5.
6.	Pakistan	153,578,000	511	197	6.
7.	Bangladesh	146,736,000	2,838	1,096	7.
8.	Russia	143,246,000	22	8	8.
9.	Japan	127,654,000	838	324	9.

The World Almanac Sections – World and Nations

Two sections – one devoted to World Facts and Figures, and one to Nation Facts and Figures – provide a wide variety of information selected from The World Almanac® and Book of Facts. The 12-page world section (pages 9-20) offers data on the world as a whole. The 57-page nations section (pages 235-291) provides data on each individual nation. Nations are arranged in alphabetical order, and are referenced to the map section for quick access to complementary information.

A concurrent reading of maps and related almanac data helps shed light on the impact of geography on the economy, culture, and other spheres of human activity.

Map Projections

Simply stated, the mapmaker's challenge is to project the earth's curved surface onto a flat plane. To achieve this elusive goal, cartographers have developed map projections — formulas that govern this conversion of geographic data. Every point on earth can be identified with the aid of a geographic coordinate grid, and this grid can be projected onto a flat surface. This section explores some of the most widely used projections. It also introduces a new projection, the Hammond Optimal Conformal.

General Principles and Terms

The earth rotates around its axis once a day. Its end points are the north and south poles; the imaginary line circling the earth midway between the poles is the equator. The arc from the equator to either pole is divided into 90 degrees of latitude. The equator represents 0° latitude. Circles of equal latitude, called parallels, are traditionally shown at every fifth or tenth degree. Circles of latitude become progressively smaller toward the poles.

The equator is divided into 360 degrees. Lines circling the globe from pole to pole through the degree points on the equator are called meridians, or great circles. All meridians are equal in length. By international agreement the meridian passing through the Greenwich Observatory near London has been chosen as the prime meridian, or 0° longitude. The distance in degrees from the prime meridian to any point east or west is its longitude.

While meridians are all equal in length, parallels become shorter as they approach the poles. Whereas one degree of latitude represents approximately 69 miles (112 km) anywhere on the globe, a degree of longitude varies from 69 miles (112 km) at the equator to zero at the poles. Each degree of latitude and longitude is divided into 60 minutes. One minute of latitude equals one nautical mile (1.15 land miles or 1.85 km).

How to Flatten a Sphere: The Art of Controlling Distortion

There is only one way to represent the earth's sphere with absolute precision: on a globe. All attempts to project our planet's surface onto a plane result in distortion. Depending upon the map projection selected, distortions appear in shapes and area sizes, angles, or distances between points on the earth.

Only the parallels or the meridians (or some other set of lines) can maintain the same length as on a globe of corresponding scale. All other lines must be either too long or too short. Accordingly, the scale on a flat map cannot be true everywhere; there will always be different scales in different parts of a map. On world maps or maps of very large areas, variations in scale may be extreme. On maps of small areas, variations in scale may be relatively insignificant. Most maps seek to preserve either true area relationships (equal area projections) or true angles and shapes (conformal projections); some attempt to achieve overall balance.

Projections: Selected Examples

Mercator Projection

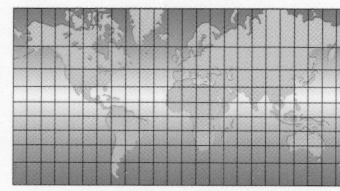

This projection is especially useful because all compass directions appear as straight lines, making it a valuable navigational tool. Moreover, it is a comformal projection – every small region conforms to its shape on a globe. But because its meridians are evenly-spaced vertical lines which never converge (unlike the meridians on a globe), the horizontal parallels must be drawn farther and farther apart at higher latitudes to maintain a correct relationship. Only the equator is true to scale, and the sizes of areas in the higher latitudes are dramatically distorted.

Robinson Projection

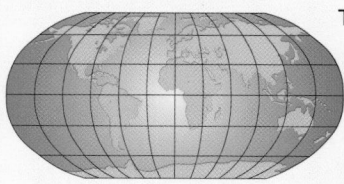

The Robinson is a compromise projection that combines elements of both conformal and equal area projections to show the whole earth with relatively true shapes and reasonably equal areas. The Robinson is used mostly for world maps. To create the World Political and World Physical maps on pages 22-25, this projection has been used.

Conic Projection

The original idea of this projection is to project lines of latitude and longitude from the planet's center onto a cone. The axis length of the cone is variable. To produce working maps, the cone is simply "cut open" and "laid flat." In the conic projection illustrated here, the cone can be made tangent to any desired parallel. One popular conic projection, the Lambert Conformal Conic, uses two standard parallels of conforming lengths near the top and the bottom of the map to further reduce errors of scale. This projection has been used to create most of the national and regional maps in this atlas.

Hammond Optimal Conformal

As its name implies, this new conformal projection presents the optimal view of an area by reducing shifts in scale over an entire region to the minimum degree possible. While conformal maps generally preserve all small shapes, large shapes can become very distorted because of varying scales, causing considerable inaccuracy in distance measurements. The concept underlying the Optimal Conformal is that for any region on the globe, there is an ideal projection for which scale variation can be made as small as possible. Consequently, unlike other projections, the Optimal Conformal does not use one standard formula to construct a map. Each map is a unique projection — the optimal projection for that particular area.

After a cartographer defines the subject area (in the illustration, left, indicated by the red outline around South America), a sophisticated computer program evaluates the size and shape of the region, and projects the most distortion-free conformal map possible. This projection has been used to create the continent maps in this atlas.

◄ *Hammond Optimal Conformal Projection*

THE WORLD ALMANAC® WORLD ATLAS

World Almanac Section

World Facts and Figures from The World Almanac®

POPULATION AND LAND AREA OF THE WORLD, 1650–20...

as of 2003 / Continent or Region	Population (estimates)							Land Area (1,000 sq mi)	(1,000 sq km)	% of Earth Land Area
	1650	1750	1850	1900	1950	1980	2003			
Asia	335,000	476,000	754,000	932,000	1,411,000	2,601,000	3,817,000	12,000	31,000	21.4
Africa	100,000	95,000	95,000	118,000	229,000	470,000	856,000	11,500	29,800	20.5
Europe	100,000	140,000	265,000	400,000	392,000	484,000	729,000	8,800	22,800	15.7
North America	5,000	5,000	39,000	106,000	221,000	372,000	505,000	8,300	21,400	
South America	8,000	7,000	20,000	38,000	111,000	242,000	364,000	6,800		
Australia, New Zealand, and the Pacific	2,000	2,000	2,000	6,000	12,000					
Antarctic	No indigenous inhabitants									
WORLD	550,000	725,000	1,170...							

WORLD FACTS AND FIGURES

About the World Almanac Sections

The information from *The World Almanac®* is presented in two parts. This first part, preceding the Map Section, contains facts and figures characterizing key aspects of the world and its population. The second part, on pages 235-291, presents detailed information on every nation of the world.

The nations in the second part are arranged in alphabetical order under the heading for the part of the world in which they are located. To find information on a particular nation, turn to the region in which it lies, as indicated by the abbreviation in parentheses below. Note that Russia is covered under Europe, as its capital and the bulk of the population are located in Europe; similarly, Turkey is covered under Asia, since that is where its capital and the majority of its population are found.

Nation Locator Guide—for pages 235-291

- **(AF)** Africa
- **(AS)** Asia
- **(AU)** Australia, New Zealand, and the Pacific
- **(E)** Europe
- **(NA)** North America, including Central America and the islands of the Caribbean
- **(SA)** South America

Afghanistan **(AS)**	Bolivia **(SA)**	of the **(AF)**	Fiji **(AU)**
Albania **(E)**	Bosnia and Herzegovina **(E)**	Congo Republic **(AF)**	Finland **(E)**
Algeria **(AF)**	Botswana **(AF)**	Costa Rica **(NA)**	France **(E)**
Andorra **(E)**	Brazil **(SA)**	Côte d'Ivoire **(AF)**	Gabon **(AF)**
Angola **(AF)**	Brunei **(AS)**	Croatia **(E)**	Gambia **(AF)**
Antigua and Barbuda **(NA)**	Bulgaria **(E)**	Cuba **(NA)**	Georgia **(AS)**
Argentina **(SA)**	Burkina Faso **(AF)**	Cyprus **(AS)**	Germany **(E)**
Armenia **(AS)**	Burma *(see Myanmar)*	Czech Republic **(E)**	Ghana **(AF)**
Australia **(AU)**	Burundi **(AF)**	Denmark **(E)**	Greece **(E)**
Austria **(E)**	Cambodia **(AS)**	Djibouti **(AF)**	Grenada **(NA)**
Azerbaijan **(AS)**	Cameroon **(AF)**	Dominica **(NA)**	Guatemala **(NA)**
Bahamas **(NA)**	Canada **(NA)**	Dominican Republic **(NA)**	Guinea **(AF)**
Bahrain **(AS)**	Cape Verde **(AF)**	East Timor **(AS)**	Guinea-Bissau **(AF)**
Bangladesh **(AS)**	Central African Republic **(AF)**	Ecuador **(SA)**	Guyana **(SA)**
Barbados **(NA)**	Chad **(AF)**	Egypt **(AF)**	Haiti **(NA)**
Belarus **(E)**	Chile **(SA)**	El Salvador **(NA)**	Honduras **(NA)**
Belgium **(E)**	China **(AS)**	Equatorial Guinea **(AF)**	Hungary **(E)**
Belize **(NA)**	Colombia **(SA)**	Eritrea **(AF)**	Iceland **(E)**
Benin **(AF)**	Comoros **(AF)**	Estonia **(E)**	India **(AS)**
Bhutan **(AS)**	Congo, Democratic Republic	Ethiopia **(AF)**	Indonesia **(AS)**

Iran **(AS)**	Malta **(E)**	Poland **(E)**	Sweden **(E)**
Iraq **(AS)**	Marshall Islands **(AU)**	Portugal **(E)**	Switzerland **(E)**
Ireland **(E)**	Mauritania **(AF)**	Qatar **(AS)**	Syria **(AS)**
Israel **(AS)**	Mauritius **(AF)**	Romania **(E)**	Taiwan **(AS)**
Italy **(E)**	Mexico **(NA)**	Russia **(E)**	Tajikistan **(AS)**
Jamaica **(NA)**	Micronesia **(AU)**	Rwanda **(AF)**	Tanzania **(AF)**
Japan **(AS)**	Moldova **(E)**	Saint Kitts and Nevis **(NA)**	Thailand **(AS)**
Jordan **(AS)**	Monaco **(E)**	Saint Lucia **(NA)**	Togo **(AF)**
Kazakhstan **(AS)**	Mongolia **(AS)**	Saint Vincent and the	Tonga **(AU)**
Kenya **(AF)**	Morocco **(AF)**	Grenadines **(NA)**	Trinidad and Tobago **(NA)**
Kiribati **(AU)**	Mozambique **(AF)**	Samoa **(AU)**	Tunisia **(AF)**
Korea, North **(AS)**	Myanmar **(AS)**	San Marino **(E)**	Turkey **(AS)**
Korea, South **(AS)**	Namibia **(AF)**	São Tomé and Príncipe **(AF)**	Turkmenistan **(AS)**
Kuwait **(AS)**	Nauru **(AU)**	Saudi Arabia **(AS)**	Tuvalu **(AU)**
Kyrgyzstan **(AS)**	Nepal **(AS)**	Senegal **(AF)**	Uganda **(AF)**
Laos **(AS)**	Netherlands **(E)**	Serbia and Montenegro **(E)**	Ukraine **(E)**
Latvia **(E)**	New Zealand **(AU)**	Seychelles **(AF)**	United Arab Emirates **(AS)**
Lebanon **(AS)**	Nicaragua **(NA)**	Sierra Leone **(AF)**	United Kingdom **(E)**
Lesotho **(AF)**	Niger **(AF)**	Singapore **(AS)**	United States **(NA)**
Liberia **(AF)**	Nigeria **(AF)**	Slovakia **(E)**	Uruguay **(SA)**
Libya **(AF)**	North Korea *(see Korea, North)*	Slovenia **(E)**	Uzbekistan **(AS)**
Liechtenstein **(E)**	Norway **(E)**	Solomon Islands **(AU)**	Vanuatu **(AU)**
Lithuania **(E)**	Oman **(AS)**	Somalia **(AF)**	Vatican City **(E)**
Luxembourg **(E)**	Pakistan **(AS)**	South Africa **(AF)**	Venezuela **(SA)**
Macedonia **(E)**	Palau **(AU)**	South Korea *(see Korea, South)*	Vietnam **(AS)**
Madagascar **(AF)**	Panama **(NA)**	Spain **(E)**	Yemen **(AS)**
Malawi **(AF)**	Papua New Guinea **(AS)**	Sri Lanka **(AS)**	Yugoslavia *(see Serbia and*
Malaysia **(AS)**	Paraguay **(SA)**	Sudan **(AF)**	*Montenegro)*
Maldives **(AS)**	Peru **(SA)**	Suriname **(SA)**	Zambia **(AF)**
Mali **(AF)**	Philippines **(AS)**	Swaziland **(AF)**	Zimbabwe **(AF)**

A WORD ABOUT THE DATA

The facts and figures given here are based on data collected for *The World Almanac®* and represent the latest information available at the time of compilation.

Data on pages 9 through 20 and pages 235 through 291 used under license from *The World Almanac® and Book of Facts*. ©2004 by World Almanac Education Group, Inc. All rights reserved.

The World Almanac® and Book of Facts is a registered trademark of World Almanac Education Group, Inc.

LOCATIONS PICTURED IN PHOTOS INTRODUCING THE REGIONS OF THE WORLD

AFRICA
page 169 right bottom, *Camel resting by the pyramids at Giza (Al Jizah), Egypt*

ASIA
page 183 left, *Tea harvesting, China*; page 183 mid bottom, *Festival celebration, Hong Kong*; page 183 mid right: *Market stall lantern, Tokyo, Japan*

AUSTRALIA, NEW ZEALAND, AND THE PACIFIC
page 198 left, *Reef formations, South Pacific*; page 198 right bottom, *Opera House, Sydney, Australia*

EUROPE
page 202 left, *Marienplatz, Munich, Germany*

NORTH AMERICA, INCLUDING CENTRAL AMERICA AND THE ISLANDS OF THE CARIBBEAN
page 214 left, *Buffalo near Grand Teton Mountains, Wyoming, United States*; page 214 right top, *Los Angeles, California, United States*

SOUTH AMERICA
page 221 left, *Machu Picchu, Peru*; page 221 mid bottom, *Rio de Janeiro, Brazil*

Chief abbreviations used in the World Almanac Section

cu	cubic	est.	estimate(d)	ft	foot, feet	in	inch(es)	km	kilometer(s)
m	meter(s)	mi	mile(s)	mm	millimeters(s)	NA	not available	Pres.	President
sq	square	yd	yard(s)						

World Facts and Figures

RANKINGS BY POPULATION AND AREA

POPULATION AND LAND AREA OF THE WORLD, 1650–2003

Population Rank as of 2003	Continent or Region	Population (estimated, in thousands)							Land Area		
		1650	1750	1850	1900	1950	1980	2003	(1,000 sq mi)	(1,000 sq km)	% of Earth Land Area
1.	Asia	335,000	476,000	754,000	932,000	1,411,000	2,601,000	3,817,000	12,000	31,000	21.4
2.	Africa	100,000	95,000	95,000	118,000	229,000	470,000	856,000	11,500	29,800	20.5
3.	Europe	100,000	140,000	265,000	400,000	392,000	484,000	729,000	8,800	22,800	15.7
4.	North America	5,000	5,000	39,000	106,000	221,000	372,000	505,000	8,300	21,400	14.8
5.	South America	8,000	7,000	20,000	38,000	111,000	242,000	364,000	6,800	17,500	12.1
6.	Australia, New Zealand, and the Pacific	2,000	2,000	2,000	6,000	12,000	23,000	32,000	3,200	8,400	5.8
7.	Antarctica	No indigenous inhabitants							5,400	14,000	9.7
	WORLD	550,000	725,000	1,175,000	1,600,000	2,556,000	4,458,000	6,302,000	56,000	145,000	100.0

Note: Areas are as defined by the U.S. Bureau of the Census and strictly apply only to 1950 and after; before then, areas may be defined differently. The Census Bureau area for Europe includes all of Russia (approximately 6,600,000 sq mi [17,100,000 sq km]); the area figure for Asia excludes Russia. Figures may not add up to totals because of rounding.

LARGEST POPULATIONS

Rank	Country	Population	Persons per sq mi	Persons per sq km
1.	China[1]	1,286,975,000	357	138
2.	India	1,065,462,000	928	358
3.	United States	288,369,000	81	31
4.	Indonesia	219,883,000	312	120
5.	Brazil	178,470,000	55	21
6.	Pakistan	153,578,000	511	197
7.	Bangladesh	146,736,000	2,838	1,096
8.	Russia	143,246,000	22	8
9.	Japan	127,654,000	838	324
10.	Nigeria	124,009,000	353	136

[1]Excluding Hong Kong and Macau.

SMALLEST POPULATIONS

Rank	Country	Population	Persons per sq mi	Persons per sq km
1.	Vatican City	900	*	*
2.	Tuvalu	11,000	1,100	425
3.	Nauru	13,000	1,625	627
4.	Palau	20,000	113	44
5.	San Marino	28,000	1,217	470
6.	Monaco	32,000	41,608	16,065
7.	Liechtenstein	33,000	550	212
8.	Saint Kitts and Nevis	39,000	386	149
9.	Marshall Islands	56,000	800	309
10.	Antigua and Barbuda	68,000	400	154

*Area only 0.17 sq mi (0.4 sq km).

LARGEST LAND AREAS

Rank	Country	Land Area sq mi	Land Area) (sq km)
1.	Russia	6,592,800	17,075,400
2.	China	3,600,900	9,326,411
3.	Canada	3,560,200	9,220,970
4.	United States	3,539,200	9,166,601
5.	Brazil	3,265,100	8,456,511
6.	Australia	2,941,300	7,617,931
7.	India	1,148,000	2,973,190
8.	Argentina	1,056,600	2,736,690
9.	Kazakhstan	1,049,200	2,717,300
10.	Algeria	919,600	2,381,741

SMALLEST LAND AREAS

Rank	Country	Land Area sq mi	Land Area (sq km)
1.	Vatican City	0.17	0.4
2.	Monaco	0.75	1.0
3.	Nauru	8	21
4.	Tuvalu	10	26
5.	San Marino	23	60
6.	Liechtenstein	62	161
7.	Marshall Islands	70	181
8.	Saint Kitts and Nevis	101	261
9.	Maldives	116	300
10.	Malta	124	321

OCEANS, OCEAN DEPTHS, AND ISLANDS

AREAS AND AVERAGE DEPTHS OF OCEANS, SEAS, AND GULFS

Geographers and mapmakers recognize four major bodies of water: the Pacific, the Atlantic, the Indian, and the Arctic oceans. The Atlantic and Pacific oceans are considered divided at the equator into the North and South Atlantic and the North and South Pacific. The Arctic Ocean is the name for waters north of the continental landmasses in the region of the Arctic Circle.

	Area (sq mi)	Area (sq km)	Average Depth (ft)	Average Depth (m)
Pacific Ocean	64,186,300	166,241,800	12,925	3,940
Atlantic Ocean	33,420,000	86,557,400	11,730	3,575
Indian Ocean	28,350,500	73,427,500	12,598	3,840
Arctic Ocean	5,105,700	13,223,700	3,407	1,038
South China Sea	1,148,500	2,974,600	4,802	1,464
Caribbean Sea	971,400	2,515,900	8,448	2,575
Mediterranean Sea	969,100	2,510,000	4,926	1,501
Bering Sea	873,000	2,261,000	4,893	1,491
Gulf of Mexico	582,100	1,508,000	5,297	1,615
Sea of Okhotsk	537,500	1,392,000	3,192	973
Sea of Japan	391,100	1,013,000	5,468	1,667
Hudson Bay	281,900	730,100	305	93
East China Sea	256,600	664,600	620	189
Andaman Sea	218,100	564,900	3,667	1,118
Black Sea	196,100	507,900	3,906	1,191
Red Sea	174,900	453,000	1,764	538
North Sea	164,900	427,100	308	94

BIGGEST ISLANDS

Island	Area (sq mi)	Area (sq km)
Greenland (Denmark)	840,000	2,180,000
New Guinea (Indonesia, Papua New Guinea)	306,000	793,000
Borneo (Indonesia, Malaysia, Brunei)	280,100	725,500
Madagascar	226,658	587,040
Baffin (Canada)	195,928	507,450
Sumatra (Indonesia)	165,000	427,350
Honshu (Japan)	87,805	227,410
Great Britain (United Kingdom)	84,200	218,080
Victoria (Canada)	83,897	217,290
Ellesmere (Canada)	75,767	196,240
Celebes (Indonesia)	69,000	178,710
South (New Zealand)	58,384	151,210
Java (Indonesia)	48,900	126,650
North (New Zealand)	44,204	114,490
Cuba	42,804	110,860
Newfoundland (Canada)	42,031	108,860
Luzon (Philippines)	40,680	105,360

PRINCIPAL OCEAN DEPTHS

Name of Area	Location (latitude)	Location (longitude)	Depth (m)	Depth (fathoms)	Depth (ft)
PACIFIC OCEAN					
Marianas Trench	11° 22′ N	142° 36′ E	10,924	5,973	35,840
Tonga Trench	23° 16′ S	174° 44′ W	10,800	5,906	35,433
Philippine Trench	10° 38′ N	126° 36′ E	10,057	5,499	32,995
Kermadec Trench	31° 53′ S	177° 21′ W	10,047	5,494	32,963
Bonin Trench	24° 30′ N	143° 24′ E	9,994	5,464	32,788
Kuril Trench	44° 15′ N	150° 34′ E	9,750	5,331	31,988
Izu Trench	31°05′ N	142°10′ E	9,695	5,301	31,808
New Britain Trench	06°19′ S	153°45′ E	8,940	4,888	29,331
Yap Trench	08°33′ N	138°02′ E	8,527	4,663	27,976
Japan Trench	36°08′ N	142°43′ E	8,412	4,600	27,599
Peru-Chile Trench	23°18′ S	71°14′ W	8,064	4,409	26,457
Palau Trench	07°52′ N	134°56′ E	8,054	4,404	26,424
Aleutian Trench	50°51′ N	177°11′ E	7,679	4,199	25,194
ATLANTIC OCEAN					
Puerto Rico Trench	19° 55′ N	65°27′ W	8,605	4,705	28,232
South Sandwich Trench	55°42′ S	25°56′ W	8,325	4,552	27,313
Romanche Gap	0°13′ S	18°26′ W	7,728	4,226	25,354

World Facts and Figures

RIVERS AND WATERFALLS

LONGEST RIVERS

River	Outflow	Length (mi)	Length (km)
AFRICA			
Congo	Atlantic Ocean	2,900	4,670
Niger	Gulf of Guinea	2,590	4,170
Nile	Mediterranean Sea	4,160	6,690
Zambezi	Indian Ocean	1,700	2,740
ASIA			
Amur	Tatar Strait	1,780	2,860
Brahmaputra	Bay of Bengal	1,800	2,900
Chang	East China Sea	3,964	6,380
Euphrates	Shatt al-Arab	1,700	2,740
Huang	Yellow Sea	3,395	5,460
Indus	Arabian Sea	1,800	2,900
Lena	Laptev Sea	2,734	4,400
Mekong	South China Sea	2,700	4,350
Ob	Gulf of Ob	2,268	3,650
Ob-Irtysh	Gulf of Ob	3,362	5,410
Yenisey	Kara Seav	2,543	4,090
AUSTRALIA			
Murray-Darling	Indian Ocean	2,310	3,720
EUROPE			
Danube	Black Sea	1,776	2,860
Volga	Caspian Sea	2,290	3,690
NORTH AMERICA			
Mississippi	Gulf of Mexico	2,340	3,770
Mississippi- Missouri- Red Rock	Gulf of Mexico	3,710	5,970
Missouri	Mississippi River	2,315	3,730
Missouri-Red Rock	Mississippi River	2,540	4,090
Rio Grande	Gulf of Mexico	1,900	3,060
Yukon	Bering Sea	1,979	3,180
SOUTH AMERICA			
Amazon	Atlantic Ocean	4,000	6,440
Japura	Amazon River	1,750	2,820
Madeira	Amazon River	2,013	3,240
Parana	Rio de la Plata	2,485	4,000
Purus	Amazon River	2,100	3,380
Sao Francisco	Atlantic Ocean	1,988	3,200

NOTABLE WATERFALLS

Name (Location)	Height (ft)	Height (m)
AFRICA		
Tugela# (South Africa)	2,014	614
Victoria, Zambezi River* (Zimbabwe-Zambia)	343	105
AUSTRALIA, NEW ZEALAND		
Wallaman, Stony Creek# (Australia)	1,137	347
Wollomombi (Australia)	1,100	335
Sutherland, Arthur River# (New Zealand)	1,904	580
EUROPE		
Krimml# (Austria)	1,312	400
Gavarnie* (France)	1,385	422
Mardalsfossen (Northern) (Norway)	1,535	468
Mardalsfossen (Southern)# (Norway)	2,149	655
Skjeggedal, Nybuai River#** (Norway)	1,378	420
Trummelbach# (Switzerland)	1,312	400
NORTH AMERICA		
Della# (Canada)	1,443	440
Niagara: Horseshoe (Canada)	173	53
Takakkaw, Daly Glacier# (Canada)	1,200	366
Niagara: American (U.S.)	182	55
Ribbon** (U.S.)	1,612	491
Silver Strand, Meadow Brook** (U.S.)	1,170	357
Yosemite#** (U.S.)	2,425	739
SOUTH AMERICA		
Iguazu (Argentina-Brazil)	230	70
Glass (Brazil)	1,325	404
Patos-Maribondo, Grande River (Brazil)	115	35
Paulo Afonso, Sao Francisco River (Brazil)	275	84
Urubupunga, Parana River (Brazil)	39	12
Great, Kamarang River (Guyana)	1,600	488
Kaieteur, Potaro River (Guyana)	741	226
Angel#*(Venezuela)	3,212	979
Cuquenan (Venezuela)	2,000	610

Note: If the river name is not shown, it is the same as that of the falls. "Height" is the total drop in one or more leaps.

#Falls of more than one leap; *falls that diminish greatly seasonally; **falls that reduce to a trickle or are dry for part of each year.

The estimated mean annual flow, in cubic feet per second (cubic meters in parentheses), of major waterfalls is as follows: Niagara, 212,200 (6,000); Paulo Afonso, 100,000 (2,800); Urubupunga, 97,000 (2,700); Iguazu, 61,000 (1,700); Patos-Maribondo, 53,000 (1,500); Victoria, 35,400 (1,000); and Kaieteur, 23,400 (660).

CONTINENTAL ALTITUDES AND LAKES

HIGHEST CONTINENTAL ALTITUDES

Continent	Highest Point	Elevation (ft)	Elevation (m)
Asia	Mount Everest, Nepal-Tibet	29,035	8,850
South America	Mount Aconcagua, Argentina	22,834	6,960
North America	Mount McKinley, Alaska, U.S.	20,320	6,194
Africa	Kilimanjaro, Tanzania	19,340	5,895
Europe	Mount Elbrus, Russia	18,510	5,642
Antarctica	Vinson Massif	16,864	5,140
Australia	Mount Kosciusko, New South Wales	7,310	2,228

LOWEST CONTINENTAL ALTITUDES

Continent	Lowest Point	Feet Below Sea Level	Meters Below Sea Level
Asia	Dead Sea, Israel-Jordan	1,348	411
South America	Valdes Peninsula, Argentina	131	40
North America	Death Valley, California, U.S.	282	86
Africa	Lake Assal, Djibouti	512	156
Europe	Caspian Sea, Russia, Azerbaijan	92	28
Antarctica	Bentley Subglacial Trench	8,327[1]	2,538[1]
Australia	Lake Eyre, South Australia	52	16

[1]Estimated level of the continental floor. Lower points that have yet to be discovered may exist further beneath the ice.

MAJOR NATURAL LAKES OF THE WORLD

Name	Continent	Area (sq mi)	Area (sq km)	Maximum Depth (ft)	Maximum Depth (m)
Caspian Sea[1]	Asia-Europe	143,244	371,000	3,363	1,025
Superior	North America	31,700	82,100	1,330	405
Victoria	Africa	26,828	69,484	270	82
Huron	North America	23,000	59,600	750	229
Michigan	North America	22,300	57,800	923	281
Aral Sea[1]	Asia	13,000[2]	33,700[2]	220	67
Tanganyika	Africa	12,700	32,900	4,823	1,470
Baykal	Asia	12,162	31,500	5,315	1,620
Great Bear	North America	12,096	31,330	1,463	446
Nyasa (Malawi)	Africa	11,150	28,880	2,280	695
Great Slave	North America	11,031	28,570	2,015	614
Erie	North America	9,910	25,670	210	64
Winnipeg	North America	9,417	24,390	60	18
Ontario	North America	7,340	19,010	802	244
Balkhash[1]	Asia	7,115	18,430	85	26
Ladoga	Europe	6,835	17,700	738	225

Note: A lake is generally defined as a body of water surrounded by land.

[1]Salt lake.

[2]Approximate figure, could be less. The diversion of feeder rivers since the 1960s has devastated the Aral—once the world's fourth-largest lake (26,000 sq mi [67,000 sq km]). By 2000, the Aral had effectively become three lakes, with the total area shown.

World Facts and Figures

RESERVOIRS AND DAMS

WORLD'S LARGEST-CAPACITY RESERVOIRS

Rank	Name	Country	Capacity (1,000 acre-ft)	Capacity (1,000,000 cu m)
1.	Kariba	Zimbabwe/ Zambia	146,400	180,600
2.	Bratsk	Russia	137,000	169,000
3.	High Aswan	Egypt	131,300	162,000
4.	Akosombo	Ghana	119,950	147,960
5.	Daniel Johnson	Canada	115,000	141,851
6.	Xinfeng	China	112,660	138,960
7.	Guri	Venezuela	109,400	135,000
8.	W. A. C. Bennett	Canada	60,235	74,300
9.	Krasnoyarsk	Russia	59,425	73,300
10.	Zeya	Russia	55,450	68,400

WORLD'S HIGHEST DAMS

Rank	Name	Country	Height Above Lowest Formation (ft)	Height Above Lowest Formation (m)
1.	Nurek	Tajikistan	984	300
2.	Grand Dixence	Switzerland	935	285
3.	Inguri	Georgia	892	272
4.	Vajont	Italy	860	262
5.	Manuel M. Torres	Mexico	856	261
6.	Alvaro Obregon	Mexico	853	260
7.	Mauvoisin	Switzerland	820	250
8.	Mica	Canada	797	243
9.	Alberto Lleras C	Colombia	797	243
10.	Sayano-Shushensk	Russia	794	242

WORLD'S LARGEST-VOLUME EMBANKMENT DAMS

Rank	Name	Country	Volume (1,000 cu yd)	Volume (1,000 cu m)
1.	Tarbela	Pakistan	194,230	148,500
2.	Fort Peck	U.S.	125,630	96,050
3.	Tucurui	Brazil	111,400	85,200
4.	Ataturk*	Turkey	111,200	85,000
5.	Yacireta*	Argentina	105,900	81,000
6.	Rogun*	Tajikistan	98,750	75,500
7.	Oahe	U.S.	92,000	70,339
8.	Guri	Venezuela	91,560	70,000
9.	Parambikulam	India	90,460	69,165
10.	High Island West	China	87,600	67,000

*Under construction.

GLOBAL TEMPERATURES

HIGHEST MOUNTAINS

Rank	Peak	Place	Height (ft)	Height (m)
1.	Everest	Nepal-Tibet	29,035	8,850
2.	K2 (Godwin Austen)	Kashmir	28,250	8,611
3.	Kanchenjunga	India-Nepal	28,208	8,598
4.	Lhotse I (Everest)	Nepal-Tibet	27,923	8,511
5.	Makalu I	Nepal-Tibet	27,824	8,481
6.	Lhotse II (Everest)	Nepal-Tibet	27,560	8,400
7.	Dhaulagiri	Nepal	26,810	8,172
8.	Manaslu I	Nepal	26,760	8,156
9.	Cho Oyu	Nepal-Tibet	26,750	8,153
10.	Nanga Parbat	Kashmir	26,660	8,126

AVERAGE GLOBAL TEMPERATURES, 1900–2000

Decade	Degrees Fahrenheit	Degrees Celsius
1900-09	56.52	13.62
1910-19	56.57	13.65
1920-29	56.74	13.74
1930-39	57.00	13.89
1940-49	57.13	13.96
1950-59	57.06	13.92
1960-69	57.05	13.92
1970-79	57.04	13.91
1980-89	57.36	14.09
1990-99	57.64	14.24
2000	57.60	14.22

HIGHEST MEASURED TEMPERATURE

Continent or Region	Temperature (degrees Fahrenheit)	Temperature (degrees Celsius)	Place	Elevation (ft)	Elevation (m)	Date
Africa	136	58	El Azizia, Libya	367	112	Sept. 13, 1922
North America	134	57	Death Valley, California (Greenland Ranch)	−178	−54	July 10, 1913
Asia	129	54	Tirat Tsvi, Israel	−722	−220	June 21, 1942
Australia	128	53	Cloncurry, Queensland	622	190	Jan. 16, 1889
Europe	122	50	Seville, Spain	26	8	Aug. 4, 1881
South America	120	49	Rivadavia, Argentina	676	206	Dec. 11, 1905
Antarctica	59	15	Vanda Station, Scott Coast	49	15	Jan. 5, 1974

LOWEST MEASURED TEMPERATURE

Continent or Region	Temperature (degrees Fahrenheit)	Temperature (degrees Celsius)	Place	Elevation (ft)	Elevation (m)	Date
Antarctica	−129.0	−89	Vostok	11,220	3,420	July 21, 1983
Asia	−90.0	−68	Oimekon, Russia	2,625	800	Feb. 6, 1933
Asia	−90.0	−68	Verkhoyansk, Russia	350	107	Feb. 7, 1892
Greenland	−87.0	−66	Northice	7,687	2,343	Jan. 9, 1954
North America	−81.4	−63	Snag, Yukon, Canada	2,120	646	Feb. 3, 1947
Europe	−67.0	−55	Ust'-Shchugor, Russia	279	85	Jan.*
South America	−27.0	−33	Sarmiento, Argentina	879	268	June 1, 1907
Africa	−11.0	−24	Ifrane, Morocco	5,364	1,635	Feb. 11, 1935
Australia	−9.4	−23	Charlotte Pass, New South Wales	5,758	1,755	June 29, 1994
Oceania	14.0	−10	Haleakala Summit, Maui, Hawaii	9,750	2,972	Jan. 2, 1961

* Exact day and year unknown.

World Facts and Figures

PRECIPITATION AND DESERTS

HIGHEST AVERAGE ANNUAL PRECIPITATION

Continent or Region	Precipitation (in)	Precipitation (mm)	Place	Elevation (ft)	Elevation (m)	Years of Data
South America	523.6[1,2]	13,300[1,2]	Lloro, Colombia	520[3]	158[3]	29
Asia	467.4[1]	11,870[1]	Mawsynram, India	4,597	1,401	38
Oceania	460.0[1]	11,680[1]	Mt. Waialeale, Kauai, Hawaii	5,148	1,569	30
Africa	405.0	10,290	Debundscha, Cameroon	30	9	32
South America	354.0[2]	8,992[2]	Quibdo, Colombia	120	37	16
Australia	340.0	8,636	Bellenden Ker, Queensland	5,102	1,555	9
North America	256.0	6,502	Henderson Lake, British Columbia	12	4	14
Europe	183.0	4,648	Crkvica, Bosnia-Herzegovina	3,337	1,017	22

[1]The value given is continent's highest and possibly the world's depending on measurement practices, procedures, and period of record variations.

[2]The official greatest average annual precipitation for South America is 354 in (8,992 mm) at Quibdo, Colombia. The 523.6 in (13,300 mm) average at Lloro, Colombia (14 mi [23 km] SE and at a higher elevation than Quibdo) is an estimated amount.

[3]Approximate elevation.

LOWEST AVERAGE ANNUAL PRECIPITATION

Continent or Region	Precipitation (in)	Precipitation (mm)	Place	Elevation (ft)	Elevation (m)	Years of Data
South America	0.03	0.8	Arica, Chile	95	29	59
Africa	< 0.1	< 3	Wadi Halfa, Sudan	410	125	39
Antarctica	0.8[1]	20[1]	Amundsen-Scott South Pole Station	9,186	2,800	10
North America	1.2	30	Batagues, Mexico	16	5	14
Asia	1.8	46	Aden, Yemen	22	7	50
Australia	4.05	103	Mulka (Troudaninna), South Australia	160[2]	49[2]	42
Europe	6.4	163	Astrakhan, Russia	45	14	25
Oceania	8.93	227	Puako, Hawaii	5	2	13

[1]The value given is the average amount of solid snow accumulating in one year as indicated by snow markers. The liquid content of the snow is undetermined.

[2]Approximate elevation.

NOTABLE DESERTS OF THE WORLD

Arabian (Eastern), 70,000 sq mi (181,000 sq km) in Egypt between the Nile River and Red Sea, extending southward into Sudan

Chihuahuan, 140,000 sq mi (363,000 sq km) in Texas, New Mexico, Arizona, and Mexico

Gibson, 120,000 sq mi (311,000 sq km) in the interior of Western Australia

Gobi, 500,000 sq mi (1,295,000 sq km) in Mongolia and China

Great Sandy, 150,000 sq mi (388,000 sq km) in Western Australia

Great Victoria, 150,000 sq mi (388,000 sq km) in South and Western Australia

Kalahari, 225,000 sq mi (583,000 sq km) in southern Africa

Kara Kum, 120,000 sq mi (311,000 sq km) in Turkmenistan

Kyzyl Kum, 100,000 sq mi (259,000 sq km) in Kazakhstan and Uzbekistan

Libyan, 450,000 sq mi (1,165,000 sq km) in the Sahara, extending from Libya through southwestern Egypt into Sudan

Nubian, 100,000 sq mi (259,000 sq km) in the Sahara in northeastern Sudan

Patagonia, 300,000 sq mi (777,000 sq km) in southern Argentina

Rub al-Khali (Empty Quarter), 250,000 sq mi (648,000 sq km) in the southern Arabian Peninsula

Sahara, 3,500,000 sq mi (9,065,000 sq km) in northern Africa, extending westward to the Atlantic; largest desert in the world

Sonoran, 70,000 sq mi (181,000 sq km) in southwestern Arizona and southeastern California extending into northwestern Mexico

Syrian, 100,000 sq mi (259,000 sq km) arid wasteland extending over much of northern Saudi Arabia, eastern Jordan, southern Syria, and western Iraq

Taklimakan, 140,000 sq mi (363,000 sq km) in Xinjiang Province, China

Thar (Great Indian), 100,000 sq mi (259,000 sq km) arid area extending 400 mi (640 km) along the India-Pakistan border

LANGUAGES, POPULATION GROWTH, AND OIL AND GAS RESERVES

TOP TEN LANGUAGES

Language	Major Countries Where Spoken	Native Speakers
Mandarin	China, Taiwan	874,000,000
Hindi	India	366,000,000
English	U.S., Canada, Britain	341,000,000
Spanish	Spain, Latin America	322,000,000
Arabic	Arabian Peninsula	207,000,000
Bengali	India, Bangladesh	207,000,000
Portuguese	Portugal, Brazil	176,000,000
Russian	Russia	167,000,000
Japanese	Japan	125,000,000
German	Germany, Austria	100,000,000

WORLD POPULATION THROUGH HISTORY

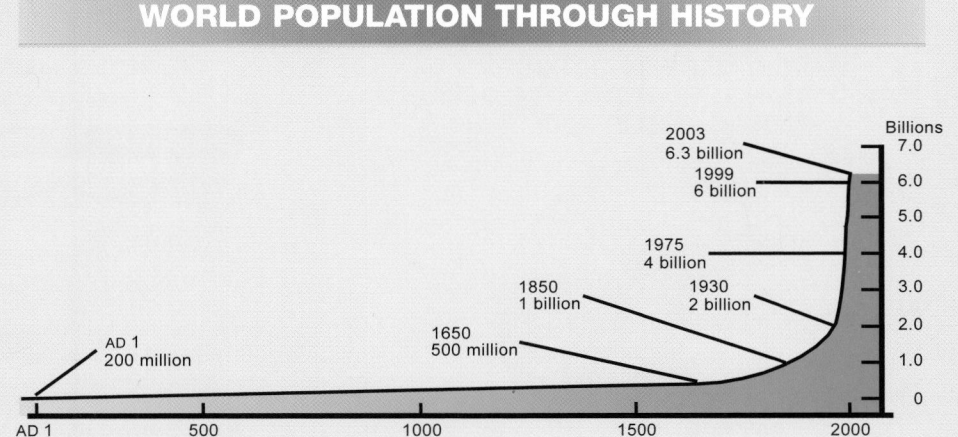

PRINCIPAL KNOWN CRUDE OIL AND NATURAL GAS RESERVES, JAN. 1, 2002

	Crude Oil (billion barrels)		Natural Gas (trillion cubic feet)			Crude Oil (billion barrels)		Natural Gas (trillion cubic feet)	
	OGJ	WO	OGJ	WO		OGJ	WO	OGJ	WO
NORTH AMERICA					Iraq	112.5	115.0	109.8	112.6
Canada	4.9	5.4	59.7	59.7	Kuwait	96.5	98.8	52.7	56.6
Mexico	26.9	23.1	29.5	39.0	Oman	5.5	5.9	29.3	30.5
United States	22.4	22.4	183.5	183.5	Qatar	15.2	13.8	508.5	757.7
SOUTH AMERICA					Saudi Arabia	261.8	261.7	219.5	228.2
Argentina	3.0	2.9	27.5	26.8	United Arab Emirates	97.8	62.8	212.1	204.1
Trinidad and Tobago	0.7	0.7	23.5	19.7	**AFRICA**				
Venezuela	77.7	50.2	147.6	149.2	Algeria	9.2	17.0	159.7	175.0
WESTERN EUROPE					Egypt	2.9	3.7	35.2	54.1
Netherlands	0.1	0.1	62.5	57.0	Libya	29.5	30.0	46.4	46.9
Norway	9.4	10.3	44.0	77.2	Nigeria	24.0	30.0	124.0	159.0
United Kingdom	4.9	4.6	26.0	24.5	**ASIA AND OCEANIA**				
EASTERN EUROPE AND FORMER USSR					Australia	3.5	3.8	90.0	80.0
Kazakhstan	5.4	NA	65.0	NA	China	24.0	29.5	48.3	42.8
Russia	48.6	53.9	1,680.0	1,700.0	India	4.8	3.8	22.9	15.4
Turkmenistan	0.5	NA	101.0	NA	Indonesia	5.0	9.2	92.5	87.5
Ukraine	0.4	NA	39.6	NA	Malaysia	3.0	4.5	75.0	82.5
Uzbekistan	0.6	NA	66.2	NA	Pakistan	0.3	0.3	25.1	24.1
MIDDLE EAST					**WORLD**				
Iran	89.7	99.1	812.3	939.4	TOTAL	1,032.0	1,018.7	5,457.1	5,930.2

OGJ = *Oil and Gas Journal*, Dec. 2001

WO = *World Oil*, Aug. 2002

NOTE: Data for Kuwait and Saudi Arabia include one-half of the reserves in the Neutral Zone between Kuwait and Saudi Arabia. All reserve figures except those for the former USSR and natural gas reserves in Canada are *proved reserves* recoverable with present technology and prices at the time of estimation. Former USSR and Canadian natural gas figures include *proved* and some *probable reserves*.

World Facts and Figures

CARBON DIOXIDE EMISSION, AND MAJOR ENERGY USERS AND PRODUCERS

WORLD CARBON DIOXIDE EMISSIONS FROM THE USE OF FOSSIL FUELS, 2001

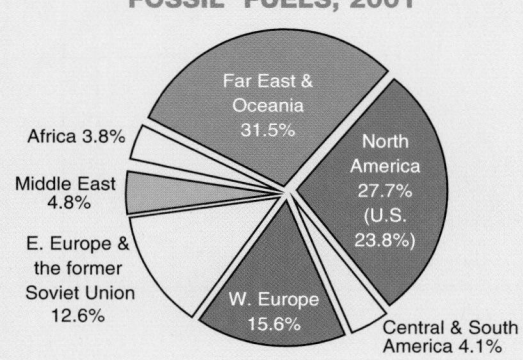

- Far East & Oceania 31.5%
- North America 27.7% (U.S. 23.8%)
- Africa 3.8%
- Middle East 4.8%
- E. Europe & the former Soviet Union 12.6%
- W. Europe 15.6%
- Central & South America 4.1%

NATIONS MOST RELIANT ON NUCLEAR ENERGY, 2002
(nuclear energy generation as % of total electricity generated)

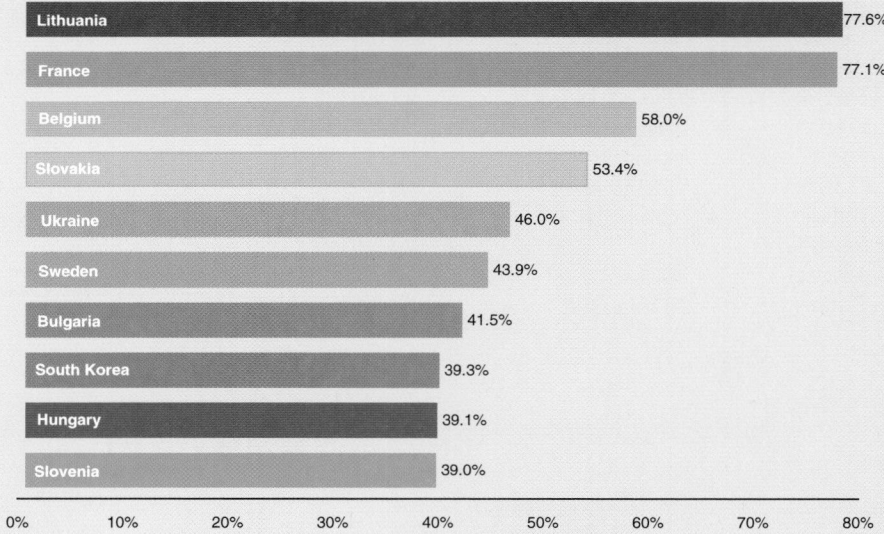

Country	%
Lithuania	77.6%
France	77.1%
Belgium	58.0%
Slovakia	53.4%
Ukraine	46.0%
Sweden	43.9%
Bulgaria	41.5%
South Korea	39.3%
Hungary	39.1%
Slovenia	39.0%

0% 10% 20% 30% 40% 50% 60% 70% 80%

WORLD'S MAJOR PRODUCERS OF PRIMARY ENERGY, 2001
(quadrillion Btu)

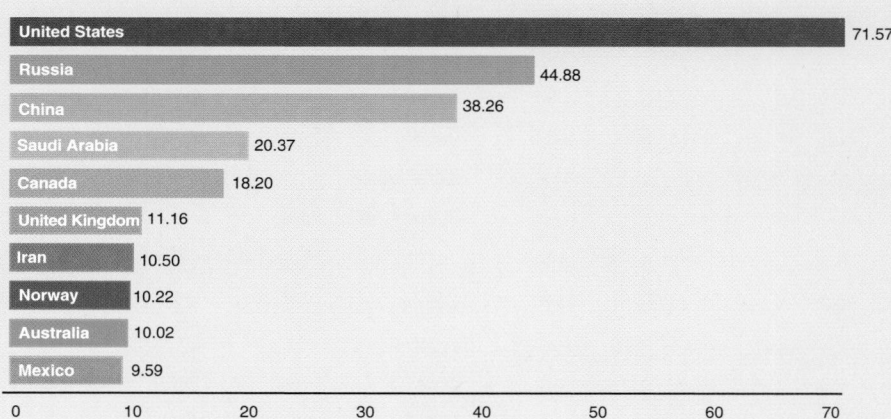

Country	quadrillion Btu
United States	71.57
Russia	44.88
China	38.26
Saudi Arabia	20.37
Canada	18.20
United Kingdom	11.16
Iran	10.50
Norway	10.22
Australia	10.02
Mexico	9.59

0 10 20 30 40 50 60 70

WORLD'S MAJOR CONSUMERS OF PRIMARY ENERGY, 2001
(quadrillion Btu)

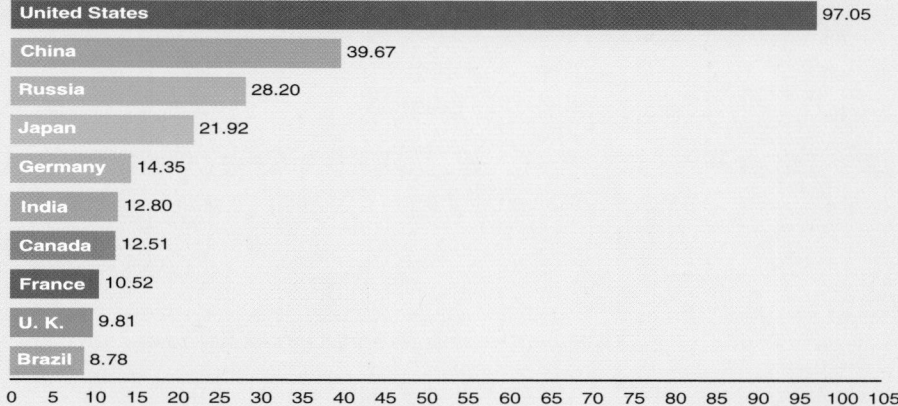

Country	quadrillion Btu
United States	97.05
China	39.67
Russia	28.20
Japan	21.92
Germany	14.35
India	12.80
Canada	12.51
France	10.52
U. K.	9.81
Brazil	8.78

0 5 10 15 20 25 30 35 40 45 50 55 60 65 70 75 80 85 90 95 100 105

THE WORLD ALMANAC®
WORLD ATLAS

World
Map Section

World

Continents

Regions / Nations

ARCTIC OCEAN

80°

Beaufort
Sea

Barrow · Pt. Barrow

GREENLAND
(KALAALLIT NUNAAT)
(DEN.)

Ellesmere I.

ASIA
CHUKCHI
SEA

Nome

ALASKA
(U.S.)

Mt. McKinley
20,320 ft. (6,194 m)
Bethel

Anchorage

Fairbanks

Whitehorse

Inuvik

Victoria I.

Yellowknife

Great Bear L.

Arctic Circle

Upernavik

Baffin
Bay

Baffin
I.

Sisimiut

Iqaluit

Nuuk

C. Chidley

Ammassalik

Qaqortoq

Reykjavik

ICELAND

Faroe Is.
(DEN.)

60°

BERING SEA

Gulf of
Alaska

Juneau

Prince Rupert

Rocky Mountains

Edmonton

Calgary

Great Slave L.

Rankin Inlet

Hudson
Bay

Churchill

Nelson

LABRADOR

Kap Farvel

ALEUTIAN IS.

Vancouver
Seattle
C. Flattery
Portland

Spokane

Great Falls

Boise

Saskatoon

Regina

Great
Plains

Winnipeg

L. Winnipeg

CANADA

Moosonee

Happy Valley -
Goose Bay

Newfoundland

St. John's
C. Race
ST. PIERRE & MIQUELON
(FR.)

SEA

NORTH

Halifax

IRELAND
C. Clear

EUROP

NORTH

Missouri

Great
Lakes

Ottawa

Québec

Montréal

Toronto

Boston

C. Fisterra

ATLANTIC

Porto
PORTUGAL

40°

NORTH

Salt Lake City

C. Mendocino

Sacramento
San Francisco

Reno

Denver

Nevada

Las
Vegas

UNITED

STATES

Minneapolis
Duluth

Fargo

Kansas
City

Cheyenne

Arkansas

St. Louis

Chicago

Indianapolis

Detroit

Cleveland

Cincinnati

Nashville

Appalachian

Mississippi

Philadelphia
Washington

New York

Norfolk

NORTH

AMERICA

AZORES
(PORT.)

Lisbon

OCEAN

Casablanca

MOROC

Los Angeles

San Diego

Tijuana

Albuquerque

Phoenix

El Paso

Memphis

Dallas

San
Antonio

Houston

New
Orleans

Savannah

C. Hatteras

C. Canaveral

Bermuda
(U.K.)

Madeira
(PORT.)

Marrakech

PACIFIC

Chihuahua

Torreón

MEXICO

Monterrey

Tampa
Gulf of Mexico

Miami

BAHAMAS

West Indies

Tropic of Cancer

CANARY IS.
(SP.)

WESTERN
SAHARA
(Mor.)

20°

I. Guadalupe
(MEX.)

Midway Is.

French
Frigate Shoals

HAWAIIAN ISLANDS

C. Falso

Guadalajara

Revillagigedo
(MEX.)

León

Tampico

Veracruz

Mérida

Havana

Greater Antilles

HAITI

DOMINICAN
REP.

Puerto Rico (U.S.)

MAURITANIA

Nouakchott

CAPE
VERDE

Saint-Louis

Honolulu

Hawaii

Johnston Atoll
(U.S.)

OCEAN

I. Clarion

Mexico

GUATEMALA
Guatemala
EL SALVADOR

Tegucigalpa

BELIZE
HONDURAS

JAMAICA

Caribbean

ANTIGUA AND BARBUDA
DOMINICA

Lesser
Antilles

BARBADOS

C. Verde

Dakar

GAMBIA

GUINEA-BISSAU

SENE

GUINEA

5

Clipperton I.
(FR.)

Managua

San José

NICARAGUA

COSTA RICA

Panama

PANAMA

SEA

Barranquilla

GRENADA

Caracas

TRINIDAD AND TOBAGO

Conakry

Freetown

SIERRA LEONE

Monrovia

LIBERIA

Palmyra (U.S.)

Teraina (Washington I.)

Tabuaeran (Fanning I.)

Kiritimati (Christmas I.)

Equator

Galápagos Is.
(ECU.)

ECUADOR

Quito

Guayaquil

Maracaibo

Medellín

Cali

COLOMBIA

Bogotá

VENEZUELA

Boa
Vista

GUYANA

Georgetown

SURINAME

Paramaribo

Cayenne

FRENCH GUIANA

St. Peter & St. Paul Rocks
(BRAZ.)

Equator

0°

Howland I. (U.S.)

Baker I. (U.S.)

Jarvis I. (U.S.)

LINE ISLANDS

International Date Line

Malden I.

Starbuck I.

Iquitos

Amazon

Manaus

Belém

São Luís

Fortaleza

C. de São Roque

Fernando de Noronha
(BRAZ.)

Natal

Ascension
(ST. IL.)

PHOENIX
IS.

KIRIBATI

6

Atafu

TOKELAU IS.
(N.Z.)

Fakaofo

Nuku Hiva

MARQUESAS IS.

Hiva Oa
Atuona

FRENCH

Punta Aguja

Trujillo

PERU

Porto
Velho

Rio
Branco

Selvas

BRAZIL

Recife

Mata
Utu

Wallis Is. (FR.)

Manihiki

Nassau

Suwarrow

Puka Puka

Rangiroa

Caroline I.

Flint I.

Disappointment Is.

Lima

Cusco

BOLIVIA

Cuiabá

Goiânia

Brasília

Salvador

SOUTH

St. Helena
(U.K.)

FUTUNA

SAMOA

Pago Pago
AMER.
SAMOA
(U.S.)

Apia

Niue
(N.Z.)

COOK
ISLANDS
(N.Z.)

Palmerston
Atoll

Manihiki

Uturoa

SOCIETY IS.

Papeete
Tahiti

Takatoto

Reao

POLYNESIA

Hikueru

Arequipa

La Paz

Sucre

Santa Cruz

PARAGUAY

Belo Horizonte

AMERICA

Rio de Janeiro

SOUTH

TONGA

Nuku'alofa

Rarotonga

Mangaia

Tubuai

TUBUAI IS.

Mururoa

GAMBIER IS.

Rikitea

Henderson I. (U.K.)

Iquique

Antofagasta

CHILE

Asunción

Paraná

Pilcomayo

Curitiba

São Paulo

C. Frio
Santos

ATLANT

20°

Tonga-
tapu

Rapa I.
(FR.)

Bass Is.

Oeno I.
(U.K.)

Pitcairn I.
(U.K.)

Ducie I. (U.K.)

Easter I.
(CHILE)

PITCAIRN IS.
(U.K.)

Sala y Gomez
(CHILE)

Tropic of Capricorn

La Serena

San Miguel
de Tucumán

Córdoba

Rosario

Porto Alegre

Is. Martín Vaz
(BRAZ.)

OCEAN

7

Kermadec Is.
(N.Z.)

International Date Line

SOUTH PACIFIC OCEAN

Cerro Aconcagua 6,959 m

Valparaíso

Is. Juan Fernández
(CHILE)

Mendoza

Santiago

Concepción

Buenos Aires
La Plata

URUGUAY

Montevideo

Pampas

R. de la Plata

ARGENTINA

St. Helena

40°

Chatham Is.
(N.Z.)

Valdivia

Bahía Blanca

Viedma

Tristan

Gou

8

Comodoro Rivadavia

C. Tres Puntas

Punta Arenas

Tierra
del Fuego

Cape Horn

Stanley

Falkland Is.
(U.K.)

Drake Passage

S. Georgia
(U.K.)

S. Sandwich Is.
(U.K.)

60°

S. Shetland
Is. (U.K.)

South Orkney Is.
(U.K.)

Antarctic Circle

Antarctic Circle

Peter I Island
(NOR.)

Antarctic
Pen.

WEDDELL SEA

C. Norvegia

9

ROSS SEA

80°

10

POPULATION OF CITIES AND TOWNS

◉ OVER 5,000,000   ◉ 500,000 - 1,999,999
◉ 2,000,000 - 4,999,999   ○ UNDER 500,000

SCALE 1:80,500,000   ROBINSON PROJECTION   STANDARD PARALLELS 38° N and 38° S

MILES   0   1000   2000   3000   4000
KILOMETERS   0   1000   2000   3000   4000

ARCTIC OCEAN

Queen Elizabeth Is.

80°

Beaufort
Sea

Wrangel I.
CHUKCHI
SEA

Pt. Barrow

60°

BERING SEA

Aleutian Is.

ALEUTIAN TRENCH

40°

MENDOCINO FRACTURE ZONE

NORTH

San Francisco

MURRAY FRACTURE ZONE

PACIFIC

20°

HAWAIIAN RIDGE

Hawaiian Is.
Honolulu

MOLOKAI FRACTURE ZONE

OCEAN

CLARION FRACTURE ZONE

CENTRAL
PACIFIC
BASIN

0°

Line Islands

CLIPPERTON FRACTURE ZONE

Equator

Phoenix
Is.

Northern
Cook Is.

Marquesas
Is.

Samoan

Tahiti
Society
Is.

Tuamotu Arch.

Southern
Cook Is.

20°

Tropic of Capricorn

Pitcairn I.

TONGA TRENCH

Tubuai Is.

KERMADEC TRENCH

7

LOUISVILLE RIDGE

SOUTH PACIFIC OCEAN

40°

Chatham Is.

SOUTHWEST
PACIFIC
BASIN

PACIFIC-ANTARCTIC RIDGE

60°

80°

ROSS SEA

9

10

Mt. McKinley
6,194

Yukon

Arctic Circle

Gulf of
Alaska

Vancouver

Seattle

Rocky Mountains

Snake

Great
Basin

Denver

Baja
California

Mexico

Clipperton I.

Galápagos Is.

EAST PACIFIC RISE

Is. Juan Fernández

Victoria I.

Great Bear L.

Great Slave L.

L. Winnipeg

Churchill

NORTH
AMERICA

Great
Plains

Missouri

Chicago

Ohio

Arkansas

Dallas

Mississippi

Rio Grande

Yucatan
Pen.

GUATEMALA
BASIN

MIDDLE-AMERICAN TRENCH

Bogotá

PERU
BASIN

PERU-CHILE TRENCH

NAZCA RIDGE

Sala y Gomez
Easter I.

CHILE
BASIN

Santiago

CHILE RISE

Cerro Aconcagua
6,959 m

Pampas

Devon I.

Ellesmere I.

Baffin
Bay

Baffin
I.

Hudson
Bay

Ungava
Pen.

Great
Lakes

Montreal

Appalachian Mts.

New York

C. Hatteras

Gulf of Mexico

Miami

Bahamas

Cuba

Hispaniola

Greater Antilles

West
Indies

Milwaukee Deep
-8,605 m

CARIBBEAN
SEA

Lesser
Antilles

Trinidad

L. Maracaibo

Llanos

Guiana Highlands

Marajó

Belém

Amazon

Selvas

Madeira

SOUTH
AMERICA

Cordillera de los Andes

Brazilian
Highlands

Gran
Choco

Paraná

R. de la Plata

ARGENTINE
BASIN

Pen.
Valdés

C. Tres Puntas

Str. of Magellan

Cape Horn

Drake Passage

Falkland Is.

Tierra
del Fuego

Antarctic
Pen.

AMUNDSEN ABYSSAL PLAIN

Greenland

Denmark
Str.

Iceland

LABRADOR
SEA

Kap Farvel

ICELAND BASIN

Ireland

Newfoundland

Gulf of
St. Lawrence

C. Race

NORTH

ATLANTIC

MID-ATLANTIC RIDGE

OCEAN

Azores

Tropic of Cancer

Madeira

Canary Is.

Cape Verde Is.

Cape
Verde

BRASIL
BASIN

ROMANCHE FRACTURE ZONE

Ascension

SOUTH

MID-ATLANTIC RIDGE

ATLANTIC

OCEAN

Rio de Janeiro

RIO GRANDE
PLATEAU

Tristan

S. Georgia

Meteor Deep
-8,325 m

S. Sandwich Is.

SCOTIA SEA

S. Shetland

WEDDELL
ABYSSAL
PLAIN

WEDDELL SEA

C. Norvegia

Rabat

Cap Blanc

20° | L 40° | M 60° | N 80° | P 100° | Q 120° | R 140° | S 160° | T 180° |

1

ARCTIC OCEAN
80°

Svalbard
Franz Josef Land
Severnaya Zemlya

New Siberian Is.
2

bergen
Nordkapp
*BARENTS
SEA*
Novaya Zemlya
Kara Sea
Yamal Pen.

Arctic Circle
60°

Kolyma Ra.
BERING SEA

Kiellen
Kola
Pen.
White
Sea
Central
Siberian
Plateau
Yenisey
Tunguska
Lena
Kamchatka
SEA OF
Sakhalin
3
EMPEROR SEAMOUNTS CHAIN

L. Ladoga
West
Siberian
Plain
Ob
OKHOTSK
Kuril Is.

Moscow
Baltic Sea
Ural Mountains
NORTHWEST
PACIFIC
BASIN
40°

EUROPE
Kirgiz Steppe
A S I A
Irtysh
Altai Mts.
Hokkaidō
NORTH

Carpathians
Dnepr
Volga
Aral
Sea
L. Balkhash
Tian Shan
Gobi Desert
Sea
of
Japan
Honshū

Black Sea
Caucasus
El'brus
5,642 m
Caspian Sea
Amu Darya
Beijing
Huang
Tōkyō
20°

İstanbul
Taurus Mts.
Zagros Mts.
Takla
Makan
Kunlun Mts.
Yellow
Sea
PACIFIC

MEDITERRANEAN SEA
Sicily
Cyprus
Tehran
Hindu Kush
Himalaya
Mt. Everest
8,848 m
Salween
East
China
Sea
RYUKYU TRENCH
Ryūkyū Is.
4

Rome
Euphrates
Tigris
Indus
Ganges
Chang
Taiwan
Tropic of Cancer

Cairo
Red Sea
Persian Gulf
Karachi
Narmada
SOUTH
PHILIPPINE
Mariana Is.
OCEAN

hara
Nile
Hejaz
Arabian
Pen.
Rub' al Khali
Mumbai
(Bombay)
BAY
OF
BENGAL
CHINA
Luzon
Manila
PHILIPPINE
BASIN
Challenger Deep
–11,033 m
CENTRAL
PACIFIC
20°

Sudan
AFRICA
ARABIAN
SEA
C. Comorin
Hainan
SEA
Mindanao
MARIANA TRENCH
Marshall
Is.
BASIN
5

L. Chad
Socotra
Gulf of Aden
Maldive
Is.
Sri Lanka
Andaman
Is.
Isthmus
of Kra
Palawan
Sulu
Sea
Celebes
Sea
Caroline Is.
MELANESIAN

Ethiopian
Plateau
CARLSBERG RIDGE
Malay
Pen.
Halmahera
Bismarck Arch.
BASIN

Blue Nile
White Nile
SOMALI
BASIN
Equator
Chagos
Arch.
INDIAN
Sumatra
Borneo
Celebes
Banda Sea
New
Guinea
New
Britain
Solomon
Is.
0°

oko
Congo
Congo
Basin
Kilimanjaro
5,895 m
Seychelles
OCEAN
JAVA TRENCH
Jakarta
Java Sea
Java
–7,450 m
Timor
Sea
Arafura
Sea
Torres Str.
Cape York
Pen.
CORAL
New
Hebrides
6

Kinshasa
L. Victoria
Tanganyika
Comoros
Is.
Cocos Is.
Gulf
of
Carpentaria
SEA
Fiji Is.

GOLA
SIN
Lusaka
Zambezi
L. Nyasa
Madagascar
Réunion
Mauritius
Great Victoria
Desert
New
Caledonia
20°

RIDGE
Namib Desert
Orange
Johannesburg
Mozambique Chan.
BROKEN
PLATEAU
AUSTRALIA
Darling
Great
Dividing Ra.
Sydney
North C.
7

Drakensberg
SOUTHWEST INDIAN RIDGE
C. Leeuwin
Great
Australian
Bight
Murray
Mt. Kosciusko
2,228 m
TASMAN
North I.

Cape of Good Hope
SOUTHEAST
INDIAN
Melbourne
Great
SEA
40°

Kerguélen
McDonald Is.
KERGUÉLEN
PLATEAU
AUSTRALIAN-ANTARCTIC BASIN
RIDGE
Tasmania
South I.
8

ENDERBY ABYSSAL PLAIN
60°

C. Batterbee
C. Adare
9

ctic Circle
ROSS SEA

A N T A R C T I C A
80°
10

20° | L 40° | M 60° | N 80° | P 100° | Q 120° | R 140° | S 160° | T 180° |

POPULATION OF CITIES AND TOWNS
- ◉ OVER 5,000,000
- ⊙ 2,000,000 - 4,999,999
- ⊚ 500,000 - 1,999,999
- ○ UNDER 500,000

SCALE 1:80,500,000   ROBINSON PROJECTION   STANDARD PARALLELS 38° N and 38° S

MILES 0   1000   2000   3000   4000
KILOMETERS 0   1000   2000   3000   4000

Europe

The terrain in this high-oblique, northwest-looking image, is indicative of the rugged, mountainous landscape characterizing most of Greece. Two major landform regions are captured in this image: the northwest to southeast-trending Mountains of Pindus in central Greece (north of the Gulf of Corinth), and the Peloponnisos Peninsula (south of the Gulf of Corinth). The Pindus, a massive continuation of the Dinaric Alps of Albania and the former Yugoslavia, make the land inhospitable and travel difficult. This rugged terrain caused the Greeks to become a seafaring people.

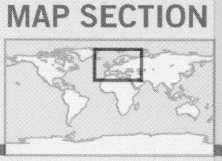
AREA OF OPTIMIZATION The red band which surrounds this map defines the "Area of Optimization." Within this bounding curve is the most accurate conformal map that can be made of the region. Outside the optimized area, distortion increases rapidly, and gaps or other irregularities in the grid may occur. (See page 8 for additional information.)

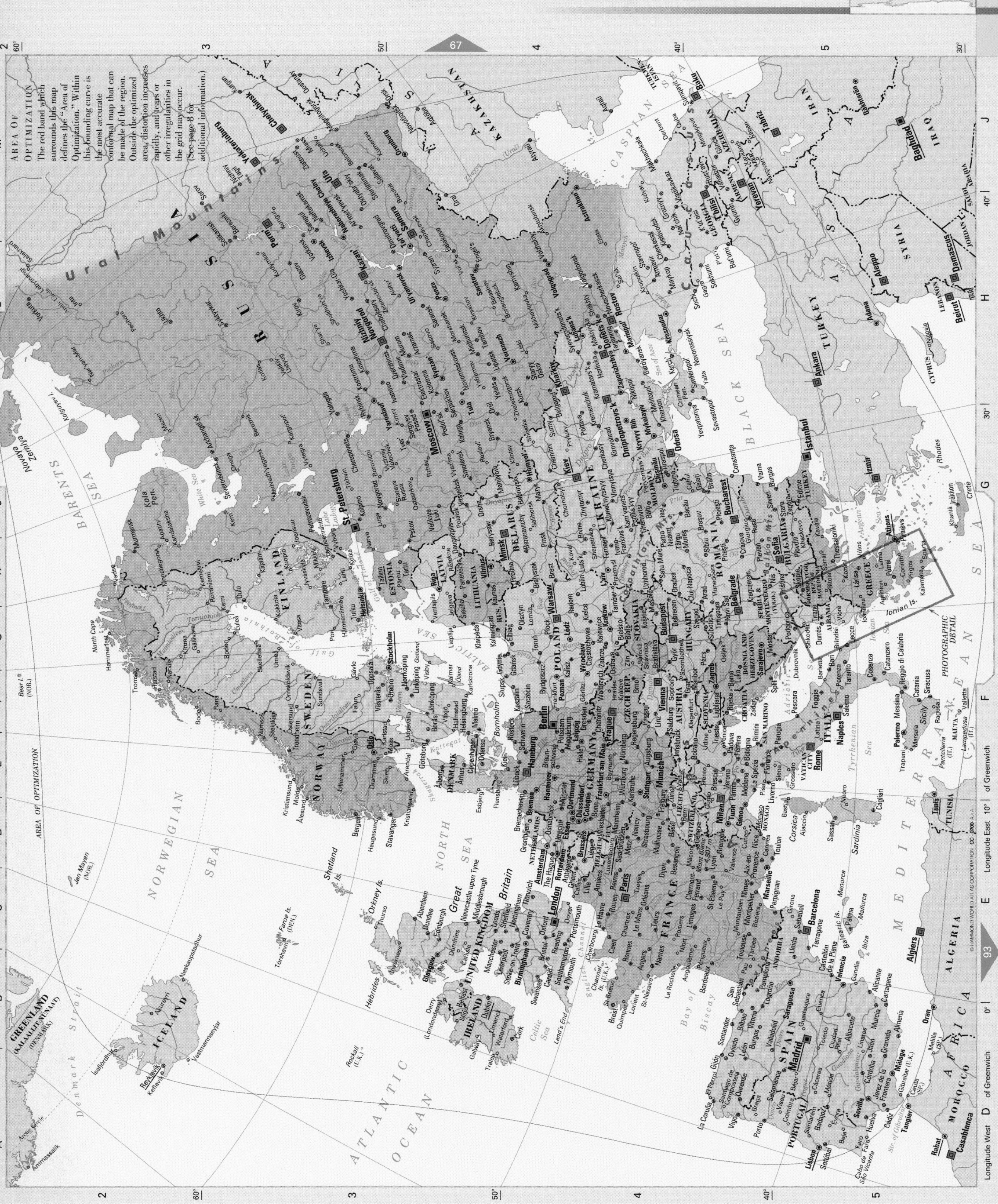

POPULATION OF CITIES AND TOWNS

■ OVER 3,000,000
■ 1,000,000 - 2,999,999
■ 500,000 - 999,999
● 100,000 - 499,999
○ UNDER 100,000

SCALE 1:20,700,000   OPTIMAL CONFORMAL PROJECTION

MILES   0   300   600   900
KILOMETERS   0   300   600   900

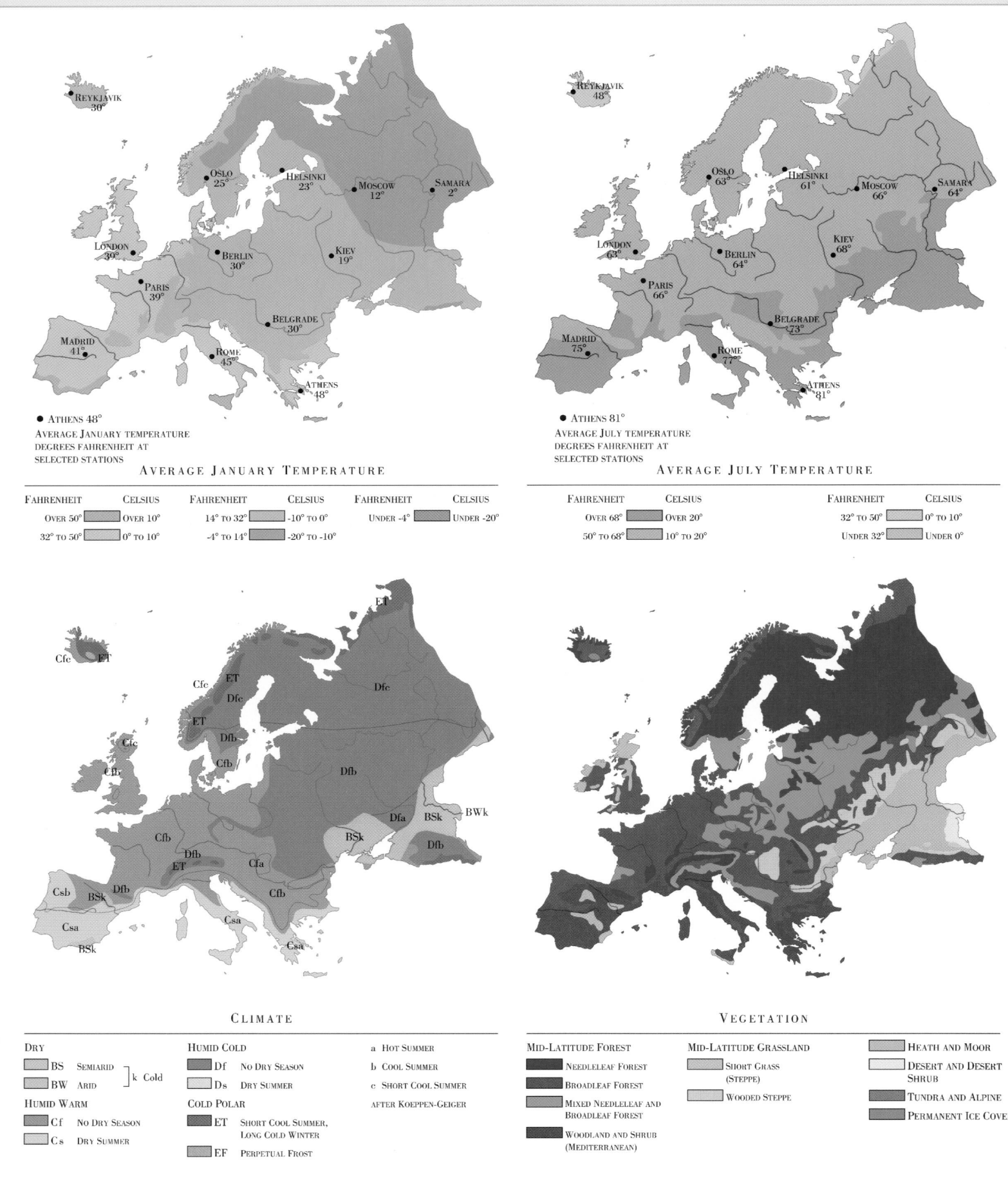

28

REYKJAVIK 30°

OSLO 25° **HELSINKI** 23° **MOSCOW** 12° **SAMARA** 2°

LONDON 39° **BERLIN** 30° **KIEV** 19°

PARIS 39°

BELGRADE 30°

MADRID 41°

ROME 45°

ATHENS 48°

● ATHENS 48°
AVERAGE JANUARY TEMPERATURE
DEGREES FAHRENHEIT AT
SELECTED STATIONS

AVERAGE JANUARY TEMPERATURE

FAHRENHEIT	CELSIUS	FAHRENHEIT	CELSIUS	FAHRENHEIT	CELSIUS
OVER 50°	OVER 10°	14° TO 32°	-10° TO 0°	UNDER -4°	UNDER -20°
32° TO 50°	0° TO 10°	-4° TO 14°	-20° TO -10°		

REYKJAVIK 48°

OSLO 63° **HELSINKI** 61° **MOSCOW** 66° **SAMARA** 64°

LONDON 63° **BERLIN** 64° **KIEV** 68°

PARIS 66°

BELGRADE 73°

MADRID 75°

ROME 77°

ATHENS 81°

● ATHENS 81°
AVERAGE JULY TEMPERATURE
DEGREES FAHRENHEIT AT
SELECTED STATIONS

AVERAGE JULY TEMPERATURE

FAHRENHEIT	CELSIUS	FAHRENHEIT	CELSIUS
OVER 68°	OVER 20°	32° TO 50°	0° TO 10°
50° TO 68°	10° TO 20°	UNDER 32°	UNDER 0°

CLIMATE

DRY
- BS SEMIARID
- BW ARID } k Cold

HUMID WARM
- Cf NO DRY SEASON
- Cs DRY SUMMER

HUMID COLD
- Df NO DRY SEASON
- Ds DRY SUMMER

COLD POLAR
- ET SHORT COOL SUMMER, LONG COLD WINTER
- EF PERPETUAL FROST

a HOT SUMMER
b COOL SUMMER
c SHORT COOL SUMMER

AFTER KOEPPEN-GEIGER

VEGETATION

MID-LATITUDE FOREST
- NEEDLELEAF FOREST
- BROADLEAF FOREST
- MIXED NEEDLELEAF AND BROADLEAF FOREST
- WOODLAND AND SHRUB (MEDITERRANEAN)

MID-LATITUDE GRASSLAND
- SHORT GRASS (STEPPE)
- WOODED STEPPE

- HEATH AND MOOR
- DESERT AND DESERT SHRUB
- TUNDRA AND ALPINE
- PERMANENT ICE COVER

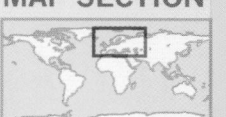
Europe – Geographical Comparisons

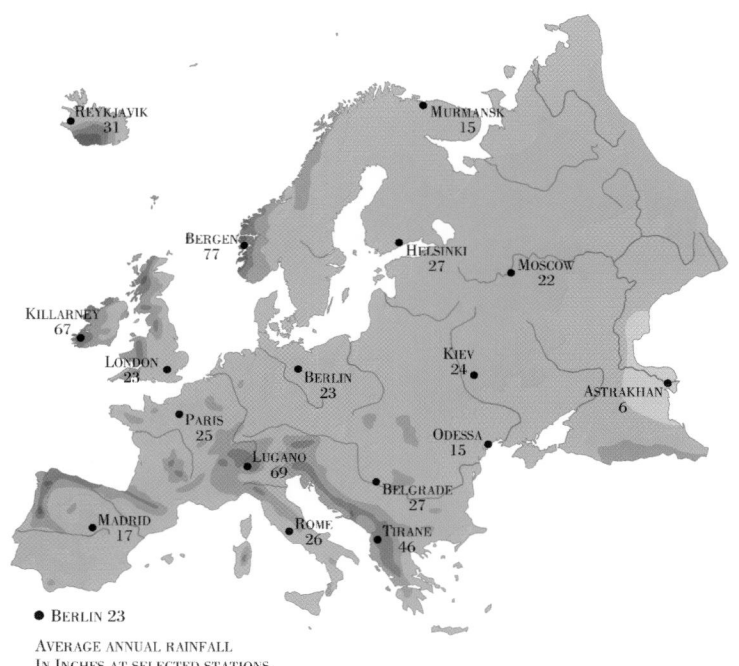

REYKJAVIK
31

MURMANSK
15

BERGEN
77

HELSINKI
27

MOSCOW
22

KILLARNEY
67

LONDON
23

BERLIN
23

KIEV
24

ASTRAKHAN
6

PARIS
25

LUGANO
69

ODESSA
15

BELGRADE
27

MADRID
17

ROME
26

TIRANE
46

● BERLIN 23

AVERAGE ANNUAL RAINFALL
IN INCHES AT SELECTED STATIONS

AVERAGE ANNUAL RAINFALL

INCHES	CM	INCHES	CM	INCHES	CM
OVER 80	OVER 200	40 TO 60	100 TO 150	10 TO 20	25 TO 50
60 TO 80	150 TO 200	20 TO 40	50 TO 100	UNDER 10	UNDER 25

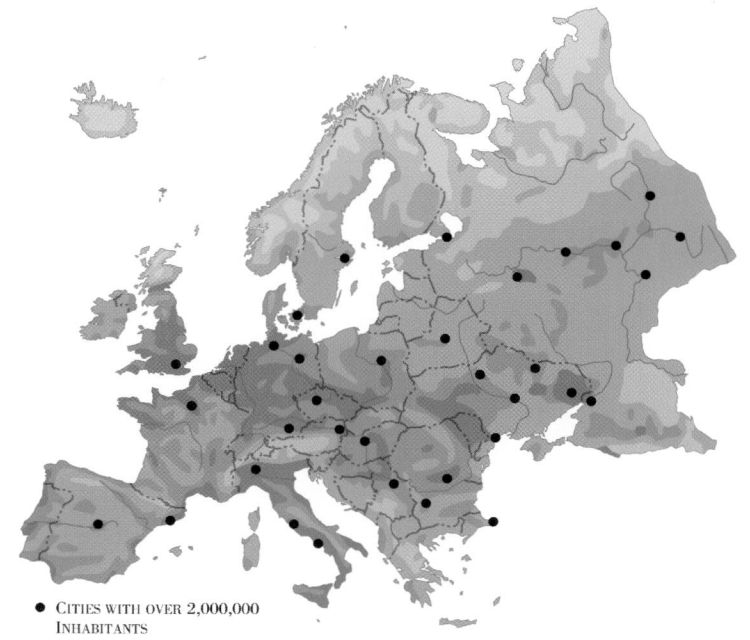

● CITIES WITH OVER 2,000,000
INHABITANTS

POPULATION DISTRIBUTION

DENSITY PER		SQ. MI.	SQ. KM.	SQ. MI.	SQ. KM.
SQ. MI.	SQ. KM.	130 TO 260	50 TO 100	3 TO 25	1 TO 10
OVER 260	OVER 100	25 TO 130	10 TO 50	UNDER 3	UNDER 1

FURS

FURS

FURS

OATS

FLAX

RYE

RYE

WHEAT

HEMP

DAIRY

DAIRY

RYE

POTATOES

RYE

POTATOES

WHEAT

DAIRY

RYE

OATS

HOGS

OATS

RYE

SUGAR BEETS

CATTLE

CORN HOGS

WHEAT

SHEEP

WHEAT

DAIRY

DAIRY

WHEAT

WINE

CORN

BARLEY

WINE

CORN

CORN

TOBACCO

TEA

WINE

WINE

WHEAT

WINE

CORN

SHEEP

TOBACCO

WINE

SHEEP

FRUIT

OLIVES

WINE

OLIVES

LAND USE

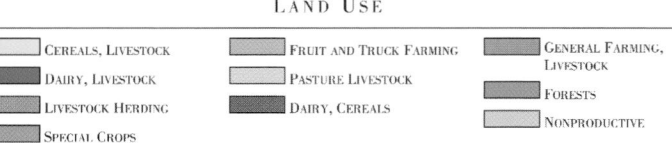

- CEREALS, LIVESTOCK
- DAIRY, LIVESTOCK
- LIVESTOCK HERDING
- SPECIAL CROPS
- FRUIT AND TRUCK FARMING
- PASTURE LIVESTOCK
- DAIRY, CEREALS
- GENERAL FARMING, LIVESTOCK
- FORESTS
- NONPRODUCTIVE

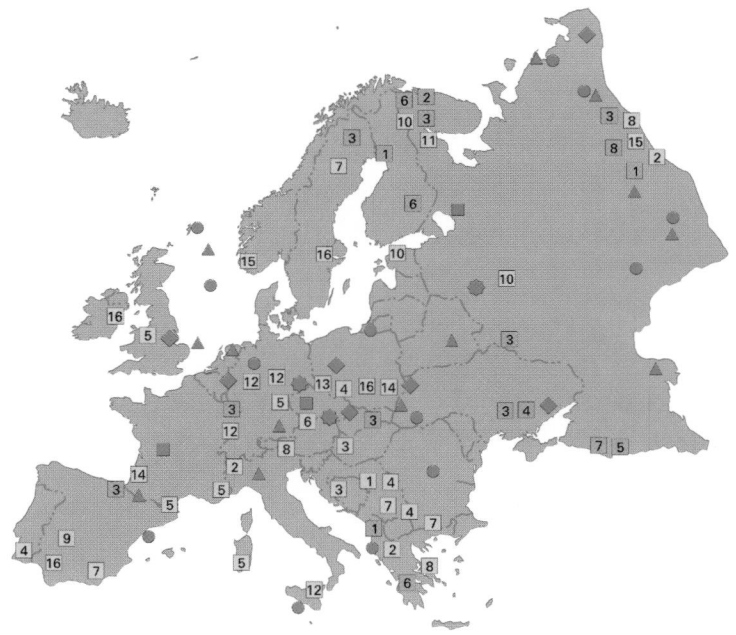

MINERAL RESOURCES

ENERGY & FUELS
- ◆ COAL
- ⬟ LIGNITE
- ▲ NATURAL GAS
- ● PETROLEUM
- ◼ URANIUM

IRON & FERROALLOYS
- 1 CHROMIUM
- 2 COBALT
- 3 IRON ORE
- 4 MANGANESE
- 5 MOLYBDENUM
- 6 NICKEL
- 7 TUNGSTEN
- 8 VANADIUM

OTHER MAJOR RESOURCES
- 1 ANTIMONY
- 2 ASBESTOS
- 3 BAUXITE
- 4 COPPER
- 5 FLORSPAR
- 6 GRAPHITE
- 7 LEAD
- 8 MAGNESITE
- 9 MERCURY
- 10 PHOSPHATES
- 11 PLATINUM
- 12 POTASH
- 13 SILVER
- 14 SULFER
- 15 TITANIUM
- 16 ZINC

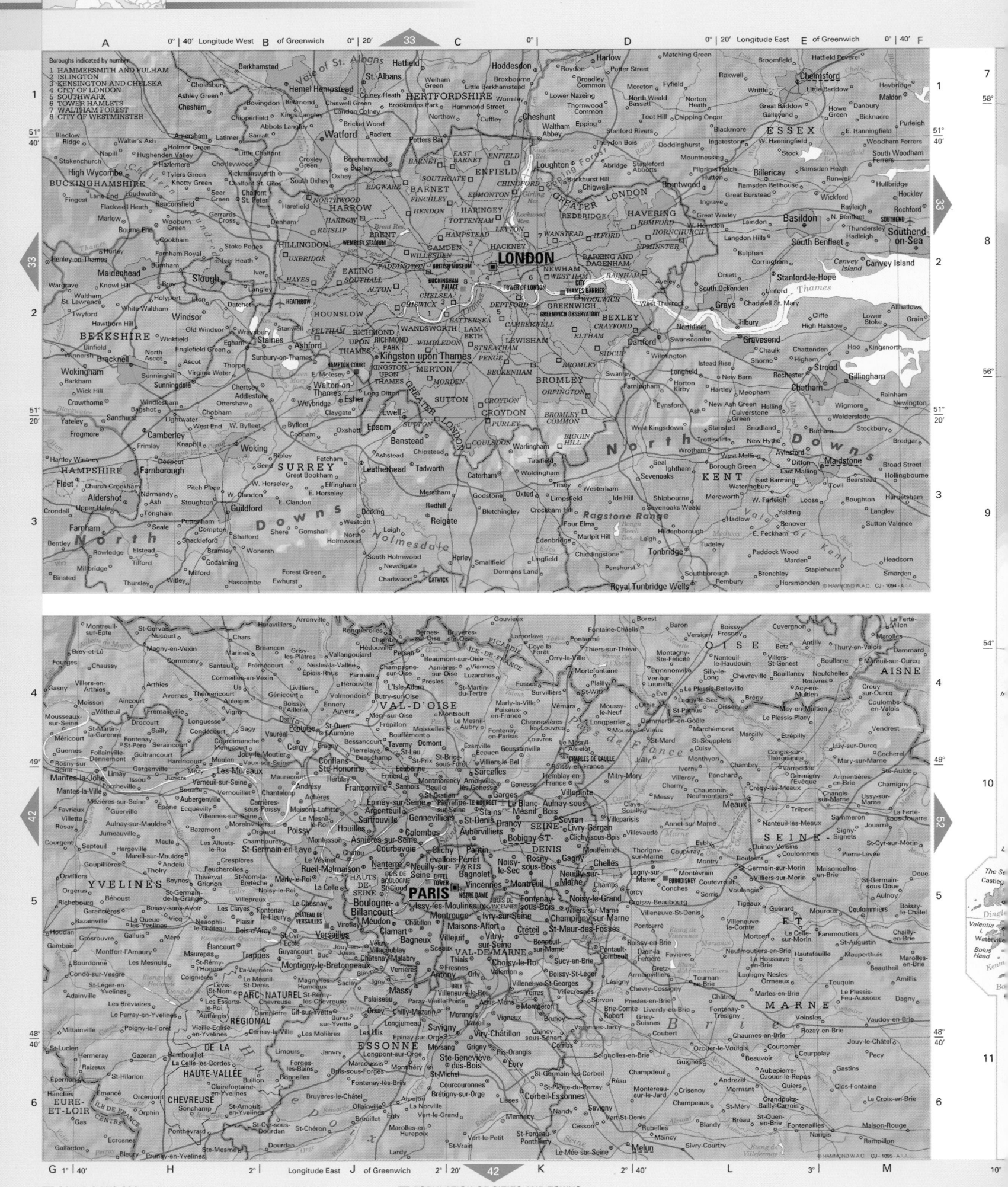

SCALE 1:570,000   LAMBERT CONFORMAL CONIC PROJECTION

MILES   0   10   20
KILOMETERS 0   10   20

POPULATION OF CITIES AND TOWNS
- ■ OVER 2,000,000
- ■ 1,000,000 - 1,999,999
- ● 500,000 - 999,999
- ● 250,000 - 499,999
- ● 100,000 - 249,999
- ● 30,000 - 99,999
- ● 10,000 - 29,999
- ○ UNDER 10,000

POPULATION OF CITIES AND TOWNS

■ OVER 2,000,000 ● 500,000 - 999,999 ● 100,000 - 249,999 ● 10,000 - 29,999
■ 1,000,000 - 1,999,999 ● 250,000 - 499,999 ● 30,000 - 99,999 ○ UNDER 10,000

SCALE 1:1,150,000   LAMBERT CONFORMAL CONIC PROJECTION

MILES 0   10   20   30   40   50
KILOMETERS 0   10   20   30   40   50

POPULATION OF CITIES AND TOWNS

- ■ OVER 2,000,000
- ■ 1,000,000 - 1,999,999
- ● 500,000 - 999,999
- ● 250,000 - 499,999
- ● 100,000 - 249,999
- ● 30,000 - 99,999
- ◉ 10,000 - 29,999
- ○ UNDER 10,000

SCALE 1:1,150,000   LAMBERT CONFORMAL CONIC PROJECTION

MILES 0 10 20 30 40 50

KILOMETERS 0 10 20 30 40 50

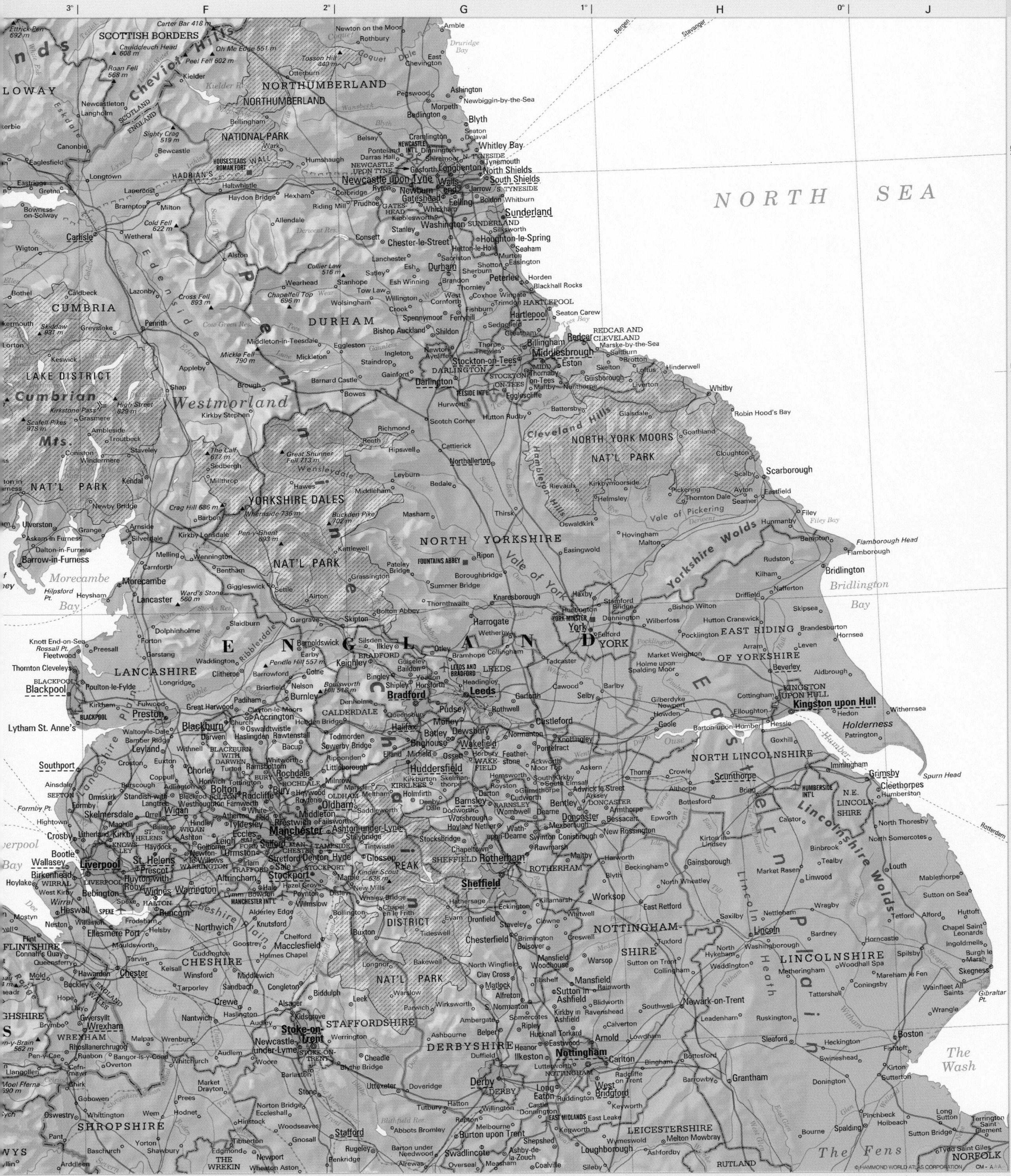

Longitude West of Greenwich

© Hammond World Atlas Corporation

Central Scotland

SCALE 1:1,150,000   LAMBERT CONFORMAL CONIC PROJECTION

MILES

KILOMETERS

POPULATION OF CITIES AND TOWNS

| ■ OVER 2,000,000 | ◉ 500,000 - 999,999 | ⊕ 100,000 - 249,999 | ○ 10,000 - 29,999 |
| □ 1,000,000 - 1,999,999 | ◎ 250,000 - 499,999 | ⊙ 30,000 - 99,999 | ∘ UNDER 10,000 |

SCALE 1:6,900,000   LAMBERT CONFORMAL CONIC PROJECTION

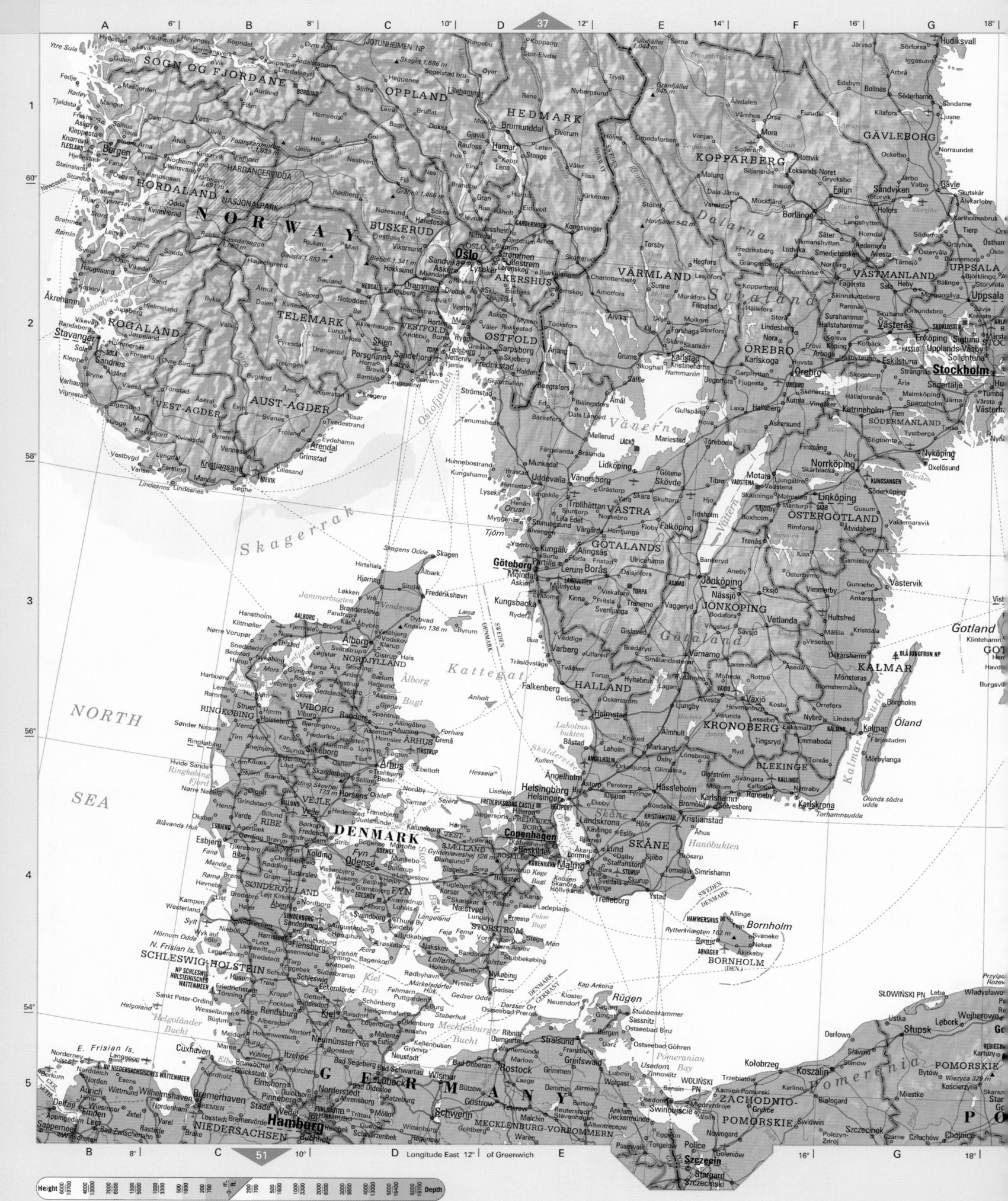

| A | 6° | B | 8° | C | 10° | D | 37 | 12° | E | 14° | F | 16° | G | 18° |

NORWAY

Ytre Sula · Hyllestad · Høyanger · Sogndal · Ringebu · Koppang

SOGN OG FJORDANE · JOTUNHEIMEN NP · Skagan 1,686 m · Fulufjället 1,044 m · Sörforsa · Hudiksvall

Fedje · Radøy · Manger · Hermansverk · Øvre Ardal · Ardalstangen · Øyer · Stor-Elvdal · Trängslet · Järvsö · Iggesund · Arbrå

HORDALAND · Folarskardnuten 1,933 m · BORGUND · Slidre · Bruflat · Rena · Nybergsund · Grönfjället 945 m · Edsbyn · Bollnäs · Söderhamn · Sandarne

OPPLAND · HEDMARK · GÄVLEBORG

N O R W A Y · BUSKERUD · Oslo · AKERSHUS

HARDANGERVIDDA NASJONALPARK · KOPPARBERG · Siljan · Dalarna

TELEMARK · VESTFOLD · ØSTFOLD · VÄRMLAND · VÄSTMANLAND · UPPSALA

ROGALAND · Stavanger · Gausta 1,883 m · SVEALAND · Uppsala

VEST-AGDER · AUST-AGDER · Vänern · ÖREBRO · Stockholm

Kristiansand · SÖDERMANLAND

SKAGERRAK · Vättern · ÖSTERGÖTLAND

NORTH SEA · Vendsyssel · Knøsen 136 m · SWEDEN/DENMARK · Kattegat · GÖTALAND · Jönköping · KALMAR · Gotland · GOT

AALBORG · NORDJYLLAND · Ålborg Bugt · Anholt · HALLAND · BLÅ JUNGFRUN NP · Öland

RINGKØBING · VIBORG · KRONOBERG · Kalmar

ÅRHUS · BLEKINGE

DENMARK · SKÅNE · Hanöbukten

RIBE · VEJLE · Fyn · Odense · STORSTRØM · SJÆLLAND · Copenhagen · Malmö · Kristianstad · Ålands södra udde

SCHLESWIG-HOLSTEIN · BORNHOLM (DEN) · Rügen

G E R M A N Y · POMORSKIE · Pomerania

Hamburg · NIEDERSACHSEN · MECKLENBURG-VORPOMMERN · ZACHODNIO-POMORSKIE · Szczecin · PO

| B | 8° | C | 51 | 10° | D | Longitude East 12° of Greenwich | E | | 16° | G | 18° |

Height 4000 3000 2000 1500 1000 500 200 0 200 500 1000 2000 3000 4000 5000 6000 7000 Depth

Baltic Region

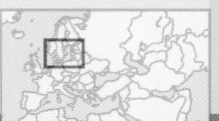

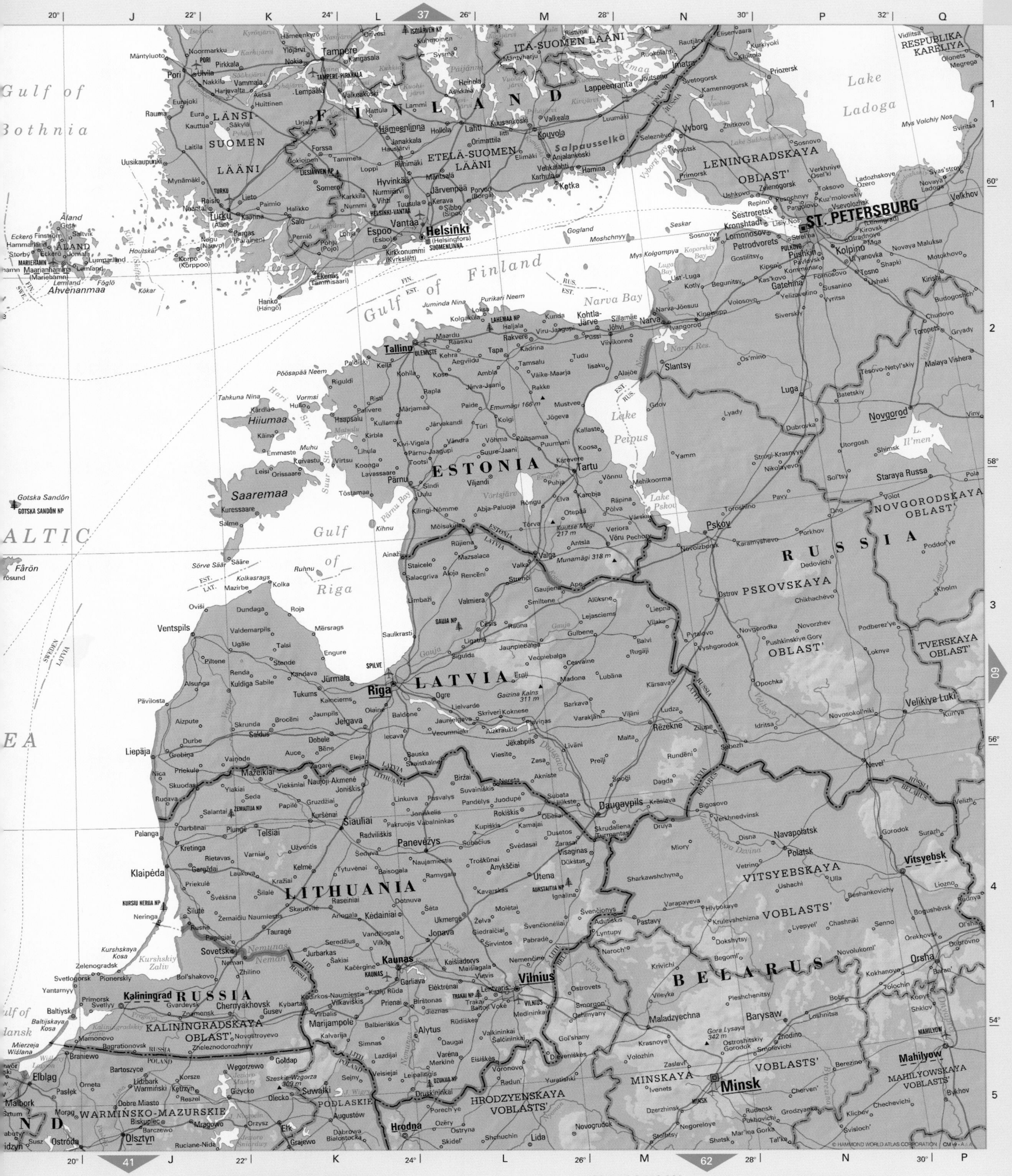

POPULATION OF CITIES AND TOWNS

- OVER 2,000,000
- 1,000,000 - 1,999,999
- 500,000 - 999,999
- 250,000 - 499,999
- 100,000 - 249,999
- 30,000 - 99,999
- 10,000 - 29,999
- UNDER 10,000

SCALE 1:3,450,000 LAMBERT CONFORMAL CONIC PROJECTION

MILES 0 50 100 150

KILOMETERS 0 50 100 150

POPULATION OF CITIES AND TOWNS

- ■ OVER 2,000,000
- ◉ 500,000 - 999,999
- ● 100,000 - 249,999
- ◉ 10,000 - 29,999
- ■ 1,000,000 - 1,999,999
- ◉ 250,000 - 499,999
- ● 30,000 - 99,999
- ○ UNDER 10,000

SCALE 1:3,450,000   LAMBERT CONFORMAL CONIC PROJECTION

MILES 0   50   100   150

KILOMETERS 0   50   100   150

© HAMMOND WORLD ATLAS CORPORATION

POPULATION OF CITIES AND TOWNS

| ■ OVER 2,000,000 | ◉ 500,000 - 999,999 | ● 100,000 - 249,999 | ⊙ 10,000 - 29,999 |
| ▣ 1,000,000 - 1,999,999 | ◉ 250,000 - 499,999 | ● 30,000 - 99,999 | · UNDER 10,000 |

SCALE 1:3,450,000   LAMBERT CONFORMAL CONIC PROJECTION

MILES   0   50   100   150

KILOMETERS   0   50   100   150

© HAMMOND WORLD ATLAS CORPORATION   CM-1015 - A.A.A.

Longitude East 8° of Greenwich

42

F G H J K L

M N P Q

U V

R S T W X Y

POPULATION OF CITIES AND TOWNS

| ■ OVER 2,000,000 | ● 500,000 - 999,999 | ⊕ 100,000 - 249,999 | ⊙ 10,000 - 29,999 |
| □ 1,000,000 - 1,999,999 | ⊛ 250,000 - 499,999 | ⊕ 30,000 - 99,999 | ○ UNDER 10,000 |

SCALE 1:3,450,000   LAMBERT CONFORMAL CONIC PROJECTION

MILES

KILOMETERS

8° A 10° B 43 12° C 14° D 16° E

CROATIA

Supetar

ADRIATIC

Marseille
Nice
Cap Corse
Rogliano
I. di Capraia

TOSCANA
Donoratico

CORSE
Monte Cinto
2,710 m

Corsica
(FRANCE)

Ajaccio

Strait of
Bonifacio

SARDEGNA

Sardinia

Cagliari

TYRRHENIAN

SEA

UMBRIA

Grosseto

LAZIO

ROME

MARCHE

Ancona

ABRUZZI

Pescara

MOLISE

Campobasso

ITALY

Foggia

CAMPANIA

Benevento

Naples
(Napoli)

BASILICATA

Potenza

Bari

PUGLIA

Taranto

CALABRIA

Cosenza

Catanzaro

Messina

Reggio di Calabria

Isole Eolie
(Lipari Islands)

Palermo

Sicily

SICILIA

Catania

Siracusa

MEDITERRANEAN

Strait of Sicily

ITALY
TUNISIA

BIZERTE

Tunis
TUNIS

NABEUL

Cap Bon

TUNISIA

ZAGHOUAN

SILIANA

KAIROUAN

MONASTIR

MAHDIA

SIDI BOU
ZID

Pantelleria

Isola di
Pantelleria
(IT.)

Isole
Pelagie
(IT.)

Linosa
I. di Linosa

Lampedusa
Isola di
Lampedusa

Gozo
Rabat (Victoria)

MALTA

Malta
Valletta

Malta Channel

MALTA

Gozo

Malta

Valletta

Sliema

10° 99 12° Longitude East of Greenwich 14° L 14° 30' M

SCALE 1:3,450,000 LAMBERT CONFORMAL CONIC PROJECTION
MILES
KILOMETERS

POPULATION OF CITIES AND TOWNS

■ OVER 2,000,000	⦿ 500,000 - 999,999	● 100,000 - 249,999	∘ 10,000 - 29,999
▣ 1,000,000 - 1,999,999	⦿ 250,000 - 499,999	∘ 30,000 - 99,999	∘ UNDER 10,000

POPULATION OF CITIES AND TOWNS

▣ OVER 2,000,000	◉ 500,000 - 999,999	⊙ 100,000 - 249,999	⊙ 10,000 - 29,999
▣ 1,000,000 - 1,999,999	◉ 250,000 - 499,999	⊙ 30,000 - 99,999	∘ UNDER 10,000

MILES
KILOMETERS

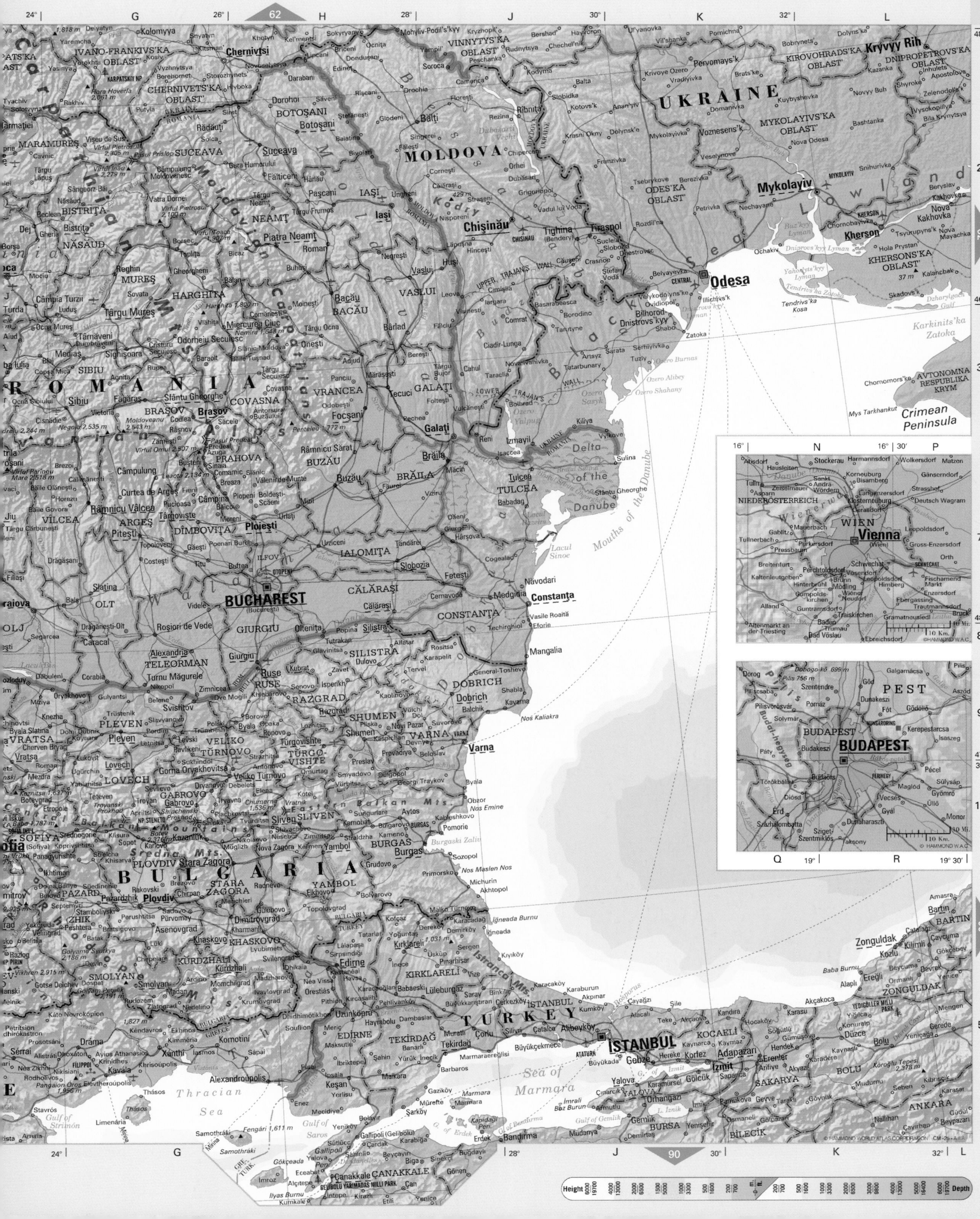

Netherlands, Northwestern Germany

NORTH SEA

West Frisian Islands

Waddenzee

GRONINGEN

FRIESLAND

DRENTHE

IJsselmeer

NOORD-HOLLAND

OVERIJSSEL

FLEVOLAND

Amsterdam

GELDERLAND

UTRECHT

The Hague

ZUID-HOLLAND

Rotterdam

NETHERLAND

ZEELAND

NOORD-BRABANT

LIMBURG

Antwerp (Antwerpen)

ANTWERPEN

BELGIUM

OOST-VLAANDEREN

Düsseldorf

Mönchengladbach

Duisburg

LIMBURG

VLAAMS-BRABANT

A 52   4°   Longitude East of Greenwich   B   5°   C   6°   D 53

Height 6000 19700 4000 13000 2000 6500 1500 5000 1000 3300 500 1600 200 700   0   0   200 700 1000 3300 2000 6500 3000 9900 4000 13000 5000 16400 6000 19700 Depth

38

Scharhörn (HAMBURG)   Neuwerk (HAMBURG)   NP SCHLESWIG-HOLSTEINISCHES WATTENMEER   Brunsbüttel   Wister
NP HAMBURGISCHES WATTENMEER   Cuxhaven   Freiburg   Krempe   Barmstedt   Quickborn   Ahrensburg   Grosshansdorf   Gudow   Zarrentin
Helgoländer   NORDHOLZ   Glückstadt   Elmshorn   Tornesch   Norderstedt   HAMBURG   Glinde   SCHLESWIG   Schwarzenbek
Grosser Knechtsand   Cadenberge   Wischhafen   Pinneberg   Schenefeld   Hamburg   FUHLSBÜTTEL   Trittau   Aumühle   HOLSTEIN   Dassendorf   Büchen
risian Islands   Wangeroog   Wangerooge   Minsener Oog   Oldoog   Mellum   NP NIEDERSÄCHSISCHES WATTENMEER   Nordholz   Otterndorf   Drochtersen   Stade   Appen   Holm   Wedel   Ostenstedt   Reinbek   Börnsen   MECKLENBURG-VORPOMMERN

Helgoländer
Bucht   Jade   Weser   Elbe

POPULATION OF CITIES AND TOWNS

■ OVER 2,000,000   ● 500,000 - 999,999   ◎ 100,000 - 249,999   ○ 10,000 - 29,999
□ 1,000,000 - 1,999,999   ◉ 250,000 - 499,999   ⊙ 30,000 - 99,999   ○ UNDER 10,000

SCALE 1:1,150,000   LAMBERT CONFORMAL CONIC PROJECTION

MILES   0   10   20   30   40   50
KILOMETERS   0   10   20   30   40   50

Belgium, Northern France, Western Germany

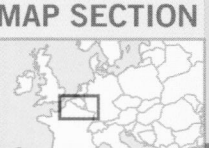

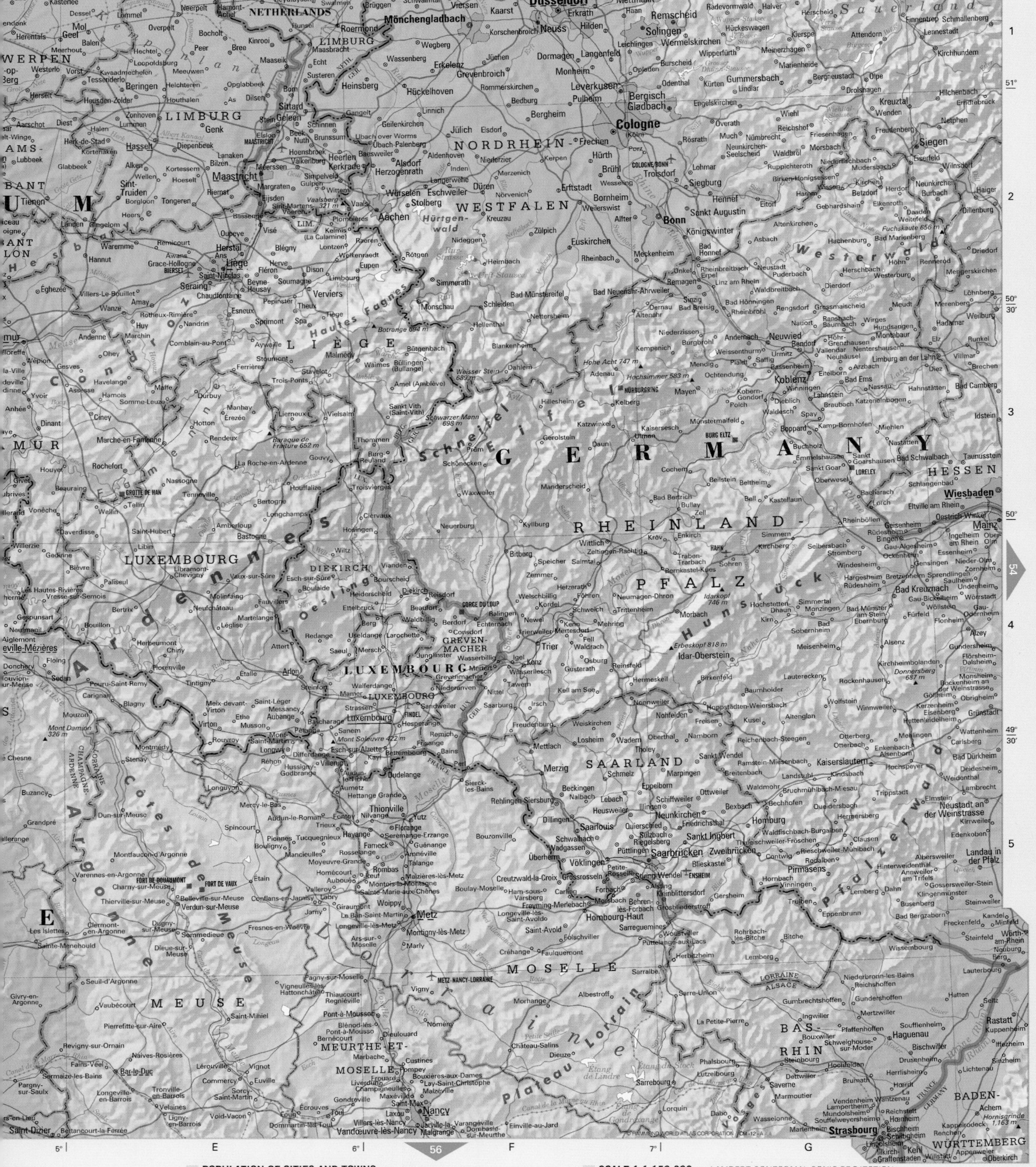

POPULATION OF CITIES AND TOWNS

■ OVER 2,000,000	⊙ 500,000 - 999,999	⊕ 100,000 - 249,999
▣ 1,000,000 - 1,999,999	◎ 250,000 - 499,999	⊘ 30,000 - 99,999
⊙ 10,000 - 29,999	○ UNDER 10,000	

SCALE 1:1,150,000 LAMBERT CONFORMAL CONIC PROJECTION

MILES 0 10 20 30 40 50
KILOMETERS 0 10 20 30 40 50

SCALE 1:1,150,000 LAMBERT CONFORMAL CONIC PROJECTION

MILES 0   10   20   30   40   50

KILOMETERS 0   10   20   30   40   50

POPULATION OF CITIES AND TOWNS

■ OVER 2,000,000   ● 500,000 - 999,999   ● 100,000 - 249,999   ○ 10,000 - 29,999

■ 1,000,000 - 1,999,999   ● 250,000 - 499,999   ● 30,000 - 99,999   ○ UNDER 10,000

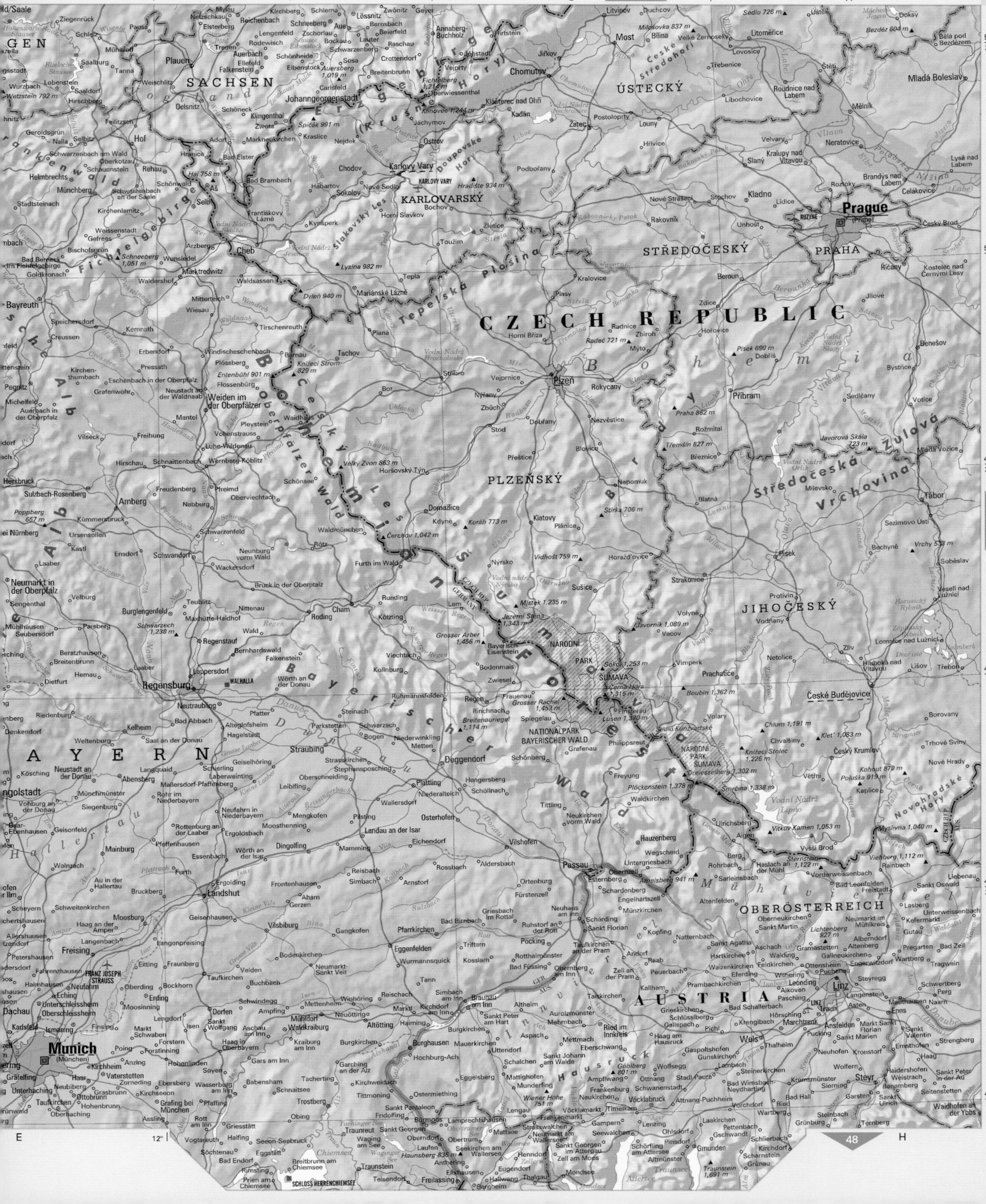

Central Alps Region

SCALE 1:1,150,000   LAMBERT CONFORMAL CONIC PROJECTION

MILES
KILOMETERS

Longitude East of Greenwich

© HAMMOND WORLD ATLAS CORPORATION   CM-1018-A A

Northern Italy

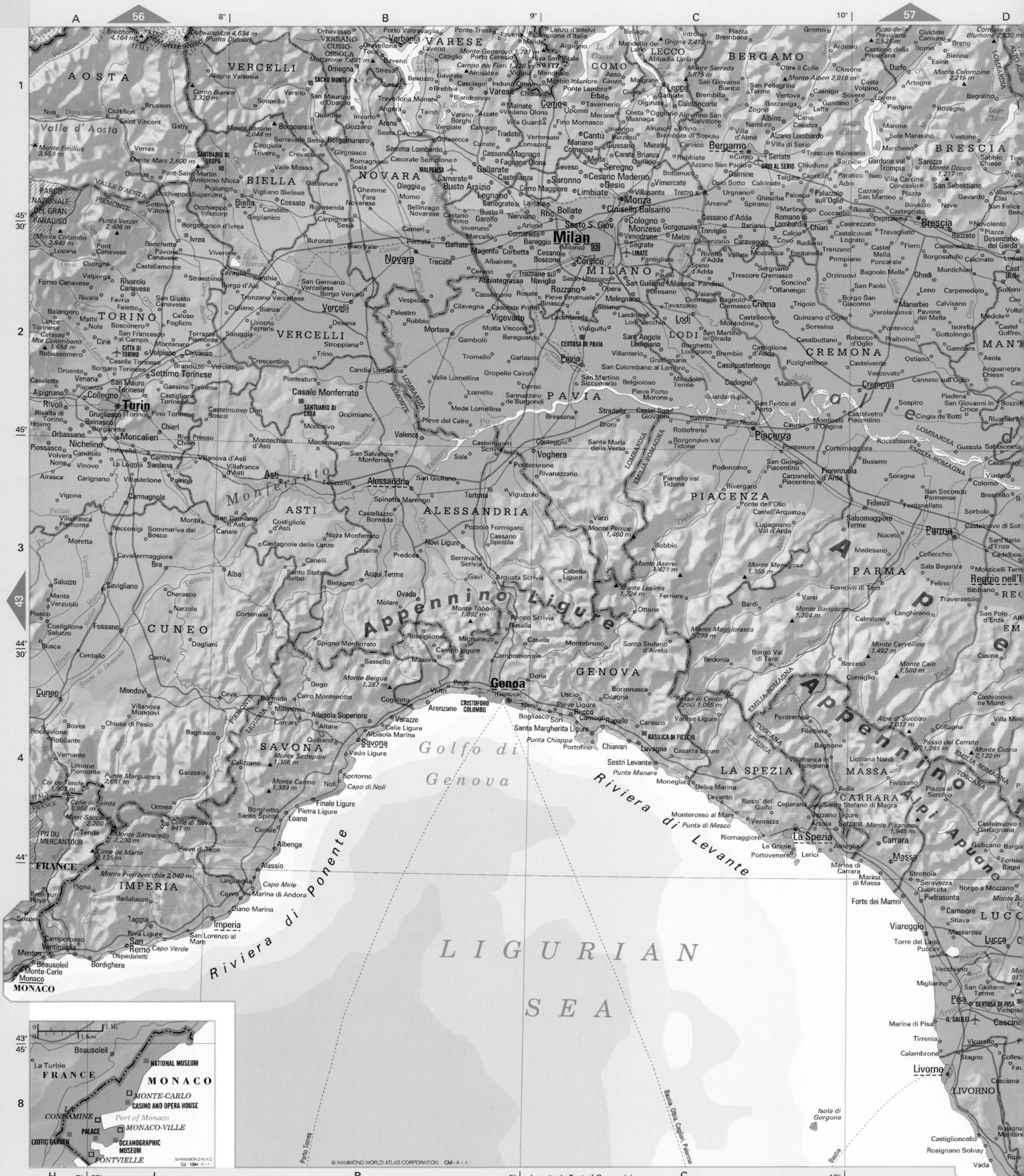

SCALE 1:1,150,000   LAMBERT CONFORMAL CONIC PROJECTION

MILES
0   10   20   30   40   50

KILOMETERS
0   10   20   30   40   50

POPULATION OF CITIES AND TOWNS

■ OVER 2,000,000	● 500,000 - 999,999	● 100,000 - 249,999	○ 10,000 - 29,999
■ 1,000,000 - 1,999,999	● 250,000 - 499,999	● 30,000 - 99,999	○ UNDER 10,000

11° E 12° F 43 UDINE G

Cornetto 2,179 m
Monte Verena 2,019 m
Dro
Aldeno
Folgaria
Arco
Nago-Torbole
Rovereto
Mori
Limone sul Garda
Malcesine
Cima Paloni 2,235 m
Avio
Idrara 218 m

VICENZA
Asiago
Arsiero
Cogollo del Cengio
Chiuppano
Piovene-Rocchette

BELLUNO
Cappella Maggiore
Monte Cesen 1,570 m
Quero
Segusino
Col San Martino
Pieve di Soligo
Valdobbiadene
Cison di Valmarino

Codroipo
Mortegliano
Talmassons

Feletto Umberto
Martignacco
Passons
Pasian di Prato
Basaldella
Buttrio
Manzano

Remanzacco
Cividale del Friuli

Premariacco
Orsaria

Corno di Rosazzo
Terenzano

UDINE
Udine

Nova Gorica
Gorizia
GORIZIA
Ajdovščina

Romans d'Isonzo
Ronchi dei Legionari
RONCHI DEI LEGIONARI
Gradisca d'Isonzo
Staranzano
Monfalcone

SLOVENIA
ITALY
SLOVENIA

GROTTA GIGANTE
Prosecco
Sežana

CROATIA

Zadar
Split
Dubrovnik

ADRIATIC

SEA

Golfo di Venezia

Golfo di Trieste

TRIESTE
Trieste

Muggia
Koper
Piran
Izola
Umag
Poreč
Rovinj
Pula
Rt Kamenjak
Pazin

Istria

SLOVENIA
CROATIA

Cortina
Negrar
Grezzana
VERONA
Verona

VICENZA
Vicenza

PADOVA
Padova

TREVISO
Treviso

VENEZIA
Venice
(Venezia)
Mestre

Chioggia

ROVIGO
Rovigo
Polesine

FERRARA
Ferrara

BOLOGNA
Bologna

RAVENNA
Ravenna

FORLÌ-CESENA
Forlì
Cesena

RIMINI
Rimini

SAN MARINO

PESARO E URBINO
Pesaro
Fano
Urbino

ANCONA
Ancona
Jesi

MACERATA

PERUGIA

AREZZO
Arezzo

SIENA
Siena

FIRENZE
Florence
(Firenze)
Prato
PRATO
Pistoia
PISTOIA

MODENA
Modena

Emiliano

Appennino Umbro-Marchigiano

Romagna

Montefeltro

Height Depth

NORWEGIAN

SEA

Arctic Circle

BARE

Poluostrov
Rybachiy

FINNMARK

Murmansk

Severomorsk

Kola

Peninsula

MURMANSKAYA OBLAST'

Monchegorsk

Apatity   Kirovsk

Kandalaksha

NORWAY

NORRBOTTEN

LAPPI

Kandalaksha Gulf

White

Sea

SWEDEN

JÄMTLAND

VÄSTERBOTTEN

Luleå

Haparanda

Rovaniemi

OULUN LÄÄNI

Oulu

FINLAND

RESPUBLIKA

KARELIYA

Onega

Pen.

Dvina

Bay

Severodvinsk   **Archangel's**

ARKHANGEL'SK

ARKHANGEL'SK

KOPPARBERG

GÄVLEBORG

LÄNSI-

SUOMEN

LÄÄNI

ITÄ-SUOMEN

LÄÄNI

Kuopio

Petrozavodsk

Lake

Onega

Petrozavodsk

Tampere

Hämeenlinna

Lahti

ETELÄ-

SUOMEN LÄÄNI

Mikkeli

Lappeenranta

Vyborg

Lake

Ladoga

Lodeynoye Pole

LENINGRADSKAYA

OBLAST'

VOLOGODSKAYA

Stockholm

Uppsala

Turku

Helsinki

Kotka

Gulf of Finland

Kronshtadt

ST. PETERSBURG

Pushkin

Gatchina

Cherepovets

Vologda

BALTIC

GOTLAND

Tallinn

ESTONIA

Tartu

Novgorod

NOVGORODSKAYA

OBLAST'

Staraya

Russa

Rybinsk

Res.

Rybinsk

KOSTROMS

SEA

Ventspils

Gulf of

Riga

Riga

Lake

Peipus

Pskov

PSKOVSKAYA

OBLAST'

Yaroslavl'

YAROSLAVSKAYA

OBLAST'

Kostroma

LATVIA

Daugavpils

Rēzekne

Velikiye

Luki

TVERSKAYA

OBLAST'

Tver'

Ivanovo

IVANOVO

OBLAST'

RUSSIA

Gdynia

Gdańsk

Kaliningrad

KALININGRADSKAYA OBL.

LITHUANIA

Kaunas

Vilnius

Vitsyebsk

SMOLENSKAYA OBLAST'

MOSCOW

Sergiyev

Posad

Vladimir

VLADIMIRSKAYA OBL.

Kovrov

Kolomna

KALUZHSKAYA

OBLAST'

Kaluga

POLAND

Hrodna

BELARUS

Minsk

MINSKAYA

VOBLASTS'

Mahilyow

Smolensk

Orsha

Ryazan

RYAZANSKAYA

OBLAST'

Height   Depth

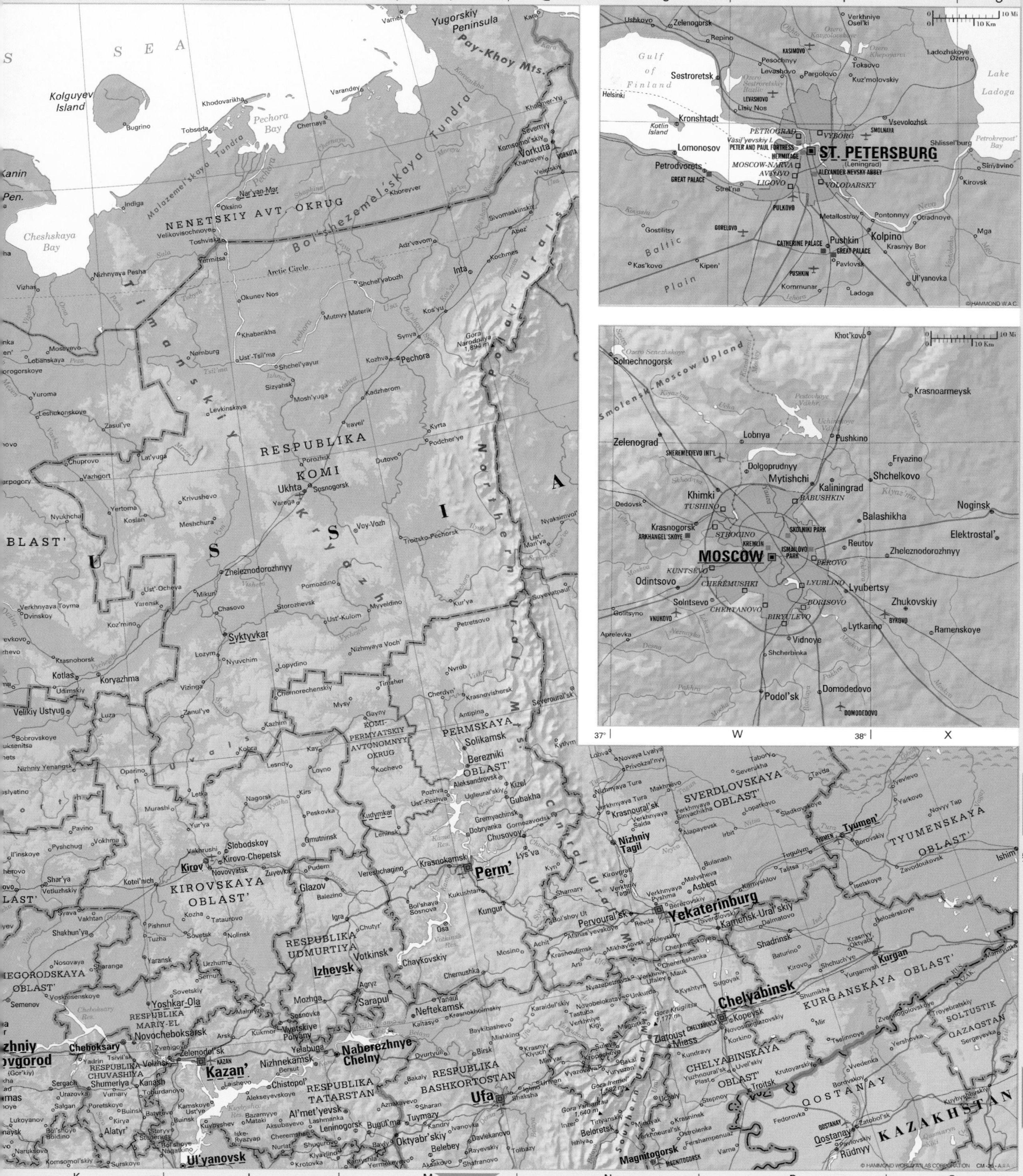

POPULATION OF CITIES AND TOWNS

- OVER 2,000,000
- 1,000,000 - 1,999,999
- 500,000 - 999,999
- 250,000 - 499,999
- 100,000 - 249,999
- 30,000 - 99,999
- 10,000 - 29,999
- UNDER 10,000

SCALE 1:6,900,000

LAMBERT CONFORMAL CONIC PROJECTION

MILES
KILOMETERS

© HAMMOND WORLD ATLAS CORPORATION   CM-61-AXA

POPULATION OF CITIES AND TOWNS

■ OVER 2,000,000	● 500,000 - 999,999	◉ 100,000 - 249,999	○ 10,000 - 29,999
■ 1,000,000 - 1,999,999	◉ 250,000 - 499,999	◉ 30,000 - 99,999	∘ UNDER 10,000

Height
Depth

Russia and Neighboring Countries

RUSSIA
(Administrative divisions are named only when they differ from their respective capitals.)

1. RESPUBLIKA ADYGEYA
2. RESPUBLIKA KARACHAYEVO-CHERKESIYA
3. RESPUBLIKA KABARDINO-BALKARIYA
4. RESPUBLIKA SEVERNAYA OSETIYA-ALANIYA
5. RESPUBLIKA INGUSHETIYA
6. RESPUBLIKA CHECHNYA
7. RESPUBLIKA DAGESTAN
8. RESPUBLIKA MORDOVIYA
9. RESPUBLIKA CHUVASHIYA
10. RESPUBLIKA MARIY EL
11. RESPUBLIKA TATARSTAN
12. RESPUBLIKA BASHKORTOSTAN
13. RESPUBLIKA UDMURTIYA
14. KOMI-PERMYATSKIY AVTONOMNYY OKRUG
15. RESPUBLIKA KHAKASIYA
16. UST'-ORDYNSKIY BURYATSKIY AVT. OKRUG
17. AGINSKIY BURYATSKIY AVT. OKRUG

© HAMMOND WORLD ATLAS CORPORATION   CM-29-A-A

POPULATION OF CITIES AND TOWNS

■ OVER 2,000,000	● 500,000 - 999,999	● 50,000 - 99,999
▣ 1,000,000 - 1,999,999	● 100,000 - 499,999	○ UNDER 50,000

SCALE 1:20,700,000 LAMBERT CONFORMAL CONIC PROJECTION

MILES
0   300   600   900

KILOMETERS
0   300   600   900

THE WORLD ALMANAC
WORLD ATLAS

Asia

The delta of the Indus River, the longest river in southwest Asia, is the highlight of this southeast-looking, low-oblique image. Fed by snowmelt and glacial meltwater from the mountains of the Tibet Plateau, the Indus River flows nearly 1800 miles (2897 km.) before emptying into the Arabian Sea. After leaving the Tibet Plateau, the river flows onto the Punjab Plains of western Pakistan and through a vast alluvial lowland where it receives its major tributary, the Panjnad (five streams). In this severely arid landscape the rivers form precarious strips of fertile land.

AREA OF OPTIMIZATION

The red band which surrounds this map defines the "Area of Optimization." Within this bounding curve is the most accurate conformal map that can be made of the region. Outside the optimized area, distortion increases rapidly, and tears or other irregularities in the grid may occur. (See page 8 for additional information.)

POPULATION OF CITIES AND TOWNS

- OVER 3,000,000
- 1,000,000 - 2,999,999
- 500,000 - 999,999
- 100,000 - 499,999
- UNDER 100,000

SCALE 1:48,300,000 OPTIMAL CONFORMAL PROJECTION

MILES 0   700   1400   2100
KILOMETERS 0   700   1400   2100

Longitude East F of Greenwich

© HAMMOND WORLD ATLAS CORPORATION CC-1000-A

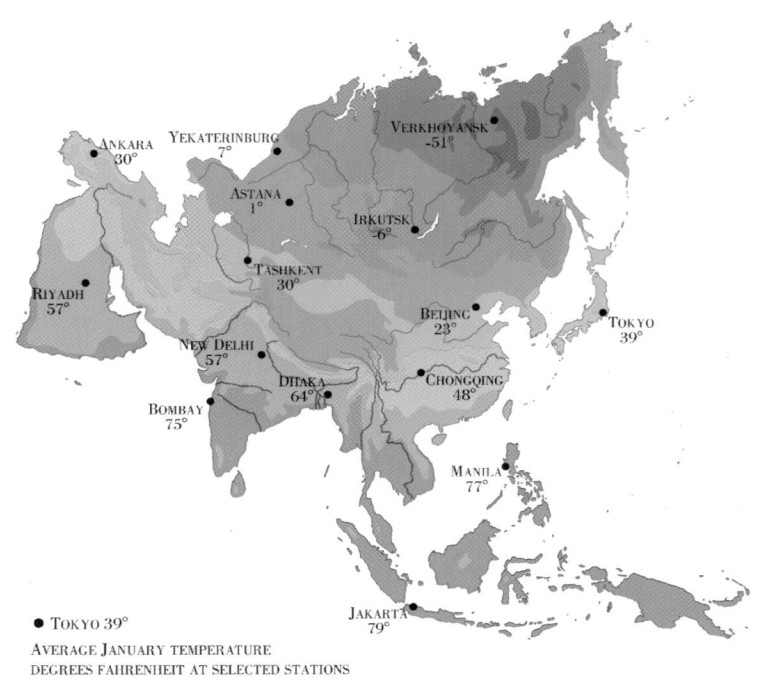

● TOKYO 39°

AVERAGE JANUARY TEMPERATURE
DEGREES FAHRENHEIT AT SELECTED STATIONS

AVERAGE JANUARY TEMPERATURE

FAHRENHEIT	CELSIUS	FAHRENHEIT	CELSIUS	FAHRENHEIT	CELSIUS
OVER 68°	OVER 20°	14° TO 32°	-10° TO 0°	-40° TO -22°	-40° TO -30°
50° TO 68°	10° TO 20°	-4° TO 14°	-20° TO -10°	UNDER -40°	UNDER -40°
32° TO 50°	0° TO 10°	-22° TO -4°	-30° TO -20°		

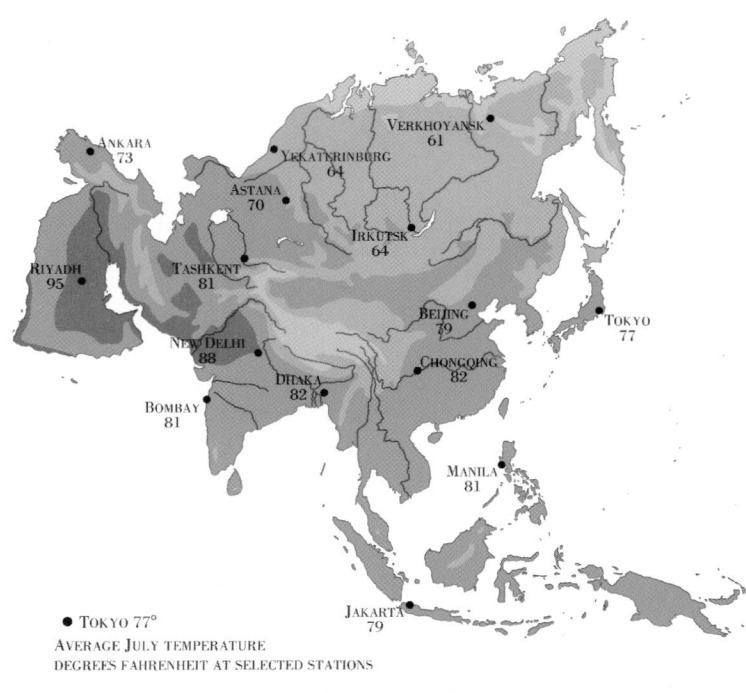

● TOKYO 77°

AVERAGE JULY TEMPERATURE
DEGREES FAHRENHEIT AT SELECTED STATIONS

AVERAGE JULY TEMPERATURE

FAHRENHEIT	CELSIUS	FAHRENHEIT	CELSIUS	FAHRENHEIT	CELSIUS
OVER 86°	OVER 30°	50° TO 68°	10° TO 20°	UNDER 32°	UNDER 0°
68° TO 86°	20° TO 30°	32° TO 50°	0° TO 10°		

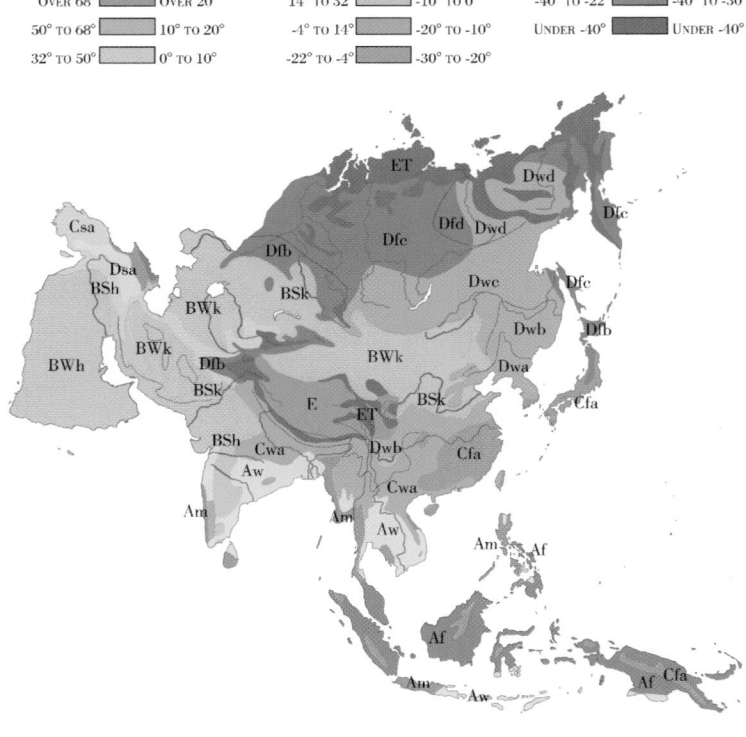

CLIMATE

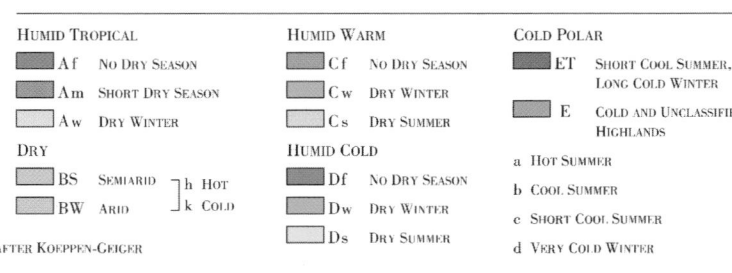

HUMID TROPICAL
- Af — NO DRY SEASON
- Am — SHORT DRY SEASON
- Aw — DRY WINTER

DRY
- BS — SEMIARID ⎤ h HOT
- BW — ARID ⎦ k COLD

HUMID WARM
- Cf — NO DRY SEASON
- Cw — DRY WINTER
- Cs — DRY SUMMER

HUMID COLD
- Df — NO DRY SEASON
- Dw — DRY WINTER
- Ds — DRY SUMMER

COLD POLAR
- ET — SHORT COOL SUMMER, LONG COLD WINTER
- E — COLD AND UNCLASSIFIED HIGHLANDS

a HOT SUMMER
b COOL SUMMER
c SHORT COOL SUMMER
d VERY COLD WINTER

AFTER KOEPPEN-GEIGER

VEGETATION

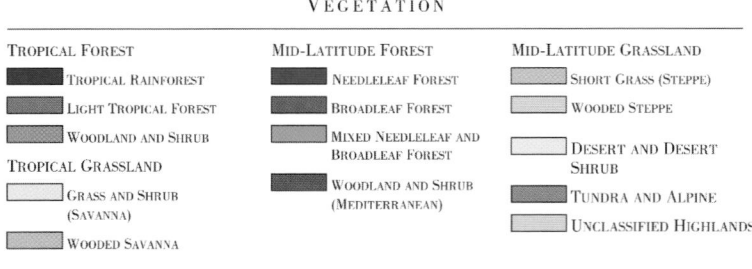

TROPICAL FOREST
- TROPICAL RAINFOREST
- LIGHT TROPICAL FOREST
- WOODLAND AND SHRUB

TROPICAL GRASSLAND
- GRASS AND SHRUB (SAVANNA)
- WOODED SAVANNA

MID-LATITUDE FOREST
- NEEDLELEAF FOREST
- BROADLEAF FOREST
- MIXED NEEDLELEAF AND BROADLEAF FOREST
- WOODLAND AND SHRUB (MEDITERRANEAN)

MID-LATITUDE GRASSLAND
- SHORT GRASS (STEPPE)
- WOODED STEPPE
- DESERT AND DESERT SHRUB
- TUNDRA AND ALPINE
- UNCLASSIFIED HIGHLANDS

Asia – Geographical Comparisons

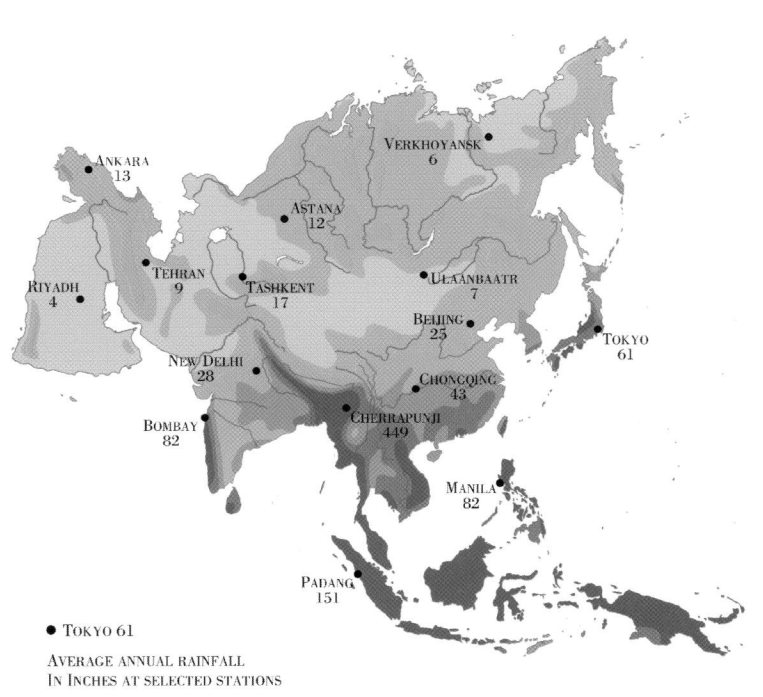

ANKARA
13

VERKHOYANSK
6

ASTANA
12

TEHRAN
9
TASHKENT
17

ULAANBAATR
7

RIYADH
4

BEIJING
25

TOKYO
61

NEW DELHI
28

CHONGQING
43

BOMBAY
82

CHERRAPUNJI
449

MANILA
82

PADANG
151

● TOKYO 61

AVERAGE ANNUAL RAINFALL
IN INCHES AT SELECTED STATIONS

AVERAGE ANNUAL RAINFALL

INCHES	CM	INCHES	CM	INCHES	CM
OVER 80	OVER 200	40 TO 60	100 TO 150	10 TO 20	25 TO 50
60 TO 80	150 TO 200	20 TO 40	50 TO 100	UNDER 10	UNDER 25

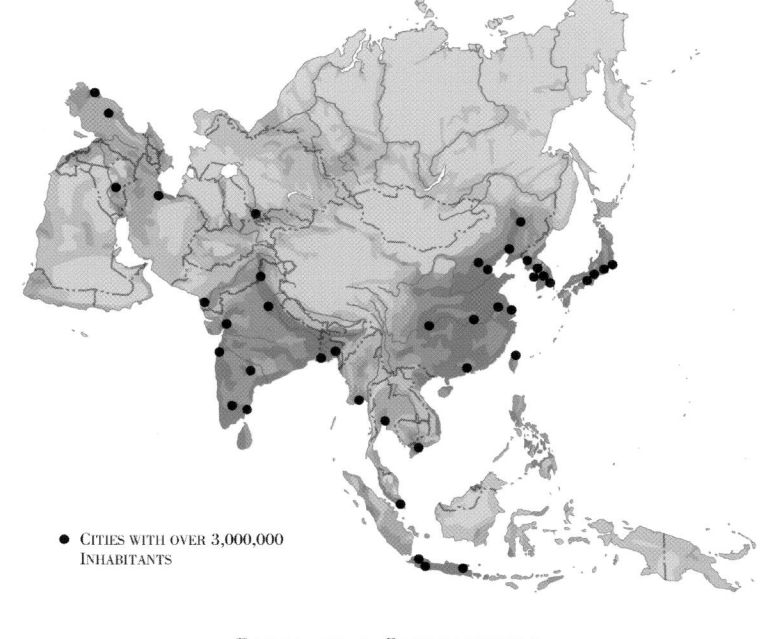

● CITIES WITH OVER 3,000,000
INHABITANTS

POPULATION DISTRIBUTION

DENSITY PER		SQ. MI.	SQ. KM.	SQ. MI.	SQ. KM.
SQ. MI.	SQ. KM.	130 TO 260	50 TO 100	3 TO 25	1 TO 10
OVER 260	OVER 100	25 TO 130	10 TO 50	UNDER 3	UNDER 1

TOBACCO
WHEAT
OLIVES
FRUIT
SHEEP
DATES
SHEEP
DATES
CATTLE
OATS
POTATOES
OATS WHEAT
WHEAT
OATS
FURS
FURS
SHEEP
COTTON
SHEEP
WHEAT
SHEEP
SHEEP
RICE
WHEAT
POTATOES
SOYBEANS
RICE FRUIT TEA
CATTLE
WHEAT
COTTON
RICE
PEANUTS
RICE
TEA
JUTE
CASSAVA
CORN
RICE
RICE
WHEAT
SOYBEANS
CORN COTTON
RICE TEA
HOGS
SUGARCANE
FRUIT
SUGARCANE
RUBBER
RUBBER
COCONUTS
RUBBER
RUBBER
SPICES
COCONUTS
SPICES
COCONUTS
COCOA
RICE
COFFEE

LAND USE

- CEREALS, LIVESTOCK
- CASH CROPS, MIXED FARMING
- DAIRY, LIVESTOCK
- DIVERSIFIED TROPICAL & SUBTROPICAL CROPS
- LIVESTOCK RANCHING & HERDING
- SPECIAL CROPS
- FORESTS
- NONPRODUCTIVE

MINERAL RESOURCES

ENERGY & FUELS
- ◆ COAL
- ⬟ LIGNITE
- ▲ NATURAL GAS
- ● PETROLEUM
- ■ URANIUM

IRON & FERROALLOYS
- 1 CHROMIUM
- 2 COBALT
- 3 IRON ORE
- 4 MANGANESE
- 5 MOLYBDENUM
- 6 NICKEL
- 7 TUNGSTEN

OTHER MAJOR RESOURCES
- 1 ANTIMONY
- 2 ASBESTOS
- 3 BAUXITE
- 4 BORAX
- 5 COPPER
- 6 DIAMONDS
- 7 GOLD
- 8 GRAPHITE
- 9 LEAD
- 10 MAGNESITE
- 11 MERCURY
- 12 MICA
- 13 PHOSPHATES
- 14 PLATINUM
- 15 POTASH
- 16 SILVER
- 17 SULFER
- 18 TIN
- 19 TITANIUM
- 20 ZINC

Northeastern China

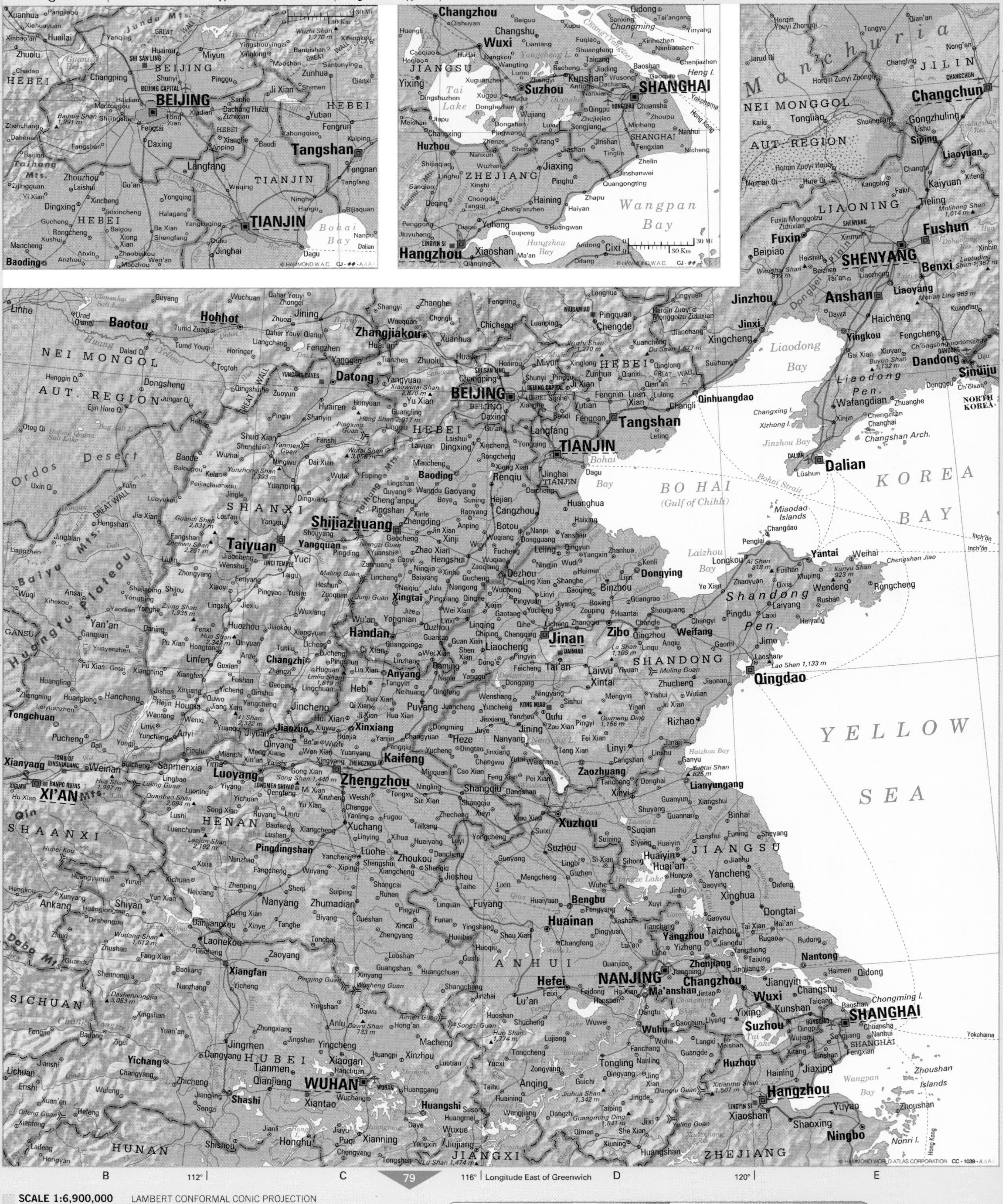

POPULATION OF CITIES AND TOWNS

- ■ OVER 2,000,000
- ▣ 1,000,000 - 1,999,999
- ● 500,000 - 999,999
- ◉ 250,000 - 499,999
- ◉ 100,000 - 249,999
- ⊙ 30,000 - 99,999
- ⊙ 10,000 - 29,999
- ○ UNDER 10,000

SCALE 1:3,450,000   LAMBERT CONFORMAL CONIC PROJECTION

MILES 0   50   100   150

KILOMETERS 0   50   100   150

Longitude East of Greenwich

SEA OF JAPAN

SOUTH
KOREA

PACIFIC

OCEAN

EAST

CHINA

SEA

Honshū

PACIFIC OCEAN

EAST CHINA SEA

Ryukyu Islands (Nansei - Shotō)

Izu Islands (JAPAN)

POPULATION OF CITIES AND TOWNS

■ OVER 2,000,000	◉ 500,000 - 999,999	◍ 100,000 - 249,999	⊕ 10,000 - 29,999
▣ 1,000,000 - 1,999,999	◐ 250,000 - 499,999	⊙ 30,000 - 99,999	· UNDER 10,000

SCALE 1:3,450,000 LAMBERT CONFORMAL CONIC PROJECTION

MILES 0   50   100   150

KILOMETERS 0   50   100   150

© HAMMOND WORLD ATLAS CORPORATION CM -1035 - A - A

© HAMMOND W.A.C. CJ -1116 - A - A

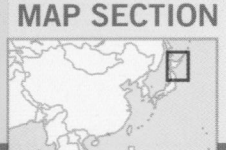
Northern Japan

138°   A   140°   B   142°   65   C   144°   D   146°   E

SAKHALINSKAYA
OBLAST'

Kril'on Pen.

Aniva Bay

Tonino-Anivskiy Pen.

Mys Aniva

46°   46°

Mys Kril'on
•Kril'on

RUSSIA
JAPAN

La Perouse Strait

*SEA OF
OKHOTSK*

Rebun-tō
•Wakkanai
Noshappu-misaki
•Rebun   *Sōya-misaki*
RISHIRI-
REBUN-SAROBETSU
NP
Rishiri-tō
•Rishiri

Sarufutsu•

Kutcharo

•Hamatombetsu

*Vulkan Chirip
1,589 m*
•Kuril'sk

1   1

•Esashi

•Teshio

•Ōmu

•Okoppe

•Etoro

SEA OF JAPAN

•Enbetsu

Kitami Mountains

Nayoro•

Mombetsu•

•Yūbetsu

Gora Tyatya
1,819 m

44°   44°

Hokkaidō

•Obira
•Rumoi

•Haboro
Teuri-tō   ▲1,032 m
•Tomamae

•Shibetsu

*Teshio-dake
1,558 m*

•Engaru

•Tokoro

Shiretoko-misaki
SHIRETOKO
NP

•Abashiri

Nemuro Strait

Occupied by Russia
since 1945: claimed
by Japan

Kunashiri-tō
•Yuzhno-Kuril'sk

Shikotan-tō

Yakishiri-tō
•Mashike

•Fukagawa
•Akabira

Kamikawa•

•Shari

Bihoro•

Gora Golovnina
547 m
•Golovnino

Habomai Islands   *Shpanberga Chan.*

Otaru• •Ishikari
Ishikari Bay
Kamui-misaki
*Shakotan
Pen.*
•Yoichi

•Takikawa
*Shokanbetsu-dake
1,492 m*
•Sunagawa

•Bibai
•Utashinai
Mikasa•

•Asahikawa

*Asahi-dake
2,290 m*
DAISETSUZAN
NAT'L PARK

Ishikari Mts.

*Me-akan-dake
1,503 m*
AKAN
NP

•Kitami

•Teshikaga

Nakashibetsu•

•Suishō-tō

•Taraku-jima

Shibetsu•

Shikotan-tō

•Yuri-tō
Shibotsu-jima

2   2

Iwanai
Benkei-misaki
•Kutchan
*Yōtei-san
1,893 m* ▲
JŌZANKEI SPA
SHIKOTSU-
TŌYA
NP

Sapporo
•Ebetsu
Iwamizawa•
Kurisawa•
Naganuma•
•Yūbari

HOKKAIDŌ

Shimukappu•
•Shimizu

•Shintoku
•Otofuke

Honbetsu•

•Ashoro

KUSHIRO-
SHITSUGEN
NP

Shibecha•

•Akkeshi

•Kushiro

*Konsen
Plateau*

•Hamanaka

•Nemuro

Nosappu-misaki
Nemuro Pen.
Ochiishi-misaki

•Eniwa
CHITOSE
•Chitose

*Hidaka-dake
2,052 m*

•Obihiro

•Ikeda

•Shiranuka

•Ūraho

Motsuta-misaki
•Suttsu
*Niseko-
Annupuri
1,308 m*
•Abuta
•Date

Okushiri-tō
•Okushiri
•Kumaishi
•Setana
•Oshamambe

*Yakumo•
Uchiura Bay
•Mori
•Shikabe
•Noboribetsu
•Shiraoi

•Tomakomai

Mukawa•
•Biratori

•Shizunai

Urakawa•
•Samani

•Taiki
•Hiro'o

42°   42°

Muroran

•Nanae

•Kamiiso

•Minamikayabe

Erimo-misaki

Ō-shima

Oshima Peninsula

•Esashi

Esan-misaki

•Kikonai

*Dai-Sengen-dake
1,072 m*

Hakodate

Tsugaru Strait

3   3

•Fukushima
•Matsumae
Shirakami-misaki
HOKKAIDŌ
TŌHOKU

•Ōma
Ōma-zaki

•Ōhata
Shiriya-zaki

*Shimokita
Pen.*

•Mutsu

Tappi-zaki
•Mimmaya

•Kodomari

•Nakasato

*Tsugaru
Pen.*

Mutsu Bay

•Hiranai

•Rokkasho

Ogawara

PACIFIC

•Goshogawara
•Ajigasawa
*Iwaki-san
1,640 m* ▲

•Itayanagi

•Namioka

Aomori
AOMORI

*Hakkōdasan
585 m*

•Noheji

•Misawa

•Momoishi

40°   40°

Henashi-zaki
•Iwasaki

•Hirosaki
•Kuroishi

•Owari
TOWADA
HACHIMANTAI
NP

•Gonohe
•Hachinohe

•Hachimori

•Ōdate

Towada

•Sannohe

•Ninohe

•Kuji

•Noshiro
•Takanosu
•Kazuno

•Ichinohe
•Kuzumaki

Honshū

Nyūdo-zaki
Oga Pen.
•Oga
•Gojōnome
TOWADA
HACHIMANTAI

•Ani

AKITA

*Iwate-san
2,041 m* ▲

•Iwate

•Iwaizumi

•Tarō

Akita

•Tazawako
•Kakunodate
•Shizukuishi

Morioka

•Miyako

•Kawabe

*Hayachine-san
1,914 m*

•Yamada
•Ōtsuchi

RIKUCHŪ-
KAIGAN
NP

•Honjō
•Ōmagari
•Yokote

IWATE

•Hanamaki

Dewa Mts.
•Yashima
•Yuzawa

•Jūmonji

•Kitakami

•Tōno

•Esashi

•Mizusawa

•Kamaishi

4   4

*Chōkai-san
2,237 m*

•Yuri

Mahiru Mts.

•Kaneyama

•Ichinoseki

•Ōfunato

•Rikuzentakata

•Kisakata
•Sakata
•Kaneyama
•Shinjō
•Mogami

•Ōgachi

*Kurikoma-yama
1,628 m*

•Kesen'numa

•Tsuruoka
•Yuza
•Murakami
•Atsumi

•Amarume

•Higashine

•Tsukidate

•Motoyoshi

•Shizugawa

Awa-shima

TŌHOKU
CHŪBU
BANDAI
ASAHI NP

YAMAGATA

•Murayama

•Obanazawa

•Ogata
•Furukawa

•Ōsaki

•Wakuya

•Onagawa

*Gas-san
1,980 m*

Yamagata

*Zaō-san
1,841 m* ▲

•Tendō
•Izumi

•Matsushima

•Ishinomaki

40°

MIYAGI

*Oshika
Pen.*

NIIGATA
•Nakajō
*Asahi-dake
1,870 m*

•Nagai
•Kaminoyama

•Wataii
•Shiogama
Sendai
Sendai Bay

A   140°   B   142°   Longitude East of Greenwich   C   144°   D   146°   E

© HAMMOND WORLD ATLAS CORPORATION

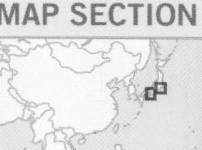
POPULATION OF CITIES AND TOWNS

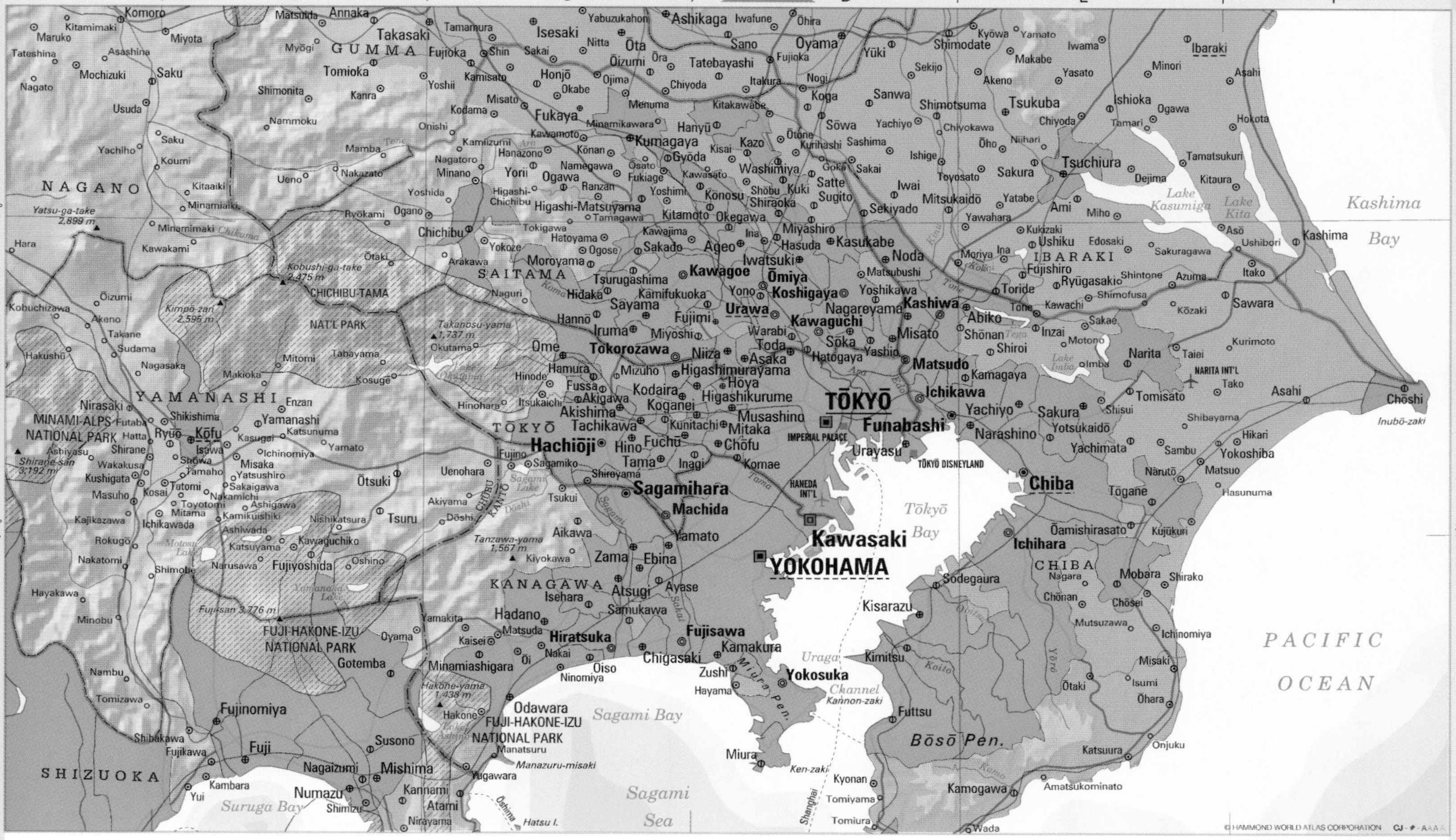

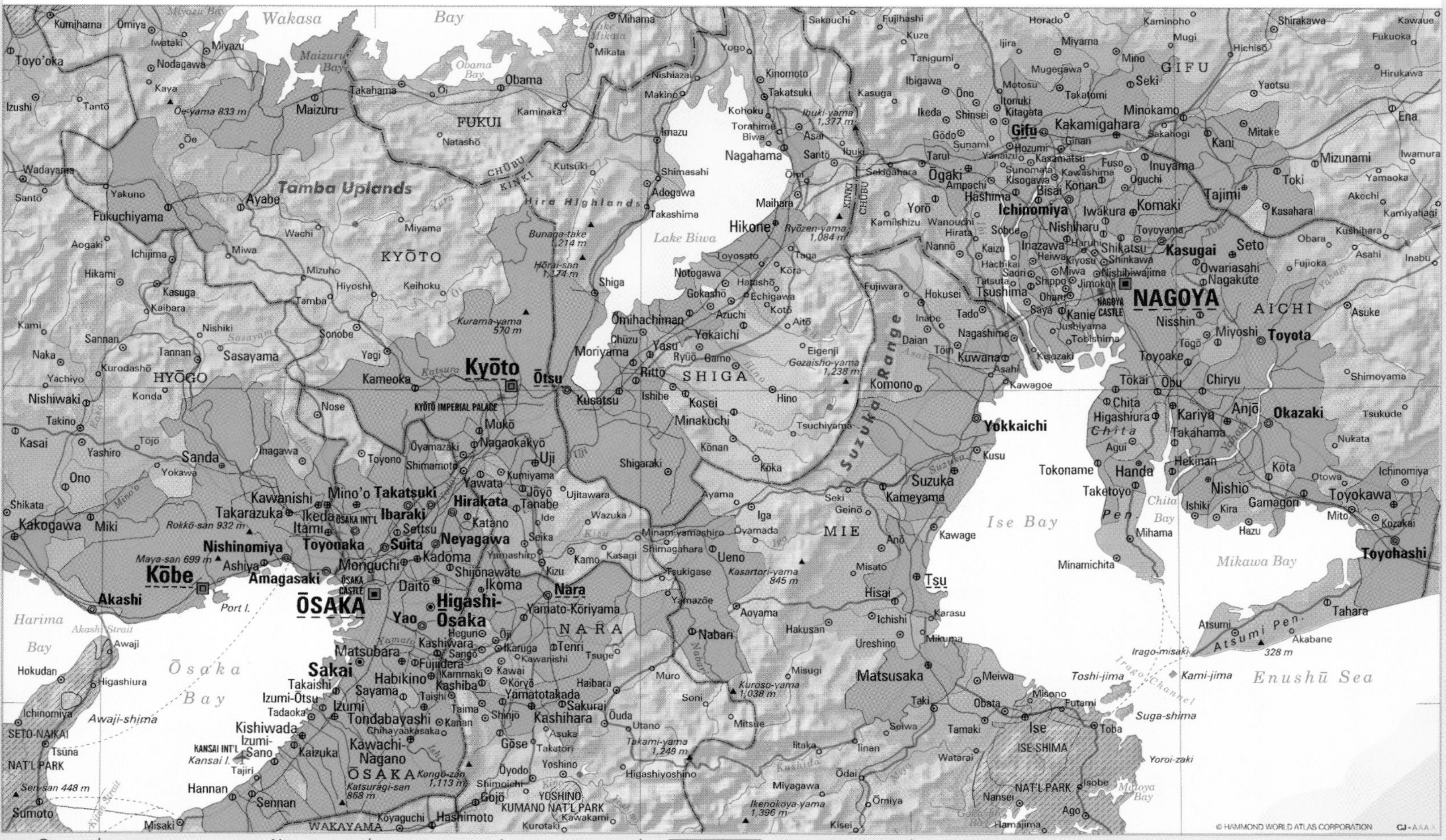

■ OVER 2,000,000　　● 500,000 - 999,999　　● 100,000 - 249,999　　○ 10,000 - 29,999
◼ 1,000,000 - 1,999,999　　◉ 250,000 - 499,999　　◦ 30,000 - 99,999　　○ UNDER 10,000

SCALE 1:1,150,000　　LAMBERT CONFORMAL CONIC PROJECTION

MILES
0　　10　　20　　30　　40　　50

KILOMETERS
0　　10　　20　　30　　40　　50

© HAMMOND WORLD ATLAS CORPORATION

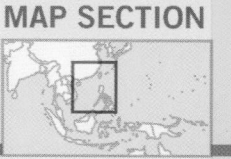

A 110° B 115° 72 C 120° D 120° E

EAST CHINA SEA

WUHAN Huangshi
Shashi Echeng Xiantao Tianmen Zhicheng Changyang Lichuan Enshi Dianjiang Huaying Luoshuikan Xuan'en
CHONGQING Fuling Xianfeng Heng Zizhou Zhijiang Songzi Jianli Jiayu Daye Xianning Honghu
Anging Guichi Jinde Taiping **Hangzhou** Haining Zhoushan Islands Yuyao
Nanchang Jingdezhen Quzhou Shaoxing **Ningbo**
Changsha Xiangtan Zhuzhou Pingxiang Linchuan Yingtan Guixi Lishui Jinhua Linhai Jiaojiang
CHINA Shaoyang Hengshan Hengyang Ji'an Nanfeng Guangchang Nanping Wenzhou Yuhuan
Guiyang Kaili Leiyang Ling Xian Lianhua Yongxin Ninggang Taihe Jianyang Taishun Fuding
Liuzhou Chenzhou Zixing Guidong Chongyi Ganzhou Longchuan Sanming **Fuzhou**
Guilin Shaoguan Lian Xian Renhua Xinfeng Anyuan Longnan Longyan Quanzhou Anxi
Nanning **GUANGZHOU** (Canton) Conghua Huizhou Meizhou Zhangzhou **Xiamen**
Foshan Dongguan Chaozhou **Shantou**
Maoming Yangjiang **Kowloon** **HONG KONG** MACAU **Victoria** Macau
VIETNAM Hong Gai **Zhanjiang** Leizhou Pen. **Haikou** Qiongshan
Gulf of Tonkin **Hainan** Wuzhi Shan 1,867 m

T'AIPEI Keelung T'aoyüan Hsinchu Ilan **TAIWAN** Hualien **T'aichung** Changhua Chiai Yü Shan 3,997 m **T'ainan** **Kaohsiung** P'ingtung Taitung
TAIWAN STRAIT Penghu Is. (Pescadores)
Tropic of Cancer
Ryukyu Islands Okinawa Is. Kume **Naha** Okinawa
Sakishima Is. Iriomote Ishigaki Miyako
PACIFIC OCEAN

TAIWAN PHILIPPINES Bashi Channel
Dongsha I. (CHINA) Itbayat Itbayat I. Batan I.

PHILIPPINE SEA

SOUTH CHINA SEA
Paracel Islands (Sovereignty disputed)

VIETNAM Hue Da Nang Hoi An Tam Ky Quang Ngai Kon Tum Pleiku (Play Cu) Qui Nhon Tuy Hoa Nha Trang Da Lat Cam Ranh Phan Rang Phan Thiet Ngoc Linh 2,600 m

Babuyan Islands Calayan I. Babuyan I. Camiguin I. C. Engaño
Laoag Abulog Aparri Claveria Fuga I.
Batac Dingras Tuao Baggao Tuguegarao
Cabugao Vigan Bangued Solana Tumauini Ilagan San Mariano
Narvacan Tabuk Bontoc Roxas Cauayan Santiago
Candon San Fernando Baguio Bayombong Luzon
Dagupan Mangaldan San Jose Baler
San Carlos Tarlac Cabanatuan Polillo I.
Iba Mabalacat Mt. Pinatubo 1,759 m San Fernando
Angeles Olongapo **Quezon City** Pasig **PHILIPPINES**
Balanga **Manila** Santa Cruz Daet
San Pablo Lucena Naga Nabua Tabaco Viga Catanduanes
Batangas Calapan Boac Santa Cruz Libon Virac Legaspi
Paluan Naujan Pinamalayan Daraga Sorsogon
Mamburao **Mindoro** Siruyan Sea Bulan Laoang Catarman Samar Oras
Tablas Romblon Masbate Uson Calbayog Catbalogan Borongan
Busuanga I. Odiongan Masbate Cataingan Daram Taft Tacloban
Calamian Group Coron Ibajay Kalibo **Roxas** Cangara Leyte Palo Burauen
Culion I. Linapacan I. Panay Bantayan Ormoc Abuyog Dinagat I.
Taytay Sibalom Silay Bogo Danao Hilongos Naasin Dinagat
San Jose de Buenavista **Iloilo** **Bacolod** **Cebu** Mandaue Surigao Siargao I.
Bago Toledo Bohol Jagna Ubay
Himamaylan Negros Tanjay Tagbilaran Mambajao Cabadbaran
Roxas Cauayan Bayawan Santa Catalina Dumaguete Butuan
Dumaran I. **Cagayan de Oro** San Francisco Prosperidad Bislig
Puerto Princesa Dapitan Dipolog Ozamiz **Iligan** Gingoog Bayugan
Quezon Sindangan Malaybalay Maramag Monkayo Baganga
Narra **Palawan** Labason Salug Tangub **Marawi** Kapalong Baganga
Brooke's Point Margosatubig Pagadian Panabo Tagum
Balabac I. **Zamboanga** Alicia Cotabato Maganoy Mt. Apo 2,954 m **Davao** Mati
Isabela Pikit Santa Cruz Mali
Bonggi I. Cagayan Sulu I. Moro Gulf Midsayap Koronadal Digos Panabo
MALAYSIA Sikuati Senaja Sulu Sea Polomolok Surallah Banga
Jolo Indanan Jolo Arch. General Santos C. San Agustin
Tawi-Tawi Siasi Pangutaran Lamitan Basilan I. Glan Jose Abad Santos
Tambisan Siasi Mindanao
CELEBES SEA

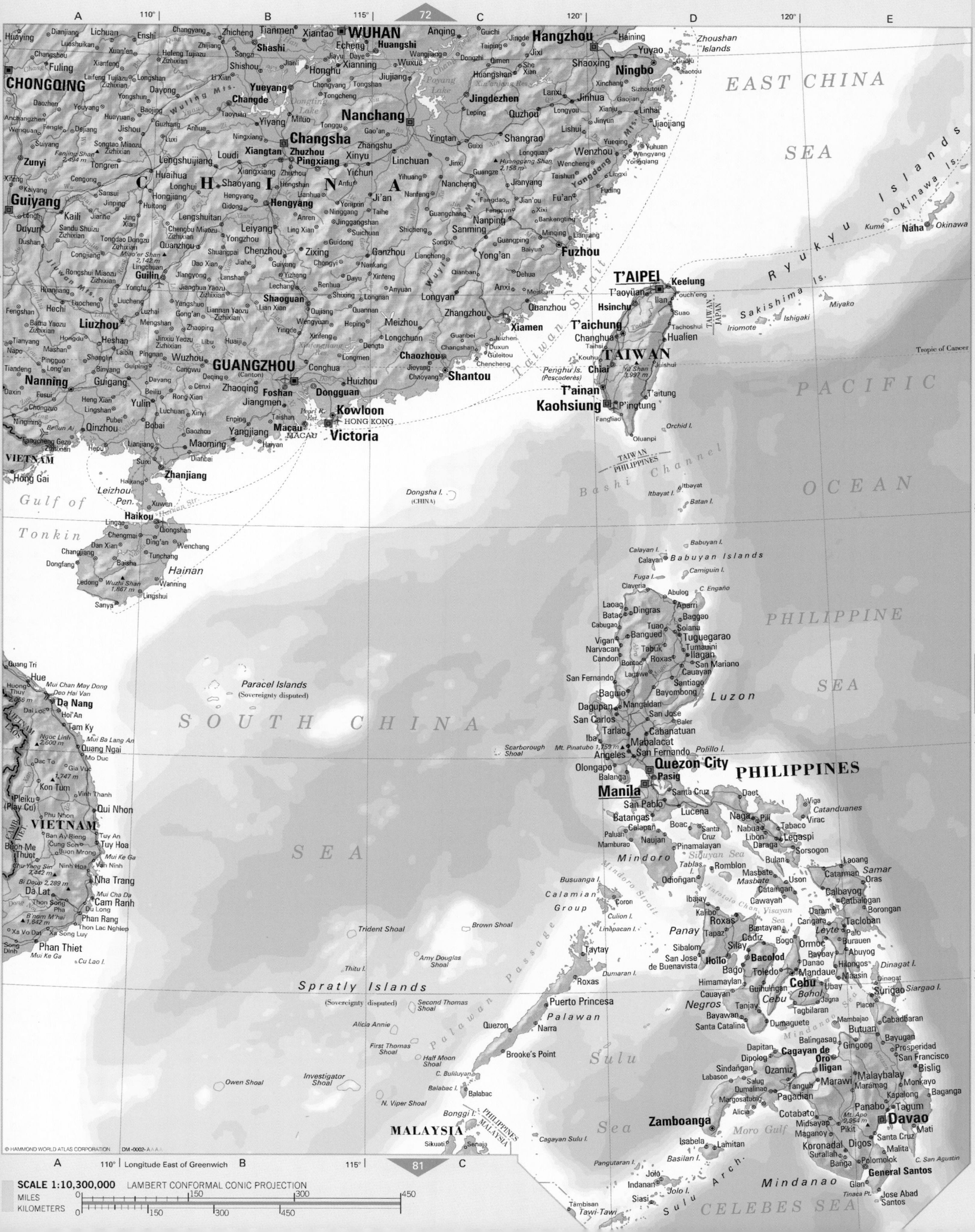

SCALE 1:10,300,000 LAMBERT CONFORMAL CONIC PROJECTION
MILES 0 150 300 450
KILOMETERS 0 150 300 450

© HAMMOND WORLD ATLAS CORPORATION DM-0002-AXX
A 110° Longitude East of Greenwich B 115° 81 C

SCALE 1:10,300,000   LAMBERT CONFORMAL CONIC PROJECTION

MILES
KILOMETERS

POPULATION OF CITIES AND TOWNS

Indonesia, Malaysia

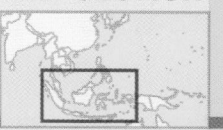

PHILIPPINES

Sulu Sea

Celebes Sea

Sulu Archipelago

Sabah

Zamboanga
Davao
General Santos

Cagayan de Oro
Iligan
Pagadian
Cotabato

Doberai Peninsula

New Guinea

Jayapura

Maoke Mountains
Irian Jaya

Van Rees Mts.

PACIFIC OCEAN

Ceram Sea

Arafura Sea

Halmahera

Manado
Gorontalo
Minahasa

Molucca Sea

Ternate
Tidore

Samarinda

Balikpapan

Celebes (Sulawesi)

Gunung Rantekombola 3,455 m

INDONESIA

Parepare

Ujung Pandang

Buru

Ceram

Ambon

Banda Sea

Flores Sea

Lesser Sunda Islands

Sumbawa
Flores
Sumba

Komodo

Timor

Kupang

EAST TIMOR

Timor Sea

Savu Sea

Aru Islands

Tanimbar Islands

Kai Islands

Wokam I.

© HAMMOND WORLD ATLAS CORPORATION CM-1047-A.A.A

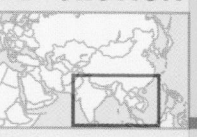
POPULATION OF CITIES AND TOWNS

- ■ OVER 2,000,000
- ■ 1,000,000 - 1,999,999
- ● 500,000 - 999,999
- ● 250,000 - 499,999
- ● 100,000 - 249,999
- ● 30,000 - 99,999
- ○ 10,000 - 29,999
- ○ UNDER 10,000

SCALE 1:10,300,000   LAMBERT CONFORMAL CONIC PROJECTION

MILES   0   150   300   450

KILOMETERS   0   150   300   450

© HAMMOND WORLD ATLAS CORPORATION

SCALE 1:3,450,000 LAMBERT CONFORMAL CONIC PROJECTION

MILES
KILOMETERS

POPULATION OF CITIES AND TOWNS

■ OVER 2,000,000	◉ 500,000 - 999,999
■ 1,000,000 - 1,999,999	◎ 250,000 - 499,999

● 100,000 - 249,999   ○ 10,000 - 29,999
◦ 30,000 - 99,999   · UNDER 10,000

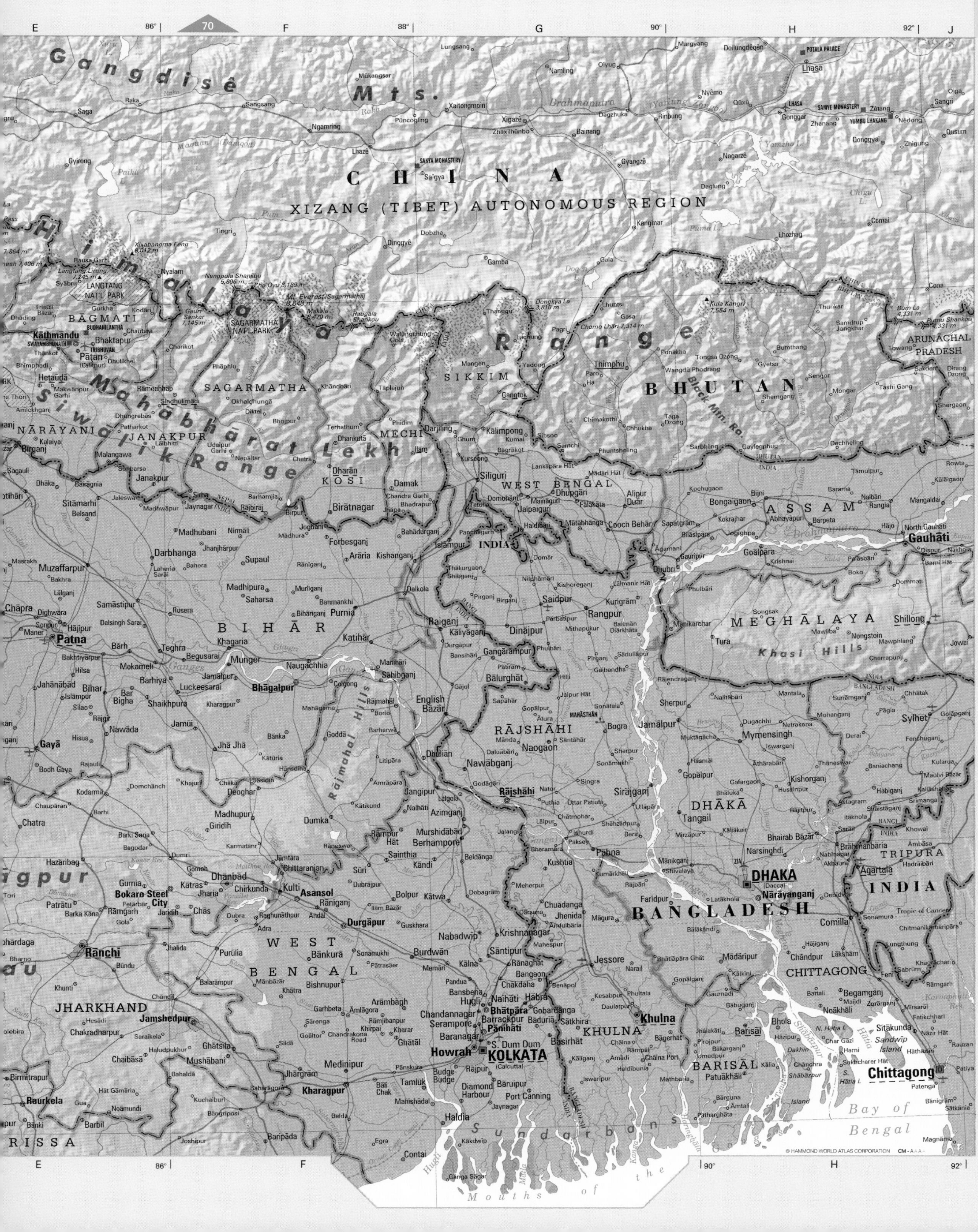

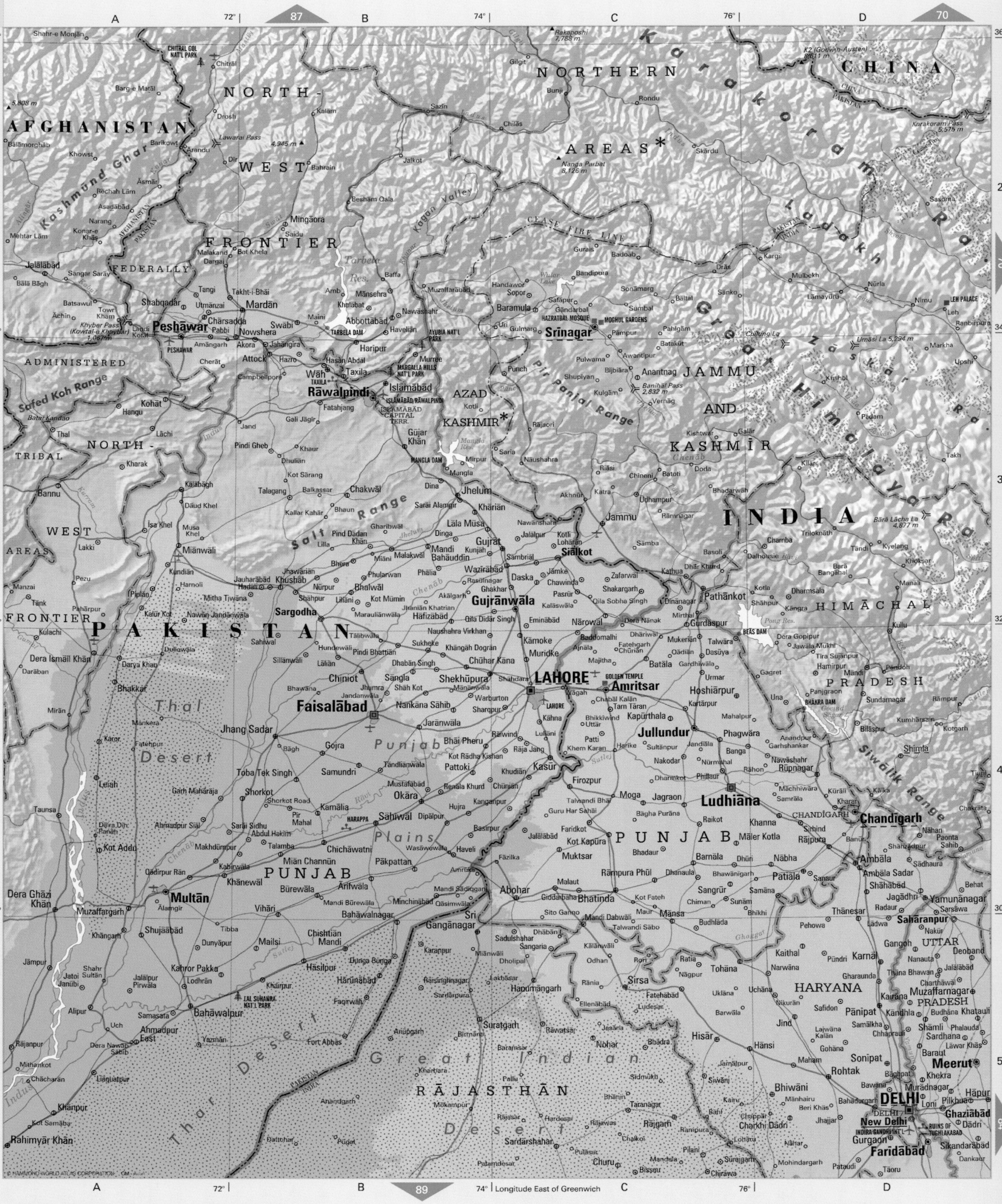

SCALE 1:3,450,000   LAMBERT CONFORMAL CONIC PROJECTION

MILES
KILOMETERS

Height Depth

* AZAD KASHMIR AND THE NORTHERN
AREAS ARE ADMINISTERED BY PAKISTAN
BUT DO NOT HAVE PROVINCIAL STATUS.

Longitude East of Greenwich

© HAMMOND WORLD ATLAS CORPORATION

POPULATION OF CITIES AND TOWNS
■ OVER 2,000,000   ● 500,000 - 999,999   ● 100,000 - 249,999   ○ 10,000 - 29,999
■ 1,000,000 - 1,999,999   ● 250,000 - 499,999   ● 30,000 - 99,999   ○ UNDER 10,000

SCALE 1:10,300,000   LAMBERT CONFORMAL CONIC PROJECTION
MILES
KILOMETERS

MEDITERRANEAN SEA

TURKEY

Antalya · Manavgat · Serik · Hadım · Taşkent
Alanya · Kumluca · Karacaл Tepe 2,339 m · Anamur · C. Anamur
Mersin · Adana · Kadirli · Kozan · Osmaniye · Gaziantep · Viranşehir
Tarsus · Ceyhan · Nizip · Birecik · Suruç · Ceylanpınar · Mardin · Cizre · Hakkâri · Yüksekova
İskenderun · Dörtyol · Yakacık · Kilis · Al Bāb · TURKEY · Al Qāmishlī · Zākhū
Antioch · Reyhanlı · İdlib · Mambij · Ar Raqqah · Al Ḥasakah · Tall 'Afar · Mosul · Irbīl
CYPRUS · Nicosia · Latakia · Ḥamāh · As Sabkhah · Dayr az Zawr · Kirkūk
Famagusta · Ṭarṭūs · Tripoli · **SYRIA** · As Sukhnah · Tadmur · PALMYRA · As Salīḥīyah · Abū Kamāl · **IRAQ** · As Sulaymānīyah · Sanandaj

Aleppo (Ḥalab)
Ḥimṣ
Beirut (Bayrūt) · **LEBANON** · **Damascus** (Dimashq) · Sāmarrā' · **Bākhtarān**
Sidon · Tyre · Qunayṭirah · An Nabk · Syrian Desert · Ar Ramādī · **Baghdad** (Baghdād) · CTESIPHON · **Karbalā'** · BABYLON · **Esfahān**
Haifa · Ṣafad · Az Zarqā' · Ar Ruṭbah · Al Fallūjah · Al Ḥillah · An Najaf · Ad Dīwānīyah
Tel Aviv-Yafo · **ISRAEL** · Ramlah · **Amman** · **JORDAN** · Al Kūt · Al 'Amārah
Jerusalem · Gaza · Al Karak · An Nāṣirīyah · **Aḥvāz**
Beersheba · Maʿān · PETRA · Ash Shawbak · **Al Baṣrah** · Ābādān

Port Said (Būr Saʿīd) · Al Manṣūrah · Ismailia · Sinai · Al 'Aqabah
CAIRO (Al Qāhirah) · Suez · **KUWAIT** · Kuwait · As Sālimīyah
AL JĪZAH · Banī Suwayf · **An Nafūd** · **SAUDI ARABIA** · Al Aḥmadī · BAHRAIN · Manama
Al Fayyūm · Tabūk · **QATAR** · **Doha**
EGYPT · Al Minyā · Al Wajh · Ad Dammām · Al Hufūf

RED SEA
Aswan · Al Ghurdaqah · Medina (Al Madīnah) · **Najd** · **Riyadh** (Ar Riyāḍ)
Luxor (Al Uqṣur) · **ARABIAN**
Jiddah · Mecca (Makkah) · Aṭ Ṭā'if
Port Sudan (Būr Sūdān)
SUDAN · **PENINSULA** · **Rub' al Khali**
Atbara · NO DEFINED BOUNDARY
Khartoum · Kassala · **ERITREA** · Keren · Asmara
Omdurman · Wad Medanī · **Sanaa** · **YEMEN**
Jizan · Al Hudaydah
ETHIOPIA · **Aden**

CASPIAN SEA
Tehran · Karaj · Qazvin · Zanjān · Qom · Shīrāz
PERSIAN GULF
Gulf of Aden

*AZAD KASHMIR AND THE NORTHERN AREAS ARE ADM... BY PAKISTAN BUT DO NOT HAVE PROVINCIAL STATUS.

TURKMENISTAN
UZBEKISTAN
TAJIKISTAN
CHINA
AFGHANISTAN
Mashhad
Ashgabat
Kabul
Peshawar
Rawalpindi
Islamabad
Srinagar
PAKISTAN
Kerman
Quetta
BALOCHISTAN
LAHORE
Amritsar
Jullundur
Ludhiana
Chandigarh
Faisalabad
Multan
Gujranwala
Zahedan
SINDH
PUNJAB
RAJASTHAN
Bikaner
Jaipur
INDIA
DELHI
New Delhi
Faridabad
Meerut
Ajmer
Jodhpur
Hyderabad
Great Indian Desert (Thar)
KARACHI
Udaipur
OMAN
Muscat
Gulf of Oman
Tropic of Cancer
AHMADABAD
Vadodara
Jamnagar
GUJARAT
Surat
MADHYA PRADESH
Indore
Kathiawar
Bhavnagar
Nasik
MAHARASHTRA
Aurangabad
MUMBAI (Bombay)
Thana
Kalyan
Pimpri-Chinchwad
Pune
Sholapur
ARABIAN SEA
Kolhapur
KARNATAKA
Belgaum
GOA
Hubli-Dharwar
Davangere

POPULATION OF CITIES AND TOWNS

- OVER 2,000,000
- 1,000,000 - 1,999,999
- 500,000 - 999,999
- 250,000 - 499,999
- 100,000 - 249,999
- 30,000 - 99,999
- 10,000 - 29,999
- UNDER 10,000

SCALE 1:10,300,000 LAMBERT CONFORMAL CONIC PROJECTION

MILES 0 150 300 450
KILOMETERS 0 150 300 450

© HAMMOND WORLD ATLAS CORPORATION

SCALE 1:6,900,000   LAMBERT CONFORMAL CONIC PROJECTION

MILES

KILOMETERS

Eastern Mediterranean Region

TURKEY

ANTALYA · Antalya · Gulf of Antalya · Manavgat · Alanya · Anamur · KONYA · KARAMAN · İÇEL · Mersin · Tarsus · **Adana** · ADANA · Ceyhan · Osmaniye · GAZIANTEP · KİLİS · İskenderun · Gulf of İskenderun · HATAY · Antioch (Antakya) · Reyhanlı · **Aleppo** (Halab) · HALAB · İdlib · IDLIB

CYPRUS · NICOSIA · Kyrenia · KYRENIA · FAMAGUSTA · Famagusta · Larnaca · LARNACA · LIMASSOL · Limassol · PAPHOS · Paphos · U.K. SOVEREIGN BASE AREA · Akrotiri · C. Gata · Turkish Cypriot-controlled area · Olympus 1,951 m

SYRIA · Latakia (Al Lādhiqīyah) · AL LĀDHIQĪYAH · Ṭarṭūs · TARTŪS · HAMĀH · Hamāh · HIMS · Hims · KRAK DES CHEVALIERS · Tripoli (Ṭarābulus) · ASH SHAMĀL · AL BIQĀ' · JABAL LUBNĀN · **Damascus** (Dimashq) · DIMASHQ · DAR'Ā · AS SUWAYDĀ'

LEBANON · **Beirut** (Bayrūt) · Sidon (Ṣaydā) · Tyre (Ṣūr) · AL JANŪB

ISRAEL · Haifa (Hefa) · HAIFA · Nazareth · Tiberias · Netanya · **Tel Aviv-Yafo** · TEL AVIV · Ramat Gan · Holon · Petah Tiqwa · Rishon LeZiyyon · **Jerusalem** (Yerushalayim) · JERUSALEM · Beersheba (Be'er Sheva') · Ashdod · Ashqelon · CENTRAL · SOUTHERN · NORTHERN · Negev · Dimona

WEST BANK (OCC. BY ISR.) · Nablus · Ram Allah · Jericho · Bethlehem (Bayt Laḥm) · Hebron (Al Khalīl) · GOLAN HTS. OCC. BY ISR.

GAZA STRIP · Gaza (Ghazzah) · Khān Yūnus · Rafah

JORDAN · **Amman** ('Ammān) · 'AMMĀN · Az Zarqā' · AZ ZARQĀ' · Irbid · IRBID · AL MAFRAQ · Al Mafraq · AL BALQĀ' · As Salt · Al Karak · AL KARAK · AT TAFILAH · Aṭ Ṭafīlah · MA'ĀN · Ma'dabā · Petra (Baṭrā) · QUEEN ALIA INT'L

EGYPT · **ALEXANDRIA** (Al Iskandarīyah) · AL ISKANDARĪYAH · Nile Delta · Damanhūr · Ṭanṭā · Al Maḥallah al Kubrā · Al Manṣūrah · Az Zaqāzīq · Port Said (Būr Sa'īd) · Ismailia (Al Ismā'īlīyah) · Suez (As Suways) · **CAIRO** (Al Qāhirah) · AL QĀHIRAH · AL JĪZAH · Shubrā al Khaymah · Al Fayyūm · AL FAYYŪM · Al 'Arīsh · SHAMĀL SĪNĀ' · JANŪB SĪNĀ' · Sinai · Gulf of Suez

SAUDI ARABIA

MEDITERRANEAN SEA

Gulf of Aqaba

Inset (Israel / West Bank)

ISRAEL · Haifa (Hefa) · NORTHERN · Nazareth · Netanya · CENTRAL · **Tel Aviv-Yafo** · TEL AVIV · Ramat Gan · Holon · Bat Yam · Rishon LeZiyyon · Rehovot · Ashdod · **Jerusalem** (Yerushalayim) · JERUSALEM · Bethlehem (Bayt Laḥm) · **WEST BANK** · Nablus · Ram Allah · SOUTHERN · BEN GURION · CASTEL · OLD CITY · EYN HEMED

0 ... 10 Mi · 0 ... 10 Km

POPULATION OF CITIES AND TOWNS

■ OVER 2,000,000	● 500,000 - 999,999	● 100,000 - 249,999	○ 10,000 - 29,999
■ 1,000,000 - 1,999,999	● 250,000 - 499,999	● 30,000 - 99,999	○ UNDER 10,000

SCALE 1:3,450,000   LAMBERT CONFORMAL CONIC PROJECTION

MILES 0 ... 50 ... 100 ... 150
KILOMETERS 0 ... 50 ... 100 ... 150

Longitude East of Greenwich

THE WORLD ALMANAC WORLD ATLAS

Africa

Several physiographic features are captured in this southeast-looking, high-oblique image. The Nile River Delta, the large, dark area at the bottom of the image, extends from the capital city of Cairo at the apex of the delta to the Suez Canal. The entire region is classified as desert (less than 10 inches [25 cm.] of rainfall per year). Desert-like areas are visible southwest of the delta and in the northwestern Sinai. Major rock outcrops (darker areas) are seen encircling the Red Sea. The two bodies of water flanking the southern end of the Sinai Peninsula are the Gulf of Suez and the Gulf of Aqaba.

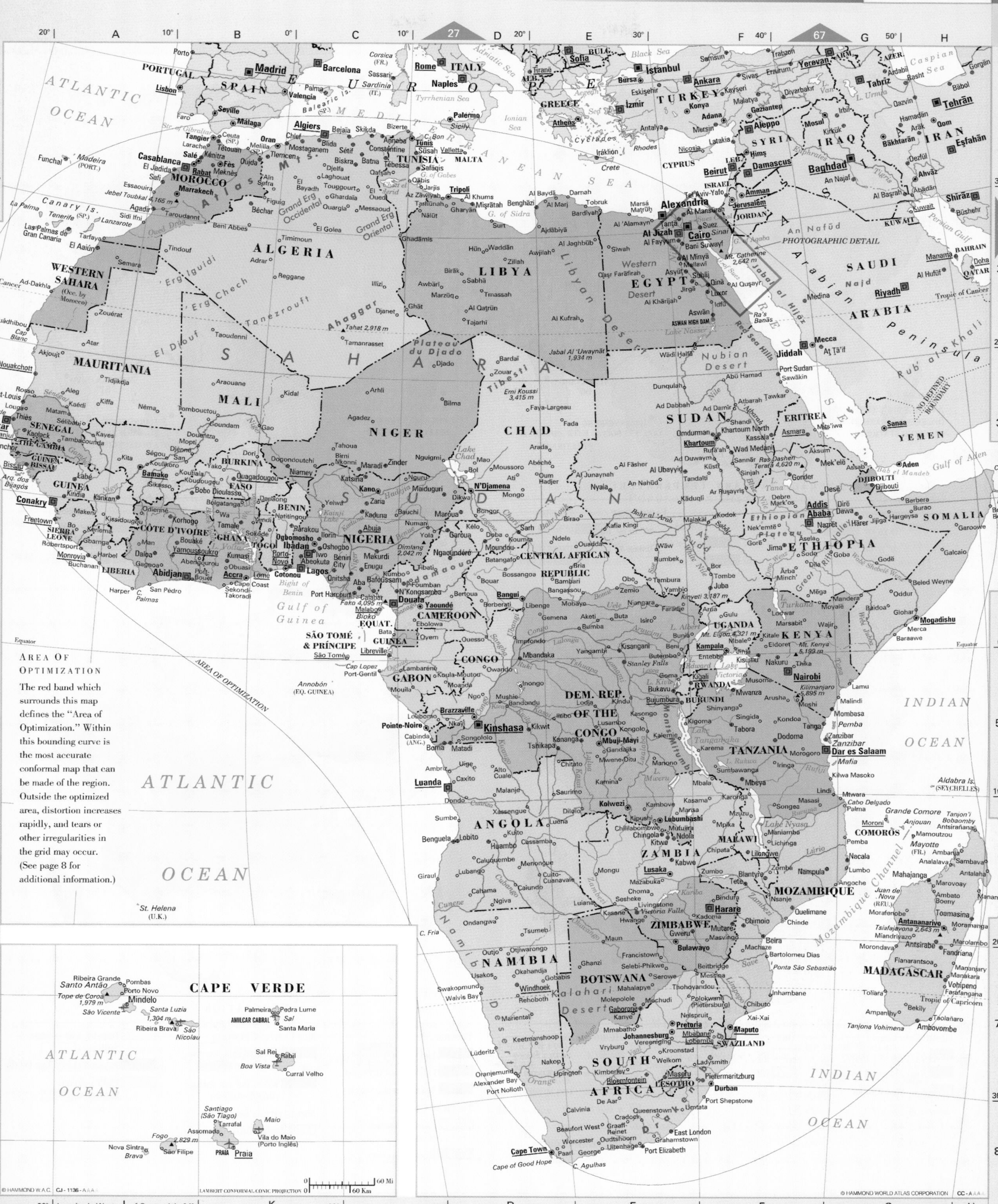

AREA OF OPTIMIZATION

The red band which surrounds this map defines the "Area of Optimization." Within this bounding curve is the most accurate conformal map that can be made of the region. Outside the optimized area, distortion increases rapidly, and tears or other irregularities in the grid may occur. (See page 8 for additional information.)

POPULATION OF CITIES AND TOWNS

- OVER 3,000,000
- 1,000,000 - 2,999,999
- 500,000 - 999,999
- 100,000 - 499,999
- UNDER 100,000

SCALE 1:34,500,000 OPTIMAL CONFORMAL PROJECTION

© HAMMOND WORLD ATLAS CORPORATION

Africa Geographical Comparisons

A 20° **B** 15° **C** 10° **D** 5°

SPAIN

Granada Cartagena
Jerez Málaga Marbella Almería
Cádiz Gibraltar (U.K.) Cerro de Mulhacén 3,478 m Algiers (El Djezair) Bizerte Cape Bon
Str. of Gibraltar Ceuta (SP.) Melilla (SP.) Nador Mostaganem Chercheli Blida Boufarik DJÉMILA Skikda Annaba Ariana Tunis Pantelleria (IT.) MALTA Valletta

Tangier El Hoceima Oran El Asnam Sétif Constantine Kairouan Sousse Pelagie Is. Mahdia
Tétouan Sidi Bel Abbès Mascara Tiaret Batna Ain Beida Tébessa El Kef Sfax MEDI

Mohammedia Fès Meknès Saïda Djelfa Biskra Djebel Mahmoud 2,321 m Gafsa Gulf of Gabes Île de Jerba Tripoli (Tarabulus)

MOROCCO Rabat Moyen Atlas Adrar bou Nassem 3,340 m El Bayadh Laghouat Touggourt El Oued Grand Gabes Zuwárah LABDAH (LEPTIS MAGNA) Misrátah

Casablanca Khouribga Oued Zem Er Rachidia Jebel Mesrouh 2,714 m Djebel Aïssa 2,236 m Ghardaïa Hassi Messaoud Nalút TUNISIA Gharyan Al Khums Tarhúnah

MAURITANIA MALI BURKINA FASO GUINEA SIERRA LEONE LIBERIA CÔTE D'IVOIRE GHANA TOGO BENIN NIGERIA NIGER ALGERIA WESTERN SAHARA

ATLANTIC OCEAN

Gulf of Guinea

Bight of Benin

Equator

B 15° **C** 10° Longitude West **D** of Greenwich 5° **E** 0° Longitude East **F** of Greenwich 5° **G** 10° **H** 15°

Height 600 16700 4000 13000 2000 6500 1500 5000 1000 3300 500 1600 200 700 0 200 700 1000 3300 2000 6500 4000 13000 6000 19600 8000 26700 Depth

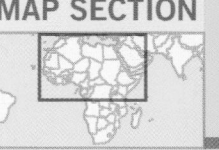
© HAMMOND WORLD ATLAS CORPORATION   CM -2103 - A - A

POPULATION OF CITIES AND TOWNS

| ■ OVER 2,000,000 | ● 500,000 - 999,999 | ⊙ 50,000 - 99,999 |
| ■ 1,000,000 - 1,999,999 | ● 100,000 - 499,999 | ○ UNDER 50,000 |

SCALE 1:17,200,000   POLYCONIC PROJECTION

MILES   0   250   500   750

KILOMETERS   0   250   500   750

MOROCCO is divided into 7 non-administrative regions shown here. Scale does not permit showing the boundaries and names of Morocco's provinces and prefectures.

ATLANTIC

OCEAN

Madeira Is.
(PORT.)

Canary Islands
(SPAIN)

SPAIN

MOROCCO

CASABLANCA

WESTERN
SAHARA
(Occupied by Morocco)

TINDOUF

TIRIS ZEMMOUR

MAURITANIA

MALI

TOMBOUC

ADRAR

HODH
ECH
CHARGUI

Tropic of Cancer

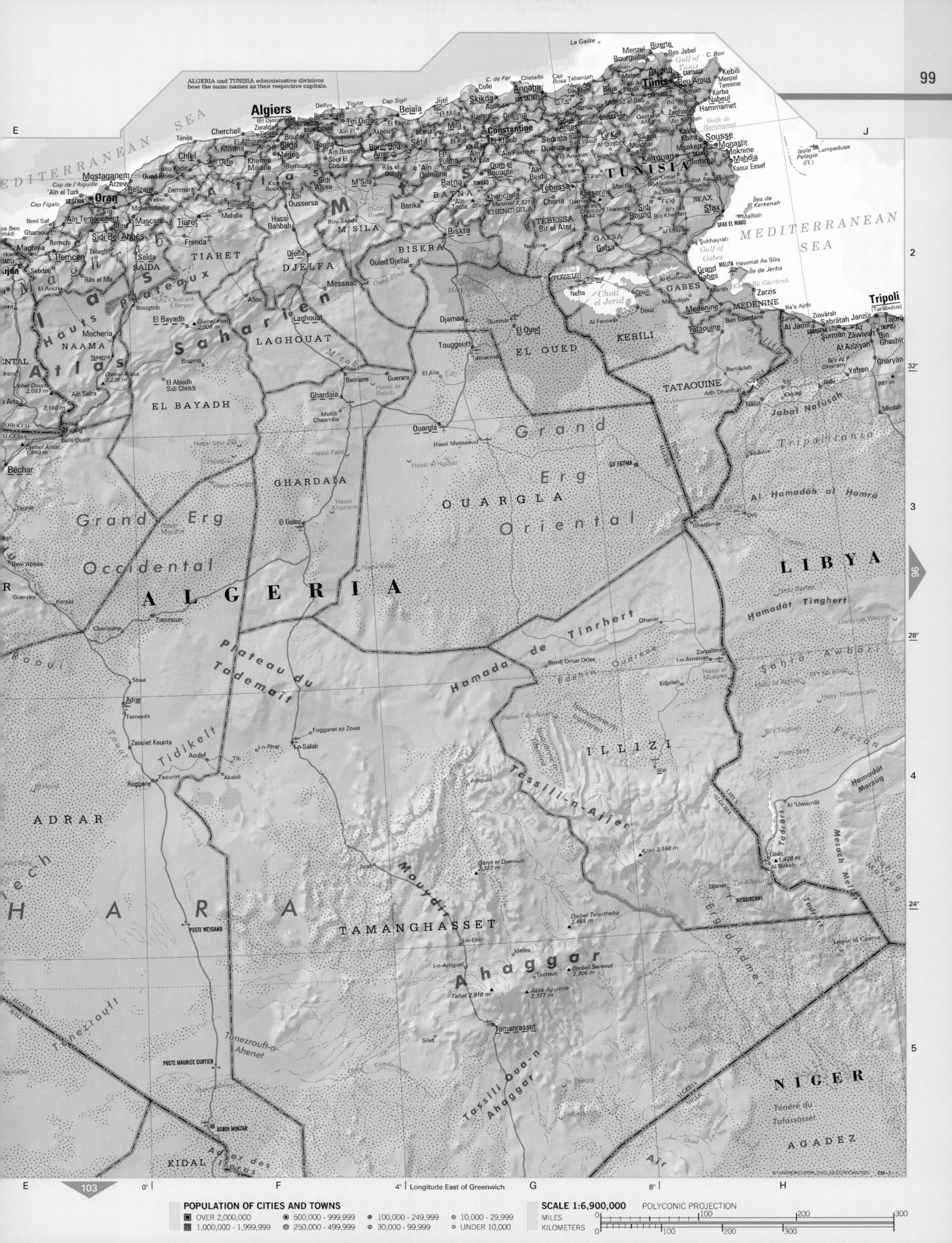

ALGERIA and TUNISIA administrative divisions
bear the same names as their respective capitals.

MEDITERRANEAN SEA

La Galite

Menzel
Bourguiba
Bizerte
Ras Jebel
Gulf of
Tunis
CARTHAGE
Kebili

C. de Fer   Chetaibi   Cap
Collo   Rosa   Tabarqah   Mateur
Annaba   Aïn   Béja
El Tarf   Mateur   Tunis   Ben Arous
Menzel
Temime
Grombalia   Nabeul
Hammamet

Algiers
(El Djezaïr)
Dellys   Tizirt   Cap Sigli   Jijel   Skikda   Azzaba
Ténès   Cherchell   Boumerdes   Tizi Ouzou   El Kseur   Mila
Chlef   Boufarik   Akbou   DJEMILA   Chelghoum   Guelma
Blida   Bouira   Aïn El   Sétif   El   M'Lila   Khroub   Sedrata   Le Kef   Siliana
Miliana   Médéa   Sour El   Ghozlane   Ras El   Aïn   El Fakroun   Ouzara   Kairouan
Oued Rhiou   Bordj Bou   Arrendj   Oulmène   Batna   TIMGAD   Khenchela   Chéria   Kasserine
Khemis   Miliana   Berrouaghia   M'Sila   Aïn   Touta   Djebel Mahmel 2,321 m   Negrine   Sbeitla   Sidi   Sfax
Mostaganem   Arzew   Relizane   Zemmora   Bou Saada   Barika   Biskra   KHENCHELA   TEBESSA   Sfax
Cap de l'Aiguille   Ksar el   Bahbah   Hassi   TÉBESSA   Bir el Ater
Oran   ES SÉNIA   Mascara   Tiaret   Frenda   Djelfa   Ouled Djellal   Gafsa
Aïn Temouchent   Sidi Bel Abbès   Saïda   TIARET   DJELFA   Messaad   BISKRA   Tozeur   GABES
Béni Saf   Tlemcen   Ras el Ma   Hauts   Plateaux   LAGHOUAT   TOZEUR   Gabes
Maghnia   Remchi   NAAMA   Laghouat   Djamaa   El Oued   KEBILI   Medenine   MEDENINE
Mecheria   El Bayadh   Touggourt   EL OUED   Zarzis
Naama   Brezina   Temacine   Douz   Matmata   Ben Guerdane

Atlas Saharien

Atlas Tellien

Grand Erg Oriental

LIBYA

ALGERIA

Tripoli
(Tarabulus)

Plateau du Tademaït

Hamada de Tinrhert

Hamadät Tinghert

Grand Erg Occidental

Tidikelt

ILLIZI

Tassili-n-Ajjer

ADRAR

TAMANGHASSET

Ahaggar

Tahat 2,918 m

Tamanrasset

NIGER

AGADEZ

SAHARA

KIDAL

POPULATION OF CITIES AND TOWNS

| ■ OVER 2,000,000 | ◉ 500,000 - 999,999 | ● 100,000 - 249,999 | ◎ 10,000 - 29,999 |
| □ 1,000,000 - 1,999,999 | ◉ 250,000 - 499,999 | ● 30,000 - 99,999 | ○ UNDER 10,000 |

SCALE 1:6,900,000   POLYCONIC PROJECTION

MILES
KILOMETERS

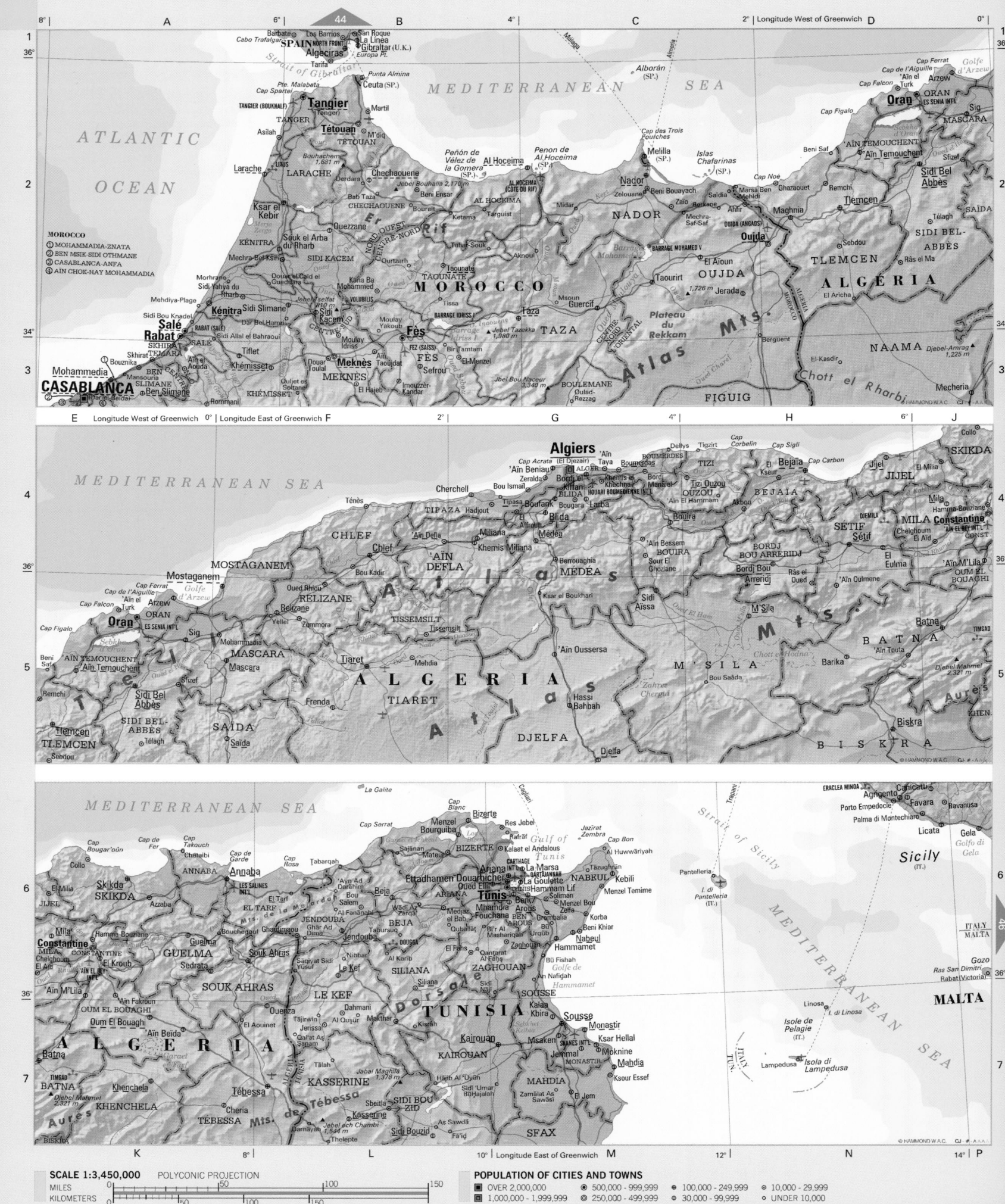

SCALE 1:3,450,000   POLYCONIC PROJECTION

MILES 0   50   100   150
KILOMETERS 0   50   100   150

POPULATION OF CITIES AND TOWNS

■ OVER 2,000,000   ● 500,000 - 999,999   ● 100,000 - 249,999   ● 10,000 - 29,999
■ 1,000,000 - 1,999,999 ● 250,000 - 499,999   ● 30,000 - 99,999   ● UNDER 10,000

POPULATION OF CITIES AND TOWNS

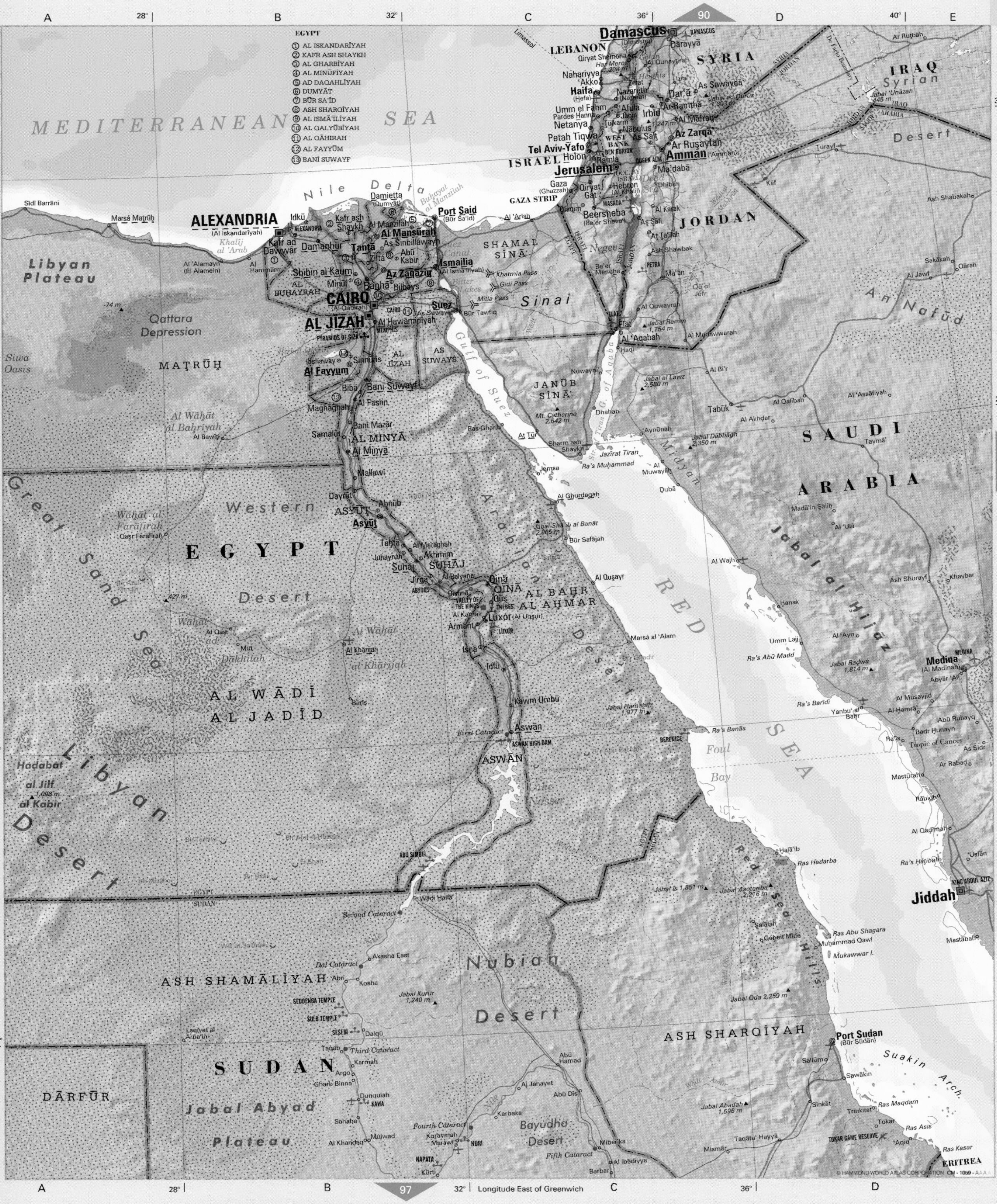

- ■ OVER 2,000,000
- ■ 1,000,000 - 1,999,999
- ● 500,000 - 999,999
- ● 250,000 - 499,999
- ● 100,000 - 249,999
- ● 30,000 - 99,999
- ● 10,000 - 29,999
- ○ UNDER 10,000

SCALE 1:6,900,000   POLYCONIC PROJECTION

MILES
KILOMETERS

Longitude East of Greenwich

Countries & regions: ALGERIA · MALI · NIGER · BURKINA FASO · GHANA · TOGO · BENIN · NIGERIA · CAMEROON

Selected labels: SAHARA · KIDAL · GAO · Adrar des Iforas · TAMANGHASSET · AIR · Ténéré · Erg de Ténéré · AGADEZ · TAHOUA · ZINDER · MARADI · Sudan · OUDALAN · SOUM · SÉNO · TILLABÉRI · Niamey · DOSSO · SOKOTO · KATSINA · KANO · JIGAWA · YOBE · DIFFA · BAUCHI · GOMBE · KEBBI · ZAMFARA · Sokoto Plains · KADUNA · Zaria · JOS · Jos Plateau · PLATEAU · GOURMA · TAPOA · BORGOU · ATAKORA · BENIN · NIGER · Kainji Lake · Abuja · ABUJA FED. CAP. TERR. · Minna · NASSARAWA · BENUE · TARABA · UPPER EAST · NORTHERN · GHANA · Tamale · BRONG-AHAFO · ASHANTI · Kumasi · EASTERN · CENTRAL · GREATER ACCRA · Accra · VOLTA · TOGO · Lomé · Cotonou · Porto-Novo · Lagos · OYO · Ibadan · Ogbomosho · Oshogbo · Ife · Abeokuta · OGUN · ONDO · EKITI · KWARA · KOGI · Ilorin · EDO · Benin City · DELTA · Warri · Onitsha · ANAMBRA · ENUGU · Enugu · EBONYI · ABIA · Aba · IMO · RIVERS · Port Harcourt · BAYELSA · AKWA IBOM · CROSS RIVER · Calabar · CAMEROON · NORD-OUEST · OUEST · SUD-OUEST

Water bodies: Slave Coast · Gold Coast · Bight of Benin · Bight of Biafra · Mouths of the Niger · Niger Delta

Longitude East of Greenwich

POPULATION OF CITIES AND TOWNS

Symbol	Population
■	OVER 2,000,000
□	1,000,000 - 1,999,999
⊙	500,000 - 999,999
⊙	250,000 - 499,999
•	100,000 - 249,999
•	30,000 - 99,999
•	10,000 - 29,999
◦	UNDER 10,000

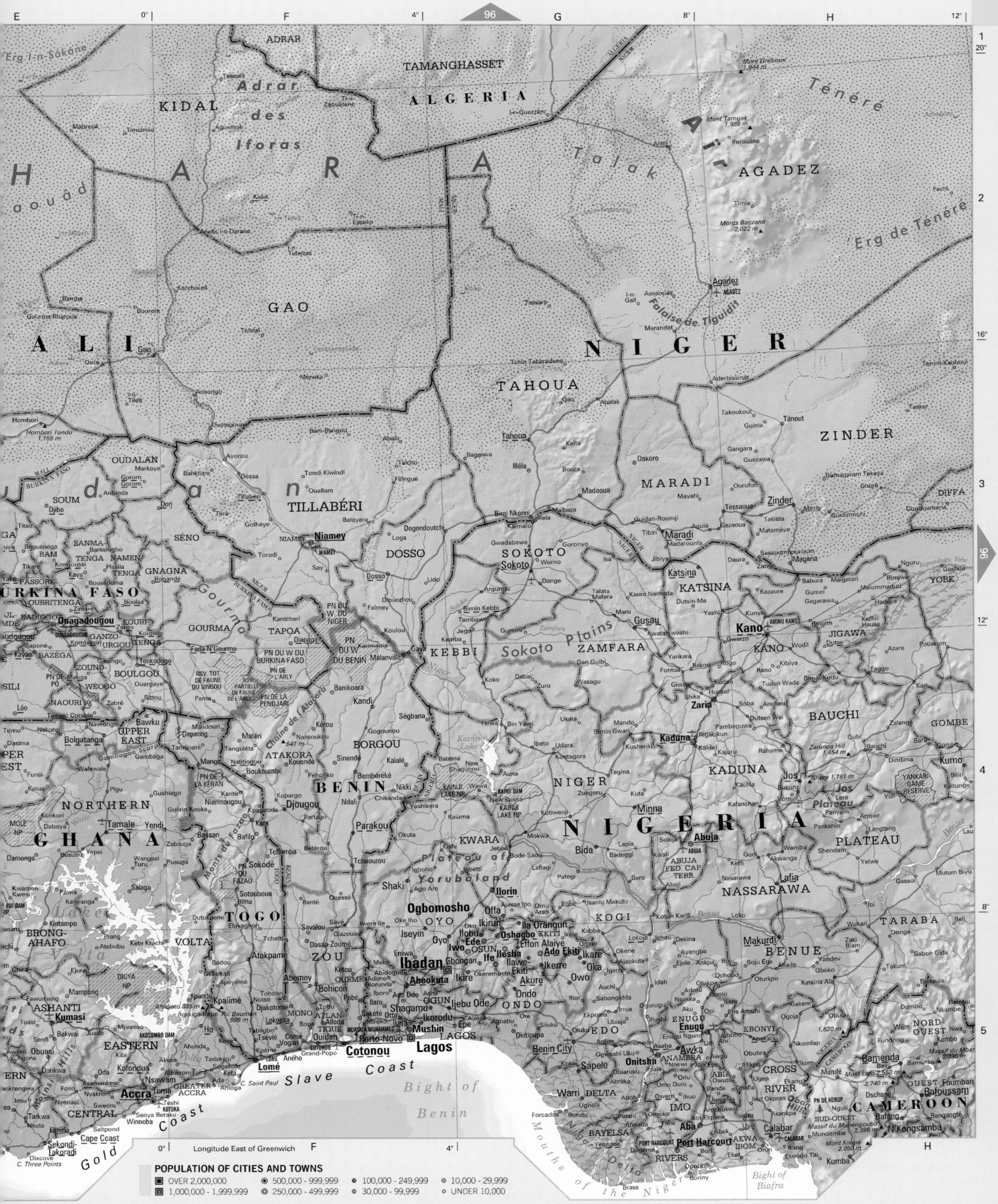

SCALE 1:6,900,000
POLYCONIC PROJECTION

MILES 0   100   200   300
KILOMETERS 0   100   200

Longitude East of Greenwich

POPULATION OF CITIES AND TOWNS

| ◼ OVER 2,000,000 | ⬤ 500,000 - 999,999 | ⦿ 100,000 - 249,999 | ○ 10,000 - 29,999 |
| ◼ 1,000,000 - 1,999,999 | ⬤ 250,000 - 499,999 | ⦿ 30,000 - 99,999 | ○ UNDER 10,000 |

© HAMMOND WORLD ATLAS CORPORATION   CC-2102-A

POPULATION OF CITIES AND TOWNS

■ OVER 2,000,000
■ 1,000,000 - 1,999,999
● 500,000 - 999,999
● 100,000 - 499,999
∘ 50,000 - 99,999
∘ UNDER 50,000

SCALE 1:17,200,000 POLYCONIC PROJECTION

MILES

KILOMETERS

© HAMMOND WORLD ATLAS CORPORATION CC - 2101 A · A · A

ATLANTIC OCEAN

BOTSWANA

NAMIBIA

SOUTH AFRICA

NORTHERN CAPE

WESTERN CAPE

EASTERN CAPE

FREE STATE

LESOTHO

Cape Town

Port Elizabeth

East London

Johannesburg

Pretoria

Soweto

Bloemfontein

Maseru

WESTERN CAPE

ATLANTIC OCEAN

SOUTH AFRICA

GAUTENG

NORTH-WEST

FREE STATE

MPUMALANGA

LIMPOPO

Johannesburg

Pretoria

Soweto

Height | Depth

Same scale as main map

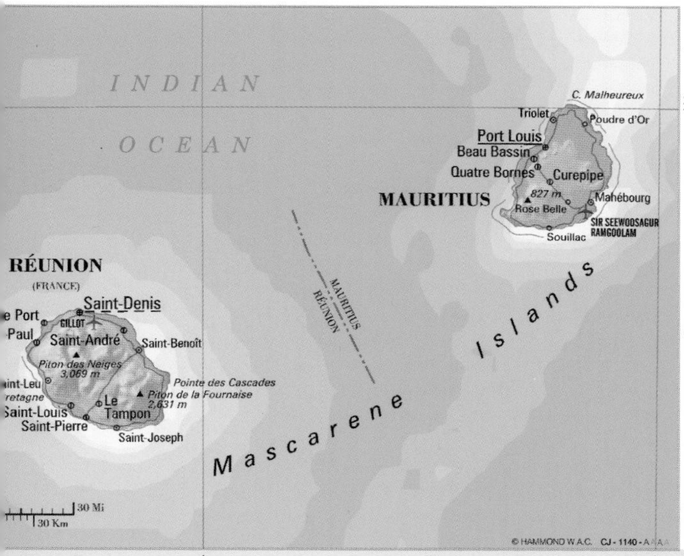

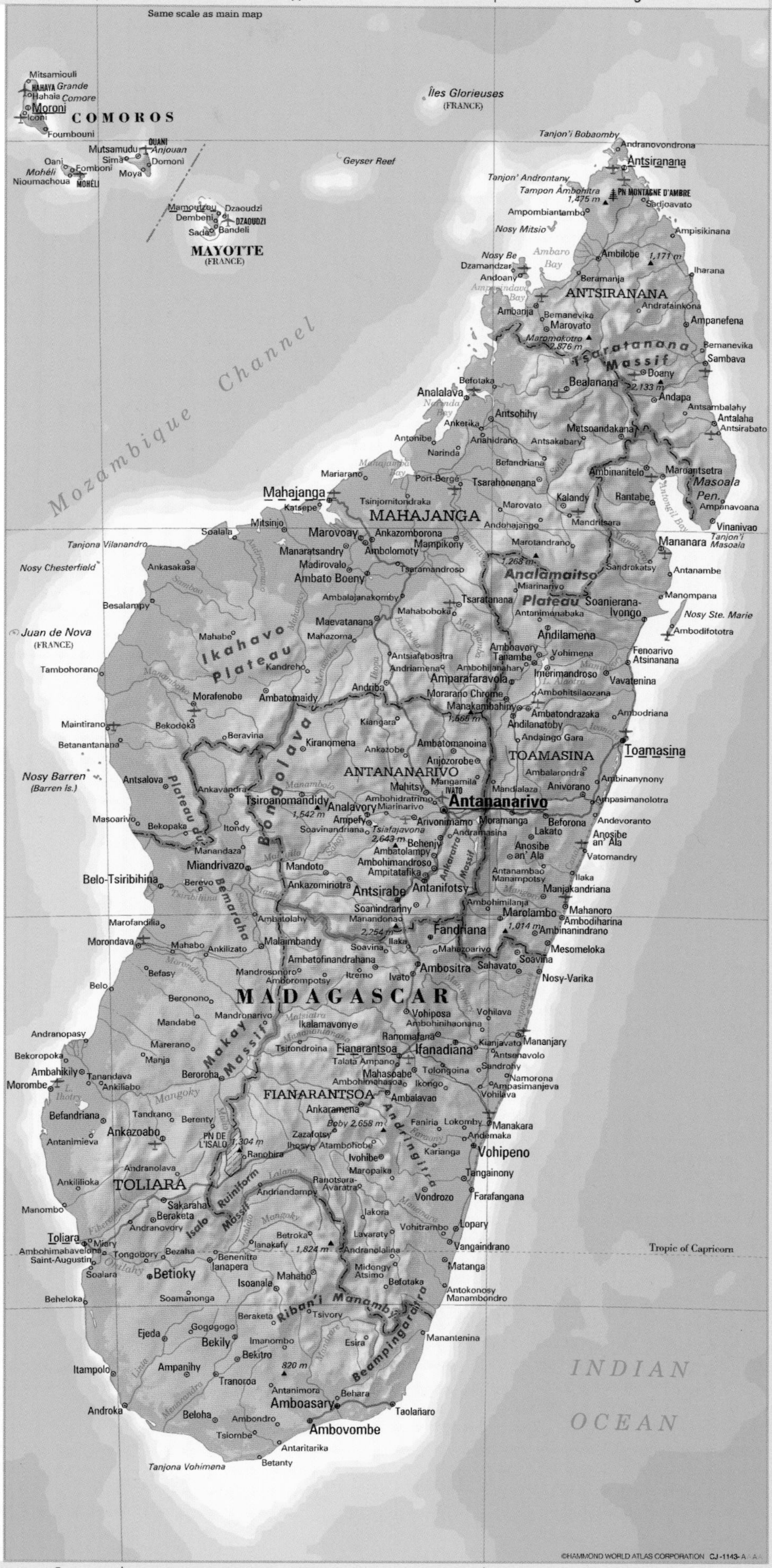

MOZAMBIQUE
INHAMBANE
GAZA
MAPUTO
Matola
Maputo
Mbabane
SWAZILAND
MALANGA
KRUGER NP

KWAZULU-NATAL
KwaMashu
Durban
DURBAN (LOUIS BOTHA)
Pinetown
Port Shepstone
Uvongo Beach
Margate

INDIAN

OCEAN

COMOROS
Moroni
MAYOTTE
(FRANCE)
Îles Glorieuses
(FRANCE)

ANTSIRANANA
PN MONTAGNE D'AMBRE
Geyser Reef
Mozambique Channel

MAHAJANGA
Mahajanga
Tsaratanana Massif

Juan de Nova
(FRANCE)

Nosy Chesterfield

Ikahavo Plateau

ANTANANARIVO
Antananarivo
TOAMASINA
Toamasina

Antsirabe
Fandriana

MADAGASCAR

FIANARANTSOA
Vohipeno

TOLIARA
Toliara

Betioky

Ambovombe

INDIAN

OCEAN

Tropic of Capricorn

INDIAN

OCEAN

RÉUNION
(FRANCE)
Saint-Denis
Saint-André
Saint-Pierre
Piton des Neiges
3,069 m
Pointe de la Cascades
Piton de la Fournaise
2,631 m

MAURITIUS
Port Louis
Beau Bassin
Quatre Bornes
Curepipe
Rose Belle
Mahébourg
SIR SEEWOOSAGUR
RAMGOOLAM

Mascarene Islands

30 Mi
30 Km

© HAMMOND W.A.C. CJ-1140-A

©HAMMOND WORLD ATLAS CORPORATION CJ-1143-A

Longitude East of Greenwich

THE WORLD ALMANAC
WORLD ATLAS

Australia, New Zealand and the Pacific

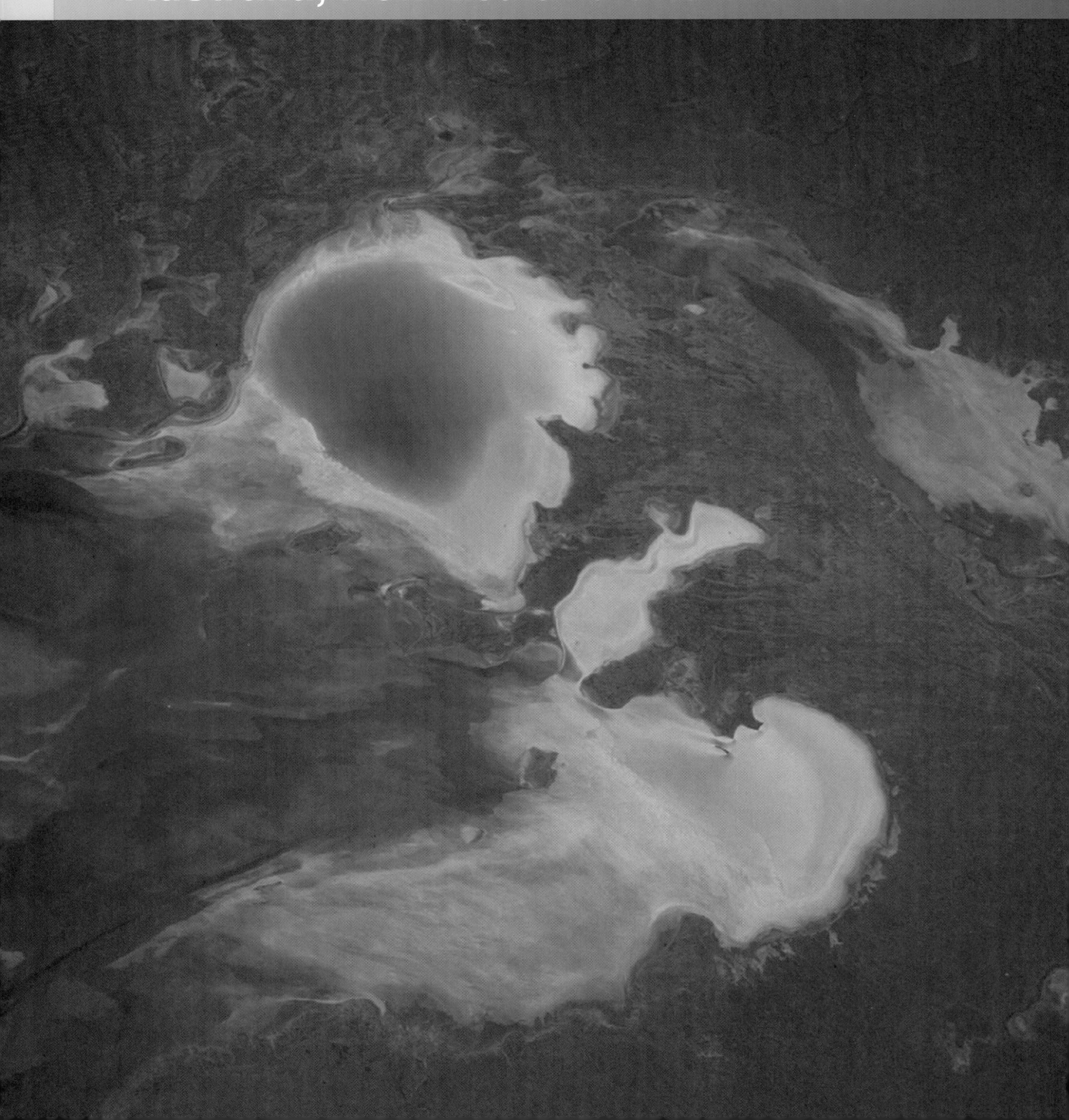

The Lake Eyre Basin is located in the arid interior of south central Australia. This basin is one of the largest areas of internal drainage in the world. It consists of two distinct, but interrelated basins: the north basin and the south basin. The much larger north basin shown here (the highly reflective areas) consists of two very large, normally dry lakebeds. The western lobe (bottom of the image) is Belt Bay, and the eastern lobe is Madigan Bay. The color change, especially in the Madigan Bay lobe, indicates that there was some water in this lobe at the time the image was taken.

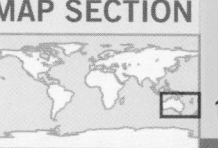
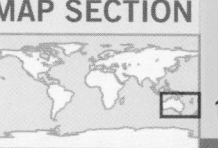

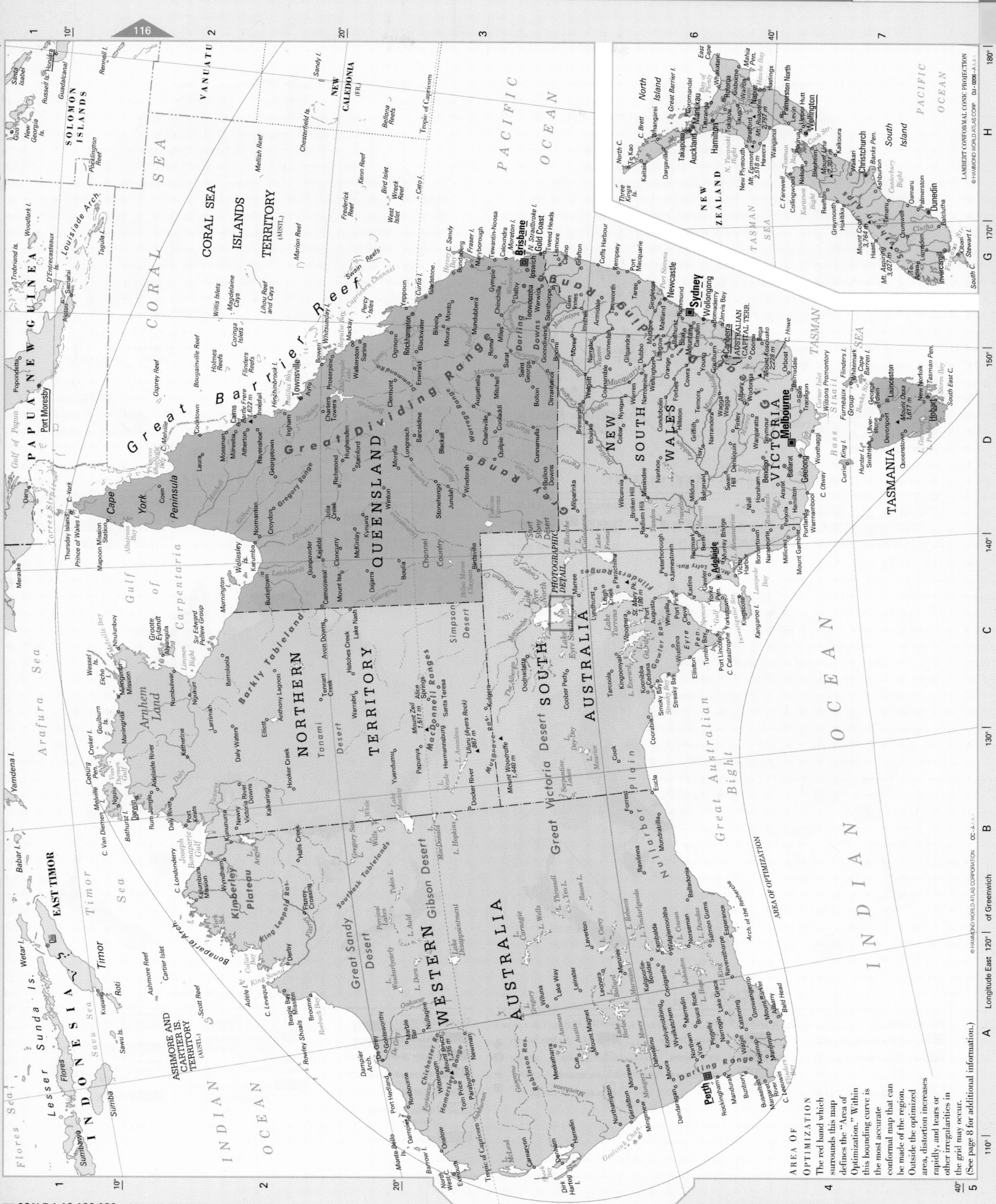

POPULATION OF CITIES AND TOWNS

■ OVER 2,000,000   ● 500,000 - 999,999   ⊕ 50,000 - 99,999
■ 1,000,000 - 1,999,999   ● 100,000 - 499,999   ○ UNDER 50,000

AREA OF OPTIMIZATION
The red band which surrounds this map defines the "Area of Optimization." Within this bounding curve is the most accurate conformal map that can be made of the region. Outside the optimized area, distortion increases rapidly, and tears or other irregularities in the grid may occur.
(See page 8 for additional information.)

Western and Central Australia

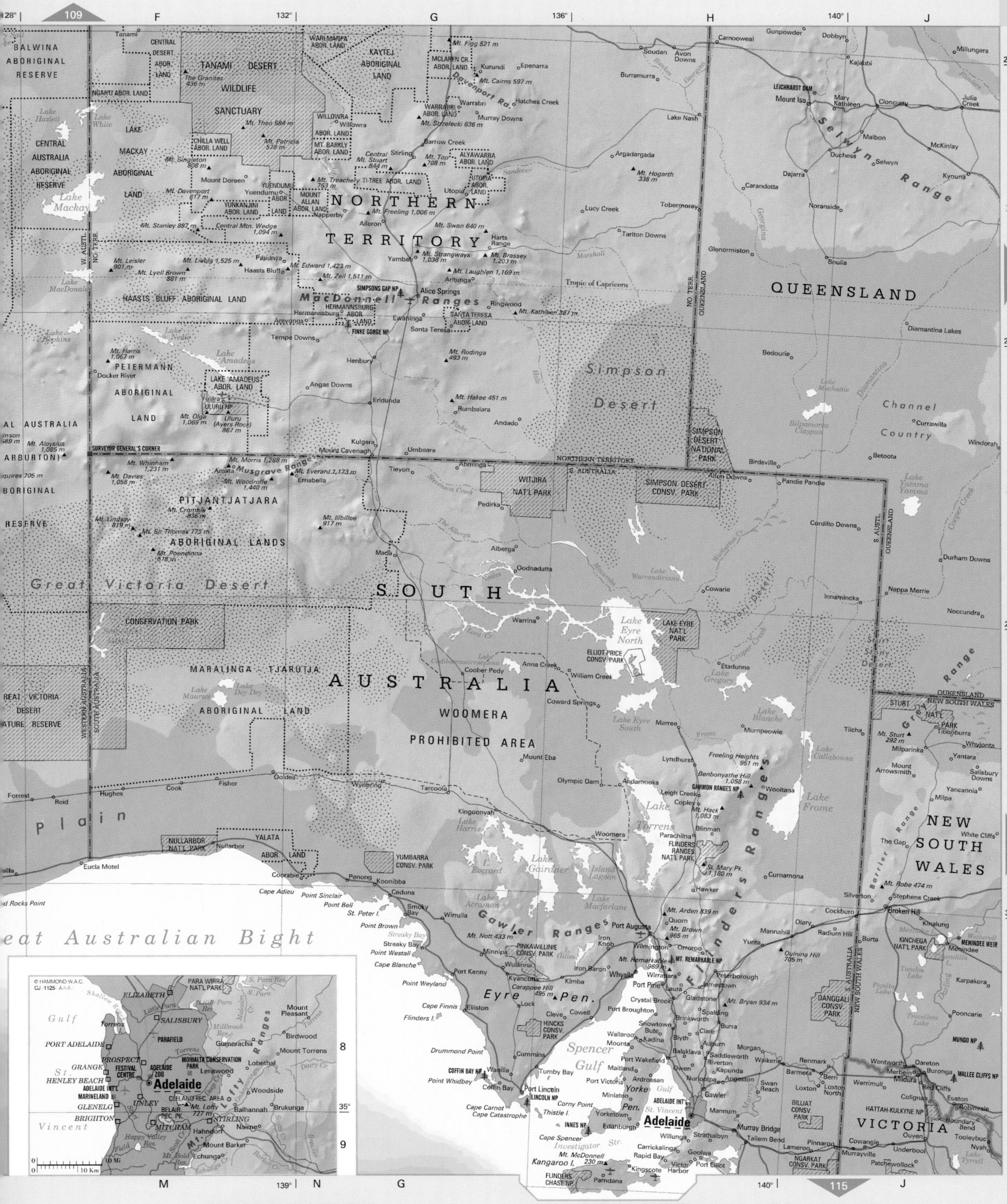

NORTHERN TERRITORY

QUEENSLAND

SOUTH AUSTRALIA

WESTERN AUSTRALIA

NEW SOUTH WALES

VICTORIA

Great Victoria Desert

Tanami Desert

Simpson Desert

Channel Country

Great Australian Bight

Nullarbor Plain

Woomera Prohibited Area

MacDonnell Ranges

Musgrave Ranges

Flinders Ranges

Gawler Ranges

Spencer Gulf

Gulf St. Vincent

Eyre Pen.

Yorke Pen.

Lake Eyre North

Lake Eyre South

Lake Torrens

Lake Gairdner

Lake Frome

Lake Blanche

Lake Callabonna

Lake Amadeus

Lake Mackay

Lake White

Lake Hopkins

Alice Springs

Uluru (Ayers Rock) 867 m

Adelaide

Port Augusta

Port Lincoln

Whyalla

Broken Hill

Coober Pedy

Tropic of Capricorn

Adelaide inset

© HAMMOND W.A.C.
CJ -1125- AAA

Gulf St. Vincent

ELIZABETH
SALISBURY
PARAFIELD
PORT ADELAIDE
PROSPECT
GRANGE
HENLEY BEACH
ADELAIDE INTL.
MARINELAND
GLENELG
BRIGHTON
UNLEY
ADELAIDE
FESTIVAL CENTRE
ADELAIDE ZOO
CLELAND REC. AREA
BELAIR REC. PK.
Mt. Lofty 727 m
STIRLING
Mount Barker

Mount Lofty Ranges

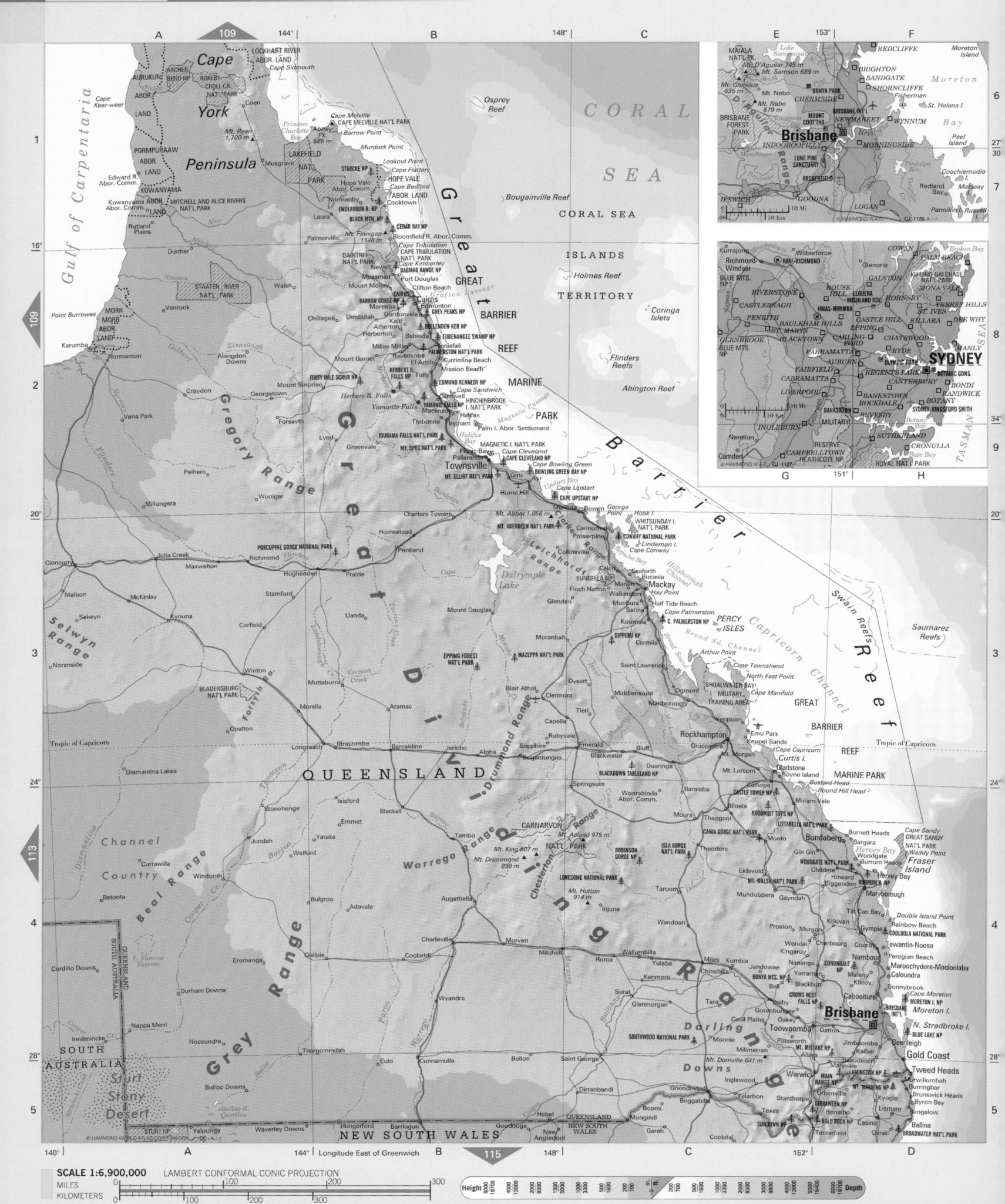

QUEENSLAND

NEW SOUTH WALES

SOUTH AUSTRALIA

VICTORIA

TASMANIA

INDIAN OCEAN

TASMAN SEA

Bass Strait

SYDNEY

MELBOURNE

Canberra

Newcastle

Wollongong

Geelong

Hobart

POPULATION OF CITIES AND TOWNS

- ■ OVER 2,000,000
- ▣ 1,000,000 - 1,999,999
- ● 500,000 - 999,999
- ◉ 250,000 - 499,999
- ● 100,000 - 249,999
- ◎ 30,000 - 99,999
- ○ 10,000 - 29,999
- ◦ UNDER 10,000

SCALE 1:6,900,000   LAMBERT CONFORMAL CONIC PROJECTION

MILES

KILOMETERS

Longitude East of Greenwich

© HAMMOND WORLD ATLAS CORPORATION   CC - A - A

HAWAIIAN ISLANDS

HAWAII (U.S.)

Kure
Midway Is.
Pearl and Hermes Reef
Lisianski I.
Laysan I.
Maro Reef
French Frigate Shoals
Necker I.
Nihoa
Niihau
Kauai
Oahu
Honolulu
Lanai
Molokai
Maui
Hilo
Hawaii

Tropic of Cancer

Johnston Atoll (U.S.)

PACIFIC OCEAN

P o l y n e s i a

Kingman Reef (U.S.)
Palmyra Atoll (U.S.)
Teraina (Washington I.)
Tabuaeran (Fanning I.)
Kiritimati (Christmas I.)

International Date Line

Equator

Jarvis I. (U.S.)

LINE ISLANDS

KIRIBATI

PHOENIX IS.
Abariringa (Canton I.)
Enderbury
Rawaki (Phoenix I.)
Birnie
Orona (Hull I.)
Manra (Sydney I.)

Malden I.

Starbuck I.

Vostok I.
Caroline I.
Flint I.

TOKELAU (N.Z.)
Atafu
Nukunono
Fakaofo
Swains I.

SAMOA
Mt. Silisili 1,858 m
Savai'i
Apia
Upolu

AMERICAN SAMOA
Pago Pago
Tutuila
Manu'a Is.
Rose I.

Rakahanga
Manihiki
Tongareva (Penrhyn)
Pukapuka
Nassau
Suwarrow

NORTHERN COOK IS.

COOK ISLANDS (N.Z.)

Bellingshausen
Palmerston Atoll
Aitutaki Atoll
Amuri
Manuae Atoll
Mitiaro
Atiu
Mauke
Maria

SOUTHERN COOK IS.

NIUE (N.Z.)
Alofi

Neiafu
Vava'u Group
Pangai
Ha'apai Group
Nuku'alofa
'Eua
Tongatapu Group

TONGA

Rarotonga
Mangaia

Îles Sous le Vent
Maupiti
Bora Bora
Tupai
Huahine
Raiatea
Tahaa
Uturoa
Moorea
Papeete
Faaa
Tahiti
Îles du Vent

SOCIETY IS.

Hereheretue
Duke of Gloucester Is.

Rimatara
Rurutu
Mataura
Tubuai
Raivavae

TUBUAI ISLANDS (Austral Islands)

Rapa

Moerai

FRENCH POLYNESIA

Tikehau
Rangiroa
Manihi
Takaroa
Tepoto
Disappointment Is.
Napuka
Pukapuka
Tiputa
Arutua
Apataki
Fangatau
Kaukura
Makatea
Toau
Fakarava
Anaa
Tahanea
Makemo
Hikueru
Marokau
Taenga
Amanu
Hao
Otepa
Vahitahi
Reao
Nukutavake
Pukarua
Vanavaro
Turela
Marutea
Mururoa
Maria
Fangataufa
Morane
Rikitea
Temoe
Mangareva

GAMBIER IS.

Marotiri Is. (Bass Is.)

TUAMOTU ARCHIPELAGO

Actaeon Group

MARQUESAS IS.

PACIFIC OCEAN

PITCAIRN ISLANDS (U.K.)
Oeno Atoll
Adamstown
Pitcairn I.
Henderson I.
Ducie I.

Tropic of Capricorn

Easter Island (Isla de Pascua) (CHILE)

International Date Line

New Zealand inset map

Three Kings Is.
C. Maria van Diemen
North C.
Te Kao
C. Kerikeri
Kaitaia
Kaikohe
C. Brett
Whangarei
Dargaville
Warkworth
Kaipara Har.
Great Barrier I.
Hauraki Gulf
Takapuna
Auckland
Coromandel Pen.
Manukau
Thames
Te Aroha
Bay of Plenty
Huntly
Tauranga
Te Araroa
Hamilton
Cambridge
Whakatane
East C.
Te Awamutu
Kawerau
Hikurangi 1,754 m
Tokoroa
Rotorua
Te Kuiti
Murupara
UREWERA NP
North Taranaki Bight
Taupo
New Plymouth
Mt. Egmont 2,518 m
Mt. Ruapehu 2,797 m
Turangi
TONGARIRO NP
Napier
Gisborne
C. Egmont
Stratford
Hawera
Mahia Pen.
Wairoa
Hawke Bay
Wanganui
Hastings
South Taranaki Bight
Dannevirke
Ashhurst
Waipukurau
Palmerston North
Levin
Masterton

NORTH ISLAND

NEW ZEALAND

TASMAN SEA

C. Farewell
Collingwood
Tasman Bay
Karamea Bight
Karamea
Motueka
Porirua
Nelson
Upper Hutt
Wellington
Lower Hutt
Mt. Owen 1,875 m
Westport
Murchison
Blenheim
NELSON LAKES NP
Mt. Una 2,301 m
Ward
Reefton
C. Palliser
Cook Strait
Greymouth
Clarence
Hokitika
Lewis Pass
Kaikoura
Otira
ARTHUR'S PASS NP
Arthur's Pass
Waikari
Rangiora
Pegasus Bay
Fox Glacier
WESTLAND NP
Mt. Cook 3,764 m
Darfield
Kaiapoi
Christchurch
MT. COOK NP
Haast
Banks Pen.
Ashburton
Geraldine
MT. ASPIRING NP
Mt. Aspiring 3,027 m
Temuka
Twizel
Timaru
Canterbury Bight
Wanaka
Cromwell
Waimate
Queenstown
Alexandra
Oamaru
FIORDLAND
Te Anau
Lumsden
Palmerston
NAT'L PARK
West C.
Mosgiel
Gore
Milton
Dunedin
Riverton
Balclutha
Invercargill
Bluff
Oban
Mt. Anglem 980 m
Stewart I.
South C.
Foveaux Strait
SOUTHERN ALPS

SOUTH ISLAND

PACIFIC OCEAN

Snares Is.

© HAMMOND W.A.C. CJ-1200-A-A-A

LAMBERT CONFORMAL CONIC PROJECTION

0   90 Mi
0   90 Km

© HAMMOND WORLD ATLAS CORPORATION   CM·A·A

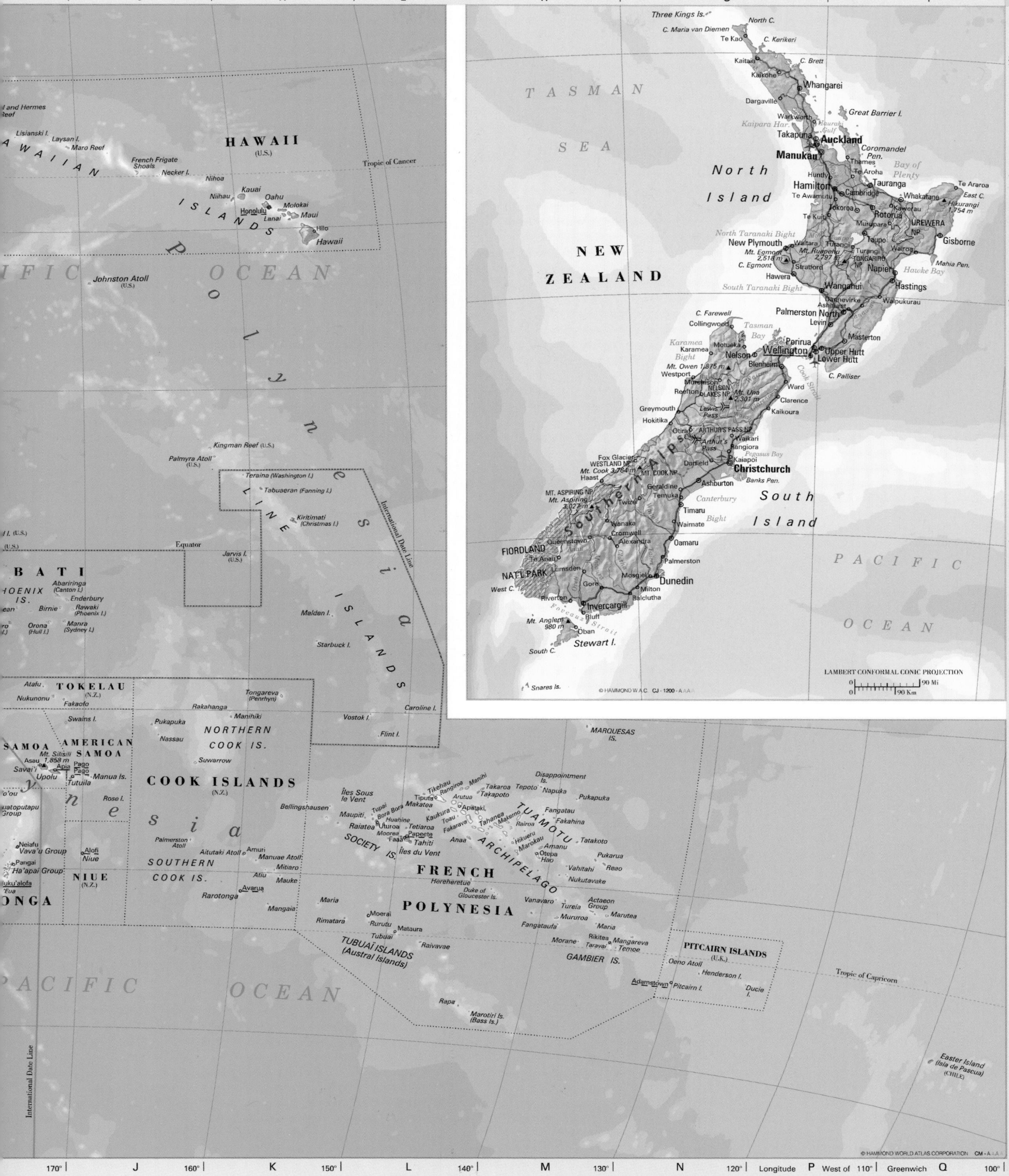

POPULATION OF CITIES AND TOWNS

■ OVER 3,000,000
◙ 1,000,000 - 2,999,999
⊕ 500,000 - 999,999
⊙ 100,000 - 499,999
○ UNDER 100,000

SCALE 1:31,000,000   LAMBERT CONFORMAL CONIC PROJECTION

MILES
0   50   100   150
KILOMETERS
0   50   100   150

THE **WORLD** ALMANAC
WORLD ATLAS

North America

The Grand Canyon, one of the deepest canyons in the world, with a depth of 1 mile (1.6 km.), can be seen in this spectacular, west-looking, low-oblique image. The Colorado River cut through rocks billions of years old to create this canyon. The Grand Canyon is 277 miles (466 km.) long and averages nearly 10 miles (16 km.) in width. The snow-covered, forested Kaibab Plateau (north of the canyon) and the Coconino Plateau (south of the canyon) are visible. Western portions of the Painted Desert can be seen east of the canyon where the Little Colorado joins the Colorado River.

AREA OF OPTIMIZATION
The red band which surrounds this map defines the "Area of Optimization." Within this bounding curve is the most accurate conformal map that can be made of the region. Outside the optimized area, distortion increases rapidly, and tears or other irregularities in the grid may occur. (See page 8 for additional information.)

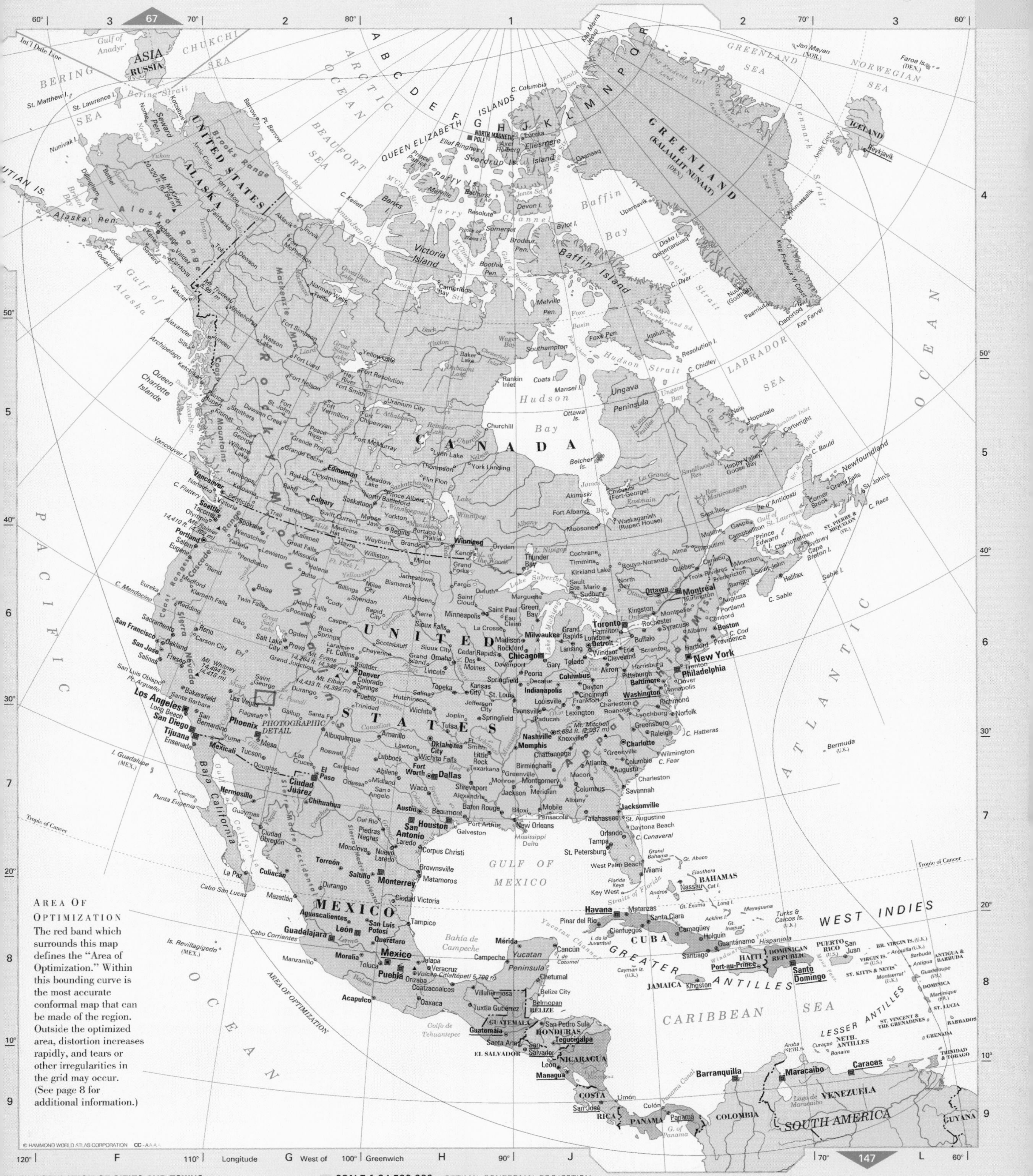

© HAMMOND WORLD ATLAS CORPORATION   CC - A.A.A.-

POPULATION OF CITIES AND TOWNS

- ■ OVER 3,000,000
- ■ 1,000,000 - 2,999,999
- ● 500,000 - 999,999
- ● 100,000 - 499,999
- ○ UNDER 100,000

SCALE 1:34,500,000   OPTIMAL CONFORMAL PROJECTION

MILES 0   500   1000   1500
KILOMETERS 0   500   1000   1500

● New York 34°
AVERAGE JANUARY TEMPERATURE
DEGREES FAHRENHEIT AT
SELECTED STATIONS

AVERAGE JANUARY TEMPERATURE

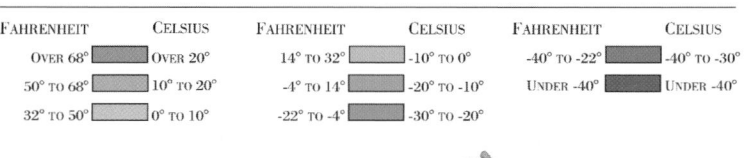

FAHRENHEIT	CELSIUS	FAHRENHEIT	CELSIUS	FAHRENHEIT	CELSIUS
OVER 68°	OVER 20°	14° TO 32°	-10° TO 0°	-40° TO -22°	-40° TO -30°
50° TO 68°	10° TO 20°	-4° TO 14°	-20° TO -10°	UNDER -40°	UNDER -40°
32° TO 50°	0° TO 10°	-22° TO -4°	-30° TO -20°		

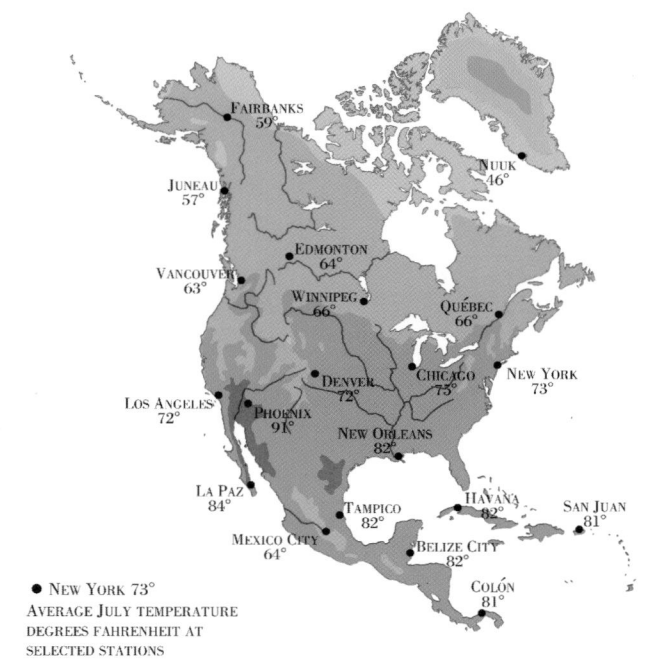

● New York 73°
AVERAGE JULY TEMPERATURE
DEGREES FAHRENHEIT AT
SELECTED STATIONS

AVERAGE JULY TEMPERATURE

FAHRENHEIT	CELSIUS	FAHRENHEIT	CELSIUS	FAHRENHEIT	CELSIUS
OVER 86°	OVER 30°	50° TO 68°	10° TO 20°	14° TO 32°	-10° TO 0°
68° TO 86°	20° TO 30°	32° TO 50°	0° TO 10°	UNDER 14°	UNDER -10°

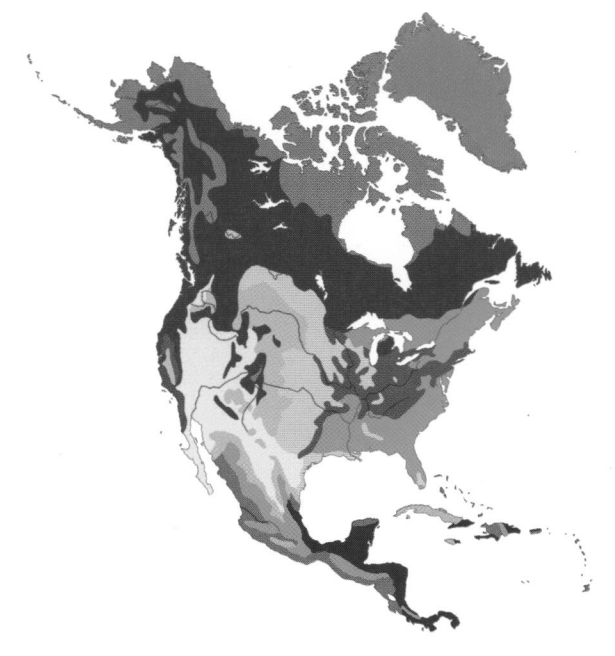

CLIMATE

HUMID TROPICAL
- Af NO DRY SEASON
- Am SHORT DRY SEASON
- Aw DRY WINTER

DRY
- BS SEMIARID ⎤ h HOT
- BW ARID   ⎦ k COLD

HUMID WARM
- Cf NO DRY SEASON
- Cw DRY WINTER
- Cs DRY SUMMER

HUMID COLD
- Df NO DRY SEASON
- Ds DRY SUMMER

COLD POLAR
- ET SHORT COOL SUMMER, LONG COLD WINTER
- EF PERPETUAL FROST
- a HOT SUMMER
- b COOL SUMMER
- c SHORT COOL SUMMER

AFTER KOEPPEN-GEIGER

VEGETATION

TROPICAL FOREST
- TROPICAL RAINFOREST
- LIGHT TROPICAL FOREST

TROPICAL GRASSLAND
- WOODED SAVANNA

MID-LATITUDE FOREST
- NEEDLELEAF FOREST
- BROADLEAF FOREST
- MIXED NEEDLELEAF AND BROADLEAF FOREST
- WOODLAND AND SHRUB (MEDITERRANEAN)

MID-LATITUDE GRASSLAND
- SHORT GRASS (STEPPE)
- TALL GRASS (PRAIRIE)
- DESERT AND DESERT SHRUB
- TUNDRA AND ALPINE
- PERMANENT ICE COVER

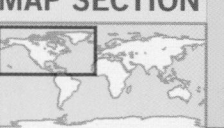
North America – Geographical Comparisons

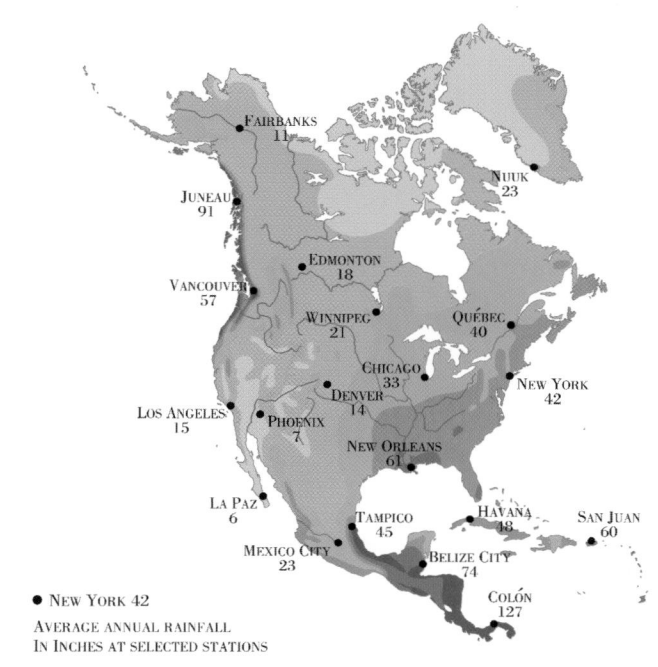

FAIRBANKS
11

NUUK
23

JUNEAU
91

EDMONTON
18

VANCOUVER
57

WINNIPEG
21

QUÉBEC
40

CHICAGO
33

DENVER
14

NEW YORK
42

LOS ANGELES
15

PHOENIX
7

NEW ORLEANS
61

LA PAZ
6

TAMPICO
45

HAVANA
48

SAN JUAN
60

MEXICO CITY
23

BELIZE CITY
74

COLÓN
127

● NEW YORK 42
AVERAGE ANNUAL RAINFALL
IN INCHES AT SELECTED STATIONS

AVERAGE ANNUAL RAINFALL

INCHES	CM	INCHES	CM	INCHES	CM
OVER 80	OVER 200	40 TO 60	100 TO 150	10 TO 20	25 TO 50
60 TO 80	150 TO 200	20 TO 40	50 TO 100	UNDER 10	UNDER 25

● CITIES WITH OVER 2,000,000
INHABITANTS

POPULATION DISTRIBUTION

DENSITY PER		SQ. MI.	SQ. KM.	SQ. MI.	SQ. KM.
SQ. MI.	SQ. KM.	130 TO 260	50 TO 100	3 TO 25	1 TO 10
OVER 260	OVER 100	25 TO 130	10 TO 50	UNDER 3	UNDER 1

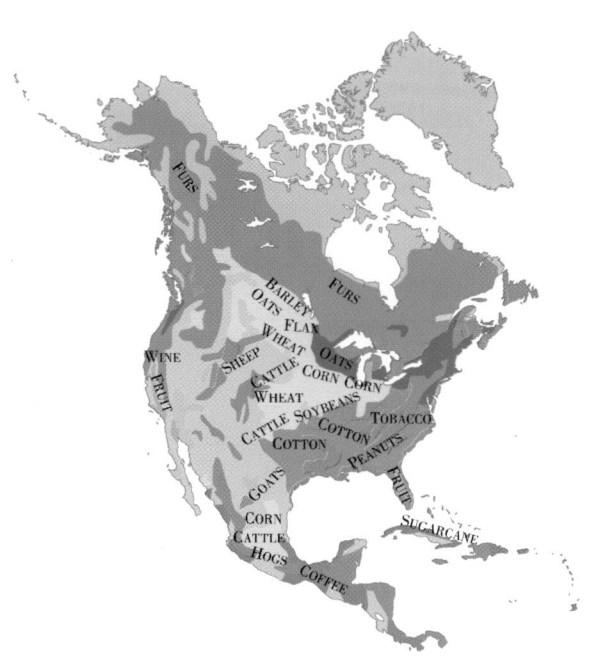

FURS

BARLEY

OATS

FLAX

WHEAT

FURS

OATS

WINE

SHEEP

CATTLE

CORN CORN

WHEAT

CATTLE SOYBEANS

COTTON

TOBACCO

COTTON

PEANUTS

GOATS

FRUIT

FRUIT

CORN

CATTLE

HOGS

COFFEE

SUGARCANE

LAND USE

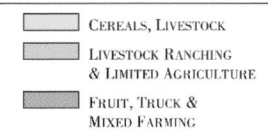 CEREALS, LIVESTOCK

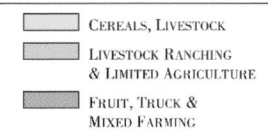 LIVESTOCK RANCHING
& LIMITED AGRICULTURE

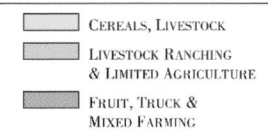 FRUIT, TRUCK &
MIXED FARMING

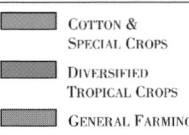 COTTON &
SPECIAL CROPS

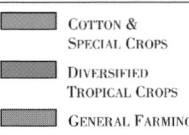 DIVERSIFIED
TROPICAL CROPS

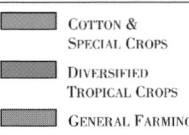 GENERAL FARMING

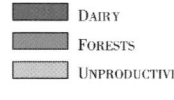 DAIRY

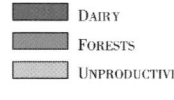 FORESTS

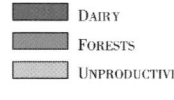 UNPRODUCTIVE

MINERAL RESOURCES

ENERGY & FUELS	IRON & FERROALLOYS	OTHER MAJOR RESOURCES		
◆ COAL	1 COBALT	1 ANTIMONY	7 GOLD	13 PLATINUM
▲ NATURAL GAS	2 IRON ORE	2 ASBESTOS	8 GRAPHITE	14 POTASH
● PETROLEUM	3 MANGANESE	3 BAUXITE	9 LEAD	15 SILVER
■ URANIUM	4 MOLYBDENUM	4 BORAX	10 MERCURY	16 SULFUR
	5 NICKEL	5 COPPER	11 MICA	17 TITANIUM
	6 TUNGSTEN	6 FLUORSPAR	12 PHOSPHATES	18 ZINC
	7 VANADIUM			

134

A 150° B

60°

ALASKA
UNITED STATES

YUKON

TERRITORY

3

Alexander

Archipelago

Queen
Charlotte
Islands

PACIFIC

50°

OCEAN

Vancouver
Island

4

BRITISH

COLUMBIA

R O C K Y   M O U N T A I N S

NORTHWEST

TERRITORIES

BEAUFORT
SEA

Banks
Island

Amundsen
Gulf

Victoria
Island

Prince Albert Sound

Coronation Gulf Dease Str.

Great Slave
Lake

Great
Bear
Lake

Boothia
Peninsula

Prince
of Wales
Island

Somerset
Island

F 110° 100° G

Parry

Resolute

King
William I.

N U N

ALBERTA

SASKATCHEWAN

MANITOBA

Edmonton

Calgary

Saskatoon

Regina

Winnipeg

Lake
Winnipeg

Churchill

WASHINGTON

Seattle

Vancouver
Portland
Salem
OREGON

U N I T E D

MONTANA

CANADA
UNITED STATES

NORTH DAKOTA

MINNESOTA

40°

CALIFORNIA

Great

Basin

IDAHO

WYOMING

S T A T E S

SOUTH DAKOTA

Minneapolis
Saint Paul

WISCON

San Francisco
San Jose

NEVADA

Salt Lake City
UTAH Provo

NEBRASKA

IOWA

5

D 120° E 110° 124 F 100° Longitude West of Greenwich G 90°

Height Depth

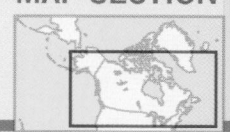
POPULATION OF CITIES AND TOWNS
- ■ OVER 2,000,000
- ■ 1,000,000 - 1,999,999
- ● 500,000 - 999,999
- ● 100,000 - 499,999
- 50,000 - 99,999
- ○ UNDER 50,000

SCALE 1:13,800,000 LAMBERT CONFORMAL CONIC PROJECTION

MILES 0 ... 200 ... 400 ... 600
KILOMETERS 0 ... 200 ... 400 ... 600

© HAMMOND WORLD ATLAS CORPORATION

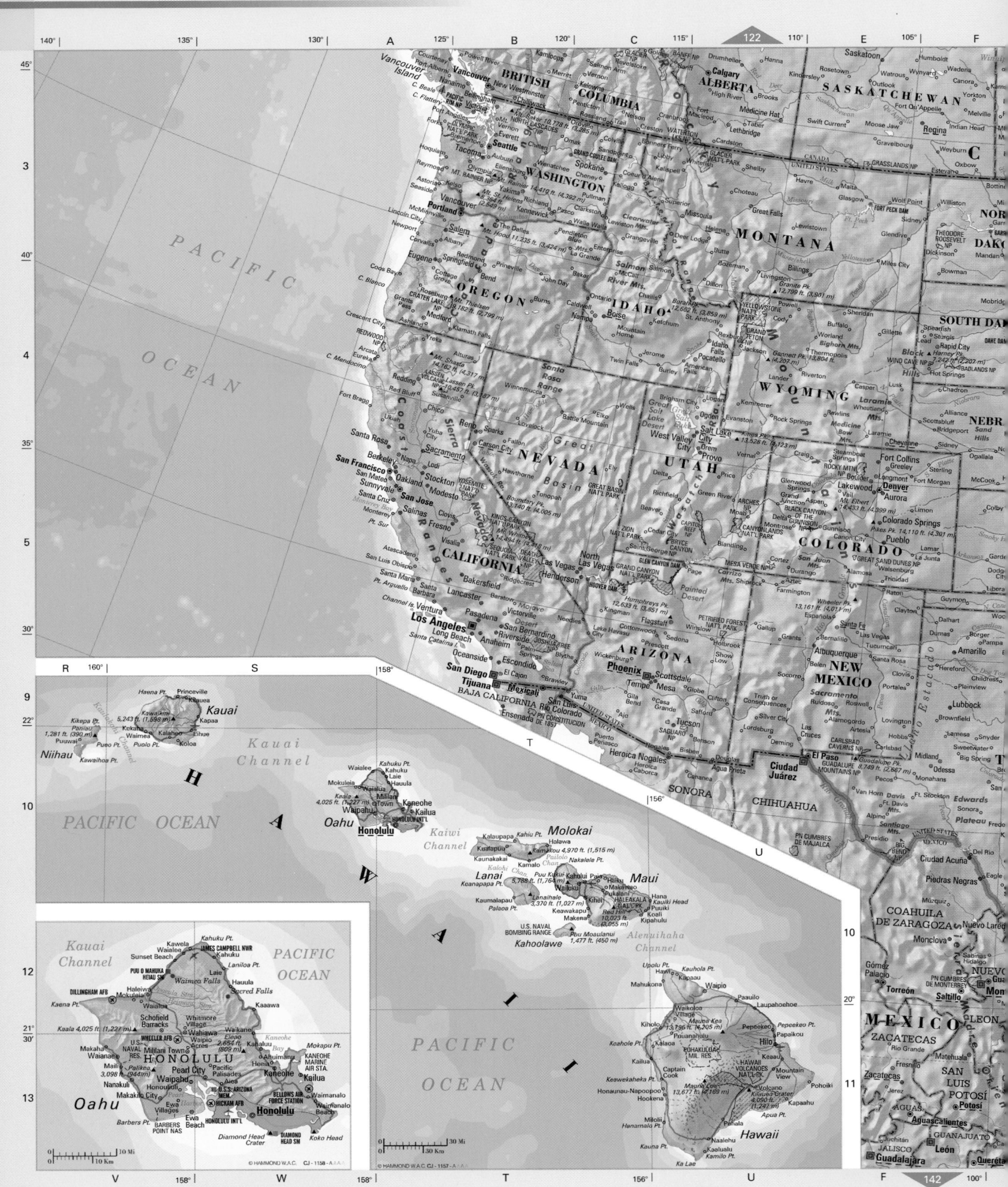

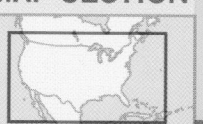
POPULATION OF CITIES AND TOWNS

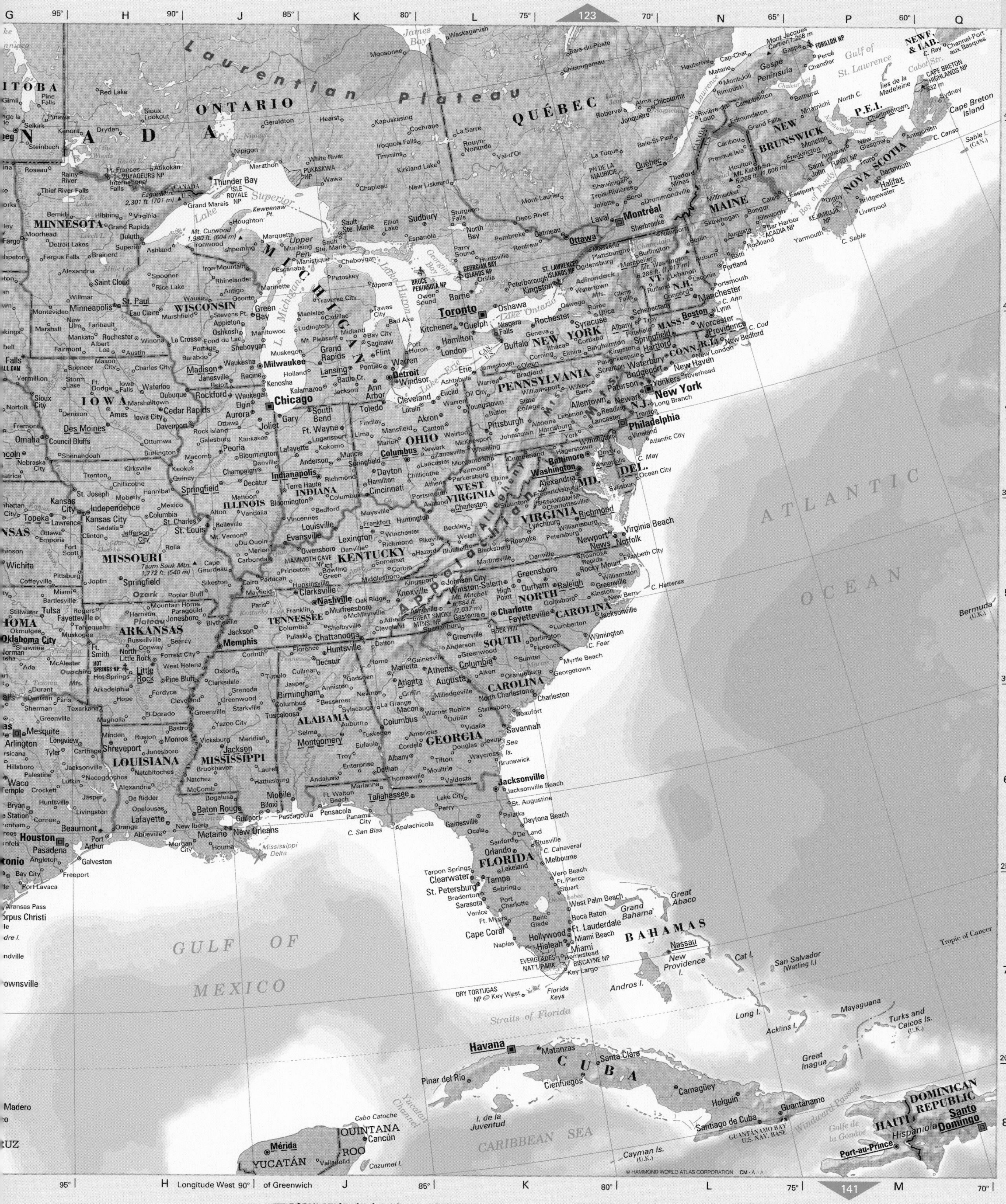

- ■ OVER 2,000,000
- ■ 1,000,000 - 1,999,999
- ● 500,000 - 999,999
- ● 100,000 - 499,999
- ◎ 50,000 - 99,999
- ○ UNDER 50,000

SCALE 1:13,800,000 LAMBERT CONFORMAL CONIC PROJECTION

MILES

KILOMETERS

© HAMMOND WORLD ATLAS CORPORATION CM-A-A-A

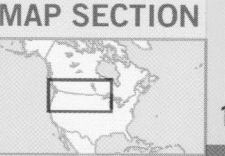
POPULATION OF CITIES AND TOWNS

■ OVER 2,000,000	◉ 500,000 - 999,999	⊕ 100,000 - 249,999	◎ 10,000 - 29,999
■ 1,000,000 - 1,999,999	◉ 250,000 - 499,999	⊕ 30,000 - 99,999	◦ UNDER 10,000

SCALE 1:6,900,000   LAMBERT CONFORMAL CONIC PROJECTION

MILES 0 — 100 — 200 — 300
KILOMETERS 0 — 100 — 200 — 300

© HAMMOND WORLD ATLAS CORPORATION

PACIFIC

OCEAN

Southwestern United States

POPULATION OF CITIES AND TOWNS

■ OVER 2,000,000
■ 1,000,000 - 1,999,999
◉ 500,000 - 999,999
◎ 250,000 - 499,999
◉ 100,000 - 249,999
◉ 30,000 - 99,999
◦ 10,000 - 29,999
• UNDER 10,000

SCALE 1:6,900,000   LAMBERT CONFORMAL CONIC PROJECTION

MILES   0   100   200   300
KILOMETERS   0   100   200   300

© HAMMOND WORLD ATLAS CORPORATION   CM-A-14

GULF OF MEXICO

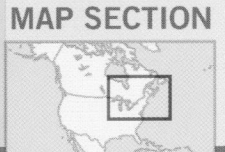
Southeastern Canada, Northeastern United States

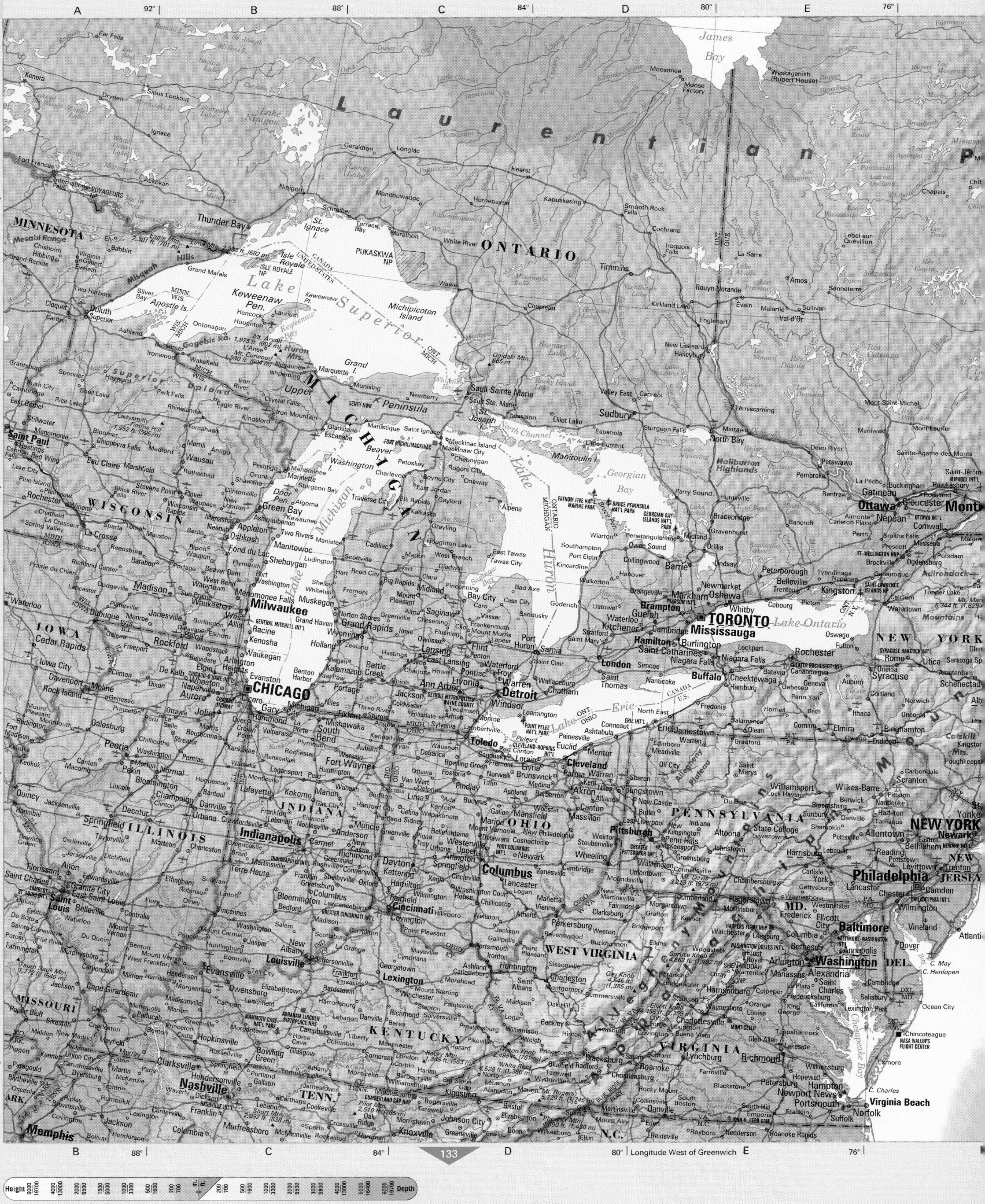

F   88°   G   84°   H   130   80°   J   76°   K

ILLINOIS
INDIANA
OHIO
WEST VIRGINIA
KENTUCKY
VIRGINIA
TENNESSEE
NORTH CAROLINA
MISSISSIPPI
ALABAMA
GEORGIA
SOUTH CAROLINA
FLORIDA

Springfield
Indianapolis
Columbus
Cincinnati
Louisville
Lexington
Richmond
Washington
Baltimore
DEL.
MD.
Virginia Beach
Norfolk
Nashville
Memphis
Knoxville
Raleigh
Charlotte
Atlanta
Birmingham
Montgomery
Columbus
Savannah
Columbia
Jacksonville
Tallahassee
Orlando
Tampa
Saint Petersburg
Miami
Key West
New Orleans

ATLANTIC
OCEAN

GULF OF MEXICO

BAHAMAS
Nassau
New Providence I.
Grand Bahama
Great Abaco
Andros Island

Mississippi
Delta

Florida
Keys

36°
3
32°
4
28°
5
24°
6

F   88°   G   84°   H   141   80°   J

© HAMMOND WORLD ATLAS CORPORATION   CM - AAA

POPULATION OF CITIES AND TOWNS
■ OVER 2,000,000
■ 1,000,000 - 1,999,999
● 500,000 - 999,999
● 250,000 - 499,999
● 100,000 - 249,999
● 30,000 - 99,999
● 10,000 - 29,999
● UNDER 10,000

SCALE 1:6,900,000   LAMBERT CONFORMAL CONIC PROJECTION
MILES   0   100   200   300
KILOMETERS   0   100   200   300

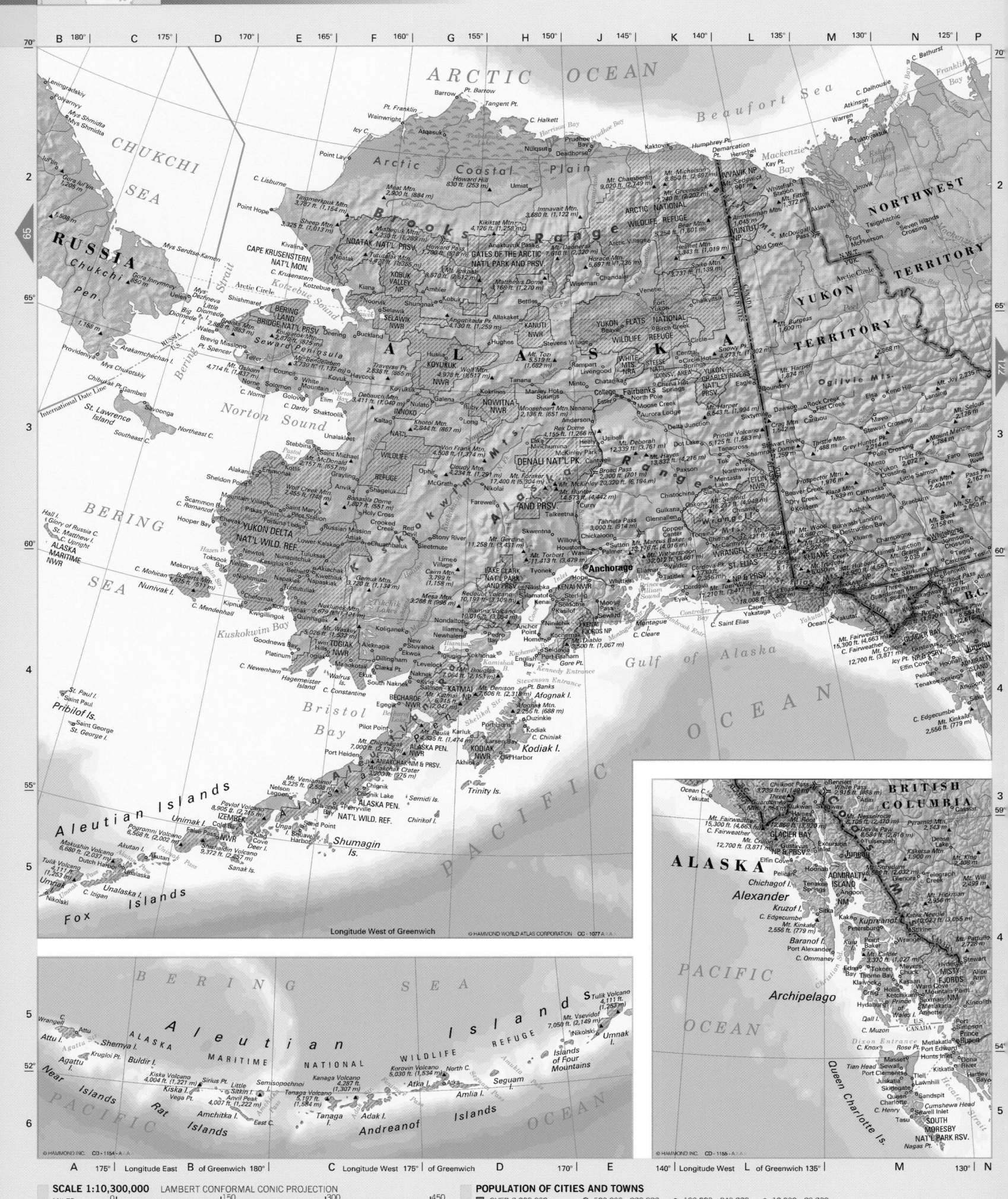

SCALE 1:1,150,000   LAMBERT CONFORMAL CONIC PROJECTION

MILES

KILOMETERS

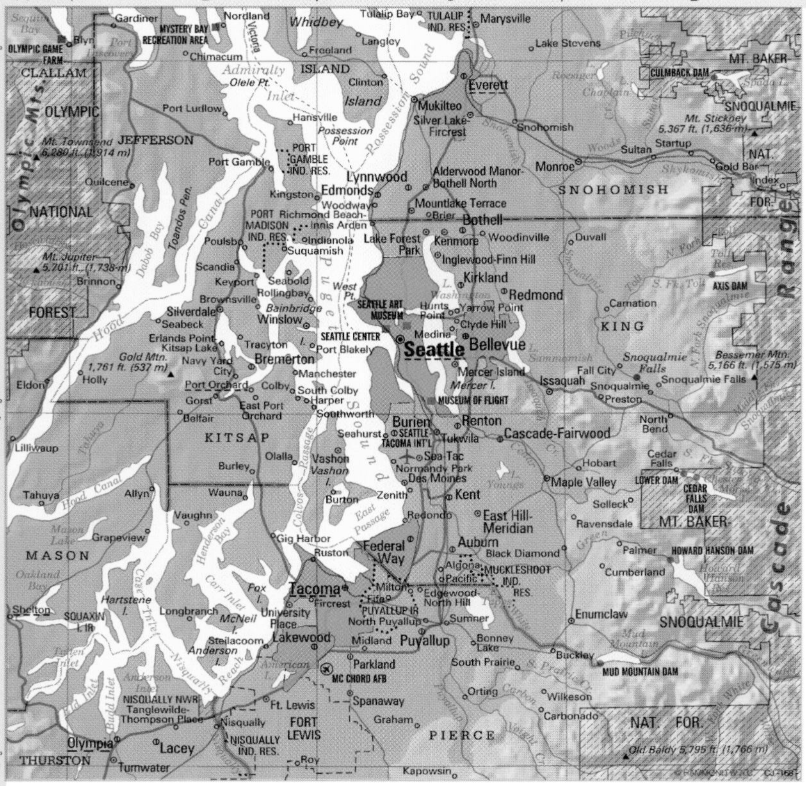

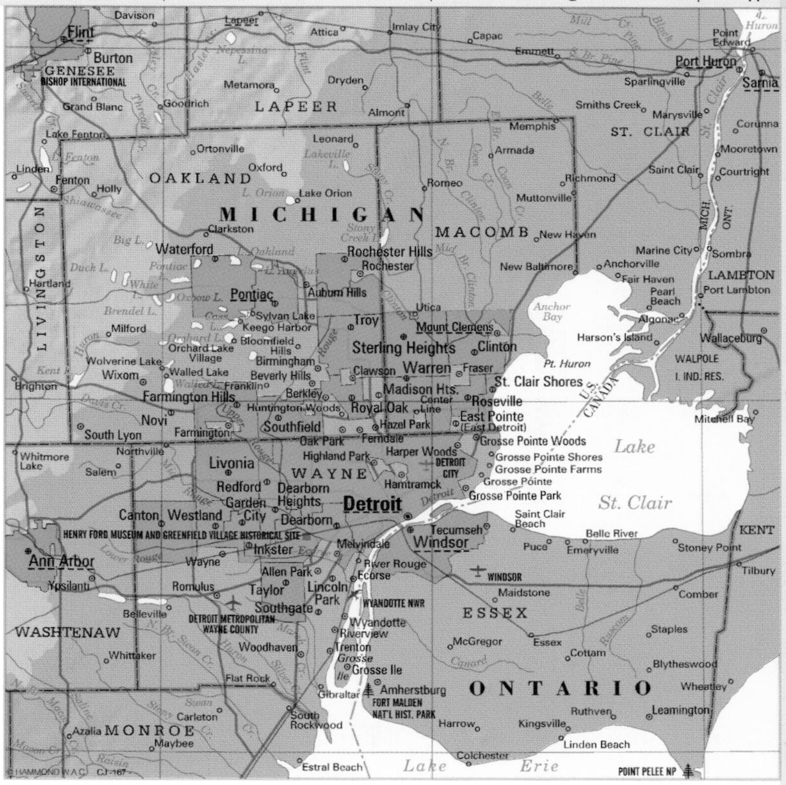

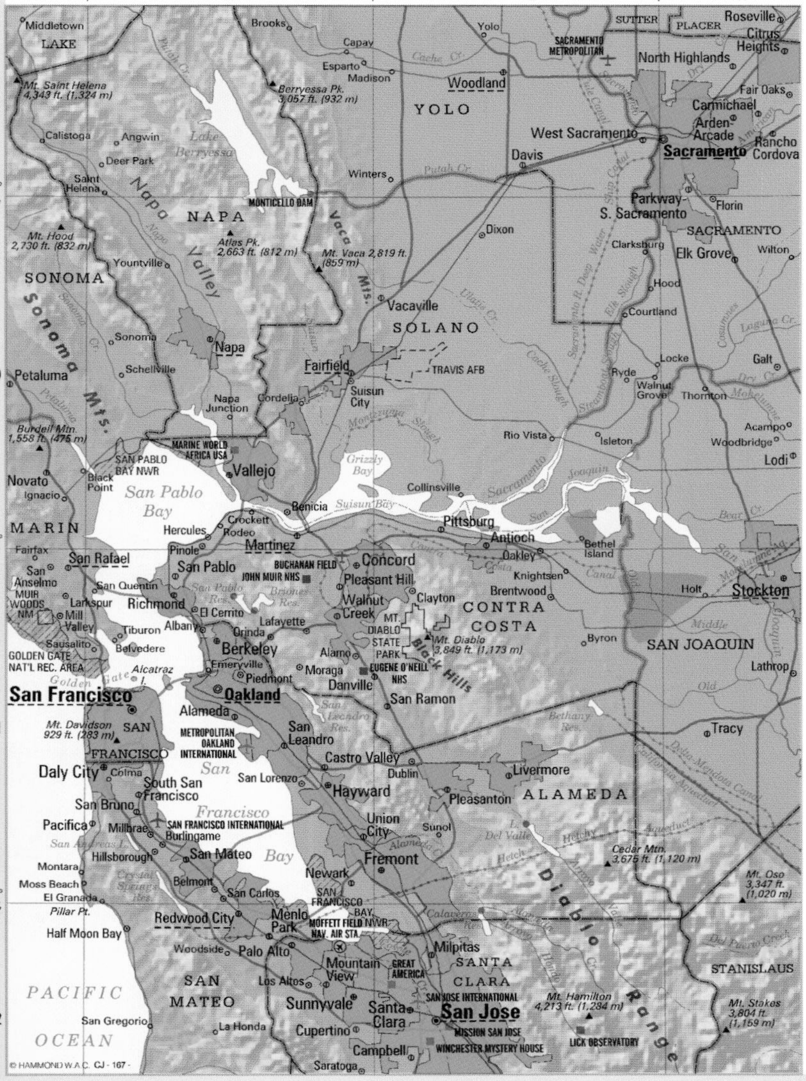

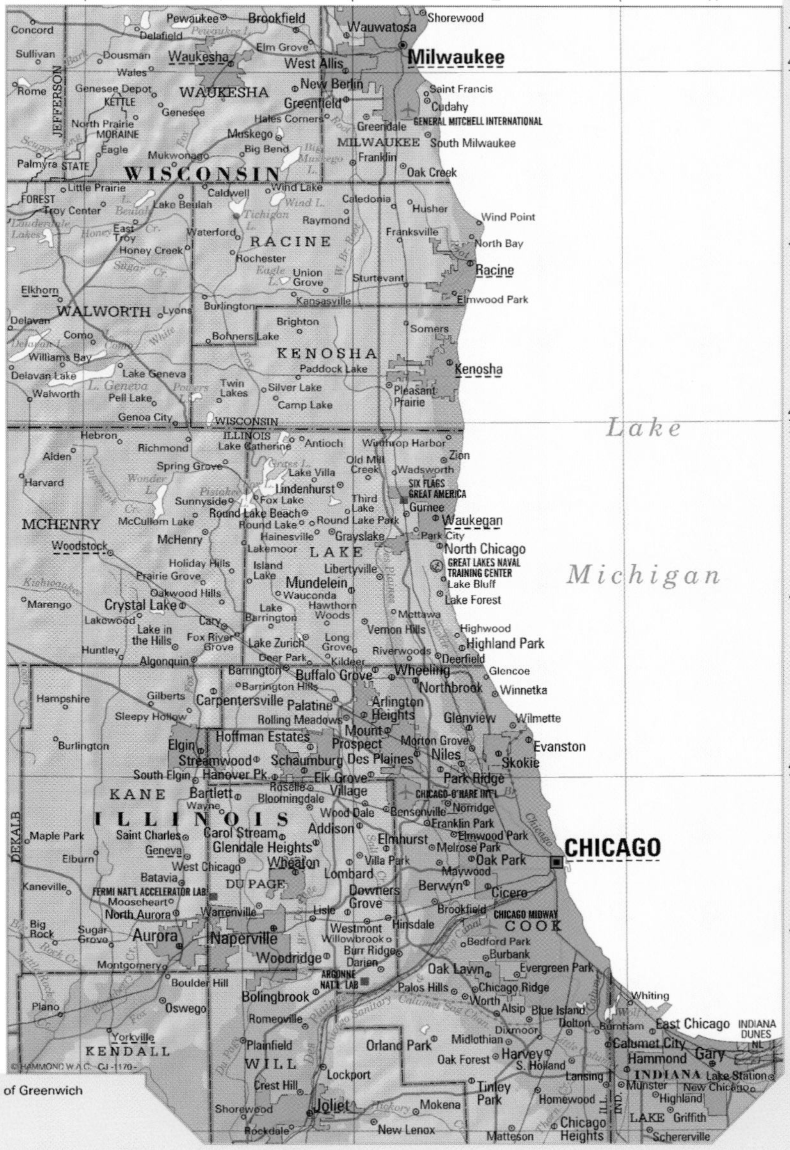

Longitude West of Greenwich

Los Angeles – San Diego

Longitude West of Greenwich

SCALE 1:1,150,000   LAMBERT CONFORMAL CONIC PROJECTION

MILES
KILOMETERS

Height   Depth

Denver, Kansas City, New Orleans, Oklahoma City, Phoenix, San Antonio, Salt Lake City, St. Louis

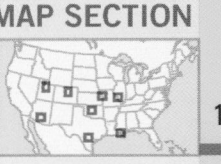

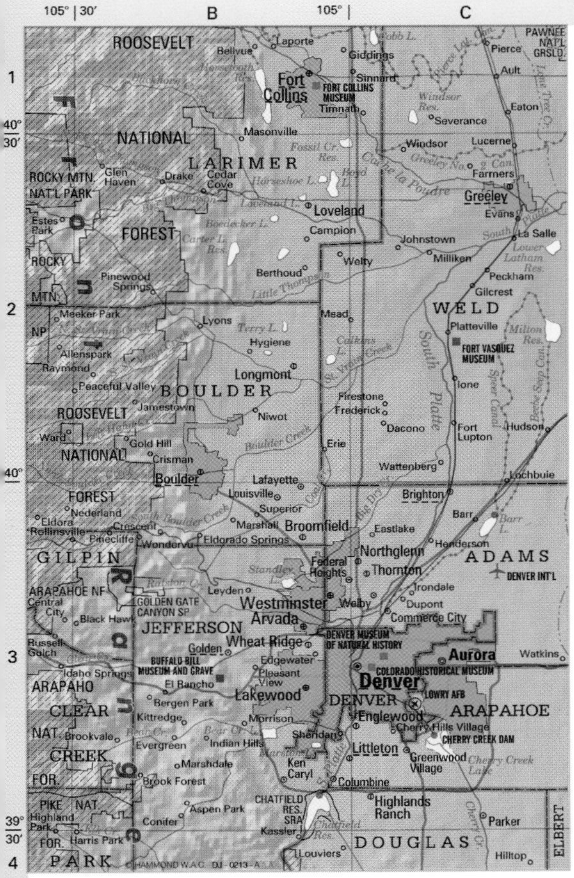

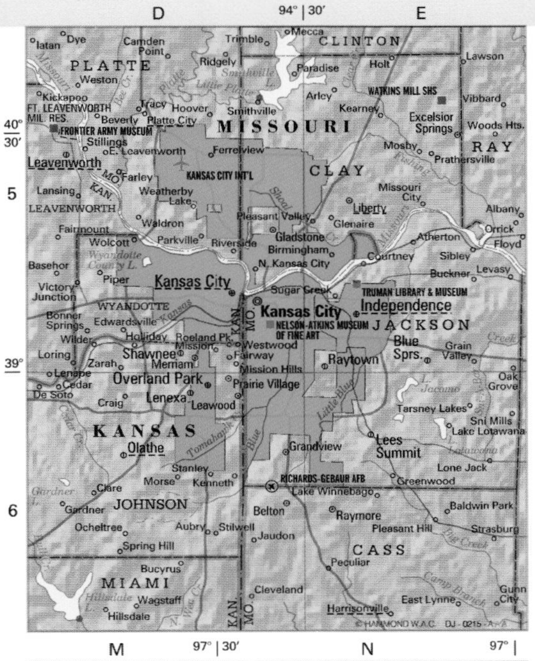

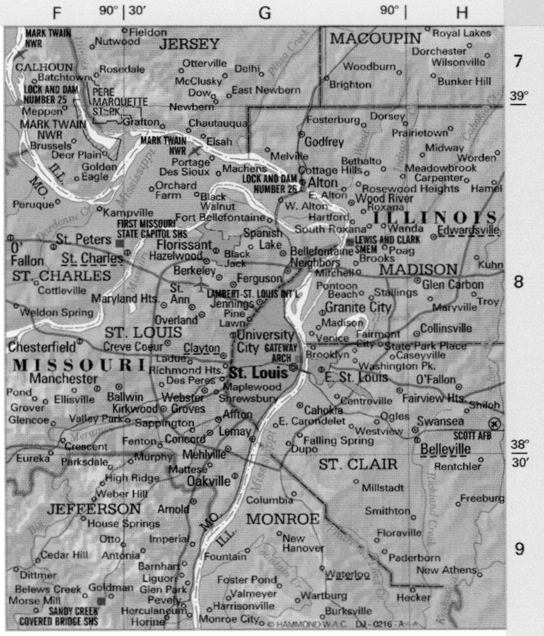

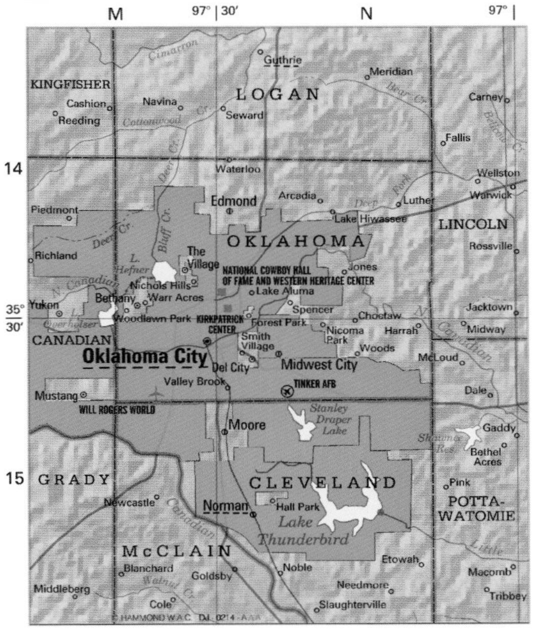

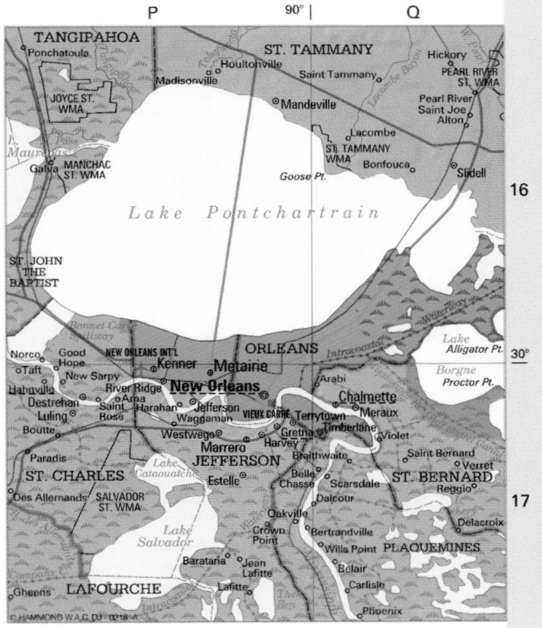

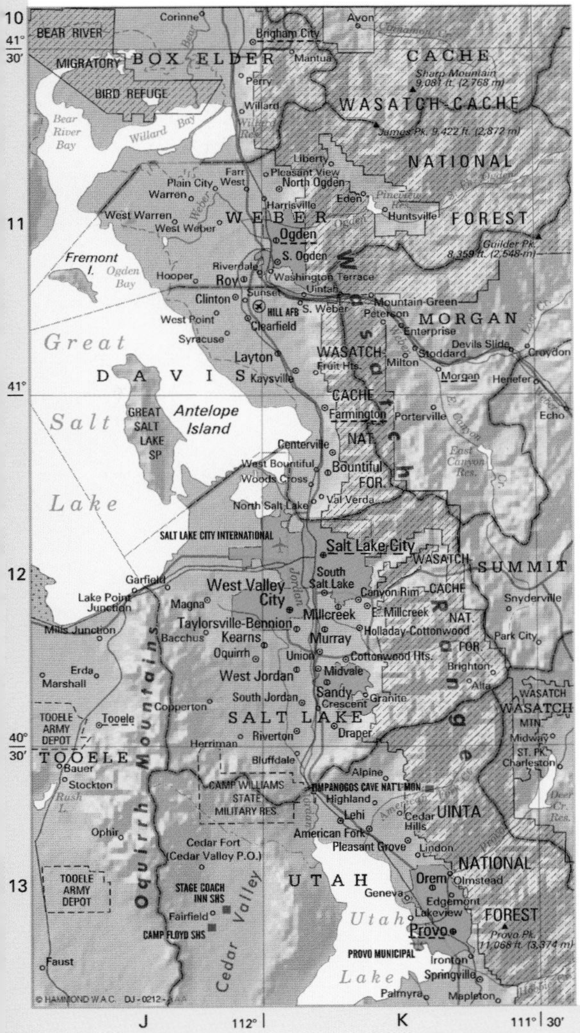

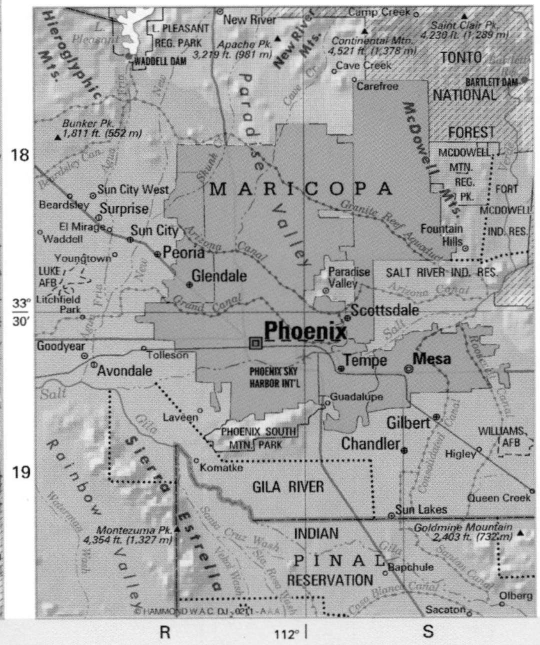

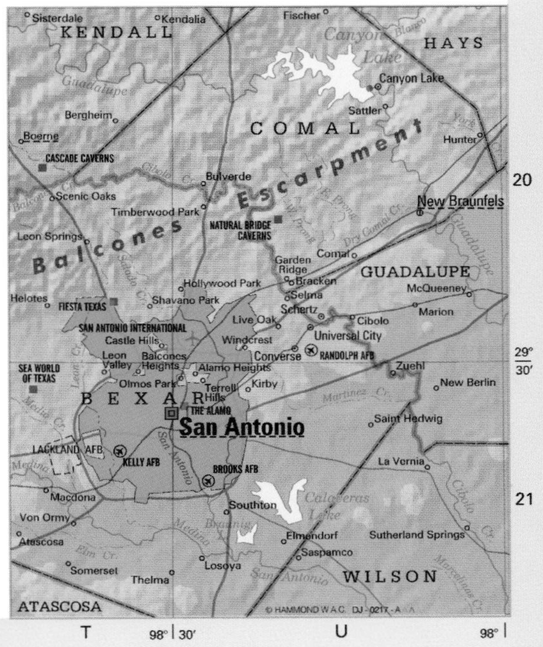

Longitude West of Greenwich

POPULATION OF CITIES AND TOWNS

- OVER 2,000,000
- 1,000,000 - 1,999,999
- 500,000 - 999,999
- 250,000 - 499,999
- 100,000 - 249,999
- 30,000 - 99,999
- 10,000 - 29,999
- UNDER 10,000

SCALE 1:1,150,000 LAMBERT CONFORMAL CONIC PROJECTION

MILES 0 10 20 30 40 50

KILOMETERS 0 10 20 30 40 50

CONNECTICUT

NEW YORK

Long Island Sound

ATLANTIC OCEAN

LONG ISLAND

SUFFOLK

NASSAU

NEW YORK

NEW JERSEY

WESTCHESTER

ROCKLAND

ORANGE

SUSSEX

PASSAIC

BERGEN

MORRIS

ESSEX

UNION

HUDSON

MIDDLESEX

MONMOUTH

RICHMOND

KINGS (BROOKLYN)

QUEENS

CONN. FAIRFIELD

© HAMMOND WORLD ATLAS CORPORATION

© HAMMOND W.A.C.

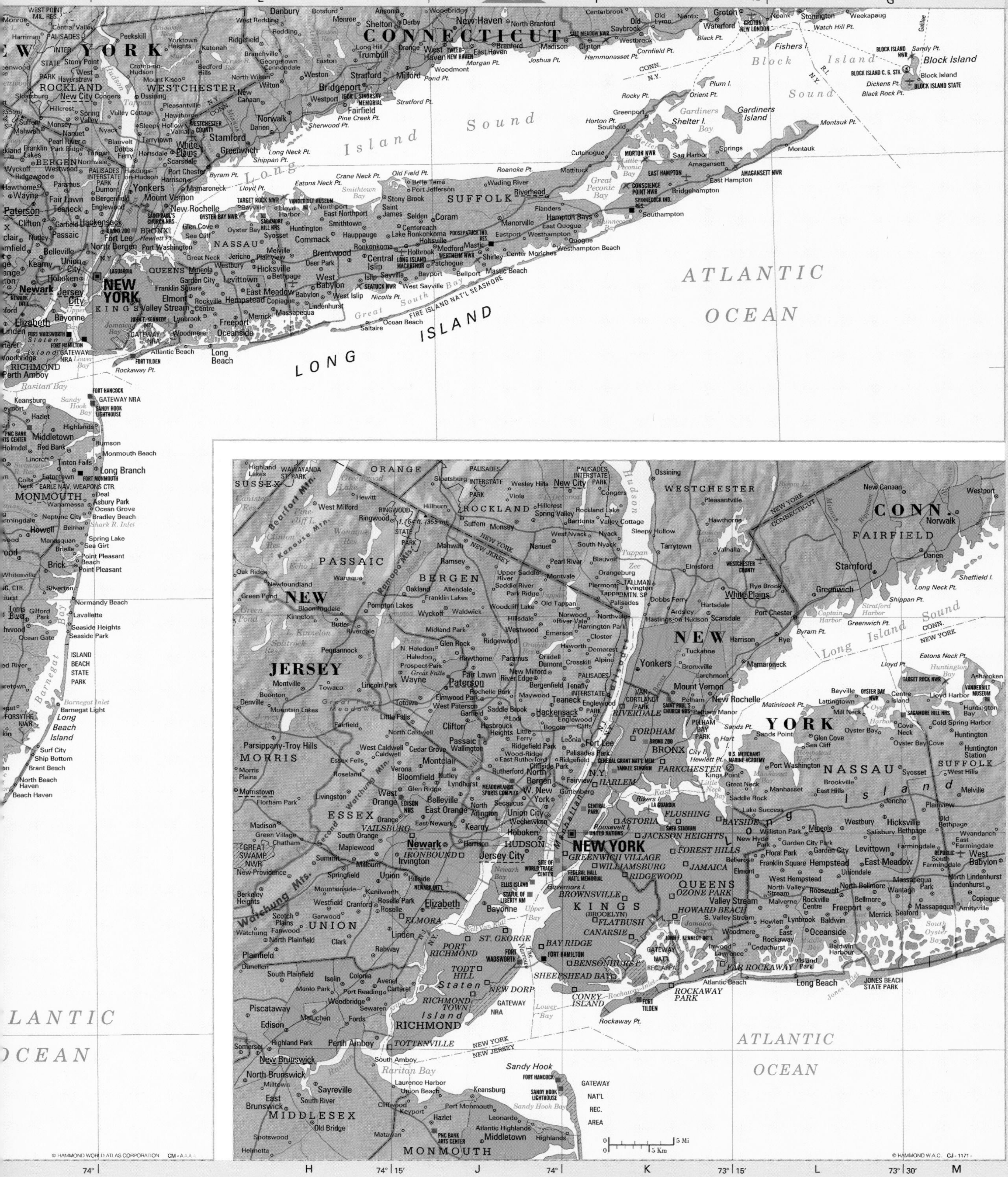

POPULATION OF CITIES AND TOWNS

■ OVER 2,000,000 ● 500,000 - 999,999 ● 100,000 - 249,999 ● 10,000 - 29,999
□ 1,000,000 - 1,999,999 ● 250,000 - 499,999 ● 30,000 - 99,999 ○ UNDER 10,000

SCALE 1:1,150,000   LAMBERT CONFORMAL CONIC PROJECTION

MILES 0 5 Mi 10 20 30 40 50

KILOMETERS 0 5 Km 10 20 30 40 50

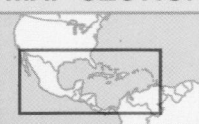

ATLANTIC OCEAN

DOMINICAN REPUBLIC

PUERTO RICO

Virgin Islands

Anegada (U.K.)
Aguadilla Isabela
San Juan
Arecibo Bayamón Carolina
Mayagüez Utuado Caguas
Hormigueros Yabucoa Fajardo
I. Mona Ponce Guayama Charlotte Amalie St. Thomas (U.S.) St. John (U.S.) V.I.
C. Rojo Yauco
El Yunque 1,065 m
US NAV. RES. (P.R.) I. de Vieques (P.R.)
St. Croix (U.S.)
Frederiksted Christiansted

Tortola I. (U.K.) Virgin Gorda (U.K.)
Road Town
The Valley Anguilla (U.K.)
Marigot St-Martin (GUAD.)
Sint Maarten (N.A.)
Gustavia St-Barthélemy (GUAD.)
Saba (N.A.) Oranjestad
Sint Eustatius (N.A.)
St. Kitts BRIMSTONE HILL NP Basseterre
ST. KITTS AND NEVIS Nevis Pk. 1,096 m
Charlestown Nevis
Boggy Pk. 402 m
Barbuda
Codrington
ANTIGUA AND BARBUDA
Saint John's
Falmouth
Antigua

Leeward Islands

Montserrat (U.K.) Plymouth

Grande-Terre
Port-Louis
Basse-Terre GUADELOUPE NP Pointe-à-Pitre Guadeloupe (FRANCE)
Soufrière 1,467 m Morne Constant 205 m
Basse-Terre Marie-Galante

Lesser Antilles

Aves I. (VEN.)

CARIBBEAN SEA

Dominica Passage
Portsmouth Marigot
Morne Diablotin 1,447 m
DOMINICA
Roseau

Martinique Passage
Mt. Pelée 1,397 m
Sainte-Marie
Saint-Pierre Martinique (FRANCE)
FORT DESAIX Fort-de-France

St. Lucia Channel
Castries Gros Islet
Mt. Gimie 958 m ST. LUCIA Micoud
Vieux Fort

Soufrière 1,234 m St. Vincent Passage
Barrouallie St. Vincent
Georgetown Mt. Hillaby 336 m Bathsheba
Kingstown BARBADOS Bridgetown
Bequia
ST. VINCENT AND THE GRENADINES

Windward Islands

Canouan
Carriacou
Sauteurs
Gouyave Mt. St. Catherine 840 m
Saint George's
GRENADA

I. Blanquilla (VEN.)

La Asunción
NUEVA ESPARTA
Porlamar
VENEZUELA SUCRE
Cariaco El Pilar Irapa
Casanay

Is. Los Testigos
Dragon's Mouths
PN PEN. DE PARIA
El Cerro del Aripo 940 m
Port-of-Spain Arima
TRINIDAD AND TOBAGO
Chaguanas Sangre Grande Tabaquite
San Fernando Rio Claro
Gulf of Paria Point Fortin Siparia Fullarton
Güiria
Carúpano Pedernales Trinidad

Tobago
Charlotteville
Scarborough

© HAMMOND W.A.C.

ATLANTIC OCEAN

Beach
Pierce
rt St. Lucie

West Palm Beach
al Springs
ort Lauderdale
Hollywood
Miami

BAYNE NP

BAHAMAS

Grand Bahama
Freeport
Great Abaco
Bimini Is.
Berry Is.
Eleuthera
Nassau
New Providence I.
Andros I.
Great Bahama Bank
Great Guana Cay
Great Exuma
Exuma Sound
Cat I.
San Salvador (Watling I.)
Long I.
Rum Cay
Clarence Town
Tropic of Cancer

CUBA

Sagua la Grande
Cabaiguán
Caibarién
Ciego de Ávila
Morón
Punta Maternillos
Sancti Spíritus
Carlos M. de Céspedes
Florida
Camagüey
Nuevitas
Victoria de las Tunas
Contramaestre
G. de Ana María
Santa Cruz del Sur
Holguín
Mayari
Jobabo
Jesús Menéndez
Sierra de Tánamo
Cabo Lucrecia
Bayamo
Julio A. Mella
San Luis
El Salvador
Cabo Maisí
Palma Soriano
Yara
Bartolomé Masó
Manzanillo
Pico Turquino 1,974 m
Santiago de Cuba
Guantánamo
GUANTANAMO BAY U.S. NAVAL BASE
Cabo Cruz

Crooked I.
Acklins I.
Abraham's Bay
Salina Pt.
Mayaguana
Kew
Northeast Pt.
BAHM. TURKS.
Turks and Caicos Is. (U.K.)
Caicos Is.
Great Inagua
Little Inagua
Matthew Town
Grand Turk
Turks Is.
Southeast Pt.

JAMAICA
Montego Bay Ocho Rios
Saint Ann's Bay
Savanna-la-Mar
Spanish Town Port Antonio
Mandeville Blue Mtn. Pk. 2,256 m
May Pen Kingston
Portland Pt.
Pedro Cays (JAM.)

Cayman Brac

Serranilla Bank (COL.)
Bajo Nuevo (COL.)
Roncador Cay (COL.)
Serrana Bank (COL.)

WEST INDIES

Windward Passage
Cap-Haïtien
Port-de-Paix
Golfe de la Gonâve
Jérémie
Dame Marie
Cap Tiburon
Anse-d'Hainault
Les Cayes
Pointe à Gravois

HAITI
Port-au-Prince
Pic de Macaya 2,300 m
Cabo Falso

Monte Cristi
St-Louis du Nord
Santiago Pico Duarte 3,175 m
Mao La Vega
Las Matas de Farfán
Bonao
San Juan Hato Mayor
Azua
Neiba Barahona
Pedernales
Cabo Beata

Hispaniola
Cabo Francés Viejo
Puerto Plata
Sosúa
Cabo Samaná
DOMINICAN REPUBLIC
El Seibo
San Francisco de Macorís
Higüey
La Romana
San Pedro de Macorís
SANTO DOMINGO
Cabo Rojo

PUERTO RICO (U.S.)
San Juan
Bayamón Carolina
Mayagüez Utuado Caguas
Aguadilla
Ponce Guayama
Christiansted
St. Croix (U.S.)

Virgin Is. (U.S.)
Anegada (U.K.)
St. Thomas
Charlotte Amalie St. John
Tortola I. (U.K.) Road Town

Lesser Antilles

Anguilla (U.K.)
St-Martin (FR.)
Sint Maarten (N.A.)
Philipsburg
Saba (N.A.)
ST. KITTS AND NEVIS
Basseterre
Charlestown Nevis
Plymouth Montserrat (U.K.)

Codrington Barbuda
ANTIGUA AND BARBUDA
Saint John's Antigua

Basse-Terre GUADELOUPE NP Grande-Terre
Soufrière 1,467 m Pointe-à-Pitre Guadeloupe (FRANCE)
Basse-Terre Marie-Galante

Aves I. (VEN.)

DOMINICA
Roseau Marigot

Mont Pelée 1,397 m
Saint-Pierre Martinique (FRANCE)
Fort-de-France

CARIBBEAN SEA

Castries Gros Islet
ST. LUCIA Micoud
Vieux Fort
Soufrière 1,234 m

ST. VINCENT AND THE GRENADINES
Kingstown BARBADOS Bridgetown
Carriacou
GRENADA
Saint George's Mt. St. Catherine 840 m

Windward Is.

Aruba (NETH.)
Oranjestad
NETH. ANTILLES
Willemstad
Curaçao Bonaire
Kralendijk

Punta Gallinas
Guajira Pen.
Cabo de la Vela Pen. de Paraguaná
Carrizal Jadacaquiva
Santa Ana
El Roque
I. La Orchila (VEN.)
Islas Los Roques (VEN.)
Las Aves (VEN.)

I. La Tortuga (VEN.)
I. Blanquilla (VEN.)

Coro
Puerto Cumarebo
Chichiriviche
Tucacas
Juangriego
La Asunción
Porlamar Guinima
Pen. de Paria
Arima
Port-of-Spain
Trinidad

Ríohacha Uribia
Santa Marta
Ciénaga
PN SIERRA NEVADA DE SANTA MARTA
Malambo Soledad
Cristóbal Colón 5,775 m
San Francisco
Maracaibo
Cabimas
Ciudad Ojeda
Barranquilla
Cartagena
Turbaco Arjona
Valledupar
Campo de la Cruz
Agustín Codazzi
Machiques
Lago de Maracaibo
Gibraltar

Puerto Cabello
Valencia
Maracay
Caracas
Los Teques
Barcelona
Puerto La Cruz
Cumaná
Maturín
Delta del Orinoco

COLOMBIA
Sincelejo Corozal
Chinú Sahagún
Planeta Rica
Cerete
Montería
San Marcos
Ayapel
El Banco
Magangué
Mompós

San Carlos del Zulia
Santa Bárbara
El Vigía
Ejido
Mérida Pico Bolívar 5,007 m
Tovar La Fría

Barinas
Guanare
San Carlos
Acarigua
Barquisimeto
Tucuyo
San Felipe

VENEZUELA
Valle de la Pascua
Calabozo
Zaraza
El Tigre
Ciudad Bolívar
Ciudad Guayana
Upata
El Palmar

Isthmus of Panama
Gulf of Panama
Panamá
PN DARIEN
Cerro Chucanti 1,439 m

Isla del Rey

POPULATION OF CITIES AND TOWNS
■ OVER 2,000,000   ● 500,000 - 999,999   ● 100,000 - 249,999   ○ 10,000 - 29,999
■ 1,000,000 - 1,999,999   ● 250,000 - 499,999   ● 30,000 - 99,999   ○ UNDER 10,000

SCALE 1:10,300,000   LAMBERT CONFORMAL CONIC PROJECTION
MILES 0   150   300   450
KILOMETERS 0   150   300   450

152   G   153   H   J

Northern and Central Mexico

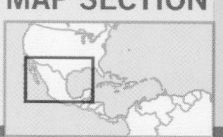

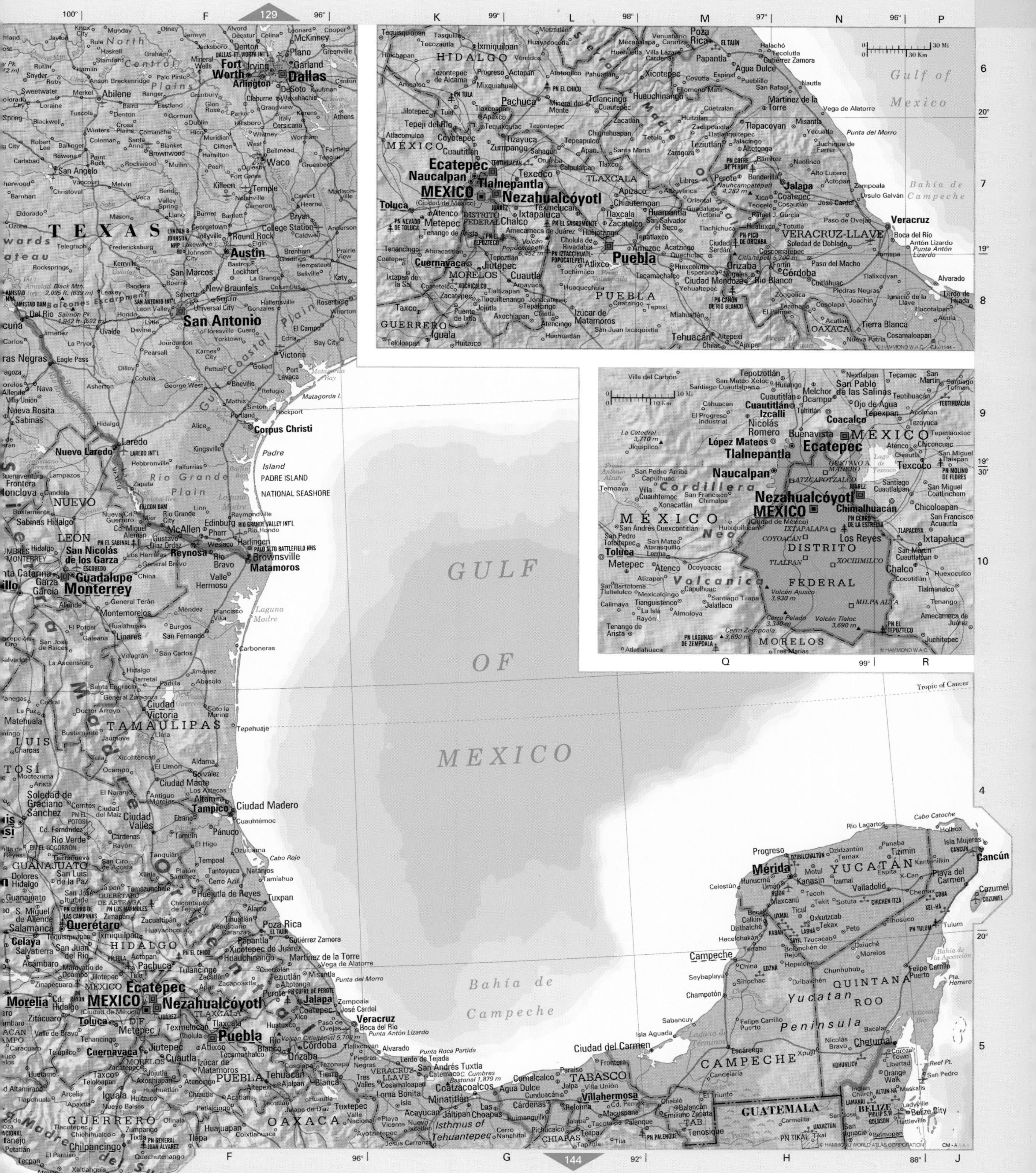

129
144

POPULATION OF CITIES AND TOWNS
- OVER 2,000,000
- 1,000,000 - 1,999,999
- 500,000 - 999,999
- 250,000 - 499,999
- 100,000 - 249,999
- 30,000 - 99,999
- 10,000 - 29,999
- UNDER 10,000

SCALE 1:6,900,000 LAMBERT CONFORMAL CONIC PROJECTION
MILES 0 100 200 300
KILOMETERS 0 100 200 300

A 100° 143 B 96° C 92° D 88° Tropic

GULF OF MEXICO

Arrecife
Alacrán

Bahía de

Campeche

Arrecifes
Triángulos

Cayos
Arcas

PACIFIC

OCEAN

Golfo de
Tehuantepec

B 96° C Longitude West of Greenwich 92° D 88°

© HAMMOND WORLD ATLAS CORPORATION   CM-1067-A-A-A

SCALE 1:6,900,000   LAMBERT CONFORMAL CONIC PROJECTION
MILES
KILOMETERS

POPULATION OF CITIES AND TOWNS

■ OVER 2,000,000	● 500,000 - 999,999	● 100,000 - 249,999	○ 10,000 - 29,999
■ 1,000,000 - 1,999,999	● 250,000 - 499,999	● 30,000 - 99,999	○ UNDER 10,000

TAMAULIPAS   SAN LUIS POTOSÍ   Tampico   Ciudad Madero   Altamira

GUANAJUATO   San Luis de la Paz   QUERETARO DE ARTEAGA   Querétaro   HIDALGO   Pachuca

Poza Rica

MEXICO   Ecatepec   Nezahualcóyotl   Toluca   Jalapa   VERACRUZ   Veracruz   Boca del Río

Cuernavaca   MORELOS   Puebla   PUEBLA   Córdoba   Orizaba   Río Blanco

TLAXCALA   GUERRERO   Iguala   Taxco

Acapulco

MEXICO

OAXACA   Oaxaca   MONTE ALBÁN

Isthmus of

Tehuantepec

Puerto Escondido   Puerto Ángel

Sierra Madre del Sur

Coatzacoalcos   Minatitlán   TABASCO   Villahermosa   Agua Dulce

CHIAPAS   Tuxtla Gutiérrez   San Cristóbal de las Casas   Comitán

Tapachula   Salina Cruz   Tehuantepec   Juchitán de Zaragoza   Tonalá

Ciudad del Carmen   CAMPECHE   Campeche   Champotón

Progreso   Mérida   YUCATÁN   Valladolid   CHICHEN ITZA

Felipe Carrillo Puerto   QUINTANA ROO   Chetumal

Cozumel

Yucatán   Peninsula

Cabo Catoche   I. Contoy   Isla Mujeres   CANCÚN   Cancún   Playa del Carmen

GUATEMALA   Quezaltenango   Guatemala   San Pedro Carchá   Cobán

BELIZE   Belize City   Turneffe Islands   Glovers Reef

HONDURAS   San Pedro Sula   La Ceiba   Tegucigalpa   Comayagua

EL SALVADOR   San Salvador   Santa Ana   San Miguel   Usulután

Islas de la Bahía   Roatán   I. de Utila

Managua   Diriamba   Chinandega   Chichigalpa   León   Corinto

Golfo de Fonseca

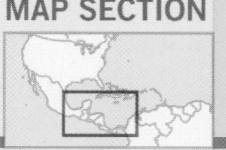
84° F 80° G ▲141 76° H 72° J

HAVANA Marianao Guanabacoa JOSÉ MARTÍ (La Habana) Punta Hicacos
Mariel Regla Cárdenas Varadero Corralillo Sagua la Grande Cayo Fragosa Arch. de Sabana
Minas de Matahambre San Cristóbal Artemisa Guanajay Colón Perico Santo Domingo Cifuentes Caibarién Cayo Coco
Guane Consolación del Sur Betancourt Santa Clara Camajuaní Cayo Sabinal
Pinar del Río Punta Gorda Pen. de Zapata Cienfuegos Placetas Chambas Taguasco Morón
Mantua Mendoza Ensenada de la Broa Sancti Spíritus Guasimal Cayo Romano
Las Martinas Nueva Gerona Golfo de Batabanó Condado La Sierpe Ciego de Ávila
Pen. de Guanahacabibes 310 m Santa Fe Arch. de los Canarreos Jardines de la Reina Punta Casilda Florida Nuevitas
Corrientes Cabo Frances Isla de la Juventud (I. de Pinos) Cayo Largo Vertientes Minas Puerto Padre
Cabo Pepe **CUBA** Golfo de Ana María Camagüey Las Tunas Holguín
Santa Cruz del Sur Jiguaní Bayamo Jobabo Jesús Menéndez Cabo Lucrecia Moa
Golfo de Guacanayabo Manzanillo Yara Palma Soriano San Luis Sagua de Tánamo
Niquero Bartolomé Pico Turquino 2,000 m Gran Piedra 1,131 m Guantánamo
Cabo Cruz Maestra **Santiago de Cuba** GUANTÁNAMO BAY UNITED STATES NAVAL BASE

BAHAMAS
Long Island Clarence Town Crooked I. Samana Northeast Pt. Mayaguana
Long Cay Plana Cays Abraham's Bay
Salina Pt. Acklins I. Providenciales W. Caicos N. Caicos Middle Caicos East Caicos
Great Inagua Little Inagua Matthew Town Kew Turks and Caicos Is. (U.K.) Grand Turk Salt Cay Southeast Pt.

20°
Mayarí San Germán Cueto Baracoa Pta. del Quemado
Môle Saint Nicolas Port-de-Paix Cap-Haïtien Monte Cristi Va. Isabela Mao
Pointe Ouest I. de la Tortue (Tortuga I.) St-Louis Cap du Nord Dajabón
Hispaniola
Golfe de la Gonâve Gonaïves Petite Rivière de l'Artibonite **DOMINICAN REPUBLIC**
Grande Saline Saint-Marc Hinche Bánica Comendador San Juan de la Maguana
Pointe Ouest I. de la Gonâve Pointe à Raquette Mirebalais Las Matas
HAITI **Port-au-Prince** PN ISLA CABRITOS Barahona
Cayman Islands (U.K.) Cayman Brac Jérémie Cap Dame Marie Dame Marie Pic de Macaya 2,300 m Petit Goâve Grand Goâve Pétionville Belle Jaragua
Little Cayman Grand Cayman Roseaux Corail Chaîne de la Selle Jacmel Sa. de Bahoruco
George Town Owen Roberts Anse-d'Hainault Les Cayes Île à Vache Pedernales Enriquillo
Chardonnière Torbeck Cabo Falso Isla Beata Cabo Beata

2
Discovery Bay Ocho Rios Port Maria
Montego Bay ANCHOVY Marbon Town Port Antonio
Negril Christiana Spanish Town Northeast Pt. Navassa I. (U.S.) Pointe à Gravois
Savanna-la-Mar Mandeville **Kingston** Blue Mtn. Pk. 2,256 m
Black River May Pen NORMAN MANLEY Morant Southeast Pt.
JAMAICA Portland Pt.

Greater **WEST** **Antilles**

16°
Swan Islands (HOND.) Cayos Cajones (HOND.) Bajo Nuevo (COL.)
Punta Patuca Barra Patuca Cayo Cocorocuma (HOND.) Serranilla Bank (COL.)
1,083 m Laguntara Bancos del Cabo Falso (HOND.)
Auas Laguna de Caratasca Arrecifes de La Media Luna (HOND.)
Auasbila (HOND.) Cabo Falso **INDIES**
940 m Waspán Cabo Gracias a Dios
1,782 m Kuyu Tingni Cabo Gracias a Dios Quita Sueño Bank (COL.) **CARIBBEAN**
Yablis Laguna Bismuna
Saslaya 50 m Cayos Miskitos London Reef Serrana Bank (COL.)
Alamikamba Prinzapolka **SEA**
kuina Puerto Cabezas Laguna Karatá Roncador Cay (COL.)
Wawasang 553 m Santa Isabel Isla de Providencia (COL.)
de Huapí La Barra

3
San Pedro de Lóvago Punta de Perlas
Villa Sandino **ICARAGUA** San Andrés Isla de San Andrés (COL.)
710 m Arrapesbarba **Bluefields** ISLA DE SAN ANDRÉS (COL.)
El Rama I. del Venado de Bluefields Cayos del Este Sudeste (COL.)
jeras Pta. Mono Pequeña Isla del Maíz Punta Gallinas
Chirripa 719 m Barra Punta Gorda Gran Isla del Maíz Cayos de Albuquerque (COL.) Cabo de la Vela
San Carlos Pta. Gorda Pen. de la Guajira
Serrs. de Yolaina Bahía de Punta Gorda Carrizal

12°
San Juan del Norte Riohacha Uribia Maicao Golfo de zuela
Colorado Cabo de la Aguja LA GUAJIRA Carraipía
CAÑO NEGRO NWR PN BARRA DEL COLORADO PN TAYRONA Maiambo Cojoro
cán Miravalles Quesada Puerto Viejo PN TORTUGUERO Santa Marta PN ISLA DE SALAMANCA PN SIERRA NEVADA DE SANTA MARTA
20 m Volcán Arenal 1,633 m **Barranquilla** Ciénaga San Carlos San Rafael
nas PN VOLCÁN POÁS PN BRAULIO CARRILLO ERNESTO CORTISSOZ Pico Cristóbal Colón 5,775 m Villanueva La Chinita
San Ramón Guácimo Limón **ATLÁNTICO** Soledad La Paz
Alajuela PN GUANACASTE **COSTA RICA** Baranoa Sabanalarga El Difícil La Concepción Machiques de
intarenas Cartago Cervantes **Cartagena** Turbaco CESAR **ZULIA** Maracaibo
San José Paraíso PN CAHUITA Rafael Núñez San Juan Nepomuceno Valledupar San Carlos del Zulia
Cerro de la Muerte 3,491 m GANDOCA-MANZANILLO NWR PN CORALES DEL ROSARIO San Jacinto El Banco **VENEZUELA**

4
Parrita Isidro Cerro Chirripó 3,820 m Pta. San Bernardo MAGDALENA La Gloria San Cristóbal
Quepos Bahía de Isthmus of Panama Golfo de Morrosquillo San Onofre El Carmen Gamarra Aguachica
Coronado Ciudad Cortés PN PORTOBELO Pta. Grande Tolú SUCRE **NORTE DE SANTANDER** Sardinata
Boruca Volcán Barú 3,476 m PN ALTOS DE CAMPANA El Porvenir Narganá Sincelejo Corozal Cereté Ciénaga de Oro La Fría
PN CORCOVADO San Vito Changuinola **PANAMÁ** Cerro Carti 792 m Ailigandí Montería San Marcos El Banco Grita
Pen. de Osa La Concepción Bocas del Toro Chagres Arraiján Tocumen Puerto Obaldía CÓRDOBA Planeta Rica Tamalameque **TÁCHIRA** San Antonio
2,826 m David Coclé del Norte La Chorrera Chepo Acandí **ANTIOQUIA** Turbo Ayapel Zaragoza Cúcuta Villa Rosario
PN VOLCÁN BARÚ Bugaba Santiago Cerro Peña Blanca 1,314 m Bahía de Panamá El Llano Yaviza PARAMILLO El Bagre Cerro El Viejo 4,000 m Pamplona
Progreso Remedios Aguadulce Antón Río Hato La Palma Chepigana Apartadó Alto de Tamar 2,350 m San José
Pen. Burica Pta. Burica La Concepción 2,238 m B. de Parita Pocrí San Miguel Golfo de San Miguel Cerro Pirre 1,515 m PN DARIÉN **SANTANDER**

5
Puerto Armuelles **PANAMÁ** MONAGRILLO Chitré Los Santos Pta. Garachiné Jurado CHOCÓ **COLOMBIA** **ANTIOQUIA** PN LOS KATÍOS PN EL TAMÁ
Golfito Golfo de Chiriquí Guararé Peninsula de Azuero Pedasí Punta Piña Riosucio Cord. Central Toledo
Punta Jabalí I. de Cébaco Cerro Canajagua 1,100 m Tonosí Punta Mala Serranía de Baudó Bahía de Humboldt
Isla de Coiba 405 m Cerro Cambutal Punta Mariato Punta Morro de Puercos Punta Marzo

84° 80° 76° ▼152 72°

ATLANTIC OCEAN

Nicholas Channel Arch. de Camagüey Old Bahama Channel

Golfo de Batabanó Nueva Gerona G u l f o f P i g s

Windward Passage Jamaica Channel

Golfo de **Panama** Gulf of Panama Bahía de Humboldt

The highest mountain peak in the Americas, Mount Aconcagua, at 22,831 feet (6959 m.) above sea level, is visible in this northeast-looking, low-oblique image. Several major snow-covered peaks with summits exceeding 20,000 feet (6100 m.) rise along the north-south axis of the cohesive and massive structure of the Andes Mountains through this area of Argentina and Chile. The narrow east-west valley immediately south of Mount Aconcagua contains a section of the American Highway that connects Mendoza, Argentina, with Santiago, Chile.

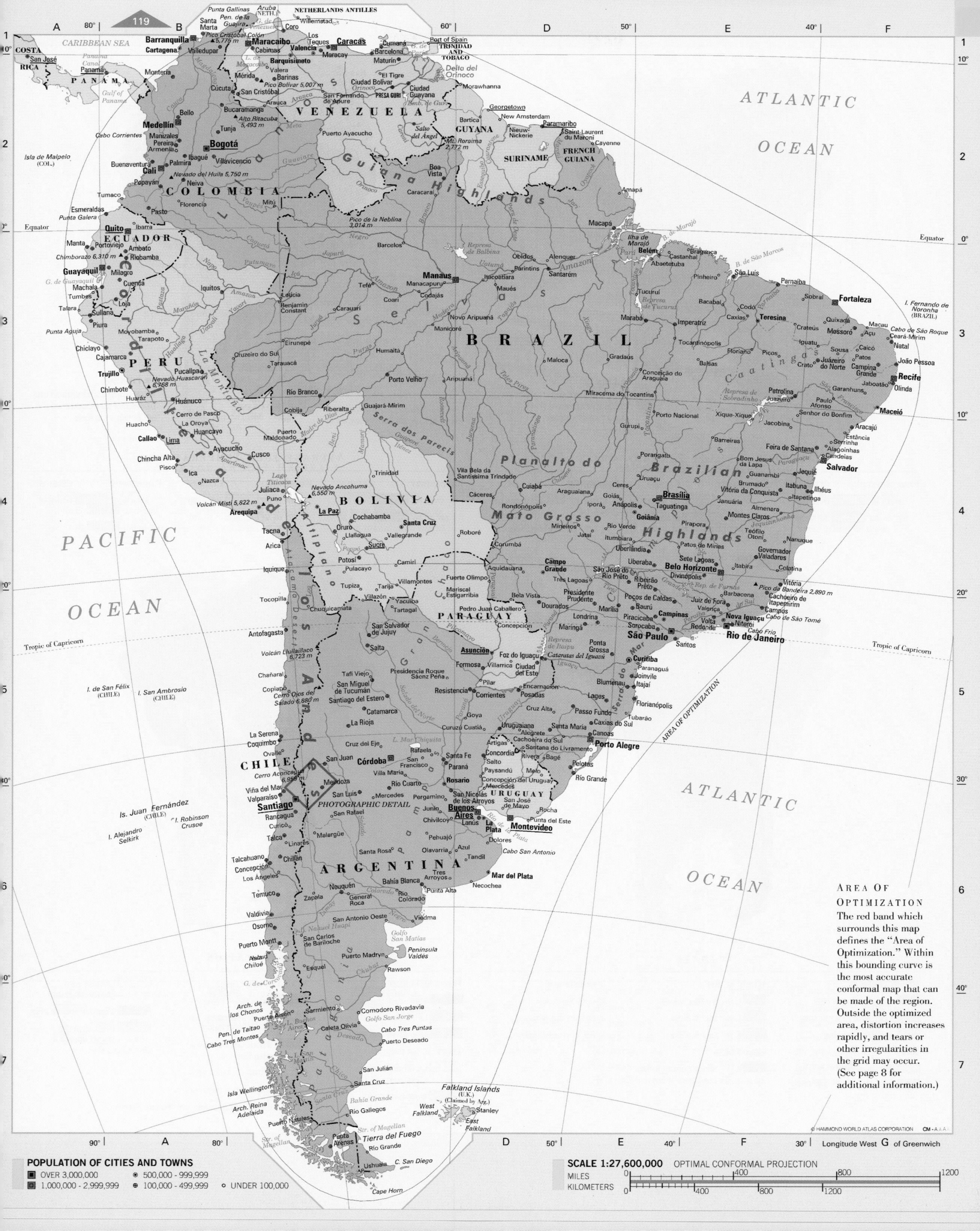

AREA OF OPTIMIZATION
The red band which surrounds this map defines the "Area of Optimization." Within this bounding curve is the most accurate conformal map that can be made of the region. Outside the optimized area, distortion increases rapidly, and tears or other irregularities in the grid may occur. (See page 8 for additional information.)

POPULATION OF CITIES AND TOWNS
■ OVER 3,000,000
■ 1,000,000 - 2,999,999
● 500,000 - 999,999
● 100,000 - 499,999
○ UNDER 100,000

SCALE 1:27,600,000 OPTIMAL CONFORMAL PROJECTION
MILES 0 400 800 1200
KILOMETERS 0 400 800 1200

Longitude West of Greenwich

© HAMMOND WORLD ATLAS CORPORATION

CARIBBEAN SEA

PACIFIC

OCEAN

PANAMA

Isthmus of Panama

Gulf of
Panama

Peninsula
de Azuero

Arch. de
las Perlas

Barranquilla

Cartagena

Medellín

Cali

COLOMBIA

Bogotá

Maracaibo

Barquisimeto

Valenc

Aruba
(NETH.)
Oranjestad

NETH. ANTILLI

Curaçao

Willemstad

FALCÓN

LARA

YARACUY

COJED

PORTUGUESA

BARINAS

APUR

ARAUCA

CASANARE

VICHADA

META

GUAINÍA

GUAVIARE

VAUPÉS

CAQUETÁ

PUTUMAYO

AMAZONAS

ECUADOR

Quito

MANABÍ

NAPO

PASTAZA

MORONA-
SANTIAGO

Guayaquil

GUAYAS

AZUAY

LORETO

PERU

Golfo de
Guayaquil

COLOMBIA
① RISARALDA
② QUINDÍO

ECUADOR
① BOLÍVAR

B Longitude West of Greenwich 76°

80°

72°

Height Depth

Colombia, Venezuela, Ecuador

CARIBBEAN SEA

ATLANTIC

OCEAN

DEPENDENCIAS FEDERALES
(VEN.)

Aves

I. El Roque
Los Roques
(VEN.)

I. La Orchila
(VEN.)

I. La Tortuga
(VEN.)

I. Blanquilla
(VEN.)

GRENADA
Victoria
Carriacou
Saint George's ● Sauteurs
Mt. St. Catherine 840 m
POINT SALINES

NUEVA ESPARTA I. de Margarita
(VEN.)
Juangriego
Porlamar
PN LAGUNA DE LA RESTINGA
La Asunción
GRAL. S. MARINO
PN CERRO EL COPEY

Tobago
576 m
Charlotteville
Roxborough
Scarborough
CROWN POINT

Caracas
Petare
Los Teques
Victoria
MIRANDA
C. Codera
Cumaná
I. Cubagua
I. Coche
Carúpano
PN PENÍNSULA
DE PARIA
Blanchisseuse
Toco Pta. Galera
El Cerro del Aripo 940 m

TRINIDAD
AND
TOBAGO

Ocumare del Tuy
San José
de Guaribe
Valle de Guanape
Pozuelos
Barcelona
Puerto La Cruz
PN MOCHIMA
SUCRE
Casanay
San Antonio
del Golfo
Cariaco
Pen. de Araya
El Pilar Irapa
Güiria
Port-of-Spain
Chaguanas PIARCO
Arima
San Fernando
Couva
Sangre Grande
Tabaquite
Rio Claro

Trinidad

Gulf of Paria

Dragon's Mouth

GUARICO
El Sombrero
Chaguaramas
Tucupido
Las Mercedes
Valle de La Pascua
Zaraza
ANZOÁTEGUI
Cachipo
El Tigre
San Tomé
San José de Guanipa
Anaco
Cantaura
Aguasay
MONAGAS
San-Antonio
de Tabasca
Maturín
Temblador
Uracoa
Tucupita
DELTA
La Horqueta

PN
AGUARO-
GUARIQUITO
Santa María de Ipire
San Mauricio
San Antonio
Santa Rita
Zuata
San Pablo
Onoto
Aragua
Areo
Caicara
Quiriquire
Caripito
Carito
Punta de Mata
Barrancas
Los Castillos
Piacoa
Santo Niño
La Esperanza
Macareo

Delta del
Orinoco

AMACURO
San José de Amacuro

Fernando de Apure
La Urbana
Escudillas
Las Lajitas
Cabruta
Caicara
Santa
Rosalía
Mapire
Aripao
Soledad
Ciudad Bolívar
Upata
Ciudad Guayana
El Pao
Las Piedras
La Margarita
La Horqueta

Mabaruma
Baramanni
Charity
POMEROON
SUPENAAM
Anna Regina
Queenstown
Suddie
ESSEQUIBO IS.-W. DEMERARA
Vreed-en-Hoop ● Paradise
Georgetown
TIMEHRI
DEMERARA-
MAHAICA
Mahaica
Mahaicony Village
Fort Wellington
New Amsterdam

VENEZUELA
Guiana

Cuatro
Santa Cruz de Orinoco
Moitaco
Almacén
Ciudad Piar
El Manteco
PRESA GURI
Embalse
de Guri
Guasipat
El Callao
Tumeremo

Mount Everard
BARIMA-WAINI

Serranía
de la
Cerbatana

Cerro Bolívar 802 m
San Pedro
de las Bocas
El Dorado
Catabobo

Cataratas de
Kamaria
Bartica
Rockstone
Linden

E. BER.
COR.
MAHAICA-
BERBICE
Calcutta
Converton
Nieuw-Amsterdam

BOLÍVAR

Las Trincheras
La Paragua
El Casabe
Salto Pará
Salto Hacha
PARQUE
Salto del Ángel
(Angel Falls)
Auyán-Tepuí
2,950 m

CUYUNI-MAZARUNI
Tumerong
Cataratas de
Surukwakuma
Kamarang
Aurora
Monte
Ayanganna
2,042 m

UPPER
DEMERARA-
BERBICE
Paradise
Ituni
Kwakwani
Epira
Orealla

Totness
CORONIE
NICKERIE
Groningen
Bitagron

SARAMACCA

Nieuw-Nickerie

Paramaribo

SURINAME

Highlands

Cerro Guanay
2,300 m
Cerro Yaví
2,441 m
Cerro Guaiquinima
2,100 m
Uriyén
Cerro Venamo
1,650 m
NACIONAL
Uriman
Chimantá-Tepuí
2,342 m
Aparurén
La Gran
Sabana
Monte Roraima
2,772 m
Aratopó

PN KAIETEUR
Cataratas de Kaieteur
POTARO-
SIPARUNI
Mahdia
Tumatumari
Kurupukari

DEMERARA-
MAHAICA
Fort Wellington
New Amsterdam
WANICA
PARA
Lelydorp
Brokopondo
ZANDERIJ
PRESA AFOBAKA

MAROWIJNE
Albina
Mana

AMAZONAS

PN
YAPACANA
PN
DUIDA
MARAHUACA
Cerro Marahuaca
2,579 m
Cerro Duida 2,400 m
La Esmeralda
Santa María
de Erebató
Yenichaña
Uriranteruri
Guaña
CANAIMA
Santa Elena de Uairén
Icabarú

Rera

GUYANA

Karasabai

BROKO-
PONDO
FRENCH
GUIANA
Grand Santi-
Papaichton

SIPALIWINI

St-Laurent-
du-Maroni
Apatou
Dépôt Lézard
Paul Isnard
Délices

Cerro Guanay
San Juan de Manapiare
Santa María
de Erebató
Marfila

Serra   Parima

Ventuari

Cerro Ovaña
1,978 m

Cuaurí
VENEZUELA
BRAZIL

Sa. parima

Uraricoera

Uraricá

Annai
Yupukari
Lethem
Kumaka

Apoteri

Kanuku
Mts.
Wichabai

Mucajaí

UPPER TAKUTU-
UPPER ESSEQUIBO
Isherton

RORAIMA

Caracaraí

Karanambu
Biloku
Kassikaityu

EAST BERBICE-
CORENTYNE

1,009 m
Serra Acaraí

Cataratas
Frederik
Willem IV

Juliana Top
1,230 m
Wilhelmina Gebergte

Alalapadu

SURINAME
GUYANA
BRAZIL

Kayser
Gebergte

Cataratas Tonckens
Hendrik Top
975 m

Eilerts de
Haan Gebergte

Oranje Gebergte
Majoli

Tumuc-Humac Mts.

Cottica
Maripasoula
Intelewa
Ouaqui

AMAPÁ
Porto
Poet

Comunidad

Solano
Guayabal
San Carlos de Río Negro
Buenos Aires
Pamoni
Capibara
Esperanza
Platanal

Parima

Platanal

BOA VISTA
Boa
Vista

Parque
Nacional
Serranía
de la Neblina
Sta. Rosa de
Amanadona
Santa Isabel
El Carmen
Cucuí
Pico de la Neblina
3,014 m

VENEZUELA
BRAZIL

Parque Nacional
do Pico da Neblina

AMAZONAS

BRAZIL

Barcelos

Rio Negro

PARÁ

Parque   Nacional
do Rio Jaú

Represa
de
Balbina

Equator

0°

Sa.
Jauaru

Orixímina
Óbidos

Alenquer Monte Alegre

Santarém

EDUARDO GOMES
Manaus

L. Grande
de Manacapuru

Itapiranga
Urucará
Urucurituba
Silves
Itacoatiara

Nhamundá
Faro

Parintins
Barreirinha
Juruti

Amazon

CM-A

POPULATION OF CITIES AND TOWNS

■ OVER 2,000,000	● 500,000 - 999,999	● 100,000 - 249,999	○ 10,000 - 29,999
■ 1,000,000 - 1,999,999	● 250,000 - 499,999	● 30,000 - 99,999	○ UNDER 10,000

SCALE 1:6,900,000   LAMBERT CONFORMAL CONIC PROJECTION

MILES 0   100   200   300
KILOMETERS 0   100   200   300

SCALE 1:6,900,000   LAMBERT CONFORMAL CONIC PROJECTION

MILES
KILOMETERS

Height / Depth

Longitude West of Greenwich

© HAMMOND WORLD ATLAS CORPORATION   CM-2104-A-A

Southeastern Brazil

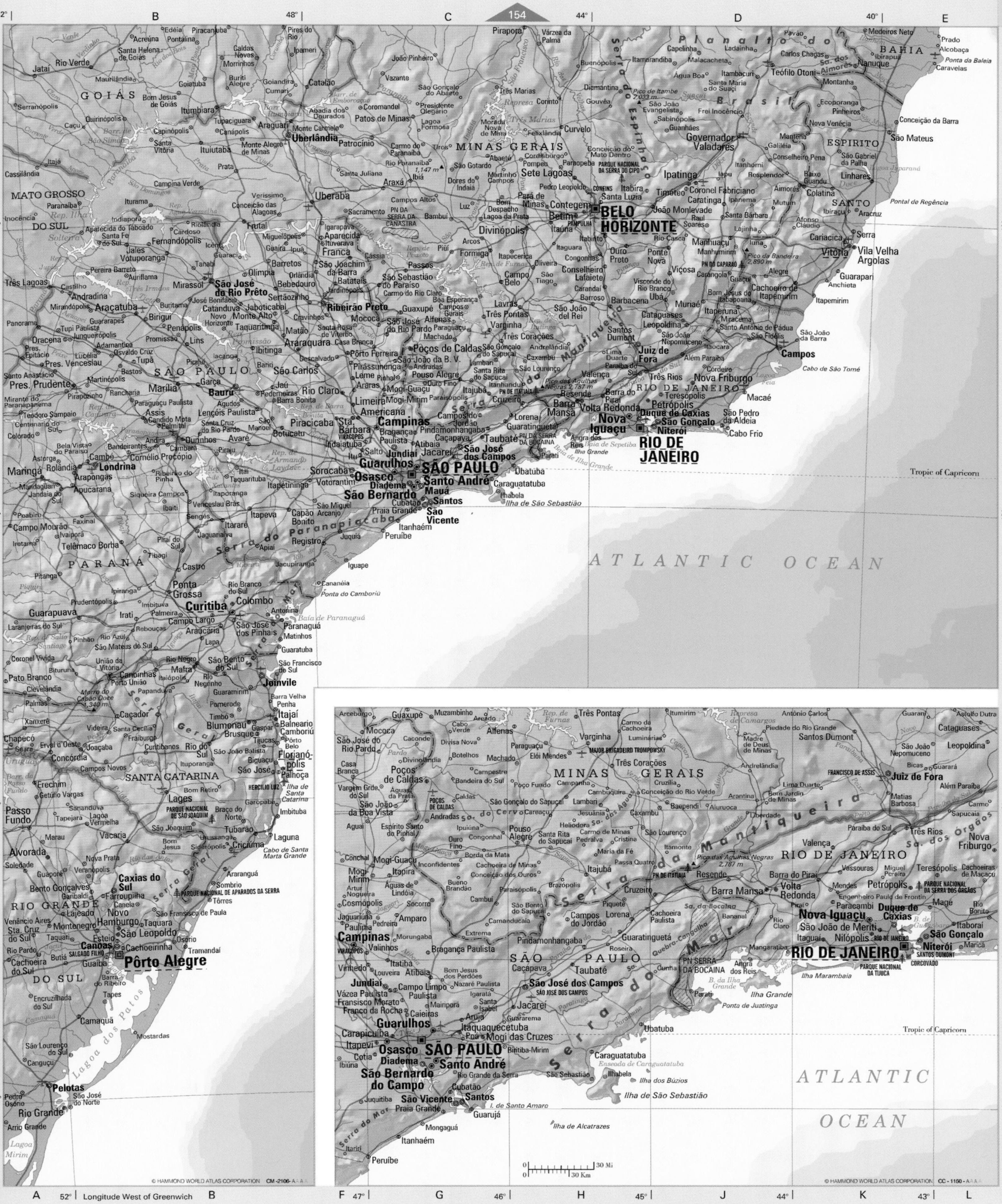

POPULATION OF CITIES AND TOWNS

- OVER 2,000,000
- 1,000,000 - 1,999,999
- 500,000 - 999,999
- 250,000 - 499,999
- 100,000 - 249,999
- 30,000 - 99,999
- 10,000 - 29,999
- UNDER 10,000

SCALE 1:6,900,000   LAMBERT CONFORMAL CONIC PROJECTION

MILES 0   100   200   300

KILOMETERS 0   100   200   300

Longitude West of Greenwich

© HAMMOND WORLD ATLAS CORPORATION

Golfo de Guayaquil

PACIFIC OCEAN

COLOMBIA

ECUADOR

BRAZIL

AMAZONAS

ACRE

PERU

Galápagos Islands (ECUADOR)

Equator

PARQUE NACIONAL GALÁPAGOS

GALÁPAGOS

PACIFIC OCEAN

© HAMMOND W.A.C.   CC-149-A-A-A   © HAMMOND WORLD ATLAS CORPORATION   CM-10/2-A-A-A

Longitude West of Greenwich

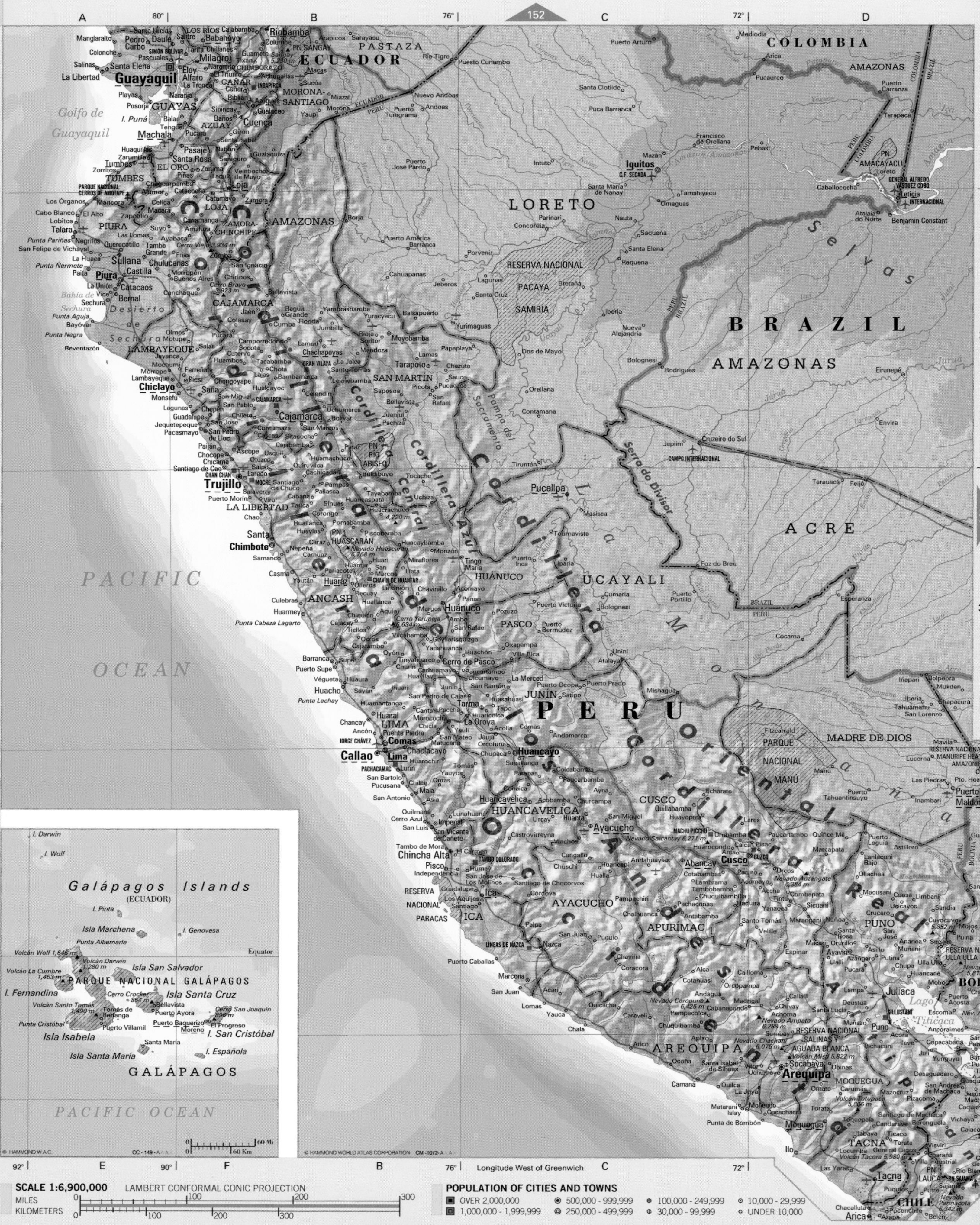

SCALE 1:6,900,000   LAMBERT CONFORMAL CONIC PROJECTION

MILES 0 · 100 · 200 · 300

KILOMETERS 0 · 100 · 200 · 300

0 · 60 Mi

POPULATION OF CITIES AND TOWNS

| ■ OVER 2,000,000 | ● 500,000 - 999,999 | ● 100,000 - 249,999 | ○ 10,000 - 29,999 |
| ■ 1,000,000 - 1,999,999 | ● 250,000 - 499,999 | ● 30,000 - 99,999 | ○ UNDER 10,000 |

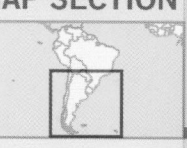

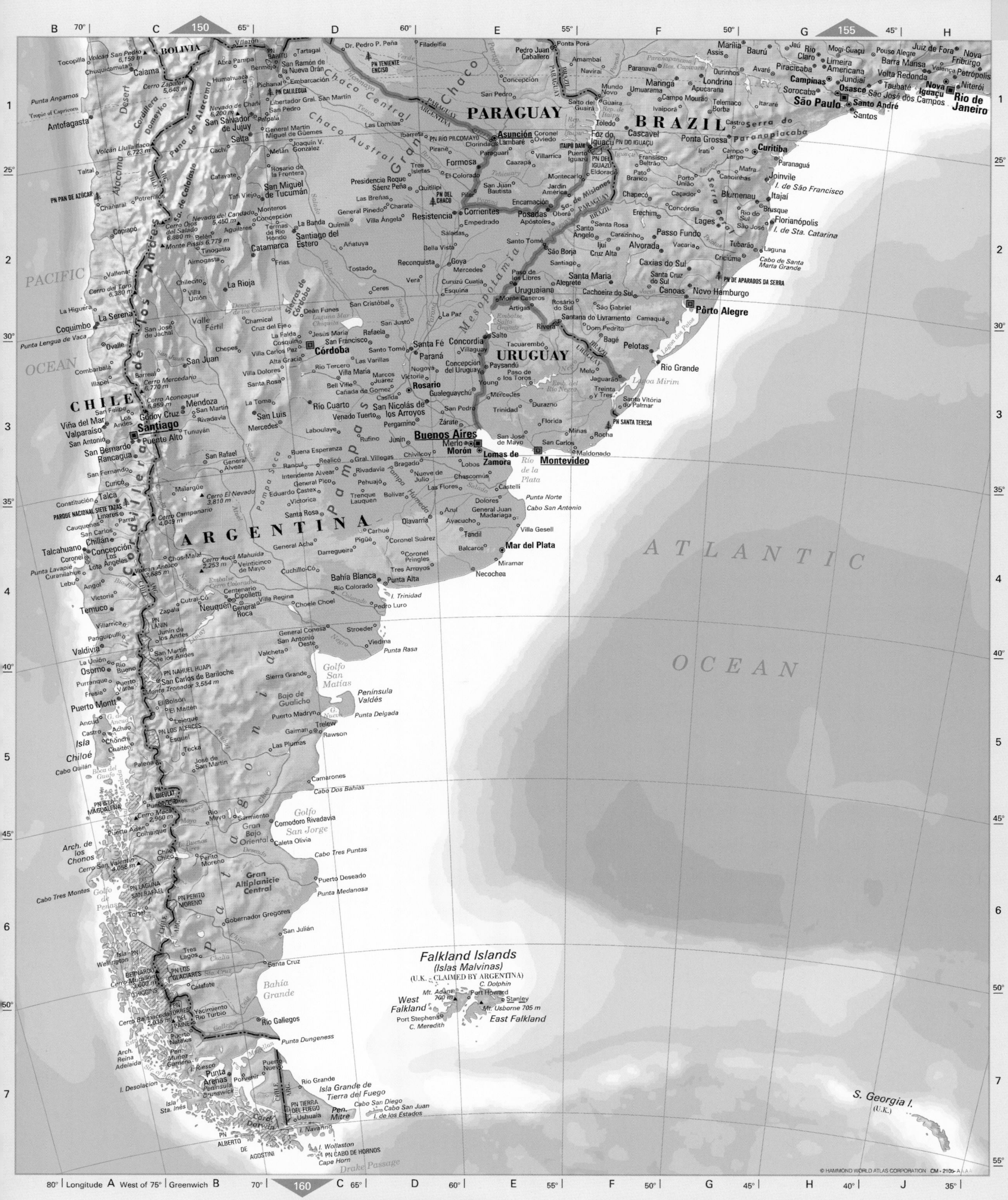

Southern Chile and Argentina

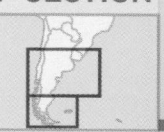

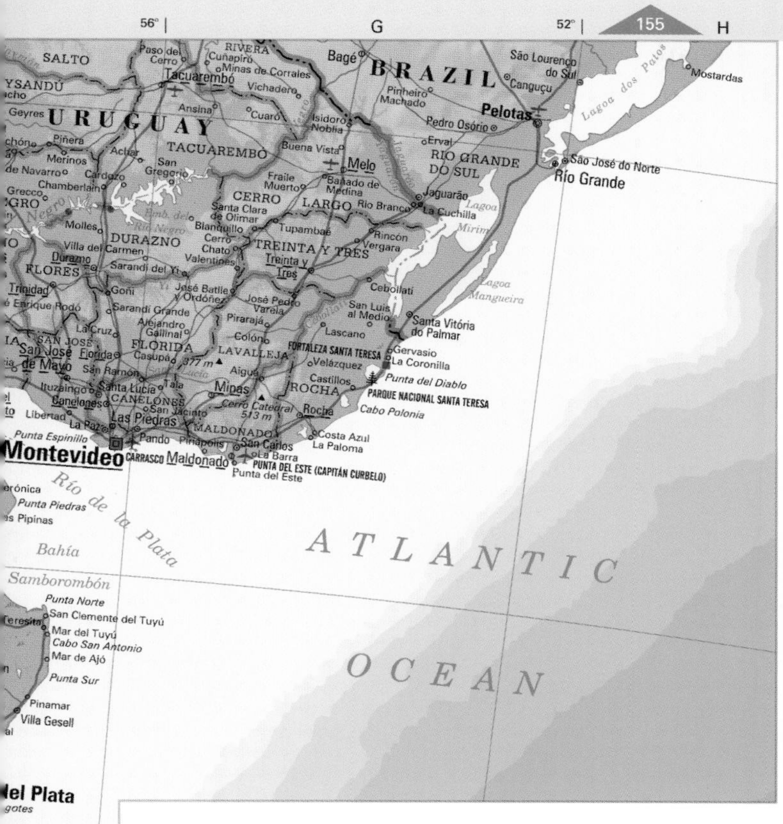
56°
G
52°
155
H
BRAZIL
URUGUAY
TACUAREMBÓ
RIO GRANDE DO SUL
CERRO
LARGO
DURAZNO
TREINTA Y TRES
FLORIDA
LAVALLEJA
ROCHA
MALDONADO
Montevideo
Pelotas
Rio Grande
Río de la Plata
ATLANTIC
OCEAN
Bahía
Samborombón
Punta Norte
San Clemente del Tuyú
Mar del Tuyú
Cabo San Antonio
Mar de Ajó
Punta Sur
Pinamar
Villa Gesell
PARQUE NACIONAL SANTA TERESA
Cabo Polonio
PUNTA DEL ESTE (CAPITÁN CURBELO)
Punta del Este

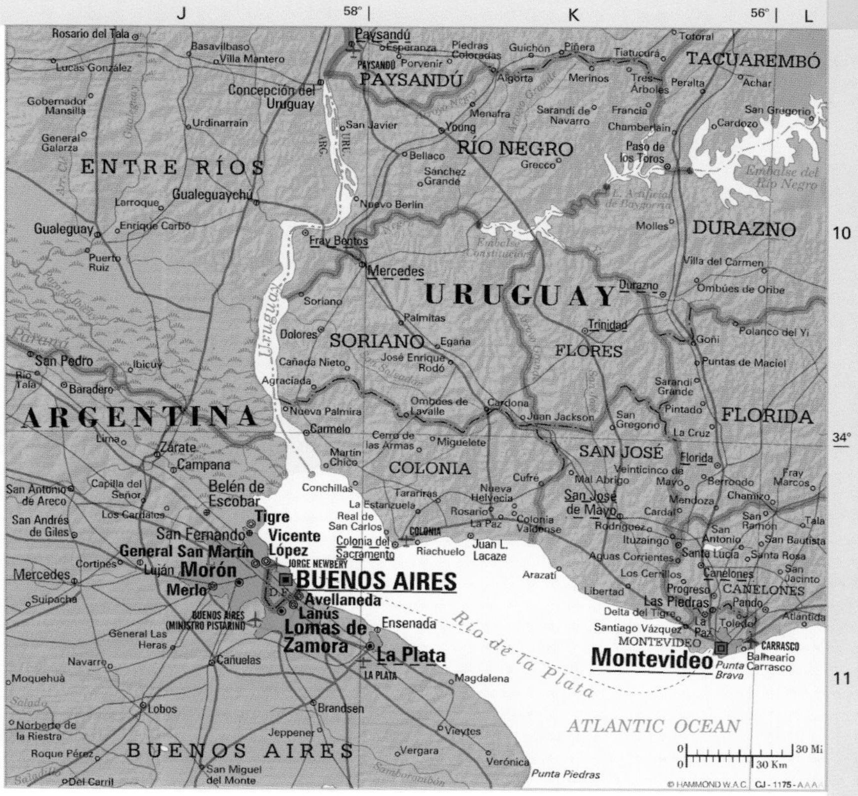
J
58°
K
56°
L
PAYSANDÚ
TACUAREMBÓ
ENTRE RÍOS
RÍO NEGRO
DURAZNO
URUGUAY
SORIANO
FLORES
ARGENTINA
COLONIA
SAN JOSÉ
FLORIDA
CANELONES
BUENOS AIRES
Tigre
Vicente López
General San Martín
Morón
Merlo
Avellaneda
Lanús
Lomas de Zamora
La Plata
Montevideo
Río de la Plata
ATLANTIC OCEAN
10
11
34°
30 Mi
30 Km
© HAMMOND W.A.C.

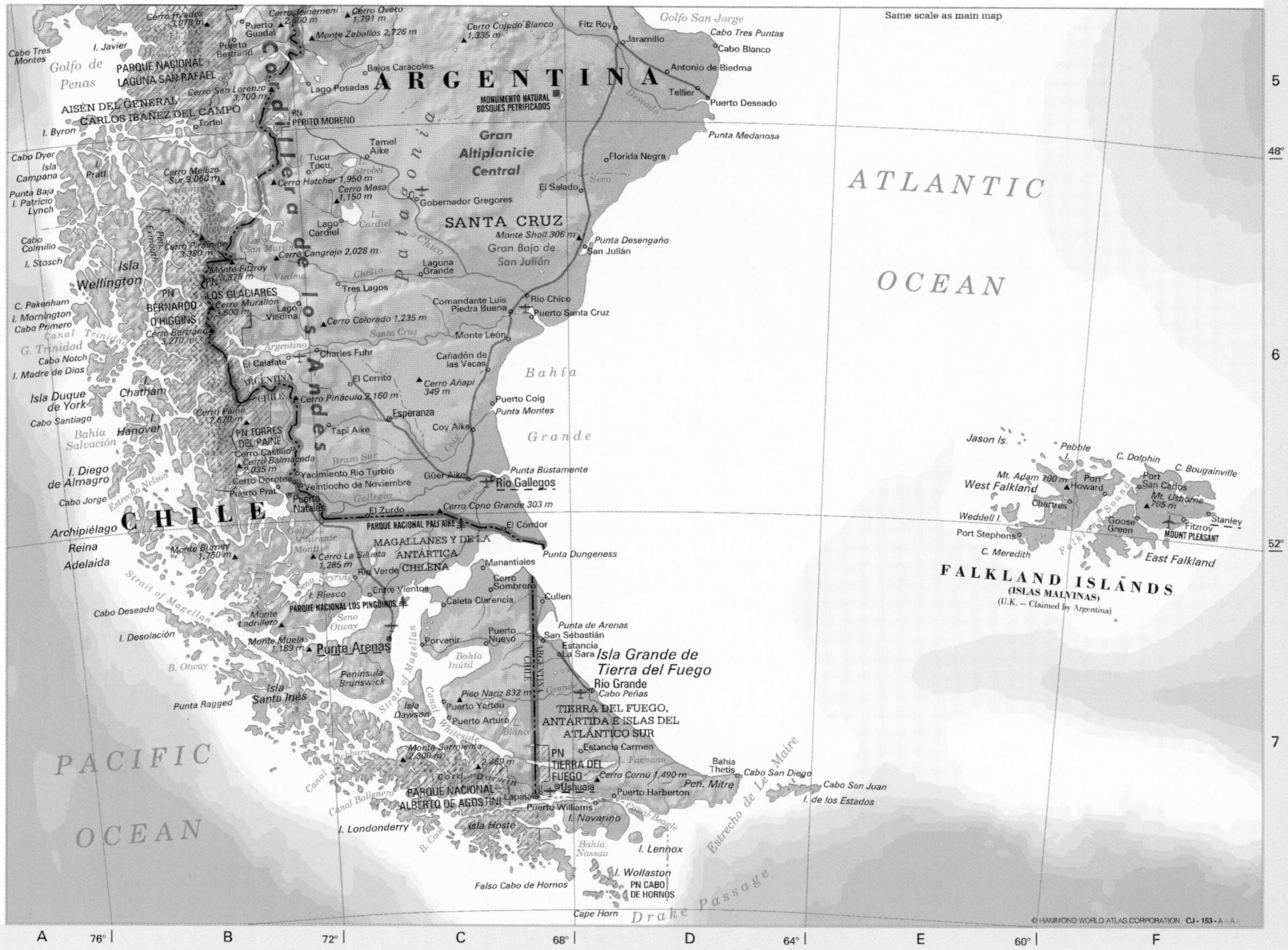
Same scale as main map
ARGENTINA
CHILE
Gran Altiplanicie Central
SANTA CRUZ
Golfo San Jorge
Puerto Deseado
Río Gallegos
Puerto Santa Cruz
Bahía Grande
ATLANTIC
OCEAN
PACIFIC
OCEAN
Isla Wellington
PN LOS GLACIARES
PN BERNARDO O'HIGGINS
PN TORRES DEL PAINE
El Calafate
Puerto Natales
MAGALLANES Y DE LA ANTÁRTICA CHILENA
Punta Arenas
Strait of Magellan
Isla Grande de Tierra del Fuego
Río Grande
TIERRA DEL FUEGO, ANTÁRTIDA E ISLAS DEL ATLÁNTICO SUR
Ushuaia
PARQUE NACIONAL ALBERTO DE AGOSTINI
I. Navarino
Estrecho de Le Maire
I. de los Estados
Cape Horn
Drake Passage
FALKLAND ISLANDS
(ISLAS MALVINAS)
(U.K. – Claimed by Argentina)
West Falkland
East Falkland
Stanley
5
6
7
48°
52°
A
76°
B
72°
C
68°
D
64°
E
60°
F
© HAMMOND WORLD ATLAS CORPORATION

POPULATION OF CITIES AND TOWNS

- OVER 2,000,000
- 1,000,000 - 1,999,999
- 500,000 - 999,999
- 250,000 - 499,999
- 100,000 - 249,999
- 30,000 - 99,999
- 10,000 - 29,999
- UNDER 10,000

SCALE 1:6,900,000 LAMBERT CONFORMAL CONIC PROJECTION

MILES 0 100 200 300

KILOMETERS 0 100 200 300

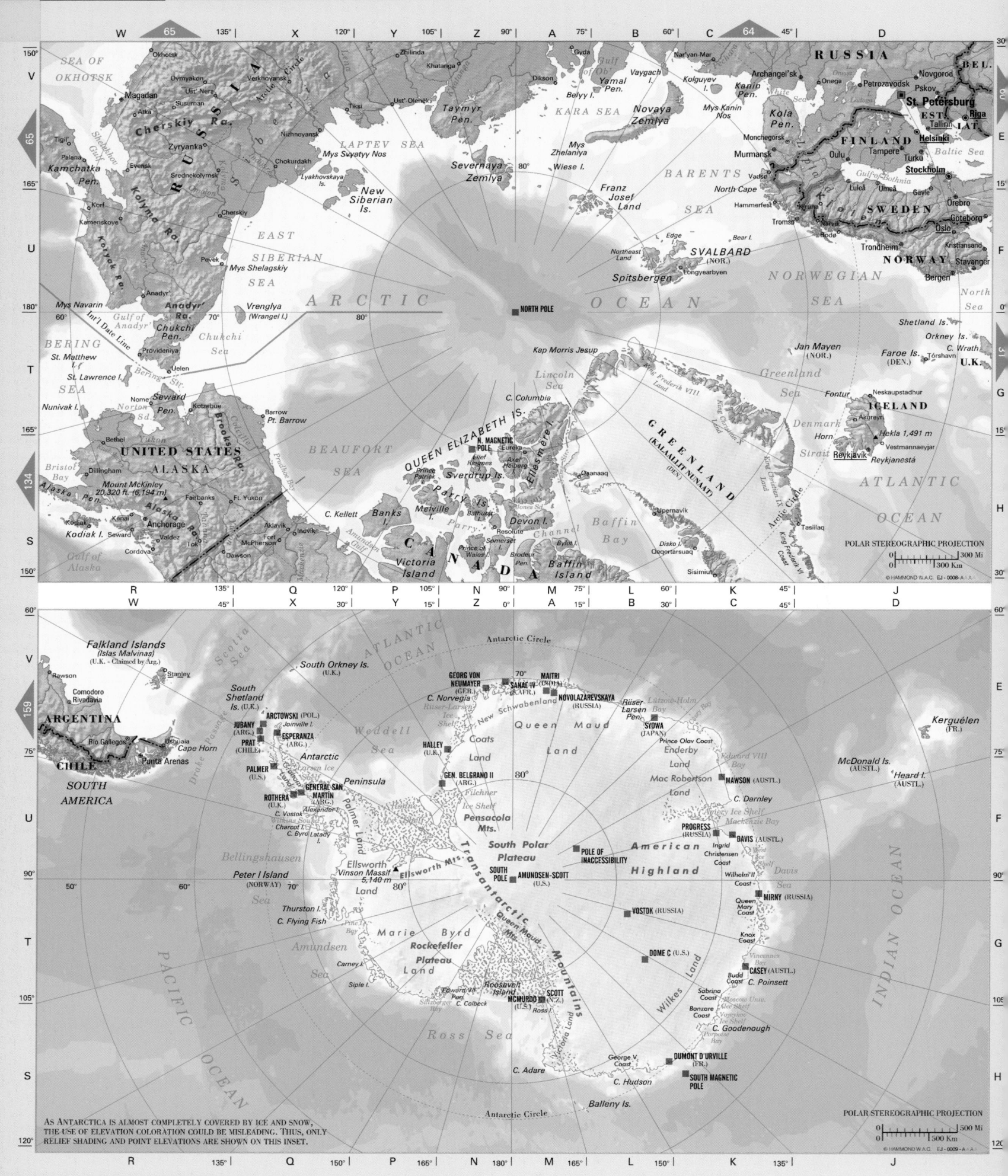

THE WORLD ALMANAC WORLD ATLAS

Index to the World Map Section

162 Using the Index

This index is a comprehensive listing of the places and geographic features found in the atlas. Names are arranged in strict alphabetical order, without regard to hyphens or spaces. Every name is followed by the country or area to which it belongs. Except for cities, towns, countries and cultural areas, all entries include a reference to feature type, such as province, river, island, peak, and so on. The page number and alpha-numeric code appear in blue to the right of each listing. The page number directs you to the largest scale map on which the name can be found, or in the case of a nation, on which the nation is depicted in its entirety. The code refers to the grid squares formed by the horizontal and vertical lines of latitude and longitude on each map. Following the letters from left to right and the numbers from top to bottom helps you to locate quickly the square containing the place or feature. Inset maps have their own alpha-numeric codes. Names that are accompanied by a point symbol are indexed to the symbol's location on the map. Other names are indexed to the initial letter of the name. When a map name contains a subordinate or alternate name, both names are listed in the index. To conserve space and provide room for more entries, many abbreviations are used in this index. The primary abbreviations are listed below.

Abbreviations

A

Ab,Can	Alberta
Abor.	Aboriginal
Acad.	Academy
ACT	Australian Capital Territory
A.F.B.	Air Force Base
Afld.	Airfield
Afg.	Afghanistan
Afr.	Africa
Ak,US	Alaska
Al,US	Alabama
Alb.	Albania
Alg.	Algeria
Amm. Dep.	Ammunition Depot
And.	Andorra
Ang.	Angola
Angu.	Anguilla
Ant.	Antarctica
Anti.	Antigua and Barbuda
Ar,US	Arkansas
Arch.	Archipelago
Arg.	Argentina
Arm.	Armenia
Arpt.	Airport
Aru.	Aruba
ASam.	American Samoa
Ash.	Ashmore and Cartier Islands
Aus.	Austria
Austl.	Australia
Aut.	Autonomous
Az,US	Arizona
Azer.	Azerbaijan
Azor.	Azores

B

Bahm.	Bahamas, The
Bahr.	Bahrain
Bang.	Bangladesh
Bar.	Barbados
BC,Can	British Columbia
Bela.	Belarus
Belg.	Belgium
Belz.	Belize
Ben.	Benin
Berm.	Bermuda
Bfld.	Battlefield
Bhu.	Bhutan
Bol.	Bolivia
Bor.	Borough
Bosn.	Bosnia and Herzegovina
Bots.	Botswana
Braz.	Brazil
BrIn.	British Indian Ocean Territory
Bru.	Brunei
Bul.	Bulgaria
Burk.	Burkina Faso
Buru.	Burundi
BVI	British Virgin Islands

C

Ca,US	California
CAfr.	Central African Republic
Camb.	Cambodia
Camr.	Cameroon
Can.	Canada
Can.	Canal
Canl.	Canary Islands
Cap.	Capital
Cap. Dist.	Capital District
Cap. Terr.	Capital Territory
Cay.	Cayman Islands

C.d'Iv. / (continued)

C.d'Iv.	Côte d'Ivoire
C.G.	Coast Guard
Chan.	Channel
Chl.	Channel Islands
Co.	County
Co,US	Colorado
Col.	Colombia
Com.	Comoros
Cont.	Continent
CpV.	Cape Verde Islands
CR	Costa Rica
Cr.	Creek
Cro.	Croatia
CSea.	Coral Sea Islands Territory
Ct,US	Connecticut
Ctr.	Center
Ctry.	Country
Cyp.	Cyprus
Czh.	Czech Republic

D

DC,US	District of Columbia
De,US	Delaware
Den.	Denmark
Depr.	Depression
Dept.	Department
Des.	Desert
DF	Distrito Federal
Dist.	District
Djib.	Djibouti
Dom.	Dominica
Dpcy.	Dependency
D.R.Congo	Democratic Republic of the Congo
DRep.	Dominican Republic

E

Ecu.	Ecuador
Emb.	Embankment
Eng.	Engineering
Eng,UK	England
EqG.	Equatorial Guinea
Erit.	Eritrea
ESal.	El Salvador
Est.	Estonia
Eth.	Ethiopia
ETim.	East Timor
Eur.	Europe

F

Falk.	Falkland Islands
Far.	Faroe Islands
Fed. Dist.	Federal District
Fin.	Finland
Fl,US	Florida
For.	Forest
Fr.	France
FrAnt.	French Southern and Antarctic Lands
FrG.	French Guiana
FrPol.	French Polynesia
FYROM	Former Yugoslav Rep. of Macedonia

G

Ga,US	Georgia
Galp.	Galapagos Islands
Gam.	Gambia, The
Gaza	Gaza Strip
GBis.	Guinea-Bissau

Geo. / (continued)

Geo.	Georgia
Ger.	Germany
Gha.	Ghana
Gib.	Gibraltar
Glac.	Glacier
Gov.	Governorate
Govt.	Government
Gre.	Greece
Grld.	Greenland
Gren.	Grenada
Grsld.	Grassland
Guad.	Guadeloupe
Guat.	Guatemala
Gui.	Guinea
Guy.	Guyana

H

Har.	Harbor
Hi,US	Hawaii
Hist.	Historic(al)
Hon.	Honduras
Hts.	Heights
Hun.	Hungary

I

Ia,US	Iowa
Ice.	Iceland
Id,US	Idaho
Il,US	Illinois
IM	Isle of Man
In,US	Indiana
Ind. Res.	Indian Reservation
Indo.	Indonesia
Int'l	International
Ire.	Ireland
Isl., Isls.	Island, Islands
Isr.	Israel
Isth.	Isthmus
It.	Italy

J

Jam.	Jamaica
Jor.	Jordan

K

Kaz.	Kazakhstan
Kiri.	Kiribati
Ks,US	Kansas
Kuw.	Kuwait
Ky,US	Kentucky
Kyr.	Kyrgyzstan

L

La,US	Louisiana
Lab.	Laboratory
Lag.	Lagoon
Lakesh.	Lakeshore
Lat.	Latvia
Lcht.	Liechtenstein
Ldg.	Landing
Leb.	Lebanon
Les.	Lesotho
Libr.	Liberia
Lith.	Lithuania
Lux.	Luxembourg

M

Ma,US	Massachusetts
Madg.	Madagascar
Madr.	Madeira

Malay. / (continued)

Malay.	Malaysia
Mald.	Maldives
Malw.	Malawi
Mart.	Martinique
May.	Mayotte
Mb,Can	Manitoba
Md,US	Maryland
Me,US	Maine
Mem.	Memorial
Mex.	Mexico
Mi,US	Michigan
Micr.	Micronesia, Federated States of
Mil.	Military
Mn,US	Minnesota
Mo,US	Missouri
Mol.	Moldova
Mon.	Monument
Mona.	Monaco
Mong.	Mongolia
Monts.	Montserrat
Mor.	Morocco
Moz.	Mozambique
Mrsh.	Marshall Islands
Mrta.	Mauritania
Mrts.	Mauritius
Ms,US	Mississippi
Mt.	Mount
Mt,US	Montana
Mtn., Mts.	Mountain, Mountains
Mun. Arpt.	Municipal Airport
Myan.	Myanmar

N

NAm.	North America
Namb.	Namibia
NAnt.	Netherlands Antilles
Nat'l	National
Nav.	Naval
NB,Can	New Brunswick
Nbrhd.	Neighborhood
NC,US	North Carolina
NCal.	New Caledonia
ND,US	North Dakota
Ne,US	Nebraska
Neth.	Netherlands
Nf,Can	Newfoundland
Nga.	Nigeria
NH,US	New Hampshire
NI,UK	Northern Ireland
Nic.	Nicaragua
NJ,US	New Jersey
NKor.	North Korea
NM,US	New Mexico
NMar.	Northern Mariana Islands
Nor.	Norway
NS,Can	Nova Scotia
Nv,US	Nevada
Nun.,Can	Nunavut
NW,Can	Northwest Territories
NY,US	New York
NZ	New Zealand

O

Obl.	Oblast
Oh,US	Ohio
Ok,US	Oklahoma
On,Can	Ontario
Or,US	Oregon

P

Pa,US	Pennsylvania
PacUS	Pacific Islands, U.S.
Pak.	Pakistan

Pan. / (continued)

Pan.	Panama
Par.	Paraguay
Par.	Parish
PE,Can	Prince Edward Island
Pen.	Peninsula
Phil.	Philippines
Phys. Reg.	Physical Region
Pitc.	Pitcairn Islands
Plat.	Plateau
PNG	Papua New Guinea
Pol.	Poland
Port.	Portugal
Poss.	Possession
Pkwy.	Parkway
PR	Puerto Rico
Pref.	Prefecture
Prov.	Province
Prsv.	Preserve
Pt.	Point

Q

Qu,Can	Quebec

R

Rec.	Recreation(al)
Ref.	Refuge
Reg.	Region
Rep.	Republic
Res.	Reservoir, Reservation
Reun.	Réunion
RI,US	Rhode Island
Riv.	River
Rom.	Romania
Rsv.	Reserve
Rus.	Russia
Rvwy.	Riverway
Rwa.	Rwanda

S

SAfr.	South Africa
Sam.	Samoa
SAm.	South America
SaoT.	São Tomé and Príncipe
SAr.	Saudi Arabia
Sc,UK	Scotland
SC,US	South Carolina
SD,US	South Dakota
Seash.	Seashore
Sen.	Senegal
Serb.	Serbia and Montenegro
Sey.	Seychelles
SGeo.	South Georgia and Sandwich Islands
Sing.	Singapore
Sk,Can	Saskatchewan
SKor.	South Korea
SLeo.	Sierra Leone
Slov.	Slovenia
Slvk.	Slovakia
SMar.	San Marino
Sol.	Solomon Islands
Som.	Somalia
Sp.	Spain
Spr., Sprs.	Spring, Springs
SrL.	Sri Lanka
Sta.	Station
StH.	Saint Helena
Str.	Strait
StK.	Saint Kitts and Nevis
StL.	Saint Lucia
StP.	Saint Pierre and Miquelon
StV.	Saint Vincent and the Grenadines

Sur. / (continued)

Sur.	Suriname
Sval.	Svalbard
Swaz.	Swaziland
Swe.	Sweden
Swi.	Switzerland

T

Tah.	Tahiti
Tai.	Taiwan
Taj.	Tajikistan
Tanz.	Tanzania
Ter.	Terrace
Terr.	Territory
Thai.	Thailand
Tn,US	Tennessee
Tok.	Tokelau
Trg.	Training
Trin.	Trinidad and Tobago
Trkm.	Turkmenistan
Trks.	Turks and Caicos Islands
Tun.	Tunisia
Tun.	Tunnel
Turk.	Turkey
Tuv.	Tuvalu
Twp.	Township
Tx,US	Texas

U

UAE	United Arab Emirates
Ugan.	Uganda
UK	United Kingdom
Ukr.	Ukraine
Uru.	Uruguay
US	United States
USVI	U.S. Virgin Islands
Ut,US	Utah
Uzb.	Uzbekistan

V

Va,US	Virginia
Val.	Valley
Van.	Vanuatu
VatC.	Vatican City
Ven.	Venezuela
Viet.	Vietnam
Vill.	Village
Vol.	Volcano
Vt,US	Vermont

W

Wa,US	Washington
Wal,UK	Wales
Wall.	Wallis and Futuna
WBnk.	West Bank
Wi,US	Wisconsin
Wild.	Wildlife, Wilderness
WSah.	Western Sahara
WV,US	West Virginia
Wy,US	Wyoming

Y

Yem.	Yemen
Yk,Can	Yukon Territory

Z

Zam.	Zambia
Zim.	Zimbabwe

A

100 Mile House, BC, Can. 126/C3
Aa (riv.), Ger. 50/D5
Aach (riv.), Ger. 57/F2
Aach, Ger. 57/E2
Aachen, Ger. 53/F2
Aalbach (riv.), Ger. 54/C3
Aalborg (int'l arpt.), Den. 38/C4
Aalburg, Neth. 50/C5
Aalen, Ger. 54/D5
Aalsmeer, Neth. 50/B4
Aalst, Belg. 52/D2
Aalten, Neth. 50/D5
Aalter, Belg. 52/C1
Aar (riv.), Ger. 53/H3
Aarau, Swi. 56/E3
Aarberg, Swi. 56/D3
Aarburg, Swi. 56/D3
Aardenburg, Neth. 52/C1
Aare (riv.), Swi. 56/E3
Aargau (canton), Swi. 57/E3
Aarred (lake), WSah. 98/B4
Aarschot, Belg. 53/D1
Aartselaar, Belg. 52/D1
Aarwangen, Swi. 56/D3
Aba, D.R. Congo 104/A2
Aba, China 70/H5
Aba, Nga. 103/G5
Abā as Su'ūd, SAr. 88/D5
Abacaxis (riv.), Braz. 150/G3
Abadab (peak), Sudan 101/C5
Abādān, Iran 88/E2
Abādeh, Iran 88/G3
Abadia dos Dourados, Braz. 155/C1
Abadla, Alg. 99/E3
Abádszalók, Hun. 48/E2
Abaeté, Braz. 155/C1
Abaetetuba, Braz. 151/J4
Abaiang (isl.), Kiri. 116/G4
Abakan, Rus. 64/K4
Abancay, Peru 156/C4
Abano Terme, It. 59/E2
Abar Kūh, Iran 88/G3
Abarán, Sp. 44/E3
Abashiri (lake), Japan 76/D1
Abashiri, Japan 76/D1
Abasolo, Mex. 143/E4
Abasolo, Mex. 143/F3
Abay, Kaz. 63/D4
Abaya Hayk (lake), Eth. 97/N6
Abbadia Lariana, It. 57/F6
Abbadia San Salvatore, It. 57/C1
Abbeville, La, US 129/J5
Abbeville, SC, US 133/H1
Abbeville, Fr. 52/A3
Abbey (peak), Austl. 114/B1
Abbeyfeale, Ire. 31/P10
Abbeyleix, Ire. 31/Q10
Abbiategrasso, It. 58/B2
Abbot (mt.), Austl. 114/B3
Abbotsinch (int'l arpt.), Sc, UK 36/A2
Abbottābād, Pak. 86/B2
Abbotstown, Pa, US 138/B4
Abcoude, Neth. 50/B4
Abdul Hakīm, Pak. 86/B4
Abdulino, Rus. 63/K1
Abéché, Chad 97/K5
Abemama (isl.), Kiri. 116/G4
Abenberg, Ger. 54/D4
Abengourou, C.d'Iv. 102/E5
Abenrā, Den. 38/C4
Abens (riv.), Ger. 40/F4
Abensberg, Ger. 55/E5
Abeokuta, Nga. 103/F5
Abercarn, Wal, UK 34/C3
Aberchirder, Sc, UK 36/C1
Aberdare, Wal, UK 36/C1
Aberdare NP, Kenya 115/D2
Aberdeen (lake), Nun., Can. 122/F2
Aberdeen, SAfr. 106/D4
Aberdeen, Md, US 36/D2
Aberdeen (pol. reg.), Sc, UK 36/D2
Aberdeen, SD, US 127/J4
Aberdeen, Ms, US 133/F3
Aberdeen, Md, US 138/B4
Aberdeen, Wa, US 126/C4
Aberdeen Proving Ground, Md, US 138/B4
Aberdeenshire, Sc, UK 36/D2
Aberdeenshire (pol. reg.), Sc, UK 36/D2
Aberdour, Sc, UK 36/C1
Aberdour (bay), Sc, UK 36/D1
Aberfeldy, Sc, UK 36/C1
Aberfoyle, Sc, UK 36/B4
Abergavenny, Wal, UK 32/C3
Abergele, Wal, UK 34/E5
Aberlour, Sc, UK 36/C2
Abernethy, Sc, UK 36/C4
Abert (lake), Or, US 126/C5
Abertillery, Wal, UK 32/B2
Aberystwyth, Wal, UK 32/B2
Abhā, SAr. 88/D5
Abhar, Iran 88/F1
Abhayāpuri, India 85/H2
Abbe Bad (lake), Djib.,Eth 97/H5
Abia (prov.), Nga. 103/G5
Abidjan, C.d'Iv. 102/D5

Abiko, Japan 77/E2
Abilene, Tx, US 129/H4
Abilene, Ks, US 129/H3
Abingdon, Eng, UK 33/E3
Abingdon, Md, US 138/B5
Abington (reef), Austl. 114/C2
Abington, Sc, UK 36/C6
Abino (pt.), On, Can. 131/R10
Abiquiu, NM, US 132/B2
Abitibi (lake), On,Qu, Can. 123/H4
Abitibi (riv.), On, Can. 123/H4
Abkhazia Aut. Rep., Geo. 63/G4
Ableiges, Fr. 30/H4
Abnūb, Egypt 101/B3
Abo (Turku), Fin. 39/K1
Abohar, India 86/C4
Aboisso, C.d'Iv. 102/E5
Abomey, Ben. 103/F5
Abondance, Fr. 56/C5
Abony, Hun. 48/D2
Aboyne, Sc, UK 36/D2
Abra (riv.), Phil. 79/D4
Abra Pampa, Arg. 157/C1
Abrantes, Port. 44/A3
Abreojos (pt.), Mex. 142/B3
Abrud, Rom. 49/F2
Abruzzi (prov.), It. 43/K5
Abruzzo, PN de, It. 46/C2
Absam, Aus. 57/H3
Absaroka (range), Mt,Wy, US 126/F4
Absecon, NJ, US 138/D5
Abtsgmünd, Ger. 54/D5
Abu el-Husein (well), Egypt 101/A2
Abū Ḩammād, Egypt 91/B4
Abu Hashim (well), Egypt 101/C4
Abū Ḩummuş, Egypt 91/B4
Abū Kabīr, Egypt 91/B4
Abū Kamāl, Syria 90/E3
Abū Qashsh, WBnk. 91/G8
Abu Shagara (cape), Sudan 101/D4
Abu Simbel (ruin), Egypt 101/B4
Abū Ẕaby (Abu Dhabi) (cap.), UAE 89/G4
Abuja (cap.), Nga. 103/G4
Abuja (int'l arpt.), Nga. 103/G4
Abuja Capital Territory, Nga. 103/G4
Abukuma (riv.), Japan 75/G2
Abukuma (plat.), Japan 75/G2
Abulog, Phil. 79/D4
Abuná (riv.), Braz. 150/E6
Abuta, Japan 76/B2
Abuyē Mēda (peak), Eth. 97/N5
Abuyog, Phil. 79/E5
Aby, Swe. 38/G2
Abydos (ruin), Egypt 101/B3
Abydro, Den. 38/C3
Acacías, Col. 152/C4
Acacoyagua, Mex. 144/C3
Acadia NP, Me, US 131/G4
Acadian Village, La, US 129/J5
Acajutiba, Braz. 154/C3
Acámbaro, Mex. 143/E4
Acampo, Ca, US 135/M10
Acandí, Col. 152/C2
Acaponeta (riv.), Mex. 142/D4
Acaponeta, Mex. 142/D4
Acapulco de Juárez, Mex. 140/B4
Acaraí (mts.), Braz.,Guy. 153/G3
Acaraú, Serra (mts.), Braz. 150/G3
Acaraú (riv.), Braz. 154/B1
Acaraú, Braz. 154/B1
Acari, Braz. 154/C2
Acari (riv.), Braz. 150/G5
Acari, Peru 156/C4
Acarigua, Ven. 152/D2
Acatlán de Osorio, Mex. 144/B2
Acatlán de Pérez Figueroa, Mex. 143/N8
Acatzingo, Mex. 143/M7
Acayucan, Mex. 144/C2
Accha, Peru 156/D4
Acciaroli, It. 46/D2
Accra (cap.), Gha. 103/E5
Accrington, Eng, UK 35/F4
Aceuchal, Sp. 44/B3
Ach (riv.), Aus. 55/G6
Achacachi, Bol. 150/E7
Achaguas, Ven. 152/D3
Achao, Chile 158/B4
Achar, Uru. 159/K10
Achegour (well), Niger 96/H4
Achen (pass), Ger. 57/H2
Acheng, China 71/N2
Achères, Fr. 30/J5
Achhnera, India 84/A2
Achicourt, Fr. 52/B3
Achill (riv.), Ire. 30/N10
Achill Head (isl.), Ire. 30/N10
Achiltibuie, Sc, UK 31/R7
Achinsk, Rus. 64/K4
Achmim (well), Mrta. 102/D2
Achnasheen, Sc, UK 36/A1
Achoma, Peru 156/D4

A'chràlaig (peak), Sc, UK 36/A2
Achuapa, Nic. 144/E3
Achupallas, Ecu. 156/B1
Acireale, It. 46/D4
Acklins (isl.), Bahm. 141/G3
Acland (mt.), Austl. 114/C4
Acobamba, Peru 156/C4
Acolla, Peru 156/C3
Acolman, Mex. 143/R9
Acomayo, Peru 156/C3
Acomayo, Peru 156/B3
Aconcagua (peak), Arg. 158/C2
Aconchi, Mex. 142/C2
Acopiara, Braz. 154/C2
Acora, Peru 156/D4
Acqualagna, It. 59/F5
Acquanegra sul Chiese, It. 58/D2
Acquapendente, It. 46/B1
Acqui Terme, It. 58/B3
Acraman (lake), Austl. 113/G5
Acrata (pt.), Alg. 100/G4
Acre (riv.), Braz. 150/E6
Acre (state), Braz. 156/D3
Acreúna, Braz. 155/B1
Acropolis, Gre. 47/N9
Actaeon Group (isls.), FrPol. 117/M7
Acton, Ca, US 136/B2
Actopan, Mex. 143/N7
Actopan, Mex. 143/L6
Acton, Mex. 143/L6
Açu, Braz. 154/C2
Açude Aratas (res.), Braz. 154/B2
Açude Banabuiu (res.), Braz. 154/C2
Acula, Mex. 143/P8
Aculeo (lag.), Chile 158/N8
Acy-en-Multien, Fr. 30/L4
Ad Dahnā' (des.), SAr. 88/D3
Ad-Dakhla, WSah. 98/B5
Ad Damazin, Sudan 97/M5
Ad Damīr, Sudan 88/B4
Ad Dammām, S.Ar. 88/F3
Ad Daqahliyah (gov.), Egypt 101/B1
Ad Dilinjāt, Egypt 91/B4
Ad Dīwānīyah, Iraq 90/F4
Ad Dujayl, Iraq 90/F3
Ad Duwaym, Sudan 97/M5
Ada, Gha. 103/F5
Ada, Serb. 48/E3
Ada, Oh, US 130/D3
Ada, Ok, US 129/H4
Adair (cape), Nun., Can. 123/J1
Adair, Bahia del (bay), Mex. 128/D5
Adaja (riv.), Sp. 44/C2
Adak (peak), Ak, US 134/C6
Adak (str.), Ak, US 134/C6
Adam (mt.), UK 159/E6
Adamantina, Braz. 155/B2
Adamaoua (plat.), Camr.,Nga. 93/D4
Adamello (peak), It. 57/G5
Adaminaby, Austl. 115/D3
Adams (lake), BC, Can. 126/D3
Adams (co.), Co, US 137/C3
Adams (co.), Pa, US 138/A4
Adams (mt.), Wa, US 126/C4
Adamstown (cap.), Pitc. 117/M7
Adamstown, Pa, US 138/B3
Adamwa (plat.), Nga. 103/H5
'Adan, Yem. 88/D6
Adana (prov.), Turk. 90/C2
Adana, Turk. 91/D1
Adana (int'l arpt.), Turk. 91/D1
Adapazarı, Turk. 49/K5
Adare, Ire. 31/P10
Adare (cape), Ant. 160/M
Adarza (peak), Fr. 44/E1
Add (riv.), Sc, UK 36/A4
Adda (riv.), It. 43/H4
Addison, Il, US 139/P16
Addlestone, Eng, UK 30/B2
Addo Elephant NP, SAfr. 106/D4
Adekeieh (Ādī K'eyih), Erit. 88/C6
Adelaide, SAfr. 106/D4
Adelaide (pen.), Nun., Can. 122/G2
Adelaide, Austl. 113/M8
Adelaide (int'l arpt.), Austl. 113/M8
Adelaide Zoo, Austl. 113/M8
Adelanto, Ca, US 136/C1
Adelboden, Swi. 98/B5
Adelebsen, Ger. 51/G5
Adelheidsdorf, Ger. 51/H3
Adelmannsfelden, Ger. 54/D5
Adelong, Austl. 115/D2
Adelschlag, Ger. 54/C4
Adelsheim, Ger. 54/C4
Adelsried, Ger. 54/C4
Adenau, Ger. 53/F2
Adendorf, Ger. 51/H2
Adh Dhirā', Jor. 91/D4
Adi (isl.), Indo. 81/H4
Adi Ugri, Erit. 88/C6
Adige (riv.), It. 43/J4
Adige (Etsch) (riv.), It. 57/H5
Ādigrat, Eth. 88/C6

Adilābād, India 82/C4
Adilcevaz, Turk. 90/E2
Adiora (well), Mali 103/E2
Adirondack (mts.), NY, US 125/L3
Adīs Ābeba (Addis Ababa) (cap.), Eth. 97/N6
Adıyaman, Turk. 90/D2
Adıyaman (prov.), Turk. 90/D2
Adjud, Rom. 49/H2
Adjuntas, Presa de la (res.), Mex. 143/F4
Adler/Sochi (int'l arpt.), Rus. 62/F4
Adliswil, Swi. 57/E3
Admiralty (inlet), Nun., Can. 123/H1
Admiralty (isl.), Ak, US 122/C3
Admiralty Island Nat'l Mon., Ak, US 134/M4
Admiralty (isls.), PNG 116/C3
Admiralty (inlet), Wa, US 135/B2
Adnan Menderes (int'l arpt.), Turk. 90/A2
Ado (riv.), Japan 77/J5
Ado Ekiti, Nga. 103/G5
Ado Odo, Nga. 103/F5
Adogawa, Japan 77/K5
Adolfo López Mateos, Mex. 142/B3
Adoni, India 82/C4
Adour (riv.), Fr. 42/C5
Adra, India 85/F4
Adra, Sp. 44/D4
Adrano, It. 46/D4
Adrar (phys. reg.), Mrta. 96/C3
Adrar, Alg. 99/E4
Adrar (pol. reg.), Mrta. 102/C1
Adrar (prov.), Alg. 99/E4
Adrar (reg.), Mrta. 96/C5
Adrar bou Nasser (peak), Mor. 98/E2
Adrar Sotuf (mts.), WSah. 98/B5
Adria, It. 59/F2
Adrian, Mi, US 130/C3
Adriatic (sea), Eur. 27/F4
Adro, It. 58/C1
Aduana del Sásabe, Mex. 128/C5
Adulis (ruin), Erit. 88/C5
Adur (riv.), Eng, UK 33/F5
Ādwa, Eth. 88/C6
Adwick le Street, Eng, UK 35/G4
Adycha (riv.), Rus. 65/P3
Adygeya, Resp., Rus. 62/F3
Adz'va (riv.), Rus. 61/P2
Aegean (sea), Gre.,Turk. 62/C5
Aero (isl.), Den. 38/D4
Aeron (riv.), Wal, UK 32/B2
Aesch, Swi. 56/D3
Aeschi bei Spiez, Swi. 56/D4
Aetsä, Fin. 39/K1
Afafdjoto (peak), Gha. 103/F5
Afándou, Gre. 90/B2
Aff (riv.), Fr. 42/B3
Affoltern im Emmental, Swi. 56/D3
Affric (lake), Sc, UK 36/A2
Affton, Mo, US 137/G8
Afghanistan (ctry.) 89/H2
Afmadow, Som. 97/P7
Afogados da Ingázeira, Braz. 154/C2
Afognak (mtn.), Ak, US 134/H4
Afognak (isl.), Ak, US 134/H4
Afollé, Massif de (phys. reg.), Mrta. 102/C2
Afonso Bezerra, Braz. 154/C2
Afonso Cláudio, Braz. 155/D2
Afragola, It. 46/D2
Afrânio, Braz. 154/B3
Africa (cont.) 93
Afrin (riv.), Turk. 91/E1
'Afrīn, Syria 91/E1
Afrique (peak), Fr. 56/A3
Afsluitdijk (dam), Neth. 50/C2
Afte (riv.), Ger. 51/F5
Afton, Wy, US 126/E5
Afuidich (lake), WSah. 98/B5
'Afula, Isr. 91/G6
Afyon, Turk. 90/B2
Afyon (prov.), Turk. 90/B2
Afzalgarh, India 84/B1
Agadès (int'l arpt.), Niger 103/G2
Agadez, Niger 96/H3
Agadez (dept.), Niger 99/H5
Agadir, Mor. 98/C3
Agago (riv.), Ugan. 104/B2
Agamor (well), Mali 103/F2
Agano (riv.), Japan 77/F2
Aganju (isl.), NMar. 116/D3
Agar, India 82/C4
Agartala, India 85/G4
Agassiz Ice Cap (ice field), Nun., Can. 123/T6
Agattu (isl.), Ak, US 134/A5
Agattu (str.), Ak, US 134/A5
Agbabu, Nga. 103/G5

Agboville, C.d'Iv. 102/D5
Ağdam, Azer. 63/H5
Agde, Fr. 42/D4
Agen, Fr. 42/D4
Ageo, Japan 77/D2
Ager (riv.), Aus. 55/G7
Agerisee (lake), Swi. 57/E3
Agger (riv.), Ger. 53/G1
Aggteleki NP, Slvk. 48/E1
Aghā Jārī, Iran 88/E2
Aghagallon, NI, UK 34/B3
Aghagower, Ire. 31/P10
Ağin, Turk. 90/D2
Aginskoye, Rus. 71/K1
Agliana, It. 59/D5
Ağlıköy, Turk. 90/C1
Agly (riv.), Fr. 42/E5
Agna, It. 59/E2
Agnanderón, Gre. 47/G3
Agnita, Rom. 49/G3
Agno (riv.), It. 59/E1
Agno (int'l arpt.), Swi. 57/E6
Agnone, It. 46/D2
Ago, Japan 77/L7
Agogna (riv.), It. 43/H4
Agordo, It. 43/K3
Agout (riv.), Fr. 42/D5
Agra, India 84/B2
Agraciada, Uru. 159/J10
Agrado, Col. 152/C4
Agreda, Sp. 44/E2
Agri (prov.), Turk. 90/E2
Agria, Gre. 47/H3
Agrigento, It. 46/C4
Agrihan (isl.), NMar. 116/D3
Agrinion, Gre. 47/G3
Agrio (riv.), Arg. 158/C3
Agropoli, It. 46/D2
Agryz, Rus. 61/M4
Agsumal (dry lake), WSah. 98/B5
Agua Boa, Braz. 154/B5
Agua Branca, Braz. 154/B2
Agua Dulce, Mex. 144/C2
Agua Dulce, Ca, US 136/B2
Agua Fria (riv.), Az, US 137/R19
Agua Fria NM, Az, US 128/E4
Agua Hedionda (lake), Ca, US 136/C4
Agua Larga, Ven. 152/D2
Agua Prieta, Mex. 128/E5
Aguachica, Col. 152/C2
Aguadilla, PR 141/M8
Aguadulce, Pan. 152/A2
Aguaí, Braz. 211/G7
Agualva-Cacém, Port. 45/P10
Aguan (riv.), Hon. 140/D4
Aguanus (riv.), Qu, Can. 131/J1
Aguapeí (riv.), Braz. 155/B2
Aguarico (riv.), Peru 152/B5
Aguas Belas, Braz. 154/C2
Aguas Corrientes, Uru. 159/K11
Aguas da Prata, Braz. 211/G6
Aguas de Lindóia, Braz. 211/G7
Aguas Formosas, Braz. 154/B5
Aguas, Serra das (hills), Braz. 211/H7
Aguasay, Ven. 153/F2
Aguascalientes, Mex. 142/E4
Aguascalientes (state), Mex. 140/A3
Aguavermelha, Represa (res.), Braz. 155/B1
Aguaytía, Peru 156/C3
Agudos, Braz. 155/B2
Agueda (riv.), Sp. 44/B2
Agueda, Port. 44/A2
Aguéraktem (well), Mali 99/E2
Aguglia, It. 59/G5
Agui, Japan 77/L6
Aguilar, Sp. 44/C4
Aguilar de Campóo, Sp. 44/C1
Aguilares, Arg. 157/C2
Aguilas, Sp. 44/E4
Aguililla, Mex. 142/E5
Aguja (pt.), Peru 156/A2
Agulhas (cape), SAfr. 106/M11
Agulhas Negras, Pico das (peak), Braz. 211/J7
Agung (vol.), Indo. 81/E5
Agusan (riv.), Phil. 79/E6
Agustín Codazzi, Col. 152/C2
Ahaggar (plat.) 93
Ahaggar, Niger 103/G2
Ahaggar (mts.), Alg. 96/G3
Ahal (pol. reg.), Trkm. 87/C5
Aham, Ger. 55/F5
Ahar, Iran 63/H5
Ahaus, Ger. 50/E4
Ahklun (mts.), Ak, US 134/E4
Ahlat, Turk. 90/E2
Ahlen, Ger. 51/E5

Ahlerstedt, Ger. 51/G2
Ahmadābād, India 89/K4
Ahmadpur East, Pak. 86/A5
Ahmadpur Siāl, Pak. 86/A4
Ahmar (mts.), Eth. 97/P6
Ahmar, 'Erg el (des.), Mali 98/D4
Ahmed (well), WSah. 98/B5
Ahmeyine (well), Mrta. 98/B5
Ahoghill, NI, UK 34/B2
Ahome, Mex. 142/C3
Ahr (riv.), Ger. 43/G1
Ahraurā, India 84/D3
Ahrensburg, Ger. 51/H1
Ahse (riv.), Ger. 51/F5
Ahuacatitlán, Mex. 143/K8
Ahuacatlán, Mex. 142/D4
Ahualulco, Mex. 143/E4
Ahuimanu, Hi, US 124/W13
Ahumada, Mex. 128/F5
Ahun, Fr. 42/E3
Ahvāz, Iran 88/E2
Ahvenanmaa (prov.), Fin. 37/F4
Ai (riv.), China 71/N4
Ai-Ais Hot Springs, Namb. 106/B2
Ai-shima (isl.), Japan 74/B3
Aibag Gol (riv.), China 72/B2
Aichach, Ger. 54/E6
Aichi (pref.), Japan 75/E3
Aidhausen, Ger. 54/D2
Aidlingen, Ger. 54/B5
Aiea, Hi, US 124/W13
Aiello del Friuli, It. 59/G1
Aigen im Mühlkreis, Aus. 55/G5
Aigle, Pic de l' (peak), Fr. 56/B4
Aiglemont, Fr. 53/D4
Aigoual (peak), Fr. 42/E4
Aiguá, Uru. 159/G2
Aigües Tortes y Lago de San Mauricio, PN de, Sp. 45/F1
Aiguille, Cap de l' (cape), Alg. 100/E5
Aiguillon, Fr. 42/D4
Aikawa, Japan 75/F2
Aikawa, Japan 77/C2
Aiken, SC, US 133/H3
Ailigandí, Pan. 152/B2
Ailinglapalap (isl.), Mrsh. 116/F4
Aillevillers-et-Lyaumont, Fr. 53/D4
Ailly-sur-Noye, Fr. 52/B4
Ailsa Craig (isl.), Sc, UK 36/A6
Ailuk (isl.), Mrsh. 116/F3
Aimen (pass), China 72/C5
Aimogasta, Arg. 157/C2
Aimorés, Braz. 155/D1
Aimorés, Serra dos (mts.), Braz. 155/D1
Aïn (riv.), Fr. 42/F4
Aïn Beïda, Alg. 100/K7
'Aïn Beniau, Alg. 100/G4
'Aïn Bessem, Alg. 100/H4
Aïn Chok-Hay Mohammadia (prov.), Mor. 98/D1
'Aïn Defla, Alg. 100/H4
'Aïn Defla (prov.), Alg. 100/H4
'Aïn el Aouda, Mor. 100/L1
'Aïn el Bey (int'l arpt.), Alg. 100/K6
'Aïn el Hammam, Alg. 100/H4
'Aïn el Turk, Alg. 100/G4
'Aïn Fakroun, Alg. 100/K6
'Aïn M'lila, Alg. 100/K6
'Aïn Oulmene, Alg. 100/H5
'Aïn Oussersa, Alg. 100/G4
'Aïn Sefra, Alg. 99/E2
'Aïn Taoujdat, Mor. 100/L1
'Aïn Taya, Alg. 100/H4
'Aïn Temouchent, Alg. 100/G4
'Aïn Touta, Alg. 100/J5
Aina Haina, Hi, US 124/W13
Aincourt, Fr. 30/H4
Ainos NP, Gre. 47/G3
Aïnsa, Sp. 44/E1
Ainos (peak), Gre. 47/G3
Aïr (plat.), Niger 96/G4
Air Force (mt.), Nun., Can. 123/J2
Airaines, Fr. 52/A4
Airdrie, Ab, Can. 126/E3
Airdrie, Sc, UK 36/C5
Aire (riv.), Fr. 42/F2
Aire, Canal d' (canal), Fr. 52/B3
Aire-sur-la-Lys, Fr. 52/B3
Aire-sur-l'Adour, Fr. 42/C5
Airolo, Swi. 57/E4
Airuno, It. 58/C1
Airvault, Fr. 42/C3
Aisch (riv.), Ger. 43/J2
Aisén del General Carlos Ibáñez del Campo (pol. reg.), Chile 158/B5
Aisne (riv.), Fr. 40/B4
Aïssa (peak), Alg. 99/E2

Aist (riv.), Aus. 55/H6
Akşehir Lake (lake), Turk. 90/B2
Akseki, Turk. 90/B1
Aksoran (peak), Kaz. 87/G3
Aksu, China 70/D3
Aksu, Turk. 91/B1
Aksu (riv.), Turk. 90/B2
Aksum, Eth. 88/C6
Aktepe, Turk. 91/E1
Akti (pen.), Gre. 62/C4
Akto, China 87/G5
Akune, Japan 74/B4
Akureyri, Ice. 37/N6
Akuse, Gha. 103/F5
Akutan (isl.), Ak, US 134/E5
Akutan, Ak, US 134/E5
Akutan Pass (chan.), Ak, US 134/E5
Akwa Ibom (state), Nga. 103/G5
Akyab (Sittwe), Myan. 83/F3
Akyazı, Turk. 49/K5
Ajaria Aut. Rep., Geo. 63/G4
Al, Nor. 38/C1
Al 'āl, Jor. 91/D4
Al 'Amārah, Iraq 88/E2
Al Anbar (gov.), Iraq 90/E3
Al 'Aqabah, Jor. 91/D5
Al 'Arīsh, Egypt 91/C4
Al 'Ayn, UAE 89/G4
Al 'Azīzīyah, Libya 96/H1
Al 'Azīzīyah, Iraq 90/F3
Al Bāb, Syria 90/D2
Al Badrashayn, Egypt 91/B5
Al Baḥr Al Aḥmar (gov.), Egypt 101/C3
Al Bājūr, Egypt 91/B4
Al Balqā' (gov.), Jor. 91/D3
Al Balyanā, Egypt 101/B3
Al Başrah, Iraq 88/E2
Al Batrūn, Leb. 91/D2
Al Baydā, Libya 97/K1
Al Biqā' (gov.), Leb. 91/E2
Al Biqā' (valley), Leb. 91/D3
Al Bīrah, WBnk. 91/G8
Al Birkah, Libya 99/H4
Al Buḩayrah (gov.), Egypt 101/B2
Al Fāsher, Sudan 97/L5
Al Faṭḩah, Iraq 90/E2
Al Fāw, Iraq 88/E2
Al Fayyum, Egypt 91/B5
Al Fayyūm (gov.), Egypt 101/B1
Al Ghurdaqah, Egypt 101/C3
Al Ḩadīthah, Iraq 90/E3
Al Ḩaḑr, Iraq 90/E2
Al Ḩaffah, Syria 91/E2
Al Ḩajar ash Sharqī (mts.), Oman 89/G4
Al Hamādah al Hamrā (upland), Libya 96/H2
Al Ḩammāmāt, Tun. 46/B4
Al Ḩasakah, Syria 90/E2
Al Ḩasakah (prov.), Syria 90/E2
Al Ḩawāmidīyah, Egypt 91/B5
Al Ḩayy, Iraq 88/E2
Al Ḩillah, Iraq 90/F3
Al Hindīyah, Iraq 90/F3
Al Hirmil, Leb. 91/E2
Al Hoceima (prov.), Mor. 100/B3
Al Hoceima, Mor. 100/C3
Al Ḩudaydah, Yem. 88/D6
Al Hufūf, SAr. 88/E3
Al Iskandarīyah, Iraq 90/F3
Al Iskandarīyah (Alexandria), Egypt 101/B1
Al Iskandarīyah (gov.), Egypt 101/B1
Al Ismā'īlīyah, Egypt 91/C4
Al Ismā'īlīyah (gov.), Egypt 91/C4
Al Jabal Akaur (mts.), Oman 89/G4
Al Jaghbūb, Libya 97/K2
Al Jamm, Tun. 46/B4
Al Jarīdah (gov.), Leb. 91/D3
Al Jīfārah (plain), Libya 99/H4
Al Jīzah, Egypt 91/B4
Al Junaynah, Sudan 97/K5
Al Kāf, Tun. 100/L6
Al Kāf (gov.), Tun. 100/L6
Al Karak, Jor. 91/D4
Al Karak (gov.), Jor. 91/D4
Al Khābūrah, Oman 89/G4
Al Khalīl (Hebron), WBnk. 91/G8
Al Khāliş, Iraq 90/F3
Al Khānkah, Egypt 91/B4
Al Khārijah, Egypt 101/B3
Al Khartūm Bahrī (Khartoum North), Sudan 97/M4
Al Khubar, SAr. 88/F3
Al Khums, Libya 96/H1
Al Kufrah, Libya 97/K3
Al Kūfah, Iraq 90/F3
Al Ladhiqīyah (prov.), Syria 90/C4
Al Ladhiqīyah (Latakia), Syria 91/D2
Al Madīnah, SAr. 88/C4
Al Madīnah al Fikrīyah, Egypt 88/B3

Al Mafraq (gov.), Jor. 91/E3
Al Mafraq, Jor. 91/E3
Al Maghrib (reg.), Mor. 96/E1
Al Maḥallah al Kubrá, Egypt 91/B4
Al Mahdīyah, Tun. 46/B5
Al Mahdīyah (prov.), Tun. 100/M7
Al Maḥmūdīyah, Egypt 91/B4
Al Mālikīyah, Syria 90/E2
Al Mansūrah, Egypt 91/B4
Al Manzilah, Egypt 91/B4
Al Marāghah, Egypt 101/B3
Al Marj, Libya 97/K1
Al Marsá, Tun. 46/B4
Al Maṭarīyah, Egypt 91/C4
Al Mawṣil (Mosul), Iraq 90/E2
Al Mayādīn, Syria 90/E3
Al Mazra'ah, Jor. 91/D4
Al Minyā (gov.), Egypt 101/B2
Al Miqdādīyah, Iraq 90/F3
Al Mubarraz, SAr. 88/E4
Al Mudawwarah, Jor. 91/D5
Al Mukallā, Yem. 88/E6
Al Muknīn, Tun. 46/B5
Al Munastīr, Tun. 46/B5
Al Munastīr (prov.), Alg. 100/M7
Al Murnāqīyah, Tun. 46/B4
Al Musayyib, Iraq 90/F3
Al Muthanná (gov.), Iraq 90/F4
Al Qābil, Oman 89/G4
Al Qaḍārif, Sudan 88/C6
Al Qādisīyah (gov.), Iraq 90/F4
Al Qāhirah (gov.), Egypt 101/B1
Al Qāhirah (Cairo) (cap.), Egypt 91/B5
Al Qā'im, Iraq 90/E3
Al Qāmishlī, Syria 90/E2
Al Qanāṭir al Khayrīyah, Egypt 91/B4
Al Qanṭarah, Egypt 91/C4
Al Qaṣr, Jor. 91/D4
Al Qaṣrayn (gov.), Tun. 100/L7
Al Qaṣrayn, Tun. 100/L7
Al Qayrawān, Tun. 46/B5
Al Qayrawān (gov.), Tun. 46/A5
Al Qunayṭirah (prov.), Syria 91/D3
Al Qunayṭirah, Syria 91/D3
Al Qurnah, Iraq 88/E2
Al Quṣayr, Syria 91/E2
Al Quṭayfah, Syria 91/E3
Al Quwayrah, Jor. 91/D5
Al Ubayyiḍ, Sudan 97/M5
Al 'Uwaynāt (peak), Sudan 97/L3
Al Wādī Al Jadīd (gov.), Egypt 101/B3
Al Wāḥāt al Baḥrīyah (oasis), Egypt 101/B2
Al Wāḥāt al Khārijah (oasis), Egypt 101/B2
Al Wāsiṭah, Egypt 91/B5
Al Yāmūn, WBnk. 91/G7
Ala (pt.), It. 46/B1
Ala, It. 59/E1
Alabama (riv.), Al,Ga, US 133/G4
Alabama (state), US 133/G3
Alabaster, Al, US 133/G3
Alaca, Turk. 90/C1
Alacalı, Turk. 49/J5
Alaçam, Turk. 49/H5
Alaçatı, Turk. 47/K3
Alachua, Fl, US 133/H4
Alacrán (reef), Mex. 141/D1
Alacranes, Cuba 145/F1
Aladağ, Turk. 50/C2
Alaejos, Sp. 44/C2
Alagir, Rus. 63/H4
Alagna Valsesia, It. 58/A1
Alagnon (riv.), Fr. 42/E4
Alagoa Grande, Braz. 154/D2
Alagoas (state), Braz. 154/C3
Alagoinhas, Braz. 154/C4
Alagón (riv.), Sp. 44/C2
Alagón, Sp. 45/E2
Alajärvi, Fin. 60/D3
Alajuela, CR 145/E4
Alakanuk, Ak, US 134/F3
Alakol' (lake), Kaz. 70/D2
Alakol (lake), Kaz. 64/J5
Alalaú (riv.), Braz. 153/F5
Alamagan (isl.), NMar. 116/D3
'Alāmarvdasht (riv.), Iran 116/D3
Alameda, Ca, US 135/K11
Alaminos, Phil. 79/C4
Alamo (lake), Az, US 128/D4
Alamo, Mex. 144/B1
Alamo, Ca, US 135/M11
Alamo Heights, Tx, US 137/U12
Alamogordo, NM, US 129/F4
Alamor, Ecu. 156/A2
Álamos, Mex. 142/C3
Åland (isl.), Fin. 37/G3
Åland (riv.), Ger. 40/F2
Alanya, Turk. 91/C1
Alaotra (lake), Madg. 107/J7

Alapaha (riv.), Fl,Ga, US 133/H4
Alaplı, Turk. 49/K5
Alarcón, Embalse de (res.), Sp. 44/D3
Alaşehir, Turk. 90/B2
Alaska (state), US 134/G2
Alaska (range), Ak, US 134/G4
Alaska (pen.), Ak, US 134/G4
Alaska, Gulf of (gulf), Ak, US 134/J4
Alassio, It. 58/B5
Alatyr', Rus. 61/K5
Alaverdi, Arm. 63/H4
Alavus, Fin. 60/D3
Alaw (riv.), Wal, UK 34/D5
Alaw, Llyn (lake), Wal, UK 34/D5
Alayor, Sp. 45/G3
Alayskiy (mts.), Kyr. 87/F5
Alazeya (riv.), Rus. 65/R3
Alb (riv.), Ger. 54/B5
Alba, It. 43/H4
Alba (prov.), Rom. 49/F2
Alba de Tormes, Sp. 44/C2
Alba Fucens (ruin), It. 46/C1
Alba Iulia, Rom. 49/F2
Albacete, Sp. 44/E3
Albaida, Sp. 45/E3
Albairate, It. 58/B2
Albæk, Den. 38/D3
Albalate del Arzobispo, Sp. 45/E2
Alban, Fr. 42/E5
Albania (lake), Qu, Can. 130/F1
Albania (ctry.)
Albany, Austl. 112/C5
Albany (riv.), On, Can. 122/H3
Albany, Ca, US 135/K11
Albany, Ga, US 133/G4
Albany, Ky, US 130/C4
Albany, Mo, US 130/F3
Albany (cap.), NY, US 130/F3
Albany, Or, US 126/C4
Albany County (int'l arpt.), NY, US 130/F3
Albarello d'Adige, It. 59/E2
Albarine (riv.), Fr. 56/B5
Albarracín, Sp. 44/E2
Albatross (bay), Austl. 109/D2
Albatross Rock (pt.), Namb. 106/A2
Albbruck, Ger. 56/E2
Albemarle (sound), NC, US 133/J2
Albemarle, NC, US 133/H3
Albemarle (pt.), Ecu. 156/E6
Alben (peak), It. 58/D4
Albenga, It. 58/B4
Alberche (riv.), Sp. 44/C2
Alberhill, Ca, US 136/C3
Alberndorf in der Riedmark, Aus. 55/H6
Alberschwende, Aus. 57/F3
Albersdorf, Ger. 38/C4
Albersweiler, Ger. 54/B4
Albert (lake), Austl. 115/A2
Albert (lake), Ugan./D.R. 93/E4
Albert, Fr. 52/B3
Albert Kanaal (canal), Belg. 53/E2
Albert Nile (riv.), Ugan. 97/M7
Alberta (prov.), Can. 122/E3
Alberti, Arg. 158/E2
Albertinia, SAfr. 106/C4
Albertirsa, Hun. 48/D2
Alberto de Agostini, PN, Chile 147/A6
Alberton, SAfr. 106/Q13
Albertshofen, Ger. 54/E4
Albertville, Al, US 133/G3
Albertville, Fr. 43/G4
Albestroff, Fr. 53/F6
Albeuve, Swi. 56/D4
Albi, Fr. 42/E5
Albignasego, It. 59/E2
Albina, Sur. 153/H3
Albinea, It. 58/D3
Albino, It. 58/C1
Albion, Mi, US 130/C4
Albisola Marina, It. 58/B4
Albisola Superiore, It. 58/B4
Alblasserdam, Neth. 50/B5
Albocácer, Sp. 45/E2
Alborán (isl.), Mor. 98/E2
Ålborg (bay), Den. 38/D3
Ålborg, Den. 38/C3
Albox, Sp. 44/D4
Albright-Knox Art Gallery, NY, US 131/S10
Albristhorn (peak), Swi. 56/D4
Albufeira, Port. 44/A4
Albula (riv.), Swi. 43/H3
Albuñol, Sp. 44/D4
Albuquerque (int'l arpt.), NM, US 128/F4
Albuquerque, NM, US 128/F4
Albuquerque, Cayos de (isls.), Col. 145/F3
Alburquerque, Sp. 44/B3
Alburtis, Pa, US 131/H4
Alby-sur-Chéran, Fr. 56/C6
Alca, Peru 156/C4
Alcabideche, Port. 45/P10
Alcácer do Sal, Port. 44/A3

Alcalá de Chivert, Sp. 45/F2
Alcalá de Guadaira, Sp. 44/C4
Alcalá de Henares, Sp. 45/N9
Alcalá de los Gazules, Sp. 44/C4
Alcalá la Real, Sp. 44/D4
Alcamo, It. 46/C4
Alcanadre (riv.), Sp. 45/E2
Alcanar, Sp. 45/E2
Alcañices, Sp. 44/B2
Alcañiz, Sp. 45/E2
Alcántara, Braz. 154/A1
Alcántara, Sp. 44/B3
Alcántara, Embalse de (res.), Sp. 44/B3
Alcantarilla, Sp. 44/D4
Alcaraz, Sp. 44/D3
Alcaraz, Sierra de (range), Sp. 44/D3
Alcatraz (isl.), Ca, US 135/K11
Alcatrazes, Ilha de (isl.), Braz. 211/H9
Alcaudete, Sp. 44/C4
Alcázar de San Juan, Sp. 44/D3
Alcira, Sp. 45/E3
Alcira, Arg. 158/D2
Alçıtepe, Turk. 47/K2
Alcoa, Tn, US 133/H3
Alcobaça, Braz. 154/C3
Alcobaça, Port. 44/A3
Alcobendas, Sp. 45/N8
Alcochete, Port. 45/Q10
Alcora, Sp. 45/E2
Alcorcón, Sp. 45/N9
Alcorisa, Sp. 45/E2
Alcoutim, Port. 44/B4
Alcoy, Sp. 45/E3
Alcúdia, Sp. 45/G3
Aldabra (isls.), Sey. 93/G5
Aldama, Mex. 132/B4
Aldama, Mex. 143/F4
Aldan (plat.), Rus. 65/N4
Aldan (riv.), Rus. 65/N4
Aldan, Rus. 65/N4
Alde (riv.), Eng, UK 33/H2
Aldeburgh, Eng, UK 33/H2
Aldeia Nova de São Bento, Port. 44/B4
Alden, Il, US 135/N15
Aldenhoven, Ger. 53/F2
Aldeno, It. 57/H6
Aldergrove (int'l arpt.), NI, UK 34/B2
Aldergrove, NI, UK 34/B2
Alderley Edge, Eng, UK 35/F5
Alderney (isl.), ChI, UK 42/B2
Aldershot, Eng, UK 33/F4
Alderwood Manor-Bothell North, Wa, US 135/C2
Aldine, Tx, US 129/J5
Aldingen, Ger. 57/E1
Aldred (lake), Pa, US 138/B4
Aldridge, Eng, UK 33/E1
Ale Water (riv.), Sc, UK 36/D6
Aleg, Mrta. 102/B2
Alegre, Braz. 155/D2
Alegrete, Braz. 157/E2
Alejandro Gallinal, Uru. 159/G2
Alejandro Roca, Arg. 158/E2
Alejandro Selkirk (isl.), Chile 147/A6
Alejo Ledesma, Arg. 158/E2
Aleksandrov, Rus. 60/H4
Aleksandrovac, Serb. 48/E4
Aleksandrovsk, Rus. 61/N4
Aleksandrów Kujawski, Pol. 41/K2
Aleksandrów Łódzki, Pol. 41/K3
Alekseyevka, Kaz. 87/F2
Alekseyevka, Kaz. 87/E2
Alekseyevka, Rus. 62/F2
Aleksin, Rus. 60/H5
Aleksinac, Serb. 48/E4
Além Paraíba, Braz. 211/L6
Alençon, Fr. 42/D2
Alenquer, Braz. 151/H4
Alenuihaha (chan.), US 124/T10
Alerce Andino, PN, Chile 158/B4
Aléria, Fr. 46/A1
Alert (pt.), Nun., Can. 123/S6
Aleşd, Rom. 49/F2
Alessandria (prov.), It. 58/B3
Alessandria, It. 58/B3
Ålestrup, Den. 38/C3
Ålesund, Nor. 37/C3
Aletschhorn (peak), Swi. 56/D5
Aleutian (range), Ak, US 134/G4
Aleutian (isls.), Ak, US 134/B5
Alexander (mt.), Austl. 112/B2
Alexander (arch.), Ak, US 134/L4
Alexander (isl.), Ant. 160/V
Alexander Bay, SAfr. 106/B3
Alexander City, Al, US 133/G3

Alexander Nevsky Abbey, Rus. 61/T7
Alexandria, Braz. 154/C2
Alexandria (int'l arpt.), Egypt 91/A4
Alexándria, Gre. 47/H2
Alexandria, NZ 117/R12
Alexandria, Rom. 49/G4
Alexandria, SAfr. 106/D4
Alexandria, La, US 129/J5
Alexandria, Mn, US 127/K4
Alexandria, Sc, UK 36/B5
Alexandria, Va, US 138/A6
Alexandrina (lake), Austl. 109/C4
Alexandroúpolis, Gre. 47/J2
Alexis Creek, BC, Can. 126/C2
Alfaro, Sp. 44/E1
Alfatar, Bul. 49/H4
Alfbach (riv.), Ger. 53/F3
Alfeld, Ger. 51/G5
Alfenas, Braz. 211/H6
Alfhausen, Ger. 51/E3
Alfiós (riv.), Gre. 47/G3
Alfonsine, It. 59/F3
Alfonso Bonilla Aragón (int'l arpt.), Col. 152/B3
Alfred NP, Austl. 115/D3
Alfreton, Eng, UK 35/G5
Alfter, Ger. 53/G2
Alga, Kaz. 63/L2
Algård, Nor. 38/A2
Algarrobo, Chile 158/N8
Algarve (reg.), Port. 44/A4
Algeciras, Sp. 44/C4
Algeciras, Col. 152/C4
Algemesí, Sp. 45/E3
Alger (prov.), Alg. 100/G4
Algeria (ctry.) 96/F2
Algermissen, Ger. 51/G4
Algete, Sp. 45/N8
Alghero, It. 46/A2
Algiers (El Djezair) (cap.), Alg. 100/G4
Algoa (bay), SAfr. 106/D4
Algodón (riv.), Peru 150/D4
Algodonales, Sp. 44/C4
Algoma, Wi, US 127/M4
Algona, Wa, US 135/C3
Algonac, Mi, US 135/G6
Algonquin, Il, US 135/P14
Algorta, Uru. 159/K10
Algueirão, Port. 45/P10
Alhama de Granada, Sp. 44/D4
Alhama de Murcia, Sp. 44/E4
Alhambra, Ca, US 136/F7
Alhandra, Braz. 154/D2
Alhandra, Port. 45/P10
Alhaurín el Grande, Sp. 44/C4
'Alī al Gharbī, Iraq 88/E2
'Alī ash Sharqī, Iraq 88/E2
Ali Bayramlı, Azer. 63/J5
Alia, It. 46/C4
Alía, Sp. 44/C3
Aliağa, Turk. 90/A2
Aliákmon (riv.), Gre. 47/G2
Aliákmonos (lake), Gre. 47/G2
Aliartos, Gre. 47/H3
Alibates Flint Quarries Nat'l Mon., Tx, US 129/G4
Alibey (lake), Ukr. 49/J3
Alibeyköy, Turk. 50/B2
Alicante (int'l arpt.), Sp. 45/E3
Alice, Tx, US 132/D5
Alice (pt.), It. 46/D3
Alice Arm, BC, Can. 134/N4
Alice Springs, Austl. 113/G2
Aliceville, Al, US 133/F3
Alicia, Phil. 79/D6
Alicudi (isl.), It. 46/D3
Alicurá (res.), Arg. 158/C4
Alife, It. 46/D2
Alīganj, India 84/B2
Aligarh, India 84/B2
Alīgūdarz, Iran 91/F3
Alima (riv.), Congo 96/J8
Alingār (riv.), Afg. 86/A1
Alingsås, Swe. 38/E3
Alīpur, Pak. 86/A5
Alīpur Duār, India 85/G2
Alirajpur, India 84/C4
Alisos (riv.), Mex. 128/C3
Alistráti, Gre. 47/H2
Alivérion, Gre. 47/J3
Aliwal North, SAfr. 106/D3
Alizay, Fr. 52/A2
Aljezur, Port. 44/A4
Aljustrel, Port. 44/A4
Alken, Belg. 53/E2
Alkmaar, Neth. 50/B3
Alkoum (well), Alg. 99/H4
Alor Setar, Malay. 82/B4
Allahābād, India 84/C3
Allakaket, Ak, US 134/H2
Allaman, Swi. 56/C5
Allan (hills), Sk, Can. 127/G3
Allan, Sk, Can. 127/G3
Alland, Aus. 49/N7
Allanmyo, Myan. 83/G4
Allanridge, SAfr. 106/D2
Allariz, Sp. 44/B1
Allāq (well), Libya 96/H1
Alle, Swi. 56/D3
Allegan, Mi, US 130/C3
Allegheny (plat.), US 130/E3
Allegheny (riv.), US 130/D3

Allegheny (mts.), US 125/K4
Allen (riv.), Eng, UK 32/B5
Allen, Arg. 158/D3
Allen Park, Mi, US 135/F7
Allendale, SC, US 133/H3
Allendale, NJ, US 139/J7
Allende, Mex. 132/C4
Allende, Mex. 143/F4
Allendorf, Ger. 51/F6
Allensbach, Ger. 57/E2
Allenspark, Co, US 137/A2
Allentown, Pa, US 138/C2
Allentsteig, Aus. 41/H4
Allenwood, Pa, US 138/B1
Alleppey, India 82/C6
Aller (riv.), Ger. 51/H3
Alliance, Ne, US 127/H5
Alliance, Oh, US 130/D3
Allier (riv.), Fr. 42/E3
Alligator NP, Austl. 115/D3
Allingabro, Den. 38/D3
Allinges, Fr. 56/C5
Alloa, Sc, UK 36/C4
Allonnes, Fr. 42/D3
Allos, Fr. 43/G4
Alloway, NJ, US 138/C4
Allstedt, Ger. 51/G5
Alm (riv.), Aus. 55/G7
Alma, Mi, US 130/C3
Alma, Qu, Can. 131/G1
Almacelles, Sp. 45/F2
Almada, Port. 45/P10
Almadén, Sp. 44/C3
Almafuerte, Arg. 158/D2
Almagro, Sp. 44/D3
Almansa, Sp. 45/E3
Almanor (lake), Ca, US 128/B2
Almanzor, Pico de (peak), Sp. 44/C2
Almanzora (riv.), Sp. 44/D4
Almas (riv.), Braz. 151/H6
Almas, Braz. 154/A3
Almas, Pico das (peak), Braz. 154/B2
Almazán, Sp. 44/D2
Almazora, Sp. 45/E3
Almeida, Port. 44/B2
Almeirim, Braz. 151/H4
Almeirim, Port. 45/P10
Almelo, Neth. 50/D4
Almenara, Braz. 154/C2
Almenara (peak), Sp. 44/D3
Almendra, Embalse de (res.), Sp. 44/B2
Almendralejo, Sp. 44/B3
Almenno San Salvatore, It. 58/C1
Almere, Neth. 50/C4
Almería, Sp. 44/D4
Almería, Golfo de (gulf), Sp. 44/D4
Al'met'yevsk, Rus. 61/M5
Almhult, Swe. 38/F3
Almina (pt.), Sp. 100/B2
Almirós, Gre. 47/H3
Almirou (gulf), Gre. 47/H5
Almodóvar del Campo, Sp. 44/C3
Almodóvar del Río, Sp. 44/C4
Almoharín, Sp. 44/B3
Almond (riv.), Sc, UK 36/L6
Almont (riv.), Fr. 30/L6
Almonte, Sp. 44/B4
Almora, India 84/B1
Almoradí, Sp. 45/E3
Almorox, Sp. 44/C2
Almte. Montt (gulf), Chile 159/B7
Almudévar, Sp. 45/E2
Almuñécar, Sp. 44/D4
Almus, Turk. 90/D1
Alness (riv.), Sc, UK 36/B1
Alness, Sc, UK 36/B1
Alnwick, Eng, UK 36/G6
Alofi, NZ 117/J6
Alofi (pt.), Wall. 116/H6
Along, India 83/G2
Alónnisos (isl.), Gre. 47/H3
Alor (isls.), Indo. 81/F5
Alor Setar, Malay. 82/B4
Alora, Sp. 44/C4
Alotau, PNG 114/E2
Aloysius (mt.), Austl. 113/F3
Alpachiri, Arg. 158/D3
Alpe di Poti (peak), It. 59/F3
Alpedrete, Sp. 45/M8
Alpena, Mi, US 130/D2
Alpercatas (riv.), Braz. 154/A2
Alpercatas, Serra das (mts.), Braz. 151/J5
Alperschällihorn (peak), Swi. 57/F4
Alpes de Provence (range), Fr. 43/G5
Alpes (range), Austl. 114/B3

Alpha, NJ, US 138/C2
Alphen aan de Rijn, Neth. 50/B4
Alpi Apuane (range), It. 43/J4
Alpi Dolomitiche (range), It.
Alpi Orobie (range), It. 43/J3
Alpiarça, Port. 44/A3
Alpine, Ut, US 137/K13
Alpine, Wy, US 126/F5
Alpirsbach, Ger. 57/E1
Alpnach, Swi. 57/E4
Alps (mts.), Eur. 27/E4
Alqôsh, Iraq 90/E2
Als (isl.), Den. 40/F1
Alsace (pol. reg.), Fr. 40/D4
Alsager, Eng, UK 35/F5
Alsask, Sk, Can. 126/F3
Alsasua, Sp. 44/D1
Alsdorf, Ger. 53/F2
Alvängen, Swe. 38/E3
Alsenz (riv.), Ger. 53/G4
Alsenz, Ger. 53/G4
Alsfeld, Ger. 43/H1
Alsip, Il, US 135/Q16
Alstahaug, Nor. 37/D3
Alster (riv.), Ger. 51/H1
Alstonville, Austl. 115/E1
Alt (riv.), Eng, UK 35/E4
Alta, Ut, US 137/K12
Alta, Nor. 37/G1
Alta Floresta, Braz. 151/G6
Alta Gracia, Arg. 157/D3
Altach, Aus. 57/F3
Altadena, Ca, US 136/F7
Altagracia, Nic. 144/E4
Altai (mts.), Asia 70/D2
Altay, China 70/E2
Altay, Mong. 70/G2
Altay, Resp., Rus. 64/J4
Altayskiy Kray, Rus. 87/G2
Altamaha (riv.), Ga, US 140/E1
Altamira, Braz. 151/H4
Altamira, Mex. 144/B1
Altamira do Maranhão, Braz. 154/A2
Altamonte Springs, Fl, US 133/H4
Altamura, It. 46/E2
Altan, Mex. 142/C2
Altar (vol.), Ecu. 152/B5
Altar de los Sacrificios (ruin), Guat. 144/D2
Altar, Desierto de (des.), Mex. 128/D4
Altare, It. 58/B4
Altavilla Vicentina, It. 59/E1
Altay, China 70/E2
Altay, Mong. 70/G2
Altdorf, Swi. 57/E4
Altdorf bei Nürnberg, Ger. 55/E4
Altea, Sp. 45/E3
Altedo, It. 59/E3
Altena, Ger. 51/E6
Altenahr, Ger. 53/G2
Altenau, Ger. 51/H5
Altenbeken, Ger. 51/F5
Altenberg bei Linz, Aus. 55/H6
Altenburg, Ger. 40/G3
Altenfelden, Aus. 55/G6
Altenglan, Ger. 51/H6
Altengottern, Ger. 51/G6
Altenkirchen, Ger. 53/G3
Altenmünster, Ger. 55/E6
Altenstadt, Ger. 54/B2
Altenstadt, Ger. 54/B2
Altensteig, Ger. 54/B5
Altentreptow, Ger. 40/G2
Alter Rhein (riv.), Ger. 50/D5
Altes Land (phys. reg.), Ger. 40/F2
Altheim, Aus. 55/G6
Althengstett, Ger. 54/B5
Althofen, Aus. 43/L3
Althütte, Ger. 54/C5
Altindere NP, Turk. 90/D1
Altınözü, Turk. 91/E1
Altıntaş, Turk. 90/B2
Altınyaka, Turk. 91/A1
Altınyayla, Turk. 90/D1
Altiplano (plat.), Bol.,Peru 147/C4
Altkirch, Fr. 56/D2
Altlandsberg, Ger. 40/Q6
Altmark (phys. reg.), Ger. 40/F2
Altmühl (riv.), Ger. 43/J2
Altmünster, Aus. 55/G7
Altnaharra, Sc, UK 31/R7
Alto (peak), It. 58/A4
Alto (peak), It. 46/D1
Alto Araguaia, Braz. 151/H7
Alto de Tamar (peak), Col. 152/C3
Alto Garças, Braz. 151/H7
Alto Lucero, Mex. 143/A3
Alto Parnaíba, Braz. 154/A3
Alto Purús (riv.), Peru 150/D6
Alto Santo, Braz. 154/A2
Alto Yuruá (riv.), Peru 156/C3
Alton, La, US 137/Q16
Alton, Il, US 137/G8
Alton, Eng, UK 33/F4
Altona, Mb, Can. 127/J3
Altoona, Pa, US 138/D5
Altopascio, It. 59/D5

Altos, Braz. 154/B2
Altos de Camapana NP, Pan. 152/B2
Altotonga, Mex. 143/M7
Altötting, Ger. 55/F6
Altrincham, Eng, UK 35/F5
Altrip, Ger. 54/B4
Altun (mts.), China 67/H6
Altun Ha (ruin), Belz. 144/D2
Alturas, Ca, US 126/C5
Altus (res.), Ok, US 129/H4
Altus, Ok, US 129/H4
Altzayanca, Mex. 143/M7
Alucra, Turk. 90/D1
Alūksne, Lat. 60/E3
Ālūs, Iraq 90/E3
Alushta, Ukr. 62/E3
Alva, Ok, US 129/H3
Alva, Sc, UK 36/C4
Alvalade, Port. 44/A4
Alvarado, Mex. 143/P8
Alvarez, Arg. 158/E2
Alvaro Obregón, Presa (dam), Mex. 142/C2
Alvdal, Nor. 37/D3
Älvdalen, Swe. 38/F1
Alverca, Port. 45/P10
Alveringem, Belg. 52/B1
Alvesta, Swe. 38/F3
Ålvik, Nor. 38/B1
Alvin, Tx, US 129/J5
Alvito, Port. 44/B3
Alvorada, Braz. 154/A4
Alvorada do Norte, Braz. 154/A4
Älvsborg (co.), Swe. 37/E4
Älvsbyn, Swe. 37/G2
Alwen (riv.), Wal, UK 34/D5
Alxa Youqi, China 70/H4
Alxa Zuoqi, China 70/H4
Alyawarra Abor. Land, Austl. 113/G2
Alyth, Sc, UK 36/C3
Alytus, Lith. 39/L4
Alz (riv.), Ger. 55/F6
Alzano Lombardo, It. 58/C1
Alzenau in Unterfranken, Ger. 54/C2
Alzette (riv.), Lux. 53/F4
Alzey, Ger. 54/B3
Am Timan, Chad 97/K5
Ama, La, US 137/P17
Amacayacú, PN, Col. 150/D4
Amacuro (riv.), Ven. 153/F2
Amacuro (delta), Ven. 153/F2
Amacuzac (riv.), Mex. 143/K8
Amadeus (lake), Austl. 109/E4
Amadjuak (lake), Nun., Can. 123/J2
Amadora, Port. 45/P10
Amagansett NWR, NY, US 139/F2
Amagasaki, Japan 77/H6
Amagi, Japan 74/B4
Amagi-san (peak), Japan 75/F3
Amaguaña, Ecu. 152/B5
Amajac (riv.), Mex. 143/N7
Åmål, Swe. 38/E2
Amalfi, Col. 152/C3
Amalfi, It. 46/D2
Amalia, SAfr. 106/D2
Amaliás, Gre. 47/G4
Amaluza, Ecu. 156/B2
Amambaí, Braz. 157/E1
Amambaí (mts.), Braz. 151/H8
Amami (isls.), Japan 67/M7
Amami-O-Shima (isl.), Japan 75/K6
Amana (lake), Braz. 150/F4
Amance, Fr. 56/C2
Amanā (lake), Braz. 150/F4
Amancay (riv.), Braz. 151/J5
Amânganj, India 84/C3
Amāngarh, Pak. 86/A2
Amantea, It. 46/E3
Amanu (isl.), FrPol. 117/L6
Amanzimtoti, SAfr. 107/E3
Amapá, Braz. 151/H3
Amapá (state), Braz. 153/H4
Amarante, Port. 44/A2
Amarante do Maranhão, Braz. 154/A2
Amarapura, Myan. 83/G3
Amareleja, Port. 44/B3
Amargosa, Braz. 154/C4
Amargosa (riv.), Ca, US 128/C3
Amarillo, Tx, US 129/G4
Amarpātan, India 84/C3
Amarume, Japan 76/A4
Amarwāra, India 84/B4
Amasra, Turk. 49/L5
Amasya, Turk. 90/C1
Amata, Austl. 113/F3
Amatlán de Cañas, Mex. 142/D4
Amatsukominato, Japan 77/E3
Amawalk (res.), NY, US 139/E1
Amazon (Amazonas) (riv.), Braz.,Per 156/C1
Amazonas, Cuba 145/G1

Amazonas (state), Braz. 152/C5
Amazonas (Amazon) (riv.), Braz.,Per 156/C1
Amazônia, PN da (Tapajós), Braz. 151/G4
Ambāh, India 84/B2
Ambahikily, Madg. 107/G8
Ambajogai, India 89/L5
Ambāla Sadar, India 86/D4
Ambalangoda, SrL. 82/D6
Ambalavao, Madg. 107/H8
Ambam, Camr. 96/H7
Ambanja, Madg. 107/J6
Ambaro (bay), Madg. 107/J6
Ambato, Ecu. 152/B5
Ambato Boeny, Madg. 107/H7
Ambatofinandrahana, Madg. 107/H8
Ambatolampy, Madg. 107/H7
Ambatomainty, Madg. 107/H7
Ambatomanoina, Madg. 107/H7
Ambatondrazaka, Madg. 107/J7
Ambazac, Fr. 42/D4
Ambelos (cape), Gre. 47/H3
Amberg, Ger. 55/E4
Ambergris Cay (isl.), Belz. 144/E2
Ambérieu-en-Bugey, Fr. 56/B6
Amberloup, Belg. 53/E3
Ambikāpur, India 84/D4
Ambilobe, Madg. 107/J6
Ambinanindrano, Madg. 107/J7
Ambinanitelo, Madg. 107/J7
Ambler, Ak, US 134/G2
Ambler, Pa, US 138/C3
Amblève (riv.), Belg. 40/C3
Ambo, Peru 156/B3
Amboasary, Madg. 107/H9
Amboavory, Madg. 107/J7
Ambodifototra, Madg. 107/J7
Ambodiharina, Madg. 107/J8
Ambohidratrimo, Madg. 107/H7
Ambohijanahary, Madg. 107/H7
Ambohimahasoa, Madg. 107/H8
Ambohimandroso, Madg. 107/H7
Ambohinihaonana, Madg. 107/H8
Ambohitsilaozana, Madg. 107/H7
Ambolomoty, Madg. 107/H7
Ambon (isl.), Indo. 81/G4
Ambon, Indo. 81/G4
Ambondro, Madg. 107/H9
Amboni Caves, Tanz. 104/C4
Amboromptsy, Madg. 107/H8
Amboseli NP, Kenya 104/C4
Ambositra, Madg. 107/H8
Ambovombe, Madg. 107/H9
Ambrym (isl.), Van. 116/F6
Amchitka (isl.), Ak, US 134/B6
Amchitka Pass (chan.), Ak, US 134/B6
Ameca, Mex. 142/D4
Amecameca de Juárez, Mex. 143/R10
Ameghino, Arg. 158/E2
Ameglia, It. 58/C4
Ameisberg (peak), Aus. 55/G5
Ameland (isl.), Neth. 50/C2
Amelia, It. 46/C1
Amelinghausen, Ger. 51/H2
Amer (chan.), Neth. 50/B5
American (lake), Wa, US 135/B3
American (riv.), Ca, US 135/M9
American Falls (mts.), Id, US 128/D2
American Fork, Ut, US 137/K13
American, North Fork (riv.), Ca, US 128/B3
American Samoa 117/H6
American, South Fork (riv.), Ca, US 128/B3
Americana, Braz. 154/A2
Americus, Ga, US 133/G3
Ameringkogel (peak), Aus. 43/L3
Amersfoort, SAfr. 107/E2
Amersfoort, Neth. 50/C4
Amersham, Eng, UK 33/F3
Amery Ice Shelf, Ant. 160/E
Amesbury, Eng, UK 33/E4
Amet, India 89/K3
Amethi, India 84/C3
Amfíklia, Gre. 47/H3
Amfilokhía, Gre. 47/G3
Amfissa, Gre. 47/H3
Amga (riv.), Rus. 65/N3
Amga, Rus. 65/N3
Amguema (riv.), Rus. 65/T3
Amgun' (riv.), Rus. 65/P4
Amherst, NS, Can. 131/H2

Amherst, NY, US 131/S10
Amherstburg, On, Can. 135/F7
Ami, Japan 77/E1
Amiata (peak), It. 43/J5
Amiens, Fr. 52/B4
Amik (lake), Turk. 90/D2
Amila (isl.), Ak, US 134/D6
Amilcar Cabral (int'l arpt.), CpV 93/K10
Amillis, Fr. 30/M5
Amindaion, Gre. 47/G2
Aminu Kano (int'l arpt.), Nga. 103/H3
Amisk (lake), Sk, Can. 127/H2
Amistad (res.), Mex.,US 140/D2
Amistad Nat'l Rec. Area, Tx, US 129/G5
Amite, La, US 129/K5
Amityville, NY, US 139/M9
Amla, India 84/B3
Amlāgora, India 85/F4
Āmli, Nor. 38/C2
'Ammān (gov.), Jor. 91/E4
Amman (state), Nga. 103/G4
Amman (riv.), Wal, UK 32/C3
Amman ('Ammān) (cap.), Jor. 91/E4
Ammanford, Wal, UK 32/C3
Ammarfjället (peak), Swe. 37/E2
Ammassalik, Grld 160/J
Ammer (riv.), Ger. 54/B5
Ammerman (mtn.), Yk, Can. 134/K2
Ammersee (lake), Ger. 43/J3
Amnéville, Fr. 53/F5
Āmol, Iran 88/F1
Amora, Port. 45/P10
Amorbach, Ger. 54/C3
Amorgós, Gre. 47/J4
Amorgós (isl.), Gre. 47/J4
Amory, Ms, US 133/F3
Amos, Qu, Can. 130/E1
Āmot, Nor. 38/B2
Amotfors, Swe. 38/E2
Amozoc, Mex. 143/L7
Ampachi, Japan 77/L5
Ampanefena, Madg. 107/J6
Ampangalana (canal), Madg. 107/J8
Ampanihy, Madg. 107/H9
Amparafaravola, Madg. 107/H6
Amparai, SrL. 82/D6
Amparo, Braz. 211/G7
Ampasindava (bay), Madg. 107/H6
Ampato (peak), Peru 156/D4
Ampefy, Madg. 107/H7
Amper (riv.), Ger. 55/E6
Ampfing, Ger. 55/F6
Ampflwang im Hausruckwald, Aus. 55/G6
Ampitatafika, Madg. 107/H7
Amposta, Sp. 45/F2
Amqui, Qu, Can. 131/H1
Amravati, India 82/C3
Amreli, India 89/K4
'Amrīt (ruin), Syria 91/D2
Amritsar, India 86/C4
Amroha, India 84/B1
Amrum (isl.), Ger. 40/E1
Amstel (riv.), Neth. 50/B4
Amstelveen, Neth. 50/B4
Amsterdam, NY, US 130/D4
Amsterdam, SAfr. 107/E2
Amsterdam (cap.), Neth. 50/B4
Amsterdam (isl.), Fr. 23/N7
Amsterdam Rijnkanaal (riv.), Neth. 50/C4
Amsterdam (Schipol) (int'l arpt.), Neth. 50/B4
Amstetten, Aus. 43/L2
Amu Darya (riv.), Asia 67/F8
Amudat, Ugan. 104/B2
Amukta Pass (chan.), Ak, US 134/D5
Amuku (mts.), Guy. 153/G4
Amund Ringnes (isl.), Nun., Can. 123/S7
Amundsen (gulf), NW, Can. 122/D1
Amundsen (bay), Ant. 160/D
Amundsen (sea), Ant. 160/S
Amundsen-Scott, US, Ant. 160/A
Amunge (lake), Swe. 38/F1
Amur (riv.), Rus. 71/P2
Amurrio, Sp. 44/D1
Amurskaya Oblast, Rus. 65/N4
Amyūn, Leb. 91/D2
An Nabk, Syria 91/E2
An Nahūd, Sudan 97/L5
An Najaf, Iraq 90/E4
An Najaf (gov.), Iraq 90/E4
An Nāşirīyah, Iraq 88/E2
An Nu'manīyah, Iraq 90/F3
An Teallach (peak), Sc, UK 36/A1
An Uaimh, Ire. 31/Q10
Ana María (gulf), Cuba 141/F3
Anaa (isl.), FrPol. 161/L6
'Anabtā, WBnk. 91/G7
Anachucuna (mtn.), Pan. 152/B2
Anaco, Ven. 153/E2

Anaconda-Deer Lodge County, Mt, US 126/E4
Anadarko, Ok, US 129/H4
Anadyr' (gulf), Rus. 67/T3
Anadyr' (range), Rus. 160/U
Anadyr' (riv.), Rus. 67/S3
Anadyr', Rus. 65/T3
Anáfi (isl.), Gre. 47/J4
Anaheim, Ca, US 136/G8
Anaham Lake, BC, Can. 126/B2
Anáhuac, Mex. 132/C5
Anahuac, Tx, US 132/E4
Anahuac, Mex. 142/D2
Anak, NKor. 73/C3
Anakāpalle, India 82/D4
Anaktuvuk Pass, Ak, US 134/H2
Analalava, Madg. 107/H6
Analamaitso (plat.), Madg. 107/H7
Analavory, Madg. 107/H7
Anambas (isls.), Indo. 80/C3
Anambra (state), Nga. 103/G5
Anamur, Turk. 90/C1
Anamur (pt.), Turk. 91/C1
Anan, Japan 74/D4
Anand, India 89/K4
Ananea, Peru 156/D4
Ananea, Bol. 156/D4
Anantapur, India 82/C5
Anantnag, India 86/C3
Anapa, Rus. 62/F3
Anápolis, Braz. 151/J7
Anapu (riv.), Braz. 151/H4
Anār, Iran 89/G2
Anārak, Iran 88/F2
Anastácio, Braz. 154/C3
'Anātā, WBnk. 91/G8
Anathan (isl.), NMar. 116/D3
Anatolia (reg.), Turk. 90/B2
Añatuya, Arg. 157/D2
Anauá (riv.), Braz. 150/F3
Ancash (dept.), Peru 156/B3
Anchieta, Braz. 155/D2
Anchor (bay), Mi, US 135/G6
Anchor Point, Ak, US 134/H4
Anchorage, Ak, US 134/J3
Anchorville, Mi, US 135/G6
Anchovy, Jam. 145/G2
Ancient City of Oc-Eo, Viet. 78/D4
Ancohuma (peak), Bol. 156/D4
Ancón, Peru 156/B3
Ancón de Sardinas (bay), Col. 152/B4
Ancona (prov.), It. 59/G5
Ancona, It. 59/G5
Ancoraimes, Bol. 156/D4
Ancre (riv.), Fr. 52/B3
Ancrum, Sc, UK 36/D5
Ancud, Chile 158/B4
Ancud, Golfo de (gulf), Chile 157/B5
Anda, China 71/N2
Andacollo, Arg. 158/C3
Andagua, Peru 156/C4
Andahuaylas, Peru 156/C4
Andal, India 85/F4
Åndalsnes, Nor. 37/C3
Andalucia (aut. comm.), Sp. 44/C4
Andalusia, Al, US 133/G4
Andalusia (reg.), Sp. 44/C4
Andaman (sea), Asia 67/J8
Andaman and Nicobar (isls.), India 83/F5
Andamarca, Peru 156/C3
Andamooka, Austl. 113/H4
Andapa, Madg. 107/J6
Andaraí, Braz. 154/B2
Andau, Aus. 43/M3
Andebu, Nor. 38/D2
Andeer, Swi. 57/F4
Andelfingen, Swi. 57/F4
Andelot-Blancheville, Fr. 56/B1
Andelsbach (riv.), Ger. 57/F2
Andelu, Fr. 30/H5
Andemaka, Madg. 107/H8
Andenne, Belg. 53/E3
Anderlues, Belg. 53/D3
Andermatt, Swi. 57/E4
Andernach, Ger. 53/G3
Anderson (riv.), NW, Can. 122/D2
Anderson, Ak, US 134/J3
Anderson, Ca, US 128/B2
Anderson, In, US 130/C3
Anderson, SC, US 133/H3
Anderson, Tx, US 129/J5
Anderson (inlet), Wa, US 135/C4
Anderson (isl.), Wa, US 135/C4
Andes (mts.), SAm. 147/D4
Andes, Cordillera de los (mts.), SAm. 157/B4
Andevoranto, Madg. 107/J7
Andfjorden (chan.), Nor. 37/F1
Andhra Pradesh (state), India 70/D8
Andijk, Neth. 50/C3
Andijon (pol. reg.), Uzb. 87/F4
Andijon, Uzb. 87/F4

Andikithira (isl.), Gre. 47/H5
Andilamena, Madg. 107/J7
Andilanatoby, Madg. 107/J7
Andīmeshk, Iran 88/E2
Andiparos (isl.), Gre. 47/J4
Andira, Braz. 155/B2
Andissa, Gre. 47/J3
Andkhvoy, Afg. 87/E5
Andoany, Madg. 107/J6
Andohajango, Madg. 107/J6
Andong, SKor. 74/A2
Andorno Micca, It. 58/B1
Andorra (ctry.) 45/F1
Andorra, Sp. 45/E2
Andorra la Vella (cap.), And. 42/D5
Andover, Eng, UK 33/E4
Andover, NJ, US 138/D2
Andøy (isl.), Nor. 37/F1
Andøya (isl.), Nor. 37/E1
Andradas, Braz. 211/G7
Andradina, Braz. 155/B2
Andraitx, Sp. 45/G3
Andramasina, Madg. 107/J7
Andranolava, Madg. 107/H8
Andranomavo (riv.), Madg. 107/H7
Andranopasy, Madg. 107/G8
Andreanof (isls.), Ak, US 134/C6
Andrelândia, Braz. 211/J6
Andrespol, Pol. 41/K3
Andrésy, Fr. 30/J5
Andrezel, Fr. 30/L6
Andria, It. 46/E2
Andriba, Madg. 107/H7
Andringitra (mts.), Madg. 107/H8
Andritsaina, Gre. 47/G4
Androka, Madg. 107/H9
Androntany (cape), Madg. 107/J6
Andros, Gre. 47/J4
Andros (isl.), Gre. 47/J4
Andros (isl.), Bahm. 141/F3
Androscoggin (riv.), US 131/G2
Andújar, Sp. 44/C3
Aneby, Swe. 38/F3
Anecón Grande (peak), Arg. 158/C4
Anegada (isl.), UK 141/J4
Anegada (bay), Arg. 158/E4
Anegada Passage (chan.), NAm. 141/J4
Aného, Togo 103/F5
Aneityum (isl.), Van. 116/F7
Añelo, Arg. 158/C3
Aneto, Pico de (peak), Sp. 45/F1
Anfu, China 83/K2
Ang Nam Ngum (res.), Laos 83/H4
Ang Thong, Thai. 78/C3
Angamos (pt.), Chile 157/B1
Angara (riv.), Rus. 67/J4
Angaston, Austl. 113/H5
Angel (riv.), Ger. 51/E5
Angel (falls), Ven. 153/F3
Angeles, Phil. 79/D4
Angeles National Forest, Ca, US 136/F7
Angelholm, Swe. 38/G4
Angelholm (int'l arpt.), Swe. 38/G4
Angelina (riv.), Tx, US 129/J5
Angels (riv.), Ger. 40/E1
Angelus (lake), Mi, US 135/F6
Angera, It. 58/B1
Angermanalven (riv.), Swe. 37/G2
Angermünde, Ger. 41/H2
Angers, Fr. 42/C3
Anghiari, It. 59/F5
Angical do Piauí, Braz. 154/B2
Angicos, Braz. 154/C2
Angkor (ruin), Camb. 78/C3
Anglem (mt.), NZ 117/R12
Anglès, Sp. 45/G2
Anglesea, Austl. 115/C4
Anglesey (isl.), Wal, UK 34/C4
Anglet, Fr. 42/C4
Angleton, Tx, US 129/J5
Angol, Chile 158/B3
Angola (ctry.) 105/C3
Angola, In, US 130/C3
Angola, Afr. 105/B2
Angoon, Ak, US 134/M4
Angostura (res.), Mex. 140/C4
Angostura, Mex. 142/C2
Angoulême, Fr. 42/D4
Angra do Heroísmo, Azor., Port. 45/S12
Angra dos Reis, Braz. 211/J7
Angren, Uzb. 87/F4
Anguilla (isl.), UK 141/J4
Anguillara Veneta, It. 59/F2
Anguli (pol. reg.), India 83/G5
Angus (pol. reg.), Sc, UK 36/C3
Angutikada (peak), Ak, US 134/G2
Anhanduí (riv.), Braz. 151/H8
Anholt (isl.), Den. 38/D3
Anhui (prov.), China 71/L5
Anhumas, Braz. 151/G7
Ani, Japan 76/B4

Aniakchak (crater), Ak, US 134/G4
Aniakchak Nat'l Mon. and Prsv., Ak, US 134/F4
Aniche, Fr. 52/C3
Animas (riv.), Co,NM, US 128/F3
Animas, Punta De Las (pt.), Mex. 142/B2
'Anīn, Isr. 91/G6
Anina, Rom. 48/E3
Aniva (cape), Rus. 71/R2
Aniva (bay), Rus. 76/C1
Anivorano, Madg. 107/J7
Anizy-le-Château, Fr. 52/C4
Anjalankoski, Fin. 39/M1
Anjār, India 89/K4
Anjō, Japan 77/M6
Anjou (reg.), Fr. 42/C3
Anjou, Qu, Can. 131/N6
Anjouan (isl.), Com. 107/H6
Anjozorobe, Madg. 107/H7
Anju, NKor. 73/C3
Ankang, China 70/J5
Ankara (cap.), Turk. 90/C2
Ankara (prov.), Turk. 90/C1
Ankaramena, Madg. 107/H8
Ankaratra (mass.), Madg. 107/H7
Ankarsrum, Swe. 38/G3
Ankavandra, Madg. 107/H7
Ankazoabo, Madg. 107/H8
Ankazobe, Madg. 107/H7
Ankazomborona, Madg. 107/H7
Ankazomiriotra, Madg. 107/H7
Ankerika, Madg. 107/H8
Ankililioka, Madg. 107/G8
Ankilizato, Madg. 107/H8
Anklam, Ger. 38/E5
Ankum, Ger. 51/E3
Anlong, China 83/J2
Anloo, Neth. 50/D2
Anlu, China 72/C5
Anma (isl.), SKor. 73/D5
Ann (cape), Ma, US 131/G3
Ann Arbor, Mi, US 130/D3
Anna, Guy. 153/G4
Anna (lake), Va, US 138/A6
Anna Bay, Austl. 115/E2
Anna Pavlowna, Neth. 50/B3
Anna Pink (bay), Chile 158/B5
Anna Regina, Guy. 153/G3
Annaba, Alg. 100/K6
Annaba (prov.), Alg. 100/K6
Annaberg-Buchholz, Ger. 55/G3
Annaclone, NI, UK 34/B3
Annai, Guy. 153/G4
Annaka, Japan 77/B1
Annalong, NI, UK 34/C3
Annan, Sc, UK 35/E2
Annan (riv.), Sc, UK 36/C6
Annandale, Mo, US 137/G9
Annandale, Va, US 138/A6
Annapolis (cap.), Md, US 138/B6
Annapurna (peak), Nepal 84/D1
Annbank Station, Sc, UK 36/B6
Anne (mt.), Austl. 115/C4
Anne Arundel (co.), Md, US 138/B6
Annean (lake), Austl. 109/A3
Annecy, Fr. 56/C6
Annecy (lake), Fr. 56/C6
Annecy-le-Vieux, Fr. 56/C6
Annemasse, Fr. 56/C5
Annet-sur-Marne, Fr. 30/L5
Annette, Ak, US 134/M4
Annezin, Fr. 52/B2
Anniston, Al, US 133/G3
Annonay, Fr. 42/F4
Annville, Pa, US 138/B4
Annweiler, Ger. 53/G5
Anō, Japan 77/K6
Ano Víannos, Gre. 47/J5
Anoia (riv.), Sp. 45/K7
Anoka, Mn, US 127/K4
Anosibe An' Ala, Madg. 107/J7
Anou-Zeggarene (riv.), Niger 103/G2
Anould, Fr. 56/C1
Anóyia, Gre. 47/J5
Anping, China 72/C3
Anren, China 72/C3
Anrochte, Ger. 51/F5
Ans, Belg. 53/E2
Ansai, China 72/B3
Ansan, SKor. 73/F7
Ansbach, Ger. 54/D4
Anse-à-Galets, Haiti 145/H2
Anse-d'Hainault, Haiti 145/G2
Anse Rouge, Haiti 145/H2
Ansfelden, Aus. 55/H6
Anshan, China 73/B2
Anshun, China 70/J6
Anson, Tx, US 129/H4
Ansŏng, SKor. 73/D4
Ansongo, Mali 103/F3
Ant (riv.), Eng, UK 33/H1
Anta, Peru 156/C4
Antakya, Turk. 91/E1
Antalaha, Madg. 107/J6
Antalya (prov.), Turk. 90/B2

Antalya (int'l arpt.), Turk. 91/B1
Antalya, Turk. 91/B1
Antalya, Gulf of (gulf), Turk. 91/B1
Antananarivo (prov.), Madg. 107/J7
Antananarivo (cap.), Madg. 107/H7
Antanifotsy, Madg. 107/H7
Antanimieva, Madg. 107/G8
Antanimora, Madg. 107/H9
Antar (peak), Alg. 99/E3
Antarctic (pen.), Ant. 160/V
Antarctic Circle 160/Z
Antarctica (cont.) 160
Antas, Braz. 154/C3
Antas, Rio das (riv.), Braz. 155/B4
Antella, It. 59/E5
Antelope (isl.), Ut, US 137/J12
Antelope Center, Ca, US 136/C1
Antequera, Sp. 44/C4
Antes Fort, Pa, US 138/A1
Anthering, Aus. 55/G7
Anthony, NM, US 128/F4
Anti-Atlas (mts.), Mor. 96/C2
Anti-Lebanon (mts.), Leb. 91/D3
Antibes, Fr. 43/G5
Anticosti, Île d' (isl.), Qu, Can. 123/K4
Antietam (riv.), Aus. 55/G6
Antifer, Cap d' (cape), Fr. 42/D2
Antigo, Wi, US 127/L4
Antigonish, NS, Can. 131/J2
Antigua, Canl.,Sp. 98/B3
Antigua (isl.), Ant. 141/N8
Antigua and Barbuda (ctry.) 141/N8
Antigua Guatemala, Guat. 148/A3
Antiguo Morelos, Mex. 143/F4
Antilly, Fr. 30/L4
Antioquia (dept.), Col. 145/H5
Antioquia, Col. 152/C3
Antipodes (isls.), NZ 23/T8
Antipolo, Phil. 81/F4
Antisana (vol.), Ecu. 152/B5
Antlers, Ok, US 129/J4
Antofagasta, Chile 157/B1
Antoing, Belg. 52/C2
Antokonosy Manambondro, Madg. 107/H8
Antón, Pan. 152/A2
Antón Lizardo, Mex. 143/P7
Antón Lizardo (pt.), Mex. 143/P7
Antonia, Mo, US 137/G9
Antonibe, Madg. 107/H6
Antoniesberg (peak), SAfr. 106/C4
Antonina, Braz. 155/B3
Antonina do Norte, Braz. 154/C2
Antônio Carlos, Braz. 211/K6
Antonito, Co, US 132/B2
Antonovo, Bul. 49/H4
Antony, Fr. 30/J5
Antrim (mts.), NI, UK 34/B1
Antrim, NI, UK 34/B2
Antrim (mts.), NI, UK 34/B1
Antronapiana, It. 58/E5
Antsalova, Madg. 107/H7
Antsambalahy, Madg. 107/J6
Antsenavolo, Madg. 107/H8
Antsirabe, Madg. 107/H7
Antsirañana, Madg. 107/J6
Antsiranana (prov.), Madg. 107/J6
Antsohihy, Madg. 107/H6
Antsohimbondrona, Madg. 107/H6
Antu, China 71/P3
Antulai (mtn.), Malay. 81/E3
Antwerp (Deurne) (int'l arpt.), Belg. 50/B6
Antwerpen, Belg. 50/B6
Anūpgarh, India 86/B2
Anūpshahr, India 84/B1
Anuradhapura, SrL. 82/D6
Anvik, Ak, US 134/F3
Anvil Peak (vol.), Ak, US 134/B6
Anxi, China 79/C2
Anxi, China 70/G3
Anyang, China 72/C3
Anyang, SKor. 73/F7
A'nyêmaqên (mts.), China 70/G4
Anyi, China 72/B4
Anyuan, China 79/C2
Anza (riv.), It. 58/E6
Anza, WBnk. 91/G7
Anze, China 72/C3
Anzegem, Belg. 52/C1
Anzhero-Sudzhensk, Rus. 64/J4
Anzin, Fr. 52/C2
Anzing, Ger. 55/E6
Anzio, It. 46/C2
Anzoátegui, Ven. 152/D2
Anzoátegui (state), Ven. 153/E2
Anzoátegui (int'l arpt.), Ven. 153/E2
Anzola dell'Emilia, It. 59/E2
Ao Kham (pt.), Thai. 78/B4
Ao Phangnga NP, Thai. 78/B4

Aoba (isl.), Van. 116/F6
Aoga (isl.), Japan 75/F4
Aogaki, Japan 77/H6
Aoiz, Sp. 44/E1
Aomori (pref.), Japan 76/B3
Aomori, Japan 76/B3
Aonla, India 84/B1
Aoral (peak), Camb. 78/D3
Aos, Gre. 47/J4
Aosta, It. 43/G4
Aosta, Valle d' (valley), It. 58/A1
Aoukar (pol. reg.), Mrta. 96/C4
Aoulef, Alg. 99/F4
Aoyama, Japan 77/K6
Apa (riv.), Braz. 150/F7
Apalachicola, Fl, US 133/G4
Apan, Mex. 143/L7
Apaporis (riv.), Col. 150/D3
Aparados da Serra, PN de, Braz. 155/B4
Aparecida, Braz. 155/C2
Aparecida do Taboado, Braz. 155/B2
Aparición, Ven. 152/D2
Aparri, Phil. 79/D4
Apatzingán de la Constitución, Mex. 142/D4
Apeldoorn, Neth. 50/C4
Apelern, Ger. 51/G4
Apen, Ger. 51/E2
Apennines (mts.), It. 27/F4
Apensen, Ger. 51/G2
Aphrodisias (ruin), Turk. 90/B2
Api (peak), Indo. 81/E5
Api (cape), Indo. 81/F4
Api (cape), Indo. 80/C3
Apiacás, Serra dos (mts.), Braz. 150/G6
Apiaí, Braz. 155/B3
Apizaco, Mex. 143/L7
Aplao, Peru 156/C5
Apo (mt.), Phil. 79/E6
Apodi, Braz. 154/C2
Apodi (riv.), Braz. 154/C2
Apollo Bay, Austl. 115/B3
Apollonia, Gre. 47/J4
Apolo, Bol. 156/D4
Aporé (riv.), Braz. 151/H7
Apore, Braz. 155/B1
Apostle (isls.), Wi, US 127/L4
Apostle Islands Nat'l Lakeshore, Wi, US 127/K3
Apóstoles, Arg. 157/E2
Apostolos Andreas (cape), Cyp. 91/D2
Apoteri, Guy. 153/G3
Appalachian (mts.), US 125/K4
Appen, Ger. 51/G1
Appennino Ligure (mts.), It. 43/H4
Appennino Tosco-Emiliano (mts.), It. 43/J4
Appennino Umbro-Marchigiano (mts.), It. 43/K5
Appenweier, Ger. 57/E1
Appenzell, Swi. 57/F3
Appenzell (canton), Swi. 57/F3
Appignano, It. 59/G6
Appingedam, Neth. 50/C2
Apple Valley, Ca, US 136/C1
Appleton, NY, US 131/S9
Aprica, It. 58/D1
Aprica, Passo dell' (pass), It. 57/G5
Aprilia, It. 46/C2
Apšeronsk, Rus. 62/F3
Apua (pt.), Hi, US 124/U11
Apucarana, Braz. 155/B3
Apuiarés, Braz. 154/C1
Apure (riv.), Ven. 150/E2
Apure (prov.), Ven. 152/D3
Apurímac (dept.), Peru 156/C4
Apurímac (riv.), Peru 147/D4
Aqaba (gulf), Asia 67/B7
Aqmola (obl.), Kaz. 87/E2
'Aqrabah, WBnk. 91/G7
'Aqrah, Iraq 90/E3
Aqsay, Kaz. 63/J4
Aqtaū, Kaz. 63/J4
Aqtöbe (int'l arpt.), Kaz. 87/D2
Aqtöbe (obl.), Kaz. 87/D2
Aqtöbe, Kaz. 87/D2
Aquanaval (riv.), Mex. 142/E3
Aquaro-Guariquito, PN Ven. 150/E2
Aquia, Peru 156/B3
Aquidauana, Braz. 151/G8
Aquidauana (riv.), Braz. 151/G8
Aquila, Swi. 57/E5
Aquileia, It. 59/H1

Aquiles Serdán, Mex. 132/B4
Aquin, Haiti 145/H2
Aquitaine (pol. reg.), Fr. 56/C6
Ar-Asgat, Mong. 70/J2
Ar Horqin Qi, China 72/E2
Ar Ramādī, Iraq 90/E3
Ar Ramthā, Jor. 91/D3
Ar Raqqah, Syria 90/D3
Ar Raqqah (prov.), Syria 90/D2
Ar Rastan, Syria 91/E2
Ar Rayyān, Qatar 88/F3
Ar Riyāḍ (Riyadh) (cap.), SAr. 88/E4
Ar Rumaythah, Iraq 90/F4
Ar Ruşayfah, Jor. 91/E3
Ar Rutbah, Iraq 90/E3
Araban, Turk. 90/D2
Arabi, La, US 137/Q17
Arabian (sea), Asia 67/H7
Arabian (des.), Egypt 97/M2
Arabian (pen.), SAr. 88/D4
Araç, Turk. 62/E4
Araç (riv.), Turk. 62/E4
Araca, Bol. 150/E7
Araçá (riv.), Braz. 153/E4
Aracaju, Braz. 154/D3
Aracataca, Col. 152/C2
Aracena, Sp. 44/B4
Araci, Braz. 154/D3
Aračinovo, FYROM 47/G1
Aracoiaba, Braz. 154/C2
Aracruz, Braz. 155/D1
Araçuaí, Braz. 155/D1
Araçuaí (riv.), Braz. 155/D1
Arad, Rom. 48/E2
Arad (prov.), Rom. 48/E2
'Arad, Isr. 91/G8
Arādān, Iran 88/F1
Arafura (sea), Austl.,Indo. 116/C5
Aragarças, Braz. 151/H7
Aragats (peak), Arm. 63/H4
Aragón (aut. comm.), Sp. 45/E2
Aragón (riv.), Sp. 45/E1
Aragua (state), Ven. 153/E2
Aragua (riv.), Braz. 147/D3
Araguaia, PN do, Braz. 151/H6
Araguaiana, Braz. 151/H7
Araguaina, Braz. 151/J5
Araguari, Braz. 155/B1
Araguari (riv.), Braz. 151/H4
Araguatins, Braz. 151/J5
Arai, Japan 75/F2
Araioses, Braz. 154/B1
Arāk, Iran 88/E2
Arakamchechan (isl.), Rus. 134/D3
Arakan (mts.), Myan. 70/F7
Arakawa, Japan 77/C2
Arakhthos (riv.), Gre. 47/G3
Araklı, Turk. 90/E1
Aral (sea), Asia 87/D1
Aral, Kaz. 87/D3
Aral Mangy Qaraqumy (des.), Kaz. 87/D3
Aralık, Turk. 90/F2
Aralsor (lake), Kaz. 63/H2
Aramac, Austl. 114/B3
Arāmbāgh, India 85/F4
Aran (isls.), Ire. 31/P10
Aran Fawddwy (peak), Wal, UK 34/E6
Aranda de Duero, Sp. 44/D2
Arandelovac, Serb. 48/E3
Arani, Bol. 82/C5
Aranjuez, Sp. 44/D2
Aransas Pass, Tx, US 132/D4
Arantina, Braz. 211/J6
Aranuka (isl.), Kiri. 161/H5
Arapiraca, Braz. 154/C3
Arapiuns (riv.), Braz. 151/H5
Arapongas, Braz. 155/B2
'Ar'ar, Isr. 91/G7
Araranguá, Braz. 155/B4
Araraquara, Braz. 155/C2
Araras, Braz. 155/C2
Ararat, Austl. 115/B3
Arari, Braz. 154/B1
Arāria, India 85/F2
Araripe, Chapada do (uplands), Braz. 154/B2
Araripina, Braz. 154/B2
Aras (riv.), Iran 63/H5
Aratane (well), Mrta. 102/C2
Arauá (riv.), Braz. 151/G5
Arauca, Col. 152/D3
Arauca (riv.), Col.,Ven. 153/E3
Araucária, Braz. 155/B3
Arauco, Chile 158/B3
Arauquita, Col. 152/D2
Aravis, Col des (pass), Fr. 56/C6
Arawa, PNG 116/E5
Arawale Nat'l Rsv., Kenya 104/D2
Araxá, Braz. 155/C1
Araya, Ven. 153/F2
'Arba Minch', Eth. 97/N6
Arbeca, Sp. 45/F2
Arbīl (gov.), Iraq 90/E3
Arbīl, Iraq 90/E3

Arboga, Swe. 38/F2
Arbois, Fr. 56/B4
Arboletas, Col. 152/B2
Arbon, Swi. 57/F2
Arborfield, Sk, Can. 127/H2
Arborg, Mb, Can. 127/J3
Arbrá, Swe. 38/G1
Arbroath, Sc, UK 36/D3
Arc (riv.), Fr. 42/F5
Arc-en-Barrois, Fr. 56/B2
Arc-et-Senans, Fr. 56/B3
Arc-lès-Gray, Fr. 56/B3
Arc-sur-Tille, Fr. 56/B3
Arcachon, Fr. 42/C4
Arcachon, Bassin d' (lag.), Fr. 42/C4
Arcachon, Pointe d' (pt.), Fr. 42/C4
Arcadia, Ca, US 136/F7
Arcadia, Fl, US 133/H5
Arcadia, Wi, US 137/N14
Arcas, Cayos (isl.), Mex. 144/D1
Arcata, Ca, US 126/B5
Arceburgo, Braz. 211/G6
Arcelia, Mex. 143/E5
Arcene, It. 58/C1
Arcen, Neth. 50/D6
Archena, Sp. 44/E3
Archer City, Tx, US 129/H4
Arches, Fr. 56/C1
Arches NP, Ut, US 128/E3
Archidona, Sp. 44/C4
Archipelago Toscano (isl.), It. 43/H5
Arcisate, It. 57/E6
Arco, It. 57/G6
Arco, Paso del (pass), Arg. 158/C4
Arcola, It. 58/C4
Arcole, It. 59/E2
Arcos, Braz. 155/C2
Arcos de Jalón, Sp. 44/D2
Arcos de la Frontera, Sp. 44/C4
Arcos de Valdevez, Port. 44/A2
Arcoverde, Braz. 154/C2
Arctic (ocean) 160/U
Arctic Bay, Nun., Can. 123/H1
Arctic Circle 160/J
Arctic Red (riv.), NW, Can. 134/M2
Arctic Village, Ak, US 134/K2
Arctowski, Pol., Ant. 160/W
Arda (riv.), Bul. 47/J1
Ardabīl, Iran 63/J5
Ardahan, Turk. 90/F1
Ardal, Iran 88/F2
Ardalstangen, Nor. 38/B1
Ardanuç, Turk. 90/E1
Ardèche (riv.), Fr. 42/F4
Ardee, Ire. 34/B4
Arden, De, US 113/H5
Arden, De, US 138/C4
Arden-Arcade, Ca, US 135/M9
Ardennes (for.), Belg. 53/D4
Ardennes (dept.), Fr. 53/D4
Ardennes, Canal des (canal), Fr. 53/D4
Ardentes, Fr. 42/D3
Ardersier, Sc, UK 36/B1
Ardeşen, Turk. 90/E1
Ardesio, It. 57/F6
Ardestān, Iran 88/F2
Ardez, Swi. 57/G4
Ardila (riv.), Sc, UK 49/G5
Ardino, Bul. 49/G5
Ardle (riv.), Sc, UK 36/C3
Ardlethan, Austl. 115/C2
Ardmore, Ok, US 129/H4
Ardmore, Pa, US 138/C4
Ardnamurchan (pt.), Sc, UK 31/Q8
Ardon, Swi. 56/D5
Ardooie, Belg. 52/C1
Ardres, Fr. 52/A2
Ardrossan, Austl. 113/H5
Ardrossan, Sc, UK 36/B5
Ards (pen.), NI, UK 34/C3
Ards (dist.), NI, UK 34/C3
Ardsley, NY, US 139/K7
Åre, Swe. 37/G3
Areado, Braz. 211/G6
Arecibo, PR 141/M8
Areia Branca, Braz. 154/C2
Arena de la Ventana Punta (pt.), Mex. 142/C3
Arenal (vol.), CR 142/E4
Arenápolis, Braz. 151/G6
Arenas de San Pedro, Sp. 44/C2
Arenas, Punta de (pt.), Arg. 159/C7
Arendal, Nor. 38/C2
Arendonk, Belg. 50/C5
Arendtsville, Pa, US 138/A4
Arenig Fawr (peak), Wal, UK 34/E6
Arenys de Mar, Sp. 45/L6
Arenzano, It. 58/B3
Areo, Ven. 153/F2
Areópolis, Gre. 47/H4
Arequipa (dept.), Peru 156/C5
Arequipa, Peru 156/D5

Arequito, Arg. 158/E2
Aresing, Ger. 54/E5
Arévalo, Sp. 44/C2
Arezzo (prov.), It. 59/E6
Arezzo (prov.), It. 59/E5
Arga (riv.), Sp. 44/E1
Argalastí, Gre. 47/H3
Arlington Heights,
Il, US 130/C3
Argamasilla de Alba,
Sp. 44/D3
Argamasilla de Calatrava,
Sp. 44/C3
Arganda, Sp. 45/N9
Argegno, It. 57/F6
Argelès-Gazost, Fr. 42/C5
Argelès-sur-Mer, Fr. 42/E5
Argen (riv.), Ger. 57/F2
Argenbühl, Ger. 57/F2
Argens (riv.), Fr. 43/G5
Argenta, It. 59/E3
Argentat, Fr. 42/C2
Argentera (peak), It. 43/G4
Argenteuil, Fr. 30/J5
Argentière, Aiguille d'
(peak), Swi. 56/D6
Argentina (ctry.), Arg. 157/C4
Argentina (riv.), It. 58/A5
Argentino (lake), Arg. 159/B6
Argenton-sur-Creuse,
Fr. 42/D3
Argentona, Sp. 45/L6
Argeş (prov.), Rom. 49/G3
Argeş (riv.), Rom. 62/C3
Arghandab (riv.), Afg. 89/J2
Argithani, Turk. 90/B2
Argolis (gulf), Gre. 47/H4
Argonne (for.), Fr. 40/C4
Argonne National
Laboratory, Il, US 135/P16
Árgos, Gre. 47/H4
Árgos Orestikón, Gre. 47/G2
Argostólion, Gre. 47/G3
Arguello (pt.), Ca, US 128/B4
Arguin, Cap d' (cape),
Mrta. 98/A5
Argun' (riv.), Rus. 65/M4
Arguut, Mong. 70/H2
Argyle (lake), Austl. 109/B2
Argyll and Bute
(pol. reg.), Sc, UK 36/A4
Arhangay (prov.),
Mong. 70/G2
Arhreijit (well), Mrta. 98/B5
Århus, Den. 38/D3
Århus (co.), Den. 38/D3
Ariano Irpino, It. 40/D2
Ariari (riv.), Col. 156/C2
Arias, Arg. 158/E2
Arica, Chile 156/D5
Aricak, Turk. 90/E2
Arid (cape), Austl. 112/D5
Aridhaía, Gre. 47/H2
Arido (peak), Ca, US 136/A1
Aridol (lake), WSah. 98/B4
Ariège (riv.), Fr. 42/D5
Arifiye, Turk. 49/K5
Arifwâla, Pak. 86/B4
Arihã, Syria 91/E2
Arikaree (riv.), Co, US 129/G3
Arilje, Serb. 48/E4
Arima, Trin. 45/X16
Arinos (riv.), Braz. 151/G6
Arinos, Braz. 154/A4
Arinthod, Fr. 56/B5
Ario de Rosales, Mex. 143/E5
Aripao, Ven. 153/E3
Aripuanã, Braz. 150/G6
Aripuanã (riv.), Braz. 147/C3
Ariquemes, Braz. 150/F5
Arish, Austl. 114/B2
Arismendi, Ven. 152/D2
Arivechi, Mex. 142/C2
Arivonimamo, Madg. 107/H7
Ariza, Sp. 44/D2
Arizona, Arg. 158/D2
Arizona (canal),
Az, US 137/R18
Arizona (state), US 137/F4
Arizpe, Mex. 142/C2
Arjäng, Swe. 38/E2
Arjeplog, Swe. 37/F2
Arjona, Sp. 44/C4
Arjona, Col. 152/C2
Arkadelphia, Ar, US 129/J4
Arkaig (lake), Sc, UK 36/A3
Arkalokhórion, Gre. 47/J5
Arkansas (riv.), US 132/E3
Arkansas (state), US 132/E3
Arkansas City, Ar, US 129/K4
Arkansas City, Ks, US 129/H4
Arkanü (peak), Libya 97/K3
Arkhángelos, Gre. 90/B2
Arkhangel'sk (int'l arpt.),
Rus. 60/J2
Arkhangel'sk (Archangel),
Rus. 60/H2
Arkhangel'skaya Oblast,
Rus. 60/H3
Arkhangel'skoye,
Rus. 61/W9
Arklow, Ire. 34/B6
Arkona (cape), Ger. 51/G1
Arkonam, India 82/C5
Arkticheskiy Institut
(isls.), Rus. 64/H2
Arla, Swe. 38/G2
Arlan (peak), Trkm. 87/B5
Arlanda (int'l arpt.),
Swe. 38/G2
Arlanza (riv.), Sp. 44/C1
Arlazón (riv.), Sp. 44/D1
Arlbergpass (pass),
Aus. 57/G3
Arles, Fr. 42/F5
Arlesheim, Swi. 56/D3
Arley, Mo, US 137/E6
Arlington, Mn, US 127/K4
Arlington, Ga, US 133/G4
Arlington, Va, US 138/A6
Arth, Swi. 58/D1
Arthies, Fr. 30/H4
Arló, Hun. 41/L4
Arthur (pt.), Austl. 114/C3
Arlon, Belg. 53/E4
Arthur (riv.), Austl. 112/C5
Arluno, It. 58/B1
Arthur Kill (riv.),
Arly (riv.), Fr. 56/C6
NJ, NY, US 139/J9
Arly, PN de l', Burk. 103/F4
Arthur's (pass), NZ 117/S11
Arthur's Pass NP, NZ 117/S11
Arly, Réserve Totale de
Faune de l', Burk. 103/F4
Artigas, Uru. 157/E3
Armada, Mi, US 135/G6
Artogne, It. 57/E5
Armadale, Sc, UK 36/C5
Artois (reg.), Fr. 40/A3
Armagh (dist.),
Artova, Turk. 90/D1
NI, UK 34/B3
Artur Nogueira, Braz. 211/F7
Armagh, NI, UK 34/B3
Arturo Merino Benitez
Armançon (riv.), Fr. 42/F3
(Santiago) (int'l arpt.),
Armando Laydner, Represa
Chile 158/N8
de (res.), Braz. 155/B2
Artux, China 87/G5
Armant, Egypt 101/C3
Artvin, Turk. 90/E1
Armavir, Rus. 63/G3
Artvin (prov.), Turk. 90/E1
Arme, Cap d' (cape), Fr. 43/G5
Aru (isls.), Indo. 81/H5
Armenia, Col. 150/C3
Arua, Ugan. 104/A2
Armenia (riv.), It. 58/A5
Aruba (isl.),
Armenia (ctry.) 63/H5
Aru., Neth. 147/B1
Armentières, Fr. 52/B2
Arucas, Canl.,Sp. 98/B3
Armentières-en-Brie,
Arudy, Fr. 42/C5
Fr. 30/M5
Arujá, Braz. 211/G8
Armería, Mex. 142/E5
Arun (riv.), China 85/F2
Armidale, Austl. 115/D1
Arunachal Pradesh
Armilla, Sp. 44/D4
(state), India 70/F6
Armstrong, Arg. 158/E2
Arundel, Eng, UK 33/F5
Armstrong, BC, Can. 126/D3
Aruppukkottai, India 82/C6
Armthorpe, Eng, UK 35/G4
Arusha, Tanz. 104/C3
Armür, India 82/C4
'Arūrah, WBnk. 91/G7
Armutlu, Turk. 49/J5
Arus (cape), Indo. 81/F3
Army Ordnance Museum,
Arusha (pol. reg.),
Md, US 138/B5
Tanz. 104/C3
Arnage, Fr. 42/D3
Arusha NP, Tanz. 104/C3
Arnager (int'l arpt.),
Arutua (isl.), FrPol. 117/L6
Den. 38/H2
Aruwimi (riv.),
Arnaía, Gre. 47/H2
D.R. Congo 93/E4
Arnaud (riv.), Qu, Can. 123/J3
Arvada, Co, US 137/B3
Aruwheer, Mong. 70/H2
Arnedo, Sp. 44/D1
Arviat, Nun., Can. 122/G2
Arnett, Ok, US 129/H3
Arvidsjaur, Swe. 37/F2
Arnhem, Neth. 50/C5
Arvika, Swe. 38/E2
Arnhem Land (reg.),
Arvon (mt.), Mi, US 127/L4
Austl. 109/C2
Aryanah, Tun. 46/B4
Arno (riv.), It. 59/D5
Aryanah, Tun. 46/B4
Arno (isl.), Mrsh. 116/G4
Arys', Kaz. 87/E4
Arnold, Eng, UK 35/G6
Aryeweig (riv.),
Arnold, Md, US 138/B5
Eng, UK 33/E1
Arnold, Mo, US 137/G9
Arz (riv.), Fr. 42/B3
Arnoldstein, Aus. 43/K3
Arzachena, It. 46/A2
Arnon (riv.), It. 59/E1
Arzamas, Rus. 61/K5
Arnouville-lès-Gonesse,
Arzberg, Ger. 53/G3
Fr. 30/K5
Arzberg, Ger. 55/F2
Arnprior, On, Can. 130/C2
Arzen, Ger. 51/G4
Arnsberg, Ger. 51/F6
Arzew, Alg. 100/E5
Arnstadt, Ger. 43/J1
Arzignano, It. 59/E1
Arnstein, Ger. 54/C3
Arzl im Pitztal, Aus. 57/G3
Arnstorf, Ger. 55/F5
Arzúa, Sp. 44/A1
Aro Usu (cape), Indo. 81/H5
Arzúa, Sp. 44/A1
Aroab, Namb. 106/C4
Aroche, Sp. 44/B4
As, Nor. 38/D2
Arolsen, Ger. 51/G6
As, Belg. 53/E1
Aron (riv.), Fr. 42/E3
Aš, Czh. 55/F2
Arona, Canl. 45/X16
Aş Sabkhah, Syria 90/D3
Arona, It. 58/B1
Aş Şaff, Egypt 91/B5
Aronde (riv.), Fr. 52/B5
Aş Şāfī, Jor. 91/D3
Arorae (isl.), Kiri. 116/G5
Aş Sālimīyah, Kuw. 88/E3
Arosa, Swi. 57/F4
As Sallūm, Egypt 97/L1
Aroser Rothern (peak),
As Salmān, Iraq 91/D3
Swi. 57/F4
Aş Salt, Jor. 91/D3
Ærøskøbing, Den. 38/D4
Aş Şanţah, Egypt 91/B4
Arpaçay, Turk. 90/E1
Aş Şarīḩ, Jor. 91/D3
Arpajon, Fr. 30/J6
As Sinbillāwayn,
Arpajon-sur-Cère, Fr. 42/E4
Egypt 91/B4
Arqalyq, Kaz. 87/F2
As Sudd (reg.), Sudan 93/F4
Arquata Scrivia, It. 58/B3
As Sulaymānīyah (gov.),
Arques, Fr. 52/B2
Iraq 90/E2
Arrabah, WBnk. 91/G7
As Sulaymānīyah,
Arrah, India 81/E3
Iraq 90/E2
Arraias, Braz. 151/H6
As Suwaydā' (prov.),
Arraias, Braz. 154/A4
Syria 90/D3
Arraiján, Pan. 152/B2
Aş Suwaydā', Syria 91/E3
Arran (isl.), Sc, UK 31/R8
Aş Suwayrah, Iraq 90/F3
Arrancabarba (peak),
As Suways (gov.),
Nic. 145/E4
Egypt 101/C4
Arras, Fr. 52/B3
As Suways, Egypt 91/C4
Arreau, Fr. 42/D5
Asaba, Nga. 103/G5
Arrecife, Canl.,Sp. 98/B3
Asadābād, Afg. 86/A2
Arrecifes, Arg. 158/E2
Asadābād, Iran 88/E2
Arrée, Monts d' (mts.),
Asagny, PN d', C.d'Iv. 102/D5
Fr. 42/B3
Asahan (riv.), Indo. 80/A3
Arriaga, Mex. 144/C2
Asahi, Japan 75/G3
Arriondas, Sp. 44/C1
Asahi (riv.), Japan 77/F1
Arroscia (riv.), It. 58/B4
Asahi, Japan 77/L5
Arroux (riv.), Fr. 42/F3
Asahi, Japan 77/M5
Arrow (riv.), Eng, UK 32/C2
Asahi-dake (peak),
Arrowbear Lake,
Japan 76/C2
Ca, US 135/N12
Asahikawa, Japan 76/C2
Arroyo de la Luz, Sp. 44/B3
Asaka, Japan 77/D2
Arroyo Grande,
Asaka, Japan 77/M3
Ca, US 128/B4
Asama-yama (peak),
Arroyo Hondo (riv.),
Japan 77/F2
Ca, US 135/L12
Asan (bay), SKor. 73/D4
Arroyo Trabuco (riv.),
Asansol, India 85/F4
Ca, US 136/C3
Asashi-dake (peak),
Ars, Den. 38/C3
Japan 75/F1
Ars-sur-Moselle, Fr. 53/F5
Asashina, Japan 77/A1
Arsen'yev, Rus. 71/P3
Asawanwah (well),
Arsiero, It. 59/E1
Libya 96/J3
Asbach, Ger. 53/G2
Arslanköy, Turk. 91/D1
Asbest-Bäumenheim,
Árta, Gre. 47/G3
Ger. 54/E3
Artá, Sp. 45/G3
Asbest, Rus. 61/P4
Asbestos (mts.), SAfr. 106/C3
Asbury Park, NJ, US 138/D3

Arteaga, Mex. 142/E5
Arteixo, Sp. 44/A1
Artem, Rus. 71/P3
Artemisa, Cuba 145/F1
Artesia, NM, US 129/F4
Artesia, Ca, US 136/F8
Arth, Swi. 58/D1
Arthies, Fr. 30/H4
Arthur (pt.), Austl. 114/C3
Arthur (riv.), Austl. 112/C5
Arthur Kill (riv.),
NJ, NY, US 139/J9
Arthur's (pass), NZ 117/S11
Arthur's Pass NP, NZ 117/S11
Artigas, Uru. 157/E3
Artogne, It. 57/E5
Artois (reg.), Fr. 40/A3
Artova, Turk. 90/D1
Artur Nogueira, Braz. 211/F7
Arturo Merino Benitez
(Santiago) (int'l arpt.),
Chile 158/N8
Artux, China 87/G5
Artvin, Turk. 90/E1
Artvin (prov.), Turk. 90/E1
Aru (isls.), Indo. 81/H5
Arua, Ugan. 104/A2
Aruba (isl.),
Aru., Neth. 147/B1
Arucas, Canl.,Sp. 98/B3
Arudy, Fr. 42/C5
Arujá, Braz. 211/G8
Arun (riv.), China 85/F2
Arunachal Pradesh
(state), India 70/F6
Arundel, Eng, UK 33/F5
Aruppukkottai, India 82/C6
'Arūrah, WBnk. 91/G7
Arus (cape), Indo. 81/F3
Arusha (pol. reg.),
Tanz. 104/C3
Arusha NP, Tanz. 104/C3
Arutua (isl.), FrPol. 117/L6
Aruwimi (riv.),
D.R. Congo 93/E4
Arvada, Co, US 137/B3
Arvayheer, Mong. 70/H2
Arviat, Nun., Can. 122/G2
Arvidsjaur, Swe. 37/F2
Arvika, Swe. 38/E2
Arvon (mt.), Mi, US 127/L4
Aryanah, Tun. 46/B4
Aryanah, Tun. 46/B4
Arys', Kaz. 87/E4
Aryeweig (riv.),
Eng, UK 33/E1
Arz (riv.), Fr. 42/B3
Arzachena, It. 46/A2
Arzamas, Rus. 61/K5
Arzberg, Ger. 53/G3
Arzberg, Ger. 55/F2
Arzen, Ger. 51/G4
Arzew, Alg. 100/E5
Arzignano, It. 59/E1
Arzl im Pitztal, Aus. 57/G3
Arzúa, Sp. 44/A1

Ascensión, Bol. 150/F7
Ascención (bay),
Mex. 140/D4
Ascensión, Mex. 128/F5
Ascensión, Arg. 158/E2
Asola, It. 59/D1
Asolo, It. 59/E1
Asosa, Eth. 97/M5
Aus. 55/H6
Aschaffenburg, Ger. 54/C3
Aschau am Inn, Ger. 55/F6
Ascheberg, Ger. 45/E3
Aschendorf, Ger. 51/E2
Aschersleben, Ger. 40/F3
Ascoli Piceno, It. 43/K5
Ascoli Satriano, It. 46/D2
Ascona, Swi. 57/E5
Ascope, Peru 156/B2
Aseda, Swe. 38/F3
Asela, Eth. 97/N6
Asele, Swe. 37/F2
Asendorf, Ger. 51/G2
Asendorf, Ger. 51/F3
Asenovgrad, Bul. 47/J1
Aséral, Nor. 38/B2
Aserei (peak), It. 58/C3
Assa Aguiene (peak),
Alg. 99/G3
Asfeld, Fr. 53/D5
Ash, Eng, UK 30/A3
Ash, Eng, UK 33/F5
Ash Shabakah, Iraq 90/E4
Ash Shamal (gov.),
Leb. 91/E2
Ash Shāmīyah, Iraq 90/F4
Ash Shāriqah, UAE 89/G3
Ash Sharqāt, Iraq 90/E3
Ash Sharqīyah (state),
Sudan 101/C5
Ash Shawbak, Jor. 91/D4
Asha, Nga. 103/F5
Ashanti (uplands),
Gha. 103/E5
Ashanti (pol. reg.),
Gha. 103/E5
Asharoken, NY, US 139/M8
Ashbourne, Ire. 34/B4
Ashbourne, Eng, UK 35/G5
Ashburton (riv.), Austl. 109/A3
Ashburton, NZ 117/S11
Ashby (canal),
Eng, UK 33/E1
Ashby-de-la-Zouch,
Eng, UK 33/E1
Ashcroft, BC, Can. 126/C3
Ashdod, Isr. 91/F8
Asheboro, NC, US 133/J3
Ashern, Mb, Can. 127/J3
Asheville, NC, US 133/H3
Asheweig (riv.),
On, Can. 127/M2
Ashford, Austl. 115/D1
Ashford, Eng, UK 33/G4
Ashford, Eng, UK 30/B2
Ashford, Ire. 34/B5
Ashgabat (cap.), Trkm. 63/J3
Ashhurst, NZ 117/T11
Ashibetsu, Japan 76/C2
Ashigawa, Japan 77/B2
Ashikaga, Japan 77/C1
Ashino (lake), Japan 77/B3
Ashiwada, Japan 77/D3
Ashiya, Japan 77/H6
Ashiyasu, Japan 77/U7
Ashizuri-misaki (cape),
Japan 74/C4
Ashkal (lake), Tun. 100/L6
Ashland, Ks, US 129/H3
Ashland, Ky, US 130/D4
Ashland, Oh, US 130/D3
Ashland, Or, US 126/C4
Ashland, Pa, US 138/B2
Ashland, Wi, US 125/L4
Ashley, Pa, US 138/C1
Ashmore (reef), Austl. 109/B2
Ashmore and Cartier
Islands Territory
(dpcy.), Austl. 109/B2
Ashoknagar, India 84/A3
Ashoro, Japan 76/C2
Asheqlon, Isr. 91/F8
Ashta, India 82/C3
Ashtabula, Oh, US 130/D3
Ashton, Id, US 126/F4
Ashton, SAfr. 106/M10
Ashton-in-Makerfield,
Eng, UK 35/F5
Ashton-under-Lyne,
Eng, UK 35/F5
Asia (cont.) 67
Asia, Peru 156/B4
Asiago, It. 57/H4
Asikkala, Fin. 39/L1
Asilah, Mor. 100/A2
Asillo, Peru 156/D4
Asinara (isl.), It. 46/A2
Asinara, Golfo dell'
(gulf), It. 46/A2
Asino, Rus. 64/J4
Asipovichy, Bela. 60/C3
'Asīr (mts.), SAr. 88/D5
Asis (cape), Sudan 101/D5
Aşkale, Turk. 90/E2
Askeaton, Ire. 31/P10
Asker, Nor. 38/D2
Askersund, Swe. 38/F2
Askim, Nor. 38/D2
Askim, Swe. 38/N6
Askion (peak), Gre. 47/G2
Aşkja (crater), Ice. 37/P6
Askov, Den. 38/C4
Askvoll, Nor. 37/C3
Asmara (cap.), Erit. 96/D4
Asnen (lake), Swe. 38/F3
Asnières-sur-Oise, Fr. 30/K4

Asnières-sur-Seine, Fr. 30/J5
Asō, Japan 77/E2
Aso NP, Japan 74/B4
Aso-san (peak), Japan 74/B4
Asola, It. 59/D1
Asolo, It. 59/E1
Asosa, Eth. 97/M5
Asoteriba (peak),
Sudan 101/D4
Aspach, Aus. 55/G6
Aspe, Sp. 45/E3
Aspen, Co, US 128/F3
Aspen Hill, Md, US 138/A5
Aspen Park, Co, US 137/B3
Aspendos (ruin), Turk. 91/B1
Asperg, Ger. 54/C5
Aspermont, Tx, US 129/G4
Aspiring (mt.), NZ 117/R11
Aspró, Gre. 47/H3
Aspró, Gre. 47/H3
Aspróprigos, Gre. 47/N9
Asquith, Sk, Can. 126/G2
Assa, Mor. 98/C3
Assaba (pol. reg.),
Mrta. 102/C2
Assaré, Braz. 154/C2
Asse, Belg. 52/D2
Assebroek, Belg. 52/C1
Assemini, It. 46/A3
Assen, Neth. 50/D3
Assendelft, Neth. 52/C1
Assenede, Belg. 52/C1
Assens, Den. 38/C4
Assens, Den. 38/C4
Assentoft, Den. 38/D3
Assesse, Belg. 53/E3
Assiniboia, Sk, Can. 127/G3
Assiniboine (mt.),
BC, Can. 126/E3
Assiniboine (riv.),
Mb, Sk, Can. 127/H3
Assinika (lake),
Qu, Can. 130/F1
Assis, Braz. 155/B2
Assling, Ger. 55/F6
Asso, It. 58/C1
Assomada, CpV. 93/K10
Astakós, Gre. 47/G3
Astana (cap.), Kaz. 87/F2
Asten, Neth. 50/C6
Asten, Aus. 55/H6
Asti (prov.), It. 58/B3
Asti, It. 43/H4
Astico (riv.), It. 59/E1
Astipálaia, Gre. 90/A2
Astolfo Dutra, Braz. 211/L6
Astorga, Braz. 155/B2
Astorga, Sp. 44/B1
Astoria, Or, US 126/C4
Astorp, Swe. 38/E3
Astrakhan' (cap.), Trkm. 63/J2
Astrakhanskaya Oblast,
Rus. 63/H3
Astros, Gre. 47/H4
Astudillo, Sp. 44/C1
Asturias (aut. comm.),
Sp. 44/B1
Asuka (riv.), Japan 77/J7
Asuke, Japan 77/M5
Asunción (cap.), Par. 157/E2
Asunción (isl.), NMar. 116/D3
Asunción Ixtaltepec,
Mex. 140/B4
Asunden (lake), Swe. 38/F2
Aswa (riv.), Ugan. 97/M7
Aswān (gov.), Egypt 101/C3
Aswān, Egypt 101/C3
Aswan High (dam),
Egypt 101/C4
Asyūţ (gov.), Egypt 101/B3
Asyūţ, Egypt 101/C3
Aszód, Hun. 49/R9
Aţ Ţafīlah, Jor. 91/D4
Aţ Ţafīlah (prov.), Jor. 91/A4
Aţ Ţā'if, SAr. 88/D4
Aţ Tall, Syria 91/E3
At Tall al Kabīr, Egypt 91/B4
Aţ Ta'mīn (gov.), Iraq 90/E3
Aţ Ţūr, WBnk. 91/G8
Atak (riv.), Iran 89/G1
Atabapo (riv.), Ven. 153/E4
Atacama (des.), Chile 147/B4
Atacames, Ecu. 152/B4
Atafu (isl.), Tok. 117/H5
Atakpamé, Togo 103/F5
Atalaia, Braz. 154/C3
Atalaia do Norte,
Braz. 156/D2
Atalándi, Gre. 47/H3
Atalaya, Peru 156/C3
Atami, Japan 77/B3
Atar, Mrta. 96/C3
Atarfe, Sp. 44/D4
Atarra, India 84/C3
Atas Bogd (peak),
Mong. 70/G3
Atascadero, Ca, US 128/B4
Atascosa (co.),
Tx, US 137/T21
Atascosa, Tx, US 137/T21
Atatürk (dam), Turk. 90/D2
Atatürk (int'l arpt.),
Turk. 49/J5
Atbara (riv.), Eth. 97/N4
Atbara, Sudan 97/M4
Atbasar, Kaz. 87/F1
Atchafalaya (riv.),
La, US 129/K5
Atchafalaya (bay),
La, US 129/K5
Atchison, Ks, US 129/J3
Atco, NJ, US 138/D4

Atebubu, Gha. 103/E5
Ateca, Sp. 44/E2
Ateelva (riv.), Nor. 37/G1
Atén, Bol. 156/D4
Atencingo, Mex. 143/L8
Atenco, Mex. 143/R9
Atengo (riv.), Mex. 142/D4
Atessa, It. 46/D1
Atglen, Pa, US 138/C4
Ath, Belg. 52/C2
Athabasca, Ab, Can. 126/E2
Athabasca (riv.),
Ab, Can. 122/E3
Athabasca (lake),
Ab, Sk, Can. 122/E3
Athapapuskow (lake),
Mb, Can. 127/H2
Athar Ţulmaythah
(Ptolemaïs)
(ruin) Libya 97/K3
Athboy, Ire. 31/Q10
Athenry, Ire. 31/P10
Athens (Athínai) (cap.),
Gre. 47/N9
Athens, Al, US 133/G3
Athens, Ga, US 133/H3
Athens, Tn, US 133/G3
Athens, Tx, US 129/J4
Atherstone, Eng, UK 33/E1
Atherton, Austl. 114/B2
Atherton, Eng, UK 35/F4
Atherton, Mo, US 137/E5
Athgarh, India 82/E3
Athi (riv.), Kenya 104/C3
Athi (Athínai) (cap.),
Gre. 47/N9
Athis-Mons, Fr. 30/K5
Athlone, Ire. 31/Q10
Atholl (for.), Sc, UK 36/B3
Áthos (peak), Gre. 47/J2
Athy, Ire. 31/Q10
Ati, Chad 96/J5
Atibaia (riv.), Braz. 211/G7
Atibaia, Braz. 211/G8
Atico, Peru 156/C5
Atienza, Sp. 44/D2
Atikokan, On, Can. 127/L3
Atil, Mex. 142/C2
Atitlán (lake), Guat. 144/D3
Atiu (isl.), CookIs. 117/K7
Atizapán, Mex. 143/Q10
Atka, Ak, US 134/D5
Atka (isl.), Ak, US 134/C5
Atkarsk, Rus. 63/H2
Atkinson (pt.),
NW, Can. 134/M2
Atlacomulco de Fabela,
Mex. 143/K7
Atlanta (cap.), Ga, US 133/G3
Atlantic (ocean) 22/G3
Atlantic (co.), NJ, US 138/D4
Atlantic Beach,
NY, US 139/L9
Atlantic City,
NJ, US 138/D5
Atlantic Highlands,
NJ, US 139/J10
Atlántico (dept.),
Col. 145/H4
Atlántida, Uru. 159/J11
Atlantique (prov.), Ben. 103/F5
Atlas (mts.), Mor. 96/E1
Atlas (cont.), US 135/K10
Atlas Saharien (mts.),
Alg. 96/E1
Atlatlahuaca, Mex. 143/Q10
Atlin, BC, Can. 134/M3
'Atlit, Isr. 91/F6
Atlixco, Mex. 143/L8
Atmore, Al, US 133/G4
Atocha, Bol. 150/E8
Atomium, The, Belg. 52/D2
Atotonilco, Mex. 143/L6
Atouila, 'Erg (des.),
Mali 98/D5
Atoyac (riv.), Mex. 144/B2
Atoyac, Mex. 144/B2
Atqasuk, Ak, US 134/G1
Atrai (riv.), Bang. 85/G3
Atrak (riv.), Iran 89/G1
Atran (riv.), Swe. 38/E3
Atrato (riv.), Col. 150/C2
Atrauli, India 84/B1
Atsugi, Japan 77/C3
Atsumi (pen.), Japan 77/M6
Atsumi, Swi. 56/C4
Attalea, Braz. 154/C3
Attalens, Swi. 56/C4
Attalla, Al, US 133/G3
Attapu, Laos 78/D3
Attawapiskat (lake),
On, Can. 127/L2
Attawapiskat (riv.),
On, Can. 123/H3
Attel (riv.), Ger. 55/F7
Attendorn, Ger. 51/E6
Atteridgeville, SAfr. 106/Q12
Attersee (lake), Aus. 43/K3
Attert, Belg. 53/E4
Attleboro, Ma, US 135/G5
Attigny, Fr. 53/D5
'Attil, WBnk. 91/G7
Attleborough,
Eng, UK 33/H1
Attock, Pak. 86/B3
Attu, Ak, US 134/A5
Attu (isl.), Ak, US 134/A5
Atuel (riv.), Arg. 157/C4
Atuntaqui, Ecu. 152/B4
Atvidaberg, Swe. 38/F2
Aua (isl.), PNG 116/D5
Aubagne, Fr. 42/F5
Aubange, Belg. 53/E4
Aube (dept.), Fr. 53/D6
Aube (riv.), Fr. 40/C4
Aubel, Belg. 53/E2
Aubenas, Fr. 42/F4
Aubepierre-Ozouer-le-Repos,
Fr. 30/L6
Aubergenville, Fr. 30/H5
Aubert (peak), Swi. 56/C4
Aubervilliers, Fr. 30/K5
Aubetin (riv.), Fr. 52/C6
Aubette (riv.), Fr. 52/A5
Aubette de Magny
(riv.), Fr. 30/H4
Aubière, Fr. 42/E4
Aubigny-en-Artois, Fr. 52/B3
Aubigny-sur-Nère, Fr. 42/E3
Aubin, Fr. 42/E4
Aubonne, Swi. 56/C5
Auboué, Fr. 53/E5
Aubrac, Monts du
(mts.), Fr. 42/E4
Aubrives, Fr. 53/D3
Aubry, Ks, US 137/D6
Auburn, Austl. 113/H5
Auburn, Al, US 133/G3
Auburn, Ca, US 128/B3
Auburn, In, US 130/C3
Auburn, Me, US 131/G2
Auburn, Ne, US 129/J2
Auburn, NY, US 130/E3
Auburn, Pa, US 138/B2
Auburn, Wa, US 126/C3
Auburn Hills, Mi, US 135/F6
Aubusson, Fr. 42/E4
Auca Mahuida (peak),
Arg. 158/C3
Auce, Lat. 42/E5
Auch, Fr. 42/D5
Auchel, Fr. 52/B3
Auchinleck, Sc, UK 36/C4
Auchterarder, Sc, UK 36/C4
Auchtermuchty,
Sc, UK 36/C4
Auchy-lès-Hesdin, Fr. 52/B3
Auckland, NZ 117/S10
Auckland (int'l arpt.),
NZ 117/S10
Auckland (isls.), NZ 23/T8
Aude (riv.), Fr. 42/E5
Auderghem, Belg. 53/D2
Audeux (riv.), Fr. 56/C3
Audierne (bay), Fr. 42/A3
Audincourt, Fr. 56/C3
Audo (range), Eth. 97/P6
Audruicq, Fr. 52/B2
Audun-le-Roman, Fr. 53/E5
Audun-le-Tiche, Fr. 53/E5
Aue (riv.), Fr. 42/A2
Aue, Ger. 55/F1
Auer (Ora), It. 57/H5
Auerbach, Ger. 55/F1
Auerbach in der Oberpfalz,
Ger. 55/F2
Auersberg (peak),
Ger. 55/F2
Aufess (riv.), Ger. 54/E3
Auffargis, Fr. 30/H5
Augathella, Austl. 114/B4
Augher, NI, UK 34/A3
Aughnacloy, NI, UK 34/B3
Aughrim, Ire. 34/B6
Augrabies Falls NP,
SAfr. 106/C3
Augrabiesvalle (falls),
SAfr. 106/C3
Augsburg, Ger. 54/D6
Augusta, Ga, US 133/H3
Augusta, Austl. 112/B5
Augusta, NJ, US 138/D2
Augusta (cap.),
Me, US 131/G2
Augusta, It. 46/D4
Augusta, Austl. 112/B5
Augusta, NJ, US 138/D2
Augusta, Golfo di (gulf),
It. 46/D4
Augustdorf, Ger. 51/F5
Augustenborg, Den. 38/C4
Augusto (mt.), Austl. 112/C3
Augustów, Pol. 39/K5
Augustus (mt.), Austl. 112/C3
Augusto César Sandino
(int'l arpt.), Nic. 144/E3
Aulla, It. 58/C4
Aulnay, Fr. 42/C4
Aulne (riv.), Fr. 42/A2
Aulnoye-Aymeries, Fr. 52/C3
Aulnut (int'l arpt.), Fr. 42/E4
Ault, Co, US 137/C1
Ault, Fr. 52/A3
Aulus-les-Bains, Fr.
Aumale, Fr. 52/A4
Aumetz, Fr. 53/E5
Aumühle, Ger. 51/H1
Aunay-sur-Odon, Fr. 32/C5
Aunette (riv.), Fr. 52/B5
Auning, Den. 38/D3
Aur (isl.), Mrsh. 116/G4
Aura, NJ, US 138/C4
Aurach, Ger. 54/D4
Aurangābād, India 85/E3
Aurangābād, India 89/L5

Au in der Hallertau,
Ger. 55/E5
Au Sable (riv.), Mi, US 130/C2
Auari (riv.), Braz. 153/E2
Aubange, Belg. 53/E4
Aubenas, Fr. 42/F4
Auburn, Pa, US 138/B2
Auray, Fr. 42/B3
Aureilhan, Fr. 42/D5
Aurich, Ger. 51/E2
Auriflama, Braz. 155/B2
Aurillac, Fr. 42/E4
Aurisina, It. 59/G1
Aurland, Nor. 38/B1
Aurolzmünster, Aus. 55/G6
Aurora, Braz. 154/C2
Aurora, Guy. 153/G3
Aurora, Co, US 137/C3
Aurora, Il, US 129/K2
Aurora, Mo, US 129/J3
Aurora Lodge, Ak, US 134/J3
Aus, Namb. 106/B2
Ausa (riv.), It. 59/G1
Aussillon, Fr. 42/E5
Aust-Agder (co.), Nor. 37/C4
Austin, Nv, US 128/C3
Austin (lake), Austl. 109/A3
Austin, Tx, US
Austral (Tubuaï Islands)
(isls.), FrPol. 117/K7
Australia (ctry.) 109
Australia (ctry.) 109
Australian Alps (range),
Austl. 115/C3
Australian Capital Territory
(cap. terr.), Austl. 109/D4
Australind, Austl. 112/B5
Austria (ctry.) 43/L3
Austurhorn (pt.), Ice. 37/P7
Auterive, Fr. 42/D5
Authie (riv.), Fr. 42/D1
Autlán de Navarro,
Mex. 142/D5
Automne (riv.), Fr. 52/B5
Autreppe, Belg. 52/C3
Autun, Fr. 42/F3
Auvergne (pol. reg.),
Fr. 42/E4
Auvers-sur-Oise, Fr. 30/J4
Auvézère (riv.), Fr. 42/D4
Aux Sables (riv.),
On, Can. 130/D2
Auxerre, Fr. 42/E3
Auxi-le-Château, Fr. 52/B3
Auxonne, Fr. 56/B3
Auyán-Tepuí (peak),
Ven. 153/F3
Auyuittuq NP,
Nun., Can. 123/K2
Auzangate (peak),
Peru 156/D4
Avaj, Iran 89/F2
Avallon, Fr. 42/E3
Avalon (pen.), Nf, Can. 123/L4
Avalon, Ca, US 136/B4
Avalon, NJ, US 138/D5
Avanne-Aveney, Fr. 56/B3
Avaré, Braz. 155/B2
Avarua, NZ 117/K7
Avdat (ruin), Isr. 91/A4
Avebury Stone Circle,
Eng, UK 33/E4
Aveiro, Port. 44/A2
Aveiro (dist.), Port. 44/A2
Aveley, Eng, UK 30/D2
Avelgem, Belg. 52/C2
Avellaneda, Arg. 159/J11
Avellino, It. 46/D2
Avelon (riv.), Fr. 52/A5
Avenal, Ca, US 128/B3
Avenches, Swi. 56/D4
Avernes, Fr. 30/H4
Avernes, Fr. 30/H4
Aversa, It. 40/D2
Avesnes-le-Comte, Fr. 52/B3
Avesnes-sur-Helpe,
Fr. 52/C3
Avesta, Swe. 38/G1
Aveyron (riv.), Fr. 42/D4
Avezzano, It. 46/C1
Avich (lake), Sc, UK 36/A4
Aviemore, Sc, UK 36/C2
Avignon, Fr. 42/F5
Avihayil, Isr. 91/F7
Avila de los Caballeros,
Sp. 44/C2
Avilés, Sp. 44/C1
Avio, It. 59/D1
Avion, Fr. 52/B3
Avisio (riv.), It. 57/H5
Aviz, Pa, US 138/A1
Avize, Fr. 52/C5
Avlum, Den. 38/C3
Avoca, Austl. 115/C4
Avoca, Ire. 34/B6
Avoca, Austl. 115/B3
Avoch, Sc, UK 36/B1
Avola, It. 46/D4
Avon (riv.), Eng, UK 32/C6
Avon, Ire. 36/C1
Avon, Fr. 42/E2
Avon Valley NP, Austl. 112/C4
Avon Water (riv.),
Sc, UK 36/B5
Avonbeg (riv.), Ire. 34/B6
Avondale, Austl. 115/D2
Avondale, Az, US 137/R19
Avonlea, Sk, Can. 127/G3
Avonmore (riv.), Ire. 34/B5
Avranches, Fr. 42/C2
Avrillé, Fr. 42/C3
Awa-shima (isl.),
Japan 76/A4
'A'waj (riv.), Syria 91/E3
Awaji, Japan 77/H6
Awans, Belg. 53/E2

Āwasa, Eth. 97/N6
Āwash, Eth. 97/P6
Āwash Wenz (riv.), Eth. 97/P5
Awaso, Gha. 103/E5
Awat, China 70/D3
Awbārī, Libya 96/H2
Awbārī (des.), Libya 99/H4
Awe (lake), Sc, UK 36/A4
Awjilah, Libya 97/K2
Awka, Nga. 103/G5
Awsīm, Egypt 91/B4
Ax-les-Thermes, Fr. 42/D5
Axamo (int'l arpt.), Swe. 38/F3
Axams, Aus. 37/H3
Axarfjördhur (inlet), Ice. 37/N6
Axel, Neth. 50/A6
Axel Heiberg (isl.), Nun., Can. 123/S7
Axim, Gha. 103/E5
Axios (riv.), Gre. 47/H2
Axis (dam), Wa, US 135/D2
Axminster, Eng, UK 32/D5
Axochiapan, Mex. 143/L8
Ay (riv.), Rus. 61/N5
Ay, Fr. 52/C5
Ayabaca, Peru 156/B2
Ayabe, Japan 77/H5
Ayacucho, Peru 156/C4
Ayacucho (dept.), Peru 156/C4
Ayacucho, Arg. 158/F3
Ayagöz, Kaz. 70/D2
Ayaguz (riv.), Kaz. 70/C2
Ayama, Japan 77/K6
Ayamé I, Barrage d' (dam), C.d'Iv. 102/E5
Ayamé II, Barrage d' (dam), C.d'Iv. 102/E5
Ayamonte, Sp. 44/B4
Ayancık, Turk. 90/C1
Ayanganna (mtn.), Guy. 153/G3
Ayapel, Col. 152/C2
Ayaş, Turk. 90/C1
Ayase, Japan 77/C3
Ayaviri, Peru 156/D4
Aybak, Afg. 87/E5
'Aybāl, Jabal (peak), WBnk. 91/G7
Aybastı, Turk. 90/D1
Aydar Köli (lake), Trkm. 87/E4
Aydın, Turk. 90/A2
Aydin (prov.), Turk. 90/B2
Aydıncık, Turk. 90/C1
Aydıncık, Turk. 91/C1
Aydınkent, Turk. 91/B1
Ayer, Swi. 56/D5
Ayers Rock (Uluru) (peak), Austl. 113/F3
Ayeyarwady (state), Myan.
Ayeyarwady (Irrawaddy), (riv.) Myan. 49/J3
Ayiá, Gre. 47/H3
Ayía Paraskeví, Gre. 47/K3
Ayiásos, Gre. 47/K3
Áyios Ioánnis (cape), Gre. 47/J5
Áyios Kírikos, Gre. 47/K4
Áyios Konstandínos, Gre. 47/J5
Áyios Matthaíos, Gre. 47/F3
Áyios Nikólaos, Gre. 47/J5
Aylesbury, Eng, UK 33/F4
Aylesford, Eng, UK 33/G4
Ayllón, Sp. 44/D2
Aylmer (lake), NW, Can. 122/F2
'Ayn al 'Arab, Syria 90/D2
'Ayn Zuwayyah (well), Libya 97/K3
Ayna, Peru 156/C4
Ayon (isl.), Rus. 65/S3
Ayora, Sp. 45/E3
Ayotzintepec, Mex. 144/B2
'Ayoûn 'Abd el Mâlek (well), Mrta. 98/D4
'Ayoûn el 'Atroûs, Mrta. 102/C2
Ayr, Austl. 114/B2
Ayr, Sc, UK 36/B6
Ayr (riv.), Sc, UK 36/B5
Aytré, Fr. 42/C3
Ayubia NP, Pak. 86/B3
Ayutla, Mex. 142/D4
Ayutla de los Libres, Mex. 140/D4
Ayutthaya (ruin), Thai. 78/C3
Ayvacık, Turk. 47/K3
Ayvalık, Turk. 90/A2
Aywaille, Belg. 53/E3
Az Zabadānī, Syria 91/E4
Az Zāhirīyah, WBnk. 91/B4
Az Zaqāzīq, Egypt 91/B4
Az Zaqāzīq (gov.), Jor. 91/E3
Az Zarqā', Jor. 91/E3
Az Zāwiyah, Libya 88/D5
Az Zaydīyah, Yem. 88/D5
Azad Kashmir (terr.), Pak. 86/B3
Azahar (coast), Sp. 45/F3
Azalea, Or, US 126/C5
Azalia, Mi, US 135/E7
Azamgarh, India 84/D2
Azángaro, Peru 156/D4
Azángaro (riv.), Peru 156/D4
Azao (peak), Alg. 99/H4
Azaouâd (phys. reg.), Mali 96/E4

Āzārān, Iran 88/E1
Āzarbāyjān-e Gharbī (prov.), Iran 90/F2
A'zāz, Syria 91/E1
Azemmour, Mor. 98/C2
Azerbaijan (ctry.) 63/H4
Azilal, Mor. 98/D3
Azimganj, India 99/H4
Azogues, Ecu. 152/B5
Azores (dpcy.), Port. 45/R12
Azourki (peak), Mor. 98/D3
Azov, Rus. 63/G2
Azov (sea), Ukr.,Rus. 64/D5
Azoyú, Mex. 144/B2
Azpeitia, Sp. 44/D1
Azrou, Mor. 98/D2
Aztec, NM, US 128/F3
Aztec Ruins Nat'l Mon., NM, US 128/E3
Azua de Compostela, DRep. 141/G4
Azuaga, Sp. 44/C3
Azuara, Sp. 45/E2
Azuay (dept.), Ecu. 152/B5
Azuchi, Japan 77/K5
Azuero, Peninsula de (pen.), Pan. 150/B2
Azuga, Rom. 49/G3
Azul (mtn.), CR 144/E4
Azul (riv.), Guat. 144/D2
Azul, Arg. 158/F3
Azul, Cordillera (mts.), Peru 156/B2
Azuma, Japan 77/E2
Azuma, Japan 77/F2
Azuma-san (peak), Japan 75/G2
Azumaya-san (peak), Japan 75/F2
Azur, Côte d' (coast), Fr. 43/G5
Azusa, Ca, US 136/C2
Azzaba, Alg. 100/K6
Azzano Decimo, It. 59/F1
Azzano San Paolo, It. 58/C1
Azzate, It. 58/B1
'Azzūn, WBnk. 91/G7

B

Ba (riv.), Viet. 79/N3
Bà (riv.), Viet. 83/J5
Ba Lang An (cape), Viet. 78/E3
Ba Quan (cape), Viet. 78/E3
Baar, Swi. 57/E3
Baarle-Hertog, Belg. 50/B6
Baarle-Nassau, Neth. 50/B6
Baarn, Neth. 50/C4
Bab el Mandeb (str.), Asia 88/D4
Baba (mts.), Afg. 89/J2
Baba (peak), Bul. 47/H1
Baba (pt.), Turk. 49/K5
Baba Burnu (pt.), Turk. 49/J3
Babadag, Rom. 49/J3
Babaeski, Turk. 49/H5
Babahoyo, Ecu. 152/B5
Babai Khola (riv.), Nepal 84/C1
Babakale, Turk. 47/J3
Babar (isls.), Indo. 67/H5
Babatorun, Turk. 91/E1
Babatpur (int'l arpt.), India 84/D3
Babbacombe (bay), Eng, UK 32/C6
Babbitt, Mn, US 127/L4
B'abdā, Leb. 91/D3
Babelthuap (isl.), Palau 116/C4
Babenhausen, Ger. 57/G1
Babenhausen, Ger. 54/B3
Babensham, Ger. 55/F6
Baberu, India 84/C3
Babia (peak), Pol. 62/A2
Babian (riv.), China 80/F3
Babīl (gov.), Iraq 90/F3
Bābil (Babylon) (ruin), Iraq 90/F3
Babīna, India 84/B3
Babinda, Austl. 114/B2
Babine (riv.), BC, Can. 122/D3
Bābol, Iran 88/F1
Babruysk, Bela. 62/D1
Babuyan (isls.), Phil. 67/M8
Babuyan (isl.), China 83/F5
Bac Giang, Viet. 78/D1
Bac Lieu, Viet. 78/D4
Bac Ninh, Viet. 83/J3
Bacabal, Braz. 154/A2
Bacadéhuachi, Mex. 142/D2
Bacajá (riv.), Braz. 151/H4
Bacalar, Mex. 144/D2
Bacalar (lag.), Mex. 144/D2
Bacan (isls.), Indo. 81/G4
Bacău, Rom. 70/H3
Bacău (prov.), Rom. 49/H2
Baccarat, Fr. 56/C1
Bacchiglione (riv.), It. 59/E2
Bacchus, Ut, US 137/J12
Bacerac, Mex. 142/D2
Bacharach, Ger. 54/B1
Bachhraon, India 84/B1
Bachíniva, Mex. 142/D2
Back (riv.), Md, US 138/B5
Back (riv.), Nun., Can. 122/F2
Bačka Palanka, Serb. 48/D3
Bačka Topola, Serb. 48/D3
Bäckefors, Swe. 38/E2
Backnang, Ger. 54/C5
Bacobampa, Mex. 142/D2

Bacolod, Phil. 81/F1
Bács-Kiskun (prov.), Hun. 48/D2
Bácsalmás, Hun. 48/D2
Bacup, Eng, UK 35/F4
Bad Abbach, Ger. 55/E5
Bad Axe, Mi, US 130/D3
Bad Bellingen, Ger. 56/D2
Bad Bergzabern, Ger. 54/A4
Bad Berneck, Ger. 55/E2
Bad Bocklet, Ger. 54/D2
Bad Brambach, Ger. 55/F2
Bad Breisig, Ger. 53/G3
Bad Brückenau, Ger. 54/C2
Bad Buchau, Ger. 57/F1
Bad Camberg, Ger. 54/B2
Bad Doberan, Ger. 38/D4
Bad Driburg, Ger. 51/G5
Bad Dürkheim, Ger. 54/B4
Bad Dürrheim, Ger. 57/E1
Bad Ems, Ger. 53/G3
Bad Endorf, Ger. 55/F7
Bad Essen, Ger. 51/F4
Bad Freienwalde, Ger. 41/H2
Bad Gandersheim, Ger. 51/H5
Bad Goisern, Aus. 43/K3
Bad Grund, Ger. 51/H5
Bad Hall, Aus. 55/H6
Bad Harzburg, Ger. 51/H5
Bad Heilbrunn, Ger. 57/H2
Bad Herrenalb, Ger. 54/B5
Bad Hersfeld, Ger. 43/H1
Bad Hofgastein, Aus. 43/K3
Bad Homburg vor der Höhe, Ger. 54/B2
Bad Honnef, Ger. 53/G2
Bad Hönningen, Ger. 53/G2
Bad Ischl, Aus. 43/K3
Bad Karlshafen, Ger. 51/G5
Bad Kissingen, Ger. 54/D2
Bad Kohlgrub, Ger. 57/H2
Bad König, Ger. 54/C3
Bad Königshofen, Ger. 54/D2
Bad Kreuznach, Ger. 53/G4
Bad Krozingen, Ger. 56/D2
Bad Langensalza, Ger. 51/H6
Bad Lauterberg, Ger. 51/H5
Bad Leonfelden, Aus. 55/H5
Bad Liebenzell, Ger. 54/B5
Bad Lippspringe, Ger. 51/F3
Bad Marienberg, Ger. 53/G2
Bad Mergentheim, Ger. 54/C4
Bad Munder am Deister, Ger. 51/G4
Bad Nauheim, Ger. 54/B2
Bad Nenndorf, Ger. 51/G4
Bad Neuenahr-Ahrweiler, Ger. 53/G2
Bad Neustadt an der Saale, Ger. 54/D2
Bad Oeynhausen, Ger. 51/F4
Bad Orb, Ger. 54/C2
Bad Peterstal-Griesbach, Ger. 56/E1
Bad Plaas, SAfr. 107/E2
Bad Pyrmont, Ger. 51/G5
Bad Ragaz, Swi. 57/F3
Bad Rappenau, Ger. 54/C4
Bad Reichenhall, Ger. 43/K3
Bad Rothenfelde, Ger. 51/F4
Bad Sachsa, Ger. 51/H5
Bad Salzdetfurth, Ger. 51/G4
Bad Salzschlirf, Ger. 54/C1
Bad Salzuflen, Ger. 51/F4
Bad Salzungen, Ger. 40/F3
Bad Sankt-Leonhard im Lavanttal, Aus. 43/L3
Bad Sassendorf, Ger. 51/F3
Bad Schallerbach, Aus. 55/G6
Bad Schwalbach, Ger. 53/H3
Bad Schwartau, Ger. 38/D5
Bad Segeberg, Ger. 38/D5
Bad Soden-Salmünster, Ger. 54/C2
Bad Sooden-Allendorf, Ger. 51/G6
Bad Tölz, Ger. 57/H2
Bad Vilbel, Ger. 54/B2
Bad Vöslau, Aus. 43/M3
Bad Waldsee, Ger. 57/F2
Bad Wildungen, Ger. 51/F6
Bad Wimpfen, Ger. 54/C4
Bad Wimsbach-Neydharting, Aus. 55/G6
Bad Windsheim, Ger. 54/D3
Bad Wörishofen, Ger. 57/G1
Bad Wurzach, Ger. 57/F2
Bad Zell, Aus. 55/H6
Bad Zwischenahn, Ger. 51/F2
Badagara, India 82/C5
Badain Jaran (des.), China 70/H3
Badajoz, Sp. 44/B3
Badalona, Sp. 45/L7
Badalucco, It. 58/A5
Badbergen, Ger. 51/F4
Baddeckenstedt, Ger. 51/H4
Baddomalhi, Pak. 86/C4
Baden, Aus. 43/M2
Baden, Swi. 57/E3
Baden-Baden, Ger. 54/B5
Baden-Württemberg (state), Ger. 43/H2
Badener (peak), Ger. 54/B5
Badenoch (reg.), Sc, UK 36/B3
Badenweiler, Ger. 56/D2

Badgastein, Aus. 43/K3
Badgingarra NP, Austl. 112/B4
Badia Polesine, It. 59/E2
Badiar, PN du, Gui. 102/B3
Badile (peak), It. 57/F5
Badīn, Pak. 89/J4
Badiraguato, Mex. 142/D3
Badlands (plat.), SD, US 127/H5
Badlands NP, SD, US 127/H5
Badonviller, Fr. 56/C1
Badou, Togo 103/F5
Badovinci, Serb. 48/D3
Bādrah, Iraq 89/J3
Badrah, Iraq 88/E2
Badua (riv.), India 85/F3
Badulla, SrL. 82/D6
Badurīa, India 85/G4
Baena, Sp. 44/C4
Baependi, Braz. 211/J6
Baerenkopf (peak), Fr. 56/C2
Baesweiler, Ger. 53/F2
Baeza, Sp. 44/D4
Baffa, Pak. 86/B2
Baffin (bay), Can.,Grld. 119/K2
Baffin (isl.), Can. 123/H1
Baffin (bay), Tx, US 132/D5
Bafia, Camr. 96/H7
Bafilo, Togo 103/F4
Bafing (riv.), Gui. 96/C5
Bafoulabé, Mali 102/C3
Bafoussam, Camr. 96/H6
Bafq, Iran 89/G2
Bafra, Turk. 90/C1
Bafra (cape), Turk. 90/C1
Bāft, Iran 89/G3
Bag Salt (lake), China 72/B3
Bagaces, CR 144/E4
Bagadó, Col. 152/B3
Bagaha, India 85/E2
Bagamoyo, Tanz. 104/C4
Baganga, Phil. 79/E6
Bagda (mts.), China 70/E3
Bagé, Braz. 157/F3
Bagenkop, Den. 38/D4
Baggao, Phil. 79/D4
Baggy (pt.), Eng, UK 32/B4
Bagh, Pak. 86/B4
Baghain (riv.), India 84/C3
Baghdād (Baghdad) (cap.), Iraq 90/F3
Bagheria, It. 46/C3
Baghlān, Afg. 89/J1
Bāghpat, India 86/D5
Bagirpaşa (peak), Turk. 90/D2
Bagley, Mn, US 127/K4
Baglun, Nepal 84/D1
Bāgmati (riv.), India 85/E3
Bāgmati (zone), Nepal 85/E2
Bagn, Nor. 38/C1
Bagnacavallo, It. 59/F4
Bagnasco, It. 58/B4
Bagnères-de-Bigorre, Fr. 42/D5
Bagnères-de-Luchon, Fr. 42/D5
Bagneux, Fr. 30/J5
Bagni di Lucca, It. 58/D4
Bagno a Ripoli, It. 59/E5
Bagnolet, Fr. 30/K5
Bagnoli Irpino, It. 46/D2
Bagnolo Cremasco, It. 58/C2
Bagnolo in Piano, It. 59/D3
Bagnolo Mella, It. 58/D2
Bagnolo San Vito, It. 59/D2
Bagnols-sur-Cèze, Fr. 42/F4
Bagnone, It. 58/C4
Bago, Phil. 79/D5
Bago (div.), Myan. 70/G8
Bago (Pegu), Myan. 83/G4
Bagoé (riv.), Mali 102/D3
Bagolino, It. 58/D1
Bagua Grande, Peru 156/B2
Baguio, Phil. 79/D4
Baguirmi (reg.), Chad 96/J5
Bagzane (peak), Niger 103/H2
Bāh, India 84/B2
Bahādurganj, India 85/F2
Bahādurgarh, India 86/D5
Bahamas, The (ctry.) 141/F2
Bahāwalnagar, Pak. 86/B5
Bahāwalpur, Pak. 86/B5
Bahçe, Turk. 90/D2
Bahçesaray, Turk. 90/F2
Baheri, India 84/B1
Bahi (swamp), Tanz. 104/B4
Bahia (state), Braz. 154/B4
Bahía Asunción, Mex. 142/B3
Bahía de Caráquez, Ecu. 152/A5
Bahía de los Angeles, Mex. 142/B2
Bahía de Tortugas, Mex. 142/B3
Bahía, Islas de la (isls.), Hon. 140/D4
Bahía Solano, Col. 152/B3
Bahār Dar, Eth. 97/N5
Bahjoi, India 84/B1
Bahlah, Oman 88/F4
Bahr al 'Arab (riv.), Sudan 97/L6
Bahr al Milḥ (lake), Iraq 90/E3
Bahraich, India 84/D2
Bahrain (ctry.) 88/F3
Bahrain, Gulf of (gulf), Asia 88/F3

Baia de Aramă, Rom. 49/F3
Baia Mare, Rom. 49/F2
Baia Sprie, Rom. 49/G2
Bălan, Rom. 49/G2
Baïbokoum, Chad 96/J6
Baicheng, China 70/D3
Baicheng, China 71/M2
Băicoi, Rom. 49/G3
Baidong (lake), China 72/D5
Baie-Comeau, Qu, Can. 131/G1
Baie-Saint-Paul, Qu, Can. 131/G2
Baienfurt, Ger. 57/F2
Baiersbronn, Ger. 54/B5
Baiersdorf, Ger. 54/E3
Baigorrita, Arg. 158/E2
Baigou (riv.), China 72/G7
Baihar, India 84/C4
Baihua (mtn.), China 72/G7
Ba'ījī, Iraq 90/E3
Baikunthpur, India 84/D4
Bailadores, Ven. 152/D2
Baildon, Eng, UK 35/G4
Băile Govora, Rom. 49/G3
Băile Herculane, Rom. 48/F3
Băile Olăneşti, Rom. 49/G3
Băile Tuşnad, Rom. 49/G2
Bailén, Sp. 44/D3
Băileşti, Rom. 48/F3
Bailieborough, Ire. 31/Q10
Bailleul, Fr. 52/B2
Bailong (riv.), China 70/H5
Bailu (riv.), China 72/C4
Baima, China 70/H5
Bain (riv.), Eng, UK 35/H5
Bainang, China 85/G1
Bainbridge, Ga, US 133/G4
Bainbridge (isl.), Wa, US 135/B2
Bainbridge Naval Training Sta., Md, US 138/B4
Baingoin, China 70/E5
Bains-les-Bains, Fr. 56/C2
Bairāgnia, India 85/E2
Baird (inlet), Ak, US 134/F3
Baird, Tx, US 129/H4
Bairin Youqi, China 71/L3
Bairnsdale, Austl. 115/C3
Baïse (riv.), Fr. 42/D5
Baixa da Banheira, Port. 45/P10
Baixa Grande, Braz. 154/B4
Baixiang, China 72/C3
Baixo Guandu, Braz. 155/D1
Baiyin, China 70/H4
Baiyu (mts.), China 72/B3
Baiyun (int'l arpt.), China 79/B3
Baja, Mex. 142/B2
Baja, Hun. 48/D2
Baja (pt.), Chile 159/B6
Baja California (state), Mex. 142/B2
Baja California (pen.), Mex. 142/B2
Baja California Sur (state), Mex. 142/B2
Bāja (gov.), Tun. 46/A4
Bâjah, Tun. 100/L6
Bajánsenye, Hun. 40/M3
Bajestän, Iran 89/G2
Bājil, Yem. 88/D5
Bajina Bašta, Serb. 48/D4
Bajmok, Serb. 48/D3
Bajo Boquete, Pan. 145/F4
Bajo de Gualicho (plain), Arg. 157/C5
Bajram Curri, Alb. 47/G1
Bakanas (riv.), Kaz. 87/D3
Bakanas, Trkm. 87/B4
Bakau, Gam. 102/A3
Bakayan (peak), Indo. 81/E3
Bakel, Sen. 102/B3
Baker (lake), Nun., Can. 122/G2
Baker (riv.), Chile 159/B5
Baker (isl.), Pac., US 117/H4
Baker, La, US 129/K5
Baker, Mt, US 127/G4
Baker City, US 126/D4
Baker Lake, Nun., Can. 122/G2
Bakersfield, Ca, US 128/C4
Bakhchysaray, Ukr. 62/E2
Bakhmach, Ukr. 62/E2
Bakhtarän, Iran 88/E2
Bakhtiyärpur, India 85/E3
Bakhuis (mts.), Sur. 153/G4
Bakkafloi (bay), Ice. 37/P6
Baklan, Turk. 90/B2
Bakonyszombathely, Hun. 48/C2
Bakora Corridor Game Rsv., Ugan. 104/B2
Bakovský Potok (riv.), Czh. 55/G2
Bakoye (riv.), Gui. 102/C4
Baku (int'l arpt.), Azer. 63/J4
Baku (cap.), Azer. 63/J4
Bala, Wal, UK 34/E6
Balā, Turk. 90/C2
Balabac (str.), Malay.,Ph 81/E2
Balabac (isl.), Phil. 81/E2
Ba'labakk, Leb. 91/E2
Bālāghāt, India 84/C5
Balaguer, Sp. 45/F2
Balaïtous (peak), Fr. 42/C5
Balaka, Malw. 105/F3
Balakhna, Rus. 63/G1
Balaklava, Austl. 113/H5

Balakovo, Rus. 63/H1
Bal'amā, Jor. 91/E3
Balancán, Mex. 144/D2
Balanga, Phil. 79/D5
Balao, Ecu. 156/B1
Bālāngīr, India 82/D3
Balarāmpur, India 85/F4
Balashikha, Rus. 61/W9
Balashov, Rus. 63/G2
Balasore (Baleshwar), India 82/E3
Balassagyarmat, Hun. 41/K4
Balaton (lake), Cro. 48/C2
Balatonföldvár, Hun. 48/C2
Balatonfüred, Hun. 48/C2
Balatonszabadi, Hun. 48/D2
Balatonszentgyörgy, Hun. 48/C2
Balbina (res.), Braz. 147/D3
Balcarce, Arg. 158/F3
Balclutha, NZ 117/R12
Balcones Escarpment (plat.), Tx, US 137/T20
Balcones Heights, Tx, US 137/T21
Bald (riv.), Austl. 112/C5
Bald Eagle Mtn. (mtn.), Pa, US 138/A1
Bald Rock NP, Austl. 115/E1
Baldock, Eng, UK 33/F3
Baldwin, NY, US 138/D5
Baldwin Harbour, NY, US 139/L9
Baldwin Park, Mo, US 137/N5
Baldwin Park, Ca, US 136/C2
Baldy (mtn.), Mb, Can. 127/H3
Baldy Beacon (peak), Belz. 144/D2
Bale Mountains NP, Eth. 97/N6
Baleares (Balearic) (isls.), Sp. 45/G3
Baleia, Ponta da (pt.), Braz. 154/C5
Baleine, Grand Rivière de la (riv.), Qu, Can. 123/J3
Baleine, Petite Rivière de la (riv.), Qu, Can. 123/J3
Baleine, Rivière à la (riv.), Qu, Can. 123/K3
Balen, Belg. 50/C6
Baler, Phil. 79/D4
Balerna, Swi. 57/E5
Balesta (riv.), Kenya 104/C2
Baleshwar (Balasore), India 82/E3
Balfour, SAfr. 106/E2
Balfron, Sc, UK 36/B4
Balgatay, Mong. 70/G2
Balhannah, Austl. 113/M8
Bali (sea), Indo. 80/D5
Bali (isl.), Indo. 67/L10
Bāli Chak, India 85/F4
Balice (int'l arpt.), Pol. 41/K3
Baliem (riv.), Indo. 81/J4
Balıkesir, Turk. 90/A2
Balıkesir (prov.), Turk. 62/C5
Balıkpapan, Indo. 81/E4
Balimbing, Phil. 81/E2
Baling, Malay. 83/H6
Balingasag, Phil. 79/D6
Bälinge, Swe. 38/G2
Balingen, Ger. 57/E1
Balk, Neth. 50/C3
Balkan (pol. reg.), Trkm. 87/B4
Balkan (mts.), Bul.,Serb. 27/F3
Balkhash (lake), Kaz. 87/D3
Ballagan (pt.), Ire. 34/B4
Ballaghaderreen, Ire. 31/P10
Ballangen, Nor. 37/F1
Ballantrae, Sc, UK 34/C1
Ballarat, Austl. 115/B3
Ballard (lake), Austl. 109/B3
Ballarpur, India 82/C4
Ballater, Sc, UK 36/C3
Ballaugh, IM, UK 34/D3
Ballens, Swi. 160/L
Ballia, India 85/E3
Ballina, Austl. 115/E1
Ballinamallard, NI, UK 34/B2
Ballinasloe, Ire. 31/P10
Ballinderry (riv.), NI, UK 34/B2
Ballingry, Sc, UK 36/C4
Ballinrobe, Ire. 31/P10
Balloch, Sc, UK 36/B4
Ballon, Col du (pass), Fr. 56/C2
Ballon d'Alsace (peak), Fr. 56/C2
Ballon de Sevance (peak), Fr. 56/C2
Ballwin, Mo, US 137/F8
Bally, Pa, US 139/
Ballycarry, NI, UK 34/C2
Ballycastle, Ire. 31/P9
Ballycastle, NI, UK 34/C2
Ballyeaston, NI, UK 34/C2
Ballygawley, NI, UK 34/A3
Ballygeary, Ire. 31/Q10
Ballygowan, NI, UK 34/C2

Ballyhaunis, Ire. 31/P10
Ballyheigue, Ire. 30/P10
Ballyliffin, Ire. 34/A1
NI, UK 34/B2
Ballymena (dist.), NI, UK 34/B2
Ballymoney (dist.), NI, UK 34/B1
Ballymoney, NI, UK 34/B1
Ballynahinch, NI, UK 34/C3
Ballynure, NI, UK 34/C2
Ballyquintin (pt.), NI, UK 34/C3
Ballyshannon, Ire. 31/P9
Balmaceda (peak), Chile 159/B6
Balmazújváros, Hun. 41/L5
Balmhorn (peak), Swi. 56/D5
Balmoral, Austl. 115/B3
Balmoral Castle, Sc, UK 36/C2
Balneário Camboriú, Braz. 155/B3
Balneario Claromecó, Arg. 158/E3
Balnearío de los Novillos, PN, Mex. 129/G5
Balochistān (reg.), Pak. 89/J3
Balonne (riv.), Austl. 109/D3
Balotra, India 89/K3
Balqash, Kaz. 87/G3
Balrāmpur, India 84/D2
Balrānald, Austl. 115/B2
Balş, Rom. 49/G3
Bálsamo (pt.), Ecu. 152/A5
Balsapuerto, Peru 156/B2
Balsas (riv.), Mex. 142/A5
Balsas (riv.), Mex. 143/F5
Balsthal, Swi. 56/D3
Baltanás, Sp. 44/C2
Bălţi, Mol. 49/J2
Baltic (sea), Swe. 37/F5
Baltic Spit (bar), Pol.,Rus. 39/H4
Baltimore, Md, US 138/B5
Baltimore (pt.), Braz. 154/C5
Baltimore-Washington (int'l arpt.), Md, US 138/B5
Baltiysk, Rus. 39/H4
Baltray, Ire. 34/B4
Baltrum (isl.), Ger. 51/E1
Balurghāt, India 85/G3
Balve, Ger. 51/E6
Balya, Turk. 62/C5
Balykshi, Kaz. 63/J3
Balzar, Ecu. 152/B5
Balzers, Lcht. 57/F3
Bam (prov.), Burk. 103/E3
Bam, Iran 89/G3
Bama Yaozu Zizhixian, China 83/J3
Bamaji (lake), On, Can. 127/K3
Bamako (cap.), Mali 102/D3
Bamako (Senou) (int'l arpt.), Mali 102/D3
Bambamarca, Peru 156/B2
Bamban, Phil. 79/D4
Bambana (riv.), Nic. 145/E3
Bambari, CAfr. 97/K6
Bamberg, Ger. 54/D3
Bamberg, SC, US 133/H3
Bamble, Nor. 38/C2
Bambui, Braz. 79/D6
Bamenda, Camr. 103/H5
Bāmīān, Afg. 87/E6
Bāmīān (prov.), Afg. 87/J6
Bamingui-Bangoran, PN de, CAfr. 97/J6
Bammental, Ger. 54/B4
Bampūr (riv.), Iran 89/H3
Bampton, Eng, UK 30/A3
Ban Boun Tai, Laos 83/H3
Ban Chiang (ruin), Thai. 78/C2
Ban Houayxay, Laos 83/H3
Ban Kantang, Thai. 78/B5
Ban Kengkok, Laos 83/J4
Ban Pak Phanang, Thai.
Banaba (isl.), Kiri. 116/F5
Banagher, Ire. 31/Q10
Banamba, Mali 102/D3
Banana, Braz. 211/J7
Bananal, Braz. 211/J7
Bananal, Ilha do (isl.), Braz. 151/H6
Banar (riv.), Bang. 85/H3
Banarli, Turk. 49/H5
Banās (pt.), Egypt 101/C4
Banās (riv.), India 84/B3
Banat (reg.), Serb. 48/E3
Banatsko Novo Selo, Serb. 48/E3
Banaz, Turk. 90/B2
Banbar, China 70/G5
Banbridge (dist.), NI, UK 34/B3
Banbridge, NI, UK 34/B3
Banbury, Eng, UK 33/E2
Banc d'Arguin, Mrta. 98/A5
Banc d'Arguin, PN du, Mrta. 96/B3
Banc d'Arguin PN du, Mrta. 102/A2
Banchory, Sc, UK 36/C2
Banco Chinchorro (isl.), Mex. 140/D4
Bānda, India 84/C3
Banda (isls.), Indo. 81/H4
Banda, India 84/C3
Banda (sea), Indo. 67/M10

Banda Aceh, Indo. 80/A2
Bandai-san (peak), Japan 75/G2
Bandama (riv.), C.d'Iv. 96/D6
Bandama Blanc (riv.), C.d'Iv. 102/D4
Bandama Rouge (riv.), C.d'Iv. 102/D4
Bandar Beheshtī, Iran 89/H3
Bandar-e 'Abbās, Iran 89/G3
Bandar-e Anzalī, Iran 88/E1
Bandar-e Deylam, Iran 88/F2
Bandar-e Lengeh, Iran 89/F3
Bandar-e Māhshahr, Iran 88/E2
Bandar-e Torkeman, Iran 88/F1
Bandar Seri Begawan (cap.), Bru. 80/D3
Bande, Sp. 44/B1
Bandeira do Sul, Braz. 211/G6
Bandeira, Pico da (peak), Braz. 155/D2
Bandeirantes, Braz. 155/B2
Bandelier Nat'l Mon., NM, US 129/F4
Banderilla, Mex. 143/N7
Bandhavgarh NP, India 84/C4
Bandholm, Den. 38/D4
Bandiagara, Mali 102/E3
Bandipura, India 86/C2
Bandırma (gulf), Turk. 49/H5
Bandırma, Turk. 49/H5
Bandon, Ire. 31/P11
Bandon (riv.), Ire. 31/P11
Bandundu, D.R. Congo 105/C1
Bandung, Indo. 80/C5
Baneh, Iran 45/E3
Banes, Cuba 145/H1
Banff, Sc, UK 36/D1
Banff NP, Ab, Can. 126/D3
Banfora, Burk. 102/D4
Bang Lang (res.), Thai. 78/C5
Bañga, Phil. 79/D6
Banga, India 86/C4
Bangalore, India 82/C5
Bangalow, Austl. 114/D5
Bangarmau, India 84/C2
Bangassou, CAfr. 97/K7
Bangau (cape), Malay. 81/E2
Banggai (isls.), Indo. 81/F4
Banggi (isl.), Malay. 67/E5
Banghiang (riv.), Laos 78/D2
Bangka (str.), Indo. 80/B4
Bangka (isl.), Indo. 67/K10
Bangkok (int'l arpt.), Thai. 78/C3
Bangkok, Bight of (bay), Thai. 83/H5
Bangkok (Krung Thep), Thai. 78/C3
Bangladesh (ctry.) 82/E3
Bangor, NI, UK 34/C2
Bangor (int'l arpt.), Me, US 131/G2
Bangor, Me, US 131/G2
Bangor, Pa, US 139/E2
Bangor, Wal, UK 34/D5
Bangued, Phil. 79/D4
Bangui (cap.), CAfr. 97/J7
Bangweulu (swamp), Zam. 104/A5
Bangweulu (lake), Zam. 105/E2
Banhã, Egypt 91/B4
Banhine, PN de, Moz. 105/F5
Bani (riv.), Mali 96/D5
Bani, DRep. 141/G4
Banī Mazār, Egypt 101/B2
Banī Suhaylah, Gaza 91/D4
Banī Suwayf (prov.), Egypt 101/B1
Banī Suwayf, Egypt 101/B1
Bánica, DRep. 145/J2
Banifing (riv.), Mali 102/D3
Banihāl (pass), India 86/C3
Banikoara, Ben. 103/F4
Banister (riv.), Va, US 133/J2
Bāniyās, Syria 91/D2
Banja Koviljača, Serb. 48/D3
Banja Luka, Bosn. 48/C3
Banjarmasin, Indo. 80/D4
Banjul (cap.), Gam. 102/A3
Bānka, India 85/F3
Bankas, Mali 102/E3
Bankeryd, Swe. 38/F3
Bankfoot, Sc, UK 36/C3
Bankhead, Sc, UK 36/C3
Bānki, India 85/E4
Banks (str.), Austl. 109/D5
Banks (str.), NI, Can. 122/D2
Banks (pen.), NZ 109/H7
Banks (pt.), Ak, US 134/H4
Banks (isl.), Van. 116/F6
Banks (isls.), Van. 116/F6
Bankya, Bul. 47/H1
Banmankhi, India 85/F3
Bann (riv.), NI, UK 31/Q10
Bann (riv.), Ire. 31/Q10
Banna (riv.), It. 58/A3
Bannu, Pak. 86/A3
Baños, Ecu. 156/B1

Banpo Ruins, China 72/B4
Bansberia, India 85/G4
Bānsdīh, India 85/E3
Bānsi, India 84/D2
Bansin, Ger. 38/F5
Banská Bystrica, Slvk. 62/A2
Banská Štiavnica, Slvk. 48/D1
Bansko, Bul. 47/H2
Banskobystrický (pol. reg.), Slvk. 41/K4
Banstead, Eng, UK 30/C3
Bānswāra, India 89/K4
Bantayan, Phil. 79/D5
Banté, Ben. 103/F4
Bantenan (cape), Indo. 80/D5
Bantong Group (isls.), Thai. 78/B5
Bantry, Ire. 31/P11
Bañuelo (peak), Sp. 44/C3
Banyak (isls.), Indo. 80/A3
Banyoles, Sp. 45/G1
Banyuwangi, Indo. 80/D5
Banzare (coast), Ant. 160/J
Banzart (gov.), Tun. 46/A4
Banzart (Bizerte), Tun. 46/A4
Baode, China 72/B3
Baoding, China 72/H7
Baofeng, China 72/C4
Baoji, China 70/J5
Baojing, China 83/J2
Baokang, China 72/D4
Baoruco (mts.), DRep. 145/J2
Baoshan, China 83/G2
Baoshan, China 72/L8
Baotou, China 72/B2
Baoulé (riv.), Mali 96/D5
Baoying, China 72/D4
Bapaume, Fr. 52/D1
Bapchule, Az, US 137/S19
Baptistown, NJ, US 138/C2
Bāqa el Gharbiyya, Isr. 91/G7
Baqên, China 70/F5
Ba'qūbah, Iraq 90/F3
Bar, Serb. 47/F1
Bar (riv.), Fr. 40/C4
Bar Bigha, India 85/E3
Bar el Ksaïb (well), Mali 98/D5
Bar Harbor, Me, US 131/G2
Bar-le-Duc, Fr. 53/E6
Bar-sur-Aube, Fr. 42/F2
Bar-sur-Seine, Fr. 42/F2
Bara, Swe. 38/E4
Bāra Banki, India 84/C2
Bārā Lācha La (pass), India 86/D3
Barabai, Indo. 80/E4
Barabinsk, Rus. 87/G1
Baraboo, Wi, US 127/L5
Baracaldo, Sp. 44/D1
Baracoa, Cuba 145/H1
Barada (riv.), Syria 91/E3
Baradero, Arg. 159/J10
Baradine, Austl. 115/C4
Baragoi, Kenya 104/C2
Baraguá, Cuba 145/G1
Baragua, Ven. 152/D1
Barajas (int'l arpt.), Sp. 45/N9
Barajevo, Serb. 48/E3
Barākar (riv.), India 85/F3
Barakī Barak, Afg. 89/J2
Baralaba, Austl. 114/C4
Baram (cape), Malay. 80/D3
Baram (riv.), Malay. 80/D3
Barama (riv.), Guy. 150/F2
Baramanni, Guy. 153/G3
Baramula, India 86/C2
Bāran, India 89/L3
Baranagar, India 85/G4
Baranavichy, Bela. 62/C1
Baranoa, Col. 152/C2
Baranof (isl.), Ak, US 122/C3
Baranya (prov.), Hun. 48/C3
Barão de Cocais, Braz. 155/D1
Barão de Grajaú, Braz. 154/B2
Baraolt, Rom. 49/G2
Baraque de Fraiture (hill), Belg. 53/E3
Barat Daya (isls.), Indo. 81/G5
Barataria, La, US 137/P17
Barauli, India 85/E2
Baraut, India 86/D5
Baraya, Col. 152/C4
Barbacena, Braz. 155/D2
Barbacoas, Col. 152/B4
Barbados (ctry.) 141/P9
Barbalha, Braz. 154/C2
Barbaros, Turk. 49/H5
Barbas (cape), Mor. 98/A5
Barbastro, Sp. 45/F1
Barbate de Franco, Sp. 44/C4
Barbeau (peak), Nun. Can. 123/T6
Barberà del Vallès, Sp. 45/L6
Barberino di Mugello, It. 59/E5
Barbers (pt.), Hi, US 133/H3
Barberton, Oh, US 130/D3
Barberton, SAfr. 107/E2
Barbona (peak), It. 58/D5
Barbosa, Col. 152/C3
Barbourville, Ky, US 130/D4
Barbuda (isl.), Anti. 141/N8
Barcaldine, Austl. 114/B3
Barcarrota, Sp. 44/B3
Barcău (riv.), Rom. 48/F2

Barcellona Pozzo di Gotto, It. 46/D3
Barcelona, Ven. 153/E2
Barcelona, Sp. 45/L7
Barcelona (int'l arpt.), Sp. 45/L7
Barcelos, Port. 44/A2
Barcelos, Braz. 153/F5
Barcin, Pol. 41/J2
Barcoo (riv.), Austl. 109/D3
Barcs, Hun. 48/C3
Barczewo, Pol. 39/J5
Bardi, It. 58/C3
Bardīyah, Libya 97/L1
Bārdoli, India 89/K4
Bardolino, It. 59/D1
Bardonia, NY, US 139/K7
Bardsdale, Ca, US 136/B2
Bardsey (isl.), Wal, UK 34/D6
Bardstown, Ky, US 130/C4
Bareggio, It. 58/B2
Bareli, India 84/B4
Barellan, Austl. 115/C2
Barendrecht, Neth. 50/B5
Barentin, Fr. 52/D5
Barents (sea), Eur. 27/H1
Barentu, Erit. 88/C5
Barfleur, Pointe de (pt.), Fr. 42/C2
Barga, It. 58/D4
Bargara, Austl. 114/D4
Bargarh, India 82/D3
Bargfeld-Stegen, Ger. 51/H1
Bargi, India 84/B4
Bargteheide, Ger. 51/H1
Bārh, India 84/D2
Barharaj, India 84/D2
Barhalganj, India 84/D2
Barham, Austl. 115/B3
Barhiya, India 85/F3
Bāri, India 84/A2
Bari, It. 46/E2
Bari Sardo, It. 46/E3
Bariano, It. 58/C1
Baricella, It. 59/E3
Barichara, Col. 152/C3
Barigazzo (peak), It. 58/D4
Barika, Alg. 100/H5
Barillas, Guat. 148/C3
Barima (riv.), Guy. 153/G2
Barima-Waini (pol. reg.), Guy. 153/F3
Barinas (state), Ven. 152/D2
Barinas, Ven. 152/D2
Barinitas, Ven. 152/D2
Bariri, Braz. 155/B2
Barīsāl (pol. reg.), Bang. 85/H4
Barisan Mountains (mts.), Indo. 80/B4
Barito (riv.), Indo. 80/D4
Bāritu, PN, Arg. 157/D1
Bark (lake), On, Can. 130/E2
Bark (riv.), Wi, US 135/N13
Barker, NY, US 131/S9
Barki Saria, India 85/E3
Barking and Dagenham (bor.), Eng, UK 30/D2
Barkley (lake), Ky,Tn, US 133/G2
Barkley East, SAfr. 106/D3
Barkly Tableland (plat.), Austl. 109/C2
Barkly West, SAfr. 106/D3
Barkol Kazak Zizhixian, China 70/F3
Barlee (lake), Austl. 109/A3
Barlee (range), Austl. 112/B2
Barlee Range Nature Rsv., Austl. 112/B2
Barletta, It. 46/E2
Barlin, Fr. 52/B3
Barlinek, Pol. 41/H2
Barmedman, Austl. 115/C2
Barmera, Austl. 113/J5
Barmstedt, Ger. 51/G1
Barnala, India 86/C4
Bärnbach, Aus. 43/L3
Barnegat (inlet), NJ, US 138/D4
Barnegat (bay), NJ, US 138/D4
Barnegat, NJ, US 138/D4
Barnegat Light, NJ, US 138/D4
Barneveld, Neth. 50/C4
Barnhart, Mo, US 137/G9
Barnoldswick, Eng, UK 35/F5
Barnsley, Eng, UK 35/G5
Barnsley (co.), Eng, UK 35/G5
Barnstable, Ma, US 131/G3
Barnstaple (Bideford) (bay), Eng, UK 32/B4
Barnstorf, Ger. 51/F3
Barnsville, Pa, US 138/C2
Barntrup, Ger. 51/G5
Barnwell, SC, US 133/H3
Baroghil (pass), Pak. 87/F5
Baron, Fr. 50/B1
Barone (peak), It. 58/B1
Barow (riv.), Ire. 34/A5
Barowghil (pass), Afg. 89/K1
Barquisimeto, Ven. 152/D2
Barquisimeto (int'l arpt.), Ven. 152/D2
Barr (lake), Co, US 137/C3

Barr, Co, US 137/C3
Barr, Fr. 56/D1
Barra, Braz. 154/C3
Barra (isl.), Sc, UK 31/Q8
Barra Bonita, Braz. 155/B2
Barra Bonita, Represa de (res.), Braz. 155/B2
Barra da Choça, Braz. 154/B4
Barra del Colorado, PN, CR 140/E5
Barra do Bugres, Braz. 150/G7
Barra do Corda, Braz. 154/A2
Barra do Garças, Braz. 151/H7
Barra do Mendes, Braz. 154/C3
Barra do Piraí, Braz. 211/K7
Barra do Ribeiro, Braz. 155/B4
Barra Head (pt.), Sc, UK 31/Q8
Barra Mansa, Braz. 211/J7
Barra Velha, Braz. 155/B3
Barraba, Austl. 115/D1
Barrackpur, India 85/G4
Barrage de Lagdo (dam), Camr. 96/H6
Barranca, Peru 156/B2
Barranca, Peru 156/B2
Barranca de Upía, Col. 152/C3
Barranca del Cobre PN, Mex. 142/D3
Barrancabermeja, Col. 152/C3
Barrancas, Ven. 153/F2
Barrancas, Col. 152/C2
Barrancas, Chile 158/N8
Barranco de Loba, Col. 152/C2
Barrancos, Port. 44/B3
Barranquilla, Col. 152/C2
Barras, Braz. 154/B2
Barreal, Arg. 157/C3
Barreiras, Braz. 154/A4
Barreirinhas, Braz. 154/B1
Barreiro, Port. 45/P10
Barreiros, Braz. 154/D3
Barren (isls.), Madg. 107/G7
Barren (isl.), India 81/F4
Barren Islands (isls.), Madg. 107/G7
Barretal, Mex. 143/F3
Barretos, Braz. 155/B2
Barrhead, Ab, Can. 126/E2
Barrhead, Sc, UK 36/B5
Barrie, On, Can. 130/E2
Barrier (range), Austl. 113/J4
Barrington, Il, US 135/P15
Barrington Hills, Il, US 135/P15
Barrington Tops (peak), Austl. 115/D1
Barrington Tops NP, Austl. 115/D1
Barro Duro, Braz. 154/B2
Barron Gorge NP, Austl. 114/B2
Barroso, Braz. 155/D2
Barrow, Ak, US 134/G1
Barrow (isl.), Austl. 109/A3
Barrow (riv.), Ire. 31/Q10
Barrow (pt.), Ak, US 134/G1
Barrow (str.), Nun., Can. 122/G1
Barrow-in-Furness, Eng, UK 35/E3
Barrow Island, Austl. 112/B2
Barrowford, Eng, UK 35/F4
Barruelo de Santullán, Sp. 44/C1
Barry, Wal, UK 32/C4
Barsakel'mes (lake), Uzb. 87/C4
Barsinghausen, Ger. 51/G4
Barssel, Ger. 51/E2
Barstow, Ca, US 136/C3
Bartang (riv.), Taj. 87/F5
Barth, Ger. 38/E4
Bartholomä, Ger. 54/C5
Bartica, Guy. 153/G2
Bartın, Turk. 49/L5
Bartle Frere (peak), Austl. 109/D2
Bartlesville, Ok, US 129/J3
Bartlett, Il, US 137/F7
Bartlett (dam), Az, US 137/S18
Bartlett (res.), Az, US 137/S18
Bartolomé Masó, Cuba 145/G1
Bartolomeu Dias, Moz. 105/G5
Bartonsville, Pa, US 138/C2
Bartoszyce, Pol. 39/J4
Bartow, Fl, US 133/H5
Barú (vol.), Pan. 145/F4
Bāruipur, India 85/G4
Barumun (riv.), Indo. 80/A3
Barus, Indo. 80/A3
Barwa Sāgar, India 84/B3
Barwāha, India 89/L4
Barwāla, India 86/C5
Barwon (riv.), Austl. 109/D3

Barycz (riv.), Pol. 41/J3
Barysaw, Bela. 39/N4
Barysh, Rus. 63/H1
Barzanò, It. 58/C1
Bas-Rhin (dept.), Fr. 56/D1
Basaldella, It. 59/G1
Basauri, Sp. 44/D1
Bascharage, Lux. 53/E4
Basehor, Ks, US 137/D5
Basel, Swi. 56/D2
Basel/Mulhouse (int'l arpt.), Fr. 56/D2
Baselga di Pinè, It. 57/H5
Baselland (canton), Swi. 56/D2
Bashee (riv.), SAfr. 106/E3
Bashi (chan.), Phil.,Tai. 79/C3
Bashkortostan, Resp., Rus. 64/Q6
Bāsht, Iran 88/F2
Basilan (isl.), Phil. 81/F2
Basilan (peak), Phil. 81/F2
Basilica di Fieschi, It. 58/C4
Basilicata (reg.), It. 46/D2
Basingstoke, Eng, UK 33/E4
Basingstoke (canal), Eng, UK 30/A4
Basīrhāt, India 85/G4
Basīrpur, Pak. 86/B4
Başkale, Turk. 90/F2
Baskatong (res.), Qu, Can. 130/F2
Baskil, Turk. 90/D2
Basoda, India 84/A4
Basodino (peak), It. 57/E5
Basoko, D.R. Congo 96/K7
Basoli, India 86/C3
Bass (str.), Austl. 109/D4
Bass Rock (isl.), Sc, UK 36/D4
Bassae (Vassés) (ruin), Gre. 47/G4
Bassano, Ab, Can. 126/E3
Bassano del Grappa, It. 59/E1
Bassari, Togo 103/F4
Basse-Normandie (pol. reg.), Fr. 42/C2
Basse Santa Su, Gam. 102/B3
Basse-Terre (isl.), Guad. 141/J4
Basse-Terre, Fr. 141/N8
Bassecourt, Swi. 56/D3
Bassein (riv.), Myan. 83/F4
Bassein (Vasai), India 89/K5
Bassenge, Belg. 53/E2
Bassenheim, Ger. 53/G3
Bassenthwaite (lake), Eng, UK 35/E2
Basseterre (cap.), StK. 141/N8
Bassum, Ger. 51/F3
Basswood (lake), Can.,US 130/B1
Båstad, Swe. 38/E3
Bastak, Iran 89/F3
Bastām, Iran 89/G1
Bastelicaccia, Fr. 46/A2
Bastheim, Ger. 54/D2
Bastī, India 84/D2
Bastogne, Belg. 53/E4
Bastos, Braz. 155/B2
Bastrop, Tx, US 129/H5
Bat Shelomo, Isr. 91/F6
Bat Yam, Isr. 91/F7
Batabanó (gulf), Cuba 140/E3
Batac, Phil. 79/D4
Batai (pass), Pak. 86/A3
Batalha, Braz. 154/B2
Batalha, Port. 44/A3
Batang, China 70/G6
Batangafo, CAfr. 96/J6
Batangas, Phil. 79/D5
Batarasa, Phil. 79/C6
Batatais, Braz. 155/C2
Batavia, NY, US 130/E3
Batavia, Il, US 135/P16
Batavia, Rus. 62/F3
Batchawana, India 86/D5
Batdâmbang, Camb. 83/C4
Batéké (plat.), Congo 96/H8
Batemans Bay, Austl. 115/D2
Batesburg-Leesville, SC, US 133/H3
Batesville, Ms, US 129/K4
Bath, Me, US 131/G3
Bath, NY, US 130/E3
Bath, Pa, US 138/C2
Bath and Northeast Somerset (co.), Eng, UK 32/D4
Bathgate, Sc, UK 36/C5
Bathinda, India 86/C4
Bathurst, NB, Can. 131/H2
Bathurst (isl.), Austl. 115/B3
Bathurst (cape), NW, Can. 134/N1
Bathurst, Turk. 90/E1

Bathurst (inlet), Nun. Can. 122/F2
Bathurst Inlet, Nun. Can. 122/F2
Batian (Mt. Kenya) (peak), Kenya 104/C3
Batiquitos (lag.), Ca, US 136/C4
Batiscan (riv.), Qu, Can. 131/F2
Batley, Eng, UK 35/G4
Batlow, Austl. 115/D2
Batman, Turk. 90/E2
Batman (dam), Turk. 90/E2
Batna (prov.), Alg. 99/G2
Batna, Alg. 100/J5
Baton Rouge (cap.), La, US 129/K5
Batopilas, Mex. 142/D3
Batouri, Camr. 96/H7
Batra' (Petra) (ruin), Jor. 91/D4
Batsfjord, Nor. 37/J1
Batsto (riv.), NJ, US 138/D4
Batsto, NJ, US 138/D4
Batsto Historic Village, NJ, US 138/D4
Battaglia Terme, It. 59/E2
Battenberg, Ger. 51/F6
Bätterkinden, Swi. 56/D3
Batticaloa, SrL. 82/D6
Battipaglia, It. 46/D2
Battle, Eng, UK 33/G5
Battle (riv.), Ab,Sk, Can. 122/E3
Battle Creek, Mi, US 130/C3
Battle Mountain, Nv, US 126/D5
Battleford, Sk, Can. 122/E2
Battock (mt.), Sc, UK 36/D3
Batu (peak), Eth. 97/N6
Batu (isls.), Indo. 80/A4
Batu (bay), Malay. 80/D3
Batu Gajah, Malay. 80/B3
Batu Pahat, Malay. 80/B3
Batu Puteh (peak), Malay. 80/D3
Batudaka (isl.), Indo. 81/F4
Batuensambang (peak), Indo. 80/D3
Baturaja, Indo. 80/B4
Baturité, Braz. 154/C2
Batys Qazaqstan, Kaz. 64/E5
Bauchi (state), Nga. 103/H4
Bauchi, Nga. 103/H4
Baudette, Mn, US 127/K3
Baudó (mts.), Col. 145/G5
Baudó (riv.), Col. 152/B3
Bauer, Ut, US 137/J13
Baulmes, Swi. 56/C4
Bauman (peak), Togo 103/F5
Baumholder, Ger. 53/G4
Baunach, Ger. 54/D2
Baunatal, Ger. 51/G6
Baunei, It. 46/A2
Baurú, Braz. 155/B2
Bautzen, Ger. 41/H3
Bavans, Fr. 56/C3
Bavarian Alps (mts.), Aus.,Ger. 57/J2
Bavay, Fr. 52/C3
Baveno, It. 57/E6
Baviácora, Mex. 142/C2
Bavilliers, Fr. 56/C2
Bavispe, Río de (riv.), Mex. 142/C2
Baw Baw (mt.), Austl. 115/C3
Baw Baw NP, Austl. 115/C3
Bawang (cape), Indo. 80/C4
Bawean (isl.), Indo. 80/D5
Bawku, Gha. 103/E4
Baxoi, China 83/G2
Bay City, Mi, US 130/D3
Bay City, Tx, US 129/H5
Bay Minette, Al, US 133/G4
Bay Roberts, Nf, Can. 131/L2
Bay Saint Louis, Ms, US 133/F4
Bayamo, Cuba 145/G1
Bayamón, PR 141/M8
Bayan, Mong. 70/D2
Bayan Har (mts.), China 70/F5
Bayan-Hongor (prov.), Mong. 70/H2
Bayan-Ölgiy (prov.), Mong. 70/E2
Bayan-Ulaan, Mong. 70/H2
Bayanaul'skiy NP, Kaz. 107/T15
Bayanhongor, Mong. 70/H2
Bayanhushuu, Mong. 70/H2
Bayannuur, Mong. 70/H2
Bayano (lake), Pan. 145/G4
Bayanteeg, Mong. 70/H2
Bayantsagaan, Mong. 70/H2
Bayard, Ne, US 127/H5
Bayawan, Phil. 81/F2
Baybach (riv.), Ger. 53/G3
Baybay, Phil. 79/D5
Bayburt, Turk. 90/E1

Bayburt (prov.), Turk. 90/E1
Baydaratskaya (bay), Rus. 64/G2
Baydhabo (Baidoa), Som. 97/P7
Bayel, Fr. 56/A1
Bayerischer Wald (hills), Ger. 55/F4
Bayerischer Wald NP, Ger. 55/G3
Bayern (state), Ger. 40/F4
Bayeux, Braz. 154/D2
Bayeux, Fr. 42/C2
Baygorria (res.), Uru. 159/K10
Baykal (mts.), Rus. 65/L4
Baykal (lake), Rus. 67/L4
Baykan, Turk. 90/E2
Bayombong, Phil. 79/D4
Bayon, Fr. 56/C1
Bayona, Sp. 44/A1
Bayonet Point, Fl, US 133/H4
Bayonne, Fr. 42/C5
Bayonne, NJ, US 139/J9
Bayport, NY, US 139/E2
Bayramaly, Trkm. 89/H1
Bayramiç, Turk. 47/K3
Bayreuth, Ger. 55/E3
Bayrūt (cap.), Leb. 91/D3
Bayt Hanina, WBnk. 91/G8
Bayt Hanina, Gaza 91/G8
Bayt Lahm (Bethlehem), WBnk. 91/G8
Bayt Sahur, WBnk. 91/G8
Baytik Shan (mts.), China,Mon 70/E2
Baytown, Tx, US 129/J5
Bayville, NY, US 139/E8
Baza, Sp. 44/D4
Bazainville, Fr. 30/G5
Bazardüzü (peak), Azer. 63/H4
Bazaruto, Ilha do (isl.), Moz. 105/G5
Bazêga (prov.), Burk. 103/E4
Bazemont, Fr. 30/H5
Bazet, Fr. 42/D5
Bazhong, China 70/J5
Bazin (riv.), Qu, Can. 130/F2
Bāzpur, India 84/B1
Bazzano, It. 59/E3
Be, Nosy (isl.), Madg. 107/H6
Beach Haven, NJ, US 138/D4
Beachport, Austl. 115/D3
Beachwood, NJ, US 138/D4
Beachy (head), Eng, UK 33/G5
Beachy Head (pt.), Eng, UK 33/G5
Beacon, NY, US 139/E1
Beaconsfield, Austl. 114/C4
Beaconsfield, Eng, UK 33/F3
Beal (range), Austl. 114/A4
Bealanana, Madg. 107/J6
Beale (cape), BC, Can. 126/B3
Beampingaratra (ridge), Madg. 107/H9
Bear (isl.), Nor. 160/E
Bear (riv.), US 128/E2
Bear (mtn.), Ak, US 134/K3
Bear, De, US 138/C4
Bear (lake), Ut, US 124/D3
Bear Creek (lake), Co, US 137/B3
Bear River (bay), Ut, US 137/J11
Bear River Migratory Bird Refuge (nat'l wild. ref.), Ut, US 137/J11
Beardsley, Az, US 137/R18
Beardsley (canal), Az, US 137/R18
Bearma (riv.), India 84/B4
Bearpaw (mts.), Mt, US 126/F4
Bearsden, Sc, UK 36/B5
Beartooth (mts.), Mt,Wy, US 126/F4
Beas de Segura, Sp. 44/D3
Beasain, Sp. 44/D1
Beata (isl.), DRep. 145/J2
Beata (cape), DRep. 145/J2
Beatenberg, Swi. 56/D4
Beatty, Nv, US 128/C3
Beattystown, NJ, US 138/D2
Beau Bassin-Rose Hill, Mrts. 107/T15
Beaucaire, Fr. 42/F5
Beaucamps-le-Vieux, Fr. 30/J4
Beauchamp, Fr. 30/J4
Beaucourt, Fr. 56/C3
Beaudesert, Austl. 114/D4
Beaufort (sea), Can.,US 119/C2
Beaufort, Fr. 56/D1
Beaufort, Lux. 53/F4
Beaufort, SC, US 133/H3
Beaufort West, SAfr. 106/C4

Beaugency, Fr. 42/D3
Beaujolais, Monts du (mts.), Fr. 42/F4
Beauly (riv.), Sc, UK 36/B2
Beauly, Sc, UK 36/B2
Beauly Firth (lake), Sc, UK 36/B2
Beaumaris, Wal, UK 34/D5
Beaume, Fr. 42/F4
Beaumont, Tx, US 129/K5
Beaumont, Ca, US 136/D3
Beaumont, Belg. 53/D3
Beaumont-de-Lomagne, Fr. 42/D5
Beaumont-sur-Oise, Fr. 30/J4
Beaune, Fr. 42/F3
Beaupréau, Fr. 42/C3
Beauquesne, Fr. 52/B2
Beauraing, Belg. 53/D3
Beaurainville, Fr. 52/A3
Beausejour, Mb, Can. 127/K3
Beautheil, Fr. 30/M5
Beautor, Fr. 52/C4
Beauvais, Fr. 52/B5
Beauval, Sk, Can. 126/E2
Beauval, Fr. 52/B3
Beauvoir, Fr. 30/L6
Beaver (lake), Ar, US 132/E2
Beaver (riv.), Yk, Can. 122/D2
Beaver (isl.), Mi, US 130/C2
Beaver (isl.), Ok, US 128/G3
Beaver (riv.), On, Can. 127/L2
Beaver, Ut, US 128/D3
Beaver Creek, Yk, Can. 134/K3
Beaver Meadows, Pa, US 138/C2
Beaver Springs, Pa, US 138/B2
Beaverhead (riv.), Mt, US 126/E4
Beaverlodge, Ab, Can. 126/D2
Beavertown, Pa, US 138/A2
Bebedouro, Braz. 155/B2
Beberibe, Braz. 154/C2
Bebington, Eng, UK 35/E5
Bebra, Ger. 51/G7
Becal, Mex. 144/D1
Beccles, Eng, UK 33/H2
Bečej, Serb. 48/E3
Becerreá, Sp. 44/B1
Bechar (prov.), Alg. 98/E3
Bechar, Alg. 99/E3
Becharof (lake), Ak, US 134/G4
Bechhofen, Ger. 53/G5
Bechtheim, Ger. 54/B3
Bechyně, Czh. 55/H4
Beckdorf, Ger. 51/G2
Beckenried, Swi. 57/E4
Beckingen, Ger. 53/F5
Beckley, WV, US 130/D4
Beckum, Ger. 51/F5
Beclean, Rom. 49/G2
Becs de Bosson (peak), Swi. 56/D5
Bedarieux, Fr. 42/E5
Bedburg, Ger. 53/F2
Bedburg-Hau, Ger. 50/D5
Beder, Den. 38/D3
Bedford (cape), Austl. 114/B2
Bedford, Qu, Can. 130/F2
Bedford, Eng, UK 33/F2
Bedford, In, US 130/C4
Bedford, SAfr. 106/D4
Bedford, Va, US 130/D4
Bedford Hills, NY, US 139/F1
Bedford Level (phys. reg.), Eng, UK 33/G2
Bedford Park, Il, US 135/Q16
Bedfordshire (co.), Eng, UK 33/F2
Bedlington, Eng, UK 35/G1
Bedonia, It. 58/C3
Bedouaram (well), Niger 96/H4
Bedretto, Swi. 57/E5
Bedsted, Den. 38/C3
Bedum, Neth. 50/D2
Bedworth, Eng, UK 33/F2
Beebe Seep (canal), Co, US 137/D3
Beechworth, Austl. 115/C3
Beek, Neth. 53/E2
Beelen, Ger. 51/F5
Beelitz, Ger. 40/P7
Beenleigh, Austl. 114/D4
Beer (pt.), Eng, UK 32/C5
Be'er Sheva', Isr. 91/D4
Beerfelden, Ger. 54/B3
Beernem, Belg. 52/C1
Beerzel, Belg. 53/D1
Beesel, Neth. 50/D6
Beeston, Eng, UK 33/F1
Beeville, Tx, US 132/D4
Befandriana, Madg. 107/J6
Befandriana, Madg. 107/J7
Beforona, Madg. 107/J7
Beg (lake), NI, UK 34/B2
Bega (riv.), Rom. 49/F3
Bega Veche (riv.), Cro. 48/E3
Bega, Austl. 115/D3
Begamganj, Bang. 85/H4
Begamganj, India 84/B4
Bégard, Fr. 42/B2
Begejci, Serb. 48/E3
Begichev (isl.), Rus. 65/M2
Begna (riv.), Nor. 37/D3

Begusarai, India 85/F3
Béhague (pt.), FrG. 151/H3
Behala (str.), Indo. 80/B4
Behāla, India 82/E3
Behamberg, Aus. 55/H6
Behat, India 86/D4
Behbahān, Iran 88/F2
Behenjy-Afovany, Madg. 107/H7
Béhoust, Fr. 30/H5
Behren-lès-Forbach, Fr. 53/F5
Behri (riv.), Nepal 84/C1
Behshahr, Iran 88/F1
Bei (riv.), China 79/A2
Bei (mts.), China 70/F3
Bei'an, China 71/N2
Beierfeld, Ger. 55/F1
Beigua (peak), It. 58/B4
Beijing (mun.), China 71/L3
Beijing (cap.), China 72/H7
Beijing Capital (int'l arpt.), China 72/H6
Beilen, Neth. 50/D3
Beiliu, China 83/K3
Beilngries, Ger. 55/E4
Beilstein, Ger. 54/C4
Beilun (pass), China 79/A3
Bein Tharsuinn (peak), Sc, UK 36/B1
Beindersheim, Ger. 54/B3
Beinn a' Chuallaich (peak), Sc, UK 36/B3
Beinn a' Ghlò (peak), Sc, UK 36/C3
Beinn a' Mheadhoin (lake), Sc, UK 36/B1
Beinn Bhàn (peak), Sc, UK 36/A3
Beinn Bheula (peak), Sc, UK 36/B4
Beinn Bhrotain (peak), Sc, UK 36/C2
Beinn Bhuidhe (peak), Sc, UK 36/B4
Beinn Bhuidhe Mhór (peak), Sc, UK 36/B2
Beinn Dearg (peak), Sc, UK 36/B1
Beinn Dearg (peak), Sc, UK 36/C3
Beinn Dòrain (peak), Sc, UK 36/B4
Beinn Eighe (peak), Sc, UK 36/A1
Beinn Heasgarnich (peak), Sc, UK 36/B3
Beinn Mholach (peak), Sc, UK 36/B3
Beinn Mhór (peak), Sc, UK 36/A4
Beinwil am See, Swi. 56/E3
Beipiao, China 72/G6
Beira, Moz. 105/F4
Beiru (riv.), China 72/C4
Beirut (int'l arpt.), Leb. 91/D3
Beitbridge, Zim. 105/E5
Beith, Sc, UK 36/B5
Beiuş, Rom. 48/F2
Beizhen, China 73/A2
Beja, Port. 44/B3
Beja (dist.), Port. 44/A4
Bejaïa (prov.), Alg. 100/H4
Bejaïa, Alg. 100/H4
Béjar, Sp. 44/C2
Bejhi (riv.), Pak. 89/J3
Bekabad, India 87/E4
Bekasi, Indo. 80/C5
Békés (prov.), Hun. 48/E2
Békés, Hun. 48/E2
Békéscsaba, Hun. 48/E2
Bekilli, Turk. 90/B2
Bekily, Madg. 107/H9
Bekitro, Madg. 107/H9
Bekwai, Gha. 103/E5
Bel Air, Md, US 138/B4
Bel Air South, Md, US 138/B4
Bela, India 84/D2
Bela, Pak. 89/J3
Bela, Slvk. 41/K4
Bela Crkva, Serb. 48/E3
Bela Cruz, Braz. 154/B2
Bela Palanka, Serb. 47/H1
Belá pod Bezdězem, Czh. 55/H1
Belá Pratāpgarh, India 84/C3
Bela Vista, Braz. 151/G8
Bela Vista, Moz. 107/F2
Bela Vista do Paraíso, Braz. 155/B2
Belair Rec. Pk., Austl. 113/M9
Belalcázar, Sp. 44/C3
Belang, Indo. 81/F3
Belarus (ctry.) 27/G3
Belaya (riv.), Rus. 64/F3
Belbo (riv.), It. 58/B3
Belchatów, Pol. 41/K3
Belchen (peak), Ger. 56/D2
Belcher (chan.), Nun. Can. 123/S7
Belcher (isls.), Nun. Can. 123/H3
Belchite, Sp. 45/E2
Belcourt, ND, US 127/H3
Beldānga, India 85/F3
Belebey, Rus. 61/M5
Beled Weyne, Som. 97/Q7
Belém, Braz. 154/D2
Belém de São Francisco, Braz. 154/C3

Belem Tower, Port. 45/P10
Belén, Arg. 157/C2
Belen, NM, US 128/F4
Belén, Chile 156/D5
Belen, Nic. 140/D5
Belen, Turk. 91/E1
Belen, Turk. 91/C1
Belén de Escobar,
Arg. 159/J11
Belene, Bul. 49/G4
Beles Wenz (riv.), Eth. 97/N5
Belesar, Embalse de
(res.), Sp. 44/B1
Belev, Rus. 62/F1
Belews Creek,
Mo, US 137/F9
Belfair, Wa, US 135/B3
Belfast (cap.), NI, UK 34/C2
Belfast (dist.), NI, UK 34/C2
Belfast, SAfr. 107/E2
Belfast, Me, US 131/G2
Belfast Lough (bay),
NI, UK 34/C2
Belfaux, Swi. 56/C4
Belfield, ND, US 127/H4
Belfort (dept.), Fr. 56/C2
Belfort, Fr. 56/C2
Belgioioso, It. 58/C2
Belgium (ctry.) 40/C3
Belgorod, Rus. 62/F2
Belgorodskaya Oblast,
Rus. 62/F2
Belgrade, Mt, US 126/F4
Belgrade (Beograd)
(cap.), Serb. 48/E4
Beli Drim (riv.), Serb. 47/G1
Beli Manastir, Cro. 48/D3
Beli Timok (riv.), Serb. 47/H2
Belitsa, Bul. 47/H2
Belitung (isl.), Indo. 80/C4
Belize (riv.), Belz. 144/D2
Belize (ctry.) 144/D2
Belize City, Belz. 144/D2
Beljanica (peak), Serb. 48/E3
Bel'kovskiy (isl.), Rus. 65/N2
Bell, Austl. 114/C4
Bell (pt.), Austl. 113/G5
Bell (pen.), Nun., Can. 123/H4
Bell (riv.), Qu., Can. 123/J4
Bell, Ca, US 136/F8
Bell, Ger. 53/G3
Bell Gardens, Ca, US 136/F8
Bell Rock (Inchcape)
(isl.), Sc, UK 36/D4
Bell Ville, Arg. 157/D3
Bella Coola, BC, Can. 126/B2
Bella Vista, Arg. 157/E2
Bellac, Fr. 42/D3
Bellaghy, NI, UK 34/B2
Bellagio, It. 57/F6
Bellano, It. 57/F6
Bellary, India 82/C4
Bellavista, Peru 156/B2
Bellavista, Peru 156/B2
Bellavista (cape), It. 46/A3
Bellavista, Ecu. 156/E7
Belle (riv.), On, Can. 135/G7
Belle-Anse, Haiti 141/D4
Belle Chasse, La, US 137/Q17
Belle Fourche (riv.),
Wy, US 127/G5
Belle Glade, Fl, US 133/H5
Belle Haven, Va, US 138/A6
Belle-Ile (isl.), Fr. 42/B3
Belle Isle (str.),
NF, Can. 131/K1
Belle Terre, NY, US 139/E2
Belleek, NI, UK 34/B3
Bellefontaine,
Oh, US 130/D3
Bellefonte, De, US 138/C3
Bellegarde-sur-Valserine,
Fr. 56/B5
Bellenberg, Ger. 57/G1
Bellenden Ker NP,
Austl. 114/B2
Belleplain, NJ, US 138/D5
Bellerive-sur-Allier,
Fr. 42/E3
Bellerose, NY, US 139/L9
Belley, Fr. 52/C5
Belleville, On, Can. 130/E2
Belleville, Fr. 56/A5
Belleville, Il, US 137/H8
Belleville, Mi, US 135/G4
Belleville, NJ, US 139/J8
Belleville-sur-Meuse,
Fr. 53/E5
Bellevue, Md, US 138/B6
Belley, Fr. 56/B6
Bellflower, Ca, US 136/F8
Bellheim, Ger. 54/B4
Bellignat, Fr. 56/B5
Bellinge, Den. 38/D4
Bellingen, Austl. 115/E1
Bellingham, Wa, US 126/C3
Bellingshausen (isl.),
FrPol. 117/K6
Bellingshausen (sea),
Ant. 160/U
Bellingwolde, Neth. 51/E2
Bellinzago Novarese,
It. 58/B1
Bellinzona, Swi. 57/F5
Bellmawr, NJ, US 138/C4
Bellmead, Tx, US 129/H5
Bellmore, NY, US 139/L9
Bello, Col. 150/C2
Bellona Reefs (reef),
NCal. 116/E7
Bellot (str.),
Nun., Can. 122/F1
Bellport, NY, US 139/F2
Bellshill, Sc, UK 36/B5

Belluno (prov.), It. 59/E1
Belluno, It. 43/K3
Bellville, Tx, US 129/H5
Bellvue, Co, US 137/B1
Bellwald, Swi. 56/E5
Belm, Ger. 51/F4
Belmar, NJ, US 138/D3
Belmez, Sp. 44/C3
Belmont, Ca, US 135/K11
Belmont, Braz. 154/C4
Belmonte, Sp. 44/D3
Belmonte, Sp. 44/D3
Belmonte, Port. 44/B2
Belmopan (cap.),
Belz. 144/D2
Belmullet, Ire. 31/P9
Belo Campo, Braz. 154/B4
Belo Horizonte, Braz. 155/C1
Belo Jardim, Braz. 154/C3
Belo-Tsiribihina,
Madg. 107/H7
Beloeil, Qu, Can. 131/P6
Beloeil, Belg. 52/C2
Belogorsk, Rus. 71/N1
Beloha, Madg. 107/H9
Beloit, Wi, US 127/L5
Beloit, Ks, US 129/H3
Belomorsk, Rus. 60/G2
Belorado, Sp. 44/D1
Belorechensk, Rus. 62/F3
Belören, Ger. 90/A2
Beloretsk, Rus. 61/N5
Belovo, Bul. 47/J1
Belovo, Rus. 64/J4
Beloye (lake), Rus. 64/D3
Belper, Eng, UK 35/G5
Belsand, India 85/E2
Belt, Mt, US 126/F4
Belterwijde (lake),
Neth. 50/D3
Beltheim, Ger. 53/G3
Belton, Tx, US 129/H5
Belton, Mo, US 137/D6
Beltsville, Md, US 138/B5
Belukha (peak), Rus. 70/E2
Belvedere, Ca, US 135/K11
Belvidere, NJ, US 138/C2
Belyando (riv.), Austl. 115/G3
Belyy (isl.), Rus. 160/A
Belzig, Ger. 40/G2
Beljyce, Pol. 41/M3
Bemaraha (plat.),
Madg. 107/H7
Bemarivo (riv.), Madg. 107/H7
Bembéréké, Ben. 103/F4
Bembibre, Sp. 44/B1
Bemboka, Austl. 115/D3
Bemetāra, India 82/D3
Bemidji, Mn, US 127/K4
Bemmel, Neth. 50/C5
Ben Aigan (hill),
Sc, UK 36/C1
Ben Alder (peak),
Sc, UK 36/B3
Ben Améra (well),
Mrta. 98/B5
Ben Avon (peak),
Sc, UK 36/C2
Ben Boyd NP, Austl. 115/D3
Ben Chonzie (peak),
Sc, UK 36/C4
Ben Cleuch (peak),
Sc, UK 36/D2
Bennan (pt.), Sc, UK 36/A6
Ben Cruachan (peak),
Sc, UK 36/A4
Ben Davis (pt.),
Sc, UK 133/J3
Ben Gurion (int'l arpt.),
Isr. 91/F7
Ben Hope (peak),
Sc, UK 31/R7
Ben Ime (peak), Sc, UK 36/B4
Ben Lawers (peak),
Sc, UK 36/B3
Ben Ledi (peak),
Sc, UK 36/B4
Ben Lomond (peak),
Sc, UK 36/B4
Ben Lomond NP,
Braz. 155/B4
Benton, Ar, US 129/J4
Benton, La, US 129/J4
Ben Lui (peak), Sc, UK 36/B4
Ben Macdui (peak),
Sc, UK 36/C2
Ben More (peak),
Sc, UK 31/Q8
Ben More (peak),
Sc, UK 36/B4
Ben More Assynt (peak),
Sc, UK 31/R7
Ben More (peak),
Sc, UK 31/R7
Ben Msik-Sidi Othmane
(prov.), Mor. 100/A2
Ben Nevis (peak),
Sc, UK 36/B3
Ben Rinnes (peak),
Sc, UK 36/C2
Ben Slimane, Mor. 98/D2
Ben Slimane (prov.),
Mor. 100/A3
Ben Starav (peak),
Sc, UK 36/B3
Ben Tee (peak),
Sc, UK 36/B2
Ben Tirran (peak),
Sc, UK 36/C3
Ben Tre, Viet. 78/D4
Ben Vane (peak),
Sc, UK 36/B4
Ben Vorlich (peak),
Sc, UK 36/B4
Ben Vrackie (peak),
Sc, UK 36/C3

Ben Wyvis (peak),
Sc, UK 36/B1
Ben Zohra (well), Alg. 98/E3
Benabarre, Sp. 45/F1
Benahmed, Mor. 98/D2
Benalla, Austl. 115/C3
Benalmádena, Sp. 44/C4
Benavente, Sp. 44/C1
Benavides, Tx, US 132/D5
Benbane (pt.), NI, UK 34/B1
Benbecula (isl.),
Sc, UK 31/Q8
Benbonyathe (peak),
Austl. 113/H4
Benburb, NI, UK 34/B3
Bend, Or, US 126/C4
Bendeleben (mt.),
Ak, US 134/F2
Bendemeer, Austl. 115/D1
Bendersville, Pa, US 138/A4
Bendigo, Austl. 115/C3
Bendorf, Ger. 38/C4
Bene Beraq, Isr. 91/F7
Benedict (mt.),
Nf, Can. 123/L3
Benediktbeuern, Ger. 57/H2
Benediktenwand (peak),
Ger. 57/H2
Beneditinos, Braz. 154/B2
Benenitra, Madg. 107/H8
Benešov, Czh. 55/H3
Benevento, It. 46/D2
Benfeld, Fr. 56/D1
Bengal (bay), Asia 67/H8
Bengal, Bay of (gulf),
Asia 70/E7
Bengbu, China 72/D4
Benghāzī, Libya 96/K1
Bengkalis, Indo. 80/B3
Bengkalis (isl.), Indo. 80/B3
Bengkayang, Indo. 80/C3
Bengkulu, Indo. 80/B4
Bengo (co.), NJ, US 138/B2
Bengough, Sk, Can. 127/G3
Bengtsfors, Swe. 38/E2
Benguela, Ang. 105/B3
Benguerir, Mor. 98/D2
Beni, D.R. Congo 104/A2
Bergkvek, Neth. 50/C6
Beni Abbes, Alg. 99/E3
Beni Bouayach, Mor. 100/C2
Beni Ensar, Mor. 100/B2
Beni Khiar, Tun. 100/M6
Beni Mellal, Mor. 98/D2
Beni Ounif, Alg. 99/E2
Benicarló, Sp. 45/F2
Benicia, Ca, US 135/K10
Benidorm, Sp. 45/E3
Benifayó, Sp. 45/E3
Benin (ctry.) 103/F4
Benin, Bight of (bay),
Afr. 93/C4
Benin City, Nga. 103/G5
Benisa, Sp. 45/F3
Benito Juárez, Mex. 142/D2
Benjamin, Tx, US 129/H4
Benjamin Constant,
Braz. 156/D2
Benjamin Hill, Mex. 142/C2
Benjamin, Isla (isl.),
Chile 158/B5
Benkei-misaki (cape),
Japan 76/B2
Benkelman, Ne, US 129/G2
Bennachie (hill),
Sc, UK 36/D2
Bennett (riv.), Rus. 65/O2
Bennettsville,
SC, US 133/J3
Bennington, Vt, US 130/F3
Bénoue, PN de la,
Camr. 96/H6
Bensensville, Il, US 135/Q16
Bensheim, Ger. 54/B3
Benson, Mn, US 127/K4
Benson, Az, US 128/E5
Benta (riv.), Hun. 49/Q10
Bentham, Eng, UK 35/F3
Bentley, Eng, UK 35/G4
Bento Gonçalves,
Braz. 155/B4
Benton, Ar, US 129/J4
Benton, La, US 129/J4
Benton, Pa, US 138/B1
Benton Harbor,
Mi, US 130/C3
Bentong, Malay. 80/B3
Benue (state), Nga. 103/H5
Benue (riv.), Nga. 93/C4
Benxi, China 73/B2
Benxi, China 73/C2
Beočin, Serb. 48/D3
Beograd (int'l arpt.),
Serb. 48/E3
Beohāri, India 84/C3
Beppu (bay), Japan 74/B4
Beppu, Japan 74/B4
Bequia (isl.), StV. 141/N9
Bequimão, Braz. 154/B1
Beraber (well), Alg. 96/E1
Beragh, NI, UK 34/A2
Beraketa, Madg. 107/H8
Berasia, India 84/A4
Berat, Alb. 47/F2
Beratus (peak), Indo. 81/E4
Beratzhausen, Ger. 55/E4
Berau (riv.), Indo. 81/E3
Berau (bay), Indo. 81/J4
Berbenno di Valtellina,
It. 57/F5
Berbera, Som. 97/Q5
Berbérati, CAfr. 96/J7
Berbice (riv.), Guy. 150/G2
Berceto, It. 58/C3

Berchem, Belg. 50/B6
Bercher, Swi. 56/C4
Berching, Ger. 55/E4
Berchtesgaden, Ger. 43/K3
Berchtesgaden, NP,
Ger. 43/K3
Berck, Fr. 52/A3
Berdorf, Lux. 53/F4
Berdsk, Rus. 87/H2
Berdyans'k, Ukr. 62/F3
Berdychiv, Ukr. 62/D2
Berea, Ky, US 130/C4
Berehove, Ukr. 41/M4
Berekum, Gha. 103/E5
Berenguela, Bol. 156/D5
Berenice (ruin), Egypt 101/C4
Beresford, SD, US 127/J5
Beresford, NB, Can. 131/H2
Berești, Rom. 49/H2
Berevo, Madg. 107/H7
Berezina (riv.), Bela. 62/D1
Berezniki, Rus. 61/N4
Berezovo, Rus. 64/G3
Bernville, Pa, US 138/B3
Beromünster, Swi. 56/E3
Beroroha, Madg. 107/H8
Beroun, Czh. 55/H3
Berounka (riv.), Czh. 41/G4
Berovo, FYROM 47/H2
Berra, It. 59/E3
Berre, Étang de (lake),
Fr. 42/F5
Berrechid, Mor. 98/D2
Berri, Austl. 113/J5
Berriane, Alg. 99/F2
Berridale, Austl. 115/D3
Berriedale, Sc, UK 31/S7
Berrigan, Austl. 115/C2
Berriozábal, Mex. 144/C2
Berrotarán, Arg. 158/D2
Berrouaghia, Alg. 100/G4
Berry, Austl. 115/D2
Berry (isls.), Bahm. 141/F2
Berry (pt.), Eng, UK 32/C6
Berry, mt.), Pa, US 138/A2
Berryessa (peak),
Ca, US 135/K9
Bersenbrück, Ger. 51/F2
Berthoud, Co, US 137/B2
Bertinoro, It. 59/F4
Bertiolo, It. 59/G1
Bertogne, Belg. 53/E3
Bertolinia, Braz. 154/B2
Bertoua, Camr. 96/H7
Bertrand (peak), Arg. 159/B6
Bertranville, La, US 137/Q17
Bertrix, Belg. 53/E4
Bertry, Fr. 52/C3
Beru (isl.), Kiri. 116/G5
Beruit (isl.), Malay. 80/B3
Berula (riv.), Malay. 80/D3
Bergues, Fr. 52/B2
Bergum, Neth. 50/D2
Bergume meer (lake),
Neth. 50/D2
Bergün-Bravuogn, Swi. 57/F4
Berguvika (lake), Swe. 38/G1
Berikat (cape), Indo. 80/C4
Bering (sea) 65/S4
Bering (str.), Rus.,US 67/U3
Bering Land Bridge
Nat'l Prsv., Ak, US 134/E2
Beringen, Belg. 53/E1
Beritarikap (cape),
Indo. 80/B4
Berja, Sp. 44/D4
Berk, Neth. 50/B5
Berkel (riv.), Ger. 40/D2
Berkeley, Ca, US 128/B3
Berkeley, Mo, US 137/G8
Berkeley Heights,
NJ, US 139/H9
Berkhamsted, Eng, UK 30/B1
Berkheim, Ger. 57/G1
Berkhout, Neth. 50/B3
Berkley, Mi, US 135/F6
Berkovitsa, Bul. 47/H1
Berks (co.), Pa, US 138/C3
Berkshire (co.),
Eng, UK 33/E3
Berkshire Downs (hills),
Eng, UK 33/E3
Berlaimont, Fr. 52/C2
Berlanga de Duero,
Sp. 44/D2
Berlare, Belg. 52/D1
Berleburg, Ger. 51/F6
Berlicum, Neth. 50/C5
Berlin (cap.), Ger. 40/Q6
Berlin (state), Ger. 40/Q6
Berlin, NH, US 131/G2
Berlin, NJ, US 138/D4
Berlin, Wi, US 127/L5
Bermagui, Austl. 115/D3
Bermejo, Bol. 157/D1
Bermejo (riv.), Arg. 147/D5
Bermeo, Sp. 44/D1
Bermillo de Sayago,
Sp. 44/B2
Bermuda (isl.), UK 119/L6
Bernalda, It. 46/E2
Bernalillo, NM, US 128/F4
Bernard (riv.),
NW, Can. 122/D1

Bernardo O'Higgins, PN,
Chile 157/B6
Bernardsville, NJ, US 138/D2
Bernau, Ger. 56/E2
Bernau, Ger. 40/Q6
Bernay, Fr. 52/A3
Bernburg, Ger. 40/F3
Berne (riv.), Ger. 51/F2
Bernes-sur-Oise, Fr. 30/J4
Bernese Alps (mtn.),
Swi. 43/G3
Bernhardswald, Ger. 55/F4
Bernice, La, US 129/J4
Bernier (isl.), Austl. 112/B3
Bernier (bay),
Nun., Can. 122/G1
Bernina (peak), Swi. 57/F5
Bernina (mtn.), Swi. 57/F5
Bernina, Passo del
(pass), Swi. 57/G5
Bernissart, Belg. 52/C3
Bernkastel-Kues, Ger. 53/G4
Betuwe (phys. reg.),
Neth. 50/C5
Betwa (riv.), India 84/B3
Betz, Fr. 30/L4
Betzdorf, Ger. 53/G2
Betzenstein, Ger. 55/E3
Beulah, Austl. 115/B2
Beulah, ND, US 127/H4
Beulah (lake),
Wi, US 135/P14
Beure, Fr. 56/C3
Beuningen, Neth. 50/C5
Beure, Fr. 56/C3
Beuvray (peak), Fr. 42/F3
Beuvron (riv.), Fr. 42/D3
Beuvronne (riv.), Fr. 30/L5
Beuvry, Fr. 52/B2
Bevensen, Ger. 51/H2
Bever (riv.), Ger. 51/G5
Beveren, Belg. 50/B6
Beveren (peak), Swi. 57/F4
Beverley, Austl. 112/C5
Beverley, Eng, UK 35/H4
Beverly, Ma, US 137/D5
Beverly Hills, Ca, US 136/F7
Beverly Hills, Mi, US 135/F6
Beverstedt, Ger. 51/F2
Beverungen, Ger. 51/G5
Beverwijk, Neth. 50/B4
Bevern (peak), Swi. 57/F4
Bewdley (riv.), Eng, UK 59/F4
Bewār, India 84/B3
Bewl Bridge (res.),
Eng, UK 33/G4
Bex, Swi. 56/D5
Bexar (co.), Tx, US 137/T21
Bexbach, Ger. 53/G5
Bexhill, Eng, UK 33/G5
Bexley (bor.), Eng, UK 30/D2
Beyçayırı, Turk. 49/H5
Beycuma, Turk. 49/K5
Beyne-Heusay, Belg. 53/E2
Beynes, Fr. 30/H5
Beyonesu-Retsugan
(isl.), Japan 75/F5
Beypazarı, Turk. 41/M7
Beysehir, Turk. 50/K3
Bezahala, Madg. 107/H8
Beypazarı, Turk. 41/M7
Bezau, Aus. 57/F3
Bezdan, Serb. 48/D3
Bezděz (peak), Czh. 55/H1
Bezdruc Rus. 62/F3
Bezhetsk, Rus. 60/H4
Béziers, Fr. 42/E5
Bhabua, India 84/D3
Bhadarwāh, India 84/D1
Bhadaur, India 86/C4
Bhadohī, India 84/C3
Bhādra, India 84/B5
Bhadrak, India 82/F3
Bhadra (riv.), India 82/F3
Bhagalpur, India 85/F3
Bhāgalpur, India 85/F3
Bhai Pheru, Pak. 86/B3
Bhairab, Bang. 85/G4
Bhairab Bāzār, Bang. 85/H3
Bhakkar, Pak. 86/A4
Bhākra (dam), India 84/C5
Bhaktapur, Nepal 86/B3
Bhalwal, Pak. 86/B3
Bhamo, Myan. 83/G3
Bhānder, India 84/A3
Bhānrer (range), India 82/A3
Bhānwad, India 82/A3
Bharatpur, Nepal 84/A3
Bhāratpur, India 84/B2
Bharthana, India 84/B2
Bharuch, India 89/K4
Bhasāwar, India 84/A3
Bhatinda, India 86/C4
Bhātpāra, India 82/D3
Bhatkal, India 84/K6
Bhātpāra, India 85/G4
Bhavāni, India 89/K5
Bhavnagar, India 89/K4
Bhawāna, Pak. 86/B4
Bhawāni Mandi, India 89/L4
Bhera, Pak. 86/C3
Bheri (zone), Nepal 84/C2
Bhilai, India 82/D3
Bhilwāra, India 84/C3
Bhīma (riv.), India 89/L5
Bhima, India 89/L5
Bhimavaram, India 82/D4
Bhimunipatnam, India 82/D4
Bhinga, India 84/C2
Bhiwandi, India 84/B4
Bhiwāni, India 86/D5
Bhojpur, Nepal 85/F3
Bhokardan, India 82/C3
Bhola, India 85/H4
Bhongaon, India 84/B2
Bhopāl, India 84/B3
Bhor, India 89/K5
Bhraoin (lake), Sc, UK 36/A1

Bhuban, India 82/E3
Bhumibol (dam), Thai. 78/B2
Bhusawal, India 89/L4
Bi Doup (peak), Viet. 78/E3
Bi (riv.), Braz. 150/E4
Biá (riv.), Braz. 156/D2
Biá (riv.), C.d'Iv. 102/E5
Biafra, Bight of (bay),
Camr. 96/G3
Biak (isl.), Indo. 81/J4
Biak (int'l arpt.), Indo. 81/J4
Biała Podlaska, Pol. 41/M2
Biała, Turk. 90/B2
Biale, UK 32/C6
Białobrzegi, Pol. 41/L3
Białowieski NP, Pol. 41/K4
Białowieski NP, Pol. 41/M2
Białystok, Pol. 41/M2
Bianca, Sp. 44/B3
Biancavilla, It. 46/D4
Biandrate, It. 58/B2
Biandronno, It. 58/B1
Bianze, It. 58/B2
Biarritz, Fr. 42/C5
Biasca, Swi. 57/E5
Bibai, Japan 76/B2
Bibbiano, It. 58/D3
Bibbiena, It. 59/E5
Biberach, Braz. 155/B5
Biberach, Ger. 57/G1
Bihać, Bosn. 43/L4
Bihār, India 85/E3
Biharamulo, Tanz. 104/A3
Biharamulo Game Rsv.,
Tanz. 104/A3
Bihāriganj, India 85/F3
Biharkeresztes, Hun. 48/E2
Bihor (co.), Rom. 41/M5
Bihorel, Fr. 42/D2
Bihoro, Japan 76/D2
Bijagós, Arquipélago
do (isl.), GBis. 102/A4
Bijar, Iran 88/E1
Bijawar, India 84/B3
Bijbiara, India 86/C3
Bijeljina, Bosn. 48/D3
Bijelo Polje, Serb. 47/F1
Bijiang, China 83/G2
Bijie, China 83/J2
Bijni, India 85/H2
Bijnor, India 84/B1
Bikaner, India 89/K3
Bikar (isl.), Mrsh. 116/G3
Bikin, Rus. 71/P2
Bikin (riv.), Rus. 71/P2
Bikini (isl.), Mrsh. 116/F3
Bikramganj, India 85/E3
Bikuar, PN do, Ang. 105/C4
Bila Tserkva, Ukr. 62/D2
Bilāra, India 82/B2
Bilāspur, India 84/B1
Bilāsipāra, India 85/H2
Bilāspur, India 84/B1
Bilāspur, India 86/D4
Bilaukraung (range),
Myan. 83/G3
Bilauktaung (range),
Myan.,Thai 78/B3
Bilba Morea Claypan
(lake), Austl. 109/C3
Bilbao, Sp. 44/D1
Bilbays, Egypt 91/B4
Bileća, Bosn. 47/F1
Bilecik, Turk. 90/B1
Bilecik (prov.), Turk. 90/B1
Bifgoraj, Pol. 41/M3
Bilgram, India 84/C2
Bilhaur, India 84/C2
Bilhorod-Dnistrovs'kyy,
Ukr. 49/K2
Bilibino, Rus. 65/S3
Bilin (riv.), Myan. 78/B2
Bilina, Czh. 55/G1
Bilina, Czh. 55/G1
Bilina (riv.), China 73/B3
Bietigheim, Ger. 54/C5
Bietschhorn (peak),
Swi. 56/D5
Bill of Portland (pt.),
Eng, UK 32/D5
Bill Williams (riv.),
Az, US 128/D4
Bille (riv.), Ger. 51/H1
Billerbeck, Ger. 51/E5
Billère, Fr. 42/C5
Billiat Conservation Park,
Austl. 115/B2
Billiat Consv. Park,
Austl. 113/J5
Billigheim, Ger. 54/C4
Billinge, Eng, UK 35/F4
Billingham, Eng, UK 35/G2
Billings, Mt, US 126/F4
Billings, Mt, US 126/F4
Billitt, Braz. 155/E2
Billiton (isl.), Indo. 67/K10
Billund (int'l arpt.),
Den. 38/C4
Billund, Den. 38/C4
Bilma, Niger 96/H4
Biloela, Austl. 115/D3
Biloku, Guy. 153/G4
Biloxi, Ms, US 133/F4
Bilpa Morea Claypan
(lake), Austl. 113/H3
Bilqas Qism Awwal,
Egypt 91/B4
Bilston, Sc, UK 36/D5
Bilthar, India 84/B1
Biltine, Chad 97/K5
Bilzen, Belg. 53/E2
Bima (riv.), Indo. 81/E5
Bimberi (peak), Austl. 115/D2
Bimini (isls.), Bahm. 141/F2
Bin 'Arūs, Tun. 46/B4

Bin 'Arus (gov.), Tun. 46/B4
Bina (riv.), Ger. 55/F6
Bina-Etawa, India 84/B3
Binalong, Austl. 115/D2
Binasco, It. 58/C2
Binbrook, On, Can. 131/Q9
Binche, Belg. 53/D3
Binchuan, China 83/H2
Bindki, India 84/C2
Bindura, Zim. 105/F4
Binéfar, Sp. 45/F2
Binga (mtn.), Moz. 105/F4
Bingara, Austl. 115/D1
Bingen, Ger. 53/G4
Bingerville, C.d'Iv. 102/C5
Binghamton, NY, US 130/F3
Bingley, Eng, UK 35/G4
Bingöl, Turk. 90/E2
Bingöl (prov.), Turk. 90/E2
Binh Son, Viet. 78/E3
Binhai, China 72/D4
Binhon (peak), Myan. 83/G4
Binisalem, Sp. 45/G3
Binjai, Indo. 80/A3
Binkılıç, Turk. 49/J5
Binnaway, Austl. 115/D1
Binningen, Swi. 56/D2
Binongko (isl.), Indo. 81/F5
Bintang (peak), Malay. 80/B2
Binyamina, Isr. 91/F6
Bio-Bio (riv.), Chile 157/B4
Bio-Bio (pol. reg.),
Chile 158/B3
Biograd, Cro. 48/B4
Biogradska Gora NP,
Serb. 47/F1
Biogradska NP, Serb. 48/D4
Bioko (isl.), EqG. 93/C4
Biougra, Mor. 98/C3
Bipoint (Bissau)
(int'l arpt.), GBis. 102/B3
Bippen, Ger. 51/E3
Bir, India 89/L5
Bir Abu Minqâr (well),
Egypt 101/A3
Bir Aïdat (well),
Mrta. 98/C4
Bir Bel Guerdâne (well),
Mrta. 98/C4
Bi'r Ghadir (well),
Egypt 101/C3
Bîr Ounâne (well),
Mali 98/E5
Bi'r Zayt, WBnk. 91/G8
Birâk, Libya 96/H2
Birao, CAfr. 97/K5
Birâtnagar, Nepal 85/F2
Biratori, Japan 76/C2
Birch (mts.), Ab, Can. 122/E3
Birch Creek, Ak, US 134/Q2
Birch Hills, Sk, Can. 127/G2
Birch River, Mb, Can. 127/H2
Birchip, Austl. 115/B2
Bird Islet (isl.), Austl. 109/E3
Birds Rock (peak),
Austl. 115/D2
Birdsboro, Pa, US 138/C3
Birdwood, Austl. 113/M8
Birecik, Turk. 90/D2
Bîrganj, Nepal 85/E2
Biritiba-Mirim, Braz. 211/G8
Bîrjand, Iran 89/G2
Birkat Qârûm (lake),
Egypt 90/B4
Birken-Honigsessen,
Ger. 53/G2
Birkenau, Ger. 54/B3
Birkenfeld, Ger. 53/G4
Birkenhead, Eng, UK 35/E5
Birkenheide, Ger. 54/B4
Birkenwerder, Ger. 40/Q6
Birkirkara, Malta 46/L7
Birkkarspitze (peak),
Aus. 57/H3
Bîrlad, Rom. 49/H2
Birmingham, Eng, UK 33/E2
Birmingham (co.),
Eng, UK 33/E2
Birmingham (int'l arpt.),
Eng, UK 33/E2
Birmingham, Al, US 133/G3
Birmingham, Mi, US 135/F6
Birmingham, Mo, US 137/E5
Birmitrapur, India 85/E4
Birnam, Sc, UK 36/C3
Birnhorn (peak), Aus. 43/K3
Birni Nkonni, Niger 103/G3
Birnie (isl.), Kiri. 117/H5
Birnin Kebbi, Nig. 103/G3
Birobijan, Rus. 71/P2
Bîrpur, India 85/F2
Birr, Ire. 31/Q10
Birs (riv.), Swi. 56/D2
Birsk, Rus. 61/M5
Birstein, Ger. 54/C2
Biruaca, Ven. 153/E3
Birżai, Lith. 39/L3
Birżebbuġa, Malta 46/M7
Bis (isl.), Rom. 49/F4
Bisa-Nadi Nat'l Rsv.,
Kenya 104/C2
Bisai, Japan 77/L5
Bisalpur, India 84/B1
Bisamberg, Aus. 49/N7
Bisbee Douglas
(int'l arpt.), Az, US 142/C4
Biscarrosse, Fr. 42/C4
Biscarrosse,Étang de
(lake), Fr. 42/C4
Biscay (bay), Fr.,Sp. 27/D4
Biscayne NP, Fl, US 141/E2
Bisceglie, It. 46/E2
Bischberg, Ger. 54/D3

Bischheim, Fr. 53/G6
Bischofsgrün, Ger. 55/E2
Bischofsheim, Ger. 84/B3
Bischofsheim an der Rhön,
Ger. 54/D2
Bischofshofen, Aus. 43/K3
Bischofszell, Swi. 57/F3
Bischwiller, Fr. 56/D2
Biscubio (riv.), It. 59/F5
Biscucuy, Ven. 152/D2
B'shah (riv.), SAr. 88/D4
Bishkek (cap.), Kyr. 87/F4
Bishnupur, India 85/F4
Bishop, Ca, US 128/C3
Bishop Auckland,
Eng, UK 35/G2
Bishopbriggs, Sc, UK 36/B5
Bishop's Falls,
Nf, Can. 131/L1
Bishop's Stortford,
Eng, UK 33/G3
Bishopton, Sc, UK 36/B5
Bisingen, Ger. 54/B6
Biskra, Alg. 100/H5
Biskupiec, Pol. 39/J3
Bislig, Phil. 79/E6
Bismarck (cap.),
ND, US 127/H4
Bismarck, On, Can. 131/Q9
Bismarck (arch.),
PNG 116/D3
Bismarck (sea), PNG 116/D3
Bismil, Turk. 90/E2
Bismuna (lag.), Nic. 145/F3
Bispgarden, Swe. 37/F3
Bispingen, Ger. 51/G2
Bissau (cap.), GBis. 102/B4
Bissau, India 86/C5
Bissendorf, Ger. 51/F4
Bissett, Mb, Can. 127/K3
Bissingen, Ger. 54/D5
Bistagno, It. 58/B3
Bistriţa, Rom. 49/G2
Bistriţa (riv.), Rom. 49/G2
Bistriţa-Năsăud
(prov.), Rom. 49/G2
Biswän, India 84/C2
Blackwell, Ok, US 129/H3
Bita (riv.), Col. 150/E2
Bitam, Gabon 96/H7
Bitburg, Ger. 53/F3
Bitche, Fr. 53/G5
Bitkin, Chad 96/J5
Bitlis (prov.), Turk. 90/E2
Bitlis, Turk. 90/E2
Bitola, FYROM 47/G2
Bitonto, It. 46/E2
Bitter (lakes), Egypt 101/C2
Bitterfontein, SAfr. 106/B3
Bitterroot (range),
Id,Mt, US 126/E4
Bitti, It. 46/A2
Bitung, Indo. 81/F3
Bituruna, Braz. 155/B3
Biwa, Japan 77/K5
Bixby, Ok, US 132/E3
Biyalä, Egypt 91/B4
Biyang, China 72/C4
Bizard (isl.), Qu, Can. 131/M7
Bjärred, Swe. 38/E4
Bjelovar, Cro. 48/C3
Bjerkvik, Nor. 37/F1
Bjerringbro, Den. 38/C3
Bjørkelangen, Nor. 38/D2
Björklinge, Swe. 38/G1
Bjørnafjorden (estu.),
Nor. 38/A1
Bjorne (pen.),
Nun., Can. 123/S7
Bjugn, Nor. 37/D3
Bjuv, Swe. 38/E3
Blå Jungfrun NP, Swe. 38/G3
Blace, Serb. 47/G1
Blachownia, Pol. 41/K3
Black (sea), Asia,Eur. 67/C5
Black (bay), On, Can. 127/L3
Black (riv.), On. Can. 127/L2
Black (mt.), Yk, Can. 134/M3
Black (riv.), China,Vie 70/H7
Black (for.), Ger. 40/D5
Black (pt.), On, US 32/A6
Black (lake),
Austl. 109/D3
Black (peak), Swi. 56/D5
Black (cape),
Austl. 113/G5
Black (mesa), Az, US 128/E3
Black (cape), Mor. 98/A5
Black (cape), Peru 150/A6
Black (lake), Chile 159/C7
Black (pt.), Ct, US 139/F1
Black (mts.), NY, US 130/F3
Black (riv.), NY, US 130/F3
Black (hills), SD, US 124/F3
Black (riv.), Wi, US 127/L4
Blanco (cape), CR 144/E4
Black Canyon of the
Gunnison Nat'l Park,
Co, US 128/F3
Black Diamond,
Ab, Can. 126/E3
Black Diamond,
Wa, US 135/C3
Black Eagle,
Mt, US 126/F4
Black Forest (Schwarzwald)
(for.), Ger. 54/B6
Black Hawk, Co, US 137/B3
Black Jack, Mo, US 137/G8
Black Mountain NP,
Austl. 114/B1
Black Mtn. (mtn.),
Wal, UK 32/C3
Black Point, Ca, US 135/K10
Black River, Jam. 145/G2
Black River Falls,
Wi, US 130/B2
Black Rock (des.),
Nv, US 128/C2

Black Rock (pt.),
RI, US 139/G1
Black Sea Lowland (reg.),
Mol.,Ukr. 49/J3
Black Sugarloaf (peak),
Austl. 115/D1
Black Volta (riv.), Burk. 93/B4
Black Walnut, Mo, US 137/G8
Black Warrior (riv.),
Al, US 133/G3
Blackadder Water (riv.),
Sc, UK 36/D5
Blackall, Austl. 114/B4
Blackburn, Eng, UK 35/F4
Blackburn, Sc, UK 36/C5
Blackburn with Darwen,
(co.), Eng, UK 35/F4
Blackbutt, Austl. 114/D4
Blackcraig (peak),
Sc, UK 36/B6
Blackdown (hills),
Eng, UK 32/C5
Blackdown (hill),
Eng, UK 33/F4
Blackdown Tableland NP,
Austl. 114/C3
Blackfoot (res.), Id, US 126/F5
Blackheath, Austl. 115/D2
Blackmoor (upland),
Eng, UK 32/B5
Blackpool, Eng, UK 35/E4
Blackpool (co.),
Eng, UK 35/E4
Blackrod, Eng, UK 35/F4
Blackshear (lake),
Ga, US 133/H3
Blackstone, Va, US 130/E4
Blackville, NB, Can. 131/H2
Blackwater (riv.), Ire. 31/P10
Blackwater (riv.),
Eng, UK 30/A2
Blackwater (res.),
Sc, UK 36/B3
Blackwater (riv.),
Mo, US 129/J3
Blackwood (riv.),
Austl. 112/B5
Blackwood, NJ, US 138/C4
Bladensburg, Md, US 138/B6
Bladensburg NP,
Austl. 114/A3
Bladnoch (riv.),
Sc, UK 34/D2
Blaenau Gwent (co.),
Wal, UK 32/C3
Blagnac, Fr. 42/D5
Blagnac (int'l arpt.),
Fr. 42/D5
Blagny, Fr. 53/E4
Blagoevgrad, Bul. 47/H1
Blagoveshchensk,
Rus. 71/N1
Blaine Lake, Sk, Can. 126/G2
Blainville, Qu, Can. 131/N6
Blair, Ne, US 127/J5
Blair (hill), Pa, US 138/C1
Blair Atholl, Sc, UK 36/C3
Blairstown, NJ, US 138/D2
Blaise (riv.), Fr. 42/F2
Blaj, Rom. 49/F2
Blakely, Ga, US 133/G4
Blakeslee, Pa, US 138/C1
Blamont, Fr. 56/C6
Blanc (cape), Fr. 43/G5
Blanc (peak), Fr. 56/C6
Blanc (cape), Mrta. 96/B3
Blanc, Cap (cape), Tun. 46/A4
Blanc Nez (cape), Fr. 52/A2
Blanca (peak),
NM, US 129/F4
Blanca (pt.), Mex. 142/B2
Blanca (bay), Arg. 147/C5
Blanca, Cordillera (mts.),
Peru 150/C3
Blanca (mt.), Yk, Can. 134/H3
Blanca, Costa (coast),
Sp. 45/E4
Blanchard, Ok, US 137/M15
Blanche (lake),
Austl. 109/D3
Blanche (peak), Swi. 56/D5
Blanche (cape),
Austl. 113/G5
Blanco (cape), CR 144/E4
Blanco (cape), Mor. 98/A5
Blanco (cape), Peru 150/A6
Blanco (lake), Chile 159/C7
Blanco (riv.), Tx, US 129/H5
Blanding, Ut, US 128/F3
Blandy, Fr. 30/L6
Blanes, Sp. 45/G2
Blangy-sur-Bresle, Fr. 52/A4
Blankenberge, Belg. 52/C1
Blankenfelde, Ger. 40/Q7
Blankenheim, Ger. 53/F3
Blankenburg (bay), Nic. 145/F4
Blanquilla (isl.), Ven. 150/F1
Blanquillo, Uru. 159/G2
Blansko, Czh. 41/J4
Blantyre, Malw. 105/G3
Blantyre, Sc, UK 36/B5
Blanzy, Fr. 42/F3
Blaricum, Neth. 50/C4
Blas (peak), Swi. 57/F4
Blatná, Czh. 55/M5
Blato, Cro. 46/E1
Blatten, Ger. 57/E2
Blau (riv.), Ger. 54/C6
Blaubeuren, Ger. 54/C5
Blaustein, Ger. 54/C5
Blauvelt, NY, US 139/K7
Blåvands (pt.), Den. 38/C4

Blavet (riv.), Fr. 42/B3
Blaye, Fr. 42/C4
Blayney, Austl. 115/D2
Bleckede, Ger. 51/H2
Bled, Slov. 40/B2
Bléfjell (peak), Nor. 38/C2
Blégny, Belg. 102/D3
Bléharies, Belg. 52/C2
Bleicherode, Ger. 51/H6
Bleik (peak), Ger. 57/G2
Bleiswijk, Neth. 50/B4
Blekinge (co.), Swe. 37/E4
Blendecques, Fr. 52/B2
Blender, Ger. 51/G3
Blenheim, NZ 117/S11
Blénod-lès-Pont-à-Mousson,
Fr. 53/F6
Bléone (riv.), Fr. 43/G4
Blesberg (peak), SAfr. 106/C4
Blessington, Ire. 34/B5
Bletterans, Fr. 56/B4
Bleus (mts.),
D.R. Congo 97/L7
Bleus, Monts (mts.),
D.R. Congo 97/L7
Blida (prov.), Alg. 100/G4
Blida, Alg. 100/G4
Blies (riv.), Ger. 53/G5
Blieskastel, Ger. 53/G5
Blik (mt.), Phil. 81/F2
Blinnenhorn
(peak), Swi. 57/E5
Blithe (riv.), Eng, UK 35/F6
Blithfield (res.),
Eng, UK 35/G6
Block (isl.), RI, US 131/G3
Block Island C. G. Sta.,
RI, US 139/G1
Block Island (New
Shoreham), RI, US 139/G1
Block Island NWR,
RI, US 139/G1
Blodelsheim, Fr. 56/D2
Bloemendaal, Neth. 50/B4
Bloemfontein
(cap.), SAfr. 106/D3
Bloemhof, SAfr. 106/D2
Bloemhofdam (res.),
SAfr. 106/D2
Blois, Fr. 42/D3
Blomberg, Ger. 51/E1
Blomberg, Ger. 51/G3
Blomstermåla, Swe. 38/G4
Blonay, Swi. 56/C5
Blönduós, Ice. 37/N6
Bloodvein (riv.),
Mb,On, Can. 122/G3
Bloody Foreland (pt.),
Ire. 31/P9
Bloomfield, NJ, US 139/J8
Bloomfield, NM, US 128/F3
Bloomfield Hills,
Mi, US 135/F6
Bloomingdale,
NJ, US 139/H7
Bloomingdale, Il, US 135/P16
Bloomington, Mn, US 127/K4
Bloomington, Il, US 127/L5
Bloomington, In, US 130/C4
Bloomsburg, Pa, US 138/C2
Bloomsbury, NJ, US 138/D2
Blora, Indo. 80/D5
Blotzheim, Fr. 56/D2
Blountstown, Fl, US 133/G4
Bloxam (pt.), Md, US 138/B3
Blue (riv.), Ok, US 132/D3
Blue (mtn.), India 83/F3
Blue (mts.), Or,Wa, US 124/C2
Blue Island, Il, US 135/Q16
Blue Lake NP, Austl. 114/D4
Blue Marsh Lake (res.),
Pa, US 138/C3
Blue Mesa (res.),
Co, US 128/F3
Blue Mountain (peak),
Jam. 145/G2
Blue Mountain (ridge),
Pa, US 138/A3
Blue Mountains,
Austl. 115/D2
Blue Mountains NP,
Austl. 115/D2
Blue Nile (riv.),
Sudan, Eth. 97/M5
Blue Ridge (mts.), US 133/H3
Blue Ridge Parkway,
US 130/D4
Blue Springs, Mo, US 137/E5
Bluefield, WV, US 130/D4
Bluefields, Nic. 145/F4
Bluejoint (lake),
Or, US 128/C2
Bluenose (lake),
Nun., Can. 122/E2
Bluff, NZ 117/R12
Bluff (cape), Austl. 109/D4
Bluff, Austl. 114/C3
Bluff (peak), Austl. 112/C5
Blufftron, In, US 130/C3
Blümlisalp (peak),
Swi. 57/E5
Bludanci, FYROM 47/H2
Blyn, Wa, US 135/B1
Blyth, Eng, UK 35/H1
Blyth (riv.), Austl. 113/H1
Blythe, Ca, US 128/D4

Blytheville, Ar, US 129/K4
Bnom Mhai (peak),
Viet. 78/E4
Bo, SLeo. 102/C5
Bo, Nor. 38/C2
Bo Hai (Chihli) (gulf),
China 72/D3
Boa Esperança, Braz. 155/G2
Boa Esperança, Reprêsa
(res.), Braz. 151/J5
Boa Viagem, Braz. 154/C2
Boa Vista, Braz. 153/F4
Boa Vista (int'l arpt.),
Braz. 153/F4
Boa Vista (isl.), CpV. 93/K10
Boac, Phil. 79/D5
Boaco, Nic. 144/E3
Boadilla del Monte,
Sp. 45/N9
Bo'ai, China 72/C4
Boano (isl.), Indo. 81/G4
Boavita, Col. 152/C3
Boaz, Al, US 133/G3
Bobai, China 83/J3
Bobally, India 82/D4
Bobbili, India 79/D6
Bobbio, It. 58/C3
Bobenheim-Roxheim,
Ger. 54/B3
Bobigny, Fr. 30/K5
Bobingen, Ger. 57/G1
Böblingen, Ger. 54/C5
Boboshevo, Bul. 47/H1
Bobotov Kuk (peak),
Serb. 47/F1
Bobovdol, Bul. 47/H1
Bóbr (riv.), Pol. 41/H3
Bobrov, Rus. 62/G2
Boby (peak), Madg. 107/H8
Boca de Aroa, Ven. 152/D2
Boca del Guafo (chan.),
Chile 158/B4
Boca del Pao, Ven. 153/E2
Boca del Rio, Mex. 143/N7
Bôca do Acre, Braz. 150/D5
Boca Raton, Fl, US 133/H5
Bocaina, Serra da
(mts.), Braz. 211/J7
Bocairente, Sp. 45/E3
Bocas del Toro, Pan. 145/F4
Bocay (riv.), Nic. 144/E3
Bochil, Mex. 144/C2
Bochnia, Pol. 41/L4
Bocholt, Ger. 50/D5
Bocholt, Belg. 53/E1
Bochum, Ger. 51/E6
Bockau, Ger. 55/F1
Bockenem, Ger. 51/H4
Bockenheim an der
Weinstrasse, Ger. 53/H4
Bockhorn, Ger. 51/F2
Bockhorn, Ger. 55/E6
Bocono, Ven. 152/D2
Bocq (riv.), Belg. 53/D3
Boda, CAfr. 96/J7
Bodafors, Swe. 38/F3
Bodalla, Austl. 115/D3
Bodaybo, Rus. 65/M4
Boddam, Sc, UK 36/E2
Boddington, Austl. 112/C5
Bode (riv.), Ger. 40/F3
Bodega (bay), Ca, US 128/B3
Bodegraven, Neth. 50/B4
Bodélé (reg.), Chad 96/J4
Bodenheim, Ger. 54/B4
Boden (riv.), Ok, US 132/D3
Bodenkirchen, Ger. 55/F5
Bodenmais, Ger. 55/G4
Bodensee (Constance)
(lake), Swi 43/H3
Bodenteich, Ger. 51/H3
Bodh Gaya, India 85/E3
Bodhan, India 82/C4
Bodinäyakkanür,
India 82/C5
Bodio, Swi. 57/E5
Bodkin (pt.), Md, US 138/B5
Bodmin, Eng, UK 32/B6
Bodmin Moor (upland),
Eng, UK 32/B6
Bodo, Swi. 81/C4
Bodocó, Braz. 154/D2
Bodor, India 84/B2
Bodrog (riv.), Hun.,Slvk. 41/L4
Bodrum, Turk. 90/D2
Bódvaszilas, Hun. 41/L4
Boedecker (lake),
Co, US 137/B2
Boëge, Fr. 56/C5
Boegoeberg (peak),
Namb. 106/C2
Boekel, Neth. 50/C5
Boende, D.R. Congo 97/K8
Boerne, Tx, US 137/T20
Boeuf (riv.), La, US 129/K4
Bog of Allen (swamp),
Ire. 34/A5
Bogalusa, La, US 133/F4
Bogan (riv.), Austl. 109/D4
Bogan Gate, Austl. 115/C2
Bogandé, Burk. 103/E3
Bogatić, Serb. 48/D3
Bogatynia, Pol. 41/H3
Bogazkale-Alacahöyük NP,
Turk. 90/C1
Boğazlıyan, Turk. 90/C2
Bogdanci, FYROM 47/H2
Bogen, Nor. 37/F1
Bogense, Den. 38/D4
Boggabilla, Austl. 114/C1

Boggabri, Austl. 115/D1
Boggy (peak), Anti. 141/N8
Boglárlelle, Hun. 48/C2
Bogliasco, It. 58/C4
Bognor Regis, Eng, UK 33/F5
Bogny-sur-Meuse, Fr. 53/D4
Bogo, Phil. 79/D5
Bogong (mt.), Austl. 115/C3
Bogong NP, Austl. 115/C3
Bogor, Indo. 80/C5
Bogotá (cap.), Col. 150/D3
Bogota, NJ, US 139/J8
Bogovino, FYROM 47/G2
Bogra (pol. reg.), Bang. 85/G3
Bogra, Bang. 85/G3
Bográ, Mrta. 102/B2
Bohain-en-Vermandois,
Fr. 52/C4
Bohemia (reg.), Czh. 41/G4
Bohemian (for.),
Czh.,Ger. 40/G4
Bohicon, Ben. 103/F5
Böhl-Iggelheim, Ger. 54/B4
Böhme (riv.), Ger. 51/G3
Böhmenkirch, Ger. 54/C5
Bohmte, Ger. 51/F4
Bohu, China 70/E3
Bohuslav, Ukr. 44/D2
Boigne, Fr. 52/A2
Boiling Springs,
US 133/A1
Boipeba, Ilha de (isl.),
Braz. 154/C4
Boiro, Sp. 44/A1
Bois-d'Amont, Fr. 56/C4
Bois-d'Arcy, Fr. 30/J5
Bois de Boulogne
(dept.), Fr. 30/J5
Bois de Vincennes
(dept.), Fr. 30/K5
Bois-des-Filion, Fr. 131/N6
Bois, Rio dos (riv.),
Braz. 155/B1
Boisbriand, Qu, Can. 131/N6
Boise (riv.), Id, US 126/E5
Boise City, Ok, US 129/G3
Boissevain, Mb, Can. 127/H3
Boissy-Fresnoy, Fr. 30/L5
Boissy-L'Aillerie, Fr. 30/J4
Boissy-le-Châtel, Fr. 30/M5
Boissy-Saint-Léger, Fr. 30/K5
Boissy-Sans-Avoir, Fr. 30/H5
Boisville, Ger. 51/G3
Boj (plain), Kenya 104/C2
Bojador (cape), Mor. 96/C2
Bojano, It. 48/B5
Bojka (plain), Kenya 104/C2
Bojkovice, Czh. 41/J4
Bojnürd, Iran 89/G1
Bojnice, Slvk. 48/B5
Boka (riv.), D.R. Congo 93/K4
Bokaro Steel City,
India 85/F4
Boké (pol. reg.), Gui. 102/B4
Boké, Gui. 102/B4
Bokhol (plain), Kenya 104/C2
Boknafjorden (estu.),
Nor. 37/C4
Bokol (peak), Kenya 104/C2
Bokoro, Chad 96/J5
Bokpyin, Myan. 78/B4
Boksburg, SAfr. 106/Q13
Bokspits, Bots. 106/C2
Bolama, GBis. 102/B4
Bolangir, India 85/D4
Bolaños de Calatrava,
Sp. 44/D3
Bolaños (river),
Qu, Can. 131/H1
Bolbec, Fr. 42/D2
Boldești-Scăeni, Rom. 49/H3
Boldon, Eng, UK 35/H2
Bole, China 70/D3
Bole, Gha. 103/E4
Bolesławiec, Pol. 41/H3
Bolgatanga, Gha. 103/E4
Boli, China 71/P2
Boliden, Swe. 37/G2
Bolingbrook, Il, US 135/P16
Bolintin-Deal, Rom. 49/H3
Bolívar, Arg. 158/E3
Bolívar (dept.), Col. 152/C2
Bolívar, Ecu. 152/A4
Bolívar, Peru 156/B2
Bolívar, Mo, US 129/J3
Bolívar (pk.), Ven. 152/D2
Bolívar (state), Ven. 153/E3
Bolivia (ctry.), Bol. 151/D7
Bollate, It. 58/C1
Bollène, Fr. 42/F4
Bolligen, Swi. 56/D4
Bollin (riv.), Eng, UK 35/F5
Bollnäs, Swe. 37/F2
Bollullos Par del Condado,
Sp. 44/B4
Bolmen (lake), Swe. 38/E3
Bolobo, D.R. Congo 96/J8
Bologna, It. 59/E4
Bologna (prov.), It. 59/E4
Bologoye, Rus. 60/D4
Bolomba, D.R. Congo 97/J7
Bolonchén de Rejón,
Mex. 144/D2
Bolovens (plain), Laos 78/E3
Bolpur, India 85/F4
Bolsena (lake), It. 46/B1
Bol'shaya Kinel' (riv.),
Rus. 63/K1

Bol'shaya Rogovaya
(riv.), Rus. 61/P2
Bol'shaya Synya (riv.),
Rus. 61/N2
Bol'shevik (isl.), Rus. 67/H2
Bol'shezemel'skaya
(tundra), Rus. 61/N2
Bol'shoy Irgiz (riv.),
Rus. 63/J1
Bol'shoy Lyakhov (isl.),
Rus. 67/P2
Bol'shoy Lyakhovskiy
(isl.), Rus. 65/Q2
Bol'shoy Uzen' (riv.),
Rus. 63/J2
Bolsover, Eng, UK 35/G5
Bolsward, Neth. 50/C2
Bolt (pt.), Eng, UK 32/C6
Boltaña, Sp. 45/F1
Boltigen, Swi. 56/D4
Bolton, Eng, UK 35/F4
Bolton (co.), Eng, UK 35/F4
Bolu, Turk. 49/K5
Bolu (prov.), Turk. 49/K5
Bolungavík, Ice. 37/M6
Bolus Head (pt.), Ire. 30/N11
Bolvadin, Turk. 90/B2
Bôly, Hun. 48/D3
Bolzano, It. 57/H5
Bolzano-Bozen (prov.),
It. 57/H5
Bom Conselho, Braz. 154/C3
Bom Despacho,
Braz. 155/C1
Bom Jardim, Braz. 154/A1
Bom Jardin de Minas,
Braz. 211/G8
Bom Jesus, Braz. 155/B4
Bom Jesus, Braz. 154/A3
Bom Jesus da Gurguéia,
Serra (mts.), Braz. 151/K5
Bom Jesus de Goiás,
Braz. 155/B1
Bom Jesus do Itabapoana,
Braz. 155/D2
Bom Jesus dos Perdões,
Braz. 211/G8
Bom Retiro, Braz. 155/B3
Boma, D.R. Congo 105/B2
Bomaderry, Austl. 115/D2
Bombala, Austl. 115/D3
Bombay Hook NWR,
De, US 138/C5
Bombay (Mumbai),
India 82/B4
Bomberai (pen.), Indo. 81/H4
Bombo, Ugan. 104/B2
Bomi, China 83/G2
Bomlitz, Ger. 51/G3
Bømlo (isl.), Nor. 38/A2
Bomu (riv.), D.R. Congo 93/K4
Bon-Encontre, Fr. 42/D4
Bona (mt.), Ak, US 134/K3
Bonaduz, Swi. 57/F4
Bonaire (isl.), NAnt. 141/M5
Bonalbo, Austl. 115/E1
Bonampak (ruin),
Mex. 144/D2
Bonao, DRep. 141/G4
Bonaparte (arch.),
Austl. 109/B2
Bonaparte (isls.),
Austl. 109/B2
Bonasila (mtn.),
Ak, US 134/K3
Bonaventure, Qu, Can. 131/H1
Bonaventure (river),
Qu, Can. 131/H1
Bonavista (bay)
Nf, Can. 131/L1
Bonavista (cape)
Nf, Can. 131/L1
Boncourt, Swi. 56/D3
Bondeno, It. 59/E3
Bondo, D.R. Congo 97/K7
Bondoukou, C.d'Iv. 102/C4
Bondowoso, Indo. 80/D5
Bone (gulf), Indo. 67/M10
Bönen, Ger. 51/E5
Bonerate (isls.), Indo. 81/F5
Bonfol, Swi. 56/D3
Bonfouca, La, US 137/Q16
Bong, Co, Libr. 102/C5
Bong (range), Libr. 102/C5
Bongabong, Phil. 81/F1
Bongaigaon, India 85/H2
Bongandanga,
D.R. Congo 97/K7
Bongao, Phil. 81/E3
Bonggi (isl.), Malay. 81/E3
Bongka (riv.), Indo. 81/F4
Bongo, Massif des (plat.),
CAfr. 97/K6
Bongolava (uplands),
Madg. 105/K10
Bongor, Chad 96/J5
Bonham, Tx, US 129/H4
Bonheiden, Belg. 53/D1
Bonhill, Sc, UK 36/B5
Bonhomme, Col du
(pass), Fr. 56/D1
Boni Nat'l Rsv., Kenya 104/D3
Bonifacio (str.), It. 46/A1
Bonifacio, It. 46/A2
Bonifay, Fl, US 133/G4
Bonin (isls.), Japan 116/C2
Bönnigen, Swi. 56/D4
Bonin, Ca, US 136/C5
Bonita Springs, Fl, US 133/H5
Bonito (peak), Hon. 144/E3
Bonn, Ger. 53/G2

Bonndorf im Schwarzwald,
Ger. 57/E2
Bonne, Fr. 56/C5
Bonnelles, Fr. 30/K5
Bonner Springs,
Ks, US 137/M15
Bonner-West Riverside,
Mt, US 126/E4
Bonners Ferry, Id, US 126/D3
Bonnet Carré Spillway,
La, US 137/P16
Bonnet Lac du (lake),
Mb, Can. 127/K3
Bonneuil-sur-Marne,
Fr. 30/K5
Bonneval, Fr. 42/D2
Bonneville (dam),
Wa,Or, US 126/C4
Bonneville, Fr. 56/C5
Bonney Lake,
Wa, US 135/C3
Bönnigheim, Ger. 54/C4
Bonnybridge, Sc, UK 36/C5
Bonorva, It. 46/A2
Bons-en-Chablais, Fr. 56/C5
Bonsall, Ca, US 136/C4
Bontberg (peak), SAfr. 106/C4
Bontebok NP, SAfr. 106/C4
Bonthain, Indo. 81/E5
Bonthe, SLeo. 102/B5
Bontoc, Phil. 79/D4
Bonyhád, Hun. 48/D3
Bonzart (lap.), Tun. 100/L6
Booker T. Washington
Nat'l Mon., Va, US 133/J2
Boom, Belg. 53/D1
Boone, Ia, US 127/K5
Boone, NC, US 130/D4
Booneville, Ms, US 133/F3
Boonton, NJ, US 139/H8
Boorabbin NP,
Austl. 112/C4
Boorama, Som. 97/N5
Booroondara (mt.),
Austl. 115/C1
Boorowa, Austl. 115/D2
Boos (int'l arpt.), Fr. 42/D2
Boos, Ger. 57/G1
Boosaaso (Bender Cassim),
Som. 97/Q5
Boostedt, Ger. 38/D4
Boothbay Harbor,
Me, US 131/G3
Boothia (pen.),
Nun., Can. 122/G1
Boothia (gulf),
Nun., Can. 122/G1
Bootle, Eng, UK 35/E5
Booué, Gabon 96/H8
Bopa, Ben. 103/F5
Bopfingen, Ger. 54/D5
Boppard, Ger. 53/G3
Boppy (mt.), Austl. 115/C1
Boqueirão, Braz. 154/C2
Boqueirão, Serra do
(mts.), Braz. 154/B3
Boquete (peak), Arg. 158/C4
Boquilla (res.), Mex. 142/D3
Boquillas del Carmen,
Mex. 132/C4
Boquira, Braz. 154/B4
Bor, Rus. 61/K4
Bor, Serb. 48/F3
Bor, Turk. 90/C2
Bor UI (mts.), China 70/G3
Bora Bora (isl.), FrPol. 117/K6
Borah (peak), Id, US 126/E4
Borås, Swe. 38/E3
Borãzjãn, Iran 88/F3
Borba, Braz. 150/G4
Borba, Port. 44/B3
Borbera (riv.), It. 58/B3
Borbore (riv.), It. 58/B3
Borborema, Planalto da
(plat.), Braz. 151/L5
Borça, Serb. 48/E3
Borcea Branch (riv.),
Rom. 49/H3
Borchen, Ger. 51/F5
Borça, Turk. 63/G4
Borculo, Neth. 50/D4
Borda da Mata, Braz. 211/G7
Bordeaux, Fr. 42/C4
Borden (isl.),
NW,Nun., Can. 123/R7
Borden (pen.),
Nun., Can. 123/H1
Bordentown, NJ, US 138/D3
Bordertown, Austl. 115/B3
Bordj Bou Arreridj,
Alg. 100/H4
Bordj Bou Arreridj
(prov.), Alg. 100/H4
Bordj el Kiffan, Alg. 100/G4
Bordj Manaïel, Alg. 100/H4
Bordj Moktar, Alg. 100/G4
Bordj Omar Driss, Alg. 99/G3
Bordj Sainte-Marie,
Alg. 98/E4
Borehamwood,
Eng, UK 30/C2
Borest, Fr. 30/L4
Boretto, It. 58/D3
Borgå (Porvoo), Fin. 39/L1
Borgaretto, It. 58/A2
Borgarnes, Ice. 37/N7
Borgaro Torinese, It. 58/A2
Børgefjell NP, Nor. 37/E2
Børgentreich, Ger. 51/G5
Borger, Tx, US 129/G4
Borger, Neth. 50/D3
Borgerhout, Belg. 50/B6

Borges Blanques, Sp. 45/F2
Borghetto Lodigiano, It. 58/C2
Borghetto Santo Spirito, It. 58/B4
Borgholm, Swe. 38/G3
Borgholzhausen, Ger. 51/F4
Borghorst, Ger. 51/E4
Borgloon, Belg. 53/E2
Borgne (lake), La, US 137/Q17
Borgne (riv.), Swi. 56/D5
Borgo (int'l arpt.), Burk. 102/B3
Borgo, Fr. 46/A1
Borgo, It. 57/H5
Borgo a Mozzano, It. 58/D5
Borgo San Dalmazzo, It. 43/G4
Borgo San Giacomo, It. 58/C2
Borgo San Lorenzo, It. 59/E5
Borgo Tossignano, It. 59/E5
Borgo Val di Taro, It. 58/C4
Borgo Vercelli, It. 58/B2
Borgofranco d'Ivrea, It. 58/A1
Borgomanero, It. 58/B1
Borgonovo Val Tidone, It. 58/C2
Borgosatollo, It. 58/D2
Borgosesia, It. 58/B1
Borgou (prov.), Ben. 103/F4
Borgund, Nor. 38/B1
Borio, India 85/F3
Borisoglebsk, Rus. 63/G2
Borispol (int'l arpt.), Ukr. 62/D2
Borja, Peru 156/B2
Borja, Sp. 44/E2
Borken, Ger. 50/D5
Borken, Ger. 51/G6
Børkop, Den. 38/C4
Borkum, Ger. 50/D1
Borkum (isl.), Ger. 50/D1
Borlänge, Swe. 38/F1
Bormida (riv.), It. 43/H4
Bormida, It. 58/B4
Bormida di Millesimo (riv.), It. 58/B4
Bormio, It. 57/G5
Born, Neth. 53/E1
Borna, Ger. 40/G3
Borndiep (chan.), Neth. 50/C2
Borne, Neth. 50/D4
Borne (riv.), Fr. 56/C6
Bornel, Fr. 52/B5
Bornem, Belg. 53/D1
Bornemouth, Eng, UK 33/E5
Bornemouth (co.), Eng, UK 33/E5
Borneo (isl.), Indo.,Malay. 67/L9
Bornheim, Ger. 53/G2
Bornholm (co.), Den. 38/F4
Bornholm (isl.), Den.,Swe. 27/F3
Bornholmsgat (chan.), Den.,Swi. 41/H1
Borno, It. 57/G6
Bornos, Sp. 44/C4
Börnsen, Ger. 51/H2
Bornu (plain), Nga. 96/H5
Boro (riv.), Sudan 96/K5
Borohoro (mts.), China 70/D3
Borongan, Phil. 79/E5
Borough Green, Eng, UK 30/D3
Borovany, Czh. 55/H5
Borovichi, Rus. 60/G4
Borovo, Bul. 49/G4
Borovo, Cro. 48/D3
Borre, Nor. 38/D2
Borrisokane, Ire. 31/P10
Borrnida (riv.), It. 58/B3
Borşa, Rom. 49/F2
Borsec, Rom. 49/G2
Borso del Grappa, It. 59/E1
Borsod-Abaúj-Zemplén (co.), Hun. 48/E1
Borssele, Neth. 50/A6
Borstel, Ger. 51/F3
Bort-les-Orgues, Fr. 42/E4
Boruca, CR 145/F4
Borūjerd, Iran 88/E2
Boryslav, Ukr. 41/M4
Borzonasca, It. 58/C4
Borzya, Rus. 71/L1
Bosa, It. 46/A2
Bosanska Dubica, Bosn. 48/C3
Bosanska Gradiška, Bosn. 48/C3
Bosanska Kostajnica, Bosn. 48/C3
Bosanska Krupa, Bosn. 48/C3
Bosanski Brod, Bosn. 48/D3
Bosanski Petrovac, Bosn. 48/C3
Bosanski Šamac, Bosn. 48/D3
Bosco Mesola, It. 59/F3
Bosconero, It. 58/A2
Bose, China 83/J3
Boshof, SAfr. 106/D3
Boskoop, Neth. 50/B4
Boskovice, Czh. 41/J4
Bosna (riv.), Bosn. 48/D3
Bosnia and Herzegovina (ctry.) 48/C3
Bošnjaci, Cro. 48/D3
Bōsō (pen.), Japan 75/G3
Bosobolo, D.R. Congo 97/J7
Bosporus (str.), Turk. 49/J5

Bosque Farms, NM, US 128/F4
Bosques Petrificados, Mon. Natural, Arg. 159/C5
Bossangoa, CAfr. 96/J6
Bossier City, La, US 129/J4
Bostān, Iran 88/E2
Bostānābād-e Bālā, Iran 88/E1
Boston (mts.), Ar, US 129/J4
Boston (cap.), Ma, US 131/G3
Boston, Eng, UK 35/H6
Bosut (riv.), Cro. 48/D3
Boswil, Swi. 57/E3
Botād, India 89/K4
Boteler (peak), NC, US 133/H3
Botelerpunt (pt.), SAfr. 107/F2
Botelhos, Braz. 211/G6
Botev (peak), Bul. 47/J1
Botevgrad, Bul. 47/H1
Bothaspas (pass), SAfr. 107/E2
Bothaville, SAfr. 106/D2
Bothel, Ger. 51/G2
Bothell, Wa, US 135/C2
Bothnia (gulf), Swe.,Fin. 160/E3
Botoşani (prov.), Rom. 49/H2
Botoşani, Rom. 49/H2
Botou, China 72/D3
Botrange (peak), Belg. 53/F3
Botrivier, SAfr. 106/L11
Botsford, Ct, US 139/E1
Botswana (ctry.) 105/D5
Bottanuco, It. 58/C1
Botte Donato (peak), It. 46/E3
Botticino, It. 58/D1
Bottineau, ND, US 127/H3
Bottrighe, It. 59/F2
Bottrop, Ger. 50/D5
Botwood, Nf, Can. 131/L1
Bou (riv.), C.d'Iv. 102/D4
Bou Arfa, Mor. 99/E2
Boû Djébéha (well), Mali 102/E2
Bou Hamdane, Oued (riv.), Alg. 100/K6
Bou Ismaïl, Alg. 100/G4
Bou Izakarn, Mor. 98/C3
Bou Kadir, Alg. 100/G4
Bou Laber (well), Alg. 98/D4
Bou Naceur (peak), Mor. 100/C3
Bou Regreg (riv.), Mor. 100/A3
Bou Salem, Tun. 100/L6
Bou Sellam, Oued (riv.), Alg. 100/H4
Bouaflé, C.d'Iv. 102/D5
Bouafle, Fr. 30/H5
Bouaké, C.d'Iv. 102/D5
Bouar, CAfr. 96/J6
Boubin (peak), Czh. 55/G5
Bouca, CAfr. 96/J6
Bouchain, Fr. 52/C3
Bouchegouf, Alg. 100/K6
Boucherville, Qu, Can. 131/P6
Boucle du Baoulé, PN de la, Mali 96/D5
Boucle Du Baoulé, PN de la, Mali 102/C3
Boudry, Swi. 56/C4
Boufarik, Alg. 100/G4
Bouffémont, Fr. 30/J4
Bougainville (reef), Austl. 109/D2
Bougainville (isl.), PNG 116/E5
Bougainville (cape), UK 159/F6
Bougara, Alg. 100/G4
Bougar'oûn (cape), Alg. 100/K6
Bough Beech (res.), Eng, UK 30/D3
Bougouni, Mali 102/D4
Bougouriba (prov.), Burk. 102/E4
Bouguenais, Fr. 42/C3
Bouhachem (peak), Mor. 100/B2
Bouhalla (peak), Mor. 100/B2
Bouillancy, Fr. 30/L4
Bouillon, Belg. 53/E4
Bouira (prov.), Alg. 100/G4
Bouira, Alg. 100/G4
Boujad, Mor. 98/D2
Boukhalf (Tangier) (int'l arpt.), Mor. 100/B2
Boukoumbé, Ben. 103/J2
Boulaide, Lux. 53/E4
Boulaouane, Mor. 98/C2
Boulay-Moselle, Fr. 53/F5
Boulazac, Fr. 42/D4
Boulder, Co, US 137/F3
Boulder (co.), Co, US 137/F3
Boulder, Mt, US 126/E4
Boulder City, Nv, US 128/D4
Boulder Hill, Il, US 135/P16
Boulemane, Mor. 98/D2
Boulemane (prov.), Mor. 98/D2
Boulgo (prov.), Burk. 103/E3

Boulia, Austl. 113/H2
Bouligny, Fr. 53/E5
Boulkiemde (prov.), Burk. 103/E3
Boullarre, Fr. 30/M4
Boulogne (riv.), Fr. 42/C3
Boulogne-Billancourt, Fr. 30/J5
Boulogne-sur-Mer, Fr. 52/A2
Boulsworth (hill), Eng, UK 35/F4
Boumalne, Mor. 98/D3
Boumerdas (prov.), Alg. 100/G4
Boumerdas, Alg. 100/G4
Boun Nua, Laos 83/H3
Bouna, C.d'Iv. 102/E4
Bound Brook, NJ, US 138/D2
Boundary (peak), Nv, US 128/C3
Boundiali, C.d'Iv. 102/D4
Bountiful, Ut, US 137/K12
Bouquet (res.), Ca, US 136/B1
Bouquet (canyon), Ca, US 136/B2
Bourbon l'Archambault, Fr. 42/E3
Bourbonnais (reg.), Fr. 42/D3
Bourbonne-les-Bains, Fr. 56/B2
Bourbourg, Fr. 52/B2
Bourdonné, Fr. 30/G5
Bourem, Mali 103/E2
Bouressa (riv.), Mali 103/F2
Bourg-en-Bresse, Fr. 56/B5
Bourg-lès-Valence, Fr. 42/F4
Bourg-Saint-Andéol, Fr. 42/F4
Bourg-Saint-Maurice, Fr. 43/G4
Bourg-Saint-Pierre, Swi. 56/D6
Bourganeuf, Fr. 42/D4
Bourges, Fr. 42/E3
Bourget (lake), Fr. 56/B6
Bourgneuf (bay), Fr. 42/B3
Bourgogne (pol. reg.), Fr. 42/F3
Bourgogne (canal), Fr. 56/B3
Bourgoin-Jallieu, Fr. 42/F4
Bourke, Austl. 115/C1
Bourmont, Fr. 56/B2
Bourne (riv.), Eng, UK 33/E4
Bourne End, Eng, UK 33/F3
Bourne, The (riv.), Eng, UK 30/B3
Bournemouth, NJ, US 138/D3
Bourscheid, Lux. 53/F4
Bourtanger Moor (reg.), Ger. 51/E3
Bousbecque, Fr. 52/C2
Bousso, Chad 96/J5
Boussois, Fr. 52/D3
Boutilimit, Mrta. 102/B2
Boutte, La, US 137/P17
Bouvard (cape), Austl. 112/B5
Bouvet (isl.), Nor. 23/K8
Bouxières-aux-Dames, Fr. 53/F6
Bouxwiller, Fr. 53/G6
Bouznika, Mor. 100/A3
Bouzonville, Fr. 53/F5
Bovalino, It. 46/E3
Bovegno, It. 58/D1
Boven Tapanahoni (riv.), Sur. 153/H4
Bovenden, Ger. 51/G5
Bovenwijde (lake), Neth. 50/D3
Boves, Fr. 52/B4
Bovezzo, It. 58/D1
Bovingdon, Eng, UK 30/A1
Bovino, It. 48/B5
Bovolone, It. 59/E2
Bow (riv.), Ab, Can. 122/E3
Bow Island, Ab, Can. 126/F3
Bowdle, SD, US 127/J4
Bowdon, Eng, UK 35/F5
Bowen, Arg. 158/D2
Bowen, Austl. 114/C3
Bowers Beach, De, US 138/C5
Bowie, Az, US 128/E4
Bowie, Md, US 138/B6
Bowling Green (cape), Austl. 114/B2
Bowling Green, Ky, US 130/C4
Bowling Green, Mo, US 129/K3
Bowling Green, Oh, US 130/D3
Bowling Green Bay NP, Austl. 114/B2
Bowman, ND, US 127/H4
Bowman (bay), Nun., Can. 123/J2
Bowmansdale, Pa, US 138/B3
Bowmanstown, Pa, US 138/C2
Bowmansville, Pa, US 138/B3
Bowmore, Sc, UK 31/Q9
Bowokan (isls.), Indo. 81/F4
Bowral, Austl. 115/D2
Bowron (riv.), BC, Can. 126/C2
Box Elder (co.), Ut, US 137/J11
Boxberg, Ger. 54/C4
Boxholm, Swe. 38/F2

Boxing, China 72/D3
Boxmeer, Neth. 50/C5
Boxtel, Neth. 50/C5
Boyabat, Turk. 90/C1
Boyaca (dept.), Col. 152/C3
Boyanup, Austl. 112/B5
Boychinovtsi, Bul. 49/F4
Boyd (lake), Co, US 137/B2
Boye, China 72/C3
Boyer (riv.), Ia, US 127/K5
Boyertown, Pa, US 138/C3
Boyle, Ab, Can. 126/E2
Boyle, Ire. 31/P10
Boyne (riv.), Ire. 31/Q10
Boyne City, Mi, US 130/C2
Boyne Island, Austl. 114/C3
Boynton Beach, Fl, US 133/H5
Boysen (res.), Wy, US 126/F5
Boyup Brook, Austl. 112/C5
Boz (pt.), Turk. 49/J5
Bozashchy Tübegi (pen.), Kaz. 63/J3
Bozcaada (isl.), Gre. 47/J3
Bozcaada, Turk. 47/K3
Bozeman, Mt, US 126/F4
Bozkir, Turk. 90/C2
Bozman, Md, US 138/B6
Bozoum, CAfr. 96/J6
Bozova, Turk. 90/D2
Bozüyük, Turk. 90/B2
Bozyazı, Turk. 91/C1
Bozzolo, It. 58/D2
Bra, It. 58/A3
Braan (riv.), Sc, UK 36/C3
Brač (isl.), Cro. 46/C1
Bracciano (lake), It. 46/B1
Bracebridge, On, Can. 130/E2
Brackel, Ger. 51/G1
Brackettville, Tx, US 129/G5
Bracken, Tx, US 137/U20
Bracknell, Eng, UK 33/F4
Bracknell Forest (co.), Eng, UK 33/F4
Braço do Norte, Braz. 155/B4
Brad, Rom. 49/F2
Bradano (riv.), It. 48/B5
Bradda (pt.), IM, UK 34/D3
Bradenton, Fl, US 133/H5
Bradford, Eng, UK 35/G4
Bradford (co.), Eng, UK 35/G4
Bradford, Pa, US 130/E3
Bradley (int'l arpt.), Ct, US 131/F3
Bradley Beach, NJ, US 138/D3
Brady, Tx, US 129/H5
Braemar (reg.), Sc, UK 36/C2
Braeriach (peak), Sc, UK 36/C2
Braga, Port. 44/A2
Braga, Port. 44/A2
Bragado, Arg. 158/E2
Bragança (dist.), Port. 44/B2
Bragança, Port. 44/B2
Brahmanbaria, Bang. 85/H4
Brahmaputra (riv.), Asia 67/J7
Braich-y-Pwll (pt.), Wal, UK 34/B3
Braid (riv.), NI, UK 34/B2
Brăila (prov.), Rom. 49/H3
Brăila, Rom. 49/H3
Brainards, NJ, US 138/C2
Braine, Fr. 52/C5
Braine-l'Alleud, Belg. 53/D2
Braine-le-Comte, Belg. 53/D2
Brainerd, Mn, US 127/K4
Braintree, Eng, UK 30/J6
Braithwaite, La, US 137/Q17
Brak (riv.), SAfr. 106/C3
Brake, Ger. 51/F2
Brakel, Belg. 52/C2
Brakel, Ger. 51/G5
Brakel, Ger. 50/C5
Brakna (pol. reg.), Mrta. 102/B2
Brålanda, Swe. 38/E2
Bram, Fr. 42/E5
Bramdrupdam, Den. 38/C4
Bramley, Eng, UK 30/B3
Brampton, On, Can. 131/D8
Bramsche, Ger. 51/F4
Bramstedt, Ger. 51/G1
Bran (riv.), Sc, UK 36/A1
Brancaleone-Marina, It. 46/E4
Branch Dale, Pa, US 138/B2
Branchville, NJ, US 138/D1
Branchville, Ct, US 139/E1
Branco (riv.), Braz. 147/C2
Brand, Aus. 57/F3
Brandberg (peak), Namb. 105/B5
Brandbu, Nor. 38/D1
Brande, Den. 38/C4
Brandenburg (state), Ger. 40/P6
Brandenburg, Ger. 40/P6
Brander, Pass of (pass), Sc, UK 36/B4
Brandfort, SAfr. 106/D3
Brandizzo, It. 58/A2
Brandon, Mb, Can. 127/J3
Brandon, Fl, US 133/H5
Brandon, Ms, US 133/F3
Brandsen, Arg. 159/J11

Brandvlei, SAfr. 106/C3
Brandýs nad Labem, Czh. 55/H2
Brandywine, Md, US 138/B6
Brandywine (riv.), Pa, US 138/C4
Branford, Ct, US 139/F1
Branges, Fr. 56/B5
Braniewo, Pol. 39/H4
Brannenburg, Ger. 43/K3
Brant Beach, NJ, US 138/D4
Branxholm, Austl. 115/C4
Branzoll (Bronzolo), It. 57/H4
Bras d'Or (lake), NS, Can. 131/K8
Brasiléia, Braz. 150/E6
Brasilia de Minas, Braz. 154/A5
Brasília, PN de, Braz. 151/J7
Braşov, Rom. 49/G3
Braşov (prov.), Rom. 49/G3
Brasschaat, Belg. 50/B6
Brassey (mt.), Austl. 113/G2
Brasstown Bald (peak), Ga, US 133/H3
Brastad, Swe. 38/D2
Bratislava (cap.), Slvk. 43/M2
Bratislava (Ivanka) (int'l arpt.), Slvk. 48/C1
Bratislavský (pol. reg.), Slvk. 41/J4
Bratsk, Rus. 65/L4
Brattleboro, Vt, US 131/F3
Bratunac, Bosn. 48/D3
Braubach, Ger. 54/B1
Braulio Carrillo, PN, CR 140/D4
Braunau am Inn, Aus. 55/G6
Braunfels, Ger. 54/B1
Braunig (lake), Tx, US 137/U21
Braunlage, Ger. 51/H5
Braunschweig, Ger. 51/H4
Brava (isl.), CpV. 93/J11
Brava (pt.), It. 159/C7
Brava (pt.), Uru. 159/K11
Brava, Costa (coast), Sp. 45/G2
Bråviken (inlet), Swe. 38/G2
Bravo (peak), Bol. 150/F5
Bravo (peak), Peru 156/B2
Bravo del Norte (riv.), Mex. 140/A2
Brawley, Ca, US 128/D4
Bray (isl.), Nun., Can. 123/J2
Bray, Ire. 34/B5
Bray (pt.), Ire. 34/B5
Bray-Dunes, Fr. 52/B1
Braye (riv.), Fr. 42/D3
Brazey-en-Plaine, Fr. 56/B3
Brazil (ctry.) 150/F5
Brazilian Highlands (uplands), Braz. 147/E4
Brazo Casiquiare (riv.), Ven. 153/E4
Brazo Sur (riv.), Arg. 159/C6
Brazópolis, Braz. 211/H7
Brazos (riv.), Tx, US 132/D3
Brazos, Salt Fork (riv.), Tx, US 132/C3
Brazzaville (cap.), Congo 105/C1
Brčko, Bosn. 48/D3
Brda (riv.), Pol. 39/H3
Brdy (mts.), Czh. 41/G4
Brea, Ca, US 136/G8
Breadalbane (dist.), Sc, UK 36/B4
Breamish (riv.), Eng, UK 36/D6
Bréancon, Fr. 30/H4
Bréau, Fr. 30/L6
Breaza, Rom. 49/G3
Brebbia, It. 58/B1
Brèche (riv.), Fr. 52/B5
Brechen, Ger. 54/B2
Brechin, Sc, UK 36/D4
Brecht, Belg. 50/B6
Breckenridge, Mn, US 127/J4
Breckenridge, Tx, US 129/H4
Breckerfeld, Ger. 51/E6
Breckland (phys. reg.), Eng, UK 33/G2
Brecknock (pen.), Chile 159/C7
Breclav, Czh. 43/M2
Brecon, Wal, UK 32/C3
Brecon Beacons (mts.), Wal, UK 32/C3
Breda, Neth. 50/B5
Bredaryd, Swe. 38/E3
Bredasdorp, SAfr. 106/M11
Bredene, Belg. 52/B1
Bredstedt, Ger. 38/C5
Breë (riv.), SAfr. 106/B4
Bree, Belg. 50/B6
Breg (riv.), Ger. 40/E5
Bregalnica (riv.), FYROM 47/H2
Breganze, It. 59/E1
Bregenz, Aus. 57/F3
Bregenzer Ache (riv.), Aus. 57/F3
Bregovo, Bul. 48/F3

Brégy, Fr. 30/L4
Breidhafjördhur (bay), Ice. 37/M6
Breil-Brigels, Swi. 57/F4
Breisach, Ger. 56/D1
Breitbrunn am Chiemsee, Ger. 55/F7
Breitenauriegel (peak), Ger. 55/G5
Breitenbach, Swi. 56/D3
Breitenburg, Ger. 55/E4
Breitenbrunn, Ger. 55/E4
Breitenfurt bei Wien, Aus. 49/N7
Breitenworbis, Ger. 51/H6
Breithorn (peak), Swi. 56/D5
Breithorn (peak), Swi. 56/D5
Brejo, Braz. 154/B1
Brejo Santo, Braz. 154/C2
Brejões, Braz. 154/C2
Brembate di Sopra, It. 58/C1
Brembilla, It. 58/C1
Brembio, It. 58/C2
Brembo (riv.), It. 57/F6
Bremen (int'l arpt.), Ger. 51/F2
Bremen, Ger. 51/F2
Bremen (state), Ger. 51/F2
Bremer (riv.), Austl. 114/E7
Bremerhaven, Ger. 51/F1
Bremerton, Wa, US 126/C4
Bremervörde, Ger. 51/G2
Bremgarten, Swi. 57/E3
Bremgarten bei Bern, Swi. 56/D4
Bremnes, Nor. 38/D3
Brend (riv.), Ger. 54/D2
Brendel (lake), Mi, US 135/E7
Brendola, It. 59/E2
Brendon (hills), Eng, UK 32/C4
Brenig, Llyn (lake), Wal, UK 34/E5
Brenne (riv.), Fr. 40/C5
Brenner (pass), Aus. 57/H3
Brenner (riv.), Austl. 113/N9
Breno, It. 57/G6
Brent (res.), Eng, UK 30/C2
Brent (bor.), Eng, UK 33/F5
Brenta (riv.), It. 43/J4
Brenta (peak), It. 57/G5
Brentwood, NY, US 139/E2
Brentwood, Ca, US 135/L11
Brentwood, Eng, UK 30/J6
Brenz (riv.), Ger. 54/D5
Brescello, It. 58/D3
Brescia, It. 58/D1
Brescia (prov.), It. 57/G6
Bresle (riv.), Fr. 42/D1
Bresles, Fr. 52/B5
Bressana, It. 58/C2
Bressanone, It. 43/J3
Bressay (isl.), Sc, UK 31/W13
Bressuire, Fr. 42/C3
Brest, Bela. 41/M2
Brest (int'l arpt.), Bela. 41/M2
Brest, Fr. 42/A2
Brestskaya Voblasts (prov.), Bela. 62/C1
Bretagne (pol. reg.), Fr. 42/B2
Bretagne, Monts de (mts.), Fr. 42/B2
Bretagne, Pointe de (pt.), Reun. 107/S15
Bretaña, Peru 156/C2
Breteuil, Fr. 52/B4
Brétigny-sur-Orge, Fr. 30/J6
Breton, Ab, Can. 126/E2
Breton (cape), NS, Can. 131/K2
Brett (cape), NZ 117/S10
Brett (riv.), Eng, UK 30/J5
Brettach (riv.), Ger. 54/C4
Bretten, Ger. 54/B4
Bretzenheim, Ger. 53/G4
Breuberg, Ger. 54/C3
Breuillet, Fr. 30/J6
Breukelen, Neth. 50/B4
Breuna, Ger. 51/G6
Breuvannes-en-Bassigny, Fr. 56/B2
Breves, Braz. 151/H4
Brevig Mission, Ak, US 134/E2
Brevik, Nor. 38/C2
Brevoort (isl.), Nun., Can. 123/K2
Brewarrina, Austl. 115/C1
Brewer, Me, US 131/G2
Brewster, Ne, US 127/J5
Brewton, Al, US 133/G4
Brey-et-Lû, Fr. 30/G4
Breyten, SAfr. 107/E2
Brežice, Slov. 43/L3
Brezina, Alg. 99/F2
Breznik, Bul. 47/H1
Brezoi, Rom. 49/G3
Brezovo, Bul. 47/J1
Bría, CAfr. 97/K6
Briançon, Fr. 43/G4
Brianne, Llyn (res.), Wal, UK 32/C2
Briar Creek, Pa, US 138/B1
Briare, Fr. 42/E3
Brickerville, Pa, US 138/B3
Bricktown, NJ, US 138/D3
Bride, IM, UK 34/D3
Bride (riv.), Ire. 31/P10
Bridge City, Tx, US 132/E4

Bridge of Allan, Sc, UK 36/C4
Bridge of Don, Sc, UK 36/D2
Bridge of Weir, Sc, UK 36/B5
Bridgehampton, NY, US 139/G2
Bridgend, Wal, UK 32/C3
Bridgeport, Ca, US 128/C3
Bridgeport, Ct, US 139/E1
Bridgeport, Ne, US 127/H5
Bridgeport, NJ, US 138/C4
Bridger, Mt, US 126/F4
Bridgeton, NJ, US 138/C4
Bridgetown, Austl. 112/C2
Bridgetown (cap.), Bar. 141/P9
Bridgeville, De, US 138/C6
Bridgewater, Austl. 115/C4
Bridgewater, NS, Can. 131/J3
Bridgnorth, Eng, UK 32/D5
Bridgton, Me, US 131/G2
Bridgwater, Eng, UK 32/D4
Bridgwater (bay), Eng, UK 32/C4
Bridlington, Eng, UK 33/H3
Bridlington (bay), Eng, UK 33/H3
Bridport, Austl. 115/C4
Bridport, Eng, UK 32/D5
Brie-Comte-Robert, Fr. 30/K5
Brieg Brzeg, Pol. 41/J3
Brielle, Neth. 50/B5
Brielle, NJ, US 138/D3
Brienz, Swi. 56/E4
Brierfield, Eng, UK 35/F4
Brieselang, Ger. 40/Q6
Brig, Swi. 56/D5
Brigach (riv.), Ger. 54/B7
Brigantine, NJ, US 138/D4
Brigend (co.), Wal, UK 32/C3
Brigham City, Ut, US 137/J10
Brighouse, Eng, UK 35/G4
Brighton and Hove (co.), Eng, UK 33/F5
Brighton, Co, US 137/H12
Brighton, Eng, UK 33/F5
Brighton, Il, US 137/U21
Brighton, Ut, US 137/K12
Brighton, Wi, US 135/P14
Brightlingsea, Eng, UK 33/H3
Brignais, Fr. 42/F4
Brignoles, Fr. 42/G5
Brihuega, Sp. 44/D2
Brikama, Gam. 102/A3
Brilhante (riv.), Braz. 150/F5
Brilon, Ger. 51/F6
Brimstone Hill NP, StK. 141/N8
Brindisi, It. 47/E2
Brinkworth, Austl. 113/H5
Brinnon, Wa, US 135/B2
Brión, Sp. 44/A1
Briones (res.), Ca, US 135/K11
Brisbane, Austl. 114/F6
Brisbane (riv.), Austl. 114/F6
Brisbane Forest Park, Austl. 114/E6
Brisbane Ranges NP, Austl. 115/C3
Brisbane Water NP, Austl. 115/D2
Brisighella, It. 59/E4
Brisnago, Swi. 57/E5
Bristol, Eng, UK 32/D4
Bristol (chan.), UK 31/V14
Bristol (co.), Eng, UK 32/D4
Bristol (bay), Ak, US 134/F4
Bristol, Pa, US 138/D3
Bristow, Ok, US 129/H4
British Columbia (prov.), Can. 122/D3
British Empire (range), Nun., Can. 123/S6
British Indian Ocean Territory (dpcy.), UK 67/G10
British Museum, Eng, UK 30/C2
Brittany (reg.), Fr. 42/B3
Brittstown, SAfr. 106/C3
Brive-la-Gaillarde, Fr. 42/D4
Brives-Charensac, Fr. 42/E4
Briviesca, Sp. 44/D1
Brněnský (pol. reg.), Slvk. 43/L2
Brnik (int'l arpt.), Slov. 43/L3
Brno, Czh. 145/F1
Broa (bay), Cuba 145/F1
Broad (pass), Ak, US 134/J3
Broad (riv.), NC,SC, US 133/H3
Broad Law (peak), Sc, UK 36/C6
Broad Sound (isls.), Austl. 114/C2
Broadback (riv.), Qu, Can. 130/E2
Broadford, Austl. 115/C3
Broadkill (riv.), De, US 138/C6
Broads NP, The, Eng, UK 33/H1

Broadstairs, Eng, UK 33/H4
Broadus, Mt, US 127/G4
Broadwater NP, Austl. 115/E1
Broadway (hill), Eng, UK 33/E3
Broadway, NJ, US 138/C2
Broc, Swi. 56/D4
Brochet, Mb, Can. 122/F3
Brock (isl.), NW, Can. 123/R7
Brocken (peak), Ger. 51/H5
Brockman (mt.), Austl. 112/C2
Brockton, Ma, US 131/G3
Brockville, On, Can. 130/F2
Brodeur (pen.), Nun., Can. 122/G1
Brodheadsville, Pa, US 138/C2
Brodnica, Pol. 41/K2
Broek in Waterland, Neth. 50/B4
Broek Op Langedijk, Neth. 50/B3
Bröhn (peak), Ger. 51/H2
Broken (bay), Austl. 115/D2
Broken Arrow, Ok, US 129/J3
Broken Bow, Ne, US 127/J5
Broken Bow (lake), Ok, US 129/J4
Broken Bow, Ok, US 129/J4
Broken Hill, Austl. 115/B1
Brokeoff (mts.), NM, US 132/B3
Brokopondo, Sur. 151/G2
Brokopondo (dist.), Sur. 153/H3
Brome, Ger. 40/F2
Bromölla, Swe. 38/F3
Bromsgrove, Eng, UK 32/D2
Bromskirchen, Ger. 51/F6
Brønderslev, Den. 38/C3
Brong-Ahafo (pol. reg.), Gha. 103/E5
Broni, It. 58/C2
Bronkhorstspruit, SAfr. 106/E2
Brønnøy, Nor. 37/E2
Brøns, Den. 38/C4
Bronschhofen, Swi. 57/F3
Bronte, It. 46/D4
Bronx (bor.), NY, US 139/E2
Bronx Zoo, NY, US 139/K8
Bronxville, NY, US 139/K8
Brook Forest, Co, US 137/G13
Brook's Point, Phil. 81/E2
Brookfield, Il, US 135/Q16
Brookhaven, Ms, US 129/K5
Brooklyn (bor.), NY, US 138/D2
Brooklyn, Il, US 137/G8
Brooklyn Park, Md, US 138/B5
Brookmans Park, Eng, UK 30/C1
Brooks, Ab, Can. 126/F3
Brooks, Il, US 137/G8
Brooks (range), Ak, US 134/F2
Brookside, De, US 138/C4
Brooksville, Fl, US 133/H4
Brookton, Austl. 112/C5
Brookvale, Co, US 137/F13
Brookville, NY, US 139/L8
Broomall, Pa, US 138/C4
Broomfield, Co, US 137/G13
Brørup, Den. 38/C4
Brösarp, Swe. 38/F4
Brossard, Qu, Can. 131/P7
Brough (pt.), Sc, UK 31/V14
Broughshane, NI, UK 34/B2
Brousseval, Fr. 56/A1
Brouwersdam (dam), Neth. 50/A5
Brouwershaven, Neth. 50/A5
Brovst, Den. 38/C3
Brown (mt.), Austl. 113/H5
Brown (pt.), Austl. 113/G5
Brown Clee (hill), Eng, UK 32/D2
Brown Shoal (bar), Asia 79/C5
Brownfield, Tx, US 129/G4
Brownhills, Eng, UK 33/E1
Browning, Mt, US 126/E3
Browns Mills, NJ, US 138/D4
Brownsea (isl.), Eng, UK 32/D5
Brownsville, Tn, US 130/B5
Brownsville, Tx, US 132/E5
Brownsville, Wa, US 135/B2
Broxburn, Sc, UK 36/C5
Broye (riv.), Swi. 56/C4
Brozas, Sp. 44/B3
Bruay-la-Buissière, Fr. 52/C3
Bruay-sur-L'Escaut, Fr. 52/C3
Bruce (pen.), On, Can. 130/D2
Bruce (mt.), Austl. 112/C2
Bruce Rock, Austl. 112/C5
Bruchberg (peak), Ger. 51/H5
Bruchhausen-Vilsen, Ger. 51/F3
Bruchköbel, Ger. 54/B2
Bruchmühlbach-Miesau, Ger. 53/G5
Bruchsal, Ger. 54/B4
Brucht (riv.), Ger. 51/E5
Bruck, Aus. 49/P7

Bruck an der Grossglocknerstrasse, Aus. 43/K3
Bruck an der Mur, Aus. 43/L3
Bruckberg, Ger. 55/F5
Bruckmühl, Ger. 43/J3
Brue (riv.), Eng, UK 32/D4
Bruflat, Nor. 38/C1
Brügg, Swi. 56/D3
Brugg, Swi. 56/E3
Brugge, Belg. 52/C1
Brüggen, Ger. 50/D6
Brugnera, It. 59/F1
Brühl, Ger. 53/F2
Bruinisse, Neth. 50/B5
Brukkaros (peak), Namb. 106/B2
Brukunga, Austl. 113/M8
Brumado, Braz. 154/B4
Brumath, Fr. 53/G6
Brummen, Neth. 50/D4
Brumunddal, Nor. 38/D1
Brune (riv.), Fr. 52/C4
Bruneau (riv.), Id,Nv, US 126/E5
Brunei (ctry.) 80/D2
Brunete, Sp. 45/N9
Brunflo, Swe. 37/E3
Brunico, It. 43/J3
Brünigpass (pass), Swi. 56/K4
Brunn am Gebirge, Aus. 49/N7
Brunoy, Fr. 30/K5
Brunsbüttel, Ger. 51/G1
Brunssum, Neth. 53/E2
Brunstatt, Fr. 56/D2
Brunswick, Ga, US 133/H4
Brunswick, Me, US 131/G3
Brunswick, Oh, US 130/D3
Brunswick Heads, Austl. 114/D5
Brunswick Junction, Austl. 112/B5
Brunswick, Península de (pen.), Chile 157/B7
Brus (lake), Nic. 145/E3
Brusartsi, Bul. 48/F4
Brushy Creek, Tx, US 129/J5
Brusio, Swi. 57/G5
Brussels, Il, US 137/F8
Brussels (int'l arpt.), Belg. 53/D2
Brussels (Bruxelles) (cap.), Belg. 53/D2
Brusson, It. 58/A1
Bruthen, Austl. 115/C3
Bruyères, Fr. 56/C1
Bruyères-le-Châtel, Fr. 30/J6
Bruyères-sur-Oise, Fr. 30/J4
Bruz, Fr. 42/C2
Bruzual, Ven. 152/D2
Bryan, Tx, US 129/H5
Bryan, Oh, US 130/C3
Bryan (mt.), Austl. 113/H5
Bryansk, Rus. 62/E1
Bryanskaya Oblast, Rus. 62/E1
Bryce Canyon NP, Ut, US 128/D3
Bryn Brawd (peak), Wal, UK 32/C2
Bryne, Nor. 38/A2
Brzeg Dolny, Pol. 41/J3
Brzesko, Pol. 41/L4
Brzozów, Pol. 41/M4
Bua, Swe. 38/E3
Buala, Sol. 116/E5
Buba, GBis. 102/B4
Bubaque, GBis. 102/B4
Bubendorf, Swi. 56/D3
Bubikon, Swi. 57/E3
Bubu (riv.), Tanz. 104/B4
Buc, Fr. 30/J5
Bucak, Turk. 90/B2
Bucakkışla, Turk. 91/C1
Bucaramanga, Col. 152/C3
Bucasia, Austl. 114/C3
Bucelas, Port. 45/P10
Buch, Ger. 57/G1
Buchan (gulf), Nun., Can. 123/J1
Buchan (reg.), Sc, UK 36/D1
Buchan Ness (pt.), Sc, UK 36/E2
Buchanan (lake), Tx, US 129/H5
Buchanan, Libr. 102/C5
Buchans, Nf, Can. 131/K1
Bucharest (Bucureşti) (cap.), Rom. 49/H4
Buchbach, Ger. 55/F6
Büchen, Ger. 51/H2
Buchen, Ger. 54/C3
Buchenberg, Ger. 57/G2
Buchholz, Ger. 53/G3
Buchholz in der Nordheide, Ger. 51/G2
Buchloe, Ger. 57/G1
Buchon (pt.), Ca, US 128/B4
Buchs, Swi. 57/F3
Bucine, It. 59/E6
Buck, The (peak), Sc, UK 36/D2
Buckden Pike (peak), Eng, UK 35/F3
Bückeburg, Ger. 51/G4
Buckie, Sc, UK 36/D2
Buckingham, Qu, Can. 130/F2
Buckingham, Hun. 33/F3
Buckingham Palace, Eng, UK 30/C2

Buckland, Ak, US 134/F2
Buckley, Wal, UK 35/E5
Buckley, Wa, US 135/C3
Buckner, Mo, US 137/E5
Bucks (co.), Pa, US 138/C3
Bucksburn, Sc, UK 36/D2
Buctouche, NB, Can. 131/H2
Bucy-le-Long, Fr. 52/C5
Bucyrus, Oh, US 130/D3
Bucyrus, Ks, US 137/D6
Budai hegy (hill), Hun. 49/Q9
Budakeszi, Hun. 49/Q9
Budaörs, Hun. 49/R10
Budapest (cap.), Hun. 49/Q9
Budapest (co.), Hun. 49/R9
Budaun, India 84/B1
Budd (coast), Ant. 160/H
Budd (inlet), Wa, US 135/B3
Budd Lake, NJ, US 138/D2
Buddon Ness (pt.), Sc, UK 36/D4
Buddusò, It. 46/A2
Bude, Eng, UK 32/B5
Bude (bay), Eng, UK 32/B5
Budějovický (pol. reg.), Slvk. 41/H4
Budel, Neth. 50/C6
Büdelsdorf, Ger. 38/C4
Budge-Budge, India 85/G4
Budhāna, India 86/D5
Budhanilantha, Nepal 85/E2
Budhlāda, India 86/C5
Budia, Sp. 44/D2
Büdingen, Ger. 54/C2
Budrio, It. 59/E3
Budva, Serb. 47/F1
Budzhak (reg.), Mol. 49/J2
Buea, Camr. 96/G7
Buellna (int'l arpt.), Mex. 142/D4
Buena, NJ, US 138/D4
Buena Esperanza, Arg. 158/D2
Buena Fe, Ecu. 152/B5
Buena Park, Ca, US 136/G8
Buena Vista, Co, US 129/F3
Buenaventura, Mex. 142/D2
Buenaventura, Col. 152/B4
Buenavista, Mex. 143/Q9
Buenavista, Phil. 79/E6
Bueno (riv.), Chile 158/B4
Bueno Brandão, Braz. 211/G7
Buenópolis, Braz. 154/A5
Buenos Aires (lake), Arg. 159/J11
Buenos Aires (prov.), Arg. 158/E3
Buenos Aires, Col. 152/B4
Buenos Aires, Peru 156/B2
Buenos Aires (lake), Arg.,Chile 147/B7
Buenos Aires (Jorge Newbery) (int'l arpt.), Arg. 159/J11
Buenos Aires (Ministro Pistarini) (int'l arpt.), Arg. 159/J11
Buerarema, Braz. 154/C4
Buesaco, Col. 152/B4
Buet (peak), Fr. 56/C5
Bueu, Sp. 44/A1
Buffalo (mt.), Austl. 115/C3
Buffalo (lake), Ab, Can. 126/E2
Buffalo (riv.), SAfr. 107/E2
Buffalo (riv.), Ar, US 132/E3
Buffalo, Mn, US 137/E2
Buffalo, NY, US 131/S10
Buffalo, Ok, US 129/H3
Buffalo, SD, US 127/H4
Buffalo, Wy, US 126/G4
Buffalo Bill Museum and Grave, Co, US 137/B3
Buffalo Narrows, Sk, Can. 126/F2
Buffalo Springs Nat'l Rsv., Kenya 104/C2
Buffelsrivier (riv.), SAfr. 106/B3
Buford, Ga, US 133/G3
Buftea, Rom. 49/G3
Bug (riv.), Pol. 41/M2
Buga, Col. 152/B4
Bugaba, Pan. 145/F4
Bugac, Hun. 48/D2
Bugala (isl.), Ugan. 104/B3
Bugalagrande, Col. 152/B3
Bugat, Mong. 70/F2
Buğdaylı, Turk. 49/H5
Bugel (pt.), Indo. 80/D5
Buggenhout, Belg. 53/D1
Bugojno, Bosn. 48/C3
Bugosa (prov.), Ugan. 104/B2
Bugsuk (isl.), Phil. 81/F1
Bugul'ma, Rus. 61/M5
Bugurusian, Rus. 63/K1
Buh (riv.), Ukr. 63/H3
Buhayrat al Asad (lake), Syria 90/D2
Buhayrat ath Tharthār (res.), Iraq 90/E3
Buhayrat Banzart (lake), Tun. 46/A4
Buhi, Phil. 79/D5
Buhl, Fr. 56/D2
Bühler (lake), Turk. 90/B2
Bühlerzell, Ger. 55/F2
Buhuşi, Rom. 49/H2

Bui (dam), Gha. 103/E4
Bui Gorge (res.), Gha. 103/E4
Bui NP, Gha. 103/E4
Buin (peak), Swi. 57/G4
Buin, Chile 158/N8
Buíque, Braz. 154/C3
Bujalance, Sp. 44/C4
Bujanovac, Serb. 47/G1
Bujumbura (cap.), Buru. 104/A3
Bujumbura (int'l arpt.), Buru. 104/A3
Buk, Pol. 41/J2
Buka (isl.), PNG 116/E5
Bukadaban (peak), China 70/F4
Bükän, Iran 88/E1
Bukasa (isl.), Ugan. 104/B3
Bukavu, D.R. Congo 104/A3
Bukene, Tanz. 104/B4
Buket Bubat (peak), Malay. 83/H6
Bukhoro (pol. reg.), Uzb. 87/D4
Bukhoro, Uzb. 87/D5
Bukhovo, Bul. 47/H1
Bukittinggi, Indo. 80/B4
Bukoba, Tanz. 104/A3
Buku (cape), Indo. 80/B4
Bülach, Swi. 57/E2
Bulahdelah, Austl. 115/E2
Bulan, Phil. 81/F1
Bulancak, Turk. 90/D1
Bulandshahr, India 84/A1
Bulanık, Turk. 90/E2
Bulawa (peak), Indo. 81/F3
Bulawayo, Zim. 105/E5
Buldan, Turk. 90/B2
Buldibuyo, Peru 156/B3
Bulgan, Mong. 70/H1
Bulgan (prov.), Mong. 70/H2
Bulgan, Mong. 70/H2
Bulgan, Mong. 70/H3
Bulgaria (ctry.) 49/H4
Bülgen, Swi. 57/F2
Bŭlgarovo, Bul. 49/H4
Bulgheria (peak), It. 46/D2
Buliluyan (cape), Phil. 81/E2
Bulk (riv.), BC, Can. 126/B2
Bull (pt.), NI, UK 34/B1
Bull Shoals (lake), Ar,Mo, US 129/J3
Bullange, Belg. 53/F3
Bullas, Sp. 44/E3
Bulle, Swi. 56/D4
Buller (isl.), NZ 117/S11
Bullerup, Den. 38/D3
Bullhead City, Az, US 128/D4
Bullion, Fr. 30/H6
Bulloo (riv.), Austl. 114/B4
Bulloo River Overflow (swamp), Austl. 114/A5
Bully-les-Mines, Fr. 52/B3
Bulnayn (mts.), Mong. 70/G2
Bulnes, Chile 158/B3
Bultfontein, SAfr. 106/D3
Bulukumba, Indo. 81/F5
Bulverde, Tx, US 137/U20
Bumba, D.R. Congo 97/K7
Bumtang (riv.), Bhu. 85/H2
Bunaga-take (peak), Japan 77/J5
Bunbury, Austl. 112/B5
Bundaberg, Austl. 114/D4
Bundarra, Austl. 115/D1
Bünde, Ger. 51/F4
Bunde, Ger. 51/E2
Bundoran, Ire. 31/P9
Bündu, India 85/E4
Bungendore, Austl. 115/D2
Bunguran (isl.), Indo. 80/C3
Bunia, D.R. Congo 104/A2
Bunker (peak), Az, US 137/R18
Bunker Hill, Il, US 135/K11
Bunkie, La, US 129/K7
Bunnell, Fl, US 133/H4
Bunnik, Neth. 50/C4
Buñol, Sp. 45/E3
Bunschoten, Neth. 50/C4
Bunya, Austl. 114/E6
Bunya Mountains NP, Austl. 114/C4
Bünyan, Turk. 90/C2
Bunyu (isl.), Indo. 81/E3
Buochs, Swi. 57/E4
Buon Me Thuot, Viet. 78/E3
Buonconvento, It. 43/J5
Buquim, Braz. 154/C3
Bür Sa'īd (gov.), Egypt 91/C4
Bür Sa'īd (Port Said), Egypt 91/B4
Bür Sūdān (Port Sudan), Sudan 101/D5
Burang, China 70/D5
Buranga (pass), Ugan. 97/M7
Burano (riv.), It. 59/F5
Burano, It. 57/J1
Buras-Triumph, La, US 133/F4
Burauen, Phil. 79/D5
Buraydah, SAr. 88/D3
Burbach, Ger. 53/H2
Burbank, Ca, US 136/F7
Burbure, Fr. 52/B2
Burco (Burao), Som. 99/Q6
Burdekin (riv.), Austl. 109/D2
Burdell (mtn.), Ca, US 135/J10
Burdur (lake), Turk. 90/B2
Burdur (prov.), Turk. 90/B2
Burdur, Turk. 90/B2

Burdwān, India 85/F4
Bure, Eng, UK 33/H1
Büren, Ger. 51/F5
Buren, Neth. 50/C5
Büren an der Aare, Swi. 56/D3
Bürengiyn (mts.), Mong. 70/H2
Bures-sur-Yvette, Fr. 30/J5
Bürewāla, Pak. 86/B4
Bureya (riv.), Rus. 65/P4
Burg, Ger. 38/C4
Burg, Ger. 40/F2
Burgas (prov.), Bul. 49/H4
Burgas (bay), Bul. 49/H4
Burgas (int'l arpt.), Bul. 49/H4
Burgau, Ger. 54/D6
Burgaw, NC, US 133/J3
Burgberg im Allgäu, Ger. 57/G2
Burgbernheim, Ger. 54/D3
Burgbrohl, Ger. 53/G3
Burgdorf, Ger. 51/H4
Burgdorf, Swi. 56/D3
Burgebrach, Ger. 54/D3
Burgenland (prov.), Aus. 41/J5
Burgeo, Nf, Can. 131/K2
Burgersdorp, SAfr. 106/D3
Burges (mt.), Austl. 112/D4
Burgess (mt.), Yk, Can. 134/L2
Burgess Hill, Eng, UK 33/F5
Burgfjället (peak), Swe. 37/F2
Burghaslach, Ger. 54/D3
Burghausen, Ger. 55/F6
Burghead, Sc, UK 36/C1
Burghead (bay), Sc, UK 36/C1
Burgheim, Ger. 54/E5
Burgkirchen, Aus. 55/G6
Burgkirchen an der Alz, Ger. 55/F6
Burgkunstadt, Ger. 54/E2
Bürglen, Swi. 57/F2
Burglengenfeld, Ger. 55/F4
Burgos, Mex. 143/F3
Burgos, Sp. 44/D1
Burgsinn, Ger. 54/C2
Burgstall (Postal), It. 57/H4
Burgsteinfurt, Ger. 50/E4
Burgsvik, Swe. 38/H3
Burgundy (reg.), Fr. 52/A3
Burgwedel, Ger. 51/G3
Burhabalang (riv.), India 85/F4
Burhan Budai (mts.), China 70/G4
Burhaniye, Turk. 90/A2
Burhānpur, India 89/L4
Burhar-Dhanpuri, India 84/C4
Burhi Gandok (riv.), India 85/E2
Burica (pen.), Pan. 140/E6
Burica (pt.), Pan. 145/F4
Buriram, Thai. 78/C3
Buriti, Braz. 155/B2
Buriti Alegre, Braz. 155/B1
Buriti Bravo, Braz. 154/B2
Buriti dos Lopes, Braz. 154/B1
Buritis, Braz. 154/A4
Buritizeiro, Braz. 154/A5
Burjasot, Sp. 45/E3
Burkardroth, Ger. 54/C2
Burke (chan.), BC, Can. 126/B2
Burketown, Austl. 114/A2
Burkina Faso (ctry.) 141/E3
Burksville, Il, US 137/G9
Burlady, Wa, US 135/B3
Burlingame, Ca, US 135/K11
Burlington, On, Can. 131/Q9
Burlington, Co, US 129/G3
Burlington, Ia, US 127/L5
Burlington, Il, US 135/N15
Burlington, NC, US 133/H3
Burlington, NJ, US 133/D3
Burlington (co.), NJ, US 138/D4
Burlington, Vt, US 130/F2
Burlington, Wi, US 130/B3
Burma (Myanmar) (ctry.) 83/G3
Bürmoos, Aus. 55/F7
Burnas (lake), Ukr. 49/J2
Burnet, Tx, US 129/H5
Burnet Heads, Austl. 114/D4
Burney, Ca, US 128/B2
Burney (peak), Chile 159/J7
Burnham, Il, US 135/Q16
Burnham-on-Sea, Eng, UK 32/D4
Burnie-Somerset, Austl. 115/C4
Burnley, Eng, UK 35/F4
Burns, Or, US 128/C2
Burns Lake, BC, Can. 126/B2
Burnside (riv.), Nun., Can. 122/E2
Burntisland, Sc, UK 36/C4
Burntwood, Eng, UK 33/E1
Burntwood (riv.), Mb, Can. 122/G3
Buronga, Austl. 115/B2
Buronzo, It. 58/B2
Burqā, WBnk. 91/G7

Burqīn, WBnk. 91/G7
Burr Ridge, Il, US 135/Q16
Burra, Austl. 113/H5
Burrel, Alb. 47/G2
Burrendong (res.), Austl. 115/D2
Burrewarra (pt.), Austl. 115/D2
Burriana, Austl. 45/E3
Burringbar, Austl. 114/D5
Burrinjuck (res.), Austl. 115/D2
Burrow (pt.), Sc, UK 34/C2
Burrowes (pt.), Austl. 114/D2
Burrum Heads, Austl. 114/D4
Burrum River NP, Austl. 114/D4
Burry (inlet), Wal, UK 32/B3
Bursa, Turk. 90/B1
Bursa (prov.), Turk. 90/B2
Burscheid, Ger. 53/G1
Bürstadt, Ger. 54/B3
Burt, NY, US 131/S9
Burtenbach, Ger. 54/D6
Burton, Wa, US 135/C3
Burton Latimer, Eng, UK 33/F2
Burton upon Trent, Eng, UK 33/E1
Buru (isl.), Indo. 67/M10
Burullus, Buḥayrat al (lake), Egypt 91/B4
Burundi (ctry.) 104/A3
Bururi, Buru. 104/A3
Buruticupu (riv.), Braz. 154/A2
Burwash Landing, Yk, Can. 134/L3
Bury, Eng, UK 35/F4
Bury (co.), Eng, UK 35/F4
Bury Saint Edmunds, Eng, UK 33/G2
Buryatiya, Resp., Rus. 65/M4
Bury Saint Edmunds, Eng, UK 33/G2
Burynshyk (pt.), Kaz. 63/J3
Busalla, It. 57/F2
Busembatia, Ugan. 104/B2
Busenberg, Ger. 53/G5
Buseno, Swi. 57/F5
Bush (riv.), Md, US 138/B5
Bush Kill (riv.), Pa, US 138/C1
Bushey, Eng, UK 30/B2
Bushkill, Pa, US 138/C1
Bushkill Falls, Pa, US 138/C1
Bushmanland (reg.), SAfr. 106/B3
Bushmills, NI, UK 34/B1
Busigny, Fr. 52/C3
Businga, D.R. Congo 97/K7
Buskerud (co.), Nor. 37/D3
Busko-Zdrój, Pol. 41/L3
Buss Craig (pt.), Sc, UK 36/D5
Busselton, Austl. 112/B5
Busseri (riv.), Sudan 97/L6
Busseto, It. 58/D3
Bussolengo, It. 57/H5
Bussum, Neth. 50/C4
Bustamante, Mex. 132/C5
Bustamante, Mex. 143/F4
Bustamante (pt.), Arg. 159/C2
Bustard (pt.), Austl. 114/C4
Busto Arsizio, It. 58/B1
Busto Garolfo, It. 58/B1
Busuanga (isl.), Phil. 79/C5
Büsum, Ger. 38/C4
Buta, D.R. Congo 97/K7
Buta Ranquil, Arg. 158/C3
Butare, Rwa. 104/A3
Butaritari (isl.), Kiri. 91/G7
Butawal, Nepal 84/D2
Bute (inlet), BC, Can. 126/B2
Bute, Austl. 113/H5
Bute (isl.), Sc, UK 36/A5
Bute, Sound of (sound), Sc, UK 36/A5
Büteeliyn (mts.), Mong. 70/H2
Butembo, D.R. Congo 104/A2
Bütgenbach, Belg. 53/F3
Buti, It. 58/D5
Butiá, Braz. 155/B4
Butiaba, Ugan. 104/A2
Butler, Ga, US 133/G3
Butler, Pa, US 130/E3
Butler (co.), NJ, US 138/D4
Butmir (int'l arpt.), Bosn. 48/D4
Butry-sur-Oise, Fr. 30/J4
Bütschelegg (peak), Swi. 56/D4
Bütschwil, Swi. 57/F3
Butt of Lewis (pt.), Sc, UK 36/Q7
Buttapietra, It. 59/D2
Butte-Silver Bow County, Mt, US 126/F4
Buttelborn, Ger. 54/B3
Butterworth, Malay. 80/B2
Buttes, Swi. 56/C4
Buttevant, Ire. 31/P10
Buttrio, It. 59/G1
Butuan, Phil. 79/E6
Butung (isl.), Indo. 67/M10
Buturlinovka, Rus. 63/G2
Butzbach, Ger. 54/B2
Bützow, Ger. 38/D5
Büech (riv.), Fr. 42/F4
Buulo Berde, Som. 99/Q7
Buuvuma (isl.), Ugan. 104/B2
Buxar, India 85/E3
Buxheim, Ger. 57/G2
Buxtehude, Ger. 51/G2
Buxton, Eng, UK 35/G5
Buy, Rus. 60/J4

Buyant-Uhaa, Mong. 71/K3
Buynaksk, Rus. 63/H4
Buyo, Barrage de (dam), C.d'Iv. 102/D5
Büyük Anafarta, Turk. 47/K2
Büyükçekmece, Turk. 90/D2
Büyükçekmece, Turk. 49/J5
Büyükceli, Turk. 49/H5
Büyükkarıştıran, Turk. 49/H5
Büyükyurt, Turk. 90/D2
Buyun Shan (peak), China 73/B2
Buzancais, Fr. 42/D3
Buzancy, Fr. 53/D5
Buzău, Rom. 49/H3
Buzău (prov.), Rom. 49/H3
Buzău (riv.), Rom. 62/C3
Buziaş, Rom. 48/E3
Búzios, Ilha dos (isl.), Braz. 211/H3
Buz'ky Lyman (estu.), Ukr. 49/K2
Buzsák, Hun. 48/C2
Buzuluk, Rus. 63/K1
Byala, Bul. 49/G4
Byala, Bul. 49/H4
Byala Slatina, Bul. 49/F4
Byam Martin (chan.), Nun., Can. 123/J1
Byam Martin (isl.), Nun., Can. 123/K1
Byarezina (riv.), Bela. 60/E5
Byaroza, Bela. 39/P5
Bydgoszcz, Pol. 41/J2
Byers, Co, US 137/C3
Byfield, Austl. 114/D3
Byford, Austl. 112/L7
Bygland, Nor. 38/B2
Bykhov, Bela. 60/E5
Bykle, Nor. 38/B2
Bykovo, Rus. 65/M4
Bylot (isl.), Nun., Can. 123/J1
Bynum Run (riv.), Md, US 138/B4
Byram (riv.), Ct, US 139/E1
Byram (pt.), Ct, US 139/L8
Byram (lake), NY, US 139/L7
Byramo, Nor. 38/B2
Byron, Ca, US 135/L11
Byron Bay, Austl. 114/D5
Byron (isl.), Chile 159/B5
Byrranga (mts.), Rus. 64/K2
Byron, Den. 38/D3
Bystrá (peak), Slvk. 41/K4
Bystrica, Czh. 55/F7
Bystřice, Czh. 55/H3
Bytantay (riv.), Rus. 65/N3
Byten, Pol. 41/K3
Bytom, Pol. 41/K3
Bytów, Pol. 38/G4

C

C.F. Secada (int'l arpt.), Peru 156/C1
Ca (riv.), Viet. 83/J3
Ca Mau, Viet. 78/D4
Ca Mau (cape), Viet. 78/D4
Caála, Ang. 105/C3
Caatingas (phys. reg.), Braz. 147/E3
Cacazapá, Par. 157/E2
Cabadbaran, Phil. 79/E6
Cabaiguán, Cuba 145/G1
Caban-Coch (res.), Wal, UK 32/C2
Cabana, Peru 156/B3
Cabanaconde, Peru 156/D4
Cabañaquinta, Sp. 44/C1
Cabanatuan, Phil. 79/D5
Cabanes, Sp. 45/F2
Cabano, Qu, Can. 131/G2
Cabella Ligure, It. 58/C2
Cabestany, Fr. 42/E5
Cabeza del Buey, Sp. 44/C3
Cabeza Lagarto (pt.), Peru 156/B4
Cabezón de la Sal, Sp. 44/C1
Cabildo, Arg. 158/E3
Cabimas, Ven. 152/D2
Cabinda, Ang. 105/B2
Cabinda (prov.), Ang. 105/B2
Cabo, Braz. 154/D2
Cabo Corrientes, Cabo (cape), Mex. 142/D4
Cabo de Hornos, PN (cape), Chile 157/C8
Cabo Delgado (prov.), Moz. 105/G4
Cabo Frio, Braz. 155/D2
Cabo Gracias a Dios, Nic. 145/F3
Cabo Orange, PN do, Braz. 151/H3
Cabo San Lucas, Mex. 142/D4
Cabo Verde, Braz. 211/G6
Cabonga (res.), Qu, Can. 123/J4
Caboolture, Austl. 114/D4
Cabora Bassa (lake), Moz. 105/F3
Cabora Bassa, Barragem de (dam), Moz. 105/F3
Cabot (str.), Can. 123/L4
Cabra de Santo Cristo, Sp. 44/D4
Cabral, Serra do (range), Braz. 154/A5

Cabras, It. 46/A3
Cabrera, Isla de (isl.), Sp. 45/G3
Cabri, Sk, Can. 126/F3
Cabriel (riv.), Sp. 44/E3
Cabrillo Nat'l Mon., Ca, US 136/C5
Cabrobó, Braz. 154/C3
Cabruta, Ven. 153/E3
Cabudare, Ven. 152/D2
Cabugao, Phil. 79/D4
Cabure, Ven. 152/D2
Caçador, Braz. 155/B3
Caçapava, Fr. 42/D3
Cacak, Serb. 48/E4
Cacalotán, Mex. 142/D4
Caccia (cape), It. 46/A2
Cáceres, Sp. 44/B3
Cáceres, Col. 152/C3
Cachapoal (riv.), Chile 158/N9
Cachari, Arg. 159/J12
Cache (peak), Id, US 126/E5
Cache (co.), Ut, US 137/K11
Cache Creek, BC, Can. 126/C3
Cache la Poudre (riv.), Co, US 137/C2
Cache Slough (riv.), Ca, US 135/L10
Cacheu, GBis. 102/A3
Cachi, Arg. 157/C2
Cachicadán, Peru 156/B3
Cachimbo, Serra do (mts.), Braz. 150/G5
Cachipo, Ven. 153/E2
Cachoeira de Minas, Braz. 211/G7
Cachoeira do Sul, Braz. 155/A4
Cachoeira Paulista, Braz. 211/H7
Cachoeiras de Macacu, Braz. 211/L7
Cachoeirinha, Braz. 155/B4
Caconde, Braz. 211/G6
Caçu, Braz. 155/B1
Caculé, Braz. 154/B4
Cadca, Slvk. 41/K4
Caddo (mts.), Ar, US 132/E3
Cadelbosco di Sopra, It. 58/D3
Cadenhorra, Sp. 44/E1
Cadelle (peak), It. 57/F5
Cadenberge, Ger. 51/G1
Cader Idris (peak), Wal, UK 32/C1
Cadillac, Mi, US 130/C2
Cadillac, Phil. 81/F1
Cadiz, Ky, US 130/C4
Cadiz, Phil. 79/D5
Cádiz, Sp. 44/B4
Cádiz, Golfo de (gulf), Port.,Sp. 44/B4
Cadolzburg, Ger. 54/D4
Cadria (peak), It. 57/G6
Caen, Fr. 42/C2
Caerano di San Marco, It. 59/F1
Caernarfon (bay), Wal, UK 34/D5
Caernarfon, Wal, UK 34/D5
Caernarfon Castle, Wal, UK 34/D5
Caerphilly, Wal, UK 32/C3
Caerphilly (co.), Wal, UK 32/C3
Caesarea (ruin), Isr. 91/G6
Caesarea (ruin), Isr. 91/D3
Caetité, Braz. 154/B4
Cafayate, Arg. 157/C2
Cafelândia, Braz. 154/B3
Cagayan Sulu (isl.), Phil. 79/C6
Cagli, It. 59/F5
Cagliari, It. 46/A3
Cagliari, Golfo di (gulf), It. 46/A3
Cagnes-sur-Mer, Fr. 43/G5
Caguán (riv.), Col. 150/D3
Caguas, PR 141/M8
Caher, Ire. 31/Q10
Cahirsiveen, Ire. 30/N11
Cahokia, Il, US 137/G8
Cahore (pt.), Ire. 31/Q10
Cahors, Fr. 42/D4
Cahuapanas, Peru 156/B2
Cahuinari (riv.), Col. 152/C5
Cahuita, PN, CR 145/F4
Cahul, Mol. 49/J3
Cai (riv.), Braz. 155/B4
Caiapó, Serra (mts.), Braz. 151/H7
Caibarién, Cuba 145/G1
Caicara, Ven. 153/E2
Caicó, Braz. 154/D2
Caicos (isls.), Uk 141/G3
Caicos Passage (chan.), Bahm. 145/H1
Cailloma, Peru 156/D4
Cailly (riv.), Fr. 52/A4
Caio (pass), It. 58/D3
Cairate, It. 58/B1
Cairn Curran (dam), Austl. 115/B3
Cairn Gorm (peak), Sc, UK 36/C2
Cairn Table (peak), Sc, UK 36/B6

Cairn Toul (peak), Sc, UK 36/C2
Cairndow, Sc, UK 36/B4
Cairngorm (mts.), Sc, UK 36/B2
Cairns (int'l arpt.), Austl. 114/B2
Cairns (mt.), Austl. 113/G2
Cairns, Austl. 114/B2
Cairnsmore of Carsphairn (peak), Sc, UK 36/B6
Cairo, Ga, US 133/G4
Cairo (peak), It. 46/C2
Cairo (int'l arpt.), Egypt 91/B4
Cairo Montenotte, It. 58/B4
Caistor Centre, On, Can. 131/Q9
Caistorville, On, Can. 131/Q9
Caiza (lake), China 72/D5
Cajabamba, Peru 156/B2
Cajabamba, Ecu. 152/B5
Cajacay, Peru 156/B3
Cajamarca (ruin), Peru 156/B2
Cajamarca, Peru 156/B2
Cajamarca (dept.), Peru 156/B2
Cajari, Braz. 154/A1
Cajatambo, Peru 156/B3
Cajazeiras, Braz. 154/C2
Cajíbio, Col. 152/B4
Cajón (pt.), Cuba 145/E1
Cajon Junction, Ca, US 136/C2
Cajuru (isl.), Hon. 140/E4
Caju (isl.), Braz. 154/B1
Çal, Turk. 90/B2
Cala d'Oliva, It. 46/A2
Calabar, Nga. 103/H5
Calabar (int'l arpt.), Nga. 103/H5
Calabasas, Ca, US 136/B2
Calabozo, Ven. 153/E2
Calabria, PN della, It. 46/D3
Calaburras (pt.), Sp. 44/C4
Calaceite, Sp. 45/F2
Calacoto, Bol. 156/D5
Calafat, Rom. 48/F4
Calahorra, Sp. 44/E1
Calais, Me, US 131/H2
Calais, Fr. 52/A2
Calais, Canal de (canal), Fr. 52/A2
Calalaste, Sierra de (mts.), Arg. 157/C2
Calama, Chile 157/C1
Calamar, Col. 152/C2
Calamian Group (isls.), Phil. 81/E1
Calamocha, Sp. 44/E2
Calamonte, Sp. 44/B3
Calañas, Sp. 44/B4
Calanda, Sp. 45/E2
Calangianus, It. 46/A2
Calapan, Phil. 79/D5
Călăraşi (prov.), Rom. 49/H3
Călăraşi, Rom. 49/H3
Calasparra, Sp. 44/E3
Calatayud, Sp. 44/E2
Calatorao, Sp. 44/E2
Calauag, Phil. 79/D5
Calaveras (lake), Tx, US 137/U21
Calaveras (res.), Ca, US 135/L12
Calayan, Phil. 79/D4
Calayan (isl.), Phil. 79/D4
Calbayog, Phil. 81/F1
Calberlah, Ger. 51/H4
Calbuco, Chile 158/B4
Calca, Peru 156/D4
Calcanhar, Ponta do (pt.), Braz. 154/D2
Calcasieu (riv.), La, US 129/J5
Calceta, Ecu. 152/A5
Calci, It. 58/D5
Calcinato, It. 58/D2
Calcinelli, It. 59/F5
Calcio, It. 58/C2
Calcium, NY, US 130/F2
Calçoene, Braz. 151/H3
Calcutta (Kolkata), India 85/G4
Calcutta (Kolkata) (int'l arpt.), India 85/G4
Calcutta, Sur. 153/H3
Caldaro (Kaltern), It. 43/J3
Caldas, Braz. 211/G7
Caldas, Col. 152/C3
Caldas da Rainha, Port. 44/A3
Caldas Novas, Braz. 155/B1
Calden, Ger. 51/G5
Calder (mt.), Ak, US 134/K4
Caldera de Taburiente, PN de la, Canl.,Sp. 98/A3
Calderara di Reno, It. 59/E3
Caldes, Venz. 152/D2
Caldercruix, Sc, UK 36/C5
Calderdale (co.), Eng, UK 35/F4
Caldes de Montbui, Sp. 45/L6
Caldew (riv.), Eng, UK 35/F2
Caldicot, Wal, UK 32/D3
Caldiero, It. 59/E2
Çaldıran, Turk. 90/F2
Caldonazzo, It. 57/H6
Caldono, Col. 152/B4

Caldwell, NJ, US 139/H8
Caldwell, Tx, US 129/H5
Caldwell, Wi, US 135/P14
Caldy (isl.), Eng., UK 32/B3
Caledon (riv.), SAfr. 106/D3
Caledon, On, Can. 131/Q8
Caledon, SAfr. 106/L11
Caledon, NI, UK 34/B3
Caledonia (hills), NB, Can. 131/H2
Caledonia, Wi, US 135/P14
Caledonian (canal), Sc, UK 36/B2
Calella, Sp. 45/G2
Calen, Austl. 114/C3
Calenzana, Fr. 46/A1
Calenzano, It. 59/E5
Calera de Tango, Chile 158/N8
Calestano, It. 58/D3
Caleta de Campos, Mex. 142/E5
Caleta Olivia, Arg. 158/D4
Calexico, Ca, US 128/D4
Calf of Man (isl.), IM, UK 34/C3
Calf, The (peak), Eng, UK 35/F3
Calgary (int'l arpt.), Ab, Can. 126/E3
Calgary, Ab, Can. 126/E3
Calheta, Azor., Port. 45/S12
Calhoun, Ga, US 133/G3
Calhoun, Ky, US 130/C4
Calhoun (co.), WV, US 137/F7
Cali, Col. 152/B4
Calicut (Kozhikode), India 82/C5
Calida, Costa (coast), Sp. 44/E4
Caliente, Nv, US 128/D3
Califon, NJ, US 138/D2
California (gulf), Mex. 142/B2
California (state), 128/B3
California, Md, US 130/E4
California, Mo, US 129/J3
Calilegua, PN, Arg. 157/D1
Călimăneşti, Rom. 49/G3
Calimaya, Mex. 143/Q10
Calimere (pt.), India 82/C5
Calimesa, Ca, US 136/C2
Calitri, It. 46/D2
Calixa-Lavallée, Qu, Can. 131/P6
Calizzano, It. 58/B4
Calkiní, Mex. 144/D1
Calkins (lake), Co, US 137/E2
Çalköy, Turk. 90/B2
Callabonna (lake), Austl. 115/A1
Callahonna (lake), Austl. 109/D3
Callalli, Peru 156/D4
Callan, Ire. 31/Q10
Callander, Sc, UK 36/B4
Callantsoog, Neth. 50/B3
Callao, Peru 156/B4
Callapa, Bol. 156/D5
Callaway, Fl, US 133/G4
Calle Larga, Chile 158/N8
Calliope, Austl. 114/C4
Callosa de Segura, Sp. 45/E3
Calne, Eng, UK 32/E4
Calolziocorte, It. 58/C1
Calonne-Ricouart, Fr. 52/B2
Calore (riv.), It. 46/D2
Caloundra, Austl. 114/D4
Calpe, Sp. 45/F3
Calpulalpan, Mex. 143/L7
Caltagirone, It. 46/D4
Caltanissetta, It. 46/D4
Caltavuturo, It. 46/C4
Caluire-et-Cuire, Fr. 42/F4
Calumet (riv.), Il, US 135/Q16
Calumet Sag (chan.), Il, US 135/Q16
Caluso, It. 58/A2
Calvello, It. 46/D2
Calvenzano, It. 58/C2
Calvert (isl.), BC, Can. 126/A3
Calvert, Tx, US 129/H5
Calverton, Md, US 138/B5
Calvi (peak), It. 59/E4
Calvi, It. 46/A1
Calviá, Sp. 45/G3
Calvillo, Mex. 142/E4
Calvinia, SAfr. 106/B3
Calvitero (peak), Sp. 44/C2
Calw, Ger. 54/B5
Calzada de Calatrava, Sp. 44/D3
Cam or Rhee (riv.), Eng, UK 33/F2
Cam Pha, Viet. 79/A3
Cam Ranh, Viet. 78/E4
Camaçari, Braz. 154/C4
Camacho, Mex. 142/E3
Camacupa, Ang. 105/C3
Camaguán, Ven. 153/E2
Camagüey (arch.), Cuba 141/F3
Camagüey, Cuba 145/G3
Camaiore, It. 58/C5
Camajuaní, Cuba 145/G1
Camalu, Mex. 142/A2
Camamu, Braz. 154/C4
Camamu, Baía de (bay), Braz. 154/C4
Camaná, Peru 156/C5
Camanducaia, Braz. 211/G7
Camaquã, Braz. 155/B4
Camaquã (riv.), Braz. 155/A4

Camargo, Sp. 44/D1
Camargos, Reprêsa de (res.), Braz. 211/J6
Camarillo, Ca, US 136/C4
Camariñas, Sp. 44/A1
Camarón (cape), Hon. 145/E3
Camarones (bay), Arg. 158/D5
Camarones, Arg. 158/D5
Camas, Sp. 44/B4
Cambará, Braz. 155/B2
Cambé, Braz. 155/B2
Camberley, Eng, UK 30/A3
Cambiano, It. 58/A3
Cambodia (ctry.) 78/D3
Camboriú, Ponta do (pt.), Braz. 155/C3
Cambrai, Fr. 52/C3
Cambrian (mts.), Wal, UK 34/E5
Cambridge (int'l arpt.), Eng, UK 33/G2
Cambridge, NZ 117/T10
Cambridge, Ma, US 131/G3
Cambridge, Md, US 130/E4
Cambridge, Oh, US 130/D3
Cambridge, On, Can. 130/D3
Cambridge Bay, Nun., Can. 122/F2
Cambridgeshire (co.), Eng, UK 33/F2
Cambrils, Sp. 45/F2
Cambuí, Braz. 211/G7
Cambuquira, Braz. 211/H6
Cambuslang, Sc, UK 36/B5
Cambutal (mtn.), Pan. 152/A3
Camden, Austl. 114/G9
Camden (co.), Eng, UK 30/C2
Camden, Al, US 133/G4
Camden, De, US 138/C5
Camden, Me, US 131/G2
Camden, NJ, US 138/C4
Camden (co.), NJ, US 138/C4
Camden, SC, US 133/H3
Camden Haven, Austl. 115/E1
Camden Point, Mo, US 137/D5
Campti, La, US 132/E4
Camrose, Ab, Can. 126/E2
Camel (riv.), Eng, UK 32/B6
Camelback (mtn.), Pa, US 138/C1
Camerano, It. 59/G5
Cameri, It. 58/B2
Cameron (isl.), Nun., Can. 123/R7
Cameron, Mo, US 129/J4
Cameron, Tx, US 129/H5
Cameroon (ctry.) 96/H7
Cametá, Braz. 151/J4
Camicia (peak), It. 46/C1
Camiguin (isl.), Phil. 79/D4
Camilla, Ga, US 133/G4
Camilo Aldao, Arg. 158/E2
Caminha, Port. 44/A2
Camiri, Bol. 150/F8
Camisano Vicentino, It. 59/E1
Çamlıdere, Turk. 90/C1
Çamlık NP, Turk. 90/C2
Çamlıyayla, Turk. 91/D1
Camoapa, Nic. 144/E3
Camogli, It. 58/C4
Camon, Fr. 52/B4
Camorta (isl.), India 83/F6
Camp Angelus (Angelus Oaks), Ca, US 136/D2
Camp Creek, Az, US 137/S18
Camp Hill, Pa, US 138/B3
Camp Lake, Wi, US 135/P14
Camp Springs, Md, US 138/B6
Campagna Lupia, It. 59/F2
Campagnola Emilia, It. 59/D3
Campana, Arg. 159/J11
Campana (isl.), Chile 159/B6
Campana, PN de la, Chile 158/N8
Campanário, Braz. 155/B1
Campanario (peak), Arg. 158/C2
Campanario (peak), Sp. 44/C3
Campanha, Braz. 211/H6
Campania (prov.), It. 46/D2
Campbell (isl.), US 135/L12
Campbell (isl.), NZ 23/T8
Campbell River, BC, Can. 126/B3
Campbell Town, Austl. 115/C4
Campbellsville, Ky, US 130/C4
Campbellton, NB, Can. 131/H1
Campbeltown, Sc, UK 31/R9
Campden, On, Can. 135/S9
Campeche (state), Mex. 140/C4
Campeche, Mex. 144/D2
Campeche (bay), Mex. 143/G5
Camperdown, Austl. 115/B3
Camperville, Mb, Can. 127/H3
Campestre, Braz. 211/G6
Campi Bisenzio, It. 59/E5

Campidano (range), It. 46/A3
Campillo de Altobuey, Sp. 44/C4
Campillos, Sp. 44/C4
Campina Verde, Braz. 155/B1
Campinas, Braz. 211/F7
Campione d'Italia, It. 57/E6
Campo (int'l arpt.) Braz. 156/C2
Campo Belo, Braz. 155/C2
Campo de Criptana, Sp. 44/D3
Campo de la Cruz, Col. 152/C2
Campo dei Fiori (peak), It. 58/B1
Campo Grande, Braz. 151/H8
Campo Ligure, It. 58/B3
Campo Limpo Paulista, Braz. 211/G8
Campo Maior, Port. 44/B3
Campo Mourão, Braz. 155/A3
Campo Tencia (peak), Swi. 57/E5
Campo Tizzoro, It. 59/D4
Campoalegre, Col. 152/C4
Campobasso, It. 46/D2
Campodarsego, It. 59/E2
Campodolcino, It. 57/F5
Campogalliano, It. 59/D3
Campomorone, It. 58/B3
Camponogara, It. 59/F2
Camporosso, It. 58/A5
Camporredondo, Peru 156/B2
Camporredondo, Embalse de (res.), Sp. 44/C1
Campos (phys. reg.), Braz. 147/D5
Campos Altos, Braz. 155/C1
Campos Belos, Braz. 154/A4
Campos de Hielo Norte (glacier), Chile 159/B5
Campos de Hielo Sur (glacier), Chile 159/B6
Campos del Puerto, Sp. 45/G3
Campos do Jordão, Braz. 211/H7
Campos Gerais, Braz. 155/C2
Campos Novos, Braz. 155/B3
Campos Sales, Braz. 154/B2
Camposampiero, It. 59/E1
Campsie Fells (hills), Sc, UK 36/B4
Can (riv.), Eng, UK 30/H5
Can, Turk. 49/H5
Can Tho, Viet. 78/D4
Canaçari (lake), Braz. 153/G5
Canada (ctry.) 122
Cañada de Gómez, Arg. 158/E2
Cañada Nieto, Uru. 159/J10
Cañada Rosquín, Arg. 158/E2
Canadensis, Pa, US 138/C1
Canadian, Tx, US 129/G4
Canadian, North (riv.), Ok, US 124/F4
Canadian (co.), Ok, US 137/M15
Canajoharie, NY, US 130/E3
Çanakkale, Turk. 47/K2
Çanakkale (prov.), Turk. 90/A2
Canal de Moraleda (chan.), Chile 157/B6
Canalbianco (riv.), It. 59/E2
Canale, It. 58/A3
Canale Cavour (canal), It. 58/A2
Canals, Sp. 45/E3
Canals, Arg. 158/E2
Canandaigua, NY, US 130/E3
Cananea, Mex. 142/C2
Cananéia, Braz. 155/C3
Canápolis, Braz. 155/B1
Cañar (dept.), Ecu. 152/B5
Cañar, Ecu. 156/B3
Canary (isls.), Sp. 93/A2
Cañas, CR 144/E4
Cañasgordas, Col. 152/B3
Canatlán de las Manzanas, Mex. 142/D3
Canaveral (cape), Fl, US 133/H4
Canberra, Austl. 115/D2
Canchaque, Peru 156/B2
Canche (riv.), Fr. 42/E1
Cancún (int'l arpt.) Mex. 144/E1
Candado, Nevado del (peak), Arg. 158/C2
Candarave, Peru 156/D5
Çandarlı (gulf), Gre.,Turk 62/C5
Candás, Sp. 44/C1
Candeias, Braz. 154/C4
Candelaria, Mex. 144/D2
Candelaria (riv.), Mex. 144/D2
Candelaria, Arg. 159/F2
Candeleda, Sp. 44/C2
Candelo, Austl. 115/D3

Candelo, It. 58/B1
Candia Lomellina, It. 58/B2
Candiac, Qu, Can. 131/N7
Candiba, Braz. 154/B4
Cândido Mota, Braz. 155/B2
Canding (cape), Indo. 80/D5
Candir, Turk. 90/C2
Candlewood, NJ, US 138/D3
Cando, ND, US 127/J3
Candon, Phil. 79/D4
Canegrate, It. 58/B1
Canela, Braz. 155/B4
Canelli, It. 58/B3
Canelones (dept.), Uru. 159/F2
Canelones, Uru. 159/K11
Cañete, Sp. 44/E2
Canete, Rio de (riv.), Peru 156/B4
Cangallo, Peru 156/C4
Cangas, Sp. 44/A1
Cangas de Narcea, Sp. 44/B1
Cangas de Onís, Sp. 44/C1
Cango Caves, SAfr. 106/C4
Cangrejo (peak), Arg. 159/B6
Cangshan, China 72/D4
Canguaretama, Braz. 154/D2
Canguçu, Braz. 155/A4
Cangwu, China 83/K3
Cangyuan (Cangyuan Vazu Zizhixian), China 83/G3
Cangzhou, China 72/D3
Canh Cuoc (isl.), Viet. 78/D1
Cania Gorge NP, Austl. 114/C4
Caniapiscau (lake), Qu, Can. 123/K3
Caniapiskau (riv.), Qu, Can. 123/J3
Canicattì, It. 46/C4
Canik (mts.), Turk. 90/C1
Caniles, Sp. 44/D4
Canindé (riv.), Braz. 151/K5
Canino, It. 46/B1
Canistear (res.), NJ, US 139/H7
Cañitas de Felipe Pescador, Mex. 142/E4
Canjáyar, Sp. 44/D4
Çankırı, Turk. 90/C1
Çankırı (prov.), Turk. 90/C1
Canlaon (vol.), Phil. 81/F1
Canmore, Ab, Can. 126/E3
Cann River, Austl. 115/D3
Canna (isl.), Sc, UK 31/Q8
Cannanore, India 82/C5
Canne (ruin), It. 46/E2
Canner (riv.), Fr. 53/F5
Cannero Riviera, It. 57/E5
Cannes, Fr. 43/G5
Canning (peak), Austl. 112/C4
Canning (dam), Austl. 112/L7
Canning (riv.), Austl. 112/K7
Cannobio, It. 57/E5
Cannock, Eng, UK 32/D1
Cannon Falls, Mn, US 127/K4
Cannonball (riv.), ND, US 127/H4
Cannondale, Ct, US 139/E1
Cannonsville, Austl. 114/C3
Cannonvale, Austl. 114/C3
Caño Guaritico (riv.), Ven. 154/E3
Caño Negro NWF, CR 145/E4
Canoas, Braz. 155/B4
Canoas (riv.), Braz. 155/B3
Canobolas (mt.), Austl. 115/D2
Canoinhas, Braz. 155/B3
Cañon de Rio Blanco, PN, Mex. 143/M8
Cañón del Sumidero, PN, Mex. 144/C2
Canora, Sk, Can. 127/H3
Canosa di Puglia, It. 46/E2
Canouan (isl.), StV. 141/N9
Canowindra, Austl. 115/D2
Cansahcab, Braz. 154/C3
Canso (cape), NS, Can. 131/J2
Canta, Peru 156/B3
Cantabria (aut. comm.), Sp. 44/C1
Cantabria, Cordillera (mts.), Sp. 44/B1
Cantal, Massif du (mass.), Fr. 42/E4
Cantalejo, Sp. 44/D2
Cantanhede, Braz. 154/A1
Cantanhede, Port. 44/A2
Cantaura, Ven. 153/E2
Canterbury, Eng, UK 33/H4
Canterbury Bight (bay), NZ 109/H7
Canterbury Cathedral, Eng, UK 33/H4
Cantillana, Sp. 44/C4
Canto do Buriti, Braz. 154/B3
Canton, Mi, US 135/E7
Canton, Ms, US 129/K4
Canton, NJ, US 138/C5
Canton, NY, US 130/F2
Canton, Oh, US 130/D3
Canton, SD, US 132/D2
Canton (Abariringa) (isl.), Kiri. 117/H5
Cantù, It. 58/C1
Cantwell, Ak, US 134/J3

Cañuelas, Arg. 159/J11
Canunda NP, Austl. 115/B3
Canvey (isl.), Eng, UK 30/E2
Canvey Island, Eng, UK 33/G3
Canwood, Sk, Can. 126/G2
Canyon, Tx, US 129/G4
Canyon (lake), Tx, US 137/U20
Canyon de Chelly Nat'l Mon., Az, US 128/E3
Canyon Lake, Tx, US 137/U20
Canyonlands Nat'l Park, Ut, US 128/E3
Canyon of the Ancients Nat'l Mon., Co, US 128/E3
Capac, Mi, US 135/G5
Capanaparo (riv.), Ven. 150/E2
Capanema, Braz. 151/J4
Capanne (peak), It. 46/B1
Capannoli, It. 58/D5
Capannori, It. 58/D5
Capão Bonito, Braz. 155/B3
Capão Doce, Morro do (hill), Braz. 155/B3
Caparaó, PN do, Braz. 155/D2
Caparica (cap.), Port. 45/P10
Caparo (riv.), Ven. 152/D3
Capdenac-Gare, Fr. 42/E4
Capdepera, Sp. 45/G3
Cape Arid NP, Austl. 112/D5
Cape Barren (isl.), Austl. 109/D5
Cape Breton (isl.), NS, Can. 131/J2
Cape Breton Highlands (uplands), NS, Can. 131/J2
Cape Breton Highlands NP, NS, Can. 131/J2
Cape Cleveland NP, Austl. 114/B2
Cape Coast, Gha. 103/F5
Cape Cod Nat'l Seashore, Ma, US 131/G3
Cape Coral, Fl, US 133/H5
Cape Dorset, Nun., Can. 123/J2
Cape Fear (riv.), NC, US 133/J3
Cape Hatteras Nat'l Seashore, NC, US 133/K3
Cape Krusenstern Nat'l Mon., Ak, US 134/D2
Cape Le Grand NP, Austl. 112/D5
Cape Lookout Nat'l Seashore, NC, US 133/J3
Cape May, NJ, US 138/D6
Cape May (co.), NJ, US 138/D5
Cape May Court House, NJ, US 138/D5
Cape May Lighthouse, NJ, US 138/D6
Cape Melville NP, Austl. 114/B1
Cape Palmerston NP, Austl. 114/C3
Cape Range NP, Austl. 112/A3
Cape Saint Claire, Md, US 138/B5
Cape Town (cap.), SAfr. 106/L10
Cape Town (D.F. Malan) (int'l arpt.), SAfr. 106/L10
Cape Tribulation NP, Austl. 114/B2
Cape Upstart NP, Austl. 114/B2
Cape Verde (ctry.) 93/A9
Cape Yakataga, Ak, US 134/K3
Cape York (pen.), Austl. 109/D2
Capel, Austl. 112/B5
Capelinha, Braz. 155/D1
Capella, Austl. 114/C3
Capellades, Sp. 45/K6
Capendu, Fr. 42/E5
Capestang, Fr. 42/E5
Capilla del Señor, Arg. 159/J11
Capim (riv.), Braz. 151/J4
Capinópolis, Braz. 155/B1
Capirara (res.), Braz. 157/F1
Capistrello, It. 46/C2
Capitan, NM, US 132/B3
Capitão de Campos, Braz. 154/B2
Capitão Poço, Braz. 151/J4

Capitol Reef NP, Ut, US 128/E3
Capivara, Reprêsa (res.), Braz. 151/H8
Capivara, Serra de (range), Braz. 154/A4
Capivari (riv.), Braz. 211/J6
Čapljina, Bosn. 47/C1
Caplone (peak), It. 58/D1
Capo di Ponte, It. 57/G5
Capo d'Orlando, It. 46/D3
Capodichino (int'l arpt.), It. 46/D2
Capolona, It. 59/E5
Capoterra, It. 46/A3
Cappella Maggiore, It. 59/F1
Cappoquin, Ire. 31/Q10
Capraia (isl.), It. 46/A1
Caprarola, It. 46/C1
Capreol, On, Can. 130/D2
Capri (isl.), It. 46/D2
Caprino Veronese, It. 59/D1
Capriolo, It. 58/C1
Caprivi Strip (reg.), Namb. 105/D4
Captain (har.), Ct, US 139/L7
Captain Cook, Hi, US 124/U11
Captainganj, India 84/D2
Captains Flat, Austl. 115/D2
Capua, It. 48/B5
Capulhuac, Mex. 143/Q10
Capulhuac, Mex. 143/Q10
Caputh, Ger. 40/D7
Caquetá (riv.), Col. 152/C5
Caquetá (dept.), Col. 152/C4
Caquiaviri, Bol. 156/D5
Car Nicobar (isl.), India 83/F6
Carabobo (state), Ven. 152/D2
Caracal, Rom. 49/G3
Caracarai, Braz. 153/F4
Caracas (cap.), Ven. 150/E1
Carache, Ven. 152/D2
Caracol, Braz. 154/B3
Caracolí, Col. 152/C3
Carácuaro de Morelos, Mex. 143/E5
Caradon (hill), Eng, UK 32/B5
Caraguatatuba, Braz. 211/H8
Caraguatatuba, Enseada de (bay), Braz. 211/H8
Carahue, Chile 158/B3
Carajás, Serra dos (mts.), Braz. 151/H5
Caranavi, Bol. 150/E7
Carandaí, Braz. 155/D2
Carangola, Braz. 155/D2
Caransebeş, Rom. 48/F3
Carapicuíba, Braz. 211/G8
Carappee Hill (peak), Austl. 113/H5
Caras Casares, Arg. 158/E2
Caraş-Severin (prov.), Rom. 48/E3
Carasco, It. 58/C4
Carate Brianza, It. 58/C1
Caratinga, Braz. 155/D1
Carauari, Braz. 150/E4
Caraúbas, Braz. 154/C2
Caravaca de la Cruz, Sp. 44/E3
Caravaggio, It. 58/C2
Caravela, Ilha (isl.), GBis. 102/A4
Caravelas, Braz. 154/C5
Caravelí, Peru 156/C4
Caraz, Peru 156/B3
Carazinho, Braz. 155/B3
Carballino, Sp. 44/A1
Carballo, Sp. 44/A1
Carberry, Mb, Can. 127/J3
Carbo, Mex. 142/C2
Carbon (cape), Alg. 100/H4
Carbon (co.), Pa, US 138/C2
Carbon (riv.), Wa, US 135/C3
Carbonara (cape), It. 46/A4
Carbonara (peak), It. 46/A4
Carbondale, Pa, US 138/C1
Carbonear, Nf, Can. 131/L2
Carbonne, Fr. 42/D5
Carbost, Sc, UK 31/Q8
Carcagente, Sp. 45/E3
Carcarañá, Arg. 158/E2
Carcare, It. 58/B4
Carcassonne, Fr. 42/E5
Carche (peak), Sp. 44/E3
Carcross, Yk, Can. 134/M3
Cardal, Uru. 159/K11
Çardak, Turk. 49/H5
Cardedeu, Sp. 45/L6
Cardeña, Sp. 44/C3
Cardenden, Sc, UK 36/C4
Cárdenas, Cuba 145/F1
Cárdenas, Mex. 144/C2
Cárdenas, Mex. 143/F4
Cardiel (lake), Arg. 159/B6
Cardiff (co.), Wal, UK 32/C4
Cardiff, Wal, UK 32/C4
Cardiff, Md, US 138/B4
Cardiff by the Sea, Ca, US 136/C5
Cardigan, Wal, UK 32/B2
Cardona, Uru. 159/K10
Cardona, Sp. 45/F2
Cardoso, Braz. 155/B2
Cardston, Ab, Can. 126/E3
Cardwell, Austl. 114/B2

Care Alto (peak), It. 57/G5
Careaçu, Braz. 211/H7
Carefree, Az, US 137/S18
Carei, Rom. 41/M5
Carentan, Fr. 42/C2
Carev vrh (peak), FYROM 47/H1
Carey (lake), Austl. 109/B3
Carhaix-Plouguer, Fr. 42/B2
Carhuamayo, Peru 156/B3
Carhué, Arg. 158/E2
Cariacica, Braz. 155/D2
Cariaco, Ven. 153/F2
Cariamanga, Ecu. 156/B2
Cariati, It. 46/E3
Cariboo (mts.), BC, Can. 126/C2
Cariboo (chan.), Austl. 109/E3
Caribou (range), Id, US 126/F5
Caribou (mts.), Ab, Can. 122/E3
Caribou, Me, US 131/G2
Carignan, Qu, Can. 131/P7
Carignan, Fr. 53/E4
Carignano, It. 58/A3
Cariñena, Sp. 44/E2
Carinhanha, Braz. 154/B4
Carinhanha (riv.), Braz. 154/A4
Carini, It. 46/C3
Caripito, Ven. 153/F2
Cariríaçu, Braz. 154/C2
Cariris Novos, Serra dos (mts.), Braz. 154/B2
Carleton (mt.), NB, Can. 131/H2
Carleton, Qu, Can. 131/H1
Carleton, Mi, US 135/F7
Carleton Place, On, Can. 130/E2
Carlin, Nv, US 126/D5
Carlindie Abor. Land, Austl. 112/C2
Carling, Fr. 53/F5
Carlingford, Ire. 34/B1
Carlingford (lake), Ire. 34/B1
Carlingford (mtn.), Ire. 34/B3
Carlinville, Il, US 129/K3
Carlisle, Pa, US 130/E3
Carlisle, La, US 137/Q17
Carlisle (inlet), Wa, US 135/F2
Carlisle Barracks Mil. Res., Pa, US 138/A3
Carlit (peak), Fr. 42/D5
Carlos Casares, Arg. 158/E2
Carlos Chagas, Braz. 154/B5
Carlos M. de Cespedes, Cuba 145/G1
Carlow (co.), Ire. 34/B6
Carlow, Ire. 31/Q10
Carloway, Sc, UK 31/Q7
Carlsbad, Ca, US 136/C4
Carlsbad, NM, US 129/F4
Carlsbad Caverns NP, NM, US 142/D1
Carlsberg, Ger. 54/B3
Carlsfeld, Ger. 55/F2
Carlton, Eng, UK 35/G6
Carluke, Sc, UK 36/C5
Carlyle, Sk, Can. 127/H3
Carlyle (lake), Il, US 129/K3
Carmacks, Yk, Can. 134/L3
Carmagnola, It. 58/A3
Carman, Mb, Can. 127/J3
Carmarthen, Wal, UK 32/B3
Carmarthen (bay), Wal, UK 32/B3
Carmarthenshire (co.), Wal, UK 32/B3
Carmaux, Fr. 42/E4
Carmel (pt.), Wal, UK 34/D5
Carmelo, Uru. 159/J11
Carmen (isl.), Mex. 144/C2
Carmen de Patagones, Arg. 158/E4
Carmen, Arg. 158/E2
Carmo, Braz. 211/L6
Carmo (peak), It. 58/B4
Carmo da Cachoeira, Braz. 211/H6
Carmo de Minas, Braz. 211/H7
Carmo do Paranaíba, Braz. 155/C1
Carmo do Rio Claro, Braz. 155/C2
Carmona, Sp. 44/C4
Carn Ban (peak), Sc, UK 36/B2
Carn Easgann Bàna (peak), Sc, UK 36/B2
Càrn Eige (peak), Sc, UK 36/B3
Carn Glas-choire (peak), Sc, UK 36/C2
Carn Kitty (hill), Sc, UK 36/C2
Carn Mairg (peak), Sc, UK 36/B3
Càrn Mòr (peak), Sc, UK 36/C2
Carn na Cailliche (hill), Sc, UK 36/C1
Carn na Saobhaidhe (peak), Sc, UK 36/B2

Carnago, It. 58/B1
Carnamah, Austl. 112/B4
Carnarvon, Austl. 109/A3
Carnarvon NP, Austl. 114/B4
Carnarvon, SAfr. 106/C3
Carnarvonleegte (riv.), SAfr. 106/C3
Carnation, Wa, US 135/D2
Carnaubal, Braz. 154/B2
Carnaxide, Port. 45/P10
Carncastle, NI, UK 34/C2
Carndonagh, Ire. 34/A1
Carnduff, Sk, Can. 127/H3
Carnedd Llewelyn (peak), Wal, UK 34/E5
Carnegie (lake), Austl. 109/B3
Carney, Ok, US 137/N14
Carney (isl.), Ant. 160/S
Carnforth, Eng, UK 35/F3
Carnlough, NI, UK 34/C2
Carnot (cape), Austl. 113/G5
Carnot, CAfr. 96/J7
Carnota, Sp. 44/A1
Carnsore (pt.), Ire. 31/Q10
Carnwath (riv.), NW, Can.
Carnwath, Sc, UK 36/C5
Caro, Mi, US 130/D3
Carol Stream, Il, US 135/P16
Carolina, Braz. 154/A2
Carolina, PR 141/M8
Carolina, SAfr. 107/E2
Carolina Beach, NC, US 133/J3
Caroline (isl.), Kiri. 117/K5
Caroline (isls.), Micr. 116/D4
Caroní (riv.), Ven. 147/C2
Carora, Ven. 152/D2
Carouge, Swi. 56/C5
Carpaneto Piacentino, It. 58/C3
Carpathian (mts.), Eur. 27/G4
Carpegna (peak), It. 59/F5
Carpegna, It. 59/F5
Carpenedolo, It. 59/D2
Carpentaria, Gulf of (gulf), Austl. 109/C2
Carpenter, Il, US 137/H8
Carpentersville, Il, US 135/P15
Carpentras, Fr. 42/F4
Carpi, It. 59/D3
Carpignano Sesia, It. 58/B1
Carpina, Braz. 154/D2
Carpinteria, Ca, US 136/A2
Carpiquet (int'l arpt.), Fr. 42/C2
Carr (inlet), Wa, US 135/B3
Carrabelle, Fl, US 133/G4
Carrantuohill (peak), Ire. 31/P10
Carrara, It. 58/D4
Carrasco (int'l arpt.), Uru. 159/K11
Carrasquero, Ven. 152/D2
Carreg Ddu (pt.), Wal, UK 34/D6
Carriacou (isl.), Gren. 150/F1
Carrick (reg.), Sc, UK 36/B6
Carrick on Shannon, Ire. 31/P10
Carrick on Suir, Ire. 31/Q10
Carrickalinga, Austl. 113/H5
Carrickfergus, NI, UK 34/C2
Carrickfergus (dist.), NI, UK 34/C2
Carrickmacross, Ire. 31/Q10
Carrickmore, NI, UK 34/A2
Carrières-sous-Poissy, Fr. 30/J5
Carrigaholt, Ire. 31/P10
Carrigaline, Ire. 31/P11
Carrington, ND, US 127/J4
Carrión (riv.), Sp. 44/C1
Carrión de los Condes, Sp. 44/C1
Carrizo (mts.), Az, US 124/D3
Carrizo Plain Nat'l Mon., Ca, US 136/B3
Carrizo Springs, Tx, US 132/D4
Carrizo Wash (riv.), Az,NM, US 128/E4
Carrizozo, NM, US 129/F4
Carroll (co.), Md, US 138/A5
Carrollton, Ky, US 130/C4
Carrollton, Ga, US 133/G3
Carron (lake), Sc, UK 36/A2
Carron (riv.), Sc, UK 36/A2
Carrot (riv.), SK, Can. 127/H2
Carrot River, Sk, Can. 127/H2
Carrowdore, NI, UK 34/C2
Carrowkeel, Ire. 34/A1
Carrù, It. 58/A4
Carrum Downs, Austl. 115/G6
Carryduff, NI, UK 34/C2
Çarşamba, Turk. 90/D1
Carse of Forth (plain), Sc, UK 36/B4
Carse of Gowrie (plain), Sc, UK 36/C4
Carson (riv.), Nv, US 128/C3
Carson, Ca, US 136/F8
Carson City (cap.), Nv, US 128/C3
Carson Sink (dry lake), Nv, US 128/C3
Cartagena, Chile 158/N8
Cartagena, Col. 152/C2

Church Hill, Md, US 138/C5
Churchill, Austl. 115/G3
Churchill (peak), BC, Can. 122/D2
Churchill, Mb, Can. 122/D3
Churchill (cape), Mb, Can. 122/G3
Churchill (riv.), Mb,Sk, Can. 122/F3
Churchill (lake), Sk, Can. 122/F3
Churchill Falls, Nf, Can. 123/K3
Churchill NP, Austl. 115/G5
Churchville, Md, US 138/B4
Churia Ghats (mts.), Nepal 85/E2
Churin, Peru 156/B3
Churnet (riv.), Eng, UK 35/G5
Churu, India 86/C5
Churuguara, Ven. 152/D2
Churumuco de Morelos, Mex. 143/E5
Churwalden, Swi. 57/F4
Chuschi, Peru 156/C4
Chuska (mts.), Az,NM, US 128/E3
Chusovaya (riv.), Rus. 61/N4
Chusovoy, Rus. 61/N4
Chutung, Tai. 79/D3
Chuvashiya, Resp., Rus. 64/Q6
Chuwang-san NP, SKor. 74/A2
Chuxiong, China 83/H2
Chüy (obl.), Kyr. 87/F4
Chuzhou, China 71/L5
Chūzu, Japan 77/K5
Ci Xian, China 72/C3
Ciadîr-Lunga, Mol. 49/J2
Ciamis, Indo. 80/C5
Ciampino (int'l arpt.), It. 46/C2
Ciampino, It. 46/C2
Cianjur, Indo. 80/C5
Cibolo, Tx, US 137/U20
Cicagna, It. 58/C4
Cicero, Il, US 130/C3
Cicero Dantas, Braz. 154/C3
Čićevac, Serb. 48/E4
Cide, Turk. 90/C1
Ciechanów, Pol. 41/L2
Ciechocinek, Pol. 41/K2
Ciego de Ávila, Cuba 145/G1
Ciénaga, Col. 152/C2
Ciénaga de Oro, Col. 152/C2
Cienfuegos, Cuba 145/F1
Cieplice Śląskie Zdrój, Pol. 41/H3
Cieszyn, Pol. 41/K4
Cieza, Sp. 44/E3
Çiftteler, Turk. 90/B2
Cifuentes, Sp. 44/D2
Cifuentes, Cuba 145/F1
Cigánd, Hun. 41/L4
Cigliano, It. 58/B2
Cigüela (riv.), Sp. 44/D3
Cihanbeyli, Turk. 90/C2
Cihuatlán, Mex. 142/D5
Cijara, Embalse de (res.), Sp. 44/C3
Cijulung, Indo. 80/C5
Cilacap, Indo. 80/C5
Cilavegna, It. 58/B2
Çıldır (lake), Turk. 90/E1
Çilfaesty (peak), Wal, UK 32/C2
Cili, China 79/B2
Cilleros, Sp. 44/B2
Cima della Laurasca (peak), It. 57/E5
Cima de'Piazzi (peak), It. 57/G5
Cima la Casina (peak), It. 57/G4
Cimarron (range), NM, US 132/B2
Cimarron (riv.), Ks,Ok, US 124/G4
Cime du Cheiron (peak), Fr. 43/G5
Cime du Diable (peak), Fr. 43/G4
Cimone (peak), It. 59/D4
Cimpeni, Rom. 49/F2
Cimpina, Rom. 49/G3
Cîmpina, Rom. 49/G3
Cimpulung, Rom. 49/G3
Cimpulung Moldovenesc, Rom. 49/G2
Çınar, Turk. 90/E2
Çınarcık, Turk. 49/J5
Cinaruco (riv.), Ven. 152/D3
Cinca (riv.), Sp. 45/F1
Cincar (peak), Bosn. 40/C4
Cincinnati, Oh, US 130/C4
Cinco Saltos, Arg. 158/C3
Cindrelu (peak), Rom. 49/F3
Çine, Turk. 90/B2
Ciney, Belg. 53/E3
Cingia de'Botti, It. 58/D2
Cingoli, It. 59/G6
Ciniselo Balsamo, It. 58/C1
Cinnaminson, NJ, US 138/D4
Cintalapa de Figueroa, Mex. 144/C2
Cinto (peak), Fr. 46/A1
Cinto Caomaggiore, It. 59/F1
Cintruénigo, Sp. 44/E1
Čiovo (isl.), Cro. 48/C4
Cipó, Braz. 154/C3

Cipolletti, Arg. 158/D3
Circeo, PN del, It. 46/C2
Circle, Ak, US 134/K2
Circle, Mt, US 127/G4
Circle Hot Springs, Ak, US 134/K2
Cirebon, Indo. 80/C5
Cirencester, Eng, UK 32/E3
Cires-lès-Mello, Fr. 52/B5
Cirò Marina, It. 47/E3
Ciron (riv.), Fr. 42/C4
Ciserano, It. 58/C1
Cisnădie, Rom. 49/G3
Cisneros, Col. 152/C3
Cisnes (riv.), Chile 158/B5
Cisse (riv.), Fr. 42/D3
Cisterna di Latina, It. 46/C2
Cistierna, Sp. 44/C1
Citlaltépetl (vol.), Mex. 143/M7
Citrus Heights, Ca, US 128/B3
Citrusdal, SAfr. 106/L10
Città del Vaticano (Vatican City) (cap.), VatC. 46/C2
Città di Castello, It. 59/F6
Città di Torino (int'l arpt.), It. 43/G4
Cittadella, It. 59/E1
Cittanova, It. 46/E3
Cittiglio, It. 57/E6
City (isl.), NY, US 139/K8
City (int'l arpt.), NI, UK 34/C2
Ciudad Acuña, Mex. 129/G5
Ciudad Altamirano, Mex. 143/E5
Ciudad Bolívar, Ven. 153/F2
Ciudad Bolivia, Ven. 152/D2
Ciudad Camargo, Mex. 142/D3
Ciudad Constitución, Mex. 142/C3
Ciudad Cortés, CR 145/F4
Ciudad Cuauhtémoc, Mex. 144/B1
Ciudad de Dolores Hidalgo, Mex. 143/E4
Ciudad de México (Mexico) (cap.), Mex. 143/Q10
Ciudad de Nutrias, Ven. 152/D2
Ciudad de Río Grande, Mex. 142/E4
Ciudad del Carmen, Mex. 144/D2
Ciudad del Maíz, Mex. 143/F4
Ciudad Delicias, Mex. 132/B4
Ciudad Fernández, Mex. 143/E4
Ciudad Frontera, Mex. 132/C5
Ciudad Guayana, Ven. 153/F2
Ciudad Guzmán, Mex. 142/E5
Ciudad Hidalgo, Mex. 143/E5
Ciudad Hidalgo, Mex. 144/C3
Ciudad Insurgentes, Mex. 142/C3
Ciudad Ixtepec, Mex. 144/C2
Ciudad Juárez, Mex. 128/F5
Ciudad Lerdo, Mex. 142/E3
Ciudad Madero, Mex. 144/B1
Ciudad Mante, Mex. 143/F4
Ciudad Mendoza, Mex. 143/M8
Ciudad Miguel Alemán, Mex. 142/D5
Ciudad Obregón, Mex. 142/C3
Ciudad Ojeda, Ven. 152/D2
Ciudad Pemex, Mex. 144/C2
Ciudad Piar, Ven. 153/F3
Ciudad, PN de la, Mex. 142/D4
Ciudad Real, Sp. 44/D3
Ciudad Rodrigo, Sp. 44/B2
Ciudad Serdán, Mex. 143/M8
Ciudad Valles, Mex. 144/B1
Ciudad Victoria, Mex. 143/F4
Ciutadela de Menorca, Sp. 45/G3
Civa Burnu (pt.), Turk. 90/D1
Civate, It. 58/C1
Civezzano, It. 57/H5
Cividale del Friuli, It. 43/K3
Cividate Camuno, It. 57/G6
Civita Castellana, It. 46/B1
Civitavecchia, It. 46/B1
Civray, Fr. 42/D3
Civril, Turk. 90/B2
Cixi, China 72/L9
Cize, Fr. 56/B4
Cizre, Turk. 90/E2
Cizur, Sp. 44/E1
Clackmannan, Sc, UK 36/C4
Clackmannanshire (pol. reg.), Sc, UK 36/C4
Claerwen (res.), Wal, UK 32/C2
Claiborne, Md, US 138/B6

Clain (riv.), Fr. 42/D3
Clair Engle (lake), Ca, US 128/B2
Claire (lake), Ab, Can. 122/E3
Clairefontaine-en-Yvelines, Fr. 30/H6
Clairvaux-les-Lacs, Fr. 56/B4
Claise (riv.), Fr. 42/D3
Clallam (co.), Wa, US 135/A2
Clamart, Fr. 30/J5
Clamecy, Fr. 42/E3
Clane, Ire. 31/Q10
Clanton, Al, US 133/G3
Clanwilliam, SAfr. 106/B4
Clara (pt.), Arg. 158/A4
Clara, Ire. 31/Q10
Clare, Austl. 113/H5
Clare (isl.), Ire. 30/N10
Clare, Ire. 31/P10
Clare, Ks, US 137/D6
Clare, Mi, US 130/C3
Claremont, NH, US 131/F3
Claremont, Ca, US 136/C2
Claremore, Ok, US 129/J3
Claremorris, Ire. 31/P10
Clarence (pt.), Nun., Can. 123/T7
Clarence, NZ 117/S11
Clarence (riv.), NZ 117/S11
Clarence, NY, US 131/S9
Clarence Town, Bahm. 141/G3
Clarendon, Tx, US 129/G4
Clarenville, Nf, Can. 131/L1
Claresholm, Ab, Can. 126/E3
Clarion (isl.), Mex. 142/B5
Clark, SD, US 127/J4
Clark, NJ, US 139/H9
Clark Fork (riv.), Mt, US 126/E3
Clark Fork (riv.), Id, US 126/E3
Clarke (isl.), Austl. 115/C4
Clarke (lake), Ca, US 128/B3
Clarks Point, Ak, US 134/G4
Clarksburg, WV, US 130/D4
Clarksburg, Ca, US 135/L10
Clarksdale, Ms, US 129/K4
Clarkston, Wa, US 126/D4
Clarkston, Mi, US 135/F6
Clarksville, Ar, US 129/J4
Clarksville, Tn, US 130/C4
Clarksville, Tx, US 129/J4
Claro (riv.), Braz. 151/H7
Claro, Swi. 57/F5
Clatteringshaws Loch (lake), Sc, UK 34/D1
Claudy, NI, UK 34/A2
Clausen, Ger. 53/G5
Clausthal-Zellerfeld, Ger. 51/H5
Claveria, Phil. 79/D4
Clawson, Mi, US 135/F6
Clay (pt.), IM, UK 34/D3
Clay (co.), Mo, US 137/E5
Clay Center, Ks, US 129/H3
Clay Cross-North Wingfield, Eng, UK 35/G5
Claye-Souilly, Fr. 30/L5
Claymont, De, US 138/C4
Clayton, Ca, US 135/L11
Clayton, De, US 138/C5
Clayton, Ga, US 133/H3
Clayton, Mo, US 137/G8
Clayton, NJ, US 138/C4
Clayton, NM, US 129/G3
Clayton, Ok, US 132/E4
Clayton-le-Moors, Eng, UK 35/F4
Clear (lake), Ca, US 128/B3
Clear (hills), Ab, Can. 122/E3
Clear (cape), Ire. 31/P11
Clear Fork (riv.), Tx, US 143/E1
Clear Fork Brazos (riv.), Tx, US 129/H4
Clear Lake, SD, US 127/J4
Cleare (cape), Ak, US 134/J4
Clearfield, Ut, US 137/J11
Clearwater, BC, Can. 126/C3
Clearwater, Fl, US 133/H5
Clearwater (mts.), Id, US 124/C2
Clearwater (riv.), Mn, US 127/K4
Cleburne, Tx, US 129/H4
Cleethorpes, Eng, UK 35/H4
Cleve, Austl. 113/H5
Clevedon, Eng, UK 32/D4
Cleveland (cape), Austl. 114/B2

Cleveland (hills), Eng, UK 35/G3
Cleveland, Mo, US 137/D6
Cleveland, Ms, US 129/K4
Cleveland (mt.), Mt, US 126/E3
Cleveland, Oh, US 130/D3
Cleveland (co.), Ok, US 137/N15
Cleveland, Tn, US 133/G3
Cleveland, Tx, US 129/K5
Cleveland-Hopkins (int'l arpt.), Oh, US 130/D3
Cleveland National Forest, Ca, US 136/C3
Clevelândia, Braz. 155/A3
Clewiston, Fl, US 133/H5
Clichy, Fr. 30/J5
Clichy-sous-Bois, Fr. 30/K5
Cliffdale Park, NJ, US 139/J10
Cliffside Park, NJ, US 139/K8
Clifton, Az, US 128/E4
Clifton, NJ, US 139/J8
Clifton Beach, Austl. 114/B2
Clifton Forge, Va, US 133/J2
Clignon (riv.), Fr. 52/C5
Clingmans (peak), NC,Tn, US 133/H3
Clinton, BC, Can. 126/C3
Clinton, Ct, US 139/F1
Clinton, Ia, US 127/L5
Clinton, La, US 129/K5
Clinton, Ms, US 129/K4
Clinton, NC, US 133/J3
Clinton, NJ, US 138/D2
Clinton (res.), NJ, US 138/D1
Clinton, Ok, US 129/H4
Clinton (co.), Pa, US 138/A3
Clinton, SC, US 133/H3
Clinton, Ut, US 137/J11
Clinton, Wa, US 135/C2
Clinton-Colden (lake), NW, Can. 122/F2
Clinton, Middle Branch (riv.), Mi, US 135/G6
Clinton, North Branch (riv.), Mi, US 135/G6
Clintonville, Wi, US 130/B2
Clints Dod (hill), Sc, UK 36/D5
Clitheroe, Eng, UK 35/F4
Clio, Mi, US 130/D3
Cloates (pt.), Austl. 112/B2
Clocolan, SAfr. 106/D3
Clogherhead, Ire. 34/B4
Clonakilty, Ire. 31/P11
Cloncurry, Austl. 114/A3
Clondalkin, Ire. 34/B5
Clonmany, Ire. 34/A1
Clonmel, Ire. 31/Q10
Cloppenburg, Ger. 51/F2
Clorinda, Arg. 157/E2
Clos-Fontaine, Fr. 30/M6
Closter, NJ, US 139/K8
Cloudcroft, NM, US 132/B3
Cloudy (mtn.), Ak, US 134/F3
Cloughmills, NI, UK 34/B2
Cloverdale, Ca, US 128/B3
Clovis, Ca, US 128/C3
Clovis, NM, US 129/G4
Cluanie (lake), Sc, UK 36/A2
Cluj (co.), Rom. 49/F2
Cluj-Napoca, Rom. 49/F2
Cluses, Fr. 56/C5
Clusone, It. 57/F6
Clutha (riv.), NZ 109/G2
Clwyd (co.), Wal, UK 35/E5
Clwyd (cape), Wal, UK 35/E5
Clwydian (range), Wal, UK 35/E5
Clyde (riv.), NS, Can. 131/G3
Clyde, Sc, UK 36/B5
Clyde, Firth of (inlet), Sc, UK 31/R8
Clyde Hill, Wa, US 135/C2
Clydesdale (valley), Sc, UK 36/C5
Clywedog (riv.), Wal, UK 32/C2
CN Tower, On, Can. 131/R8
Co Loa Citadel, Viet. 78/D1
Coa (riv.), Port. 44/B2
Coacalco, Mex. 143/Q9
Coachella, Ca, US 128/C4
Coagh, NI, UK 34/B2
Coahuayana de Hidalgo, Mex. 142/D5
Coahuila (state), Mex. 132/C5
Coahuila, Mex. 142/B1
Coalburn, Sc, UK 36/C5
Coalcomán de Matamoros, Mex. 142/E5
Coaldale, Ab, Can. 126/E3
Coaldale, Pa, US 138/C2
Coalhurst, Ab, Can. 126/E3
Coalisland, NI, UK 34/B2
Coalville, Eng, UK 33/F1
Coalville, Ut, US 137/J11
Coaraci, Braz. 154/C4
Coari, Braz. 150/F4
Coari (riv.), Braz. 150/F5

Coasa, Peru 156/D4
Coast (mts.), Can.,US 122/C2
Coast (prov.), Kenya 104/C3
Coast (ranges), Ca, US 144/C2
Coatbridge, Sc, UK 36/B5
Coatepec, Mex. 143/N7
Coatepec Harinas, Mex. 143/K8
Coatesville, Pa, US 138/C4
Coatetelco, Mex. 143/K8
Coaticook, Qu, Can. 131/G2
Coats (isl.), Nun., Can. 123/H2
Coats Land (pol. reg.), Ant. 160/Y
Coatzacoalcos, Mex. 144/C2
Coatzingo, Mex. 143/L8
Coba (ruin), Mex. 144/C2
Coba de Serpe, Sierra de (peak), Sp. 44/B1
Cobar, Austl. 115/C1
Cobb (lake), Co, US 137/C1
Cobberas (mt.), Austl. 115/D3
Cobblestone (mtn.), Ca, US 136/B1
Cóbh, Ire. 31/P11
Cobham (riv.), Mb,On, Can. 127/K2
Cobija, Bol. 150/E6
Cobourg, On, Can. 130/E3
Cobquecura, Chile 158/B3
Coburg (pen.), Austl. 109/C2
Coburg (isl.), Nun., Can. 123/T7
Coburg, Ger. 54/D2
Coca, Ecu. 152/B5
Coca (riv.), Ecu. 152/B5
Cocachacra, Peru 156/D5
Cocal, Braz. 154/B1
Coccaglio, It. 58/C1
Cocentaina, Sp. 45/E3
Cochabamba, Bol. 150/D7
Coche (isl.), Ven. 153/F2
Cochem, Ger. 53/G3
Cocherel, Fr. 30/M4
Cochin, India 82/C6
Cochran, Ga, US 133/H3
Cochrane, Ab, Can. 126/E3
Cochrane, On, Can. 130/D1
Cock Cairn (peak), Sc, UK 36/D3
Cockatoo, Austl. 115/G5
Cockburn (sound), Austl. 112/K7
Cockburn (chan.), Chile 159/B7
Cockeysville, Md, US 138/B5
Cockscomb (peak), SAfr. 106/D4
Coclé del Norte, Pan. 145/F4
Coco (riv.), Hon. 140/E5
Coco, Cayo (isl.), Cuba 145/G1
Coco, Isla del (isl.), CR 150/A2
Cocoa, Fl, US 133/H4
Coconino (plat.), Az, US 128/D4
Cocoparra NP, Austl. 115/C2
Cocorocuma, Cayo (isl.), Hon. 145/F3
Cocos (isls.), Austl. 67/J11
Côcos, Braz. 154/A4
Cocotitlán, Mex. 143/R10
Cocula, Mex. 142/E4
Cod (isl.), Nf, Can. 123/K3
Codajás, Braz. 150/F4
Codegua, Chile 158/N9
Codigoro, It. 59/F3
Codlea, Rom. 49/G3
Codogno, It. 58/C2
Codsall, Eng, UK 32/D1
Coelemu, Chile 158/B3
Coelho Neto, Braz. 154/B2
Coesfeld, Ger. 51/E3
Coeur d'Alene (lake), Id, US 126/D4
Coeur d'Alene, Id, US 126/D4
Coevorden, Neth. 50/D3
Coffin Bay, Austl. 113/G5
Coffin Bay NP, Austl. 113/G5
Coffs Harbour, Austl. 115/E1
Cofre de Perote, PN, Mex. 143/M7
Coggiola, It. 58/B1
Coghinas (lake), It. 46/A2
Cognac, Fr. 42/C4
Cogoleto, It. 58/B4
Cogolin, Fr. 43/G5
Cogollo del Cengio, It. 59/E1
Cogolludo, Sp. 44/D2
Cohansey (riv.), NJ, US 138/C5
Cohuna, Austl. 115/C2
Cohunu NP, Austl. 112/L7
Coiba, Isla de (isl.), Pan. 150/B2
Coig (riv.), Arg. 157/C7
Coignières, Fr. 30/H5
Coihaique, Chile 158/B5
Coihueco, Chile 158/B3
Coimbatore, India 82/C5
Coimbra (dist.), Port. 44/A2
Coimbra, Port. 44/A2

Coín, Sp. 44/C4
Coina (riv.), Port. 45/P10
Coise (riv.), Fr. 42/F4
Cojedes (riv.), Ven. 150/E2
Cojedes (state), Ven. 152/D2
Cojímies, Ecu. 152/A4
Cojudo Blanco (peak), Arg. 158/C5
Cojutepeque, ESal. 144/D3
Čoka, Serb. 48/E3
Cokeville, Wy, US 126/F5
Col d'Ispéguy (pass), Fr. 42/C5
Col San Martino, It. 59/F1
Colac, Austl. 115/B3
Colares, Port. 45/P10
Colasay, Peru 156/B2
Colatina, Braz. 155/D1
Colbeck (cape), Ant. 160/Y
Colby, Wa, US 135/B3
Colca (riv.), Peru 156/D4
Colcabamba, Peru 156/C4
Colchester, Eng, UK 33/G3
Cold Bay, Ak, US 134/F4
Cold Fell (peak), Eng, UK 35/F2
Cold Lake, Ab, Can. 126/F2
Cold Spring, Mn, US 127/K4
Cold Spring Harbor, NY, US 139/M8
Coldstream, Sc, UK 36/D5
Coldwater, Ks, US 129/H3
Coldwater, Mi, US 130/C3
Cole, Ok, US 137/M15
Cole (riv.), Eng, UK 33/E3
Coleambally, Austl. 115/C2
Coleman, Tx, US 129/H5
Çölemerik, Turk. 90/E2
Colenso, SAfr. 107/E3
Coleraine (dist.), NI, UK 34/B1
Coleraine, NI, UK 34/B1
Colesberg, SAfr. 106/D3
Colfax, Wa, US 126/D4
Colgate (cape), Nun., Can. 123/S6
Colgong, India 85/F3
Colhué Huapí (lake), Arg. 158/C5
Colico, It. 57/F5
Coligny, SAfr. 106/D2
Coligny, Fr. 56/B5
Colima, Mex. 142/E5
Colima (state), Mex. 142/D5
Colima, Nevado de (peak), Mex. 142/E5
Colina, Chile 158/N8
Coliseum, Ca, US 136/F8
Coll (isl.), Sc, UK 31/Q8
Collagna, It. 58/D4
Collarenebri, Austl. 115/D1
Colle di Val d'Elsa, It. 59/E6
Collecchio, It. 58/D3
College, Ak, US 134/J3
College Park, Md, US 138/B6
College Station, Tx, US 129/H5
Collegeville, Pa, US 138/C3
Collegno, It. 43/G4
Collesalvetti, It. 58/D5
Colletorto, It. 46/D2
Collie, Austl. 112/C5
Collier (bay), Austl. 109/B2
Collier (range), Austl. 112/C3
Collier Range NP, Austl. 112/C3
Collierville, Tn, US 129/K4
Colliford (res.), Eng, UK 32/B5
Collingwood, On, Can. 130/D2
Collins, Ms, US 133/F4
Collins (int'l arpt.), Ire. 34/B5
Collinsville, Austl. 114/B3
Collinsville, Ca, US 135/L10
Collinsville, Il, US 137/H8
Collinsville, Ok, US 132/E2
Collo, Alg. 100/K6
Collombey, Swi. 56/C5
Collon, Ire. 34/B4
Collonges, Fr. 56/B5
Colma, Ca, US 135/K11
Colmar, Fr. 56/D1
Colmar, Pa, US 138/C3
Colmberg, Ger. 54/D4
Colmenar, Sp. 44/C4
Colmenar de Oreja, Sp. 44/D2
Colmenar Viejo, Sp. 44/D2
Colmillo (cape), Chile 159/B6
Colne (riv.), Eng, UK 35/G4
Colne, Eng, UK 35/F4
Cologna Veneta, It. 59/E2
Cologne, It. 58/C1
Cologne, Ger. 53/E2
Cologne/Bonn (int'l arpt.), Ger. 53/G2
Cologno Monzese, It. 58/C1
Colombes, Fr. 30/J5
Colombey-les-Belles, Fr. 56/B1
Colombia (ctry.) 150/D3

Colombia, Col. 152/C4
Colombier, Swi. 56/C4
Colombine (peak), It. 58/D1
Colombo, Braz. 155/B3
Colombo (cap.), SrL. 82/C6
Colomiers, Fr. 42/D5
Colomoncagua, Hon. 144/D3
Colón, Arg. 158/E2
Colón, Cuba 145/F1
Colón (mts.), Hon. 144/D3
Colón, Pan. 145/G4
Colón, Uru. 159/K11
Colonche, Ecu. 156/A1
Colonelganj, India 84/C2
Colonia, Micr. 116/C4
Colonia (dept.), Uru. 158/F2
Colonia, NJ, US 139/H9
Colonia Barón, Arg. 158/D3
Colonia del Sacramento, Uru. 159/K11
Colonia Juárez, Mex. 142/C2
Colonia Las Heras, Arg. 158/C5
Colonial Park, Pa, US 138/B3
Colonsay (isl.), Sc, UK 31/Q8
Colorado (peak), Arg. 158/C6
Colorado (riv.), Arg. 157/C4
Colorado, Braz. 155/B2
Colorado (plat.), US 128/E3
Colorado (riv.), US 128/D4
Colorado (state), US 128/F3
Colorado City, Tx, US 129/G4
Colorado Historical Museum, Co, US 137/C3
Con Son (isl.), Viet. 83/F2
Colorno, It. 58/D3
Colotlán, Mex. 142/E4
Colquiri, Bol. 150/E7
Colson (riv.), Belz. 144/D2
Colstrip, Mt, US 126/G4
Colt (hill), Sc, UK 36/B6
Coltauco, Chile 158/N9
Colton, Ca, US 136/C2
Colts Neck, NJ, US 138/D3
Coluene (riv.), Braz. 147/D4
Columbia (riv.), Can.,US 126/C4
Columbia (plat.), US 126/C4
Columbia, Il, US 137/G9
Columbia, Ky, US 130/C4
Columbia, La, US 129/J4
Columbia, Md, US 138/B5
Columbia, Ms, US 133/F4
Columbia, NJ, US 138/C2
Columbia, Pa, US 138/B3
Columbia (co.), Pa, US 138/B1
Columbia (cap.), SC, US 133/H3
Columbia, Tn, US 130/C5
Columbia Falls, Mt, US 126/E3
Columbine (cape), SAfr. 106/K10
Columbus, Ga, US 133/G3
Columbus, In, US 130/C4
Columbus, Ms, US 133/F3
Columbus, Mt, US 126/F4
Columbus, Ne, US 127/J5
Columbus, NM, US 132/B4
Columbus (cap.), Oh, US 130/D4
Columbus, Tx, US 129/H5
Colunga, Sp. 44/C1
Colusa, Ca, US 128/B3
Colville (riv.), Ak, US 134/G2
Colville, Wa, US 126/D3
Colville (lake), NW, Can. 122/D2
Colvos (passg.), Wa, US 135/B3
Colwyn Bay, Wal, UK 34/C5
Comacchio, It. 59/F3
Comacchio, Valli di (lag.), It. 43/K4
Comai, China 85/H1
Comal, Tx, US 137/U20
Comal (co.), Tx, US 137/U20
Comala, Mex. 142/E5
Comalcalco, Mex. 144/C2
Comanche, Tx, US 129/H5
Comandante Luis Piedra Buena, Arg. 159/C6
Comandante Nicanor Otamendi, Arg. 158/F3
Comănești, Rom. 49/H2
Comarnic, Rom. 49/G3
Comas, Peru 156/B3
Comayagua, Hon. 144/D3
Comayagua (mts.), Hon. 144/D3

Comines, Fr. 52/C2
Comines, Belg. 52/B2
Comino (isl.), Malta 46/L6
Comitán de Domínguez, Mex. 144/C2
Commack, NY, US 139/E2
Commentry, Fr. 42/E3
Commenay, Fr. 30/H4
Commerce, Ca, US 136/F7
Commerce City, Co, US 137/C3
Commercy, Fr. 53/E6
Commewijne (dist.), Sur. 153/H3
Committee (bay), Nun., Can. 123/H2
Como (lake), It. 43/H3
Como, It. 57/F6
Como, Wi, US 135/P14
Comodoro Rivadavia, Arg. 158/D5
Comoé (prov.), C.d'Iv. 102/D4
Comoé, PN de la, C.d'Iv. 96/E6
Comoé, PN de la, C.d'Iv. 102/D4
Comorin (cape), India 82/C6
Comoros (ctry.) 107/G5
Comox, BC, Can. 126/B3
Compiègne, Fr. 52/B5
Compostela, Phil. 79/E6
Compostela, Mex. 142/D4
Compton, Ca, US 136/F8
Comrat, Mol. 49/J2
Comrie, Sc, UK 36/C4
Comstock, Tx, US 132/C4
Cona, China 83/F2
Conaica, Peru 156/C4
Conakry (pol. reg.), Gui. 102/B4
Conakry (cap.), Gui. 102/B4
Conakry (int'l arpt.), Gui. 102/B4
Conambo (riv.), Ecu. 152/B5
Conca (riv.), It. 59/F5
Concarneau, Fr. 42/B3
Conceição da Barra, Braz. 155/E1
Conceição das Alagoas, Braz. 155/B1
Conceição do Araguaia, Braz. 151/J5
Conceição do Coité, Braz. 154/C3
Conceição do Mato Dentro, Braz. 155/D1
Conceição do Rio Verde, Braz. 211/H6
Conceição dos Ouros, Braz. 211/H7
Concepción (lake), Bol. 150/F7
Concepción, Arg. 157/C2
Concepción, Bol. 150/F7
Concepción, Chile 158/B3
Concepción (pt.), Mex. 142/C3
Concepción, Par. 157/E1
Concepción, Peru 156/C4
Concepción (bay), Mex. 142/B3
Concepción de La Vega, DRep. 141/G4
Concepción del Oro, Mex. 143/E3
Concepción del Uruguay, Arg. 159/J10
Conception (pt.), Ca, US 128/B4
Concesio, It. 58/D1
Conchal, Braz. 211/F7
Conchas (lake), NM, US 129/F4
Conches, Fr. 30/L5
Conchillas, Uru. 159/J11
Concho (riv.), Tx, US 129/G5
Conchos (riv.), Mex. 142/D3
Concord, Ca, US 128/B3
Concord, NC, US 133/H3
Concord (cap.), NH, US 131/G3
Concord, Wi, US 135/N13
Concordia, Arg. 159/J9
Concórdia, Braz. 155/A3
Concordia, Mex. 142/D4
Concordia, Peru 150/C6
Concordia Sagittaria, It. 59/F1
Concordia sulla Secchia, It. 59/D3
Concrete, Wa, US 126/C3
Condado, Cuba 145/G1
Condamine, Austl. 109/E3
Condamine (riv.), Austl. 115/D1
Condé, Braz. 154/B4
Condé-sur-L'Escaut, Fr. 52/C2
Condé-sur-Noireau, Fr. 42/C2
Condé-sur-Vesgre, Fr. 30/G5
Condé-sur-Vire, Fr. 42/C2
Condécourt, Fr. 30/H4
Condeúba, Braz. 154/B4
Condino, It. 57/G6
Condobolin, Austl. 115/C2
Condom, Fr. 42/D5
Condon, Or, US 126/C4
Condroz (plat.), Belg. 40/C3
Conecuh (riv.), Al, US 133/G4
Conegliano, It. 59/F1
Conejos, Co, US 129/F3

Conesa, Arg. 158/E2
Conestoga (riv.), Pa, US 138/D2
Conewago (lake), Pa, US 138/A3
Confins (int'l arpt.), Braz. 155/D1
Conflans-en-Jarnisy, Fr. 53/E5
Conflans-Sainte-Honorine, Fr. 30/J5
Congaree Swamp Nat'l Mon., SC, US 133/H3
Congers, NY, US 139/K7
Congis-sur-Thérouanne, Fr. 30/L4
Congjiang, China 83/J2
Congleton, Eng, UK 35/F5
Congo (basin), D.R. Congo 97/K3
Congo, Rep. of the (ctry.) 93/D4
Congo (riv.), Afr. 93/D4
Congo, Democratic Republic of the (ctry.) 93/E5
Congonhal, Braz. 211/G7
Congonhas, Braz. 155/D2
Congonhas (int'l arpt.), Braz. 211/G8
Conguillío, PN, Chile 158/C3
Conic (hill), Sc, UK 36/B4
Cónico (peak), Arg. 158/C4
Conifer, Co, US 137/B3
Conil de la Frontera, Sp. 44/C5
Conisbrough, Eng, UK 35/H5
Conlig, NI, UK 34/C2
Conn (lake), Nun., Can. 123/J1
Connah's Quay, Wal, UK 35/E5
Connantre, Fr. 52/C6
Conneaut, Oh, US 130/D3
Connecticut (riv.), US 131/G2
Connecticut (state), US 131/F3
Connellsville, Pa, US 130/E3
Connemara NP, Ire. 31/P10
Connersville, In, US 133/C3
Cono Grande (peak), Arg. 159/C6
Conocoto, Ecu. 152/B5
Conon, Falls of (falls), Sc, UK 36/B1
Cononbridge, Sc, UK 36/B1
Conondale NP, Austl. 114/D4
Conoplja, Serb. 48/D3
Conrad, Mt, US 126/F3
Conroe, Tx, US 129/J5
Consandolo, It. 59/E3
Conscience Point NWR, NY, US 139/F2
Consdorf, Lux. 53/F2
Conselheiro Pena, Braz. 155/D1
Conselice, It. 59/E3
Conselve, It. 59/E2
Conservation Park, Austl. 113/H4
Consett, Eng, UK 35/G2
Conshohocken, Pa, US 138/C3
Consolación del Sur, Cuba 145/F1
Consolidated (canal), Az, US 137/S19
Constance (lake), Swi. 43/H3
Constance (Bodensee) (lake), Swi. 43/H3
Constant, Mt (mtn.), Fr. 141/N9
Constanța (prov.), Rom. 49/J3
Constanța, Rom. 49/J3
Constantí, Sp. 45/F2
Constantina, Sp. 44/C4
Constantine (cape), Ak, US 134/G4
Constantine, Alg. 100/K6
Constitución, Chile 158/B2
Constitución (res.), Uru. 159/K10
Constitución de 1857, PN, Mex. 128/C5
Consuegra, Sp. 44/D3
Contai, India 85/F5
Contamana, Peru 156/C2
Contarina, It. 59/F2
Contas, Rio de (riv.), Braz. 151/J7
Contegem, Braz. 155/C1
Contes, Fr. 43/G5
Conthey, Swi. 56/D5
Continental (range), Ab,BC, Can. 126/C2
Continental (mtn.), Az, US 137/S18
Contoy (isl.), Mex. 144/E1
Contra Costa (canal), Ca, US 135/L10
Contra Costa (co.), Ca, US 135/L11
Contramaestre, Cuba 145/G1
Contratación, Col. 152/C3
Contrecoeur, Qu, Can. 131/P6
Contreras, Embalse de (res.), Sp. 44/E3
Contrexéville, Fr. 56/B1
Controller (bay), Ak, US 134/G4

Contulmo, Chile 158/B3
Contumazá, Peru 156/B2
Contwig, Ger. 53/G5
Contwoyto (lake), Nun., Can. 122/F2
Conty, Fr. 52/B4
Convención, Col. 152/C2
Conversano, It. 47/E2
Conway, Ar, US 129/J4
Conway, NH, US 131/G3
Conway, SC, US 133/J3
Conway (cape), Austl. 114/C3
Conway NP, Austl. 114/C3
Conwy (bay), Wal, UK 34/E5
Conwy (co.), Wal, UK 34/E5
Conwy (riv.), Wal, UK 34/E5
Conwy, Vale of (valley), Wal, UK 34/E5
Conyngham, Pa, US 138/B2
Coober Pedy, Austl. 113/G4
Cooch Behär, India 85/G2
Coochiemudlo (isl.), Austl. 114/F7
Cook (bay), Chile 159/C7
Cook (mt.), NZ 117/S11
Cook (str.), NZ 109/H7
Cook (inlet), Ak, US 122/A3
Cook (co.), Il, US 135/Q16
Cook Islands (dpcy.), NZ 117/J6
Cooke (mt.), Austl. 112/C5
Cookeville, Tn, US 130/C4
Cookham, Eng, UK 30/A2
Cookhouse, SAfr. 106/D4
Cookstown, NI, UK 34/B2
Cookstown (dist.), NI, UK 34/B2
Cooksville, Md, US 138/A5
Cooktown, Austl. 114/B1
Coola Coola (swamp), Austl. 115/B3
Coolah, Austl. 115/D1
Coolamon, Austl. 115/C2
Coolangatta, Austl. 115/E1
Cooley (pt.), Ire. 34/B4
Coolgardie, Austl. 112/D4
Cooloola NP, Austl. 114/D4
Cooloongup (lake), Austl. 112/K7
Cooma, Austl. 115/D3
Coonabarabran, Austl. 115/D1
Coonalpyn, Austl. 115/A2
Coonamble, Austl. 115/D1
Coonana Abor. Land, Austl. 112/D4
Coondapoor (Kundapura), India 89/K6
Coongan Abor. Land, Austl. 112/C2
Coonoor, India 82/C5
Cooper, Tx, US 129/J4
Coopersburg, Pa, US 138/C2
Cooperstown, ND, US 127/J4
Coordewandy (peak), Austl. 112/C3
Coorong NP, Austl. 115/A3
Coorow, Austl. 112/C4
Cooroy, Austl. 114/D4
Coosa (riv.), Al, US 133/G3
Cootamundra, Austl. 115/C2
Coot'tha (mt.), Austl. 114/E6
Copacabana, Bol. 156/D4
Copainalá, Mex. 144/C2
Copala, Mex. 140/B4
Copán (ruin), Hon. 144/D3
Cope (cape), Sp. 44/E4
Copeland (isl.), NI, UK 34/C2
Copenhagen (København) (cap.), Den. 38/E4
Copertino, It. 47/F2
Copeton (dam), Austl. 115/D1
Copiague, NY, US 139/M9
Copiapó, Chile 157/B2
Coplay, Pa, US 138/C2
Copparo, It. 59/E3
Coppename (riv.), Sur. 153/H3
Coppenbrügge, Ger. 51/G4
Copper Center, Ak, US 134/K3
Copperas Cove, Tx, US 129/...
Coppermine (riv.), NW,Nun., Can. 122/F2
Copperopolis, Ca, US 137/J12
Copperton, Ut, US 137/J12
Coppet, Swi. 56/C5
Copşa Mică, Rom. 49/G2
Coqên, China 70/D5
Coquet (riv.), Eng, UK 36/D6
Coquet Dale (valley), Eng, UK 35/G1
Coquimbo, Chile 157/B2
Coquitlam, BC, Can. 135/C3
Corabia, Rom. 49/G4
Coração de Jesus, Braz. 154/A5
Coracora, Peru 156/C4
Corail, Haiti 145/H2
Coraki, Austl. 115/E1
Coral (sea) 109/G2
Coral Gables, Fl, US 133/H5

Coral Harbour, Nun., Can. 123/H2
Coral Sea Islands Territory (dpcy.), Austl. 109/G2
Coral Springs, Fl, US 133/H5
Corales del Rosario, PN, Col. 152/C2
Coram, NY, US 139/E2
Corato, It. 46/E2
Corbeil-Essonnes, Fr. 30/K6
Corbelin (cape), Alg. 100/H4
Corbenay, Fr. 56/C2
Corbet (peak), Swi. 57/F5
Corbetta, It. 58/B2
Corbie, Fr. 52/B4
Corbieres (mts.), Fr. 42/C5
Corbin, Ky, US 130/C4
Corbin City, NJ, US 138/D5
Corby, Eng, UK 33/F2
Corcovado, Braz. 211/K7
Corcovado, CR 145/E4
Corcovado (vol.), Chile 158/B4
Corcovado (gulf), Chile 147/B7
Corcovado, PN, CR 140/E6
Cordeiro, Braz. 155/D2
Cordele, Ga, US 133/H4
Cordell, Ok, US 129/H4
Cordenons, It. 43/K4
Cordignano, It. 59/F1
Cordillera de Los Picachos, PN, Col. 150/D3
Cordillera Oriental (mts.), SAm. 152/B5
Cordisburgo, Braz. 155/C1
Córdoba (dept.), Col. 145/H4
Córdoba, Sp. 44/C4
Córdoba, Mex. 144/D2
Córdoba (plain), SAm. 158/E2
Córdoba, Sierra de (mts.), Arg. 157/D3
Cordova, Ak, US 134/K3
Cordova (peak), Ak, US 134/K3
Cordova, Md, US 138/C6
Coreaú, Braz. 154/B1
Coremas, Braz. 154/C2
Corentyne (riv.), Guy. 150/G3
Corfu (Kérika) (isl.), Gre. 47/F3
Corgémont, Swi. 56/D3
Corgo, Sp. 44/B1
Coria, Sp. 44/B3
Coria del Río, Sp. 44/B4
Coriano, It. 59/F5
Coribe, Braz. 154/A4
Coricudgy (mt.), Austl. 115/D2
Corigliano Calabro, It. 46/E3
Coringa Islets (isls.), Austl. 114/C2
Corinne, Ut, US 137/J10
Corinth, Ms, US 133/F3
Corinth (gulf), Gre. 47/H3
Corinth (Kórinthos) (ruin), Gre. 47/H4
Corinto, Braz. 155/C1
Corinto, Nic. 144/E3
Cork, Ire. 31/P11
Corleone, It. 46/C4
Corleto Perticara, It. 46/E2
Çorlu, Turk. 49/H5
Cormeilles-en-Vexin, Fr. 30/J4
Cormons, It. 59/G1
Cormontreuil, Fr. 52/D5
Cormorant (lake), Mb, Can. 127/H2
Cornacchia (peak), It. 46/D2
Cornaredo, It. 58/B2
Cornberg, Ger. 51/G6
Corndon (peak), Wal, UK 32/C1
Cornedo Vicentino, It. 59/E1
Cornélio Procópio, Braz. 155/B2
Cornelius Grinnell (bay), Nun., Can. 123/K2
Cornell, Ca, US 136/B2
Cornella, Sp. 45/L7
Corner (inlet), Austl. 109/D4
Corner Brook, Nf, Can. 131/K1
Cornetto (peak), It. 57/H6
Cornfield (pt.), Ct, US 139/F1
Corniglio, It. 58/D4
Cornimont, Fr. 56/C2
Corning, NY, US 130/E3
Corno alle Scale (peak), It. 43/J4
Corno di Rosazzo, It. 59/G1
Cornone di Blumone (peak), It. 57/G6
Cornú (peak), Arg. 159/D7
Cornuda, It. 59/F1
Cornwall (isl.), Nun., Can. 123/S7
Cornwall (co.), Eng, UK 32/A6
Cornwall, On, Can. 131/F2
Cornwall, PE, Can. 131/J2
Cornwall (cape), Eng, UK 32/A6
Cornwall (co.), Eng, UK 32/A6
Cornwall, Pa, US 138/B3

Cornwallis (isl.), Nun., Can. 123/S7
Corny (pt.), Austl. 113/H5
Coro, Ven. 152/D2
Coroatá, Braz. 154/A2
Corocoro, Bol. 156/D5
Coromandel, Braz. 155/C1
Coromandel (pen.), NZ 117/T10
Coromandel (coast), India 82/D5
Coron, Phil. 81/F1
Corona, Ca, US 136/C3
Corona (bay), CR 140/E6
Coronado, Ca, US 136/C5
Coronation, Ab, Can. 126/F2
Coronation (gulf), Nun., Can. 122/E2
Coronel, Chile 158/B3
Coronel Dorrego, Arg. 158/E3
Coronel Fabriciano, Braz. 155/D1
Coronel Moldes, Arg. 158/D2
Coronel Murta, Braz. 154/B5
Coronel Oviedo, Par. 157/E2
Coronel Pringles, Arg. 158/E3
Coronel Suárez, Arg. 158/E3
Coronel Vidal, Arg. 158/F3
Coronel Vivida, Braz. 155/A3
Coronie, Peru 156/B3
Coropuna (peak), Peru 156/C4
Corovodë, Alb. 47/G2
Corozal, Col. 152/C2
Corozal, Belz. 144/D2
Corpach, Sc, UK 36/A3
Corpus Christi, Tx, US 132/D5
Corpus Christi (int'l arpt.), Tx, US 143/F3
Corral, Chile 158/B3
Corral de Almaguer, Sp. 44/D3
Corral de Bustos, Arg. 158/E2
Corrales, Col. 152/C3
Corralillo, Cuba 145/F1
Corre, Fr. 56/C2
Correa, Arg. 158/E2
Corredor, CR 145/F4
Correggio, It. 59/D3
Corrente (riv.), Braz. 154/A4
Corrente, Braz. 154/A3
Correntina, Braz. 154/A4
Corrib (lake), Ire. 31/P10
Corrientes (riv.), Peru 150/C4
Corrientes, Arg. 157/E2
Corrientes (cape), Cuba 145/E1
Corrientes (pt.), Col. 152/B3
Corrientes (pt.), Ecu. 152/B5
Corrigan, Tx, US 129/J5
Corrigin, Austl. 112/C5
Corriverton, Guy. 153/G3
Corryhabbie (peak), Sc, UK 36/C2
Corryong, Austl. 115/C3
Corse (hill), Sc, UK 36/B5
Corse (cape), Fr. 43/H5
Corse (dept.), Fr. 43/H5
Corserine (peak), Sc, UK 34/D1
Corsewall (pt.), NI, UK 34/C1
Corsham, Eng, UK 32/D4
Corsica (isl.), Fr. 27/E4
Corsicana, Tx, US 129/H4
Corsico, It. 58/C2
Corsons (inlet), NJ, US 138/D5
Cortaillod, Swi. 56/C4
Cortegana, Sp. 44/B4
Cortemaggiore, It. 58/C3
Cortemilia, It. 58/B3
Cortez, Co, US 128/E3
Cortina d'Ampezzo, It. 43/K3
Cortines, Arg. 159/J11
Cortland, NY, US 130/E3
Corubal (riv.), GBis. 102/B3
Coruche, Port. 44/A3
Çoruh (riv.), Turk. 63/G4
Çorum, Turk. 90/C1
Çorum (prov.), Turk. 90/C1
Corumbá (riv.), Braz. 151/J7
Corumbá, Braz. 150/G7
Corumbaú (pt.), Braz. 154/C5
Coruripe, Braz. 154/C3
Corvallis, Or, US 126/C4
Corve (riv.), Eng, UK 32/D2
Corvo (peak), It. 46/C1
Corvo (isl.), Azor., Port. 45/R12
Corzoneso, Swi. 57/E5
Cosalá, Mex. 142/D3
Cosamaloapan, Mex. 143/P8
Cosautlán, Mex. 143/N7
Coscomatepec, Mex. 143/M7
Cosenza, It. 46/E3
Coshocton, Oh, US 130/D3
Cosigüina (pt.), Nic. 144/E3
Coslada, Sp. 45/N9
Cosmo Newberry Abor. Rsv., Austl. 112/D3
Cosmópolis, Braz. 211/F7

Cosne-Cours-sur-Loire, Fr. 42/E3
Cosne d'Allier, Fr. 42/E3
Cosolapa, Mex. 143/N8
Cospeito, Sp. 44/B1
Cosquín, Arg. 157/D3
Cossato, It. 58/B1
Cosson (riv.), Fr. 42/D3
Cossonay, Swi. 56/D4
Costa Azul, Uru. 159/G2
Costa Brava (int'l arpt.), Sp. 45/G2
Costa da Caparica, Port. 45/P10
Costa de Mosquitos (phys. reg.), Nic. 145/E4
Costa di Rovigo, It. 59/E2
Costa Masnaga, It. 58/C1
Costa Mesa, Ca, US 136/G8
Costa Rica (ctry.) 145/F4
Costa Smeralda (int'l arpt.), It. 46/A2
Costa Volpino, It. 58/D1
Costabissara, It. 59/E1
Costești, Rom. 49/G3
Costigliole d'Asti, It. 58/B3
Cotabambas, Peru 156/C3
Cotabato, Phil. 81/F2
Cotacachi (peak), Ecu. 152/B4
Cotahuasi, Peru 156/C4
Cotatumbo (riv.), Col. 145/H4
Côte d'Azur (int'l arpt.), Fr. 43/G5
Côte de Hautmont (hill), Fr. 56/B1
Côte d'Ivoire (ctry.) 102/D5
Côte d'Or (uplands), Fr. 42/F3
Côte du Rif (Al Hoceima) (int'l arpt.), Mor. 100/C2
Côte-Saint-Luc, Qu, Can. 131/N7
Coteau des Prairies (plat.), SD, US 127/J4
Coteau-du-Lac, Qu, Can. 131/M7
Coteau du Missouri (plat.), ND, US 127/H3
Coteau-Landing, Qu, Can. 131/M7
Cotegipe, Braz. 154/A4
Cotentin (pen.), Fr. 42/C2
Côtes de Meuse (uplands), Fr. 42/F2
Cothi (riv.), Wal, UK 32/B3
Cotia, Braz. 211/G8
Cotignola, It. 59/E4
Cotonou, Ben. 103/F5
Cotonou (int'l arpt.), Ben. 103/F5
Cotopaxi (dept.), Ecu. 152/B5
Cotopaxi (peak), Ecu. 152/B5
Cotopaxi (vol.), Ecu. 152/B5
Cotopaxi, PN, Ecu. 152/B5
Cotswolds (hills), Eng, UK 32/D3
Cottage Grove, Or, US 126/C3
Cottage Hills, Il, US 137/G8
Cottam, On, Can. 135/G7
Cottbus, Ger. 41/H3
Cottian Alps (mts.), Fr. 43/G4
Cottleville, Mo, US 137/F8
Cottonport, La, US 129/J5
Cottonwood, Az, US 128/D4
Cottonwood (riv.), Tx, US 129/F5
Cotulla, Tx, US 132/C2
Coubert, Fr. 30/L6
Coubre, Pointe de la (pt.), Fr. 42/C4
Couchey, Fr. 56/A3
Coudekerque-Branche, Fr. 52/B1
Coulee City, Wa, US 126/D3
Coulee Dam Nat'l Rec. Area, Wa, US 126/D3
Coulogne, Fr. 52/A2
Coulombe (riv.), GBis. 102/B3
Coulombs-en-Valois, Fr. 30/M4
Coulommes, Fr. 30/L5
Coulommiers, Fr. 52/C6
Coulonge (riv.), Qu, Can. 130/E2
Coulounieix-Chamiers, Fr. 42/D4
Council, Ak, US 134/F3
Council, Id, US 126/D4
Council Grove, Ks, US 129/H3
Coupar Angus, Sc, UK 36/C3
Courantyne (riv.), Guy.,Sur. 147/D2
Courbevoie, Fr. 30/J5
Courcelles, Belg. 52/D3
Courcouronnes, Fr. 30/K6
Courdimanche, Fr. 30/H4
Courgenay, Swi. 56/D3
Courgent, Fr. 30/H5
Courmayeur, It. 56/C6
Cournon-d'Auvergne, Fr. 42/E4
Couronne (pt.), Fr. 30/L6
Coursan, Fr. 42/E5
Courtelary, Swi. 56/D3

Courtepin, Swi. 56/D4
Courtice, On, Can. 131/S8
Courtisols, Fr. 53/D6
Courtland, Ca, US 135/L10
Courtmacsherry, Ire. 31/P11
Courtney, Mo, US 137/E5
Courtomer, Fr. 30/L6
Cousance, Fr. 56/B4
Coushatta, La, US 129/J4
Cousolre, Fr. 53/D3
Creil, Fr. 52/B5
Coutances, Fr. 42/C2
Coutevroult, Fr. 30/L5
Coutras, Fr. 42/C4
Coutts, Ab, Can. 126/F3
Couva, Trin. 153/F2
Couvet, Swi. 56/C4
Couvin, Belg. 53/D3
Couzeix, Fr. 42/D4
Covadonga NP, Sp. 44/C1
Covasna, Rom. 49/H3
Covasna (prov.), Rom. 49/G3
Cove Bay, Sc, UK 36/D2
Cove Neck, NY, US 139/L8
Coventry, Eng, UK 33/E2
Coventry (canal), Eng, UK 33/E2
Covilhã, Port. 44/B2
Covina, Ca, US 136/G7
Covington, Ga, US 133/H3
Covington, Tn, US 129/K4
Covington, Ky, US 130/C3
Covo, It. 58/C2
Cow Bay, Sc, UK 36/A4
Cow Green (res.), Eng, UK 35/F2
Cowal (reg.), Sc, UK 36/A4
Cowan (lake), Austl. 109/B4
Cowdenbeath, Sc, UK 36/C4
Cowell, Austl. 113/H5
Cowes, Eng, UK 33/E5
Cowie, Sc, UK 36/C4
Cowlitz (riv.), Wa, US 126/C4
Cowra, Austl. 115/D2
Coxim, Braz. 151/H7
Cox's Bãzãr, Bang. 83/F3
Coyame, Mex. 129/F5
Coye-la-Forêt, Fr. 30/K4
Coyotepec, Mex. 143/K7
Coyuca de Benítez, Mex. 143/E5
Coyutla, Mex. 143/M6
Cozumel, Mex. 144/E1
Cozumel (int'l arpt.), Mex. 144/E1
Cozumel (isl.), Mex. 144/E1
Cradle Mountain-Lake Saint Clair NP, Austl. 115/C4
Cradock, SAfr. 106/D4
Crag (mtn.), Yk, Can. 134/K3
Crag (peak), Eng, UK 35/F3
Craig, Co, US 128/F2
Craig, Ak, US 134/M4
Craig, Ks, US 137/D6
Craig Point, Austl. 115/C3
Craigavon (dist.), NI, UK 34/B3
Craigavon, NI, UK 34/B3
Craigieburn, Austl. 115/F5
Craik, Sk, Can. 127/G3
Crail, Sc, UK 36/D4
Crailsheim, Ger. 54/D4
Craiova, Rom. 49/F3
Cramalina (peak), Swi. 57/E5
Cramlington, Eng, UK 35/G1
Cran-Gevrier, Fr. 56/C6
Crana (riv.), Ire. 34/A1
Cranberry Portage, Mb, Can. 127/H2
Cranborne Chase (for.), Eng, UK 32/D5
Cranbourne, Austl. 115/G6
Cranbrook, BC, Can. 126/E3
Cranbrook, Austl. 112/C5
Cranbury, NJ, US 138/D3
Crane, Tx, US 132/C4
Crane Neck (pt.), NY, US 139/E2
Crane River, Mb, Can. 127/H2
Cranford, NJ, US 139/H9
Cranleigh, Eng, UK 33/F4
Craponne, Fr. 42/F4
Crasna (riv.), Rom. 48/F2
Crater (lake), Or, US 128/B2
Crater Lake NP, Or, US 128/B2
Craters of the Moon Nat'l Mon., Id, US 128/D2
Crateús, Braz. 154/B2
Crati (riv.), It. 46/E3
Crato, Braz. 154/B3
Cravinhos, Braz. 155/C2
Crawford, Sc, UK 36/C3
Crawfordsville, In, US 130/C3
Crawfordville, Fl, US 133/G4
Crawley, Eng, UK 33/F4
Cray (riv.), Eng, UK 30/C2
Crazy (mts.), Mt, US 126/F4
Creag Meagaidh (peak), Sc, UK 36/B3
Creagerstown, Md, US 138/A4
Creasy (Mifflinville), Pa, US 138/B2
Creazzo, It. 59/E2
Crèches-sur-Saône, Fr. 56/A5
Crécy-sur-Serre, Fr. 52/C4
Credit (riv.), On, Can. 131/Q8

Cree (lake), Sk, Can. 122/F3
Cree (riv.), Sk, Can. 122/F3
Cree (riv.), Sc, UK 34/D2
Creel, Mex. 142/D3
Creglingen, Ger. 54/D4
Creil, Fr. 52/B5
Crema, It. 58/C2
Crémieu, Fr. 56/B6
Cremlingen, Ger. 51/H4
Cremona (prov.), It. 58/D2
Cremona, It. 58/D2
Crepaja, Serb. 48/E3
Crépy, Fr. 52/C4
Creran (lake), Sc, UK 36/A3
Cres (isl.), Cro. 48/B3
Crescent, Mo, US 137/F8
Crescent, Co, US 137/B3
Crescent, Ut, US 137/K12
Crescent City, Ca, US 126/B5
Crescentino, It. 58/B2
Cresco, Pa, US 138/C1
Crespano del Grappa, It. 59/E1
Crespellano, It. 59/E3
Crespières, Fr. 30/H5
Crespin, Fr. 52/C3
Cresskill, NJ, US 139/K8
Cressona, Pa, US 138/B2
Cressy, Austl. 115/C4
Crest, Fr. 42/F4
Crest Hill, Il, US 135/P16
Crestline, Ca, US 136/C2
Creston, BC, Can. 126/D3
Creston, Ia, US 127/K5
Crestview, Fl, US 133/G4
Crestwood Village, NJ, US 138/D4
Creswell, Austl. 115/C4
Creswick, Austl. 115/B3
Crete (sea), Gre. 47/J4
Crete, Il, US 135/P16
Crete (isl.), Gre. 27/G5
Creuch (hill), Sc, UK 36/B5
Creus (cape), Sp. 45/G1
Creuse (riv.), Fr. 42/D3
Creussen, Ger. 55/E3
Creutzwald-la-Croix, Fr. 53/F5
Crevalcore, It. 59/E3
Creve Coeur, Mo, US 137/F8
Crèvecœur-le-Grand, Fr. 52/B4
Crevillente, Sp. 45/E3
Crevoladossola, It. 58/B1
Crewe, Eng, UK 35/F5
Crewkerne, Eng, UK 32/D5
Criciúma, Braz. 155/B4
Crikvenica, Cro. 48/B3
Crillon (mt.), Ak, US 134/L4
Crimean (pen.), Ukr. 49/L3
Crimeanpen (pen.), Ukr. 62/E3
Crimond, Sc, UK 36/D2
Crisenoy, Fr. 30/L6
Crisman, Co, US 137/B2
Cristal, Monts de (mts.), Gabon 105/B1
Cristalina, Braz. 154/A5
Cristina, Braz. 211/G7
Cristóbal (pt.), Ecu. 156/E7
Cristóbal Colón (peak), Col. 152/C2
Cristoforo Colombo (int'l arpt.), It. 58/B4
Cristuru Secuiesc, Rom. 49/G2
Crişul Alb (riv.), Rom. 48/F2
Crişul Negru (riv.), Rom. 48/F2
Crixás-Açu (riv.), Braz. 151/H6
Crna Reka (riv.), FYROM 47/G2
Črnomelj, Slov. 43/L4
Croagh Patrick (peak), Ire. 31/P10
Croajingolong NP, Austl. 115/D3
Croatia (ctry.) 48/B3
Croce (peak), It. 57/H5
Croce, Pico di (peak), It. 57/H4
Croche (peak), Fr. 56/C6
Croche (riv.), Qu, Can. 131/P2
Crocker (range), Malay. 81/E3
Crocker (peak), Ecu. 156/D4
Crockett, Tx, US 129/J5
Crockett, Ca, US 135/K10
Crocodile Head (pt.), Austl. 115/D2
Crofton, Md, US 138/B6
Croghan (mtn.), Ire. 34/B6
Croisette (cape), Fr. 42/C2
Croissy-Beaubourg, Fr. 30/K5
Croker (isl.), Austl. 109/C2
Cromarty Firth (bay), Sc, UK 36/B1

Cromdale (hills), Sc, UK 36/C2
Cromwell, NZ 117/R12
Crong A Na (riv.), Viet. 78/D3
Crooked Creek, Ak, US 134/G3
Crooked (isl.), Bahm. 141/G3
Crooked Island Passage (chan.), Bahm. 145/H1
Crookston, Mn, US 127/J3
Crookwell, Austl. 115/D2
Croom, Ire. 31/P10
Crosby, ND, US 127/H3
Crosby, Eng, UK 35/E5
Crosbyton, Tx, US 129/G4
Cross City, Fl, US 133/H4
Cross Fell (peak), Eng, UK 35/F2
Cross Plains, Tx, US 129/H4
Cross River (state), Nga. 103/H5
Cross River (res.), NY, US 139/E1
Cross Roads, Pa, US 138/B4
Crossford, Sc, UK 36/C4
Crosshouse, Sc, UK 36/B5
Crossroads, Ire. 31/P9
Crossville, Tn, US 133/G3
Crostolo (riv.), It. 59/D3
Croton-on-Hudson (Croton-Harmon), NY, US 139/E1
Crottendorf, Ger. 55/F1
Croult (riv.), Fr. 30/K5
Crouy, Fr. 52/C5
Crouy-sur-Ourcq, Fr. 30/M4
Crow Agency, Mt, US 126/G4
Crowborough, Eng, UK 33/F4
Crowdy Bay NP, Austl. 115/E1
Crowe (riv.), On, Can. 130/E2
Crowell, Tx, US 129/G4
Crowley, La, US 137/P17
Crowley's (ridge), Ar, US 133/F3
Crown Point, In, US 130/C3
Crown Point, La, US 137/P17
Crown Point (int'l arpt.), Trin. 153/F2
Crown Prince Frederik (isl.), Nun., Can. 123/H1
Crownpoint, NM, US 128/E4
Crows Nest Falls NP, Austl. 114/D4
Crowthorne, Eng, UK 33/F4
Croydon, Austl. 114/A2
Croydon (bor.), Eng, UK 30/C2
Croydon, Pa, US 138/D3
Croydon, Ut, US 137/K11
Crozet (isls.), Fr. 23/M8
Crozon, Fr. 42/A2
Cruach Mhór (peak), Ire. 31/P11
Cruach nan Capull (peak), Sc, UK 36/A5
Crucero, Peru 156/D4
Cruden Bay, Sc, UK 36/E2
Cruick Water (riv.), Sc, UK 36/D3
Crumlin, NI, UK 34/B2
Crummock Water (lake), Eng, UK 35/E2
Crumpton, Md, US 138/C5
Cruseilles, Fr. 56/C5
Crusnes, Fr. 53/E5
Cruz (cape), Cuba 145/G2
Cruz Alta, Braz. 157/F2
Cruz Alta, Arg. 158/E2
Cruz Alta (peak), Port. 45/P10
Cruz das Almas, Braz. 154/C4
Cruz del Eje, Arg. 157/D3
Cruz Grande, Mex. 144/B2
Cruzeiro, Braz. 211/J7
Cruzeiro do Sul, Braz. 156/C2
Cruzeta, Braz. 154/C2
Cruzília, Braz. 211/H6
Crvenka, Serb. 48/D3
Cryn-y-Brain, Wal, UK 35/E5
Crystal (lake), Pa, US 138/C1
Crystal Bay, Nv, US 128/C3
Crystal Brook, Austl. 113/H5
Crystal Cave, Pa, US 138/C2
Crystal City, Tx, US 132/D4
Crystal Springs, Ms, US 129/K5
Crystal Springs (res.), Ca, US 135/K11
Csenger, Hun. 41/M5
Csepreg, Hun. 43/M3
Csongrád, Hun. 48/E2
Csorna, Hun. 48/D2
Csorvás, Hun. 48/E2
Csóványos (peak), Hun. 48/D2
Csurgó, Hun. 57/L5
Cu Lao (isl.), Viet. 79/A5
Cuale (riv.), Ang. 105/C2
Cualedro, Sp. 44/B2
Cuamba, Moz. 105/G3
Cuando (riv.), Ang. 105/D4
Cuango (riv.), Ang. 105/C2
Cuanza (riv.), Ang. 93/D6
Cuart de Poblet, Sp. 45/E3
Cuarto (riv.), Arg. 158/E2

Cuatrociénagas de Carranza, Mex. 132/C5
Cuauhtémoc, Mex. 142/E5
Cuauhtémoc, Mex. 142/D2
Cuautepec, Mex. 143/L6
Cuautitlán, Mex. 143/Q9
Cuautitlán Izcalli, Mex. 143/Q9
Cuautla, Mex. 143/L8
Cuba, Mo, US 129/K3
Cuba, Port. 44/B3
Cuba (ctry.) 145/F1
Cubagua (isl.), Ven. 153/E2
Cuballing, Austl. 112/C5
Cubango (riv.), Ang. 93/D6
Çubuk, Turk. 90/C1
Cucamonga (Rancho Cucamonga), Ca, US 136/C2
Cuccurano, It. 59/F5
Cuchivero (riv.), Ven. 150/E2
Cuchumatanes (mts.), Guat. 144/D3
Cuckmere (riv.), Eng, UK 33/G5
Cucq, Fr. 42/D1
Cúcuta, Col. 152/C3
Cucuyagua, Hon. 144/D3
Cudahy, Ca, US 136/F8
Cuddapah, India 82/C5
Cudgewa, Austl. 115/C3
Cudillero, Sp. 44/B1
Cudrefin, Swi. 56/D4
Cudworth, Eng, UK 35/G4
Cue, Austl. 112/C3
Cuéllar, Sp. 44/C2
Cuéllar-Baza, Sp. 44/D4
Cuenca, Sp. 44/D2
Cuenca, Ecu. 152/B5
Cuenca, Sierra de (range), Sp. 44/E2
Cuencamé de Ceniceros, Mex. 142/E3
Cuernavaca, Mex. 143/K8
Cuero, Tx, US 129/H5
Cuers, Fr. 42/G5
Cueto, Cuba 145/H1
Cuetzalán, Mex. 143/M6
Cueva de los Guácharos, PN, Col. 150/C3
Cuevas de Vinromá, Sp. 45/F2
Cuevas del Almanzora, Sp. 44/E4
Cuffley, Eng, UK 30/C1
Cufré, Uru. 159/K11
Cugir, Rom. 49/F3
Cuglieri, It. 46/A2
Cugnaux, Fr. 42/D5
Cuiabá (riv.), Braz. 151/G7
Cuiabá, Braz. 151/G7
Cuicas, Ven. 152/D2
Cuijk, Neth. 50/C5
Cuilapa, Guat. 144/D3
Cuilco (riv.), Guat. 144/C3
Cuillin (sound), Sc, UK 31/Q8
Cuilo (riv.), Ang. 105/C2
Cuisance (riv.), Fr. 56/B4
Cuise-la-Motte, Fr. 52/C5
Cuiseaux, Fr. 56/B5
Cuisery, Fr. 56/A4
Cuisy, Fr. 30/L4
Cuité, Braz. 154/C2
Cuitláhuac, Mex. 143/N8
Cuito (riv.), Ang. 105/C4
Cuiuni (riv.), Braz. 150/F4
Culcairn, Austl. 115/C2
Culdaff (riv.), Ire. 34/A1
Culemborg, Neth. 50/C5
Culgoa (riv.), Austl. 109/D3
Culiacán Rosales, Mex. 142/D3
Culion (isl.), Phil. 79/D5
Cullen, Sc, UK 36/D1
Cullera, Sp. 45/E3
Culleredo, Sp. 44/A1
Cullman, Al, US 133/G3
Culloden Battlesite, Sc, UK 36/B2
Cully, Swi. 56/C5
Cullybackey, NI, UK 34/B2
Culmback (dam), Wa, US 135/D2
Culmore, NI, UK 34/A1
Culoz, Fr. 56/B6
Culpeper, Va, US 130/E4
Culross, Sc, UK 36/C4
Cults, Sc, UK 36/D2
Culver (pt.), Austl. 112/E5
Culver City, Ca, US 136/F7
Culvers (lake), NJ, US 138/D1
Cumaná, Ven. 153/E2
Cumari, Braz. 155/B1
Cumba, Peru 156/B2
Cumbal, Col. 152/B4
Cumbal, Nevado de (peak), Col. 152/B4
Cumberland (pen.), Nun., Can. 123/K2
Cumberland (sound), Nun., Can. 123/K2
Cumberland (lake), Sk, Can. 127/H2
Cumberland (plat.), US 133/G3
Cumberland (isl.), Ga, US 133/H4
Cumberland (falls), Ky, US 133/G2
Cumberland (lake), Ky, US 130/C4
Cumberland (riv.), Ky,Tn, US 125/J4
Cumberland, Md, US 130/E4
Cumberland (co.), NJ, US 138/A3
Cumberland, Wa, US 135/D3
Cumberland House, Sk, Can. 127/H2
Cumbernauld, Sc, UK 36/C5
Cumbres Bastonal, Cerro (peak), Mex. 144/C2
Cumbres de Majalca, PN, Mex. 142/D2
Cumbres de Monterrey, PN de, Mex. 143/E3
Cumbria (co.), Eng, UK 35/E2
Cumbrian (mts.), Eng, UK 35/E2
Cumbum, India 82/C4
Cummins, Austl. 113/G5
Cumnock, Austl. 115/D2
Cumpas, Mex. 142/C2
Çumra, Turk. 90/C2
Cumshewa (pt.), BC, Can. 134/M5
Cunaviche, Ven. 153/E3
Cunco, Chile 158/B3
Cundeelee Abor. Rsv., Austl. 112/D4
Cunderdin, Austl. 112/C4
Cundinamarca (dept.), Col. 152/C3
Cunduacán, Mex. 144/C2
Cunene (riv.), Ang. 93/D6
Cuneo (prov.), It. 58/A3
Cuneo, It. 43/G4
Cunha, Braz. 211/J8
Cunnamulla, Austl. 114/B5
Cunninghame (reg.), Sc, UK 36/B5
Čuokkaraš'ša (peak), Nor. 37/H1
Cuorgnè, It. 43/G4
Cupar, Sc, UK 36/C4
Cupertino, Ca, US 135/K12
Cupra Marittima, It. 43/K5
Cupramontana, It. 59/G6
Ćuprija, Serb. 48/E4
Ćuprija, Serb. 48/E4
Cuquenán (riv.), Ven. 153/F3
Curaçá, Braz. 154/C3
Curaçao (isl.), NAnt. 150/E1
Curacautín, Chile 158/C3
Curacaví, Chile 158/N8
Curahuara de Carangas, Bol. 156/D5
Curanilahue, Chile 158/B3
Curaray (riv.), Ecu. 150/C4
Curaray (riv.), Ecu.,Peru 152/C5
Curarén, Hon. 144/E3
Curaumilla (pt.), Chile 158/N8
Curcubăta (peak), Rom. 49/F2
Cure (riv.), Fr. 40/B5
Curecanti Nat'l Rec. Area, Co, US 132/B2
Curepipe, Mrts. 107/T15
Curepto, Chile 158/B2
Curicó, Chile 158/C2
Curimatá, Braz. 154/A3
Curitibanos, Braz. 155/B3
Curno, It. 58/C1
Curone (riv.), It. 58/C3
Curral Velho, CpV. 93/K10
Current (riv.), Ar,Mo, US 129/K3
Currie, Austl. 115/B3
Currie, Sc, UK 36/C5
Curry, Ak, US 134/H3
Curtea de Argeş, Rom. 49/G3
Curtici, Rom. 48/E2
Curtis (riv.), Austl. 114/D4
Curtis (isl.), NZ 116/G8
Curtis, Sp. 44/A1
Curtis (pt.), Md, US 138/B6
Curú NWR, CR 145/E4
Curuá (riv.), Braz. 151/G4
Curuá Una (riv.), Braz. 153/H5
Curuçú (riv.), Braz. 150/D5
Curup, Indo. 80/B4
Cururupu, Braz. 151/K4
Curuzú Cuatiá, Arg. 157/E2
Curvelo, Braz. 155/C1
Cusco (dept.), Peru 156/C4
Cusco, Peru 156/C4
Cusher (riv.), NI, UK 34/B3
Cushet Law (peak), Eng, UK 36/D6
Cushing, Ok, US 129/H4
Cusna (peak), It. 58/D4
Cusset, Fr. 42/E3
Cusseta, Ga, US 133/G3
Custer, Mt, US 126/G4
Custer, SD, US 127/H5
Custines, Fr. 53/F6
Custódia, Braz. 154/C3
Cut (hill), Eng, UK 32/C5
Cut Bank, Mt, US 126/E3
Cut Knife, Sk, Can. 126/F2
Cutchogue, NY, US 139/F2
Cutervo, Peru 156/B2
Cuthbert, Ga, US 133/G4
Cutral-Có, Arg. 158/C3
Cutro, It. 47/E3
Cuttack, India 82/E3
Cuvergnon, Fr. 30/L4
Cuvier (cape), Austl. 112/B3
Cuxhaven, Ger. 51/F1
Cuyabeno, Ecu. 152/C5
Cuyama (riv.), Ca, US 128/C4
Cuyo (isls.), Phil. 81/F1
Cuyo, Phil. 81/F1
Cuyocuyo, Peru 156/D4
Cuyuni (riv.), Ven. 150/F2
Cuyuni (riv.), Guy., Ven. 153/G3
Cuyuni-Mazaruni (pol. reg.), Guy. 153/F3
Cuzco (ruin), Peru 156/D4
Cwmbran, Wal, UK 32/C3
Cyangugu, Rwa. 104/A3
Cyclades (isls.), Gre. 47/J4
Cypress (hills), Ab,Sk, Can. 126/F3
Cypress, Ca, US 136/F8
Cyprus (ctry.) 91/C2
Cyrenaica (reg.), Libya 97/K1
Cysoing, Fr. 52/C2
Cywyn (riv.), Wal, UK 32/B3
Czaplinek, Pol. 41/J2
Czarna Białostocka, Pol. 41/M2
Czarnków, Pol. 41/J2
Czech Republic (ctry.) 41/H4
Częstochowa, Pol. 41/K3
Człuchów, Pol. 38/G5

D

Da (riv.), China 79/D2
Da Hinggan (mts.), China 67/M5
Da Lat, Viet. 78/E4
Da Nang (cape), Viet. 78/E2
Da Nang, Viet. 78/E2
Da Xian, China 70/J5
Daaden, Ger. 53/G2
Da'an, China 71/M2
Daanbantayan, Phil. 79/D5
Daba (mts.), China 70/J5
Dabajuro, Ven. 152/D2
Dabakala, C.d'Iv. 102/D4
Dabas, Hun. 48/D2
Dabbāgh, Jabal (peak), SAr. 88/C3
Dabeiba, Col. 152/B3
Dabo, Fr. 53/G6
Dabob (bay), Wa, US 135/B2
Dabou, C.d'Iv. 102/D5
Daboya, Gha. 103/E4
Dabra, India 84/B3
Dąbrowa Białostocka, Pol. 39/K5
Dąbrowa Górnicza, Pol. 41/K3
Dabu, China 79/C3
Dachang Huizu Zizhixian, China 72/H7
Dachau, Ger. 55/E6
Dacono, Co, US 137/C2
Dade City, Fl, US 133/H4
Dades, Oued (riv.), Mor. 98/D3
Dadi (cape), Indo. 81/H4
Dādra and Nagar Haveli (state), India 82/B4
Dādri, India 86/D5
Dādu, Pak. 89/J3
Daduru (riv.), SrL. 82/C6
Daen Noi (peak), Thai. 78/B4
Daet, Phil. 79/D5
Dafang, China 83/J2
Dafeng, China 72/E4
Dagana, Sen. 102/B2
Dağardı, Turk. 90/B2
Dağbaşı, Turk. 90/D2
Dagestan, Resp., Rus. 63/H4
Daggaboersnek (pass), SAfr. 106/D4
Dagmar Range NP, Austl. 114/B2
Dagneux, Fr. 56/B6
Dagny, Fr. 30/M5
Dagu, China 72/H7
Daguan, China 83/H2
D'Aguilar (range), Austl. 114/E6
D'Aguilar (mt.), Austl. 114/E6
Dagupan, Phil. 79/D4
Dahana (des.), SAr. 67/D7
Daharki, Pak. 82/A2
Dahei (riv.), China 72/B2
Dahlak (arch.), Erit. 97/N4
Dahlem, Ger. 53/F3
Dahlenburg, Ger. 51/H2
Dahlonega, Ga, US 133/G3
Dahmani, Tun. 100/L7
Dahme (riv.), Ger. 41/G3
Dahn, Ger. 53/G5
Dahūk, Iraq 90/E2
Dahūk (gov.), Iraq 90/E2
Dahuofang (res.), China 72/D2
Dai (lake), China 72/C2
Dai-Segen-dake (peak), Japan 76/B3
Dai-sen (peak), Japan 74/C3
Dai Xian, China 72/C3
Daian, Japan 77/L5
Daicheng, China 72/D3
Daigo, Japan 75/G2
Dailekh, Nepal 84/C1
Dailly, Sc, UK 36/B6
Daimiao, China 72/D3
Daimiel, Sp. 44/D3
Daingerfield, Tx, US 129/J4
Daiō-zaki (pt.), Japan 75/E3
Dāira Dīn Panāh, Pak. 86/A4
Daireaux, Arg. 158/E3
Daisen-Oki NP, Japan 74/C3
Daisetsuzan NP, Japan 76/C2
Daishan, China 79/D1
Daito (isl.), Japan 67/N7
Daitō, Japan 77/J6
Daiyun (peak), China 71/L6
Dajabón, DRep. 145/J2
Dakar (cap.), Sen. 102/A3
Dakar (pol. reg.), Sen. 102/A3
Dākhilah, Wāḥāt ad (oasis), Egypt 101/B3
Dakhin Shābāzpur (isl.), Bang. 85/H4
Dakhlet Nouadhibou (pol. reg.), Mrta. 98/A5
Dakoro, Niger 103/G3
Dakota City, Ne, US 127/J5
Dakovica, Serb. 47/G1
Dakovo, Cro. 48/D3
Dal (falls), Sudan 101/B4
Dal (riv.), Swe. 64/B3
Dala-Järna, Swe. 38/F1
Dalaas, Aus. 57/F3
Dalad Qi, China 72/B2
Dalaman, Turk. 90/B2
Dalaman (int'l arpt.), Turk. 90/B2
Dalandzadgad, Mong. 70/H3
Dalarna (reg.), Swe. 37/E3
Dalatangi (pt.), Ice. 37/Q6
Dalbeattie, Sc, UK 34/E2
Dalby, Austl. 114/C4
Dalby, Swe. 38/E4
Dalcour, La, US 137/Q17
Dalcross (int'l arpt.), Sc, UK 36/B1
Dale, Ok, US 137/N15
Dale, Nor. 38/A1
Dalen, Neth. 50/D3
Dalen, Nor. 38/C2
Dalfsen, Neth. 50/D3
Dalgaranger (mt.), Austl. 112/C3
Dalhart, Tx, US 129/G3
Dalhousie (cape), NW, Can. 134/N1
Dalhousie, NB, Can. 131/H1
Dalhousie, India 86/C3
Dali, China 83/H2
Dali, China 72/B4
Dalian (bay), China 73/A3
Dalian, China 73/A3
Dalian (int'l arpt.), China 72/E3
Dalías, Sp. 44/D4
Dalidag (peak), Azer. 63/H5
Dāliyat el Karmil, Isr. 91/G6
Dalj, Cro. 48/D3
Dalkeith, Sc, UK 36/C5
Dalkola, India 85/F3
Dall (lake), Ak, US 134/F3
Dall (isl.), Ak, US 122/C3
Dallas, Tx, US 129/H4
Dallas-Fort Worth (int'l arpt.), Tx, US 129/H4
Dallastown, Pa, US 138/B4
Dallgow, Ger. 40/Q6
Dallol Bosso (riv.), Niger,Mali 103/F3
Dalmatia (reg.), Cro. 48/B3
Dalmatia, Pa, US 138/B2
Dalmellington, Sc, UK 36/B6
Dalmeny, Austl. 115/D3
Dalmine, It. 58/C1
Dal'negorsk, Rus. 71/Q3
Dal'nerechensk, Rus. 71/P2
Daloa, C.d'Iv. 102/D5
Dalry, Sc, UK 36/B5
Dalrymple (lake), Austl. 109/D3
Dalrymple, Sc, UK 36/B6
Dals Långed, Swe. 38/E2
Dalsingh Sarai, India 85/E3
Dalsjöfors, Swe. 38/E3
Dalton, Ga, US 133/G3
Daltonganj, India 85/E3
Dalvík, Ice. 37/N6
Dalwallinu, Austl. 112/C4
Daly (riv.), Austl. 109/C2
Daly (bay), Nun., Can. 122/G2
Damak, Nepal 85/F2
Damān, India 82/B3
Damān and Diu (state), India 82/B3
Damanhūr, Egypt 91/B4
Damar (isl.), Indo. 81/G5
Damascus (int'l arpt.), Syria 91/E3
Damascus, Md, US 138/A5
Damascus (Dimashq) (cap.), Syria 91/E3
Damaturu, Nga. 96/H5
Damavand (mtn.), Iran 88/F1
Dambach-la-Ville, Fr. 56/D1
Dambaslar, Turk. 49/H5
Dame Marie (cape), Haiti 145/H2
Dame Marie, Haiti 145/H2
Dāmghān, Iran 89/F1
Damietta (riv.), Egypt 91/B4
Damietta (Dumyāṭ), Egypt 91/B4
Daming, China 72/C3
Damion (peak), Fr. 53/D4
Dammard, Fr. 30/M4
Dammartin-en-Goële, Fr. 30/L4
Dammastock (peak), Swi. 57/E4
Damme, Ger. 51/F3
Damme, Belg. 52/C1
Dāmodar (riv.), India 82/E3
Damoh, India 84/B4
Damongo, Gha. 103/E4
Damparis, Fr. 56/B3
Dampier (str.), Indo. 81/H4
Dampier (arch.), Austl. 109/A2
Dampier, Austl. 112/C2
Dampierre, Fr. 30/H5
Dampierre-sur-Salon, Fr. 56/B2
Damprichard, Fr. 56/C3
Damrei (mts.), Camb. 78/C4
Damsterdiep (riv.), Neth. 50/D2
Damvant, Swi. 56/C3
Damxung, China 70/F5
Dan (riv.), NC,Va, US 133/H2
Dan Xian, China 83/J4
Đānā, Jor. 91/D4
Dana Point, Ca, US 136/C4
Danané, C.d'Iv. 102/C5
Danao, Phil. 79/D5
Danba, China 70/H5
Danbury, Eng, UK 33/G3
Dancheng, China 72/C4
Dandaragan, Austl. 112/B4
Dandeldhurā, Nepal 84/C1
Dandenong (mt.), Austl. 115/G5
Danderhall, Sc, UK 36/C5
Dandong, China 73/C2
Dane (riv.), Eng, UK 35/F5
Daneel (pt.), SAfr. 106/L11
Danggali Conservation Park, Austl. 115/B2
Dangriga, Belz. 144/D2
Dangshan, China 72/D4
Dangtu, China 72/D5
Dangyang, China 71/K5
Danielskuil, SAfr. 106/C3
Danielsville, Pa, US 138/C2
Danilov, Rus. 60/J4
Daning, China 72/B3
Danjoutin, Fr. 56/C2
Dankaur, India 86/D5
Dankov, Rus. 62/F1
Dankova (peak), Kyr. 87/G4
Danlí, Hon. 144/E3
Dannelly (res.), Al, US 133/G3
Dannemora, Swe. 38/G1
Dannenberg, Ger. 40/F2
Dannes, Fr. 52/A2
Dannevirke, NZ 117/T11
Dannhauser, SAfr. 107/E3
Danube (riv.), Eur. 27/F4
Danube, Delta of the (delta), Rom. 49/J3
Danube (Donau) (riv.), Ger. 43/H2
Danube, Mouths of the (delta), Rom.,Ukr. 62/D3
Danville, Il, US 130/C3
Danville, Ky, US 130/C4
Danville, Pa, US 138/B2
Dao Xian, China 83/K2
Daoura, Oued ed (riv.), Alg. 98/D3
Daozhen, China 83/J2
Dapaong, Togo 103/F4
Daphne, Al, US 133/G4
Dapitan, Phil. 79/D6
Daqing, China 71/N2
Daqing (riv.), China 72/H7
Dar-el-Beida (Casablanca), Mor. 98/D2
Dar es Salaam (int'l arpt.), Tanz. 104/C4
Dar es Salaam (pol. reg.), Tanz. 104/C4
Dar es Salaam (cap.), Tanz. 104/C4
Dar Rounga (reg.), CAfr. 97/K6
Dar'ā (prov.), Syria 90/C3
Dar'ā (prov.), Syria 91/E3
Dar'ā, Syria 91/E3
Dārāb, Iran 89/F3
Darabani, Rom. 49/H1
Daraga, Phil. 81/F1
Daram, Phil. 79/D5
Dārān, Iran 88/F2
Đaravica (peak), Serb. 47/G1
Dārayyā, Syria 91/E3
Darbhanga, India 85/E2
Darby (cape), Ak, US 134/F3
Darby, Pa, US 138/C4
Darda, Cro. 48/D3
Dardanelle (lake), Ar, US 129/J4
Dardanelles (str.), Turk. 90/A2
Darent (riv.), Eng, UK 30/D3
Dareton, Austl. 115/B2
Darfield, NZ 117/S11
Darfo, It. 57/G6
Dārfūr (state), Sudan 101/A5
Dargaville, NZ 117/S10
Dargle (riv.), Ire. 34/B5
D'Arguin (bay), Mrta. 102/A1
Darhan, Mong. 70/J2
Darie (hills), Som. 97/Q6
Darien, Ga, US 133/H4
Darien, Ct, US 139/M7
Darien, Il, US 135/P16
Darién, PN, Pan. 150/C2
Darién, Serranía del (mts.), Pan. 150/C2
Darkan, Austl. 112/C5
Darlag, China 70/G5
Darling (range), Austl. 109/A4
Darling (riv.), Austl. 109/D4
Darling, SAfr. 106/L10
Darling Downs (reg.), Austl. 109/D3
Darling Downs (range), Austl. 114/C3
Darlington, Eng, UK 35/G2
Darlington (co.), Eng, UK 35/G2
Darlington, Md, US 138/B4
Darlington, SC, US 133/J3
Darlington Point, Austl. 115/C2
Darłowo, Pol. 38/G4
Darmstadt, Ger. 54/B3
Darnah, Libya 97/K1
Darney, Fr. 56/C1
Darnley (bay), NW, Can. 122/D2
Darnley (cape), Ant. 160/E
Daroca, Sp. 44/E2
Darregueira, Arg. 158/E3
Darsser (cape), Ger. 38/E4
Dart (riv.), Eng, UK 32/C6
Dart, West (riv.), Eng, UK 32/C6
Dartford, Eng, UK 30/D2
Dartmoor (upland), Eng, UK 32/B5
Dartmoor NP, Eng, UK 42/A1
Dartmouth (dam), Austl. 115/C3
Dartmouth (res.), Austl. 115/C3
Dartmouth, NS, Can. 131/J2
Dartmouth, Eng, UK 32/C6
Darton, Eng, UK 35/G4
Dartuch (cape), Sp. 45/G3
Daruvar, Cro. 48/C3
Darvel (bay), Malay. 81/E3
Darvel, Sc, UK 36/B5
Darwen, Eng, UK 35/F4
Darwin (bay), Chile 158/B5
Darwin (isl.), Ecu. 156/E6
Darwin (vol.), Ecu. 156/E7
Darwin, Cordillera (mts.), Chile 157/B7
Darya Khan, Pak. 86/A4
Daryābād, India 84/C2
Dashennongjia (peak), China 72/B5
Dashhowuz, Trkm. 87/C4
Dashhowuz (pol. reg.), Trkm. 87/C4
Dashhowuz (int'l arpt.), Trkm. 87/C4
Dasht-e Kavīr (des.), Iran 89/F2
Dasht-e Lūt (des.), Iran 89/G2
Dasht-e Mārgow (des.), Afg. 89/H2
Dasht Kaur (riv.), Pak. 89/H3
Dasing, Ger. 54/E6
Daska, Pak. 86/C3
Dassa-Zoumé, Ben. 103/F5
Dassel, Ger. 51/G5
Dassendorf, Ger. 51/H1
Dasseneiland (isl.), SAfr. 106/B4
Dasūya, India 86/C4
Dātāganj, India 84/B1
Datchet, Eng, UK 30/B2
Date, Japan 76/B3
Datia, India 84/B3
Datian, China 79/C2
Datil, NM, US 132/B3
Datong (mts.), China 70/G4
Datong, China 70/H4
Datong, China 72/C2
Datteln, Ger. 51/E5
Datu (cape), Indo. 80/C3
Datuk (cape), Indo. 80/B3
Daugava (riv.), Lat. 39/L3
Daugavpils, Lat. 39/M4
Daule, Ecu. 152/B5
Daule (riv.), Ecu. 152/B5
Daun, Ger. 53/F3
Daund, India 89/K5
Daung (isl.), Myan. 78/B3
Dauphin, Mb, Can. 127/H3
Dauphin (lake), Mb, Can. 127/J3
Dauphin, Pa, US 138/B3
Dauphin (co.), Pa, US 138/B3
Dauphiné (reg.), Fr. 42/F4
Dauphiné, Alpes du (range), Fr. 42/F4
Dāvangere, India 89/L6
Davao, Phil. 79/E6
Davel, SAfr. 107/E2
Davenport, Wa, US 126/D4
Davenport, Ia, US 127/L5
Davenport (mt.), Austl. 113/F2
Daventry, Eng, UK 33/E2
Daverdisse, Belg. 53/E3
Daveyton, SAfr. 106/E2
Davgaard-Jensen Land (phys. reg.), Grld. 123/T6
David, Pan. 145/F4
David City, Ne, US 127/J5
Davidson, Sk, Can. 127/G3
Davidson (mt.), Ca, US 135/J11
Davies (mt.), Austl. 113/F3
Davis (sea), Ant. 160/F
Davis, Austl., Ant. 160/F
Davis, Ca, US 128/B3
Davis (mt.), Pa, US 130/E4
Davis (mts.), Tx, US 132/B4
Davis (str.), Can.,Grld. 123/L2
Davlekanovo, Rus. 61/M5
Davo (riv.), C.d'Iv. 102/D5
Davos, Swi. 57/F4
Dawa, China 73/B2
Dawa Wenz (riv.), Eth. 97/N7
Dawangja (isl.), China 73/B3
Dawson, Yk, Can. 134/L3
Dawson, Ga, US 133/G4
Dawson (riv.), Austl. 109/D3
Dawson (isl.), Chile 159/C7
Dawson Creek, BC, Can. 126/C2
Dawu, China 70/H5
Dawu (mtn.), China 72/C5
Dawu, China 72/C5
Dax, Fr. 42/C5
Daxing, China 72/H7
Daxue (mts.), China 70/H5
Dayang (riv.), China 73/B2
Dayao, China 83/H2
Daye, China 79/B1
Daying (riv.), China 83/G3
Daylesford, Austl. 115/C3
Dayong, China 79/B2
Dayr al Balaḩ, Gaza 91/D4
Dayr al Ghuşūn, WBnk. 91/G7
Dayr Az Zawr (prov.), Syria 90/E3
Dayr Ballūţ, WBnk. 91/G7
Dayr Sharaf, WBnk. 91/G7
Dayrūţ, Egypt 101/B3
Daysland, Ab, Can. 126/E2
Dayton, Wa, US 126/D4
Dayton, Tn, US 133/G3
Dayton, NJ, US 138/D3
Daytona Beach, Fl, US 133/H4
Dayu, China 83/K2
Dazhizhu Dau (isl.), China 71/T11
D.C. (fed. dist.), US 138/A6
De Aar, SAfr. 106/D3
De Bilt, Neth. 50/C4
De Doorns, SAfr. 106/L10
De Funiak Springs, Fl, US 133/G4
De Grey (riv.), Austl. 109/A3
De Haan, Belg. 52/C1
De Hart (res.), Pa, US 138/B3
De Hoge Veluwe, NP, Neth. 50/C4
De Kalb (co.), Il, US 135/N16
De Land, Fl, US 133/H4
De Leijen (lake), Neth. 50/D2
De Lier, Neth. 50/B5
De Luz, Ca, US 136/C4
De Panne, Belg. 52/B1
De Peel (phys. reg.), Neth. 50/C6
De Pinte, Belg. 52/C2
De Ridder, La, US 129/J5
De Soto, Ks, US 137/D6
De Soto, Mo, US 129/K3
De Wijk, Neth. 50/D3
Dead Sea (sea), Isr.,Jor. 90/C4
Deadhorse, Ak, US 134/J1
Deadman (peak), Austl. 112/C2
Deadwood, SD, US 127/H4
Deal (isl.), Austl. 115/C3
Deal, NJ, US 138/D3
Deale, Md, US 138/B6
Dean (riv.), BC, Can. 126/B2
Dean (chan.), BC, Can. 126/B2
De'an, China 79/C2
Dean (for.), Eng, UK 32/D3
Deán Funes, Arg. 157/D3
Deanmill, Austl. 112/C5
Dearborn Heights, Mi, US 135/F7
Dearne, Eng, UK 35/G4
Dease (str.), Nun., Can. 122/F2
Dease (riv.), BC, Can. 122/D3
Dease Lake, BC, Can. 134/M4
Death Valley NP, Ca, US 128/C3
Debar, FYROM 47/G2
Debauch (mtn.), Ak, US 134/G3
Debe Habe, Nga. 96/H5
Debelets, Bul. 47/J1
Deben (riv.), Eng, UK 33/H2
Dębica, Pol. 41/L3
Dęblin, Pol. 41/L3
Dębno, Pol. 41/H2
Débo (lake), Mali 102/E3
Deborah (mt.), Ak, US 134/J3
Debre Birhan, Eth. 97/N6
Debre Mark'os, Eth. 97/N5
Debre Tabor, Eth. 97/N5
Debre Zeyit, Eth. 97/N6
Debrecen, Hun. 41/L5
Decatur, Al, US 133/G3
Decatur, Il, US 127/L6
Decatur, In, US 130/C3
Decatur, Ga, US 133/G3
Decatur, Tx, US 129/H4
Decazeville, Fr. 42/E4
Deccan (plat.), India 82/C5
Decima, It. 59/E3
Děčín, Czh. 41/H3
Décines-Charpieu, Fr. 56/A6
Decize, Fr. 42/E3
Dedemsvaart, Neth. 50/D3
Dedo (peak), Arg. 158/C5
Dédougou, Burk. 102/E3
Dedza, Malw. 105/F3
Dee (riv.), Sc, UK 36/C3
Deel (riv.), Ire. 34/A4
Deep Fork (riv.), Ok, US 137/N14
Deep River, On, Can. 130/E2
Deepcut, Eng, UK 30/F3
Deepwater, Austl. 115/D1
Deepwater, NJ, US 138/C4
Deepwater (pt.), De, US 138/C5
Deer (isl.), Ak, US 134/F5
Deer Creek (res.), Ut, US 137/L13
Deer Lake, Nf, Can. 131/K1
Deer Lake, Pa, US 138/B2
Deer Lodge, Mt, US 126/E4
Deer Park, Il, US 135/P15
Deer Park, Md, US 138/B5
Deer Park, NY, US 139/E2
Deer Park, Wa, US 126/D4
Deer Plain, Il, US 137/F8
Deerfield, Il, US 135/P15
Deering, Ak, US 134/F2
Deerlijk, Belg. 52/C2
Deeside (valley), Sc, UK 36/D2
Deex Nugaaleed (riv.), Som. 97/Q6
Defensores del Chaco, PN, Par. 150/F8
Defiance, Oh, US 130/C3
Dégelis, Qu, Can. 131/G2
Degerfors, Swe. 38/F2
Degersheim, Swi. 57/F3
Deggendorf, Ger. 55/F5
Deggingen, Ger. 54/C5
Dego, It. 58/B4
DeGrey (riv.), Austl. 112/C2
Deh Bīd, Iran 88/F2
Dehalak (isl.), Erit. 97/P4
Dehalak Marine NP, Erit. 97/P4
Deheq, Iran 88/F2
Dehra Dūn, India 89/L2
Dehri, India 85/E3
Dehua, China 79/C2
Deidesheim, Ger. 54/B4
Deinste, Ger. 51/G1
Deinze, Belg. 52/C2
Deister (mts.), Ger. 51/G4
Deiva Marina, It. 58/C4
Dej, Rom. 49/F2
Deje, Swe. 38/E2
Dejiang, China 83/J2
Dejima, Japan 77/E1
Dekemhare (Dek'emhāre), Erit. 88/C5
Del Campillo, Arg. 158/D2
Del Carril, Arg. 159/J11
Del City, Ok, US 137/N15
Del Dios, Ca, US 136/C4
Del Gran Paradiso, It. 58/A2
Del Mar, Ca, US 136/C5
Del Norte, Co, US 129/F3
Del Rio, Tx, US 129/G5
Del Valle, Arg. 158/E2
Del Valle (lake), Ca, US 135/L11
Delacroix, La, US 137/Q17
Delafield, Wi, US 135/P13
Delano, Ca, US 128/C4
Delareyville, SAfr. 106/D2
Delarode (lake), Sk, Can. 126/G2
Delavan, Wi, US 129/K2
Delavan (lake), Wi, US 135/P14
Delavan Lake, Wi, US 135/N14
Delaware (riv.), US 130/F3
Delaware (state), US 130/F4
Delaware, NJ, US 138/C2
Delaware (bay), NJ, US 130/F4
Delaware, Oh, US 130/D3
Delaware (co.), Pa, US 138/C4
Delaware (pass), Pa, US 138/C2
Delaware City, De, US 138/C4
Delaware Water Gap Nat'l Rec. Area, Pa, US 130/F3
Delbrück, Ger. 51/F5
Delčevo, FYROM 47/H2
Delden, Neth. 50/D4
Delebio, It. 57/F5
Delegate, Austl. 115/D3
Delémont, Swi. 56/D3
Delft, Neth. 50/B4
Delfzijl, Neth. 50/D2
Delgada (pt.), Arg. 158/E4
Delgado (cape), Moz. 104/D5
Delhi, India 86/D5
Delhi (state), India 82/C2
Delhi, Il, US 137/G7
Delhi, La, US 129/K4

Delice, Turk. 90/C2
Delice (riv.), Turk. 62/E5
Delījān, Iran 88/F2
Déljne, NW, Can. 122/D2
Delisle, Sk, Can. 126/G3
Dell Rapids, SD, US 127/L5
Delligsen, Ger. 51/G5
Delmas, SAfr. 106/Q13
Delme (riv.), Ger. 51/F3
Delmenhorst, Ger. 51/F2
Delmiro Gouveia, Braz. 154/C3
Delmont, NJ, US 138/D5
Delnice, Cro. 48/B3
Deloraine, Austl. 115/C4
Deloraine, Mb, Can. 127/H3
Delphi (Dhelfoi) (ruin), Gre. 47/H3
Delphos, Oh, US 130/C3
Delportshoop, SAfr. 106/D3
Delran, NJ, US 138/D4
Delray Beach, Fl, US 133/H5
Delson, Qu, Can. 131/N7
Delta, Ut, US 128/D3
Delta (state), Nga. 103/G5
Delta, Pa, US 138/B4
Delta del Tigre, Uru. 159/K11
Delta du Saloum, PN du, Sen. 102/A3
Delta Junction, Ak, US 134/J3
Delta-Mendota (canal), Ca, US 135/M11
Deltona, Fl, US 133/H4
Delvinë, Alb. 47/G3
Dēma (riv.), Rus. 87/C2
Demanda, Sierra de la (range), Sp. 44/D1
Demarcation (pt.), Ak, US 134/K2
Demarest, NJ, US 139/K8
Demba, D.R. Congo 105/D2
Dembī Dolo, Eth. 97/M6
Demer (riv.), Belg. 40/C3
Demerara (riv.), Guy. 153/G3
Demerara-Mahaica (pol. reg.), Guy. 153/G3
Demerval Lobão, Braz. 154/B2
Deming, NM, US 132/B3
Demini (riv.), Braz. 150/F3
Demirci, Turk. 90/B2
Demirkent, Turk. 90/C2
Demirköprü (dam), Turk. 90/B2
Demirköy, Turk. 49/H5
Demirtaş, Turk. 90/C2
Demmin, Ger. 38/E5
Democratic Republic of the Congo (ctry.) 93/C3
Demone (valley), It. 46/D4
Demopolis, Al, US 133/G3
Dempo (peak), Indo. 80/B4
Dempster (pt.), Austl. 112/D5
Den Burg, Neth. 50/A4
Den Ham, Neth. 50/D4
Den Helder, Neth. 50/B3
Den Oever, Neth. 50/C3
Denain, Fr. 52/C3
Denakil (reg.), Djib.,Eth. 97/P5
Denali NP and Prsv., Ak, US 134/H3
Denare Beach, Sk, Can. 127/H2
Denbigh, Wal, UK 35/E5
Denbighshire (co.), Wal, UK 35/E5
Dender (riv.), Belg. 40/B3
Denderleeuw, Belg. 53/D2
Dendermonde, Belg. 53/D1
Denekamp, Neth. 50/E4
Deng Xian, China 72/C4
Dengfeng, China 72/C4
Dengkou, China 70/C3
Dengta, China 79/B3
Denham (sound), Austl. 112/B3
Denham, Austl. 112/B3
Denholme, Eng, UK 35/G4
Denia, Sp. 45/F3
Deniliquin, Austl. 115/C2
Denio, Nv, US 126/D5
Denison (mt.), Ak, US 134/H4
Denison, Ia, US 127/K5
Denison, Tx, US 129/H4
Denizli, Turk. 90/B2
Denizli (prov.), Turk. 90/B2
Denkendorf, Ger. 57/E2
Denklingen, Ger. 57/G2
Denman, Austl. 115/D2
Denmark, Austl. 112/C5
Denmark (str.), Grld.,Ice. 119/R3
Denmark (ctry.) 38/C4
Dennisville, NJ, US 138/D5
Denpasar, Indo. 80/E5
Dent de Lys (peak), Swi. 56/C4
Dent d'Hérens (peak), It. 56/D4
Dentergem, Belg. 52/C2
Dentlein am Forst, Ger. 54/D4
Denton, Eng, UK 35/F5
Denton, Md, US 138/D4
Denton, Tx, US 129/H4

D'Entrecasteaux (pt.), Austl. 112/B5
Deua NP, Austl. 115/D2
Deuil-la-Barre, Fr. 30/J5
Deûle (riv.), Fr. 52/B2
Deurne, Belg. 50/B6
Deurne, Neth. 50/C6
Deustua, Peru 156/D4
Deutsch Evern, Ger. 51/H2
Deutsch Wagram, Aus. 49/P7
Deutschkreutz, Aus. 43/M3
Deutschlandsberg, Aus. 43/L3
Deux-Montagnes, Qu, Can. 131/N6
Deux-Montagnes (co.), Qu, Can. 131/M6
Deux-Montagnes, Lac des (lake), Qu, Can. 131/N6
Deva, Rom. 48/F3
Dévaványa, Hun. 48/E2
Develi, Turk. 90/C2
Deventer, Neth. 50/D4
Deveron (riv.), Sc, UK 36/D2
Deville, Fr. 53/D4
Devil's (isl.), FrG. 151/H2
Devils (riv.), Mex. 143/E2
Devil's Elbow (pass), Sc, UK 36/C3
Devils Lake, ND, US 127/J3
Devils Creek, NJ, US 138/D5
Devils Paw (peak), Ak, US 134/M4
Devils Postpile Nat'l Mon., Ca, US 128/C3
Devils Slide, Ut, US 137/K11
Devine, Tx, US 129/H5
Devizes, Eng, UK 32/E4
Devnya, Bul. 49/H4
Devoll (riv.), Alb.,Gre. 48/E5
Devon, Ab, Can. 126/E2
Devon (isl.), Nun., Can. 123/S7
Devon (co.), Eng, UK 32/C5
Devon (riv.), Sc, UK 36/C4
Devon-Berwyn, Pa, US 138/C3
Devonport, Austl. 115/C4
Devore, Ca, US 136/C2
Devrek, Turk. 49/K5
Devrek (riv.), Turk. 49/K5
Devrez (riv.), Turk. 62/E4
Dewa (pt.), Indo. 80/A3
Dewa (mts.), Japan 76/B4
Dewas, India 89/L4
Dewetsdorp, SAfr. 106/D3
Dewsbury, Eng, UK 35/G4
Dexter, Me, US 131/G2
Dey-Dey (lake), Austl. 109/C3
Deyang, China 70/H5
Dez (riv.), Iran 64/E6
Dezfūl, Iran 88/E2
Dezhneva (cape), Rus. 134/C2
Dezhou, China 72/D3
Dhaban Singh, Pak. 86/B4
Dhāka (div.), Bang. 85/H4
Dhāka, India 85/E2
Dhaleswari (riv.), Bang. 85/H4
Dhali, Cyp. 91/C2
Dhāmpur, India 84/B1
Dhamtari, India 82/D3
Dhanaula, India 86/C4
Dhanaura, India 84/B1
Dhānbād, India 85/F4
Dhangadhi, Nepal 84/C1
Dhankutā, Nepal 85/F2
Dhār, India 89/L4
Dharampur, India 89/K4
Dharan, Nepal 85/F2
Dhāri, India 89/K4
Dhāriwāl, India 86/C4
Dharmapuri, India 82/C5
Dharmavaram, India 82/C5
Dharmjaygarh, India 84/D4
Dharmsāla, India 86/D3
Dhasan (riv.), India 84/B3
Dhaulāgiri (peak), Nepal 84/D1
Dhaulāgiri (zone), Nepal 84/D1
Dhaurahra, India 84/C1
Dhelfoí, Gre. 47/H3
Dhelvinákion, Gre. 47/G3
Dheskáti, Gre. 47/G3
Dheune (riv.), Fr. 56/A4
Dhībān, Jor. 91/D4
Dhidhimótikhon, Gre. 47/K2
Dhíkaia, Gre. 47/K2
Dhílos (ruin), Gre. 47/K4
Dhimitsána, Gre. 47/H4
Dhirfis (peak), Gre. 47/H3
Dhistomon, Gre. 47/H3
Dhofar (reg.), Oman 88/G5
Dhokímion, Gre. 47/G3
Dholka, India 89/K4
Dhomokós, Gre. 47/H3
Dhonoúsa (isl.), Gre. 47/J4
Dhorāji, India 89/K4
Dhronbach (riv.), Ger. 53/F4
Dhūlia, India 89/K4
Dhulián, India 85/F3
Dhulikhel, Nepal 85/E2
Dhupgāri, India 85/G2
Dhūri, India 86/C4

Di Linh, Viet. 78/E4
Dia (isl.), Gre. 47/J5
Diablo (mt.), Ak, US 134/H4
Diablo (range), Ca, US 128/B3
Diablo (plat.), Tx, US 132/B4
Diablo, Punta del (pt.), Uru. 159/G2
Diablotin (peak), Dom. 141/N9
Diadema, Braz. 211/G8
Diadema Argentina, Arg. 158/D5
Diamante, Arg. 158/D2
Diamantina, Braz. 154/B5
Diamantina (riv.), Austl. 109/D3
Diamantina, Chapada (hills), Braz. 151/K6
Diamantino, Braz. 151/G6
Diamond Bar, Ca, US 136/G8
Diamond Harbour, India 85/G4
Diamond Head (pt.), Hi, US 124/W13
Dianalund, Den. 38/D4
Dianbai, China 83/K3
Dianjiang, China 79/A1
Diano Marina, It. 58/B5
Dianshan (lake), China 72/L8
Diapaga, Burk. 103/F3
Dias Creek, NJ, US 138/D5
Diavolezza (peak), Swi. 57/F5
Dibai, India 84/B1
Dibeng, SAfr. 106/C2
Dibiápur, India 84/B2
Dibis (well), Egypt 101/B4
Dibis, Iraq 90/F3
Dickens, Tx, US 129/G4
Dickens (pt.), RI, US 139/G1
Dickinson, ND, US 127/H4
Dickson, Tn, US 130/C4
Dicle (dam), Turk. 90/E2
Dicomano, It. 59/E5
Didam, Neth. 50/D5
Didcot, Eng, UK 33/E3
Didsbury, Ab, Can. 126/E3
Didwāna, India 89/K3
Didyma (ruin), Turk. 90/A2
Die (riv.), Indo. 80/A3
Dieblich, Ger. 53/G3
Diébougou, Burk. 102/E4
Dieburg, Ger. 54/D2
Diedersdorf, Ger. 40/Q7
Diefenbaker (lake), Sk, Can. 126/G3
Diego de Almagro (isl.), Chile 159/B6
Diego Garcia (isl.), UK 67/G10
Diekirch (dist.), Lux. 53/E4
Diekirch, Lux. 53/F4
Diemen, Neth. 50/B4
Diemtigen, Swi. 56/D4
Diepenbeek, Belg. 53/E2
Diepenveen, Neth. 50/D4
Diepholz, Ger. 51/F3
Dieppe, Fr. 42/D2
Dierdorf, Ger. 53/G2
Diespeck, Ger. 54/D3
Diessen am Ammersee, Ger. 57/H2
Diest, Belg. 53/E2
Dietenheim, Ger. 57/G1
Dietenhofen, Ger. 54/D3
Dietersheim, Ger. 54/D3
Dietfurt an der Altmühl, Ger. 55/E4
Dietikon, Swi. 57/E3
Dietmannsried, Ger. 57/G2
Dietzenbach, Ger. 54/B2
Dieue-sur-Meuse, Fr. 53/E5
Dieulouard, Fr. 53/F6
Dieuze, Fr. 53/F6
Diever, Neth. 50/D3
Diez, Ger. 54/B2
Diffa, Niger 96/H3
Diffa (dept.), Niger 96/H3
Differdange, Lux. 53/E4
Difficult (mt.), Austl. 115/B3
Dīg, India 84/A2
Digboi, India 83/G2
Digby, NS, Can. 131/H2
Dighwāra, India 85/E3
Digne-les-Bains, Fr. 43/G4
Digoin, Fr. 42/E3
Digor, Turk. 90/E1
Digul (riv.), Indo. 81/K5
Digya NP, Gha. 103/E5
Dijon, Fr. 42/F3
Dikirnis, Egypt 91/B4
Diklosmta (peak), Geo. 63/H4
Diksmuide, Belg. 52/B1
Dila, Eth. 97/N6
Dilbeek, Belg. 53/D2
Dilek Yarımadası NP, Turk. 90/A2
Dili (cap.), ETim. 81/G5
Dillenburg, Ger. 53/H2
Dillingen, Ger. 53/F5
Dillingen an der Donau, Ger. 54/D5
Dillingham, Ak, US 134/G4
Dillon, Mt, US 126/E4
Dillon, SC, US 133/J3
Dillsburg, Pa, US 138/A3

Dilolo, D.R. Congo 105/D3
Dilsen, Belg. 53/E1
Dimāpur, India 83/F2
Dimaro, It. 57/G5
Dimas, Mex. 142/D4
Dimashq (prov.), Syria 90/D3
Diu, India 82/B3
Dimbokro, C.d'Iv. 102/D5
Dimboola, Austl. 115/B3
Dive (riv.), Fr. 42/D3
Dimbovița (prov.), Rom. 49/G3
Dimbulah, Austl. 114/B2
Dimitriya Lapteva (str.), Rus. 65/P2
Dimitrovgrad, Bul. 47/J1
Dimitrovgrad, Serb. 47/H1
Dimitrovgrad, Rus. 63/J1
Dimlang (peak), Nga. 96/H6
Dimmitt, Tx, US 129/G4
Dimona, Isr. 91/D4
Dimovo, Bul. 49/F4
Dina, Pak. 86/B3
Dinagat (isl.), Phil. 79/E5
Dinagat, Phil. 79/E6
Dinājpur (pol. reg.), Bang. 85/G3
Dinan, Fr. 42/B2
Dīnānagar, India 86/C4
Dinant, Belg. 53/D3
Dinar, Turk. 90/B2
Dinard, Fr. 42/B2
Dinaric Alps (mts.), Cro. 46/B3
Dinas (pt.), Wal, UK 32/B2
Dinder NP, Sudan 97/N5
Dindigul, India 82/C5
Dindori, India 84/C4
Dinga, Pak. 86/B3
Ding'an, China 83/K4
Dingbian, China 70/J4
Dingelstädt, Ger. 51/H6
Dinggyê, China 85/F1
Dingle, Ire. 30/F10
Dingle (bay), Ire. 30/N10
Dingmans Ferry, Pa, US 139/G1
Dingnan, China 79/C3
Dingolfing, Ger. 55/F5
Dingras, Phil. 79/D4
Dingtao, China 72/C4
Dingwall, Sc, UK 36/B1
Dingxi, China 70/H4
Dingxiang, China 72/C3
Dingxing, China 72/G7
Dinguiraye, Gui. 102/B3
Dinkel (riv.), Ger. 51/E4
Dinkelsbühl, Ger. 54/D4
Dinkelscherben, Ger. 54/D5
Dinklage, Ger. 51/F3
Dinosaur Nat'l Mon., US 128/E2
Dinslaken, Ger. 50/D5
Dinsmore, Sk, Can. 126/G3
Dintel Mark (riv.), Neth. 50/B5
Dinuba, Ca, US 128/C3
Dinxperlo, Neth. 50/E5
Dioïla, Mali 102/D3
Dion (riv.), Gui. 102/C4
Diósd, Hun. 49/Q10
Diourbel (pol. reg.), Sen. 102/A3
Diourbel, Sen. 102/A3
Dipalpur, Pak. 86/B4
Diphu, India 83/F2
Diplo, Pak. 89/J4
Dipni (dam), Turk. 90/E2
Dipolog, Phil. 79/D6
Dipperz, Ger. 57/H2
Dipperz, Ger. 54/C1
Dique (canal), Col. 145/H4
Diré, Mali 102/E2
Dirē Dawa, Eth. 97/P6
Diriamba, Nic. 144/E4
Dirj, Libya 99/H3
Dirk Hartog (isl.), Austl. 109/A3
Dirksland, Neth. 50/B5
Dirlewang, Ger. 57/G2
Dirranbandi, Austl. 114/C5
Dirrington Great Law (hill), Sc, UK 36/D5
Dirty Devil (riv.), Ut, US 128/E3
Disappointment (lake), Austl. 109/B3
Disappointment (isls.), FrPol. 117/L6
Discovery (bay), Austl. 115/B3
Discovery Bay, Jam. 145/G2
Disentis-Mustér, Swi. 57/E4
Disgrazi (peak), It. 57/F5
Disko (isl.), Grld. 119/M3
Disko (Qeqertarsuaq) (isl.), Grld. 123/L2
Disneyland, Ca, US 136/C3
Dison, Belg. 53/E2
Dispur, India 83/F3
Disraëli, Qu, Can. 131/G2
Dissen am Teutoburger Wald, Ger. 51/F4
District of Colombia (fed. dist.), US 138/A6
Distrito Federal (fed. dist.), Braz. 154/A4
Distrito Federal (fed. dist.), Mex. 140/A5
Distrito Federal (fed. dist.), Ven. 153/E2
Distrito Federal (fed. dist.), Col. 152/C3
Disūq, Egypt 91/B4

Ditchling Beacon (hill), Eng, UK 33/F5
Dittaino (riv.), It. 46/D4
Dittelbrunn, Ger. 54/D2
Dittmer, Mo, US 137/F9
Dittwiler, Fr. 53/G6
Ditzingen, Ger. 54/C5
Diva (riv.), Serb. 48/C4
Dive (riv.), Fr. 42/D3
Dividing Creek, NJ, US 138/C5
Dimboola, Austl. 115/B3
Divinolândia, Braz. 211/G6
Divinópolis, Braz. 155/C2
Divisa Nova, Braz. 211/G6
Divisor, Serra do (mts.), Braz. 151/K5
Divo, C.d'Iv. 102/D5
Divonne-les-Bains, Fr. 56/C5
Divriği, Turk. 90/D2
Dīwānīyah, Iraq 90/F3
Diyadin, Turk. 90/E2
Diyāla (gov.), Iraq 90/F3
Diyarb Najm, Egypt 91/B4
Diyarbakir (prov.), Turk. 90/E2
Diyarbakır, Turk. 90/E2
Djakotomé, Ben. 103/F5
Djamaa, Alg. 99/G2
Djambala, Congo 96/H8
Djebel-Amrag (mtn.), Alg. 100/D3
Djebel Tichka (peak), Mor. 98/C3
Djedi, Oued (riv.), Alg. 99/G2
Djelfa, Alg. 96/F1
Djema, CAfr. 97/L6
Djemila (ruin), Alg. 100/G4
Djénné, Mali 102/D3
Djibo, Burk. 103/E3
Djibouti (ctry.) 97/P5
Djibouti (cap.), Djib. 97/P5
Djougou, Ben. 103/F4
Djúpivogur, Ice. 37/P7
Djura, CAfr. 97/J5
Doba, Chad 96/J6
Dobbs Ferry, NY, US 139/K7
Dobele, Lat. 39/K3
Döbeln, Ger. 40/Q7
Doberai (pen.), Indo. 81/H4
Dobiegniew, Pol. 41/N2
Dobogo-kó (peak), Hun. 44/Q9
Doboj, Bosn. 48/D3
Dobřany, Czh. 55/G3
Dobre Miasto, Pol. 39/J5
Dobrich, Bul. 49/H4
Dobřiš, Czh. 55/H3
Dobruja (reg.), Bul. 49/H4
Dobrush, Bela. 62/D1
Dobryanka, Rus. 61/N4
Doce (riv.), Braz. 151/K7
Dochart (riv.), Sc, UK 36/C4
Dock Junction, Ga, US 133/H4
Docker River, Austl. 113/F3
Doctor Arroyo, Mex. 143/E4
Doctor Pedro P. Peña, Par. 157/D1
Doctor Petru Groza, Rom. 48/F2
Doda (lake), Qu, Can. 131/F1
Doda, India 86/D3
Doda (riv.), India 86/D3
Dodder (riv.), Ire. 34/B5
Doddinghurst, Eng, UK 30/D2
Dodecanese (isl.), Gre. 90/A2
Dodge City, Ks, US 129/G3
Dodger Stadium, Ca, US 136/F7
Dodgeville, Wi, US 127/J5
Dodman (pt.), Eng, UK 32/B6
Dodoma (pol. reg.), Tanz. 104/B4
Dodoma (cap.), Tanz. 104/B4
Dodori Nat'l Rsv., Kenya 105/C2
Dodsland, Sk, Can. 126/F3
Doesburg, Neth. 50/D4
Doetinchem, Neth. 50/D5
Doğankent, Turk. 90/D1
Doğanhisar, Turk. 90/B2
Doğanşar, Turk. 90/D1
Doğanşehir, Turk. 90/D2
Doğanyurt, Turk. 90/C1
Döger, Turk. 90/B2
Dogliani, It. 58/A3
Dogondoutchi, Niger 103/G3

Doğubayazıt, Turk. 90/F2
Doğukaradeniz (mts.), Turk. 90/D1
Dohad, India 89/K4
Dohrīghāt, India 84/D2
Doi, India 82/B3
Doi Khun Tan NP, Thai. 78/B2
Doilungdêqên, China 82/C2
Doiras, Embalse de (res.), Sp. 44/B1
Dois de Julho (int'l arpt.), Braz. 154/C4
Dois Irmãos, Serra (mts.), Braz. 151/K5
Doische, Belg. 53/D3
Dokka, Nor. 38/D1
Dokkum, Neth. 50/D2
Dokkumer Ee (riv.), Neth. 50/C2
Doksy, Czh. 55/H1
Dolbeau, Qu, Can. 131/F1
Dolcedorme (peak), It. 46/E2
Dole, Fr. 56/B3
Dolent (peak), Swi. 56/D6
Dolgellau, Wal, UK 32/C1
Dolgoprudnyy, Rus. 61/W9
Dolianova, It. 46/A3
Dolinsk, Rus. 71/R2
Dolj (prov.), Rom. 49/F3
Dolj, Serb. 48/C4
Dollar Law (peak), Sc, UK 36/C5
Dollard-des-Ormeaux, Qu, Can. 131/N7
Dollar (Dollart) (bay), Neth.,Ger. 51/E2
Dolmar (peak), Ger. 54/D1
Dolmen (ruin), It. 46/E2
Dolni Banya, Bul. 47/H1
Dolní Dübnik, Bul. 49/G4
Dolnoślaskie (prov.), Pol. 41/J3
Dolo, Eth. 97/P7
Dolo, It. 59/F2
Dolok, Indo. 81/J4
Dolomites (mts.), It. 46/D1
Dolores, Arg. 158/F3
Dolores (riv.), Co, US 128/E3
Dolores, Guat. 144/D2
Dolores, Uru. 159/J10
Dolores, Ven. 152/D2
Dolphin (cape), UK 159/F6
Dolphin and Union (str.), Nun., Can. 122/F2
Dölsach, Aus. 43/K3
Dolton, Il, US 135/Q16
Dom (peak), Swi. 56/D1
Dom (peak), Indo. 81/J4
Dom Noi (riv.), Thai. 78/C3
Do Rāh (pass), Afg. 89/K1
Do Son, Viet. 78/D1
Doany, Madg. 107/J6
Doba, Chad 96/J6
Döbeln, Ger. 40/Q7
Döbern, Ger. 40/D3
Doberai (pen.), Indo. 81/H4
Dobiegniew, Pol. 41/N2
Dom Pedrito, Braz. 157/F2
Dom Pedro, Braz. 154/B2
Domat-Ems, Swi. 57/F4
Domažlice, Czh. 55/F3
Dombasle-sur-Meurthe, Fr. 53/F6
Dombay-Ul'gen (peak), Geo. 63/G4
Dombás, Nor. 38/C1
Dombóvár, Hun. 48/D2
Dombrád, Hun. 48/E1
Dombra, India 84/C3
Dome C, US, Ant. 160/J
Domeyko, Cordillera (mts.), Chile 157/C1
Domérat, Fr. 42/E3
Dominica Passage (chan.), Dom.,Guad. 141/N9
Dominican Republic (ctry.) 141/H4
Dommartin-lès-Remiremont, Fr. 53/F6
Dommartin-lès-Toul, Fr. 53/E6
Dommel (riv.), Belg. 53/E1
Domodedovo (int'l arpt.), Rus. 61/W9
Domodossola, It. 57/E5
Domohāni, India 85/G2
Domont, Fr. 30/J4
Dompu, Indo. 81/F5
Domrémy-la-Pucelle, Fr. 56/B1
Domsjö, Swe. 38/G3
Domusnovas, It. 46/A3
Domvík (mt.), Austl. 114/C5
Domžale, Slov. 43/L3
Don (riv.), Eng, UK 35/G5
Don (ridge), Rus. 64/E5
Don Benito, Sp. 44/C3
Don Carlos, Phil. 79/E6
Don Noi (riv.), Thai. 78/D2
Donaghadee, NI, UK 34/B2
Donaghmore, NI, UK 34/B2
Donald, Austl. 115/B3
Donaldsonville, La, US 129/K5
Doñana NP, Sp. 44/B4
Donau (Danube) (riv.), Ger. 43/H2
Donaueschingen, Ger. 57/E2
Donauwörth, Ger. 54/D5
Doncaster, Eng, UK 35/G4
Doncaster (co.), Eng, UK 35/G4
Donchery, Fr. 53/D4

Dondra Head (pt.), SrL. 82/D6
Donegal, Ire. 31/P9
Donegal (dist.), Ire. 34/A1
Donegal (bay), Ire. 31/P9
Donets (riv.), Rus., Ukr. 63/G2
Donets'k, Ukr. 62/F2
Donets'k (int'l arpt.), Ukr. 62/F2
Donets'ka Oblasti, Ukr. 62/F3
Dong (riv.), Viet. 83/J5
Dong Ha, Viet. 78/D2
Dong Hoi, Viet. 78/D2
Dong Noi, Viet. 79/A5
Donga (riv.), Nga. 103/H4
Dongar Parāsia, India 84/B4
Dongara, Austl. 112/B4
Dongbei (plain), China 72/E2
Dongchuan, China 83/H2
Dong'e, China 72/D3
Dongen, Neth. 50/B5
Dongfang, China 83/J4
Donggou, China 73/C3
Dongguan, China 83/K3
Dongguang, China 72/D4
Donghai, China 72/D4
Dongio, Swi. 57/E5
Dongkya (pass), China 85/G2
Dongkou, China 79/B3
Dongliao, China 72/F2
Dongming, China 72/C4
Dongola, China 72/C4
Dongou, China 57/F5
Dongsha (isl.), China 79/C3
Dongshan, China 79/C3
Dongtai, China 72/E4
Dongting (lake), China 79/B2
Dongyang, China 79/D2
Donihue, Chile 158/N9
Donji Komren, Serb. 47/G1
Donji Vakuf, Bosn. 48/C3
Donna, Tx, US 129/H5
Donnersberg (peak), Ger. 53/G4
Donnybrook, Austl. 114/C4
Donnybrook, Austl. 112/B5
Donon (peak), Fr. 56/D1
Donoratico, It. 46/C1
Donon, Mong. 71/K2
Donzdorf, Ger. 54/C5
Donzy, Fr. 42/E3
Dooleena (peak), Austl. 112/C2
Doon (riv.), Sc, UK 36/B6
Doon (lake), Sc, UK 36/B6
Doonerak (mt.), Ak, US 134/H2
Door (pen.), Wi, US 127/M4
Doorn (riv.), SAfr. 106/B3
Doorn, Neth. 50/C4
Doppo (peak), It. 58/D1
Doqên (lake), China 85/G1
Dora (lake), Austl. 109/B3
Dora Riparia (riv.), It. 43/G4
Dorada (coast), Sp. 45/F2
Dorchester, NB, Can. 131/H2
Dorchester, II, US 137/H7
Dorchester, Eng, UK 32/D5
Dorchester (cape), Nun., Can. 123/J2
Dorchester, NJ, US 138/D5
Dordogne (riv.), Fr. 42/D4
Dordrecht, SAfr. 106/D3
Dordrecht, Neth. 50/B5
Dore (lake), Sk, Can. 126/F2
Dore, Monts (mts.), Fr. 42/E4
Dores do Indaiá, Braz. 155/C1
Dorfen, Ger. 55/F6
Dorfen (riv.), Ger. 55/F6
Dorgali, It. 46/A2
Dori, Burk. 103/E3
Dorion, Qu, Can. 131/M7
Dorking, Eng, UK 30/C3
Dorlisheim, Fr. 56/D1
Dormagen, Ger. 53/F1
Dormans, Fr. 53/D5
Dornbirn, Aus. 57/F3
Dorney Park/ Wildwater Kingdom, Pa, US 138/C2
Dornhan, Ger. 57/E1
Dorno, It. 58/B2
Dornoch Firth (inlet), Sc, UK 36/B1
Dornod (prov.), Mong. 71/K2
Dornogovī (prov.), Mong. 71/J3
Dornstetten, Ger. 54/B6
Dornum, Ger. 51/F1
Doronuevo, Ger. 57/E2
Dorothy, NJ, US 138/D5
Dörpen, Ger. 51/E3
Dorre (isl.), Austl. 115/E1
Dorrigo, Austl. 115/E1
Dorsale (mts.), Tun. 46/A5
Dorsbach (riv.), Ger. 54/B2

Dorset (co.), Eng, UK 32/D5
Dorsey, Il, US 137/G8
Dorsten, Ger. 50/D5
Dortan, Fr. 56/B5
Dortmund, Ger. 51/E5
Dortmund-Ems (canal), Ger. 51/E4
Dortmund (Wickede) (int'l arpt.), Ger. 51/E5
Dörtyol, Turk. 91/E1
Dorum, Ger. 51/F1
Dorval, Qu, Can. 131/N7
Dörverden, Ger. 51/G3
Dos Bahias (cape), Arg. 158/D5
Dos de Mayo, Peru 156/C2
Dos Hermanas, Sp. 44/C4
Döşemealtı, Turk. 91/B1
Dosewallips (riv.), Wa, US 135/A2
Dōshi, Japan 77/C2
Dōshi (riv.), Japan 77/C2
Dosse (riv.), Ger. 40/G2
Dosso, Niger 103/F3
Dosso (dept.), Niger 103/F3
Dosson, It. 59/F1
Dossor, Kaz. 63/K3
Dot Lake, Ak, US 134/K3
Dothan, Al, US 133/G4
Dötlingen, Ger. 51/F3
Döttingen, Swi. 57/E2
Douai, Fr. 52/C3
Douala, Camr. 96/G7
Douar el Câid el Gueddara, Mor. 100/A2
Douar Toulal, Mor. 100/B3
Douarnenez, Fr. 42/A2
Douarnenez, Baie de (bay), Fr. 42/A2
Double Island (pt.), Austl. 114/D4
Double Mountain Fork Brazos (riv.), Tx, US 129/G4
Double Mtn. Fork (riv.), Tx, US 143/E1
Doubs (riv.), Fr. 42/F3
Doubs (dept.), Fr. 56/C3
Doubs, Fr. 56/C4
Doubtful Island (bay), Austl. 112/C5
Douchy-les-Mines, Fr. 52/C3
Doue, Fr. 30/M5
Doué-la-Fontaine, Fr. 42/C3
Douentza, Mali 102/E3
Dougga (ruin), Tun. 100/L6
Douglas, SAfr. 106/C3
Douglas (cap.), IM, UK 34/D3
Douglas, Sc, UK 36/C5
Douglas (mt.), Ak, US 134/H4
Douglas (co.), Co, US 137/C4
Douglas, Ga, US 133/H4
Douglas, Wy, US 127/G5
Douglassville, Pa, US 138/C3
Doulaincourt-Saucourt, Fr. 56/B1
Doullens, Fr. 52/B3
Doune, Sc, UK 36/B4
Doune (peak), Sc, UK 36/B4
Doupovské Hory (mts.), Czh. 43/K1
Dour, Belg. 52/C3
Dourados, Braz. 151/H8
Dourdan, Fr. 30/J6
Dourdou (riv.), Fr. 42/E4
Dourh (peak), Mor. 99/E2
Douro (riv.), Port. 44/B2
Dousman, Wi, US 135/P13
Doussard, Fr. 56/C6
Douvaine, Fr. 56/C5
Douvrin, Fr. 52/B2
Doux (riv.), Fr. 42/F4
Douze (riv.), Fr. 42/C4
Dove Creek, Co, US 128/E3
Dover, Austl. 115/C4
Dover (pt.), Austl. 112/E5
Dover, Eng, UK 33/H4
Dover (cap.), De, US 138/C5
Dover, NJ, US 138/D2
Dover, Pa, US 138/B4
Dover-Foxcroft, Me, US 131/G2
Dover, Strait of (str.), Fr.,UK 42/D1
Dovrefjell NP, Nor. 37/D3
Dow, Il, US 137/G7
Dowerin, Austl. 112/C4
Dowlatābād, Iran 89/G3
Down (dist.), NI, UK 34/C3
Downers Grove, Il, US 135/P16
Downey, Ca, US 136/F8
Downieville, Ca, US 128/B3
Downingtown, Pa, US 138/C4
Downpatrick, NI, UK 34/C3
Doylestown, Pa, US 138/C3
Dōzen (isl.), Japan 74/C3
Dozois (res.), Qu, Can. 130/E2
Drâa (cape), Mor. 98/C3
Drâa, Oued (riv.), Mor. 93/B2
Drac (riv.), Fr. 42/F4
Dracena, Braz. 155/B2
Drachten, Neth. 50/D2
Drăgănești-Olt, Rom. 49/G3
Dragoman, Bul. 47/H1
Dragon's Mouth (str.), Trin.,Ven. 153/F2
Draguignan, Fr. 43/G5
Drake (passg.) 157/C8
Drake, Co, US 137/B2
Drake (passg.), SAm. 159/D8
Drakensberg (mts.), SAfr. 93/E8
Dráma, Gre. 47/J2
Drammen, Nor. 38/D2
Drance (riv.), Swi. 56/D5
Drancy, Fr. 30/K5
Drangedal, Nor. 38/C2
Dranse (riv.), Fr. 56/C5
Dransfeld, Ger. 51/G5
Draper, Ut, US 137/K12
Drau (riv.), Aus. 43/K3
Dráva (riv.), Aus. 48/C3
Drava (riv.), Slov. 43/L3
Draveil, Fr. 30/K5
Drawa (riv.), Pol. 41/H2
Drawienski NP, Pol. 41/H2
Drawsko Pomorskie, Pol. 41/H2
Drayton, ND, US 127/J3
Drayton Valley, Ab, Can. 126/E2
Dreghorn, Sc, UK 36/B5
Drei Zinnen (peak), PNG 81/K4
Dreiesselberg (peak), Ger. 55/G5
Dreisam (riv.), Ger. 56/D2
Drensteinfurt, Ger. 51/E5
Drenthe (prov.), Neth. 50/D3
Drentse Hoofdvaart (riv.), Neth. 50/D3
Drentwede, Ger. 51/F3
Dresano, It. 58/C2
Dresden, Ger. 41/G3
Drezdenko, Pol. 41/H2
Driebergen, Neth. 50/C4
Driedorf, Ger. 53/H2
Drigh Road, Pak. 89/J4
Drimoleague, Ire. 31/P11
Drin (gulf), Alb. 47/F2
Drin (riv.), Alb. 47/F1
Drina (riv.), Bosn. 48/D4
Drniš, Cro. 48/C4
Dro, It. 57/G6
Drøbak, Nor. 38/D2
Drobeta-Turnu Severin, Rom. 48/F3
Drochtersen, Ger. 51/G1
Drocourt, Fr. 30/H4
Drogheda, Ire. 34/B4
Drohobych, Ukr. 62/B2
Droitwich, Eng, UK 32/D2
Drolshagen, Ger. 53/G1
Dromiskin, Ire. 34/B4
Dromore (riv.), Ire. 34/A3
Dromore, NI, UK 34/B3
Dronero, It. 43/G4
Dronfield, Eng, UK 35/G5
Drongan, Sc, UK 36/B6
Dronne (riv.), Fr. 42/D4
Dronten, Neth. 50/C3
Dropt (riv.), Fr. 42/D4
Drouette (riv.), Fr. 52/A6
Drowning (riv.), On, Can. 130/C1
Drumbeg, NI, UK 34/C2
Drumcar, Ire. 34/B4
Drumheller, Ab, Can. 126/E3
Drumleck (pt.), Ire. 34/B5
Drummond (range), Austl. 109/D3
Drummond (pt.), Austl. 113/G5
Drummond (mt.), Austl. 114/B4
Drummondville, Qu, Can. 131/F2
Drumochter, Pass of (pass), Sc, UK 36/B3
Drunen, Neth. 50/C5
Druridge (bay), Eng, UK 35/G1
Drusenheim, Fr. 53/G6
Druskininkai, Lith. 39/K4
Druten, Neth. 50/C5
Drvar, Bosn. 48/C3
Drwęca (riv.), Pol. 41/K2
Dry Fork Cheyenne (riv.), Wy, US 129/F2
Dry Tortugas (isl.), Fl, US 133/H5
Dry Tortugas NP, Fl, US 133/H5
Dryanovo, Bul. 47/J1
Dryden, On, Can. 127/K3
Dryden, Tx, US 132/C4
Dryden, Mi, US 135/F6
Drygarn Fawr (peak), Wal, UK 32/C2
Du Bois, Pa, US 130/E3
Du Page (co.), Il, US 135/P16
Du Page (riv.), Il, US 135/P16
Du Page, East Br. (riv.), Il, US 135/P16
Du Quoin, Il, US 129/K3
Duaringa, Austl. 114/C3
Duarte (peak), DRep. 141/G4
Duarte, Ca, US 136/G7
Dubawnt (riv.), NW, Can. 122/F2
Dubawnt (lake), Nun., Can. 122/F2
Dubayy, UAE 89/G3
Dubbo, Austl. 115/D2
Dübendorf, Swi. 57/E3
Dübener Heide (phys. reg.), Ger. 40/G3
Dubino, It. 57/F5
Dublin (cap.), Ire. 34/B5
Dublin (co.), Ire. 34/B5
Dublin, Ca, US 135/L11
Dublin, Ga, US 133/H3
Dublin, Md, US 138/B4
Dublin, Pa, US 138/C3
Dubna, Rus. 60/H4
Dubnica nad Váhom, Slvk. 41/K4
Dubno, Ukr. 62/C2
Dubois, Wy, US 126/F5
Duboistown, Pa, US 138/A1
Dubossary (res.), Mol. 49/J2
Dubrājpur, India 85/F4
Dubrovnik, Cro. 47/F1
Dubrovnik (int'l arpt.), Cro. 47/F1
Dubuque, Ia, US 127/L5
Duchang, China 79/C2
Duchcov, Czh. 55/G1
Duchesne (riv.), Ut, US 128/E2
Duchesne, Ut, US 128/E2
Ducie (isl.), Pitc. 117/N7
Duck (riv.), Tn, US 130/C5
Duck (lake), Mi, US 135/E7
Duckabush (riv.), Wa, US 135/A2
Duda (riv.), Col. 152/C4
Duddon (riv.), Eng, UK 35/E3
Dudelange, Lux. 53/F5
Dudenhofen, Ger. 54/B4
Duderstadt, Ger. 51/H5
Dudh Kosi (riv.), Nepal 85/F2
Dūdhi, India 84/D3
Dudhwa NP, India 84/C1
Dudignac, Arg. 158/E2
Düdingen, Swi. 56/D4
Dudinka, Rus. 64/J3
Dudley, Eng, UK 32/D1
Dudley (co.), Eng, UK 32/D2
Dueñas, Sp. 44/C2
Duero (riv.), Sp. 44/C2
Dueville, It. 59/E1
Dufaja (riv.), Kenya 104/C3
Duff (isls.), Sol. 116/F5
Duffel, Belg. 53/D1
Dufftown, Sc, UK 36/C2
Dufour (Dufourspitze) (peak), Swi. 58/A1
Dufourspitze (peak), Swi. 43/G4
Dugi Otok (isl.), Cro. 48/B3
Dugny-sur-Meuse, Fr. 53/E5
Dugo Selo, Cro. 48/C3
Dugway, Ut, US 128/D2
Duich (lake), Sc, UK 36/A2
Duida (peak), Ven. 153/E4
Duida Marahuaca, PN, Ven. 150/E3
Duingen, Ger. 51/G4
Duisburg, Ger. 50/D6
Duitama, Col. 152/C3
Duiven, Neth. 50/D5
Duke of Gloucester (isls.), FrPol. 117/L7
Duke's (pass), Sc, UK 36/B4
Dukielska (Dukla Pass) (pass), Pol. 41/L4
Dulan, China 70/G4
Dulce (riv.), Arg. 157/D2
Dulce, NM, US 128/F3
Dulce (gulf), Pan. 145/F4
Dulce Nombre de Culmí, Hon. 144/E3
Duleek, Ire. 34/B4
Dŭlgopol, Bul. 49/H4
Duliu (riv.), China 83/J2
Dullewāla, Pak. 86/A4
Dülmen, Ger. 51/E5
Dulnain (riv.), Sc, UK 36/C2
Dulovo, Bul. 49/H4
Dumalinao, Phil. 79/D6
Dumaran (isl.), Phil. 81/E1
Dumaresq (riv.), Austl. 115/D1
Dumas, Ar, US 129/K4
Dumas, Tx, US 129/G4
Dumbarton, Sc, UK 36/B5
Ďumbier (peak), Slvk. 41/K4
Dumbleyung, Austl. 112/C5
Dumbrăveni, Rom. 49/G2
Dume (pt.), Ca, US 136/B2
Dumfries, Sc, UK 34/E1
Dumfries and Galloway (pol. reg.), Sc, UK 36/C6
Dumka, India 85/F3
Dumlu, Turk. 63/G4
Dümmer (lake), Ger. 51/F3
Dumoine (riv.), Qu, Can. 130/E2
Dumoine (lake), Qu, Can. 123/J4
Dumont, NJ, US 139/K8
Dumont d'Urville, Fr., Ant. 160/K
Dumraon, India 85/E3
Dumyāt (gov.), Egypt 101/B1
Dún Laoghaire, Ire. 34/B5
Dun Rig (peak), Sc, UK 36/C5
Dunaföldvár, Hun. 48/D2
Dunaharaszti, Hun. 49/R10
Dunajec (riv.), Pol. 41/L4
Dunakeszi, Hun. 49/R9
Dunany (pt.), Ire. 34/B4
Dunaszekcső, Hun. 48/D2
Dunaújváros, Hun. 48/D2
Dunavecse, Hun. 48/D2
Dunavtsi, Bul. 48/F4
Dunbar, Sc, UK 36/D5
Dunblane, Sc, UK 36/C4
Dunboyne, Ire. 34/B5
Duncan, BC, Can. 126/C3
Duncan, Ok, US 129/H4
Duncannon, Pa, US 138/A3
Duncansby Head (pt.), Sc, UK 31/V14
Duncanville, Tx, US 132/D3
Dund-Us, Mong. 70/F2
Dundalk (bay), Ire. 31/Q10
Dundalk, Md, US 138/B5
Dundalk, Ire. 34/B4
Dundas (lake), Austl. 109/B4
Dundas, On, Can. 131/Q9
Dundas (pen.), NW, Can. 123/R7
Dundee, SAfr. 107/E3
Dundee, Sc, UK 36/D4
Dundee (pol. reg.), Sc, UK 36/D4
Dundgovi (prov.), Mong. 70/J2
Dundonald, Sc, UK 36/B5
Dundrum, NI, UK 34/C3
Dundrum (bay), NI, UK 34/C3
Dundurn, Sk, Can. 126/G3
Dundwa (range), Nepal 84/D2
Dundwārāganj, India 84/B2
Dunedin, Fl, US 133/H4
Dunedin, NZ 117/S12
Dunedoo, Austl. 115/D2
Dunellen, NJ, US 139/H9
Dunfanaghy, Ire. 31/Q9
Dunfermline, Sc, UK 36/C4
Dunga Bunga, Pak. 86/B5
Dungannon, NI, UK 34/B3
Dungannon (co.), NI, UK 34/B3
Dungarpur, India 89/K4
Dungarvan, Ire. 31/Q10
Dungau (reg.), Ger. 55/F5
Dungeness (pt.), Eng, UK 33/G5
Dungeness (pt.), Arg. 159/C7
Dungiven, NI, UK 34/B2
Dunglow, Ire. 31/P9
Dungog, Austl. 115/D2
Dungu, D.R. Congo 104/A2
Dungu (riv.), D.R. Congo 104/A2
Dunhua, China 71/N3
Dunhuang, China 70/F3
Dunkeld, Sc, UK 36/C3
Dunkery (hill), Eng, UK 32/C4
Dunkirk (Dunkerque), Fr. 42/E1
Dunkwa, Gha. 103/E5
Dunleer, Ire. 34/B4
Dunloy, NI, UK 34/B2
Dunmanway, Ire. 31/P11
Dunmurry, NI, UK 34/B2
Dunn, NC, US 133/J3
Dunnamanagh, NI, UK 34/A2
Dünnern (riv.), Swi. 56/D3
Dunnet Head (pt.), Sc, UK 31/V14
Dunningen, Ger. 57/E1
Dunnville, On, Can. 131/Q10
Dunolly, Austl. 115/B3
Dunoon, Sc, UK 36/B5
Dunqulah, Sudan 101/B5
Duns, Sc, UK 36/D5
Dunsborough, Austl. 112/B5
Dunseith, ND, US 127/H3
Dunshaughlin, Ire. 34/B4
Dunsmuir, Ca, US 128/B2
Dunstable, Eng, UK 33/F3
Dunyāpur, Pak. 86/A5
Duolun, China 71/L3
Dupo, Il, US 137/G8
Dupont, Pa, US 138/C1
Dupree, SD, US 127/H4
Dupuy (cape), Austl. 112/B2
Duque de Caxias, Braz. 211/K7
Duque de York (isl.), Chile 159/A6
Dūrā, WBnk. 91/D4
Durağan, Turk. 90/C1
Durak, Turk. 91/D1
Durance (riv.), Fr. 42/F5
Durango (state), Mex. 140/A3
Durango, Sp. 44/D1
Durango de Victoria, Mex. 142/D3
Durant, Ok, US 129/H4
Durazno (dept.), Uru. 159/F2
Durazno, Uru. 159/K10
Durban, SAfr. 107/E3
Durbanville, SAfr. 106/L10
Durbion (riv.), Fr. 56/C1
Durbuy, Belg. 53/E3
Dúrcal, Sp. 44/D4
Durdevac, Cro. 48/C2
Durdevo, Serb. 48/E3
Düren, Ger. 53/F2
Durg, India 82/D3
Durgāpur, India 85/F4
Durham, NH, US 131/G3
Durham, NC, US 133/J3
Durham, Eng, UK 35/G2
Durham (co.), Eng, UK 35/F2
Durlston (pt.), Eng, UK 32/E5
Durmitor NP, Serb. 47/F1
Durnford (pt.), WSah. 98/B5
Dürrenroth, Swi. 56/D3
Durrës, Alb. 47/F2
Dürrlauingen, Ger. 54/D6
Dürrwangen, Ger. 54/D4
Dursunbey, Turk. 90/B2
Durūz (peak), Syria 91/E3
D'Urville (cape), Indo. 81/J4
Dusanovo, Serb. 47/G1
Dusey (riv.), On, Can. 127/M3
Dushan, China 83/J2
Dushanbe (cap.), Taj. 87/E5
Dushanbe (int'l arpt.), Taj. 87/E5
Düsseldorf (int'l arpt.), Ger. 50/D6
Düsseldorf, Ger. 50/D6
Duszniki-Zdrój, Pol. 41/J3
Dutch (riv.), Eng, UK 35/H4
Dutch Harbor, Ak, US 134/E5
Dutch Wonderland, Pa, US 138/B3
Dutoitspiek (peak), SAfr. 106/L10
Dutse, Nga. 103/H4
Duvall, Wa, US 135/D2
Duvno, Bosn. 48/C4
Duyun, China 83/J2
Düzce, Turk. 49/K5
Düzici, Turk. 90/D2
Dve Mogili, Bul. 49/G4
Dvina (bay), Rus. 60/H2
Dvořiště (lake), Czh. 55/H4
Dwārka, India 89/J4
Dwārkeswar (riv.), India 85/F4
Dworshak (res.), Id, US 126/D4
Dwyfor (riv.), Wal, UK 34/D6
Dwyka (riv.), SAfr. 106/C4
Dyat'kovo, Rus. 62/E1
Dybvad, Den. 38/D3
Dyce (int'l arpt.), Sc, UK 36/D2
Dyce, Sc, UK 36/D2
Dye, Mo, US 137/D5
Dyer (cape), Nun., Can. 123/K2
Dyer (cape), Chile 159/B6
Dyer, In, US 130/C3
Dyfi (riv.), Wal, UK 32/C1
Dyje (riv.), Czh. 41/J4
Dykh-tau (peak), Rus. 63/G4
Dyle (riv.), Belg. 40/C3
Dyleň (peak), Czh. 55/F3
Dylewska (peak), Pol. 41/K2
Dysart, Austl. 114/C3
Dysseldorp, SAfr. 106/C4
Dyul'tydag (peak), Rus. 63/H4
Dzaoudzi (cap.), May. 107/H6
Dzaoudzi (int'l arpt.), May. 107/H6
Dzavhan (prov.), Mong. 70/G2
Dzavhan (riv.), Mong. 70/F2
Dzenzik (pt.), Ukr. 62/F3
Dzerzhinsk, Rus. 60/J4
Dzhankoy, Ukr. 62/E3
Dzharylgach (gulf), Ukr. 49/L2
Dzhebel, Bul. 47/J2
Dzhugdzhur (range), Rus. 67/N4
Działdowo, Pol. 41/L2
Dzibalchén, Mex. 144/D2
Dzibilchaltún (ruin), Mex. 144/D1
Dzidzantún, Mex. 144/D1
Dzierżoniów, Pol. 41/J3
Dzitbalché, Mex. 144/D1
Dziuché, Mex. 144/D2
Dzukija NP, Lith. 39/L4
Dzungarian (basin), China 70/E3
Dzur, Mong. 70/G2
Dzüünbayan, Mong. 71/K3
Dzüünbulag, Mong. 71/K2
Dzüünharaa, Mong. 70/J2
Dzuunmod, Mong. 70/J2

E

Eads, Co, US 129/G3
Eagle (riv.), Nf, Can. 123/L3
Eagle (lake), On, Can. 130/A1
Eagle, Ak, US 134/K3
Eagle (lake), Ca, US 126/C5
Eagle, Co, US 128/F3
Eagle (mtn.), Mn, US 127/L4
Eagle, Wi, US 135/P14
Eagle (lake), Wi, US 127/K3
Eagle Butte, SD, US 127/H4
Eagle Pass, Tx, US 132/C4
Eagle River, Wi, US 127/L4
Eaglesham, Sc, UK 36/B5
Ealing (bor.), Eng, UK 30/B2
Ear Falls, On, Can. 127/K3
Earle Naval Weapons Center, NJ, US 138/D3
Earlimart, Ca, US 128/C4
Earl's Seat (peak), Sc, UK 36/B4
Earlston, Sc, UK 36/D5
Earn (riv.), Sc, UK 36/C4
Earn (lake), Sc, UK 36/B4
Easley, SC, US 133/H3
East (mt.), Austl. 112/D4
East (cape), NZ 117/T10
East (cape), Ak, US 134/B6
East (pt.), NJ, US 138/C5
East (riv.), NY, US 139/K8
East (passg.), Wa, US 135/C3
East Alton, Il, US 137/G8
East Anglia (reg.), Eng, UK 33/H2
East Angus, Qu, Can. 131/G2
East Ayrshire (pol. reg.), Sc, UK 36/B6
East Bangor, Pa, US 138/C2
East Berbice-Corentyne (pol. reg.), Guy. 153/G3
East Berlin, Pa, US 138/B4
East Berwick, Pa, US 138/B1
East Brunswick, NJ, US 139/H10
East Caicos (isl.), UK 145/J1
East Canyon (res.), Ut, US 137/K12
East Carondelet, Il, US 137/G8
East China (sea), Asia 67/M6
East Dart (riv.), Eng, UK 32/C5
East Dereham, Eng, UK 33/G1
East Dunbartonshire (pol. reg.), Sc, UK 36/B5
East Falkland (isl.), UK 147/D8
East Farmingdale, NY, US 139/M9
East Frisian (isls.), Ger. 40/D2
East Glen (riv.), Eng, UK 35/H6
East Greenville, Pa, US 138/C3
East Grinstead, Eng, UK 33/F4
East Hampton, NY, US 139/F2
East Haven, Ct, US 139/F1
East Helena, Mt, US 126/F4
East Hill-Meridian, Wa, US 135/C3
East Hills, NY, US 139/L8
East Jordan, Mi, US 130/C2
East Kilbride, Sc, UK 36/B5
East Korea (bay), NKor. 71/N4
East Lamma (chan.), China 71/U11
East Lansing, Mi, US 130/C3
East Leavenworth, Mo, US 137/D5
East Linton, Sc, UK 36/D5
East Liverpool, Oh, US 130/D3
East London, SAfr. 106/D4
East Los Angeles, Ca, US 136/F7
East Lothian (pol. reg.), Sc, UK 36/D5
East Lynne, Mo, US 137/E6
East Meadow, NY, US 139/L9
East Midlands (int'l arpt.), Eng, UK 35/G6
East Millcreek, Ut, US 137/K12
East Millinocket, Me, US 131/G2
East Newark, NJ, US 139/J9
East Newbern, Il, US 137/G7
East Nishnabotna (riv.), Ia, US 129/J2
East Northport, NY, US 139/E2
East Orange, NJ, US 139/J8
East Peckham, Eng, UK 30/E3
East Petersburg, Pa, US 138/B3
East Point, Ga, US 133/G3
East Pointe (East Detroit), Mi, US 135/G7
East Port Orchard, Wa, US 135/B2
East Prospect, Pa, US 138/B4
East Quogue, NY, US 139/F2
East Renfrewshire (pol. reg.), Sc, UK 36/B5
East Retford, Eng, UK 35/H5
East Riding of Yorkshire (co.), Eng, UK 35/H4
East Rockaway, NY, US 139/L9
East Rutherford, NJ, US 139/J8
East Saint Louis, Il, US 137/G8
East Siberian (sea), Rus. 65/S2
East Side, Pa, US 138/C1
East Stroudsburg, Pa, US 138/C2
East Sussex (co.), Eng, UK 33/G5
East Tawas, Mi, US 130/D2
East Timor (ctry.) 81/G5
East Troy, Wi, US 135/P14
East Wemyss, Sc, UK 36/C4
East Wenatchee, Wa, US 126/C4
East Windsor, NJ, US 138/D3
East York, Can. 131/R8
Eastbourne, Eng, UK 33/G5
Eastern (plain), Eng, UK 35/H4
Eastern (pol. reg.), Gha. 103/E5
Eastern (chan.), Japan 74/A4
Eastern (prov.), SLeo. 102/C4
Eastern (bay), Md, US 138/B6
Eastern (prov.), Zam. 104/B5
Eastern Ghats (mts.), India 82/C5
Eastern Neck Island NWR, Md, US 138/B5
Eastern Sayans (mts.), Rus. 64/K4
Easterville, Mb, Can. 127/J2
Eastlake, Co, US 137/C3
Eastleigh (int'l arpt.), Eng, UK 33/E5
Eastleigh, Eng, UK 33/E5
Eastmain (riv.), Qu, Can. 123/J3
Eastman, Ga, US 133/H3
Easton, Ct, US 139/E1
Easton (res.), Ct, US 139/E1
Easton, Pa, US 138/C2
Eastport, Me, US 131/H2
Eastport, NY, US 139/F2
Eastriggs, Sc, UK 35/E2
Eastwood, Eng, UK 35/G6
Eaton, Co, US 137/C1
Eatonia, Sk, Can. 126/F3
Eatons Neck (pt.), NY, US 139/M8
Eatontown, NJ, US 138/D3
Eau (riv.), Eng, UK 35/H5
Eau Claire (lake), Qu, Can. 123/J3
Eau d'Heure (riv.), Belg. 53/D3
Eau d'Heure, Barrage de l' (dam), Belg. 53/D3
Eaubonne, Fr. 30/J5
Eaulne (riv.), Fr. 52/A4
Eauripik (isl.), Micr. 116/D4
Eauze, Fr. 42/D5
Ebano, Mex. 144/B1
Ebble (riv.), Eng, UK 33/E4
Ebbw Vale, Wal, UK 32/C3
Ebebiyín, EqG. 96/H7
Ebeggi (well), Alg. 99/G5
Ebeleben, Ger. 51/H6
Ebeltoft, Den. 38/D3
Ebensee, Aus. 43/K3
Eberbach, Ger. 54/B4
Ebergassing, Aus. 49/P7
Ebergötzen, Ger. 51/H5
Ebermannstadt, Ger. 54/E3
Ebern, Ger. 54/D2
Ebersbach an der Fils, Ger. 54/C5
Ebersberg, Ger. 55/E6
Eberschwang, Aus. 55/G6
Ebersheim, Fr. 56/D1
Eberswalde-Finow, Ger. 41/G2
Ebetsu, Japan 76/B2
Ebian, China 83/H2
Ebina, Japan 77/C3
Ebnat-Kappel, Swi. 57/F3
Eboli, It. 46/D2
Ebolowa, Camr. 96/H7
Ebon (isl.), Mrsh. 116/F4
Ebonyi (state), Nga. 103/H5
Ebrach, Ger. 54/D3
Ebreichsdorf, Aus. 49/N8
Ebro (riv.), Sp. 27/D4
Ebstorf, Ger. 51/H2
Ecatepec, Mex. 143/Q9
Ecclefechan, Sc, UK 35/E1
Eccles, Eng, UK 35/F5
Eceabat, Turk. 49/H5
Echallens, Swi. 56/C4
Echarate, Peru 156/C4
Echaz (riv.), Ger. 54/C6
Éché Fadadinga (riv.), Niger 103/H3
Echigawa, Japan 77/K5
Eching, Ger. 55/E6
Échirolles, Fr. 42/F4
Echo (lake), NJ, US 138/D1
Echo, Ut, US 137/L12
Echoing (riv.), Mb,On, Can. 127/L2
Echt, Neth. 53/E1
Echterdingen (int'l arpt.), Ger. 54/C5
Echternach, Lux. 53/F4
Echuca, Austl. 115/C3
Echunga, Austl. 113/M9
Echzell, Ger. 54/B2
Écija, Sp. 44/C4
Ečka, Serb. 48/E3
Eckernförde, Ger. 38/C4
Eckerö (isl.), Fin. 39/H1
Eckerö, Fin. 39/H1
Eclipse Sound (bay), Nun., Can. 123/H1
Écommoy, Fr. 42/D3
Ecoporanga, Braz. 154/B5
Ecorse (riv.), Mi, US 135/F7
Ecorse, Mi, US 135/F7
Écouen, Fr. 30/K4
Ecquevilly, Fr. 30/H5
Ecrins, PN des, Fr. 43/G4
Écrosnes, Fr. 30/H6
Écrouves, Fr. 53/E6
Ecuador (ctry.) 150/C4
Ecublens, Swi. 56/C4
Ed, Swe. 38/D2
Eday (isl.), Sc, UK 31/V14
Eddystone (pt.), Austl. 115/D4
Eddystone Rocks (isls.), Eng, UK 32/B6
Ede, Nga. 103/G5
Ede, Neth. 50/C4
Edéa, Camr. 96/H7
Edegem, Belg. 53/D1
Edehin Ouarene (des.), Alg. 99/G4
Edéia, Braz. 155/B1
Edelény, Hun. 41/L4
Edemissen, Ger. 51/H4
Eden, Austl. 115/D3
Eden (riv.), Sc, UK 36/D4
Eden, NC, US 130/E4
Eden, Ut, US 137/K11
Edenbridge, Eng, UK 30/D3
Edenburg, SAfr. 106/D3
Edendale, SAfr. 107/E3
Edenhope, Austl. 115/B3
Edenkoben, Ger. 54/B4
Edenside (valley), Eng, UK 35/F2
Edenton, NC, US 133/J2
Eder (riv.), Ger. 40/E3
Eder-Stausee (lake), Ger. 51/F6
Edewecht, Ger. 51/E2
Edgar (mt.), Austl. 112/D2
Edge (isl.), Sval. 160/E
Edgecumbe (cape), Ak, US 134/L4
Edgell (isl.), Nun., Can. 123/K2
Edgemere, Md, US 138/B5
Edgemont, Ut, US 137/K13
Edgerton, Wy, US 127/G5
Edgewater, Co, US 137/B3
Edgewater Park, NJ, US 138/D3
Edgewood, Pa, US 138/B2
Edgewood, Md, US 138/B5
Edgewood Arsenal, Md, US 138/B5
Edgewood-North Hill, Wa, US 135/C3
Édhessa, Gre. 47/H2
Edinboro, Pa, US 130/D3
Edinburg, Tx, US 132/D5
Edinburgh (cap.), Sc, UK 36/C5
Edinburgh (pol. reg.), Sc, UK 36/C5
Edirne (prov.), Turk. 49/H5
Edirne, Turk. 49/H5
Edison, NJ, US 139/H9
Edison International Field, Ca, US 136/G8
Edison Nat'l Hist. Site, NJ, US 139/J8
Edisto Island, SC, US 133/H3
Edisto, South Fork (riv.), SC, US 133/H3
Edithburgh, Austl. 113/H5
Edjérir (riv.), Mali 103/F2
Edmond, Ok, US 137/N14
Edmonds, Wa, US 126/C4
Edmonton (int'l arpt.), Ab, Can. 126/E2
Edmonton (cap.), Ab, Can. 126/E2
Edmund Kennedy NP, Austl. 114/B2
Edmundston, NB, Can. 131/G2
Edna, Tx, US 129/H5
Edna Bay, Ak, US 134/M4
Edo (state), Nga. 103/G5
Edo (riv.), Japan 77/D2
Edolo, It. 57/G5
Edosaki, Japan 77/E2
Edremit, Turk. 90/A2
Edremit (gulf), Gre.,Turk 90/A2
Edsbyn, Swe. 38/F1
Edson, Ab, Can. 126/D2
Eduardo Castex, Arg. 158/D2
Edward (mt.), Austl. 113/F2
Edward (lake), D.R. Congo 93/E5
Edward River Aboriginal Community, Austl. 114/A1
Edward VII (pen.), Ant. 160/P
Edward VIII (bay), Ant. 160/D
Edwards (riv.), Il, US 129/K2
Edwards (plat.), Tx, US 124/F5
Edwardsville, Il, US 137/H8
Edwardsville, Ks, US 137/D5

Edwardsville, Pa, US 138/C1
Edzell, Sc, UK 36/D3
Edzná (ruin), Mex. 144/D2
Eek, Ak, US 134/F3
Eeklo, Belg. 52/C1
Eel (riv.), Ca, US 128/B3
Eelde-Paterswolde, Neth. 50/D2
Eem (riv.), Neth. 50/C4
Eemenes, Neth. 50/C4
Eems (Ems) (riv.), Ger., Neth 50/D2
Eemshaven (har.), Neth. 50/D2
Eemskanaal (riv.), Neth. 50/D2
Eersel, Neth. 50/C6
Efate (isl.), Van. 116/F6
Eferding, Aus. 55/H6
Effigy Mounds Nat'l Mon., Ia, US 127/L5
Effingham, Il, US 129/R9
Effingham, On, Can. 131/R9
Effon Alaiye, Nga. 103/G5
Effort, Pa, US 138/C2
Eforie, Rom. 49/J3
Efringen-Kirchen, Ger. 56/D2
Efyrnwy, Llyn (lake), Wal, UK 34/E6
Egadi (isls.), It. 46/B3
Egan (range), Nv, US 128/D3
Egan (riv.), Ger. 51/N8
Egaña, Uru. 159/K10
Egegik, Ak, US 134/G4
Eger (lake), Ger. 40/G3
Eger, Hun. 41/L5
Egeskov, Den. 38/D4
Egestorf, Ger. 51/H2
Egg, Aus. 57/F3
Egg, Swi. 57/E3
Egg Harbor City, NJ, US 138/D4
Egg Island (pt.), NJ, US 138/C5
Eggebek, Ger. 38/C4
Eggegebirge (ridge), Ger. 51/F5
Eggelsberg, Aus. 55/F6
Eggenburg, Aus. 43/L2
Eggenfelden, Ger. 55/F6
Eggenstein-Leopoldshafen, Ger. 54/B4
Eggesin, Ger. 38/F5
Eggiwil, Swi. 56/D4
Egglescliffe, Eng, UK 35/G3
Eggstätt, Ger. 55/F7
Egham, Eng, UK 30/B2
Eghezée, Belg. 53/D2
Egilsstadhir, Ice. 37/P6
Egletons, Fr. 42/E4
Eglinton (isl.), NW, Can. 123/R7
Eglinton, NI, UK 34/A1
Eglisau, Swi. 57/E2
Egly, Fr. 30/J6
Egmond aan Zee, Neth. 50/B3
Egmont (cape), NZ 117/S10
Egmont (mt.), NZ 117/S10
Egna (Neumarkt), It. 57/G2
Egnach, Swi. 57/F2
Eğridir, Turk. 90/B2
Eğridir (lake), Turk. 90/B2
Eguas, Rio das (riv.), Braz. 154/A4
Egypt (ctry.) 97/C2
Ehebach (riv.), Ger. 54/D3
Ehekirchen, Ger. 54/D5
Ehime (pref.), Japan 74/C4
Ehingen, Ger. 57/F1
Ehingen, Ger. 54/D4
Ehringshausen, Ger. 54/B1
Ehrwald, Aus. 57/G3
Eibar, Sp. 44/D1
Eibelstadt, Ger. 54/C3
Eibenstock, Ger. 55/F1
Eibergen, Neth. 50/D4
Eich, Ger. 54/B3
Eichel (riv.), Fr. 53/G6
Eichenau, Ger. 54/E6
Eichenbühl, Ger. 54/C3
Eichendorf, Ger. 55/F5
Eichenzell, Ger. 54/C2
Eichstätt, Ger. 54/E5
Eichwalde, Ger. 40/Q7
Eicklingen, Ger. 51/H3
Eid, Nor. 37/C3
Eidfjord, Nor. 38/B1
Eidsvold, Austl. 114/C4
Eidsvoll, Nor. 38/D1
Eifel (plat.), Ger. 40/D3
Eiffel Tower, Fr. 30/J5
Eigenji, Japan 77/K5
Eiger (peak), Swi. 56/D4
Eigersund, Nor. 38/A2
Eigg (isl.), Sc, UK 31/Q8
Eight Degree (chan.), India,Mal 82/B6
Eijerlandse Gat (chan.), Neth. 50/B2
Eijsden, Neth. 53/E2
Eikelandsosen, Nor. 38/A1
Eil, Loch (inlet), Sc, UK 36/A3
Eildon (lake), Austl. 115/C3
Eildon, Austl. 115/C3
Eilerts de Haan (mts.), Sur. 153/G4
Einbeck, Ger. 51/G5
Eindhoven (int'l arpt.), Neth. 50/C6

Eindhoven, Neth. 50/C6
Einsiedeln, Swi. 57/E3
Einville-au-Jard, Fr. 53/E6
Eirunepé, Braz. 156/D2
Eisch (riv.), Lux. 53/E4
Eisenach, Ger. 51/H7
Eisenberg, Ger. 54/B3
Eisenhower Nat'l Hist. Site, Pa, US 138/A4
Eisenhüttenstadt, Ger. 41/H2
Eiserfeld, Ger. 53/G2
Eisfeld, Ger. 54/D2
Eisingen, Ger. 54/C3
Eislingen, Ger. 54/C5
Eitelborn, Ger. 53/G3
Eiter (riv.), Ger. 51/F3
Eitorf, Ger. 53/G2
Eitting, Ger. 55/E6
Ejea de los Caballeros, Sp. 45/E1
Ejeda, Madg. 107/H9
Ejido, Ven. 152/D2
Ejin Horo Qi, China 72/B3
Ejin Qi, China 70/H3
Ejutla de Crespo, Mex. 144/B2
Ekeby, Swe. 38/E3
Ekenäs (Tammisaari), Fin. 39/K2
Ekeren, Belg. 50/B6
Ekhinos, Gre. 47/J2
Ekibastuz, Kaz. 87/G2
Eksjö, Swe. 38/F3
Ekwan (riv.), On, Can. 123/H3
Ekwok, Ak, US 134/G4
El Aaiún, WSah. 98/B4
El Abiodh Sidi Chrikh, Alg. 99/F2
El 'Açâba (mass.), Mrta. 102/C2
El Affroun, Alg. 100/G4
El Aguila, Mex. 132/B5
El Aïoun, Mor. 100/C2
El Alto, Peru 156/A2
El Amparo de Apure, Ven. 152/D3
El Anegado, Ecu. 152/A5
El Aouinet, Alg. 100/K7
El Arahal, Sp. 44/C4
El Arhlaf (well), Mrta. 102/D2
El Astillero, Sp. 44/D1
El Bagre, Col. 152/C3
El Banco, Col. 152/C2
El Barco, Sp. 44/B1
El Barco de Ávila, Sp. 44/C2
El Baúl, Ven. 152/D2
El Bayadh (prov.), Alg. 99/F2
El Bayadh, Alg. 99/F2
El Bolsón, Arg. 158/C4
El Bonillo, Sp. 44/D3
El Borouj, Mor. 98/D2
El Burgo de Osma, Sp. 44/D2
El Cajón, Ca, US 136/D5
El Cajón (res.), Hon. 144/E3
El Callao, Ven. 153/F3
El Capitan (peak), Mt, US 126/E4
El Carmen, Chile 158/B3
El Carmen, Col. 152/B3
El Carmen, Peru 156/B3
El Carmen de Bolívar, Col. 152/B2
El Casar de Talamanca, Sp. 45/N8
El Centro, Ca, US 128/D4
El Cerrito, Col. 152/C3
El Cerrito, Ca, US 135/K11
El Cerro del Aripo (peak), Trin. 153/F2
El Cerrón (peak), Ven. 152/D2
El Chico, PN, Mex. 143/L6
El Cocuy, Col. 152/C3
El Cocuy, PN, Col. 150/D2
El Colorado, Arg. 157/E2
El Dificil, Col. 152/C2
El Djouf (des.), Mrta. 96/D3
El Dorado, Mex. 142/D3
El Dorado, Ar, US 129/J4
El Dorado, Ks, US 129/H3
El Dorado, Ven. 153/F3
El Eglab (plat.), Alg. 96/D2
El Empedrado, Ven. 152/D2
El Escorial, Sp. 45/M8
El Espinar, Sp. 44/C2
El Eulma, Alg. 100/H4
El Fahs, Tun. 100/L6
El Ferrol, Sp. 44/A1
El Fuerte, Mex. 142/C3
El Fureidīs, Isr. 91/F6
El Gogorrón, PN, Mex. 142/E4
El Golea, Alg. 96/F2
El Golfete (lake), Guat. 144/D3
El Granada, Ca, US 135/K11
El Grullo, Mex. 142/D4
El Guachara, PN, Ven. 153/F2
El Hajeb, Mor. 100/D3
El Hank (cliff), Mali 98/D4
El Harino, Mex. 152/A2
El Harta (well), Alg. 99/E4
El Higo, Mex. 144/B1
El Indio, Tx, US 132/C4
El Jadida, Mor. 98/C2

El Kelaâ des Srarhna, Mor. 98/D2
El Khatt (cliff), Mrta. 96/C3
El Khatt (depr.), Mrta. 102/C2
El Khnâchich (cliff), Mali 98/E5
El Kroub, Alg. 100/K6
El Kseur, Alg. 100/H4
El Libertador General Bernardo O'Higgins (pol. reg.), Chile 158/N8
El Limón, Mex. 143/F4
El Mahia (phys. reg.), Mali 99/E5
El Maitén, Arg. 158/C4
El Malpais Nat'l Mon., NM, US 128/F4
El Manteco, Ven. 153/F3
El-Menzel, Mor. 100/B3
El Miamo, Ven. 153/F3
El Milia, Alg. 100/J4
El Mirage, Az, US 137/R18
El Mirage, Ca, US 136/C1
El Montcau (peak), Sp. 45/K6
El Monte, Ca, US 136/F7
El Morrito (pt.), Chile 158/C1
El Mräyer (well), Mrta. 98/C5
El Mreyyé (phys. reg.), Mrta. 102/C2
El Mzereb (well), Mali 98/D4
El Naranjo de Carlos Sarabia, Mex. 143/F4
El Nayar, Mex. 142/D4
El Nevado (peak), Arg. 158/C2
El Nido, Phil. 81/E1
El Olivar Alto, Chile 158/N9
El Oro (prov.), Ecu. 156/A1
El Oued (prov.), Alg. 99/G2
El Oued, Alg. 99/G2
El Palmar, Ven. 153/F3
El Pao, Ven. 153/F2
El Pao, Ven. 153/E2
El Paraíso, Mex. 143/E5
El Paraíso, Hon. 144/E3
El Paso, Tx, US 128/F5
El Paso International (int'l arpt.), Tx, US 129/F5
El Pilar, Ven. 153/F2
El Porvenir, Mex. 129/F5
El Porvenir, Pan. 152/B2
El Potosí, Mex. 143/E3
El Potosí, PN, Mex. 140/B3
El Prat de Llobregat, Sp. 45/L7
El Progreso, Hon. 144/E3
El Progreso, Guat. 144/D3
El Progreso, Ecu. 156/F7
El Progreso Industrial, Mex. 143/Q9
El Puerto de Santa María, Sp. 44/B4
El Quelite, Mex. 142/D4
El Quisco, Chile 158/N8
El Rama, Nic. 145/E3
El Rancho, CR, US 137/B3
El Reno, Ok, US 129/H4
El Río, Ca, US 136/B3
El Roble, Pan. 152/A2
El Rosario de Arriba, Mex. 142/B2
El Sacromonte, PN, Mex. 143/L7
El Salto, Mex. 142/D4
El Salvador (ctry.) 144/D3
El Salvador, Mex. 143/E3
El Salvador, Cuba 145/H1
El Salvador (int'l arpt.), ESal. 144/D3
El Samán de Apure, Ven. 152/D3
El Sauz, Mex. 129/F5
El Sauzal, Mex. 142/A2
El Segundo, Ca, US 136/E8
El Shab (well), Egypt 101/B4
El Tabo, Chile 158/N8
El Tajín (ruin), Mex. 143/M6
El Tama, PN, Ven. 152/C3
El Tambo, Ecu. 152/B5
El Tarf (prov.), Alg. 100/K6
El Tarf, Alg. 100/L6
El Teleno (peak), Sp. 44/B1
El Tepozteco, PN, Mex. 143/R10
El Tiemblo, Sp. 44/C2
El Tocuyo, Ven. 152/D2
El Toro, CR, US 136/C3
El Triunfo, Ecu. 152/B5
El Triunfo, Mex. 142/C3
El Tucuche (peak), Trin. 153/F2
El Tuito, Mex. 142/D4
El Tuparro, PN, Col. 150/D2
El Valle, Pan. 152/A2
El Viejo, Nic. 144/E3
El Viejo (peak), Col. 152/C3
El Yagual, Ven. 152/D3
El Yunque (peak), PR 141/M8
El Zacatón, Mex. 142/E4
Elan (riv.), Wal, UK 32/C2
Elancourt, Fr. 30/H5
Elandsrivier (riv.), SAfr. 106/Q12
Elassón, Gre. 47/H3
Elat (int'l arpt.), Isr. 91/D5
Elat, Isr. 91/D5
Elátia, Gre. 47/H3

Elato (isl.), Micr. 116/D4
Elazığ, Turk. 90/D2
Elazig (prov.), Turk. 90/D2
Elba, Al, US 133/G4
Elba (isl.), It. 43/H5
Elbasan, Alb. 47/G2
Elbbach (riv.), Ger. 53/G2
Elbe (riv.), Ger. 27/F3
Elbe (Labe) (riv.), Czh.,Ger. 41/H2
Elbe-Seitenkanaal (canal), Ger. 51/H2
Elbert (co.), Co, US 137/C4
Elberton, Ga, US 133/H3
Elbeuf, Fr. 42/D2
Elbigenalp, Aus. 57/G3
Elbistan, Turk. 90/D2
Elbląg, Pol. 39/H4
Elbow, Sk, Can. 126/G3
El'brus (peak), Rus. 63/G4
Elburg, Neth. 50/C3
Elburn, Il, US 135/N16
Elburz (mts.), Iran 88/E1
Elche, Sp. 45/E3
Elche de la Sierra, Sp. 44/D3
Elchingen, Ger. 54/D6
Elcho (isl.), Austl. 109/C2
Eld (inlet), Wa, US 135/A3
Elda, Sp. 45/E3
Elde (riv.), Ger. 40/G2
Eldersburg, Md, US 138/B3
Eldivan, Turk. 90/C1
Eldon, Wa, US 135/A2
Eldora, Co, US 137/A3
Eldora, NJ, US 138/D5
Eldorado, Arg. 157/F2
Eldorado, Tx, US 129/G5
Eldorado Springs, Co, US 137/B3
Eldoret, Kenya 104/B2
Eleao (peak), Hi, US 124/W13
Elefsís, Gre. 47/N9
Elek, Hun. 41/L5
Elektrostal', Rus. 61/X9
Elena, Arg. 158/D2
Elesbão Veloso, Braz. 154/B2
Eleşkirt, Turk. 90/E2
Eleuthera (isl.), Bahm. 141/F2
Eleven Point (riv.), Mo, US 129/K3
Elevsis (ruin), Gre. 47/N8
Elevtheroúpolis, Gre. 47/J2
Elfershausen, Ger. 54/C2
Elgg, Swi. 57/E3
Elgin, ND, US 127/H4
Elgin, Il, US 127/L5
Elgin, Sc, UK 36/C1
Elgóibar, Sp. 44/D1
Elgon (Wagagai) (peak), Ugan. 104/B2
Élida, NM, US 132/C3
Elrose, Sk, Can. 126/F3
Elim, Ak, US 134/F3
Elimäki, Fin. 39/M1
Elista, Rus. 63/H4
Elixhausen, Aus. 55/G7
Elizabeth (bay), Namb. 106/A2
Elizabeth, NJ, US 130/J9
Elizabeth City, NC, US 133/J2
Elizabethan Village Hist. Site, Austl. 112/L7
Elizabethton, Tn, US 130/D4
Elizabethtown, Pa, US 138/B3
Elizabethville, Pa, US 138/B3
Elk (mts.), Co, US 132/B2
Elk (riv.), WV, US 133/H2
Elk, Pol. 39/K5
Elk City, Ok, US 129/H4
Elk Grove, Ca, US 135/M10
Elk Grove Village, Il, US 135/P16
Elk Island NP, Ab, Can. 126/E2
Elk Mills, Md, US 138/C4
Elk Point, Ab, Can. 126/F2
Elk Rapids, Mi, US 130/C2
Elk Ridge, Md, US 138/B5
Elk River, Mn, US 127/K4
Elk Slough (riv.), Ca, US 135/L10
Elkenroth, Ger. 53/G2
Elkhart, In, US 130/C3
Elkhart, Ks, US 129/G3
Elkhart, Tx, US 129/J5
Elkhorn, Mb, Can. 127/H3
Elkhorn, Wi, US 130/B3
Elkhorn (riv.), Ne, US 125/G3
Elkhovo, Bul. 47/K1
Elkin, NC, US 133/H3
Elko, Nv, US 126/E5
Elkton, Md, US 138/C4
Ellamar, Ak, US 134/J3
Elland, Eng, UK 35/G4
Elle (riv.), Fr. 42/B3
Ellef Ringnes (isl.), Nun., Can. 123/R7
Ellen (riv.), Eng, UK 35/E2
Ellenberg, Ger. 54/D4
Ellendale, ND, US 127/J4
Ellendale, De, US 138/C6
Ellensburg, Wa, US 126/C4
Eller (riv.), Ger. 51/H5
Ellero (riv.), It. 58/A4
Ellery (mt.), Austl. 115/D3

Ellesmere (isl.), Nun., Can. 123/S6
Ellesmere Port, Eng, UK 35/F5
Ellezelles, Belg. 52/C2
Ellice (riv.), Nun., Can. 122/F2
Ellice (riv.), Sp. 53/G2
Ellicott City, Md, US 138/B5
Ellinikón (int'l arpt.), Gre. 47/N9
Elliot, SAfr. 106/D3
Elliot Lake, On, Can. 130/D2
Elliot Price Consv. Park, Austl. 113/H4
Elliott (peak), Va, US 133/J2
Ellis Island, NJ,NY, US 139/J8
Ellisras, SAfr. 105/E5
Elliston, Austl. 113/G5
Ellisville, Mo, US 137/F8
Ellon, Sc, UK 36/D2
Ellrich, Ger. 51/H5
Ellsworth (mts.), Ant. 160/U
Ellsworth, Ks, US 129/H3
Ellsworth, Me, US 131/G2
Ellsworth, Wi, US 130/A3
Ellsworth Land (phys. reg.), Ant. 160/U
Ellwangen, Ger. 54/D5
Elm, Swi. 57/F4
Elm Grove, Wi, US 135/P13
Elma, NY, US 131/S10
Elmadağ, Turk. 62/C5
Elmalı, Turk. 91/A1
Elmer, NJ, US 138/C4
Elmendorf, Tx, US 137/U21
Elmer, NJ, US 138/C4
Elmhurst, Il, US 135/Q16
Elmina, Gha. 103/E5
Elmira, NY, US 130/E3
Elmont, NY, US 139/L9
Elmore, Austl. 115/C3
Elmsford, NY, US 139/K7
Elmshorn, Ger. 51/G1
Elmstein, Ger. 53/G5
Elmwood Park, Wi, US 135/Q14
Elmwood Park, NJ, US 139/J8
Elmwood Park, Il, US 135/Q16
Elmonak, Ak, US 134/F3
Elne, Fr. 42/E5
Eloi Mendes, Braz. 211/H6
Élorn (riv.), Fr. 42/A2
Elortondo, Arg. 158/E2
Elorza, Ven. 152/D3
Elouera Nat'l Rsv., Austl. 114/H8
Eloy, Az, US 128/E4
Eloy Alfaro, Ecu. 152/B2
Eloyes, Fr. 56/C1
Elpitiya, SrL. 82/D6
Elroy, Sk, Can. 126/F3
Elsa, Yk, Can. 134/L3
Elsa (riv.), It. 43/J5
Elsah, Il, US 137/G8
Elsdorf, Ger. 51/G2
Elsdorf, Ger. 53/F2
Else (riv.), Ger. 51/F2
Elsenfeld, Ger. 54/C3
Elsenz (riv.), Ger. 54/B4
Elsfleth, Ger. 51/F2
Elsinore (lake), Ca, US 136/C3
Elsmere, De, US 138/C4
Elst, Neth. 50/C5
Elstal, Ger. 40/Q6
Elstead, Eng, UK 30/B3
Elsterberg, Ger. 55/F1
Elster (riv.), Ger. 40/F2
El'ton (lake), Rus. 63/H2
Eltville am Rhein, Ger. 54/B2
Elūru, India 82/D4
Elvanlı, Turk. 91/D1
Elvas, Port. 44/B3
Elverum, Nor. 38/D1
Elvire (mt.), Austl. 112/C2
Elvo (riv.), It. 58/B2
Elwell (lake), Mt, US 126/E4
Elwood, In, US 130/C3
Elwood-Magnolia, NJ, US 138/D4
Elwy (riv.), Wal, UK 34/E5
Ely, Nv, US 128/D3
Ely, Eng, UK 33/G2
Elyaqim, Isr. 91/F7
Elyashiv, Isr. 91/F7
Elyria, Oh, US 130/D3
Elysburg, Pa, US 138/B2
Elysian Park, Ca, US 136/F7
Elz, Ger. 54/B2
Elz (riv.), Ger. 54/B5
Elzach, Ger. 56/E1
Elzbach (riv.), Ger. 53/G3
Elze, Ger. 51/G4
Emajõgi (riv.), Est. 39/M2
Emämshahr (Shähröd) Iran 89/F1
Emån (riv.), Swe. 38/F3
Emancé, Fr. 30/H6
Emanuel, PN das, Braz. 154/B2
Emba (riv.), Kaz. 62/K3
Embarcación, Arg. 157/D1
Embarras (riv.), Il, US 133/F2
Embi (riv.), Kaz. 63/J2
Embi, Kaz. 62/K3
Embira (riv.), Braz. 150/D5

Embira (riv.), Braz. 150/D5
Emborcação, Barragem de (res.), Braz. 155/C1
Embrach, Swi. 57/E2
Embrun, Fr. 43/G4
Embsen, Ger. 51/H2
Embu, Kenya 104/C3
Emden, Ger. 51/E2
Emeishan, China 83/H2
Engi, China 83/H2
Emerald, Austl. 114/C3
Emerald, Austl. 115/G5
Emerson, Mb, Can. 127/J3
Emerson, NJ, US 139/J8
Emeryville, Ca, US 135/K11
Emet, Turk. 90/B2
Emigsville, Pa, US 138/B3
Emilia-Romagna (pol. reg.), It. 43/J4
Emiliano Zapata, Mex. 144/D2
Emin, China 70/D2
Eminábäd, Pak. 85/G3
Eminence, Mo, US 129/K3
Emir Pasha (gulf), Tanz. 104/A3
Emirdağ, Turk. 90/B2
Emirgazi, Turk. 90/C2
Emlembe (peak), Swaz. 107/E2
Emlichheim, Ger. 50/D3
Emma, Swi. 57/F4
Emmaboda, Swe. 38/F3
Emmanuel Head (pt.), Eng, UK 36/F5
Emmaus, Pa, US 138/C3
Emme (riv.), Swi. 56/D4
Emmeloord, Neth. 50/C3
Emmen, Neth. 50/D3
Emmendingen, Ger. 56/D1
Emmental (valley), Swi. 56/D3
Emmer (riv.), Ger. 51/F5
Emmerbach (riv.), Ger. 51/E5
Emmerich, Ger. 50/D5
Emmett, Mi, US 135/G6
Emminga-Liptingen, Ger. 57/E2
Emmitsburg, Md, US 138/A4
Emmonak, Ak, US 134/F3
Emneth, Eng, UK 33/G1
Emőd, Hun. 48/E2
Emory, Tx, US 129/J5
Emosson (lake), Swi. 56/C4
Empalme, Mex. 142/C3
Empangeni, SAfr. 107/E2
Empedrado, Arg. 157/E2
Empedrado, Chile 158/B2
Empoli, It. 59/D5
Emporia, Ks, US 129/H3
Emporia, Va, US 133/J2
Emsbüren, Ger. 51/E2
Emsdetten, Ger. 51/E4
Emskirchen, Ger. 54/D3
Emsland (reg.), Ger. 40/D2
Emstek, Ger. 51/F2
Emu Park, Austl. 114/C3
Ena, Japan 76/B1
Ems-Jade (canal), Ger. 50/D2
Enshi, China 79/A1
Entebbe (int'l arpt.), Ugan. 104/B2
Entebbe, Ugan. 104/B2
Entenbühl (peak), Ger. 55/F3
Enterprise, Al, US 133/G4
Enterprise, Ut, US 137/K11
Entlebuch, Swi. 56/D4
Entre Rios, Braz. 154/C2
Entre Ríos (mts.), Mex. 144/E3
Entroncamento, Port. 44/A3
Enugu, Nga. 103/G5
Enugu (state), Nga. 103/G5
Enumclaw, Wa, US 135/D3
Enxu, Japan 77/M6
Envira, Braz. 156/D2
Enz (riv.), Ger. 43/J2
Enza (riv.), It. 58/D4
Enzan, Japan 75/F3
Enzersdorf an der Fischa, Aus. 49/P7
Enzklösterle, Ger. 54/B5
Epalinges, Swi. 56/C4
Épáno Arkhánai, Gre. 47/H5
Epanomí, Gre. 47/H2
Epe, Nga. 103/F5
Epe, Neth. 50/C4
Epehy, Fr. 52/C3
Épernay, Fr. 42/E2
Épfig, Fr. 56/D1
Epi (isl.), Van. 116/F6
Epidhavros (Epidaurus) (ruin), Gre. 47/H4
Epila, Sp. 44/E2
Epinay-sur-Orge, Fr. 30/J6
Épinay-sur-Seine, Fr. 30/J5
Epinal, Fr. 56/C1
Épira, Guy. 153/G3
Epirus (reg.), Gre. 47/G3
Epône, Fr. 30/H5
Eppelborn, Ger. 53/F4
Eppenbrunn, Ger. 53/F5
Eppeville, Fr. 52/C4
Eppingen, Ger. 54/B4
Eppishausen, Ger. 54/D6
Engelhartszell, Aus. 55/G5
Engel's, Rus. 63/H2
Engelskirchen, Ger. 50/D1
Engelsmanplaat (isl.), Neth. 50/D2
Engen, Ger. 57/E2
Engenheiro Navarro, Braz. 154/B5

Engenheiro Paulo de Frontin, Braz. 211/K7
Enger, Fr. 53/G1
Engerwitzdorf, Aus. 55/H6
Enghershatu (peak), Erit. 88/C5
Enghien, Belg. 52/D2
England, UK 32/D2
Englefontaine, Fr. 52/C3
Englehart, On, Can. 130/E2
Englewood, Co, US 137/C3
Englewood, NJ, US 139/K8
Englewood Cliffs, NJ, US 138/D4
English (riv.), On, Can. 127/K3
English Bay, Ak, US 134/H4
English Bāzār, India 85/G3
English Creek, NJ, US 138/D4
Englishtown, NJ, US 138/D4
Enguera, Sp. 45/E3
Enguri (riv.), Geo. 63/G4
Enid, Ok, US 129/H3
Eniwa, Japan 76/B2
Enkenbach-Alsenborn, Ger. 53/G5
Enkhuizen, Neth. 50/C3
Enkirch, Ger. 53/G4
Enköping, Swe. 38/G2
Enna, It. 46/D4
Ennedi (plat.), Chad 97/K4
Ennepe (riv.), Ger. 51/E6
Ennepetal, Ger. 51/E6
Ennery, Fr. 30/J4
Ennis, Mt, US 126/F4
Ennis, Tx, US 129/H4
Ennis, Ire. 31/P10
Enniscorthy, Ire. 31/Q10
Enniskerry, Ire. 34/B5
Enniskillen, NI, UK 31/Q9
Ennistimon, Ire. 31/P10
Enns, Aus. 55/H6
Enns (riv.), Aus. 55/H6
Enogger (res.), Austl. 114/E6
Enonkoski, Fin. 37/U3
Enontekiö, Fin. 37/U3
Enping, China 83/K3
Enrile, Phil. 82/C2
Enrique Carbó, Arg. 159/Q10
Enriquillo, DRep. 145/J2
Enschede, Neth. 50/D4
Ensdorf, Ger. 55/E4
Ensenada, Mex. 142/A2
Ensenada, Arg. 159/K11
Enseleni, SAfr. 107/E2
Ensisheim, Fr. 56/D2
'Erg Chech (des.), Mali,Alg. 93/B2
'Erg Iguidi (des.), Alg.,Mrta. 98/D4
Ergene Nehri (riv.), Turk. 49/H5
Erguig (riv.), Chad 96/J5
Ergun Youqi, China 71/M1
Ergun Zuoqi, China 71/M1
Ericeira, Port. 45/P10
Ericht (lake), Sc, UK 36/B3
Ericht (riv.), Sc, UK 36/B3
Erickson, Mb, Can. 127/J3
Erickson, BC, Can. 126/D3
Erie (lake), Can.,US 130/D3
Erie, Co, US 137/B2
Erie (canal), NY, US 131/S9
Erie (co.), NY, US 131/S10
Erie, Pa, US 130/D3
Eriksdale, Mb, Can. 127/J3
Eriksmålä, Swe. 38/F3
Erikub (isl.), Mrsh. 116/F4
Erimanthos (mts.), Gre. 47/G4
Erimo, Japan 76/C2
Erimo-misaki (cape), Japan 76/C3
Erithraí, Gre. 47/H3
Eritrea (ctry.) 97/N5
Erkelenz, Ger. 53/F1
Erken (isl.), Swe. 39/H1
Erkheim, Ger. 57/G1
Erkner, Ger. 40/Q7
Erkrath, Ger. 50/D6
Erlach, Ger. 54/B3
Erlands Point-Kisap Lake, Wa, US 135/B2
Erlangen, Ger. 54/E3
Erlau (riv.), Ger. 55/F5
Erlenbach, Ger. 54/C3
Erlenbach am Main, Ger. 54/C3
Erlenbach bei Marktheidenfeld, Ger. 54/C3
Erlenbach im Simmental, Swi. 56/D4
Erlinsbach, Swi. 56/D3
Erlongshan (res.), China 72/F2
Ermelo, Eng, UK 32/C6
Ermelo, SAfr. 107/E2
Ermelo, Neth. 50/C4
Ermenek (riv.), Turk. 91/C1
Ermenek, Turk. 91/C1
Ermenonville, Fr. 30/L4
Ermióni, Gre. 47/H4

Ermont, Fr. 30/J5
Ermoúpolis, Gre. 47/J4
Erms (riv.), Ger. 54/C6
Erndtebrück, Ger. 53/H2
Ernée (riv.), Fr. 42/C2
Ernée, Fr. 42/C2
Ernesto Cortissoz (int'l arpt.), Col. 152/C2
Ernsthofen, Aus. 55/H6
Erode, India 82/C5
Erolzheim, Ger. 57/G1
Erowal Bay, Austl. 115/D2
Erpel, Ger. 53/G2
Erquelinnes, Belg. 53/D3
Errigal (mtn.), Ire. 31/P9
Erris Head (pt.), Ire. 31/P9
Erro (riv.), It. 58/B4
Errochty (lake), Sc, UK 36/B3
Erromango (isl.), Van. 116/F6
Erse (riv.), Ger. 51/H4
Ersekë, Alb. 47/G2
Erstein, Fr. 56/D1
Erstfeld, Swi. 57/E4
Ertis (riv.), Kaz. 64/H4
Ertix (riv.), China 70/E2
Eruh, Turk. 90/E2
Eruwa, Nga. 103/F5
Erwin, Tn, US 130/D4
Erwitte, Ger. 51/F5
Eryuan, China 83/G2
Erzgebirge (Krušné Hory) (mts.), Czh.,Ger. 43/K1
Erzen (riv.), Alb. 47/F2
Erzhausen, Ger. 54/B3
Erzincan, Turk. 90/D2
Erzin, Turk. 90/E2
Erzurum, Turk. 90/E1
Erzurum (prov.), Turk. 90/E1
Es Senia (int'l arpt.), Alg. 100/E5
Esan-misaki (cape), Japan 76/B3
Esashi, Japan 76/C1
Esashi, Japan 76/B3
Esashi, Japan 76/B4
Esbiye, Turk. 90/D1
Esbjerg, Den. 38/C4
Esbjerg (int'l arpt.), Den. 38/C4
Esbly, Fr. 30/L5
Esbo (Espoo), Fin. 39/L1
Escada, Braz. 154/D3
Escalante (riv.), Ut, US 128/E3
Escalón, Mex. 142/D3
Escalona, Sp. 44/C2
Escambia (riv.), Fl, US 133/G4
Escaudain, Fr. 52/C3
Escaut (riv.), Fr. 40/B3
Esch (riv.), Ger. 53/E6
Esch-sur-Alzette, Lux. 53/E4
Esch-sur-Sure, Lux. 53/E4
Eschach (riv.), Ger. 57/E1
Eschau, Fr. 56/D1
Eschborn, Ger. 54/B2
Eschede, Ger. 51/H3
Eschen, Lcht. 57/F3
Eschenbach, Ger. 54/C5
Eschenbach in der Oberpfalz, Ger. 55/E3
Eschershausen, Ger. 51/G5
Esches (riv.), Fr. 30/B5
Escholzmatt, Swi. 56/D4
Eschwege, Ger. 51/H6
Eschweiler, Ger. 53/F2
Escobedo (int'l arpt.), Mex. 132/C5
Escoma, Bol. 156/D4
Escondido, Ca, US 136/C4
Escuinapa de Hidalgo, Mex. 142/D4
Escuintla, Guat. 144/D3
Esdraelon, Plain of (plain), Isr. 91/G6
Eséka, Camr. 96/H7
Esenboga (int'l arpt.), Turk. 90/C1
Esence (peak), Turk. 90/D2
Esens, Ger. 51/E1
Esera (riv.), Sp. 45/F1
Esfahān, Iran 88/F2
Esfandak, Iran 89/H3
Esgair Ddu (peak), Wal, UK 32/C1
Esha Ness (cape), Sc, UK 31/W13
Esher, Eng, UK 30/B4
Eshowe, SAfr. 107/E3
Esil, Kaz. 87/E2
Esil (riv.), Kaz. 67/H4
Esine, It. 57/G6
Esino (riv.), It. 59/G6
Esk (riv.), Eng, UK 35/E2
Eskdale (valley), Sc, UK 36/C6
Eskifjördhur, Ice. 37/G6
Eskil, Turk. 90/C2
Eskilstuna, Swe. 38/G2
Eskimalatya, Turk. 90/D2
Eskimo (lakes), NW, Can. 122/G4
Eskipazar, Turk. 90/C1
Eskişehir, Turk. 90/B2
Eskişehir (prov.), Turk. 90/B2
Esla (riv.), Eng, UK 35/E2
Eslāmābād, Iran 88/E2
Eslohe, Ger. 51/F6
Eslöv, Swe. 38/E4

Eşme, Turk. 90/B2
Esmeralda, Cuba 145/G1
Esmeraldas, Ecu. 152/B4
Esmeraldas (dept.), Ecu. 152/B4
Espada (pt.), Col. 152/D1
Espalion, Fr. 42/E4
Española, NM, US 129/F4
Española, Can. 130/D2
Española (isl.), Ecu. 156/F7
Esparraguera, Sp. 45/K6
Esparta, Hon. 144/E3
Esparto, Ca, US 135/K9
Espejo, Sp. 44/C4
Espelkamp, Ger. 51/F4
Esperança, Braz. 154/D2
Esperance (bay), Austl. 112/D5
Esperance, Austl. 112/D5
Esperantina, Braz. 154/B1
Esperantinópolis, Braz. 154/A2
Esperanza, Arg., Ant. 160/W
Esperanza (inlet), BC, Can. 126/B3
Esperanza (mts.), Hon. 144/E3
Esperanza, Mex. 142/C3
Esperanza, Mex. 143/M8
Esperanza, Peru 156/D3
Espichel (cape), Port. 45/P11
Espinal, Mex. 143/M6
Espinal, Col. 152/C3
Espinar, Peru 156/D4
Espinhaço, Serra do (mts.), Braz. 151/J5
Espinho, Port. 44/A2
Espinillo (pt.), Uru. 159/F2
Espinosa, Braz. 154/B4
Espírito Santo (state), Braz. 155/D2
Espíritu Santo (isl.), Van. 116/F6
Espíritu Santo (bay), Cuba 144/E2
Espita, Mex. 144/D1
Esplanada, Braz. 154/C3
Espluga de Francolí, Sp. 45/F2
Esplugues, Sp. 45/L7
Esposende, Port. 44/A2
Espungabera, Moz. 105/F5
Espy, Pa, US 139/H4
Esqueda, Mex. 142/C2
Esquel, Arg. 158/C4
Esquina, Arg. 157/E3
Essaouira, Mor. 98/B2
Esse (riv.), Ger. 51/G5
Essen, Belg. 52/C3
Essen, Ger. 50/E6
Essenbach, Ger. 55/F5
Essendon (mt.), Austl. 112/D3
Essenheim, Ger. 53/H4
Essequibo (riv.), Guy. 147/D2
Essequibo Island-West Demerara (pol. reg.), Guy. 153/G3
Essex, On, Can. 135/G7
Essex (co.), On, Can. 135/G7
Essex, Eng, UK 30/E1
Essex, Md, US 138/B5
Essex (co.), NJ, US 138/D2
Essex Fells, NJ, US 139/H8
Esslingen, Ger. 54/C5
Essômes-sur-Marne, Fr. 52/C5
Essonne (riv.), Fr. 42/E2
Est, Canal de l' (canal), Fr. 53/E5
Estaca de Bares, Punta de la (cape), Sp. 44/B1
Estación Santa Engracia, Mex. 143/F3
Estados, Isla de los (isl.), Arg. 157/D7
Eşţahbān, Iran 88/F3
Estaires, Fr. 52/B2
Estância, Braz. 154/C3
Estancia, NM, US 142/B3
Estats, Pico de (peak), Sp. 45/F1
Estavayer-le-Lac, Swi. 56/C4
Estcourt, SAfr. 107/E3
Este, It. 59/E2
Este, Punta del (pt.), Cuba 140/D3
Este Sudeste, Cayos del (isls.), Col. 146/E4
Esteio, Braz. 155/B4
Estelí, Nic. 144/E3
Estell Manor (Risley), NJ, US 138/D5
Estella, Sp. 44/D1
Estelle (mtn.), Ca, US 136/B5
Estelle, La, US 137/P17
Estepa, Sp. 44/C4
Estepona, Sp. 44/C4
Ester, Ak, US 134/J3
Esterhazy, Sk, Can. 127/H3
Esterias (cape), Gabon 96/G7
Esternay, Fr. 52/C6
Estero de Agiabampo (lag.), Mex. 142/C3
Estéron (riv.), Fr. 43/G5
Esterwegen, Ger. 51/E3

Estes Park, Co, US 137/A2
Estevan, Sk, Can. 127/H3
Estinnes-au-Mont, Belg. 52/C3
Eston, Sk, Can. 126/F3
Estonia (ctry.) 39/L2
Estoril, Port. 45/P10
Estral Beach, Mi, US 135/F8
Estrela, Serra da (mts.), Port. 44/A3
Estrela, Serra da (peak), Port. 44/B2
Estrella (pt.), Mex. 142/B2
Estrello, Serra do (range), Braz. 154/B3
Estremoz, Serra do (mts.), Braz. 151/J5
Estremoz, Port. 44/B3
Et Taiyiba, Isr. 91/G7
Eţ Ţira, Isr. 91/F7
Etah, India 84/B2
Etal (isl.), Micr. 116/E4
Étalle, Belg. 53/E4
Étaples, Fr. 52/A2
Etawah, India 84/B2
Etawah Branch (riv.), India 84/B2
Etchojoa, Mex. 142/C3
Ethelbert, Mb, Can. 127/H3
Ethiopia (ctry.) 97/N5
Ethiopian (plat.), Eth. 97/N6
Eti (riv.), Japan 77/K5
Etili, Turk. 49/H6
Étival-Clairefontaine, Fr. 56/C1
Etive, Loch (inlet), Sc, UK 36/A4
Etna (peak), It. 46/D4
Etna, Monte (Mount Etna) (vol.), It. 46/D4
Etne, Nor. 38/A2
Etobicoke, Can. 131/Q8
Etolin (str.), Ak, US 134/E3
Eton, Eng, UK 30/B4
Etorofu (isl.), Japan 71/S2
Etorofu (isl.), Rus. 67/P5
Etosha (salt pan), Namb. 105/C4
Etosha NP, Namb. 105/C4
Etowah, Ok, US 137/N15
Étrépilly, Fr. 30/L4
Étropole, Bul. 47/J1
Etroubles, It. 56/D6
Ettadhamen Douarhicher, Tun. 100/M6
Ettelbruck, Lux. 53/F4
Etten-Leur, Neth. 50/B5
Ettenheim, Ger. 56/D1
Etterbeek, Belg. 53/D2
Etters (Goldsboro), Pa, US 138/B4
Ettrick Pen (peak), Sc, UK 36/C6
Ettrick Water (riv.), Sc, UK 36/C5
Ettringen, Ger. 57/G1
Eu, Fr. 52/A3
'Eua (isl.), Tonga 117/H7
Eubenangee Swamp NP, Austl. 114/B2
Euclid, OH, US 130/D3
Euclides da Cunha, Braz. 154/C3
Eudora, Ar, US 129/K4
Eudunda, Austl. 115/A2
Euerbach, Ger. 54/D2
Eufaula, Al, US 133/G4
Eufaula (lake), Ok, US 125/D4
Eugendorf, Aus. 55/G7
Eugene, Or, US 126/C4
Eugene O'Neill NHS, Ca, US 135/L11
Eugenia (pt.), Mex. 142/B3
Eugowra, Austl. 115/D2
Eume, Embalse de (res.), Sp. 44/B1
Eungella NP, Austl. 114/C3
Eunice, La, US 129/J5
Eunice, NM, US 129/G4
Eupen, Belg. 53/F2
Euphrates (riv.), Iraq,Syria 67/D6
Eura, Fin. 39/K1
Eurajoki, Fin. 39/J1
Eure (riv.), Fr. 42/D2
Eure (dept.), Fr. 52/A5
Eure-et-Loir (dept.), Fr. 52/A6
Eureka (sound), Nun., Can. 123/S7
Eureka, Ca, US 126/B5
Eureka, Mo, US 137/F9
Eureka, Mt, US 126/D3
Eureka, Nv, US 128/D3
Eureka, SD, US 127/J3
Euro, Austl. 115/C3
Euroa, Austl. 115/C3
Eurodisney, Fr. 30/L5
Euron (riv.), Fr. 56/C1
Europa (pt.), Gib. 44/C4
Europabrücke, Aus. 57/H3
Europe (cont.) 27
Europoort, Neth. 50/B5
Euskirchen, Ger. 53/F2

Eussenheim, Ger. 54/C3
Eustis, Fl, US 133/H4
Euston, Austl. 115/B2
Eutin, Ger. 38/D4
Eutini, Malw. 104/B5
Eutsuk (lake), BC, Can. 126/B2
Euville, Fr. 53/E6
Évain, Qu, Can. 130/E1
Evander, SAfr. 106/C2
Evans (mt.), Co, US 129/F3
Evans (lake), Qu, Can. 130/E1
Evans, Co, US 137/C2
Evans (str.), Nun., Can. 123/H4
Evans Head, Austl. 115/E1
Evanston, Wy, US 126/F5
Evansville, In, US 130/C4
Evansville, Wy, US 126/F5
Evaporation (basin), Ut, US 126/E5
Evart, Mi, US 130/C3
Evaton, SAfr. 106/D2
Evaz, Iran 88/F3
Eve, Fr. 30/L4
Even Yehuda, Isr. 91/F7
Evenlode (riv.), Eng, UK 33/E3
Evenkiyskiy Aut. Okrug, Rus. 64/K3
Everard (cape), Austl. 115/D3
Everard (lake), Austl. 109/C4
Everard (mt.), Austl. 113/G3
Everest (peak), China, Nepal 82/E2
Everest (Sagarmatha) (mtn.), China,Nepal 85/F2
Everett, Wa, US 135/J11
Evergem, Belg. 52/C1
Everglades (swamp), Fl, US 133/H5
Everglades NP, Fl, US 133/H5
Evergreen, Al, US 133/G4
Evergreen, Co, US 137/B3
Evergreen Park, Il, US 135/Q16
Everswinkel, Ger. 51/E5
Evesham, Eng, UK 33/E2
Evesham, Vale of (valley), Eng, UK 33/E2
Evian-les-Bains, Fr. 56/C5
Evinos (riv.), Gre. 47/G3
Evje, Nor. 38/B2
Evolène, Swi. 56/D5
Évora, Port. 44/B3
Évora (dist.), Port. 44/A3
Évreux, Fr. 42/D2
Evron, Fr. 42/C2
Évrótas (riv.), Gre. 47/H4
Evry, Fr. 30/K6
Évvoia (gulf), Gre. 47/H3
Évvoia (gulf), Gre. 62/B5
Évvoia (isl.), Gre. 47/H3
Évvoia (isl.), Gre. 62/B5
Evxinoúpolis, Gre. 47/H3
Ewa Beach, Hi, US 124/V13
Ewa Villages, Hi, US 124/V13
Ewan, NJ, US 138/C4
Ewarton, Jam. 145/G2
Ewaso Ng'iro (riv.), Kenya 104/C2
Ewell, Eng, UK 30/C3
Ewing, NJ, US 138/D3
Exaltános, Gre. 47/H2
Excelsior Springs, Mo, US 137/E6
Excursion Inlet, Ak, US 134/L4
Exeter, Eng, UK 32/C4
Exeter, NH, US 131/G3
Exmoor (upland), Eng, UK 32/C4
Exmoor NP, Eng, UK 32/C4
Exmore, Va, US 138/C5
Exmouth, Austl. 112/A3
Exmouth (gulf), Austl. 112/B2
Exmouth (pen.), Austl. 115/A2
Exmouth, Eng, UK 32/C4
Exu, Braz. 154/C2
Exuma (sound), Bahm. 141/F3
Eyach (riv.), Ger. 54/B6
Eyak, Ak, US 134/J3
Eyasi (lake), Tanz. 105/F1
Eyb, Ger. 54/C5
Eydehamn, Nor. 38/C2
Eyemouth, Sc, UK 36/D5
Eyguières, Fr. 42/F5
Eyn Hemed (ruin), Isr. 91/G8
Eyre (pen.), Austl. 109/C4
Eyre North (lake), Austl. 109/C3
Eyre South (lake), Austl. 109/C3
Ezanville, Fr. 30/K4
Ezel, US 159/E7
Ezhou, China 79/B1
Ezine, Turk. 49/H3
Ezequiel Ramos Mexía (res.), Arg. 158/C3
Ezzane (well), Alg. 96/H3

F.E. Walter (res.), Pa, US 138/C1
Fabbrico, It. 59/D3
Fabens, Tx, US 132/B4

Fabero, Sp. 44/B1
Fåborg, Den. 38/D4
Fabriano, It. 59/E4
Facatativá, Col. 150/D3
Faches-Thumesnil, Fr. 52/C2
Fada (lake), Sc, UK 36/A1
Fada-N'Gourma, Burk. 103/F3
Faenza, It. 59/E4
Fafa (riv.), CAfr. 97/J6
Fafe, Port. 44/A2
Fafen Shet' (riv.), Eth. 97/P6
Făgăraş, Rom. 49/G3
Fagersta, Swe. 38/F2
Faggiola (peak), It. 59/E4
Fagnano (lake), Arg. 159/D7
Fagnano Olona, It. 58/B1
Fagnières, Fr. 53/D6
Faguibine (lake), Mali 96/D4
Fahl (well), Alg. 96/D4
Fahrenzhausen, Ger. 55/E6
Faial (isl.), Azor., Port. 45/S12
Faido, Swi. 56/D4
Failsworth, Eng, UK 35/F4
Fains-Véel, Fr. 53/E6
Fair Haven, Mi, US 135/G6
Fair Haven, Vt, US 130/F3
Fair Hill, Md, US 138/C4
Fair Isle (isl.), Sc, UK 31/W14
Fair Lawn, NJ, US 139/J8
Fair Oaks, Ca, US 135/M9
Fairbanks, Ak, US 134/J3
Fairfax, Ca, US 135/J11
Fairfax, Va, US 138/A6
Fairfax (co.), Va, US 138/A6
Fairfield, Ca, US 128/B3
Fairfield, Ct, US 139/E1
Fairfield (co.), Ct, US 139/L7
Fairfield, Mt, US 126/F4
Fairfield, NJ, US 139/H8
Fairfield, Pa, US 138/A4
Fairfield, Tx, US 129/G4
Fairfield, Ut, US 137/J13
Fairfield, Md, US 138/B5
Fairlee, Md, US 138/B5
Fairless Hills, Pa, US 138/D3
Fairmont, WV, US 130/D4
Fairmont City, Il, US 137/G8
Fairmount, Ks, US 137/D5
Fairplay, Co, US 132/B2
Fairton, NJ, US 138/C5
Fairview, NJ, US 139/K8
Fairview, Ok, US 129/N3
Fairview Heights, Il, US 137/G8
Fairway, Ks, US 137/F8
Fairweather (mt.), Ak, US 134/L4
Fairweather (cape), Ak, US 134/L4
Fairweather (mt.), BC, Can. 122/C3
Fareham, Eng, UK 32/E5
Faremoutiers, Fr. 52/C6
Faistós (ruin), Gre. 47/J5
Faizābād, India 84/D2
Fajardo, PR 141/M8
Fakahina (isl.), FrPol. 117/M6
Fakaofo (isl.), Tok. 117/H5
Fakarava (isl.), FrPol. 117/L6
Faku, China 72/E2
Fakse, Den. 38/E4
Fakse Ladeplads, Den. 38/E4
Fal (riv.), Eng, UK 32/B6
Fālākāta, India 85/G2
Fálanna, Gre. 47/H3
Falces, Sp. 154/C2
Falcon (res.), Mex.,US 140/B2
Falcon (cape), Alg. 100/D2
Falcón (state), Ven. 152/D2
Falconara Marittima, It. 59/E4
Falémé (riv.), Mali 96/C5
Falfurrias, Tx, US 132/D5
Falher, Ab, Can. 126/D2
Falkenberg, Swe. 38/E3
Falkensee, Ger. 40/Q6
Falkenstein, Ger. 55/F4
Falkenstein, Ger. 55/F4
Falkirk, Sc, UK 36/C5
Falkland (isls.), UK 147/C8
Falkland, Sc, UK 36/C5
Falkland Sound (str.), UK 159/E7
Falköping, Swe. 38/E2
Fall City, Wa, US 134/M3
Fall River, Ma, US 131/G3
Fallbrook, Ca, US 136/C4
Falling Spring, Il, US 137/S16
Fallingbostel, Ger. 51/G3
Fallis, US 137/N14
Fallon, Nv, US 128/C3
Falls Church, Va, US 138/A6
Fallston, Md, US 138/B4
Falmouth, Anti. 141/N8

Falmouth, Eng, UK 32/A6
Falmouth (bay), Eng, UK 32/A6
False Pass, Ak, US 134/F5
Falshöft (pt.), Ger. 38/C4
Falso (cape), Hon. 145/F3
Falso, Cabo (cape), Mex. 142/C4
Falso Cabo de Hornos (cape), Chile 159/C7
Falster (isl.), Den. 37/E5
Falterona (peak), It. 59/E5
Fălticeni, Rom. 49/H2
Falun, Swe. 38/F1
Famagusta (bay), Cyp. 91/C2
Famagusta (dist.), Cyp. 91/C2
Famagusta, Cyp. 91/C2
Fameck, Fr. 53/F5
Famenne (reg.), Belg. 53/E3
Fammau, Moel (peak), Wal, UK 35/E5
Fan Si Pan (peak), Viet. 83/H3
Fana, Nor. 38/A1
Fanchang, China 72/D4
Fandriana, Madg. 107/H8
Fang Xian, China 72/B4
Fangataufa (isl.), FrPol. 117/L7
Fangcheng, China 72/C4
Fangcheng Gezu Zizhixian, China 83/J3
Fangshan, China 72/D1
Fanjing (peak), China 83/J2
Fannich (lake), Sc, UK 36/A1
Fanning (Tabuaeran) (isl.), Kiri. 117/K4
Fano, It. 59/G5
Fanshi, China 72/C3
Fanwood, NJ, US 139/H9
Faqīrwāli, Pak. 86/B5
Fāqūs, Egypt 91/B4
Faradje, D.R. Congo 104/A2
Farafangana, Madg. 107/H9
Farāfirah, Wāḩāt al (oasis), Egypt 101/A3
Farāh, Afg. 89/H2
Farāh (riv.), Afg. 89/H2
Farallon (isls.), Ca, US 128/B3
Farallon de Medinilla (isl.), NMar. 116/B2
Farallon de Pajaros (isl.), NMar. 116/B2
Farallones de Cali, PN, Col. 150/C3
Faranah (pol. reg.), Gui. 102/C4
Faranah, Gui. 102/C4
Farángi Samariás NP, Gre. 47/H5
Faraony (riv.), Madg. 107/H8
Faraulep (isl.), Micr. 116/C4
Farciennes, Belg. 53/D3
Fareham, Eng, UK 32/E5
Farewell, Ak, US 134/H3
Farewell (cape), NZ 117/S11
Fargo, ND, US 127/J4
Faribault, Mn, US 127/K4
Farīdābād, India 86/C5
Faridkot, India 86/C4
Farīdpur, Bang. 85/G4
Farīdpur (pol. reg.), Bang. 85/G4
Farīdpur, India 84/B1
Fāriskūr, Egypt 91/B4
Färjestaden, Swe. 38/G3
Farkadhón, Gre. 47/H3
Farkasgyepü, Hun. 48/C2
Farley, Mo, US 137/C2
Farmers, Co, US 137/C2
Farmingdale, NJ, US 138/D3
Farmingdale, NY, US 139/M9
Farmington, De, US 138/C4
Farmington, Mi, US 135/F7
Farmington, Mo, US 131/G2
Farmington, NM, US 128/E3
Farmington, Ut, US 137/K12
Farmington Hills, Mi, US 135/E6
Farnborough, Eng, UK 33/F4
Farnham, Eng, UK 33/F4
Farnham Royal, Eng, UK 30/B2
Farnworth, Eng, UK 35/F4
Faro, Yk, Can. 134/M3
Faro (dist.), Port. 44/A4
Faro, Port. 44/A4
Faro (int'l arpt.), Port. 44/A4
Faro, PN du, Camr. 96/H6
Faroe (isl.), Den. 160/G2
Fåron (riv.), Swe. 39/H3
Farösund, Swe. 39/H3
Farquhar (cape), Austl. 112/B2
Farr West, Ut, US 137/J11
Farroupilha, Braz. 155/B4

Farrukhābād, India 84/B2
Fársala, Gre. 47/H3
Farsø, Den. 38/C3
Farson, Wy, US 126/F5
Farsund, Nor. 38/B2
Fartak, Ras (pt.), Yem. 88/F5
Farwell, Tx, US 129/G4
Fasā, Iran 88/F3
Fasano, It. 47/E2
Faşıkan (pass), Turk. 91/C1
Fassberg, Ger. 51/H3
Fast Castle (pt.), Sc, UK 36/D5
Fastiv, Ukr. 62/D2
Fatagar Tuting (cape), Indo. 81/H4
Fatahjang, Pak. 86/B3
Fatehābād, India 86/C5
Fatehpur, India 84/C3
Fatehpur, India 84/C2
Fatehpur, India 89/K3
Fatick (pol. reg.), Sen. 102/A3
Fatick, Sen. 102/A3
Fátima, Port. 44/A3
Fatsa, Turk. 90/D1
Fatu Hiva (isl.), FrPol. 117/M6
Faucille, Col de la (pass), Fr. 56/C5
Faughan (riv.), NI, UK 34/A2
Fauldhouse, Sc, UK 36/C5
Faulkton, SD, US 127/J4
Faulquemont, Fr. 53/F5
Fauquier, It. 58/B1
Faure (riv.), Austl. 112/B3
Fäurei, Rom. 49/H3
Fauske, Nor. 37/E2
Faust, Ut, US 137/J13
Fauvillers, Belg. 53/E4
Faux, Tête de (peak), Fr. 56/D1
Favalto (peak), It. 59/F6
Favara, It. 46/C4
Fave (riv.), Fr. 56/C1
Faverges, Fr. 56/C6
Faverney, Fr. 56/C2
Favières, Fr. 30/L5
Favignana, It. 46/C4
Favria, It. 58/A2
Favrieux, Fr. 30/G5
Fawn (riv.), On, Can. 127/L2
Fawn Grove, Pa, US 138/B4
Faxafloi (bay), Ice. 37/M7
Faya-Largeau, Chad 97/J4
Fayal-la-Forêt, Fr. 56/B2
Fazao, Monts du (mts.), Togo 103/F4
Fazao, PN du, Togo 103/F4
Fdérik, Mrta. 98/B5
Fear (cape), NC, US 133/J3
Feale (riv.), Ire. 31/P10
Feasterville-Trevose, Pa, US 138/D3
Feather (riv.), Ca, US 128/C2
Featherstone, Eng, UK 35/F4
Fécamp, Fr. 42/D2
Fecht (riv.), Fr. 56/D1
Federal Hall Nat'l Mem., NY, US 139/K9
Federal Heights, Co, US 137/B3
Federally Admin. Tribal Areas, Pak. 86/A2
Federsee (lake), Ger. 54/C6
Fedje, Nor. 38/A1
Feeny, NI, UK 34/A2
Fegersheim, Fr. 54/A6
Fehérgyarmat, Hun. 48/F2
Fehmarn (isl.), Ger. 38/D4
Fehmarn Belt (str.), Den. 38/D4
Fehring, Aus. 40/F1
Fei Huang (riv.), China 72/D4
Fei Xian, China 72/D4
Feia, Lagoa (lake), Braz. 155/D2
Feicheng, China 72/D3
Feidong, China 72/C5
Feignies, Fr. 52/C3
Feijó, Braz. 156/D3
Feillans, Fr. 56/A5
Feira, Port. 44/A2
Feira de Santana, Braz. 154/C4
Feistritz (riv.), Aus. 43/L3
Feixi, China 72/D5
Fejér (co.), Hun. 48/D2
Fejø (isl.), Ger. 38/D4
Feke, Turk. 90/C2
Feketić, Serb. 48/D3
Felanitx, Sp. 45/G3
Feldafing, Ger. 57/H2
Feldaist (riv.), Aus. 55/H6
Feldberg, Ger. 39/H3
Feldkirch, Aus. 57/F3
Feldkirchen an der Donau, Aus. 55/H6
Feldkirchen bei Graz, Aus. 48/B2

Feldkirchen in Kärnten, Aus. 43/L3
Feletto, It. 58/A2
Feletto Umberto, It. 59/G1
Felino, It. 58/D3
Felipe Carillo Puerto, Mex. 144/D2
Felixdorf, Aus. 48/C2
Felixlândia, Braz. 155/C1
Felixstowe, Eng, UK 33/H3
Felizzano, It. 58/B3
Fell, Ger. 53/F4
Fellbach, Ger. 54/C5
Felling, Eng, UK 35/G2
Felsberg, Ger. 51/G6
Felsberg, Swi. 57/F4
Felton, Ca, US 138/C5
Felton, De, US 138/C5
Fema (peak), It. 43/K5
Femø (isl.), Den. 38/D4
Femundsmarka NP, Nor. 37/D3
Fénay, Fr. 56/B3
Fene, Sp. 44/A1
Fener (pt.), Turk. 91/D1
Fénérive, Madg. 105/K10
Feng Xian, China 72/D4
Fengari (peak), Gre. 47/J2
Fengcheng, China 71/L6
Fengcheng, China 73/C2
Fenghuang, China 83/J2
Fengle (riv.), China 72/D5
Fengnan, China 72/D2
Fengning, China 72/D2
Fengqing, China 83/G3
Fengqiu, China 72/C4
Fengrun, China 72/D2
Fengshan, Tai. 79/D3
Fengtai, China 72/H7
Fengxian, China 72/L9
Fengyang, China 72/D4
Fengyüan, Tai. 79/D3
Fengzhen, China 72/C2
Fenimore Pass (chan.), Ak, US 134/C4
Fenoarivo Atsinanana, Madg. 107/J7
Fens (phys. reg.), Eng, UK 33/G1
Fensmark, Den. 38/D4
Fensterbach (riv.), Ger. 55/F4
Fenton, Mi, US 130/D3
Fenton, Mo, US 137/G8
Fenton (lake), Mi, US 135/F7
Fenxi, China 72/B3
Feodosiya, Ukr. 62/E3
Fer, Cap de (cape), Alg. 100/K6
Ferbane, Ire. 31/O10
Ferdinandshof, Ger. 41/G2
Fère-Champenoise, Fr. 52/C5
Fère-en-Tardenois, Fr. 52/C5
Ferentino, It. 46/C2
Ferento (ruin), It. 46/C1
Fergus Falls, Mn, US 127/J4
Ferguson, Mo, US 137/G8
Ferguson (lake), Nun., Can. 122/F2
Ferihegy (int'l arpt.), Hun. 48/D2
Ferkéssédougou, C.d'Iv. 102/D4
Ferlach, Aus. 43/L3
Fermanagh (dist.), NI, UK 34/A3
Fermi National Accelerator Laboratory, Il, US 135/P16
Fermignano, It. 59/F5
Fermin (pt.), Ca, US 136/F8
Fermo, It. 43/K5
Fermoselle, Sp. 44/B2
Fermoy, Ire. 31/P10
Fernán-Núñez, Sp. 44/C4
Fernandina (isl.), Ecu. 156/E7
Fernandina Beach, Fl, US 133/H4
Fernando de Noronha (isl.), Braz. 147/F3
Fernandópolis, Braz. 155/B2
Ferndale, Md, US 138/B5
Ferndale, Mi, US 135/F7
Ferney-Voltaire, Fr. 56/C5
Fernie, BC, Can. 126/E3
Fernpass (pass), Aus. 57/G3
Ferntree Gully NP, Austl. 115/C3
Ferrandina, It. 46/E2
Ferrara (prov.), It. 59/E3
Ferrara, It. 59/E3
Ferrat (cape), Alg. 100/E5
Ferreira do Alentejo, Port. 44/A3
Ferrelview, Mo, US 137/D5
Ferreñafe, Peru 156/B2
Ferret (cape), Fr. 42/C4
Ferrette, Fr. 56/D3
Ferriday, La, US 129/K5
Ferriere, It. 58/C3
Ferrière-la-Grande, Fr. 52/D3
Ferrières, Belg. 53/E3
Ferryden, Sc, UK 36/D3
Ferryfield (int'l arpt.), Eng, UK 33/G5
Ferryhill, Eng, UK 35/G2
Fertő (Neusiedler See) (lake), Aus. 43/M3
Ferté-Bernard, Fr. 42/C2

Fértil (valley), Arg. 157/C3
Ferwerd, Neth. 50/C2
Fès, Mor. 100/B2
Fès (prov.), Mor. 100/B3
Fesches-le-Châtel, Fr. 56/C2
Feshie (riv.), Sc, UK 36/C2
Fessenheim, Fr. 56/D2
Festival Centre, Austl. 113/M8
Fethaland (pt.), Sc, UK 31/W13
Fethiye, Turk. 90/B2
Feucherolles, Fr. 30/H5
Feucht, Ger. 54/E4
Feuchtwangen, Ger. 54/D4
Feuilles (lake), Qu, Can. 123/J3
Feuilles, Rivière aux (riv.), Qu, Can. 123/J3
Feuquières, Fr. 52/A4
Feuquières-en-Vimeu, Fr. 52/A3
Feurs, Fr. 42/F4
Fevzipaşa, Turk. 91/E1
Feyzābād, Afg. 89/K1
Fez (Saiss) (int'l arpt.), Mor. 100/B3
Fezzan (reg.), Libya 96/H2
Fferna, Moel (peak), Wal, UK 34/B3
Ffestiniog, Wal, UK 34/C6
Fianarantsoa (prov.), Madg. 107/H8
Fianarantsoa, Madg. 107/H8
Fianga, Chad 96/J6
Ficarolo, It. 59/E3
Fichtelberg (peak), Ger. 55/F2
Fichtelgebirge (mts.), Ger. 40/F3
Fichtelnaab (riv.), Ger. 55/E3
Ficksburg, SAfr. 106/D3
Fidenza, It. 58/D3
Fié (riv.), Gui. 102/C4
Field (riv.), Austl. 113/M9
Fieldon, Il, US 137/D7
Fieni, Rom. 49/G3
Fier (riv.), Fr. 56/B6
Fierzë (lake), Alb. 47/G1
Fiesch, Swi. 56/E5
Fiesole, It. 59/E5
Fiesso, It. 59/E2
Fiesso Umbertiano, It. 59/E3
Fiesta Texas, Tx, US 137/T20
Fife, Wa, US 135/C3
Fife (pol. reg.), Sc, UK 36/D4
Fifth Cataract (falls), Sudan 101/C5
Figalo (cape), Alg. 100/D3
Figari, Fr. 46/A2
Figeac, Fr. 42/E4
Figline Valdarno, It. 59/E5
Figueira da Foz, Port. 44/A2
Figueres, Sp. 45/G1
Figuig, Mor. 99/E2
Figuig (prov.), Mor. 100/C3
Fiherenana (riv.), Madg. 107/G8
Fiji (ctry.) 116/G6
Filadelfia, Par. 157/D2
Filadélfia, Braz. 154/A2
Filattiera, It. 58/C4
Filchner Ice Shelf, Ant. 160/T
Filey (bay), Eng, UK 35/H4
Fili, Gre. 47/N8
Filiaşi, Rom. 49/F3
Filiátai, Gre. 47/G3
Filiatrá, Gre. 47/G4
Filicudi (isl.), It. 46/D3
Filingué, Niger 103/F3
Filippiás, Gre. 47/G3
Filippoi (ruin), Gre. 47/J2
Filipstad, Swe. 38/F2
Filisur, Swi. 57/F4
Fillière (riv.), Fr. 56/C6
Fillmore, Ut, US 128/D3
Fillmore, Ca, US 136/B2
Filomeno Mata, Mex. 143/M6
Filótion, Gre. 47/J4
Filottrano, It. 59/G6
Fils, Fr. 54/C5
Filsum, Ger. 51/E2
Fimi (riv.), D.R. Congo 96/J8
Fina, Forêt Classée de, Mali 102/C3
Finale Emilia, It. 59/E3
Finale Ligure, It. 58/B4
Fiñana, Sp. 44/D4
Finch Hatton, Austl. 114/C3
Findel (int'l arpt.), Lux. 53/F4
Findhorn (riv.), Sc, UK 36/C1
Findhorn, Sc, UK 36/C1
Findlay, Oh, US 130/D3
Finesville, NJ, US 138/C2
Fingal, Austl. 115/C4
Finger (lake), On, Can. 127/K2
Finhaut, Swi. 56/C5
Finike, Turk. 91/B1
Finisterre, Sp. 44/A1
Finisterre (cape), Sp. 44/A1
Finke, Austl. 113/G3
Finke Gorge NP, Austl. 113/G3
Finkenstein, Aus. 43/K3

Finksburg, Md, US 138/B5
Finland (ctry.) 37/H2
Finland (gulf), Eur. 37/H2
Finlay (mts.), Tx, US 132/B4
Finlay (riv.), BC, Can. 122/D3
Finley, Austl. 115/C2
Finn (riv.), Ire. 31/Q9
Finnentrop, Ger. 51/E6
Finnigan (mt.), Austl. 114/B1
Finnis (cape), Austl. 113/G5
Finnmark (co.), Nor. 37/G1
Fino Mornasco, It. 58/C1
Finsing, Ger. 55/E6
Finspång, Swe. 38/F2
Finsteraarhorn (peak), Swi. 56/E4
Finström, Fin. 39/H1
Fintel, Ger. 51/G2
Fintona, NI, UK 34/A3
Fionn Loch (lake), Sc, UK 36/A1
Fiora (riv.), It. 43/J5
Fiorano, It. 59/D3
Fiordland NP, NZ 117/R12
Fiorenzuola d'Arda, It. 58/C3
Fircrest, Wa, US 135/C3
Fire Island Nat'l Seashore, NY, US 139/E2
Firenze (prov.), It. 59/E5
Firenze (Florence), It. 59/E5
Firenzuola, It. 59/E4
Firestone, Co, US 137/C2
Firmat, Arg. 158/E2
Firmi, Fr. 42/E4
Firminy, Fr. 42/F4
Firozābād, India 84/B2
Firozpur, India 86/C4
First Cataract (falls), Egypt 101/C3
Firūz Kūh, Iran 88/F1
Firūzābād, Iran 88/F3
Fischa (riv.), Aus. 49/P7
Fischach, Ger. 55/E3
Fischamend Markt, Aus. 49/P7
Fischbacher Alpen (mts.), Aus. 43/L3
Fischen im Allgäu, Ger. 57/G3
Fischer, Tx, US 137/U20
Fish (riv.), Namb. 105/C5
Fisher (bay), Mb, Can. 127/J3
Fisher (str.), Nun., Can. 123/H2
Fisher Branch, Mb, Can. 127/J3
Fisherman (isl.), Austl. 114/F6
Fishers (isl.), NY, US 139/G1
Fishguard, Wal, UK 32/B3
Fisht (peak), Rus. 62/F4
Fismes, Fr. 52/C5
Fitful Head (pt.), Sc, UK 31/W14
Fitjar, Nor. 38/A2
Fitton (mt.), Yk, Can. 134/L2
Fitzgerald, Ga, US 133/H4
Fitzgerald River NP, Austl. 112/C5
Fitzroy (riv.), Austl. 109/B2
Fitzroy (peak), Arg. 159/B6
Fitzwilliam (str.), NW, Can. 123/R7
Fiume Veneto, It. 59/F1
Fiumicino, It. 46/C2
Five Sisters (peak), Sc, UK 36/A2
Fivemiletown, NI, UK 34/A3
Fivizzano, It. 58/D4
Fjell, Nor. 38/A1
Fjerritslev, Den. 38/C3
Fjugesta, Swe. 38/F2
Flå, Nor. 38/C1
Flachslanden, Ger. 54/D4
Fladungen, Ger. 54/D1
Flagler, Co, US 129/G3
Flagler Beach, Fl, US 133/H4
Flagstaff, Az, US 128/E4
Flambeau (riv.), Wi, US 127/L4
Flamborough, Eng, UK 35/H3
Flamborough Head (pt.), Eng, UK 35/H3
Flaming Gorge (res.), Ut,Wy, US 126/F5
Flaming Gorge Nat'l Rec. Area, Ut,Wy, US 128/E2
Flamingo Field (int'l arpt.), NAnt. 152/D1
Flanagan (riv.), On, Can. 127/K2
Flanders (reg.), Fr. 42/E1
Flanders, NY, US 139/F2
Flat Holm (isl.), Eng, UK 32/C4
Flat Keys (isls.), Fl, US 133/H5
Flathead (riv.), Mt, US 126/E4
Flathead (lake), Mt, US 126/E4
Flathead, South Fork (riv.), Mt, US 126/E4
Flattery (cape), Austl. 114/B1
Flattery (cape), Wa, US 126/B3
Flavio Alfaro, Ecu. 152/B3
Flawil, Swi. 57/F3
Flaxlanden, Fr. 56/D2
Fleet, Eng, UK 33/F4

Fleetwood, Pa, US 138/C3
Fleetwood, Eng, UK 35/E4
Flekkefjord, Nor. 38/B2
Flemington, NJ, US 138/D2
Flemington Racecourse, Austl. 115/F5
Flemish Brabant (prov.), Belg. 53/D2
Flen, Swe. 38/G2
Flensburg, Ger. 38/C4
Flero, It. 58/D2
Fleron, Belg. 53/E2
Flers, Fr. 42/C2
Flesland (int'l arpt.), Nor. 38/A1
Fletschhorn (peak), Swi. 56/D5
Fleurance, Fr. 42/D5
Fleurier, Swi. 56/C4
Fleurus, Belg. 53/E2
Fleury-les-Aubrais, Fr. 42/D3
Flevoland (prov.), Neth. 50/C4
Flevoland (isl.), Neth. 40/C2
Flexenpass (pass), Aus. 57/G3
Flieden, Ger. 54/C2
Flieden (riv.), Ger. 54/C2
Fliess, Aus. 57/G3
Flims, Swi. 57/F4
Flin Flon, Mb, Can. 127/H2
Flinders (ranges), Austl. 109/C4
Flinders (bay), Austl. 109/A4
Flinders (reef), Austl. 109/D2
Flinders (riv.), Austl. 109/C2
Flinders (reefs), Austl. 109/D4
Flinders (range), Austl. 113/H5
Flinders Chase NP, Austl. 113/H5
Flinders Ranges NP, Austl. 113/H4
Flinders Reefs (isls.), Austl. 114/C2
Flines-lez-Raches, Fr. 52/C3
Flint (hills), Ks, US 129/H3
Flint (riv.), Ga, US 133/G4
Flint (isl.), Kiri. 117/K6
Flint (lake), Nun., Can. 123/J2
Flint, South Branch (riv.), Mi, US 135/F5
Flintbek, Ger. 38/D4
Flintshire (co.), Wal, UK 35/E5
Flisa, Nor. 38/E1
Flix, Sp. 45/F2
Flixecourt, Fr. 52/B3
Flize, Fr. 53/D4
Floby, Swe. 38/E2
Floda, Swe. 38/E3
Flögelner See (riv.), Ger. 51/F1
Flöha (riv.), Ger. 41/G3
Floing, Fr. 53/D4
Flonheim, Ger. 54/B3
Flora, Il, US 129/K3
Flora (mt.), Austl. 112/C2
Flora, Nor. 37/C3
Floral Park, NY, US 139/L9
Florange, Fr. 53/F5
Florânia, Braz. 154/C2
Floraville, It. 137/G9
Floreffe, Belg. 53/D3
Florence, SC, US 133/J3
Florence, Al, US 133/G3
Florence, Az, US 128/E4
Florence (Firenze), It. 43/J5
Florence-Graham, Ca, US 136/F8
Florencia, Col. 152/C4
Florennes, Belg. 53/D3
Florenville, Belg. 53/E4
Flores (sea), Indo. 67/K10
Flores (isl.), Indo. 67/M10
Flores, Guat. 144/D2
Flores (dept.), Uru. 159/F2
Flores do Piauí, Braz. 154/B2
Floresta, Braz. 154/C3
Florham Park, NJ, US 139/H8
Floriano, Braz. 154/B2
Florianópolis, Braz. 155/B3
Florida, Peru 156/B2
Florida (bay), Fl, US 133/H5
Florida, Hon. 144/D3
Florida, Cuba 145/G1
Florida, Col. 152/B4
Florida (dept.), Uru. 159/F2
Florida, Uru. 159/K11
Florida (state), US 133/H4
Florida, NY, US 138/D1
Florida (str.), Cuba, US 125/K7
Florida Keys (isls.), Fl, US 133/H5
Floridablanca, Col. 152/C3
Floridia, It. 46/D4
Florin, Ca, US 135/M10
Flórina, Gre. 47/G2
Florissant, Mo, US 137/G8
Florissant Fossil Beds Nat'l Mon., Co, US 132/B2
Flörsbachtal, Ger. 54/C2
Flörsheim am Main, Ger. 54/B2
Flörsheim-Dalsheim, Ger. 54/B3
Florstadt, Ger. 54/B2
Flossenbürg, Ger. 55/F3

Floyd, Mo, US 137/E5
Floydada, Tx, US 129/H4
Fluchthorn (peak), Aus. 57/G4
Flüelapass (pass), Swi. 57/F4
Flüelen, Swi. 57/E4
Flums, Swi. 57/F4
Flushing, Mi, US 130/D3
Fly (riv.), PNG 116/D5
Flying Fish (cape), Ant. 160/T
Fnjóská (riv.), Ice. 37/P6
Foam Lake, Sk, Can. 127/H3
Foča, Bosn. 48/D4
Fochabers, Sc, UK 36/C1
Fochville, SAfr. 106/P13
Fockbek, Ger. 38/C4
Focşani, Rom. 49/H3
Fogang, China 83/K3
Foggia, It. 46/D2
Foglia (riv.), It. 59/F5
Foglizzo, It. 58/A2
Föglö (isl.), Fin. 39/J3
Fogo (isl.), CpV. 93/J10
Fohnsdorf, Aus. 43/L3
Föhren, Ger. 53/F4
Foix, Fr. 42/D5
Folarskardnuten (peak), Nor. 38/B1
Folda (inlet), Nor. 37/E2
Földeák, Hun. 48/E2
Folégandros (isl.), Gre. 47/J4
Folembray, Fr. 52/C4
Foley (isl.), Nun., Can. 123/J2
Folgaria, It. 57/H6
Foligno, It. 43/H5
Folkestone, Eng, UK 33/H4
Folkston, Ga, US 133/H4
Follainville-Dennemont, Fr. 30/H4
Follonica, Golfo di (gulf), It. 43/J5
Folschviller, Fr. 53/F5
Folsom, NJ, US 138/D5
Fomboni, Com. 107/G6
Fond du Lac, Wi, US 127/L5
Fond du Lac, Sk, Can. 122/F3
Fond du Lac (riv.), Sk, Can. 122/F3
Fondi, It. 46/C2
Fondo, It. 57/H5
Fongen (peak), Nor. 38/D1
Fonni, It. 46/A2
Fonsagrada, Sp. 44/B1
Fonseca (gulf), Nic. 140/D5
Fonseca, Col. 152/C2
Font Sancte, Pic de la (peak), Fr. 43/G4
Fontaine, Fr. 42/F4
Fontaine-Châalis, Fr. 30/L4
Fontaine-lès-Dijon, Fr. 56/A3
Fontaine-lès-Luxeuil, Fr. 56/C2
Fontaine-L'Evêque, Belg. 53/D3
Fontainebleau, Fr. 42/E2
Fontana, Ca, US 136/C2
Fontanarossa (int'l arpt.), It. 46/D4
Fontanella, It. 58/C2
Fontanellato, It. 58/D3
Fontaniva, It. 59/E1
Fonte Boa, Braz. 153/E5
Fontenailles, Fr. 30/L6
Fontenais, Swi. 56/D3
Fontenay-en-Parisis, Fr. 30/K4
Fontenay-le-Comte, Fr. 42/C3
Fontenay-le-Fleury, Fr. 30/J5
Fontenay-les-Briis, Fr. 30/J6
Fontenay-Saint-Père, Fr. 30/H4
Fontenay-sous-Bois, Fr. 30/K5
Fontenay-Trésigny, Fr. 30/L5
Fontenelle (res.), Wy, US 126/F5
Fontoy, Fr. 53/F5
Fontur (pt.), Ice. 37/P6
Foping, China 70/J3
Foraker (mt.), Ak, US 134/H3
Forbach, Fr. 53/F5
Forbach, Ger. 54/B4
Forbes, Austl. 115/D2
Forbesganj, India 85/F2
Forcarey, Sp. 44/A1
Forchheim, Ger. 54/E3
Forclaz, Col de la (pass), Swi. 56/D5
Fords, NJ, US 139/H9
Foreland (pt.), Eng, UK 32/C4
Foreland, The (pt.), Eng, UK 33/E5
Foremost, Ab, Can. 126/F3
Foreness (pt.), Eng, UK 33/H4
Forest, Ms, US 133/F3
Forest Hill, Md, US 138/B4
Forest Park, Ok, US 137/N14
Forestier (pen.), Austl. 115/D4
Forestville, Qu, Can. 131/G1
Forestville, Md, US 138/B6
Forez, Monts du (mts.), Fr. 42/E4
Forfar, Sc, UK 36/D3
Forges-les-Bains, Fr. 30/J6

Forggensee (lake), Ger. 57/G2
Forillon NP, Qu, Can. 131/H1
Forked River, NJ, US 138/D4
Forkill, NI, UK 34/B3
Forks, Wa, US 126/B4
Forli, It. 59/F4
Forli-Cesena (prov.), It. 59/F4
Forlimpopoli, It. 59/F4
Formartine (reg.), Sc, UK 36/D2
Formby, Eng, UK 35/E4
Formby (pt.), Eng, UK 35/E4
Formentera, Isla de (isl.), Sp. 45/F3
Formentor (cape), Sp. 45/G3
Formerie, Fr. 52/A4
Formia, It. 46/C2
Formiga, Braz. 155/C2
Formigine, It. 59/D3
Formignana, It. 59/E3
Formosa, Arg. 157/E2
Formosa, Braz. 154/A4
Formosa (peak), SAfr. 106/C4
Formosa (isl.), GBis. 102/B4
Formosa do Rio Prêto, Braz. 154/A3
Formosa, Serra (mts.), Braz. 155/B1
Formoso (riv.), Braz. 151/J6
Fornacelle, It. 59/E5
Fornaci di Barga, It. 58/D4
Fornæs (cape), Den. 38/D3
Fornebu (int'l arpt.), Nor. 38/D2
Fornovo di Taro, It. 59/D3
Forres, Sc, UK 36/C1
Forrest City, Ar, US 129/K4
Forsand, Nor. 38/A2
Forshaga, Swe. 38/F2
Forssa, Fin. 39/K1
Forstern, Ger. 55/E6
Forstinning, Ger. 55/E6
Forsyth, Mt, US 126/G4
Forsyth, Ga, US 133/H3
Forsyth (range), Austl. 114/A3
Forsythe NWR, NJ, US 138/D5
Fort Abbâs, Pak. 86/B5
Fort Augustus, Sc, UK 36/B2
Fort Beaufort, SAfr. 106/D4
Fort Belvoir, Va, US 138/A6
Fort Benton, Mt, US 126/F4
Fort Bragg, Ca, US 126/C6
Fort Chambly Nat'l Hist. Park, Qu, Can. 131/P7
Fort Chipewyan, Ab, Can. 122/E3
Fort Cobb (res.), Ok, US 129/H4
Fort Collins, Co, US 137/B1
Fort Collins Museum, Co, US 137/B1
Fort Davis, Tx, US 129/G5
Fort de Douaumont, Fr. 53/E5
Fort-de-France, Guad. 141/N9
Fort de Vaux, Fr. 53/E5
Fort Desaix Mil. Res., Fr. 141/N9
Fort Dodge, Ia, US 127/K5
Fort Erie, On, Can. 131/S10
Fort Frances, On, Can. 127/K3
Fort Frederica Nat'l Mon., Ga, US 133/J4
Fort George Nat'l Hist. Park, On, Can. 131/R9
Fort Gibson (lake), Ok, US 132/E3
Fort Good Hope, NW, Can. 122/D2
Fort Hancock, Tx, US 129/J10
Fort Howard, Md, US 138/B5
Fort Kent, Me, US 131/G2
Fort Lauderdale, Fl, US 133/H5
Fort Lauderdale-Hollywood (int'l arpt.), Fl, US 133/H5
Fort Lee, NJ, US 139/K8
Fort Lewis, Wa, US 135/C3
Fort Liard, NW, Can. 122/D2
Fort Liberté, Haiti 145/J2
Fort Lupton, Co, US 137/C2
Fort Macleod, Ab, Can. 126/E3
Fort Madison, Ia, US 127/L5
Fort-Mahon-Plage, Fr. 52/A3
Fort Malden Nat'l Hist. Park, On, Can. 135/F7
Fort-Mardyck, Fr. 52/B2
Fort Matanzas Nat'l Mon., Fl, US 133/H4
Fort McDowell Ind. Res., Az, US 137/S18
Fort McHenry Nat'l Mon., Md, US 138/B5
Fort McMurray, Ab, Can. 122/E3
Fort McPherson, NW, Can. 134/M2
Fort Meade, Md, US 138/B5
Fort Morgan, Co, US 137/C2
Fort Myers, Fl, US 133/H5
Fort Nelson, BC, Can. 122/D3
Fort Nelson (riv.), BC, Can. 122/D3
Fort Nottingham, SAfr. 107/E3

Fort Payne, Al, US 133/G3
Fort Peck (dam), Mt, US 127/G4
Fort Peck (lake), Mt, US 126/G4
Fort Pierce, Fl, US 133/H5
Fort Portal, Ugan. 104/A2
Fort Providence, NW, Can. 122/E2
Fort Qu'Appelle, Sk, Can. 127/H3
Fort Randall (dam), SD, US 127/J5
Fort Resolution, NW, Can. 122/E2
Fort Saint James, BC, Can. 126/B2
Fort Saint John, BC, Can. 122/D3
Fort Saskatchewan, Ab, Can. 126/E2
Fort Scott, Ks, US 129/J3
Fort-Shevchenko, Kaz. 63/J3
Fort Simpson, NW, Can. 122/D2
Fort Smith, Ar, US 129/J4
Fort Smith, NW, Can. 122/E2
Fort Stanwix Nat'l Mon., NY, US 130/E3
Fort Stockton, Tx, US 129/G5
Fort Sumner, NM, US 129/F4
Fort Sumter, SC, US 133/J4
Fort Tilden, NY, US 139/K9
Fort Totten, ND, US 127/H4
Fort Vasquez Museum, Co, US 137/C2
Fort Vermilion, Ab, Can. 122/E3
Fort Wadsworth, NY, US 139/J9
Fort Walton Beach, Fl, US 133/G4
Fort Wayne, In, US 130/C3
Fort Wellington, Cuba 145/F1
Fort William, Sc, UK 36/A3
Fort Yates, ND, US 127/H4
Fort Yukon, Ak, US 134/J2
Fortaleza, Braz. 154/C1
Fortaleza dos Nogueiras, Braz. 154/A2
Fortaleza Santa Teresa, Uru. 159/G2
Forte dei Marmi, It. 58/D5
Fortescue, NJ, US 138/C5
Fortescue (riv.), Austl. 112/C2
Forth, Sc, UK 36/C5
Forth (riv.), Sc, UK 36/B4
Forth, Firth of (inlet), Sc, UK 36/D4
Fortin, Mex. 143/N8
Fortore (riv.), It. 46/D2
Fortrose, Sc, UK 36/B1
Fortuna, Braz. 154/A4
Fortuna, Arg. 158/D2
Fortuna Ledge, Ak, US 134/F3
Fortune (bay), Nf, Can. 131/L2
Fortune, Nf, Can. 131/L2
Forty Fort, Pa, US 138/C1
Forty Mile Scrub NP, Austl. 114/B2
Foshan, China 83/K3
Fosheim (pen.), Nun., Can. 123/S7
Foss (riv.), Eng, UK 35/G4
Fossalta di Piave, It. 59/F1
Fossalta di Portogruaro, It. 59/F1
Fossano, It. 58/A3
Fosses, Fr. 30/K4
Fosses-la-Ville, Belg. 53/D3
Fossil, NJ, US 126/C4
Fossil Creek (res.), Co, US 137/B2
Fossò, It. 59/F1
Fossombrone, It. 59/F5
Foster, Austl. 115/C3
Foster Pond, Il, US 137/G9
Fosterburg, Il, US 137/G8
Fostoria, Oh, US 130/D3
Fót, Hun. 49/R9
Foucarmont, Fr. 52/A4
Foucherans, Fr. 56/B3
Foug, Fr. 53/E6
Fougères, Fr. 42/C2
Fougerolles, Fr. 56/C2
Fouilloy, Fr. 52/B4
Foul (bay), Egypt, Su 101/D3
Foula (isl.), Sc, UK 31/V13
Foulness (pt.), Eng, UK 33/G3
Foulness (isl.), Eng, UK 33/G3
Foum Zguid, Mor. 98/D3
Foumban, Camr. 96/H6
Foundiougne, Sen. 102/A3
Fountain, Co, US 137/C3
Fountain Hill, Pa, US 138/C2
Fountain Hills, Az, US 137/S18
Fountain Valley, Ca, US 136/C3
Fountains Abbey, Eng, UK 35/G4
Fourchambault, Fr. 42/E3
Fourche La Fave (riv.), Ar, US 129/J4
Fourges, Fr. 30/G4
Fourmies, Fr. 52/D4

Fourth Cataract (falls), Sudan 101/C5
Fouta Djallon (phys. reg.), Gui. 96/C5
Foveaux (str.), NZ 109/G7
Fowey (riv.), Eng, UK 32/B6
Fowman, Iran 88/E1
Fox (isls.), Ak, US 134/K5
Fox (mtn.), Yk, Can. 134/M3
Fox (isl.), Il,Wi, US 127/L5
Fox (isl.), Wa, US 135/B3
Fox Creek, Ab, Can. 126/D2
Fox Glacier, NZ 117/S11
Fox Lake, Il, US 135/P15
Fox River Grove, Il, US 135/P15
Fox Valley, Sk, Can. 126/F3
Foxe (pen.), Nun., Can. 123/J2
Foxe (chan.), Nun., Can. 123/H2
Foxe Basin (chan.), Nun., Can. 123/J2
Foxen (lake), Swe. 38/D2
Foyle (riv.), NI, UK 34/A2
Foz, Sp. 44/B1
Foz do Iguaçu, Braz. 157/F2
Frackville, Pa, US 138/B2
Fraga, Sp. 45/F2
Fragosa, Cayo (isl.), Cuba 145/G1
Fraiburgo, Braz. 155/B3
Frailes, Cordillera de los (mts.), Ven. 150/F2
Fraisans, Fr. 56/B3
Fraize, Fr. 56/D1
Frameries, Belg. 52/C3
Framlingham, Eng, UK 33/H2
Frammersbach, Ger. 54/C2
Francavilla al Mare, It. 46/D1
Francavilla Fontana, It. 47/E2
Francavilla in Sinni, It. 46/E2
France (ctry.) 42/D3
Frances (cape), Cuba 145/F1
Frances (lake), Yk, Can. 122/C2
Francés Viejo (cape), DRep. 145/H4
Franceville, Gabon 96/H8
Franche-Comté (pol. reg.), Fr. 56/B5
Franche-Comté Austl. 109/E3
Francis Case (lake), SD, US 127/J5
Francisco de Orellana, Peru 156/C1
Francisco Escárcega, Mex. 144/D2
Francisco Javier Mina, Mex. 142/C3
Francisco Sá, Braz. 154/B5
Francisco Zarco, Mex. 142/A1
Francistown, Bots. 105/E5
Franco da Rocha, Braz. 211/G8
Francolino, It. 59/E3
Franconville, Fr. 30/J5
Franeker, Neth. 50/C2
Frangy, Fr. 56/B5
Frank Hahn NP, Austl. 112/C5
Franken Wald (for.), Ger. 55/E2
Frankenau, Ger. 51/F6
Frankenberg-Eder, Ger. 51/F6
Frankenburg am Hausruck, Aus. 55/G6
Frankenhöhe (mts.), Ger. 54/D4
Frankenmarkt, Aus. 55/G7
Frankenmuth, Mi, US 130/D3
Frankenthal, Ger. 54/B3
Frankfort (cap.), Ky, US 130/C4
Frankfort, SAfr. 106/E2
Frankfurt (int'l arpt.), Ger. 54/B2
Frankfurt am Main, Ger. 54/B2
Fränkische Alb (mts.), Ger. 40/E4
Fränkische Rezat (riv.), Ger. 54/D4
Fränkische Saale (riv.), Ger. 54/D2
Fränkische Schweiz (reg.), Ger. 40/E4
Fränkische Schweiz (reg.), Ger. 40/F4
Frankland (cape), Austl. 115/C3

Franklin D. Roosevelt (lake), Wa, US 126/D3
Franklin Lakes, NJ, US 139/J7
Franklin-Lower Gordon Wild Rivers NP, Austl. 115/C4
Franklin Mineral Museum, NJ, US 138/D1
Franklin Park, Il, US 135/Q16
Franklin Square, NY, US 139/L9
Franksville, Wi, US 135/Q14
Franois, Fr. 56/B3
Franschhoek, SAfr. 106/L10
Fransisco Beltrão, Braz. 157/F2
Fransisco Morato, Braz. 211/G8
Františkovy Lázně, Czh. 55/F2
Franz Josef Land (isls.), Rus. 160/C
Franz Joseph Strauss (int'l arpt.), Ger. 55/E6
Franzburg, Ger. 38/E4
Fraser (riv.), BC, Can. 126/C2
Fraser (isl.), Austl. 109/E3
Fraser (mt.), Austl. 112/C3
Fraser, Mi, US 135/G6
Fraser Lake, BC, Can. 126/B2
Fraser NP, Austl. 115/C3
Fraserburg, SAfr. 106/C4
Fraserburgh, Sc, UK 36/D1
Frasne, Fr. 56/C4
Frassine (riv.), It. 59/E2
Frassino, It. 59/D2
Frastanz, Aus. 57/F3
Frati, Monte dei (peak), It. 59/F5
Frauenfeld, Swi. 57/E2
Fraunberg, Ger. 55/E6
Fray Bentos, Uru. 159/J10
Fray Marcos, Uru. 159/L11
Frazier Park, Ca, US 128/C4
Frechen, Ger. 53/F2
Freckenfeld, Ger. 54/B4
Frederica, De, US 138/C6
Fredericia, Den. 38/C4
Frederick (reef), Austl. 109/E3
Frederick, Co, US 137/C2
Frederick, Md, US 130/E4
Frederick (co.), Md, US 138/A5
Frederick, Ok, US 129/H4
Fredericksburg, Md, US 138/A5
Fredericksburg, Va, US 138/A6
Frederickton, Austl. 115/E1
Fredericton (cap.), NB, Can. 131/H2
Frederik Willem IV (falls), Sur. 153/G4
Frederiks, Den. 38/C3
Frederiksberg, Den. 38/E4
Frederiksborg Slot (Frederiksborg Castle), Den. 38/E4
Frederikshavn, Den. 38/D3
Frederiksted, USVI 141/M8
Fredersdorf bei Berlin, Ger. 40/Q7
Fredonia, Az, US 128/D3
Fredonia, NY, US 130/E3
Fredrikberg, Swe. 38/F1
Fredrikstad, Nor. 38/D2
Free State (prov.), SAfr. 106/P13
Freeburg, Il, US 137/H9
Freeburg, Pa, US 138/B2
Freedom, Ok, US 132/D3
Freehold, NJ, US 138/D2
Freeland, Pa, US 138/C1
Freeland, Md, US 138/B4
Freeland, Wa, US 135/B1
Freeling, Mt., Austl. 113/G2
Freeling Heights (peak), Austl. 113/H4
Freemansburg, Pa, US 138/C2
Freeport, Il, US 127/L5
Freeport, Tx, US 129/J5
Freeport, Bahm. 141/F2
Freeport, NY, US 139/L9
Freer, Tx, US 132/D5
Freetown (cap.), SLeo. 102/B4
Fregenal de la Sierra, Sp. 44/B3
Fréhel (cape), Fr. 42/B2
Frei Inocêncio, Braz. 155/D1
Freib Mulde (riv.), Ger. 40/G3
Freiberg, Ger. 41/G3
Freiburg, Ger. 51/G1
Freiburg, Ger. 40/B5
Freienbach, Swi. 57/E3
Freilassing, Ger. 55/F7
Freinsheim, Ger. 54/B3
Freire, Chile 158/B3
Freisen, Ger. 53/G4
Freising, Ger. 55/E6
Freistadt, Aus. 55/H5
Freital, Ger. 41/G3

Freixo de Espada à Cinta, Port. 44/B2
Frejorgues (int'l arpt.), Fr. 42/E5
Fréjus, Fr. 43/G5
Frekhaug, Nor. 38/A1
Frémainfille, Fr. 30/H4
Fremdingen, Ger. 54/D5
Frémécourt, Fr. 30/J4
Fremont (riv.), Ut, US 128/E3
Fremont, Oh, US 130/D3
Fremont, Mi, US 130/C3
Fremont, Ca, US 128/B3
Fremont (isl.), Ut, US 137/J11
French (riv.), On, Can. 130/D2
French Creek State Park, Pa, US 138/C3
French Frigate Shoals (bar), Hi, US 117/C2
French Guiana (dpcy.), Fr. 151/H3
French Polynesia (terr.), Fr. 117/L6
Frenchman (riv.), Can., US 122/F4
Frenchman's (bay), On, Can. 131/R8
Frenchmans Cap (peak), Austl. 115/C4
Frenchtown, NJ, US 138/C2
Frenda, Alg. 100/F5
Frépillon, Fr. 30/H4
Freren, Ger. 51/E4
Fresco, Braz. 151/H5
Fresco, C.d'Iv. 102/D5
Fresia, Chile 158/B4
Fresnes, Fr. 30/J5
Fresnes-en-Woëvre, Fr. 53/E5
Fresno, Ca, US 128/C3
Fresnoy-le-Grand, Fr. 52/C4
Fresse-sur-Moselle, Fr. 56/C2
Fressenneville, Fr. 52/A3
Fretin, Fr. 52/C2
Freuchie (lake), Sc, UK 36/C3
Freudenberg, Ger. 55/E4
Freudenberg, Ger. 53/G2
Freudenburg, Ger. 53/F4
Freudenstadt, Ger. 57/E1
Frévent, Fr. 52/B2
Freycinet (har.), Austl. 112/B3
Freycinet NP, Austl. 115/D4
Freyming-Merlebach, Fr. 53/F5
Freyung, Ger. 55/G5
Fria (cape), Namb. 105/B4
Frias, Arg. 157/C2
Frias, Peru 156/B2
Fribourg, Swi. 56/D4
Fribourg (canton), Swi. 56/D4
Frick, Swi. 56/D3
Frickenhausen am Main, Ger. 55/F2
Fridingen an der Donau, Ger. 57/E1
Fridolfing, Ger. 55/F6
Friedberg, Ger. 54/B2
Friedberg, Ger. 54/D6
Friedeburg, Ger. 51/E2
Friedrichsdorf, Ger. 54/B2
Friedrichshafen, Ger. 57/F2
Friedrichstadt, Ger. 38/C4
Friedrichsthal, Ger. 53/G5
Frielendorf, Ger. 51/F2
Friesenhagen, Ger. 53/G2
Friesenheim, Ger. 56/D1
Friesland (prov.), Neth. 50/C2
Friesoythe, Ger. 51/E2
Frignicourt, Fr. 53/D5
Frio (riv.), Tx, US 143/F2
Friockheim, Sc, UK 36/D3
Friol, Sp. 44/B1
Frisange, Lux. 53/F4
Fristad, Swe. 38/E3
Fritsla, Swe. 38/E3
Fritzlar, Ger. 51/G6
Friuli-Venezia Giula (prov.), It. 43/K3
Friville-Escarbotin, Fr. 52/A3
Frobisher (bay), Nun., Can. 123/K2
Frogmore, Eng, UK 30/A3
Frohavel (inlet), Nor. 37/D3
Frohnleiten, Aus. 43/L3
Froid-Chapelle, Belg. 52/C5
Froideconche, Fr. 56/C2
Froissy, Fr. 52/B3
Froland, Nor. 38/C2
Frolovo, Rus. 63/G2
Frome (lake), Austl. 109/D4
Frome (riv.), Eng, UK 32/C5
Frome, Eng, UK 32/C4
Frome (riv.), Austl. 113/H4
Froncles, Fr. 53/D6
Fronteira, Port. 44/B3
Frontenhausen, Ger. 55/F5
Frontera, Mex. 144/C2
Frontera Comalapa, Mex. 144/C3
Frontier Army Museum, Ks, US 137/D5
Frontignan, Fr. 42/E5
Fronton, Fr. 42/D5
Frosinone, It. 46/C2
Frösö, Swe. 37/E3
Frotey-lès-Vesoul, Fr. 56/C2
Frouard, Fr. 53/F6

Frövi, Swe. 38/F2
Freya (isl.), Nor. 37/D3
Frozen (str.), Nun., Can. 123/H2
Fruges, Fr. 52/B2
Fruit Heights, Ut, US 137/K11
Fruska Gora NP, Cro. 48/D3
Frutal, Braz. 155/B1
Frutigen, Swi. 56/D4
Frutillar, Chile 158/B4
Fryazino, Rus. 61/X9
Frýdek-Mistek, Czh. 41/K4
Fu Xian, China 72/B4
Fu'an, China 72/D5
Fucecchio, It. 59/D5
Fucheng, China 72/D3
Fuchskaute (peak), Ger. 43/H1
Fuchū, Japan 77/C2
Fuchū, Japan 77/C2
Fuchun (riv.), China 72/D5
Fuding, China 72/D5
Fuengirola, Sp. 44/C4
Fuenlabrada, Sp. 45/N9
Fuensalida, Sp. 45/N8
Fuente, Sp. 45/N8
Fuente de Cantos, Sp. 44/B3
Fuente del Maestre, Sp. 44/B3
Fuente Obejuna, Sp. 44/C3
Fuentelapeña, Sp. 44/C2
Fuentes de Oñoro, Sp. 44/B2
Fuentesaúco, Sp. 44/C2
Fuerte (riv.), Mex. 142/C3
Fuerte Olimpo, Par. 150/G8
Fuerteventura (isl.), Sp. 45/Y16
Fuga (isl.), Phil. 79/D4
Fuglebjerg, Den. 38/D4
Fugong, China 83/G2
Fugou, China 72/C4
Fuhai, China 70/E2
Fuhne (riv.), Ger. 40/F3
Fuhse (riv.), Ger. 51/H4
Fuji (riv.), Japan 75/F3
Fuji, Japan 75/F3
Fuji-Hakone-Izu NP, Japan 75/F3
Fuji-san (peak), Japan 75/F3
Fujieda, Japan 75/F3
Fujihashi, Japan 77/K4
Fujiidera, Japan 77/J6
Fujikawa, Japan 77/B3
Fujimi, Japan 77/D2
Fujino, Japan 77/C2
Fujinomiya, Japan 77/B3
Fujioka, Japan 75/F2
Fujioka, Japan 77/D1
Fujioka, Japan 77/M5
Fujisawa, Japan 75/F3
Fujishiro, Japan 77/K5
Fujiwara, Japan 77/K5
Fujiyoshida, Japan 75/F3
Fukagawa, Japan 76/C2
Fukaya, Japan 77/C1
Fukiage, Japan 77/C1
Fukuchiyama, Japan 77/H5
Fukue, Japan 74/A4
Fukui (pref.), Japan 74/E3
Fukui, Japan 74/E3
Fukuoka, Japan 74/B4
Fukuoka (int'l arpt.), Japan 74/B4
Fukuoka (pref.), Japan 74/B4
Fukuoka, Japan 77/M4
Fukuroi, Japan 75/G2
Fukushima, Japan 75/G2
Fukushima (pref.), Japan 75/F2
Fukushima, Japan 76/B3
Fukuyama, Japan 74/C3
Fūlādī (mtn.), Afg. 89/J2
Fulda (riv.), Ger. 40/E3
Fulda, Ger. 51/G6
Fullerton, Ca, US 136/G8
Fullerton (Whitehall), Pa, US 138/C2
Fully, Swi. 56/D4
Fulpmes, Aus. 57/H3
Fulton, Mo, US 129/K3
Fulton, NY, US 130/E3
Fulton, Ky, US 130/B4
Fulufjället (peak), Swe. 38/E1
Fumaiolo (peak), It. 59/F5
Fumay, Fr. 53/D4
Fumel, Fr. 42/D5
Fumin, China 83/H2
Funabashi, Japan 75/G2
Funafuti (cap.), Tuv. 116/G5
Funafuti (isl.), Tuv. 116/G5
Funan, China 72/C4
Funchal, Port. 98/A2
Funchal (int'l arpt.), Port. 98/A2
Fundão, Col. 152/C2
Fundão, Port. 44/B2
Fundy NP, NB, Can. 131/H2
Funhalouro, Moz. 105/D3
Funing, China 83/J3
Funing, China 72/D3
Fuorn, Pass dal (Ofenpass) (pass), Swi. 57/G4
Fuping, China 72/C3
Fuqing, China 79/C2
Fuquan, China 83/J2
Fur (riv.), China 73/C2

Furan (riv.), Fr. 56/B6
Furano, Japan 76/C2
Fürfeld, Ger. 53/G4
Furmanov, Rus. 60/J4
Furnas (res.), Braz. 147/E5
Furneaux Group (isls.), Austl. 109/D4
Fürstenau, Ger. 51/E3
Fürstenfeld, Aus. 43/M3
Fürstenfeldbruck, Ger. 54/E6
Fürstenwalde, Ger. 41/H2
Fürth, Ger. 55/E4
Fürth, Ger. 54/D4
Fürth, Ger. 55/F5
Furth im Wald, Ger. 55/F4
Furtwangen im Schwarzwald, Ger. 56/E1
Furudal, Swe. 38/F1
Furukawa, Japan 76/B4
Fury and Hecla (str.), Nun., Can. 123/H2
Fushan, China 72/B4
Fushan, China 72/E3
Fushun, China 73/B2
Fushun, China 83/J2
Fusignano, It. 59/E4
Fusin, China 73/B2
Fusong, China 73/D2
Füssen, Ger. 57/G2
Fusui, China 78/D1
Futaba, Japan 77/A2
Futog, Serb. 48/D3
Futrono, Chile 158/B4
Futtsu, Japan 75/F3
Futuna (isl.), Wall. 116/H6
Fuwah, Egypt 91/B4
Fuxian (lake), China 83/H3
Fuxin, China 130/D3
Fuxin Monggolzu Zizhixian, China 72/E2
Fuyang, China 72/E4
Fuyi (riv.), China 79/B2
Fuyu, China 71/M2
Fuyu, China 71/M2
Fuyuan, China 70/E2
Fuzhou, China 79/C2
Füzesabony, Hun. 48/E2
Fuzhou, China 79/C2
Fyn (co.), Den. 38/D4
Fyn (isl.), Den. 37/D5
Fyne, Loch (inlet), Sc, UK 36/A5
Fyresdal, Nor. 38/C2

G
Ga Vache (isl.), Haiti 145/H2
Gaast, Neth. 50/C2
Gabas (riv.), Fr. 42/C5
Gabela, Ang. 105/B3
Gabes (gulf), Tun. 93/D1
Gabicce Mare, It. 59/F5
Gablingen, Ger. 54/D6
Gablitz, Aus. 49/N7
Gabon (ctry.) 96/H7
Gaborone (cap.), Bots. 105/E5
Gabriel Leyva Solano, Mex. 142/C3
Gabrovo, Bul. 47/J1
Gaby, It. 58/A1
Gacko, Bosn. 47/F1
Gādarwāra, India 84/B4
Gaddy, Ok, US 137/N15
Gadmen, Swi. 57/E4
Gadsden, Al, US 133/G3
Gaeta, It. 46/C2
Gaeta, Golfo di (gulf), It. 46/C2
Gaffney, SC, US 133/H3
Gagarin, Rus. 60/G5
Gaggenau, Ger. 54/B5
Gaggio Montano, It. 59/B1
Gaglianico, It. 58/B1
Gagnoa, C.d'Iv. 102/D5
Gagny, Fr. 30/K5
Gagra, Geo. 63/G4
Gagret, India 86/D4
Gai Xian, China 73/B2
Gaichtpass (pass), Aus. 57/G3
Gaildorf, Ger. 54/C5
Gaillac, Fr. 42/D5
Gailtaler (mts.), Aus. 43/K3
Gaiman, Arg. 158/D4
Gaimersheim, Ger. 55/E5
Gainesville, Ga, US 133/H3
Gainesville, Fl, US 133/H4
Gainsborough, Eng, UK 35/H5
Gairdner (lake), Austl. 109/C4
Gairn (riv.), Sc, UK 36/C3
Gais, Swi. 57/F3
Gaiserwald, Swi. 57/F3
Gaizina (peak), Lat. 39/L3
Gakarosa (peak), SAfr. 106/C2
Gakona, Ak, US 134/J3
Galana (riv.), Kenya 105/B3
Galand, Iran 89/G1

Galapagar, Sp. 45/M8
Galápagos (isls.), Ecu. 156/E6
Galápagos (dept.), Ecu. 156/E7
Galápagos, PN, Ecu. 156/E7
Galashiels, Sc, UK 36/D5
Galati (prov.), Rom. 49/H3
Galati, Rom. 49/J3
Galatina, It. 47/F2
Galatini, Gre. 47/G2
Galátista, Gre. 47/H2
Galatone, It. 47/F2
Galb Azefal (hill), WSah. 98/B5
Galbiate, It. 58/C1
Galdácano, Sp. 44/D1
Gáldar, Canl.,Sp. 98/B3
Galeana, Mex. 143/E3
Galena, Ak, US 134/G3
Galena, Md, US 138/C5
Galeota (pt.), Trin. 153/F2
Galera (pt.), Ecu. 152/A4
Galera (pt.), Trin. 153/F2
Galera (pt.), Chile 158/B3
Galesburg, Il, US 127/L5
Galey (riv.), Ire. 31/P10
Galga (riv.), Hun. 49/R9
Galgamácsa, Hun. 49/R9
Galgorm, NI, UK 34/B2
Galich, Rus. 60/J4
Gangi, It. 46/D4
Galiçica NP, FYROM 48/D3
Galiléia, Braz. 155/D1
Galileo Galilei (int'l arpt.), It. 58/D5
Galinakopf (peak), Aus. 57/F4
Galion, Oh, US 130/D3
Gallan Head (pt.), Sc, UK 31/Q7
Gallarate, It. 58/B1
Gallatin, Tn, US 130/C4
Galle, SrL. 82/D6
Gallegos (riv.), Arg. 157/B7
Gallicano, It. 58/D4
Galliera Veneta, It. 59/E1
Gallinas (mts.), NM, US 132/B3
Gallinas (pt.), Col. 152/D1
Gallipoli, It. 47/E2
Gallipoli (pen.), Turk. 49/H5
Gällivare, Swe. 37/G2
Gallneukirchen, Aus. 55/H6
Gallo (cape), It. 46/C3
Gallo (lake), It. 57/G4
Gallspach, Aus. 55/G6
Galluis, Fr. 30/H5
Gallup, NM, US 128/E4
Gallur, Sp. 44/E2
Gally (riv.), Fr. 30/H5
Galston, Sc, UK 36/B5
Galten, Ger. 38/C3
Galtymore (peak), Ire. 31/P10
Galva, La, US 137/P16
Galvarino, Chile 158/B3
Galveston, Tx, US 129/J5
Galveston (bay), Tx, US 140/C2
Galveston (isl.), Tx, US 140/C2
Gálvez, Sp. 44/C3
Galway, Ire. 31/P10
Galway (bay), Ire. 31/P10
Galzignano, It. 59/E2
Gam (riv.), Viet. 83/J3
Gamaches, Fr. 52/A4
Gamagara (riv.), SAfr. 106/C2
Gamagōri, Japan 77/M6
Gamarra, Col. 152/C2
Gamba, China 85/G1
Gambaga, Gha. 103/E4
Gambaga Scarp (cliff), Gha. 103/E4
Gambais, Fr. 30/H5
Gambara, It. 58/D2
Gambat, Pak. 82/A2
Gambela NP, Eth. 97/M6
Gambell, Ak, US 134/D3
Gambellara, It. 59/E2
Gambettola, It. 59/F4
Gambia (riv.), Gam. 102/A3
Gambia, The (ctry.) 102/A3
Gambier (isls.), FrPol. 117/M7
Gambo, Nf, Can. 131/L1
Gambolò, It. 58/B2
Gambsheim, Fr. 54/A5
Gaming, Aus. 43/L3
Gamka (riv.), SAfr. 106/C4
Gamkab (riv.), Namb. 106/B3
Gamleby, Swe. 38/G3
Gammelstad, Swe. 60/D2
Gammertingen, Ger. 57/F1
Gammon Ranges NP, Austl. 113/H4
Gamo, Japan 77/K5
Gampern, Aus. 55/G6
Gamud (peak), Eth. 105/D2
Gan (riv.), China 71/L6
Gan, Fr. 42/C5
Gananoque, On, Can. 131/H2
Gäncä, Azer. 63/H4
Ganda, Ang. 105/B3

Gandajika, D.R. Congo 105/D2
Gandak (riv.), India 85/E2
Gandaki (zone), Nepal 84/D1
Gander (lake), Nf, Can. 131/L1
Gander, Nf, Can. 131/L1
Ganderkesee, Ger. 51/F2
Gandesa, Sp. 45/F2
Gāndhī Sāgar (res.), India 82/B3
Gāndhīdhām, India 89/K4
Gandhinagar, India 89/K4
Gandia, Sp. 45/E3
Gandino, It. 58/C1
Gandoca-Manzanillo NWR, CR 145/K4
Gandu, Braz. 154/C4
Ganeb (well), Mrta. 102/C2
Ganesh (mtn.), China 85/E1
Gangapur, India 85/L1
Gangārāmpur, India 85/G3
Gangaw, Myan. 83/F3
Gangca, China 70/H4
Gangdisê (mts.), China 70/D5
Gangelt, Ger. 53/F2
Ganges, Fr. 42/E5
Ganges (riv.), Asia 67/G5
Ganges (Ganga) (riv.), India 84/B1
Ganges, Mouths of the (delta), Bang. 70/E7
Gangkofen, Ger. 55/F6
Gangoh, India 84/D2
Gangtok, India 85/G2
Ganluo, China 83/H2
Gannat, Fr. 42/E3
Ganquan, China 72/B3
Gansbaai, SAfr. 106/L11
Gänserndorf, Aus. 49/P7
Gansu (prov.), China 70/H4
Ganyu, China 72/D3
Ganzhou, China 79/B2
Ganzlin, Ger. 40/G2
Gao (pol. reg.), Mali 103/E2
Gao, Mali 103/E2
Gao'an, China 79/C2
Gaocheng, China 72/C3
Gaochun, China 72/D3
Gaogou, China 72/D3
Gaoping, China 72/C4
Gaotai, China 70/G4
Gaotang, China 72/D3
Gaoua, Burk. 102/E4
Gaoyao, China 72/C3
Gaoyi, China 72/C3
Gaoyou, China 72/D4
Gaozhou, China 83/K3
Gap, Fr. 43/G4
Gar, China 70/B5
Garabogazköl Aylagy (gulf), Trkm. 63/K4
Garachiné, Pan. 145/G4
Garachiné (pt.), Pan. 145/G4
Garai (riv.), Bang. 82/E3
Garajonay, PN de, Canl.,Sp. 98/A3
Garamba, PN de la, D.R. Congo 97/L7
Garancières, Fr. 52/A6
Garanhuns, Braz. 154/C3
Garbsen, Ger. 51/G4
Garça, Braz. 155/B2
Garças (riv.), Braz. 151/H7
Garching an der Alz, Ger. 55/F6
Garcia de Sota, Embalse de (res.), Sp. 44/C3
Gard (riv.), Fr. 42/F4
Garda (lake), It. 43/J1
Garda, It. 59/D1
Garde, Cap de (cape), Alg. 100/K3
Gardelegen, Ger. 40/F2
Garden City, Ga, US 133/H3
Garden City, Ks, US 129/G3
Garden City, Mi, US 135/E7
Garden City Park, NY, US 135/H9
Garden Grove, Ca, US 136/G8
Garden Ridge, Tx, US 137/U20
Garden View, Pa, US 138/A1
Gardena, Ca, US 136/F8
Gardēz, Afg. 89/J2
Gardiner, Mt, US 126/F4
Gardiner, Qu, Can. 131/G2
Gardiner, Wa, US 136/C2
Gardiners (isl.), NY, US 139/F1
Gardiners (bay), NY, US 139/F1
Gardner (lake), Austl. 113/H4
Gardner, Ks, US 137/D6
Gardone val Trompia, It. 58/D1
Gare Loch (inlet), Sc, UK 36/B4
Gareat el Tarf (salt pan), Alg. 100/K7

Garelochhead, Sc, UK 36/B4
Garessio, It. 58/B4
Garet el Djenoun (peak), Alg. 99/G4
Garfield (mtn.), Mt, US 126/E4
Garfield, Ut, US 137/J12
Garfield, NJ, US 139/J8
Garforth, Eng, UK 35/G4
Gargano (peak), It. 42/D4
Gargaliánoi, Gre. 47/G4
Gargenville, Fr. 52/A6
Garges-lès-Gonesse, Fr. 30/K5
Gargnano, It. 58/D1
Garh Mahārāja, Pak. 86/A4
Garhākotā, India 84/B4
Garhbeta, India 85/F4
Garhmuktesar, India 84/B1
Garibaldi, Braz. 155/B4
Garies, SAfr. 106/B3
Garioch (reg.), Sc, UK 36/D2
Garissa, Kenya 104/C3
Garland, Tx, US 129/H4
Garlasco, It. 58/B2
Garmisch-Partenkirchen, Ger. 57/H3
Garmsār, Iran 88/F1
Garnpung (lake), Austl. 115/B2
Garonne (riv.), Fr. 42/D4
Garopaba, Braz. 155/B4
Garou (lake), Mali 103/E2
Garoua, Camr. 96/H6
Garphyttan, Swe. 38/F2
Garraf (mts.), Sp. 45/K7
Garrel, Ger. 51/F3
Garrison (dam), ND, US 127/H4
Garrison, ND, US 127/H4
Garron (pt.), NI, UK 34/C1
Garrovillas, Sp. 44/B3
Garry (bay), Nun., Can. 123/H2
Garry (lake), Nun., Can. 122/F2
Garry (lake), Sc, UK 36/B2
Garry (riv.), Sc, UK 36/A2
Gars am Inn, Ger. 55/F6
Garsten, Aus. 55/H6
Garte (riv.), Ger. 51/H6
Gärtringen, Ger. 54/B5
Garut, Indo. 80/C5
Garvagh, NI, UK 34/B2
Garwolin, Pol. 41/L3
Garwood, NJ, US 139/H8
Gary, In, US 130/C3
Garza García, Mex. 143/E3
Garzón, Col. 152/C4
Garzón, Uru. 159/F3
Garzê, China 70/H5
Gas, Fr. 30/G6
Gas City, In, US 130/C3
Gas-san (peak), Japan 76/B4
Gæsafjöll (peak), Ice. 37/P6
Gaschurn, Aus. 57/G4
Gasconade (riv.), Mo, US 129/K3
Gascony (reg.), Fr. 42/C5
Gascoyne (riv.), Austl. 109/A3
Gascoyne (mt.), Austl. 112/C3
Gaspar (str.), Indo. 80/C4
Gaspar, Braz. 155/B3
Gaspé (pen.), Qu, Can. 131/H1
Gaspé, Cap de (cape), Qu, Can. 131/H1
Gaspoltshofen, Aus. 55/G6
Gasport, NY, US 131/S9
Gassino Torinese, It. 58/A2
Gastins, Fr. 30/M6
Gaston (lake), NC, US 133/J2
Gastonia, NC, US 133/H3
Gastoúni, Gre. 47/G4
Gata (cape), Sp. 44/D4
Gata (cape), Cyp. 91/C2
Gata de Gorgos, Sp. 45/F3
Gata, Sierra de (mts.), Sp. 44/B2
Gatchina, Rus. 39/P7
Gatehouse-of-Fleet, Sc, UK 34/D2
Gates of the Arctic NP and Prsv., Ak, US 134/G2
Gateshead (isl.), Nun., Can. 122/F1
Gateshead (co.), Eng, UK 35/G2
Gateshead, Eng, UK 35/G2
Gatesville, Tx, US 132/D4
Gateway Arch (arch), Mo, US 137/G8
Gateway NRA, NJ,NY, US 139/K9
Gatineau (riv.), Qu, Can. 123/J4
Gatineau, Qu, Can. 123/J4
Gatow, Ger. 40/Q7
Gattaran, Phil. 79/D4
Gattendorf, Aus. 43/M2
Gattianara, It. 58/B1
Gatún (dam), Pan. 145/G4
Gatún (lake), Pan. 145/G4
Gatwick (int'l arpt.), Eng, UK 30/D5
Gau Algesheim, Ger. 54/B3
Gau Bischofsheim, Ger. 54/B3

Gau Odernheim, Ger. 54/B3
Gaubickelheim, Ger. 53/H4
Gauchy, Fr. 52/C4
Gaucín, Sp. 44/C4
Gauja (riv.), Est.,Lat. 39/L3
Gauja NP, Lat. 39/L3
Gaukönigshofen, Ger. 54/C3
Gaunless (riv.), Eng, UK 35/G2
Gaupne, Nor. 37/C3
Gaur (riv.), Sc, UK 36/B3
Gauri Sankar (peak), Nepal 85/F2
Gauripur, India 85/G2
Gausta (peak), Nor. 38/C2
Gauting, Ger. 55/E6
Gavà, Sp. 45/L7
Gávdhos (isl.), Gre. 47/J5
Gavere, Belg. 52/C2
Gavi, It. 58/B3
Gavião, Port. 44/B3
Gavirate, It. 58/B1
Gävle, Swe. 38/G1
Gävleborg (co.), Swe. 37/E3
Gawler (ranges), Austl. 109/C4
Gawler, Austl. 113/H5
Gay (riv.), WV, US 130/D4
Gay, Rus. 63/L2
Gaya, Niger 103/F4
Gaya, India 85/F3
Gayaza, Ugan. 104/A3
Gaylord, Mi, US 130/C2
Gayndah, Austl. 114/C4
Gaza Strip, Isr. 90/C4
Gazeran, Fr. 30/H6
Gaziantep (prov.), Turk. 90/D2
Gaziantep, Turk. 90/D2
Gaziköy, Turk. 49/H5
Gazipaşa, Turk. 91/C1
Gazon de Faing (peak), Fr. 56/D1
Gazzaniga, It. 58/C1
Gbadolite, D.R. Congo 97/K7
Gbarnga, Libr. 102/C5
Gbongan, Nga. 103/G5
Gdansk (gulf), Pol. 41/K1
Gdańsk, Pol. 38/H4
Gdynia, Pol. 38/H4
Ge (lake), China 72/D5
Geal Charn (peak), Sc, UK 36/C2
Geal Charn (peak), Sc, UK 36/A3
Gebaberg (peak), Ger. 54/D1
Gebe (isl.), Indo. 81/G3
Gebhardshain, Ger. 53/G2
Gebiz, Turk. 91/B1
Gebze, Turk. 49/J5
Gedi Ruins Nat'l Mon., Kenya 104/D3
Gedikbulak, Turk. 90/D2
Gedinne, Belg. 53/D4
Gediz (riv.), Turk. 90/A2
Gedser (cape), Den. 38/D4
Gedser, Den. 38/D4
Gedsted, Den. 38/C3
Geel, Belg. 53/E1
Geelong, Austl. 115/C3
Geelvink (chan.), Austl. 109/A3
Geertruidenberg, Neth. 50/B5
Geeste (riv.), Ger. 51/F1
Geeste, Ger. 51/E3
Geesthacht, Ger. 51/H2
Gefrees, Ger. 55/E2
Geg̃yai, China 70/D5
Gehrde, Ger. 51/F3
Gehrden, Ger. 51/G4
Geifas (reg.), Wal, UK 32/C2
Geikie (riv.), Sk, Can. 122/F3
Geilenkirchen, Ger. 53/F2
Geilo, Nor. 38/C1
Geinō, Japan 77/K6
Geiselhöring, Ger. 55/F5
Geiselwind, Ger. 54/D3
Geisenfeld, Ger. 55/E5
Geisenhausen, Ger. 55/F5
Geisenheim, Ger. 53/G4
Geislingen, Ger. 57/F1
Geislingen an der Steige, Ger. 54/C5
Geita, Tanz. 104/B3
Gejiu, China 83/H3
Gela, It. 46/D4
Gela, Golfo di (gulf), It. 46/D4
Gelai (peak), Tanz. 104/C3
Gelderland (prov.), Neth. 50/C4
Geldermalsen, Neth. 50/C5
Geldern, Ger. 53/E1
Geldrop, Neth. 50/C6
Geleen, Neth. 53/E2
Gelendost, Turk. 91/B1
Gelendzhik, Rus. 62/F3
Gelibolu (Gallipoli), Turk. 49/H5
Gelibolu Yarımadas NP, Turk. 47/K2
Gelincik (peak), Turk. 90/E2
Gelnhausen, Ger. 54/C2
Gelsenkirchen, Ger. 50/E5

Geltendorf, Ger. 57/H1
Gelterkinden, Swi. 56/D3
Gelting, Ger. 38/C4
Gemas, Malay. 80/B3
Gembloux, Belg. 53/D2
Gemena, D.R. Congo 97/J7
Gemert, Neth. 50/C5
Gemlik (gulf), Turk. 49/J5
Gemlik, Turk. 49/J5
Gemona del Friuli, It. 43/K3
Gemsbok NP, Bots. 105/D6
Gemuk (mtn.), Ak, US 134/G3
Gemünden am Main, Ger. 54/C2
Genalê Wenz (riv.), Eth. 97/N6
Genappe, Belg. 53/D2
Genay, Fr. 56/A6
Genç, Turk. 90/E2
Gendringen, Neth. 50/D5
Gendt, Neth. 50/C5
Genemuiden, Neth. 50/D3
General Abelardo L. Rodríguez (int'l arpt.), Mex. 128/C4
General Alfredo Vasquez Cobo (int'l arpt.), Col. 156/D2
General Alvear, Arg. 158/D2
General Alvear, Arg. 158/D3
General Arenales, Arg. 158/E2
General Belgrano, Arg. 158/F2
General Belgrano II, Arg., Ant. 160/X
General Cabrera, Arg. 158/E2
General Carrera (lake), Chile 157/B6
General Cepeda, Mex. 143/E3
General Conesa, Arg. 158/D4
General Deheza, Arg. 158/E2
General Edward Lawrence Logan (Logan Int'l), (int'l arpt.), Ma, US 131/G3
General Enrique Godoy, Arg. 158/D3
General Francisco Villa, Mex. 143/F3
General Galarza, Arg. 159/J10
General Grant Nat'l Mem., NY, US 139/K8
General Juan Álvarez, PN, Mex. 143/F5
General Juan José Ríos, Mex. 142/C3
General Juan Madariaga, Arg. 159/F3
General La Madrid, Arg. 158/E3
General Lagos, Chile 156/D5
General Las Heras, Arg. 159/J11
General Lavalle, Arg. 159/K12
General Martín Miguel de Güemes, Arg. 157/C1
General Pico, Arg. 158/E2
General Pinedo, Arg. 157/D2
General Pinto, Arg. 158/E2
General Roca, Arg. 158/D3
General San Martín, Arg. 158/E2
General San Martín, Arg. 159/J11
General San Martín, Arg., Ant. 160/V
General Santiago Marino (int'l arpt.), Ven. 153/F2
General Terán, Mex. 143/F3
General-Toshevo, Bul. 49/J4
General Viamonte, Arg. 158/E2
General Villalobos, Arg. 158/E2
General Villegas, Arg. 158/E2
General Zaragoza, Mex. 143/F3
Generoso (peak), Swi. 57/F6
Genesee (co.), Mi, US 135/E6
Genesee (riv.), NY, US 130/E3
Genesee, Wi, US 135/P14
Genesee Depot, Wi, US 135/P14
Geneseo, Il, US 130/E3
Geneseo, NY, US 130/E3
Geneva (Léman) (lake), Swi. 43/G3
Geneva (Genève), Swi. 43/G3
Geneva (int'l arpt.), Swi. 56/C5
Geneva, Al, US 133/G4
Geneva, Ne, US 129/H2
Geneva, NY, US 130/E3
Geneva, Oh, US 130/D3
Geneva, Ut, US 137/K13
Genève (canton), Swi. 56/C5
Genève (Geneva), Swi. 56/C5
Gengenbach, Ger. 56/E1
Génicourt, Fr. 30/J4
Genk, Belg. 53/E2
Genlis, Fr. 56/B3
Gennargentu (mts.), It. 46/A2
Gennep, Neth. 50/C5

Gennevilliers, Fr. 30/J5
Genoa (Genova), It. 43/H4
Genoa City, Wi, US 135/P14
Genova (prov.), It. 58/C4
Genova (Genoa), It. 58/B4
Genova, Golfo di (gulf), It. 43/H4
Genovesa (isl.), Ecu. 156/F6
Gensingen, Ger. 53/G4
Gent-Brugge Kanaal (canal), Belg. 52/C1
Gent (Ghent), Belg. 52/C1
Genteng (cape), Indo. 80/C5
Genteng, Indo. 80/D5
Geographe (bay), Austl. 112/B5
Geographe (chan.), Austl. 112/B3
Georg von Neumayer, Ger., Ant. 160/Z
George (lake), Austl. 113/D2
George (pt.), Austl. 114/C3
George (riv.), Qu, Can. 123/K3
George, SAfr. 106/C4
George (lake), Ugan. 104/A3
George (lake), Fl, US 133/H4
George Land (isl.), Rus. 64/E2
George Town, Austl. 115/C4
George Town (cap.), Cay. 145/F2
George Town, Malay. 80/B2
George V (coast), Ant. 160/L
George Washington Birthplace Nat'l Mon., Va, US 133/J2
George West, Tx, US 132/D4
Georgensmünd, Ger. 54/E4
Georges (riv.), Austl. 114/G9
Georgetown, Austl. 114/A2
Georgetown, Gam. 102/B3
Georgetown (cap.), Guy. 153/G3
Georgetown, StV. 141/N9
Georgetown, Ct, US 139/E1
Georgetown, Ga, US 133/H4
Georgetown, Ky, US 130/C4
Georgetown, SC, US 133/J3
Georgetown, Tx, US 129/H5
Georgi Traykov, Bul. 49/H4
Georgia (ctry.) 63/G4
Georgia, Strait of (str.), BC, Can. 126/B3
Georgia (state), US 133/G3
Georgian (bay), On, Can. 123/H4
Georgian Bay Islands NP, On, Can. 130/D2
Georgina (riv.), Austl. 109/C3
Georgsmarienhütte, Ger. 51/F4
Gepatsch (lake), Aus. 57/G4
Gera, Ger. 40/G3
Geraardsbergen, Belg. 52/C2
Geral de Goiás, Serra (mts.), Braz. 151/J6
Geral, Serra (mts.), Braz. 157/F2
Geraldine, NZ 117/S11
Geraldton, Austl. 112/B4
Gérardmer, Fr. 56/C1
Gerasdorf bei Wien, Aus. 49/N7
Gerbéviller, Fr. 56/C1
Gerbier de Jonc (peak), Fr. 42/F4
Gerbrunn, Ger. 54/C3
Gerdau (riv.), Ger. 51/H3
Gerdine (mt.), Ak, US 134/H3
Gerede, Turk. 49/L5
Geretsried, Ger. 57/H2
Gérgal, Sp. 44/D4
Gerger, Turk. 90/D2
Gerlach, Nv, US 126/D5
Gerlachovský Štít (peak), Slvk. 41/L4
Gerlafingen, Swi. 56/D3
Germantown, Tn, US 129/K4
Germantown, Md, US 138/A5
Germany (ctry.) 40/E3
Germering, Ger. 55/E6
Germersheim, Ger. 54/B4
Germigny-l'Evêque, Fr. 30/L5
Germinaga, It. 57/E6
Germiston, SAfr. 106/E2
Gernsbach, Ger. 54/B5
Geroldsgrün, Ger. 55/E2
Gerolsbach, Ger. 55/E5
Gerolstein, Ger. 53/F3
Gerolzhofen, Ger. 54/D3
Gerpinnes, Belg. 53/D3
Gerra (Verzasca), Swi. 57/E5
Gerringong, Austl. 115/D2
Gers (riv.), Fr. 42/D5
Gersau, Swi. 57/E4
Gersfeld, Ger. 54/C2
Gersheim, Ger. 53/G5
Gerspenz (riv.), Ger. 54/B3
Gerstetten, Ger. 54/E5
Gerstheim, Fr. 56/D1
Gersthofen, Ger. 54/D6
Gerstungen, Ger. 51/H7
Gêrzê, China 70/D5
Gerze, Turk. 62/E4
Gescher, Ger. 50/E5
Geseke, Ger. 51/F5
Gespunsart, Fr. 53/D4
Gessertshausen, Ger. 54/D6
Gestro Wenz (riv.), Eth. 97/P6
Gesves, Belg. 53/E3
Geta, Fin. 39/H1
Getafe, Sp. 45/N9
Gete (riv.), Belg. 53/E2
Getinge, Swe. 38/E3
Gettorf, Ger. 38/C4
Gettysburg, SD, US 127/J4
Gettysburg, Pa, US 130/E4
Gettysburg Nat'l Mil. Park, Pa, US 138/A4
Getúlio Vargas, Braz. 155/A3
Geul (riv.), Neth. 53/E2
Geureudong (peak), Indo. 80/A3
Geurie, Austl. 115/D2
Gevaş, Turk. 90/E2
Gevelsberg, Ger. 51/E6
Gevgelija, FYROM 47/H2
Gex, Fr. 56/C5
Geyer, Ger. 55/F1
Geyersberg (peak), Ger. 54/C3
Geyikli, Turk. 47/K3
Geyser (reef), Madg. 107/H6
Geyve, Turk. 49/K5
Gez (riv.), China 87/F5
Ghadāmis, Libya 99/H3
Ghaggar (riv.), India 86/C5
Ghaghara (riv.), India 84/C2
Ghakhar, Pak. 86/C3
Ghana (ctry.) 103/E4
Ghanzi, Bots. 105/D5
Gharaunda, India 86/D5
Ghardaïa, Alg. 99/F2
Ghardaïa (prov.), Alg. 99/F3
Ghardimaou, Tun. 100/L6
Gharghoda, India 84/D4
Gharyān, Libya 96/H1
Ghāt, Libya 99/H4
Ghātāl, India 85/F4
Ghātampur, India 84/C2
Ghātsīla, India 85/F4
Ghazal, Bahr el (riv.), Chad 96/J5
Ghazaouet, Alg. 100/D2
Ghāzīpur, India 84/D3
Ghaznī, Afg. 89/J2
Ghedi, It. 58/D2
Gheens, La, US 137/P17
Ghemme, It. 58/B1
Ghenghis Khan, Wall of, Mong. 71/K2
Gheorghe Gheorghiu-Dej, Rom. 49/H2
Gheorgheni, Rom. 49/G2
Gherla, Rom. 49/F2
Ghilarza, It. 46/A2
Ghinda (Gīnda), Erit. 88/C5
Ghio (lake), Arg. 158/C5
Ghirārah (gulf), Gabon 99/H2
Ghisalba, It. 58/C1
Ghisonaccia, Fr. 46/A1
Ghotki, Pak. 82/A2
Ghugri (riv.), India 85/F3
Ghūrīān, Afg. 89/H2
Ghuzayyil, Bi'r al (well), Libya 96/H2
Giannutri (isl.), It. 46/B1
Giant's Castle (peak), SAfr. 106/E3
Giant's Causeway, NI, UK 34/B1
Giant Sequoia Nat'l Mon., Ca, US 128/C4
Giarre, It. 46/D4
Gibbons, Ab, Can. 126/E2
Gibbstown, NJ, US 138/C4
Gibloux (peak), Swi. 56/D4
Gibraleón, Sp. 44/B4
Gibraltar (pt.), Eng, UK 35/J5
Gibraltar (cap.), Gib. 44/C4
Gibraltar (str.), Mor.,Sp. 27/D5
Gibraltar (res.), Ca, US 136/A1
Gibraltar, Mi, US 135/F7
Gibraltar, Ven. 141/G6
Gibraltar Range NP, Austl. 115/E1
Gibson (des.), Austl. 109/B3
Gibson Desert Nature Reserve, Austl. 112/E3
Giddarbāha, India 86/C4
Giddings, Tx, US 129/H5
Giddings, Co, US 137/B1
Gidi (pass), Egypt 91/C4
Giebelstadt, Ger. 54/C3
Gieboldehausen, Ger. 51/H5
Gien, Fr. 42/E3
Giengen an der Brenz, Ger. 54/D5
Gier (riv.), Fr. 42/F4
Giessbachfälle (falls), Swi. 56/E4
Giessen (riv.), Fr.,Ger. 56/D1
Giessen, Ger. 54/B1
Giessendam, Neth. 50/B5
Gieten, Neth. 50/D2
Gif-sur-Yvette, Fr. 30/J5
Gīfān, Iran 63/L5
Gifford, Fl, US 133/H5
Gifford (riv.), Nun., Can. 123/H1
Giffre (riv.), Fr. 56/C5
Gifhorn, Ger. 51/H4
Gifu, Japan 77/L5
Giganta, Sierra de la (mts.), Mex. 142/C3
Gigante, Col. 152/C4
Giglio (isl.), It. 46/B1
Gijón, Sp. 44/C1
Gil de Vilches, PN, Chile 158/C2
Gila (riv.), Az, US 128/D4
Gila Bend, Az, US 128/D4
Gila Cliff Dwellings Nat'l Mon., NM, US 128/E4
Gila River Ind. Res., Az, US 137/R19
Gilbert, Mn, US 130/A2
Gilbert (riv.), Austl. 109/D2
Gilbert, Az, US 137/S19
Gilbert (isls.), Kiri. 116/G5
Gilberts, Il, US 135/P15
Gilbués, Braz. 154/A3
Gilching, Ger. 54/E6
Gilcrest, Co, US 137/C2
Gilford, NI, UK 34/B3
Gilford Park, NJ, US 138/D4
Gilgandra, Austl. 115/D1
Gilgil, Kenya 104/C3
Gilgit (riv.), Pak. 87/F5
Gilles (lake), Austl. 113/H5
Gillette, Wy, US 127/G4
Gillies Bay, BC, Can. 126/B3
Gillingham, Eng, UK 33/G4
Gillot (int'l arpt.), Reun. 107/S15
Gilly, Swi. 56/C5
Gilman Hot Springs, Ca, US 136/D3
Gilmer, Tx, US 129/J4
Gilpin, Co, US 137/A3
Gilgit (riv.), Pak. 89/K1
Gilze, Neth. 50/B5
Gīmbī, Eth. 97/N6
Gimbsheim, Ger. 54/B3
Gimel, Swi. 56/C4
Gimie (mt.), StL. 141/N9
Gimli, Mb, Can. 127/J3
Gimo, Swe. 38/H1
Gin Gin, Austl. 114/C4
Ginan, Japan 77/L5
Gingelom, Belg. 53/E2
Gingin, Austl. 112/B4
Gingindlovu, SAfr. 107/E3
Gingoog, Phil. 79/E6
Gingst, Ger. 38/E4
Ginosa, It. 46/E2
Ginowan, Japan 75/J7
Gioia (gulf), It. 46/D3
Gioia del Colle, It. 46/E2
Gioia Tauro, It. 46/D3
Giornico, Swi. 57/E5
Gioüra (isl.), Gre. 47/J3
Gioveretto (peak), It. 57/G5
Giovi (peak), It. 59/E5
Gipping (riv.), Eng, UK 33/G2
Girardot, Col. 150/D3
Girardville, Pa, US 138/B2
Giraumont, Fr. 53/E5
Girdle Ness (pt.), Sc, UK 36/D2
Giresun (prov.), Turk. 90/D1
Giresun, Turk. 90/D1
Girgnasco, It. 58/B1
Girīdīh, India 85/F3
Girifalco, It. 46/E3
Girling (res.), Eng, UK 30/C2
Giromagny, Fr. 56/C2
Girón, Ecu. 152/B5
Girón, Col. 152/C3
Girona, Sp. 45/G2
Gironcourt-sur-Vraine, Fr. 56/B1
Gironde (riv.), Fr. 42/C4
Gironella, Sp. 45/F1
Girraween NP, Austl. 115/D1
Giru, Austl. 114/B2
Girvan, Sc, UK 34/D1
Gisborne, NZ 117/T10
Gisenyi, Rwa. 104/A3
Gislaved, Swe. 38/E3
Gisors, Fr. 52/A5
Gistel, Belg. 52/B1
Gistrup, Den. 38/D3
Gitega, Buru. 104/A3
Gittsfjället (peak), Swe. 37/E2
Giubiasco, Swi. 57/F5
Giugliano in Campania, It. 48/B5
Giulianova, It. 43/K5
Giurgiu (prov.), Rom. 49/G3
Giurgiu, Rom. 49/G4
Giussano, It. 58/C1
Giv'at Brenner, Isr. 91/F8
Giv'at Ḥayyim, Isr. 91/F7
Giv'atayim, Isr. 91/F7
Give, Den. 38/C4
Givet, Fr. 53/D3
Givors, Fr. 42/F4
Givrine, Col de la (pass), Swi. 56/C5
Giyani, SAfr. 105/F5
Gizhiga (bay), Rus. 65/R3
Gizo, Sol. 116/E5
Giżycko, Pol. 39/J4
Gjerdrum, Nor. 38/D1
Gjerlev, Den. 38/D3
Gjerstad, Nor. 38/C2
Gjirokastër, Alb. 47/G2
Gjoa Haven, Nun., Can. 122/G2
Gjøvik, Nor. 38/D1
Glabbeek, Belg. 53/E2
Glace Bay, NS, Can. 131/K2
Glacier (peak), Wa, US 126/C3
Glacier Bay NP and Prsv., Ak, US 134/L4
Glacier NP, BC, Can. 126/D3
Gladbeck, Ger. 50/D5
Gladewater, Tx, US 129/J4
Gladstone, Mo, US 137/D5
Gladstone, Austl. 114/C3
Gladstone, Austl. 113/H5
Gladwin, Mi, US 130/C3
Glafsfjorden (lake), Swe. 38/D2
Glåma (riv.), Nor. 37/D3
Glamis, Sc, UK 36/D3
Glamsbjerg, Den. 38/D4
Glan, Phil. 79/E6
Glan (riv.), Ger. 40/D4
Glanamman, Wal, UK 32/C3
Gland, Swi. 56/C5
Gland (riv.), Fr. 53/D4
Glandorf, Ger. 51/F4
Glärnisch (range), Swi. 57/E3
Glarus, Swi. 57/F3
Glarus (canton), Swi. 57/E4
Glarus Alps (range), Swi. 43/H3
Glas Maol (peak), Sc, UK 36/C3
Glasgow, Mt, US 126/G3
Glasgow, Ky, US 130/C4
Glasgow, De, US 138/C4
Glasgow, Sc, UK 36/B5
Glashütten, Ger. 54/B2
Glaslyn (riv.), Wal, UK 34/D6
Glass (mts.), Ok, US 132/D2
Glass (lake), Sc, UK 36/B1
Glass (riv.), Sc, UK 36/B2
Glassboro, NJ, US 138/C4
Glastonbury, Eng, UK 32/D4
Glatt (riv.), Ger. 54/B6
Glattbach, Ger. 54/C3
Glattfelden, Swi. 57/E2
Glavinitsa, Bul. 49/H4
Glazoué, Ben. 103/F5
Glazov, Rus. 61/M4
Glems (riv.), Ger. 54/C5
Glen (riv.), Eng, UK 35/H6
Glen Burnie, Md, US 138/B5
Glen Canyon (dam), Az, US 128/E3
Glen Canyon Nat'l Rec. Area, US 128/E3
Glen Carbon, Il, US 137/H8
Glen Coe (pass), Sc, UK 36/B3
Glen Cove, NY, US 139/L8
Glen Gardner, NJ, US 138/D2
Glen Haven, Co, US 137/B2
Glen Innes, Austl. 115/D1
Glen Lyon, Pa, US 138/B1
Glen Mòr (valley), Sc, UK 36/B2
Glen Park, Mo, US 137/G9
Glen Ridge, NJ, US 139/J8
Glen Rock, Pa, US 138/B4
Glen Rock, NJ, US 139/J8
Glen Ullin, ND, US 127/H4
Glenaire, Mo, US 137/E5
Glenan, Îles de (isls.), Fr. 42/A3
Glenarm, NI, UK 34/C2
Glenarm (riv.), NI, UK 34/C2
Glenavy, NI, UK 34/B2
Glenbawn (dam), Austl. 115/D2
Glenboro, Mb, Can. 127/J3
Glencoe, SAfr. 107/E3
Glencoe, Mo, US 137/E8
Glencoe, Il, US 135/Q15
Glencoe, Sc, UK 36/A3
Glendale, Or, US 126/C5
Glendale, Az, US 137/R18
Glendale, Ca, US 136/F7
Glendale Heights, Il, US 135/P16
Glenden, Austl. 114/C3
Glendive, Mt, US 127/G4
Glendo (res.), Wy, US 127/G5
Glendora, Ca, US 136/C2
Glendun (riv.), NI, UK 34/B1
Glenealy, Ire. 34/B6
Glenelg (riv.), Austl. 115/B3
Glenelg, Md, US 138/B5
Glenelg, Sc, UK 31/R8
Glenelly (riv.), NI, UK 34/A2
Glengarry (range), Austl. 112/C3
Glenluce, Sc, UK 34/D2
Glenmere (lake), NY, US 138/D1
Glennallen, Ak, US 134/J3
Glenolden, Pa, US 138/C4
Glenorie, Austl. 114/H8
Glenpool, Ok, US 129/H4
Glenrothes, Sc, UK 36/C4
Glens Falls, NY, US 130/F3
Glenshane (pass), NI, UK 34/B2
Glenside, Pa, US 138/C3
Glenties, Ire. 31/P9
Glenveagh NP, Ire. 31/Q9
Glenview, Il, US 135/Q15
Glenwood, NJ, US 138/D1
Glenwood Springs, Co, US 128/F3
Gleouraich (peak), Sc, UK 36/A2
Glifádha, Gre. 47/N9
Glimåkra, Swe. 38/F3
Glina, Cro. 48/C3
Glinde, Ger. 51/H1
Glindow, Ger. 40/P7
Gliwice, Pol. 41/K3
Globe, Az, US 128/E4
Glockturm (peak), Aus. 57/G4
Gloggnitz, Aus. 41/H5
Głogów, Pol. 41/J3
Głogówek, Pol. 41/J3
Glonn (riv.), Ger. 54/E6
Gloria (bay), Cuba 145/G1
Glorieuses, Îles (isls.), Reun. 107/H5
Glorious (mt.), Austl. 114/E6
Glory of Russia (cape), Ak, US 134/D3
Glossop, Eng, UK 35/G5
Gloster, Ms, US 129/K5
Gloucester, Austl. 115/D1
Gloucester, On, Can. 130/F2
Gloucester, Eng, UK 32/D3
Gloucester (co.), NJ, US 138/C4
Gloucester City, NJ, US 138/C4
Gloucestershire (co.), Eng, UK 32/D3
Glovers (reef), Belz. 144/E2
Glovertown, Nf, Can. 131/L1
Głowno, Pol. 41/K3
Głubczyce, Pol. 41/J3
Głuchołazy, Pol. 41/J3
Glücksburg, Ger. 38/C4
Glückstadt, Ger. 51/G1
Glyndon, Md, US 138/B5
Glyngøre, Den. 38/C3
Glynn, NI, UK 34/C2
Gmünd, Aus. 41/H4
Gmunden, Aus. 55/G7
Gnagna (prov.), Burk. 103/E3
Gnarrenburg, Ger. 51/G2
Gniew, Pol. 39/H5
Gniezno, Pol. 41/J2
Gnjilane, Serb. 47/G1
Gnowangerup, Austl. 112/C5
Gō (riv.), Japan 74/C3
Go Cong, Viet. 78/D4
Goa (state), India 82/B4
Goālpāra, India 85/H2
Goat Fell (peak), Sc, UK 36/A5
Goba, Eth. 97/N6
Gobabis, Namb. 105/C5
Gobardānga, India 85/G4
Gobernador Castro, Arg. 158/F2
Gobernador Costa, Arg. 158/C5
Gobernador Gregores, Arg. 159/C6
Gobernador Mansilla, Arg. 159/J10
Gobi (des.), China,Mon 67/K5
Göblberg (peak), Aus. 55/G6
Gobō, Japan 74/D4
Goch, Ger. 50/D5
Gochsheim, Ger. 54/D2
Godalming, Eng, UK 33/F4
Godāvari (riv.), India 67/G8
Goddā, India 85/F3
Godeanu (peak), Rom. 48/F3
Godech, Bul. 47/H1
Goderich, On, Can. 130/D3
Godfrey, Il, US 137/G8
Gōdo, Japan 77/L5
Gödöllő, Hun. 41/K5
Godoy Cruz, Arg. 158/C2
Gods (riv.), Mb, Can. 122/G3
Gods (lake), Mb, Can. 122/G3
Gods Mercy (bay), Nun., Can. 123/H2
Godthåb (Nuuk), Grld. 119/M3
Godwin Austen (K2) (peak), Pak. 86/D2
Goéland (lake), Qu, Can. 130/E1
Goeree (isl.), Neth. 50/A5
Goes, Neth. 50/A5
Gogebic (range), Mi, US 127/L4
Göggingen, Ger. 54/D6
Gogland (isl.), Rus. 39/M1
Gogōme, Japan 76/B4
Gogounou, Ben. 103/F4
Gogra (riv.), India 82/D2
Gohad, India 84/B2
Gohāna, India 86/D5
Gohbach (riv.), Ger. 51/G3
Goiana, Braz. 154/D2
Goiandira, Braz. 155/B1
Goiânia, Braz. 151/J7
Goianinha, Braz. 154/D2
Goiás, Braz. 151/H7
Goiás (state), Braz. 154/A5
Goiatuba, Braz. 155/B1
Goil (lake), Sc, UK 36/B4
Goirle, Neth. 50/C5
Góis, Port. 44/A2
Goito, It. 59/D2
Gojō, Japan 74/D3
Gojra, Pak. 86/B4
Gök (riv.), Turk. 62/E4
Goka, Japan 77/D1
Gokase (riv.), Japan 74/B4
Gokashō, Japan 77/K5
Gokasho (bay), Japan 77/L7
Gökçeada (isl.), Turk. 90/A1
Gökçebey, Turk. 49/L5
Gökçekaya (dam), Turk. 90/B1
Göksu (riv.), Turk. 90/D2
Göksun, Turk. 90/D2
Göktepe, Turk. 91/C1
Gol, Nor. 38/C1
Gola Gokarannāth, India 84/C1
Golan Hts. (reg.), Syria 91/D3
Golasecca, It. 58/B1
Gölbaşı, Turk. 90/D2
Golbey, Fr. 56/C1
Golborne, Eng, UK 35/F5
Gölcük, Turk. 49/J5
Gold (coast), Gha. 96/E7
Gold (mtn.), Wa, US 135/B2
Gold Bar, Wa, US 135/D2
Gold Beach, Or, US 126/B5
Gold Coast, Austl. 114/D5
Gold Hill, Co, US 137/B2
Gold River, BC, Can. 126/B3
Goldach, Swi. 57/F3
Gołdap, Pol. 39/K4
Goldbach, Ger. 54/C3
Goldberg, Ger. 38/E5
Golden, BC, Can. 126/D3
Golden, Co, US 137/B3
Golden Eagle, Il, US 137/F8
Golden Gate (chan.), Ca, US 135/J11
Golden Gate Highlands NP, SAfr. 106/D3
Golden Hinde (peak), BC, Can. 126/B3
Golden Temple, India 86/C4
Goldendale, Wa, US 126/C4
Goldene Aue (reg.), Ger. 40/F3
Goldenstedt, Ger. 51/F3
Goldkronach, Ger. 55/E2
Goldman, Mo, US 137/F9
Goldmine (mtn.), Az, US 137/S19
Goldsboro, NC, US 133/J3
Goldsboro, Md, US 138/C5
Goldsby, Ok, US 137/N15
Goldsworthy, Austl. 112/C2
Goldthwaite, Tx, US 132/D4
Göle, Turk. 90/E1
Goleniów, Pol. 38/F5
Golfito NWR, CR 145/F4
Golfo Aranci, It. 46/A2
Golfo de Santa Clara, Mex. 142/B2
Gölhisar, Turk. 91/A1
Goliad, Tx, US 129/H5
Gölköy, Turk. 90/D1
Gollach (riv.), Ger. 54/D3
Göllheim, Ger. 54/B3
Gölmarmara, Turk. 90/A2
Golmud, China 70/F4
Golovin, Ak, US 134/F3
Golovnina (peak), Rus. 76/D2
Golpāyegān, Iran 88/F2
Gölpazarı, Turk. 49/K5
Gols, Aus. 43/M3
Golts, Md, US 138/C5
Golub-Dobrzyń, Pol. 41/K2
Golubovci (int'l arpt.), Serb. 47/F1
Golyam Perelik (peak), Bul. 47/J2
Golyama Kamchiya (riv.), Bul. 49/H4
Golyama Syutkya (peak), Bul. 47/J2
Goma, D.R. Congo 104/A3
Goma (int'l arpt.), D.R. Congo 104/A3
Gomaringen, Ger. 54/C6
Gomati (riv.), India 84/C2
Gombe (state), Nga. 103/H4
Gombe (riv.), Tanz. 104/A4
Gombe NP, Tanz. 104/A4
Gomera (isl.) Canl.,Sp. 98/A4
Gómez Farías, Mex. 142/D2
Gómez Palacio, Mex. 142/E3
Gomīshān, Iran 88/F1
Gommern, Ger. 40/F2
Gomoh, India 85/F4
Goms (valley), Swi. 56/E5
Gonābād, Iran 89/G2
Gonaïves, Haiti 145/H2
Gonarezhou NP, Zim. 105/F5
Gonâve (gulf), Haiti 141/G4
Gonâve (isl.), Haiti 145/H2
Gonbad-e Qābūs, Iran 89/G1
Gonbadī, Iran 87/D5
Gönc, Hun. 41/L4
Gonçalves Dias, Braz. 154/A2
Gondelsheim, Ger. 54/B4
Gonder, Eth. 97/N5
Gondia, India 82/D3
Gondomar, Sp. 44/A1
Gondomar, Port. 44/A2
Gondrecourt-le-Château, Fr. 56/B1
Gondreville, Fr. 53/E6
Gondrexange (lake), Fr. 53/F6
Gönen, Turk. 49/H5
Gonesse, Fr. 30/K5
Gong Xian, China 83/H2
Gong Xian, China 72/C4
Gong'an, China 83/K3
Gongbo'gyamda, China 83/F2
Gongcheng, China 79/B3
Gongga (peak), China 83/H2
Gonggar, China 85/H1
Gonghe, China 70/H4
Gongliu, China 70/D3
Gongola (riv.), Nga. 96/H5
Gongshan Drungzu Nuzu Zizhixian, China 83/G2
Gongzhuling, China 72/F2
Goñi, Uru. 159/K10
Gonjo, China 70/G5
Gónnoi, Gre. 47/H3
Gonohe, Japan 76/B3
Gonubie, SAfr. 106/D4
Gonyű, Hun. 48/C2
Gonzaga, It. 59/D3
Gonzales, Tx, US 129/H5
González, Mex. 143/F4
Good Hope, La, US 137/P17
Good Hope, Cape of (cape), SAfr. 106/L11
Goodenough (cape), Ant. 160/J
Goodnews Bay, Ak, US 134/F4
Goodooga, Austl. 115/C1
Goodrich, Mi, US 135/F6
Goodwick, Wal, UK 32/B2
Goodwood, SAfr. 106/L10
Goodyear, Az, US 137/R19
Gooimeer (lake), Neth. 50/C4
Goole, Eng, UK 35/H4
Goolgowi, Austl. 115/C2
Gooloogong, Austl. 115/D2
Goolwa, Austl. 113/H5
Goomalling, Austl. 112/C4
Goombungee, Austl. 114/C4
Goondiwindi, Austl. 114/C5
Goongarrie NP, Austl. 112/D4
Goor, Neth. 50/D4
Goose (lake), Mb, Can. 127/H2
Goose (pt.), La, US 137/Q16
Goose (lake), Ca, US 124/B3
Goose (pt.), De, US 138/C5
Gopālganj, India 85/E2
Gopālpur, Bang. 85/G3
Gopat (riv.), India 84/D3
Göppingen, Ger. 54/C5
Góra, Pol. 41/J3
Góra Kalwaria, Pol. 41/L3
Goražde, Bosn. 48/D4
Gorczański NP, Pol. 41/L4
Gorda (pt.), Nic. 145/F3
Gorda (pt.), Cuba 145/F1
Gorda (pt.), Nic. 145/F4
Gordevio, Swi. 57/E5
Gørding, Den. 38/C4
Gordola, Swi. 57/E5
Gordon, Austl. 115/C4
Gordon (lake), Austl. 109/D5
Gordonsbaai, SAfr. 106/L11
Gordonvale, Austl. 114/B2
Gore (pt.), Ak, US 134/H4
Goré, Chad 96/J6
Gorē, Eth. 97/N6
Gore, NZ 117/R12
Gorebridge, Sc, UK 36/C5
Görele, Turk. 90/D1
Goresbridge, Ire. 31/Q10
Gorey, Chl, UK 42/B2
Gorey, Ire. 31/Q10
Gorgān, Iran 89/F1
Gorges du Loup, Lux. 53/F4
Gorges du Ziz, Mor. 98/D2
Gorgol (pol. reg.), Mrta. 102/B3
Gorgol (riv.), Mrta. 102/B2
Gorgona, Isola di (isl.), It. 58/C6
Gorgonzola, It. 58/C1
Gori, Geo. 63/H4
Gorinchem, Neth. 50/B5
Gorizia, It. 59/G1
Gorizia (prov.), It. 59/G1
Gorj (prov.), Rom. 49/F3
Gorki, Bela. 62/D1
Gor'kiy (res.), Rus. 60/J4
Gorlice, Pol. 41/L4
Görlitz, Ger. 41/H3
Gorllwyn (peak), Wal, UK 32/C2
Gorman, Tx, US 129/H4
Gormanstown, Ire. 34/B4
Gormī, India 84/B2
Gorner (glacier), Swi. 56/D6
Gornji Milanovac, Serb. 48/E3
Gornji Vakuf, Bosn. 48/C4
Gorno-Altay Aut. Rep., Rus. 64/J4
Goro, It. 59/F3
Gorodets, Rus. 61/J4
Gorom Gorom, Burk. 103/E3
Gorong (isl.), Indo. 81/H4
Gorongoza, Moz. 105/F4
Gorontalo, Indo. 81/F3
Gorssel, Neth. 50/D4
Gorst, Wa, US 135/B2
Gortin, NI, UK 34/A2
Görwihl, Ger. 56/E2
Goryn' (riv.), Ukr. 62/C2
Gorzano (peak), It. 43/K5
Gorzów Wielkopolski, Pol. 41/H2
Gosainganj, India 84/D2
Göschenen, Swi. 57/E4
Gōse, Japan 77/J7
Gosen, Japan 75/F2
Gosford, Austl. 115/D2
Gosforth, Eng, UK 35/G2
Goshen, NJ, US 138/D5
Goshogawara, Japan 76/B3
Goslar, Ger. 51/H5
Gospić, Cro. 48/B3
Gosport, Eng, UK 33/E5
Gossas, Sen. 102/A3
Gossau, Swi. 57/F3
Gossersweiler-Stein, Ger. 53/G5
Gostivar, FYROM 47/G2
Gostyń, Pol. 41/J3
Gostynin, Pol. 41/K2
Göta (riv.), Swe. 38/G2
Götaland (reg.), Swe. 38/E3
Göteborg, Swe. 38/D3
Göteborg Och Bohus (co.), Swe. 37/D4
Gotel (mts.), Nga. 96/H6
Gotemba, Japan 75/F3
Götene, Swe. 38/E2
Gotha, Ger. 51/H7
Gotland (co.), Swe. 37/F4
Gotland (isl.), Swe. 37/F4
Gotse Delchev, Bul. 47/H2
Gotska Sandön (isl.), Swe. 39/H2
Gotska Sandön NP, Swe. 39/H2
Götsu, Japan 74/C3
Gottenheim, Ger. 56/D1
Göttingen, Ger. 51/G5
Gottmadingen, Ger. 57/E2
Gottolengo, It. 58/D2
Götzis, Aus. 57/F3
Gouda, Neth. 50/B4
Gouda, SAfr. 106/L10
Gough (isl.), StH 22/J7
Gouin (res.), Qu, Can. 123/J4
Goulais (riv.), On, Can. 130/C2
Goulburn (riv.), Austl. 115/D2
Goulburn, Austl. 115/D2
Goulburn (isls.), Austl. 109/C2
Gould, Ar, US 132/F3
Gould (mt.), Austl. 112/C3
Gouldsboro, Pa, US 138/C1
Goulimine, Mor. 98/C3
Goulmima, Mor. 98/D3
Goundam, Mali 102/E2
Goupillières, Fr. 30/H5
Gourdon, Fr. 42/D4
Gouré, Niger 103/H3
Gourin, Fr. 42/B2
Gourits (riv.), SAfr. 106/C4
Gourma (phys. reg.), Burk. 103/F3
Gourma (prov.), Burk. 103/F3
Gourma Rharous, Mali 103/E2
Gournay-en-Bray, Fr. 52/A5
Gourock, Sc, UK 36/B5
Goussainville, Fr. 30/K4
Gouvêa, Braz. 155/D1
Gouveia, Port. 44/B2
Gouvieux, Fr. 30/K4
Gouvy, Belg. 53/E3
Gouyave, Gren. 141/N9
Govardhan, India 84/A2
Goverla (peak), Ukr. 49/G1
Governador Archer, Braz. 154/A2
Governador Dix-Sept Rosado, Braz. 154/C2
Governador Eugênio Barros, Braz. 154/A2
Governador Valadares, Braz. 155/D1
Governor Generoso, Phil. 79/E6
Governors (isl.), NY, US 139/J9
Govi-Altay (prov.), Mong. 70/F2
Govĭ Altayn (mts.), Mong. 70/G3
Govind Sāgar (res.), India 86/D4
Govindgarh, India 84/C3
Gower (pen.), Wal, UK 32/B3
Goya, Arg. 157/E2
Goyllarisquizga, Peru 156/B3
Göynük, Turk. 49/K5
Goyt (riv.), Eng, UK 35/F5
Gozaisho-yama (peak), Japan 77/K5
Gözeli, Turk. 90/D2
Gozo (isl.), Malta 46/D4
Gozzano, It. 58/B1
Graaff-Reinet, SAfr. 106/D4
Graafschap (phys. reg.), Neth. 50/D4
Graben, Ger. 57/G1

Graberberg (peak), Namb. 106/B2
Grabouw, SAfr. 106/L11
Grabow, Ger. 40/F2
Graça Aranha, Braz. 154/A2
Gračac, Cro. 48/B3
Gračanica, Bosn. 48/D3
Gracemere, Austl. 114/C3
Graceville, Fl, US 133/G4
Grächen, Swi. 56/D5
Gracias, Hon. 144/D3
Gracias a Dios (cape), Hon. 145/F3
Graciosa (isl.), Azor., Port. 45/S12
Grad Sofiya (prov.), Bul. 47/H1
Gradačac, Bosn. 48/D3
Gradisca d'Isonzo, It. 59/G1
Grado, It. 59/G1
Grado, Sp. 44/B1
Grady (co.), Ok, US 137/M15
Gräfelfing, Ger. 55/E6
Grafenau, Ger. 55/G5
Gräfenberg, Ger. 54/E3
Grafenrheinfeld, Ger. 54/D3
Gräfentonna, Ger. 51/H6
Grafenwöhr, Ger. 55/E3
Graffignana, It. 58/C2
Grafing bei München, Ger. 55/E6
Gräfjell (peak), Nor. 38/C1
Grafrath, Ger. 57/H1
Grafton, Austl. 115/E1
Grafton, ND, US 127/J3
Grafton, WV, US 130/D4
Grafton, Il, US 137/G8
Grafton Passage, Austl. 114/B2
Graham, Tx, US 129/H4
Graham (isl.), Nun., Can. 123/S7
Graham (isl.), BC, Can. 122/C3
Graham Bell (isl.), Rus. 64/G1
Graham Land (phys. reg.), Ant. 160/V
Grahamstown, SAfr. 106/L11
Graian Alps (range), It. 43/G4
Grain (coast), Libr. 96/D6
Grain Valley, Mo, US 137/E5
Grainau, Ger. 57/H3
Grajaú (riv.), Braz. 151/J5
Grajaú, Braz. 154/A2
Grajewo, Pol. 39/K5
Gram, Den. 38/C4
Gramada, Bul. 48/F4
Gramastetten, Aus. 55/H6
Gramat, Fr. 42/D4
Gramat, Causse de (plat.), Fr. 42/D4
Gramatneusiedl, Aus. 49/N7
Grampian (pol. reg.), Sc, UK 36/C2
Grampian (mts.), Sc, UK 36/B3
Grampians NP, Austl. 115/B3
Grampians, The (phys. reg.), Austl. 115/B3
Gramsbergen, Neth. 50/D3
Gramsh, Alb. 47/G2
Gran, Nor. 38/D1
Gran Altiplanicie Central (plat.), Arg. 157/C6
Gran Bajo de San Julián (plain), Arg. 159/C6
Gran Bajo Oriental (plain), Arg. 157/C6
Gran Canaria (isl.), Canl.,Sp. 98/B4
Gran Canaria (int'l arpt.), Canl.,Sp. 98/B4
Gran Chaco (plain), SAm. 147/C5
Gran Isla del Maíz (isl.), Nic. 145/F3
Gran Laguna Salada (lag.), Arg. 158/D5
Gran Paradiso, PN del, It. 43/G4
Gran Piedra (hill), Cuba 145/H2
Gran Pilastro (peak), It. 43/J3
Gran Vilaya (ruin), Peru 156/B2
Granada, Sp. 44/D4
Granada, Nic. 144/E4
Granada, Co, US 152/C4
Granadilla de Abona, Canl.,Sp. 98/A3
Granados, Mex. 142/C2
Granard, Ire. 31/Q10
Granarolo dell'Emilia, It. 59/E3
Granbury, Tx, US 129/H4
Grand (co.), Ut, US 137/D4
Grand (canal), China 72/D4
Grand (falls), Kenya 104/C3
Grand (canal), Az, US 137/R18
Grand (isl.), NY, US 127/M4
Grand (isl.), Mi, US 130/C2
Grand (riv.), Mo, US 132/E2
Grand (riv.), SD, US 127/H4
Grand Bahama (isl.), Bahm. 141/F2
Grand Bank, Nf, Can. 131/L2
Grand Bassa (co.), Libr. 102/C5

Grand-Bassam, C.d'Iv. 102/E5
Grand Bay, NB, Can. 131/H2
Grand Canal d'Alsace (canal), Fr. 56/D2
Grand Canyon, Az, US 128/D3
Grand Canyon Nat'l Park, Az, US 128/D3
Grand Canyon-Parashant Nat'l Mon., Az, US 128/D3
Grand Cape Mount (co.), Libr. 102/C5
Grand Cayman (isl.), Cay. 140/E4
Grand Centre, Ab, Can. 126/F2
Grand-Charmont, Fr. 56/C2
Grand Colombier (peak), Fr. 56/B6
Grand Combine (peak), Swi. 56/D6
Grand Coulee, Wa, US 126/D4
Grand Coulee (dam), Wa, US 126/D4
Grand Drumont (peak), Fr. 56/C2
Grand Erg de Bilma (des.), Niger 96/H4
Grand Erg Occidental (des.), Alg. 93/C1
Grand Erg Oriental (des.), Alg. 93/C1
Grand Falls, NB, Can. 131/H2
Grand Falls, Nf, Can. 131/L1
Grand Forks, ND, US 127/J4
Grand Forks, BC, Can. 126/D3
Grand-Fort-Philippe, Fr. 42/E5
Grand Goâve, Haiti 145/H2
Grand Haven, Mi, US 130/C3
Grand Isle, La, US 133/F4
Grand Jide (co.), Libr. 102/D5
Grand Junction, Co, US 128/E3
Grand-Iahou, C.d'Iv. 102/D5
Grand Lake o' the Cherokees (lake), Ok, US 129/J3
Grand Manan (isl.), NB, Can. 131/H2
Grand-Mère, Qu, Can. 131/F2
Grand Mont Ruan (peak), Fr. 56/C5
Grand Muveran (peak), Swi. 56/D5
Grand-Popo, Ben. 103/F5
Grand Portage Nat'l Mon., Mn, US 127/L4
Grand Rapids, Mb, Can. 127/J2
Grand Rapids, Mi, US 130/C3
Grand Rhône (riv.), Fr. 42/F5
Grand Saint-Bernard, Col du (pass), Swi. 56/D6
Grand Staircase-Escalante Nat'l Mon., Ut, US 128/E3
Grand Taureau (peak), Fr. 56/C4
Grand Teton NP, Wy, US 128/E2
Grandcour, Swi. 56/C4
Grande (riv.), Braz. 150/J7
Grande (isl.), Braz. 155/B2
Grande (peak), It. 46/C1
Grande (peak), It. 46/C1
Grande (pt.), Pan. 145/G4
Grande (bay), Arg. 147/C8
Grande (lake), Braz. 153/H5
Grande Cache, Ab, Can. 126/D2
Grande Comore (isl.), Com. 93/G6
Grande de Gurupá, Ilha (isl.), Braz. 151/H4
Grande de Manacapuru, Lago (isl.), Braz. 150/F4
Grande de Matagalpa (riv.), Nic. 140/D5
Grande de Santiago (riv.), Mex. 142/D4
Grande de Tierra del Fuego (isl.), Arg.,Chil 157/C7
Grande Dixence, Barrage de la (dam), Swi. 56/D5
Grande do Curuaí (lake), Braz. 153/H5
Grande Miquelon (isl.), StP. 131/K2
Grande Prairie, Ab, Can. 126/D2
Grande Saline, Haiti 145/H2
Grande, Serra (mts.), Braz. 153/F4
Grande-Synthe, Fr. 52/B1
Grande-Terre (isl.), Guad. 141/J4
Grandes Jorasses (peak), It. 56/D5
Grandfresnoy, Fr. 52/B5
Grândola, Port. 44/A3
Grandpuits-Bailly-Carrois, Fr. 30/L6
Grandson, Swi. 56/C4
Grandview, Wa, US 126/D4
Grandview, Mb, Can. 127/H3

Grandview, Tx, US 129/H4
Grandview, Mo, US 137/D6
Grandvillars, Fr. 56/C2
Grandvilliers, Fr. 52/A4
Graneros, Chile 158/N9
Granfjället (peak), Swe. 38/E1
Grange, Mont de (peak), Fr. 56/C5
Grangemouth, Sc, UK 36/C4
Granger (mt.), Yk, Can. 134/L3
Granges-sur-Vologne, Fr. 56/C1
Grängesberg, Swe. 38/F1
Grangeville, Id, US 126/D4
Granisle, BC, Can. 126/B2
Granite (peak), Mt, US 126/F4
Granite, Ut, US 137/K12
Granite City, Il, US 137/G8
Granite Reef Aqueduct, Az, US 137/S18
Granites, The (peak), Austl. 113/F4
Granja, Braz. 154/B1
Granollers, Sp. 45/L6
Grantham, Eng, UK 35/H6
Grantown-on-Spey, Sc, UK 36/C2
Grants, NM, US 128/F4
Grants Pass, Or, US 126/C5
Granville, Fr. 42/C2
Granville (lake), Mb, Can. 122/F3
Grão Mogol, Braz. 154/B5
Grapeview, Wa, US 135/B3
Gras-Ellenbach, Ger. 54/B5
Grasberg, Ger. 51/F2
Grasbrunn, Ger. 55/E6
Grasø (isl.), Swe. 38/H1
Grasonville, Md, US 138/B5
Grass (lake), Il, US 135/P15
Grasse, Fr. 46/C6
Grassie, On, Can. 131/Q9
Grasslands NP, Sk, Can. 126/G3
Grassy, Austl. 115/C4
Grassy Park, SAfr. 106/L11
Grästorp, Swe. 38/E2
Gratkorn, Aus. 43/L3
Gratz, Pa, US 138/B2
Graubünden (canton), Swi. 57/F4
Graulhet, Fr. 42/E5
Graus, Fr. 45/F1
Gravatá, Braz. 154/D3
Grave, Neth. 50/C5
Gravedona, It. 57/F5
Gravelbourg, Sk, Can. 126/G3
Gravelines, Fr. 52/B2
Gravellona Toce, It. 57/E6
Gravenhurst, On, Can. 130/E2
Grävenwiesbach, Ger. 54/B2
Gravesend, Eng, UK 30/E2
Gravina di Puglia, It. 46/E2
Gravois (pt.), Haiti 145/H2
Gray, Fr. 56/B3
Grayling, Ak, US 134/F3
Grayling, Mi, US 130/C2
Grays (har.), Wa, US 126/B4
Grays (lake), Id, US 126/F5
Grays, Eng, UK 30/E2
Grayslake, Il, US 135/P15
Grayson, Sk, Can. 127/H3
Graz, Aus. 43/L3
Grazalema, Sp. 44/C4
Great (lake), Austl. 115/C4
Great (plain), Can., US 127/G3
Great (plain), Nv, US 124/C3
Great (isl.), NJ, US 139/J8
Great Abaco (isl.), Bahm. 141/F2
Great Alfold (plain), Serb. 48/D2
Great America, Ca, US 135/L12
Great Australian Bight (bay), Austl. 109/B4
Great Barrier (reef), Austl. 109/D2
Great Barrier (isl.), NZ 109/H6
Great Basin NP, Nv, US 128/D3
Great Bear (lake), NW, Can. 122/D2
Great Bend, Ks, US 129/H3
Great Bitter (lake), Egypt 91/C4
Great Brak (riv.), SAfr. 106/C3
Great Britain (isl.), UK 27/D3
Great Cedar (swamp), NJ, US 138/D5
Great Coco (isl.), Myan. 83/F5
Great Cumbrae (isl.), Sc, UK 36/B5
Great Divide (basin), Wy, US 126/F5
Great Dividing (range), Austl. 109/D2
Great Egg (har.), NJ, US 138/D5
Great Egg Harbor (riv.), NJ, US 138/D4
Great Exuma (isl.), Bahm. 141/F3
Great Falls, Mt, US 126/F4

Great Fish (riv.), SAfr. 106/D4
Great Fish (pt.), SAfr. 106/D4
Great Guana Cay (isl.), Bahm. 141/F3
Great Harwood, Eng, UK 35/F4
Great Himalaya (range), Asia 70/D6
Great Inagua (isl.), Bahm. 141/G3
Great Indian (des.), India, Pak. 82/B2
Great Karoo (plat.), SAfr. 106/C3
Great Kei (riv.), SAfr. 106/D4
Great Mis Tor (hill), Eng, UK 32/B5
Great Missenden, Eng, UK 33/F3
Great Neck, NY, US 139/L8
Great Nicobar (isl.), India 83/F6
Great Ouse (riv.), Eng, UK 33/G2
Great Oyster (bay), Austl. 115/C4
Great Palace, Rus. 61/T7
Great Palace, Rus. 61/T7
Great Peconic (bay), NY, US 139/F2
Great Pee Dee (riv.), SC, US 133/J3
Great Piece Meadows (swamp), NJ, US 139/H8
Great Rift (valley), Afr. 105/F1
Great Ruaha (riv.), Tanz. 105/F2
Great Salt (lake), Ut, US 128/D2
Great Salt Lake (lake), Ut, US 137/J11
Great Salt Lake (des.), Ut, US 124/D3
Great Sand Dunes Nat'l Park Co, US 129/F3
Great Sand Sea (des.), Egypt, Li 97/K2
Great Sandy (des.), Austl. 109/B2
Great Scarcies (riv.), SLeo. 102/B4
Great Shunner Fell (peak), Eng, UK 35/F3
Great Slave (lake), NW, Can. 122/E2
Great Smoky Mountains NP, NC,Tn, US 133/H3
Great South (bay), NY, US 139/F2
Great Stour (riv.), Eng, UK 33/G4
Great. Tenasserim (riv.), Myan. 78/B3
Great Victoria (des.), Austl. 109/B3
Great Victoria Desert Nature Rsv., Austl. 113/C4
Great Wall, China 70/J4
Great Western Tiers (mts.), Austl. 115/C4
Great Winterhoek (mts.), SAfr. 106/L10
Great Yarmouth, Eng, UK 33/H1
Great Zab (riv.), Iraq 90/E2
Great Zimbabwe (ruin), Zim. 105/F5
Greater Accra (pol. reg.), Gha. 103/F5
Greater Antilles (isls.), NAm. 141/F2
Greater Buffalo (int'l arpt.), NY, US 131/S10
Greater Cincinnati (int'l arpt.), Ky, US 130/C4
Greater London (co.), Eng, UK 30/D2
Greater Manchester (co.), Eng, UK 35/F4
Greater Pittsburgh (int'l arpt.), Pa, US 130/D3
Greater Rochester (int'l arpt.), NY, US 130/E3
Greater Sunda (isls.), Indo. 80/C4
Grebenhain, Ger. 54/C2
Grebenstein, Ger. 51/G6
Grébon (peak), Niger 96/H4
Grecco, Uru. 159/K10
Greco (peak), It. 46/C2
Greco (cape), Cyp. 91/C2
Gredos, Sierra de (mts.), Sp. 44/C2
Greece (ctry.) 47/G3
Greeley, Co, US 137/C2
Greeley Number 2 (canal), Co, US 137/C2
Greely (fjord), Nun., Can. 123/S6
Green (cape), Austl. 115/D3
Green (riv.), Ky, US 130/C4
Green (mts.), Vt, US 130/F3
Green (bay), Mi,Wi, US 127/M4
Green (riv.), Wy, US 128/E2
Green (range), Austl. 109/D3
Green (riv.), Nf, Can. 131/K2
Green Cove Springs, Fl, US 133/H4
Green Creek, NJ, US 138/D5

Green Haven, Md, US 138/B5
Green Lane (res.), Pa, US 138/C3
Green Lowther (peak), Sc, UK 36/C6
Green Pond, NJ, US 138/D1
Green River, Wy, US 126/F5
Green Valley, Az, US 128/E5
Green Valley, Ca, US 136/B1
Green Valley Lake, Ca, US 136/C2
Green Village, NJ, US 139/H9
Greenbelt, Md, US 138/B6
Greenbushes, Austl. 112/C5
Greencastle, In, US 130/C4
Greencastle, Eng, UK 34/B1
Greencastle, Wi, US 135/Q14
Greendale, Wi, US 135/P14
Greeneville, Tn, US 130/D4
Greenfield, Ma, US 131/F3
Greenfield, In, US 130/C4
Greenfield, Wi, US 135/P14
Greenfield Park, Qu, Can. 131/P7
Greenisland, NI, UK 34/C2
Greenland (sea) 119/R2
Greenmount, Md, US 138/B4
Greenock, Sc, UK 36/B5
Greenough (mt.), Ak, US 134/K2
Greenport, NY, US 139/F1
Greensboro, NC, US 133/H3
Greensboro, Al, US 133/G3
Greensburg, In, US 130/C4
Greensburg, Pa, US 130/E3
Greenvale, Austl. 114/B2
Greenville, Ca, US 126/C5
Greenville, SC, US 133/H3
Greenville, Al, US 133/G4
Greenville, Ms, US 133/F3
Greenville, NC, US 133/J3
Greenville, Tx, US 129/H4
Greenville, Ms, US 129/K4
Greenville, Oh, US 130/C3
Greenville, Li 102/C5
Greenwater (riv.), Wa, US 135/D3
Greenwell Point, Austl. 115/D2
Greenwich, Ct, US 139/L7
Greenwich (bor.), Eng, UK 30/D2
Greenwich (pt.), Ct, US 139/L8
Greenwich Observatory, Eng, UK 30/D2
Greenwood (lake), SC, US 133/H3
Greenwood, SC, US 133/H3
Greenwood, Ms, US 133/F3
Greenwood, Mo, US 137/E6
Greenwood, De, US 138/D6
Greenwood Lake, NY, US 138/D1
Greers Ferry (lake), Ar, US 129/J4
Grefrath, Ger. 50/D6
Gregório (riv.), Braz. 150/D5
Gregory, SD, US 127/J3
Gregory (range), Austl. 109/D2
Gregory (lake), Austl. 109/B3
Greifswald, Ger. 38/E4
Greifswalder Bodden (bay), Ger. 41/G2
Greimberg (peak), Aus. 43/L3
Greiz, Ger. 43/K1
Gremyachinsk, Rus. 61/N4
Grená, Den. 38/D3
Grenada, Ms, US 129/K4
Grenade, Fr. 42/D5
Grenay, Fr. 52/B3
Grenchen, Swi. 56/D3
Grenfell, Austl. 115/D2
Grenfell, Sk, Can. 127/H3
Grennach (riv.), Ger. 54/D6
Grenoble, Fr. 42/F4
Grenzach-Wyhlen, Ger. 56/D2
Gressåmoen NP, Nor. 37/E2
Greta (riv.), Eng, UK 35/E2
Gretna, Mb, Can. 127/J3
Gretna, La, US 137/P17
Gretna, Sc, UK 35/E2
Gretna, Fl, US 133/G4
Gretz-Armainvilliers, Fr. 30/L5
Greve (riv.), It. 59/E5
Greve in Chianti, It. 59/E5
Grevelingen (dam), Neth. 50/B5
Greven, Ger. 51/E4
Grevená, Gre. 47/G2
Grevená (cape), Gre. 53/F1
Grevenbroich, Ger. 54/B3
Grevenmacher (dist.), Lux. 53/F4
Grevenmacher, Lux. 53/F4
Grevesmühlen, Ger. 40/F2
Grevlingen (chan.), Neth. 50/A5
Grey (range), Austl. 109/D3
Grey (riv.), Nf, Can. 131/K2
Grey (pt.), NI, UK 34/C2
Grey Abbey, NI, UK 34/C2

Grey Hunter (peak), Yk, Can. 134/L3
Grey Peaks NP, Austl. 114/B2
Greybull, Wy, US 126/F4
Greylingstad, SAfr. 106/E2
Greymouth, NZ 117/S11
Greystones, Ire. 31/R10
Greytown, SAfr. 107/E3
Grez-Doiceau, Belg. 53/D2
Grezzana, It. 59/E1
Gribbin (pt.), Eng, UK 32/B6
Griefensee (lake), Swi. 57/E3
Griekwastad, SAfr. 106/C3
Griend (isl.), Neth. 50/C2
Gries am Brenner, Aus. 57/H3
Griesheim, Ger. 54/B3
Grieskirchen, Aus. 55/G6
Griesskogel (peak), Aus. 57/H3
Griesstätt, Ger. 55/F7
Griffin, Ga, US 133/G3
Griffith, Austl. 115/C2
Griffith, In, US 135/R16
Griffith Park, Ca, US 136/F7
Grigna (peak), It. 57/F6
Grignano Polesine, It. 59/D2
Grigny, Fr. 30/K6
Grijalva (riv.), Mex. 144/C2
Grijpskerk, Neth. 50/D2
Grim (cape), Austl. 115/C4
Grimbergen, Belg. 53/D2
Grimes, Ca, US 136/B3
Grimmen, Ger. 38/E4
Grimisuat, Swi. 56/D5
Grimma, Ger. 43/J1
Grimsby, On, Can. 131/Q9
Grimsby, Eng, UK 35/H4
Grimselpass (pass), Swi. 57/F4
Grimsey (isl.), Ice. 37/N6
Grimstad, Nor. 38/C2
Grindavík, Ice. 37/M7
Grindelwald, Swi. 56/E4
Grindsted, Den. 38/C4
Grinnell (pen.), Nun., Can. 123/S7
Grintavec (peak), Slov. 43/L3
Griqualand East (reg.), SAfr. 106/E3
Griqualand West (reg.), SAfr. 106/C2
Gris-Nez (cape), Fr. 52/A2
Grise Fiord, Nun., Can. 123/S7
Grisslehamn, Swe. 39/H1
Grisy-les-Plâtres, Fr. 30/J4
Grisy-Suisnes, Fr. 30/L5
Grivette (riv.), Fr. 30/L4
Grizzly (bay), Ca, US 135/K10
Grmeč (mts.), Bosn. 48/C3
Groairas, Braz. 154/B1
Grobbendonk, Belg. 50/B6
Gröbenzell, Ger. 55/E6
Groblershoop, SAfr. 106/C3
Grodkow, Pol. 41/J3
Grodzisk Wielkopolski, Pol. 41/H2
Groenlo, Neth. 50/D4
Groesbeek, Neth. 50/C5
Groix (isl.), Fr. 42/B3
Grójec, Pol. 41/L3
Grömitz, Ger. 38/D4
Gromo, It. 57/F6
Gronau, Ger. 51/E4
Gronau, Ger. 51/G4
Groningen (prov.), Neth. 50/D2
Groningen, Neth. 50/D2
Grönlait (peak), It. 57/H5
Grono, Swi. 57/F5
Groot (riv.), SAfr. 105/D7
Groot-Marico (riv.), SAfr. 106/D2
Groote Eylandt (isl.), Austl. 109/C2
Grootegast, Neth. 50/D2
Grootfontein, Namb. 105/C4
Grootvloer (salt pan), SAfr. 106/C3

Grosse Aue (riv.), Ger. 51/F4
Grosse Ile, Mi, US 135/F7
Grosse Laber (riv.), Ger. 55/F5
Grosse Mühl (riv.), Aus. 55/G6
Grosse Münzenberg (peak), Namb. 106/A2
Grosse Nister (riv.), Ger. 53/G2
Grosse Pointe, Mi, US 135/G7
Grosse Pointe Farms, Mi, US 135/G7
Grosse Pointe Park, Mi, US 135/G7
Grosse Pointe Shores, Mi, US 135/G7
Grosse Pointe Woods, Mi, US 135/G7
Grosse Rodl (riv.), Aus. 55/H6
Grossengottern, Ger. 51/H6
Grossenkneten, Ger. 51/F3
Grossenlüder, Ger. 54/C1
Grossenwiehe, Ger. 38/C4
Grosser Ahrensberg (peak), Ger. 51/G5
Grosser Aletsch (glacier), Swi. 56/D5
Grosser Arber (peak), Ger. 55/G4
Grosser Beer-Berg (peak), Ger. 43/J1
Grosser Bösenstein (peak), Aus. 43/L3
Grosser Daumen (peak), Ger. 57/G3
Grosser Feldberg (peak), Ger. 54/B2
Grosser Gleichberg (peak), Ger. 54/D2
Grosser Heuberg (mts.), Ger. 54/B6
Grosser Knechtsand (isl.), Ger. 51/F1
Grosser Peilstein (peak), Aus. 43/J1
Grosser Plessower (lake), Ger. 40/P7
Grosser Priel (peak), Aus. 43/L3
Grosser Rachel (peak), Ger. 55/G5
Grosser Seddiner (lake), Ger. 40/P7
Grosser Selchower (lake), Ger. 40/Q7
Grosses Meer (lake), Ger. 51/E2
Grosses Moor (swamp), Ger. 51/H3
Grosseto, It. 43/J5
Grossgerau, Ger. 54/B3
Grossglockner (peak), Aus. 43/K3
Grosshansdorf, Ger. 51/H1
Grossheubach, Ger. 54/C3
Grosskrotzenburg, Ger. 54/B2
Grossmaischeid, Ger. 53/G3
Grosso (cape), Fr. 46/D5
Grossrosseln, Ger. 53/F5
Grosssiegharts, Aus. 41/H4
Grosswallstadt, Ger. 54/C3
Grosswangen, Swi. 56/E3
Grosuplje, Slov. 43/L4
Grote Gete (riv.), Belg. 53/D2
Groton, SD, US 127/J4
Grottaglie, It. 47/E2
Grottammare, It. 43/K5
Grotte de Han, Belg. 53/D3
Grouard Mission, Ab, Can. 126/D2
Groundhog (riv.), On, Can. 130/D1
Grouw, Neth. 50/C2
Grovdageaidnu-Kautokeino, Nor. 37/G1
Grove, Ok, US 129/J3
Grove, Pa; Md, US 138/B5
Grover, Mo, US 137/F8
Grover City, Ca, US 128/B4
Groveton, Tx, US 129/J5
Groznyy, Rus. 63/H4
Grubišno Polje, Cro. 48/D2
Grudovo, Bul. 49/H4
Grudziądz, Pol. 41/K2
Grumeti (riv.), Tanz. 104/B3
Grums, Swe. 38/E2
Grünau im Almtal, Aus. 49/P7
Grünberg, Aus. 55/H7
Gründau, Ger. 54/C2
Grune (pt.), Eng, UK 35/E2
Grünstadt, Ger. 54/B3
Gruyères, Swi. 56/D4
Gryazi, Rus. 62/F1
Gryfice, Pol. 38/F5
Gryfino, Pol. 41/H2
Gryon, Swi. 56/D5
Gschwandt, Aus. 55/G7
Gschwend, Ger. 54/C5

Gsteig, Swi. 56/D5
Gua, India 85/E4
Guabún (pt.), Chile 158/B4
Guaca, Col. 152/C3
Guacanayabo (gulf), Cuba 141/F3
Guacarí, Col. 152/B4
Guachochi, Mex. 142/D3
Guácimo, CR 145/F4
Guaçuí, Braz. 155/D2
Guadalajara, Mex. 142/E4
Guadalajara, Sp. 44/D2
Guadalcanal, Sp. 44/C3
Guadalcanal (isl.), Sol. 116/E6
Guadalentín (riv.), Sp. 44/D4
Guadalimar (riv.), Sp. 44/D3
Guadalix (riv.), Sp. 45/N8
Guadalope (riv.), Sp. 45/E2
Guadalquivir (riv.), Sp. 44/C4
Guadalupe, Braz. 154/B2
Guadalupe, Col. 152/C4
Guadalupe, Mex. 142/E4
Guadalupe, Mex. 143/E3
Guadalupe (isl.), Mex. 119/E7
Guadalupe, Pan. 152/B2
Guadalupe, Peru 156/C4
Guadalupe, Sp. 44/C3
Guadalupe (mts.), NM,Tx, US 132/D3
Guadalupe (co.), Tx, US 137/U20
Guadalupe (peak), Tx, US 129/F5
Guadalupe (riv.), Tx, US 140/B2
Guadalupe Mountains NP, Tx, US 129/F5
Guadalupe, Sierra de (mts.), Sp. 44/C3
Guadalupe Victoria, Mex. 142/B1
Guadalupe Victoria, Mex. 142/D3
Guadalupe Victoria, Mex. 143/M7
Guadarrama (riv.), Sp. 44/C3
Guadarrama, Ven. 152/D2
Guadarrama, Sierra de (mts.), Sp. 44/C2
Guadeloupe (isl.), Fr. 141/N8
Guadeloupe NP, Fr. 141/N8
Guadeloupe Passage (chan.), Fr. 141/J4
Guadiana (riv.), Port.,Sp. 44/B3
Guadiana Menor (riv.), Sp. 44/D4
Guadix, Sp. 44/D4
Guafo (isl.), Chile 158/B4
Guafo, Boca del (mouth) 157/B5
Guagua Pichincha (peak), Ecu. 152/B5
Guaíba, Braz. 155/B4
Guaíba (riv.), Braz. 155/B4
Guáimaro, Cuba 145/G1
Guainía (riv.), Col. 150/E3
Guainía (dept.), Col. 152/D4
Guaiquinima (peak), Ven. 153/F1
Guaira, Braz. 157/F1
Guaíra, Braz. 155/B2
Guaiteca (isl.), Chile 158/B4
Guajará-Mirim, Braz. 150/E6
Guajira (pen.), Col. 147/B1
Gualaceo, Ecu. 152/B5
Gualán, Guat. 144/D3
Gualeguay, Arg. 159/J10
Gualeguaychú, Arg. 159/J10
Gualtieri, It. 58/D3
Guam (isl.), Pac., US 116/D3
Guamal, Col. 152/C2
Guamblín, Isla (isl.), Chile 158/A5
Guamote, Ecu. 156/B1
Guamúchil, Mex. 142/C3
Gu'an, China 72/H7
Guan Xian, China 70/H5
Guan Xian, China 72/H5
Guanabacoa, Cuba 145/F1
Guanabara (bay), Braz. 211/K7
Guanahacabibes (gulf), Cuba 144/E1
Guanahacabibes (pen.), Cuba 145/E1
Guanaja (isl.), Hon. 144/E2
Guanaja, Hon. 144/E2
Guanajay, Cuba 145/F1
Guanajuato, Mex. 143/E4
Guanajuato (state), Mex. 140/A3
Guanambi, Braz. 154/B4
Guanapalo (riv.), Ven. 152/D2
Guanare, Ven. 152/D2
Guanare (riv.), Ven. 152/D2
Guanarito, Ven. 152/D2
Guandi (mtn.), China 72/B3
Guane, Cuba 145/E1
Guangchang, China 79/C2
Guangde, China 72/D5
Guangdong (prov.), China 71/K7
Guangfeng, China 79/C2

Guangling, China 72/C3
Guanglu (isl.), China 73/B3
Guangnan, China 83/J3
Guangping, China 79/C2
Guangping, China 72/C3
Guangrao, China 72/C4
Guangshan, China 72/C4
Guangxi Zhuangzu (aut. reg.), China 70/J7
Guangyuan, China 70/J5
Guangze, China 79/C2
Guangzhou, China 83/K3
Guanhães, Braz. 155/D1
Guanipa (riv.), Ven. 150/F2
Guannan, China 72/C4
Guantánamo, Cuba 145/H1
Guantánamo Bay U.S. Naval Base, Cuba 145/H2
Guantao, China 72/C3
Guanting (res.), China 72/G6
Guanujo, Ecu. 152/B5
Guanyun, China 72/D4
Guapi, Col. 152/B4
Guaporé, Braz. 155/B4
Guaporé (riv.), Braz. 147/C4
Guaqui, Bol. 156/D5
Guarabira, Braz. 154/D2
Guaraci, Braz. 155/B2
Guaraciaba do Norte, Braz. 154/B2
Guaraí, Braz. 151/J5
Guaramirim, Braz. 155/B3
Guaranda, Ecu. 152/B5
Guarani, Braz. 211/K6
Guarapari, Braz. 155/D2
Guarapuava, Braz. 155/B3
Guararé, Braz. 211/K6
Guararapes (int'l arpt.), Braz. 154/D3
Guararapes, Braz. 155/B2
Guararema, Braz. 211/G8
Guaratinga, Braz. 154/C5
Guaratinguetá, Braz. 211/H7
Guaratuba, Braz. 155/B3
Guarda (dist.), Port. 44/B2
Guarda, Port. 44/B2
Guardamar, Sp. 45/E3
Guardiamiglio, It. 58/C2
Guardarrama (riv.), Sp. 45/N8
Guardia Alta (peak), It. 57/H4
Guardia Mitre, Arg. 158/E4
Guardia Sanframondi, It. 48/B5
Guardiagrele, It. 46/D1
Guareña, Sp. 44/B3
Guarico (pt.), Cuba 145/H1
Guárico (riv.), Ven. 141/H6
Guárico (state), Ven. 153/F2
Guárico, Embalse de (res.), Ven. 150/F2
Guarujá, Braz. 211/G9
Guarulhos (int'l arpt.), Braz. 211/G8
Guarulhos, Braz. 211/G8
Guarumal, Pan. 152/A3
Guasave, Mex. 142/C3
Guasdualito, Ven. 152/D3
Guasimal, Cuba 145/G1
Guasipati, Ven. 153/F3
Guastalla, It. 58/D2
Guatemala (ctry.) 144/D3
Guatemala (cap.), Guat. 144/D3
Guateque, Col. 152/C3
Guaviare (dept.), Col. 152/C4
Guaviare (riv.), Col. 147/C2
Guaxupé, Braz. 211/G6
Guayabero (riv.), Col. 152/C4
Guayabo, Cayo (isl.), Cuba 145/G1
Guayalejo (riv.), Mex. 143/E4
Guayama, PR 141/M8
Guayape (riv.), Hon. 144/E3
Guayaquil (gulf), Ecu.,Peru 147/A3
Guayaquil, Ecu. 152/B5
Guayaquil, Gulf of (gulf), Ecu.,Peru 156/A1
Guayaramerin, Bol. 150/E6
Guayas, Ecu. 152/B5
Guayas (prov.), Ecu. 152/C5
Guayas (riv.), Col. 152/C4
Guaymas, Mex. 142/C3
Gubakha, Rus. 61/N4
Gubbio, It. 59/F6
Guben, Ger. 41/H3
Gubin, Pol. 41/H3
Gubkin, Rus. 62/F2
Gucheng, China 72/B4
Gucheng, China 72/C3
Gúdar, Sierra de (range), Sp. 45/E2
Gudenå (riv.), Den. 38/D3
Gudensberg, Ger. 51/G6
Gudermes, Rus. 63/H4
Gudivāda, India 85/D2
Gudow, Ger. 51/H1
Güdül, Turk. 49/L5
Gudūr, India 82/C5
Guebli (lake), Mrta. 98/B5
Guebwiller, Fr. 56/D2
Guecho, Sp. 44/D1
Guelb Azefal (hill), Mrta. 98/B5
Guelb er Rîchât (peak), Mrta. 98/B4
Guelma, Alg. 100/K6
Guelma (prov.), Alg. 100/K6
Guelph, On, Can. 130/D3

Guémené-Penfao, Fr. 42/C3
Guénange, Fr. 53/F5
Guérande, Fr. 42/B3
Guerara, Alg. 99/G2
Guérard, Fr. 30/L5
Guercif, Mor. 100/C2
Guéret, Fr. 42/D3
Guernes, Fr. 30/G4
Guernsey (int'l arpt.), ChI, UK 42/B2
Guernsey (isl.), ChI, UK 42/B2
Gümüşhane (prov.), Turk. 90/D1
Guerville, Fr. 30/H5
Guesle (riv.), Fr. 30/H5
Gueugnon, Fr. 42/F3
Gueux, Fr. 52/C5
Gugē (peak), Eth. 97/N6
Guggisberg, Swi. 56/D4
Gugielmo Marconi (int'l arpt.), It. 59/E3
Güglingen, Ger. 54/B4
Guguletu, SAfr. 106/L11
Gui (riv.), China 79/B3
Guiana Highlands (uplands), SAm. 147/C2
Guichen, Fr. 42/C3
Guichón, Uru. 159/K10
Guidder, Camr. 96/H6
Guidimaka (pol. reg.), Mrta. 102/B3
Guiding, China 83/J2
Guidizzolo, It. 58/D2
Guidong, China 83/K2
Guidonia, It. 46/C2
Guiglo, C.d'Iv. 102/D5
Guignes-Rabutin, Fr. 30/L6
Guihulngan, Phil. 81/F1
Guija, Moz. 105/F5
Guijuelo, Sp. 44/C2
Guilder (peak), Ut, US 137/L11
Guilderton, Austl. 112/B4
Guildford, Eng, UK 30/B3
Guilherand, Fr. 42/F4
Guilin (int'l arpt.), China 79/B2
Guilin, China 83/K2
Guillaume-Delisle (lake), Qu, Can. 123/J3
Guillena, Sp. 44/B4
Guimarães, Braz. 154/A1
Guimarães, Port. 44/A2
Guimba, Phil. 79/D4
Guimeng (mtn.), China 72/D4
Guinan, China 70/H4
Guinard (riv.), Sc, UK 34/A3
Guinea (ctry.) 102/C4
Guinea (gulf), Afr. 93/C4
Guinea-Bissau (ctry.) 102/B3
Guînes, Fr. 52/A2
Guingamp, Fr. 42/B2
Guinguinéo, Sen. 102/B3
Guiones (pt.), CR 144/E4
Guipavas, Fr. 42/A2
Guipavas (int'l arpt.), Fr. 42/A2
Guir, Oued (riv.), Alg. 98/E2
Guiratinga, Braz. 151/H7
Güira, Ven. 153/F2
Güiria, Ven. 153/F2
Guisborough, Eng, UK 35/G2
Guiscard, Fr. 52/C4
Guise, Fr. 52/C4
Guitiriz, Sp. 44/B1
Guitrancourt, Fr. 30/H4
Guiuan, Phil. 79/E5
Güiza (riv.), Col. 152/B4
Guizhou (prov.), China 70/J6
Gujan-Mestras, Fr. 42/C4
Gujar Khān, Pak. 86/B3
Gujarāt (state), India 82/B3
Gujrānwala, Pak. 86/C3
Gujrāt, Pak. 86/C3
Gukovo, Rus. 62/F2
Gulaothi, India 84/A1
Gulargambone, Austl. 115/D1
Gulbarga, India 85/D1
Guldenbach (riv.), Ger. 53/G2
Güldüzü, Turk. 91/E1
Gülistow, Ger. 38/E5
Gulen, Nor. 38/A1
Gulf Coastal (plain), Tx, US 132/D5
Gulf Islands Nat'l Seashore, US 133/F4
Gulf Shores, Al, US 133/G4
Gulfport, Ms, US 133/F4
Gulgong, Austl. 115/D2
Guliston, Uzb. 87/E4
Gulkana, Ak, US 134/J3
Gull Lake, Sk, Can. 126/F3
Gullane, Sc, UK 36/C4
Gullane (pt.), Sc, UK 36/C4
Gullspång, Swe. 38/F3
Gulmarg, India 86/C2
Gülnar, Turk. 91/C1
Gulpen, Neth. 53/E2
Gulu, Uga. 104/B2
Gulyantsi, Bul. 49/G4
Gumal (riv.), Pak. 86/A4
Gumare, Bots. 105/D4
Gumbrechtshoffen, Fr. 53/G6
Gumdag, Trkm. 63/K5
Gumeracha, Austl. 113/M8

Gumia, India 85/E4
Gumla, India 85/E4
Gumma (pref.), Japan 75/F2
Gummersbach, Ger. 53/G1
Gumpoldskirchen, Aus. 49/N7
Gumti (riv.), India 85/H4
Gümüşhacıköy, Turk. 62/E4
Gümüşhane, Turk. 90/D1
Gümüşhane (prov.), Turk. 90/D1
Guna (peak), Eth. 97/N5
Gunbower, Austl. 115/C2
Gundagai, Austl. 115/D2
Gundelfingen, Ger. 56/D1
Gundelfingen, Ger. 54/D5
Gundelfingen an der Donau, Ger. 54/C4
Gundelsheim, Ger. 54/C4
Gundershoffen, Fr. 53/G6
Gündoğmuş, Turk. 91/C1
Güneydoğu Toroslar (mts.), Turk. 90/D2
Gunisao (riv.), Mb, Can. 127/J2
Gunisao (lake), Mb, Can. 127/J2
Gunja, Cro. 48/D3
Gunn City, Mo, US 137/E6
Gunnaur, India 84/B1
Gunnebo, Swe. 38/G3
Gunnedah, Austl. 115/D1
Gunning, Austl. 115/D2
Gunnison (riv.), Co, US 128/F3
Gunnison, Ut, US 128/E3
Gunpowder (riv.), Md, US 138/B5
Gunpowder Falls State Park, Md, US 138/B5
Gunskirchen, Aus. 55/G6
Guntersblum, Ger. 54/B3
Guntersville, Al, US 133/G3
Guntersville (lake), Al, US 133/G3
Guntramsdorf, Aus. 49/N7
Guntūr, India 82/D4
Günz (riv.), Ger. 40/F4
Günzburg, Ger. 54/D6
Gunzenhausen, Ger. 54/D4
Guoyang, China 72/D4
Gura Humorului, Rom. 49/G2
Guragē (peak), Eth. 97/N6
Gurbantünggut (des.), China 70/E2
Gurdāspur, India 86/C3
Gurgaon, India 86/D5
Gürgentepe, Turk. 90/D1
Gurguéia (riv.), Braz. 151/K6
Guri (res.), Ven. 147/C2
Guri (dam), Ven. 153/F3
Gurk (riv.), Aus. 43/L3
Gurkthaler Alpen (mts.), Aus. 43/K3
Guro, Moz. 105/F4
Gürpınar, Turk. 90/E2
Gursarai, India 84/B3
Gürsu, Turk. 90/B1
Guru Sikhar (peak), India 89/K4
Gürün, Turk. 90/D2
Gurupi, Braz. 151/J6
Gurupi (riv.), Braz. 151/J4
Gurupi, Serra do (mts.), Braz. 151/J4
Gus'-Khrustal'nyy, Rus. 60/J5
Gusau, Nga. 103/G3
Gushi, China 72/C4
Gushikawa, Japan 75/J7
Gusinje, Serb. 47/F1
Guskhara, India 85/F4
Guspini, It. 46/A3
Gussola, It. 58/D2
Gustavo Díaz Ordaz, Mex. 142/C3
Gustavo Díaz Ordaz, Mex. 142/B3
Gusterath, Ger. 53/F4
Güstrow, Ger. 38/E5
Gusum, Swe. 38/G2
Gutau, Aus. 55/H6
Gütersloh, Ger. 51/F5
Guthrie, Tx, US 129/G4
Guthrie, Ok, US 137/N14
Gutiérrez Zamora, Mex. 143/M6
Guttannen, Swi. 57/E4
Guttenberg, NJ, US 139/K8
Gutulia NP, Nor. 37/E3
Guwāhāti, India 83/F2
Guxhagen, Ger. 51/G6
Guxian, China 72/B3
Guy Fawkes River NP, Austl. 115/E1
Guyana (ctry.) 153/G3
Guyancourt, Fr. 30/J5
Guyandotte (riv.), WV, US 133/H2
Guyang, China 72/B2
Guyenne (riv.), Fr. 42/C4
Guymon, Ok, US 129/G3
Guyra, Austl. 115/D1
Güzelbağ, Turk. 91/B1
Güzeloba, Turk. 91/B1
Güzelsu, Turk. 91/E1
Guzhang, China 83/J2

Guzhen, China 72/D4
Guzmán (lake), Mex. 142/D2
Gwādar, Pak. 89/H3
Gwaii Haanas NP, BC, Can. 122/C3
Gwalior, India 84/B2
Gwanda, Zim. 105/E5
Gwandalan, Austl. 115/D2
Gwash (riv.), Eng, UK 33/F1
Gwaunceste (peak), Wal, UK 32/C2
Gwda (riv.), Pol. 41/J2
Gwersyllt, Wal, UK 35/E5
Gweru, Zim. 105/E4
Gwydir (riv.), Austl. 115/D1
Gwynedd (co.), Wal, UK 34/D5
Gwyrfai (riv.), Wal, UK 34/D5
Gy, Fr. 56/B3
Gya (pass), China 85/E1
Gyaca, China 83/F3
Gyál, Hun. 49/R10
Gyasikan, Gha. 103/F5
Gyda (pen.), Rus. 55/F5
Gyhum, Ger. 51/G2
Gyirong, China 85/E1
Gyldenløveshøj (peak), Den. 38/D4
Gympie, Austl. 114/D4
Gyōda, Japan 77/C1
Gyoma, Hun. 48/E2
Gyömrő, Hun. 49/R10
Győr, Hun. 48/C2
Győr-Moson-Sopron (co.), Hun. 41/J5
Győrújbarát, Hun. 48/C2
Gyumri, Arm. 63/G4
Gyyzylarbat, Trkm. 63/L5
Gžira, Malta 46/L7

H

Hå, Nor. 38/A2
Ha Giang, Viet. 83/H3
Ha Noi (Hanoi) (cap.), Viet. 83/J3
Haacht, Belg. 53/D2
Haag, Aus. 55/H6
Haag am Hausruck, Aus. 55/G6
Haag an der Amper, Ger. 55/E6
Haag in Oberbayern, Ger. 55/E6
Haaksbergen, Neth. 50/D4
Haaltert, Belg. 52/D2
Haamstede, Neth. 50/A5
Ha'apai Group (isl.), Tonga 117/H7
Haapavesi, Fin. 60/G2
Haapsalu, Est. 39/K2
Haar, Ger. 55/E6
Haardt (mts.), Ger. 53/G5
Haarlem, Neth. 50/B4
Haast, NZ 117/R11
Haasts Bluff Abor. Land, Austl. 113/F2
Hab (riv.), Pak. 89/J3
Habahe, China 70/E2
Habartov, Czh. 55/F2
Habbānīyah, Iraq 90/E3
Habicht (peak), Aus. 57/H3
Habiganj, Bang. 85/H3
Habikino, Japan 77/J6
Habomai (isls.), Rus. 76/D2
Habonim, Isr. 91/F6
Haboro, Japan 76/B1
Hacha (falls), Ven. 153/F3
Hache (riv.), Ger. 51/F3
Hachenburg, Ger. 53/G2
Hachijō, Japan 75/F4
Hachikai, Japan 77/L5
Hachimori, Japan 76/B3
Hachinohe, Japan 76/B3
Hachiōji, Japan 75/F3
Hacıbektaş, Turk. 90/C2
Hacienda Heights, Ca, US 136/G8
Hacılar, Turk. 90/C2
Hack (mt.), Austl. 113/H4
Hackensack, NJ, US 139/J8
Hackensack (riv.), NJ, US 139/J9
Hackettstown, NJ, US 138/D2
Hackney (bor.), Eng, UK 30/C4
Haddenham, Eng, UK 30/D3
Haddington, Sc, UK 36/D5
Haddonfield, NJ, US 138/C4
Hadejia (riv.), Nga. 93/D3
Hadelner (canal), Ger. 51/F1
Hadera, Isr. 91/F7
Haderslev, Den. 38/D4
Hadhramaut (reg.), Yem. 88/E6

Hadım, Turk. 91/C1
Hadjout, Alg. 100/G4
Hadleigh, Eng, UK 30/E2
Hadley (bay), Nun., Can. 122/F1
Hadlow, Eng, UK 30/E3
Haka, Myan. 83/F3
Hadrian's Wall, Eng, UK 35/F1
Hadselfjorden (inlet), Nor. 37/E1
Hadsten, Den. 38/D3
Hadsund, Den. 38/D3
Haeju (bay), NKor. 73/C4
Haeju, NKor. 73/C3
Haena (pt.), Hi, US 124/S9
Haenam, SKor. 73/D5
Hafik, Turk. 90/D2
Hāfizābād, Pak. 86/B3
Hāflong, India 83/F2
Hafnarfjördhur, Ice. 37/N7
Hafnarhreppur, Ice. 37/N7
Haft Gel, Iran 88/E2
Hafun (riv.), Som. 97/R5
Hagåtña (cap.), Guam 116/D3
Hagelstadt, Ger. 55/F5
Hagemeister (isl.), Ak, US 134/F4
Hagen, Ger. 51/E6
Hagen am Teutoburger Wald, Ger. 51/F4
Hagen im Bremischen, Ger. 51/F2
Hagenow, Ger. 51/J2
Hagerman, NM, US 132/B3
Hagerstown, Md, US 130/E4
Hagetmau, Fr. 42/C5
Hagfors, Swe. 38/F1
Hagi, Japan 74/B3
Hagnau am Bodensee, Ger. 57/F2
Hags (pt.), Ire. 31/P10
Hague, Sk, Can. 127/G2
Hague, Cap de la (cape), Fr. 42/C2
Haguenau, Fr. 53/G6
Hahashima (isls.), Japan 116/D2
Hahaya (int'l arpt.), Com. 107/G5
Hahle (riv.), Ger. 51/H5
Hahndorf, Austl. 113/M9
Hahnenbach (riv.), Ger. 53/G4
Hahnstätten, Ger. 53/G3
Hahnville, La, US 137/P17
Haïbā Awbārī (des.), Libya 96/H2
Hai (riv.), China 72/C3
Hai Duong, Viet. 78/D1
Hai Phong, Viet. 83/J3
Hai Van (pass), Viet. 78/E2
Hai'an, China 72/E4
Haibach, Ger. 54/C3
Haibara, Japan 77/J6
Haicheng, China 73/B2
Haidenaab (riv.), Ger. 55/E3
Haidershofen, Aus. 55/H6
Haifa (dist.), Isr. 91/F7
Haifeng, China 79/C3
Haiger, Ger. 43/H1
Haikou (int'l arpt.), China 79/B3
Haikou, China 83/K3
Hailar-Pauwela, Hi, US 124/T10
Hailey, Id, US 124/T10
Hailong, China 71/L2
Hailsham, Eng, UK 30/E5
Hailun, China 71/N2
Haimen, China 72/E4
Haimhausen, Ger. 55/E6
Haiming, Aus. 57/G3
Haiming, Ger. 55/F6
Haina, Ger. 51/F6
Hainan (prov.), China 70/J8
Hainan (str.), China 79/B3
Hainan (isl.), China 67/L8
Hainaut (prov.), Belg. 52/B2
Hainburg, Ger. 54/C1
Haines, Ak, US 134/L4
Haines City, Fl, US 133/H4
Haines Junction, Yk, Can. 134/L3
Hainesville, NJ, US 138/D1
Hainesville, Il, US 135/P15
Hainich (mts.), Ger. 40/F3
Haining, China 72/L9
Haiti (ctry.) 145/H2
Haixia (str.), China 71/K7
Haixing, China 72/C3
Haiyan, China 79/B3
Haiyan, China 70/H4
Haiyang (isl.), China 73/B3
Haiyang, China 73/B3
Haiyuan, China 70/J4
Haizhou (bay), China 72/D4
Hadd, Ra's al (pt.), Oman 89/G4
Hajdu-Bihar (co.), Hun. 49/F2
Hajdúböszörmény, Hun. 49/F2
Hajdúdorog, Hun. 41/L5
Hajdúhadház, Hun. 41/L5
Hajdúnánás, Hun. 41/L5
Hajdúszoboszló, Hun. 41/L5
Hajiki-zaki (pt.), Japan 75/F1
Hājīpur, India 85/F3
Hajjah, Yem. 88/D5

Hajnówka, Pol. 41/M2
Hājo, India 85/H2
Hajós, Hun. 49/D2
Haka, Myan. 83/F3
Hakee (mt.), Austl. 113/G3
Hakkari (prov.), Turk. 90/E2
Hakken-san (peak), Japan 74/D3
Hakkōda-san (peak), Japan 76/B3
Hakodate, Japan 76/B3
Hakone, Japan 77/C3
Hakone-yama (peak), Japan 77/C3
Haku-san (peak), Japan 75/E2
Hakui, Japan 75/E2
Hakusan, Japan 77/K6
Hakusan NP, Japan 75/E2
Hakushū, Japan 77/C2
Hāla, Pak. 89/J3
Halab (prov.), Syria 90/D2
Halab (Aleppo), Syria 91/E1
Halabjah, Iraq 88/E1
Halachó, Mex. 143/M6
Halawa, Hi, US 124/T10
Halcon (mt.), Phil. 81/F1
Halden, Nor. 38/D2
Haldensleben, Ger. 40/F2
Haldenwang, Ger. 57/G2
Haldia, India 85/G4
Haldībāri, India 85/G2
Haldimand, On, Can. 131/Q10
Haldimand-Norfolk On, Can. 131/Q10
Hale (riv.), Austl. 113/G3
Hale (mt.), Austl. 113/G3
Hale, Eng, UK 35/F5
Haleakala NP, Hi, US 124/T11
Haledon, NJ, US 139/J8
Haleiwa, Hi, US 124/V12
Halen, Belg. 53/E2
Hales Corners, Wi, US 135/P14
Halesowen, Eng, UK 30/D2
Haleyville, Al, US 133/G3
Half Assini, Gha. 102/C5
Half Falls (mt.), Pa, US 138/A3
Half Moon Bay, Ca, US 135/K12
Half Tide Beach, Austl. 114/C2
Halfing, Ger. 55/F7
Halfway, Sk, Can. 126/D2
Halfweg, Neth. 50/B4
Haliburton Highlands (uplands), On, Can. 130/E2
Halifax (cap.), NS, Can. 131/J2
Halifax, Austl. 114/B2
Halifax, Eng, UK 35/G4
Halifax (bay), Austl. 109/D2
Halifax (int'l arpt.), NS, Can. 131/J2
Halifax (co.), On, Can. 131/J2
Halkett (cape), Ak, US 134/H1
Hall, Austl. 115/C2
Hall (isl.), Ak, US 134/F4
Hall (isls.), Micr. 116/E4
Hall (pen.), Nun., Can. 123/K2
Hall Beach, Nun., Can. 123/H2
Hall Park, Ok, US 137/N15
Halladale (riv.), Sc, UK 31/S7
Hallam (Hellam), Pa, US 138/B4
Halland (co.), Swe. 37/E4
Hällbybrunn, Swe. 38/F2
Halle, Ger. 41/G3
Halle, Belg. 52/D2
Halle-Neustadt, Ger. 40/F3
Hälleforsnäs, Swe. 38/F2
Hallein, Aus. 43/K3
Hallenberg, Ger. 51/F6
Hallertau (reg.), Ger. 54/D5
Hallettsville, Tx, US 129/H5
Halle, Ger. 51/F6
Halle, Belg. 53/D2
Hallingdalselvi (riv.), Nor. 38/C1
Hallock, Mn, US 127/J3
Hallsberg, Swe. 38/F2
Hallstahammar, Swe. 38/F2
Hallstavik, Swe. 38/H1
Hallu (riv.), Fr. 30/A1
Halluin, Fr. 52/C2
Hallwilersee (lake), Swi. 56/E3
Hallyŏ Haesang NP, SKor. 74/A3
Halmahera (sea), Indo. 81/G4
Halmahera (isl.), Indo. 67/M9
Halmstad, Swe. 38/E4
Halq al Wādi, Tun. 46/B4
Hals, Den. 38/D3
Halsteren, Neth. 50/B5
Haltern, Ger. 51/E5
Halton (co.), On, Can. 131/Q8
Halton Hills, On, Can. 131/Q8

Halver, Ger. 51/E6
Halverder Aa (riv.), Ger. 51/E4
Ham, Fr. 52/C4
Ham, Oued El (riv.), Alg. 100/G3
Ham-sous-Varsberg, Fr. 53/F5
Ham-sur-Heure, Belg. 53/D3
Hamada, Japan 74/C3
Hamada de Tinrhert (plat.), Alg. 99/G4
Hamada du Drâa (plat.), Alg. 96/D2
Hamada du Tinrhert (plat.), Alg. 99/G4
Hamada Safia (plat.), Mali 98/D5
Hamadān, Iran 88/E2
Hamadat Marzūq (plat.), Libya 99/H3
Hamadat Tinghert (uplands), Libya 96/H2
Hamadat Tinghert (uplands), Libya 99/H3
Hamāh (prov.), Syria 91/E2
Hamāh, Syria 90/D2
Hamajima, Japan 77/C1
Hamakita, Japan 75/E3
Hamam, Turk. 91/E1
Hamamatsu, Japan 75/E3
Hamami (reg.), Mrta. 98/D5
Hamanaka, Japan 76/D2
Hamar, Nor. 38/D1
Hamāt (peak), Egpt 101/C3
Hamath Tiberias NP, Isr. 91/D3
Hamatombetsu, Japan 76/C1
Hambantota, SrL. 82/C6
Hambergen, Ger. 51/F2
Hambleton (hills), Eng, UK 35/G3
Hambühren, Ger. 51/G3
Hamburg, Ger. 51/G1
Hamburg, NY, US 130/E3
Hamburg, NJ, US 138/D1
Hamburg, Pa, US 138/C3
Hamburg (state), Ger. 38/D5
Hamburg-Fuhlsbüttel (int'l arpt.), Ger. 51/G1
Häme (prov.), Fin. 37/G3
Hämeenkyrö, Fin. 39/K1
Hämeenlinna, Fin. 39/L1
Hamel, Il, US 137/H8
Hamelin Pool (bay), Austl. 112/B3
Hameln, Ger. 51/G4
Hamersley (range), Austl. 109/A3
Hamersley Range NP, Austl. 112/C2
Hamford Water (inlet), Eng, UK 33/H2
Hamgyŏng-bukto (prov.), NKor. 73/E2
Hamgyŏng-namdo (prov.), NKor. 73/D2
Hamh, Syria 90/D3
Hamhŭng, NKor. 73/D3
Hamhŭng-si (prov.), NKor. 73/D3
Hami, China 70/F3
Hamilton, Austl. 115/B3
Hamilton, Mt, US 126/F4
Hamilton, Tx, US 129/H5
Hamilton, Al, US 133/G3
Hamilton (har.), Hamilton, NZ 117/T10
Hamilton, On, Can. 131/Q9
Hamilton, NZ 117/T10
Hamilton (inlet), Nf, Can. 123/J2
Hamilton (mt.), Ca, US 135/L12
Hamilton, Sc, UK 36/B5
Hamilton Mil. Res., NY, US 139/J9
Hamilton-Wentworth On, Can. 131/Q9
Hamina, Fin. 39/M1
Hamīrpur, India 84/B3
Hamīrpur, India 86/D4
Hamlin, Tx, US 129/G4
Hamm, Ger. 51/E5
Hamm, Ger. 54/B3
Hamm, Belg. 53/D2
Hamm-Bouziane, Alg. 100/A1
Hammām Al Anf, Tun. 46/B4
Hammāmāt (gulf), Tun. 46/B4
Hamman-Bouziane, Alg. 100/A1
Hammarland, Fin. 39/H1
Hammarön (isl.), Swe. 38/F2
Hammarstrand, Swe. 37/F3
Hamme, Belg. 52/D1
Hamme, Ger. 51/E2
Hammelburg, Ger. 54/C2
Hammerfest, Nor. 37/G1
Hammershus, Den. 38/F4
Hammersmith and Fulham (bor.), Eng, UK 30/A4
Hamminkeln, Ger. 50/D5
Hammonasset (pt.), Ct, US 139/F1
Hammond, La, US 137/P16
Hammond, In, US 135/P16
Hammond, NJ, US 138/C4
Hamont-Achel, Belg. 50/C6
Hampshire Downs (hills), Eng, UK 33/G4

Hampstead, Md, US 138/B4
Hampton, Pa, US 138/A4
Hampton Bays, NY, US 139/F2
Hampton Court, Eng, UK 30/C2
Hampton Nat'l Hist. Site, Md, US 138/B5
Hamp'yŏng, SKor. 73/D5
Hamtramck, Mi, US 135/F7
Hamura, Japan 77/C2
Hamyang, SKor. 73/D5
Hamyŏl, SKor. 73/D4
Han (riv.), China 67/M6
Hana, Hi, US 124/U10
Hana (pt.), Hi, US 124/U10
Hanak, Tur. 90/E1
Hanamaki, Japan 76/B4
Hanamalo (pt.), Hi, US 124/U11
Hanang (peak), Tanz. 104/B4
Hanau, Ger. 54/B2
Hancocks Bridge, NJ, US 138/C5
Handa, Japan 77/L6
Handan, India 86/C2
Handeni, Tanz. 104/C4
Handjila, India 82/C3
Handlová, India 84/D3
Hanford, Ca, US 128/C3
Hanford Reach Nat'l Mon., Wa, US 126/D4
Hangayn (mts.), Mong. 70/G2
Hangingstone (hill), Eng, UK 32/C5
Hangklip (cape), SAfr. 106/L11
Hangu, Pak. 86/A3
Hangzhou (bay), China 72/L9
Hanhöhiy (mts.), Mong. 70/F2
Hani, Turk. 90/G1
Haninge, Swe. 38/H2
Hankensbüttel, Ger. 51/H3
Hankey, SAfr. 106/D4
Hankinson, ND, US 127/J4
Hanko (Hangö), Fin. 39/K2
Hanley, Sk, Can. 127/G3
Hanna, Ab, Can. 126/F3
Hannan, Japan 77/H7
Hanningfield (res.), Eng, UK 30/E4
Hannō, Japan 77/C2
Hannover (int'l arpt.), Ger. 51/G4
Hannover, Ger. 51/G4
Hannut, Belg. 53/E2
Hanöbukten (bay), Swe. 37/E5
Hanover, NH, US 131/F3
Hanover, On, Can. 130/D2
Hanover, SAfr. 106/D3
Hanover, Pa, US 138/B4
Hanover (isl.), Chile 159/B6
Hanover Park, Il, US 135/P16
Hansen (dam), Ca, US 136/F7
Hanshan, China 72/B5
Hanshou, China 79/B2
Hänsi, India 86/C5
Hanstedt, Ger. 51/H2
Hanstholm, Den. 38/C3
Hansville, Wa, US 135/B2
Hantzsch (riv.), Nun., Can. 123/J2
Hanumāngarh, India 86/C5
Hanwood, Austl. 115/C2
Hanyū, Japan 77/D1
Hanyuan, China 83/H2
Hanzhong, China 70/J5
Hao (isl.), FrPol. 117/L6
Haparanda, Swe. 60/G2
Happy Valley (res.), Austl. 113/M9
Happy Valley-Goose Bay, Nf, Can. 123/K3
Haptŏk, SKor. 73/D4
Hāpur, India 84/A1
Haquira, Peru 156/C4
Har Karmel (Mount Carmel) (peak), Isr. 91/F7
Har Meron (peak), Isr. 91/D3
Har Ramon (peak), Isr. 91/D4
Hara, Japan 77/C3
Harahan, La, US 137/P17
Haramachi, Japan 75/G2
Harappa (ruin), Pak. 86/B4
Harare (cap.), Zim. 105/F4
Harash, Bi'r al (well), Libya 97/K2
Haravilliers, Fr. 30/J4
Harbel, Libr. 102/C5
Harbeson, De, US 138/C6
Harbin, China 71/N2
Harbiye, Turk. 91/E1
Harbonnières, Fr. 52/B4
Harbour Breton, Nf, Can. 131/L2
Harbour Grace, Nf, Can. 131/L2
Hard, Aus. 57/F3
Hardā, India 89/L4

Har-Ayrag, Mong. 156/C4

Hardangervidda NP, Nor. 38/B1
Hardau (riv.), Ger. 51/H3
Hardegsen, Ger. 51/G5
Hardenberg, Neth. 50/D3
Harderwijk, Neth. 50/C4
Hardheim, Ger. 54/C3
Hardin, Mt, US 126/G4
Harding, SAfr. 107/E3
Hardoi, India 84/C2
Hardoi Branch (riv.), India 84/C2
Hardricourt, Fr. 30/H4
Hardy (pen.), Chile 159/C7
Hare (bay), Nf, Can. 131/L1
Hare Dimona (peak), Isr. 91/D4
Harefield, Eng, UK 30/B2
Harelbeke, Belg. 52/C2
Haren, Ger. 51/E3
Haren, Neth. 50/D2
Härer, Eth. 97/P6
Harford (co.), Md, US 138/B4
Hargesheim, Ger. 53/G4
Hargeville, Fr. 30/H5
Hargeysa, Som. 97/P6
Harghita (prov.), Rom. 49/G2
Harghita (peak), Rom. 49/G2
Hari (riv.), Indo. 80/B4
Hari (str.), Est. 39/K2
Harihar, India 89/L6
Harim, Syria 91/E1
Harima (sea), Japan 74/D3
Harima, Jor. 91/D3
Harima, Japan 77/G6
Harima (bay), Japan 77/G6
Haringey (bor.), Eng, UK 30/C2
Haringhata (riv.), Bang. 85/G4
Haringvliet (chan.), Neth. 50/B5
Haringvlietdam (dam), Neth. 50/B5
Haripur, Pak. 86/B3
Harirud (riv.), Afg. 67/F6
Haris, WBnk. 91/G7
Harjavalta, Fin. 39/K1
Harlan, Ky, US 130/D4
Harlech, Wal, UK 34/D6
Harlingen, Tx, US 132/D5
Harlingen, Neth. 50/C2
Harlow, Eng, UK 30/D1
Harlowton, Mt, US 126/F4
Harmannsdorf, Aus. 49/N7
Harmelen, Neth. 50/C3
Harnes, Fr. 52/B3
Harney (basin), Or, US 128/C2
Harney (lake), Or, US 126/D5
Harney (peak), SD, US 127/H5
Harney (valley), Or, US 126/D5
Harney, Md, US 138/A4
Harnoli, Pak. 86/A3
Haro (cape), Mex. 142/C3
Haro, Sp. 44/D1
Harold, Ca, US 136/B1
Harpenden, Eng, UK 33/F3
Harper (mtn.), Yk, Can. 134/L3
Harper (mt.), Ak, US 134/K3
Harper, Ks, US 129/H3
Harper, Libr. 102/D5
Harper Woods, Mi, US 135/F7
Harpstedt, Ger. 51/F3
Harqin Zuoyi Monggolzu Zizhixian, China 72/D2
Harrah, Ok, US 137/N15
Harrai, India 84/B4
Harran, Turk. 90/D2
Harricana (riv.), Qu, Can. 123/J4
Harriman, Tn, US 130/C5
Harriman, NY, US 138/D1
Harrington, Austl. 115/E1
Harrington, De, US 138/C6
Harrington Park, NJ, US 139/K8
Harris (mt.), Austl. 113/F3
Harris (lake), Austl. 113/G4
Harris (isls.), Sc, UK 31/Q8
Harris Park, Co, US 137/E4
Harrisburg, Ne, US 127/H5
Harrisburg, Il, US 130/B4
Harrisburg (cap.), Pa, US 138/B3
Harrislee, Ger. 38/C4
Harrismith, SAfr. 106/E3
Harrison (bay), Ak, US 134/H1
Harrison, Ar, US 129/J3
Harrison, Mi, US 130/C2
Harrison, NY, US 139/L8
Harrison, NJ, US 139/J9
Harrison (cape), Nf, Can. 123/L3
Harrison (lake), BC, Can. 126/C3
Harrisonville, Il, US 137/G9
Harrisonville, Mo, US 137/E6
Harrisville, Ut, US 137/K11
Harrodsburg, Ky, US 130/C4
Harrow (bor.), Eng, UK 30/B2
Harry S Truman (res.), Mo, US 129/J3
Harsefeld, Ger. 51/G2
Harsewinkel, Ger. 51/F5

Harson's Island, Mi, US 135/G6
Hart (lake), Or, US 128/C2
Hart, Mi, US 130/C3
Hart (riv.), Yk, Can. 122/C1
Hart (isl.), NY, US 139/K8
Hart Fell (peak), Sc, UK 36/C6
Hartbeesrivier (riv.), SAfr. 106/C3
Hårteigen (peak), Nor. 38/B1
Hartelkanaal (riv.), Neth. 50/B5
Hartford (cap.), Ct, US 131/F3
Hartford, Il, US 137/G8
Hartford, NJ, US 138/D4
Hartford City, In, US 130/C3
Hartheim, Ger. 54/B1
Hartington, Ne, US 129/H2
Hartkirchen, Aus. 55/H6
Hartland (pt.), Eng, UK 32/B4
Hartland, Mi, US 135/E6
Hartlepool, Eng, UK 35/G2
Hartlepool (co.), Eng, UK 35/G2
Hartleton, Pa, US 138/A2
Hartley Wintney, Eng, UK 30/A3
Hartly, De, US 138/C5
Hartney, Mb, Can. 127/H3
Hartsdale, NY, US 139/K7
Hartselle, Al, US 133/G3
Hartshill, Eng, UK 33/E1
Hartstene (isl.), Wa, US 135/B3
Hartwell, Ga, US 133/H3
Hartwell (lake), Ga,SC, US 133/H3
Hartz Mountain NP, Austl. 115/C4
Haruhi, Japan 77/L5
Harun (peak), Indo. 81/E3
Hārūnabād, Pak. 86/C2
Hārūt (riv.), Afg. 89/H2
Harvey, ND, US 127/J4
Harvey, La, US 137/P17
Harvey, Austl. 112/B5
Harvey, Il, US 135/Q16
Harveys (lake), Pa, US 138/B1
Harwich, Eng, UK 33/H3
Haryana (state), India 82/C2
Harz (mts.), Ger. 40/F3
Hasan, Turk. 90/C2
Hasan Abdāl, Pak. 86/B3
Hasanpur, India 84/B1
Hasbrouck Heights, NJ, US 139/J8
Hasdo (riv.), India 84/D4
Hase (riv.), Ger. 40/D2
Hasel (riv.), Ger. 51/E3
Haselünne, Ger. 51/E3
Hasenmatt (peak), Swi. 56/D3
Hashima, Japan 77/L5
Hashimoto, Japan 74/D3
Hasi el Farsía (well), WSah. 98/C4
Hasilpur, Pak. 86/B5
Haslach an der Mühl, Aus. 55/H5
Haslach im Kinzigtal, Ger. 56/E1
Hasle bei Burgdorf, Swi. 56/D3
Haslemere, Eng, UK 33/F4
Haslingden, Eng, UK 35/F4
Hasloh, Ger. 51/G1
Haspres, Fr. 52/C3
Hassa, Turk. 91/E1
Hassan, India 82/C5
Hassan (El Aaiún) (int'l arpt.), WSah. 98/B4
Hassberge (hills), Ger. 54/D2
Hassel, Ger. 51/G3
Hassel Sound (str.), Nun., Can. 123/S7
Hasselt, Neth. 50/D3
Hasselt, Belg. 53/E2
Hassfurt, Ger. 54/D2
Hassi Bahbah, Alg. 100/G5
Hassi bou Zid (well), Alg. 99/F3
Hassi el Hadjar (well), Alg. 99/G3
Hassi el Mislane (well), Alg. 99/H4
Hassi er Rebib (well), Alg. 99/G3
Hässleholm, Swe. 38/E3
Hasslo (int'l arpt.), Swe. 38/G2
Hassloch, Ger. 51/G4
Haste, Ger. 51/G4
Hastings, Austl. 115/C3
Hastings, Ne, US 129/H2
Hastings, Mi, US 130/C3
Hastings, NZ 117/T10
Hastings, Eng, UK 33/G5
Hastings Battlesite, Eng, UK 33/G5
Hastings-On-Hudson, NY, US 139/K7
Hasuda, Japan 77/D2
Hasunuma, Japan 77/E2
Hasvik, Nor. 37/G1

Hat Chao Mai NP, Thai. 78/B5
Hat Head, Austl. 115/E1
Hat Head NP, Austl. 115/E1
Hat Nai Yang NP, Thai. 78/B5
Hat Yai, Thai. 78/C5
Hat Yai (int'l arpt.), Thai. 78/C5
Hatashō, Japan 77/K5
Hatavch, Mong. 71/K2
Hatay (prov.), Turk. 90/C2
Hatboro, Pa, US 138/C3
Hatch, NM, US 124/F4
Hatcher (peak), Arg. 159/B6
Hateg, Rom. 48/F3
Hatfield, Pa, US 138/C3
Hatfield, Eng, UK 30/C1
Hatfield Peverel, Eng, UK 30/E1
Hatfield, Il, US 130/C3
Hathras, India 84/B2
Hātia, North (isl.), Bang. 85/H4
Hātia, South (isl.), Bang. 85/H4
Hātibah, Ras (pt.), SAr. 88/C4
Hato (int'l arpt.), NAnt. 152/D1
Hato Corozal, Col. 152/D3
Hato Mayor, DRep. 141/H4
Hatoyama, Japan 77/C2
Hatsu (isl.), Japan 77/C3
Hatta, India 84/B3
Hatta, Japan 77/A2
Hattah-Kulkyne NP, Austl. 113/J5
Hattem, Neth. 50/D3
Hatten, Ger. 51/F2
Hatten, Fr. 53/G6
Hatteras, NC, US 133/K3
Hatteras (cape), NC, US 133/K3
Hattersheim am Main, Ger. 54/B2
Hattiesburg, Ms, US 133/F4
Hattieville, Belz. 144/D2
Hattingen, Ger. 51/E6
Hattula, Fin. 39/L1
Hatvan, Hun. 48/D2
Hatzenbühl, Ger. 54/B4
Hatzfeld, Ger. 51/F6
Hau Giang (riv.), Viet. 78/D4
Haubourdin, Fr. 52/B2
Haud (reg.), Eth. 97/Q6
Hauge, Nor. 38/B2
Haugesund, Nor. 38/A2
Haukipudas, Fin. 60/E2
Haune (riv.), Ger. 40/E3
Haunsberg (peak), Aus. 55/H7
Hauppauge, NY, US 139/E2
Hauraki (gulf), NZ 117/S10
Haus, Nor. 38/A1
Hausach, Ger. 56/E1
Hausjärvi, Fin. 39/L1
Hausleiten, Aus. 49/N7
Hausstock (peak), Swi. 57/F4
Haut Atlas (mts.), Mor. 96/D1
Haut-Rhin (dept.), Fr. 56/D2
Haute-Normandie (pol. reg.), Fr. 42/D2
Haute-Saône (dept.), Fr. 56/B2
Haute-Savoie (dept.), Fr. 56/C5
Hautefeuille, Fr. 30/L5
Hautes Fagnes (uplands), Belg. 53/E3
Hauteville-Lompnes, Fr. 56/B6
Hautmont, Fr. 52/C3
Hauts (plat.), Alg. 99/C2
Hauula, Hi, US 124/W12
Havant, Eng, UK 33/F5
Havdhem, Swe. 38/H3
Havel (canal), Ger. 40/P6
Havel (riv.), Ger. 41/G2
Havelange, Belg. 53/E2
Haveli, Pak. 86/B2
Haveliān, Pak. 86/B2
Havelländischer Grosser Hauptkanal (canal), Ger. 40/P6
Havelock, NC, US 133/J3
Havelte, Neth. 50/D3
Havencore (isl.), Eng, UK 33/G3
Haverfordwest, Wal, UK 32/B3
Haverhill, Ma, US 131/G3
Haverhill, Eng, UK 33/G2
Havering (bor.), Eng, UK 30/D2
Havířov, Czh. 41/K4
Havixbeck, Ger. 51/E5
Havlíčkuv Brod, Czh. 41/H4
Havneby, Den. 38/C4
Havre, Mt, US 126/F3
Havre de Grace, Md, US 138/B4

Havre-Saint-Pierre, Qu, Can. 131/J1
Havsa, Turk. 47/K2
Havza, Turk. 90/C1
Haw (riv.), NC, US 133/J3
Hawaii (state), US 124/S10
Hawaii (isl.), Hi, US 124/U11
Hawaiian (isls.), Hi, US 117/H2
Hawaii Kai, Hi, US 124/W13
Hawaii Volcanoes NP, Hi, US 124/U11
Hawaiian Gardens, Ca, US 136/F8
Hawallī, Kuw. 88/E3
Hawarden, Wal, UK 35/E5
Hawera, NZ 117/S10
Haweswater (res.), Eng, UK 35/F2
Hawi, Hi, US 124/U10
Hawick, Sc, UK 36/D6
Hawke (cape), Austl. 115/E2
Hawke (bay), NZ 109/H6
Hawker, Austl. 113/H4
Hawkesbury (isl.), BC, Can. 126/A2
Hawkesbury (riv.), On, Can. 130/D2
Hawkesbury, Austl. 114/G8
Hawks Nest, Austl. 115/E2
Haworth, NJ, US 139/K8
Hawston, SAfr. 106/L11
Hawthorn Woods, Il, US 135/P15
Hawthorne, Nv, US 128/C3
Hawthorne, Ca, US 136/F8
Hawthorne, NJ, US 139/J8
Hawthorne, NY, US 139/K8
Hawwārah, Jor. 91/D3
Haxby, Eng, UK 35/G3
Hay, Austl. 115/C2
Hay (pt.), Austl. 114/C3
Hay (riv.), Ab,BC, Can. 122/E2
Hay River, NW, Can. 122/E2
Hay, Austl. 113/H4
Hayachine-san (peak), Japan 76/B4
Hayakawa, Japan 77/A3
Hayama, Japan 77/D3
Hayange, Fr. 53/F5
Haybes, Fr. 53/D4
Haycock, Ak, US 134/F2
Haydock, Eng, UK 35/F5
Hayes (mt.), Ak, US 134/J3
Hayes (pen.), Grld. 123/T7
Hayes (riv.), Mb, Can. 122/G3
Hayingen, Ger. 57/F1
Haylaastay, Mong. 71/K2
Hayle (riv.), Eng, UK 32/A6
Hayling (isl.), Eng, UK 33/F5
Haymana, Turk. 90/C2
Haynesville, La, US 129/J4
Hayrabolu, Turk. 49/H5
Hays, Ks, US 129/H3
Hays (co.), Tx, US 137/U20
Haysyn, Ukr. 62/D2
Hayward, Wi, US 127/L4
Hazārā (mtn.), Iran 89/G3
Hazard, Ky, US 130/D4
Hazāribag, India 85/E4
Hazebrouck, Fr. 52/B2
Hazel Park, Mi, US 135/F7
Hazelwood, Mo, US 137/G8
Hazen (bay), Ak, US 134/E3
Hazen (str.), NW,Nun., Can. 123/R7
Hazlehurst, Ms, US 129/K5
Hazlemere, Eng, UK 30/A2
Hazlet, NJ, US 139/J10
Hazleton, Pa, US 138/C2
Hazlett (lake), Austl. 113/F2
Hazratbal Mosque, India 86/C2
Hazro, Pak. 86/B3
Hazu, Japan 77/M6
He (riv.), China 79/B3
He Xian, China 72/D5
Headcorn, Eng, UK 33/G4
Heads of Ayr (pt.), Sc, UK 36/B6
Healdsburg, Ca, US 128/B3
Healesville, Austl. 115/G5
Healy, Ak, US 134/J3
Heanor, Eng, UK 35/G6
Heard (isl.), Austl. 160/E
Hearst, On, Can. 130/D1
Heart (riv.), ND, US 127/H4
Heart Law (hill), Sc, UK 36/B6
Heath (pt.), Qu, Can. 131/J1
Heathcote NP, Austl. 114/G9
Heathrow (int'l arpt.), Eng, UK 30/B2
Hebbronville, Tx, US 132/D5
Hebei (prov.), China 71/K4
Hebertshausen, Ger. 55/E6
Hebrides (isls.), UK 27/D3
Hebrides (sea), UK 31/G4
Hebron, Ne, US 129/H2
Hebron, Il, US 135/P15
Hebron (vol.), Ice. 37/M7
Hecate (str.), BC, Can. 122/C3
Hecelchakán, Mex. 144/D1
Hechi, China 83/J3
Hechingen, Ger. 54/B6

Hechtel, Belg. 53/E1
Hechthausen, Ger. 51/G1
Hecker, Il, US 137/H9
Hecla, SD, US 127/J4
Hecla and Griper (bay), NW,Nun., Can. 123/R7
Hector (mt.), Ab, Can. 126/D3
Heddal, Nor. 38/C2
Hedel, Neth. 50/C5
Hedemora, Swe. 38/F1
Hedensted, Den. 38/C4
Hedmark (co.), Nor. 37/D3
Hedo-misaki (cape), Japan 75/K7
Hédouville, Fr. 30/J4
Heede, Ger. 51/E2
Heek, Ger. 51/E4
Heemskerk, Neth. 50/B3
Heemstede, Neth. 50/B3
Heerenveen, Neth. 50/C3
Heerhugowaard, Neth. 50/B3
Heerlen, Neth. 53/E2
Heers, Belg. 53/E2
Heesch, Neth. 50/C5
Heeslingen, Ger. 51/G2
Heeze, Neth. 50/C6
Hefa (Haifa), Isr. 91/F6
Hefei, China 72/D5
Hefeng Tujiazu Zizhixian, China 79/B2
Hegang, China 71/P2
Hegau (mts.), Ger. 43/H3
Hegau (reg.), Ger. 40/E5
Heggenes, Nor. 38/C1
Hegins, Pa, US 138/B2
Heguri, Japan 77/J6
Heide, Ger. 38/C4
Heidelberg, Ms, US 133/F4
Heidelberg, SAfr. 106/C4
Heidelberg, SAfr. 106/E2
Heidelberg, Ger. 54/B4
Heiden, Ger. 50/D5
Heiden, Swi. 57/F3
Heidenheim, Ger. 54/D4
Heidenreichstein, Aus. 41/H4
Heigenbrücken, Ger. 54/C2
Heikendorf, Ger. 38/D4
Heilbron, SAfr. 106/D2
Heilbronn, Ger. 54/D4
Heiligenberg, Ger. 57/F2
Heiligenblut, Aus. 43/H3
Heiligenhafen, Ger. 38/D4
Heiligenhaus, Ger. 50/D6
Heiligenstadt, Ger. 51/H6
Heilong (Amur) (riv.), China,Rus. 65/N5
Heilongjiang (prov.), China 71/N2
Heiloo, Neth. 50/B3
Heimaey (isl.), Ice. 37/N7
Heimbach, Ger. 53/F2
Heimberg, Swi. 56/D4
Heimsheim, Ger. 54/B5
Heino, Neth. 50/D4
Heinola, Fin. 39/M1
Heinsberg, Ger. 53/F1
Heishan, China 73/A2
Heist-op-den-Berg, Belg. 53/D1
Heitersheim, Ger. 56/D2
Heiwa, Japan 77/L5
Hejian, China 72/D4
Hejin, China 72/C4
Hejing, China 70/E3
Hekimhan, Turk. 90/D2
Hekinan, Japan 77/C4
Hekla (vol.), Ice. 37/N7
Hekou, China 83/H3
Hel, Pol. 39/H4
Helan (mts.), China 70/J4
Helbe (riv.), Ger. 51/H6
Helden, Neth. 50/D6
Helena (cap.), Mt, US 126/E4
Helena (riv.), Austl. 112/L6
Helensburgh, Austl. 115/C2
Helensburgh, Sc, UK 36/B4
Helgasjön (lake), Swe. 38/F3
Helgoland (isl.), Ger. 38/B4
Helgoländer (bay), Wa, US 135/B3
Helgoländer (bay), Ger. 38/B4
Heliport (int'l arpt.), Austl. 114/G9
Hellas (see Greece) 27/G5
Helleh (riv.), Iran 88/F3
Hellenthal, Ger. 53/F3
Hellertown, Pa, US 138/C2
Hellevoetsluis, Neth. 50/B5
Hellín, Sp. 44/E3
Hells (canyon), 126/D4
Hells Canyon Nat'l Rec. Area, US 128/D4
Helmand (riv.), Afg. 67/F6
Helmbrechts, Ger. 55/E2

Helmet (mtn.), Ak, US 134/K2
Helmetta, NJ, US 139/H10
Helmond, Neth. 50/C6
Helmstadt, Ger. 54/C4
Helmstedt, Ger. 40/F2
Helmstedt, Md, US 138/B4
Helong, China 71/N3
Helotes, Tx, US 137/T20
Helper, Ut, US 128/E3
Helsenhorn (peak), Swi. 56/E5
Helsingør, Den. 38/E3
Helsinki (Helsingfors) (cap.), Fin. 37/H3
Helsinki-Vantaa (int'l arpt.), Fin. 39/L1
Hem (riv.), Fr. 52/B2
Hemau, Ger. 55/E4
Hemel Hempstead, Eng, UK 30/B1
Hemer, Ger. 51/E6
Hemet, Ca, US 136/D3
Hemmingen, Ger. 51/G4
Hemmoor, Ger. 51/G1
Hemphill, Tx, US 132/E4
Hempstead, Tx, US 129/H5
Hempstead (har.), NY, US 139/L8
Hempstead, NY, US 139/L9
Hemse, Swe. 38/H3
Hemsedal, Nor. 38/C1
Hemsworth, Eng, UK 35/H4
Henan (prov.), China 71/K5
Hénan, Swe. 38/D2
Henares (riv.), Sp. 44/D2
Henashi-zaki (pt.), Japan 76/A3
Hendaye, Fr. 42/C5
Hendek, Turk. 49/K5
Henderson, NC, US 130/E4
Henderson, Nv, US 128/D3
Henderson, Tn, US 130/B5
Henderson, Ky, US 130/C4
Henderson, Co, US 137/C3
Henderson (isl.), Pitc. 117/N7
Henderson, Arg. 158/E3
Henderson, Md, US 138/C5
Hendersonville, Tn, US 130/C4
Hendersonville, NC, US 133/H3
Hendrik-Ido-Ambacht, Neth. 50/B5
Hendrik Verwoerdam (res.), SAfr. 106/D3
Hendrina, SAfr. 107/E2
Henefer, Ut, US 137/L11
Heng (mtn.), China 72/C3
Heng Xian, China 83/J3
Hengduan (mts.), China 70/G6
Hengelo, Neth. 50/D4
Hengersberg, Ger. 55/G5
Hengoed, Wal, UK 32/C3
Hengshan, China 79/B2
Hengshan, China 72/B3
Hengshui, China 72/C3
Hengyang, China 79/B2
Henichés'k, Ukr. 62/E3
Hénin-Beaumont, Fr. 52/B3
Henley-on-Thames, Eng, UK 33/F3
Henlopen (cape), De, US 138/C6
Henlopen Acres, De, US 138/C6
Hennef, Ger. 51/F6
Hennebont, Fr. 42/B3
Henneman, SAfr. 106/D2
Hennigsdorf, Ger. 40/G6
Henrietta, Tx, US 129/H4
Henrietta Maria (cape), On, Can. 123/H3
Henry (cape), BC, Can. 134/M5
Henry (mts.), Ut, US 128/E3
Henry Ford Museum and Greenfield Village Historical Site, Mi, US 135/E7
Henryetta, Ok, US 129/J4
Henryville, Pa, US 138/C1
Hensies, Belg. 52/C3
Hentiy (prov.), Mong. 71/L2
Hentiyn (mts.), Mong. 70/J2
Henty, Austl. 115/C2
Henzada, Myan. 83/G4
Heping, China 79/B3
Heppenheim an der Bergstrasse, Ger. 54/B3
Hepu, China 83/J3
Heqing, China 83/H2
Hequ, China 72/C3
Heradhsvötn (riv.), Ice. 37/N6
Herāt, Afg. 89/H2
Herbert (riv.), Austl. 114/B2
Herbert River Falls NP, Austl. 114/B2
Herberton, Austl. 114/B2
Herbeumont, Belg. 53/E4
Herblay, Fr. 30/J5
Herbolzheim, Ger. 56/D1
Herbrechtingen, Ger. 54/D5
Herbstein, Ger. 51/G6
Hercegnovi, Serb. 47/F1
Hercílio Luz (int'l arpt.), Braz. 155/B3
Herculaneum, Mo, US 137/G9
Herculaneum (ruin), It. 46/D2
Hercules, Ca, US 135/K10

Herdecke, Ger. 51/E6
Herdorf, Ger. 53/G2
Heredia, CR 145/E4
Hereford, Eng, UK 32/D2
Hereford, Md, US 138/B4
Hereford (inlet), NJ, US 138/D5
Hereford, Pa, US 138/C3
Hereford, Tx, US 129/G4
Herefordshire (co.), Eng, UK 32/D2
Hereke, Turk. 49/J5
Herencia, Sp. 44/C3
Herentals, Belg. 50/B6
Herford, Ger. 51/F4
Héricourt, Fr. 56/C3
Hérimoncourt, Fr. 56/C3
Herington, Ks, US 129/H3
Herisau, Swi. 57/F3
Herk (riv.), Belg. 53/E2
Herk-de-Stad, Belg. 53/E2
Hèrlèn Gol (Kerulen) (riv.), Mong. 71/K2
Herleshausen, Ger. 51/H6
Herma Ness (cape), Sc, UK 31/W13
Hermann, Mo, US 129/K3
Hermannsburg, Ger. 51/H3
Hermannsburg, Austl. 113/G2
Hermannsburg Abor. Land, Austl. 113/G2
Hermansverk, Nor. 38/B1
Hermanus, SAfr. 106/L11
Hermeray, Fr. 30/G6
Hermersberg, Ger. 53/G5
Hermes, Fr. 52/B5
Hermeskeil, Ger. 53/F4
Hermiston, Or, US 126/D4
Hermitage, Rus. 61/T7
Hermosa Beach, Ca, US 136/F8
Hermosillo, Mex. 142/C2
Hermsdorf, Ger. 40/G6
Hernández, Mex. 142/E4
Hernando, Ms, US 129/K4
Hernani, Sp. 44/E1
Herndon, Pa, US 138/B2
Herne, Ger. 51/E5
Herne, Belg. 52/D2
Herne Bay, Eng, UK 33/H4
Herning, Den. 38/C3
Heroes de la Independencia, Mex. 142/B2
Heroica Caborca, Mex. 142/B2
Heroica Ciudad de Tlaxiaco, Mex. 144/B2
Heroica Matamoros, Mex. 132/D5
Heroica Nogales, Mex. 128/E5
Heroldsberg, Ger. 54/E3
Hérouville, Fr. 30/J4
Hérouville-Saint-Clair, Fr. 42/C2
Heroy, Nor. 37/C3
Herpf (riv.), Ger. 54/D1
Herre, Ger. 38/C2
Herrenberg, Ger. 54/B5
Herrera, Sp. 44/C4
Herrera de Pisuerga, Sp. 44/C1
Herrera del Duque, Sp. 44/C3
Herrero (pt.), Mex. 144/E2
Herrestad, Swe. 38/D2
Herrieden, Ger. 54/D4
Herriman, Ut, US 137/J12
Herrlisheim, Fr. 53/G6
Herrnhut, Ger. 41/G3
Herrsching am Ammersee, Ger. 57/H2
Hers (riv.), Fr. 42/D5
Hersbruck, Ger. 55/E3
Herschbach, Ger. 53/G2
Herscheid, Ger. 51/E6
Herselt, Belg. 53/D1
Hershey, Pa, US 138/B3
Hersheypark, Pa, US 138/B3
Herstal, Belg. 53/E2
Herten, Ger. 51/E5
Hertford, NC, US 133/J2
Hertford, Eng, UK 30/C1
Herval d'Oeste, Braz. 155/B3
Hervás, Sp. 44/C2
Hervey (bay), Austl. 114/D3
Hervey Bay, Austl. 114/D3
Hervey Bay (reef), Austl. 114/D3
Herxheim bei Landau, Ger. 54/B4
Herzberg am Harz, Ger. 51/H5
Herzbrock-Clarholz, Ger. 51/F5
Herzele, Belg. 52/C2
Herzliyya, Isr. 91/F7
Herzogenaurach, Ger. 54/D3
Herzogenbuchsee, Swi. 56/D3
Herzogenburg, Aus. 48/B1
Hesbaye (plat.), Belg. 40/C3
Hesdin, Fr. 52/B3
Hesel, Ger. 51/E2
Hesperange, Lux. 53/F4
Hesperia, Ca, US 136/C2

Hesselø (isl.), Den. 38/D3
Hessen (state), Ger. 43/H1
Hessen, Ger. 51/H4
Hessisch Lichtenau, Ger. 51/G6
Hessisch Oldendorf, Ger. 51/G4
Hetaudā, Nepal 85/E2
Heteren, Neth. 50/C5
Hettenleidelheim, Ger. 54/B3
Hettingen, ND, US 127/H4
Hetton-le-Hole, Eng, UK 35/G2
Hettstadt, Ger. 54/C3
Hetzerath, Ger. 53/F4
Heubach (riv.), Ger. 51/E5
Heubach, Ger. 54/C5
Heuchelheim, Ger. 54/B1
Heukuppe (peak), Aus. 41/H5
Heusden, Neth. 50/C5
Heusden-Zolder, Belg. 53/E1
Heusenstamm, Ger. 54/B2
Heusweiler, Ger. 53/F5
Hève, Cap de la (cape), Fr. 42/D2
Heves, Hun. 48/E2
Heves (co.), Hun. 41/L5
Hewitt, NJ, US 139/H7
Hewlett (pt.), US 139/L8
Hewlett, NY, US 139/L9
Hex River (mts.), SAfr. 106/L10
Hex River (pass), SAfr. 106/L10
Hexenkopf (peak), Aus. 57/G2
Heyerode, Ger. 51/H6
Heythuysen, Neth. 50/C6
Heywood, Austl. 115/B3
Heywood, Eng, UK 35/F4
Heze, China 72/C4
Hialeah, Fl, US 133/H5
Hiawatha, Ks, US 129/J3
Hibbing, Mn, US 127/K4
Hibbs (pt.), Austl. 115/C4
Hicacos (pt.), Cuba 145/E1
Hichisō, Japan 77/M4
Hickman, BC, Can. 134/M4
Hickory, NC, US 133/H3
Hickory, La, US 137/Q16
Hickory Run State Park, Pa, US 138/C1
Hicks, NY, US 139/L8
Hicksville, NY, US 139/L8
Hico, Tx, US 129/H4
Hida (riv.), Japan 75/E3
Hidaka (riv.), Japan 74/D4
Hidaka (mts.), Japan 76/C2
Hidaka, Japan 77/C2
Hidalgo, Mex. 143/F3
Hidalgo (state), Mex. 140/B3
Hidalgo del Parral, Mex. 142/D3
Hidden Hills, Ca, US 136/B2
Hiddenhausen, Ger. 51/F4
Hidrolândia, Braz. 154/B2
Hierapolis (ruin), Turk. 90/B2
Hieroglyphic (mtn.), Az, US 137/R18
Hierro (isl.), Sp. 98/A4
Hieve (lake), Ger. 51/E2
Higashi-Chichibu, Japan 77/C1
Higashi-Matsuyama, Japan 77/C1
Higashi-Ōsaka, Japan 77/J6
Higashikurume, Japan 77/D2
Higashimurayama, Japan 77/C2
Higashine, Japan 76/B4
Higashiura, Japan 77/B4
Higashiyoshino, Japan 77/J7
High (des.), Or, US 126/C5
High (isl.), China 71/V10
High Bridge, NJ, US 138/D2
High Island, Tx, US 132/E4
High Level, Ab, Can. 122/E3
High Point, NC, US 133/H3
High Ridge, Mo, US 137/F9
High River, Ab, Can. 126/E3
High Street (peak), Eng, UK 35/F2
High Willhays (hill), Eng, UK 32/C5
High Wycombe, Eng, UK 33/F3
Higham, Eng, UK 30/E2
Higham Ferrers, Eng, UK 33/F2
Highland, Ca, US 136/C2
Highland, Ut, US 137/K12
Highland, In, US 135/R16
Highland (pol. reg.), Sc, UK 36/A2
Highland Lakes, NJ, US 138/D1
Highland Park, Co, US 137/A4
Highland Park, Mi, US 135/F7
Highland Park, NJ, US 139/H10
Highlands, NJ, US 139/L10
Highrock (lake), Mb, Can. 127/H2
Highspire, Pa, US 138/B3
Hightstown, NJ, US 138/D3
Highwood, Il, US 135/Q15
Higley, Az, US 137/S19

Higuera de Zaragoza, Mex. 142/C3
Hihyā, Egypt 91/B4
Hiidenportin NP, Fin. 60/F3
Hiiumaa (isl.), Est. 60/D4
Híjar, Sp. 45/E2
Hijāz, Jabal al (mts.), SAr. 88/C3
Hiji, Japan 74/B4
Hijuelas de Conchali, Chile 158/N8
Hikami, Japan 77/J5
Hikari, Japan 77/F2
Hikone, Japan 77/K5
Hikueru (isl.), FrPol. 117/L6
Hikurangi (peak), NZ 117/T10
Hildburghausen, Ger. 54/D2
Hilden, Ger. 53/F1
Hilders, Ger. 54/C1
Hildesheim, Ger. 51/G4
Hilgermissen, Ger. 51/G3
Hill (isl.), Pa, US 138/B3
Hill City, Ks, US 129/H3
Hill of Fare (hill), Sc, UK 36/C2
Hill of Stake (hill), Sc, UK 36/B5
Hillaby (mt.), Bar. 141/P9
Hillburn, NY, US 139/J7
Hillcrest, NY, US 139/J7
Hille, Ger. 51/F4
Hillegom, Neth. 50/B4
Hillerød, Den. 38/E4
Hillesheim, Ger. 53/F3
Hillingdon (bor.), Eng, UK 30/B2
Hillsboro, Md, US 138/C6
Hillsboro, ND, US 127/J4
Hillsboro, Oh, US 130/D4
Hillsboro, Or, US 126/C4
Hillsboro, Tx, US 129/H4
Hillsborough (chan.), Austl. 114/C3
Hillsborough, Ca, US 135/K11
Hillsborough, NJ, US 138/D3
Hillsdale, Mi, US 130/C3
Hillsdale, Ks, US 137/D6
Hillsdale (lake), Ks, US 137/D6
Hillsdale, NJ, US 139/J7
Hillside, Md, US 139/J9
Hillside, Sc, UK 36/D3
Hillston, Austl. 115/C2
Hillswick, Sc, UK 31/W13
Hilltop, Co, US 135/C3
Hilltown, NI, UK 32/B2
Hilo, Hi, US 124/U11
Hilongos, Phil. 79/D5
Hilpoltstein, Ger. 54/E4
Hilpsford (pt.), Eng, UK 35/E3
Hilsa, India 85/E3
Hilterfingen, Swi. 56/D4
Hilton Head (isl.), SC, US 133/H3
Hilton Head Island, SC, US 133/H3
Hilvarenbeek, Neth. 50/C6
Hilversum, Neth. 50/C4
Hilzingen, Ger. 57/E2
Himáchal Pradesh (state), India 70/C3
Himalaya (range), Asia 67/G6
Himálchuli (peak), Nepal 85/E1
Himamaylan, Phil. 79/D5
Himanka, Fin. 60/D2
Himeji, Japan 49/N7
Himeji Castle, Japan 74/D3
Himi, Japan 75/E2
Himmelpforten, Ger. 51/G1
Hims (prov.), Syria 90/D3
Hims, Syria 91/E2
Hinche, Haiti 145/H2
Hinchinbrook (isl.), Austl. 109/D2
Hinchinbrook Entrance (chan.), Ak, US 134/J3
Hinchinbrook Island, Austl. 114/B2
Hinckley, Eng, UK 35/E1
Hincks Conservation Park, Austl. 113/H5
Hindan (riv.), India 84/A1
Hindaun, India 84/A2
Hindelang, Ger. 57/G3
Hindeloopen, Neth. 50/C3
Hindley, Eng, UK 35/F4
Hindmarsh (lake), Austl. 115/B3
Hindu Kush (mts.), Asia 67/F6
Hindupur, India 82/C5
Hinesville, Ga, US 133/H4
Hinganghāt, India 82/C4
Hingol (riv.), Pak. 89/J3
Hingoli, India 82/C4
Hingorja, Pak. 89/J3
Hnis, Turk. 90/E2
Hino, Japan 77/K5
Hino, Japan 77/C2
Hino (riv.), Japan 77/K5
Hino-misaki (cape), Japan 74/C3
Hinode, Japan 77/K5
Hinohara, Japan 77/K5
Hinojosa del Duque, Sp. 44/C3
Hinsdale, Il, US 135/Q16
Hinte, Ger. 51/E2
Hinterbrühl, Aus. 49/N7
Hinterrhein (riv.), Swi. 57/F4

Hinterrugg (peak), Swi. 57/F3
Hinterweidenthal, Ger. 53/G5
Hinton, Ab, Can. 126/D2
Hinton, WV, US 130/D4
Hinwil, Swi. 57/E3
Hipólito Bouchard, Arg. 158/E2
Hippolytushoef, Neth. 50/B3
Hipswell, Eng, UK 35/G3
Hira Highlands (uplands), Japan 77/J5
Hirado, Japan 74/A4
Hirakata, Japan 77/F2
Hirakud (res.), India 82/D3
Hiraman (riv.), Kenya 104/C3
Hiran (riv.), India 84/B4
Hiranai, Japan 76/B3
Hirara, Japan 75/H8
Hirata, Japan 74/C3
Hirata, Japan 77/L5
Hiratsuka, Japan 77/C3
Hirfanli (dam), Turk. 90/C2
Hîrlău, Rom. 49/H2
Hiro'o, Japan 76/C2
Hirosaki, Japan 76/B3
Hiroshima, Japan 74/C3
Hiroshima (pref.), Japan 74/C3
Hofgeismar, Ger. 51/G6
Hofheim am Taunus, Ger. 54/B2
Hofheim in Unterfranken, Ger. 54/D2
Hofmeyr, SAfr. 106/D3
Hofong Qagan Salt (lake), China 72/B3
Hofors, Swe. 38/G1
Hofsá (riv.), Ice. 37/P6
Hofsjökull (glacier), Ice. 37/N7
Hōfu, Japan 74/B3
Hogarth (mt.), Austl. 113/H2
Hogyész, Hun. 48/D2
Hoh Xil (mts.), China 70/E4
Höhbürd, Mong. 70/H2
Hohe Acht (peak), Ger. 53/G3
Hohe Geige (peak), Aus. 57/G4
Hohe Tauern (mts.), Aus. 43/K3
Hohe Tauern NP, Aus. 43/K3
Hohegrass (peak), Ger. 51/G6
Hohen Neuendorf, Ger. 40/Q6
Hohenbrunn, Ger. 55/E6
Hohenems, Aus. 57/F3
Hohenhameln, Ger. 51/H4
Hohenlinden, Ger. 55/F6
Hohenlockstedt, Ger. 40/E2
Hohenloher Ebene (plain), Ger. 40/E4
Hohenpeissenberg, Ger. 57/G2
Hohenroth, Ger. 54/D2
Hoher Dachstein (peak), Aus. 43/K3
Hoher Ifen (peak), Ger. 57/G3
Hoher Randen (peak), Ger. 57/E2
Hohgant (peak), Swi. 56/D4
Hohhot, China 71/K3
Hohneck (peak), Fr. 56/D1
Hohnstorf, Ger. 51/H2
Hohokam Pima Nat'l Mon., Az, US 128/E4
Höhr-Grenzhausen, Ger. 53/G3
Hoi An, Viet. 78/E3
Hoima, Ugan. 104/A2
Hoisington, Ks, US 129/H3
Hojby, Den. 38/D4
Højer, Den. 38/C4
Hōjō, Japan 74/C4
Hokitika, NZ 117/S11
Hokkaidō (isl.), Japan 67/P5
Hokksund, Nor. 38/C2
Hokota, Japan 75/G2
Hokudan, Japan 77/G6
Hokusei, Japan 77/L5
Hol, Nor. 38/C1
Holbox, Mex. 144/E1
Holbrook, Austl. 115/C2
Holbrook, Az, US 128/E4
Holbrook, NY, US 139/E2
Holderness (pen.), Eng, UK 35/H4
Holdorf, Ger. 51/F3
Holdrege, Ne, US 129/H2
Holeby, Den. 38/D4
Holguin, Cuba 145/G1
Holiday Hills, Il, US 135/P15
Holitna (riv.), Ak, US 134/G3
Höljes, Swe. 38/E1
Holladay-Cottonwood, Ut, US 137/K12
Holland, Mi, US 130/C3
Holland (pt.), Md, US 138/B6
Hollandale, Ms, US 129/K4
Hollandse IJssel (riv.), Neth. 50/B4
Hollandstoun, Sc, UK 31/V14
Hollenstedt, Ger. 51/G2
Hollfeld, Ger. 54/E2
Holliday, Ks, US 137/D5
Hollis, Ak, US 134/M4
Hollister (mt.), Austl. 112/B2
Hollogne-aux-Pierres, Belg. 53/E2
Hollola, Fin. 39/L1
Höllviksnäs, Swe. 38/E4
Holly, Wa, US 135/B2

Hodal, India 84/A2
Hodder (riv.), Eng, UK 35/F4
Hoddesdon, Eng, UK 30/D1
Hodenhagen, Ger. 51/G3
Hodges (lake), Ca, US 136/C4
Hodgeville, Sk, Can. 126/G3
Hodh (phys. reg.), Mrta. 102/C2
Hódmezővásárhely, Hun. 48/E2
Hodonín, Czh. 41/J4
Hoeske Waard (isl.), Neth. 50/B5
Hoensbroek, Neth. 53/E2
Hoeselt, Belg. 53/E2
Hoevelaken, Neth. 50/C4
Hoeven, Neth. 50/B5
Hoeybuktmoen (int'l arpt.), Nor. 37/J1
Hof, Ger. 55/E2
Hofbieber, Ger. 54/C1
Höfdhakaupstadhur, Ice. 37/N6
Hoffman Estates, Il, US 135/P15
Holm, Ger. 51/G1
Holman, NW, Can. 122/E1
Hólmavik, Ice. 37/N6
Holmdel, NJ, US 138/D3
Holmes (reefs), Austl. 109/D2
Holmesdale (valley), Eng, UK 30/C3
Holmestrand, Nor. 38/D2
Holmfirth, Eng, UK 35/G4
Holmsjön (lake), Swe. 37/F3
Holmsund, Swe. 37/G3
Holon, Isr. 91/F7
Holstebro, Den. 38/C3
Holston (riv.), Tn, US 133/H2
Holt, Mo, US 137/E5
Holtålen, Nor. 37/D3
Holten, Neth. 50/D4
Holtland, Ger. 51/E2
Holton, Ks, US 129/J3
Holtsville, NY, US 139/E2
Holy (isl.), Sc, UK 36/A5
Holy Cross, Ak, US 134/G3
Holyhead, Wal, UK 34/D5
Holyoke, Co, US 129/G2
Holyoke, Ma, US 131/F3
Holywell, Wal, UK 35/E5
Holywood, NI, UK 34/C2
Holzkirchen, Ger. 43/J3
Holzminden, Ger. 51/G5
Holzwickede, Ger. 51/E5
Hom (riv.), Namb. 106/B3
Homberg, Ger. 51/G6
Homberg, Ger. 50/D6
Hombori Tondo (peak), Mali 103/E3
Hombourg-Haut, Fr. 53/F5
Homburg, Ger. 53/G5
Home (bay), Nun., Can. 123/K2
Home Hill, Austl. 114/B2
Homécourt, Fr. 53/E5
Homeland, Ca, US 136/C3
Homer, Ak, US 134/H4
Homer, La, US 129/J4
Homestead, Fl, US 133/H5
Homestead Nat'l Mon. of America, Ne, US 129/H2
Homewood, Al, US 133/G3
Homewood, Il, US 135/Q16
Homib (riv.), Erit. 88/C5
Hommersåk, Nor. 38/A2
Homochitto (riv.), Ms, US 132/F4
Homyel', Bela. 62/D1
Homyel'skaya Voblasts Bela. 62/D1
Hon Quan, Viet. 78/D4
Honaunau-Napoopoo, Hi, US 124/U11
Honbetsu, Japan 76/C2
Hondo (riv.), Wal, UK 32/C2
Hondeklipbaai, SAfr. 106/B3
Hondo (riv.), Belz. 144/D2
Hondo, Japan 74/B4
Hondo, Tx, US 129/H5
Hondschoote, Fr. 52/B2
Hondsrug (reg.), Neth. 50/D3
Hondsrug (hills), Neth. 40/D2
Honduras (gulf), NAm. 144/E2
Honduras (ctry.) 144/E3
Honey (lake), Ca, US 126/C5
Honey Brook, Pa, US 138/C3
Honey Creek, Wi, US 135/P14
Hong (isl.), SKor. 73/C5
Hong (lake), China 72/C5
Hong (riv.), China 72/C4
Hong Gai, Viet. 78/E2
Hong Kong (dpcy.), China 67/L7
Hong Kong (isl.), China 71/U10
Hong'an, China 72/C5
Hongch'ŏn, SKor. 73/D4
Hongdu (riv.), China 83/J2
Honghu, China 72/C5
Hongjiang, China 83/J2
Hongqiao (int'l arpt.), China 72/L8
Hongshui (riv.), China 70/J6
Hongsŏng, SKor. 73/D4
Hongtong, China 72/B3
Honguedo (passg.), Qu, Can. 131/H1
Hongwŏn, NKor. 73/D2
Hongze, China 72/D4
Hœnheim, Fr. 53/G6
Honiara (cap.), Sol. 116/E5
Honjō, Japan 76/B4
Honjō, Japan 77/C1
Honkajoki, Fin. 42/D3
Honokohau, Hi, US 124/T10
Honolulu (cap.), Hi, US 124/V13
Honolulu (int'l arpt.), Hi, US 124/W13
Honouliuli, Hi, US 124/V13
Hōnow, Ger. 40/Q6
Honshū (isl.), Japan 67/N5
Hood (pt.), Austl. 112/C5
Hood, Ca, US 135/L10
Hood (mt.), Ca, US 135/J10
Hood (mt.), Or, US 126/C4
Hood Canal (str.), Wa, US 126/C4
Hoofddorp, Neth. 50/B4
Hoogeloon, Neth. 50/C6

Hoogeveen, Neth. 50/D3
Hoogeveense Vaart (canal), Neth. 50/D3
Hoogezand, Neth. 50/D2
Hooghly (riv.), India 85/F5
Hooghly-Chinsura, India 85/G4
Hoogkarspel, Neth. 50/C3
Hooglede, Belg. 52/C2
Hoogstraten, Belg. 50/B6
Hook (pt.), Ire. 31/Q10
Hook (sound), Austl. 114/C3
Hookena, Hi, US 124/U11
Hoonah, Ak, US 134/L4
Hooper, Ut, US 137/J11
Hooper Bay, Ak, US 134/F3
Hoopeston, Il, US 130/C3
Hoopstad, SAfr. 106/D2
Hoorn, Neth. 50/C3
Hoornse Hop (bay), Neth. 50/C3
Hoover (dam), Az, US 128/D3
Hoover, Mo, US 137/D5
Hopa, Turk. 90/E1
Hopatcong, NJ, US 138/D2
Hopatcong (lake), NJ, US 138/D2
Hope (lake), Austl. 109/A4
Hope, BC, Can. 126/C3
Hope, Ak, US 134/J3
Hope, NJ, US 138/D2
Hope Vale Aboriginal Community, Austl. 114/A1
Hopedale, Nf, Can. 123/J3
Hopelchén, Mex. 144/D2
Hopeman, Sc, UK 36/C1
Hopes Advance (cape), Qu, Can. 123/K2
Hope's Nose (pt.), Eng, UK 32/C6
Hopetown, SAfr. 106/D3
Hopewell, NJ, US 138/D3
Hopewell Furnace NHS, Pa, US 138/C3
Hopkins (riv.), Austl. 115/B3
Hopkins (lake), Austl. 109/B3
Hopkinsville, Ky, US 130/C4
Hoppecke (riv.), Ger. 51/F6
Hoppegarten, Ger. 40/Q6
Hoppstädten-Weiersbach, Ger. 53/G4
Hopsten, Ger. 51/E4
Hoquiam, Wa, US 126/C4
Horace (mtn.), Ak, US 134/J2
Horado, Japan 77/L4
Hōrai-san (peak), Japan 77/L4
Horasan, Turk. 90/E1
Horažďovice, Czh. 55/G4
Horb am Neckar, Ger. 54/B6
Horbourg-Wihr, Fr. 56/D1
Hörbranz, Aus. 57/F2
Horche, Sp. 44/D2
Hordaland (co.), Nor. 37/C3
Hördt, Ger. 54/B4
Hørdt, Fr. 56/D1
Horezu, Rom. 49/G3
Horgau, Ger. 54/D6
Horgen, Swi. 57/E3
Horine, Mo, US 137/E6
Horinger, China 72/B2
Horley, Eng, UK 30/C3
Horlivka, Ukr. 62/F2
Hormigueros, PR 141/M8
Hormuz (str.), Oman 89/G3
Horn (cape), Chile 159/D7
Horn, Neth. 50/C3
Horn (isl.), Ice. 37/L2
Horn (pt.), Ice. 160/H
Horn-Bad Meinberg, Ger. 51/F5
Hornachuelos, Sp. 44/C4
Hornád (riv.), Slvk. 41/L4
Hornavan (lake), Swe. 37/F2
Hornbach, Ger. 53/G5
Hornberg, Ger. 57/E1
Horndal, Swe. 38/G1
Horneburg, Ger. 51/G2
Hornell, NY, US 130/E3
Horní Bříza, Czh. 55/G3
Horní Slavkov, Czh. 55/F2
Hornisgrinde (peak), Ger. 54/B5
Hornos (cape), Chile 159/D7
Hornoy-le-Bourg, Fr. 52/A4
Hornslet, Den. 38/D3
Hørnum (cape), Ger. 38/C4
Horoshiri-dake (peak), Japan 76/C2
Horovice, Czh. 55/G3
Horqin Zuoyi Houqi, China 72/E2
Horqin Zuoyi Zhongqi, China 72/E2
Hörsching, Aus. 55/H6
Horse Cave, Ky, US 130/C4
Horsefly (lake), BC, Can. 126/C2
Horsens, Den. 38/C4
Horseshoe (pt.), Sc, UK 31/V14
Horseshoe, Il, US 137/G8
Horseshoe (lake), Co, US 137/B2
Horsetooth (res.), Co, US 137/B2
Horsey (isl.), Eng, UK 33/H3
Horsforth, Eng, UK 35/G4
Horsham, Austl. 115/B3
Horsham, Eng, UK 33/F4
Horsham, Pa, US 138/D3
Horst, Neth. 50/D6

Hörstel, Ger. 51/E4
Horstmar, Ger. 51/E4
Horta, Azor., Port. 45/S12
Horten, Nor. 38/D2
Hortes, Fr. 56/B2
Hortobágyi NP, Hun. 62/B3
Horton (pt.), NY, US 139/F1
Horton (riv.), NW, Can. 122/D2
Høruphav, Den. 38/C4
Horusický Rybník (lake), Czh. 55/H4
Hørve, Den. 38/D4
Hørvot Dor, Isr. 91/F6
Horw, Swi. 57/E3
Horwich, Eng, UK 35/F4
Horwood (lake), On, Can. 130/D2
Hösbach, Ger. 54/C2
Hosenfeld, Ger. 54/C1
Hoshiārpur, India 84/C2
Hosingen, Lux. 53/F3
Hospental, Swi. 57/E4
Hosszúpereszteg, Hun. 48/C2
Hoste (isl.), Chile 159/C7
Hot Springs, SD, US 127/H5
Hot Springs NP, Ar, US 129/J4
Hotaka, Japan 75/E2
Hotaka-dake (peak), Japan 75/E2
Hotan, China 70/D4
Hotan (riv.), China 70/D4
Hotazel, SAfr. 106/C2
Hotont, Mong. 70/H2
Hottah (lake), NW, Can. 122/E2
Hotton, Belg. 53/E3
Houari Boumedienne (int'l arpt.), Alg. 100/G4
Houdain, Fr. 52/B3
Houdan, Fr. 30/G5
Houet (prov.), Burk. 102/D4
Houffalize, Belg. 53/E3
Houghton (riv.), Austl. 115/B3
Houghton Lake, Mi, US 130/C2
Houghton-le-Spring, Eng, UK 35/G2
Houilles, Fr. 30/J5
Houlton, Me, US 131/H2
Houma, China 72/B4
Houplines, Fr. 52/B2
Hourdel (pt.), Fr. 52/A3
Hourn, Loch (inlet), Sc, UK 36/A2
Hourtin, Fr. 42/C4
Housatonic (riv.), Ct, US 139/E1
House (range), Ut, US 128/D3
House Springs, Mo, US 137/F9
Houssen, Fr. 56/D1
Houston, BC, Can. 126/B2
Houston, Ak, US 134/J3
Houston, De, US 138/C6
Houston, Mo, US 129/K3
Houston, Ms, US 133/F3
Houston, Tx, US 129/J5
Houtbaai, SAfr. 106/L11
Houten, Neth. 50/C4
Houthulst, Belg. 52/B2
Houtman Abrolhos (isl.), Austl. 112/A4
Houtribdijk (dam), Neth. 50/C3
Houtskär (isl.), Fin. 39/J1
Houyet, Belg. 53/E3
Hova, Swe. 38/E2
Hovd (prov.), Mong. 70/F2
Hovd, Mong. 70/F2
Hövelhof, Ger. 51/F5
Hovenweep Nat'l Mon., Ut, US 128/E3
Hovfjället (peak), Swe. 38/E1
Hovmantorp, Swe. 38/F3
Hövsgöl (prov.), Mong. 70/G1
Hovsta, Swe. 38/F2
Howard, Austl. 114/D4
Howard (hill), Ak, US 134/H2
Howard (pass), Ak, US 134/G2
Howard (co.), Md, US 138/B5
Howard Hanson (res.), Wa, US 135/D3
Howard Hanson (dam), Wa, US 135/D3
Howe (cape), Austl. 115/D3
Howell, Mi, US 130/D3
Howell, NJ, US 138/D3
Howick, SAfr. 107/E3
Howland (isl.) 117/H4
Höxter, Ger. 51/G5
Hoxud, China 70/E3
Hoy (isl.), Sc, UK 31/V14
Høyanger, Nor. 38/C1
Hoya, Japan 77/D2
Høydalsmo, Nor. 38/C2
Hoylake, Eng, UK 35/E5
Hoyland Nether, Eng, UK 35/G4
Hoyos, Sp. 44/B2
Hoyoux (riv.), Belg. 53/E3
Hozumi, Japan 77/L5

Hracholusky (res.), Czh. 55/F3
Hradec Králové, Czh. 41/H3
Hradiště (peak), Czh. 55/G2
Hranice, Bosn. 48/D4
Hrasnica, Bosn. 48/D4
Hrazdan, Arm. 71/K5
Hrodna, Bela. 39/K5
Hrodzyenskaya Voblasts Bela. 60/B3
Hrolleifsborg (peak), Ice. 37/M6
Hron (riv.), Slvk. 62/A2
Hronov, Czh. 41/H3
Hrubieszów, Pol. 41/M3
Hrubý Jeseník (mts.), Czh.,Pol. 41/J3
Hrútafjöll (peak), Ice. 37/P6
Hsinchu, Tai. 79/K3
Hua (pt.), China 72/B4
Hua (lake), China 72/B4
Hua Hin, Thai. 78/B4
Hua Xian, China 72/C4
Hua'an, China 79/C2
Huacabamba, Peru 156/B3
Huachi, China 72/B4
Huacho, Peru 156/B3
Huachón, Peru 156/B3
Huachuca City, Az, US 128/E5
Huacrachuco, Peru 156/B3
Huade, China 72/B3
Huahine (isl.), FrPol. 117/K6
Huai'an, China 72/C2
Huai'an, China 72/C2
Huaibei, China 71/L5
Huaibin, China 72/C4
Huaiji, China 83/K3
Huainan, China 72/D4
Huairen, China 72/B3
Huairou, China 72/H6
Huaiyang, China 72/C4
Huaiyin, China 72/D4
Huaiyuan, China 72/D4
Huajicori, Mex. 142/D4
Huajuapan de León, Mex. 144/B2
Hualahuises, Mex. 143/F3
Hualañé, Chile 158/C2
Hualgayoc, Peru 156/B2
Hualien, Tai. 79/D3
Hualla, Peru 156/C4
Huallaga (riv.), Peru 147/B3
Huallanca, Peru 156/B3
Huallanca, Peru 156/C4
Huamachuco, Peru 156/B3
Huamantanga, Peru 156/B3
Huamantla, Mex. 143/M7
Huambos, Peru 156/B2
Huan (riv.), China 72/B3
Huan Xian, China 70/J4
Huancané, Peru 156/C4
Huancapi, Peru 156/C4
Huancaspata, Peru 156/B3
Huancavelica (dept.), Peru 156/C4
Huancavelica, Peru 156/C4
Huancayo, Peru 156/C4
Huanchaca (peak), Bol. 150/E8
Huang (riv.), China 67/L6
Huangchuan, China 72/C4
Huanggang (peak), China 79/C2
Huanghua, China 72/D3
Huangling, China 72/B4
Huanglong, China 72/B4
Huanglong, China 72/B4
Huangqi (lake), China 79/C2
Huangshan, China 79/C2
Huangtang (lake), China 72/C5
Huangtu (plat.), China 72/B3
Huangueién, Arg. 158/E3
Huangyan, China 79/D2
Huangzhong, China 70/H4
Huanren, China 73/C2
Huanta, Peru 156/C4
Huántar, Peru 156/B3
Huánuco (dept.), Peru 156/C4
Huánuco, Peru 156/B3
Huanuni, Bol. 150/E7
Huapi (mts.), Nic. 144/E4
Huaquechula, Mex. 143/L8
Huaquillas, Ecu. 156/A1
Huaral, Peru 156/C4
Huaraz, Peru 156/B3
Huari, Peru 156/C4
Huaricolca, Peru 156/C4
Huarina, Bol. 150/D7
Huarmey, Peru 156/C4
Huarochiri, Peru 156/C4
Huarocondo, Peru 156/C4
Huásabas, Mex. 142/C2
Huasahuasi, Peru 156/C4
Huascarán, Peru 156/B3
Huatabampo, Mex. 142/C3
Huatunas (lake), Bol. 150/E6
Huatusco, Mex. 143/N7
Huauchinango, Mex. 143/N7
Huautla de Jiménez, Mex. 144/B2
Huayacocotla, Mex. 143/L6
Huayanay (riv.), Belg. 53/E3
Huaylas, Peru 156/B3
Huayllay, Peru 156/B3

Huayopata, Peru 156/C4
Huayuan, China 83/J2
Huazhou, China 83/K3
Hubbard (mt.), Ak, US 134/L3
Hubbard Creek (res.), Tx, US 129/H4
Hubei (prov.), China 71/K5
Hubei (pass), China 72/B4
Hubli-Dhārwār, India 89/L5
Huch'ang, NKor. 73/D2
Hückelhoven, Ger. 53/F1
Hückeswagen, Ger. 53/G1
Hucknall, Eng, UK 35/G5
Huddersfield, Eng, UK 35/G4
Huddinge, Swe. 38/G2
Hude, Ger. 51/F2
Hudiksvall, Swe. 38/G1
Hudson (cape), Ant. 160/L
Hudson (bay), Can. 123/H2
Hudson (str.), Nun., Qu, Can. 123/J2
Hudson, Qu, Can. 131/M7
Hudson, Co, US 137/C2
Hudson (co.), NJ, US 139/J9
Hudson (riv.), NJ,NY, US 130/F3
Hudson, NY, US 130/F3
Hudson Bay, Sk, Can. 127/H2
Hudson's Hope, BC, Can. 122/D3
Hue, Viet. 78/D2
Huedin, Rom. 49/F2
Huehuetenango, Guat. 144/A1
Huehuetlán, Mex. 143/L6
Huejotzingo, Mex. 143/L7
Huejuquilla el Alto, Mex. 142/E4
Huejutla de Reyes, Mex. 144/B1
Huelma, SAfr. 44/A4
Huelva, Sp. 44/B4
Huelva (riv.), Sp. 44/B4
Huequi (vol.), Chile 158/B4
Huercal-Overa, Sp. 44/E4
Huerfano (riv.), Co, US 129/F3
Huesca, Sp. 45/E1
Huéscar, Sp. 44/D4
Huetamo de Nuñez, Mex. 143/E5
Huete, Sp. 44/D2
Huexoculco, Mex. 143/R10
Hüfingen, Ger. 57/E2
Hugh Town, Eng, UK 31/Q12
Hughenden, Austl. 114/A3
Hughenden Valley, Eng, UK 30/A2
Hughes, Ak, US 134/H2
Hughes, Arg. 158/E2
Hughesville, Pa, US 138/B1
Huglfing, Ger. 57/H2
Hugo, Ok, US 129/J4
Huguan, China 72/C3
Hui Xian, China 72/C4
Hui'an, China 79/C2
Huib-Hock (plat.), Namb. 106/B2
Huichang, China 79/C2
Huichapan, Mex. 143/K6
Hüich'ŏn, NKor. 73/D2
Huila (dept.), Col. 152/C4
Huila, Nevado del (peak), Col. 152/C4
Huilai, China 79/C3
Huilango, Mex. 143/Q9
Huili, China 83/H2
Huimanguillo, Mex. 144/C2
Huimin, China 72/D3
Huinca Renancó, Arg. 158/D2
Huining, China 70/J4
Hüisaek-pong (peak), NKor. 73/D2
Huishui, China 83/J2
Huisne (riv.), Fr. 42/D2
Huissen, Neth. 50/C5
Huitong, China 83/J2
Huitzilan, Mex. 143/N7
Huitzilan, Mex. 143/M7
Huitzilac, Mex. 143/K8
Huixcolotla, Mex. 143/M8
Huixquilucan, Mex. 143/Q10
Huixtla, Mex. 144/C3
Huize, China 83/H2
Huizen, Neth. 50/C4
Hujra, Bel. 86/B4
Hulan, China 71/N2
Hulett, Wy, US 127/G5
Hulin, China 71/P2
Hullbridge, Eng, UK 30/E2
Hüllhorst, Ger. 51/F4
Hulst, Neth. 50/B6
Hultsfred, Swe. 38/F3
Huma, China 71/N1
Humay, Peru 156/B3
Humber (riv.), Nf, Can. 131/K1
Humber (bay), On, Can. 131/R8
Humber (riv.), Eng, UK 35/H4
Humberto de Campos, Braz. 154/B1
Humble, Tx, US 129/J5
Humboldt, Sk, Can. 127/H2
Humboldt (range), Nv, US 128/C2
Humboldt, Tn, US 130/B3
Humboldt (bay), Col. 145/G3
Humboldt, Nv, US 124/C3

Hume (lake), Austl. 115/C2
Húmeda, Pampa (plain), Arg. 158/E2
Humenné, Slvk. 41/L4
Humida, Pampa (plain), Arg. 157/D4
Humlum, Den. 38/C3
Hummels Wharf, Pa, US 138/B2
Hummelstown, Pa, US 138/B3
Humphrey (pt.), Ak, US 134/K2
Humphreys (peak), Az, US 128/E4
Hūn, Libya 96/J2
Húnaflói (bay), Ice. 37/N6
Hunan (prov.), China 71/K6
Hundsangen, Ger. 53/G3
Hunedoara, Rom. 48/F3
Hunedoara (prov.), Rom. 48/F3
Hünenberg, Swi. 57/E3
Hünfeld, Ger. 43/H1
Hung Yen, Viet. 78/D1
Hungaroring, Hun. 49/R9
Hungary (ctry.) 48/D2
Hungen, Ger. 54/B2
Hüngnam, NKor. 73/D3
Hunjiang, China 73/D2
Hunnebostrand, Swe. 38/D2
Hunsel, Neth. 50/C6
Hunsrück (mts.), Ger. 40/D4
Hunte (isl.), Austl. 109/D5
Hunter (isl.), Austl. 115/D2
Hunter (mt.), Ak, US 134/H3
Hunter, Tx, US 137/U20
Hunterdon (co.), NJ, US 138/C2
Huntingburg, In, US 130/C4
Huntingdon, Eng, US 33/F2
Huntington, In, US 130/C3
Huntington, NY, US 139/M8
Huntington (bay), NY, US 139/M8
Huntington Bay, NY, US 139/M8
Huntington Beach, Ca, US 136/G8
Huntington Park, Ca, US 136/F8
Huntington Station, NY, US 139/M8
Huntington Woods, Mi, US 135/F7
Huntley, Il, US 135/P15
Huntly, NZ 117/T10
Huntly, Sc, UK 36/D2
Hunts Inlet, BC, Can. 134/M4
Hunts Point, Wa, US 135/C2
Huntsville, Al, US 133/G3
Huntsville, On, Can. 136/E2
Huntsville, Ut, US 137/K11
Huntsville (res.), Pa, US 138/B1
Hunucmá, Mex. 144/D1
Hünxe, Ger. 50/D5
Hunyuan, China 72/C3
Huo (mtn.), China 72/D5
Huo (prov.), China 72/D5
Huocheng, China 70/D3
Huojia, China 72/C4
Huolin Gol, China 71/L2
Huoqiu, China 72/D4
Huoshan, China 72/D5
Huozhou, China 72/B3
Hurdal, Nor. 38/D1
Hure Qi, China 72/E2
Hurepoix (reg.), Fr. 30/H6
Hurley, NM, US 128/E4
Hurley, Eng, UK 30/A2
Hurley (riv.), Ire. 34/B4
Hurlford, Sc, UK 36/B3
Huron (lake), Can.,US 130/D2
Huron (riv.), Mi, US 130/B2
Huron (pt.), Mi, US 135/G6
Huron (riv.), Mi, US 135/E7
Hurricane, WV, US 130/D4
Hurtaut (riv.), Fr. 52/D4
Hürtgenwald (reg.), Ger. 53/E2
Hürth, Ger. 53/F2
Hurup, Den. 38/C3
Husainābād, India 85/E3
Húsavík, Ice. 37/P6
Huscarán, PN, Peru 150/C5
Husher, Wi, US 135/Q14
Huşi, Rom. 49/J2
Huskisson, Austl. 115/D2
Huslia, Ak, US 134/G2
Husnes, Nor. 38/A2
Hussigny-Godbrange, Fr. 53/E5
Husum, Ger. 38/C4
Husum, Swe. 37/F3
Hutag, Mong. 70/H2
Hutchinson, Mn, US 127/K4
Hutchinson, Ks, US 129/H3
Hüttisheim, Ger. 57/F1
Hüttlingen, Ger. 57/F2
Hutton (mt.), Austl. 114/C4
Hutton, Eng, UK 30/E2
Huttwil, Swi. 56/D3
Hutuo (riv.), China 72/C3
Ḫuwwārāh, WBnk. 91/G7
Huy, Belg. 53/E2
Huyton-with-Roby, Eng, UK 35/F5
Huzhou, China 72/L9
Hvammstangi, Ice. 37/N6
Hvannadalshnúkur (peak), Ice. 37/P7

Hvar (isl.), Cro. 46/E1
Hvide Sande, Den. 38/C4
Hvítá (riv.), Ice. 37/N7
Hvolsvöllur, Ice. 37/N7
Hwange, Zim. 105/E4
Hwange (Wankie) NP, Zim. 105/E4
Hwanghae-bukto (prov.), NKor. 73/D3
Hwanghae-namdo (prov.), NKor. 73/C3
Hwangju, NKor. 73/C3
Hwangju (riv.), NKor. 73/C3
Hwasun, SKor. 73/D5
Hyades (peak), Chile 158/B5
Hyattstown, Md, US 138/A5
Hyattsville, Md, US 138/B6
Hydaburg, Ak, US 134/M4
Hyde, Eng, UK 35/F5
Hyder, Ak, US 134/M4
Hyderābād, India 82/C4
Hyderābād, Pak. 89/J3
Hyères, Fr. 43/G5
Hyères, Îles d' (isls.), Fr 43/G5
Hyesan, NKor. 73/E2
Hygiene, Co, US 137/B2
Hyland (riv.), Yk, Can. 122/D2
Hyllestad, Nor. 38/A1
Hyltebruk, Swe. 38/E3
Hylton (hill), Ky, US 130/D4
Hyō-no-sen (peak), Japan 74/D3
Hyōgo (pref.), Japan 74/D3
Hyŏndũng-san (peak), SKor. 73/G6
Hyrum, Ut, US 128/E2
Hythe, Eng, UK 33/H4
Hyūga, Japan 74/B5
Hyvinkää, Fin. 39/L1
Hywel, Moel (peak), Wal, UK 32/C2

I

I-n-Amenas, Alg. 99/H3
I-n-Azaoua, Oued (riv.), Niger 99/H5
I-n-Dagouber (well), Mali 99/E5
I-n-Echaï (well), Mali 103/E1
I-n-Gall, Niger 99/G5
I-n-Guezzâm, Alg. 103/G2
I-n-Milach (well), Mali 103/E2
I-n-Sâkâne, 'Erg (des.), Mali 103/E1
I-n-Salah, Alg. 99/F4
I-n-Tassik (well), Mali 103/F2
Iacanga, Braz. 155/B2
Iaciara, Braz. 154/A4
Iaco (riv.), Braz. 150/E6
Iaçu, Braz. 154/B4
Iāf di Montasio (peak), It. 43/K3
Iakora, Madg. 107/H8
Ialomiţa (riv.), Rom. 62/C3
Ialomiţa (prov.), Rom. 49/H3
Ianapera, Madg. 107/H8
Iapu, Braz. 155/D1
Iaşi (riv.), Rom. 49/H2
Iaşi, Rom. 49/H2
Iasmos, Gre. 47/J2
Iatan, Mo, US 137/D5
Iba, Phil. 79/C4
Ibadan, Nga. 103/F5
Ibagué, Col. 150/C3
Ibaiti, Braz. 155/B2
Ibajay, Phil. 79/D5
Ibanda, Ugan. 104/A3
Ibanga, Ugan. 104/A3
Ibaporã, Braz. 154/B4
Ibapaba, Serra da (range), Braz. 154/B1
Ibar (riv.), Serb. 48/E4
Ibara, Japan 74/C3
Ibaraki (pref.), Japan 75/F2
Ibaraki, Japan 77/M1
Ibaraki, Japan 77/E1
Ibarra, Ecu. 150/C3
Ibarreta, Arg. 157/E2
Ibb, Yem. 88/D6
Ibba (riv.), Sudan 97/L6
Ibbenbüren, Ger. 50/D4
Ibdekkene (riv.), Mali 103/F2
Iberia, Peru 156/D3
Iberia, Peru 156/C2
Ibérico, Sistema (range), Sp. 44/D2
Iberville, Qu, Can. 131/P7
Ibiá, Braz. 155/C1
Ibiapina, Braz. 154/B1
Ibicaraí, Braz. 154/C4
Ibicuy, Arg. 159/J10
Ibigawa, Japan 77/L5
Ibimirim, Braz. 155/D2
Ibiraçu, Braz. 155/D1
Ibirapuã, Braz. 155/D1
Ibitinga, Braz. 155/B2
Ibiúna, Braz. 211/F8
Ibiza (isl.), Sp. 45/F3
Ibiza, Sp. 45/F3
Ibó, Moz. 105/H3
Ibo (riv.), Japan 74/D3
Iboro, Nga. 103/F5
Ibotirama, Braz. 154/B4
Iboundji (peak), Gabon 96/H8
Ibrány, Hun. 41/L4
Ibshawāy, Egypt 91/B5
Ibuki, Japan 77/K5

Ibuki-yama (peak), Japan 77/K5
Ica (dept.), Peru 156/C4
Ica, Peru 156/C4
Içana (riv.), Braz. 150/D3
Icel (prov.), Turk. 90/C2
Icém, Braz. 155/B2
Ichalkaranji, India 89/K5
Ichāmati (riv.), Bang. 85/G3
Ichchāpuram, India 82/D4
Ichenhausen, Ger. 54/D6
Ichhāwar, India 84/A4
Ichihara, Japan 75/F3
Ichijima, Japan 77/H5
Ichikawa, Japan 77/D2
Ichikawada, Japan 77/B2
Ichinohe, Japan 76/B3
Ichinomiya, Japan 77/E3
Ichinomiya, Japan 77/E3
Ichinomiya, Japan 77/L7
Ichinomiya, Japan 77/M6
Ichinoseki, Japan 76/B4
Ichishi, Japan 77/K6
Ichishi, Japan 77/K6
Ich'ŏn, SKor. 73/D4
Ichtegem, Belg. 52/C1
Ickesburg, Pa, US 138/A3
Icó, Braz. 154/C2
Icod de los Vinos, Canl.,Sp. 98/A3
Icy (cape), Ak, US 134/F1
Icy (pt.), Ak, US 134/L4
Icy (str.), Ak, US 134/L4
Icy (bay), Ak, US 122/B3
Idabel, Ok, US 129/J4
Idaho (state), US 126/E5
Idaho Springs, Co, US 137/A3
Idanha-a-Nova, Port. 44/B3
Idar, India 82/B3
Idar-Oberstein, Ger. 53/G4
Idarkopf (peak), Ger. 53/G4
Idaville, Pa, US 138/A3
Ide, Japan 77/J6
Ideles, Alg. 99/G5
Idfū, Egypt 101/C3
Idhi (peak), Gre. 47/J5
Idhra, Gre. 47/H4
Idice (riv.), It. 59/E4
Idjwe, Île (isl.), D.R. Congo 104/A3
Idkū, Egypt 91/B4
Idle (riv.), Eng, UK 35/H5
Idlewild, Japan 77/K7
Idlib (prov.), Syria 90/D3
Idlib, Syria 91/E2
Idna (riv.), WBnk. 91/D4
Idrija, Slo. 43/L4
Idriss I (dam), Mor. 100/B2
Idriss I, Barrage (res.), Mor. 100/B2
Idro, Lago d' (lake), It. 58/D1
Idstein, Ger. 54/B2
Idzikowice, Japan 75/J7
Ieper, Belg. 52/B2
Ierápetra, Gre. 47/J5
Ierissós, Gre. 47/H2
Iesolo, It. 59/F1
Ifalik (isl.), Micr. 116/D4
Ifanadiana, Madg. 107/H8
Ife, Nga. 103/F5
Iferles (well), Libya 99/H3
Iffeldorf, Ger. 57/H2
Iffezheim, Ger. 54/B5
Iflora, Adrar des (upland), Alg.,Mali 96/F4
Iframe, Mor. 98/D2
Iga (riv.), Japan 77/K6
Iga, Japan 77/K6
Igal, Hun. 48/C2
Iganga, Ugan. 104/A3
Igaporã, Braz. 154/B4
Igara Paraná (riv.), Col. 152/C5
Igarapava, Braz. 155/C2
Igarapé Grande, Braz. 154/A2
Igarapé-Miri, Braz. 151/J4
Igaratá, Braz. 211/J3
Igarka, Rus. 64/J3
Igatpuri, India 82/B4
Igdet (peak), Mor. 98/C3
Iğdır, Turk. 90/F2
Igel, Ger. 53/F4
Iggesund, Swe. 38/G1
Ightham, Eng, UK 30/D3
Igikpak (mt.), Ak, US 134/H2
Igis, Swi. 57/F4
Igli, Alg. 99/E3
Igloolik, Nun., Can. 123/H2
Ignace, On, Can. 127/L3
Ignacio, Ca, US 135/J10
Ignacio de la Llave, Mex. 143/P8
Ignacio Zaragoza, Mex. 142/D2
Iğneada Burnu (cape), Turk. 49/J5
Iğney, Fr. 56/C1
Ignon (riv.), Fr. 56/A1
Igny, Fr. 30/J5
Igombe (riv.), Tanz. 104/B5
Igora Paraná (riv.), Col. 156/C1
Igoumenítsa, Gre. 47/G3
Igra, Rus. 61/M4
Igreja, Morro da (peak), Braz. 155/B4
Iguaçu (riv.), Braz. 147/D5
Iguaçu, PN do, Braz. 155/B4
Iguaí, Braz. 154/B4

Iguala, Mex. 143/K8
Igualada, Sp. 45/C2
Iguape, Braz. 155/C3
Iguape (riv.), Braz. 155/B3
Iguatu, Braz. 154/C2
Iguazú, PN del, Arg. 157/D2
Iguetti (lake), Mrta. 98/C4
Iheya (isl.), Japan 75/J7
Ihhayrhan, Mong. 70/J2
Ihosy, Madg. 107/H8
Ihotry (lake), Madg. 107/G8
Ihuari, Peru 156/B3
Ii, Fin. 60/E2
Ii (riv.), Fin. 60/E2
Iida, Japan 75/E3
Iijima, Japan 77/E3
Iijoki (riv.), Fin. 60/F2
Iinan, Japan 77/K7
Iisalmi, Fin. 37/H3
Iitaka, Japan 77/K7
Iitti, Fin. 39/M1
Iiyama, Japan 75/F2
Iizuka, Japan 74/B4
Ijebu Ode, Nga. 103/F5
Ijill, Mrta. 98/B5
Ijill (lake), Mrta. 98/B5
IJmeer (bay), Neth. 50/C4
IJmuiden, Neth. 50/B4
Ijnaoun (well), Mrta. 102/B2
Ijoki (riv.), Fin. 37/H2
Ijoubbane, 'Erg (des.), Mali 98/D5
IJssel (riv.), Neth. 50/D4
IJsselmeer (lake), Neth. 40/C2
IJsselmuiden, Neth. 50/C4
IJsselstein, Neth. 50/C4
Ik (riv.), Rus. 61/M5
Ikahavo (plat.), Madg. 107/H7
Ikalamavony, Madg. 107/H8
Ikare, Nga. 103/G5
Ikaría, Gre. 90/A2
Ikaría (isl.), Gre. 47/J4
Ikaruga, Japan 77/J6
Ikast, Den. 38/C3
Ikeda, Japan 74/C3
Ikeda, Japan 76/C2
Ikeda, Japan 77/H6
Ikeja, Nga. 103/F5
Ikenokoya-yama (peak), Japan 77/K6
Ikerre, Nga. 103/G5
Ikhtiman, Bul. 47/H1
Iki (isl.), Japan 74/A4
Iki (chan.), Japan 74/A4
Ikire, Nga. 103/G5
Ikirun, Nga. 103/G5
Ikizce, Turk. 90/C2
Ikizdere, Turk. 90/E1
Ikoma, Japan 77/J6
Ikongo, Madg. 107/H7
Ikopa (riv.), Madg. 107/H7
Ikorodu, Nga. 103/F5
Ikuno, Japan 74/D3
Ila Orangun, Nga. 103/G4
Ilabaya, Peru 156/D5
Ilagan, Phil. 79/D4
Ilam, Nepal 85/F2
Ilām, Iran 79/D3
Ilan, Tai. 79/D3
Ilanz, Swi. 57/E4
Ilaro, Braz. 103/F5
Ilave, Peru 156/D4
Iława, Pol. 41/K2
Ilawe-Ekiti, Nga. 103/G5
Île-à-la-Crosse, Sk, Can. 126/G2
Île-a-la-Crosse (lake), Sk, Can. 126/G2
Île-de-France (pol. reg.), Fr. 52/A6
Ilebo, D.R. Congo 105/D4
Ilek (riv.), Rus. 63/K2
Îles Ehotilés, PN des, C.d'Iv. 102/E5
Îles Tristao, Îles (isls.), Gui. 102/B4
Ilesha, Nga. 103/G5
Ilfis (riv.), Swi. 56/D4
Ilgaz, Turk. 90/D1
Ilgın, Turk. 90/B2
Ilha Grande (bay), Braz. 211/J8
Ilha Grande, Baía de (bay), Braz. 155/C2
Ilha Solteira, Reprêsa (res.), Braz. 151/H7
Ilhabela, Braz. 211/H8
Ilhavo, Port. 44/A2
Ilhéus, Braz. 154/C4
Iliamna, Ak, US 134/H4
Iliamna (lake), Ak, US 134/H4
Iliamna (vol.), Ak, US 134/G4
Iliç, Turk. 90/D2
Ilijaš, Bosn. 48/D4
Iliniza (peak), Ecu. 152/B5
Ilinsk, Sp. 45/G3
Ilírska Bistrica, Slov. 43/L4
Ilisu (dam), Turk. 90/E2
Ilium (Troy) (ruin), Turk. 47/K3
Ilkeston, Eng, UK 35/G6
Ilkley, Eng, UK 35/G5
Illampu (pt.), Turk. 90/E1
Illana, Sp. 45/D3
Illapel, Chile 157/B3
Illasi (riv.), It. 59/E1
Illbillee (mt.), Austl. 113/G3
Illéla, Niger 103/H4

Iller (riv.), Ger. 43/J2
Illertissen, Ger. 57/G1
Illescas, Sp. 44/D2
Illiers-Combray, Fr. 42/D2
Illimani (peak), Bol. 150/E7
Illingen, Ger. 53/G5
Illinois (riv.), Il, US 130/B3
Illinois (state), US 130/B4
Illizi, Alg. 99/H4
Illizi (prov.), Alg. 99/H4
Illkirch-Graffenstaden, Fr. 56/D1
Illmensee, Ger. 57/F2
Illnau, Swi. 57/E3
Illora, Sp. 44/D4
Illovo, SAfr. 107/E3
Illovy (riv.), Rus. 63/H2
Illzach, Fr. 56/D2
Ilmenau, Ger. 40/F4
Ilmenau (riv.), Ger. 51/H2
Il'men (lake), Rus. 64/D4
Ilmenau, Ger. 43/J1
Ilo, Peru 156/D5
Ilobu, Nga. 103/G4
Ilorin, Nga. 103/G4
Ilovlya (riv.), Rus. 63/H2
Ilpendam, Neth. 50/B4
Ilse (riv.), Ger. 51/H4
Ilsenburg, Ger. 51/H5
Ilshofen, Ger. 54/C4
Ilyas Burnu (pt.), Turk. 49/H5
Ilych (riv.), Rus. 61/N3
Ilz (riv.), Ger. 41/G4
Imabari, Japan 74/C3
Imaichi, Japan 75/F2
Imaloto (riv.), Madg. 107/H8
Imamoğlu, Turk. 90/C2
Imandra (lake), Rus. 37/J2
Imari, Japan 74/A4
Imatra, Fin. 39/N1
Imazu, Japan 77/K5
Imba (lake), Japan 77/E2
Imba, Japan 77/E2
Imbabura (prov.), Ecu. 152/B4
Imbituba, Braz. 155/B4
Imbituva, Braz. 155/B3
Imeni Moskvy (canal), Rus. 61/W9
Imerimandroso, Madg. 107/J7
Imi n'tanout, Mor. 98/C3
Imişli, Azer. 63/J5
Imja (isl.), SKor. 73/C5
Imlay, Nv, US 126/D5
Immendingen, Ger. 57/E2
Immenhausen, Ger. 51/G4
Immenstaad am Bodensee, Ger. 57/F2
Immenstadt im Allgäu, Ger. 57/G2
Imola, It. 59/E4
Imouzzèr-Kandar, Mor. 100/B3
Imperatriz, Braz. 154/B2
Imperia, It. 58/B5
Imperial, Sk, Can. 127/G3
Imperial, Peru 156/B4
Imperial, Ne, US 129/G2
Imperial Beach, Ca, US 136/C5
Imperial Palace, Japan 77/B2
Impero (riv.), It. 58/B5
Impfondo, Congo 96/J7
Imphal, India 83/F3
Imphy, Fr. 42/E3
Impruneta, It. 59/E5
Imrali (isl.), Turk. 90/B1
Imranlı, Turk. 90/D2
Imroz, Gre. 47/J2
Imshil, SKor. 73/D4
Imst, Aus. 57/G3
Imuris, Mex. 142/C2
Ina, Japan 75/E3
Ina (riv.), Pol. 41/H2
Inabe, Japan 77/L5
Inabu, Japan 77/L6
Inagawa, Japan 77/H6
Inagi, Japan 77/D2
Inajá, Braz. 151/H7
Inambari (riv.), Peru 156/D4
Inanwatan, Indo. 116/E3
Inaouene (riv.), Mor. 100/B2
Inari (lake), Fin. 37/H1
Inarijärvi (lake), Fin. 37/H1
Inawashiro (lake), Japan 75/F2
Inazawa, Japan 77/L5
Inca, Sp. 45/G3
Incesu, Turk. 90/C2
Incheville, Fr. 52/A3
Inchinnan, Sc, UK 36/A6
Inchkeith (isl.), Sc, UK 36/C4
Inchnadamph, Sc, UK 31/R7
Inch'ŏn, SKor. 73/F7
Inch'ŏn-Gwangyŏksi, SKor. 73/D4
Incirliova, Turk. 90/A2
Incisa in Val d'Arno, It. 59/E5
Inconfidentes, Braz. 211/G7

Incudine, Mont l' (peak), Fr. 46/A2
Indaiá (riv.), Braz. 155/C1
Indaiatuba, Braz. 155/C2
Indalsälven (riv.), Swe. 37/E3
Indanan, Phil. 81/F2
Independence (mts.), Nv, US 126/E5
Independence, Ks, US 129/J3
Independence, Ca, US 128/C3
Independence, Mo, US 137/E5
Independence, Belz. 144/D2
Independence Nat'l Hist. Park, Pa, US 138/C4
Independência, Braz. 154/B2
Independencia, Peru 156/B4
Index, Wa, US 135/D2
India (ctry.) 67/D7
Indian (ocean) 23/N6
Indian Echo Caverns, Pa, US 138/B3
Indian Head, Sk, Can. 127/H3
Indian Hills, Co, US 137/B3
Indian Peaks Wilderness Area, Co, US 137/A2
Indiana (state), US 130/C3
Indiana, Pa, US 130/E3
Indianapolis (int'l arpt.), In, US 130/C4
Indianapolis (cap.), In, US 130/C4
Indianola, Ms, US 129/K4
Indianola, Wa, US 135/B2
Indiantown, Fl, US 133/H5
Indiaporã, Braz. 155/B1
Indigirka (riv.), Rus. 67/P3
Indija, Serb. 48/E3
Indio, Ca, US 128/C4
Indira Gandhi (int'l arpt.), India 80/B4
Indochina (reg.), Laos 78/E3
Indonesia (ctry.) 81/E4
Indore, India 89/L4
Indragiri (riv.), Indo. 80/B4
Indramayu (cape), Indo. 80/C0
Indrāvati (riv.), India 70/D8
Indre Arna, Nor. 38/A1
Indre (riv.), Fr. 42/D3
Indrois (riv.), Fr. 42/D3
Induno Olona, It. 57/E6
Indus (riv.), Asia 67/G6
Industry, Ca, US 136/C2
Inebolu, Turk. 90/C1
Inca (state), Nga. 103/G5
Inegöl, Turk. 90/B1
Iner (riv.), Rus. 54/C3
Inesu, Mor. 98/D3
Ineu, Rom. 48/E2
Inezgane, Mor. 98/C3
Inezgane (Agadir) (int'l arpt.), Mor. 98/C3
Infanta (cape), SAfr. 106/C4
Infiernillo (res.), Mex. 140/A4
Infiernillo, Presa del (dam), Mex. 142/E7
Infiesto, Sp. 44/C1
Ingapirca (ruin), Ecu. 152/B5
Ingatestone, Eng, UK 30/E2
Ingelmunster, Belg. 52/C1
Ingeniero Jacobacci, Arg. 158/C4
Ingeniero Luiggi, Arg. 158/D2
Ingenio, Canl.,Sp. 98/B4
Ingersheim, Fr. 56/D1
Ingettolgoy, Mong. 70/H2
Ingham, Austl. 114/B2
Ingleside, Md, US 138/C4
Inglewood, Austl. 115/B3
Inglewood, Austl. 114/C5
Inglewood-Finn Hill, Wa, US 135/C2
Inglis, Fl, US 133/H4
Ingoda (riv.), Rus. 65/M4
Ingolstadt, Ger. 55/E5
Ingrid Christianson (coast), Ant. 160/F
Ingushetia, Resp., Rus. 53/G5
Ingwavuma, SAfr. 107/E2
Ingwiller, Fr. 53/G6
Inhambane, Moz. 105/G5
Inhambupe, Braz. 154/C3
Inharrime, Moz. 105/G5
Inhuma, Braz. 154/C2
Inhumas, Braz. 151/J7
Iniesta, Sp. 44/E3
Inírida (riv.), Col. 150/D3
Inirida (riv.), Col. 152/C3
Inishbofin (isl.), Ire. 30/N10
Inishowen (pen.), Ire. 34/A1
Inje, SKor. 73/E3
Injune, Austl. 114/C4
Inkeroinen, Fin. 39/M1
Inkster, Mi, US 135/F7
Inland (sea), Japan 74/C4
Inle (lake), Myan. 83/G3
Inn (riv.), Aus. 40/F4
Inn (riv.), Swi. 57/F4
Inn (riv.), Aus. 43/L2
Innbach, Aus. 55/H6
Innellan, Sc, UK 36/A5
Inner (chan.), Belz. 144/D2
Inner (sound), Sc, UK 31/Q8

Inner Hebrides (isls.), Sc, UK 31/Q8
Inner Mongolia (reg.), China 67/L5
Innerdouny (hill), Sc, UK 36/C4
Innerleithen, Sc, UK 36/C5
Innerste (riv.), Ger. 51/G4
Innertkirchen, Swi. 56/E4
Innes NP, Austl. 113/H5
Innichen (San Candito), It. 43/K3
Innisfail, Ab, Can. 126/E2
Innisfail, Austl. 114/B2
Innoko (riv.), Ak, US 134/G3
Innsbruck, Aus. 57/H3
Innviertel (reg.), Aus. 55/G6
Inny (riv.), Eng, UK 32/B5
Ino, Japan 74/C4
Inocência, Braz. 155/B1
Inongo, D.R. Congo 97/J8
Inönü, Turk. 90/B2
Inowrocław, Pol. 41/K2
Insch, Sc, UK 36/D2
Inscription (cape), Austl. 112/B3
Insein, Myan. 83/G4
Inside (passg.), BC, Can. 126/A2
Insjön, Swe. 38/F1
Inta, Rus. 61/N2
Intendente Alvear, Arg. 158/E2
Intepe, Turk. 47/K2
Intercourse, Pa, US 138/B3
Interior (plat.), BC, Can. 126/B2
Interlaken, Swi. 56/D4
Internacional (int'l arpt.), Braz. 156/D2
Internacional (int'l arpt.), Braz. 156/D2
International Peace Garden, ND, US 127/H2
Inthanon (peak), Thai. 83/G4
Intorsura Buzăului, Rom. 49/H3
Intragna, Swi. 57/E5
Inubō-zaki (pt.), Japan 75/G3
Inujima, Japan 74/C3
Inukjuak, Qu, Can. 123/J3
Inutil (bay), Chile 159/C7
Inuvik, NW, Can. 134/M2
Inuyama, Japan 77/L5
Inver (bay), Sc, UK 36/C1
Inver Arna, Nor. 38/A1
Inveraray, Sc, UK 36/A4
Inverbervie, Sc, UK 36/D3
Invercargill, NZ 117/R10
Inverclyde (pol. reg.), Sc, UK 36/B5
Inverell, Austl. 115/D1
Invergordon, Sc, UK 36/B1
Inverie, Sc, UK 31/R8
Inverigo, It. 57/E6
Inverkeithing, Sc, UK 36/C4
Inverloch, Austl. 115/C3
Invermay, Sk, Can. 127/H3
Inverness, Sc, UK 36/B2
Inverness, Al, US 133/G3
Inverness, Fl, US 133/H4
Inveruno, It. 57/E6
Inverurie, Sc, UK 36/D2
Invorio, It. 58/B1
Inwood, NY, US 139/L9
Inyanga, Zim. 105/F4
Inyangani (peak), Zim. 105/F4
Inymney (peak), Rus. 67/T3
Inyo (mts.), Ca, US 128/C3
Inza, Rus. 63/H1
Inzai, Japan 77/E2
Inzigkofen, Ger. 57/F2
Inzing, Aus. 57/H3
Iō-shima (isl.), Japan 74/A5
Ioánnina (int'l arpt.), Gre. 47/G3
Ioánnina, Gre. 47/G3
Iolotan', Trkm. 89/H1
Iona (isl.), Sc, UK 31/Q8
Iona, PN da, Ang. 105/B4
Ione, Co, US 137/C2
Ionia, Mi, US 130/C3
Ionian (sea), Gre. 47/F3
Ionian (isls.), Gre. 27/F5
Ios (isl.), Gre. 47/J4
Iouik (cape), Mrta. 102/A2
Iowa (state), US 129/J2
Iowa (riv.), Ia, US 127/L5
Iowa Falls, Ia, US 127/L5
Ipameri, Braz. 155/B1
Ipanema, Braz. 155/D1
Iparia, Peru 156/C3
Ipatinga, Braz. 155/D1
Ipeľ (riv.), Slvk. 41/K4
Iphofen, Ger. 54/D3
Ipiales, Col. 152/B4
Ipiaú, Braz. 154/C4
Ipirá, Braz. 154/C4
Ipiranga, Braz. 155/B3
Ipoh, Malay. 80/B3
Ipoly (riv.), Hun. 41/K4
Iporá, Braz. 151/H7
Ipsala, Turk. 47/K2
Ipsheim, Ger. 54/D3
Ipswich, SD, US 127/H4
Ipswich, Eng, UK 33/H2
Ipu, Braz. 154/B2
Ipuã, Braz. 155/B2
Ipubi, Braz. 154/C2
Ipueiras, Braz. 154/B2

Ipuiúna, Braz. 211/G7
Ipumba (hill), Tanz. 104/A4
Ipun, Isla (isl.), Chile 158/B5
Ipupiara, Braz. 154/B3
Iqaluit (cap.), Nun, Can. 123/K2
Iquique, Chile 150/D8
Iquitos, Peru 156/C1
Irago (chan.), Japan 77/L6
Irago-misaki (cape), Japan 77/M6
Iráklia, Gre. 47/J4
Iráklia (isl.), Gre. 47/J4
Iráklion, Gre. 47/J5
Iráklion (int'l arpt.), Gre. 47/J5
Iramaia, Braz. 154/B4
Iran (riv.), Indo.,Mal 80/D3
Iran (ctry.) 67/E6
Irapa, Ven. 153/F2
Irapuato, Mex. 143/E4
Irará, Braz. 154/C4
Irati, Braz. 155/B3
Iraúcuba, Braz. 154/C1
Irbid (gov.), Jor. 91/D3
Irbid, Jor. 91/D3
Irbīl, Iraq 90/F2
Irecê, Braz. 154/B3
Ireland (ctry.) 31/P10
Ireland's Eye (isl.), Ire. 34/B5
Iremel' (peak), Rus. 61/N5
Iretama, Braz. 155/A3
Irfon (riv.), Wal, UK 32/C2
Irharhar, Oued (riv.), Alg. 99/G4
Irhazer Oua-n-Agadez (riv.), Niger 103/G2
Iri, SKor. 73/D5
Irian Jaya (reg.), Indo. 81/H4
Iricoume (mts.), Braz. 153/G4
Irig, Serb. 48/E3
Irigui (phys. reg.), Alg. 99/G4
Iriklinskiy (res.), Rus. 63/L2
Iringa (prov.), Tanz. 104/B5
Iringa, Tanz. 104/B4
Iriomote (isl.), Japan 79/D3
Iriri (riv.), Braz. 151/H4
Irish (sea), Ire.,UK 34/C4
Irlam, Eng, UK 35/F5
Irō-zaki (pt.), Japan 75/F3
Iroise (bay), Fr. 42/A2
Iron Baron, Austl. 113/H5
Iron Knob, Austl. 113/H5
Iron Mountain, Mi, US 127/L4
Irondale, Co, US 137/C3
Ironton, Oh, US 130/D4
Ironwood, Mi, US 127/L4
Ironwood Forest Nat'l Mon., Az, US 128/E4
Irput' (riv.), Rus. 62/E1
Irrawaddy (Ayeyarwady) (riv.), Myan. 67/G2
Irrawaddy, Mouths of the (delta), Myan. 83/F4
Irsch, Ger. 53/F4
Irsen (riv.), Ger. 53/F3
Irsina, It. 46/E2
Irt (riv.), Eng, UK 35/E3
Irthing (riv.), Eng, UK 35/F1
Irthlingborough, Eng, UK 33/F2
Irtysh (riv.), Rus. 67/G4
Iruma, Japan 77/C2
Irumu, D.R. Congo 104/A2
Irún, Sp. 44/E1
Irvine, Ca, US 136/G8
Irvine, Sc, UK 36/B5
Irvine (bay), Sc, UK 36/B5
Irvine, Sc, UK 36/B5
Irving, Tx, US 132/D3
Irvington, NJ, US 139/J9
Irvington, NY, US 139/K7
Is (peak), Sudan 101/C4
Is-sur-Tille, Fr. 56/B2
Ísa Khel, Pak. 86/A3
Isaac (riv.), Austl. 109/D3
Isabela, Phil. 81/F2
Isabela, PR 141/M8
Isabela (isl.), Ecu. 156/E7
Isabela (mts.), Nic. 144/E3
Isabella (bay), Nun., Can. 123/K2
Isaccea, Rom. 49/J3
Isachsen (cape), Nun., Can. 123/G1
Isafjardhardjúp (inlet), Ice. 37/M6
Isafjördhur, Ice. 37/M6
Isahaya, Japan 74/B4
Isalo, PN de l', Madg. 107/H8
Isalo Ruiniform (mass.), Madg. 107/H8
Isana (riv.), Col. 152/D4
Isandhlwana Battlesite, SAfr. 107/E2
Isangano NP, Zam. 104/B5
Isaouanne-n-Irarraren (des.), Alg. 99/G4
Isaouanne-n-Tifernine (des.), Alg. 99/G4
Isarco (Eisack) (riv.), It. 57/H4
Isaszeg, Hun. 49/R9
Isawa, Japan 77/B2
Isbergues, Fr. 52/B2
Iscar, Sp. 44/C2
Ischgl, Aus. 57/G3
Ischia, It. 48/A5
Ise (bay), Japan 75/F3
Ise (riv.), Eng, UK 33/F2

Ise, Japan 77/L7
Ise-Shima NP, Japan 75/E3
Isehara, Japan 75/F3
Iselin, NJ, US 139/H9
Isen, Ger. 55/F6
Isen (riv.), Ger. 40/G4
Isenthal, Swi. 57/E4
Iseo (lake), It. 43/J4
Iseo, It. 58/D1
Iseo, Lago d' (lake), It. 58/C1
Isère (riv.), Fr. 42/F4
Isère (dept.), Fr. 56/B6
Iserlohn, Ger. 51/E6
Isernia, It. 46/D2
Isesaki, Japan 75/F2
Iset' (riv.), Rus. 87/D1
Iseyin, Nga. 103/F5
'Isfiyā, Isr. 91/G6
Ishi (riv.), Japan 77/J7
Ishibashi, Japan 75/F2
Ishibe, Japan 77/K5
Ishidoriya, Japan 76/B4
Ishigaki (isl.), Japan 79/D3
Ishige, Japan 75/F2
Ishikari, Japan 76/B2
Ishikari (bay), Japan 76/B2
Ishikari (mts.), Japan 76/C2
Ishikari (riv.), Japan 76/B2
Ishikawa (pref.), Japan 75/E2
Ishikawa, Japan 75/G2
Ishiki, Japan 77/M6
Ishim (riv.), Rus. 64/H4
Ishim, Rus. 61/R4
Ishimbay, Rus. 63/L1
Ishinomaki, Japan 76/B4
Ishioka, Japan 75/G2
Ishizuchi-san (peak), Japan 74/C4
Isiboro Sécure, PN, Bol. 150/E7
Isigny-sur-Mer, Fr. 42/C2
Isil'kul', Rus. 87/F2
Isiolo, Kenya 104/C2
Isiro, D.R. Congo 97/L7
Isisford, Austl. 114/B4
İskenderun, Turk. 91/E1
İskenderun, Gulf of (gulf), Turk. 91/D1
İskilip, Turk. 90/C1
Iskŭr (riv.), Aus. 49/G4
Iskŭr (res.), Bul. 49/F4
Iskŭr (riv.), Bul. 47/H1
Isla, Mex. 144/C2
Isla (riv.), Sc, UK 36/C3
Isla Aguada, Mex. 144/D2
Isla Cabritos, PN, DRep. 145/J2
Isla Cedros, Mex. 142/B2
Isla Cristina, Sp. 44/B4
Isla de Maipo, Chile 158/N8
Isla de Salamanca, PN, Col. 152/C2
Isla de San Andrés (int'l arpt.), Col. 145/F3
Isla Gorge NP, Austl. 114/C4
Isla Guamblin, PN, Chile 158/B5
Isla Isabela, PN, Mex. 142/D4
Isla Magdalena, PN, Chile 157/B5
Isla Mujeres, Mex. 144/E1
Islâhiye, Turk. 91/E1
Islām Kot, Pak. 89/K4
Islāmābād (cap. terr.), Pak. 86/B3
Islāmābād (cap.), Pak. 86/B3
Islāmābād/Rāwalpindi (int'l arpt.), Pak. 86/B3
Islāmnagar, India 84/B1
Islamorada, Fl, US 133/H5
Islāmpur, India 85/G2
Islāmpur, India 85/E3
Island (lake), Mb, Can. 122/G3
Island (co.), Wa, US 135/B2
Island Beach State Park, NJ, US 138/D4
Island Lagoon (lake), Austl. 113/H4
Island Lake, Mb, Can. 127/K2
Island Lake, Il, US 135/P15
Island Park, NY, US 139/L9
Islands (bay), Nf, Can. 131/K1
Islay, Peru 156/C5
Islay (isl.), Sc, UK 31/Q9
Isle (riv.), Fr. 42/D4
Isle of Anglesey (co.), Wal, UK 34/D5
Isle of Ely (phys. reg.), Eng, UK 33/G2
Isle of Portland (pen.), Eng, UK 32/D5
Isle of Thanet (phys. reg.), Eng, UK 33/H4
Isle of Wight (co.), Eng, UK 33/E5
Isle Royale NP, Mi, US 130/B2
Isleton, Ca, US 135/L10
Islington (bor.), Eng, UK 30/A1
Islip, NY, US 139/E2
Ismailovo Park, Rus. 61/W9
Ismaning, Ger. 55/E6
Isny, Ger. 57/G2
Isoanala, Madg. 107/H8
Isobe, Japan 77/L7
Isojärven NP, Fin. 39/L1
Isojärvi (lake), Fin. 39/J1
Isoka, Zam. 104/B5
Isola del Liri, It. 46/C2
Isola della Scala, It. 59/D2
Isola di Capo Rizzuto, It. 47/E3
Isola Vicentina, It. 59/E1
Isonzo (riv.), It. 59/G1
Isorella, It. 58/D2
Isparta, Turk. 90/B2
Isparta (prov.), Turk. 90/B2
Isperikh, Bul. 49/H4
İspir, Turk. 63/G4
Israel (ctry.) 91/C3
Issaquah, Wa, US 135/C2
Issel (riv.), Ger. 50/D5
Isselburg, Ger. 50/D5
Issenheim, Fr. 56/D2
Issia, C.d'Iv. 102/D5
Issoire, Fr. 42/E4
Issou, Fr. 30/H5
Issoudun, Fr. 42/E3
Issum, Ger. 50/D5
Issy-les-Moulineaux, Fr. 30/J5
Istállós-kó (peak), Hun. 48/E1
İstanbul (prov.), Turk. 49/J5
İstanbul, Turk. 49/J5
Istead Rise, Eng, UK 30/E2
Istiaía, Gre. 47/H3
Istmina, Col. 152/B3
Istok, Serb. 47/G1
Istra (riv.), Rus. 61/W9
Istrana, It. 59/F1
Istranca (mts.), Turk. 49/H5
Istres, Fr. 42/F5
Istria (pen.), Cro. 48/A3
Isulan, Phil. 81/F2
Isumi, Japan 77/E3
Itabaiana, Braz. 154/C3
Itabaiana, Braz. 154/D2
Itabaianinha, Braz. 154/C3
Itabapoana (riv.), Braz. 155/D2
Itaberaba, Braz. 154/B4
Itabira, Braz. 155/D1
Itabirito, Braz. 155/D2
Itaboraí, Braz. 211/L7
Itabuna, Braz. 154/C4
Itacaiunas (riv.), Braz. 151/H5
Itacarambi, Braz. 154/A4
Itacoatiara, Braz. 150/G4
Itacuaí (riv.), Braz. 150/D5
Itacuruba, Braz. 154/C3
Itaguaí, Braz. 211/K7
Itaguara, Braz. 155/C2
Itaguatins, Braz. 154/A2
Itagüí, Col. 150/C2
Itaí, Braz. 155/B2
Itaíba, Braz. 154/C3
Itaiçaba, Braz. 154/C2
Itainópolis, Braz. 154/B2
Itaiópolis, Braz. 155/B3
Itaipu (dam), Par. 157/F2
Itaipú (res.), Braz.,Par. 147/D5
Itaipu, Represa do (res.), Braz. 157/F1
Itaituba, Braz. 151/G4
Itajá, Braz. 155/B1
Itajaí, Braz. 155/B3
Itajaí (riv.), Braz. 155/B3
Itajubá, Braz. 211/H7
Itajuípe, Braz. 154/C4
Itako, Japan 75/G3
Itakura, Japan 77/D1
Italy, Tx, US 129/H4
Italy (ctry.) 27/F4
Itamaraju, Braz. 154/C5
Itamarandiba, Braz. 155/D1
Itambacuri, Braz. 154/B5
Itambé, Braz. 154/B4
Itambé, Pico de (peak), Braz. 154/B5
Itami, Japan 77/H6
Itamonte, Braz. 211/J7
Itampolo, Madg. 107/G9
Itanhaém, Braz. 211/G9
Itanhandu, Braz. 155/C2
Itanhém, Braz. 154/B5
Itanhém (riv.), Braz. 155/D1
Itanhomi, Braz. 155/D1
Itaobim, Braz. 154/B5
Itaocara, Braz. 155/D2
Itapagé, Braz. 154/C1
Itaparica (isl.), Braz. 154/C4
Itapé, Braz. 154/C4
Itapebi, Braz. 154/C4
Itapecerica, Braz. 155/C2
Itapecuru-Mirim, Braz. 154/A1
Itapemirim, Braz. 155/D2
Itaperuna, Braz. 155/D2
Itapetim, Braz. 154/C3
Itapetinga, Braz. 154/B4
Itapetininga, Braz. 155/B2
Itapeva, Braz. 155/B2
Itapevi, Braz. 211/G8
Itapicuru (riv.), Braz. 154/C3
Itapicuru (riv.), Braz. 151/K5
Itapipoca, Braz. 154/C1
Itapira, Braz. 211/G7
Itapitanga, Braz. 154/C4
Itaporanga, Braz. 155/B2
Itaquaquecetuba, Braz. 211/G8
Itarantim, Braz. 154/B4
Itararé, Braz. 155/B3
Itariri, Braz. 211/F9
Itārsi, India 84/A4
Itatiaia, PN de, Braz. 211/J7
Itatiba, Braz. 211/G7
Itaueira (riv.), Braz. 151/K5
Itaueira, Braz. 154/B2
Itaúna, Braz. 155/C2
Itayanagi, Japan 76/B3
Itbayat, Phil. 79/D3
Itbayat (isl.), Phil. 79/D3
Itchen (riv.), Eng, UK 33/E4
Itéa, Gre. 47/H3
Iténez (riv.), Bol. 147/C4
Itezhi-Tezhi (dam), Zam. 105/E4
Ith (hills), Ger. 51/G4
Ithaca, NY, US 130/E3
Ithaca, (Itháki) (isl.), Gre. 47/G3
Itháki, Gre. 47/G3
Ithon (riv.), Wal, UK 32/C2
Itimbiri (riv.), D.R. Congo 97/K7
Itinga, Braz. 154/B5
Itiruçu, Braz. 154/B4
Itō, Japan 75/F3
Itogon, Phil. 79/D4
Itoigawa, Japan 75/E2
Itoman, Japan 75/J7
Iton (riv.), Fr. 42/D2
Itonuki, Japan 77/L5
Itororó, Braz. 154/B4
Itsukaichi, Japan 77/C2
Itter (riv.), Ger. 51/F6
Itterbeck, Ger. 50/D3
Ittiri, It. 46/A2
Itu, Braz. 155/C2
Ituango, Col. 152/C3
Ituberá, Braz. 154/C4
Ituí (riv.), Braz. 150/D5
Ituiutaba, Braz. 155/B1
Itumbiara, Braz. 155/B1
Itumbiara, Barragem (res.), Braz. 155/B1
Itumirim, Braz. 211/J6
Ituna, Sk, Can. 127/H3
Itupiranga, Braz. 151/J5
Ituporanga, Braz. 155/B3
Iturama, Braz. 155/B1
Ituri (riv.), D.R. Congo 104/A2
Itutinga, Represa de (res.), Braz. 155/C2
Ituverava, Braz. 155/C2
Ituxi (riv.), Braz. 150/E5
Ituzaingó, Uru. 159/K11
Ityāy al Bārūd, Egypt 91/B4
Itz (riv.), Ger. 40/F3
Iul'tin (peak), Rus. 134/C2
Iúna, Braz. 155/D2
Ivaí (riv.), Braz. 155/B3
Ivaiporã, Braz. 155/B3
Ivalojoki (riv.), Fin. 37/H1
Ivančice, Czh. 43/M2
Ivanec, Cro. 43/M3
Ivangrad, Serb. 47/G1
Ivanhoe, Austl. 115/C2
Ivanhoe (riv.), On, Can. 130/D1
Ivanjica, Serb. 48/E4
Ivanjska, Bosn. 48/C3
Ivankovo, Cro. 48/D3
Ivano-Frankivs'k, Ukr. 62/C2
Ivano-Frankivs'ka Oblasti, Ukr. 62/C2
Ivanof Bay, Ak, US 134/G4
Ivanovo, Rus. 60/J4
Ivanovovskaya Oblast, Rus. 60/J4
Ivato, Madg. 107/H8
Ivato (int'l arpt.), Madg. 107/H7
Ivaylovgrad (res.), Bul. 47/J2
Ivaylovgrad, Bul. 47/K2
Ivdel, Rus. 64/G3
Iveragh (pen.), Ire. 30/P11
Iverny, Fr. 30/L5
Ivindo (riv.), Gabon 96/H7
Ivohibe, Madg. 107/H8
Ivondro (riv.), Madg. 107/J7
Ivory (coast), C.d'Iv. 96/D7
Ivösjön (lake), Swe. 38/F3
Ivrea, It. 58/A2
İvrindi, Turk. 90/A2
Ivry-sur-Seine, Fr. 30/K5
Ivujivik, Qu, Can. 123/J2
Ivvavik NP, Yk, Can. 122/B2
Iwafune, Japan 77/D1
Iwai, Japan 75/F2
Iwaizumi, Japan 76/B4
Iwaki, Japan 75/G2
Iwaki-san (peak), Japan 76/B3
Iwakuni, Japan 74/C3
Iwakura, Japan 77/L5
Iwama, Japan 77/E1
Iwami, Japan 74/D3
Iwamizawa, Japan 76/B2
Iwamura, Japan 77/M5
Iwanai, Japan 76/B2
Iwanuma, Japan 75/G1
Iwasaki, Japan 76/A3
Iwata, Japan 75/E3
Iwataki, Japan 77/H4
Iwate (pref.), Japan 76/B4
Iwate, Japan 76/B4
Iwate-san (peak), Japan 76/B4
Iwatsuki, Japan 77/D2
Iwere Ile, Nga. 103/F5
Iwo, Nga. 103/G5
Iwo Jima (isl.), Japan 116/D2
Iwŏn, NKor. 73/E2
Iwuy, Fr. 52/C3
Ixcán (riv.), Guat. 144/D3
Ixelles, Belg. 53/D2
Ixmiquilpan, Mex. 143/K6
Ixopo, SAfr. 107/E3
Ixtapaluca, Mex. 143/L7
Ixtapan de la Sal, Mex. 143/K8
Ixtlán del Río, Mex. 142/D4
Iyo (sea), Japan 74/B4
Iyo, Japan 74/C4
Izabal (lake), Guat. 140/D4
Īzad Khvāst, Iran 88/F2
Izamal, Mex. 144/D1
Izberbash, Rus. 63/H4
Izegem, Belg. 52/C2
Izhevsk, Rus. 61/M4
Izhma (riv.), Rus. 61/M2
Izhora (riv.), Rus. 61/T7
Izi (well), Alg. 99/F3
Izigan (cape), Ak, US 134/E5
Izkī, Oman 89/G4
Izmayil, Ukr. 49/J3
İzmir, Turk. 90/A2
İzmir (prov.), Turk. 90/A2
İzmit (gulf), Turk. 49/J5
İzmit, Turk. 49/J5
Iznájar, Sp. 44/C4
İznik, Turk. 49/J5
İznik (lake), Turk. 49/J5
Izola, Slov. 59/G1
Izra', Syria 91/E3
Izsák, Hun. 48/D2
Iztaccíhuatl-Popocatépetl, PN, Mex. 143/L7
Izu (pen.), Japan 75/F3
Izu (isls.), Japan 75/F4
Izúcar de Matamoros, Mex. 143/L8
Izuhara, Japan 74/A3
Izumi, Japan 74/B4
Izumi, Japan 76/B4
Izumi, Japan 77/H7
Izumi-Ōtsu, Japan 77/H7
Izumi-Sano, Japan 77/H7
Izumo, Japan 74/C3
Izunagaoka, Japan 77/B3
Izushi, Japan 77/G5
Izyum, Ukr. 62/F2

J

J. Paul Getty Museum, Ca, US 136/E7
Jääsjärvi (lake), Fin. 39/M1
Jaba', WBnk. 91/G7
Jabal 'Abd al 'Azīz (mts.), Syria 90/D2
Jabal Abu Rujmayn (mts.), Syria 90/D3
Jabal Abyad (plat.), Sudan 101/B5
Jabal al 'Arab (mts.), Syria 91/E3
Jabal an Nusayriyah (mts.), Syria 91/E2
Jabal ar Ruwaq (mts.), Syria 90/D3
Jabal as Sawdā' (hills), Libya 96/H2
Jabal ash Shaykh (peak), Leb. 91/D3
Jabal Lubnān (gov.), Leb. 91/D2
Jabal Ramm (peak), Jor. 91/D5
Jabal 'Unāzah (peak), SAr. 90/D3
Jabalí (pt.), Pan. 145/F5
Jabalón (riv.), Sp. 44/D3
Jabalpur, India 84/B4
Jabālyah, Gaza 91/D4
Jabbeke, Belg. 52/C1
Jablah, Syria 91/D2
Jablanica (mts.), Alb. 47/G2
Jablonec nad Nisou, Czh. 41/H3
Jaboatão dos Guararapes, Braz. 154/D3
Jaboticabal, Braz. 155/B2
Jabuka, Serb. 48/E3
Jabung (cape), Indo. 80/B4
Jaca, Sp. 45/E1
Jacaré (riv.), Braz. 154/B3
Jacareí, Braz. 211/H8
Jaceel (riv.), Som. 97/Q5
Jáchymov, Czh. 55/F2
Jacinto, Braz. 154/B5
Jacinto Arauz, Arg. 158/E3
Jackman, Me, US 131/G2
Jackpot, Nv, US 126/E5
Jacks Mountain (ridge), Pa, US 138/A2
Jacksboro, Tx, US 129/H4
Jackson, Al, US 133/G4
Jackson, Ca, US 128/B3
Jackson, La, US 129/K5
Jackson, Mi, US 130/C3
Jackson, Mo, US 129/K3
Jackson (co.), Mo, US 137/E5
Jackson (cap.), Ms, US 129/K4
Jackson (mts.), Nv, US 126/D5
Jackson, Tn, US 130/B5
Jackson, Wy, US 126/F5
Jackson (lake), Wy, US 128/E2
Jacksonville, Al, US 133/G3
Jacksonville, Ar, US 129/J4
Jacksonville, Fl, US 133/H4
Jacksonville (int'l arpt.), Fl, US 133/H4
Jacksonville, Il, US 129/K3
Jacksonville, NC, US 133/J3
Jacksonville Beach, Fl, US 133/H4
Jacktown, Ok, US 137/N14
Jacmel, Haiti 145/H2
Jacobābād, Pak. 89/J3
Jacobina, Braz. 154/B3
Jacobsdal, SAfr. 106/D3
Jacobstown, NJ, US 138/D3
Jacobus, Pa, US 138/B4
Jacomo (lake), Mo, US 137/E6
Jacona de Plancarte, Mex. 142/E5
Jacques-Cartier (riv.), Qu, Can. 131/G2
Jacques Cartier (peak), Qu, Can. 131/H1
Jacuí (riv.), Braz. 157/F2
Jacuípe (riv.), Braz. 151/L6
Jacupiranga, Braz. 155/B3
Jacura, Ven. 152/D2
Jadacaquiva, Ven. 152/D2
Jaddi (pt.), Pak. 89/H3
Jade, Ger. 51/F2
Jade (riv.), Ger. 51/F1
Jade (bay), Ger. 40/E2
Jadebusen (bay), Ger. 51/F2
Jaén, Peru 156/B2
Jaén, Sp. 44/D4
Jaffa (cape), Austl. 115/A3
Jaffna, SrL. 82/C6
Jagādhri, India 86/D4
Jagdīspur, India 85/E3
Jagersfontein, SAfr. 106/D3
Jægerspris, Den. 38/D4
Jagna, Phil. 79/D6
Jagraon, India 86/C4
Jagst (riv.), Ger. 43/J2
Jagtiāl, India 82/C4
Jaguaquara, Braz. 154/C4
Jaguarão, Braz. 157/F3
Jaguarão (riv.), Braz. 159/G2
Jaguarari, Braz. 154/B3
Jaguaretama, Braz. 154/C2
Jaguariaíva, Braz. 155/B3
Jaguaribara, Braz. 154/C2
Jaguaribe (riv.), Braz. 151/L5
Jaguaribe, Braz. 154/C2
Jaguariúna, Braz. 211/G7
Jaguaruana, Braz. 154/C2
Jagungal (mt.), Austl. 115/D3
Jahānābād, India 85/E3
Jahāngīra, India 86/B3
Jahāngīrābād, India 84/B1
Jahrom, Iran 88/F3
Jaicós, Braz. 154/B2
Jailolo, Indo. 81/G3
Jailu (riv.), China 72/C4
Jainca, China 70/H4
Jāis, India 84/C2
Jaisalmer, India 89/K3
Jaisinghnagar, India 84/C4
Jājapur, India 82/E3
Jājarm, Iran 89/G1
Jajce, Bosn. 48/C3
Jakarta (cap.), Indo. 80/C5
Jakobstad (Pietarsaari), Fin. 60/D3
Jal, NM, US 129/G4
Jala, Mex. 142/E4
Jalacingo, Mex. 143/M7
Jalaid Qi, China 71/M2
Jalal-Abad, Kyr. 87/F4
Jalal-Abad (obl.), Kyr. 87/F4
Jalālābād, India 84/B2
Jalālābād, India 86/C4
Jalālābād, Afg. 86/A2
Jalālābād, India 86/D5
Jalāli, India 84/B2
Jalālpur, India 84/D2
Jalālpur, Pak. 86/B3
Jalālpur Pīrwāla, Pak. 86/A5
Jalamah, WBnk. 91/G6
Jalangi (riv.), India 85/G3
Jalapa, Mex. 143/N7
Jalapa, Mex. 144/C2
Jalapa, Guat. 144/D3
Jalatlaco, Mex. 143/Q10
Jālaun, India 84/B2
Jaldhāka (riv.), India 85/G2
Jales, Braz. 155/B2
Jalesar, India 84/B2
Jalingo, Nga. 96/H6
Jalisco, Mex. 142/D4
Jaliṭah, Jazīrat (isl.), Tun. 46/A4
Jallouvre, Pic de (peak), Fr 56/C6
Jalon (riv.), Sp. 44/E2
Jalostotitlán, Mex. 142/E4
Jalpa, Mex. 142/E4
Jalpa de Méndez, Mex. 144/C2
Jalpan de Serra, Mex. 143/F4
Jaltenango de la Paz, Mex. 144/C3
Jaltepec (riv.), Mex. 144/C2
Jáltipan de Morelos, Mex. 144/C2
Jālūd, WBnk. 91/G7
Jaluit (isl.), Mrsh. 116/F4
Jalūlā', Iraq 90/F3
Jam, Iran 88/F3
Jamaame, Som. 97/P7
Jamaare (riv.), Nga. 96/H5
Jamaica (ctry.) 145/G2
Jamaica (chan.), Jam. 145/H2
Jamaica (bay), NY, US 138/K9
Jamālpur, Bang. 85/G3
Jamanxim (riv.), Braz. 151/G5
Jamapa, Mex. 143/N7
Jamari (riv.), Braz. 150/F5
Jambi, Indo. 80/B4
Jambuair (cape), Indo. 80/A2
James (pt.), Chile 158/B5
James (bay), Qu, Can. 123/H3
James (peak), Ut, US 137/K11
James (riv.), Va, US 127/J4
James Campbell NWR, Hi, US 124/V12
James M. Cox Dayton (int'l arpt.), Oh, US 130/C4
James Ross (str.), Nun., Can. 122/G1
Jamesburg, NJ, US 138/D3
Jamestown, ND, US 127/J4
Jamestown, NY, US 130/E3
Jamestown, Tn, US 130/C4
Jamestown, Co, US 137/B2
Jamestown, Austl. 113/H5
Jamīrāpāt (range), India 84/D4
Jāmke, Pak. 86/C3
Jammāl, Tun. 46/B5
Jammerbugt (bay), Den. 38/C3
Jammu and Kashmīr (state), India 70/C5
Jāmpur, Pak. 86/A5
Jāmtāra, India 85/F4
Jämtland (co.), Swe. 37/E3
Jamūi, India 85/E3
Jamuna (riv.), Bang. 85/G3
Jan (lake), Sk, Can. 127/H2
Jan Kempdorp, SAfr. 106/D2
Jan Mayen (isl.), Nor. 160/G
Jan Smuts (Johannesburg) (int'l arpt.), SAfr. 106/E2
Janakkala, Fin. 39/L1
Janakpur, Nepal 85/E2
Janakpur (zone), Nepal 85/E2
Janaúba, Braz. 154/B4
Janaucu, Ilha (isl.), Braz. 151/H3
Jandaia do Sul, Braz. 155/B2
Jandaq, Iran 89/F2
Jandowae, Austl. 114/C4
Jándula (riv.), Sp. 44/C4
Jangaon, India 82/C4
Jangipur, India 85/G3
Janikowo, Pol. 41/K2
Janīn, WBnk. 91/G7
Janja, Bosn. 48/D3
Janjevo, Serb. 47/G1
Janos, Mex. 142/C2
Jánoshalma, Hun. 48/D2
Jánosháza, Hun. 48/C2
Janów Lubelski, Pol. 41/M3
Jansenville, SAfr. 106/D4
Januária, Braz. 154/A4
Janvry, Fr. 30/J6
Janzé, Fr. 42/C3
Japan (sea), Asia 67/N5
Japan (ctry.) 71/Q4
Japan, Sea of (sea), Asia 71/P3
Japanese Alps NP, Japan 75/E2
Japurá (riv.), Braz. 147/C3
Jaqué, Pan. 152/B3
Jarābulus, Syria 90/D2
Jaraíz de la Vera, Sp. 44/C2
Jarama (riv.), Sp. 44/D2
Jaramānah, Syria 91/E3
Jarandilla de la Vera, Sp. 44/C2
Jarānwāla, Pak. 86/B4
Jarash, Jor. 91/D3
Jarbah (isl.), Tun. 96/H1
Järbo, Swe. 38/G1
Jarby (pt.), IM, UK 34/D3
Jardim, Braz. 154/C2
Jardín América, Arg. 157/E2
Jardines de la Reina (arch.), Cuba 145/G1
Jardinópolis, Braz. 155/C2
Jargalant, Mong. 70/G2
Jari (riv.), Braz. 147/D2
Jaridih, India 85/F4
Jarjīs, Tun. 96/H1
Jarmen, Ger. 38/E5
Järna, Swe. 38/G2
Jarny, Fr. 53/E5
Jarocin, Pol. 41/J3
Jaroměř, Czh. 41/H3
Jarosław, Pol. 41/M3
Jarrettsville, Md, US 138/B4
Jarrow, Eng, UK 35/G2
Jars (plain), Laos 78/C2
Jarud Qi, China 72/E1
Järvenpää, Fin. 39/L1
Jarville-la-Malgrange, Fr. 53/F6
Jarvis (isl.), Pac., US 117/J5
Järvsö, Swe. 38/G1
Jáse-Nagykun-Szolnok (prov.), Hun. 48/E2
Jashpurnagar, India 85/E4
Jasidih, India 85/F3
Jāsk, Iran 89/G3
Jasło, Pol. 41/L4
Jason (isl.), Mald. 159/E6
Jasper, Ab, Can. 126/D2
Jasper, Al, US 133/G3
Jasper, Fl, US 133/H4
Jasper, Tx, US 129/J5
Jasper, Ga, US 133/G3
Jasper, In, US 130/C4
Jasper NP, Ab, Can. 126/D2
Jaspur, India 84/B1
Jastrebarsko, Cro. 48/B3
Jastrowie, Pol. 41/J2
Jastrzębie Zdrój, Pol. 41/K4
Jaswantnagar, India 84/B2
Jászapáti, Hun. 41/L5
Jászárokszállás, Hun. 48/D2
Jászberény, Hun. 41/K5
Jataí, Braz. 155/B1
Jatapu (riv.), Braz. 150/G3
Jatāra, India 84/B3
Jatāt (riv.), Mex. 144/D2
Jāti, Pak. 89/J4
Jatibonico, Cuba 145/G1
Játiva, Sp. 45/E3
Jatoi Janūbi, Pak. 86/A5
Jaú (riv.), Braz. 150/F4
Jaú, Braz. 155/B2
Jaua Sarisarinama, PN, Ven. 150/F3
Jauaperi (riv.), Braz. 150/F3
Jauaperi (riv.), Braz. 153/F5
Jauaru, Serra (mts.), Braz. 151/H4
Jaudon, Mo, US 137/D6
Jauharābād, Pak. 86/B3
Jauja, Peru 156/C3
Jaumave, Mex. 143/F4
Jaun, Swi. 56/D4
Jaunay-Clan, Fr. 42/D3
Jaunpass (pass), Swi. 56/D4
Java (sea), Indo. 67/K10
Java (isl.), Indo. 67/K10
Javari (riv.), Braz. 150/D5
Jávea, Sp. 45/F3
Javier (isl.), Chile 159/B5
Javorie (peak), Slvk. 48/D1
Javornice (riv.), Czh. 55/G2
Javorník (peak), Czh. 55/G4
Javorová Skála (peak), Czh. 55/H3
Jawāla Mukhi, India 86/D4
Jawor, Pol. 41/J3
Jayanca, Peru 156/B2
Jayapura, Indo. 81/K4
Jaynagar, India 85/F2
Jaynagar, India 85/G4
Jayton, Tx, US 129/G4
Jbel Bani (mts.), Mor. 98/D3
Jean Lafitte, La, US 137/P17
Jeberos, Peru 156/B2
Jebjerg, Den. 38/C3
Jed Water (riv.), Sc, UK 36/D6
Jedburgh, Sc, UK 36/D6
Jedlicze, Pol. 41/L4
Jędrzejów, Pol. 41/L3
Jeetze (riv.), Ger. 40/F2
Jefferson (co.), Co, US 137/B3
Jefferson (parish), La, US 137/P17
Jefferson (riv.), La, US 137/P17
Jefferson (co.), Mo, US 137/F9
Jefferson (mt.), Or, US 126/C4
Jefferson, Tx, US 129/J4
Jefferson (co.), Wi, US 135/N14
Jefferson City (cap.), Mo, US 129/J3
Jeffersonville, In, US 130/C4
Jeffrey City, Wy, US 128/F2
Jeffreys Bay, SAfr. 106/D4
Jegenstorf, Swi. 56/D3
Jeinemeni (peak), Chile 158/B5
Jēkabpils, Lat. 39/L4
Jelcz-Laskowice, Pol. 41/J3
Jelenia Góra, Pol. 41/H3
Jelep (pass), China 82/E2
Jelgava, Lat. 39/K3
Jemaa Sahim, Mor. 98/C2
Jemappes, Belg. 52/D3
Jember, Indo. 80/D5
Jemez Pueblo, NM, US 128/F4
Jeminay, China 70/E2
Jempang (lake), Indo. 81/E4
Jena, La, US 129/J5
Jena, Ger. 40/F3
Jenaz, Swi. 57/F4
Jenbach, Aus. 43/J3
Jendouba, Tun. 100/L6
Jendouba (gov.), Tun. 100/L6
Jeneponto, Indo. 81/E5
Jengen, Ger. 57/G2
Jenkintown, Pa, US 138/C3
Jennings, La, US 129/J5
Jennings, Mo, US 137/G8
Jenny Lind (isl.), Nun., Can. 122/F2
Jens Munk (isl.), Nun., Can. 123/H2
Jeppener, Arg. 159/J11
Jequetepeque, Peru 156/B2
Jequié, Braz. 154/B4
Jequitaí, Braz. 155/C1
Jequitinhonha, Braz. 154/B5
Jequitinhonha (riv.), Braz. 147/E4
Jerada, Mor. 100/C2
Jérémie, Haiti 145/H2
Jeremoabo, Braz. 154/C3
Jerez de García Salinas, Mex. 142/E4
Jerez de la Frontera, Sp. 44/B4
Jerez de los Caballeros, Sp. 44/B3
Jericho, Austl. 114/B3
Jericho, NY, US 139/L8
Jericho (Arīḥā), Isr. 91/D4
Jericó, Braz. 154/C2
Jerilderie, Austl. 115/C2
Jerissa, Tun. 100/L7
Jerramungup, Austl. 112/C5
Jersey (isl.), Chl, UK 42/B2
Jersey (co.), Il, US 137/G7
Jersey City, NJ, US 139/J9
Jersey City (res.), NJ, US 139/H8
Jersey Shore, Pa, US 138/A1
Jerumenha, Braz. 154/B2
Jerusalem (dist.), Isr. 91/D4
Jerusalem (Yerushalayim) (cap.), Isr. 91/G8
Jervis (inlet), BC, Can. 126/C3
Jervis Bay, Austl. 115/D2
Jerzu, It. 46/A3
Jesberg, Ger. 51/G6
Jesenice, Slov. 43/L3
Jesenice (res.), Czh. 55/F2
Jesi, It. 59/G5
Jessheim, Nor. 38/D1
Jessore (pol. reg.), Bang. 85/G4
Jesuânia, Braz. 211/H6
Jesup, Ga, US 133/H4
Jésus (isl.), Qu, Can. 131/N6
Jesús Carranza, Mex. 144/C2
Jesús de Machaca, Bol. 156/D5
Jesús María, Arg. 157/D3
Jesús Menéndez, Cuba 145/G1
Jeta, Ilha de (isl.), GBis. 102/A4
Jetmore, Ks, US 129/H3
Jetpur, India 89/K4
Jettingen-Scheppach, Ger. 54/D6
Jetzendorf, Ger. 55/E6
Jeumont, Fr. 53/D3
Jevenstedt, Ger. 40/E1
Jever, Ger. 51/E1
Jevnaker, Nor. 38/D1
Jewar, India 84/A1
Jewel Cave Nat'l Mon., SD, US 127/H5
Jezerce (peak), Alb. 47/F1
Jezerní Stěna (peak), Czh. 55/G4
Jeziorak (lake), Pol. 41/K2
Jhā Jhā, India 85/F3
Jhajjar, India 86/D5
Jhālawār, India 89/L4
Jhalida, India 85/E4
Jhālū, India 84/B1
Jhang Sadar, Pak. 86/B4
Jhanjhārpur, India 85/F2
Jhānsi, India 84/B3
Jhārgrām, India 85/F4
Jharia, India 85/F4
Jharkhand (state), India 85/E4
Jhārsuguda, India 85/E5
Jhawāriān, Pak. 86/B3
Jhelum, Pak. 86/B3
Jhelum (riv.), Pak. 89/K2
Jhenida, Bang. 85/G4
Jhumra, Pak. 86/B4
Ji Xian, China 72/C4
Ji Xian, China 72/H6
Jia Xian, China 72/B3
Jiading, China 72/L8
Jiahe, China 83/K2
Jialing (riv.), China 67/K6
Jiamusi, China 71/P2
Jian (riv.), China 79/B3
Jianchang, China 72/D2
Jiang (riv.), China 78/E1
Jiang Xian, China 72/B4
Jiang'an, China 83/J2
Jiangcheng Hanizu Yizu Zizhixian, China 83/H3
Jiangchuan, China 83/H3
Jiangdu, China 72/D4
Jianghua Yaozu Zizhixian, China 83/K3
Jiangjin, China 83/J2
Jiangmen, China 83/K3
Jiangning, China 72/D5
Jiangsu (prov.), China 71/L5
Jiangxi (prov.), China 71/K6
Jiangyin, China 72/E5
Jiangyong, China 83/K3
Jiangyou, China 70/H5
Jianhe, China 83/J2
Jianhu, China 72/D4
Jianli, China 79/B2
Jian'ou, China 79/C2
Jianshi, China 71/J5
Jianshui, China 83/H3
Jianyang, China 79/C2
Jiaocheng, China 72/C3
Jiaohe, China 71/N3
Jiaojiang, China 79/D2
Jiaokou, China 72/C3
Jiaoling, China 79/C3
Jiaonan, China 72/D4
Jiaozuo, China 72/C4
Jiashan, China 72/D4
Jiashan, China 72/L9
Jiashi, China 87/G5
Jiaxiang, China 72/D4
Jiaxing, China 72/L9
Jiayin, China 71/P2
Jiayu, China 79/B2
Jiayuguan, China 70/G4
Jibou, Rom. 49/F2
Jibsh, Ra's (pt.), Oman 89/G4
Jicarón (isl.), Pan. 145/F5
Jičín, Czh. 41/H3
Jiddah, SAr. 88/C4
Jieshou, China 72/C4
Jiexiu, China 72/B3
Jieyang, China 79/C3
Jifnā, Isr. 91/G8
Jigalong Abor. Land, Austl. 112/D2
Jigawa (prov.), Nga. 103/H4
Jigüaní, Cuba 145/G1
Jigzhi, China 70/H5
Jihlava (riv.), Czh. 43/L2

Jihlava, Czh. 41/H4
Jihlavský (pol. reg.), Czh. 41/H4
Jijel, Alg. 100/H4
Jijel (prov.), Alg. 100/H4
Jijia (riv.), Rom. 62/C3
Jijiga, Eth. 97/P6
Jijona, Sp. 45/E3
Jilhã, Reprêsa (res.), Braz. 155/B2
Jihlava (riv.), Czh. 41/H4
Jilib, Som. 97/P7
Jilin, China 71/N3
Jilin (prov.), China 71/N3
Jiloca (riv.), Sp. 44/E2
Jilotepec, Mex. 143/K7
Jilové u Prahy, Czh. 55/H3
Jim Thorpe, Pa, US 138/C2
Jima, Eth. 97/N6
Jimani, DRep. 145/J2
Jimbolia, Rom. 48/E3
Jimboomba, Austl. 114/D4
Jimena de la Frontera, Sp. 44/C4
Jiménez, Mex. 129/G5
Jiménez, Mex. 142/D3
Jimo, China 72/E3
Jimokuji, Japan 77/L5
Jimsar, China 70/E3
Jin (riv.), China 83/K2
Jin Xian, China 72/C3
Jin Xian, China 72/D3
Jinchang, China 70/H4
Jincheng, China 72/C4
Jinchuan, China 70/H5
Jinci Temple, China 72/C3
Jīnd, India 86/D5
Jindabyne (dam), Austl. 115/D3
Jindabyne, Austl. 115/D3
Jindřichuv Hradec, Czh. 41/H4
Jing Xian, China 71/L5
Jing Xian, China 83/J2
Jingbian, China 72/B3
Jingde, China 79/C1
Jingdezhen, China 79/C2
Jingdong, China 83/K2
Jinggangshan, China 83/K2
Jinghai, China 72/H7
Jinghe, China 70/D3
Jinghong, China 83/H3
Jingjiang, China 72/E4
Jingle, China 72/B3
Jingmen, China 72/C5
Jingshan, China 72/C5
Jingxi, China 83/J3
Jingyuan, China 70/H4
Jinhu, China 72/D4
Jinhua, China 79/C2
Jining, China 72/C2
Jining, China 72/D4
Jinja, Ugan. 104/B2
Jinkou, China 83/H2
Jinotega, Nic. 144/E4
Jinotepe, Nic. 144/E4
Jinping, China 83/J2
Jinsha, China 83/J2
Jinsha (riv.), China 67/J7
Jinshan, China 72/L9
Jinshi, China 83/K2
Jintan, China 79/C2
Jintotolo (chan.), Phil. 79/D5
Jintūr, India 89/L5
Jinxi, China 79/C2
Jinxi, China 72/E1
Jinxian, China 79/C2
Jinxiang, China 72/D4
Jinyun, China 79/D2
Jinzhai, China 72/C5
Jinzhou (bay), China 73/A3
Jinzhou, China 72/E2
Jiparana (riv.), Braz. 150/F5
Jipijapa, Ecu. 152/A5
Jiquilpan de Juárez, Mex. 142/E4
Jiquipilco, Mex. 143/J9
Jiřkov, Czh. 55/G1
Jishan, China 72/B4
Jishou, China 83/J2
Jishui, China 79/C2
Jisr ash Shughūr, Syria 91/E2
Jiu (riv.), Rom. 62/B3
Jiujiang, China 79/C2
Jiujiang, China 79/C2
Jiulong, China 83/H2
Jiutai, China 71/N3
Jiutepec, Mex. 143/K8
Jiuwan (mts.), China 70/J6
Jixi, China 71/P2
Jixi, China 79/C1
Jiyang, China 72/D3
Jiyuan, China 72/C4
Jīzān, SAr. 88/D5
Jize, China 72/C3
Jizera (riv.), Czh. 41/H3
Jizō-zaki (pt.), Japan 74/C3
Jizzakh, Uzb. 87/G4
Jizzakh (pol. reg.), Uzb. 87/G4
Joaçaba, Braz. 155/B3
Joachin, Mex. 143/N8
Joaíma, Braz. 154/D2
João Câmara, Braz. 154/C2
João Lisboa, Braz. 154/A2
João Monlevade, Braz. 155/D1
João Pessoa, Braz. 154/D2
João Pinheiro, Braz. 154/A5
Joaquín V. González, Arg. 157/D2
Jobabo, Cuba 145/G1
Jockgrim, Ger. 54/B4
Jocón, Hon. 144/E3

Jódar, Sp. 44/D4
Jodhpur, India 89/K3
Jodoigne, Belg. 53/D2
Joensuu, Fin. 60/F3
Jõetsu, Japan 75/F2
Jogbani, India 85/F2
Johannesburg, Ger. 54/C2
Johannesburg, SAfr. 106/E2
Johanngeorgenstadt, Ger. 55/F2
Johilla (riv.), India 84/C4
John Day, Or, US 126/C2
John Day (riv.), Or, US 124/B2
John Day Fossil Beds Nat'l Mon., Or, US 126/C4
John Day, Middle Fork (riv.), Or, US 126/D4
John Day, North Fork (riv.), Or, US 126/D4
John F. Kennedy (int'l arpt.), NY, US 139/K9
John Forrest NP, Austl. 112/K6
John H. Kerr (res.), NC,Va, US 133/J2
John Martin (res.), Co, US 132/C2
John Wayne/Orange County (int'l arpt.), Ca, US 136/G8
Johnson (co.), Ks, US 137/D6
Johnson City, Tn, US 130/D4
Johnsonburg, NJ, US 138/D2
Johnsons Crossing, Yk, Can. 134/M3
Johnston (falls), Zam. 104/A5
Johnston, Austl. 109/B4
Johnston Atoll (isl.), Pac., US 117/J3
Johnstone, Sc, UK 36/B5
Johnstown, Pa, US 130/E4
Johnstown, Co, US 137/C2
Johnsville, Md, US 138/A4
Johor Baharu, Malay. 80/B3
Jõhstadt, Ger. 55/G1
Joigny, Fr. 42/E3
Joinvile, Braz. 155/B3
Joinville, Fr. 56/B1
Jojutla, Mex. 143/K8
Jokioinen, Fin. 39/K1
Jokkmokk, Swe. 37/F2
Jökulsárgljufur NP, Ice. 37/P6
Jolanda di Savoia, It. 59/E3
Joliette, Qu, Can. 130/F2
Jollyville, Tx, US 129/H5
Jolo (isl.), Phil. 81/F2
Jolo, Phil. 81/F2
Jomala, Fin. 39/H1
Jombang, Indo. 80/D5
Jomda, China 70/G5
Jomo Kenyatta (int'l arpt.), Kenya 104/C3
Jona, Swi. 57/E3
Jonacatepec, Mex. 143/L8
Jonava, Lith. 39/L4
Jonchery-sur-Vesle, Fr. 52/C5
Jones, Ok, US 137/N14
Jones (inlet), NY, US 139/L9
Jones (mtn.), Pa, US 138/A2
Jones (sound), Nun., Can. 121/S7
Jonesboro, Ar, US 129/K4
Jonesboro, La, US 129/J4
Jönköping, Swe. 38/F3
Jönköping (co.), Swe. 37/E4
Jonquière, Qu, Can. 131/G1
Jonuta, Mex. 140/C4
Joondalup (lake), Austl. 112/K6
Joplin, Mo, US 129/J3
Joppatowne (Joppa), Md, US 138/B5
Jora, India 84/A2
Jordan, Mt, US 126/G4
Jordan, On, Can. 131/R9
Jordan (riv.), Isr.,Jor. 91/D4
Jordan (ctry.) 88/C2
Jordan Valley, Or, US 126/D5
Jordânia, Braz. 154/B4
Jorge (cape), Chile 159/B6
Jorge Chavez (int'l arpt.), Peru 156/B4
Jork, Ger. 51/G1
Jornada del Muerto (valley), NM, US 132/B3
Jørpeland, Nor. 38/B2
Jos (plat.), Nga. 96/G6
Jos, Nga. 103/H4
Jose Abad Santos, Phil. 81/G2
José Batlle y Ordóñez, Uru. 159/G2
José Bonifácio, Braz. 155/B2
José Cardel, Mex. 143/N7
José de Freitas, Braz. 154/B2
José de San Martín, Arg. 157/B5
José Enrique Rodó, Uru. 159/K10
José María Morelos, Mex. 144/D2
Jose Marti (int'l arpt.), Cuba 145/F1
José Pedro Varela, Uru. 159/G2
José, South (dept.), Uru. 159/F2
Josefa Camejo (int'l arpt.), Ven. 152/D2

Joseph Bonaparte (gulf), Austl. 109/B2
Joshin-Etsu Kogen NP, Japan 75/F2
Joshua (pt.), Ct, US 139/F1
Joshua Tree NP, Ca, US 128/D4
Jossa (riv.), Ger. 54/C2
Jotunheimen NP, Nor. 38/C1
Jouanne (riv.), Fr. 42/C2
Jouarre, Fr. 30/M5
Joué-lès-Tours, Fr. 42/D3
Jœuf, Fr. 53/F5
Jourama Falls NP, Austl. 114/B2
Jourdanton, Tx, US 129/H5
Joure, Neth. 50/C3
Joutseno, Fin. 39/N1
Joux (lake), Swi. 56/C4
Jouy-en-Josas, Fr. 30/A6
Jouy-le-Châtel, Fr. 30/M6
Jouy-le-Moutier, Fr. 30/A4
Jouy-sur-Morin, Fr. 52/C6
Jovellanos, Cuba 145/F1
Joveyn (riv.), Iran 89/G1
Jowai, India 83/F2
Joy (mt.), Yk, Can. 134/M3
Jōyō, Japan 77/J6
Jozankei Spa, Japan 76/B2
Ju Xian, China 72/D4
Juan Aldama, Mex. 142/E3
Juan de Fuca (str.), BC, Can.,US 122/D4
Juan de Fuca, Strait of (str.), Can.,US 126/B3
Juan de Nova (isl.), Fr. 93/G6
Juan Fernández (isls.), Chile 147/A6
Juan Fernández, Arg. 158/F3
Juan José Paso, Arg. 158/E2
Juan L. Lacaze, Uru. 159/K11
Juan Santamaria (int'l arpt.), CR 145/E4
Juancheng, China 72/C4
Juangriego, Ven. 153/F2
Juanjui, Peru 156/B2
Juárez, Braz. 158/F3
Juarez, Sierra de (mts.), Mex. 128/D4
Juatinga, Ponta de (pt.), Braz. 211/J8
Juazeirinho, Braz. 154/C2
Juazeiro, Braz. 154/B3
Juazeiro do Norte, Braz. 154/C2
Juba, Sudan 97/M7
Jubany, Arg., Ant. 160/W
Jubba (riv.), Som. 99/P7
Jübek, Ger. 40/E1
Jubones (riv.), Ecu. 156/B1
Juby (cape), Mor. 98/B4
Júcar (riv.), Sp. 44/D3
Jucás, Braz. 154/C2
Jūchen, Ger. 53/F1
Juchipila, Mex. 142/E4
Juchique de Ferrer, Mex. 143/N7
Juchitán de Zaragoza, Mex. 144/C2
Juchitepec, Mex. 143/R10
Jucurutu, Braz. 154/C2
Judaberg, Nor. 38/A2
Judenburg, Aus. 43/L3
Judith (riv.), Mt, US 126/F4
Juelsminde, Den. 38/D4
Juhaynah, Egypt 101/B3
Juigalpa, Nic. 144/E3
Juilly, Fr. 30/L4
Juine (riv.), Fr. 42/E2
Juist, Ger. 50/D1
Juist (isl.), Ger. 50/E1
Juiz de Fora, Braz. 211/K6
Jujurieux, Fr. 56/B5
Julbach, Ger. 55/F6
Julesburg, Co, US 137/H6
Juli, Peru 156/D4
Julia Creek, Austl. 114/A3
Juliaca, Peru 156/D4
Julian Alps (mts.), It. 43/K3
Juliana Top (peak), Sur. 151/G3
Jülich, Ger. 53/F2
Julio A. Mella, Cuba 145/H1
Juliustown, NJ, US 138/D3
Jullundur, India 86/H4
Julu, China 72/C3
Jumbilla, Peru 156/B2
Jumeauville, Fr. 30/H5
Jumilla, Sp. 44/E3
Juminda (pt.), Est. 39/L2
Jumla, Nepal 84/D1
Jūmonji, Japan 76/B4
Junāgadh, India 89/K4
Junan, China 72/D4
Juncal (peak), Chile 158/N8
Junction, Ut, US 128/B2
Junction, Tx, US 129/H5
Junction City, Or, US 126/C4
Jundiaí, Braz. 211/G8
Jundu (mts.), China 73/A1
Juneda, Sp. 45/F2
Jungar Qi, China 72/B3
Jungfrau (peak), Swi. 56/D4
Jungfraujoch, Swi. 56/D4
Junglinster, Lux. 53/F4
Juniata (riv.), Pa, US 138/A2
Juniata, On, Can. 131/P16
Junik, Serb. 47/G1
Junín (dept.), Peru 156/B3
Junín, Ecu. 152/A5

Junín, Arg. 158/C2
Junin, Arg. 158/E2
Junin de los Andes, Arg. 158/C3
Juniper Hills, Ca, US 136/C2
Junji (pass), China 72/C3
Juno Beach, Fl, US 133/H5
Junqueirópolis, Braz. 155/B2
Junsele, Swe. 37/F3
Juparanã, Lagoa (lake), Braz. 155/D1
Jupiter (riv.), Qu, Can. 131/J1
Jupiter, Fl, US 133/H5
Jupiter (mt.), Wa, US 135/A2
Juquiá, Braz. 155/B3
Juquitiba, Braz. 211/F8
Jur (riv.), Sudan 97/L6
Jur pri Bratislave, Slvk. 124/V12
Jura (mts.), Fr. 78/B3
Jura (dept.), Fr. 56/B4
Jura (isl.), Sc, UK 31/R8
Jura (isl.), Sc, UK 31/Q9
Juradó, Col. 152/B3
Jurançon, Fr. 44/C5
Jurbise, Belg. 52/C2
Jurien, Austl. 112/B4
Jūrmala, Lat. 39/K3
Juruá, Braz. 147/E3
Juruá (riv.), Braz. 147/D4
Juruena (riv.), Braz. 147/D4
Juruti, Braz. 151/G4
Jushiyama, Japan 77/L5
Juskatla, BC, Can. 134/M5
Jussey, Fr. 56/B3
Jussy, Swi. 56/C5
Jussy, Fr. 52/C4
Justo Daract, Arg. 158/D2
Jutaí, Braz. 150/E5
Jutaí (riv.), Braz. 150/E4
Jutiapa, Guat. 144/D3
Juticalpa, Hon. 144/E3
Jutland, NJ, US 138/D2
Jutland (pen.), Den. 37/D4
Juventud, La (isl.), Cuba 145/E1
Juye, China 72/D4
Juzhang (riv.), China 72/C5
Juziers, Fr. 30/H4
Južna Morava (riv.), Serb. 48/E4
Juzur Qarqannah (isl.), Congo 99/H2
Jyderup, Den. 38/D4

K

Ka (riv.), Nga. 96/F5
Ka (isl.), NKor. 73/C3
Ka Lae (cape), Hi, US 124/T11
Kaawawa, Hi, US 124/W12
Kaala (peak), Hi, US 124/U11
Kaalualu, Hi, US 124/U11
Kaap Plato (plat.), SAfr. 106/C3
Kaarina, Fin. 39/K1
Kaarst, Ger. 50/D6
Kaba, Hun. 48/E2
Kabadak (riv.), Bang. 85/G4
Kabaena (isl.), Indo. 81/F5
Kabah (ruin), Mex. 144/D1
Kabala, SLeo. 102/C4
Kabalega (falls), Ugan. 104/A2
Kabalega NP, Ugan. 97/M7
Kabalo, D.R. Congo 105/E2
Kabamba, Lac (lake), D.R. Congo 105/E2
Kabankalan, Phil. 81/F2
Kabardino-Balkaria, Resp., Rus. 63/G4
Kabare, D.R. Congo 105/E1
Kaberamaido, Ugan. 104/B2
Kabinakagani (lake), On, Can. 130/C1
Kabinda, D.R. Congo 105/D2
Kabir, Oued el (riv.), Alg. 100/H4
Kabīrwāla, Pak. 86/A4
Kabīyah, Sabkhat al (swamp), Tun. 46/A5
Kableshkovo, Bul. 49/H4
Kābol (Kabul) (cap.), Afg. 89/J2
Kabompo (riv.), Zam. 105/D3
Kabinach (riv.), Aus. 48/B2
Kabongo, D.R. Congo 105/E2
Kabrai, India 84/C3
Kabri'i (riv.), Afg. 89/J2
Kabul (Kābol) (cap.), Afg. 89/J2
Kaburuang (isl.), Indo. 81/G3
Kačanik, Serb. 47/G1
Kachalola, Zam. 105/F3
Kachemak (bay), Ak, US 134/H4
Kachemak, Ak, US 134/H4
Kachin (div.), Myan. 70/G6
Kaçkar Dai (peak), Turk. 90/E1
Kadaianallur, India 82/C6
Kadam (peak), Ugan. 104/B2
Kadam (isl.), Myan. 78/B3
Kadan (isl.), Myan. 78/B3
Kadavu (isl.), Fiji 116/G6
Kadeï (riv.), CAfr.,Cam 96/J7
Kadina, Austl. 113/H5

Kadınhanı, Turk. 90/C2
Kadiogo (prov.), Burk. 103/E3
Kadiolo, Mali 102/D4
Kadiri, India 82/C5
Kadırli, Turk. 90/D2
Kadışehri, Turk. 90/C1
Kadoma, Zim. 105/E4
Kadoma, Japan 77/J6
Kaduna (state), Nga. 103/G4
Kaduna, Nga. 103/G4
Kaduna (riv.), Nga. 93/C4
Kāduqli, Sudan 97/L5
Kaech'ŏn, NKor. 73/C3
Kaedi, Mrta. 102/B2
Kaélé, Camr. 96/H5
Kaena (pt.), Hi, US 124/V12
Kafar Jar Ghar (mts.), Afg. 89/J2
Kaffraria (reg.), SAfr. 106/D4
Kaffrine, Sen. 102/B3
Kafr Ash Shaykh (gov.), Egypt 101/B1
Kafr ash Shaykh, Egypt 91/B4
Kafr az Zayyāt, Egypt 91/B4
Kafr Kannā, Isr. 91/G6
Kafr Mandā, Isr. 91/G6
Kafr Qari', Isr. 91/G6
Kafr Qāsim, Isr. 91/F7
Kafu (riv.), Ugan. 104/A2
Kafue (riv.), Zam. 105/E4
Kafue NP, Zam. 105/E3
Kaga, Japan 74/E2
Kaga Bandoro, CAfr. 97/J6
Kagan, Uzb. 87/D5
Kagawa (pref.), Japan 74/D3
Kagera (riv.), Tanz. 104/A3
Kağızman, Turk. 90/E1
Kagoshima (int'l arpt.), Japan 74/B5
Kagoshima, Japan 74/B5
Kagoshima (bay), Japan 74/B5
Kagoshima (dept.), Japan 75/L5
Kahaluu, Hi, US 124/W13
Kahama, Tanz. 104/B1
Kahayan (riv.), Indo. 80/D4
Kahiu (pt.), Hi, US 124/T10
Kahl am Main, Ger. 54/C2
Kāhna, Pak. 86/B2
Kahoka, Mo, US 127/L5
Kahoolawe (isl.), Hi, US 124/T10
Kahperusvaara (peak), Fin. 37/G1
Kahraman Maraş (prov.), Turk. 90/D2
Kahramanmaraş, Turk. 90/D2
Kahror Pakka, Pak. 86/A5
Kâhta, Turk. 90/D2
Kahuku, Hi, US 124/W12
Kahuku (pt.), Hi, US 124/W12
Kahului, Hi, US 124/T10
Kahuzi-Biega, PN de, D.R. Congo 105/E1
Kai (isls.), Indo. 81/H5
Kai Besar (isl.), Indo. 81/H5
Kai Kecil (isl.), Indo. 81/H5
Kaiapoi, NZ 117/S11
Kaibab (plat.), Az, US 128/D3
Kaibola, Japan 81/F1
Kaieteur (falls), Guy. 153/G3
Kaieteur NP, Guy. 153/G3
Kaifeng, China 71/K5
Kaihua, China 79/C2
Kaikohe, NZ 117/S10
Kaikoura, NZ 117/S11
Kaili, China 83/J2
Kailu, China 72/E2
Kailua, Hi, US 124/U11
Kailua, Hi, US 124/W13
Kaimganj, India 84/B2
Kaimur (range), India 84/C3
Kainab (riv.), Namb. 106/B3
Kainach (riv.), Aus. 48/B2
Kainan, Japan 74/D3
Kainji (riv.), Nga. 103/G4
Kainji (lake), Nga. 93/C3
Kainji Lake NP, Nga. 103/F4
Kaipara (har.), NZ 117/S10
Kairāna, India 84/C2
Kairi, Austl. 114/B2
Kairouan, Tun. 96/H1
Kaiseregg (peak), Swi. 56/D4
Kaisersesch, Ger. 53/G2
Kaiserslautern, Ger. 54/B4
Kaisheim, Ger. 54/D5
Kaitaia, NZ 117/S10
Kaithal, India 86/D5
Kaiwi (chan.), Hi, US 124/T10
Kaiyang, China 83/J2
Kaiyuan, China 72/F2
Kaizuka, Japan 77/H7
Kajaani, Fin. 37/N3
Kaji-san (peak), SKor. 74/A3
Kajiado, Kenya 104/C3

Kajikazawa, Japan 77/A2
Kakamas, SAfr. 106/C3
Kakamega, Kenya 104/B2
Kakamigahara, Japan 77/L5
Kakanj, Bosn. 48/D3
Kake, Ak, US 134/M4
Kaketsa (mtn.), BC, Can. 134/M4
Kakhovka, Ukr. 49/L2
Kakhovs'ke Vodoskhovyshche (res.), Ukr. 62/E3
Kākināda, India 82/D5
Kakiri, Ugan. 104/B2
Kako (riv.), Japan 77/G6
Kakogawa, Japan 77/G6
Kakoma, D.R. Congo 105/E1
Kakrāla, India 84/C2
Kaktovik, Ak, US 134/K1
Kakuda, Japan 75/G2
Kakunodate, Japan 76/B4
Kalaa Kebira, Tun. 46/B5
Kālābāgh, Pak. 86/A3
Kalabo, Zam. 105/D3
Kalach, Rus. 63/G2
Kalach-na-Donu, Rus. 63/G2
Kaladan (riv.), Myan. 83/F3
Kalahari (des.), Namb. 93/D7
Kalahari-Gemsbok NP, SAfr. 106/C3
Kalaheo, Hi, US 124/S10
Kalaiya, Nepal 85/E2
Kalalé, Ben. 103/F4
Kalamákion, Gre. 47/N8
Kalamariá, Gre. 47/H2
Kalamáta, Gre. 47/H4
Kalamazoo, Mi, US 130/C3
Kalampáka, Gre. 47/G3
Kalandy, Madg. 107/A6
Kalaoa, Hi, US 124/U11
Kalasin, Thai. 78/C2
Kalāswāla, Pak. 86/C3
Kalat, Pak. 89/J3
Kalaupapa, Hi, US 124/T10
Kalávrita, Gre. 47/H3
Kalbach, Ger. 54/B2
Kalbar, Austl. 114/D4
Kalbarri, Austl. 112/B3
Kalbarri NP, Austl. 112/B3
Kaldakvísl (riv.), Ice. 37/P6
Kale, Turk. 62/F4
Kale, Turk. 90/B2
Kalefeld, Ger. 51/H5
Kalemie (int'l arpt.), D.R. Congo 105/E2
Kalemie, D.R. Congo 104/A4
Kalemyo, Myan. 83/F3
Kalety, Pol. 41/K3
Kalewa, Myan. 83/F3
Kalgoorlie-Boulder, Austl. 112/D4
Kāli (riv.), India 84/B1
Kāli (riv.), India 84/D2
Kāli (riv.), Nepal 84/D2
Kalima, D.R. Congo 97/L8
Kalimantan (reg.), Indo. 80/D4
Kálimnos, Gre. 90/A2
Kálimnos (isl.), Gre. 90/A2
Kālimpong, India 85/G2
Kaliningrad, Rus. 61/W9
Kaliningrad, Rus. 39/J4
Kaliningradskaya Oblast, Rus. 60/D5
Kalininsk, Rus. 63/G1
Kalinkavichy, Bela. 62/D1
Kaliro, Ugan. 104/A3
Kalisizo, Ugan. 104/A3
Kalispell, Mt, US 126/D3
Kalisz, Pol. 41/K3
Kaliua, Tanz. 104/A3
Kalix, Swe. 60/D2
Kalixälven (riv.), Swe. 37/G2
Kaliyāganj, India 85/G3
Kalkaska, Mi, US 130/C2
Kalkfeld, Namb. 105/C3
Kallinge, Swe. 38/F3
Kallinge (int'l arpt.), Swe. 38/F3
Kallithéa, Gre. 47/N8
Kallsjön (lake), Swe. 37/E3
Kalmar, Swe. 38/G3
Kalmar (co.), Swe. 37/F4
Kalmarsund (sound), Swe. 38/G3
Kalmthout, Belg. 50/B6
Kalmykia, Resp., Rus. 63/H3
Kālna, India 85/F3
Kalocsa, Hun. 48/D2
Kalofer, Bul. 49/H4
Kalohi (chan.), Hi, US 124/T10
Kalokhórion, Gre. 47/H3
Kālol, India 85/F3
Kalomo, Zam. 105/E4
Kalongo, Ugan. 104/B2
Kālpi, India 84/B2
Kalsdorf bei Graz, Aus. 43/L3
Kaltag, Ak, US 134/G2
Kaltbrunn, Swi. 57/F3
Kaltenleutgeben, Aus. 49/N7

Kaltennordheim, Ger. 54/D1
Kaltern (Caldaro), It. 43/J3
Kalu (riv.), SrL. 82/D6
Kaluga, Rus. 60/H5
Kalundborg, Den. 38/D4
Kalungu, Ugan. 104/A3
Kalungwishi (riv.), Zam. 104/A5
Kalur Kot, Pak. 86/A3
Kalush, Ukr. 49/J3
Kalutara, SrL. 82/C6
Kalyān, India 89/K5
Kama (riv.), D.R. Congo 105/E1
Kama, D.R. Congo 105/E1
Kama (res.), Rus. 61/M4
Kama (riv.), Rus. 27/K3
Kamaishi, Japan 76/B4
Kamakou (peak), Hi, US 124/T10
Kamakura, Japan 77/T9
Kamālia, Pak. 86/B4
Kamalo, Hi, US 124/T10
Kāman, India 84/A2
Kamango (lake), Mali 102/E2
Kamanjab, Namb. 105/B4
Kamarang, Guy. 153/F3
Kāmāreddi, India 82/C4
Kamarhāti, India 82/E3
Kamaniwa (falls), Guy. 153/G3
Kambalda, Austl. 112/D4
Kambam, Japan 77/J3
Kambar, Pak. 82/A2
Kambaia, Nepal 85/E2
Kambia, SLeo. 102/B4
Kambove, D.R. Congo 105/E3
Kambuno (peak), Indo. 81/F4
Kamchatka (pen.), Rus. 67/Q3
Kamchatskaya Oblast, Rus. 65/R4
Kamchiya (riv.), Bul. 49/H4
Kamen, Ger. 51/E5
Kamen'-na-Obi, Rus. 87/J2
Kamenka, Rus. 63/H1
Kamenka, Rus. 49/M4
Kamen', Rus. 62/G2
Kamensk-Shakhtinskiy, Rus. 62/G2
Kamensk-Ural'skiy, Rus. 61/P4
Kameoka, Japan 77/J5
Kameyama, Japan 77/K6
Kami, Japan 77/J5
Kami (isl.), Japan 77/M6
Kami-koshiki (isl.), Japan 74/A5
Kamiah, Id, US 126/D4
Kamień Pomorski, Pol. 38/F5
Kamieskroon, SAfr. 106/B3
Kamifukuoka, Japan 77/M5
Kamiiso, Japan 76/B3
Kamiishizu, Japan 77/L5
Kamikawa, Japan 76/C2
Kamikuishiki, Japan 77/B2
Kamilo (pt.), Hi, US 124/U11
Kamina, D.R. Congo 105/E2
Kaminaka, Japan 77/J5
Kaminoho, Japan 77/M4
Kaminoyama, Japan 75/G2
Kamisato, Japan 77/L1
Kamishak (bay), Ak, US 134/H4
Kamiyahagi, Japan 77/M5
Kamiyaku, Japan 74/B5
Kamla (riv.), India 85/F2
Kamloops, BC, Can. 126/C3
Kammaki, Japan 77/J6
Kamnik, Slov. 43/L3
Kamo, Japan 75/F2
Kamo, Japan 77/G5
Kamo (riv.), Japan 77/J5
Kamogawa, Japan 75/G3
Kamojima, Japan 74/D3
Kamouraska, Qu, Can. 131/K1
Kamp (riv.), Aus. 41/H4
Kamp-Bornhofen, Ger. 53/G2
Kamp-Lintfort, Ger. 50/D5
Kampala (cap.), Ugan. 104/B2
Kampar, Malay. 80/B3
Kampar (riv.), Indo. 80/B3
Kampen, Neth. 50/C3
Kampen, Ger. 38/C4
Kamphaeng Phet, Thai. 78/C5
Kamphaeng Phet (ruin), Thai. 78/B3
Kampinoski NP, Pol. 62/B1
Kamp'o, SKor. 73/E5
Kampong Kuala Besut, Malay. 80/B2
Kampong Saom (bay), Camb. 80/B1
Kampong Saom, Camb. 78/B2
Kampville, Mo, US 139/H7
Kamsack, Sk, Can. 127/H1
Kamsdorf, Ger. 55/E2
Kamuchawie (lake), Mb,Sk, Can. 127/H1
Kamui-misaki (cape), Japan 76/B2
Kámuk (mtn.), CR 145/E5
Kamuli, Ugan. 104/B2
Kam'yanets'-Podil's'kyy, Ukr. 62/C2
Kamyshin, Rus. 63/H1

Kanan, Japan 77/J7
Kananga, D.R. Congo 105/D2
Kanangra-Boyd NP, Austl. 115/D2
Kanash, Rus. 61/K5
Kanasin, Mex. 144/D1
Kanawake Ind. Res., Qu, Can. 131/N7
Kanawha (riv.), WV, US 133/H2
Kanazawa, Japan 75/E2
Kanchanaburi, Thai. 78/B3
Kānchenjunga (peak), Nepal 82/E2
Kānchīpuram, India 82/C5
Kandahār, Afg. 89/J2
Kandalaksha, Rus. 60/G2
Kandalaksha (gulf), Rus. 37/K2
Kándanos, Gre. 47/H5
Kandé, Togo 103/F4
Kandel (peak), Ger. 56/E1
Kandel, Ger. 54/B4
Kandel (riv.), Swi. 56/D5
Kandern, Ger. 56/D2
Kandersteg, Swi. 56/D5
Kandhkot, Pak. 89/J3
Kāndhla, India 86/D5
Kandi (cape), Indo. 81/F3
Kandi, Ben. 103/F4
Kāndi, India 85/G4
Kandıra, Turk. 49/K5
Kandos, Austl. 115/D2
Kandukūr, India 82/C4
Kandy, SrL. 82/D6
Kane (basin), Grld. 123/K7
Kane (co.), Il, US 135/P16
Kanem (prov.), Chad 96/H5
Kaneohe, Hi, US 124/W13
Kaneohe (bay), Hi, US 124/W13
Kaneohe Marine Air Corps Station, Hi, US 124/W13
Kaneville, Il, US 135/N16
Kaneyama, Japan 76/B4
Kang, Bots. 105/D5
Kanga (riv.), Bang. 85/G5
Kangaba, Mali 102/C4
Kangal, Turk. 90/C2
Kangān, Iran 88/F3
Kangan Abor. Land, Austl. 112/C2
Kanganpur, Pak. 86/C4
Kangar, Malay. 78/C5
Kangaroo (isl.), Austl. 109/C4
Kangasala, Fin. 39/L1
Kangāvar, Iran 88/E2
Kangbao, China 71/K3
Kangding, China 70/H5
Kangean (isls.), Indo. 81/E5
Kanggye, NKor. 73/D2
Kanggyŏng, SKor. 73/D4
Kanghwa, SKor. 73/F6
Kangiqsualujjuaq, Qu, Can. 123/K3
Kangiqsujuaq, Qu, Can. 123/J2
Kangirsuk, Qu, Can. 123/J2
Kangjin, SKor. 73/D5
Kangmar, China 85/G1
Kangnam (mts.), NKor. 73/C3
Kangning, SKor. 74/A2
Kangping, China 72/E2
Kāngra, India 86/D3
Kangrinboqê (peak), China 70/D5
Kangshan, Tai. 79/D3
Kangto (peak), China 83/F2
Kangwŏn-do (prov.), SKor. 74/A2
Kanha NP, India 84/C4
Kanhān (riv.), India 82/C3
Kani, India 77/M5
Kanie, Japan 77/L5
Kanin (riv.), Rus. 160/C
Kanin Nos (pt.), Rus. 64/E3
Kaniva, Austl. 115/B3
Kanjiza, Serb. 48/E2
Kankakee (riv.), Il, US 130/C3
Kankan, Gui. 102/C4
Kanmuri-yama (peak), Japan 74/C3
Kannami, Japan 77/B3
Kannapolis, NC, US 133/H3
Kannauj, India 84/B2
Kannon-zaki (pt.), Japan 77/D3
Kannus, Fin. 60/N3
Kano, Nga. 103/H4
Kano (state), Nga. 103/H4
Kan'onji, Japan 74/C3
Kanouse (mtn.), NJ, US 139/H7
Kanoya, Japan 74/B5
Kanra, Japan 77/B1
Kansai (int'l arpt.), Japan 77/H7
Kansai (isl.), Japan 77/M7
Kansas (riv.), Ks, US 129/H3
Kansas City (int'l arpt.), Mo, US 129/J3
Kansas City, Ks, US 137/D5
Kansas City, Mo, US 137/D5
Kansasville, Wi, US 135/P14
Kansk, Rus. 64/K4
Kansŏng, SKor. 73/E3
Kantabānji, India 82/D3
Kānth, India 84/B1
Kantō (prov.), Japan 75/F2
Kantunilkin, Mex. 144/E1

Kanuku (mts.), Guy. 150/G3
Kanuma, Japan 75/F2
Kanye, Bots. 105/E5
Kaohsiung, Tai. 79/D3
Kaohsiung (int'l arpt.), Tai. 79/D3
Kaokoveld (mts.), Namb. 105/B4
Kaolack, Sen. 102/A3
Kaolack (pol. reg.), Sen. 102/B3
Kaolinovo, Bul. 49/H4
Kaoma, Zam. 105/D3
Kapaa, Hi, US 124/S9
Kapaahu, Hi, US 124/U11
Kapaau, Hi, US 124/U10
Kapalong, Phil. 79/E6
Kapan, Arm. 63/H5
Kapchorwa, Ugan. 104/B2
Kapellen, Belg. 50/B6
Kapenguria, Kenya 104/B2
Kapidaği (pen.), Turk. 49/H5
Kapingamarangi (isl.), Micr. 116/E2
Kapiri Mposhi, Zam. 105/E3
Kapiskau (riv.), On, Can. 123/H3
Kaplice, Czh. 55/H5
Kapos (riv.), Hun. 48/C2
Kaposvár, Hun. 48/C2
Kappl, Aus. 57/G3
Kapsan, NKor. 73/E2
Kapuas (riv.), Indo. 80/C4
Kapuas Hulu (mts.), Indo.,Mal 80/D3
Kapunda, Austl. 113/H5
Kapūrthala, India 86/C4
Kapuskasing, On, Can. 130/D1
Kapuskasing (riv.), On, Can. 130/D1
Kapuvár, Hun. 43/M3
Kapydzhik (peak), Azer. 63/H5
Kap'yŏng, SKor. 73/D4
Kara, Togo 103/F4
Kara (sea), Rus. 160/A4
Kara (riv.), Rus. 61/Q1
Kara-saki (pt.), Japan 77/J2
Karaali, Turk. 90/C2
Karabiğa, Turk. 49/H5
Karabük, Turk. 90/C1
Karaburun, Turk. 49/J5
Karaca (peak), Turk. 90/D2
Karacabey, Turk. 90/B1
Karacaköy, Turk. 49/K5
Karaçal (peak), Turk. 91/C1
Karacaoğlan, Turk. 82/B5
Karachayevo-Cherkesiya, Resp., Rus. 63/G4
Karachev, Rus. 62/E1
Karāchi, Pak. 89/J4
Karadere, Turk. 49/K5
Karaginskiy (isl.), Rus. 67/R4
Karaj, Iran 88/F1
Karakax (riv.), China 89/L1
Karakaya (dam), Turk. 90/D2
Karakelong (isl.), Indo. 81/G3
Karakhoto (ruin), China 70/H3
Karakol, Kyr. 87/G4
Karakoram (range), India 70/C4
Karakoram (pass), India 86/D2
Karakoro (riv.), Mali 102/C3
Karakorum (ruin), Mong. 70/H2
Karakorum (ruin), Mong. 87/G3
Karakorum (pass), China 89/L1
Karaköse, Turk. 90/E2
Karaköy, Turk. 90/E2
Karakul' (lake), Taj. 87/F5
Karakumy (des.), Trkm. 64/F5
Karakyon (peak), Trkm. 87/B4
Karakyr (peak), Trkm. 89/H1
Karam (riv.), Indo. 81/E4
Karaman (prov.), Turk. 90/C2
Karaman, Turk. 90/C2
Karamay, China 70/D2
Karamea Bight (bay), NZ 109/H7
Karamoja (prov.), Ugan. 104/B2
Karamürsel, Turk. 49/J5
Karangasem, Indo. 81/E5
Karanginskiy (isl.), Rus. 65/S4
Karanginskiy (bay), Rus. 65/S4
Kāranja, India 82/C3
Karanpur, India 86/B5
Karapınar, Turk. 90/C2
Karasabai, Guy. 153/G3
Karaşar, Turk. 49/L5
Karasburg, Namb. 106/B3
Karasjohka-Karasjok, Nor. 37/H1
Karasu, Turk. 49/K5
Karasu, Japan 77/L6
Karasuk, Rus. 46/H1
Karatá (lag.), Nic. 145/F3
Karataş, Turk. 91/D1
Karatoya (riv.), Bang. 85/G3
Karatsu, Japan 74/A4

Karauli, India 84/A2
Karaurgan, Turk. 90/E1
Karáva (peak), Gre. 47/G3
Karawang, Indo. 80/C5
Karayaka, Turk. 62/F4
Karayazı, Turk. 90/E2
Karazhal, Kaz. 64/H4
Karbalā' (gov.), Iraq 90/F3
Karbalā', Iraq 90/F3
Karben, Ger. 54/B2
Karcag, Hun. 48/E2
Kardhámila, Gre. 47/K3
Kāsai, India 85/F4
Kardhítsa, Gre. 47/G3
Kasai, Japan 74/D3
Kardhitsomagoúla, Gre. 47/G3
Kareha (riv.), India 85/E3
Karelī, India 84/B4
Karelia (reg.), Rus. 37/J2
Karelia, Resp., Rus. 64/D3
Karera, India 84/B3
Karesuando, Swe. 37/G1
Karēt (reg.), Mrta. 98/D4
Karf Ash Shaykh (gov.), Egypt 90/B4
Kargı, Turk. 90/C1
Karhal, India 84/B2
Karhijärvi (lake), Fin. 39/K1
Karhula, Fin. 39/M1
Kariá, Gre. 47/G3
Kariaí, Gre. 47/J2
Karianga, Madg. 107/H8
Kariba (dam), Zam. 105/E4
Kariba, Zim. 105/E4
Kariba (lake), Zim. 93/E6
Kariba-yama (peak), Japan 76/A4
Karibib, Namb. 105/C5
Karimama, Ben. 103/F3
Karimata (isl.), Indo. 80/D4
Karimata (str.), Indo. 80/C4
Karīmnagar, India 82/C4
Karimunjawa (isls.), Indo. 80/D5
Kariótissa, Gre. 47/H2
Karise, Den. 38/E4
Karisimbi (vol.), Kenya 104/C3
Karisimbi (vol.), Rwa. 105/E1
Káristos, Gre. 47/J3
Kariya, Japan 77/L6
Karkaar (mts.), Som. 97/Q6
Kārkäl, India 82/B5
Karkar (isl.), PNG 116/D5
Karkinits'ka Zatoka (gulf), Ukr. 62/D3
Kárkkila, Fin. 39/L1
Karkonski NP, Pol. 41/H3
Karla Marksa (peak), Taj. 89/K1
Karlholmsbruk, Swe. 38/G1
Karlino, Pol. 38/F4
Karlovac, Cro. 48/B3
Karlovarský (pol. reg.), Czh. 55/F2
Karlovo, Bul. 47/J1
Karlovy Vary, Czh. 55/F2
Karlsdorf-Neuthard, Ger. 54/B4
Karlsfeld, Ger. 55/E6
Karlshamn, Swe. 38/F3
Karlshuld, Ger. 54/E5
Karlskoga, Swe. 38/F2
Karlskron, Ger. 55/E5
Karlskrona, Swe. 38/F3
Karlsruhe, Ger. 54/B4
Karlstad, Swe. 38/E2
Karlstadt, Ger. 54/C3
Karlstein am Main, Ger. 54/C2
Karluk, Ak, US 134/H4
Karmāla, India 85/L5
Karnali (riv.), Nepal 70/D6
Karnali (zone), Nepal 84/C1
Karnaphuli (res.), Bang. 85/H4
Karnataka (state), India 82/C4
Karnes City, Tx, US 129/H5
Karnobat, Bul. 47/K1
Kärnten (prov.), Aus. 57/J3
Karonga, Malw. 104/B5
Karoo NP, SAfr. 106/C4
Katanga (reg.), D.R. Congo 105/D2
Karoonda, Austl. 115/A2
Karor, Pak. 86/A4
Karoso (cape), Indo. 81/E5
Kárpathos, Gre. 47/K5
Kárpathos (isl.), Gre. 90/A3
Karpatskiy NP, Ukr. 49/G1
Karratha, Austl. 112/C2
Kars (prov.), Turk. 90/E1
Kars, Turk. 90/E1
Kärsämäki, Fin. 39/L1
Kārsiyāng, India 85/F3
Karşıyaka, Turk. 90/C2
Karshi (int'l arpt.), Uzb. 87/E5
Kartaly, Rus. 63/M1
Kārtārpur, India 86/C4
Kartuzy, Pol. 38/H4
Karuah, Austl. 115/D2
Karuma (falls), Ugan. 104/B2

Karumba, Austl. 114/A2
Karūn (riv.), Iran 88/E2
Karup, Den. 38/C3
Karviná, Czh. 41/K4
Kaş, Turk. 91/A1
Kås, Den. 38/C3
Kasaan, Ak, US 134/M4
Kasabonika (lake), On, Can. 127/L2
Kasagi, Japan 77/J6
Kasahara, Japan 77/M5
Kāsai, Japan 85/F4
Kasai, Japan 74/D3
Kasai, D.R. Congo 93/D5
Kasama, Zam. 104/A5
Kasama, Japan 75/G2
Kasamatsu, Japan 77/L5
Kasane, Bots. 105/E4
Kasaoka, Japan 74/C3
Kasar (cape), Sudan 101/D5
Kāsaragod, India 82/C5
Kasartori-yama (peak), Japan 77/K6
Kasba (lake), NW,Nun., Can. 122/F2
Kasba Tadla, Mor. 98/D2
Kaseda, Japan 74/B5
Kasese, Ugan. 104/A2
Kashaf (riv.), Iran 89/H1
Kāshān, Iran 88/F2
Kashi, China 87/G5
Kashiba, Japan 77/J6
Kashihara, Japan 77/J6
Kashima, Japan 74/B4
Kashima, Japan 75/G3
Kashima (bay), Japan 77/F1
Kashin, Rus. 60/H4
Kāshīpur, India 84/B1
Kashiwa, Japan 77/D2
Kashiwazaki, Japan 75/F2
Kashmīr (reg.), India,Pak 87/G3
Kashmūng Ghar (range), Afg. 86/A2
Kasigau (peak), Kenya 104/C3
Kasigluk, Ak, US 134/F3
Kasilof, Ak, US 134/H3
Kasimov, Rus. 60/J5
Kasiruta (isl.), Indo. 81/G4
Kasiui (isl.), Indo. 81/H4
Kaskaskia (riv.), Il, US 129/K3
Kaslo, BC, Can. 126/D3
Kasongo, D.R. Congo 105/E1
Kásos (isl.), Gre. 90/A3
Kaspichan, Bul. 49/H4
Kaspiysk, Rus. 63/H4
Kassala, Sudan 88/C5
Kassándra (pen.), Gre. 62/B5
Kassándria, Gre. 47/H2
Kassel, Ger. 51/G6
Kassikaityu (riv.), Guy. 153/G4
Kassler, Co, US 137/B4
Kasson, Mn, US 127/K4
Kastamonu, Turk. 90/C1
Kastamonu (prov.), Turk. 90/C1
Kastanéai, Gre. 47/K2
Kaštel Stari, Cro. 48/C4
Kaštel Sućurac, Cro. 48/C4
Kastellaun, Ger. 53/G3
Kastéllion, Gre. 47/J5
Kasterlee, Belg. 50/B6
Kastl, Ger. 55/E4
Kastoria, Gre. 47/G2
Kastrakíou (lake), Gre. 47/G3
Kasuga, Japan 77/H5
Kasugai, Japan 77/K5
Kasugai, Japan 77/B2
Kasukabe, Japan 75/F3
Kasumiga (lake), Japan 75/G2
Kasungu, Malw. 105/F3
Kasūr, Pak. 86/C4
Kat O Chau (isl.), China 71/V9
Katahdin (mt.), Me, US 131/G2
Katákolon, Gre. 47/G4
Katangi, India 84/B4
Katanning, Austl. 112/C5
Katano, Japan 77/J6
Katastárion, Gre. 47/G4
Katavi NP, Tanz. 105/F2
Katchall (isl.), India 83/M7
Katerini, Gre. 47/H2
Kates Needle (peak), Ak, US 134/M4
Katete, Zam. 105/F3
Katghora, India 84/D4
Kāthgodām, India 84/B1
Kathiawar (pen.), India 89/K4
Kathleen (mt.), Austl. 113/G2
Kāthmāndu (cap.), Nepal 85/E2
Kathua, India 86/C3
Kati, Mali 102/C3

Katiola, C.d'Iv. 102/D4
Katlehong, SAfr. 106/E2
Katlenburg-Lindau, Ger. 51/H5
Katmai (vol.), Ak, US 134/H4
Katmai NP, Ak, US 134/G4
Káto Akhaía, Gre. 47/G3
Katokhí, Gre. 47/G3
Katonah, NY, US 139/E1
Katonga (riv.), Ugan. 104/A2
Katoúna, Gre. 47/G3
Katowice, Pol. 41/K3
Katra, India 86/C3
Kātrās, India 85/F4
Katrine (lake), Sc, UK 36/B4
Katrineholm, Swe. 38/G2
Katsikás, Gre. 47/G3
Katsina (state), Nga. 103/G3
Katsina, Nga. 103/G3
Katsina Ala (riv.), Nga. 103/H5
Katsunuma, Japan 77/B2
Katsura (riv.), Japan 77/J5
Katsuragi, Japan 74/D3
Katsuragi-san (peak), Japan 77/H7
Katsuta, Japan 75/G2
Katsuura, Japan 75/G3
Katsuyama, Japan 74/E2
Katsuyama, Japan 77/B3
Kattakurgan, Uzb. 87/E5
Kattegat (str.), Den. 27/F3
Katumbi, Malw. 104/B5
Kātwa, India 85/G4
Katwe-Kabatooro, Ugan. 104/A3
Katwijk aan Zee, Neth. 50/B4
Katy, Tx, US 129/J5
Katzenbach (riv.), Ger. 54/B4
Katzenbuckel (peak), Ger. 54/C4
Katzenelnbogen, Ger. 53/G3
Katzhütte, Ger. 54/D1
Katzwinkel, Ger. 53/F3
Kau-ye (isl.), Myan. 78/B4
Kauai (chan.), Hi, US 124/S10
Kauai (isl.), Hi, US 124/S9
Kaufbeuren, Ger. 57/G2
Kaufering, Ger. 57/G1
Kaufungen, Ger. 51/G6
Kauhajoki, Fin. 60/D3
Kauhola (pt.), Hi, US 124/U10
Kauiki (pt.), Hi, US 124/U10
Kaukaveld (uplands), Namb. 105/C5
Kaukura (isl.), FrPol. 117/L6
Kaulakahi (chan.), Hi, US 124/R9
Kaulsdorf, Ger. 55/L1
Kaumalapau, Hi, US 124/T10
Kaunakakai, Hi, US 124/T10
Kauna (isl.), Hi, US 124/U11
Kaunas (int'l arpt.), Lith. 39/K4
Kaunas (res.), Lith. 39/L4
Kaunas, Lith. 39/L4
Kaupanger, Nor. 38/B1
Kauttua, Fin. 39/K1
Kavadarci, FYROM 47/H2
Kavajë, Alb. 47/F2
Kavála, Gre. 47/J2
Kavalerovo, Rus. 71/Q3
Kāvali, India 82/C5
Kavangel (isls.), Palau 116/C4
Kavaratti, India 82/B5
Kavarna, Bul. 49/J4
Kavgolovskoye (lake), Rus. 61/T6
Kavieng, PNG 116/E5
Kavīr-e Namak (dry lake), Iran 89/E3
Kävlinge, Swe. 38/E4
Kaw (lake), Ok, US 129/H3
Kawa (ruin), Sudan 101/B5
Kawabe, Japan 76/B4
Kawachi, Japan 77/E2
Kawachi-Nagano, Japan 77/J7
Kawage, Japan 77/L6
Kawagoe, Japan 75/F3
Kawagoe, Japan 77/L5
Kawaguchi, Japan 75/F3
Kawaguchiko, Japan 77/B3
Kawai, Japan 77/J6
Kawaihoa (pt.), Hi, US 124/R10
Kawaikini (peak), Hi, US 124/S9
Kawajima, Japan 77/J6
Kawakami, Japan 77/B2
Kawakami, Japan 77/B3
Kawamata, Japan 75/G2
Kawambwa, Zam. 104/A5
Kawamoto, Japan 77/C1
Kawanishi, Japan 77/H6
Kawanishi, Japan 77/B2
Kawardha, India 84/C4
Kawartha (lakes), On, Can. 130/E2
Kawasaki, Japan 75/F3
Kawasato, Japan 77/D1
Kawashima, Japan 77/M4
Kawaue, Japan 77/M4
Kawela (Kawela Bay), Hi, US 124/V12

Kawerau, NZ 117/T10
Kawlin, Myan. 83/G3
Kawthaung, Myan. 78/B4
Kax (riv.), China 70/D3
Kay (pt.), Yk, Can. 134/L2
Kaya, SKor. 73/E5
Kaya, Japan 77/H5
Kaya-san (peak), SKor. 73/D4
Kayadibi, Turk. 90/C2
Kayagangiri (peak), CAfr. 96/J6
Kayah (div.), Myan. 78/C2
Kayah (state), Myan. 83/G4
Kayan (riv.), Indo. 67/U9
Kayanga (riv.), Sen. 102/B3
Kaycee, Wy, US 126/G5
Kayenta, Az, US 128/E3
Kayes, Mali 102/C3
Kayes, Chad 96/H5
Kayes (pol. reg.), Mali 102/C3
Kayin (state), Myan. 83/G4
Kayl, Lux. 53/F5
Kaymaz, Turk. 49/K5
Kaynarca, Turk. 49/K5
Kaynaşlı, Turk. 49/K5
Kayoa (isl.), Indo. 81/G3
Kayser (mts.), Sur. 153/G4
Kayseri, Turk. 90/C2
Kayseri (prov.), Turk. 90/C2
Kaysersberg, Fr. 53/G4
Kaysville, Ut, US 137/K11
Kayuagung, Indo. 80/B3
Kazakhstan (ctry.), 64/G5
Kazan', Rus. 61/L5
Kazan (int'l arpt.), Rus. 61/L5
Kazan (riv.), Nun., Can. 122/F2
Kazancı, Turk. 91/C1
Kazanlı, Turk. 91/D1
Kazanlŭk, Bul. 47/J1
Kazbek (peak), Geo. 63/H4
Kāzerūn, Iran 88/F3
Kazgar (riv.), China 70/C4
Kazimierza Wielka, Pol. 41/L3
Kāzımkarabekir, Turk. 90/C2
Kazincbarcika, Hun. 41/L4
Kazo, Japan 77/D1
Kazuno, Japan 76/B3
Ke Ga (cape), Viet. 78/E3
Ké Macina, Mali 102/E3
Kéa, Gre. 47/J4
Kéa (isl.), Gre. 47/J4
Keaau, Hi, US 124/U11
Keady, NI, UK 34/B3
Keahole (pt.), Hi, US 124/T11
Keanapapa (pt.), Hi, US 124/T10
Keansburg, NJ, US 139/J10
Kearney, Ne, US 129/H2
Kearney, Mo, US 137/E6
Kearns, Ut, US 137/K12
Kearny, NJ, US 139/J8
Kearny (pt.), NI, UK 34/C3
Keawakapu, Hi, US 124/T10
Keawekaheka (pt.), Hi, US 124/U11
Keban (dam), Turk. 90/D2
Kebbi (state), Nga. 103/G4
Kébémer, Sen. 102/A3
Kebnekaise (peak), Swe. 37/G2
Kebumen, Indo. 80/C5
Kecel, Hun. 40/E5
Keçiborlu, Turk. 90/B2
Kecskemét, Hun. 48/D2
Kedah (state), Malay. 78/C5
Kédainiai, Lith. 39/K4
Kediri, Indo. 80/D5
Kedougou, Sen. 102/B3
Kędzierzyn-Koźle, Pol. 41/K3
Keego Harbor, Mi, US 135/F6
Keele (riv.), NW, Can. 122/D2
Keele (peak), Yk, Can. 122/C2
Keelung, Tai. 79/D2
Keelung, Japan 75/G8
Keen (mt.), Sc, UK 36/D3
Keene, D.R. Congo 105/C1
Keene, NH, US 131/F3
Keepit (dam), Austl. 115/D2
Keer-Weer (cape), Austl. 114/A1
Keetmanshoop, Namb. 106/B2
Kefallinía (isl.), Gre. 47/G3
Kefar Sava, Isr. 91/F7
Kefar Vitkin, Isr. 91/F7
Keflavik, Ice. 37/M7
Keflavik (int'l arpt.), Ice. 37/M7
Kehl, Ger. 56/D1
Kehrsatz, Swi. 53/F4
Keighley, Eng, UK 35/G4
Keihoku, Japan 77/J5
Keimoes, SAfr. 106/C3
Keïta (riv.), Chad 97/J6
Keith, Austl. 115/A3
Keith, Sc, UK 36/D1
Kejimkujik NP, NS, Can. 131/H2

Kekaha, Hi, US 124/S10
Kékes (peak), Hun. 41/K5
Kelan, China 70/J3
Kelang (isl.), Indo. 81/G4
Kelang, Malay. 80/B3
Kelberg, Ger. 53/F3
Keles, Turk. 62/D5
Kelheim, Ger. 55/E5
Kelkit, Turk. 90/C2
Kelkit (riv.), Turk. 90/D1
Kell, Ger. 53/F4
Kellenhusen, Ger. 38/D4
Keller (lake), 122/D2
Keller (peak), Ca, US 136/C2
Kellerberrin, Austl. 112/C4
Kellogg, Id, US 126/D4
Kells, NI, UK 34/B2
Kelowna, BC, Can. 126/D3
Kelsey (pt.), Wi, US 135/P14
Kelso, Wa, US 126/C4
Kelso, Sc, UK 36/D5
Kelvington, Sk, Can. 127/H2
Kem' (riv.), Rus. 64/D3
Kem', Rus. 60/G2
Kemah, Turk. 62/F5
Kemaliye, Turk. 90/D2
Kemalpaşa, Turk. 62/B5
Kemasik, Malay. 80/B3
Kematen an der Ybbs, Aus. 55/H6
Kematen in Tirol, Aus. 57/J3
Kembs, Fr. 56/D2
Kemecse, Hun. 41/L4
Kemena (riv.), Malay. 80/D3
Kemence, Hun. 41/K4
Kemer (dam), Turk. 91/B1
Kemer, Turk. 91/B1
Kemerhisar, Turk. 90/C2
Kemerovo, Rus. 64/J4
Kemerovskaya Oblast, Rus. 64/J4
Kemijärvi, Fin. 37/H2
Kemijoki (riv.), Fin. 37/H2
Kemmerer, Wy, US 126/F5
Kemnath, Ger. 55/E3
Kemnay, Sc, UK 36/D2
Kemp (lake), Tx, US 129/H4
Kempele, Fin. 60/E2
Kempen, Ger. 50/D5
Kempenich, Ger. 53/G3
Kempenland (phys. reg.), Belg. 50/C6
Kempisch Kanaal (canal), Belg. 53/E2
Kempsey, Austl. 115/C4
Kempston, Eng, UK 33/F2
Kempt (res.), Qu, Can. 130/F2
Kempten, Ger. 57/G2
Kempton, Austl. 115/C4
Kempton Park, SAfr. 106/E2
Kemptown, Md, US 138/A5
Kemri, India 84/B1
Kemul (peak), Indo. 81/E3
Ken (riv.), India 84/C3
Ken (lake), Sc, UK 34/D1
Ken-zaki (pt.), Japan 77/D1
Kenadsa, Alg. 99/E3
Kenai, Ak, US 134/H3
Kenai Fjords NP, Ak, US 134/H4
Kendal, Eng, UK 35/F3
Kendalia, Tx, US 137/T20
Kendall, Austl. 115/E1
Kendall (co.), Il, US 135/P16
Kendall (co.), Tx, US 137/T20
Kendall Park, NJ, US 138/D3
Kendallville, In, US 130/C3
Kendari, Indo. 81/F4
Kendrāpāra, India 82/E3
Kendel (riv.), Ger. 50/D5
Kenedy, Tx, US 129/H5
Kenedougou (prov.), Burk. 102/D4
Kenema, SLeo. 102/C4
Kenge, D.R. Congo 105/C1
Kenhardt, SAfr. 106/C3
Kenhorst, Pa, US 138/C3
Kenié-Baoulé, Réserve de, Mali 102/C3
Kenilworth, Eng, UK 33/E2
Kenilworth, NJ, US 139/H9
Kénitra (prov.), Mor. 100/A2
Kénitra, Mor. 100/A2
Kenli, China 72/D3
Kenmare, ND, US 127/E3
Kenmare, Ire. 31/P11
Kenmore, NY, US 137/S2
Kenmore, Wa, US 135/C2
Kenn (reef), Austl. 53/F4
Kenn, Ger. 53/F4
Kennebec (riv.), Me, US 131/G2
Kennebunk, Me, US 131/G3
Kennedy (range), Austl. 112/B3

Kennedy Entrance (chan.), 134/H4
Kennedyville, Md, US 138/C3
Kennelbach, Aus. 57/F3
Kenner, La, US 137/P17
Kennet (riv.), Eng, UK 33/E4
Kennet and Avon (canal), Eng, UK 32/D4
Kennesaw, Ga, US 137/D6
Kennett, Mo, US 129/K3
Kennett Square, Pa, US 138/C3
Kennewick, Wa, US 126/D4
Keno Hill, Yk, Can. 134/L3
Kenogami (riv.), On, Can. 123/H3
Kenora, On, Can. 127/K3
Kenosha, Wi, US 135/Q14
Kenosha (co.), Wi, US 135/P14
Kensico (res.), NY, US 139/K7
Kensington and Chelsea (bor.), Eng, UK 30/A1
Kent (pen.), Nun., Can. 122/F2
Kent (co.), On, Can. 135/G6
Kent (riv.), Eng, UK 35/F3
Kent (pt.), Md, US 138/B6
Kent, Oh, US 130/D3
Kent, Wa, US 126/C4
Kent County (int'l arpt.), Mi, US 130/C3
Kent Group (isls.), Austl. 115/C3
Kenton, De, US 138/C5
Kenton, Oh, US 130/D3
Kentucky (state), US 133/G2
Kentucky (riv.), Ky, US 130/C4
Kentucky (lake), Ky, US 133/F2
Kentville, NS, Can. 131/H2
Kenya (ctry.), 104/C2
Kenzingen, Ger. 56/D1
Keonjhar, India 82/E3
Kep i Gjuhëzës (cape), Alb. 47/F2
Kep i Rodonit (cape), Alb. 47/F2
Kepno, Pol. 41/J3
Keppel Sands, Austl. 114/C3
Kerala (state), India 82/C5
Kéran, PN de la, Togo 103/F4
Kerang, Austl. 115/B3
Keratéa, Gre. 47/J4
Kerava, Fin. 39/L1
Kerch' (str.), Rus.,Ukr. 62/F3
Kerch', Ukr. 62/F3
Keremeos, BC, Can. 126/D3
Kerempe Burnu (cape), Turk. 90/C1
Kerepestarcsa, Hun. 49/R9
Kerguélen (isl.), Fr. 23/N8
Kericho, Kenya 104/B3
Kerinci (peak), Indo. 80/B4
Kerio (riv.), Kenya 104/C2
Kerio Valley Nat'l Rsv., Kenya 104/B2
Kerkdriel, Neth. 50/C5
Kerken, Ger. 50/D6
Kerkini (lake), Gre. 47/H2
Kérkira, Gre. 47/F3
Kerkrade, Neth. 50/F2
Kerkwijk, Neth. 50/C5
Kermadec (isls.), NZ 116/G8
Kermān, Iran 89/G2
Kern (riv.), Ca, US 128/C4
Kern, South Kern (riv.), Ca, US 128/D4
Kerns, Swi. 57/E4
Kérou, Ben. 103/F4
Kerpen, Ger. 50/D6
Kerr (lake), Ok, US 129/J4
Kerrobert, Sk, Can. 126/F3
Kerrville, Tx, US 129/G5
Kerry (riv.), Mor. 100/C2
Kerulen (riv.), Mong. 67/L5
Kerzaz, Alg. 99/E3
Kerzers, Swi. 56/D4
Kesagami (riv.), On, Can. 130/D1
Keşan, Turk. 47/K2
Kesen (peak), Swi. 57/F4
Kesen'numa, Japan 76/B4
Keshan, China 71/N2
Keshod, India 82/B3
Keski-Suomi (prov.), Fin. 37/H3
Kesselbach (riv.), Ger. 54/C1
Kessenich, Belg. 50/D5
Kestel, Turk. 90/B1
Kesten'ga, Rus. 64/D2
Keszthely, Hun. 48/C2
Ket' (riv.), Rus. 64/J4
Ketapang, Indo. 80/D4

Ketelmeer (lake), Neth. 50/C3
Kétou, Ben. 103/F5
Kętrzyn, Pol. 39/J4
Ketsch, Ger. 54/B4
Kettering, Eng, UK 33/F2
Kettle (riv.), Mn, US 126/D3
Kettle Moraine State Forest, Wi, US 135/P14
Ketzin, Ger. 40/P7
Keukenhof, Neth. 50/B4
Kevelaer, Ger. 50/D5
Kewaunee, Wi, US 130/C2
Keweenaw (pen.), Mi, US 127/L4
Keweenaw (pt.), Mi, US 127/M4
Keweenaw (bay), Mi, US 127/L4
Keymar, Md, US 138/A4
Keyport, NJ, US 139/J10
Keyport, Wa, US 135/B2
Keystone (lake), Ok, US 129/H3
Kežmarok, Slvk. 41/L4
Khaanziir (cape), Som. 97/Q5
Khabarovsk, Rus. 71/Q2
Khabarovskiy Kray, Rus. 65/P4
Khagaria, India 85/F3
Khair, India 84/A2
Khairābād, India 84/C2
Khairpur, Pak. 86/B5
Khairpur, Pak. 89/J3
Khakasiya, Resp., Rus. 65/P6
Khalándrion, Gre. 47/N8
Khalīj al Hammāmāt (gulf), Tun. 46/B4
Khalīlābād, India 85/E3
Khalkhāl, Iran 88/E1
Khalkhidhiki (pen.), Gre. 47/H2
Khalkidhón, Gre. 47/H2
Khalkís, Gre. 47/H3
Khamar-Daban (mts.), Rus. 70/H1
Khambhāliya, India 89/J4
Khambhat, India 89/K4
Khamis Mushayt, SAr. 88/D5
Khammam, India 82/D4
Khamr, Yem. 88/D5
Khānābād, Afg. 89/J1
Khānaqīn, Iraq 90/F3
Khanem (well), Alg. 99/F3
Khānewāl, Pak. 86/A4
Khāngāh Dogrān, Pak. 86/B4
Khāngarh, Pak. 86/A5
Khaniá, Gre. 47/J5
Khanka (lake), China,Rus 67/N5
Khanna, India 86/D3
Khanpur, Pak. 86/A5
Khanty-Mansiysk, Rus. 64/G3
Khanty-Mansiyskiy Aut. Okrug, Rus. 64/G3
Khao Chamao-Khao Wong NP, Thai. 78/C3
Khao Khitchakut NP, Thai. 78/C3
Khao Laem (res.), Thai. 83/G4
Khao Sam Roi Yot NP, Thai. 78/B3
Khao Yai NP, Thai. 78/C3
Kharagpur, India 85/F4
Kharagpur, India 85/F4
Khārān, Pak. 86/A3
Kharar, India 86/D4
Kharar, India 86/D4
Khārdah, India 81/J8
Khargon, India 89/L4
Khargon, India 86/B3
Kharkiv (int'l arpt.), Ukr. 62/F2
Kharkiv, Ukr. 62/F2
Kharkivs'ka Oblasti, Ukr. 62/F2
Kharmanli, Bul. 47/J2
Kharovsk, Rus. 60/J4
Kharrour (riv.), Mor. 100/B2
Kharsia, India 84/D5
Khartoum (Khartūm) (cap.), Sudan 88/B5
Khasavyurt, Rus. 63/H4
Khāsh (riv.), Afg. 89/H2
Khashuri, Geo. 63/G4
Khaskovo (pol. reg.), Bul. 47/J2
Khaskovo (prov.), Bul. 47/J2
Khatanga (riv.), Rus. 160/Z
Khatanga (gulf), Rus. 65/L2
Khatauli, India 86/D3
Khātegaon, India 84/A4
Khatlon (obl.), Taj. 87/E3
Khatmia (pass), Egypt 91/C4
Khātra, India 85/F4
Khatt Atoui (riv.), Mrta. 96/B3

Khaur, Pak. 86/B3
Khaybar (pass), Afg. 86/A2
Khazzān Dūkān (res.), Iraq 90/F3
Khazzān Jabal Al Awliyā (dam), Sudan 97/M4
Khekra, India 86/D5
Khemis el Khechna, Alg. 100/G4
Khemis Miliana, Alg. 100/G4
Khémisset (prov.), Mor. 100/A3
Khémisset, Mor. 100/A3
Khenchela (prov.), Alg. 99/G2
Khenchela, Alg. 100/K7
Khénifra, Mor. 98/D2
Khepoyarvi (lake), Rus. 61/T6
Kheri, India 84/C2
Khersān (riv.), Iran 88/F2
Kherson (int'l arpt.), Ukr. 49/L2
Kherson, Ukr. 49/L2
Khersons'ka Oblasti, Ukr. 62/E3
Khilok, Rus. 71/K1
Khimki, Rus. 61/W9
Khíos, Gre. 47/K3
Khíos (isl.), Gre. 62/C5
Khirpai, India 85/F4
Khisarya, Bul. 47/J1
Khiva, Uzb. 87/D4
Khlebarovo, Bul. 49/H4
Khmel'nyts'ka Oblasti, Ukr. 62/C2
Khmel'nytskyy, Ukr. 62/C2
Kho Sawai (plat.), Thai. 83/H4
Khodzheyli, Uzb. 87/C4
Khojak (pass), Afg. 89/J2
Kholm, Afg. 89/J1
Kholmsk, Rus. 71/R2
Khomeynīshahr, Iran 88/F2
Khon Kaen, Thai. 78/C2
Khopër (riv.), Rus. 64/E4
Khor (riv.), Rus. 65/P5
Khóra Sfakíon, Gre. 47/J5
Khorazm (pol. reg.), Uzb. 87/D4
Khorion, Gre. 90/A2
Khorramābād, Iran 88/E2
Khorramshahr, Iran 88/E2
Khorugh, Taj. 89/K1
Khotol (mtn.), Ak, US 134/G3
Khouribga, Mor. 98/D2
Khowai, India 83/F3
Khrisoúpolis, Gre. 47/J2
Khromtaū, Kaz. 63/L2
Khrysí (isl.), Gre. 47/J5
Khuan Ubon Ratana (lake), Thai. 78/C2
Khudiān, Pak. 86/C4
Khuis, Bots. 106/C2
Khujand, Taj. 87/E4
Khulna (pol. div.), Bang. 85/G4
Khünjerāb (pass), Pak. 89/L1
Khunjerab NP, Pak. 87/G5
Khunti, India 85/E4
Khurai, India 84/B3
Khurda, India 82/E3
Khurja, India 84/A1
Khushāb, Pak. 89/L3
Khust, Ukr. 41/M4
Khūtār, India 84/C1
Khuzdār, Pak. 89/J3
Khvalynka, Rus. 71/P3
Khvor, Iran 89/G2
Khvoy, Iran 63/H5
Khwaja Rawash (int'l arpt.), Afg. 87/E6
Khyber (pass), Pak. 86/A2
Kia, Sol. 116/S5
Kiama, Austl. 115/D2
Kiamichi (mts.), Ok, US 132/E3
Kiana, Ak, US 134/F2
Kibæk, Den. 38/C3
Kibali (riv.), D.R. Congo 104/A2
Kibergneset (pt.), Nor. 37/J1
Kibo (Kilimanjaro) (peak), Tanz. 104/C3
Kiboga, Ugan. 104/A2
Kibrıscık, Turk. 49/K5
Kibwezi, Kenya 104/C3
Kičevo, FYROM 47/G2
Kichha, India 84/B1
Kickapoo, Ks, US 137/D5
Kidal, Mali 103/F2
Kidal (reg.), Mali 103/F2
Kidapawan, Phil. 81/G2
Kidderminster, Eng, UK 32/D2
Kidepo Valley NP, Ugan. 97/M7
Kidsgrove, Eng, UK 35/F5
Kiel (bay), Den. 37/D5
Kiel, Ger. 38/D4
Kielce, Pol. 41/L3
Kielder (res.), Eng, UK 35/F1
Kien An, Viet. 78/D1
Kierspe, Ger. 53/G1
Kiev (Kyyiv) (cap.), Ukr. 62/D2
Kiffa, Mrta. 102/C2
Kifisiá, Gre. 47/N8

Kigali (cap.), Rwa. 104/A3
Kigali (Gregoire Kayibanda) (int'l arpt.), Rwa. 104/A3
Kigi, Turk. 90/E2
Kigoma (pol. reg.), Tanz. 104/A4
Kigoma, Tanz. 104/A4
Kigye, SKor. 73/E4
Kihei, Hi, US 124/T10
Kihnu (isl.), Est. 39/L4
Kiholo, Hi, US 124/U11
Kihti (str.), Fin. 39/J1
Kii (chan.), Japan 74/D4
Kii (mts.), Japan 74/D4
Kijang, SKor. 73/E5
Kikai (isl.), Japan 75/L6
Kikepa (pt.), Hi, US 124/R9
Kikiktat (mtn.), Ak, US 134/H2
Kikinda, Serb. 48/E3
Kikonai, Japan 76/B3
Kikuchi, SKor. 73/E4
Kikwit, D.R. Congo 105/C2
Kil, Swe. 38/E2
Kilafors, Swe. 38/G1
Kilauea, Hi, US 124/S9
Kilbarchan, Sc, UK 36/B5
Kilberry, Ire. 31/Q10
Kilbirnie, Sc, UK 36/B5
Kilbrannan (sound), Sc, UK 36/A5
Kilchoan, Sc, UK 31/Q8
Kilchu, NKor. 73/E2
Kilcoole, Ire. 34/B5
Kilcormac, Ire. 31/Q10
Kildare, Ire. 31/Q10
Kildare (co.), Ire. 31/Q10
Kildeer, Il, US 135/P15
Kil'den (isl.), Rus. 60/G1
Kilembe Estates, Ugan. 104/A2
Kilgarvan, Ire. 31/P11
Kilgore, Tx, US 129/J4
Kilian (riv.), Nun., Can. 122/E1
Kili, Kenya 104/C3
Kilimanjaro (pol. reg.), Tanz. 104/C3
Kilimanjaro (int'l arpt.), Tanz. 104/C3
Kilimanjaro NP, Tanz. 104/C3
Kilimli, Turk. 49/K5
Kilinochchi, SrL. 82/D6
Kilis, Turk. 91/E1
Kiliya, Ukr. 49/J3
Kilkee, Ire. 31/P10
Kilkeel, NI, UK 34/B3
Kilkenny, Ire. 31/Q10
Kilkenny (co.), Ire. 34/A6
Kilkieran (riv.), Ire. 34/B1
Kilkis, Gre. 47/H2
Kilkivan, Austl. 114/D4
Kilküsh, Turk. 49/K1
Kill Van Kull (riv.), NJ,NY, US 139/J9
Killam, Ab, Can. 126/F2
Killarney, Austl. 115/E1
Killarney, Mb, Can. 127/J3
Killarney, Ire. 31/P10
Killarney NP, Ire. 31/P10
Killdeer, ND, US 127/H4
Killearn, Sc, UK 36/B4
Killeen, Tx, US 129/H5
Killenaule, Ire. 31/Q10
Killiecrankie, Pass of (pass), Sc, UK 36/C3
Killin, Sc, UK 36/B4
Killinchy, NI, UK 34/C3
Killinek (isl.), Nun., Can. 123/K2
Killini (peak), Gre. 47/H4
Killini, Gre. 47/G4
Killough, NI, UK 34/C3
Killybegs, Ire. 31/P9
Killyclogher, NI, UK 34/A2
Killyleagh, NI, UK 34/C3
Kilmacanogue, Ire. 34/B5
Kilmacolm, Sc, UK 36/B5
Kilmacow, Ire. 31/Q10
Kilmallock, Ire. 31/P10
Kilmar Tor (hill), Eng, UK 32/B5
Kilmarnock, Sc, UK 36/B5
Kilmaurs, Sc, UK 36/B5
Kilmichael (pt.), Ire. 34/B6
Kilmore, Austl. 115/C3
Kilmore Quay, Ire. 31/Q10
Kilombero (riv.), Tanz. 104/C5
Kilosa, Tanz. 104/C4
Kilraghts, NI, UK 34/B1
Kilrea, NI, UK 34/B1
Kilrush, Ire. 31/P10
Kilsyth, Sc, UK 36/C5
Kilwa Kivinje, Tanz. 104/C5
Kilwinning, Sc, UK 36/B5
Kimba, Austl. 113/H5
Kimball, SD, US 127/J5
Kimbe, PNG 116/E5
Kimberley, BC, Can. 126/E3
Kimberley (plat.), Austl. 109/B2
Kimberley, SAfr. 106/D3
Kimberley (cape), Austl. 114/B2
Kimch'aek, NKor. 73/E2
Kimch'ŏn, SKor. 73/E4
Kimhae, SKor. 74/A3
Kimhae (int'l arpt.), SKor. 74/A3
Kimi, Gre. 47/H3
Kimina, Gre. 47/H2
Kimitsu, Japan 75/F3
Kimje, SKor. 73/D5
Kimméria, Gre. 47/J2

Kimmirut, Nun., Can. 123/K2
Kimolos (isl.), Gre. 47/J4
Kimovsk, Rus. 62/F1
Kimp'o, SKor. 73/F6
Kimp'o (int'l arpt.), SKor. 73/F6
Kimpō-zan (peak), Japan 77/B2
Kimry, Rus. 60/H4
Kinabalu (peak), Malay. 81/E2
Kinabatangan (riv.), Malay. 81/E2
Kinango, Kenya 104/C4
Kinbasket (lake), BC, Can. 126/D2
Kinbrace, Sc, UK 31/S7
Kincaid, Sk, Can. 126/G3
Kincardine, On, Can. 130/D2
Kincardine, Sc, UK 36/C4
Kinchega NP, Austl. 115/B2
Kinder Scout (peak), Eng, UK 35/G5
Kindersley, Sk, Can. 126/F3
Kindia, Gui. 102/B4
Kindia (pol. reg.), Gui. 102/B4
Kinding, Ger. 55/E5
Kindsbach, Ger. 53/G5
Kindu, D.R. Congo 105/E1
Kinel', Rus. 63/J1
Kineshma, Rus. 60/J4
King (lake), Austl. 109/A4
King (mt.), Austl. 114/B4
King (sound), Austl. 109/B2
King (isl.), BC, Can. 126/B2
King (isl.), NZ 109/H6
King (co.), Wa, US 135/D2
King Christian (isl.), Nun., Can. 123/R7
King Christian IX Land (reg.), Grld. 119/P3
King Christian X Land (reg.), Grld. 119/Q2
King City, Ca, US 128/B3
King Cove, Ak, US 134/F4
King Frederik VI Coast (reg.), Grld. 119/N3
King Frederik VIII Land (reg.), Grld. 119/P1
King George (isls.), FrPol. 117/L6
King George Is. (isls.), Qu, Can. 123/J3
King George's (res.), Eng, UK 30/C2
King Leopold (ranges), Austl. 109/C2
King of Prussia, Pa, US 138/C3
King Salmon, Ak, US 134/G4
King William (isl.), Nun., Can. 122/G2
King William's Town, SAfr. 106/D4
Kingaroy, Austl. 114/C4
Kingfisher, Ok, US 137/M14
Kinghorn, Sc, UK 36/C4
Kinglake NP, Austl. 115/C3
Kinglake NP, Austl. 115/G5
Kingman, Ks, US 129/H3
Kingman, Az, US 128/D4
Kingman (reef), Pac., US 117/J4
Kings (riv.), Ca, US 128/C3
Kings (co.), NY, US 139/K9
Kings (peak), Ut, US 128/E2
Kings Canyon NP, Ca, US 128/C3
Kings Langley, Eng, UK 30/B1
King's Lynn, Eng, UK 33/G1
Kings Park, Austl. 112/K6
Kings Point, NY, US 139/L8
King's Seat (hill), Sc, UK 36/C4
Kingsbridge, Eng, UK 32/C6
Kingscote, Austl. 113/H5
Kingscourt, Ire. 31/Q10
Kingsford, Mi, US 130/B2
Kingsport, Tn, US 130/D4
Kingston, Austl. 116/F7
Kingston, On, Can. 130/E2
Kingston, NY, US 130/F3
Kingston (cap.), Jam. 145/G2
Kingston, Wa, US 135/B2
Kingston S.E., Austl. 115/A3
Kingston upon Hull, Eng, UK 35/H4
Kingston upon Hull (co.), Eng, UK 35/H4
Kingston upon Thames (bor.), Eng, UK 30/C2
Kingston upon Thames, SKor. 74/A3
Kingstown, SC, US 133/J3
Kingstree, SC, US 133/J3
Kingsville, Tx, US 129/H6

Kingsville, Md, US 138/B5
Kingswood, Eng, UK 32/D4
Kingussie, Sc, UK 36/B2
Kınık, Turk. 90/A2
Kinkaid (mt.), Ak, US 134/L4
Kinkala, Congo 105/B1
Kinki (prov.), Japan 74/D3
Kinlochewe, Sc, UK 36/A1
Kinlochleven, Sc, UK 36/B1
Kinloss, Sc, UK 36/C1
Kinna, Swe. 38/E3
Kinnairds (pt.), Sc, UK 36/D1
Kinnelon, NJ, US 139/H8
Kinnelon (lake), NJ, US 139/H8
Kinnitty, Ire. 31/Q10
Kino (riv.), Japan 74/D3
Kinoje (riv.), On, Can. 130/D1
Kinomoto, Japan 77/K5
Kinrooi, Belg. 53/E1
Kinross, Sc, UK 36/C4
Kinsale, Ire. 31/P11
Kinsarvik, Nor. 38/B1
Kinshasa (cap.), D.R. Congo 105/C1
Kinston, NC, US 133/J3
Kintampo, Gha. 103/E4
Kintnersville, Pa, US 138/C2
Kintore, Sc, UK 36/D2
Kintyre (isl.), Sc, UK 31/R8
Kinu (riv.), Japan 75/F2
Kinvarra, Ire. 31/P10
Kinyeti (peak), Sudan 97/M7
Kinzig (riv.), Ger. 40/E4
Kipahulu, Hi, US 124/T10
Kiparissia (gulf), Gre. 47/G4
Kiparissia, Gre. 47/G4
Kipawa (lake), Qu, Can. 130/E2
Kipkarren (riv.), Kenya 104/B2
Kipling, Sk, Can. 127/H3
Kipnuk, Ak, US 134/F4
Kippel, Swi. 56/D5
Kippen, Sc, UK 36/B4
Kippure (peak), Ire. 34/B5
Kipushi, D.R. Congo 105/E3
Kira, Japan 77/M6
Kira Panayia (isl.), Gre. 47/H3
Kirakira, Sol. 116/T7
Kiranomena, Madg. 107/H7
Kiratpur, India 84/B1
Kirazlı, Turk. 49/H5
Kircasalih, Turk. 49/H5
Kirchberg, Swi. 56/D3
Kirchberg, Swi. 57/F3
Kirchberg, Ger. 53/G4
Kirchberg, Ger. 55/F1
Kirchberg an der Iller, Ger. 57/G1
Kirchberg an der Jagst, Ger. 54/F3
Kirchdorf, Ger. 51/F3
Kirchdorf an der Krems, Aus. 55/H7
Kirchenlamitz, Ger. 55/E2
Kirchenthumbach, Ger. 55/E3
Kirchheim, Ger. 57/G1
Kirchheim bei München, Ger. 55/E6
Kirchheim unter Teck, Ger. 54/C5
Kirchheimbolanden, Ger. 53/G3
Kirchhundem, Ger. 51/F4
Kirchlengern, Ger. 51/F3
Kirchlinteln, Ger. 51/G3
Kirchsee (lake), Ger. 57/H2
Kirchseeon, Ger. 55/E6
Kirchweidach, Ger. 55/F6
Kirchzarten, Ger. 56/D2
Kirchzell, Ger. 54/C3
Kircudbright (bay), Sc, UK 34/D2
Kirensk, Rus. 65/L4
Kirgiz Steppe (upland), Kaz. 64/F5
Kirgizskiy (mts.), Kyr. 70/B3
Kiriákion, Gre. 47/H3
Kiribati (ctry.) 116/H5
Kırıkhan, Turk. 91/E1
Kırıkkale, Turk. 90/C2
Kırıkkale (prov.), Turk. 90/C2
Kirishi, Rus. 39/Q2
Kirishima-Yaku NP, Japan 74/B5
Kirishima-yama (peak), Japan 74/B5
Kiritimati (Christmas) (isl.), Kiri. 117/K4
Kırkağaç, Turk. 90/A2
Kıthira (isl.), Gre. 47/H4
Kithíra, Gre. 47/H4
Kíthnos, Gre. 47/J4
Kíthnos (isl.), Gre. 47/J4
Kitimat Arm (lake), BC, Can. 126/C2
Kitkatla, Ak, US 135/B3
Kirkby in Ashfield, Eng, UK 35/G5
Kirkcaldy, Sc, UK 36/C4
Kirkconnel, Sc, UK 36/C6
Kirkcudbright, Sc, UK 34/D2
Kirkee, India 89/K5
Kirkenær, Nor. 38/E1
Kirkintilloch, Sc, UK 36/B5
Kirklees (co.), Eng, UK 35/G4

Kirkkonummi (Kyrkslätt), Fin. 39/L1
Kirkland, Qu, Can. 131/N7
Kirkland (hill), Sc, UK 36/C6
Kirkland Lake, On, Can. 130/D1
Kirklar (peak), Turk. 90/A2
Kirklareli, Turk. 49/H5
Kirklareli (prov.), Turk. 49/H5
Kirkliston, Sc, UK 36/C5
Kirkstone (pass), Eng, UK 35/F3
Kirkwall, Sc, UK 31/V14
Kirkwood, De, US 138/C4
Kirn, Ger. 53/G4
Kirov, Rus. 62/F1
Kirov, Rus. 61/L4
Kirovo-Chepetsk, Rus. 61/L4
Kirovohrad, Ukr. 62/E2
Kirovohrads'ka Oblasti, Ukr. 62/D2
Kirovs'ke, Ukr. 60/G2
Kırrıemuir, Sc, UK 36/D3
Kirrweiler, Ger. 54/B4
Kirsanov, Rus. 63/G1
Kırşehir (prov.), Turk. 90/C2
Kırşehir, Turk. 90/C2
Kiruna, Swe. 37/G2
Kiryū, Japan 75/F2
Kisa, Swe. 38/F3
Kisai, Japan 77/D1
Kisakata, Japan 76/A4
Kisarazu, Japan 75/F3
Kisber, Hun. 41/K5
Kisei, Japan 77/K7
Kiselevsk, Rus. 64/J4
Kishanganj, India 85/F2
Kishangarh, India 89/K3
Kishiwada, Japan 77/H7
Kishorganj, Bang. 85/H3
Kishtwar, India 86/C3
Kisii, Kenya 104/B3
Kisigo (riv.), Tanz. 104/C4
Kiska (vol.), Ak, US 134/B5
Kiska (isl.), Ak, US 134/B6
Kiskatinaw (riv.), Ca, US 126/C2
Kiskitto (lake), Mb, Can. 127/J2
Kiskőrös, Hun. 48/D2
Kiskunfélegyháza, Hun. 48/D2
Kiskunhalas, Hun. 48/D2
Kiskunmajsa, Hun. 48/D2
Kiskunsági Nemzeti NP, Hun. 48/D2
Kislovodsk, Rus. 63/G4
Kismaayo (Chisimayu), Som. 97/P8
Kiso (riv.), Japan 75/E3
Kisogawa, Japan 77/L5
Kisozaki, Japan 77/L6
Kissamos, Gre. 47/H5
Kissimmee (lake), Fl, US 133/H4
Kissimmee, Fl, US 133/H4
Kissing, Ger. 54/D6
Kississing (lake), Mb, Can. 127/H2
Kisslegg, Ger. 57/F2
Kist, Ger. 54/C3
Kisújszállás, Hun. 48/E2
Kisumu, Kenya 104/B3
Kisvárda, Hun. 41/M4
Kita, Mali 102/C3
Kita (lake), Japan 75/E3
Kita-Ibaraki, Japan 75/G2
Kitaaiki, Japan 77/B1
Kitadaitō (isl.), Japan 75/L8
Kitagata, Japan 77/L5
Kitakami (mts.), Japan 76/B3
Kitakami (riv.), Japan 76/B3
Kitakata, Japan 75/F2
Kitakawabe, Japan 77/D1
Kitakyūshū, Japan 74/B4
Kitale, Kenya 104/B2
Kitami, Japan 76/C2
Kitamimaki, Japan 77/A1
Kitamoto, Japan 77/D1
Kitan (str.), Japan 77/G7
Kitangiri (lake), Tanz. 104/B3
Kitchener, On, Can. 130/D2
Kitgum, Ugan. 104/B2
Kithira (isl.), Gre. 47/H4
Kíthira, Gre. 47/H4
Kíthnos, Gre. 47/J4
Kíthnos (isl.), Gre. 47/J4
Kitimat Arm (lake), BC, Can. 126/C2
Kitkatla, Ak, US 135/B3
Kittanning, Pa, US 135/B3
Kittatinny (mts.), NJ, US 138/C1
Kittery, Me, US 131/G3
Kittredge, Co, US 137/K3
Kitui, Kenya 104/C3

Kitumbeine (peak), Tanz. 104/C3
Kitwe, Zam. 105/E3
Kitzbühel, Aus. 43/K3
Kitzingen, Ger. 54/D3
Kiunga Marine Nat'l Rsv., Kenya 104/D3
Kiuruvesi, Fin. 60/E3
Kiuyu (pt.), Tanz. 104/C4
Kivalina, Ak, US 134/F2
Kivalo (mts.), Fin. 37/H2
Kivijärvi (lake), Fin. 39/M1
Kiviõli, Est. 39/M2
Kivu (lake), D.R. Congo 93/E5
Kıyıköy, Turk. 49/J5
Kiyosu, Japan 77/L5
Kizil (riv.), China 64/H6
Kizilcadağ, Turk. 91/A1
Kızılcahamam, Turk. 90/B2
Kızılhisar, Turk. 90/B2
Kızılırmak (riv.), Turk. 90/C1
Kızıltepe, Turk. 90/E2
Kızılyaka, Turk. 91/C1
Kizlyar, Rus. 63/H4
Kizu (riv.), Japan 74/E3
Kizu, Japan 77/J6
Kizukuri, Japan 76/B3
Kjerkestinden (peak), Nor. 37/F1
Kjevik (int'l arpt.), Nor. 38/C2
Kjølen (mts.), Nor. 37/G2
Klabava (riv.), Czh. 55/G3
Kladanj, Bosn. 48/D3
Kladno, Czh. 55/H2
Klagenfurt, Aus. 43/K3
Klaipėda, Lith. 39/J4
Klamath (mts.), Ca,Or, US 126/C5
Klamath Falls, Or, US 126/C5
Klangenan, Indo. 80/C5
Klarälven (riv.), Swe. 38/E2
Klarup, Den. 38/D2
Klášterec nad Ohří, Czh. 55/G2
Klatovy, Czh. 55/G3
Klaus, Aus. 57/F3
Klaus, Ger. 53/G3
Klausenpass (pass), Swi. 57/F4
Klawock, Ak, US 135/B3
Klazienaveen, Neth. 50/E3
Kleinblittersdorf, Ger. 53/G5
Kleine Elster (riv.), Ger. 41/G3
Kleine Emme (riv.), Swi. 56/E4
Kleine Gete (riv.), Belg. 53/D2
Kleine Laber (riv.), Ger. 55/F5
Kleine Nete (riv.), Belg. 52/D3
Kleinheubach, Ger. 54/C3
Kleinlützel, Swi. 56/D3
Kleinmachnow, Ger. 40/G7
Kleinmond, SAfr. 106/L11
Kleinolifants (riv.), SAfr. 106/Q12
Kleinrinderfeld, Ger. 54/C3
Kleinsee, SAfr. 106/A3
Kleinwallstadt, Ger. 54/C3
Kleinwinternheim, Ger. 54/B3
Kleppestø, Nor. 38/A1
Klerksdorp, SAfr. 106/D2
Kleve, Ger. 51/E3
Klina, Serb. 47/G1
Klingenberg am Main, Ger. 54/C3
Klingenmünster, Ger. 54/B4
Klingenthal, Ger. 55/F2
Klínovec (peak), Czh. 55/F2
Klintehamn, Swe. 38/H3
Klintsy, Rus. 62/E1
Klip (riv.), SAfr. 106/E2
Klippan, Swe. 38/E3
Klipplaat, SAfr. 106/D4
Klisura, Bul. 47/J1
Klíštětěrang, Czh. 55/G2
Klitmøller, Den. 38/C2
Kljajićevo, Serb. 48/D3
Ključ, Bosn. 40/C3
Kłodawa, Pol. 41/K2
Kłodzko, Pol. 41/J3
Klöntaler-See (lake), Swi. 57/F3
Klosterbach (riv.), Ger. 51/F1
Klosterlechfeld, Ger. 57/G1
Klosterneuburg, Aus. 49/N7
Klosters, Swi. 57/F3
Klosterwappen (peak), Aus. 41/H5
Kloten, Swi. 57/E3
Klötze, Ger. 51/G2
Kluane NP, Yk, Can. 134/K3
Klukwan, Ak, US 134/K3
Klundert, Neth. 50/C3
Klyaz'ma (riv.), Rus. 60/J4
Klyuchevskaya (peak), Rus. 65/S4
Knäred, Swe. 38/E3

Knaresborough, Eng, UK 35/G3
Knee (lake), Mb, Can. 127/K2
Knetzgau, Ger. 54/D3
Knezha, Bul. 49/G4
Knight (inlet), BC, Can. 126/B3
Knighton, Wal, UK 32/C2
Knightsen, Ca, US 135/L11
Knin, Cro. 48/C3
Knittelfeld, Aus. 43/L3
Knittlingen, Ger. 54/B4
Knivsta, Swe. 38/G2
Kniežecí Stolec (peak), Czh. 55/H5
Knižecí Strom (peak), Czh. 55/G3
Knjaževac, Serb. 48/F4
Knob (peak), Phil. 81/F1
Knob (cape), Austl. 112/C5
Knobby (pt.), Austl. 112/B4
Knoch (hill), Sc, UK 36/D1
Knockcloghrim, NI, UK 34/B2
Knosós (Knossos) (ruin), Gre. 47/J5
Knottingley, Eng, UK 35/G4
Knott's Berry Farm, Ca, US 136/G8
Knowsley (co.), Eng, UK 35/F5
Knox (coast), Ant. 160/G
Knox (cape), BC, Can. 134/M4
Knox City, Tx, US 129/H4
Knoxville, Tn, US 130/D5
Knutsford, Eng, UK 35/F5
Knysna, SAfr. 106/C4
Ko (riv.), Sen. 102/B3
Ko-saki (pt.), Japan 74/A3
Ko Samui NP, Thai. 78/C3
Koali, Hi, US 124/T10
Koani, Tanz. 104/C4
Koāth, India 85/E3
Kobayashi, Japan 74/B5
Kōbe, Japan 77/H6
Kōbe (int'l arpt.), Japan 77/H6
København (int'l arpt.), Den. 38/E4
Kobern-Gondorf, Ger. 53/G3
Kobipato (peak), Indo. 81/G4
Koblach, Aus. 57/F3
Koblenz, Swi. 57/E2
Koblenz, Ger. 53/G3
Kobryn, Bela. 41/N2
Kobuchizawa, Japan 77/A2
Kobuk (riv.), Ak, US 134/G2
Kobuk, Ak, US 134/G2
Kobuk Valley NP, Ak, US 134/G2
Kobushi-ga-take (peak), Japan 75/F3
Kocába (riv.), Czh. 55/H3
Kocaeli (prov.), Turk. 49/J5
Koçalı, Turk. 90/D2
Koçani, FYROM 47/H2
Kocapınar, Turk. 90/E2
Kočevje, Slov. 43/L4
Koch (isl.), Nun., Can. 123/J2
Koch'ang, SKor. 73/D5
Koch'ang, SKor. 73/D5
Kochel am See, Ger. 57/H2
Kocherinovo, Bul. 47/H1
Kōchi, Japan 74/C4
Kōchi (pref.), Japan 74/C4
Kodaira, Japan 77/C2
Kodala, India 82/E4
Kodama, Japan 77/C1
Kodarmā, India 85/E3
Kodiak, Ak, US 134/H4
Kodiak (isl.), Ak, US 134/H4
Kodinār, India 86/B4
Kodomari, Japan 76/B3
Kodry (hills), Mol. 49/H2
Koekelare, Belg. 52/B1
Koel (riv.), India 82/D3
Koes, Namb. 106/B2
Koesan, SKor. 73/D4
Koetari (riv.), Sur. 153/G4
Kofa (mts.), Az, US 128/D4
Kofarnihon (riv.), Taj. 87/E5
Kofçaz, Turk. 49/H5
Koffiefontein, SAfr. 106/D3
Kofiau (isl.), Indo. 81/G4
Koforidua, Gha. 103/E5
Kōfu, Japan 75/F3
Koga, Japan 77/D1
Koganei, Japan 77/D2
Køge (bay), Den. 38/E4
Kogi, Nga. 103/G4
Kogon (riv.), Gui. 96/C5
Kōgum (isl.), SKor. 73/D5
Kohāt, Pak. 89/L2
Kohīma, India 83/F2
Kohoku, Japan 77/K5
Kohout (peak), Czh. 55/H3
Kohtla-Järve, Est. 39/M2
Kohunlich (ruin), Mex. 144/D2
Koimisis, Gre. 47/H2
Koito (riv.), Japan 75/F3
Koiva (riv.), Lat. 39/M3
Kojonup, Austl. 112/C5
Kōjō (isl.), SKor. 73/D5
Komür (pt.), Turk. 47/K3
Kon Tum, Viet. 78/D3
Konakovo, Rus. 60/H4
Kōnan, Japan 77/C1

Kōka, Japan 77/K6
Kokai (riv.), Japan 77/E2
Kōkar (isl.), Fin. 39/J3
Kokemäenjoki (riv.), Fin. 39/J1
Kokhonak, Ak, US 134/H4
Kokkola (Karleby), Fin. 60/D3
Koko Head (pt.), Hi, US 124/W13
Kokomo, In, US 130/C3
Kokrajhar, India 85/H2
Kokrines, Ak, US 134/H3
Koksan, NKor. 73/D3
Kökshetaū, Kaz. 87/F2
Kökshetaū (obl.), Kaz. 87/E2
Koksijde, Belg. 52/B1
Koksoak (riv.), Qu, Can. 123/K3
Kokstad, SAfr. 106/E3
Kokubu, Japan 74/B5
Kola (pen.), Rus. 160/D
Kola (riv.), Rus. 60/G1
Kolaka, Indo. 81/F4
Kolār, India 82/C5
Kolāras, India 84/A3
Kolašin, Serb. 47/F1
Kolback, Swe. 38/G2
Kol'bay (peak), Kaz. 87/B4
Kolbermoor, Ger. 43/K3
Kolbuszowa, Pol. 41/L3
Kolda (pol. reg.), Sen. 102/B3
Kolda, Sen. 102/B3
Kolding, Den. 38/C4
Kolgompya (cape), Rus. 39/N2
Kolguyev (isl.), Rus. 160/C
Kolhāpur, India 89/K5
Koliba (riv.), Gui. 102/B3
Koliganek, Ak, US 134/G4
Kolín, Czh. 41/H3
Kolkasrags (pt.), Lat. 39/K3
Kolkata (Calcutta), India 85/G4
Kolkata (Calcutta) (int'l arpt.), India 85/G4
Kollbach (riv.), Ger. 55/F5
Kollnburg, Ger. 55/F4
Kollum, Neth. 50/D2
Köln (Cologne), Ger. 53/F2
Kolno, Pol. 41/L2
Kofo, Pol. 62/A1
Koloa, Hi, US 124/S10
Kořobrzeg, Pol. 38/F4
Kolokani, Mali 102/C3
Kolomna, Rus. 60/H5
Kolomyya, Ukr. 49/G1
Kolondiéba, Mali 102/D4
Kolossa (riv.), Mali 102/D3
Kolpashevo, Rus. 64/J4
Kolpino, Rus. 61/T7
Kolsva, Swe. 38/F2
Kolubara (riv.), Serb. 48/D3
Koluszki, Pol. 41/K3
Kolva (riv.), Rus. 61/N2
Kolwezi, D.R. Congo 105/E3
Kolyma (riv.), Rus. 67/Q3
Kolyma (range), Rus. 67/Q3
Kolyma Lowland (plain), Rus. 65/Q2
Kom (peak), Bul. 47/H1
Koma (riv.), Japan 77/C2
Komádi, Hun. 48/E2
Komaduga Gana (riv.), Niger.,Ng 96/H5
Komadugu Yobe (riv.), Nga. 103/H3
Komae, Japan 77/D2
Komagane, Japan 75/E3
Komaki, Japan 77/L5
Komandorskiye (isls.), Rus. 67/R4
Komárno, Slvk. 48/D3
Komárom, Hun. 48/D2
Komárom-Esztergom (prov.), Hun. 48/D2
Komatirivier (riv.), SAfr. 106/Q13
Komatke, Az, US 137/N19
Komatsu, Japan 74/E2
Komatsu (int'l arpt.), Japan 74/E2
Komatsushima, Japan 74/D3
Kombissiri, Burk. 103/E3
Kome (isl.), Tanz. 104/B3
Komi, Resp., Rus. 61/M2
Komi-Permyatskiy Aut. Okrug, Rus. 61/M2
Komló, Hun. 48/D2
Kommetjie, SAfr. 106/L11
Kommunizma (peak), Taj. 87/F5
Komodo (isl.), Indo. 81/E5
Komodo Island NP, Indo. 81/E5
Komoé (riv.), C.d'Iv. 96/E6
Komono, Japan 77/K5
Komoran (isl.), Indo. 81/J5
Komoro, Japan 77/A1
Komornosi, Japan 77/K5
Kompasberg (peak), SAfr. 106/D3
Komsomolets (isl.), Rus. 67/J1
Komsomol'skiy, Rus. 61/P2
Komsomol'sk (int'l arpt.), Rus. 65/P3
Komür (pt.), Turk. 47/K3
Kon Tum, Viet. 78/D3
Konakovo, Rus. 60/H4
Kōnan, Japan 77/C1
Kōnan, Japan 77/K6
Kōnan, Japan 77/L5
Kōnan, Japan 77/K6

Konār (riv.), India 85/E4
Konār (res.), India 85/E4
Konar (str.), Afg. 86/A2
Konaweha (riv.), Indo. 81/F4
Konda, Japan 77/H6
Kondagaon, India 82/D4
Kondinin, Austl. 112/C5
Kondoa, Tanz. 104/B4
Kondopoga, Rus. 60/G3
Kondūz, Afg. 87/E5
Kong, C.d'Iv. 102/D4
Kong (riv.), Laos 78/D3
Kong (isl.), Camb. 78/C4
Kong Miao, China 72/D4
Kongiganak, Ak, US 134/F4
Kongju, SKor. 73/D4
Kongō-zan (peak), Japan 77/J7
Kongolo, D.R. Congo 105/E2
Kongoussi, Burk. 103/E3
Kongsberg, Nor. 38/C2
Kongsvinger, Nor. 38/D1
Kongur (peak), China 87/G5
Koniecpol, Pol. 41/K3
Königs Wusterhausen, Ger. 40/Q7
Königsberg in Bayern, Ger. 54/E2
Königsberg-Stein, Ger. 54/B5
Königsbronn, Ger. 54/D5
Königsbrunn, Ger. 57/G1
Königsdorf, Ger. 57/E1
Königsfeld im Schwarzwald, Ger. 57/E1
Königslutter am Elm, Ger. 51/H4
Königstein im Taunus, Ger. 54/B2
Königswinter, Ger. 53/G2
Kónitsa, Gre. 47/G2
Köniz, Swi. 56/D4
Konjic, Bosn. 48/C4
Könkämäeno (riv.), Fin. 38/D2
Konkouré (riv.), Gui. 102/B4
Konnevesi, Fin. 60/E3
Konolfingen, Swi. 56/D4
Kōnosu, Japan 77/D1
Konotop, Ukr. 62/E2
Konqi (riv.), China 64/J5
Konsen (plat.), Japan 76/D2
Końskie, Pol. 41/L3
Konstancin-Jeziorna, Pol. 41/K3
Konstantynów Łódzki, Pol. 41/K3
Konstanz, Ger. 57/F2
Kontich, Belg. 53/D1
Kontiolahti, Fin. 60/F3
Konuralp, Turk. 49/K5
Kóny, Hun. 48/C2
Konya, Turk. 90/C2
Konya (prov.), Turk. 90/C2
Konz, Ger. 53/F4
Koondrook, Austl. 115/C2
Koorawatha, Austl. 115/D2
Koorda, Austl. 112/C4
Kootenai (riv.), Id, US 126/D3
Kootenay (lake), BC, Can. 122/E3
Kootenay NP, BC, Can. 126/D3
Kootingal, Austl. 115/D1
Kop-Geјdi (pass), Turk. 90/E2
Kopāganj, India 84/D2
Kopargaon, India 89/K5
Kópavogur, Ice. 37/N7
Kope (peak), C.d'Iv. 102/D5
Köpenick, Ger. 40/Q7
Koper, Slov. 43/K4
Kopervik, Nor. 38/C2
Kopeysk, Rus. 61/P5
Kopfing im Innkreis, Aus. 55/G6
Köping, Swe. 38/C2
Kopondei (cape), Indo. 81/F5
Koporskiy (bay), Rus. 39/N2
Koppang, Nor. 38/D1
Kopparberg, Swe. 38/F2
Kopparberg (co.), Swe. 37/E3
Koppies, SAfr. 106/D2
Koprivnica, Cro. 48/C2
Koprivshtitsa, Bul. 47/J1
Köprü (riv.), Turk. 91/B1
Köprülü, Turk. 91/C1
Köprülü Kanyon NP, Turk. 90/B2
Kor (riv.), Iran 88/F2
Kora, India 84/C2
Kōra, India 77/K5
Kora NP, Kenya 104/C3
Korab (peak), Alb. 47/G2
Koráb (peak), Czh. 55/G4
Korakuen Garden, Japan 74/C3
Koraluk (riv.), Nf, Can. 123/K3
Korana (riv.), Cro. 43/L4
Koraput, India 82/D4
Korba, India 84/D4
Korbach, Ger. 51/F6
Korçë, Alb. 47/G2
Korčula (isl.), Cro. 46/E1
Korčulanski Kanal (chan.), Cro. 46/E1
Kord Kūy, Iran 88/F1
Kordel, Ger. 53/F4

Korea (bay), China,NKor. 73/B3
Korea (str.), Japan,SKor. 74/A4
Korea, North (ctry.) 73/D2
Korea, South (ctry.) 73/D4
Korean Folk Village, SKor. 73/G7
Korenovsk, Rus. 62/F3
Korhogo, C.d'Iv. 102/D4
Korinós, Gre. 47/H2
Kórinthos (Corinth), Gre. 47/H4
Kő ris-hegy (peak), Hun. 48/C2
Kōriyama, Japan 75/G2
Korizo, Passe de (pass), Chad 96/J3
Korkodon (riv.), Rus. 65/R3
Korkuteli, Turk. 91/B1
Korla, China 70/E3
Kormakiti (cape), Cyp. 91/C2
Körmend, Hun. 43/M3
Körner, Ger. 51/H6
Korneuburg, Aus. 49/N7
Korntal-Münchingen, Ger. 54/C5
Kornwestheim, Ger. 54/C5
Koro (sea), Fiji 116/G6
Köroğlu (peak), Turk. 49/K5
Korogwe, Tanz. 104/C4
Koroit, Austl. 115/B3
Koronadal, Phil. 81/F2
Korónia (lake), Gre. 47/H2
Koronowo, Pol. 41/J2
Koropion, Gre. 47/N9
Koror (cap.), Palau 116/C4
Körös (riv.), Hun. 48/E2
Korosten', Ukr. 62/D2
Korostyshiv, Ukr. 62/D2
Korotaikha (riv.), Rus. 61/P1
Korovin (vol.), Ak, US 134/D5
Korpo (Korppoo), Fin. 39/J1
Korsakov, Rus. 71/R2
Korschenbroich, Ger. 50/D6
Korsør, Den. 38/D4
Korsze, Pol. 39/J4
Kortemark, Belg. 52/C1
Kortenaken, Belg. 53/E2
Kortenberg, Belg. 53/D2
Kortessem, Belg. 53/E2
Kortrijk, Belg. 52/C2
Korup, PN de, Camr. 103/H5
Koryak (range), Rus. 67/R3
Koryakskiy Aut. Okrug, Rus. 65/S3
Koryazhma, Rus. 61/K3
Kōryō, Japan 77/J6
Koryŏng, SKor. 73/E5
Kós (isl.), Gre. 90/A2
Kós, Gre. 90/A2
Kosai, Japan 75/E3
Kosai, Japan 77/A2
Kösching, Ger. 55/E5
Kościan, Pol. 41/J2
Kościerzyna, Pol. 38/G4
Kosciusko (mt.), Austl. 115/D3
Kosciusko, Ms, US 133/F3
Kosciusko NP, Austl. 115/D3
Köse, Turk. 90/D1
Kosei, Japan 77/K6
Koshigaya, Japan 75/F3
Kōshim (riv.), Kaz. 87/B3
Koshiki (isls.), Japan 75/K5
Kosi, India 84/A2
Kosi (zone), Nepal 85/F2
Kosi (riv.), India 82/E2
Košice, Slvk. 41/L4
Košický (pol. reg.), Slvk. 41/L4
Koskinoú, Gre. 90/B2
Kosoba (peak), Kaz. 87/G3
Kosŏng, SKor. 73/E5
Kosŏng, NKor. 73/E3
Kosovo (reg.), Serb. 47/G1
Kosovo (prov.), Serb. 48/E4
Kosovo Polje, Serb. 47/G1
Kosovska Kamenica, Serb. 47/G1
Kosovska Mitrovica, Serb. 47/G1
Kosový (riv.), Czh. 55/G4
Kosrae (isl.), Micr. 116/F4
Kossi (prov.), Burk. 102/D3
Kossou, Barrage de (dam), C.d'Iv. 102/D5
Kossou, Lac de (lake), C.d'Iv. 96/D6
Kosta, Swe. 38/F3
Kostelec nad Černými Lesy, Czh. 55/H3
Koster, SAfr. 106/D2
Kostinbrod, Bul. 47/H1
Kostopil', Ukr. 62/C2
Kostroma (riv.), Rus. 60/J4
Kostroma, Rus. 60/J4
Kostromskaya Oblast, Rus. 60/J4
Kostrzyn, Pol. 41/H2
Kostyantynivka, Ukr. 62/E2
Kosuge, Japan 77/B2
Kos'va (riv.), Rus. 61/N2
Kos'yu (riv.), Rus. 61/N2
Koszalin, Pol. 38/G4
Kőszeg, Hun. 43/M3
Kot Addu, Pak. 86/A4

Kot Kapūra, India 86/C4
Kot Mūmin, Pak. 86/C3
Kot Rādha Kishan, Pak. 86/C4
Kot Samāba, Pak. 86/A5
Kota, India 84/D4
Kota, India 89/L3
Kōta, Japan 77/M6
Kota Baharu, Malay. 83/H6
Kota Kinabalu, Malay. 81/E2
Kotaagung, Indo. 80/B5
Kotabaru, Indo. 81/E4
Kotabumi, Indo. 80/B4
Kotapād, India 82/D4
Kotdwāra, India 84/B1
Kotel, Bul. 47/K1
Kotel'nich, Rus. 61/L4
Kotel'nikovo, Rus. 63/G3
Kotel'nyy (isl.), Rus. 65/P2
Köthen, Ger. 40/F3
Kotido, Ugan. 104/B2
Kotka, Fin. 39/M1
Kotlas, Rus. 61/K3
Kotli Lohārān, Pak. 86/C3
Kotlik, Ak, US 134/F3
Kotlin (isl.), Rus. 61/S7
Kotō, Japan 77/K5
Kotoka (int'l arpt.), Gha. 103/E5
Kotor, Serb. 47/F1
Kotor Varoš, Bosn. 48/C3
Kotovo, Rus. 63/H2
Kotovsk, Rus. 63/G1
Kotri, India 89/J3
Kottayam, India 82/C6
Kotto (riv.), CAfr. 97/K6
Kotuy (riv.), Rus. 67/K3
Kotzebue, Ak, US 134/F2
Kotzebue (sound), Ak, US 134/E2
Kötzting, Ger. 55/F4
Kouandé, Ben. 103/F4
Kouchibouguac NP, NB, Can. 131/H2
Koudougou, Burk. 103/E3
Koufonísion (isl.), Gre. 47/J5
Kougarok (mtn.), Ak, US 134/E2
Koukdjuak (riv.), Nun., Can. 123/J2
Koula-Moutou, Gabon 96/H8
Koulikoro, Mali 102/D3
Koulikoro (pol. reg.), Mali 102/C3
Koulountou (riv.), Sen. 102/B3
Koumbi Saleh (ruin), Mrta. 102/C3
Koumi, Japan 77/A1
Koumra, Chad 96/J6
Koundara, Gui. 102/B3
Kounradskiy, Kaz. 87/G3
Kountze, Tx, US 129/J5
Koupela, Burk. 103/E3
Kouritenga (prov.), Burk. 103/E3
Kourou, FrG. 151/H2
Koussi (peak), Chad 96/J4
Koutiala, Mali 102/D3
Kouvola, Fin. 39/M1
Kovačica, Serb. 48/E3
Kovada Gölü NP, Turk. 90/B2
Kovashi (riv.), Rus. 61/S7
Kovdozero (lake), Rus. 37/J2
Kovel', Ukr. 62/C2
Kovilj, Serb. 48/E3
Kovilpatti, India 82/C6
Kovrov, Rus. 60/J4
Kovür, India 82/C5
Kovylkino, Rus. 63/G1
Kowanyama Aboriginal Community, Austl. 114/A1
Kowkcheh (riv.), Afg. 89/J1
Kowl-e Namaksār (lake), Afg. 87/D6
Kowloon, China 79/B3
Kowt-e 'Ashrow, Afg. 89/J2
Kōyaguchi, Japan 77/J7
Kōyama, Japan 74/B5
Koynare, Bul. 49/G4
Koyuk, Ak, US 134/F2
Koyukuk (riv.), Ak, US 134/H2
Koyukuk, Ak, US 134/G3
Koyukuk, South Fork (riv.), Ak, US 134/H2
Kozakai, Japan 77/M6
Kōzaki, Japan 77/F6
Kozan, Turk. 90/C2
Kozáni, Gre. 47/G2
Kozara NP, Serb. 48/C3
Kozhikode (Calicut), India 82/C5
Kozhozero (lake), Rus. 60/H3
Kozienice, Pol. 41/M2
Kozloduy, Bul. 49/F4
Kozlu, Turk. 49/J5
Kozluk, Turk. 50/D2
Koznitsa (peak), Bul. 47/H1
Kōzu (isl.), Japan 75/F3
Kōzu, Japan 77/H3
Kozyatyn, Ukr. 62/D2
Kpalimé, Togo 103/F5
Kpandu, Gha. 103/F5
Kpémé, Togo 103/F5

Kra (isth.), Myan. 83/G6
Kraai (riv.), SAfr. 106/D3
Kraaifontein, SAfr. 106/L10
Krabi, Thai. 78/B4
Kragerø, Nor. 38/C2
Kragujevac, Serb. 48/E3
Kraiburg am Inn, Ger. 55/F6
Kraichbach (riv.), Ger. 54/B4
Kraichgau (reg.), Ger. 43/H2
Krailling, Ger. 55/E6
Krakatau (vol.), Indo. 80/C5
Kraków, Pol. 41/K3
Kralendijk, NAnt. 152/D1
Kraljevo, Serb. 48/E4
Kralkızı (dam), Turk. 90/E2
Královéhradecký (pol. reg.), Czh. 41/H3
Kralovice, Czh. 55/G3
Kralupy nad Vltavou, Czh. 55/H2
Kramators'k, Ukr. 62/F2
Kramfors, Swe. 37/F3
Krammer (chan.), Neth. 50/B5
Kranéa Elassónos, Gre. 47/G3
Kranebitten (int'l arpt.), Aus. 57/H3
Kranenburg, Ger. 50/D5
Kranidhion, Gre. 47/H4
Kranj, Slov. 43/L3
Kranskop, SAfr. 107/E3
Krapkowice, Pol. 41/J3
Kraslice, Czh. 55/F2
Kraśnik, Pol. 41/M3
Kraśnik Fabryczny, Pol. 41/M3
Krasnoarmeysk, Rus. 63/H2
Krasnodar, Rus. 62/F3
Krasnodar (int'l arpt.), Rus. 38/C1
Krasnodarskiy Kray, Rus. 64/D3
Krasnogorsk, Rus. 61/W9
Krasnohrad, Ukr. 62/F2
Krasnokamensk, Rus. 71/L1
Krasnokamsk, Rus. 61/M4
Krasnoslobodsk, Rus. 63/H2
Krasnotur'insk, Rus. 61/P4
Krasnoural'sk, Rus. 61/P4
Krasnovodsk (int'l arpt.), Trkm. 63/K4
Krasnovodsk (Trkmenbashi), Trkm. 63/K5
Krasnoyarsk, Rus. 64/K4
Krasnoyarskiy Kray, Rus. 64/J4
Krasnyy Kut, Rus. 63/H2
Krasnyy Luch, Ukr. 62/F2
Krasnyy Sulin, Rus. 62/G3
Kratovo, FYROM 47/H1
Krautheim, Ger. 54/C4
Kravanh (mts.), Camb. 83/H5
Kreb en Nâga (cliff), Mali 98/D5
Kreck (riv.), Ger. 54/D5
Krefeld, Ger. 50/D6
Kreiensen, Ger. 51/G5
Kremastón (lake), Gre. 47/G3
Křemelná (riv.), Czh. 55/G4
Kremenchuts'ke Vodoskhovyshche (res.), Ukr. 62/E2
Kremlin, Rus. 61/W9
Kremmen, Ger. 40/G6
Kremmling, Co, US 128/F2
Krempe, Ger. 51/G1
Krems an der Donau, Aus. 41/H4
Kremsmünster, Aus. 55/H6
Krenglbach, Aus. 55/H6
Kresgeville, Pa, US 138/C2
Kresna, Bul. 47/H1
Kressbronn am Bodensee, Ger. 57/F2
Kresta (gulf), Rus. 65/T3
Kréstena, Gre. 47/G4
Kretinga, Lith. 39/J4
Kreuzau, Ger. 53/F2
Kreuzberg (peak), Ger. 54/C2
Kreuzlingen, Swi. 57/F2
Kreuztal, Ger. 53/G2
Kreuzwertheim, Ger. 54/C3
Kria Vrisi, Gre. 47/H2
Kribi, Camr. 96/G7
Krieglach, Aus. 45/L3
Kriens, Swi. 57/F3
Kriftel, Ger. 54/A2
Kril'on (pen.), Rus. 76/B1
Kril'on (cape), Rus. 76/C1
Krimpen aan de IJssel, Neth. 50/B5
Krindhes, Gre. 47/J2
Kriós (cape), Gre. 47/H5
Krishna (riv.), India 67/G8
Krishnagiri, India 82/C5
Krishnanagar, India 85/G4
Kristdala, Swe. 38/G3
Kristiansand, Nor. 38/C2
Kristiansand (int'l arpt.), Swe. 38/F4
Kristianstad, Swe. 38/F3
Kristianstad (co.), Swe. 37/E4
Kristianstad (int'l arpt.), Swe. 38/F4
Kristinehamn, Swe. 38/E2
Kriva Palanka, FYROM 47/H1
Krk (isl.), Cro. 48/B3

Krk, Cro. 48/B3
Krnov, Czh. 41/J3
Krokom, Swe. 37/E3
Krókos, Gre. 47/G2
Kroměříž, Czh. 41/J4
Kronberg im Taunus, Ger. 54/B2
Kronoberg (co.), Swe. 37/E4
Kronshtadt, Rus. 61/S6
Kronstorf, Aus. 55/H6
Kroombit Tops NP, Austl. 114/C4
Kroonstad, SAfr. 106/D2
Kropotkin, Rus. 63/G3
Kropp, Ger. 38/C4
Krosno, Pol. 41/L4
Krosno Odrzańskie, Pol. 41/H2
Krotoszyn, Pol. 41/J3
Krottenkopf (peak), Aus. 57/G3
Krousón, Gre. 47/J5
Krško, Slov. 43/L4
Kruckau (riv.), Ger. 51/G1
Kruger NP, SAfr. 105/F5
Krugersdorp, SAfr. 106/P13
Kruibeke, Belg. 50/B6
Kruisfontein, SAfr. 106/D4
Krujë, Alb. 47/F2
Krummenau, Swi. 57/G1
Krumovgrad, Bul. 47/H2
Krün, Ger. 57/H3
Krupina, Slvk. 48/D1
Kruså, Den. 38/C4
Krusenstern (cape), Ak, US 134/E2
Kruševac, Serb. 48/E4
Kruševo, FYROM 47/G2
Krušné Hory (Erzgebirge) (mts.), Czh.,Ger. 43/K1
Kruzof (isl.), Ak, US 134/L4
Krychaw, Bela. 62/D1
Krym, Aut. Rep., Ukr. 62/E3
Krymsk, Rus. 62/F3
Krynica, Pol. 41/L4
Kryvvy Rih, Ukr. 49/L2
Krzna (riv.), Pol. 41/M2
Krzyż, Pol. 41/J2
Ksar el Kebir, Mor. 100/B2
Ksel (peak), Alg. 99/F2
Ktima, Cyp. 91/C2
Ku-Ring-Gai NP, Austl. 114/H8
Ku Sathan (peak), Thai. 78/C2
Kuah, Malay. 78/B5
Kuala Belait, Bru. 80/D3
Kuala Dungun, Malay. 80/B3
Kuala Kerai, Malay. 83/H6
Kuala Lipis, Malay. 83/H6
Kuala Lumpur (cap.), Malay. 80/B3
Kuala Pilah, Malay. 80/B3
Kuala Selangor, Malay. 80/B3
Kuala Terengganu, Malay. 83/H6
Kualapu'u, Hi, US 124/T10
Kuancheng, China 72/D2
Kuandian, China 73/C2
Kuantan, Malay. 80/B3
Kuban' (riv.), Rus. 64/D5
Kubaysah, Iraq 90/E3
Kubenskoye (lake), Rus. 60/H4
Kubokawa, Japan 74/B4
Kubrat, Bul. 49/H4
Kučevo, Serb. 48/E3
Kuchen, Ger. 54/C5
Kuching, Malay. 80/D3
Kuchino (isl.), Japan 75/K6
Kuchinoerabu (isl.), Japan 74/A5
Kuchl, Aus. 43/K3
Kücükbahçe, Turk. 90/A2
Kücükkuyu, Turk. 47/K3
Kudamatsu, Japan 74/B3
Kudat, Malay. 81/E2
Kudus, Indo. 80/D5
Kudymkar, Rus. 61/M4
Kuei (oasis), Libya 97/K3
Kufrinjah, Jor. 49/D3
Kufstein, Aus. 43/K3
Kugluktuk, Nun., Can. 122/D1
Kühbach, Ger. 54/E6
Kuhmo, Fin. 60/F2
Kuhmoinen, Fin. 39/L1
Kuhn, II, US 137/H8
Kühpäyeh, Iran 88/F2
Kuinder of Tjonger (riv.), Neth. 50/C3
Kuito, Ang. 105/C3
Kuiu (isl.), Ak, US 134/L4
Kujawsko-Pomorskie (prov.), Pol. 41/K2
Kujawy (reg.), Pol. 41/K2
Kuji, Japan 76/B3
Kujū-san (peak), Japan 74/B4

Kujūkuri, Japan 77/E2
Kukalaya (riv.), Nic. 145/E3
Kuki, Japan 75/F2
Kukizaki, Japan 77/E2
Kukkia (lake), Fin. 39/L1
Kül (riv.), Iran 88/C3
Kula, Serb. 48/D3
Kula, Bul. 48/F4
Kula Kangri (peak), Bhu. 85/H1
Kulachi, Pak. 86/A4
Kulai, Malay. 80/B3
Kulal (mt.), Kenya 104/C2
Kulaly (isl.), Kaz. 63/J3
Kulandag (mts.), Kaz. 87/B4
Kuldīga, Lat. 39/J3
Kulebaki, Rus. 60/J5
Kulgām, India 86/C3
Kulin, Austl. 112/C5
Kulob, Taj. 89/J1
Kuloy (riv.), Rus. 61/J2
Kulpahār, India 84/C2
Kulpmont, Pa, US 138/B2
Kulpsville, Pa, US 138/C2
Kul'sary, Kaz. 63/K3
Külsheim, Ger. 54/C4
Kulti, India 85/F4
Kullu, India 86/D4
Kulmbach, Ger. 55/E2
Kulunda (lake), Rus. 87/G1
Kulunda, Rus. 87/G2
Kuma, Japan 74/B4
Kuma (riv.), Rus. 64/E5
Kumagaya, Japan 75/F2
Kumaishi, Japan 76/A2
Kumamoto, Japan 74/B4
Kumamoto (int'l arpt.), Japan 74/B4
Kumamoto (pref.), Japan 74/B4
Kumano (riv.), Japan 74/D4
Kumano, Japan 77/G4
Kumanovo, FYROM 47/G1
Kumār (riv.), Bang. 85/G4
Kumasi, Gha. 103/E5
Kumatori, Japan 77/H7
Kumba, Camr. 96/G7
Kumbia, Austl. 114/C4
Kümch'on, SKor. 73/F6
Kumé (isl.), Japan 79/E2
Kumertau, Rus. 63/K1
Kumgang-san (peak), NKor. 73/E3
Kumho (riv.), SKor. 73/D5
Kumi, Ugan. 104/B2
Kumi, SKor. 73/D4
Kumihama, Japan 77/G4
Kumiyama, Japan 77/J6
Kumkale, Turk. 49/H6
Kumköy, Turk. 49/J5
Kumla, Swe. 38/F2
Kumluca, Turk. 91/B1
Kümmersbruck, Ger. 55/E4
Kumo, Nga. 96/H5
Kumon (range), Myan. 70/G6
Kümsan, SKor. 73/D4
Kumta, India 89/K6
Kunashiri (isl.), Rus. 76/D1
Künch, India 84/B3
Kunda, India 84/B3
Kundapura (Coondapoor), India 89/K6
Kundarkhi, India 84/B1
Kundelungu, PN de, D.R. Congo 105/E3
Kundiān, Pak. 86/A3
Kundla, India 89/K4
Kungälv, Swe. 38/D2
Kungsängen (int'l arpt.), Swe. 38/G2
Kungsbacka, Swe. 38/E3
Kungshamn, Swe. 38/D2
Kungur, Rus. 61/N4
Kunhegyes, Hun. 48/E2
Kunimi-dake (peak), Japan 74/B4
Kuningan, Indo. 80/C4
Kunisaki, Japan 74/B3
Kunitachi, Japan 77/F5
Kunjah, Pak. 86/C3
Kunjirap (pass), China 89/L1
Kunkletown, Pa, US 138/C2
Kunlun (mts.), China 67/H6
Kunmadaras, Hun. 41/L5
Kunming, China 70/D3
Kunsan, SKor. 73/D5
Kunshan, China 72/E5
Kunszentmárton, Hun. 48/E2
Kunu (riv.), India 84/A2
Kunwāri (riv.), India 84/A2
Kunwi, SKor. 73/D4
Kunyu (mtn.), China 73/C3
Künzell, Ger. 54/C1
Kunžvartské (pass), Czh. 55/G4
Kuohijärvi (lake), Fin. 39/L1
Kuolimo (riv.), Fin. 39/L1
Kuopio, Fin. 60/E3
Kuopio (prov.), Fin. 60/E3
Kupa (riv.), Cro. 48/B3
Kupang, Indo. 81/F2
Kupino, Rus. 87/G2
Kupiškis, Lith. 39/L3
Kupreanof (isl.), Ak, US 134/L4
Kup"yans'k, Ukr. 62/F2
Kuqa, China 71/L3

Kür (riv.), Azer. 63/J5
Kürälī, India 86/D4
Kurama-yama (peak), Japan 77/J5
Kurashiki, Japan 74/C3
Kurayoshi, Japan 74/C3
Kurdistan (reg.), Asia 64/E6
Kürdzhali, Bul. 47/J2
Kürdzhali (res.), Bul. 47/J2
Kure, Japan 74/C3
Kure (mts.), Turk. 90/C1
Kure (isl.), Hi, US 116/H2
Kuressaare, Est. 39/K2
Kureyka (riv.), Rus. 64/K3
Kurganskaya Oblast, Rus. 61/P5
Kuri, SKor. 73/G6
Kurigrām, Bang. 85/G3
Kurihashi, Japan 77/D1
Kurikoma-yama (peak), Japan 76/B4
Kuril (isls.), Rus. 67/G5
Kuril'sk, Rus. 76/D1
Kurinwas (riv.), Nic. 145/E3
Kurisawa, Japan 76/B2
Kuriyama, Japan 77/L5
Kurkçü, Turk. 91/C1
Kurrimine Beach, Austl. 114/B2
Kurnool, India 82/C4
Kuro-shima (isl.), Japan 74/A4
Kurodashō, Japan 77/G5
Kuroiso, Japan 75/G2
Kuroso-yama (peak), Japan 77/K6
Kurotaki, Japan 77/H7
Kurrajong, Austl. 114/G8
Kurram (riv.), Afg.,Pak. 89/K2
Kuršėnai, Lith. 39/K3
Kurseong, India 85/F3
Kuršių Nerija NP, Lith. 39/J4
Kurskaya Oblast, Rus. 62/E1
Kurskaya Spit (bar), Lith.,Rus. 39/J4
Kurskiy (lag.), Rus. 39/J4
Kuršumlija, Serb. 47/G1
Kurşunlu, Turk. 90/C1
Kurtalan, Turk. 90/E2
Kürten, Ger. 53/G1
Kuru (riv.), Sudan 97/G7
Kuruca (pass), Turk. 90/E2
Kuruçay, Turk. 90/D2
Kurume, Japan 74/B4
Kurunegala, SrL. 82/D6
Kurupukari, Guy. 153/G3
Kurur (peak), Sudan 101/D4
Kurwongbah (lake), Austl. 114/E6
Kurye, SKor. 73/D5
Kur'ya (riv.), NKor. 73/D3
Kuş Cenneti NP, Turk. 90/B1
Kuşadası, Turk. 90/A2
Kusatsu, Japan 77/J5
Kusel, Ger. 53/G4
Kushālgarh, India 89/K4
Kushida (riv.), Japan 77/K7
Kushigata, Japan 77/G2
Kushihara, Japan 77/M5
Kushima, Japan 74/B5
Kushimoto, Japan 74/D4
Kushiro, Japan 76/D2
Kushiro-Shitsugen NP, Japan 76/D2
Kushtia (pol. reg.), Bang. 85/G4
Kushtia, Bang. 85/G4
Kusŏng, NKor. 73/C3
Küssnacht am Rigi, Swi. 57/E3
Küstenkanal (canal), Ger. 51/F2
Küstī, Sudan 97/H6
Kusu, Japan 77/L6

Kut (isl.), Thai. 83/H5
Kütahya, Turk. 90/B2
K'ut'aisi (int'l arpt.), Geo. 63/G4
K'ut'aisi, Geo. 63/G4
Kutch (reg.), India 89/J4
Kutch, Gulf of (gulf), India 89/J4
Kutchan, Japan 76/B1
Kutcharo (lake), Japan 76/C1
Kutenholz, Ger. 51/G2
Kutná Hora, Czh. 41/H4
Kutno, Pol. 41/K2
Kutsuki, Japan 77/J5
Küttigen, Swi. 56/E3
Kutu, D.R. Congo 96/J8
Kutzenhausen, Ger. 54/D2
Kutztown, Pa, US 138/C2
Kuujjua (riv.), NW, Can. 122/E1
Kuujjuaq, Qu, Can. 123/K3
Kuusamo, Fin. 37/J2
Kuusankoski, Fin. 39/M1
Kuutse (hill), Est. 39/M2
Kuvandyk, Rus. 63/L2
Kuwait (ctry.) 88/E3
Kuwait (cap.), Kuw. 88/E3
Kuwāna (riv.), India 82/D2
Kuwana, Japan 77/L5
Kuybyshev (res.), Rus. 64/E4
Kuyto (lake), Rus. 37/J2
Kuytun, China 70/E3
Kuyuwini (riv.), Guy. 153/G4
Kuze, Japan 77/K4
Kuzitrin (riv.), Ak, US 134/E2
Kuznetsk, Rus. 63/H1
Kuzucubelen, Turk. 91/C1
Kuzumaki, Japan 76/B3
Kvaløy (isl.), Nor. 37/F1
Kværndrup, Den. 38/D4
Kvarner (gulf), Cro. 48/B3
Kvarnerić (chan.), Cro. 48/B3
Kvigtinden (peak), Nor. 37/E2
Kvinesdal, Nor. 38/B2
Kvinnherad, Nor. 38/B2
Kviteseid, Nor. 38/C2
Kwa (riv.), D.R. Congo 93/D5
Kwach'on, SKor. 73/F7
Kwajalein (isl.), Mrsh. 116/F4
Kwale, Kenya 104/C4
KwaMashu, SAfr. 107/E3
Kwanak-san (peak), SKor. 73/F7
Kwangch'ŏn, SKor. 73/D4
Kwangju, SKor. 73/D5
Kwangju-Gwangyŏksi (prov.), SKor. 73/D5
Kwangmyŏng, SKor. 73/F7
Kwango (riv.), D.R. Congo 93/D5
Kwangyang, SKor. 73/D5
Kwania (lake), Ugan. 97/M7
Kwansan, SKor. 73/D5
Kwara (state), Nga. 103/G4
Kwaraha (peak), Tanz. 104/B4
Kwataboahegan (riv.), On, Can. 130/D1
Kwazulu Natal (prov.), SAfr. 107/E3
Kwekwe, Zim. 105/E4
Kwethluk, Ak, US 134/F3
Kwidzyn, Pol. 39/H5
Kwigillingok, Ak, US 134/F4
Kwili (riv.), D.R. Congo 105/C1
Kwilu (riv.), D.R. Congo 93/D5
Kwinana, Austl. 112/K7
Kyabé, Chad 97/J6
Kyabram, Austl. 115/C3
Kyaikto, Myan. 78/B2
Kyaiktiyo Pagoda, Myan. 78/B2
Kyaukpyu, Myan. 83/G4
Kyaukse, Myan. 83/G3
Kyenjojo, Ugan. 104/A2
Kyeryong-san NP, SKor. 73/D4
Kyjov, Czh. 41/J4
Kyle, SK, Can. 126/F3
Kyle (riv.), Sc, UK 36/B5
Kyll (riv.), Ger. 53/F3
Kymi (prov.), Fin. 39/M1
Kymi, Gre. 47/H3
Kymijoki (riv.), Fin. 39/M1
Kymore, India 84/B4
Kyneton, Austl. 115/C3
Kynšperk nad Ohří, Czh. 55/F2
Kyoga (lake), Ugan. 97/M7
Kyōga-misaki (cape), Japan 74/D3
Kyogle, Austl. 114/D4
Kyonan, Japan 75/F3
Kyŏngbok Palace, SKor. 73/F6
Kyŏnggi (bay), SKor. 73/C4

Kyŏnggi-do (prov.), SKor. 73/D4
Kyŏngju, SKor. 74/A3
Kyŏngju NP, SKor. 74/A3
Kyŏngsan, SKor. 74/A3
Kyŏngsang-bukto (prov.), SKor. 73/E4
Kyŏngsang-namdo (prov.), SKor. 73/E5
Kyōto (pref.), Japan 74/D3
Kyōto, Japan 77/J5
Kyōto Imperial Palace, Japan 77/J6
Kyōwa, Japan 77/E1
Kyrenia (dist.), Cyp. 91/C2
Kyrenia, Cyp. 91/C2
Kyrgyzstan (ctry.) 87/F4
Kyritz, Ger. 40/G2
Kyrösjärvi (lake), Fin. 39/K1
Kythrea, Cyp. 91/C2
Kyūshū (isl.), Japan 67/M6
Kyūshū Highlands (uplands), Japan 74/B4
Kyustendil, Bul. 47/H1
Kywebwe, Myan. 83/F4
Kyyivs'ka Oblasti, Ukr. 62/D2
Kyyivs'ke Vodoskhovyshche (res.), Ukr. 62/D2
Kyzyl, Rus. 70/F1

L

La Algaba, Sp. 44/B4
La Almunia de Doña Godina, Sp. 44/E2
La Amistad Int'l Park, CR 140/E6
La Araucanía (pol. reg.), Chile 158/B3
La Ascensión, Mex. 143/F3
La Asunción, Ven. 153/F2
La Aurora (int'l arpt.), Guat. 144/D3
La Babia, Mex. 132/C4
La Baie, Qu., Can. 131/G1
La Banda, Arg. 157/D2
La Bañeza, Sp. 44/C1
La Bassée, Fr. 52/B2
La Baule-Escoublac, Fr. 42/B3
La Belle, Fl, US 133/H5
La Birse (riv.), Swi. 56/D3
La Blanquilla (isl.), Ven. 153/E2
La Bocana, Mex. 142/B3
La Bresse, Fr. 56/C2
La Broque, Fr. 56/D1
La Calera, Chile 158/N8
La Campana, Sp. 44/C4
La Cañada (peak), Cuba 145/F1
La Canada-Flintridge, Ca, US 136/F7
La Capelle, Fr. 52/C4
La Carlota, Sp. 44/C4
La Carlota, Arg. 158/E2
La Carolina, Sp. 44/D3
La Catedral (peak), Mex. 143/Q9
La Ceiba, Hon. 144/E3
La Ceiba (int'l arpt.), Hon. 144/E3
La Celle-les-Bordes, Fr. 30/H6
La Celle-Saint-Cloud, Fr. 30/J5
La Celle-sur-Morin, Fr. 30/L5
La Chapelle-de-Guinchay, Fr. 46/A5
La Chapelle-Saint-Luc, Fr. 42/F2
La Chaux-de-Bonds, Swi. 56/C3
La Chinita (int'l arpt.), Ven. 152/D2
La Chorrera, Pan. 150/C2
La Cienega, NM, US 129/F4
La Ciotat, Fr. 42/F5
La Clusaz, Fr. 56/C6
La Concepción, Ven. 152/D2
La Concepción, Nic. 144/E4
La Concepción, Pan. 145/H4
La Coronilla, Uru. 159/G2
La Coruña, Sp. 44/A1
La Couronne, Fr. 42/D4
La Crèche, Fr. 42/C3
La Crescenta-Montrose, Ca, US 136/F7
La Croix-en-Brie, Fr. 30/M6
La Croix, Lac (lake), On, Can. 127/L3
La Cruz, CR 144/E4
La Cruz, Col. 152/B4
La Cruz, Chile 158/N8
La Cruz, Mex. 142/D4
La Cruz, Mex. 159/K10
La Cumbre (vol.), Ecu. 156/E7
La Dôle (peak), Swi. 56/C5
La Dorada, Col. 152/C3
La Dormida, Arg. 158/D2
La Esperanza, Hon. 144/D3
La Estrada, Sp. 44/A1
La Estrella, Chile 158/N9
La Falda, Arg. 157/D3
La Fayette, Ga, US 133/G3
La Fère, Fr. 52/C4
La Ferté-Gaucher, Fr. 52/C6
La Ferté-Macé, Fr. 30/H6
La Ferté-Milon, Fr. 30/M7
La Ferté-Sous-Jouarre, Fr. 52/C6

La Flèche, Fr. 42/C3
La Fría, Ven. 152/C2
La Garamba NP, D.R. Congo 104/A2
La Garita (mts.), US 132/B2
La Garriga, Sp. 45/L6
La Gineta, Sp. 44/E3
La Gloria, Col. 152/C2
La Gran Sabana (plain), Ven. 150/F2
La Grande, Or, US 126/D4
La Grande (riv.), Qu, Can. 123/J3
La Grande Ruine (peak), Fr. 43/G4
La Grange, Ga, US 133/G3
La Grange, Tx, US 129/H5
La Grita, Ven. 145/J4
La Gruyère (lake), Swi. 56/D4
La Guajira (dept.), Col. 145/H4
La Guajira (pen.), Col. 145/H4
La Guardia, Sp. 44/A2
La Guardia (int'l arpt.), NY, US 139/K8
La Habana (Havana) (cap.), Cuba 140/E3
La Habra, Ca, US 136/G8
La Have (riv.), NS, Can. 131/H2
La Higuera, Chile 157/B2
La Honda, Ca, US 135/K12
La Houssaye-en-Brie, Fr. 30/L5
La Huaca, Peru 156/A2
La Huacana, Mex. 143/E5
La Huerta, Mex. 142/D5
La Isla, Mex. 143/Q10
La Jalca, Peru 156/B2
La Joya, Peru 156/D5
La Joya de los Sachas, Ecu. 152/B5
La Junta, Co, US 129/G3
La Junta, Mex. 142/D2
La Laguna, Canl.,Sp. 98/A3
La Libertad (dept.), Peru 156/B2
La Libertad, Hon. 144/E3
La Libertad, Guat. 144/D3
La Libertad, Ecu. 152/A5
La Ligua, Chile 158/N8
La Línea de la Concepción, Sp. 44/C4
La Llagosta, Sp. 45/L6
La Loche, Sk, Can. 126/F1
La Louvière, Belg. 53/D3
La Luisiana, Sp. 44/C4
La Luz, NM, US 129/F4
La Machine, Fr. 42/E3
La Maddalena, It. 46/A2
La Madeleine, Fr. 52/C2
La Malbaie, Qu, Can. 131/G2
La Martre (lake), NW, Can. 122/E2
La Masica, Hon. 144/E3
La Mauricie NP, Qu., Can. 130/F2
La Mensura (peak), Col. 152/C4
La Merca, Sp. 44/C4
La Merced, Peru 156/C3
La Mesa, Ca, US 136/C5
La Mesa (int'l arpt.), Hon. 144/E3
La Mesa, Ven. 152/D2
La Mira, Mex. 142/E5
La Mirada, Ca, US 136/F8
La Moine (riv.), Il, US 130/B3
La Montaña (phys. reg.), Peru 156/C3
La Moure, ND, US 127/J4
La Neuveville, Swi. 56/D3
La Norville, Fr. 30/J6
La Orchila (isl.), Ven. 141/H5
La Orotava, Canl.,Sp. 98/A3
La Oroya, Peru 156/C3
La Palma, Pan. 145/G4
La Palma (isl.), Sp. 93/A2
La Paloma, Uru. 159/G2
La Pampa (prov.), Arg. 158/D3
La Paz, Arg. 158/D3
La Paz (cap.), Bol. 150/E7
La Paz (dept.), Bol. 150/E7
La Paz (bay), Mex. 142/C3
La Paz, Mex. 142/C3
La Paz, Hon. 144/E3
La Paz, Col. 152/C3
La Paz, Uru. 159/K11
La Pèche, Qu, Can. 130/F2
La Peña, Mex. 142/E3
La Perla, Mex. 132/B4
La Pérouse (str.), Gui. 102/B4
La Pérouse (str.), Japan,Rus. 71/R2
La Petite-Raon, Fr. 56/C1
La Piedad Cavadas, Mex. 142/E4
La Plata, Md, US 130/E4
La Plata, Arg. 159/K11
La Pobla de Lillet, Sp. 45/F1
La Pocatière, Qu, Can. 131/G2
La Pola de Gordón, Sp. 44/C1
La Ponge (lake), Sk, Can. 126/G2

La Porte, In, US 130/C3
La Prairie, Qu, Can. 131/P7
La Pryor, Tx, US 129/H5
La Puebla, Sp. 45/G3
La Puebla de Almoradiel, Sp. 44/D3
La Puebla de Cazalla, Sp. 44/C4
La Puebla de Montalbán, Sp. 44/C4
La Puente, Ca, US 136/G7
La Puntilla (pt.), Ecu. 152/A5
La Quebrada, Ven. 152/D2
La Queue-les-Yvelines, Fr. 30/J5
La Quiaca, Arg. 150/E8
La Rambla, Sp. 44/C4
La Reforma, Mex. 142/C3
La Rinconada, Sp. 44/C4
La Rioja (dept.), Arg. 157/C2
La Rioja (aut. comm.), Sp. 44/D1
La Rioja (prov.), Sp. 44/D1
La Roda, Sp. 44/D3
La Roche (lake), Sk, Can. 126/F1
La Roche-en-Ardenne, Belg. 53/E3
La Roche-sur-Foron, Fr. 56/C5
La Roche-sur-Yon, Fr. 42/C3
La Rochelle, Fr. 42/C3
La Romana, DRep. 141/H4
La Ronge, Sk, Can. 127/G2
La Rúa, Sp. 44/B1
La Salle, Co, US 137/C2
La Sarraz, Swi. 56/C4
La Sarre, Qu, Can. 130/E1
La Sauveterre (peak), Fr. 43/G5
La Scie, Nf, Can. 131/L1
La Serena, Chile 157/B2
La Seu d'Urgell, Sp. 45/F1
La Seyne-sur-Mer, Fr. 42/F5
La Sierpe, Cuba 145/G1
La Sila (mts.), It. 46/E3
La Silueta (peak), Chile 159/B7
Lacroix-Saint-Ouen, Fr. 52/B5
Ladainha, Braz. 154/B5
Ladakh (mts.), India 89/L2
Lähijän, Iran 88/F1
Ladbergen, Ger. 51/E4
Ladder (hills), Sc, UK 36/C2
Ładek-Zdrój, Pol. 41/J3
Ladenburg, Ger. 54/B4
Ladera Heights, Ca, US 136/F8
Ladismith, SAfr. 106/C4
Ladispoli, It. 46/C2
Ladoga (lake), Rus. 160/D
Ladoix-Serrigny, Fr. 56/A3
Ladrillero (mtn.), Chile 159/B7
Ladue, Mo, US 137/G8
Lādwa, India 86/D5
Lady Isle (isl.), Sc, UK 36/B3
Ladybank, Sc, UK 36/C4
Ladybower (res.), Eng, UK 35/G5
Ladybrand, SAfr. 106/D3
Ladysmith, SAfr. 107/E3
Lae (isl.), Mrsh. 116/F4
Laer, Ger. 51/E4
Lafayette, In, US 130/C3
Lafayette, La, US 129/J5
Lafayette, Co, US 137/B3
Lafayette, NJ, US 138/D1
Lafayette, La, US 135/K11
Lafia, Nga. 103/H4
Lafitte, La, US 137/P17
Laflamme (riv.), Qu, Can. 130/E1
Lafnitz (riv.), Aus. 43/L3
Lafontaine, Qu, Can. 131/M6
Lafourche (parish), La, US 137/T17
Laga Balal (riv.), Kenya 104/D2
Laga Mado Gali (riv.), Kenya 104/D2
Laga Merille (riv.), Kenya 104/C2
Lajinha, Braz. 155/D2
Lajosmizse, Hun. 40/D2
L'Akagera, PN de, Rwa. 104/A3
Lakato, Madg. 107/J7
Lagawe, Phil. 79/D4
Lagdo, Lac de (lake), Camr. 96/H6
Lage, Ger. 51/F5
Lage Vaart (canal), Neth. 50/C4
Lågen (riv.), Nor. 38/C1
Laggan (lake), Sc, UK 36/B3
Laghouat (prov.), Alg. 99/F2
Laghouat, Alg. 99/F2
Lagny-le-Sec, Fr. 30/L4
Lagny-sur-Marne, Fr. 30/L5
Lago da Pedra, Braz. 154/A2

Lago de Atitlán, PN, Guat. 144/D3
Lago Puelo, PN, Arg. 158/C4
Lago Verde, Chile 158/C5
Lagoa, Port. 44/A4
Lagoa da Prata, Braz. 155/C2
Lagoa Formosa, Braz. 155/C1
Lagoa Vermelha, Braz. 155/B4
Lagoda (lake), Rus. 37/J3
Lagord, Fr. 42/C3
Lagos, Nga. 103/F5
Lagos (state), Nga. 103/F5
Lagos, Port. 44/A4
Lagos de Moreno, Mex. 142/E4
Lagosanto, It. 59/F3
Lagonegro, It. 46/D2
Laguardia, Sp. 44/D1
Laguna, Braz. 155/B4
Laguna Beach, Ca, US 136/C4
Laguna Blanca, PN, Arg. 158/C3
Laguna de Duero, Sp. 44/C2
Laguna de la Restinga, PN, Ven. 153/E2
Laguna del Laja, PN, Chile 158/C3
Laguna del Rey, Mex. 142/E3
Laguna Hills, Ca, US 136/C4
Laguna San Rafael, PN, Chile 157/B6
Lagunas, Peru 156/C2
Lagunas, Peru 156/B2
Lagunas de Chacahua, PN, Mex. 144/B3
Lagunas de Montebello, Mex. 140/C4
Lagunas de Zempoala, PN, Mex. 143/Q10
Lagunillas, Ven. 152/D2
Laguntara (lag.), Hon. 145/E3
Lahad Datu, Malay. 81/E2
Lahar, India 84/D2
Lāharpur, India 84/C2
Lahat, Indo. 80/B4
Lähijän, Iran 88/F1
Lahn (riv.), Ger. 40/C3
Lahnstein, Ger. 53/G3
Laholm, Swe. 38/E4
Laholms (bay), Den. 38/E4
Lahore, Pak. 86/C4
Lahore (int'l arpt.), Pak. 86/C4
Lahti, Fin. 39/L1
Lai Chau, Viet. 78/C1
Lai'an, China 72/D4
Laibin, China 79/A3
Laichingen, Ger. 54/F3
Laidon (lake), Sc, UK 36/B3
Laie, Hi, US 134/W12
Laifeng Tujiazu Zizhixian, China 79/A2
Laiguegila, It. 58/B5
Laihia, Fin. 37/G3
Laingsburg, SAfr. 106/C4
Lainioälven (riv.), Swe. 37/G1
Laishui, China 72/C3
Laisvall, Swe. 37/F2
Laitila, Fin. 39/J1
Laives (Leifers), It. 57/H5
Laiwu, China 72/D3
Laixi, China 73/H5
Laiyang, China 72/C3
Laizhou (bay), China 72/D3
Lajas, Peru 156/B2
Lajeado, Braz. 155/B4
Lajedo, Braz. 154/D2
Lajes, Braz. 154/C2
Lajes, Azor., Port. 45/S12
Lajes (int'l arpt.), Azor., Port. 45/S12
Lajing (pass), Nepal 85/E1
Lakamane, Mali 102/C3
Lakemoor, Il, US 135/P15
Lakeport, Ca, US 128/B3
Lakes Entrance, Austl. 115/D3
Lakhimpur, India 84/C2
Lakhnädon, India 84/B4
Lakki, Pak. 86/A3
Lakkion, Gre. 90/A2
Lakonía (gulf), Gre. 47/H4
Lakshadweep (terr.), India 82/B6
Lakshadweep (isls.), India 67/F8
Lal Suhanra NP, Pak. 86/B5
Lāla Mūsa, Pak. 86/B3
Lalana (riv.), Madg. 107/H8
Lalang (riv.), Indo. 80/B4
Lālganj, India 85/G3
Lālgola, India 85/G3
Lalín, Sp. 44/A1
Lalitpur, India 84/D3
Lalitpur (Pāṭan), Nepal 85/E2
Lalla Rookh Abor. Land, Austl. 112/C2
Lamachan (peak), Sc, UK 34/D1

Lago Chelan Nat'l Rec. Area, Wa, US 126/C3
Lake City, Fl, US 133/H4
Lake Clark NP and Prsv., Ak, US 134/C3
Lake District NP, Eng, UK 35/E2
Lake Elsinore, Ca, US 136/C3
Lake Forest, Il, US 135/Q15
Lake Forest Park, Wa, US 135/C2
Lake Fork (res.), Tx, US 129/H5
Lake Grace, Austl. 112/C5
Lake Havasu City, Az, US 128/D4
Lake Hiwassee, Ok, US 137/N14
Lake in the Hills, Il, US 135/P15
Lake Jackson, Tx, US 129/J5
Lake Lotawana, Mo, US 137/E6
Lake Louise, Ab, Can. 126/D3
Lake Malawi NP, Malw. 105/F3
Lake Manyara NP, Tanz. 104/B3
Lake Mburo NP, Ugan. 104/A3
Lake Mead Nat'l Rec. Area, US 128/D4
Lake Meredith Nat'l Rec. Area, Tx, US 129/G4
Lake Minchumina, Ak, US 134/H3
Lake Mohawk, NJ, US 138/D1
Lake Nakuru NP, Kenya 104/C3
Lake of the Woods (lake), Can.,US 127/K3
Lake Orion, Mi, US 135/F6
Lake Point Junction, Ut, US 137/J12
Lake Providence, La, US 129/K4
Lake Ronkonkoma, NY, US 139/E2
Lake Shore, Md, US 138/B5
Lake Station, In, US 135/R16
Lake Success, NY, US 139/L8
Lake Villa, Il, US 135/P15
Lake Wales, Fl, US 133/H5
Lake Winnebago, Mo, US 137/E6
Lake Worth, Fl, US 133/H5
Lake Zurich, Il, US 135/P15
Lakehurst, NJ, US 138/D3
Lakehurst Naval Air Eng. Ctr., NJ, US 138/D3
Lakeland, Fl, US 133/H4
Lakeland Village, Ca, US 136/C4
Lakemoor, Il, US 135/P15
Lakeport, Ca, US 128/B3
Lakeside, Ca, US 136/D5
Lakeview, Or, US 126/C4
Lakeview, Ut, US 137/K13
Lakeville (lake), Mi, US 135/F6
Lakeway, Tx, US 129/H5
Lakewood, Wa, US 126/C4
Lakewood, Co, US 137/B3
Lakewood, NJ, US 138/D3
Lakewood, Ca, US 135/P15
Lakhemaa NP, Est. 42/G4
Lakhimpur, India 84/C2
Lakhnädon, India 84/B4
Lakki, Pak. 86/A3
Lakkion, Gre. 90/A2
Lakonía (gulf), Gre. 47/H4
Lakshadweep (terr.), India 82/B6
Lakshadweep (isls.), India 67/F8
Lal Suhanra NP, Pak. 86/B5
Lalapaşa, Turk. 47/K3

Lamarche-sur-Saône, Fr. 56/B3
Lamarque, Arg. 158/D3
Lamas, Peru 156/B2
Lambach, Aus. 55/G6
Lamballe, Fr. 42/B2
Lambaré, Par. 157/E2
Lambaréné, Gabon 96/H6
Lambari, Braz. 211/H6
Lambay (isl.), Ire. 31/Q10
Lambayeque (dept.), Peru 156/A2
Lambayeque, Peru 156/B2
Lambé Coba (riv.), Mali 102/C3
Lambert-St. Louis (int'l arpt.), Mo, US 129/K3
Lambert's Bay, SAfr. 106/B4
Lambertville, Mi, US 130/D3
Lambertville, NJ, US 138/D2
Lambesc, Fr. 42/F5
Lambeth (bor.), Eng, UK 30/C2
Lambrama, Peru 156/C4
Lambrecht, Ger. 54/B4
Lambro (riv.), It. 58/C2
Lambsheim, Ger. 54/B3
Lambton (co.), On, Can. 135/F6
Lamego, Port. 44/B2
Lamèque (isl.), NB, Can. 131/H2
Lameroo, Austl. 113/J5
Lamesa, Tx, US 129/G4
Lamia, Gre. 47/H3
Lamington (riv.), NJ, US 138/D2
Lamington NP, Austl. 114/D5
Lamitan, Phil. 81/F2
Lamlash, Sc, UK 36/A5
Lamma (isl.), China 71/U11
Lammermuir (hills), Sc, UK 36/D5
Lammhult, Swe. 38/F3
Lammi, Fin. 39/L1
Lamon (riv.), It. 43/J4
Lamone (riv.), It. 57/E4
Lamont, Ca, US 128/C4
Lamont, Ab, Can. 126/E2
Lamongan (vol.), Indo. 80/K4
Lamotrek (isl.), Micr. 116/D4
Lampa, Peru 156/D4
Lampa, Chile 158/N8
Lampang, Thai. 78/B2
Lampasas, Tx, US 129/H5
Lampasas (riv.), Tx, US 143/F2
Lampazos de Naranjo, Mex. 132/C3
Lampedusa, It. 46/C5
Lampedusa (isl.), It. 27/F5
Lampertheim, Ger. 54/B3
Lampeter, Pa, US 138/B4
Lampeter, Wal, UK 32/B3
Lamphun, Thai. 78/B2
Lampman, Sk, Can. 127/H3
Lamporecchio, It. 59/D5
Lamstedt, Ger. 51/G1
Lamu, Kenya 104/D3
Lamud, Peru 156/B2
Lamwa (peak), Ugan. 104/B2
Lan Sang NP, Thai. 78/B2
Lana, It. 57/H4
Lana, Río de la (riv.), Mex. 144/C2
Lanai (isl.), Hi, US 124/T10
Lanaihale (peak), Hi, US 124/T10
Lanaken, Belg. 53/E2
Lanark, Sc, UK 36/C5
Lanbi (isl.), Myan. 83/G6
Lancang Lahuzu Zizhixian, China 83/G3
Lancashire (co.), Eng, UK 35/F4
Lancashire (plain), Eng, UK 35/E4
Lancaster (sound), Nun., Can. 123/H1
Lancaster, Eng, UK 35/F4
Lancaster, Ca, US 128/C4
Lancaster, NY, US 131/S10
Lancaster, Pa, US 138/B3
Lancaster, SC, US 133/H3
Lanciano, It. 46/D1
L'Ancienne-Lorette, Qu, Can. 131/G2
Lanco, Chile 158/B3
Lançut, Pol. 41/M3
Lancy, Swi. 56/C5
Land Kehdingen (reg.), Ger. 51/G1
Landau an der Isar, Ger. 55/F5
Landau in der Pfalz, Ger. 54/B4
Landeck, Aus. 57/G3
Landerneau, Fr. 42/A2
Landes (reg.), Fr. 42/C4
Landes de Lanvaux (mts.), Fr. 42/B3
Landesbergen, Ger. 51/G3
Landis, Sk, Can. 126/F2
Landis Valley Museum, Pa, US 138/B3
Lamarche, Fr. 56/B1

Landivisiau, Fr. 42/A2
Landrecies, Fr. 52/C3
Landri Sales, Braz. 154/B2
Landriano, It. 58/C2
Land's End (pt.), Eng, UK 32/A6
Landsberg, Ger. 57/G1
Landser, Fr. 56/D2
Landshut, Ger. 55/F5
Landskrona, Swe. 38/E4
Landsmeer, Neth. 50/B4
Landstuhl, Ger. 53/G5
Landvetter (int'l arpt.), Swe. 38/E3
Lane End, Eng, UK 30/A2
Lanester, Fr. 42/B3
Lanett, Al, US 133/G3
Lang Craig (pt.), Sc, UK 36/D3
Lang Kha Tuk (peak), Thai. 78/B4
Lang Son, Viet. 83/J3
Lang Suan, Thai. 78/B4
Langadhás, Gre. 47/H2
Langdon, ND, US 127/J3
Langeac, Fr. 42/E4
Langebaanweg, SAfr. 106/L10
Langeberg (mts.), SAfr. 106/L10
Langeland (isl.), Den. 38/D4
Langelsheim, Ger. 51/H3
Langen, Ger. 51/F1
Langen, Ger. 54/B3
Langenaltheim, Ger. 54/D5
Langenargen, Ger. 57/F2
Langenau, Ger. 54/D5
Langenbach, Ger. 55/E6
Langenberg, Ger. 51/E6
Langenburg, Sk, Can. 127/H3
Längenfeld, Aus. 57/G3
Langenfeld, Ger. 53/E2
Langenhagen, Ger. 51/G4
Langenhorn, Ger. 38/C4
Langenlois, Aus. 41/H4
Langenpreising, Ger. 55/E6
Langenselbold, Ger. 54/C2
Langenstein, Aus. 55/H6
Langenthal, Swi. 56/D3
Langenzenn, Ger. 54/D3
Langenzersdorf, Aus. 49/N7
Langeoog, Ger. 51/E1
Langeoog (isl.), Ger. 51/E1
Langerringen, Ger. 57/G1
Langeskov, Den. 38/D4
Langesund, Nor. 38/C2
Langeten (riv.), Swi. 56/D3
Langfang, China 72/H7
Langfurth, Ger. 54/D4
Langham, Sk, Can. 126/G2
Langhirano, It. 58/D3
Langholm, Sc, UK 35/F1
Langhorne, Pa, US 138/D3
Langjökull (glacier), Ice. 37/N7
Langkawi (isl.), Malay. 83/G6
Langley, Wa, US 135/C1
Langnau im Emmental, Swi. 56/D4
Langney (pt.), Eng, UK 33/G5
Langogne, Fr. 42/E4
Langon, Fr. 42/C4
Langøya (isl.), Nor. 37/E1
Langquaid, Ger. 55/F5
Langres, Fr. 56/B2
Langres, Plateau de (plat.), Fr. 42/F3
Langsa, Indo. 80/A3
Langshyttan, Swe. 38/F1
Langtang Lirung (peak), Nepal 85/E1
Langtang NP, Nepal 85/E1
Langtry, Tx, US 132/C4
Languedoc (reg.), Fr. 42/E5
Languedoc-Roussillon (pol. reg.), Fr. 42/E5
Langwedel, Ger. 51/G3
Langweid an Lech, Ger. 54/E6
Langwies, Swi. 57/F4
Langxi, China 72/D5
Lanham-Seabrook, Md, US 138/B6
Lanigan, Sk, Can. 127/G3
Laniloa (pt.), Hi, US 124/W12
Lanin (vol.), Arg. 158/C3
Lanín, PN, Arg. 158/C3
Länkäran, Azer. 51/J2
Lanlacuni Bajo, Peru 156/D4
Lannemezan (plat.), Fr. 42/C5
Lannion (bay), Fr. 42/B2
Lannion, Fr. 42/B2
Lansdale, Pa, US 138/C3
Lansdowne, India 84/B1
Lansdowne-Baltimore Highlands, Md, US 138/B5
Lansford, Pa, US 138/C3
Lanshan, China 79/E5
Lansing (cap.), Mi, US 130/C3
Lansing, Ks, US 137/E6
Lansing, Il, US 135/Q16
Lanta, Thai. 83/G6
Lantau (chan.), China 71/T11
Lantau (peak), China 71/T11
Lantau (isl.), China 71/T10
Lanterne (riv.), Fr. 56/C2
Lanús, Arg. 159/J11
Lanusei, It. 46/A3

Lanxi, China 79/C2
Lanzarote (int'l arpt.), Canl.,Sp. 98/B3
Lanzarote (isl.), Canl.,Sp. 93/A2
Lanžhot, Czh. 41/J4
Lanzhou, China 70/H4
Lao (mts.), China 73/D2
Lao (peak), China 72/E3
Lao Cai, Viet. 70/H7
Laoag, Phil. 79/D4
Laoang, Phil. 79/E5
Laohekou, China 72/B4
Laojun (mtn.), China 72/B4
Laon, Fr. 52/C4
Laos (ctry.) 78/C2
Laoshan, China 72/E3
Laotuding (peak), China 73/C2
Laou (riv.), Mor. 100/B2
Lapa, Braz. 155/B3
Lapeer, Mi, US 130/D3
Lapeer (co.), Mi, US 135/F6
Lapinlahti, Fin. 60/E3
Lapithos, Cyp. 91/C2
Lapland (reg.), Swe. 160/D
Laporte, Co, US 137/E1
Lappeenranta, Fin. 39/N1
Lappersdorf, Ger. 55/F4
Lappi (prov.), Fin. 37/H2
Laptev (sea), Rus. 67/M2
Lapua, Fin. 60/D3
Lapy, Pol. 41/M2
L'Aquila, It. 46/C1
Lār, Iran 89/F3
Lara, Austl. 115/C3
Lara (state), Ven. 152/D2
Laracha, Sp. 44/A1
Larache, Mor. 100/A2
Larache (prov.), Mor. 100/B2
Laragne-Montéglin, Fr. 42/F4
Laramie, Wy, US 127/G5
Laramie, Wy, US 127/G5
Laramie (mts.), Wy, US 124/E3
Laranjeiras do Sul, Braz. 155/A3
Larat (isl.), Indo. 81/K5
Larba, Alg. 100/G4
Larchmont, NY, US 139/K8
Lærdalsøyri, Nor. 38/B1
Laredo, Peru 156/B3
Laredo (int'l arpt.), Tx, US 132/D5
Laredo, Tx, US 132/D5
Laredo, Sp. 44/D1
Laren, Neth. 50/C4
Lares, Peru 156/C4
Largo, Fl, US 133/H5
Largo, Md, US 138/D5
Largo (bay), Sc, UK 36/D4
Largo, Cayo (isl.), Cuba 145/F1
Largs, Sc, UK 36/B5
Largue (riv.), Fr. 56/D2
Lariang (riv.), Indo. 81/E4
Larino, It. 46/D2
Lárisa, Gre. 47/H3
Lark (riv.), Eng, UK 33/G2
Lärkäna, Pak. 89/J3
Larkhall, Sc, UK 36/C5
Larkspur, Ca, US 135/J11
Larmor-Plage, Fr. 42/B3
Larnaca (int'l arpt.), Cyp. 91/C2
Larnaca (dist.), Cyp. 91/C2
Larnaca, Cyp. 91/C2
Larne, NI, UK 34/C2
Larne (dist.), NI, UK 34/C2
Larne Lough (inlet), NI, UK 34/C2
Larned, Ks, US 129/H3
Larochette, Lux. 51/F4
Laroque-d'Olmes, Fr. 42/D5
Larose, La, US 133/G4
Larreynaga, Nic. 144/E3
Larroque, Arg. 159/J10
Larsen Bay, Ak, US 134/H4
Larsen Ice Shelf, Ant. 160/V
Larsen Sound (bay), Nun., Can. 122/G1
L'Artois, Collines de (hills), Fr. 40/A3
Laruns, Fr. 42/C5
Larvik, Nor. 38/D2
Las Animas, Co, US 129/G3
Las Aves (isls.), Ven. 141/H5
Las Breñas, Arg. 157/D2
Las Cabezas de San Juan, Sp. 44/C4
Las Cabras, Chile 158/N9
Las Cruces, NM, US 128/F4
Las Cruces (int'l arpt.), NM, US 142/D1
Las Delicias, Ven. 132/C4
Las Eutimias, Mex. 132/C4
Las Flores, Arg. 158/F3
Las Guacamayas, Mex. 142/E5
Las Hermosas, PN, Col. 152/C4
Las Higueras, Arg. 158/F2
Las Lajas, Arg. 158/C3
Las Lajas (peak), Arg. 158/A2
Las Lomas, Peru 156/A2
Las Lomitas, Arg. 157/D1
Las Margaritas, Mex. 144/D2

Las Martinas, Cuba 145/E1
Las Mercedes, Ven. 153/E2
Las Minas (peak), Hon. 144/D3
Las Nieves, Mex. 142/D3
Las Orquídeas, PN, Col. 152/B3
Las Palmas, Pan. 145/F4
Las Palmas de Cocalán, PN, Chile 158/N9
Las Palmas de Gran Canaria, Canl.,Sp. 98/B3
Las Pedroñeras, Sp. 44/D3
Las Perdices, Arg. 158/E2
Las Perlas (arch.), Pan. 145/G4
Las Piedras, Peru 156/D4
Las Piedras, Ven. 152/C2
Las Piedras, Uru. 159/K11
Las Pipinas, Arg. 159/F2
Las Rosas, Mex. 144/C2
Las Rozas de Madrid, Sp. 45/N9
Las Tablas, Pan. 152/A3
Las Varas, Mex. 142/D4
Las Varillas, Arg. 157/D3
Las Vegas, NM, US 129/F4
Las Vegas, Nv, US 128/D3
Lasalle, Qu, Can. 131/N7
Lasberg, Aus. 55/H6
Lascano, Uru. 159/G2
Lashio, Myan. 83/G3
Lashkar Gāh, Afg. 89/H2
Lasne-Chapelle-Saint-Lambert, Belg. 53/D2
Læsø (isl.), Den. 38/D3
Lasolo (riv.), Indo. 81/F4
Lassen (peak), Ca, US 126/C5
Lassen Volcanic NP, Ca, US 128/B2
L'Assomption, Qu, Can. 131/P6
L'Assomption (co.), Qu, Can. 131/N6
L'Assomption (riv.), Qu, Can. 131/P6
Last Mountain (lake), Sk, Can. 127/G3
Lastovo (isl.), Cro. 46/E1
Lastovski (chan.), Cro. 48/C4
Lastovski Kanal (chan.), Cro. 46/E1
Lastra a Signa, It. 59/E5
Lastrup, Ger. 51/E3
Lata, SD. 116/F6
Latacunga, Ecu. 152/B5
Latady (isl.), Ant. 160/U
L'Atakora (prov.), Ben. 103/F4
Lätehär, India 85/E4
Laterza, It. 46/E2
Lathan (riv.), Fr. 42/C3
Lathrop, Ca, US 135/M11
Latina, It. 46/C2
Latisana, It. 59/G1
Latorica (riv.), Slvk.,Ukr. 41/M4
Latrobe (riv.), Austl. 115/C3
Latrobe (mt.), Tn, US 133/G3
Latrobe, Austl. 115/C4
Latrobe, Austl. 115/C4
Lattes, Fr. 42/E5
Lattingtown, NI, US 34/B3
Lātūr, India 89/L5
Latvia (ctry.) 39/L3
Lau Group (isl.), Fiji 116/H6
Laubach, Ger. 54/B1
Lauca, PN, Chile 150/D7
Lauchheim, Ger. 54/D5
Lauchheim, Ger. 54/D5
Lauda-Königshofen, Ger. 54/C4
Lauder, Sc, UK 36/D5
Lauderdale (lakes), Wi, US 135/N14
Lauenbrück, Ger. 51/G2
Lauenburg, Ger. 51/H2
Lauenen, Swi. 56/D5
Lauenförde, Ger. 51/H5
Lauer (riv.), Ger. 54/D2
Lauf, Ger. 54/C3
Laufach, Ger. 54/C2
Laufen, Swi. 56/D3
Laufen, Ger. 55/F7
Laufenburg, Swi. 56/E2
Lauffen am Neckar, Ger. 54/C4
Laughlen (mt.), Austl. 113/G2
Lauhanvuoren NP, Fin. 60/D3
Lauingen, Ger. 54/D5
Launceston, Austl. 115/C4
Launette (riv.), Fr. 52/B4
Laupahoehoe, Hi, US 124/U11
Laupen, Swi. 56/D4
Laupersiwl, Swi. 56/D4
Laupheim, Ger. 57/F1
Laura, Austl. 113/H6
Laureana di Borrello, It. 46/E3
Laurel, Mt, US 126/F4
Laurel, Ms, US 133/F4
Laurel Springs, NJ, US 138/C4
Laureldale, Pa, US 138/B5

Laurelton, Pa, US 138/A2
Laurence Harbor, NJ, US 139/J10
Laurencekirk, Sc, UK 36/D3
Laurens, SC, US 133/H3
Laurentian (plat.), On, Can. 122/G2
Laurentides, Qu, Can. 131/N6
Laurinburg, NC, US 133/J3
Laurium, Mi, US 127/L4
Lausanne, Swi. 56/C4
Lauscha, Ger. 54/E2
Laut (isl.), Indo. 81/E4
Lautaro, Chile 158/B3
Lauter, Ger. 55/F1
Lauter (riv.), Ger. 40/E3
Lauterach (riv.), Ger. 57/F1
Lauterbach (riv.), Ger. 54/E2
Lauterbach, Ger. 54/C1
Lauterbourg, Fr. 54/B5
Lauterbrunnen, Swi. 56/D4
Lauterecken, Ger. 53/G4
Lauve, Nor. 38/D2
Lauwers (chan.), Neth. 50/D1
Lauwersmeer (lake), Neth. 50/D2
Lava Beds Nat'l Mon., Ca, US 126/C5
Lavagna (riv.), It. 58/C4
Lavagna, It. 58/C4
Laval, Fr. 42/C2
Laval, Qu, Can. 131/N6
Lavalleja (dept.), Uru. 159/G2
Lavallette, NJ, US 138/D4
Lavans-lès-Saint-Claude, Fr. 56/B5
Lavant (riv.), Aus. 43/L3
Lavapié (pt.), Chile 158/B3
Lavaur, Fr. 42/D5
Laveen, Az, US 137/H4
Lavelanet, Fr. 42/D5
Lavello, It. 46/D2
Laveno, It. 57/E6
Laverton, Austl. 112/D4
Lavey, Swi. 56/D5
Lavezzola, It. 59/E3
Lavino (riv.), It. 59/E4
Lavis, It. 57/H5
Lavos, Port. 44/A2
Lavras, Braz. 155/C2
Lavras da Mangabeira, Braz. 154/C2
Lávrion, Gre. 47/J4
Lawa (riv.), FrG. 153/H4
Lāwar Khās, India 84/A1
Lawarai (pass), Pak. 86/A2
Lawit (mtn.), Indo. 80/D3
Lawit (peak), Malay. 83/H6
Lawndale, Ca, US 136/F8
Lawnhill, BC, Can. 134/M5
Lawra, Gha. 102/E4
Lawrence, Ma, US 131/G3
Lawrence, Ks, US 129/J3
Lawrence, NY, US 139/L9
Lawrenceburg, In, US 130/C4
Lawrenceburg, Tn, US 133/G3
Lawrenceburg, Ky, US 36/D5
Lawrencetown, NI, UK 34/B3
Lawrenceville, Ga, US 133/H3
Lawrenceville, NJ, US 138/D3
Lawson, Mo, US 137/E5
Lawu (peak), Indo. 80/D5
Lawz, Jabal al (peak), SAr. 88/C3
Laxå, Swe. 38/F2
Laxey, IM, UK 34/D3
Laxou, Fr. 53/F6
Lay (riv.), Fr. 42/C3
Lay-Saint-Christophe, Fr. 53/F6
Laya (riv.), Rus. 61/N2
Layar (cape), Indo. 81/E4
Laylän, Iraq 90/F3
Layon (riv.), Fr. 42/C3
Laysan (isl.), Hi, US 117/H2
Layton, Ut, US 137/K11
Layton, NJ, US 138/D1
Lazarevac, Serb. 48/E3
Lázaro Cárdenas, Mex. 128/D5
Lázaro Cárdenas, Mex. 142/B2
Lázaro Cárdenas, Mex. 142/E5
Lazio (prov.), It. 43/J5
Łbrikterpe, Turkm. 47/K2
Le Ban-Saint-Martin, Fr. 53/F5
Le Blanc, Fr. 42/D3
Le Blanc-Mesnil, Fr. 30/K5
Le Breuil, Fr. 42/F3
Le Cannet, Fr. 43/G5
Le Cateau-Cambrésis, Fr. 30/E1
Le Chasseral (peak), Swi. 56/D3
Le Chasseron (peak), Swi. 56/C4
Le Chesnay, Fr. 30/J5
Le Chesne, Fr. 53/D4
Le Cheval Blanc (peak), Fr. 56/C5
Le Cheylard, Fr. 42/F4
Le Cornate (peak), It. 43/J5

Le Creusot, Fr. 42/F3
Le Crotoy, Fr. 52/A3
Le Gore, Md, US 138/A4
Le Grammont (peak), Swi. 56/C5
Le Grand (cape), Austl. 112/D5
Le Grand Ballon (peak), Fr. 56/D2
Le Grand Ballon (peak), Fr. 56/D2
Le Grau-du-Roi, Fr. 42/F5
Le Grazie, It. 58/C4
Le Havre, Fr. 42/D2
Le Landeron, Swi. 56/D3
Le Lavandou, Fr. 41/M3
Le Locle, Swi. 56/C3
Le Luc, Fr. 43/G5
Le Mans, Fr. 42/D2
Le Mée-sur-Seine, Fr. 30/K6
Le Mesnil-Amelot, Fr. 30/K4
Le Mesnil-Aubry, Fr. 30/K4
Le Mesnil-Esnard, Fr. 52/A5
Le Mesnil-le-Roi, Fr. 30/J5
Le Mesnil-Saint-Denis, Fr. 30/H5
Le Mesnil-sur-Oger, Fr. 52/D6
Le Môle (peak), Fr. 56/C4
Le Morond (peak), Fr. 56/C4
Le Moure de la Gardille (peak), Fr. 42/E4
Le Murge (mts.), It. 46/E2
Le Noirmont (peak), Fr. 56/C4
Le Noirmont (peak), Swi. 56/C5
Le Noirmont, Swi. 56/C3
Le Nouvion-en-Thiérache, Fr. 52/C3
Le Palais, Fr. 42/B3
Le Palais-sur-Vienne, Fr. 42/D4
Le Passage, Fr. 42/D4
Le Perray-en-Yvelines, Fr. 30/H5
Le Petit Ballon (peak), Fr. 56/D2
Le Plessis-Belleville, Fr. 30/L4
Le Plessis-Feu-Aussoux, Fr. 30/M5
Le Plessis-Placy, Fr. 30/L4
Le Port, Reun. 107/S15
Le Portel, Fr. 52/A2
Le Puy-en-Velay, Fr. 42/E4
Le Quesnoy, Fr. 52/C3
Le Russey, Fr. 56/C3
Le Suchet (peak), Swi. 56/C4
Le Tampon, Reun. 107/S15
Le Teil, Fr. 42/F4
Le Tholy, Fr. 56/C2
Le Touquet-Paris-Plage, Fr. 52/A2
Le Tréport, Fr. 52/A3
Le Val-d'Ajol, Fr. 56/C2
Le Vésinet, Fr. 30/J5
Le Vigan, Fr. 42/E5
Lea (riv.), Eng, UK 33/F3
Leach (lake), Ca, US 127/K4
Leach (riv.), Eng, UK 33/E3
Leacock-Leola-Bareville, Pa, US 138/B3
Lead, SD, US 127/H4
Leader, Sk, Can. 126/F3
Leader Water (riv.), Sc, UK 36/D5
Leadon (riv.), Eng, UK 32/D3
Leadville, Co, US 132/B2
Leaf (riv.), Ms, US 133/F4
Leaghur (lake), Austl. 115/B2
League City, Tx, US 129/J5
Leakey, Tx, US 129/H5
Leam (riv.), Eng, UK 33/E2
Leamington, On, Can. 130/D3
Le'an, China 79/C2
Leander (pt.), Austl. 112/B4
Leaota (peak), Rom. 49/G3
Learmonth, Austl. 112/B2
Leatherhead, Eng, UK 30/C3
Leavenworth, Ks, US 137/D5
Leavenworth (co.), Ks, US 137/D5
Leavenworth, Wa, US 126/C4
Leawood, Ks, US 137/D6
Leba, Pol. 38/G4
Lebach, Ger. 53/F5
Lebak, Phil. 79/D6
Lebane, Serb. 47/G1
Lebanon (ctry.) 91/D3
Lebanon (mts.), Leb. 91/D3
Lebanon, In, US 130/C3
Lebanon, Ky, US 50/B4
Lebanon, NH, US 131/F3
Lebanon, NJ, US 138/D2
Lebanon, Or, US 126/C4
Lebanon, Pa, US 138/B3
Lebanon, Tn, US 130/C4
Lebbeke, Belg. 53/D1
Lebedyn, Ukr. 62/E2
Lebel-sur-Quévillon, Qu, Can. 130/E1
Lebène (riv.), Mor. 48/C2
Lébény, Hun. 48/C2
Lębork, Pol. 38/G4
Lebrija, Sp. 44/B4
Lebu, Chile 157/B3
Lebu, Chile 158/B3
Leça da Palmeira, Port. 44/A2
Lecce, It. 47/F2
Lecco, It. 58/C1
Lecco (prov.), It. 58/C1

Lecco, Lago di (lake), It. 58/C1
Lech, Aus. 57/G3
Lech (riv.), Ger. 43/K2
Lechang, China 83/K2
Lechbruck, Ger. 57/G2
Leche (lake), Cuba 145/G1
Lechtaler Alps (mts.), Aus. 57/G3
Leck, Ger. 38/C4
Lectoure, Fr. 42/D5
Łęczna, Pol. 41/M3
Leda (riv.), Ger. 51/E2
Ledang (peak), Malay. 80/B3
Lede, Belg. 52/C2
Ledegem, Belg. 52/C2
Ledesma, Sp. 44/B2
Ledong, China 83/J4
Ledro (lake), It. 57/G6
Ledu (peak), It. 57/F5
Leduc, Ab, Can. 126/E2
Lee (riv.), Ire. 31/P11
Lee (mtn.), Pa, US 138/B1
Leech (lake), Mn, US 125/H2
Leeds, Eng, UK 35/G4
Leeds (co.), Eng, UK 35/G4
Leeds, Ms, US 35/G4
Leeds and Bradford (int'l arpt.), Eng, UK 35/H7
Leeds and Liverpool (canal), Eng, UK 35/G4
Leeds Point, NJ, US 138/D5
Leegebruch, Ger. 40/Q6
Leek, Eng, UK 35/F5
Leek, Neth. 50/D2
Leeman, Austl. 112/B4
Leer, Ger. 51/E2
Leerdam, Neth. 50/C5
Leersum, Neth. 50/C5
Lees Summit, Mo, US 137/E6
Leesburg, Fl, US 133/H4
Leesburg, NJ, US 138/C5
Leese, Ger. 51/G4
Leesport, Pa, US 138/C3
Leesville, La, US 129/J5
Leeton, Austl. 115/C4
Leeu (riv.), SAfr. 106/L10
Leeuwarden, Neth. 50/C2
Leeuwin (cape), Austl. 112/B5
Leeuwin-Naturaliste NP, Austl. 112/B5
Leeward (isls.), NAm. 141/J4
Leff (riv.), Fr. 42/B2
Lefka, Cyp. 91/C2
Lefo (peak), Camr. 103/H5
Lefroy (lake), Austl. 112/D4
Legana, Austl. 115/C4
Leganés, Sp. 45/N9
Legaspi, Phil. 79/D5
Legau, Ger. 57/G2
Legazpia, Sp. 44/D1
Legges Tor (peak), Austl. 115/C4
Léglise, Belg. 53/E4
Legnago, It. 59/E2
Legnano, It. 59/E2
Legnaro, It. 59/E2
Legnica, Pol. 41/J3
Legnone (peak), It. 57/F5
Leh, India 86/D2
Leh Palace, India 86/D2
Lehi, Ut, US 137/K13
Lehigh (co.), Pa, US 138/C2
Lehigh Acres, Fl, US 133/H5
Lehighton, Pa, US 138/C2
Lehinch, Ire. 31/P10
Lehrberg, Ger. 54/D4
Lehrte, Ger. 51/G4
Leiblfing, Ger. 55/F5
Leibo, China 83/H2
Leicester, Eng, UK 33/E1
Leicester (co.), Eng, UK 33/E1
Leicestershire (co.), Eng, UK 35/H6
Leichhardt (dam), Austl. 113/H2
Leichhardt (riv.), Austl. 113/G2
Leichlingen, Ger. 53/G1
Leiden, Neth. 50/B4
Leiderdorp, Neth. 50/B4
Leidschendam, Neth. 50/B4
Leie (riv.), Belg. 42/E1
Leifers (Laives), It. 57/H5
Leigh, Eng, UK 35/F5
Leigh Creek, Austl. 113/H4
Leimebamba, Peru 156/B4
Leimen, Ger. 54/B4
Leine (riv.), Ger. 40/D3
Leinefelde, Ger. 51/H6
Leinster (mt.), Ire. 31/Q10
Leinster, Austl. 112/C3
Leinster (reg.), Ire. 34/A5
Leipheim, Ger. 54/D6
Leipsic, Oh, US 130/E2
Leipsic (riv.), De, US 138/D5
Leipzig, Ger. 42/G3
Leira, Nor. 38/C1

Leiria, Port. 44/A3
Leiria (dist.), Port. 44/A3
Leisler (mt.), Austl. 113/F2
Leith (hill), Eng, UK 30/B3
Leitha (riv.), Aus. 41/J5
Leixlip, Ire. 34/B5
Leizhou (pen.), China 83/J3
Lek (riv.), Neth. 40/C3
Lekhainá, Gre. 47/G4
Lekkerkerk, Neth. 50/B5
Lekki (lag.), Nga. 103/G5
Leksands-Noret, Swe. 38/F1
Leksozero (lake), Rus. 37/J3
Lelai (cape), Indo. 81/G3
Leland, Ms, US 129/K4
Lelång (lake), Swe. 38/E2
Leling, China 72/D3
Lelystad, Neth. 50/C3
Lem, Den. 38/C3
Lema (peak), It. 57/E5
Léman (Geneva) (lake), Fr. 43/G3
Lemberg (peak), Ger. 57/F2
Lemberg, It. 53/G5
Lembu (peak), Indo. 80/D3
Lemgo, Ger. 51/F4
Lemhi (isl.), Fin. 39/H2
Lemland, Fin. 39/J1
Lemmer, Neth. 50/C3
Lemmon, SD, US 127/H4
Lemon Grove, Ca, US 136/C5
Lempa (riv.), ESal. 144/D3
Lempäälä, Fin. 39/K1
Lempdes, Fr. 42/E4
Lemvig, Den. 38/C3
Lemvik (riv.), Rus. 61/P2
Lemwerder, Ger. 51/F2
Lena (riv.), Rus. 67/M3
Lena, Nor. 38/D1
Lenape, Ks, US 137/D6
Lenape (lake), NJ, US 138/D5
Lençóis Maranhenses, PN dos, Braz. 151/K4
Lençóis Paulista, Braz. 155/B2
Lendinara, It. 59/E2
Lenexa, Ks, US 137/D6
Lengau, Aus. 55/G6
Lengdorf, Ger. 55/F6
Lengede, Ger. 51/H4
Lengenfeld, Ger. 55/F1
Lengerich, Ger. 51/E4
Lenggries, Ger. 57/H2
Lengnau, Swi. 56/D3
Lengshuitan, China 83/K2
Lengua de Vaca (pt.), Chile 157/B3
Lenhartsville, Pa, US 138/C2
Lenina (peak), Taj. 87/F5
Leninabad (int'l arpt.), Taj. 87/E4
Leningradskaya Oblast, Rus. 60/G3
Leninobod (obl.), Taj. 87/E5
Leninogorsk, Rus. 61/M5
Leninsk-Kuznetskiy, Rus. 64/J4
Leninváros, Hun. 41/L5
Lenk, Swi. 56/D5
Lenne (riv.), Ger. 53/G1
Lennestadt, Ger. 51/F6
Lenningen, Ger. 57/F1
Lennox (isl.), Chile 159/D7
Lennox, Ca, US 136/F8
Lennox (hills), Sc, UK 36/B5
Lennoxtown, Sc, UK 36/B5
Leno, It. 57/G1
Lenoir, NC, US 133/H3
Lenoir City, Tn, US 133/G3
Lens, Swi. 56/D5
Lens, Fr. 52/B3
Lens, Belg. 52/C2
Lensahn, Ger. 38/D4
Lensk, Rus. 67/M3
Lenting, Ger. 55/E5
Lentini, It. 46/D4
Lenvik, Nor. 37/F1
Leny, Pass of (pass), Sc, UK 36/B4
Lenzburg, Swi. 56/E3
Lenzkirch, Ger. 57/E2
Léo, Burk. 103/E4
Leoben, Aus. 43/L3
Leográ (riv.), It. 59/E1
Leola, SD, US 127/J4
Leominster, Eng, UK 32/D2
León, Mex. 143/E4
León (int'l arpt.), Mex. 142/C3
León, Sp. 44/C1
León, Nic. 144/E3
Léon, Étang de (lake), Fr. 42/C4
Leon-Guanajuato (int'l arpt.), Mex. 143/E4
Leon Valley, Tx, US 137/T20
Leona Valley, Ca, US 136/C1
Leonard, Tx, US 129/H4
Leonard, Mi, US 135/F6
Leonard, NJ, US 139/J10
Leonardo da Vinci (int'l arpt.), It. 46/B2
Leonberg, Ger. 54/C4

Leonding, Aus. 55/H6
Leone (peak), It. 56/E5
Leones, Arg. 158/E2
Leonforte, It. 46/D4
Leongatha, Austl. 115/C3
Leonidhion, Gre. 47/H4
Leonora, Austl. 112/D4
Leopoldina, Braz. 211/L6
Leopoldkanaal (riv.), Belg. 52/C1
Leopoldsburg, Belg. 52/C1
Leopoldsdorf, Aus. 49/N7
Leopoldsdorf im Marchfelde, Aus. 49/P7
Leopoldshöhe, Ger. 51/F4
Leoville, Sk, Can. 126/G2
Lepaera, Hon. 144/D3
Lépanges-sur-Vologne, Fr. 56/C2
Lepenoú, Gre. 47/G3
Lepe, Sp. 44/B4
L'Épiphanie, Qu, Can. 131/P6
Lepontine Alps (mts.), Swi 43/H3
Leptokariá, Gre. 47/H2
Léraba (riv.), Burk. 102/D3
Lercara Friddi, It. 46/C4
Lerdo de Tejada, Mex. 144/C2
Leribe, Les. 106/E3
Lerici, It. 58/C4
Lérin, Sp. 44/E1
Lerma, Sp. 44/D1
Lerma, Mex. 143/Q10
Lerma (riv.), Mex. 143/E4
Lérouville, Fr. 53/E6
Lerum, Swe. 38/E3
Lerwick, Sc, UK 31/W13
Léry (lake), La, US 137/Q17
Les Allues-le-Roi, Fr. 30/H5
Les Bois, Fr. 56/C4
Les Breuleux, Swi. 56/C4
Les Bréviaires, Fr. 30/H5
Les Cayes, Haiti 145/H2
Les Cèdres, Qu, Can. 131/M7
Les Clayes-sous-Bois, Fr. 30/H5
Les Contamines-Montjoie, Fr. 56/C6
Les Diablerets (range), Swi. 56/D5
Les Essarts-le-Roi, Fr. 30/H5
Les Gets, Fr. 56/C5
Les Hautes-Rivières, Fr. 53/D4
Les Herbiers, Fr. 42/C3
Les Islettes, Fr. 53/E5
Les Molières, Fr. 30/J6
Les Mesnuls, Fr. 30/H5
Les Mureaux, Fr. 52/A6
Les Ponts-de-Martel, Swi. 56/C4
Les Rousses, Fr. 56/C5
Les Sables-d'Olonne, Fr. 42/C3
Les Salines (int'l arpt.), Alg. 100/C4
Les Ulis, Fr. 30/J6
Les Verrières, Swi. 56/C4
Lesa, It. 58/B1
Leshan, China 83/H2
Lésigny, Fr. 30/K5
Lesima (peak), It. 58/C3
Lesja, Nor. 37/D3
Lesjöfors, Swe. 38/F2
Lesko, Pol. 41/M4
Leskovac, Serb. 47/G1
Leslie, Sc, UK 36/C4
Lesmahagow, Sc, UK 36/C5
Lesneven, Fr. 42/A2
Lešnica, Serb. 46/E3
Lesotho (ctry.) 106/E6
Lesozavodsk, Rus. 71/P2
Lesparre-Médoc, Fr. 42/C4
Lesquin (int'l arpt.), Fr. 52/C2
Lessay, Fr. 42/C2
Lessebo, Swe. 38/F3
Lesser Antilles (isls.), NAm. 141/M4
Lesser Caucasus (mts.), Asia 63/G4
Lesser Slave (lake), Ab, Can. 122/E3
Lesser Sunda (isls.), Indo. 81/E5
Lessines, Belg. 52/C2
Lessunga (peak), Indo. 80/D3
Lésvos (isl.), Gre. 62/C5
Leszno, Pol. 41/J3
Létavértes, Hun. 48/E2
Letchworth, Eng, UK 33/F3
Letham, Sc, UK 36/D4
Lethbridge, Ab, Can. 126/E3
Lethe (riv.), Ger. 51/F2
Leti (isls.), Indo. 81/G5
Leticia, Col. 152/D5
Leting, China 72/D3
Letlhakane, Bots. 105/D4
Letlhakeng, Bots. 105/D5
L'Étoile, Fr. 52/B3
Letpadan, Myan. 83/G4
Letschin, Ger. 41/H2
Letsôk-Aw (isl.), Myan. 80/A1
Letterkenny, Ire. 34/A2
Leucate, Fr. 42/E5
Leuchars, Sc, UK 36/D4
Leuk, Swi. 56/D5

Leukerbad, Swi. 56/D5
Leun, Ger. 54/B1
Leuser (peak), Indo. 80/A3
Leutershausen, Ger. 54/D4
Leutkirch im Allgäu, Ger. 57/G2
Levádhia, Gre. 47/H3
Levallois-Perret, Fr. 30/J5
Levanger, Nor. 37/D3
Levante, Riviera di (coast), It. 58/C4
Levanto, It. 58/C4
Level (isl.), Chile 158/B5
Level, Md, US 138/B4
Levelland, Tx, US 129/G4
Levelock, Ak, US 134/H4
Leven (pt.), SAfr. 107/F2
Leven (lake), Sc, UK 36/A3
Leven, Sc, UK 36/C4
Leven (riv.), Sc, UK 36/C4
Leveque (cape), Austl. 109/B2
Leverburgh, Sc, UK 31/Q8
Leverkusen, Ger. 53/F1
Levico Terme, It. 57/H5
Levier, Fr. 56/C4
Levin, NZ 117/T11
Lévis, Qu, Can. 131/G2
Lévis-Saint-Nom, Fr. 30/H5
Levittown, Pa, US 138/D3
Levittown, NY, US 139/L9
Levkás, Gre. 47/G3
Levkás (isl.), Gre. 47/G3
Levkímmi, Gre. 47/G3
Levrier (bay), Mrta. 98/A5
Levski, Bul. 49/G4
Lewes (riv.), Yk, Can. 126/C4
Lewes, Eng, UK 33/G5
Lewin Brzeski, Pol. 41/J3
Lewis (range), Mt, US 126/E3
Lewis (hills), Nf, Can. 131/L1
Lewis (pass), NZ 117/S11
Lewis and Clark (lake), Ne,SD, US 127/J5
Lewis Smith (lake), Al, US 133/G3
Lewisburg, Tn, US 133/G3
Lewisburg, WV, US 130/D4
Lewisburg, Pa, US 138/B2
Lewisham (bor.), Eng, UK 30/C2
Lewisporte, Nf, Can. 131/L1
Lewiston, Id, US 126/D4
Lewiston, Me, US 131/G2
Lewiston, NY, US 131/R9
Lewiston, Mt, US 126/F4
Lewistown, Pa, US 130/E3
Lewotobi (peak), Indo. 81/F5
Lexington, Ne, US 127/J5
Lexington, Tn, US 130/D5
Lexington, Ky, US 130/C4
Lexington, NC, US 133/H3
Lexington Park, Md, US 130/E4
Leyburn, Eng, UK 35/G3
Leyden, Co, US 137/B3
Leyland, Eng, UK 35/F4
Leye, China 83/J3
Leysin, Swi. 56/D5
Leyte (isl.), Phil. 67/M8
Leytron, Swi. 56/D5
Lez (riv.), Fr. 42/F4
Leżajsk, Pol. 41/M3
Lézignan-Corbières, Fr. 42/E5
Lezuza, Sp. 44/D3
L'gov, Rus. 62/E2
Lhanbryd, Sc, UK 36/C1
Lhari, China 70/F5
Lhasa, China 82/F2
Lhazê, China 85/F1
L'Hongrin (lake), Swi. 56/D5
Lhorong, China 70/G4
L'Hospitalet de Llobregat, Sp. 45/L7
Lhozhag, China 85/H1
Lhünzê, China 83/G2
Li (riv.), China 79/B2
Li (riv.), China 83/K2
Li (mtn.), China 79/B2
Li Xian, China 79/B2
Lian (riv.), China 79/B2
Lian Xian, China 83/K3
Liancourt, Fr. 52/B2
Liancourt Rocks (isl.), Asia 74/B2
Liangcheng, China 72/C3
Liangpran (peak), Indo. 80/D3
Lianhua, China 83/K2
Lianjiang, China 83/K3
Liannan Yaozu Zizhixian, China 79/B3
Lianshui, China 79/D2
Lianyuan, China 79/B2
Lianyungang, China 72/D4
Liao (riv.), China 67/M5
Liaocheng, China 72/C3
Liaodong (pen.), China 73/A3

Liaodong (isls.), China 72/E3
Liaodong, Gulf of (gulf), China 71/M3
Liaoning (prov.), China 71/M3
Liaoyang, China 73/B2
Liaoyuan, China 71/N3
Liaozhong, China 73/B2
Liäquatpur, Pak. 86/A5
Liard (riv.), NW, Can. 122/D2
Libby, Mt, US 126/E3
Libenge, D.R. Congo 97/J7
Libercourt, Fr. 52/C3
Liberdade (riv.), Braz. 151/H6
Liberdade, Braz. 211/J7
Liberec, Czh. 41/H3
Liberecký (pol. reg.), Czh. 41/H3
Liberia, CR 144/E4
Liberia (ctry.) 102/C5
Libertad, Belz. 144/D2
Libertad, Ven. 152/D2
Libertad, Uru. 159/K11
Libertador General San Martín, Arg. 157/D1
Liberty, Tx, US 129/J5
Liberty, Ky, US 130/C4
Liberty, Ms, US 129/K5
Liberty, Mo, US 137/E5
Liberty, Wa, US 137/K11
Liberty (res.), Md, US 138/B5
Liberty Grove, Md, US 138/B4
Libertyville, Il, US 135/P15
Libin, Belg. 53/E4
Libo, China 83/J2
Libobo (cape), Indo. 81/G4
Liboc (riv.), Czh. 41/G3
Libochovice, Czh. 55/H2
Libon, Phil. 79/D5
Librazhd, Alb. 47/G2
Libres, Mex. 143/M7
Libreville (cap.), Gabon 96/G7
Libya (ctry.) 97/J2
Libyan (plat.), Libya 97/K1
Libyan (des.), Egypt,Libya 97/K2
Licantén, Chile 158/B2
Licata, It. 46/C4
Lice, Turk. 90/E2
Lich, Ger. 54/B1
Licheng, China 72/C3
Licheng, China 72/D3
Lichfield, Eng, UK 33/E1
Lichinga, Moz. 105/G3
Lichtenau, Ger. 51/F5
Lichtenau, Ger. 54/D4
Lichtenau, Ger. 54/B5
Lichtenburg, SAfr. 106/D2
Lichtenfels, Ger. 54/D2
Lichtenrade, Ger. 40/Q7
Lichtensteig, Swi. 57/F3
Lichtenvoorde, Neth. 50/D5
Lichtervelde, Belg. 52/C1
Lichuan, China 79/A1
Licinio de Almeida, Braz. 154/B4
Lick Observatory, Ca, US 135/L12
Licking (riv.), Ky, US 130/C4
Licosa (cape), It. 46/D2
Licques, Fr. 52/A2
Lida, Bela. 39/L5
Liddell Water (riv.), Sc, UK 36/D6
Liddes, Swi. 57/G4
Liddon (gulf), NW, Can. 123/R7
Lidhorikion, Gre. 47/H3
Lidingö, Swe. 38/H2
Lidköping, Swe. 38/E2
Lido, It. 59/F2
Lido di Iesolo, It. 59/F1
Lido di Ostia, It. 46/C2
Lidzbark, Pol. 41/K2
Lidzbark Warmiński, Pol. 39/J4
Liebenau, Aus. 55/H5
Liebenbergsvlei (riv.), SAfr. 106/F2
Liebig (mt.), Austl. 113/F2
Liechtenstein (ctry.) 57/F3
Liedekerke, Belg. 53/D2
Liège, Belg. 53/E2
Liège (prov.), Belg. 53/E3
Lieksa, Fin. 60/F3
Lienden, Neth. 50/C5
Lienen, Ger. 51/E4
Lienz, Aus. 43/K3
Liepāja, Lat. 39/J3
Lier, Belg. 53/D1
Lierneux, Belg. 53/E3
Lieser (riv.), Ger. 53/F3
Liesjärven NP, Fin. 39/K1
Liesse-Notre-Dame, Fr. 52/C4
Liestal, Swi. 57/E2
Lieto, Fin. 39/K1
Liévin, Fr. 52/B2
Lièvre (riv.), Qu, Can. 130/F2
Liez (lake), Fr. 56/B2
Liezen, Aus. 43/L3
Liffey (riv.), Ire. 34/B5
Liffol-le-Grand, Fr. 56/B1
Lifford, Ire. 31/Q9
Ligao, Phil. 81/F1
Lightning Ridge, Austl. 115/C1
Lightwater, Eng, UK 30/B3

Lignano Sabbiadoro, It. 59/G1
Ligny-en-Barrois, Fr. 53/E6
Ligoncio (peak), It. 57/F5
Ligoúrion, Gre. 47/H4
Liguori, Mo, US 137/G9
Liguria (pol. reg.), It. 58/B4
Liguria (prov.), It. 43/H4
Ligurian (sea), Fr.,It. 43/H5
Lihou (reefs), Austl. 109/E2
Lihue, Hi, US 124/S10
Lijiang Naxizu Zizhixian, China 83/H2
Lijin, China 72/D3
Likasi, D.R. Congo 105/E3
Likely, BC, Can. 126/C2
Likoma (isl.), Malw. 105/F3
Likouala (riv.), Congo 96/H7
Likova (riv.), Rus. 61/W9
L'Île-Perrot, Qu, Can. 131/N7
L'Île-Rousse, Fr. 46/A1
Liliāni, Pak. 86/B3
Lilienthal, Ger. 51/F2
Liling, China 83/K2
Lilla Edet, Swe. 38/E2
Lille, Belg. 53/C2
Lille, Fr. 52/C2
Lille Bælt (chan.), Ger. 38/C4
Lillehammer, Nor. 38/D1
Lillers, Fr. 52/B2
Lillesand, Nor. 38/C2
Lillestrøm, Nor. 38/D2
Lilliwaup, Wa, US 135/A3
Lillo, Sp. 44/D3
Lillooet, BC, Can. 126/C3
Lillooet (riv.), BC, Can. 126/C3
Lilongwe (cap.), Malw. 105/F3
Liloy, Phil. 79/D6
Lim (riv.), Serb. 47/F1
Lima (dept.), Peru 156/C4
Lima (cap.), Peru 156/B4
Lima, Oh, US 130/C3
Lima (riv.), Port. 45/A2
Lima, Arg. 159/J11
Lima Duarte, Braz. 211/K6
Limache, Chile 158/N8
Limanowa, Pol. 41/L4
Limassol, Cyp. 91/C2
Limassol (dist.), Cyp. 91/C2
Limay (riv.), Arg. 147/C7
Limbach, Ger. 54/C4
Limbani, Peru 156/D4
Limbara (peak), It. 46/A2
Limbdi, India 89/K4
Limbé, Haiti 145/H2
Limbiate, It. 58/C1
Limbourg, Belg. 53/E2
Limburg (prov.), Belg. 53/E1
Limburg an der Lahn, Ger. 54/B2
Limburgerhof, Ger. 54/B4
Lime Village, Ak, US 134/G3
Limedsforsen, Swe. 38/E1
Limeira, Braz. 155/C2
Limekilns, Sc, UK 36/C4
Limena, It. 59/E2
Limenária, Gre. 47/J2
Limerick, Íre. 31/P10
Limfjorden (chan.), Den. 38/C3
Limidario (peak), It. 57/E5
Limite, It. 59/D5
Limmat (riv.), Swi. 57/E3
Limmen Bight (bay), Austl. 109/C2
Limni, Gre. 47/H3
Límnos (isl.), Gre. 47/H3
Limoeiro, Braz. 154/D2
Limoeiro do Norte, Braz. 154/C2
Limoges, Fr. 42/D4
Limogne, Causse de (plat.), Fr. 42/D4
Limón, Hon. 144/E3
Limón, CR 145/F4
Limours, Fr. 30/J6
Limousin (mts.), Fr. 42/D4
Limousin (pol. reg.), Fr. 42/D4
Limoux, Fr. 42/E5
Limpopo (riv.), Moz. 93/F7
Lin Xian, China 79/C1
Lin'an, China 79/C1
Linapacan (isl.), Phil. 79/D6
Linard (peak), Swi. 57/G4
Linares, Mex. 143/F4
Linares, Chile 158/B2
Linaria, Gre. 47/J3
Linate (int'l arpt.), It. 58/C2
Lincang, China 83/H3
Lincheng, China 72/C3
Linchuan, China 79/C2
Lincoln, Arg. 158/E2
Lincoln (sea) 119/L1
Lincoln, Can.,Grld. 119/L1
Lincoln, Eng, UK 35/H5
Lincoln, De, US 139/R9
Lincoln, Il, US 137/L5
Lincoln, Me, US 131/G2
Lincoln (cap.), Ne, US 137/E2
Lincoln (co.), Ok, US 137/N14
Lincoln Beach, Or, US 138/B3
Lincoln City, Or, US 126/B4

Lincoln Heath (woodld.), Eng, UK 35/H5
Lincoln NP, Austl. 113/G5
Lincoln Park, Mi, US 135/F7
Lincoln Park, NJ, US 139/H8
Lincolnshire (co.), Eng, UK 35/H5
Lincolnshire Wolds (grsld.), Eng, UK 35/H4
Lincroft, NJ, US 138/D3
Lind, Den. 38/C3
Lind NP, Austl. 115/D3
Lindau, Ger. 57/F2
Lindau, Swi. 57/F1
Linde (riv.), Neth. 50/D3
Lindeman (chan.), Austl. 114/C3
Linden, Al, US 133/G3
Linden, Tx, US 129/J4
Linden, Guy. 153/G3
Linden, NJ, US 139/J9
Linden, Mi, US 135/E6
Linden, Ger. 54/B1
Linden Beach, On, Can. 135/G7
Lindenberg im Allgäu, Ger. 57/F2
Lindenfels, Ger. 54/B3
Lindenhurst, Ger. 51/E5
Lindenhurst, NY, US 139/E2
Lindenhurst, Il, US 135/P15
Lindenwold, NJ, US 138/D4
Lindern, Ger. 51/E3
Lindesberg, Swe. 38/F2
Lindesnes (cape), Nor. 38/B3
Lindewitt, Ger. 38/C3
Lindhorst, Ger. 51/E5
Lindi (pol. reg.), Tanz. 104/C5
Lindi, Tanz. 104/C5
Lindlar, Ger. 53/G1
Lindley, SAfr. 106/D2
Lindome, Swe. 38/E3
Lindon, Ut, US 137/K13
Lindre (lake), Fr. 53/F6
Lindsay, On, Can. 130/E2
Lindsay (mt.), Austl. 113/F3
Lindsay (mt.), Austl. 115/E1
Lindsdal, Swe. 38/G3
Line Mountain (mtn.), Pa, US 138/B2
Líneas de Nazca, Peru 156/C4
Lineboro, Md, US 138/B4
Linfen, China 72/B3
Ling (riv.), Sc, UK 36/A2
Ling Xian, China 83/K2
Ling Xian, China 72/D3
Lingbao, China 72/B4
Lingbi, China 72/D4
Lingchuan, China 83/H2
Lingchuan, China 72/C4
Linge (riv.), Neth. 50/C5
Lingen, Ger. 51/E3
Lingfield, Eng, UK 30/C3
Lingga (isls.), Indo. 80/B3
Linglestown, Pa, US 138/B3
Lingolsheim, Fr. 56/D1
Lingqiu, China 72/C3
Lingshan, China 83/J3
Lingshan, China 72/C3
Lingshi, China 72/B3
Lingshui, China 83/K4
Linguère, Sen. 102/B3
Lingyin Si, China 72/L9
Lingyuan, China 72/D2
Lingyun, China 83/J3
Linhai, China 79/C2
Linhares, Braz. 155/D1
Linhe, China 70/J3
Linli, China 79/B2
Linliu (mtn.), China 72/C3
Linne (lake), Sc, UK 36/A3
Linnich, Ger. 53/F2
Linntown, Pa, US 138/B2
Linosa (isl.), It. 100/N7
Linqing, China 72/C3
Linqu, China 72/D3
Linru, China 72/C4
Lins, Braz. 155/B2
Linschoten, Neth. 50/B4
Linshu, China 72/D4
Linta (riv.), Madg. 107/H9
Linth (riv.), Swi. 57/F3
Linthal, Swi. 57/F4
Linton, ND, US 137/J4
Linwood, Eng, UK 35/H5
Linwu, China 83/K2
Linxi, China 72/B4
Linyi, China 72/D4
Linyi, China 72/D4
Linyi, China 72/B4
Linz (int'l arpt.), Aus. 55/H6
Linz am Rhein, Ger. 53/G2
Linzhang, China 72/C3
Lion (gulf), Fr.,Sp. 45/G1
Lipa, Phil. 79/D5
Lipari, It. 46/D3
Lipari (isls.), It. 46/D3
Liperi, Fin. 60/F3

Lipetsk, Rus. 62/F1
Lipetsk (int'l arpt.), Rus. 62/F1
Lipetskaya Oblast, Rus. 62/F1
Lipez, Cordillera de (mts.), Bol. 150/E8
Lipez (riv.), Bol. 150/E8
Liping, China 83/J2
Lipljan, Serb. 47/G1
Lipno (res.), Czh. 55/H5
Lipno, Pol. 41/K2
Lipno, Údolní nádrž (lake), Czh. 43/L2
Lipova, Rom. 48/E2
Lipovka, NY, US 139/K8
Lippe (riv.), Ger. 40/D3
Lippstadt, Ger. 51/F5
Liptovský Svätý Mikuláš, Slvk. 41/K4
Liptrap (cape), Austl. 115/C3
Lira, Ugan. 104/C3
Lircay, Peru 156/C4
Liri (riv.), It. 46/C2
Liria, Sp. 45/E3
Liro (riv.), It. 54/B1
Lisboa, Port. 44/A3
Lisboa (dist.), Port. 44/A3
Lisboa (int'l arpt.), Port. 45/P10
Lisboa (Lisbon) (cap.), Port. 45/P10
Lisbon, ND, US 127/J4
Lisbon, Me, US 131/G2
Lisbon, Oh, US 138/A5
Lisburn, NI, UK 34/B2
Lisburn (dist.), NI, UK 34/B3
Lisburne (cape), Ak, US 134/E2
Lisdoonvarna, Ire. 31/P10
Liseleje, Den. 38/D3
Lisha (riv.), China 83/H2
Lishu, China 72/F2
Lishui, China 79/C2
Lisianski (isl.), Hi, US 117/H2
Lisieux, Fr. 42/D2
Liski, Rus. 62/F2
Lisle, Il, US 135/P16
L'Isle-Adam, Fr. 30/J4
L'Isle-en-Dodon, Fr. 42/D5
L'Isle-sur-la-Sorgue, Fr.
L'Isle-sur-le-Doubs, Fr. 56/C3
L'Isle-sur-Tarn, Fr. 42/D5
Lismore, Austl. 115/E1
Lismore, NI, UK 34/B3
Lišov, Czh. 55/H4
Lispeszentadorján, Hun. 48/C2
Lisse, Neth. 50/B4
Lisses, Fr. 30/K6
List, Ger. 38/C4
Lister (riv.), Ger. 51/E6
Listowel, On, Can. 130/D3
Listowel, Ire. 31/P10
Lit. Scarcies (riv.), SLeo. 102/B4
Litang, China 70/H6
Litang, China 83/H2
Liṭāni (riv.), Leb. 91/D3
Litava (riv.), Czh. 55/H2
Litchfield, Mn, US 127/K4
Litchfield, Il, US 129/K3
Litchfield Park, Az, US 137/R19
Lith, Neth. 50/C5
Litherland, Eng, UK 35/F5
Lithgow, Austl. 115/D2
Lithuania (ctry.) 39/K4
Litija, Slov. 43/L3
Lititz, Pa, US 138/B3
Litókhoron, Gre. 47/H2
Litoměřice, Czh. 55/H1
Littabella NP, Austl. 114/D3
Littau, Swi. 57/E3
Little (riv.), Ar, US 129/J4
Little (riv.), Ga, US 133/H4
Little (riv.), Tx, US 132/D4
Little (riv.), NC, US 133/J3
Little (riv.), Ok, US 137/N15
Little Abitibi (riv.), On, Can. 130/D1
Little Andaman (isl.), India 83/F5
Little Belt (mts.), Mt, US 126/F4
Little Bighorn Battlefield Nat'l Mon., Mt, US 126/G4
Little Bitter (lake), Egypt 91/C4
Little Blue (riv.), Ks,Ne, US 129/H2
Little Calumet (riv.), Il, US 135/Q16
Little Cayman (isl.), Cay. 141/E4
Little Colorado (riv.), Az, US 128/E4
Little Creek, De, US 138/C5
Little Cumbrae (isl.), Sc, UK 36/A5
Little Current (riv.), On, Can. 130/D1
Little Current, On, Can. 130/D2
Little Desert NP, Austl. 115/B3
Little Diomede (isl.), Ak, US 134/E2
Little Egg (har.), NJ, US 139/J8
Little Falls, Mn, US 127/K4
Little Falls, NJ, US 139/J8
Little Ferry, NJ, US 139/J8

Little Fork (riv.), Mn, US 127/K3
Little Inagua (isl.), Bahm. 141/G3
Little Karoo (valley), SAfr. 106/C4
Little Lehigh (riv.), Pa, US 138/C3
Little Minch (str.), Sc, UK 31/Q8
Little Missouri (riv.), Ar, US 129/J4
Little Neck (bay), NY, US 139/K8
Little Nicobar (isl.), India 83/F6
Little Para (res.), Austl. 113/M8
Little Para (riv.), Austl. 113/M8
Little Patuxent (riv.), Md, US 138/B5
Little Peconic (bay), NY, US 139/F2
Little Platte (riv.), Mo, US 137/D5
Little Prairie, Wi, US 135/N14
Little Red (riv.), Ar, US 129/K4
Little Rock (cap.), Ar, US 129/J4
Little Schuylkill (riv.), Pa, US 138/B2
Little Sioux (riv.), Ia, US 125/G3
Little Smoky (riv.), Ab, Can. 126/D2
Little Snake (riv.), Co, US 128/E2
Little Stour (riv.), Eng, UK 33/H4
Little Wabash (riv.), Il, US 129/K3
Little White (riv.), SD, US 129/G2
Little Wood (riv.), Id, US 126/E5
Little Zab (riv.), Iraq 90/E3
Littleborough, Eng, UK 35/F4
Littlefield, Tx, US 129/G4
Littlehampton, Eng, UK 33/F5
Littlerock, Ca, US 136/C1
Littlestown, Pa, US 138/A4
Littleton, NH, US 131/G2
Littleton, Co, US 137/B3
Littleton, Ma, US 139/L7
Litvínov, Czh. 55/G1
Liu (riv.), China 79/A3
Liu (riv.), China 72/E2
Liuba, China 70/J5
Liucheng, China 83/J3
Liulin, China 72/B3
Liuwa Plain NP, Zam. 105/D3
Liuyang, China 83/H2
Liuzhou, China 83/J3
Livádhion, Gre. 47/H3
Livanátai, Gre. 47/H3
Liverdun, Fr. 53/F6
Liverdy-en-Brie, Fr. 30/L5
Livermore (mt.), US 159/J11
Livermore, Ca, US 136/C4
Liverpool (cape), Nun., Can. 123/J1
Liverpool, NS, Can. 131/H2
Liverpool (bay), NW, Can. 122/C1
Liverpool, Eng, UK 35/F5
Liverpool (co.), Eng, UK 35/F5
Liverpool (bay), Wal, UK 34/E5
Liverpool, Pa, US 138/B2
Livigno, It. 57/G4
Livilliers, Fr. 30/J4
Livingston, Guat. 144/D3
Livingston (co.), Mi, US 135/G6
Livingston, Mt, US 126/F4
Livingston, NJ, US 139/H8
Livingston, Tx, US 129/J5
Livingston (lake), Tx, US 129/J5
Livingstone, Zam. 105/E4
Livingstone (falls), Congo 105/B2
Livingstone (mts.), Ab, Can. 126/E3
Livno, Bosn. 48/C4
Livny, Rus. 62/F1
Livojoki (riv.), Fin. 37/H7
Livonia, Mi, US 130/D3
Livorno, It. 58/D6
Livorno (prov.), It. 58/D6
Livorno, Ca, US 135/L10
Livorno Ferraris, It. 58/B2
Livramento do Brumado, Braz. 155/L10
Livron-sur-Drôme, Fr. 42/F4
Livry-Gargan, Fr. 30/K5
Lixin, China 72/D4
Lixnaw, Ire. 31/P10
Lixoúrion, Gre. 47/G3
Lizard (pt.), Eng, UK 32/A7
Lizard, The (pen.), Eng, UK 32/A6

Lizy-sur-Ourcq, Fr. 52/C5
Ljubic, Serb. 48/E4
Ljubija, Bosn. 48/C3
Ljubinje, Bosn. 47/F1
Ljubljana (cap.), Slov. 43/L3
Ljubuški, Bosn. 47/E1
Ljungan (riv.), Swe. 37/F3
Ljungby, Swe. 38/E3
Ljungsbro, Swe. 38/F2
Ljungskile, Swe. 38/D2
Ljusnan (riv.), Swe. 37/E3
Ljusne, Swe. 38/G1
Ljustera (isl.), Swe. 39/H2
Lkst (peak), Mor. 98/C3
Llabanere (int'l arpt.), Fr. 42/E5
Llaillay, Chile 158/N8
Llallagua, Bol. 150/E7
Llalli, Peru 156/D4
Llanberis, Pass of (pass), Wal, UK 34/D5
Llancañelo (lake), Arg. 158/C2
Llandovery, Wal, UK 32/C3
Llandrindod Wells, Wal, UK 32/C2
Llandudno, Wal, UK 34/D5
Llanes, Sp. 44/C1
Llanfairfechan, Wal, UK 34/E5
Llangollen, Wal, UK 35/E6
Llanidloes, Wal, UK 32/C2
Llano (riv.), Tx, US 129/H5
Llano, Tx, US 129/H5
Llano Estacado (plain), US 129/G4
Llanos (plain), Col.,Ven. 147/D2
Llanquihue (lake), Chile 158/B4
Llata, Peru 156/B3
Lleida, Sp. 45/F2
Llera de Canales, Mex. 143/F4
Llerena, Sp. 44/B3
Lleyn (pen.), Wal, UK 34/D6
Llívia, Sp. 45/F1
Llobregat (riv.), Sp. 45/F1
Llodio, Sp. 44/D1
Lloret de Mar, Sp. 45/G2
Llorona (pt.), CR 140/E6
Lloyd (pt.), NY, US 139/M8
Lloyd Harbor, NY, US 139/M8
Lloydminster, Sk, Can. 126/F2
Lloyds (riv.), Nf, Can. 131/K1
Lluchmayor, Sp. 45/H3
Llullaillaco (vol.), Arg.,Chile 157/C1
Llwchwr (riv.), Wal, UK 32/C3
Llynfi (riv.), Wal, UK 32/C3
Loa, Ut, US 128/E3
Loa (riv.), Chile 147/C5
Loanhead, Sc, UK 36/C5
Loano, It. 58/B4
Loaoya (canal), Sp. 45/N8
Lobatse, Bots. 105/D5
Lobbes, Belg. 53/D3
Loberia, Arg. 158/F3
Lobethal, Austl. 113/M8
Lobez, Pol. 41/H2
Lobito, Ang. 105/B3
Lobitos, Peru 156/A2
Lobo (riv.), C.d'Iv. 102/D5
Lobos, Arg. 159/J11
Lobos de Tierra, Isla (isl.), Peru 150/B5
Lobos, Punta de (pt.), Chile 158/M9
Locarno, Swi. 57/E5
Loch na Sealga (lake), Sc, UK 36/A1
Loch Raven (res.), Md, US 138/B5
Lochaber (reg.), Sc, UK 36/A3
Locharbriggs, Sc, UK 34/E1
Lochau, Aus. 57/F3
Lochboisdale, Sc, UK 31/Q8
Lochbuie (co.), Sc, UK 137/C2
Lochem, Neth. 50/D4
Loches, Fr. 42/D3
Lochgelly, Sc, UK 36/C4
Lochgilphead, Sc, UK 36/A4
Lochindorb (lake), Sc, UK 36/C2
Lochmaben, Sc, UK 34/E1
Lochmaddy, Sc, UK 31/Q8
Lochnagar (mt.), Sc, UK 36/C3
Lochristi, Belg. 52/C1
Lochwinnoch, Sc, UK 36/B5
Lochy (riv.), Sc, UK 36/B3
Lochy (riv.), Sc, UK 36/B3
Lock, Austl. 113/F5
Lock Haven, Pa, US 138/B2
Locke, Ca, US 135/L10
Lockerbie, Sc, UK 35/E1
Lockhart, Austl. 115/C2
Lockington, Austl. 115/C3
Locknitz (riv.), Ger. 40/D2
Lockport, NY, US 131/S9
Lockport, Il, US 135/P16
Lockwood (res.), Eng, UK 30/C2
Locon, Fr. 52/B2
Locri, It. 46/E3
Locust Fork (riv.), Al, US 133/G3

Lod, Isr. 91/F8
Loddon (riv.), Austl. 115/A1
Loddon (riv.), Eng, UK 33/A4
Lodenice (riv.), Czh. 55/H2
Lodève, Fr. 42/E5
Lodeynoye Pole, Rus. 60/G3
Lodhrān, Pak. 86/A5
Lodi, It. 58/C2
Lodi (prov.), It. 58/C2
Lodi, Ca, US 128/B3
Lodi, NJ, US 139/J8
Lodi Vecchio, It. 58/C2
Lodja, D.R. Congo 105/D1
Lodosa, Sp. 44/D1
Lodrino, Swi. 57/E5
Łódź, Pol. 41/K3
Łódzkie (prov.), Pol. 41/K3
Loei, Thai. 78/C2
Loenen, Neth. 50/D4
Loeriesfontein, SAfr. 106/B3
Lofa (co.), Libr. 102/C5
Lofa (riv.), Libr. 102/C5
Löffingen, Ger. 57/E2
Lofoten (isle.), Nor. 37/D2
Lofty (range), Austl. 112/C3
Lofty (mt.), Austl. 113/M8
Logan (mt.), Yk, Can. 134/K3
Logan, NM, US 132/C3
Logan, Oh, US 130/D4
Logan (co.), Ok, US 137/N14
Logan, Ut, US 126/F5
Logan, WV, US 130/D4
Logan (isl.), NY, US 139/J8
Logan (mtn.), Wal, UK 32/C1
Loganton, Pa, US 138/A1
Logansport, In, US 130/A1
Logatec, Slov. 43/L4
Logone (riv.), Chad 93/D3
Lograto, It. 58/D2
Logroño, Sp. 44/D1
Logrosán, Sp. 44/C3
Løgstør, Den. 38/C3
Løgten, Den. 38/D3
Lohals, Den. 38/D4
Lohārdaga, India 85/E4
Lohfelden, Ger. 51/G6
Lohja, Fin. 39/L1
Lohjanjärvi (lake), Fin. 39/K1
Lohmar, Ger. 53/G2
Löhnberg, Ger. 54/B1
Löhne, Ger. 51/F4
Lohne, Ger. 51/F4
Lohr, Ger. 54/C3
Loi-kaw, Myan. 83/G4
Loi Lun (range), China,Mya 70/G7
Loing (riv.), Fr. 40/B5
Loir (riv.), Fr. 42/D3
Loire (riv.), Fr. 27/E4
Loisin (riv.), Fr. 53/E5
Loita (hills), Kenya 97/N8
Loja (prov.), Ecu. 156/B2
Loja, Ecu. 156/B2
Loja, Sp. 44/C4
Løjt Kirkeby, Den. 38/C4
Lokeren, Belg. 52/D1
Lokitaung, Kenya 104/B1
Løkken, Den. 38/C3
Lokoja, Nga. 103/G5
Lokolo (riv.), D.R. Congo 97/K8
Lokomby, Madg. 107/H8
Lokoro (riv.), D.R. Congo 97/J8
Lőkösháza, Hun. 48/E2
Loks (isl.), Nun., Can. 123/K2
Lol (riv.), Sudan 97/L6
Lolland (isl.), Den. 37/D5
Lollar, Ger. 54/B3
Lolo (peak), Mt, US 126/F4
Lolui (isl.), Ugan. 104/B3
Lom, Nor. 37/D3
Lom Sak, Thai. 78/C2
Loma (mts.), SLeo. 96/C6
Loma (pt.), Ca, US 136/C5
Loma Bonita, Mex. 144/C2
Loma Linda, Ca, US 136/C2
Loma Mansa (peak), SLeo. 102/C4
Loma Negra, Arg. 158/E3
Lomami (riv.), D.R. Congo 93/G6
Lomas de Zamora, Arg. 159/J11
Lomazzo, It. 58/C1
Lombard, Il, US 135/P16
Lombardia, Serra (mts.), Braz. 151/H3
Lombardia, Mex. 142/E5
Lombardia (pol. reg.), It. 43/H4
Lomblen (isl.), Indo. 81/F5
Lombok (isl.), Indo. 67/L10
Lomé (int'l arpt.), Togo 103/F5
Lomé (cap.), Togo 103/F5
Lomello, It. 58/B2
Lometa, Tx, US 132/C4
Lomma, Swe. 38/E4
Lomme, Fr. 52/B2
Lommel, Belg. 50/C6
Lomnice, Czh. 55/G4
Lomnice nad Lužnicí, Czh. 55/H4
Lomond (lake), Sc, UK 36/B4
Lomond (hills), Sc, UK 36/C4
Lomonosov, Rus. 61/S7
Lompobatang (peak), Indo. 81/E5

Lompoc, Ca, US 128/B4
Łomża, Pol. 41/M2
Lonato, It. 58/D2
Lonāvale, India 89/K5
Loncoche, Chile 158/B3
Loncopué, Arg. 158/C3
Londerzeel, Belg. 53/D2
London, On, Can. 130/D3
London (reef), Nic. 145/F3
London (cap.), UK 30/C2
London, Ky, US 130/C4
London, City of (bor.), Eng, UK 30/A1
Londonderry (cape), Austl. 109/B2
Londonderry (isl.), Chile 159/C7
Londonderry (dist.), NI, UK 34/A2
Londonderry, NI, UK 34/A2
Londrina, Braz. 155/B2
Lone (riv.), Ger. 54/C5
Lone Grove, Ok, US 129/H4
Lone Jack, Mo, US 137/E6
Lone Pine Sanctuary, Austl. 114/E7
Lonesome NP, Austl. 114/C4
Long, Ak, US 134/G3
Long (lake), On, Can. 127/M3
Long (lake), Sc, UK 36/A2
Long (riv.), China 79/A3
Long (isl.), Bahm. 141/F3
Long (isl.), NY, US 131/F3
Long (mtn.), Wal, UK 32/C1
Long (str.), Rus. 65/T2
Long Beach, Wa, US 126/B4
Long Beach, On, Can. 131/R10
Long Beach (isl.), NJ, US 138/D4
Long Beach, Ca, US 136/F8
Long Beach, NY, US 139/L9
Long Branch, NJ, US 138/E3
Long Cay (isl.), India 145/H1
Long Crag (hill), Eng, UK 36/F6
Long Eaton, Eng, UK 35/G6
Long Grove, Il, US 135/P15
Long Hill, Ct, US 139/E1
Long, Loch (inlet), Sc, UK 36/B4
Long Mynd, The (hill), Eng, UK 32/D1
Long Neck (pt.), Ct, US 139/M7
Long Range (mts.), Nf, Can. 131/K2
Long Valley, NJ, US 139/H1
Long Xuyen, Viet. 78/D4
Longá (riv.), Braz. 154/B1
Longare, It. 59/E2
Longarone, It. 59/F1
Longboat Key, Fl, US 133/H6
Longbranch, Wa, US 135/B3
Longchang, China 83/J2
Longchuan, China 83/G3
Longchuan, China 83/G3
Longde, China 70/J4
Longeau (riv.), Fr. 53/E5
Longeville-en-Barrois, Fr. 53/E6
Longeville-lès-Metz, Fr. 53/F5
Longeville-lès-Saint-Avold, Fr. 53/F5
Longfellow (mts.), Me, US 131/G2
Longfield, Eng, UK 30/D2
Longford, Austl. 115/D4
Longford, Ire. 31/Q10
Longhua, China 72/D2
Longhui, China 83/J2
Longhui, China 83/K3
Longjumeau, Fr. 30/J5
Longkou, China 72/E3
Longlac, On, Can. 127/M3
Longli, China 83/J2
Longmen, China 79/B3
Longmen Shiyao, China 72/C4
Longmont, Co, US 137/B2
Longnan, China 79/B3
Longniddry, Sc, UK 36/D5
Longperrier, Fr. 30/K4
Longpont-sur-Orge, Fr. 30/J6
Longport, NJ, US 138/D5
Longpré-les-Corps-Saints, Fr. 52/A3
Longquan, China 79/C2
Longreach, Austl. 114/B3
Longshan, China 79/A2
Longshou (mts.), China 70/H4
Longueau, Fr. 52/B4
Longueil-Annel, Fr. 52/B5
Longuenesse, Fr. 52/B2
Longuesse, Fr. 30/H4
Longueuil, Qu, Can. 131/P6
Longuyon, Fr. 53/E5
Longvic, Fr. 56/B3
Longview, Wa, US 126/B4
Longview, Tx, US 129/J4
Longwood Gardens, Pa, US 138/C4
Longwy, Fr. 53/E4
Longyan, China 79/C2
Longyearbyen, Nor. 64/B2
Longyou, China 79/C2
Longzhou, China 78/D1
Loni, India 89/K5
Lonigo, It. 59/E2
Löningen, Ger. 51/E3
Lonquimay, Arg. 158/E3

Lons, Fr. 42/C5
Lons-le-Saunier, Fr. 56/B4
Lönsboda, Swe. 38/F3
Lontzen, Belg. 53/F2
Lonza (riv.), Swi. 56/D5
Looe (isl.), Eng, UK 32/B6
Lookout (cape), NC, US 133/J3
Lookout (pt.), Austl. 114/B1
Loolmalasin (peak), Tanz. 104/B3
Loon Lake, Sk, Can. 126/F1
Loon op Zand, Neth. 50/C5
Loop Head (pt.), Ire. 30/P10
Loos, Fr. 52/C2
Lop Buri, Thai. 78/C3
Lopary, Madg. 107/H8
Lopez (cape), Gabon 96/G8
López Mateos, Mex. 143/Q9
Lopik, Neth. 50/B5
Lopori (riv.), D.R. Congo 97/K7
Lopphavet (bay), Nor. 37/G1
Loppi, Fin. 39/L1
Lora del Río, Sp. 44/C4
Lorain, Oh, US 130/D3
Loralai, Pak. 89/J2
Lorca, Sp. 44/E4
Lord Howe (isl.), Austl. 116/E8
Lordsburg, NM, US 128/E4
Lorelei, Ger. 53/G3
Lorena, Braz. 211/H7
Lorengau, PNG 116/D5
Lørenskog, Nor. 38/D2
Lorentz (riv.), Indo. 81/J5
Lorentzsluizen (dam), Neth. 50/C2
Loreo, It. 59/F2
Loreto, Braz. 154/A2
Loreto, It. 59/G6
Loreto, Mex. 142/C3
Loreto (int'l arpt.), Mex. 142/C3
Loreto, Mex. 142/E4
Loreto, Ecu. 152/B5
Loreto (state), Peru 152/C5
Lorette, Mb, Can. 127/J3
Lorgues, Fr. 43/G5
Lorian (swamp), Kenya 97/N7
Lorica, Col. 152/C2
Lorient, Fr. 42/B3
L'Oriental (pol. reg.), Mor. 99/E2
Lorillard (riv.), Nun., Can. 122/G2
Lorinci, Hun. 41/K5
Loring, Ks, US 137/D5
Loriol-sur-Drôme, Fr. 42/F4
Lorn, Firth of (inlet), Sc, UK 31/Q8
Lorne, Austl. 115/B3
Lorosuk (peak), Kenya 104/B2
Lorquin, Fr. 53/G6
Lörrach, Ger. 56/D2
Lorrain (plat.), Fr. 40/D4
Lorraine (pol. reg.), Fr. 42/G2
Lorraine (pol. reg.), Fr. 56/C1
Lorraine, Qu, Can. 131/N6
Lorraine (reg.), Fr. 53/E5
Lorsch, Ger. 54/B3
Lorup, Ger. 51/E3
Los Alamitos, Ca, US 136/F8
Los Alamos, NM, US 129/F4
Los Alerces, PN, Arg. 157/B5
Los Altos, Ca, US 135/K12
Los Amates, Guat. 144/D3
Los Andes, Chile 158/N8
Los Andes, Col. 152/B4
Los Angeles, Chile 158/B3
Los Angeles, Ca, US 136/F7
Los Angeles (co.), Ca, US 136/B2
Los Angeles (int'l arpt.), Ca, US 136/F8
Los Angeles (riv.), Ca, US 136/B2
Los Angeles Outer (har.), Ca, US 136/F8
Los Aquijes, Peru 156/C4
Los Aztecas, Mex. 143/F4
Los Banos, Ca, US 128/B3
Los Barrios, Sp. 44/C4
Los Canarreos (arch.), Cuba 145/F1
Los Cardales, Arg. 159/J11
Los Cerrillos, Uru. 159/K11
Los Chonos (arch.), Chile 147/B7
Los Corrales de Buelna, Sp. 44/C1
Los Glaciares, PN, Arg. 157/B6
Los Katios, PN, Col. 152/B3
Los Lagos, Chile 158/B3
Los Lagos (pol. reg.), Chile 158/B4
Los Llanos de Aridane, Canl.,Sp. 98/A3
Los Lunas, NM, US 128/F4
Los Mármoles, PN, Mex. 144/B1
Los Menucos, Arg. 158/C4
Los Mochis, Mex. 142/C3
Los Mosquitos (gulf), Pan. 145/F4
Los Muermos, Chile 158/B4
Los Navalmorales, Sp. 44/C3
Los Navalucillos, Sp. 44/C3
Los Órganos, Peru 156/A2
Los Padres National Forest, Ca, US 136/A1
Los Palacios y Villafranca, Sp. 44/C4
Los Pingüinos, PN, Chile 159/C7
Los Planes, Mex. 142/C3
Los Reyes, Mex. 143/R10
Los Reyes de Salgado, Mex. 142/E5
Los Ríos (prov.), Ecu. 156/B1
Los Roques, Islas (isls.), Ven. 150/E1
Los Santos, Pan. 152/A3
Los Santos de Maimona, Sp. 44/B3
Los Sauces, Chile 158/B3
Los Taques, Ven. 152/D2
Los Teques, Ven. 150/E1
Los Testigos (isls.), Ven. 153/F2
Los Vilos, Chile 158/C1
Los Yébenes, Sp. 44/D3
Losai Nat'l Rsv., Kenya 104/C2
Losheim, Ger. 53/F4
Losice, Pol. 41/M2
Lošinj (isl.), Cro. 48/B3
Losne, Fr. 56/B3
Losone, Swi. 57/E5
Losoya, Tx, US 137/U21
Lossburg, Ger. 57/E1
Losser, Neth. 50/E4
Lossie (riv.), Sc, UK 36/C1
Lössnitz, Ger. 55/F1
Lossoganeu (hill), Tanz. 104/C4
Lost River (range), Id, US 128/D1
Lost River Caverns, Pa, US 138/C2
Lostallo, Swi. 57/F5
Lot (riv.), Fr. 42/D4
Lota, Chile 158/B3
Lotawana (lake), Mo, US 137/E6
Løten, Nor. 38/D1
Lotte, Ger. 51/E4
Lotuke (peak), Sudan 104/B1
Lotung, Tai. 79/D3
Lou (riv.), China 72/B5
Louang Namtha, Laos 83/H3
Louangphrabang, Laos 83/H4
Loubomo, Congo 105/B1
Loudéac, Fr. 42/B2
Loudi, China 83/K2
Loudun, Fr. 42/D3
Loue (riv.), Fr. 42/F3
Loufan, China 72/B3
Louga (pol. reg.), Sen. 102/B3
Louga, Sen. 102/A3
Lough Foyle (lake), UK 34/A1
Loughborough, Eng, UK 33/E1
Loughbrickland, NI, UK 34/B3
Lougheed (isl.), Nun., Can. 123/R7
Loughgall, NI, UK 34/B3
Loughrea, Ire. 31/P10
Loughton, Eng, UK 30/D2
Louhans, Fr. 56/B4
Louis Botha (Durban) (int'l arpt.), SAfr. 107/E3
Louisiade (arch.), PNG 116/E6
Louisiana (state), US 132/E4
Louisville, Co, US 137/B3
Louisville, Ky, US 130/C4
Louisville, Ms, US 133/F3
Loukkos (riv.), Mor. 100/A2
Loulé, Port. 44/A4
Louny, Czh. 55/G2
Loup (riv.), Ne, US 127/J5
Loup, Middle (riv.), Ne, US 127/H5
Loup, North (riv.), Ne, US 127/H5
Loup, South (riv.), Ne, US 127/J5
Lourches, Fr. 52/C3
Lourdes, Fr. 42/C5
Lourdes/Tarbes (int'l arpt.), Fr. 42/D5
Loures, Port. 45/P10
Louriçal, Port. 44/A3
Lourinhã, Port. 44/A3
Lousã, Port. 44/A2
Lousa, Port. 45/Q10
Louth, Eng, UK 35/H5
Louth (co.), Ire. 34/B4
Louth, Ire. 34/B4
Loutrá Aidhipsoú, Gre. 47/H3
Loutrákion, Gre. 47/H4
Loútsa, Gre. 47/P9
Louvain (Leuven), Belg. 53/D2
Louveira, Braz. 211/G8
Louviers, Fr. 42/D2
Louviers, Co, US 137/B4
Louvigné-du-Désert, Fr. 42/C2
Louvres, Fr. 30/K4
Louvroil, Fr. 52/C3
Lovaart (riv.), Belg. 52/B1
Lovat' (riv.), Rus. 60/F4
Lovat' (riv.), Bela.,Rus. 39/P3
Lovćen NP, Serb. 47/F1
Lovćenac, Serb. 48/D3
Love Point, Md, US 138/B5
Lovech (prov.), Bul. 47/J1
Loveland, Co, US 137/B2
Loveland (lake), Co, US 137/B2
Lovell, Wy, US 126/F4
Lovelock, Nv, US 128/C2
Lovere, It. 58/D1
Loving, NM, US 129/F4
Lovington, NM, US 129/G4
Lovios, Sp. 44/A2
Lövő, Hun. 43/M3
Lovosice, Czh. 55/H1
Lovozero (lake), Rus. 60/G2
Low (cape), Nun., Can. 123/H2
Lowa (riv.), D.R. Congo 93/E5
Lowell, Ma, US 131/G3
Löwen (riv.), Namb. 106/B2
Löwenstein, Ger. 54/C4
Lower (bay), NJ, US 138/D2
Lower (dam), Wa, US 135/D3
Lower Arrow (lake), BC, Can. 126/D3
Lower Engadine (valley), Swi. 57/G4
Lower Ganges (canal), India 84/B2
Lower Glenelg NP, Austl. 115/B3
Lower Hutt, NZ 117/S11
Lower Kalskag, Ak, US 134/F3
Lower Latham (res.), Co, US 137/C2
Lower Otay (lake), Ca, US 136/D5
Lower Red (lake), Mn, US 127/K4
Lower Rhine (riv.), Neth. 50/C5
Lower Rouge (riv.), Mi, US 135/E7
Lower Trajan's Wall, Mol.,Ukr. 62/D3
Lower Tunguska (riv.), Rus. 67/J3
Lower Zambezi NP, Zam. 105/E4
Lowestoft, Eng, UK 33/H2
Lowi (riv.), D.R. Congo 105/E1
Łowicz, Pol. 41/K2
Lowther (hills), Sc, UK 36/C6
Loxstedt, Ger. 51/F2
Loxton, SAfr. 106/C3
Loxton, Austl. 113/J5
Loyalton, Pa, US 138/B2
Loyalty (isls.), NCal. 116/F7
Loyettes, Fr. 56/B6
Loyne (lake), Sc, UK 36/A2
Loysville, Pa, US 138/A3
Loznica, Serb. 48/D3
Loznitsa, Bul. 49/H4
Lozova, Ukr. 62/F2
Lozovik, Serb. 48/E3
Lu (mtn.), China 72/D3
Lu (riv.), China 72/C5
Lu Xian, China 83/J2
Lualaba (riv.), D.R. Congo 93/E5
Luan (riv.), China 72/D2
Lu'an, China 72/D5
Luan Xian, China 72/D3
Luanchuan, China 72/B4
Luanco, Sp. 44/C1
Luanda (cap.), Ang. 105/B2
Luang (peak), Thai. 78/B4
Luang Lagoon (lag.), Thai. 83/H6
Luangwa (riv.), Zam. 105/F2
Luangwe, Zam. 104/A5
Luanping, China 72/D2
Luanshya, Zam. 105/E3
Luapula (prov.), Zam. 104/A5
Luarca, Sp. 44/B1
Luba, EqG. 96/G7
Lubaantun (ruin), Belz. 144/D2
Lubaczów, Pol. 41/M3
Lubań, Pol. 41/H3
Lubango, Ang. 105/B3
Lubansenshi (riv.), Zam. 104/A5
Lubartów, Pol. 41/M3
Lubawa, Pol. 41/K2
Lübbecke, Ger. 51/F4
Lubbeek, Belg. 53/D2
Lubbock, Tx, US 129/G4
Lubelska (uplands), Pol. 41/M3
Lubelskie (prov.), Pol. 41/M3
Lubero (riv.), D.R. Congo 104/A3
Lubień Kujawski, Pol. 41/K2
Lubin, Pol. 41/J3
Lublin, Pol. 41/M3
Lubliniec, Pol. 41/K3
Lubmin, Ger. 38/E4
Lubnaig (lake), Sc, UK 36/B4
Lubny, Ukr. 62/E2
Luboń, Pol. 41/J2
Lubrín, Sp. 44/D4
Lubsko, Pol. 41/H3
Lubudi, D.R. Congo 105/E2
Lubuklinggau, Indo. 80/B4
Lubuksikaping, Indo. 80/B3
Lubumbashi, D.R. Congo 105/E3
Lubuskie (prov.), Pol. 41/H2
Lucan, Ire. 34/B5
Lucania (mt.), Yk, Can. 134/K3
Lucas González, Arg. 159/J10
Lucca (prov.), It. 58/D5
Lucca, It. 58/D5
Lucciana, Fr. 46/A1
Luce (bay), Sc, UK 34/D2
Lucedale, Ms, US 133/F4
Lucélia, Braz. 155/B2
Lucena, Phil. 79/D5
Lucena, Sp. 44/C4
Lucena del Cid, Sp. 45/E2
Lučenec, Slvk. 41/K4
Lucens, Swi. 56/C4
Lucerne, Co, US 137/C2
Lucerne (lake), Swi. 43/H3
Lucerne (Vierwaldstättersee) (lake), Swi. 57/E3
Lucheng, China 72/C3
Lüchow, Ger. 40/F2
Lucindale, Austl. 115/B3
Luckeesarai, India 85/F3
Luckenwalde, Ger. 41/G2
Lucknow, India 84/C2
Lucky Lake, Sk, Can. 126/G3
Luco dei Marsi, It. 46/C2
Lucomagno, Passo del (pass), Swi. 57/E4
Lucrecia (cape), Cuba 145/H1
Lucrezia, It. 59/F5
Luda Kamchiya (riv.), Bul. 47/K1
Lüdenscheid, Ger. 51/E6
Lüderitz, Namb. 106/A2
Ludesch, Aus. 57/F3
Ludhiāna, India 86/C4
Ludian, China 83/H2
Ludinghausen, Ger. 51/E5
Ludington, Mi, US 130/C3
Ludogorie (reg.), Bul. 49/H4
Ludvika, Swe. 38/F1
Ludwigs (canal), Ger. 55/E4
Ludwigsburg, Ger. 54/C5
Ludwigsfelde, Ger. 40/Q7
Ludwigshafen, Ger. 57/F2
Ludwigshafen, Ger. 54/B4
Ludwigslust, Ger. 40/F2
Ludwigsstadt, Ger. 55/E2
Luebo, D.R. Congo 105/D2
Luena, Ang. 105/C3
Lufeng, China 79/C3
Lufkin, Tx, US 129/J5
Luga (bay), Rus. 39/N2
Luga, Rus. 39/N2
Luga (riv.), Rus. 39/N2
Lugagnano, It. 59/D2
Lugagnano Val d'Arda, It. 58/C3
Lugano, Swi. 57/E6
Lugano (lake), It. 57/E6
Luganville, Van. 116/F6
Lugards (falls), Kenya 104/C3
Lugavčina, Serb. 48/E3
Lügde, Ger. 51/G5
Lugenda (riv.), Moz. 105/G3
Lugg (riv.), Eng, UK 32/D2
Lugg (riv.), Wal, UK 32/C2
Lugnaquillia (peak), Ire. 34/B6
Lugo, It. 59/E4
Lugo, Sp. 44/B1
Lugogo (riv.), Ugan. 104/B2
Lugoj, Rom. 48/E3
Lugrin, Fr. 56/C5
Lugunga (peak), Tanz. 104/C4
Luhan (int'l arpt.), Ukr. 62/F2
Luhans'k, Ukr. 62/F2
Luhans'ka Oblasti, Ukr. 62/F2
Lühe (riv.), Ger. 51/H2
Luhe, China 72/D4
Luhe (riv.), Ger. 55/F3
Luhe-Wildenau, Ger. 55/F3
Luhombero (peak), Tanz. 104/C4
Luichart (lake), Sc, UK 36/B1
Luino, It. 57/E6
Luis B. Sánchez, Mex. 142/B1
Luís Correia, Braz. 154/B1
Luján, Arg. 159/J11
Lujiang, China 72/D5
Lukácsháza, Hun. 43/M3
Lukang, Tai. 79/D3
Lukavac, Bosn. 48/D3
Luke (mt.), Austl. 112/C3
Lukenie (riv.), D.R. Congo 105/C1
Lukovit, Bul. 47/J1
Łuków, Pol. 41/M3
Lukuga (riv.), D.R. Congo 104/A4
Lukulu, Zam. 105/D3
Lukulu (riv.), Zam. 104/A5
Lukunor (isl.), Micr. 116/E4
Luleå, Swe. 60/D2
Luleälven (riv.), Swe. 37/G2
Luliang, China 83/H2
Luling, La, US 137/P17
Luling (pass), China 72/B4
Lulong, China 72/D3
Lulonga (riv.), D.R. Congo 93/E4
Lulsgate (int'l arpt.), Eng, UK 32/D4
Lulua (riv.), D.R. Congo 93/E5
Lumangwe (falls), Zam. 104/A5
Lumberton, Tx, US 129/J5
Lumberton, NC, US 133/J3
Lumberton, NJ, US 138/D4
Lumbini (zone), Nepal 84/D2
Lumbo, Moz. 105/H4
Lumbrales, Sp. 44/B2
Lumbrein, Swi. 57/F4
Lumbres, Fr. 52/B2
Lumby, BC, Can. 126/D3
Lumding, India 83/F2
Lumigny-Nesles-Ormeaux, Fr. 30/L5
Luminárias, Braz. 211/J6
Lummen, Belg. 53/E2
Lumparland, Fin. 39/J1
Lumsden, Sk, Can. 127/G3
Lumsden, NZ 117/R12
Lumut, Malay. 80/B3
Luna (mtn.), Ca, US 136/C2
Lunahuaná, Peru 156/B4
Lund, Swe. 38/E4
Lundazi, Zam. 105/F3
Lundby, Den. 38/D4
Lundi (riv.), Zim. 105/F5
Lundy (isl.), Eng, UK 32/B4
Lune (riv.), Ger. 51/F2
Lune (riv.), Eng, UK 35/F2
Lüneburg, Ger. 51/H2
Lüneburger Heide (reg.), Ger. 40/F2
Lunel, Fr. 42/F5
Lünen, Ger. 51/E5
Lunenburg, NS, Can. 131/H2
Lunestedt, Ger. 51/F2
Lunéville, Fr. 43/G2
Lung Kwu Chau (isl.), China 71/T10
Lunga (riv.), Zam. 105/E3
Lungern, Swi. 56/E4
Lungi, SLeo. 102/B4
Lungi (Freetown) (int'l arpt.), SLeo. 102/B4
Lunglei, India 83/F3
Lungue-Bungo (riv.), Ang. 105/C3
Luni (riv.), India 89/K3
Lünne, Ger. 51/E4
Luocheng, China 83/J3
Luodian, China 83/J2
Luoding, China 83/K3
Luohe, China 72/C4
Luoma (lake), China 72/D4
Luongo (riv.), Zam. 104/A5
Luoning, China 72/B4
Luoshan, China 72/C4
Luoshuikan, China 79/A1
Luoyang, China 72/C4
Luoyuan, China 79/C2
Luozi, D.R. Congo 105/B1
Lupanshui, China 83/H2
Luqa (int'l arpt.), Malta 46/L7
Luqu, China 70/H5
Luquan, China 83/H2
Lūrah (riv.), Afg. 89/J2
Lure, Fr. 56/C2
Lurgan, NI, UK 34/B3
Luri, Fr. 43/H5
Lurín, Peru 156/B4
Lúrio, Moz. 105/H3
Lúrio (riv.), Moz. 93/F6
Lurnfeld, Aus. 43/K3
Lurøy, Nor. 37/E2
Lusaka (cap.), Zam. 105/E4
Lusambo, D.R. Congo 105/D1
Lusen (peak), Ger. 55/G5
Lusenga NP, Zam. 104/A5
Lushan, China 72/C4
Lushi, China 72/B4
Lushnjë, Alb. 47/F2
Lushoto, Tanz. 104/C4
Lushui, China 83/G2
Lusignan, Fr. 42/D3
Lusk, Wy, US 127/G5
Lusk, Ire. 34/B4
Lustenau, Aus. 57/F3
Lutanga (riv.), D.R. Congo 97/J7
Luther, Ok, US 137/N14
Luthern, Swi. 56/D3
Lutherville, Md, US 138/B5
Lütjehorn (isl.), Ger. 50/D1
Lütjenburg, Ger. 38/D4
Luton, Eng, UK 33/F3
Luton (co.), Eng, UK 33/F3
Luton (int'l arpt.), Eng, UK 33/F3
Lutry, Swi. 56/C5
Lutselk'e, NW, Can. 122/E2
Luts'k, Ukr. 62/C2
Lutter (riv.), Ger. 51/F5
Lutterbach, Fr. 56/D2
Lutz (riv.), Aus. 57/F3
Lützow-Holm (bay), Ant. 160/C
Luumäki, Fin. 39/M1
Luverne, Mn, US 127/J5
Luvua (riv.), D.R. Congo 104/A4
Luwegu (riv.), Tanz. 105/G2
Luwero, Ugan. 104/B2
Luwingu, Zam. 104/A5
Lux, Fr. 56/A4
Luxembourg (ctry.) 53/E4
Luxembourg (prov.), Belg 53/E4
Luxembourg (cap.), Lux. 53/F4
Luxeuil-les-Bains, Fr. 56/C2
Luxi, China 83/H3
Luxi, China 83/K2
Luxi, China 83/G3
Luxor (int'l arpt.), Egypt 101/C3
Luyi, China 72/C4
Luz, Braz. 155/C1
Luz (coast), Port.,Sp. 44/B4
Luza (riv.), Rus. 61/L3
Luzarches, Fr. 30/K4
Luzein, Swi. 57/F4
Luzern, Swi. 57/E3
Luzern (canton), Swi. 56/E3
Luzerne (co.), Pa, US 138/B1
Luzhai, China 83/J3
Luzhi, China 83/J2
Luzhou, China 83/J2
Luziânia, Braz. 154/A5
Luzilândia, Braz. 154/B1
Lužnice (riv.), Czh. 41/H4
Luzon (isl.), Phil. 79/D4
Luzon (str.), Phil. 116/A3
Lužuice (riv.), Czh. 43/L2
Luzzara, It. 59/D3
Luzzi, It. 46/E3
L'viv, Ukr. 62/C2
L'vivs'ka Oblasti, Ukr. 62/B2
Lwala (peak), Ugan. 104/B2
Lwi (riv.), Myan. 78/C1
Lyantonde, Ugan. 104/A3
Lyapin (riv.), Rus. 61/P2
Lycksele, Swe. 37/F2
Lycoming (co.), Pa, US 138/A1
Lyell Brown (mt.), Austl. 113/F2
Lykens, Pa, US 138/B2
Lyman, Wy, US 126/F5
Lyme (bay), Eng, UK 42/B1
Lymington, Eng, UK 33/E5
Lymm, Eng, UK 35/F5
Łyna (riv.), Pol. 41/L1
Lynas (pt.), Wal, UK 34/D5
Lynbrook, NY, US 139/L9
Lynch, Md, US 138/B5
Lynches (riv.), SC, US 133/H3
Lyndhurst, NJ, US 139/J8
Lyne (riv.), Eng, UK 35/F1
Lyngdal, Nor. 38/B2
Lyngen (inlet), Nor. 37/G1
Lynn, Ma, US 131/G3
Lynn Haven, Fl, US 133/G4
Lynn Lake, Mb, Can. 122/F3
Lynwood, Ca, US 136/F8
Lynx (lake), NW, Can. 122/F2
Lyon, Fr. 42/F4
Lyon (riv.), Sc, UK 36/B3
Lyon (lake), Sc, UK 36/B3
Lyon (Satolas) (int'l arpt.), Fr. 56/B6
Lyons, Ks, US 129/H3
Lyons, Co, US 137/B2
Lyons (riv.), Austl. 112/C3
Lyons, Wi, US 135/P14
Lyra (reef), PNG 116/E5
Lys (riv.), It. 58/A1
Lys (riv.), Fr. 42/E1
Lys-lez-Lannoy, Fr. 52/C2
Lysá (peak), Czh. 41/K4
Lysá nad Labem, Czh. 55/H2
Lysaker, Nor. 38/D2
Lysaya (hill), Bela. 39/M4
Lysekil, Swe. 38/D2
Lysica (peak), Pol. 41/L3
Lysina (peak), Czh. 55/G2
Lyss, Swi. 56/D3
Lystrup, Den. 38/D3
Lys'va, Rus. 61/N4
Lysychans'k, Ukr. 62/F2
Lytham Saint Anne's, Eng, UK 35/E4
Lytle, Tx, US 129/H5
Lytle Creek, Ca, US 136/C2
Lytton, BC, Can. 126/C3
Lyubertsy, Rus. 61/W9
Lyubotyn, Ukr. 62/E2
Lyudinovo, Rus. 62/E1
Lywd (riv.), Wal, UK 32/C3

M

M. Aleman (res.), Mex. 140/B4
Ma-Ubin, Myan. 83/G4
Ma'alot-Tarshiha, Isr. 91/D3
Ma'ān, Jor. 91/D4
Ma'an (gov.), Jor. 91/E4
Maanīt, Mong. 70/H2
Maanīt, Mong. 70/J2
Maanselkä (mts.), Fin. 37/H1
Ma'anshan, China 72/D5
Maarheeze, Neth. 50/C6
Maarianhamina (Mariehamn), Fin. 39/H1
Ma'arrat an Nu'mān, Syria 91/E2
Maarssen, Neth. 50/C4
Maartensdijk, Neth. 50/C4
Maas (riv.), Belg. 42/F1
Maasbracht, Neth. 53/E1
Maasbree, Neth. 50/D6
Maaseik, Belg. 53/E1
Maassluis, Neth. 50/B5
Maastricht, Neth. 53/E2
Maastricht (int'l arpt.), Neth. 53/E2
Mabalacat, Phil. 79/D4
Mabalane, Moz. 105/F5
Mabaruma, Guy. 153/G2
Mabechi (riv.), Japan 76/B3
Mabian, China 83/H2
Mabinay, Phil. 79/D6
Mabopane, SAfr. 106/Q12
Mabote, Moz. 105/F5
Mabule, Bots. 106/D2
Mac Robertson Land (phys. reg.), Ant. 160/D
Macá (peak), Chile 158/B5
Macachín, Arg. 158/E3
Macaé, Braz. 155/D2
Macael, Sp. 44/D4
Macaíba, Braz. 154/D2
Mação, Port. 44/A3
Macapá, Braz. 151/H3
Macará, Ecu. 156/B2
Macarani, Braz. 154/B4
Macaravita, Col. 152/C3
Macari, Peru 156/D4
Macarthur, Austl. 115/B3
Macas, Ecu. 152/B5
Macau, Braz. 154/C2
Macau, China 83/K3
Macau (dpcy.), China 67/L7
Macaúbas, Braz. 154/B4
Macauley (isl.), NZ 116/G7
Macaya (riv.), Col. 150/D3
Macaya, Pic de (peak), Haiti 145/H2
Maccagno, It. 57/E5
Macclenny, Fl, US 133/H4
Macclesfield (canal), Eng, UK 35/F5
Macclesfield, Eng, UK 35/F5
Macdhui (peak), SAfr. 106/D3
Macdona, Tx, US 137/T21
MacDonald (lake), Austl. 109/B3
Macdonnell (ranges), Austl. 109/C3
Macduff, Sc, UK 36/D1
Maceda, Sp. 44/B1
Macedonia (reg.), Gre. 47/G2
Macedonía (int'l arpt.), Gre. 47/H2
Macedonia (Former Yugoslav Republic of Macedonia) (ctry.) 47/G2
Maceió (pt.), Braz. 154/C2
Maceió, Braz. 154/D3
Macerata (prov.), It. 59/G6
Macerata, It. 43/K5
Macfarlane (lake), Austl. 113/H5
Machacalis, Braz. 154/B5
Machacamarca, Bol. 150/E7
Machache (peak), Les. 106/D3
Machachi, Ecu. 152/B5
Machado, Braz. 211/H6
Machado (swamp), Col. 145/H4
Machadodorp, SAfr. 107/E2
Machakos, Kenya 104/C3
Machala, Ecu. 156/B1
Machali, Chile 158/N9
Machalilla, PN, Ecu. 152/A5
Machanga, Moz. 105/F5
Machaquilá (riv.), Guat. 144/D2
Machars, The (pen.), Sc, UK 34/D2
Machattie (lake), Austl. 113/H3
Machaze, Moz. 105/F5
Machecoul, Fr. 42/C3
Machemma (ruin), SAfr. 105/E5
Macheng, China 72/C5
Machens, Mo, US 137/G8
Machhlīshahr, India 84/D3
Machias, Me, US 131/H2
Machichaco (cape), Sp. 44/D1
Machida, Japan 77/C2
Machilipatnam, India 82/D4
Machiques, Ven. 152/C2
Machovo Jezero (lake), Czh. 55/H1
Machu Picchu (ruin), Peru 156/C4
Machupo (riv.), Bol. 150/F6
Machynlleth, Wal, UK 32/C1
Măcin, Rom. 49/J3
Macina (phys. reg.), Mali 96/E4
Macintyre (riv.), Austl. 109/E3
Mackay (lake), Austl. 109/B3
Mackay, Austl. 114/C3
Mackenzie, BC, Can. 126/C2
Mackenzie, Austl. 114/C3
Mackenzie (bay), NW,Yk, Can. 122/C2
Mackenzie (mts.), NW, Can. 122/C2
Mackenzie (riv.), NW, Can. 122/E2
Mackenzie King (isl.), NW, Can. 123/R7
Mackinac Island, Mi, US 130/C2
Mackinaw City, Mi, US 130/C2
Macklin, Sk, Can. 126/F2
Macknade, Austl. 114/B2
Macksville, Austl. 115/E1
Maclean, Austl. 115/E1
Maclear, SAfr. 106/E3
Macleay (isl.), Austl. 114/F7
Macleod (lake), Austl. 112/B3
Macmillan (riv.), Yk, Can. 134/L3
Macomb, Il, US 127/L5
Macomb (co.), Mi, US 135/G6
Macomb, Ok, US 137/N15
Macomer, It. 46/A2
Mâcon, Fr. 42/F3
Macon, Ga, US 133/H3
Macon, Mo, US 129/J3
Macondes, Planalto dos (plat.), Moz. 104/C5
Macosquin, NI, UK 34/B1
Macotera, Sp. 44/C2
Macoupin (co.), Il, US 137/G7
Macquarie (har.), Austl. 115/C4
Macquarie (isl.), Austl. 23/S8
Macquarie (riv.), Austl. 109/D4
Macroom, Ire. 31/P11
Macuelizo, Hon. 144/D3
Macuim (riv.), Braz. 150/F5
Macuira, PN, Col. 152/D1
Macuma (riv.), Ecu. 156/B1
Macumba (riv.), Austl. 109/C3
Macungie, Pa, US 138/C2
Macusani, Peru 156/D4
Macuspana, Mex. 144/C2
Macuzari, Presa (dam), Mex. 142/C3
Mādabā, Jor. 91/D4
Madagascar (ctry.) 107/H8
Madan, Bul. 47/J2
Madanapalle, India 82/C5
Madanīyīn, Tun. 96/H1
Madanīyīn (gov.), Tun. 99/H2
Madaoua, Niger 103/G3
Madaras, Hun. 48/D2
Madauk, Myan. 83/G4
Madawaska, Me, US 131/G2
Madawaska (riv.), On, Can. 130/E2
Madden (dam), Pan. 152/B2
Madeira (aut. reg.), Port. 45/U14
Madeira (riv.), Braz. 147/C3
Mädelegabel (peak), Ger. 57/G3
Madeleine, Îles de la (isls.), Qu, Can. 131/J2
Madeline (isl.), Wi, US 127/L4
Maden, Turk. 90/D2
Mäder, Aus. 57/F3
Madera, Mex. 142/C2
Maderas (vol.), Nic. 144/E4
Madgaon (Margao), India 89/K5
Madhipura, India 85/F3
Madhubani, India 85/F2
Madhumati (riv.), Bang. 85/G4
Madhupur, India 85/F3
Madhya Pradesh (state), India 70/D7
Madidi (riv.), Bol. 150/E6
Madīnat ath Thawrah, Syria 90/D3
Madirovalo, Madg. 107/H7
Madison, Al, US 133/G3
Madison, Ca, US 135/K9
Madison, Ct, US 139/F1
Madison, Fl, US 133/H4
Madison, Il, US 137/G8
Madison, In, US 130/C4
Madison, Ms, US 133/F3
Madison (riv.), Mt, US 124/D2
Madison, Ne, US 127/J5
Madison, NJ, US 139/H9
Madison (co.), Oh, US 137/G8
Madison, SD, US 127/J4
Madison Heights, Mi, US 135/F6
Madisonville, Tx, US 129/J5
Madisonville, Ky, US 130/C4
Madisonville, La, US 137/P16
Madiun, Indo. 80/D5
Mado Gashi, Kenya 104/C2
Madoi, China 70/G5
Madon (riv.), Fr. 40/D4
Madrakah, Ra's al (pt.), Oman 89/G5
Madre (lag.), Tx, US 140/B2
Madre de Deus de Minas, Braz. 211/J6
Madre de Dios (riv.), Bol. 150/E6
Madre de Dios (dept.), Peru 156/C4
Madre de Dios (isl.), Chile 159/A6
Madre del Sur, Sierra (mts.), Mex. 140/A4
Madre Occidental, Sierra (mts.), Mex. 142/D3
Madre Oriental, Sierra (mts.), Mex. 143/F4
Madrid (aut. comm.), Sp. 44/C2
Madrid (cap.), Sp. 45/N9
Madridejos, Sp. 44/D3
Madrigal, Peru 156/D4

Madri – Maqui

Madrigal de las Altas Torres, Sp. 44/C2
Madrigalejo, Sp. 44/C3
Madrisahorn (peak), Swi. 57/F4
Madroñera, Sp. 44/C3
Madugula, India 82/D4
Madura (isl.), Indo. 67/L10
Madurai, India 82/C6
Mae Hong Son, Thai. 83/G4
Mae Ping NP, Thai. 78/B2
Mae Tho (peak), Thai. 78/B2
Mae Ya (mtn.), Thai. 78/B2
Maebashi, Japan 75/F2
Maella, Sp. 45/F2
Maep'o, SKor. 73/E4
Maerne, It. 59/F1
Maestra, Sierra (mts.), Cuba 145/G2
Maevatanana-Ambanivohitra, Madg. 107/H7
Maewo (isl.), Van. 116/F6
Mafeteng, Les. 106/D3
Maffra, Austl. 115/C3
Mafia (isl.), Tanz. 105/G2
Mafia (chan.), Tanz. 104/C5
Mafikeng, SAfr. 106/D2
Mafou (riv.), Gui. 102/C4
Mafra, Braz. 155/B3
Mafra, Port. 45/P10
Magadan, Rus. 65/R4
Magadino, Swi. 57/E5
Magalies Berg (mts.), SAfr. 106/P12
Magaliesburg, SAfr. 106/P12
Magallanes y Antártica Chilena (prov.), Chile 159/C7
Magangué, Col. 152/C2
Mağara, Turk. 91/C1
Magaria, Niger 103/H3
Magat (riv.), Phil. 79/D4
Magazine (mtn.), Ar, US 129/J4
Magdalena, Bol. 150/F6
Magdalena (peak), Malay. 81/E3
Magdalena (riv.), Col. 147/B2
Magdalena (dept.), Col. 145/H4
Magdalena, Arg. 159/K11
Magdalena de Kino, Mex. 142/C2
Magdeburg, Ger. 40/F2
Magdelaine Cays (isls.), Austl. 109/E2
Magé, Braz. 211/K7
Mage-shima (isl.), Japan 74/B5
Magee, Ms, US 133/F4
Magee (isl.), NI, UK 34/C2
Magelang, Indo. 80/D5
Magellan (str.), Arg.,Chile 147/B8
Magenta, It. 58/B2
Magenta (lake), Austl. 112/C5
Magerøya (isl.), Nor. 37/H1
Maggia, Swi. 57/E5
Maggia (riv.), Swi. 57/E5
Maggio (peak), It. 59/E6
Maggiorasca (peak), It. 58/C3
Maggiore (peak), It. 59/E5
Maggiore (lake), It. 43/H4
Maghāghah, Egypt 101/B2
Maghar, India 84/D2
Maghera, NI, UK 34/B2
Magherafelt (co.), NI, UK 34/B2
Magherafelt, NI, UK 34/B2
Maghīla (peak), Tun. 100/L7
Maghnia, Alg. 100/D2
Magilligan (pt.), NI, UK 34/B1
Maglaj, Bosn. 48/D3
Maglić (peak), Serb. 47/F1
Maglie, It. 47/F2
Maglod, Hun. 49/R10
Magna, Ut, US 137/J12
Magnac-Laval, Fr. 42/D3
Magnetawan (riv.), On, Can. 130/D2
Magnetic Passage, Austl. 114/B2
Magnitogorsk, Rus. 61/N5
Magnitogorsk (int'l arpt.), Rus. 61/N5
Magnolia, Ar, US 129/J4
Magnolia, De, US 138/C5
Magny-en-Vexin, Fr. 52/A5
Magny-les-Hameaux, Fr. 30/J5
Mago NP, Eth. 97/N6
Mágoè, Moz. 105/F4
Magog, Qu, Can. 131/F2
Magpie (riv.), Qu, Can. 131/H1
Magpie (lake), Qu, Can. 131/H1
Magpie Ouest (riv.), Qu, Can. 131/H1
Magra (riv.), It. 58/C4
Magreta, It. 59/D3
Maguan, China 78/D1
Magude, Moz. 105/F6
Magugnano, It. 59/D1
Magway (div.), Myan. 70/F8
Magway (Magwe), Myan. 83/F3
Magwe (Magway), Myan. 83/F3
Maha Sarakham, Thai. 78/C2
Mahābād, Iran 88/E1
Mahabe, Madg. 107/H8
Mahābhārat (range), Nepal 84/C1
Mahabo, Madg. 107/H8
Mahaboboka, Madg. 107/H7
Mahād, India 89/K5
Mahadeo (range), India 84/A4
Mahaica, Guy. 153/G3
Mahaica-Berbice (pol. reg.), Guy. 153/G3
Mahaicony Village, Guy. 153/G3
Mahajamba (riv.), Madg. 107/H7
Mahajamba (bay), Madg. 107/H6
Mahajanga (prov.), Madg. 107/H6
Mahajanga, Madg. 107/H6
Mahajilo (riv.), Madg. 107/H7
Mahakali (zone), Nepal 84/C1
Mahakam (riv.), Indo. 81/E3
Mahalapye, Bots. 105/E5
Mahale Mountains NP, Tanz. 104/A4
Maḩallāt, Iran 88/F2
Maham, India 86/D5
Māhān (riv.), India 84/D4
Māhān, Iran 89/G2
Mahānadī (riv.), India 70/D7
Mahananda (riv.), India 85/F3
Mahandiabani (riv.), C.d'Iv. 102/D4
Mahanoro, Madg. 107/J7
Mahanoy City, Pa, US 138/B2
Mahantango (mtn.), Pa, US 138/B2
Mahārājganj, India 85/E2
Mahārājganj, India 84/D2
Mahārajpur, India 82/C2
Mahārāshtra (state), India 82/B4
Mahāsamund, India 82/D3
Mahāshān (ruin), Bang. 85/G3
Mahasoabe, Madg. 107/H8
Mahavavy (riv.), Madg. 107/H7
Mahawa (riv.), India 84/B1
Mahazoarivo, Madg. 107/H8
Mahazoma, Madg. 107/H7
Mahbubnagar, India 82/C4
Mahdia, Guy. 153/G3
Mahébourg, Mrts. 107/T15
Mahendranagar, Nepal 84/C1
Mahesāna, India 89/K4
Mahgawān, India 84/B2
Mahia (pen.), NZ 109/H6
Mahilyow (int'l arpt.), Bela. 39/P5
Mahilyow, Bela. 39/P5
Mahilyowskaya Voblasts Bela. 60/F5
Mahīshādal, India 85/F4
Mahitsy, Madg. 107/H7
Mahlaing, Myan. 83/G3
Mahlberg, Ger. 56/D1
Mahleur (lake), Or, US 126/D5
Mahlow, Ger. 40/Q7
Mahmel (peak), Alg. 96/G1
Maḩmūd-e 'Erāqī, Afg. 89/J1
Mahmūdābād, India 84/C2
Mahón, Sp. 45/H3
Mahroni, India 84/B3
Mahukona, Hi, US 124/U10
Mahuva, India 89/K4
Mahwah, India 84/A2
Mahwah, NJ, US 139/J7
Mai-Ndombe (lake), D.R. Congo 96/J8
Maia, Port. 44/A2
Maiala NP, Austl. 114/E6
Maials, Sp. 45/F2
Maiana (isl.), Kiri. 116/G4
Maicao, Col. 152/C2
Maîche, Fr. 56/C3
Maicuru (riv.), Braz. 151/H3
Maidenhead, Eng, UK 33/F3
Maidens, Sc, UK 36/B6
Maidstone, Sk, Can. 126/F2
Maidstone, Eng, UK 33/G4
Maidstone, On, Can. 135/G7
Maiduguri, Nga. 96/H5
Maienfeld, Swi. 57/F4
Maigue (riv.), Ire. 31/P10
Maihar, India 84/C3
Maihara, Japan 77/K5
Maikala (range), India 84/C4
Maiko, PN de la, D.R. Congo 97/L8
Mailāni, India 84/C1
Maili, Hi, US 124/V13
Mailly-le-Camp, Fr. 53/D6
Mailsi, Pak. 86/B5
Main (riv.), NI, UK 34/B2
Main (riv.), Ger. 40/E4
Main-Donau (canal), Ger. 54/D3
Main Range NP, Austl. 114/C5
Maināguri, India 85/G2
Mainbernheim, Ger. 54/D3
Maincy, Fr. 30/L6
Maine (state), US 131/G2
Maine (riv.), Ire. 31/P10
Maine (reg.), Fr. 42/C2
Maine, Collines du (hills), Fr. 42/C2
Maine, Gulf of (gulf), Me, US 131/G3
Mainhardt, Ger. 54/C4
Mainhausen, Ger. 54/B2
Mainland (isl.), Sc, UK 31/V14
Mainling, China 83/F2
Mainpurī, India 84/B2
Mainstockheim, Ger. 54/D3
Maintirano, Madg. 107/H7
Mainz, Ger. 54/B3
Maio (isl.), CpV. 93/K10
Maipo (vol.), Chile 158/P9
Maipo (riv.), Chile 158/N8
Maipú, Arg. 158/F3
Maipú, Chile 158/N8
Maira (riv.), It. 43/G4
Maire (str.), Arg. 159/D7
Mairiporã, Braz. 211/G8
Mairwa, India 85/E2
Mais Gate (int'l arpt.), Haiti 145/H2
Maisach, Ger. 54/E6
Maisí (cape), Cuba 141/G3
Maisome (isl.), Tanz. 104/A3
Maison-Rouge, Fr. 30/M6
Maisons-Alfort, Fr. 30/K5
Maisons-Laffitte, Fr. 30/J5
Maithon (res.), India 85/F4
Maitland, Austl. 115/D2
Maitland (riv.), On, Can. 130/D3
Maitland, Austl. 113/H5
Maitri, India, Ant. 160/A
Maizhokunggar, China 83/F2
Maizières-lès-Metz, Fr. 53/F5
Maizuru, Japan 77/H5
Maizuru (bay), Japan 77/H4
Maja e Zezë (peak), Alb. 47/G2
Majadahonda, Sp. 45/N9
Majagual, Col. 152/C2
Majardah (mts.), Alg. 100/K6
Majāz Al Bāb, Tun. 100/L6
Majdanpek, Serb. 48/E3
Majene, Indo. 81/E4
Majia (riv.), China 72/D3
Majiang, China 79/A2
Majorca (isl.), Sp. 45/G3
Majur, Serb. 48/D3
Majuro (cap.), Mrsh. 116/G4
Makabe, Japan 77/E1
Makaha, Hi, US 124/V13
Makakilo City, Hi, US 124/V13
Makālu (peak), China 85/F2
Makālu (peak), Nepal 82/E2
Makarska, Cro. 47/E1
Makassar (str.), Indo. 67/L10
Makatea (isl.), FrPol. 117/L6
Makawao, Hi, US 124/T10
Makay (mass.), Madg. 107/H8
Makemo (isl.), FrPol. 117/L6
Makena, Hi, US 124/T10
Makeni, SLeo. 102/B4
Makgadikgadi (salt pans), Bots. 105/D5
Makhachkala, Rus. 63/H4
Makhdūmpur, Pak. 86/B4
Makhfar al Busayyah, Iraq 88/E2
Makhmūr, Iraq 90/E3
Makian (isl.), Indo. 81/G3
Makin (isl.), Kiri. 116/G4
Makino, Japan 77/K5
Makinsk, Kaz. 87/F2
Makioka, Japan 77/B2
Makiyivka, Ukr. 62/F2
Makkah, SAr. 88/C4
Makkovik, Nf, Can. 123/L3
Makó, Hun. 48/E2
Makokou, Gabon 96/H7
Makonde (plat.), Tanz. 104/C5
Maków Mazowiecki, Pol. 41/L2
Makrakómi, Gre. 47/H3
Makran (coast), Iran 89/G3
Makran (reg.), Iran 89/H3
Makrokhórion, Gre. 47/H2
Maksutlu, Turk. 47/K2
Makteir (reg.), Mrta. 98/C5
Makthar, Tun. 100/L7
Makurazaki, Japan 74/B5
Makurdi, Nga. 103/H5
Makushin (vol.), Ak, US 134/E5
Mal Abrigo, Uru. 159/K11
Mala, Peru 156/B4
Mala (pt.), CR 144/E4
Mala (pt.), Pan. 152/B3
Malabar (coast), India 82/B5
Malabata (pt.), Mor. 100/B2
Malabo (cap.), EqG. 96/G7
Malacacheta, Braz. 154/B5
Malacca (str.), Asia 67/J9
Malacky, Slvk. 41/J4
Maladers, Swi. 57/F4
Maladzyechna, Bela. 39/M4
Málaga (int'l arpt.), Sp. 44/C4
Málaga, Sp. 44/C4
Malaga, NJ, US 138/C4
Malaga Cove (bay), Ca, US 136/F8
Malagarasi (riv.), Tanz. 104/A4
Malagón, Sp. 44/D3
Malagueta (bay), Cuba 145/G1
Malahide, Ire. 34/B5
Malaimbandy, Madg. 107/H8
Malaita (isl.), Sol. 116/F5
Malakāl, Sudan 97/M6
Malakangiri, India 82/D4
Malakwāl, Pak. 86/B3
Malambo, Col. 152/C2
Malang, Indo. 80/D5
Malangawa, Nepal 85/E2
Malanje, Ang. 105/C2
Malans, Swi. 57/F4
Malanville, Ben. 103/F4
Malargüe, Arg. 158/C2
Malartic, Qu, Can. 130/E1
Malasoro (pt.), Indo. 81/E5
Malatya (prov.), Turk. 90/D2
Malatya, Turk. 90/D2
Malaut, India 86/C4
Malawi (ctry.) 105/F3
Malawi (Nyasa) (lake), Malw. 104/B5
Malay (pen.), Thai. 83/G6
Malaya (reg.), Malay. 80/B3
Malaya Vishera, Rus. 39/Q2
Malaybalay, Phil. 79/E6
Malāyer, Iran 88/E2
Malaysia (ctry.) 80/C2
Malazemel'skaya (tundra), Rus. 61/L2
Malazgirt, Turk. 90/E2
Malbaie (riv.), Qu, Can. 131/G1
Malbork, Pol. 39/H4
Malcesine, It. 59/D1
Malchin, Ger. 38/E5
Malcontenta, It. 59/F2
Maldegem, Belg. 52/C1
Malden, Mo, US 129/K3
Malden (isl.), Kiri. 117/K5
Maldive (isls.), Mald. 82/B6
Maldives (ctry.) 67/G9
Maldon, Austl. 115/C3
Maldon, Eng, UK 33/G3
Maldonado, Uru. 159/G2
Maldonado (dept.), Uru. 159/G2
Male (cap.), Mald. 67/G9
Maléa (cape), Gre. 47/H4
Mālegaon, India 89/K4
Malekula (isl.), Van. 116/F6
Malemort-sur-Corrèze, Fr. 42/D4
Malente, Ger. 38/D4
Maleny, Austl. 114/D4
Maleo, It. 58/C2
Malesína, Gre. 47/H3
Malfa, It. 46/D3
Malgobek, Rus. 63/H4
Malgrat de Mar, Sp. 45/G2
Malgrate, It. 58/C1
Malheur (lake), Or, US 128/C2
Malheur (riv.), Or, US 126/D5
Malheureux (cape), Mrts. 107/T14
Mali (riv.), Myan. 83/G2
Mali (isl.), Myan. 78/B3
Mali (ctry.) 96/E4
Mali Lošinj, Cro. 48/B3
Málía, Gre. 47/J5
Malibu, Ca, US 136/B2
Malīhābād, India 84/C2
Målilla, Swe. 38/F3
Malin Head (pt.), Ire. 31/Q9
Malinau, Indo. 81/E3
Malindang (mt.), Phil. 81/F2
Malindi, Kenya 104/D3
Maling (pass), China 72/C3
Malio (riv.), Madg. 107/H8
Malipo, China 78/D1
Malīr Cantonment, Pak. 89/J4
Malka Mari NP, Kenya 97/P7
Malkara, Turk. 49/H5
Malko Tŭrnovo, Bul. 49/H5
Mallacoota, Austl. 115/D3
Mallaig, Sc, UK 31/R8
Mallānwān, India 84/C2
Mallasvesi (lake), Fin. 39/K1
Mallee Cliffs NP, Austl. 115/B2
Mallén, Sp. 44/E2
Malleray, Swi. 56/D3
Mallero (riv.), It. 57/F5
Mallersdorf-Pfaffenberg, Ger. 55/F5
Malles (Mals), It. 57/G4
Malloa, Chile 158/N9
Mallow, Ire. 31/P10
Malmberget, Swe. 37/G2
Malmédy, Belg. 53/F3
Malmesbury, SAfr. 106/L10
Malmköping, Swe. 38/G2
Malmö, Swe. 38/E4
Malmöhus (co.), Swe. 37/E5
Malmslätt, Swe. 38/F2
Malnate, It. 58/B1
Malo, It. 59/E1
Maloelap (isl.), Mrsh. 116/G4
Malone, NY, US 130/F2
Malong, China 83/H2
Malonje (peak), Tanz. 104/A5
Malonno, It. 57/G5
Małopolska (uplands), Pol. 41/K3
Małopolskie (prov.), Pol. 41/K4
Malpartida de Cáceres, Sp. 44/B3
Malpartida de Plasencia, Sp. 44/B3
Malpelo (isl.), Col. 147/A2
Malpensa (int'l arpt.), It. 58/B1
Malpica, Sp. 44/A1
Malsch (riv.), Aus. 55/H5
Malsch, Ger. 54/B5
Malše (riv.), Czh. 41/H4
Mälstek (peak), Czh. 55/G4
Malta, Mt, US 126/G3
Malta, Braz. 154/C2
Malta (chan.), Malta 46/C4
Malta (ctry.) 46/L7
Maltahöhe, Namb. 105/C5
Maltby, Eng, UK 35/G5
Malters, Swi. 56/E3
Maltorne (riv.), Fr. 30/G6
Malung, Swe. 38/E1
Malvaglia, Swi. 57/E5
Malvan, India 89/K5
Malveira, Port. 45/P10
Malvern, Pa, US 138/C3
Malverne, NY, US 139/L9
Malvinas (Falkland) (isls.), UK 160/W
Malvy Uzen' (riv.), Rus. 63/H2
Malyn, Ukr. 62/D2
Malyy Yenisey (riv.), Rus. 70/G1
Malzéville, Fr. 53/F6
Mamanguape, Braz. 154/D2
Mamaroneck, NY, US 139/L8
Mamba, Zam. 105/E4
Mamba, Japan 77/B1
Mambajao, Phil. 79/D6
Mambasa, D.R. Congo 104/A2
Mamberamo (riv.), Indo. 81/J4
Mambéré (riv.), CAfr. 96/J7
Mambij, Syria 90/D2
Mamburao, Phil. 81/F1
Mamer, Lux. 53/F4
Mamers, Fr. 42/D2
Mamfé, Camr. 103/H5
Mammendorf, Ger. 57/H1
Mamming, Ger. 55/F5
Mammoth, Az, US 128/E4
Mammoth Cave NP, Ky, US 133/G2
Mamoré (riv.), Braz. 150/E6
Mamou, La, US 129/J5
Mamoutzou, May. 107/H6
Mampikony, Madg. 107/H7
Mampong, Gha. 103/E5
Mamry (lake), Pol. 39/J4
Mamuju, Indo. 81/E4
Mamuri (riv.), Braz. 151/G4
Mamwera (peak), Tanz. 104/C4
Man, C.d'Iv. 102/D5
Man, Isle of (isl.), IM, UK 34/D3
Man Mia (peak), Thai. 78/B4
Mana (riv.), FrG. 153/H3
Manabl (prov.), Ecu. 152/A5
Manacapuru, Braz. 150/F4
Manacle (pt.), Eng, UK 32/A6
Manacor, Sp. 45/G3
Manado, Indo. 81/F3
Manage, Belg. 53/D3
Managua (lake), Nic. 140/D5
Managua (cap.), Nic. 144/E3
Manahawkin, NJ, US 138/D4
Manakambahiny, Madg. 107/J7
Manakara, Madg. 107/J8
Manalapan, NJ, US 138/D3
Manāli, India 86/D3
Manambaho (riv.), Madg. 107/H7
Manambolo (riv.), Madg. 107/H7
Mananantanana (riv.), Madg. 107/H8
Mananara, Madg. 107/J7
Mananara (riv.), Madg. 107/H8
Mananjary, Madg. 107/J8
Mananjary (riv.), Madg. 107/H8
Manara (pt.), It. 58/C4
Manaratsandry, Madg. 107/H7
Manas, China 70/E3
Manas (int'l arpt.), Kyr. 87/F4
Manas (peak), Kyr. 87/F4
Manās (riv.), India 85/H2
Manas (riv.), China 70/E2
Manāslu (peak), Nepal 85/E1
Manasquan, NJ, US 138/D3
Manasquan (riv.), NJ, US 138/D3
Manassa, Co, US 132/B2
Manastir Dečani, Serb. 47/G1
Manastir Gračanica, Serb. 47/G1
Manastir Sopoćani, Serb. 47/G1
Manatsuru, Japan 77/C3
Manaus, Braz. 150/F4
Manawatu (riv.), NZ 117/T11
Mañazo, Peru 156/D4
Manazuru-misaki (cape), Japan 77/C3
Mance (riv.), Fr. 56/B2
Mancha Real, Sp. 44/D4
Mancheng, China 72/G7
Mancherāl, India 82/C4
Manchester (lake), Austl. 114/E7
Manchester, Eng, UK 35/F5
Manchester (co.), Eng, UK 35/F5
Manchester (Ringway) (int'l arpt.), Eng, UK 35/F5
Manchester, Ky, US 130/D4
Manchester, Mo, US 137/F8
Manchester, Md, US 138/B4
Manchester, NH, US 131/G3
Manchester, Pa, US 138/B3
Manchester, Tn, US 133/G3
Manchester, Wa, US 135/B2
Manchuria (reg.), China 71/M3
Mancieulles, Fr. 53/E5
Máncora, Peru 156/A2
Mand (riv.), Iran 89/F3
Manda, PN de, Chad 96/J6
Mandabe, Madg. 107/H8
Mandaguari, Braz. 155/B2
Mandal, India 82/B3
Mandal, Nor. 38/B2
Mandal-Ovoo, Mong. 70/H3
Mandala (peak), Indo. 81/K4
Mandalay (div.), Myan. 70/F7
Mandalay, Myan. 83/G3
Mandalgovĭ, Mong. 70/J2
Mandalī, Iraq 88/E2
Mandan, ND, US 127/H4
Mandasavu (peak), Indo. 81/F5
Mandaue, Phil. 79/D5
Mandeb (str.), Afr.,Asia 93/G3
Mandello del Lario, It. 57/F6
Mandera, Kenya 97/P7
Mandeure, Fr. 56/C3
Mandeville, La, US 137/P16
Mandeville, Jam. 145/G2
Mandi Bahāuddīn, Pak. 86/B3
Mandi Dabwāli, India 86/C5
Mandi Sādiqganj, Pak. 86/B4
Mandié, Moz. 105/F4
Mandiola (isl.), Indo. 81/G4
Mandira (res.), India 85/E4
Mandla, India 84/C4
Mandø (isl.), Den. 38/C4
Mándok, Hun. 41/M4
Mandoto, Madg. 107/H7
Mandoúdhion, Gre. 47/H3
Mándra, Gre. 47/N8
Mandrare (riv.), Madg. 107/H9
Mandritsara, Madg. 107/J6
Mandsaur, India 89/L4
Mandurah, Austl. 112/B5
Manduria, It. 47/E2
Māndvi, India 89/J4
Mandya, India 82/C5
Mane (pass), Nepal 84/D1
Manéngouba, Massif du (peak), Camr. 103/H5
Maner, India 85/E3
Manerbio, It. 58/D2
Manfalūt, Egypt 88/B3
Manfredonia, It. 46/D2
Manfredonia, Golfo di (gulf), It. 46/D2
Mang (riv.), China 72/B4
Manga, Braz. 154/B4
Manga, Burk. 103/E4
Mangabeiras, Chapada das (hills), Braz. 151/J6
Mangai, D.R. Congo 105/C1
Mangaia (isl.), Cookls. 117/K7
Mangaldai, India 83/F2
Mangaldan, Phil. 79/D4
Mangalia, Rom. 49/J4
Mangalisa (peak), Tanz. 104/C4
Mangalore, India 82/B5
Mangaratiba, Braz. 211/J7
Mangareva (isl.), FrPol. 117/M7
Manger, Nor. 38/A1
Mangghystaū (obl.), Kaz. 64/F5
Mangghystaū Tübegi (pen.), Kaz. 63/J3
Mangghystaū Üstirti (plat.), Kaz. 63/K4
Mangkalihat (cape), Indo. 81/E3
Mangla (dam), Pak. 86/B3
Mangla, Pak. 86/B3
Mangla (res.), Pak. 86/B3
Manglaralto, Ecu. 156/A1
Manglares (pt.), Col. 152/B4
Manglaur, India 84/A1
Mangles (bay), Austl. 112/K7
Mango, Togo 103/F4
Mangoche, Malw. 105/G3
Mangoky (riv.), Madg. 105/J11
Mangole (isl.), Indo. 81/G4
Mangoro (riv.), Madg. 107/J7
Mangotsfield, Eng, UK 32/D4
Māngrol, India 89/K4
Mangualde, Port. 44/B2
Mangueira (lake), Braz. 159/G2
Mangum, Ok, US 129/H4
Manhasset, NY, US 139/L8
Manhasset (bay), NY, US 139/L8
Manhattan, Mt, US 126/F4
Manhattan (isl.), NY, US 139/K9
Manhattan Beach, Ca, US 136/F8
Manhay, Belg. 53/E3
Manheim, Pa, US 138/B3
Manhiça, Moz. 105/F6
Manhuaçu, Braz. 155/D2
Manhumirim, Braz. 155/D2
Mania (riv.), Madg. 107/H7
Maniamba, Moz. 105/G3
Maniāri (riv.), India 84/C4
Manicoré (riv.), Braz. 150/F5
Manicoré, Braz. 150/F5
Manicouagan (riv.), Qu, Can. 123/K3
Manicouagan (res.), Qu, Can. 131/G1
Manifold (cape), Austl. 114/C3
Manigotagan, Mb, Can. 127/J3
Manihāri, India 85/F3
Manihi (isl.), FrPol. 117/L6
Manihiki (isl.), Cookls. 117/J6
Manikarchar, India 85/G3
Manila (cap.), Phil. 79/D5
Manilla, Austl. 115/D1
Maningory (riv.), Madg. 107/J7
Manipa (str.), Indo. 81/G4
Manipat (hills), India 84/D4
Manipur (state), India 70/F7
Manisa (prov.), Turk. 90/B2
Manistee (riv.), Mi, US 130/C2
Manistee, Mi, US 130/C2
Manistique, Mi, US 130/C2
Manitoba (prov.), Can. 122/G3
Manitoba (lake), Mb, Can. 127/J3
Manitou (riv.), Qu, Can. 131/H1
Manitou Springs, Co, US 129/F3
Manitoulin (isl.), On, Can. 130/D2
Manitowoc, Wi, US 127/M4
Maniwaki, Qu, Can. 130/F2
Manizales, Col. 150/C2
Manja, Madg. 107/H8
Manjakandriana, Madg. 107/J7
Manjimup, Austl. 112/C5
Mankono, C.d'Iv. 102/D4
Manley Hot Springs, Ak, US 134/H2
Manlleu, Sp. 44/D1
Manlyutka, Rus. 61/R4
Manmād, India 89/K4
Mannar, SrL. 82/C6
Mannar (gulf), SrL.,India 67/G9
Männedorf, Swi. 57/E3
Mannetjiesberg (peak), SAfr. 106/C4
Mannheim, Ger. 54/B4
Manning, SC, US 133/H3
Manning (cape), NW, Can. 123/Q7
Manning, Ab, Can. 122/E3
Mannington Meadow (lake), NJ, US 138/C4
Männlifluh (peak), Swi. 56/D4
Mannum, Austl. 113/H5
Mano (riv.), Libr. 96/C6
Manokotak, Ak, US 134/G4
Manolo Fortich, Phil. 79/D6
Manombo, Madg. 107/G8
Manono, D.R. Congo 105/E2
Manorville, NY, US 139/F2
Manosque, Fr. 42/F5
Manouane (riv.), Qu, Can. 131/G1
Manouane (lake), Qu, Can. 131/G1
Manp'o, NKor. 73/D2
Manra (Sydney) (isl.), Kiri. 117/H5
Manresa, Sp. 45/K6
Mansa, Zam. 104/A5
Mānsa, India 86/C5
Mansa Konko, Gam. 102/B3
Mansalay, Phil. 81/F1
Mānsehra, Pak. 86/B2
Mansel (isl.), Nun., Can. 123/H2
Mansfield, Austl. 115/C3
Mansfield, Oh, US 130/D3
Mansfield, La, US 129/J4
Mansfield, Eng, UK 35/G5
Mansfield Woodhouse, Eng, UK 35/G5
Mansilla de las Mulas, Sp. 44/C1
Manta, Ecu. 152/A5
Mantalingajan (mt.), Phil. 81/E2
Mantaro (riv.), Peru 150/C6
Manteca, Ca, US 128/B3
Mantecal, Ven. 152/D3
Manteigas, Port. 44/B2
Mantena, Braz. 155/D1
Manthani, India 82/C4
Manti, Ut, US 128/E3
Mantiqueira, Serra da (mts.), Braz. 151/K8
Mantorp, Swe. 38/F2
Mantova (prov.), It. 58/D2
Mantova, It. 59/D2
Mäntsälä, Fin. 39/L1
Mantua, Ut, US 137/K11
Mantua, Cuba 145/E1
Mantua, NJ, US 138/C4
Manturovo, Rus. 61/K4
Mäntyharju, Fin. 39/M1
Manu (riv.), India 150/D6
Manú, Peru 156/D4
Manú, PN, Peru 150/D6
Manua (isls.), ASam. 117/J6
Manuae Atoll (atoll), Cookls. 117/K6
Manuel Alves da Natividade (riv.), Braz. 151/J6
Manuel Benavides, Mex. 132/C4
Manuel J. Cobo, Arg. 159/K11
Manui (isl.), Indo. 81/F4
Manuk (riv.), Indo. 80/C5
Manukau, NZ 117/S10
Manumuskin (riv.), NJ, US 138/D5
Manuripe (riv.), Bol. 150/E6
Manuripe Heath Amazonica, Reserva Nacional, Bol. 156/D4
Manus (isl.), PNG 116/D5
Manville, NJ, US 138/D2
Many, La, US 129/J5
Many Farms, Az, US 128/E3
Manyara (lake), Tanz. 104/B3
Manych (riv.), Rus. 64/E5
Manych-Gudilo (lake), Rus. 63/G3
Manzanares, Sp. 44/D3
Manzanares (riv.), Sp. 45/N8
Manzanares el Real, Sp. 45/N8
Manzanillo, Mex. 142/D5
Manzanillo (int'l arpt.), Mex. 142/D5
Manzanillo, Cuba 145/G1
Manzano (mts.), NM, US 132/B3
Manzano, It. 59/G1
Manzhouli, China 71/L2
Manzil Bū Zalafah, Tun. 46/B4
Manzil Tamīn, Tun. 46/B4
Manzilah, Buḩayrat al (lake), Egypt 91/B4
Manzini, Swaz. 107/E2
Mao, Chad 96/J5
Maoke (mts.), Indo. 81/J4
Maoming, China 83/K3
Mapastepec, Mex. 144/C3
Mapi (riv.), Indo. 81/J5
Mapimí, Bolsón de (depr.), Mex. 142/D3
Mapire, Ven. 153/E3
Maple (riv.), ND, US 127/J4
Maple Creek, Sk, Can. 126/F3
Maple Grove, Qu, Can. 131/N7
Maple Park, Il, US 135/N16
Maple Shade, NJ, US 138/D4
Maple Valley, Wa, US 135/C3
Mapleton, Ut, US 137/K13
Maplewood, Mo, US 137/G8
Maplewood, NJ, US 139/H9
Maporal, Ven. 152/D3
Mapuera (riv.), Braz. 150/G3
Maputo (int'l arpt.), Moz. 107/F2
Maputo (cap.), Moz. 107/F2
Maqdam (cape), Sudan 101/D5
Maqên Gangri (peak), China 70/G5
Maquan (Damqog) (riv.), China 84/E1
Maquinchao, Arg. 158/C4

Maquoketa (riv.), Ia, US 129/K2
Mar (mts.), Braz. 147/E5
Mar (reg.), Sc, UK 36/D2
Mar Chiquita (lake), Arg. 157/D3
Mar de Ajó, Arg. 159/F3
Mar del Plata, Arg. 158/F3
Mar del Tuyú, Arg. 159/F3
Mara (pol. reg.), Tanz. 104/B3
Mara (riv.), Tanz. 104/B3
Marabá, Braz. 151/J5
Maracá, Ilha de (isl.), Braz. 151/H3
Maracaibo, Ven. 152/D2
Maracaibo (lake), Ven. 147/B2
Maracaju, Serra de (mts.), Braz. 151/G8
Maracás, Braz. 154/B4
Maracás, Chapada de (hills), Braz. 154/B4
Maracay, Ven. 150/E1
Maracena, Sp. 44/D4
Marādah, Libya 96/J2
Maradi, Niger 103/G3
Maradi (dept.), Niger 103/G3
Marāgheh, Iran 88/E1
Mārahra, India 84/B2
Marahuaca (peak), Ven. 153/E4
Marais de St-Gond (swamp), Fr. 52/C6
Marais des Cygnes (riv.), Ks,Mo, US 129/J3
Marajó (bay), Braz. 147/E3
Marajó, Ilha de (isl.), Braz. 147/D3
Maralal, Kenya 104/C2
Maralinga-Tjarutja Abor. Land, Austl. 113/F4
Maramag, Phil. 79/E6
Marambaia, Ilha (isl.), Braz. 211/K8
Maramureş (co.), Rom. 41/M5
Marana, Az, US 128/E4
Marana (lag.), Cro. 59/G1
Marand, Iran 63/H5
Marang, Malay. 80/B2
Marangani, Peru 156/D4
Maranguape, Braz. 154/C1
Maranhão (riv.), Braz. 151/J6
Maranhão (state), Braz. 154/A2
Marano Lagunare, It. 59/G1
Marano sul Panaro, It. 59/D4
Marano Vicentino, It. 59/E1
Maranoa (riv.), Austl. 109/D3
Marañón (riv.), Peru 147/B3
Marans, Fr. 42/C3
Maraoue, PN de la, C.d'Iv. 102/D5
Marapi (peak), Indo. 80/B4
Maras (peak), Indo. 80/C4
Mărăşeşti, Rom. 49/H3
Marathon, On, Can. 127/M3
Marathon, Fl, US 133/H5
Marathon, Tx, US 132/C4
Marathón, Gre. 47/N8
Marau, Braz. 155/A4
Maraulianwāla, Pak. 86/B3
Maravatío de Ocampo, Mex. 143/E5
Marawi, Phil. 81/F2
Marbach, Swi. 56/D4
Marbach am Neckar, Ger. 54/C5
Marbache, Fr. 53/F6
Marbella, Sp. 44/C4
Marble Bar, Austl. 112/C2
Marbleton, Wy, US 126/F5
Marburg, Ger. 43/H1
Marburg (lake), Pa, US 138/B4
Marca, Ponta da (pt.), Ang. 105/B4
Marcali, Hun. 48/C2
Marcallo, It. 58/B2
Marcapata, Peru 156/D4
March, Eng, UK 33/G1
Marche (prov.), It. 43/K5
Marche (mts.), Fr. 42/D3
Marche-en-Famenne, Belg. 53/E3
Marchémoret, Fr. 30/L4
Marchena, Sp. 44/C4
Marchena (isl.), Ecu. 156/E6
Marcheno, It. 58/D1
Marchiennes, Fr. 52/C3
Marchin, Belg. 53/E3
Marchtrenk, Aus. 55/H6
Marciana Marina, It. 46/B1
Marcilly, Fr. 30/L4
Marcilly-sur-Tille, Fr. 56/B2
Marck, Fr. 52/A2
Marckolsheim, Fr. 56/D1
Marco, Braz. 154/B1
Marco, Fl, US 133/H5
Marco Polo (int'l arpt.), It. 59/F2
Marcoing, Fr. 52/C3
Marcon, It. 59/F1
Marcona, Peru 156/C4
Marconi (mt.), BC, Can. 126/E3
Marcos Juárez, Arg. 158/E2
Marcoussis, Fr. 30/J6
Marcovia, Hon. 144/E3
Marcq-en-Barœul, Fr. 52/C2
Marcus Baker (mt.), Ak, US 134/J3
Marcy (mt.), NY, US 130/F2
Mardān, Pak. 86/B2
Marden, Eng, UK 30/E3
Mardeuil, Fr. 52/C5
Mardin (town), Turk. 90/E2
Marecchia (riv.), It. 59/F5
Maree (lake), Sc, UK 31/R8
Mareeba, Austl. 114/B2
Mareil-sur-Mauldre, Fr. 30/H5
Marengo, Il, US 135/N15
Marennes, Fr. 42/C4
Mareuil-sur-Ourcq, Fr. 30/M4
Marfa, Tx, US 129/F5
Margalla Hills NP, Pak. 86/B3
Marganets', Ukr. 62/E3
Margao (Madgaon), India 89/K5
Margaret (mt.), Austl. 112/C2
Margaret River, Austl. 112/B5
Margarita (peak), Ca, US 136/C4
Margarita, Isla de (isl.), Ven. 150/F1
Margaritíon, Gre. 47/G3
Margate, SAfr. 107/E3
Margate, Eng, UK 33/H4
Margate City, NJ, US 138/D5
Margeride, Monts de la (mts.), Fr. 42/E4
Margherita (peak), Ugan. 104/A2
Marghilon, Uzb. 87/E4
Marghita, Rom. 48/F2
Margny-lès-Compiègne, Fr. 52/B5
Margos, Peru 156/B3
Margosatubig, Phil. 81/F2
Margraten, Neth. 53/E2
Mari, Braz. 154/D2
Maria (mt.), Austl. 115/D4
María Cleófas (isl.), Mex. 142/D4
Maria da Fé, Braz. 211/H7
Maria Island NP, Austl. 115/D4
María Madre (isl.), Mex. 142/D4
María Magdalena (isl.), Mex. 142/D4
Maria van Diemen (cape), NZ 117/S9
Mariāhū, India 84/D3
Marian, Austl. 114/C3
Marianao, Cuba 145/F1
Marianna, Fl, US 133/G4
Marianna, Ar, US 129/K4
Mariano Comense, It. 58/C1
Mariano Marcos, Phil. 79/D6
Mariánské Lázně, Czh. 55/F3
Marias (riv.), Mt, US 126/F3
Mariato (pt.), Pan. 152/A3
Maribo, Den. 38/D4
Maribor, Slov. 43/L3
Maricá, Braz. 211/L7
Maricopa (co.), Az, US 137/R18
Marié (riv.), Braz. 150/E4
Marie Byrd Land (phys. reg.), Ant. 160/S
Marie-Galante (isl.), Dom. 141/J4
Mariehamn (int'l arpt.), Fin. 39/H1
Mariel, Cuba 145/F1
Marienhafe, Ger. 51/E1
Marienheide, Ger. 53/G1
Mariental, Namb. 105/C5
Mariestad, Swe. 38/E2
Marietta, Ok, US 129/H4
Marietta, Ga, US 133/G3
Marietta, Pa, US 138/B3
Marignane, Fr. 42/F5
Marigot, Dom. 141/N9
Marijampolė, Lith. 39/K4
Marília, Braz. 155/B2
Marín, Sp. 44/A1
Marin (co.), Ca, US 135/J10
Marin-Epagnier, Swi. 56/D3
Marina, It. 46/D3
Marina del Rey, Ca, US 136/F8
Marina del Rey (har.), Ca, US 136/F8
Marina di Andora, It. 58/B5
Marina di Montemarciano, It. 59/G5
Marina di Ravenna, It. 59/F4
Marine Nat'l Rsv., Kenya 104/D3
Marine World Africa USA, Ca, US 135/K10
Marineland, Austl. 113/M8
Marines, Fr. 30/H4
Marinette, Wi, US 127/M4
Maringá, Braz. 155/B2
Marinha Grande, Port. 44/A3
Marinhas, Port. 44/A2
Marion, Ky, US 130/B4
Marion, Mi, US 130/C2
Marion, In, US 130/C3
Marion, Oh, US 130/D3
Marion (reef), Austl. 109/E2
Marion, Al, US 133/G3
Marion (lake), SC, US 125/K5
Maripa, Ven. 153/E3
Mariposa, Ca, US 128/C3
Mariscal Estigarribia, Par. 150/F8
Mariscal Sucre (int'l arpt.), Ecu. 152/B5
Maritime Alps (mts.), Fr. 43/G4
Maritsa (riv.), Bul. 62/C4
Mariupol' (int'l arpt.), Ukr. 62/F3
Mariupol', Ukr. 62/F3
Mariy-El, Resp., Rus. 64/Q6
Marj 'Uyūn, Leb. 91/D3
Mark (riv.), Belg. 50/B6
Mark Twain NWR, Il, US 137/F7
Mark Twain (lake), Mo, US 129/J3
Mark Twain NWR, Mo, US 137/G8
Marka (riv.), Ger. 51/E3
Marka (Merca), Som. 97/P7
Markam, China 83/G2
Markaryd, Swe. 38/E3
Markdorf, Ger. 57/F2
Markelsdorfer (pt.), Ger. 38/D4
Marken (isl.), Neth. 50/C4
Markerwaard (polder), Neth. 50/C3
Market Harborough, Eng, UK 33/F2
Markgroningen, Ger. 54/C5
Markham, On, Can. 131/R8
Markham (bay), Nun., Can. 123/J2
Marki, Pol. 41/L2
Markinch, Sc, UK 36/C4
Markit, China 87/G5
Markleeville, Ca, US 128/C3
Markneukirchen, Ger. 55/F2
Markópoulon, Gre. 47/N9
Markovac, Serb. 48/E3
Marks, Rus. 63/H2
Marksville, La, US 129/J5
Markt Bibart, Ger. 54/D3
Markt Erlbach, Ger. 54/D4
Markt Indersdorf, Ger. 55/E6
Markt Rettenbach, Ger. 57/G2
Markt Sankt Florian, Aus. 55/H6
Markt Schwaben, Ger. 55/E6
Marktbreit, Ger. 54/D3
Marktheidenfeld, Ger. 54/C3
Marktl, Ger. 55/F6
Marktoberdorf, Ger. 57/G2
Marktredwitz, Ger. 55/F3
Marl, Ger. 51/E5
Marla, Austl. 113/G3
Marlboro, NJ, US 138/D3
Marlboro (Upper Marlboro), Md, US 138/B6
Marle, Fr. 52/C4
Marlengo (Marling), It. 57/H4
Marlenheim, Fr. 53/G6
Marles-en-Brie, Fr. 30/L5
Marles-les-Mines, Fr. 52/B3
Marlow, Eng, UK 33/F3
Marlow, Ger. 38/E4
Marlton, NJ, US 138/D4
Marly, Swi. 56/D4
Marly, Fr. 53/F5
Marly, Fr. 52/C3
Marly-la-Ville, Fr. 30/K4
Marly-le-Roi, Fr. 30/J5
Marmagao, India 89/K5
Marmande, Fr. 42/D4
Marmara, Turk. 49/H5
Marmara (isl.), Turk. 49/H5
Marmara (sea), Turk. 49/J5
Marmaraereğlisi, Turk. 49/H5
Marmaris, Turk. 90/B2
Marmelos (riv.), Braz. 150/F5
Marmion (lake), Austl. 109/A3
Marmirolo, It. 59/D2
Marmolada (peak), It. 43/J3
Marmolejo, Sp. 44/C3
Marmontana (peak), It. 57/F5
Marmora, NJ, US 138/D5
Marmoutier, Fr. 53/G6
Marnay, Fr. 56/B3
Marnaz, Fr. 56/C5
Marne (riv.), Fr. 42/F2
Marne, Ger. 38/C5
Marne (dept.), Fr. 52/C6
Marne au Rhin, Canal de la (canal), Fr. 53/D6
Maro (reef), Hi, US 117/H2
Maroa, Ven. 153/E4
Maroantsetra, Madg. 107/J6
Marokau (isl.), FrPol. 117/L6
Marolambo, Madg. 107/J8
Maroldsweisach, Ger. 54/D2
Marolles-en-Brie, Fr. 30/M5
Marolles-en-Hurepoix, Fr. 30/J6
Maromokotro (peak), Madg. 107/J6
Marondera, Zim. 105/F4
Marone, It. 58/D1
Maroni (riv.), FrG.,Sur. 147/D2
Maroochydore-Mooloolaba, Austl. 114/D4
Maroon Town, Jam. 145/G2
Marostica, It. 59/E1
Marotandrano, Madg. 107/J7
Marotiri (Bass Is.) (isls.), FrPol. 117/L7
Marotta, It. 59/G5
Maroua, Camr. 96/H5
Marouini (riv.), FrG. 153/H4
Marovato, Madg. 107/J6
Marovoay, Madg. 107/H7
Marowijne (dist.), Sur. 153/H3
Marpingen, Ger. 53/G5
Marple, Eng, UK 35/F5
Marquan (riv.), China 82/E2
Marquard, SAfr. 106/D3
Marquarie (riv.), Austl. 115/C1
Marquesas (isls.), FrPol. 117/M5
Marquise, Fr. 52/A2
Marracuene, Moz. 107/F2
Marradi, It. 59/E4
Marrah (mts.), Sudan 97/K5
Marrah (peak), Sudan 97/K5
Marrakech, Mor. 98/D3
Marrero, La, US 137/P17
Marromeu, Moz. 105/G4
Marrupa, Moz. 105/G3
Mars (peak), It. 58/A1
Marsá al Burayqah, Libya 96/J1
Marsá Maţrūḩ (cap.), Egypt 101/A2
Marsabit, Kenya 104/C2
Marsabit Nat'l Rsv., Kenya 104/C2
Marsala, It. 46/C4
Marsange (riv.), Fr. 30/L5
Marsannay, Fr. 56/A3
Marsberg, Ger. 51/F6
Marsciano, It. 43/K5
Marsdiep Texelstroom (chan.), Neth. 50/B3
Marseille, Fr. 42/F5
Marseille-en-Beauvaisis, Fr. 52/A4
Marsh (isl.), La, US 140/C2
Marshall, Sk, Can. 126/F2
Marshall, Mn, US 127/K4
Marshall, Tx, US 129/J4
Marshall, Mo, US 129/J3
Marshall, Co, US 137/B3
Marshall, Ut, US 137/J12
Marshall (riv.), Austl. 113/H2
Marshall Islands (ctry.) 116/G3
Marshallton, De, US 138/C4
Marshalltown, Ia, US 127/K5
Marshdale, Co, US 137/B3
Marshfield, Mo, US 129/J3
Märsta, Swe. 38/G2
Marston (lake), Co, US 137/B3
Marsyandi (riv.), Nepal 85/E1
Marta, It. 46/B1
Marta (mts.), Col. 145/H4
Martaban, Myan. 78/B2
Martaban (gulf), Myan. 78/B2
Martapura, Indo. 80/D4
Marte R. Gomez, Mex. 142/C3
Martelange, Belg. 53/E4
Martellago, It. 59/F1
Martensville, Sk, Can. 126/G2
Martfeld, Ger. 51/G3
Martha's Vineyard (isl.), Ma, US 131/G3
Martignacco, It. 59/G1
Martigny, Swi. 56/D5
Martigny-les-Bains, Fr. 56/B1
Martigues, Fr. 42/F5
Martil, Mor. 100/B2
Martin, Tn, US 130/B4
Martin (lake), Al, US 133/G3
Martin Vaz (isls.), Braz. 151/N8
Martina Franca, It. 47/E2
Martinengo, It. 58/C1
Martinez, Ga, US 133/H3
Martínez de la Torre, Mex. 143/M6
Martinho Campos, Braz. 155/C1
Martinique (isl.), Fr. 141/N9
Martinique Passage (chan.), Dom.,Mart. 141/J4
Martinon, Gre. 47/H3
Martinópole, Braz. 154/B1
Martinópolis, Braz. 155/B2
Martins, Braz. 154/C2
Martins Creek, Pa, US 138/C2
Martinsburg, WV, US 130/E4
Martinsville, Va, US 130/E4
Martorell, Sp. 45/K7
Martos, Sp. 44/D4
Martre (riv.), Qu, Can. 130/F1
Martres-Tolosane, Fr. 42/D5
Marty, SD, US 127/J5
Marugame, Japan 74/C3
Maruim, Braz. 154/C3
Maruko, Japan 75/F2
Marum, Neth. 50/D2
Maruoka, Japan 74/E2
Marutea (isl.), FrPol. 117/M7
Marv Dasht, Iran 88/F3
Marxheim, Ger. 54/D5
Mary, Trkm. 89/H1
Mary Anne Passage, Austl. 112/B2
Mary Esther, Fl, US 133/G4
Mary-sur-Marne, Fr. 30/M4
Maryborough, Austl. 115/B3
Maryborough, Austl. 114/D4
Marydale, SAfr. 106/C3
Marydel, Md, US 138/C5
Maryfield, Sk, Can. 127/H3
Maryland (co.), Libr. 102/C5
Maryland (state), US 130/E4
Maryland City, Md, US 138/B5
Maryland Heights, Mo, US 137/G8
Maryland Line, Md, US 138/B4
Marystown, Nf, Can. 131/L2
Marysville, Ks, US 129/H3
Marysville, Pa, US 138/B3
Maryville, Tn, US 133/H3
Maryville, Il, US 137/H8
Marzabotto, It. 59/E4
Marzano (peak), It. 46/D2
Marzo (pt.), Col. 152/B3
Marzūq, Libya 96/H2
Masada (ruin), Isr. 91/D4
Masai Mara Nat'l Rsv., Kenya 105/F1
Masai Steppe (grsld.), Tanz. 104/C4
Masaka, Ugan. 104/A3
Masākin, Tun. 46/B5
Masamagrell, Sp. 45/E3
Masamba, Indo. 81/F4
Masan, SKor. 73/E5
Masangwe (hill), Tanz. 104/A4
Masaya, Nic. 144/E4
Masbate (isl.), Phil. 79/D5
Mascara, Alg. 100/F5
Mascarene (isls.), Mrts 107/T15
Mascota, Mex. 142/D4
Mascouche, Qu, Can. 131/N6
Maselheim, Ger. 57/F1
Maserà di Padova, It. 59/E2
Maseru (cap.), Les. 106/D3
Masevaux, Fr. 56/D2
Masfjorden, Nor. 38/A1
Mashan, China 79/A3
Mashhad (int'l arpt.), Iran 87/C5
Mashike, Japan 76/B2
Māshkīd (riv.), Iran 89/H3
Mashtūl as Sūq, Egypt 91/B4
Mashū (lake), Japan 76/D2
Masiaca, Mex. 142/C3
Maside, Sp. 44/A1
Masim (peak), Rus. 63/L1
Masindi, Ugan. 104/A2
Maşīrah, Jazīrat (isl.), Oman 67/F5
Masisea, Peru 156/C3
Masjed-e Soleymān, Iran 88/E2
Mask (lake), Ire. 31/P10
Masker (peak), Mor. 98/D2
Masnou, Sp. 45/L7
Masoala (cape), Madg. 107/J6
Masoala (pen.), Madg. 105/L10
Masoarivo, Madg. 107/H7
Mason, Mi, US 130/C3
Mason, Tx, US 129/H5
Mason (co.), Wa, US 135/A3
Mason (lake), Wa, US 135/B3
Mason and Dixon Line, Pa, US 138/B4
Masone, It. 58/B4
Masonville, Co, US 137/B2
Masquefa, Sp. 45/K6
Massa, It. 58/D4
Massa-Carrara (prov.), It. 58/C4
Massa Finalese, It. 59/E3
Massa Fiscaglia, It. 59/F3
Massa Lombarda, It. 59/E4
Massa Marittima, It. 43/J5
Massa Martana, It. 43/K5
Massachusetts (state), US 131/F3
Massachusetts (bay), Ma, US 131/G3
Massaciuccoli, Lago di (lake), It. 58/D5
Massafra, It. 47/E2
Massangena, Moz. 105/F5
Massapê, Braz. 154/B1
Massapequa, NY, US 139/M9
Massapequa Park, NY, US 139/M9
Massarosa, It. 58/D5
Massbach, Ger. 54/D2
Massena, NY, US 130/F2
Masset, BC, Can. 134/M4
Massey (sound), Nun., Can. 123/S7
Massey, Md, US 138/C5
Massillon, Oh, US 130/D3
Massy, Fr. 30/J5
Masterton, NZ 117/T11
Mastgat (chan.), Neth. 50/B5
Mastic, NY, US 139/F2
Mastic Beach, NY, US 139/F2
Mastník (riv.), Czh. 55/H3
Mastūj (riv.), Pak. 86/A2
Mastung, Pak. 89/J3
Masuda, Japan 74/B3
Masuho, Japan 77/A2
Masurai (peak), Indo. 80/B4
Masvingo, Zim. 105/F5
Maswa Game Rsv., Tanz. 104/B3
Maşyāf, Syria 91/E2
Mat (riv.), Alb. 47/F2
Mata Grande, Braz. 154/C3
Mata Utu, Fr. 117/H6
Matābhānga, India 85/G2
Matadi, D.R. Congo 105/B2
Matador, Tx, US 129/G4
Matagalpa, Nic. 144/E3
Matagami (lake), Qu, Can. 130/E1
Matagorda (bay), Tx, US 140/B2
Matagorda (isl.), Tx, US 140/B2
Matale, SrL. 82/D6
Matam, Sen. 102/B3
Matamoras, Pa, US 138/D1
Matamoros, Mex. 142/E3
Ma'ṭan as Sarra (well), Libya 97/K3
Matandu (riv.), Tanz. 104/C5
Matane (riv.), Qu, Can. 131/H1
Matane, Qu, Can. 131/H1
Matanga, Madg. 107/H8
Matanzas, Cuba 140/E3
Matão, Braz. 155/B2
Matape (riv.), Mex. 142/C2
Matapedia (riv.), Qu, Can. 131/H1
Mataquito (riv.), Chile 158/C2
Matara (ruin), Erit. 88/C6
Matara, SrL. 82/D6
Mataram, Indo. 81/E5
Matarànga, Gre. 47/G3
Mataró, Sp. 45/L7
Matatiele, SAfr. 106/E3
Mataura (riv.), NZ 117/R12
Matawan, NJ, US 139/J10
Matehuala, Mex. 143/E4
Matéri, Ben. 103/F4
Maternillos (pt.), Cuba 141/F3
Mátészalka, Hun. 41/M5
Mathay, Fr. 56/C3
Matheniko Game Rsv., Ugan. 104/B2
Mathew's (peak), Kenya 104/C2
Mathews (lake), Ca, US 136/C3
Mathis, Tx, US 132/D4
Mathoura, Austl. 115/C2
Mathurā, India 84/A2
Mati, Phil. 79/E6
Matias Barbosa, Braz. 211/K6
Matias Olímpio, Braz. 154/B1
Matías Romero, Mex. 144/C2
Matiguas, Nic. 144/E3
Matilija (dam), Ca, US 136/A2
Matinha, Braz. 154/A2
Matinhos, Braz. 155/B3
Matinicock (pt.), NY, US 139/L8
Mātir, Tun. 46/A4
Matiyuri (riv.), Ven. 152/D3
Mātla (riv.), India 85/G5
Matlock, Eng, UK 35/G5
Mato Grosso (plat.), Braz. 147/D4
Mato Grosso do Sul (state), Braz. 155/A1
Mato Grosso, Planalto do (plat.), Braz. 151/H6
Mato Verde, Braz. 154/B4
Matopos, Zim. 105/E5
Matosinhos, Port. 44/A2
Matoya (bay), Japan 77/L7
Maţraḩ, Oman 89/G4
Matrei am Brenner, Aus. 57/H3
Matrei in Osttirol, Aus. 43/K3
Matriz de Camaragibe, Braz. 154/D3
Matroosberg (peak), SAfr. 106/L10
Matsalu (gulf), Est. 39/K2
Matsapa (Manzini) (int'l arpt.), Swaz. 107/E2
Matsiatra (riv.), Madg. 107/H8
Matsoandakana, Madg. 107/J6
Matsubara, Japan 77/J6
Matsubushi, Japan 77/D2
Matsuda, Japan 77/C3
Matsudo, Japan 77/D2
Matsue, Japan 74/C3
Matsuida, Japan 77/B1
Matsumae, Japan 76/B3
Matsumoto, Japan 75/E2
Matsuo, Japan 77/E2
Matsusaka, Japan 77/L6
Matsushima, Japan 76/B4
Matsutō, Japan 74/E2
Matsuyama, Japan 74/C4
Matt, Swi. 57/F4
Mattagami (riv.), On, Can. 130/D1
Mattarello, It. 57/H6
Mattawa, On, Can. 130/E2
Matterhorn (peak), It.,Swi. 56/D6
Mattertal (valley), Swi. 56/D5
Mattese, Mo, US 137/G9
Matthews (mtn.), Ak, US 134/H2
Mattig (riv.), Aus. 55/G6
Mattighofen, Aus. 55/G6
Mattituck, NY, US 139/F2
Mattmarksee (lake), Swi. 56/D5
Mattō, Japan 74/E2
Mattock (riv.), Ire. 34/B4
Mattsee, Aus. 55/G7
Matucana, Peru 156/B3
Maturín, Ven. 153/F2
Matusadona NP, Zim. 105/E4
Matzen, Aus. 49/P7
Maú (riv.), Guy. 150/G3
Mau (peak), Kenya 104/B3
Mau Aimma, India 84/C3
Mau Rānīpur, India 84/B3
Mauá, Braz. 155/C2
Maubert-Fontaine, Fr. 53/D4
Maubeuge, Fr. 52/C3
Maubourguet, Fr. 42/D5
Mauchline, Sc, UK 36/B5
Maud (pt.), Austl. 112/B2
Maud, Sc, UK 36/D1
Maudaha, India 84/C3
Mauerbach, Aus. 49/N7
Mauerkirchen, Aus. 55/G6
Maués, Braz. 150/G4
Maués Açu (riv.), Braz. 150/G4
Maug (isls.), NMar. 116/D2
Mauganj, India 84/C3
Maughold, IM, UK 34/D3
Maughold (pt.), IM, UK 34/D3
Mauguio, Fr. 42/F5
Maui (isl.), Hi, US 124/T10
Mauke (isl.), Cookls. 117/K7
Maulbronn, Ger. 54/B5
Mauldre (riv.), Fr. 52/A6
Maule (pol. reg.), Chile 158/B2
Maule (riv.), Chile 158/C2
Maule, Fr. 30/H5
Mauléon, Fr. 42/C3
Maullín, Chile 158/B4
Maumee (riv.), In,Oh, US 130/C3
Maun, Bots. 105/D4
Mauna Kea (peak), Hi, US 124/U11
Mauna Loa (peak), Hi, US 124/U11
Maunath Bhanjan, India 84/D3
Maungdaw, Myan. 83/F3
Mauperthuis, Fr. 30/M5
Maupertus (int'l arpt.), Fr. 42/C2
Maupiti (isl.), FrPol. 117/K6
Maur, Swi. 57/E3
Maurāwān, India 84/C2
Maurecourt, Fr. 30/J5
Maurepas (lake), La, US 137/P16
Maurepas, Fr. 52/A6
Mauriac, Fr. 42/E4
Maurice (lake), Austl. 109/C3
Maurice (riv.), NJ, US 138/C5
Mauricetown, NJ, US 138/D5
Maurienne (valley), Fr. 43/G4
Maurilândia, Braz. 155/B1
Mauritania (ctry.) 96/C4
Mauriti, Braz. 154/C2
Mauritius (ctry.) 107/T15
Mauston, Wi, US 127/L5
Mauthausen, Aus. 55/H6
Mauvoisin, Barrage de (dam), Swi. 56/D6
Mavrommátion, Gre. 47/H3
Mavrovo NP, FYROM 47/G2
Maw Daung (pass), Thai. 78/B4
Mawāna, India 84/A1
Mawlaik, Myan. 83/F3
Mawlamyine (Moulmein), Myan. 78/B2
Mawson, Austl., Ant. 160/E
Maxaranguape, Braz. 154/D2
Maxcanú, Mex. 144/D1
Maxdorf, Ger. 54/B4
Maxéville, Fr. 53/F6
Maxhütte-Haidhof, Ger. 55/F4
May (cape), NJ, US 138/D5
May-en-Multien, Fr. 30/M4
May, Isle of (isl.), Sc, UK 36/D4
May Pen, Jam. 145/G2
Maya (isl.), Indo. 80/C4
Maya (riv.), Rus. 67/N4
Maya (mts.), Guat. 144/D2
Maya-san (peak), Japan 77/H6
Mayaguana (isl.), Bahm. 141/G3
Mayaguana Passage (chan.), Bahm. 145/H1
Mayagüez, PR 141/M8
Mayakovskogo (peak), Taj. 89/K1
Mayang, China 83/J2
Mayari, Cuba 145/H1
Maybee, Mi, US 135/E8
Maybole, Sc, UK 36/B6
Maydān, Iraq 88/E2
Mayen, Ger. 53/G3
Mayenne, Fr. 42/C2
Mayenne (riv.), Fr. 42/C3
Mayerthorpe, Ab, Can. 126/E2
Mayfield, Ky, US 130/B4
Mayfield, Sc, UK 36/C5
Maykop, Rus. 62/G3
Maymyo, Myan. 83/G3
Maynooth, Ire. 31/Q10
Mayo (riv.), Arg. 157/B6
Mayo, Yk, Can. 134/L3
Mayo, Md, US 138/B6
Mayotte (isl.), May. 107/H6
Mays Landing, NJ, US 138/D5
Maysville, Ky, US 130/D4
Maythalūn, WBnk. 91/G7
Mayville, ND, US 127/J4
Maywood, NJ, US 139/J8
Maywood, Il, US 135/Q16
Maywood, Ca, US 136/F8
Mazabuka, Zam. 105/E4
Mazagão, Braz. 151/H4
Mazamet, Fr. 42/E5
Mazán, Peru 156/C1
Mazār-e Sharīf, Afg. 89/J1
Mazara del Vallo, It. 46/C4
Mazara, Val di (valley), It. 46/C4
Mazarrón, Sp. 44/E4
Mazaruni (riv.), Guy. 150/G2
Mazatán, Mex. 142/C2
Mazatenango, Guat. 144/D3
Mazatlán, Mex. 142/D4
Mažeikiai, Lith. 39/K3
Mazeppa NP, Austl. 114/B3
Mazgirt, Turk. 90/D2
Mazıkıran (pass), Turk. 90/D2
Mazingarbe, Fr. 52/B3
Mazocruz, Peru 156/D5
Mazong (peak), China 70/G3
Mazowieckie (prov.), Pol. 41/L2
Mazury (reg.), Pol. 41/L2
Mazyr, Bela. 62/D1
Mbabala (isl.), Zam. 104/A5
Mbabane (cap.), Swaz. 107/E2
Mbabo (peak), Camr. 96/H6
Mbacké, Sen. 102/B3
Mbaïki, CAfr. 96/J7
Mbakaou, Lac de (lake), Camr. 96/H6
Mbala, Zam. 104/A5
Mbale, Ugan. 104/B2
Mbalmayo, Camr. 96/H7
Mbandaka, D.R. Congo 97/J7
Mbarangandu (riv.), Tanz. 104/C5
Mbarara, Ugan. 104/A3
Mbata, CAfr. 97/J7
Mbeya (peak), Tanz. 104/B5
Mbeya (range), Tanz. 105/F2
Mbeya, Tanz. 104/B5
Mbeya (pol. reg.), Tanz. 104/B5
Mbini, EqG. 96/G7
Mbini (riv.), EqG.,Gabo 96/H7
Mbirizi, Ugan. 104/A3
Mbomou (riv.), CAfr. 97/K7
M'Bour, Sen. 102/A3
Mbuji-Mayi, D.R. Congo 105/D2
Mbwemburu (riv.), Tanz. 104/C5
McAdoo, Pa, US 138/C2
McAfee, NJ, US 138/D1
McAlester, Ok, US 129/J4
McAlisterville, Pa, US 138/A2
McAllen, Tx, US 132/D5
McBride, BC, Can. 126/C2
McCall, Id, US 126/D4
McCarran (int'l arpt.), Nv, US 128/D3
McCarthy, Ak, US 134/K3

McClain (co.), Ok, US 137/M15
McClure, Pa, US 138/A2
McClusky, Il, US 137/G7
McClusky, ND, US 127/H4
McComb, Ms, US 129/K5
McConaughy (lake), Ne, US 127/H5
McCook, Ne, US 129/G2
McCormick, SC, US 133/H3
McCreary, Mb, Can. 127/J3
McCullom Lake, Il, US 135/P15
McDaniel, Md, US 138/B6
McDermitt, Nv, US 126/D5
McDonald (mt.), Ak, US 134/F3
McDonald (isls.), Austl. 23/N8
McDonnell (mt.), Austl. 113/H5
McDougall (pass), NW,Yk, Can. 134/L2
McDowell (mts.), Az, US 137/S18
McElhattan, Pa, US 138/A1
McGhee Tyson (int'l arpt.), Tn, US 133/H3
McGrath, Ak, US 134/G3
McGregor (riv.), BC, Can. 126/C2
McGregor, On, Can. 135/G7
McHenry (co.), Il, US 135/N15
McKean (isl.), Kiri. 117/H5
McKeand (riv.), Nun., Can. 123/K2
McKee City, NJ, US 138/D5
McKeesport, Pa, US 130/E3
McKenzie, Tn, US 130/B4
McKinlay, Austl. 114/A3
McKinley (mt.), Ak, US 134/H3
McKinleyville, Ca, US 126/B5
McLaughlin, SD, US 127/H4
McLean, Va, US 138/A6
McLennan, Ab, Can. 126/D2
McLeod (riv.), BC, Can. 126/D2
McLeod (lake), Austl. 109/A3
McLeod (bay), NW, Can. 122/E2
McLeod Lake, BC, Can. 126/C2
M'Clintock (chan.), Nun., Can. 122/F1
McLoud, Ok, US 137/N15
M'Clure (str.), NW, Can. 123/Q7
McMinnville, Or, US 126/C4
McMinnville, Tn, US 130/C5
McMurdo, US, Ant. 160/M
McNeil (isl.), Wa, US 135/C2
McPherson, Ks, US 129/H3
McQueeney, Tx, US 137/U20
Mdantsane, SAfr. 106/D4
M'diq, Mor. 100/B2
Me-akan-dake (peak), Japan 76/C2
Mead, Co, US 137/C2
Mead (lake), Az,Nv, US 128/D3
Meade (riv.), Ak, US 134/G2
Meadow Lake, Sk, Can. 126/F2
Meadow Valley Wash (riv.), Nv, US 128/D3
Meadowbrook, Il, US 137/G8
Meadowlands Sports Complex, NJ, US 139/J8
Meadows, Md, US 138/B6
Meadville, Ms, US 133/F4
Meadville, Pa, US 130/D3
Mealhada, Port. 44/A2
Meall a' Bhuiridh (peak), Sc, UK 36/B3
Meall Buidhe (peak), Sc, UK 36/B3
Meall Dearg (peak), Sc, UK 36/C3
Meall Dubh (peak), Sc, UK 36/B2
Meall nam Fuaran (peak), Sc, UK 36/C4
Meall Tairneachan (peak), Sc, UK 36/C3
Mearim (riv.), Braz. 151/J5
Meat (mtn.), Ak, US 134/F2
Meath (co.), Ire. 34/B4
Meath Park, Sk, Can. 127/G2
Méaulte, Fr. 52/B4
Meaux, Fr. 30/L5
Mecapalapa, Mex. 143/M6
Mecatina, Rivière du Petit (riv.), Nf,Qu, Can. 123/J3
Mecca, US 137/D5
Mechanicsburg, Pa, US 138/A3
Mechanicsburg Naval Rsv., Pa, US 138/A3
Mechelen, Belg. 53/D1
Mecheria, Alg. 99/E2
Mechi (zone), Nepal 85/F2
Mechra-Bel-Ksiri, Mor. 100/B2
Mecidiye, Turk. 47/K2
Mecitözü, Turk. 90/C1
Meckenbeuren, Ger. 57/F2
Meckenheim, Ger. 53/G2
Mecklenburg-Vorpommern (state), Ger. 38/E5

Mecklenburger (bay), Ger. 40/F1
Mecúa (peak), Moz. 105/G3
Meda, It. 58/C1
Medak, India 82/C4
Medan, Indo. 80/A3
Médanos, Arg. 158/E3
Medanos de Coro, PN, Ven. 152/D2
Medanosa (pt.), Arg. 159/D6
Mede Lomellina, It. 58/B2
Médéa, Alg. 100/G4
Médéa (prov.), Alg. 100/G4
Medebach, Ger. 51/F6
Medeiros Neto, Braz. 154/B5
Medel (peak), Swi. 57/E4
Medellín, Col. 150/C2
Medemblik, Neth. 50/C3
Medesano, It. 58/D3
Medetsiz (peak), Turk. 90/C2
Medford, Or, US 126/C5
Medford, NY, US 139/E2
Medford Lakes, NJ, US 138/D4
Medgidia, Rom. 49/J3
Media, Pa, US 138/C4
Media Luna, La (isls.), Hon. 145/F3
Mediaş, Rom. 49/G2
Medical Lake, Wa, US 126/D4
Medicine Bow, Wy, US 127/G5
Medicine Bow (range), Wy, US 128/F2
Medicine Hat, Ab, Can. 126/F3
Medina, ND, US 127/J4
Medina (riv.), Tx, US 129/H5
Medina, Braz. 154/B5
Medina, Oh, US 130/D3
Medina, Col. 152/C3
Medina, Wa, US 135/C2
Medina de Pomar, Sp. 44/D1
Medina de Rioseco, Sp. 44/C2
Medina del Campo, Sp. 44/C2
Medina-Sidonia, Sp. 44/C4
Medinaceli, Sp. 44/D2
Medinipur, India 85/F4
Mediouna, Mor. 98/D2
Mediterranean (sea) 27/E5
Mednogorsk, Rus. 63/L2
Medole, It. 58/D2
Medolla, It. 59/E3
Međugorje, Bosn. 48/C4
Medvedítsa (riv.), Rus. 64/E5
Medvezh'i (isls.), Rus. 65/S2
Medvezh'yegorsk, Rus. 60/G3
Medvode, Slov. 43/L3
Medway (co.), Eng, UK 33/G4
Meekatharra, Austl. 112/C3
Meeker, Co, US 128/F2
Meeker Park, Co, US 137/A2
Meerbusch, Ger. 50/D6
Meerhout, Belg. 53/E1
Meersburg, Ger. 57/F2
Meerssen, Neth. 53/F2
Meerut, India 84/A1
Meeteetse, Wy, US 126/F4
Megála Kalívia, Gre. 47/G3
Megáli Panayía, Gre. 47/H2
Megálon Khórion, Gre. 90/A2
Megalópolis, Gre. 47/H4
Megantic (peak), Qu, Can. 139/E3
Mégara, Gre. 47/H3
Megève, Fr. 56/C6
Meghálaya (state), India 70/F6
Meghalaya (state), India 83/F2
Meghna (riv.), Bang. 85/H4
Megiddo, Isr. 91/G6
Mégiscane (lake), Qu, Can. 130/E1
Mégiscane (riv.), Qu, Can. 130/E1
Megista (isl.), Greece 91/A1
Mehaigne (riv.), Belg. 53/E2
Mehamn, Nor. 37/H1
Meharry (mt.), Austl. 112/C2
Mehdia, Alg. 100/F5
Mehdiya-Plage, Mor. 100/B2
Mehe (riv.), Ger. 51/F1
Mehedinți (prov.), Rom. 48/F3
Mehlingen, Ger. 53/G4
Mehlville, Mo, US 137/G9
Mehndāwal, India 84/D2
Mehrān (riv.), Iran 89/F3
Mehring, Ger. 53/G4
Mehrnbach, Aus. 55/G6
Mehtar Lām, Afg. 86/A2
Mei (riv.), China 79/C3
Meia Ponte (riv.), Braz. 155/B1
Meiganga, Camr. 96/H6
Meighen (isl.), Nun., Can. 123/R7
Meigu, China 83/H2
Meihekou, China 71/N3
Meikle Bin (peak), Sc, UK 36/B4

Meikle Black Law (hill), Sc, UK 36/D5
Meikle Says Law (peak), Sc, UK 36/D5
Meiktila, Myan. 83/G3
Meilen, Swi. 57/E3
Meine, Ger. 51/H4
Meiners Oaks, Ca, US 136/A2
Meinersen, Ger. 51/H4
Meinerzhagen, Ger. 53/G1
Meiningen, Ger. 54/D1
Meiringen, Swi. 56/E4
Meisenheim, Ger. 53/G4
Meishan (res.), China 72/C5
Meissen, Ger. 41/G3
Meissner (peak), Ger. 51/G6
Meitan, China 79/A2
Meitingen, Ger. 54/D5
Meiwa, Japan 77/L6
Meix-devant-Virton, Belg. 53/E4
Meizhou, China 79/C3
Mejaniga, It. 59/E2
Mejaouda (well), Mrta. 98/D5
Mejorada del Campo, Sp. 45/N9
Mek'elē, Eth. 97/N5
Meknès (prov.), Mor. 100/B3
Meknès, Mor. 100/B3
Mekong (riv.), Asia 70/G5
Mekong, Mouths of the (delta), Viet. 83/J6
Mekongga (peak), Indo. 81/F4
Mekoryuk, Ak, US 134/E3
Melaka, Malay. 80/B3
Melanesia (reg.) 116/C5
Melappālaiyam, India 82/C6
Melawi (riv.), Indo. 80/D4
Melbeck, Ger. 51/H2
Melbourne, Fl, US 133/H4
Melbourne (isl.), Nun., Can. 123/J3
Melbourne, Austl. 115/G5
Melbu, Nor. 37/E1
Melchor (isl.), Chile 158/B5
Melchor Múzquiz, Mex. 132/C5
Melchor Ocampo, Mex. 143/Q9
Meldola, It. 59/F4
Meldorf, Ger. 38/C4
Mele (cape), It. 58/B5
Melegnano, It. 58/C2
Melenci, Serb. 48/E3
Melenki, Rus. 60/J5
Melesse, Fr. 42/C2
Meleuz, Rus. 63/K1
Mélèzes (riv.), Qu, Can. 123/J3
Melezza (riv.), It. 57/E5
Melfi, It. 46/D2
Melfort, Sk, Can. 127/G2
Melgar de Fernamental, Sp. 44/C1
Melhus, Nor. 37/D3
Melibocus (peak), Ger. 54/B3
Melide, Swi. 57/E6
Meligalás, Gre. 47/G4
Meliki, Gre. 47/H2
Melili (peak), Kenya 104/C3
Melilla, Sp. 100/C2
Melimoyu (peak), Chile 158/B5
Melipilla, Chile 158/N8
Mélisey, Fr. 56/C2
Melissano, It. 47/F3
Melita, Mb, Can. 127/H3
Melito di Porto Salvo, It. 46/D4
Melitopol', Ukr. 62/E3
Melitota, Md, US 138/B5
Melkbosstrand, SAfr. 106/L10
Melksham, Eng, UK 32/D4
Mella (riv.), It. 58/D2
Mellan Fryken (lake), Swe. 38/F1
Melle, Ger. 51/F4
Melle, Belg. 52/C2
Mellea (riv.), It. 58/A3
Mellègue, Oued (riv.), Alg. 100/K7
Mellerud, Swe. 38/E2
Mellid, Sp. 44/A1
Mellieħa, Malta 46/L7
Mellingen, Swi. 57/E3
Mellrichstadt, Ger. 54/D2
Mellum (isl.), Ger. 51/F1
Melmoth, SAfr. 107/E3
Melnik, Bul. 47/H2
Mělník, Czh. 55/H2
Melo, Uru. 157/F3
Melocheville, Qu, Can. 131/N7
Melrose, Md, US 138/B4
Melrose, Sc, UK 36/D5
Melrose Abbey, Sc, UK 36/D5
Melrose Park, Il, US 135/Q16
Mels, Swi. 57/F3
Melsungen, Ger. 51/G6
Meltham, Eng, UK 35/G4
Melton, Austl. 115/C3
Melton Mowbray, Eng, UK 33/F1
Melun, Fr. 30/K6

Melville (cape), Phil. 81/E2
Melville, Sk, Can. 127/H3
Melville (isl.), Austl. 109/C2
Melville (bay), Austl. 109/C2
Melville, Il, US 137/G8
Melville (cape), Austl. 114/B1
Melville (lake), Nf, Can. 123/L3
Melville (pen.), Nun., Can. 123/H2
Melville, NY, US 139/M8
Melvindale, Mi, US 135/F7
Mélykút, Hun. 48/D2
Melzo, It. 58/C2
Mēmāri, India 85/G4
Memmert (isl.), Ger. 50/D1
Memmingen, Ger. 57/G2
Memphis (int'l arpt.), Tn, US 129/K4
Memphis, Mo, US 127/K5
Memphis, Tx, US 129/G4
Memphis, Tn, US 129/K4
Memphis (ruin), Egypt 91/B5
Memphis, Mi, US 135/G6
Mena, Ar, US 129/J4
Menaggio, It. 57/F5
Menai (str.), Wal, UK 34/C1
Menai Bridge, Wal, UK 34/C1
Ménaka, Mali 103/F3
Menaldum, Neth. 50/C2
Menarandra (riv.), Madg. 107/H9
Menard, Tx, US 129/H5
Menasalbas, Sp. 44/C3
Menavava (riv.), Madg. 107/H7
Mendawai (riv.), Indo. 80/D4
Mende, Fr. 42/E4
Menden, Ger. 51/E6
Mendenhall (cape), Ak, US 134/E4
Mendes, Braz. 211/K4
Méndez, Mex. 143/F3
Mendham, NJ, US 138/D2
Mendig, Ger. 53/G3
Mendip (hills), Eng, UK 32/D4
Mendocino, Ca, US 128/B3
Mendocino (cape), Ca, US 124/A3
Mendooran, Austl. 115/D1
Mendoza, Peru 156/B2
Mendoza, Cuba 145/E1
Mendoza (prov.), Arg. 158/C2
Mendoza, Arg. 158/C2
Mendoza (El Plumerillo) (int'l arpt.), Arg. 158/C2
Mendrisio, Swi. 57/E6
Mene Grande, Ven. 152/D2
Menegosa (peak), It. 58/C3
Menemen, Turk. 62/C5
Menen, Belg. 52/C2
Menengai Crater, Kenya 104/C3
Menengiyn (plain), Mong. 71/L2
Menfi, It. 46/C4
Meng Xian, China 72/C4
Mengcheng, China 72/D4
Mengen, Ger. 57/F1
Mengersgereuth-Hämmern, Ger. 54/D2
Mengerskirchen, Ger. 54/B1
Mengeš, Slov. 43/L3
Menggala, Indo. 80/C4
Menghai, China 78/C1
Mengíbar, Sp. 44/D4
Mengkofen, Ger. 55/F5
Mengla, China 78/C1
Menglian Daizu Lahuzu Vazu Zizhixian, China 83/G3
Mengyin, China 72/D4
Mengzi, China 83/H3
Menindee, Austl. 115/B2
Menindee (dam), Austl. 115/B2
Menindee (lake), Austl. 113/J5
Meningie, Austl. 115/A2
Menlo Park, Ca, US 135/K12
Menlo Park, NJ, US 139/H9
Menlonlat (peak), Chile 158/B5
Mennecy, Fr. 30/K6
Menomonee Falls, Wi, US 127/L4
Menomonie, Wi, US 127/L4
Menorca (int'l arpt.), Sp. 45/H3
Menorca (Minorca) (isl.), Sp. 45/H2
Mentasta Lake, Ak, US 134/K3
Mentawai (str.), Indo. 80/A4
Mentawai (isls.), Indo. 67/J10
Menteroda, Ger. 51/H6
Menthon-Saint-Bernard, Fr. 56/C6
Mentone, Tx, US 129/G5
Mentone, Ca, US 136/C2

Mentor, Oh, US 130/D3
Mentue (riv.), Swi. 56/C4
Menucourt, Fr. 30/H4
Menuma, Japan 77/C1
Menyapa (peak), Indo. 81/E3
Menzel Bourguiba, Tun. 46/A4
Menzie (mt.), Yk, Can. 134/M3
Menzies, Austl. 112/C4
Menziken, Swi. 56/E3
Menzingen, Swi. 57/E3
Menznau, Swi. 56/E3
Meolo, It. 59/F1
Meon (riv.), Eng, UK 33/G5
Meoqui, Mex. 132/B4
Mepistskaro (peak), Geo. 63/G4
Meppel, Neth. 50/D3
Meppen, Il, US 137/F8
Meppen, Ger. 51/E3
Mequinenza, Embalse de (res.), Sp. 45/G2
Mer, Fr. 42/D3
Mera (riv.), It. 57/F5
Meramec (riv.), Mo, US 129/K3
Merano, It. 57/H4
Merate, It. 58/C1
Meratus (mts.), Indo. 80/D4
Meraux, La, US 137/O17
Mercaderes, Col. 152/B4
Mercantour, PN du, Fr. 43/G4
Mercatello sul Metauro, It. 59/F5
Mercato Saraceno, It. 59/F5
Merced (riv.), Ca, US 128/B3
Merced, Ca, US 128/B3
Mercedario (peak), Arg. 157/B3
Mercedes, Arg. 157/E2
Mercedes, Arg. 158/D2
Mercedes, Arg. 159/J11
Mercedes, Uru. 159/J10
Mercer (co.), NJ, US 138/D3
Mercer (isl.), Wa, US 135/C2
Mercer Island, Wa, US 135/C2
Mercerville-Hamilton Square, NJ, US 138/D3
Merchtem, Belg. 53/D2
Mercier, Qu, Can. 131/N7
Mercoal, Ab, Can. 126/D2
Mercy (cape), Nun., Can. 123/K2
Mercy-le-Bas, Fr. 53/E5
Méré, Fr. 30/H5
Meredith (lake), Tx, US 129/G4
Meredith (cape), UK 159/E7
Merefa, Ukr. 62/F2
Mergozzo, It. 57/E5
Mergui (arch.), Myan. 83/G5
Mergui (Myeik), Myan. 78/B3
Meriç, Turk. 49/H5
Méricourt, Fr. 30/G4
Mérida, Sp. 44/B3
Mérida, Ven. 152/D2
Mérida (state), Ven. 152/D2
Mérida, Mex. 144/D1
Mérida, Cordillera de (mts.), Ven. 150/D2
Meridian, Ms, US 133/F3
Meridian, Ok, US 137/N14
Mérignac (int'l arpt.), Fr. 42/C4
Mérignac, Fr. 42/C4
Merimbula, Austl. 115/D3
Merinda, Austl. 114/C3
Mering, Ger. 54/D6
Merinos, Uru. 159/K10
Merja Zerga (lake), Mor. 100/A2
Mérk, Hun. 48/F2
Merkendorf, Ger. 54/D4
Merksem, Belg. 50/B6
Merksplas, Belg. 50/B6
Merlimont, Fr. 52/A3
Merlo, Arg. 159/J11
Merone, It. 58/C1
Merredin, Austl. 112/C4
Merriam, Ks, US 137/D5
Merrick, NY, US 139/L9
Merrick (peak), Sc, UK 36/B5
Merrill, Wi, US 127/L4
Merrill Creek (res.), NJ, US 138/D2
Merrimack (riv.), NH, US 131/G3
Merritt, BC, Can. 126/C3
Merritt Island, Fl, US 133/H4
Merriwa, Austl. 115/D2
Mers-les-Bains, Fr. 52/A3
Mersch, Lux. 53/F4
Merseburg, Ger. 54/E1
Mersey (riv.), Eng, UK 35/F5
Merseyside (co.), Eng, UK 35/F5
Mersin, Turk. 90/C2
Mersing, Malay. 80/B3
Merta, India 89/K3
Mertert, Lux. 53/F4
Mertesdorf, Ger. 53/F4
Merthyr Tydfil, Wal, UK 32/C3

Merthyr Tydfil (co.), Wal, UK 32/C3
Mértola, Port. 44/B4
Merton (bor.), Eng, UK 30/C2
Mertzon, Tx, US 129/G5
Mertzwiller, Fr. 53/G6
Meru (mt.), Tanz. 104/C3
Meru, Kenya 104/C2
Méru, Fr. 52/B5
Meru NP, Kenya 104/C2
Merville, Fr. 50/C5
Méry-sur-Oise, Fr. 30/J4
Merzen, Ger. 51/E4
Merzenich, Ger. 53/F2
Merzifon, Turk. 90/C1
Merzig, Ger. 53/F5
Mesa (mtn.), Ak, US 134/G3
Mesa, Az, US 137/S19
Mesa, Mo, US 129/K3
Mesa (peak), Arg. 159/C6
Mesa Verde NP, Co, US 128/E3
Mesabi (range), Mn, US 127/K4
Mesach Mellet (hills), Libya 99/H4
Mesagne, It. 47/F5
Mesarás (gulf), Gre. 47/J5
Mescalero (ridge), NM, US 132/C3
Meschede, Ger. 51/F6
Mesco, Punta di (pt.), It. 58/C4
Mescolino (peak), It. 59/F5
Meseta de Montemayor (plat.), Arg. 158/D5
Mesgouez (lake), Qu, Can. 130/F1
Mesola, It. 59/F3
Mesolóngion, Gre. 47/G3
Mesomeloka, Madg. 107/J8
Mesopotamia (reg.), Arg. 157/E3
Mesoraca, It. 46/E3
Mespelbrunn, Ger. 54/C3
Mesquite, Tx, US 129/H4
Mesrouh (peak), Mor. 98/E2
Messaad, Alg. 96/F1
Messancy, Belg. 53/E4
Messel, Ger. 54/B3
Messina, SAfr. 105/F5
Messina (str.), It. 46/D4
Messina, It. 46/D3
Messini (gulf), Gre. 47/H4
Messini, It. 47/H4
Messíni, Gre. 47/H4
Messkirch, Ger. 57/F2
Messstetten, Ger. 57/E1
Messy, Fr. 30/L5
Mesta (riv.), Bul. 49/F5
Mestre, It. 59/F2
Mesudiye, Turk. 62/F4
Mesumba (peak), Tanz. 104/C4
Mesurado (cape), Libr. 102/C5
Meta (dept.), Col. 152/C4
Meta (riv.), Col.,Ven. 147/C2
Meta Incognita (pen.), Nun., Can. 123/K2
Metabetchouan, Qu, Can. 131/G1
Metabetchouane (riv.), Qu, Can. 131/F1
Metairie, La, US 137/P17
Metallifere, Colline (mts.), It. 59/D6
Metamora, Mi, US 135/F6
Metán, Arg. 157/D2
Metapontum (ruin), It. 46/E2
Metauro (riv.), It. 43/K5
Metelen, Ger. 51/E4
Metéora, Gre. 47/G3
Metepec, Mex. 143/Q10
Methven, Sc, UK 36/C4
Metica (riv.), Col. 152/C4
Metković, Cro. 47/E1
Metlakatla, Ak, US 134/M4
Metlatonoc, Mex. 144/B2
Metlili Chaamba, Alg. 99/F2
Metnitz, Aus. 43/L3
Metro Toronto Zoo, On, Can. 131/R8
Metropolis, Il, US 130/B4
Metropolitan Oakland (int'l arpt.), Ca, US 128/B3
Metropolitana de Santiago (pol. reg.), Chile 158/N8
Métsovon, Gre. 47/G3
Mettawa, Il, US 135/Q15
Mettenheim, Ger. 55/F6
Mettet, Belg. 53/E2
Mettingen, Ger. 51/E4
Mettlach, Ger. 53/F5
Mettmach, Aus. 55/G6
Mettmann, Ger. 53/G1
Mettuchen, NJ, US 139/H9
Mettula, Isr. 91/D3
Metz, Fr. 53/F5
Metz-Nancy-Lorraine (int'l arpt.), Fr. 53/F6
Metzingen, Ger. 54/C6
Metztitlán, Mex. 143/L6
Meudon, Fr. 30/J5
Meudt, Ger. 53/G3
Meulan, Fr. 30/H4
Meulebeke, Belg. 52/C2

Meurthe (riv.), Fr. 56/C1
Meurthe-et-Moselle (dept.), Fr. 53/E6
Meuse (dept.), Fr. 53/E6
Meuse (riv.), Fr. 40/C4
Meuzin (riv.), Fr. 56/A3
Mevasseret Ziyyon, Isr. 91/G8
Mexborough, Eng, UK 35/G5
Mexia, Tx, US 129/H5
Mexiana, Ilha (isl.), Braz. 151/J3
Mexicalcingo, Mex. 143/Q10
Mexicali, Mex. 128/D4
Mexico (ctry.) 119/G7
México (cap.), Mex. 143/Q10
México (state), Mex. 140/A5
Mexico (gulf), NAm. 140/C2
Mexico, Mo, US 129/K3
Meximieux, Fr. 56/B6
Meybod, Iran 88/F2
Meyers Chuck, Ak, US 134/M4
Meyerton, SAfr. 106/Q13
Meymaneh, Afg. 89/H1
Meyrin, Swi. 56/C5
Meythet, Fr. 56/C6
Meyzieu, Fr. 56/A6
Mezdra, Bul. 47/H1
Mèze, Fr. 42/E5
Mezen' (riv.), Rus. 64/E3
Mezen' (bay), Rus. 61/J2
Mezha (riv.), Bela. 39/P4
Mezhdurechensk, Rus. 64/J4
Mezhdusharskiy (isl.), Rus. 64/E2
Mézières-sur-Seine, Fr. 30/H5
Mezőberény, Hun. 48/E2
Mezőkovácsháza, Hun. 48/E2
Mezőkövesd, Hun. 41/L5
Mezőtúr, Hun. 48/E2
Mezquital (riv.), Mex. 142/D4
Mezzana (peak), It. 57/G5
Mezzocorona, It. 57/H5
Mezzogoro, It. 59/F3
Mezzolombardo, It. 57/H5
Mfangano (isl.), Kenya 104/B3
Mga (riv.), Rus. 61/U7
Mhamdia Fūshānah, Tun. 46/B4
Mhow, India 89/L4
Mi (riv.), China 79/B2
Mi-shima (isl.), Japan 74/B3
Miahuatlán de Porfirio Diaz, Mex. 144/B2
Miajadas, Sp. 44/C3
Mie (pref.), Japan 74/E3
Mie, Japan 74/B4
Miechów, Pol. 41/K3
Międzychód, Pol. 41/H2
Międzylesie, Pol. 41/J3
Międzyrzec Podlaski, Pol. 41/M3
Międzyrzecz, Pol. 41/H2
Międzyzdroje, Pol. 38/F5
Miehlen, Ger. 53/G3
Mielec, Pol. 41/L3
Miercurea Ciuc, Rom. 49/G2
Mieres, Sp. 44/C1
Miesbach, Ger. 43/J3
Mifflin, Pa, US 138/A2
Mifflinburg, Pa, US 138/A2
Migdal Ha'emeq, Isr. 91/G6
Migennes, Fr. 42/E3
Migliarino, It. 58/B5
Mignano, It. 58/B3
Mignovillard, Fr. 56/C4
Migori, Kenya 104/B3
Migori (riv.), Kenya 104/B3
Miguel Alemán, Mex. 142/C2
Miguel Aleman, Presa (dam), Mex. 143/M8
Miguel Alves, Braz. 154/B2
Miguel Auza, Mex. 142/E3
Miguel Calmon, Braz. 154/B3
Miguel Hidalgo (int'l arpt.), Mex. 142/K4
Miguel Hidalgo (res.), Mex. 142/C2
Miguel Pereira, Braz. 211/K7
Miguel Riglos, Arg. 158/...
Miguelete, Uru. 159/K11
Miguelópolis, Braz. 155/B2
Miguelturra, Sp. 44/D3
Migūm, SKor. 73/G6
Mihama, Japan 74/D3
Mihama, Japan 77/L6
Mihara, Japan 77/J6
Miharu, Japan 77/J6
Mihla, Ger. 51/H6
Miho, Japan 77/E2
Mihrābpur, Pak. 89/J3
Mijares (riv.), Sp. 45/E2
Mijas, Sp. 44/C4
Mijdrecht, Neth. 50/B4
Mikasa, Japan 76/B2
Mikata, Japan 77/J4
Mikata (lake), Japan 77/J4

Middle (bay), NY, US 139/L9
Middle Alkali (lake), Ca, US 128/C2
Middle Andaman (isl.), India 83/G5
Middle Caicos (isl.), UK 145/J1
Middle Concho (riv.), Tx, US 132/C4
Middle Raccoon (riv.), Ia, US 129/J2
Middle River, Md, US 138/B5
Middle Sister (peak), Or, US 126/C4
Middleberg, Ok, US 137/M15
Middleburg, Md, US 138/A4
Middleburg, Pa, US 138/A3
Middleburg, Vt, US 130/F2
Middlemount, Austl. 114/C4
Middleport, Pa, US 138/B2
Middlesboro, Ky, US 130/C4
Middlesbrough, Eng, UK 35/G2
Middlesbrough (co.), Eng, UK 35/G2
Middlesex (co.), Eng, UK 33/H4
Middlesex, NJ, US 138/D2
Middleton, Eng, UK 35/F4
Middletown, De, US 138/C5
Middletown, NJ, US 139/J10
Middletown, Pa, US 138/B3
Midelt, Mor. 98/D2
Midi (canal), Fr. 42/D5
Midi-Pyrénées (pol. reg.), Fr. 42/D4
Midland, Mi, US 130/C3
Midland, On, Can. 130/E2
Midland, Tx, US 129/G5
Midland (int'l arpt.), Tx, US 142/J1
Midland, Wa, US 135/C3
Midland Park, NJ, US 139/H8
Midleton, Ire. 31/P13
Midlothian, Il, US 135/Q16
Midlothian (pol. reg.), Sc, UK 36/C5
Midlum, Ger. 51/F1
Midongy Atsimo, Madg. 107/H8
Midou (riv.), Fr. 42/C5
Midsayap, Phil. 79/D6
Midu, China 83/H2
Midvale, Ut, US 137/K12
Midway (isls.), Pac., US 116/H2
Midway, De, US 138/C6
Midway, Il, US 137/H8
Midway, Ok, US 137/N15
Midway, Ut, US 137/L12
Midyan (reg.), SAr. 88/C3
Midyat, Turk. 90/E2
Midžor (peak), Serb. 49/F4
Mie, Japan 74/B4
Miesbach, Ger. 43/J3
Mihama, Japan 77/L6
Mihara, Japan 75/G2
Miharu, Japan 77/J6
Mihla, Ger. 51/H6
Miho, Japan 77/E2
Mikasa, Japan 76/B2
Mikata, Japan 77/J4
Mikata (lake), Japan 77/J4

INDEX SECTION
Mikaw – Monsc 203

Mikawa (bay), Japan 77/M6
Mikhaylovka, Rus. 63/G2
Mikhmoret, Isr. 91/F7
Miki, Japan 77/G6
Mikínai, Gre. 47/H4
Mikínai (Mycenae) (ruin), Gre. 47/H4
Mikkeli (prov.), Fin. 37/H3
Míkonos, Gre. 47/J4
Míkonos (isl.), Gre. 47/J4
Mikri Prespa (lake), Alb.,Gre. 47/G2
Mikri Prespa NP, Gre. 47/G2
Mikuma, Japan 77/L6
Mikumi NP, Tanz. 105/G2
Mikuni, Japan 74/E2
Mikuni-tōge (pass), Japan 75/F2
Mikura (isl.), Japan 75/F4
Mila (prov.), Alg. 100/H4
Milagro, Ecu. 152/B5
Milak, India 84/B1
Milan (Milano), It. 43/H4
Milang, Austl. 115/A2
Milano (prov.), It. 58/C2
Milano (Milan), It. 43/H4
Milas, Turk. 90/A2
Milazzo, It. 46/D3
Milbank, SD, US 127/J4
Mildura, Austl. 115/B2
Miles, Tx, US 132/C4
Miles, Austl. 114/C4
Miles City, Mt, US 127/G4
Milešovka (peak), Czh. 55/G1
Milestone, Sk, Can. 127/G3
Miletto (peak), It. 46/D2
Milevsko, Czh. 55/H4
Milford (lake), Ks, US 132/D2
Milford, Ut, US 128/D3
Milford, NJ, US 138/C2
Milford, Ct, US 139/E1
Milford, De, US 138/C6
Milford, Mi, US 135/E6
Milford Haven, Wal, UK 32/A3
Milford Haven (inlet), Wal., UK 32/A3
Milgis (riv.), Kenya 104/C2
Mili (isl.), Mrsh. 116/G4
Miliana, Alg. 100/G4
Milicz, Pol. 41/J3
Mililani Town, Hi, US 124/V13
Milk (hill), Eng, UK 33/E4
Milk (riv.), Can.,US 122/F4
Milk River, Ab, Can. 126/E3
Mill (isl.), Nun., Can. 123/J2
Mill (riv.), Ct, US 139/E1
Mill Neck, NY, US 139/L8
Millaa Millaa, Austl. 114/B2
Millau, Fr. 42/E4
Millbrae, Ca, US 135/K11
Millbrook (res.), Austl. 113/M8
Millburn, NJ, US 139/H9
Millcreek, Ut, US 137/K12
Mille Îles (riv.), Qu, Can. 131/N6
Mille Lacs (lake), Mn, US 125/H2
Milledgeville, Ga, US 133/H3
Miller, SD, US 127/J4
Miller (int'l arpt.), Tx, US 143/F3
Millerovo, Rus. 63/G2
Millers Ferry (dam), Al, US 133/G3
Millersburg, Pa, US 138/B2
Millerstown, Pa, US 138/A2
Millersville, Pa, US 138/B4
Millesimo, It. 58/B4
Milleur (pt.), Sc, UK 34/C1
Millevaches (plat.), Fr. 42/D4
Millgrove, On, Can. 131/Q9
Millicent, Austl. 115/B3
Milliken, Co, US 137/C2
Millingen aan de Rijn, Neth. 50/D5
Millington, Md, US 138/C5
Millinocket, Me, US 131/G2
Millisle, NI, UK 34/C2
Millmerran, Austl. 114/C4
Millmont, Pa, US 138/A2
Millport, Sc, UK 36/B5
Mills Junction, Ut, US 137/J12
Millstadt, Il, US 137/G9
Millstone (riv.), NJ, US 138/D3
Millstream-Chichester NP, Austl. 112/C2
Millthorpe, Austl. 115/D2
Milltown, NJ, US 139/H10
Milltown Malbay, Ire. 31/P10
Millville, Pa, US 138/B1
Millville, NJ, US 138/C5
Millwood (lake), Ar, US 132/E3
Milmay, NJ, US 138/D5
Milnathort, Wal, UK 35/E5
Milne (bay), PNG 116/E5
Milngavie, Sc, UK 36/B5
Milnrow, Eng, UK 35/F4
Milo, Me, US 131/G2
Milo (riv.), Gui. 102/C4
Milolii, Hi, US 124/U11
Mílos (isl.), Gre. 47/J4
Mílos, Gre. 47/J4
Milseburg (peak), Ger. 54/C1
Miltenberg, Ger. 54/C3
Milton, Austl. 115/D2
Milton, On, Can. 131/Q8
Milton, NZ 117/R12
Milton (res.), Co, US 137/C2
Milton, Fl, US 133/G4
Milton, NH, US 131/G3
Milton, Pa, US 138/B1
Milton, Ut, US 137/K11
Milton, Wa, US 135/C3
Milton-Freewater, Or, US 126/D4
Milton Keynes, Eng, UK 33/F2
Milton Keynes (co.), Eng, UK 33/F2
Milton Ness (pt.), Sc, UK 36/D3
Milton of Campsie, Sc, UK 36/B5
Milwaukee, Wi, US 127/M5
Milwaukee (co.), Wi, US 135/P14
Milz (riv.), Ger. 54/D2
Mimi (riv.), Japan 74/B4
Mimizan, Fr. 42/C4
Mimmaya, Japan 76/B3
Min (riv.), China 70/H5
Min Xian, China 70/H5
Mīna (riv.), Alg. 100/F5
Mīnāb, Iran 89/G3
Minahasa (pen), Indo. 81/F3
Minakuchi, Japan 77/K6
Minamata, Japan 74/B4
Minami Alps NP, Japan 75/F3
Minami-tori-shima (isl.), Japan 116/E2
Minamiaiki, Japan 77/B1
Minamiashigara, Japan 77/C3
Minamichita, Japan 77/L6
Minamidaitō (isl.), Japan 75/L8
Minamiiō (isl.), Japan 116/D2
Minamikawara, Japan 77/K7
Minamimaki, Japan 77/A2
Minamiyamashiro, Japan 77/J6
Minano, Japan 77/C1
Minas (peak), Ecu. 152/B5
Minas, Cuba 145/G1
Minas, Uru. 159/G2
Minas de Matahambre, Cuba 145/F1
Minas de Ríotinto, Sp. 44/B4
Minas Gerais (state), Braz. 154/A5
Minas Novas, Braz. 154/B5
Minatitlán, Mex. 144/C2
Minbu, Myan. 83/F3
Minbya, Myan. 83/F3
Minch, The (North Minch) (str.), Sc, UK 31/Q8
Minchinābād, Pak. 86/B4
Minchinmávida (vol.), Chile 158/B4
Mincio (riv.), It. 59/D2
Mindanao (sea), Phil. 81/F2
Mindanao (isl.), Phil. 67/M9
Mindel (riv.), Ger. 40/F4
Mindelheim, Ger. 57/G1
Mindelo, CpV. 93/J10
Minden, La, US 129/J4
Minden, Ne, US 129/H2
Minden, Ger. 51/F4
Mindoro (str.), Phil. 79/C5
Mindoro (isl.), Phil. 67/L8
Mine (pt.), Ire. 31/Q10
Mineiros, Braz. 151/H7
Mineola, Tx, US 129/J4
Mineola, NY, US 139/L8
Mineral del Monte, Mex. 143/L6
Mineral Wells, Tx, US 129/H4
Mineral'nye Vody (int'l arpt.), Rus. 63/G3
Mineral'nye Vody, Rus. 63/G3
Minerbe, It. 59/E2
Minerbio, It. 59/E3
Minerbio (pt.), Fr. 43/H5
Minersville, Pa, US 138/B2
Minfeld, Ger. 54/B4
Minfeng, China 70/D4
Ming (riv.), China 83/J3
Mingäçevir, Azer. 63/H4
Mingäçevir Su Anbari (res.), Azer. 63/H4
Mingan (riv.), Qu, Can. 131/J1
Mingāora, Pak. 86/B2
Mingenew, Austl. 112/B4
Minglanilla, Sp. 44/E3
Mingshui, China 71/N2
Mingxi, China 79/C2
Minhe, China 70/H4
Minhla, Myan. 83/G4
Minho (riv.), Sp. 44/A1
Minidoka Internment Nat'l Mon., Id, US 126/E6
Minigwal (lake), Austl. 112/D4
Minitonas, Mb, Can. 127/H2
Minlaton, Austl. 113/H5
Minle, China 70/H4
Minna, Nga. 103/G4
Minneapolis, Mn, US 127/K4
Minneapolis-St. Paul (Wold-Chamberlain) (int'l arpt.), Mn, US 127/K4
Minnedosa, Mb, Can. 127/J3
Minnesota (state), US 127/K4
Minnesota (riv.), Mn, US 127/K4
Minnigaff, Sc, UK 34/D2
Minnis (lake), On, Can. 130/B1
Minnitaki (lake), On, Can. 127/K3
Miño (riv.), Port.,Sp. 44/A1
Mino, Japan 77/L4
Minobu, Japan 75/F3
Minokamo, Japan 77/M5
Mino'o, Japan 77/H6
Mino'o (riv.), Japan 77/H6
Minori, Japan 77/E1
Minot, ND, US 127/H3
Minqin, China 70/H4
Minqing, China 79/C2
Minquan, China 72/C4
Minsener Oog (isl.), Ger. 51/F1
Minsk (cap.), Bela. 39/M5
Minsk (int'l arpt.), Bela. 39/M5
Mińsk Mazowiecki, Pol. 41/L2
Minskaya Voblasts Bela. 62/C1
Mintaka (pass), Pak. 87/F5
Mintaka (pass), China 89/K1
Mintlaw, Sc, UK 36/E1
Minto, Ak, US 134/J2
Minto, NB, Can. 131/H2
Minto (inlet), NW, Can. 122/E1
Minūf, Egypt 91/B4
Minusinsk, Rus. 64/K4
Minusio, Swi. 57/E5
Minyā al Qamḩ, Egypt 91/B4
Minyip, Austl. 115/B3
Miquan, China 70/E3
Mira, Port. 44/A2
Mira (riv.), Col. 152/B4
Mira Loma, Ca, US 136/C2
Mira Monte, Ca, US 136/A2
Mira Taglio, It. 59/F2
Mirabel (int'l arpt.), Qu, Can. 131/M6
Mirabel, Qu, Can. 131/M6
Mirabela, Braz. 154/A5
Mirabello, It. 59/E3
Miracema, Braz. 155/D2
Miracema do Norte, Braz. 151/J5
Miradolo Terme, It. 58/C2
Mirador, Braz. 154/A2
Mirador (pass), Chile 158/C4
Miraflores, Peru 156/B3
Miraflores, Mex. 142/C4
Miraflores, Col. 152/C4
Miraflores, Col. 152/C3
Miragoâne, Haiti 145/H2
Miraj, India 89/K5
Miramar, Ca, US 136/C5
Miramar, Arg. 158/F3
Miramar Naval Air Station, Ca, US 136/C5
Mirambéllou (gulf), Gre. 47/J5
Miramichi, NB, Can. 131/H2
Miramont-de-Guyenne, Fr. 42/D4
Miranda (riv.), Braz. 151/G8
Miranda de Ebro, Sp. 44/D1
Miranda do Corvo, Port. 44/A2
Miranda do Douro, Port. 44/B2
Mirande, Fr. 42/D5
Mirandela, Port. 44/B2
Mirandola, It. 43/J4
Mirandópolis, Braz. 155/B2
Mirano, It. 59/F2
Mīrānpur, India 84/A1
Mirante do Paranapanema, Braz. 155/B2
Mirassol, Braz. 155/B2
Miravalles (peak), Sp. 44/B1
Miravalles (vol.), CR 144/E4
Mirebalais, Haiti 145/H2
Mirebeau, Fr. 56/B3
Mirecourt, Fr. 56/C1
Mirfield, Eng, UK 35/G4
Miri, Malay. 80/D3
Miriam Vale, Austl. 114/C4
Mirim (lake), Braz. 157/F3
Mirimire, Ven. 152/D2
Mirina, Gre. 47/J3
Miritiparaná (riv.), Col. 152/D5
Mirna (riv.), Cro. 59/G2
Mirnyy, Rus. 65/M3
Mirnyy, Rus., Ant. 160/G
Mirond (lake), Sk, Can. 127/H2
Mirow, Ger. 40/G2
Mirror (lake), NJ, US 138/D4
Mirtóön (sea), Gre. 47/H4
Miryang, SKor. 74/A3
Mirzāpur, India 84/D3
Misa (riv.), It. 59/G5
Misāha (well), Egypt 101/A4
Misaka, Japan 77/B2
Misaki, Japan 74/D3
Misaki, Japan 77/E3
Misano Adriatico, It. 59/F5
Misantla, Mex. 143/N7
Misato, Japan 77/C1
Misato, Japan 77/D2
Misato, Japan 77/K6
Misawa, Japan 76/B3
Mishan, China 71/P2
Mishawaka, In, US 130/C3
Misheguk (mtn.), Ak, US 134/F2
Mishima, Japan 75/F3
Misilmeri, It. 46/C3
Misiones, Sierra de (mts.), Arg. 157/E2
Miskitos, Cayos (isls.), Nic. 140/E5
Miskolc, Hun. 41/L4
Misono, Japan 77/L6
Misool (isl.), Indo. 81/H4
Misquah (hills), Mn, US 127/L4
Mişrātah (pt.), Libya 97/L1
Mişrātah, Libya 96/J1
Missinaibi (lake), On, Can. 130/D1
Missinaibi (riv.), On, Can. 123/H3
Mission, Tx, US 132/D5
Mission (bay), Ca, US 136/C5
Mission, Ks, US 137/D5
Mission Beach, Austl. 114/B2
Mission Hills, Ks, US 137/D5
Mission Ind. Res., Ca, US 136/C4
Mission San Buenaventura, Ca, US 136/A2
Mission San Jose, Ca, US 135/L12
Mission San Juan Capistrano, Ca, US 136/C3
Mission Viejo, Ca, US 136/C3
Missisa (lake), On, Can. 127/M2
Missisicabi (riv.), Qu, Can. 130/E1
Mississauga, On, Can. 131/Q8
Mississippi (pt.), Austl. 112/D5
Mississippi (state), US 133/F3
Mississippi (riv.), US 125/H5
Mississippi (delta), La, US 133/F4
Mississippi River Gulf Outlet (canal), La, US 137/Q17
Missoula, Mt, US 126/E4
Missouri (state), US 129/J3
Missouri (riv.), US 125/G3
Missouri City, Tx, US 129/J5
Missouri City, Mo, US 137/E5
Mistaken (pt.), Nf, Can. 131/L2
Mistassibi (riv.), Qu, Can. 131/F1
Mistassibi Nord-Est (riv.), Qu, Can. 131/G1
Mistassini, Qu, Can. 131/F1
Mistassini (riv.), Qu, Can. 131/F1
Mistassini (lake), Qu, Can. 123/J3
Mistelbach an der Zaya, Aus. 43/M2
Misti (vol.), Peru 156/D5
Mistissini, Qu, Can. 130/F1
Mistrás (ruin), Gre. 47/H4
Mistretta, It. 46/D4
Misty Fjords Nat'l Mon., US 134/M4
Misty Fjords Nat'l Mon., Ak, US 122/C3
Misugi, Japan 77/K6
Mita, Punta de (pt.), Mex. 142/D4
Mitaka, Japan 77/D2
Mitake, Japan 77/M5
Mitama, Japan 77/B2
Mitare, Ven. 152/D2
Mitchell, SD, US 127/J5
Mitchell (mt.), NC, US 133/H3
Mitchell (riv.), Austl. 109/D2
Mitchell, Il, US 137/G8
Mitchell, Austl. 114/B4
Mitchell River NP, Austl. 115/C3
Mitha Tiwāna, Pak. 86/B3
Mithankot, Pak. 86/A5
Mithi, Pak. 89/J4
Míthimna, Gre. 47/K3
Mitiaro (isl.), CookIs. 117/K6
Mitilíni, Gre. 47/K3
Mitla (pass), Egypt 91/C4
Mitla (ruin), Mex. 144/B2
Mito, Japan 75/G2
Mito, Japan 77/M6
Mitomi, Japan 77/B2
Mitra (peak), EqG. 96/G7
Mitre (pen.), Arg. 157/C7
Mitry-Mory, Fr. 30/K5
Mitsamiouli, Com. 107/G5
Mitsinjo, Madg. 107/H7
Mitsio, Nosy (isl.), Madg. 107/J6
Mits'iwa, Erit. 97/N4
Mitsue, Japan 77/K7
Mitsukaidō, Japan 75/F2
Mitsuke, Japan 75/F2
Mittagong, Austl. 115/D2
Mittagspitze (peak), Aus. 57/F3
Mittainville, Fr. 30/G5
Mittelberg, Aus. 57/G3
Mittelland (canal), Ger. 51/F4
Mittelradde (riv.), Ger. 51/E3
Mittenwald, Ger. 57/H3
Mittersill, Aus. 43/K3
Mitterteich, Ger. 55/F3
Mittlere-Isar (canal), Ger. 55/E6
Mittweida, Ger. 40/G3
Mitú, Col. 152/D4
Mitumba, Monts (mts.), D.R. Congo 105/E1
Mitwitz, Ger. 54/E2
Miura (pen.), Japan 77/D3
Miura, Japan 77/D3
Miwa, Japan 77/H5
Miwa, Japan 77/L5
Mixco Viejo (ruin), Guat. 144/D3
Mixquiahuala, Mex. 143/K6
Mixteco (riv.), Mex. 144/B2
Miya (riv.), Japan 77/K7
Miyagawa, Japan 77/K7
Miyagi (pref.), Japan 76/B4
Miyake (isl.), Japan 75/F3
Miyako (isl.), Japan 79/E3
Miyako, Japan 76/B4
Miyako (isls.), Japan 75/H8
Miyakonojō, Japan 74/B5
Miyama, Japan 77/J5
Miyama, Japan 77/L4
Miyanojō, Japan 74/B5
Miyashiro, Japan 77/D2
Miyazaki (pref.), Japan 74/B4
Miyazaki, Japan 74/B5
Miyazu, Japan 77/H4
Miyazu (bay), Japan 77/H4
Miyi, China 83/H2
Miyoshi, Japan 74/C3
Miyoshi, Japan 77/D2
Miyoshi, Japan 77/D3
Miyoshi, Japan 77/M5
Miyota, Japan 77/B1
Miyun (res.), China 72/H6
Miyun, China 72/H6
Mizen (pt.), Ire. 34/B6
Miziya, Bul. 49/F4
Mizoram (state), India 70/F7
Mizpah, NJ, US 138/D5
Mizpe Ramon, Isr. 91/D4
Mizuho, Japan 77/C2
Mizuho, Japan 77/H5
Mizunami, Japan 77/M5
Mizusawa, Japan 76/B4
Mjölby, Swe. 38/F2
Mjøndalen, Nor. 38/D2
Mjörn (lake), Swe. 38/E3
Mjøsa (lake), Nor. 37/D3
Mkata (plain), Tanz. 104/C4
Mkokotoni, Tanz. 104/C4
Mkomazi Game Rsv., Tanz. 104/C4
Mkombo (riv.), Tanz. 104/A4
Mkondoa (riv.), Tanz. 104/C4
Mkorn (peak), Mor. 98/D3
Mkumbi (pt.), Tanz. 104/C4
Mkushi, Zam. 105/E3
Mkuze (riv.), SAfr. 107/F2
Mladá Boleslav, Czh. 55/H2
Mladá Vožice, Czh. 55/H3
Mladenovac, Serb. 48/E3
Mlala (hills), Tanz. 104/A4
Mława, Pol. 41/L2
Mljet (isl.), Cro. 47/E1
Mljet NP, Cro. 47/E1
Mmabatho, SAfr. 106/D2
Mnyera (riv.), Tanz. 104/B5
Mo Duc, Viet. 78/E3
Moa (isl.), Indo. 81/G5
Moa (riv.), SLeo. 102/C5
Moa, Cuba 145/H1
Moab, Ut, US 128/E3
Moala Group (isl.), Fiji 116/G6
Moama, Austl. 115/C1
Moamba, Moz. 107/F2
Moaña, Sp. 44/A1
Moanda, Gabon 96/H8
Moate, Ire. 31/Q10
Mobara, Japan 77/E3
Mobaye, CAfr. 97/K7
Moberly, Mo, US 129/J3
Moberly Lake, BC, Can. 126/C2
Mobile, Al, US 133/F4
Mobridge, SD, US 127/H4
Moca (pass), Turk. 91/C1
Mocache, Ecu. 152/B5
Mocajuba, Braz. 151/J4
Moçambique, Moz. 105/H4
Mocanaqua, Pa, US 138/B1
Mocha (riv.), Rus. 61/W9
Moche (ruin), Peru 156/B3
Mochima, PN, Ven. 153/E2
Mochizuki, Japan 77/A1
Mochudi, Bots. 105/E5
Mochumí, Peru 156/B2
Mocímboa da Praia, Moz. 104/D5
Möckeln (lake), Swe. 38/E3
Mockfjärd, Swe. 38/F1
Möckmühl, Ger. 54/C4
Moclín, Sp. 44/D4
Mocoa, Col. 152/B4
Mococa, Braz. 211/F6
Mocorito, Mex. 142/D3
Moctezuma, Mex. 143/E4
Moctezuma, Mex. 142/C2
Mocuba, Moz. 105/G4
Modāsa, India 89/K4
Modderrivier (riv.), SAfr. 106/D3
Modena (prov.), It. 59/D3
Modena, It. 59/D3
Moder (riv.), Fr. 43/G2
Modesto, Ca, US 128/B3
Modica, It. 46/D4
Modigliana, It. 59/E4
Modjeska, Ca, US 136/C3
Modjigo (reg.), Niger 96/H4
Mödling, Aus. 49/N7
Modot, Mong. 71/J2
Modriča, Bosn. 48/D3
Modugno, It. 46/E2
Moe, Austl. 115/C3
Moeb (bay), Namb. 106/A2
Moel-y-Llyn (peak), Wal, UK 32/C2
Moëlan-sur-Mer, Fr. 42/B3
Moelfre (peak), Wal, UK 32/C1
Moen, Nor. 37/F1
Moenkopi (riv.), US 128/E3
Moerai (isl.), FrPol. 117/K7
Moerbeke, Belg. 52/C1
Moers, Ger. 50/D6
Moervaart (riv.), Belg. 52/C1
Moesa (riv.), Swi. 57/F5
Moffat, Sc, UK 36/C6
Moffett Field Naval Air Sta., Ca, US 135/K12
Moga, India 86/C4
Mogadouro, Port. 44/B2
Mogami (riv.), Japan 76/B4
Mogami, Japan 76/B4
Mogaung, Myan. 83/G2
Mogent (riv.), Sp. 45/L6
Mogglingen, Ger. 54/C5
Moghul Gardens, India 86/C3
Mogi das Cruzes, Braz. 211/G8
Mogi-Guaçu, Braz. 211/G7
Mogi-Guaçu (riv.), Braz. 211/G7
Mogi-Mirim, Braz. 211/G7
Mogilno, Pol. 41/J2
Moglia, It. 59/D3
Mogliano Veneto, It. 59/F1
Möglingen, Ger. 54/C5
Mogoro, It. 46/A3
Mogotes (pt.), Arg. 158/F3
Mogotón (peak), Nic. 144/E3
Moguer, Sp. 44/B4
Mohács, Hun. 48/D3
Mohaeli (isl.), Com. 107/G6
Mohales Hoek, Les. 106/D3
Mohall, ND, US 127/H3
Mohamed V (dam), Mor. 100/C2
Mohamed V, Barrage (res.), Mor. 100/C2
Mohamed V (Casablanca) (int'l arpt.), Mor. 98/D2
Mohammadia, Alg. 100/F5
Mohammadia-Znata (prov.), Mor. 100/A2
Mohammedia, Mor. 100/A3
Mohawk (lake), NJ, US 138/D1
Moheda, Swe. 38/F3
Mohembo, Bots. 105/D4
Mohican (cape), Ak, US 134/E3
Möhlin, Swi. 56/D2
Möhne (riv.), Ger. 51/F6
Möhnestausee (lake), Ger. 51/F5
Mohnton, Pa, US 138/C3
Moho, Peru 156/D4
Mohrsville, Pa, US 138/C3
Mohyliv-Podil's'kyy, Ukr. 49/H1
Moi (int'l arpt.), Kenya 104/C4
Moi, Nor. 38/B2
Moie, It. 59/G5
Moinești, Rom. 49/H2
Moinkum (des.), Kaz. 64/H5
Moinsi (hills), Gha. 103/E5
Moira (riv.), On, Can. 130/E2
Moirans, Fr. 42/F4
Moirans-en-Montagne, Fr. 56/B5
Moisie (riv.), Qu, Can. 123/K3
Moislains, Fr. 52/B4
Moissac, Fr. 42/D4
Moisselles, Fr. 30/K4
Moisson, Fr. 30/H4
Moita, Port. 45/Q10
Moitaco, Ven. 153/E3
Mojácar, Sp. 44/E4
Mojave (riv.), Ca, US 128/C4
Mojave (des.), Ca, US 124/C5
Mojiang Hanizu Zizhixian, China 83/H3
Mojikit (lake), On, Can. 127/L3
Mojkovac, Serb. 47/F1
Mojos, Llanos de (plain), Bol. 150/E6
Moju (riv.), Braz. 151/J4
Mōka, Japan 75/F2
Mokameh, India 85/E3
Mokapu (pt.), Hi, US 124/W13
Mokau (riv.), NZ 117/S10
Mokelumne (riv.), Ca, US 128/B3
Mokelumne (aqueduct), Ca, US 135/M11
Mokena, Il, US 135/Q16
Mokil (isl.), Micr. 116/E4
Mokochu (peak), Thai. 78/B3
Mokokchūng, India 83/F2
Mokolo, Camr. 96/H5
Mokp'o, SKor. 73/D5
Mokrin, Serb. 48/E3
Moksha (riv.), Rus. 63/G1
Mokuleia, Hi, US 124/V12
Mol, Serb. 48/E3
Mol, Belg. 50/C6
Moláoi, Gre. 47/H4
Molare, It. 58/B3
Molas, Punta (pt.), Mex. 144/E1
Molat (isl.), Cro. 48/B3
Molatón (peak), Sp. 44/E3
Molbergen, Ger. 51/E3
Mold, Wal, UK 35/E5
Moldavia (reg.), Rom. 49/H2
Moldavian Carpathians (range), Rom. 49/G2
Molde, Nor. 37/C3
Moldova (ctry.) 49/H2
Moldova (riv.), Rom. 49/G2
Moldova Nouă, Rom. 48/E3
Moldoveanu (peak), Rom. 49/G3
Mole (riv.), Eng, UK 32/C5
Mole NP, Gha. 103/E4
Môle Saint-Nicolas, Haiti 145/H2
Molepolole, Bots. 105/E5
Molina, Sp. 44/E2
Molina, Chile 158/B3
Molina de Segura, Sp. 44/E3
Moline, Il, US 127/L5
Molinella, It. 59/E3
Molinicos, Sp. 44/D3
Molino de Flores, PN, Mex. 143/R9
Molins de Rei, Sp. 45/L7
Molise (reg.), It. 46/D2
Molkom, Swe. 38/E2
Möll (riv.), Aus. 43/K3
Møllebjerg (peak), Den. 37/D5
Mollendo, Peru 156/C5
Mollendruz, Col du (pass), Swi. 56/C4
Mollerussa, Sp. 45/F2
Molles (pt.), Chile 158/C2
Molles, Uru. 159/K10
Mollet del Vallès, Sp. 45/L6
Mollis, Swi. 57/F3
Mölndal, Swe. 38/E3
Mölnlycke, Swe. 38/E3
Molodezhnaya, Rus., Ant. 160/D
Mologa (riv.), Rus. 60/G4
Molokai (isl.), Hi, US 124/T10
Moloma (riv.), Rus. 61/L4
Molong, Austl. 115/D2
Molopo (riv.), Bots. 93/E7
Mólos, Gre. 47/H3
Molsheim, Fr. 56/D1
Molteno, SAfr. 106/D3
Molu (isl.), Indo. 81/H5
Molucca (isls.), Indo. 67/M10
Molucca (sea), Asia 67/M10
Moluccas (arch.), Indo. 81/G3
Molveno (lake), It. 57/G5
Molveno, It. 57/G5
Mombaça, Braz. 154/C2
Mombasa, Kenya 104/C4
Mombetsu, Japan 76/C1
Mombetsu, Japan 76/C2
Mömbris, Ger. 54/C2
Momchilgrad, Bul. 47/J2
Momfafa (cape), Indo. 81/H4
Momignies, Belg. 53/D3
Mömlingen, Ger. 54/C3
Momo, It. 58/B1
Momoishi, Japan 76/B3
Mompós, Col. 152/C2
Mon (state), Myan. 83/G4
Mon (riv.), Myan. 83/F3
Møn (isl.), Den. 37/E5
Mona (isl.), PR 141/M8
Mona (passg.), NAm. 141/L8
Monaco (ctry.) 58/J8
Monaco (cap.), Mona. 58/J8
Monaco, Port of (har.), Mona. 58/J8
Monadhliath (mts.), Sc, UK 36/B2
Monagas (state), Ven. 153/F2
Monaghan (co.), Ire. 34/A3
Monagrillo, Pan. 152/A3
Monagrillo (ruin), Pan. 152/A2
Monar (lake), Sc, UK 36/A2
Monashee (mts.), BC, Can. 126/D3
Moncada, Sp. 45/E3
Moncalieri, It. 43/G4
Moncalvo, It. 58/B2
Monção, Braz. 154/A1
Moncayo, Sierra del (range), Sp. 44/E2
Mönch (peak), Swi. 56/D4
Monchegorsk, Rus. 60/G2
Mönchengladbach, Ger. 50/D6
Monchique, Serra de (mts.), Port. 44/A4
Monchique, Port. 44/A4
Moncks Corner, SC, US 133/H3
Monclova, Mex. 132/C5
Moncton, NB, Can. 131/H2
Mondego (cape), Port. 44/A2
Mondego (riv.), Port. 44/A2
Mondéjar, Sp. 44/D2
Mondolfo, It. 59/G5
Mondoñedo, Sp. 44/B1
Mondorf-les- Bains, Lux. 53/F4
Mondovì, It. 58/A4
Mondragón, Sp. 44/D1
Mondragone, It. 46/C2
Mondsee (lake), Aus. 55/G7
Mondsee, Aus. 55/G7
Moneglia, It. 58/C4
Monemvasía, Gre. 47/H4
Mones Cazón, Arg. 158/E3
Monesterio, Sp. 44/B3
Money (pt.), Sc, UK 34/C2
Moneyreagh, NI, UK 34/C2
Monferrato (reg.), It. 43/H4
Monforte, Sp. 44/B1
Monforte, Port. 44/B3
Mongaguá, Braz. 211/G9
Mongers (lake), Austl. 109/A3
Monghidoro, It. 59/E4
Mongo, Chad 97/J5
Mongo (riv.), Gui. 102/C4
Mongolia (ctry.) 70/G2
Mongu, Zam. 105/D4
Mönh Hayrhan (peak), Mong. 70/F2
Mönh Sarĭdag (peak), Mong. 70/H1
Monheim, Ger. 54/D5
Monheim, Ger. 53/F1
Monifieth, Sc, UK 36/D4
Moniquirá, Col. 152/C3
Monistrol de Montserrat, Sp. 45/K6
Monistrol-sur-Loire, Fr. 42/F4
Monitor (range), Nv, US 128/C3
Monkayo, Phil. 79/E6
Monkey (pt.), Nic. 145/F4
Monkey River Town, Belz. 144/D2
Mońki, Pol. 41/M2
Monks (isl.), Md, US 138/B5
Monmouth, Il, US 127/L5
Monmouth, Or, US 126/C4
Monmouth Beach, NJ, US 138/E3
Monmouth Junction, NJ, US 138/D3
Monmouth Mil. Res., NJ, US 138/D3
Monmouthshire (co.), Wal, UK 32/D3
Monmow (riv.), Eng, UK 32/C2
Monnickendam, Neth. 50/C4
Mono (riv.), Togo 96/F6
Mono (lake), Ca, US 128/C3
Mono (prov.), Ben. 103/F5
Monocacy (riv.), Md, US 138/A4
Monor, Hun. 48/D2
Monóvar, Sp. 45/E3
Monreal del Campo, Sp. 44/E2
Monreale, It. 46/C3
Monroe, Wi, US 127/L5
Monroe, Ut, US 128/D3
Monroe, Ga, US 133/H3
Monroe (lake), Fl, US 133/G2
Monroe, La, US 129/J4
Monroe, NC, US 133/H3
Monroe, Mi, US 130/D3
Monroe, Ct, US 139/E1
Monroe, NY, US 138/D1
Monroe, Wa, US 135/C2
Monroe City, Il, US 137/G9
Monroeville, Al, US 133/G4
Monroeville, NJ, US 138/C4
Monrovia (cap.), Libr. 102/C5
Monrovia, Ca, US 136/G7
Mons, Belg. 52/C3
Monsanto, Port. 44/B2
Monschau, Ger. 53/F2

Monsefú, Peru 156/B2
Monselice, It. 43/J4
Monsenhor Tabosa,
Braz. 154/B2
Monsey, NY, US 139/J7
Monsheim, Ger. 54/B3
Monster, Neth. 50/B4
Mönsteras, Swe. 38/G3
Monsummano Terme,
It. 59/D5
Mont-de-Marsan, Fr. 42/C5
Mont-Joli, Qu, Can. 131/G1
Mont-Laurier,
Qu, Can. 130/F2
Mont Peko, PN du,
C.d'Iv. 102/D5
Mont-Royal,
Qu, Can. 131/N6
Mont-Saint-Martin, Fr. 53/E4
Mont-Saint-Michel,
Qu, Can. 130/F2
Mont Sangbé, PN du,
C.d'Iv. 102/D4
Mont-Sous-Vaudrey,
Fr. 56/B4
Montà, It. 58/A3
Monta Fon (mts.),
Aus. 57/F3
Montabaur, Ger. 53/G3
Montagnana, It. 59/E2
Montagne d'Ambre NP,
Madg. 107/J6
Montagny-Sainte-Félicité,
Fr. 30/L4
Montagu, SAfr. 106/M10
Montague (str.),
Ak, US 134/J4
Montague, Ca, US 129/H4
Montague, Tx, US 129/H4
Montague, PE, Can. 131/J2
Montague, NJ, US 138/D1
Montague (isl.),
Ak, US 122/B2
Montaigu, Fr. 42/C3
Montaione, It. 59/D5
Montalbán, Sp. 45/E2
Montalbano Jonico, It. 46/E2
Montale, It. 59/E5
Montale, It. 59/D3
Montalieu-Vercieu, Fr. 56/B6
Montalvão, Port. 44/B3
Montalvo, Ca, US 136/C2
Montana (prov.), Bul. 47/H1
Montana, Bul. 49/F4
Montana, Swi. 56/D5
Montana (state), US 126/F4
Montanaro, It. 58/A2
Montanha, Braz. 154/B5
Montara, Ca, US 135/J11
Montargis, Fr. 42/E2
Montataire, Fr. 52/B5
Montauban, Fr. 42/D4
Montauk, NY, US 139/G1
Montauk (pt.), NY, US 139/G1
Montbard, Fr. 42/F3
Montbéliard, Fr. 56/C2
Montblanc, Sp. 45/F2
Montcada i Reixac,
Sp. 45/L7
Montceau-les-Mines,
Fr. 42/F3
Montclair, Ca, US 136/C2
Montclair, NJ, US 139/J8
Montcornet, Fr. 52/C5
Montdidier, Fr. 52/B4
Monte Albán (ruin),
Mex. 144/B2
Monte Alegre,
Braz. 151/H4
Monte Alegre de Goiás,
Braz. 154/A4
Monte Alegre de Minas,
Braz. 155/B1
Monte Alegre do Piauí,
Braz. 154/A3
Monte Alto, Braz. 155/B2
Monte Azul, Braz. 154/B4
Monte Carmelo, Braz. 155/C1
Monte Carmelo, Ven. 152/D2
Monte Caseros, Arg. 157/E3
Monte Comán, Arg. 158/D2
Monte Escobedo,
Mex. 142/E4
Monte Maíz, Arg. 158/E2
Monte Pascoal, PN de,
Braz. 151/L7
Monte Pascoal, PN de,
Braz. 154/C5
Monte Rosa (mts.), It. 56/D6
Monte San Savino, It. 59/E6
Montealegre, Sp. 44/E3
Montebello (isls.),
Austl. 109/A3
Montebello, Ca, US 136/F7
Montebello
Vicentino, It. 59/E2
Montebelluna, It. 59/F1
Montebruno, It. 58/C3
Montecarlo, Arg. 157/F2
Montecassino, It. 59/G6
Montecatini Terme, It. 59/D5
Montecavolo, It. 58/D3
Montecchio, It. 59/F5
Montechiaro d'Asti, It. 58/B2
Montecito, Ca, US 136/D4
Montecristo (isl.), It. 46/B1
Montecristo, PN,
ESal. 144/D3
Montefeltro (reg.), It. 59/F5
Monteforte d'Alpone, It. 59/E2
Montefrío, Sp. 44/C4
Montego Bay, Jam. 145/G2
Montegranaro, It. 43/K5
Montegrotto Terme, It. 59/E2
Montehermoso, Sp. 44/B2

Monteiro, Braz. 154/C2
Montelavar, Port. 45/P10
Montellano, Sp. 44/C4
Montello, Nv, US 126/E5
Montelupo Fiorentino,
It. 59/E5
Montemagno, It. 58/B3
Montemarciano, It. 59/G5
Montemor-o-Novo,
Port. 44/A3
Montemor-o-Velho,
Port. 44/A3
Montemorelos, Mex. 143/F3
Montemuro (peak),
Port. 44/A2
Montendre, Fr. 42/C4
Montenegro di
Bisaccia, It. 46/D2
Montepulciano, It. 43/J5
Montereau-Faut-Yonne,
Fr. 42/E2
Montereau-sur-le-Jard,
Fr. 30/K5
Monterey, Ca, US 128/B3
Monterey (bay),
Ca, US 124/B4
Monterey Park,
Ca, US 136/F7
Montería, Col. 152/C2
Montero, Bol. 150/F7
Monteros, Arg. 157/C2
Monterosso (peak), It. 57/G4
Monterosso al Mare,
It. 58/C4
Monterotondo, It. 46/C1
Monterrey, Mex. 143/E3
Monterrey, Sp. 44/B2
Montes (pt.), Arg. 159/C6
Montes Altos, Braz. 154/B5
Montes Claros, Braz. 154/B5
Montese, It. 59/D4
Montespertoli, It. 59/E5
Montesson, Fr. 30/J5
Monteux, Fr. 42/F4
Montevarchi, It. 59/E5
Montevideo, Mn, US 127/K4
Montevideo (cap.),
Uru. 159/K11
Montevideo (dept.),
Uru. 159/K11
Montévrain, Fr. 30/L5
Montezuma (peak),
Az, US 137/R19
Montezuma Castle
Nat'l Mon., Az, US 128/E4
Montfermeil, Fr. 30/K5
Montferrand-le-Château,
Fr. 56/B3
Montfoort, Neth. 50/B4
Montfort-L'Amaury,
Fr. 52/A6
Montgeron, Fr. 30/K5
Montgomery, Wal, UK 32/C1
Montgomery (cap.),
Al, US 133/G3
Montgomery,
Il, US 135/P16
Montgomery (co.),
Md, US 138/A5
Montgomery,
Pa, US 138/B1
Montgomery,
WV, US 130/D4
Montgomery Village,
Md, US 138/A5
Montgomeryville,
Pa, US 138/C2
Montgrand (peak), Fr. 42/E5
Monthermé, Fr. 53/D4
Monthey, Swi. 56/C5
Monthureux-sur-Saône,
Fr. 56/B1
Monthyon, Fr. 30/L4
Monti Sabini (mts.), It. 46/C1
Monticelli d'Ongina,
It. 58/C2
Monticelli Terme, It. 58/D3
Monticello, Mo, US 127/L5
Monticello, Ky, US 130/C4
Monticello, In, US 130/C3
Monticello, Ia, US 129/K4
Monticello, Fl, US 133/H4
Monticello, Va, US 133/J2
Monticello Conte Otto,
It. 59/E1
Montichiari, It. 58/D2
Montier-en-Der, Fr. 56/A1
Montignies-le-Tilleul,
Belg. 52/C2
Montigny-en-Gohelle,
Fr. 52/B3
Montigny-le-Bretonneux,
Fr. 30/J5
Montigny-le-Roi, Fr. 56/B1
Montijo, Sp. 44/B3
Montijo, Port. 45/Q10
Montilla, Sp. 44/C4
Montivilliers, Fr. 42/D2
Montlebon, Fr. 56/C3
Montlhéry, Fr. 30/J6
Montluel, Fr. 56/B6
Montmagny,
Qu, Can. 131/G2
Montmédy, Fr. 53/E4
Montmerle-sur-Saône,
Fr. 56/A5
Montmirail, Fr. 52/C6
Montmorency, Fr. 30/K5
Montmorillon, Fr. 42/D3
Montmorot, Fr. 56/B4

Monto, Austl. 114/C4
Montodine, It. 58/C2
Montoir-de-Bretagne,
Fr. 42/B3
Montois-la-Montagne,
Fr. 53/F5
Montone (riv.), It. 59/E4
Montopoli, It. 59/D5
Montorio Veronese, It. 59/E2
Montoro, Sp. 44/C3
Montour (ridge),
Pa, US 138/B2
Montour, Pa, US 138/B1
Montoursville,
Pa, US 138/B1
Montpelier (cap.),
Vt, US 131/F2
Montpellier, Fr. 42/E5
Montreal (lake),
Sk, Can. 127/G2
Montreal (riv.),
On, Can. 130/C2
Montréal, Qu, Can. 131/N6
Montréal-Est,
Qu, Can. 131/N6
Montréal-la-Cluse, Fr. 56/B5
Montréal-Nord,
Qu, Can. 131/N6
Montréjeau, Fr. 42/D5
Montreuil, Fr. 30/K5
Montreuil, Fr. 52/A3
Montreuil-Bellay, Fr. 42/C3
Montreuil-sur-Epte, Fr. 30/G4
Montreux, Swi. 56/C5
Montreux-Château, Fr. 56/C2
Montrevel-en-Bresse,
Fr. 56/B5
Montricher, Swi. 56/C5
Montrose, Co, US 128/F3
Montrose (basin),
Sc, UK 36/D3
Montrose, Sc, US 36/D3
Montrouge, Fr. 30/J5
Montry, Fr. 30/L5
Monts, Fr. 42/D3
Montseny, PN, Sp. 45/L6
Montserrat (co.),
Libr. 102/C5
Montserrat (peak), Sp. 45/F2
Montserrat
(dpcy.), UK 141/N8
Montsoult, Fr. 30/J4
Montvale, NJ, US 139/J7
Montville, NJ, US 139/H8
Monywa, Myan. 83/G3
Monza, It. 58/C1
Monze, Zam. 105/E4
Monzingen, Ger. 53/G4
Monzón, Peru 156/B3
Monzón, Sp. 45/F2
Mooirivier, SAfr. 107/E3
Mool (riv.), SAfr. 106/P13
Moonta, Austl. 113/H5
Moora, Austl. 112/C4
Moorcroft, Wy, US 127/G4
Moordrecht, Neth. 50/B5
Moore (lake), Austl. 109/A3
Moore, Ok, US 137/N15
Moore Haven,
Fl, US 133/H5
Moore River NP,
Austl. 112/B4
Moorea (isl.),
FrPol. 117/K6
Moorenweis, Ger. 57/H1
Moorestown,
NJ, US 138/D4
Mooresville,
NC, US 133/H3
Mooretown,
On, Can. 135/H6
Moorfoot (hills),
Sc, UK 36/C3
Moorhead, Mn, US 127/J4
Moorook, Austl. 115/B2
Moorpark, Ca, US 136/B2
Moorreesburg,
SAfr. 106/L10
Moorslede, Belg. 52/C2
Moosburg, Ger. 55/E6
Moose (mtn.),
Sk, Can. 127/G3
Moose (riv.), On, Can. 130/D1
Moose Creek,
Ak, US 134/J3
Moose Jaw,
Sk, Can. 127/G3
Moose Pass,
Ak, US 134/J3
Moosehead (lake),
Me, US 125/N2
Mooseheart (mtn.),
Ak, US 134/H3
Mooseheart,
Il, US 135/P16
Moosinning, Ger. 55/E6
Moosomin,
Sk, Can. 127/H3
Moosonee,
On, Can. 130/D1
Mooseedorf, Swi. 56/D3
Mopti (pol. reg.),
Mali 102/D3
Mopti, Mali 102/D3
Moquegua (dept.),
Peru 156/D5
Moquegua, Peru 156/D5
Moquehuà, Arg. 159/J11
Mor (riv.), India 85/F4
Mór, Hun. 48/D2
Mora, Camr. 96/H5
Mora (riv.), NM, US 129/F4
Mora, NM, US 129/F4

Mora, Sp. 44/D3
Mora, Port. 44/A3
Mora, Swe. 38/F1
Mora de Rubielos, Sp. 45/E2
Morača (riv.), Serb. 47/F1
Morada Nova,
Braz. 154/C2
Morada Nova de Minas,
Braz. 155/C1
Morādābād, India 84/B1
Morin Dawa Daurzu Zizhiqi,
China 71/M2
Morafenobe, Madg. 107/H7
Morag, Pol. 39/H5
Moraga, Ca, US 135/K11
Mórahalom, Hun. 48/D2
Morainvilliers, Fr. 30/H5
Moral de Calatrava,
Sp. 44/D3
Moraleja, Sp. 44/B2
Morales, Guat. 144/D3
Moramanga, Madg. 107/J7
Moranbah, Austl. 114/C3
Morane (isl.),
FrPol. 117/M7
Morangis, Fr. 30/K5
Morano Calabro, It. 46/E3
Morant Bay, Jam. 145/G2
Morar (lake), Sc, UK 31/R8
Mörarano Chrome,
Madg. 107/J7
Morat (lake), Swi. 56/D4
Morata de Tajuña,
Sp. 45/N9
Moratalla, Sp. 44/D3
Moratuwa, SrL. 82/C6
Morava (riv.), Czh. 41/J4
Moravia (reg.), Czh. 41/J4
Moravská Třebová,
Czh. 41/J4
Moravské Budějovice,
Czh. 41/H4
Morawa, Austl. 112/C4
Morawhanna, Guy. 150/G2
Moray (pol. reg.),
Sc, UK 36/C2
Moray Firth (inlet),
Sc, UK 36/B1
Morbach, Ger. 53/G4
Morbegno, It. 57/F5
Morbier, Fr. 56/C4
Morbio Inferiore,
Swi. 57/F6
Morbras (riv.), Fr. 30/K5
Mörbylånga, Swe. 38/G3
Morcenx, Fr. 42/C4
Morciano di Romagna,
It. 59/F5
Morclan, Pic de
(peak), Fr. 56/C5
Morden, Mb, Can. 127/J3
Mordoviya, Resp.,
Rus. 64/Q6
Møre Og Romsdal (co.),
Nor. 37/C3
Moreau (riv.),
SD, US 127/H4
Morecambe (bay),
Eng, UK 35/E3
Moree, Austl. 115/D1
Morehead, Ky, US 130/D4
Morehead City,
NC, US 133/J3
Morelia, Mex. 143/E5
Morella, Sp. 45/E2
Morelos (state),
Mex. 140/A5
Morena, Sierra (range),
Sp. 44/C4
Morelos (isl.),
Ca, US 136/C2
Moresby (isl.),
BC, Can. 122/C3
Moreton (isl.),
Austl. 109/E3
Moreton (cape),
Austl. 114/D4
Moreton (bay),
Austl. 114/F6
Moreton Island NP,
Austl. 114/D4
Moreuil, Fr. 52/B4
Moreyu (riv.), Rus. 61/P2
Morez, Fr. 56/C4
Mørs (isl.), Den. 38/C3
Morgan, Austl. 113/H5
Morgan (co.),
Ut, US 137/K11
Morgan City,
La, US 133/F4
Morganfield,
Ky, US 130/C4
Morgantina (ruin), It. 46/D4
Morganton,
NC, US 133/H3
Morgantown,
Ky, US 130/C4
Morgantown,
WV, US 130/E4
Morge (riv.), Fr. 42/E3
Morgenzon, SAfr. 107/E2
Morges, Swi. 56/C4
Morghāb (riv.), Afg. 89/H1
Morgongåva, Swe. 38/G2
Morguilla (pt.),
Chile 158/B3
Morhange, Fr. 53/F5
Morhar (riv.), India 85/E3
Mori, It. 43/J4
Mori, Japan 76/B2

Mori Kazak Zizhixian,
China 70/F3
Morton NWR,
NY, US 139/F2
Morialta Conservation Park,
Austl. 113/M8
Moriarty, NM, US 129/F4
Morice (lake),
BC, Can. 122/D3
Morie (lake), Sc, UK 36/B1
Moriguchi, Japan 77/J6
Morin Dawa Daurzu Zizhiqi,
China 71/M2
Moringen, Ger. 51/G5
Morinville, Ab, Can. 126/E2
Morioka, Japan 76/B4
Morisset, Austl. 115/D2
Moriston (riv.),
Sc, UK 36/B2
Moriya, Japan 77/D2
Moriyama, Japan 77/J5
Morlaix, Fr. 42/B2
Morlanwelz, Belg. 53/D3
Mörlenbach, Ger. 54/B3
Morley, Eng, UK 35/G4
Mormant, Fr. 30/L6
Mormoiron (hill),
Fr. 30/K5
Mörnsheim, Ger. 54/D5
Moro, Pak. 89/J3
Moro (gulf), Phil. 79/D6
Morocco, Port. 98/D2
Morocelí, Hon. 144/E3
Morococha, Peru 156/B3
Morogoro (pol. reg.),
Tanz. 104/C4
Morogoro, Tanz. 104/C4
Morombe, Madg. 107/G8
Morón, Ven. 152/D2
Morón, Arg. 159/J11
Morón, Cuba 145/G1
Morón de la Frontera,
Sp. 44/C4
Morona (riv.), Peru 150/C4
Morona-Santiago (dept.),
Ecu. 152/B5
Morondara (riv.),
Madg. 107/H8
Morondava, Madg. 107/H8
Morón, Com. 107/G5
Morotai (str.), Indo. 81/G3
Morotai (isl.), Indo. 67/M9
Moroto, Ugan. 104/B2
Moroto (mt.), Ugan. 104/B2
Moroyama, Japan 77/C2
Morpará, Braz. 154/B4
Morpeth, Eng, UK 35/G1
Morphou, Cyp. 91/C2
Morphou (bay), Cyp. 91/C2
Morra (lake), Neth. 50/C3
Morrinhos, Braz. 155/B1
Morris (mt.), Austl. 113/F3
Morris, Mb, Can. 127/J3
Morris (res.),
Ca, US 136/C2
Morris, Mn, US 127/K4
Morris (co.), NJ, US 138/D2
Morris Jesup (cape),
Grld 160/J
Morris Plains,
NJ, US 139/H8
Morrison, Co, US 137/B3
Morristown,
NJ, US 138/D2
Morristown NHP,
NJ, US 138/D2
Morrisville, Pa, US 138/D3
Morro Bay, Ca, US 128/B4
Morro de Môco (peak),
Ang. 105/C3
Morro de Puercos (pt.),
Pan. 145/F5
Morro do Chapéu,
Braz. 154/B3
Morro, Punta del (pt.),
Mex. 143/N7
Morrocoy, PN,
Ven. 152/D2
Mórrope, Peru 156/A2
Morropón, Peru 156/A2
Morros, Braz. 154/A1
Morrosquillo (gulf),
Col. 145/G4
Morshansk, Rus. 64/B3
Morskoy (isl.), Kaz. 63/J3
Morsum, Ger. 38/B1
Mortagne (riv.), Fr. 56/C1
Mortagne-sur-Sèvre,
Fr. 42/C3
Mortara, It. 58/B2
Mortcerf, Fr. 30/L5
Morte (pt.), Eng, UK 32/B4
Morteau, Fr. 56/B4
Mortefontaine, Fr. 30/K4
Mortegliano, It. 59/G1
Mortes, Rio das (riv.),
Braz. 151/H6
Mortlake, Austl. 115/B3
Morton, Austl. 115/B3
Morton, Il, US 129/K2
Morton Grove,
Il, US 135/Q15

Morton NP, Austl. 115/D2
Morton NWR,
NY, US 139/F2
Mortsel, Belg. 50/B6
Moruya, Austl. 115/D2
Morvan (plat.), Fr. 42/E3
Morven, Austl. 114/B4
Morven (peak),
Sc, UK 133/J3
Morvi, India 89/K4
Morvillars, Fr. 56/C2
Morwell, Austl. 115/C3
Morzine, Fr. 56/C5
Mos, Sp. 44/A1
Mosbach, Ger. 54/C4
Mosby, Mo, US 137/E5
Moscow (Moskva) (cap.),
Rus. 62/F1
Moscow (upland),
Rus. 60/F5
Moscow, Id, US 126/D3
Moscow University
Ice Shelf, Ant. 160/J
Moselle (riv.), Fr. 43/G2
Moselle (dept.), Fr. 53/F5
Moselotte (riv.), Fr. 56/C2
Moses Lake,
Wa, US 126/D4
Mosfellsbær, Ice. 37/N7
Mosgiel, NZ 117/S12
Moshaweng (riv.),
SAfr. 106/C2
Moshchnyy (isl.), Rus. 39/M2
Moshi, Tanz. 104/C4
Moshoeshoe (Maseru)
(int'l arpt.), Les. 106/D3
Mosina, Pol. 41/J2
Moskovskaya Oblast,
Rus. 60/H5
Moskva (riv.),
Rus. 60/G5
Moskva (Moscow) (cap.),
Rus. 62/F1
Mosonmagyaróvár,
Hun. 48/C2
Mosquera, Col. 152/B4
Mosquero,
NM, US 129/G4
Mosquitia (phys. reg.),
Hon. 145/E3
Mosquito (pt.),
Pan. 145/G4
Mosquitos, Golfo de los
(gulf), Pan. 150/B2
Moss, Nor. 38/D2
Moss Beach,
Ca, US 135/J11
Moss Bluff, La, US 129/J5
Moss Point,
Ms, US 133/F4
Moss-Side, NI, UK 34/B1
Moss Vale, Austl. 115/D2
Mosselbaai, SAfr. 106/C4
Mosses, Col des (pass),
Swi. 56/D5
Mossi Highlands (uplands),
Burk. 102/E4
Mössingen, Ger. 54/C6
Mossman, Austl. 114/B2
Mossoró, Braz. 154/C2
Most, Czh. 55/G1
Mostaganem (prov.),
Alg. 100/F4
Mostaganem, Alg. 100/F5
Mostar, Bosn. 47/E1
Mostardas, Braz. 155/B4
Móstoles, Sp. 45/N9
Mota del Cuervo,
Sp. 44/D3
Motagua (riv.), Guat. 140/D4
Motherwell, Sc, UK 36/C5
Motian (mtn.),
China 72/C3
Motīhāri, India 85/E2
Motilla del Palancar,
Sp. 44/E3
Motobu, Japan 75/J7
Motomiya, Japan 75/G4
Motosu (lake),
Japan 77/B3
Motosu, Japan 77/L5
Motovskiy (gulf),
Rus. 37/K1
Motoyoshi, Japan 76/B4
Motozintla de Mendoza,
Mex. 144/C3
Motril, Sp. 44/D4
Motsuta-misaki (cape),
Japan 76/B4
Mott, ND, US 127/H4
Motta di Livenza, It. 59/F1
Motta Visconti, It. 58/B2
Mottarone (peak), It. 58/B1
Motueka, NZ 117/S11
Motul de Carrillo Puerto,
Mex. 144/D1
Motupe, Peru 156/B2
Motygino, Rus. 64/K4
Mouchard, Fr. 56/B4
Mouchoir Passage
(chan.), UK 145/J1
Moúdhros, Gre. 47/J3
Moudon, Swi. 56/C4
Mougins (well), Mrta. 102/B2
Mouhoun (prov.),
Burk. 102/E3
Mouila, Gabon 96/H8
Mouína (well), Alg. 99/F3
Moul (well), Niger 96/H4

Moulamein (riv.),
Austl. 115/C2
Moulamein, Austl. 115/C2
Moulay Idriss, Mor. 100/B2
Moulins, Fr. 42/E3
Moulouya (riv.), Mor. 100/C2
Moultrie, Ga, US 133/H4
Moultrie (lake),
SC, US 133/J3
Moundou, Chad 96/J6
Moundsville,
WV, US 130/D4
Morwell, Austl. 115/D1
Mourenx, Fr. 42/C5
Mouse (riv.), US 136/G3
Mouscron, Belg. 52/C2
Mouths of the Niger,
Nga. 96/G6
Mouzákion, Gre. 47/G3
Mouzon, Fr. 53/E4
Moxotó (riv.), Braz. 154/C3
Moy, NI, UK 34/B3
Moy (riv.), Ire. 34/A2
Moyamba, SLeo. 102/B4
Moye (isl.), China 73/B4
Moyen Atlas (mts.),
Mor. 96/D1
Moyenmoutier, Fr. 56/C1
Moyeuvre-Grande, Fr. 53/F5
Moyle (dist.),
NI, UK 34/B1
Moyo (isl.), Indo. 81/E5
Moyo, Ugan. 104/A2
Moyobamba, Peru 156/B2
Moyowosi (riv.),
Tanz. 104/A3
Moyu, China 70/C4
Moyuta, Guat. 144/D3
Mozambique (ctry.) 105/G3
Mozambique (chan.).
Afr. 105/G5
Mozhaysk, Rus. 60/H5
Mozhga, Rus. 61/M4
Mozzanica, It. 58/C2
Mozzecane, It. 59/D2
Mpanda, Tanz. 104/A4
Mpigi, Ugan. 104/A2
Mpika, Zam. 104/A5
Mporokoso, Zam. 104/A5
Mpraeso, Gha. 103/E5
Mpulungu, Zam. 104/A5
Mpumalanga (prov.),
SAfr. 107/E2
Mpwapwa, Tanz. 104/C4
Mrągowo, Pol. 39/J5
Mrkonjić Grad,
Bosn. 48/C3
M'Sila (prov.), Alg. 99/F2
M'sila, Alg. 100/H5
M'sila (riv.), Alg. 100/H5

Msoun (riv.), Mor. 100/C2
Msta (riv.), Rus. 60/G4
Mszana Dolna, Pol. 41/L4
Mtorwi (peak), Tanz. 104/B5
Mtsensk, Rus. 62/F1
Mtubatuba, SAfr. 107/E3
Mtunzini, SAfr. 107/E3
Mtwara, Tanz. 104/D5
Mtwara (pol. reg.), Tanz. 104/C5
Mu-kawa (riv.), Japan 76/C2
Mu Ko Similan NP, Thai. 78/B4
Mu Ko Surin NP, Thai. 78/B4
Mualama, Moz. 105/G4
Muan, SKor. 73/D5
Muang Hinboun, Laos 78/D2
Muang Khammouan, Laos 78/D2
Muang Khong, Laos 78/D3
Muang Khongxedon, Laos 78/D3
Muang Pak-lay, Laos 78/C2
Muang Paksan, Laos 78/D2
Muang Sing, Laos 83/H3
Muang Vangviang, Laos 78/C2
Muang Xaignabouri, Laos 78/C2
Muang Xay, Laos 83/H3
Muar, Malay. 80/B3
Muarabungo, Indo. 80/B4
Muâri (pt.), Pak. 89/J4
Mubârakpur, India 84/D2
Mubende, Ugan. 104/A2
Mucajaí (riv.), Braz. 150/F3
Much, Ger. 53/G2
Muchinga (mts.), Zam. 104/B5
Muck (isl.), Sc, UK 31/G8
Muckleshoot Ind. Res., Wa, US 135/C4
Mucojo, Moz. 105/H3
Mucupina (mtn.), Hon. 144/E3
Mucur, Turk. 90/C2
Mucuri (riv.), Braz. 151/K7
Mud Mountain (dam), Wa, US 135/D3
Mud Mountain (lake), Wa, US 135/D3
Mudanjiang, China 71/N3
Mudanya, Turk. 49/J5
Mudau, Ger. 54/C3
Mudbach (riv.), Ger. 54/C3
Muddan (riv.), China 71/N2
Muddas NP, Swe. 37/G2
Muddy Run (res.), Pa, US 138/B4
Müden, Ger. 51/H3
Mudersbach, Ger. 53/G2
Mudgee, Austl. 115/D2
Mudjatik (riv.), Sk, Can. 122/F3
Mudon, Myan. 78/B2
Mudurnu, Turk. 49/M4
Muela (peak), Chile 159/B7
Muerte, Cerro de la (peak), CR 145/F4
Muff, Ire. 34/A1
Mufulira, Zam. 105/E3
Mugardos, Sp. 44/A1
Mugegawa, Japan 77/L4
Mughal Sarai, India 84/D3
Mugi, Japan 77/L4
Mugia, Sp. 44/A1
Muğla, Turk. 90/B2
Muğla (prov.), Turk. 90/B2
Mughalzhar Taüy (mts.), Kaz. 87/C3
Muhamdi, India 84/C2
Muhammad (pt.), Egypt 101/C2
Muhammadâbad, India 84/D3
Muhavura (vol.), Rwa. 104/A3
Muhila, Monts (mts.), D.R. Congo 105/E3
Mühlacker, Ger. 54/B5
Mühlbach (riv.), Ger. 54/A2
Mühldorf, Ger. 55/F6
Mühleberg, Swi. 56/D4
Mühlenbeck, Ger. 40/Q6
Mühlhausen, Ger. 55/E4
Mühlheim am Main, Ger. 54/B2
Mühlheim an der Donau, Ger. 57/F1
Mühltroff, Ger. 55/E1
Mühlviertel (reg.), Aus. 41/G4
Munising, Mi, US 127/M4
Muhos, Fin. 60/G2
Muhu (isl.), Est. 60/D3
Muiden, Neth. 50/B4
Muir of Ord, Sc, UK 36/B1
Muir Woods Nat'l Mon., Ca, US 128/B3
Muir Woods Nat'l Mon., Ca, US 135/J11
Muirkirk, Sc, UK 36/B5
Muizon, Fr. 52/C5
Muju, SKor. 73/D4
Mukacheve, Ukr. 41/M4
Mukawa, Japan 76/B2
Mukawar (isl.), Sudan 101/D4
Mukden, Bol. 156/D3
Mukeriān, India 86/C4

Mukhayyam al Yarmūk, Syria 91/E3
Mukhmās, Isr. 91/G8
Mukinbudin, Austl. 112/C4
Mukō, Japan 77/J6
Mukono, Ugan. 104/B2
Mukoshima (isls.), Japan 116/D2
Muktsar, India 86/C4
Mukwonago, Wi, US 135/P14
Mula, Sp. 44/E3
Mulanje, Malw. 105/G4
Mulchatna (riv.), Ak, US 134/G4
Mulchén, Chile 158/B3
Mulde (riv.), Ger. 40/G3
Mulegé, Mex. 142/C3
Muleshoe, Tx, US 129/G4
Mulhacén, Cerro de (peak), Sp. 44/D4
Mülhausen, Ger. 51/H6
Mülheim an der Ruhr, Ger. 50/D6
Mulhouse, Fr. 56/D2
Muli (riv.), Indo. 81/J5
Muli Zangzu Zizhixian, China 83/H2
Muling (pass), China 72/D3
Mull (isl.), Sc, UK 31/R8
Mull of Galloway (pt.), Sc, UK 34/D2
Mull of Kintyre (pt.), Sc, UK 34/C1
Mull of Logan (pt.), Sc, UK 34/D2
Mullach Coire Mhic Fhearchair (peak), Sc, UK 36/A1
Mullaghcleevaun (peak), Ire. 34/B5
Mullaghmore (peak), NI, UK 34/B2
Mullaittivu, SrL. 82/D6
Mullardoch (lake), Sc, UK 36/A2
Muller (mts.), Indo. 80/D4
Mullewa, Austl. 112/B4
Müllheim, Ger. 56/D2
Müllheim, Swi. 57/F2
Mullica (riv.), NJ, US 138/D4
Murdock (riv.), De, US 138/C6
Mullingar, Ire. 31/Q10
Mullins, SC, US 133/J3
Mullumbimby, Austl. 115/E1
Mulobezi, Zam. 105/E4
Multai, India 84/B5
Multan, Pak. 86/A4
Multnomah (falls), Or, US 126/C4
Mulu (peak), Malay. 80/D3
Mulwala, Austl. 115/A3
Mum Nauk (pt.), Thai. 78/B5
Mumbai (Bombay), India 89/K6
Mumbwa, Zam. 105/E3
Mümling (riv.), Ger. 54/B3
Mumoni (peak), Kenya 104/C3
Mun (riv.), Thai. 83/H4
Muna (isl.), Indo. 81/F4
Muna, Mex. 144/D1
Munamägi (hill), Est. 39/M3
Muñani, Peru 156/D4
Muncar, Indo. 80/D5
Münchberg, Ger. 55/E2
München (Munich), Ger. 55/E6
Münchenstein, Swi. 56/D2
Munchique (peak), Col. 152/B4
Munchique, PN, Col. 152/B4
Münchmünster, Ger. 55/E5
Muncie, In, US 130/C3
Muncy, Pa, US 138/B1
Mundaring, Austl. 112/L6
Munday, Tx, US 129/H4
Mundelein, Il, US 135/O15
Mundemba, Camr. 103/H5
Münden, Ger. 51/G6
Munderfing, Aus. 55/G6
Munderkingen, Ger. 57/F1
Mundo Novo, Braz. 157/F1
Mundubbera, Austl. 114/C4
Munera, Sp. 44/D3
Mungaolī, India 84/B3
Munger, India 85/F3
Mungo NP, Austl. 115/B2
Mun'gyŏng, SKor. 73/E4
Munising, Mi, US 127/M4
Munkebo, Den. 38/D4
Munkedal, Swe. 38/D2
Munkfors, Swe. 38/E2
Munku-Sardyk (peak), Rus. 70/H1
Münnerstadt, Ger. 54/D2
Muñoz Gamero (pen.), Chile 157/B7
Munsan, SKor. 73/F6
Münsingen, Swi. 56/D4
Münster (reg.), Ire. 31/P10
Münster, Ger. 51/E5
Münster, Ger. 51/E5
Münster, Ger. 51/H3
Munster, Swi. 57/F3
Munster, Fr. 56/D1
Münster, Swi. 57/F3
Munster, In, US 135/R16

Münster, Ger. 54/B3
Münster/Osnabrück (int'l arpt.), Ger. 51/E4
Münstereifel, Ger. 53/F2
Münsterhausen, Ger. 54/D6
Münsterland (reg.), Ger. 40/D2
Münstermaifeld, Ger. 53/G3
Muntele Mare (peak), Rom. 49/F2
Muntendam, Neth. 50/D2
Muntok, Indo. 80/C4
Müntschemier, Swi. 56/D4
Münzenberg, Ger. 54/B2
Münzkirchen, Aus. 55/G6
Munzur Vadisi NP, Turk. 90/D2
Muonio, Fin. 37/G2
Muonioälven (riv.), Swe. 37/G1
Muotathal, Swi. 57/E4
Mupa, PN da, Ang. 105/C4
Muqdisho (Mogadishu) (cap.), Som. 97/Q7
Muqeibila, Isr. 91/G6
Mur (riv.), Aus. 43/L3
Mura (riv.), Slov.,Hun 48/C2
Muradiye, Turk. 90/E2
Murādnagar, India 86/D5
Murakami, Japan 75/F1
Murallón (peak), Chile 159/B6
Murano, It. 59/F2
Murat (peak), Turk. 90/B2
Muratlı, Turk. 90/E2
Muratlı, Turk. 49/H5
Murayama, Japan 76/B4
Murchison, Austl. 115/C3
Murchison (riv.), Austl. 109/A3
Murchison, NZ 117/S11
Murchison (mt.), Austl. 112/C3
Murcia, Sp. 45/E4
Murcia (aut. comm.), Sp. 44/E4
Murderkill (riv.), De, US 138/C6
Murdochville, Qu, Can. 131/H1
Murdock, Austl. 114/B1
Mürefte, Turk. 49/H5
Mureş (riv.), Rom. 62/B3
Mureş (prov.), Rom. 49/G2
Muret, Fr. 42/D5
Murfreesboro, Ar, US 129/J4
Murg (riv.), Ger. 53/H6
Murgab (riv.), Turk. 87/D5
Murgap (riv.), Trkm. 64/G6
Murgon, Austl. 114/C4
Muri, Swi. 57/E3
Muri bei Bern, Swi. 56/D4
Muria (peak), Indo. 80/D5
Muriaé, Braz. 155/D2
Murias de Paredes, Sp. 44/B1
Murici, Braz. 154/C4
Murīdke, Pak. 86/C4
Müritz (lake), Ger. 40/G2
Murlīganj, India 85/F3
Murmansk, Rus. 60/G1
Murmansk (int'l arpt.), Rus. 60/G1
Murmanskaya Oblast, Rus. 37/J1
Murnau, Ger. 57/H2
Muro, Sp. 45/G3
Muro, Japan 77/K6
Muro Lucano, It. 46/D2
Murom, Rus. 60/J5
Muroran, Japan 76/B2
Muros, Sp. 44/A1
Muroto, Japan 74/D4
Muroto-zaki (pt.), Japan 74/D4
Murowana Goślina, Pol. 41/J2
Murphy, NC, US 133/G3
Murphy, Mo, US 137/G9
Murr (riv.), Ger. 54/C5
Ak, US 134/M4
Murramarang NP, Austl. 115/D2
Murray (lake), SC, US 133/H3
Murray (riv.), Austl. 109/D4
Murray, Ky, US 130/D4
Murray, Ut, US 137/K12
Murray Bridge, Austl. 113/H5
Murraysburg, SAfr. 106/C3
Murrayville, Austl. 115/B2
Murrieta, Ca, US 136/C3
Murrieta Hot Springs, Ca, US 136/C3
Murrumbidgee (riv.), Austl. 109/D4
Murrumburrah, Austl. 115/D1
Murrurundi, Austl. 115/D1
Murshidābād, India 85/G3
Murtala Muhammed (int'l arpt.), Nga. 103/F5
Murtaröl (peak), Swi. 57/G4
Murten, Swi. 56/D4
Murtoa, Austl. 115/B3
Murtosa, Port. 44/A2
Murupara, NZ 117/T10

Mururoa (isl.), FrPol. 117/M7
Murwāra, India 84/C4
Murwillumbah, Austl. 114/D5
Mürz (riv.), Aus. 41/H5
Mürzzuschlag, Aus. 41/H5
Muş (prov.), Turk. 90/E2
Muş, Turk. 90/E2
Musabeyli, Turk. 91/E1
Musá'firkhāna, India 84/C2
Musala (peak), Bul. 47/H1
Musan, NKor. 73/E1
Musashino, Japan 77/D2
Musconetcong (riv.), NJ, US 138/C2
Muscoot (res.), NY, US 139/E1
Muscoy, Ca, US 136/C2
Musekwapoort (pass), SAfr. 105/E5
Museum of Flight, Wa, US 135/C2
Musgrave (ranges), Austl. 109/C3
Musgrave Harbour, Nf, Can. 131/L1
Mushābani, India 85/F4
Mushie, D.R. Congo 96/J3
Mushin, Nga. 103/F5
Musi (riv.), Indo. 80/B4
Musile di Piave, It. 59/F1
Musinga (peak), Col. 152/B3
Muskego, Wi, US 135/P14
Muskegon, Mi, US 130/C3
Muskegon (riv.), Mi, US 130/C3
Muskingum (riv.), Oh, US 130/D4
Muskoka (lake), On, Can. 130/E2
Musoma, Tanz. 104/B3
Musone (riv.), It. 59/G6
Musquaro (riv.), Qu, Can. 131/J1
Mussau (isl.), PNG 116/D5
Musselburgh, Sc, UK 36/C5
Musselshell (riv.), Mt, US 124/E2
Mussomeli, It. 46/C4
Musson, Belg. 53/E4
Mustafābād, Pak. 86/B4
Mustafakemalpaşa, Turk. 90/B1
Müstair, Swi. 57/G4
Mustang, Ok, US 137/M15
Musters (lake), Arg. 158/C5
Musu-dan (pt.), NKor. 73/E2
Musún (mtn.), Nic. 144/E3
Mušutište, Serb. 47/G1
Muswellbrook, Austl. 115/D2
Müt, Egypt 101/B3
Mut, Turk. 91/C1
Mutá, Ponta do (pt.), Braz. 154/C4
Mutare, Zim. 105/F4
Muthill, Sc, UK 36/C4
Mutis (peak), Indo. 81/F5
Mutsamudu, Com. 107/H6
Mutsu (bay), Japan 76/B3
Mutsu, Japan 76/B3
Mutsuzawa, Japan 77/F3
Muttekopf (peak), Aus. 57/G3
Muttenz, Swi. 56/D2
Mutters, Aus. 57/H3
Mutterstadt, Ger. 54/B4
Muttler (peak), Swi. 57/G4
Muttonville, Mi, US 135/G6
Mutum, Braz. 155/D1
Mutzig, Fr. 56/D1
Müynoq, Uzb. 63/L4
Muzaffargarh, Pak. 86/A4
Muzaffarnagar, India 86/D5
Muzaffarpur, India 85/E2
Muzambinho, Braz. 211/G6
Muzon (cape), Ak, US 134/M4
Muztag (peak), China 70/D4
Muztagata (peak), China 87/G5
Muzzana del Turgnano, It. 59/G1
Mwadui (riv.), Tanz. 104/B3
Mwana (cape), Kenya 104/D3
Mwanza (pol. reg.), Tanz. 104/B3
Mwanza, Tanz. 104/B3
Mweelrea (peak), Ire. 31/P10
Mweka, D.R. Congo 105/D1
Mwene-Ditu, D.R. Congo 105/D2
Mwense, Zam. 104/A5
Mweru (lake), D.R. Congo 93/E5
Mweru-Wantipa NP, Zam. 104/A5
Mwesi (mtn.), Tanz. 104/A4
Mwinilunga, Zam. 105/D3
My Son Temples (ruin), Viet. 78/E3
My Tho, Viet. 78/D4
Myall Lakes NP, Austl. 115/E2
Myanaung, Myan. 83/G4

Myanmar (Burma) (ctry.), 83/G3
Myebon, Myan. 83/F3
Myerstown, Pa, US 138/B3
Myggenäs, Swe. 38/D2
Myingyan, Myan. 83/G3
Myitkyinā, Myan. 83/G2
Myjava, Slvk. 41/J4
Mykolayiv, Ukr. 49/L2
Mykolayiv (int'l arpt.), Ukr. 49/L2
Mykolayivs'ka Oblasti, Ukr. 62/D3
Mylau, Ger. 55/F1
Mymensingh (pol. reg.), Bang. 85/H3
Mynämäki, Fin. 39/J1
Mynydd Eppynt (mts.), Wal, UK 32/C2
Mynydd Pencarreg (peak), Wal, UK 32/B2
Mynydd Preseli (mtn.), Wal, UK 32/B3
Myōgi, Japan 77/B1
Myohaung, Myan. 83/F3
Myōkō-san (peak), Japan 77/L5
Myŏngch'ŏn, NKor. 73/E2
Myrhorod, Ukr. 62/E2
Myrtle Beach, SC, US 133/J3
Myrtle Creek, Or, US 126/C5
Myrtleford, Austl. 115/C3
Mysen, Nor. 38/D2
Myślenice, Pol. 41/K4
Myślibórz, Pol. 41/H2
Mysliv (peak), Czh. 55/H5
Mysore, India 82/C5
Mystery Bay Rec. Area, Wa, US 135/B1
Mystic Island, NJ, US 138/D4
Myszków, Pol. 41/K3
Mytishchi, Rus. 61/W9
Mže (riv.), Czh. 40/G4
Mzimba, Malw. 104/B5
Mzuzu, Malw. 104/B5

N

Na (riv.), Viet. 78/C1
Naab (riv.), Ger. 43/J2
Naaldwijk, Neth. 50/B5
Naalehu, Hi, US 124/U11
Naama, Alg. 76/B3
Naantali, Fin. 39/K1
Naarden, Neth. 50/C4
Naarn im Machlande, Aus. 55/H6
Naas, Ire. 31/Q10
Nababeep, SAfr. 106/B3
Nabari, Japan 77/K6
Nabari (riv.), Japan 77/K6
Nabberu (lake), Austl. 112/D3
Nabburg, Ger. 55/F4
Naberezhnye Chelny, Rus. 61/M5
Nābha, India 86/D4
Nabiac, Austl. 115/E2
Nabisipi (riv.), Qu, Can. 131/J1
Nabón, Ecu. 156/B1
Nabua, Phil. 79/D5
Nābul, Tun. 46/B4
Nābul (gov.), Tun. 46/B4
Nacala, Moz. 105/H3
Nacaome, Hon. 144/E3
Nachi-Katsuura, Japan 74/D4
Nachingwea, Tanz. 104/C5
Náchod, Czh. 41/J3
Nachrodt-Wiblingwerde, Ger. 51/E6
Nacimiento, Chile 158/B3
Naco, Mex. 128/E5
Nacogdoches, Tx, US 129/J5
Nácori Chico, Mex. 142/C2
Nacozari de García, Mex. 142/C2
Nādbai, India 84/A2
Nadder (riv.), Eng, UK 32/D4
Nadiād, India 89/K4
Nādlac, Rom. 49/E2
Nador (prov.), Mor. 100/C2
Nador, Malta 46/L6
Naejang-san NP, SKor. 73/D5
Nafüsah, Jabal (mts.), Libya 99/H3
Naga, Phil. 79/D5
Nagagami, On, Can. 130/C1
Nāgāland (state), India 70/F6
Nagambie, Austl. 115/C3
Nagano, Japan 75/F2
Nagano (pref.), Japan 75/E2
Nagaoka, Japan 76/B2
Nagaokakyō, Japan 77/J6
Nagaon (Nowgong), India 83/F2
Nagar, India 84/B2
Nagara (riv.), Japan 75/E3

Nagara, Japan 77/E3
Nagareyama, Japan 77/D2
Nāgārjuna Sāgar (res.), India 82/C4
Nagarote, Nic. 140/D5
Nagarze, China 85/H1
Nagas (pt.), BC, Can. 134/M5
Nagasaka, Japan 77/B1
Nagasaki, Japan 74/A4
Nagasaki (pref.), Japan 74/A4
Nagasaki Peace, Japan 74/A4
Nagashima, Japan 85/H2
Nagato, Japan 74/B3
Nagato, Japan 77/C1
Nāgaur, India 89/K3
Nāgda, India 89/K4
Nāgercoil, India 82/C6
Nagīna, India 84/B1
Nago, Japan 75/J7
Nago-Torbole, It. 57/G6
Nāgod, India 84/C3
Nagold, Ger. 54/B5
Nagorno-Karabakh (prov.), Azer. 63/H5
Nagoya, Japan 77/L5
Nagoya Castle, Japan 77/L5
Nagpula (pass), China 85/F1
Nāgpur, India 82/C3
Nags Head, NC, US 133/K3
Naguri, Japan 77/C2
Nagy-Milic (peak), Hun. 41/L4
Nagyatád, Hun. 48/C2
Nagyecsed, Hun. 41/M5
Nagyhalász, Hun. 48/E1
Nagykanizsa, Hun. 48/C2
Nagykáta, Hun. 48/D2
Nagykőrös, Hun. 48/D2
Naha, Japan 75/J7
Nahal Shillo (riv.), Isr.,WBnk 91/G7
Nāhan, India 86/D4
Nahanni NP, NW, Can. 122/D2
Nahariyya, Isr. 91/D3
Nahāvand, Iran 88/E2
Nahe (riv.), Ger. 43/G2
Nahel Soreq (riv.), Isr.,WBnk 91/F8
Nahouri (prov.), Burk. 103/E4
Nahr 'Atbarah (riv.), Sudan 97/M4
Nahr Mufjir (riv.), Isr.,WBnk 91/G7
Nahr Ouassel (riv.), Alg. 100/F5
Nahuel Huapi (lake), Arg. 147/B7
Nahuel Huapi, PN, Arg. 158/C4
Nahuelbuta, PN, Chile 158/B3
Naica, Mex. 142/D3
Naihāti, India 85/G4
Naila, Ger. 55/E2
Naiman Qi, China 72/E2
Na'īn, Iran 88/G2
Nainital, India 84/B1
Nainpur, India 84/C4
Naintré, Fr. 42/D3
Nairn (riv.), Sc, UK 36/C1
Nairn, Sc, UK 36/C1
Nairne, Austl. 113/M9
Nairobi (cap.), Kenya 104/C3
Nairobi NP, Kenya 104/C3
Naivasha, Kenya 104/C3
Naives-Rosières, Fr. 53/E6
Najafābād, Iran 88/F2
Nájera, Sp. 44/D1
Najin, NKor. 71/P3
Naju, SKor. 73/D5
Naka (riv.), Japan 77/D4
Naka, Japan 77/G5
Nakadōri (isl.), Japan 74/A4
Nakai, Japan 77/B2
Nakajō, Japan 77/E1
Nakalele (pt.), Hi, US 124/T10
Nakamichi, Japan 77/B2
Nakaminato, Japan 77/G2
Nakamura, Japan 74/C4
Nakano, Japan 75/F2
Nakano (lag.), Japan 74/C3
Nakasato, Japan 77/B1
Nakashibetsu, Japan 76/D2
Nakasongola, Ugan. 104/B2
Nakatane, Japan 75/L5
Nakatomi, Japan 77/B2
Nakatsu, Japan 74/B4
Nakatsugawa, Japan 75/E2
Nakazato, Japan 77/B1
Nakhodka, Rus. 77/M4
Nakhon Nayok, Thai. 78/C3
Nakhon Pathom, Thai. 78/C3
Nakhon Phanom, Thai. 78/D2
Nakhon Ratchasima, Thai. 78/C3
Nakhon Sawan, Thai. 78/C3
Nakhon Si Thammarat, Thai. 78/B4
Nakina, On, Can. 123/S6
Nakkila, Fin. 39/J1

Nakło nad Notecią, Pol. 41/J2
Naknek, Ak, US 134/G4
Nakodar, India 86/C4
Nakonde, Zam. 104/B5
Nakskov, Den. 38/D4
Naktong, SKor. 73/E4
Naktong (riv.), SKor. 74/A3
Nakuru, Kenya 104/C3
Nakusp, BC, Can. 126/D3
Nāl (riv.), Pak. 89/J3
Nalayh, Mong. 70/J2
Nalbach, Ger. 53/F5
Nalbāri, India 85/H2
Nalbaugh NP, Austl. 115/D3
Nal'chik (int'l arpt.), Rus. 63/G4
Nal'chik, Rus. 63/G4
Nalda, India 82/C4
Nalhāti, India 85/F3
Nālīya, India 89/J4
Nallıhan, Turk. 49/K5
Nalón (riv.), Sp. 44/B1
Nālūt, Libya 99/H3
Nam Dinh, Viet. 83/J3
Nam Nao NP, Thai. 78/C2
Nam Un (res.), Thai. 78/C2
Namangan (pol. reg.), Uzb. 87/F4
Namangan, Uzb. 87/F4
Namaqualand (reg.), SAfr. 106/B3
Namaripí (cape), Indo. 81/J4
Namasagali, Ugan. 104/B2
Namatanai, PNG 116/E5
Namborn, Ger. 53/G4
Nambour, Austl. 114/D4
Nambu, Japan 77/A3
Nambucca Heads, Austl. 115/E1
Nambung NP, Austl. 112/B4
Namdae (riv.), NKor. 73/E2
Namdalseid, Nor. 37/D2
Namegawa, Japan 77/C1
Namekagon (riv.), Wi, US 127/L4
Namentenga (prov.), Burk. 103/E3
Namerikawa, Japan 75/E2
Nametil, Moz. 105/G3
Namhae, SKor. 73/D5
Namib (des.), Namb. 105/B4
Namibe, Ang. 105/B3
Namibia (ctry.), 105/C5
Namie, Japan 75/G2
Namioka, Japan 77/C1
Namja (pass), Nepal 82/D2
Namjagbarwa (peak), China 83/G2
Namling, China 82/D2
Namloser Wetterspitze (peak), Aus. 57/G3
Nammoku, Japan 77/B1
Namnoi (peak), Myan. 78/B4
Napf (peak), Swi. 56/D4
Napier, NZ 117/T10
Napier, SAfr. 106/L11
Micr. 116/F4
Naples, Fl, US 133/H5
Naples (Napoli), It. 46/D2
Nampʼo, NKor. 73/C4
Nampula, Moz. 105/G4
Namsê (pass), China 82/D2
Namsos, Nor. 37/D2
Namu (riv.), Sc, UK 36/C1
Namur, Belg. 53/D3
Namur (prov.), Belg. 53/D3
Namwon, SKor. 73/D5
Namysłów, Pol. 41/J3
Napuka (isl.), FrPol. 117/L6
Nan (riv.), Thai. 78/C2
Nan, Thai. 78/C2
Nanae, Japan 76/B3
Nanakuli, Hi, US 124/V13
Nanam, NKor. 73/E2
Nanango, Austl. 114/D4
Nanao, Japan 75/E2
Nanay (riv.), Peru 156/B3
Nanchang, China 79/C2
Nancheng, China 79/C3
Nanchong, China 79/A2
Nancy, Fr. 53/F6
Nanda Devi (peak), India 70/C5
Nandan, China 83/J3
Nānded, India 82/C4
Nandrin, Belg. 53/E3
Nandurbār, India 89/K4
Nandy, Fr. 30/K6
Nanfeng, China 79/C2
Nang Xian, China 83/G2
Nanga Parbat (peak), Can.,Grld. 123/T6
Nangapinoh, Indo. 80/D4
Nangnim (mts.), NKor. 73/D2
Nangong, China 72/C3
Nangtud (mt.), Phil. 81/F1
Nanhui, China 72/L8
Nanjian Yizu Zizhixian, China 83/H2

Nankāna Sāhib, Pak. 86/B4
Nankang, China 79/B2
Nankoku, Japan 74/C4
Nanle, China 72/C3
Nanliu (riv.), China 83/J3
Nanning, China 83/J3
Nannô, Japan 77/L5
Nannup, Austl. 112/B5
Nanny (riv.), Ire. 34/B4
Nānpāra, India 84/C2
Nanpi, China 72/D3
Nanping, China 79/C2
Nansei, Japan 77/L7
Nansen (sound), Nun., Can. 123/S6
Nant (lake), Sc, UK 36/A4
Nantai-san (peak), Japan 75/F2
Nanterre, Fr. 30/J5
Nantes, Fr. 42/C3
Nanteuil-le-Haudouin, Fr. 30/L4
Nanteuil-lès-Meaux, Fr. 52/B6
Nanticoke, On, Can. 130/D3
Nanticoke, Pa, US 138/B1
Nanton, Ab, Can. 126/E3
Nantong, China 72/E4
Nantua, Fr. 56/B5
Nantucket (isl.), Ma, US 123/S6
Nantwich, Eng, UK 35/F5
Nanuet, NY, US 139/J7
Nanumanga (isl.), Tuv. 116/G5
Nanumea (isl.), Tuv. 116/G5
Nanuque, Braz. 154/B5
Nanwon (riv.), China 72/C4
Nanxi, China 83/H2
Nanxiong, China 79/B2
Nanyang, China 72/C4
Nanyang, China 72/D4
Nanyuki, Kenya 104/C2
Nanzhang, China 72/B5
Nanzhao, China 72/C4
Nao, Cabo de la (cape), Sp. 45/F3
Naococane (lake), Qu, Can. 123/J3
Naogaon, Bang. 85/G3
Naolinco, Mex. 143/N7
Náousa (falls), C.d'Iv. 47/J4
Náousa, Gre. 47/H2
Napa, Ca, US 128/B3
Napa (co.), Ca, US 135/K10
Napa (riv.), Ca, US 135/K10
Napa (valley), Ca, US 135/K9
Napa Junction, Ca, US 135/K10
Napak (peak), Ugan. 104/B2
Napanee, On, Can. 130/E2
Napaskiak, Ak, US 134/F3
Naperville, Il, US 130/B3
Napf (peak), Swi. 56/D4
Napier, NZ 117/T10
Napier, SAfr. 106/L11
Naples, Fl, US 133/H5
Naples (Napoli), It. 46/D2
Napo (riv.), Peru 152/C5
Napo (riv.), Ecu.,Peru 147/B3
Napo (prov.), Ecu. 152/C5
Napoleon, ND, US 127/J4
Napoleonville, La, US 129/K5
Napoli, Golfo di (gulf), It. 46/C2
Napuka (isl.), FrPol. 117/L6
Naqʼl Sumārah (pass), Yem. 88/D6
Nara, Mali 102/D3
Nara (riv.), Pak. 89/J4
Nara, Japan 77/J6
Naracoorte, Austl. 115/B3
Naraini, India 84/C3
Naranbulag, Mong. 70/F2
Naranjal, Ecu. 152/B5
Naranjo, Mex. 156/B1
Naranjos, Mex. 144/B1
Narāq, Iran 88/F2
Narasannapeta, India 82/D4
Narashino, Japan 77/E2
Narathiwat, Thai. 78/C5
Nārāyanganj, Bang. 85/H4
Nārāyani (zone), Nepal 85/E2
Narayan (riv.), Nepal 85/E2
Nārāyanpet, India 82/C4
Narbonne, Fr. 42/E5
Narceo (riv.), Sp. 44/B1
Nardò, It. 47/F2
Nare (pt.), Eng, UK 32/B6
Narellan, Austl. 114/G9
Narembeen, Austl. 112/C5
Nares (str.), Can.,Grld. 123/T6
Narganá, Pan. 152/D2
Nari (riv.), Pak. 89/H6
Nariño (dept.), Col. 152/B4
Narita, Japan 77/E2
Narita (int'l arpt.), Japan 75/G3
Nariz (peak), Chile 159/C7
Narkatiāganj, India 85/E2
Narman, Turk. 63/G4

Narni, It. 46/C1
Narodnaya (peak), Rus. 61/P2
Narok, Kenya 104/B3
Narón, Sp. 44/A1
Narooma, Austl. 115/D3
Nārowāl, Pak. 86/C3
Nærøy, Nor. 37/D2
Narra, Phil. 81/E2
Narrabri, Austl. 115/D1
Narrandera, Austl. 115/C2
Narrogin, Austl. 112/C5
Narromine, Austl. 115/D2
Narrows (riv.), NY, US 139/J9
Narsimhapur, India 84/B4
Narsingarh, India 89/L4
Narsinghdi, Bang. 85/H4
Narusawa, Japan 77/B3
Naruto, Japan 74/D3
Narutō, Japan 77/E2
Narva (res.), Rus. 60/E4
Narva (riv.), Est.,Rus. 60/E4
Narva (bay), Est.,Rus. 39/M2
Narva, Est. 39/N2
Narvacan, Phil. 79/D4
Narvik, Nor. 37/F1
Narwāna, India 86/D5
Nar'yan-Mar, Rus. 61/M2
Naryn, Kyr. 87/G4
Naryn (obl.), Kyr. 87/G4
Naryn (riv.), Kyr. 64/H5
Naryn Qum (plain), Kaz. 63/J2
Narzole, It. 58/A3
Năsăud, Rom. 49/G2
Naschel, Arg. 158/D2
Nash (pt.), Wal, UK 32/C4
Nashua, NH, US 131/G3
Nashville (int'l arpt.), Tn, US 130/C4
Nashville (cap.), Tn, US 130/C4
Našice, Cro. 48/D3
Nasielsk, Pol. 41/L2
Nasijärvi (lake), Fin. 39/K1
Nāsik, India 89/K5
Nasīrābād, India 89/K3
Naso (pt.), Phil. 81/F1
Nāsriganj, India 85/E3
Nass (riv.), BC, Can. 134/N4
Nassach (riv.), Ger. 54/D2
Nassarawa (state), Nga. 103/G4
Nassau (cap.), Bahm. 141/F2
Nassau (bay), Chile 159/D7
Nassau (isl.), Cook Is. 117/J6
Nassau, Ger. 53/G3
Nassau, De, US 138/C6
Nassau (co.), NY, US 139/E2
Nasser (lake), Egypt 93/C2
Nassereith, Aus. 57/G3
Nässjö, Swe. 38/F3
Nassogne, Belg. 53/E3
Nastapoka (isls.), Qu, Can. 123/J3
Nastätten, Ger. 53/G3
Næstved, Den. 38/D4
Nasu-dake (peak), Japan 75/F2
Nat (peak), Myan. 83/G4
Nata, Bots. 105/E5
Natá, Pan. 152/A2
Natagaima, Col. 152/C4
Natal, Braz. 154/D2
Natanz, Iran 88/F2
Natashō, Japan 77/J5
Natashquan (riv.), Qu, Can. 123/K3
Natchez, Ms, US 129/K5
Natchez Trace Nat'l Parkway, US 130/C5
Natchitoches, La, US 129/J5
Naters, Swi. 56/D5
Nāthdwāra, India 89/K4
Natimuk, Austl. 115/B3
Nation (riv.), BC, Can. 126/B2
National Agriculture Research Center, Md, US 138/B6
National Aquarium, Md, US 138/B5
National Archaeological Museum, Gre. 47/N8
National City, Ca, US 136/C5
National Cowboy Hall of Fame and Western Heritage Center, Ok, US 137/N14
National Exhibition Centre, Eng, UK 33/E2
National Institutes of Health, Md, US 138/A6
National Museum, Mona. 58/J8
National Security Agency, Md, US 138/B5
Natitingou, Ben. 103/F4
Natl, Ir. 91/D4
Natron (lake), Tanz. 104/B3
Natternbach, Aus. 55/G6
Nattheim, Ger. 54/D5
Nättraby, Swe. 38/F3
Natuna (isls.), Indo. 67/K9
Natural Bridge Caverns, Tx, US 137/U20
Natural Bridges Nat'l Mon., Ut, US 128/E3
Naturaliste (cape), Austl. 115/D4
Naturaliste (chan.), Austl. 112/B3
Naturaliste (cape), Austl. 112/B5
Naturno (Naturns), It. 57/G4
Naucalpan, Mex. 143/Q10
Naucelle, Fr. 42/E4
Né (riv.), Fr. 42/C4
Néa Alikarnassós, Gre. 47/J5
Néa Ankhíalos, Gre. 47/H3
Néa Artáki, Gre. 47/H3
Néa Ionía, Gre. 47/H3
Néa Ionía, Gre. 47/N8
Néa Kallikrátia, Gre. 47/H2
Néa Kíos, Gre. 47/H4
Néa Mikhanióna, Gre. 47/H2
Néa Moudhaniá, Gre. 47/H2
Néa Potídhaia, Gre. 47/H2
Néa Tríglia, Gre. 47/H2
Néa Zíkhni, Gre. 47/H2
Nä'ūr, Jor. 91/D4
Nauru (ctry.) 116/F5
Náushahra, India 86/C3
Naushahra Virkhan, Pak. 86/B4
Nauta, Peru 156/C2
Nautla, Mex. 143/N6
Nauvo (Nagu), Fin. 39/J1
Nava, Mex. 132/C4
Nava, Colle di (pass), It. 58/A4
Nava del Rey, Sp. 44/C2
Navajo (res.) 128/F3
Navajo Nat'l Mon., Az, US 128/E3
Navalcarnero, Sp. 45/M9
Navalmoral de la Mata, Sp. 44/C3
Navalvillar de Pela, Sp. 44/C3
Navapolatsk, Bela. 39/N4
Navarino (isl.), Chile 157/C3
Navarra (aut. comm.), Sp. 44/D1
Navarro, Arg. 159/J11
Navàs, Sp. 45/F2
Navas de San Juan, Sp. 44/D3
Navasota (riv.), Tx, US 143/F2
Navassa (isl.), Myan. 145/H2
Navax (pt.), Eng, UK 32/A6
Nave, It. 58/D1
Navenne, Fr. 56/C2
Navia, Sp. 44/B1
Navia (riv.), Sp. 44/B1
Navidad, Chile 158/N8
Navina, Ok, US 137/M14
Naviraí, Braz. 158/F3
Năvodari, Rom. 49/J3
Navojoa, Mex. 142/D3
Navolato, Mex. 142/D3
Návpaktos, Gre. 47/G3
Návplion, Gre. 47/H4
Navsāri, India 89/K4
Navy Board (inlet), Nun., Can. 123/H1
Navy Yard City, Wa, US 135/B2
Nawābganj, India 84/B1
Nawābganj, India 84/C2
Nawābganj, Bang. 85/G3
Nawābshāh, Pak. 89/J3
Nawāda, India 85/E3
Nawān Jandānwāla, Pak. 86/A3
Nawāshahr, India 86/D4
Nawāshahr, Pak. 86/B2
Nawoiy, Uzb. 87/E4
Nawoiy (pol. reg.), Uzb. 87/D4
Nawş, Ra's (pt.), Oman 89/G5
Naxçivan, Azer. 63/H5
Naxçivan Aut. Rep., Azer. 63/H5
Naxi, China 83/J2
Náxos, Gre. 47/J4
Náxos (isl.), Gre. 47/J4
Nayarit (state), Mex. 142/D4
Nayong, China 83/J2
Nayoro, Japan 76/C1
Nayramadlín (peak), Mong. 70/E2
Nayzatash (pass), Taj. 87/F5
Nazaré, Braz. 154/C4
Nazaré, Port. 44/A3
Nazaré do Piauí, Braz. 154/D3
Nazaré Paulista, Braz. 211/G8
Nazareth, Pa, US 138/C2
Nazareth, Belg. 52/C2
Nazas (riv.), Mex. 142/D3
Nazas, Mex. 142/D3
Nazca, Peru 156/C4
Naze, Japan 75/K6
Naze, The (pt.), Eng, UK 33/H3
Nazerat (Nazareth), Isr. 91/G6
Nazilli, Turk. 90/B2
Nazrēt, Eth. 97/N6
Nazyvayevsk, Rus. 87/F1
Nchelenge, Zam. 104/A5
Ncheu, Malw. 105/F3
Ndalatando, Ang. 105/B2
Ndali, Ben. 103/F4
Ndele, CAfr. 97/K6
Ndende (isl.), Sol. 116/F6
N'djamena (cap.), Chad 96/J5
Ndola, Zam. 105/E3
Ndrhamcha (lake), Mrta. 102/B2
Neagh (lake), NI, UK 34/B2
Neale (lake), Austl. 109/C3
Neales (riv.), Austl. 113/G3
Neamţ (prov.), Rom. 49/H2
Neaophli-le-Château, Fr. 30/H5
Neápolis, Gre. 47/J2
Neápolis, Gre. 47/G2
Neápolis, Gre. 47/J5
Near (isl.), Ak, US 134/A5
Neath, Wal, UK 32/C3
Neath (riv.), Wal, UK 32/C3
Neath Port Talbot (co.), Wal, UK 32/C3
Neavitt, Md, US 138/B6
Nebbi, Ugan. 104/A2
Nebel-Horn (peak), Ger. 57/G3
Nebikon, Swi. 56/D3
Nebitdag, Trkm. 63/K5
Neblina (peak), Braz. 150/F3
Nebo (mt.), Austl. 114/E6
Nebraska (state), US 129/G2
Nebrodi (mts.), It. 46/C4
Nechako (riv.), BC, Can. 122/D3
Neches (riv.), Tx, US 125/G5
Nechisar NP, Eth. 97/N6
Nechranice (res.), Czh. 55/G2
Neckar (riv.), Ger. 40/D4
Neckarbischofsheim, Ger. 54/B4
Neckargemünd, Ger. 54/B4
Neckarsteinach, Ger. 54/B4
Neckarsulm, Ger. 54/C4
Necker (isl.), Hi, US 117/J2
Necochea, Arg. 158/F3
Necoclí, Col. 152/B2
Neda, Sp. 44/A1
Nedelino, Bul. 47/J2
Nedelišće, Cro. 43/M3
Nederland, Tx, US 129/J5
Nederland, Co, US 137/A3
Nederweert, Neth. 50/C6
Neede, Neth. 50/D4
Needles, Ca, US 128/D4
Needles, The, Eng, UK 33/E5
Needmore, Ok, US 137/N15
Neepawa, Mb, Can. 127/J3
Neerabup NP, Austl. 112/K6
Neerpelt, Belg. 50/C6
Neetze, It. 51/H2
Neetze, Ger. 51/H2
Neffelbach (riv.), Ger. 53/F2
Neftekamsk, Rus. 61/M4
Nefud (des.), SAr. 89/E3
Nefyn, Wal, UK 34/D6
Negēlē, Eth. 97/N6
Negev (reg.), Isr. 91/D5
Negoiu (peak), Rom. 49/G3
Negombo, SrL. 82/C6
Negotin, Serb. 48/F3
Negotino, FYROM 47/H2
Negra (pt.), Peru 156/A2
Negra (range), Braz. 154/A3
Negra (pt.), Belz. 144/D2
Negrais (cape), Myan. 83/F4
Negrar, It. 59/D1
Negreira, Sp. 44/A1
Negreşti, Rom. 49/H2
Negritos, Peru 156/A2
Negro (riv.), Uru. 157/E3
Negro (riv.), Arg. 157/D5
Negro (peak), Arg. 158/C3
Negros (isl.), Phil. 67/M9
Nehbandān, Iran 89/H2
Nei Monggol (aut. reg.), China 71/K3
Nei Monggol (plat.), China 71/K3
Neiafu, Tonga 117/H6
Neiba, DRep. 141/G4
Neiba (mts.), DRep. 145/J2
Neiderösterreich (prov.), Aus. 43/L2
Neige, Crêt de la (peak), Fr. 56/B5
Neihuang, China 72/C4
Neijiang, China 70/J6
Neilston, Sc, UK 36/B3
Neiqiu, China 72/C3
Neiva, Col. 152/C4
Neixiang, China 72/B4
Nejanilini (lake), Mb, Can. 122/G3
Nejdek, Czh. 55/F2
Nejrab (int'l arpt.), Syria 91/E1
Nek'emtē, Eth. 97/N6
Neksø, Den. 38/F4
Nelas, Port. 44/B2
Nelidovo, Rus. 60/G4
Nellingen, Ger. 54/C5
Nellore, India 82/C5
Nelson (cape), Austl. 115/B3
Nelson (isl.), Ak, US 134/E3
Nelson (str.), Chile 157/A7
Nelson, BC, Can. 126/D3
Nelson, NZ 117/S11
Nelson, Eng, UK 35/F4
Nelson Bay, Austl. 115/E2
Nelson Lagoon, Ak, US 134/F4
Nelson Lakes NP, NZ 117/S11
Nelson-Atkins Museum of Fine Art, Mo, US 137/D5
Nelspruit, SAfr. 105/F6
Néma, Mrta. 102/D2
Néma, Dhar (cliff), Mrta. 102/D2
Neman (riv.), Rus. 41/M1
Nembro, It. 58/C1
Neméa, Gre. 47/H4
Nemingha, Austl. 115/D1
Nemira (peak), Rom. 49/H2
Nemours, Fr. 42/E2
Nemunas (riv.), Lith. 60/D5
Nemuro (pen.), Japan 76/D2
Nemuro, Japan 76/D2
Nen (riv.), China 67/M5
Nenagh, Ire. 31/P10
Nenana, Ak, US 134/J3
Nendaz, Swi. 56/D5
Nene (riv.), Eng, UK 35/J6
Nenetskiy Aut. Okrug, Rus. 61/J2
Nenjiang, China 71/N2
Nentershausen, Ger. 51/G6
Nentershausen, Ger. 51/G3
Nenzing, Aus. 57/F3
Neo Volcanica, Cordillera (mts.), Mex. 143/Q10
Néon Petrítsion, Gre. 47/H2
Neoria Husainpur, India 84/B1
Néos Marmarás, Gre. 47/H2
Neosho (riv.), Ks,Ok, US 129/J3
Nepal (ctry.) 84/D1
Nepālganj, Nepal 84/C1
Nepanagar, India 89/L4
Nepean, On, Can. 130/F2
Nepean (riv.), Austl. 114/G8
Nepeña, Peru 156/B3
Nepessing (lake), Mi, US 135/F6
Nephi, Ut, US 128/E3
Nepisiguit (riv.), NB, Can. 131/H2
Nepomuk, Czh. 55/G4
Neptune City, NJ, US 138/D3
Nera (riv.), It. 43/K5
Nérac, Fr. 42/D4
Neratovice, Czh. 55/H2
Nerekhta, Rus. 60/J4
Neresheim, Ger. 54/D5
Neretva (riv.), Bosn. 57/H5
Neris (riv.), Lith. 60/D5
Nerja, Sp. 44/D4
Nermete (pt.), Peru 156/A2
Nerokoúros, Gre. 47/J5
Nerone (peak), It. 59/F5
Nerpio, Sp. 44/D3
Nersingen, Ger. 54/D6
Nerva, Sp. 44/B4
Nervesa della Battaglia, It. 59/F1
Nerviano, It. 58/B1
Nes, Neth. 38/D1
Nes, Nor. 38/D1
Nes Ziyyona, Isr. 91/F8
Nesbyen, Nor. 38/D1
Nesebŭr, Bul. 47/K1
Nesher, Isr. 91/G6
Neskaupstadhur, Ice. 37/Q6
Nesle, Fr. 52/B4
Nesles-la-Vallée, Fr. 30/J4
Nesquehoning, Pa, US 138/C2
Ness (riv.), Sc, UK 36/B2
Ness (lake), Sc, UK 36/B2
Nesselrode (mt.), Ak, US 134/M4
Nesselwang, Ger. 57/G2
Nesslau, Swi. 57/F3
Neston, Eng, UK 35/E5
Nestório, Gre. 47/G2
Néstos (riv.), Gre. 49/G5
Netanya, Isr. 91/F7
Netarhāt, India 85/E4
Netcong, NJ, US 138/D2
Nethe (riv.), Ger. 51/G5
Netherlands (ctry.) 40/C3
Netherlands Antilles (dpcy.), Neth. 141/H5
Netolice, Czh. 55/H2
Netphen, Ger. 53/H2
Netstal, Swi. 57/F3
Nette (riv.), Ger. 50/D6
Nettebach (riv.), Ger. 53/G3
Nettersheim, Ger. 53/F3
Nettetal, Ger. 50/D6
Nettilling (lake), Nun., Can. 123/J2
Nettuno, It. 46/C2
Netzschkau, Ger. 55/F1
Neu Darchau, Ger. 51/H2
Neu-Isenburg, Ger. 54/B2
Neu-Ulm, Ger. 54/D6
Neu Zittau, Ger. 40/Q7
Neubiberg, Ger. 55/E6
Neubrandenburg, Ger. 41/G2
Neubulach, Ger. 54/B5
Neuburg, Ger. 54/B5
Neuburg an der Donau, Ger. 54/E5
Neuburg an der Kammel, Ger. 57/G1
Neuchâtel, Swi. 56/C4
Neuchâtel (canton), Swi. 56/C4
Neuchâtel, Lac de (lake), Swi. 56/C4
Neuenbürg, Ger. 54/B5
Neuenburg am Rhein, Ger. 56/D2
Neuendettelsau, Ger. 54/D4
Neuenhagen, Ger. 40/Q6
Neuenhaus, Ger. 50/D3
Neuenkirchen, Ger. 51/F3
Neuenkirchen, Ger. 51/E4
Neuenkirchen, Ger. 51/E4
Neuenrade, Ger. 51/E6
Neuenstadt am Kocher, Ger. 54/C4
Neuenstein, Ger. 54/C4
Neuerburg, Ger. 53/F3
Neufahrn bei Freising, Ger. 55/E6
Neufchâteau, Belg. 53/E4
Neufchâtel-en-Bray, Fr. 42/D2
Neufchâtel-Hardelot, Fr. 52/A2
Neufchelles, Fr. 30/M4
Neufmanil, Fr. 53/D4
Neufmoutiers-en-Brie, Fr. 30/L5
Neuhaus am Inn, Ger. 55/G6
Neuhaus am Rennweg, Ger. 54/E1
Neuhaus-Schierschnitz, Ger. 54/E2
Neuhäusel, Ger. 53/G3
Neuhausen am Rheinfall, Swi. 57/E2
Neuhof, Ger. 54/C2
Neuhof an der Zenn, Ger. 54/D4
Neuhofen, Ger. 54/B4
Neuhofen an der Krems, Aus. 55/H6
Neuilly-en-Thelle, Fr. 52/B5
Neuilly-L'Évêque, Fr. 56/B2
Neuilly-sur-Marne, Fr. 30/K5
Neuilly-sur-Seine, Fr. 30/J5
Neukirchen, Ger. 38/C4
Neukirchen an der Vöckla, Aus. 55/G6
Neukirchen vorm Wald, Ger. 55/G5
Neumarkt am Wallersee, Aus. 55/G6
Neumarkt (Egna), It. 57/H5
Neumarkt im Mühlkreis, Aus. 55/H6
Neumarkt in der Oberpfalz, Ger. 55/E4
Neumarkt-Sankt Veit, Ger. 55/F6
Neumünster, Ger. 38/C4
Neunburg, Ger. 55/F4
Neunkirchen, Aus. 43/M3
Neunkirchen, Ger. 53/F2
Neunkirchen, Ger. 53/G5
Neunkirchen-Seelscheid, Ger. 53/G2
Neupotz, Ger. 54/B4
Neuquén (riv.), Arg. 157/C3
Neuquén (prov.), Arg. 158/C3
Neuquén, Arg. 158/C3
Neuruppin, Ger. 54/D1
Neusäß, Ger. 54/D6
Neuse (riv.), NC, US 133/J3
Neusiedl am See, Aus. 43/M3
Neusiedler (lake), Aus. 41/J5
Neusiedler See (lake), Aus. 48/C2
Neuss, Ger. 53/F1
Neustadt am Rübenberge, Ger. 51/G3
Neustadt an der Aisch, Ger. 54/D4
Neustadt an der Donau, Ger. 55/E5
Neustadt an der Waldnaab, Ger. 55/F4
Neustadt an der Weinstrasse, Ger. 53/G4
Neustadt bei Coburg, Ger. 54/E2
Neustadt in Holstein, Ger. 38/D4
Neustift im Stubaital, Aus. 57/H3
Neustrelitz, Ger. 40/G2
Neutraubling, Ger. 55/F5
Neuves-Maisons, Fr. 42/F2
Neuvic, Fr. 42/E4
Neuville-sur-Saône, Fr. 56/A6
Neuwied, Ger. 53/G3
Neuzelle, Ger. 41/H2
Neva (riv.), Rus. 39/P2
Nevada (state), US 128/C3
Nevada, Mo, US 129/J3
Nevada (mts.), Col. 145/H4
Nevada, Sierra (mts.), Sp. 44/D4
Nevado de Colima PN, Mex. 142/D5
Nevado de Toluca, PN, Mex. 143/K7
Nevado del Huila, PN, Col. 150/D3
Nevado, Sierra del (mts.), Arg. 158/C3
Nevel', Rus. 39/N3
Nevele, Belg. 52/C1
Nevel'sk, Rus. 71/R2
Nevers, Fr. 42/E3
Nevesinje, Bosn. 47/F1
Nevinnomyssk, Rus. 63/G3
Nevis (peak), StK. 141/N8
Nevis (isl.), UK 141/J4
Nevola (riv.), It. 59/G5
Nevşehir (prov.), Turk. 90/C2
Nevşehir, Turk. 90/C2
New (riv.), Guy. 150/G3
New (riv.), WV, US 130/D4
New Albany, In, US 130/C4
New Albany, Ms, US 133/F3
New Amsterdam, Guy. 153/G3
New Ancholme (riv.), Eng, UK 35/H4
New Athens, Il, US 137/H9
New Baltimore, Mi, US 135/G6
New Bataan, Phil. 79/E6
New Bedford, Ma, US 131/G3
New Berlin, Tx, US 137/U21
New Berlin, Pa, US 138/B2
New Berlin, Wi, US 135/P14
New Berlinville, Pa, US 138/C2
New Bern, NC, US 133/J3
New Braunfels, Tx, US 137/U20
New Britain, Ct, US 131/F3
New Britain (isl.), PNG 116/D5
New Britain, Pa, US 138/C3
New Brunswick (prov.), Can. 131/H2
New Brunswick, NJ, US 139/H10
New Buffalo, Pa, US 138/B3
New Buildings, NI, UK 34/A2
New Caledonia (isl.), NCal. 116/F7
New Caledonia (terr.), Fr. 116/F6
New Canaan, Ct, US 139/M7
New Castle (co.), De, US 138/C6
New Castle, In, US 130/C4
New Castle, Pa, US 130/D3
New Chicago, In, US 135/R16
New City, NY, US 139/K7
New Columbia, Pa, US 138/B2
New Columbus, Pa, US 138/B1
New Cumberland, NJ, US 139/J9
New Cumnock, Sc, UK 36/B6
New Delhi (cap.), India 86/D5
New Denver, BC, Can. 126/D3
New Egypt, NJ, US 138/D3
New England NP, Austl. 115/E1
New Freedom, Pa, US 138/B4
New Galloway, Sc, UK 34/D1
New Georgia (isls.), Sol. 116/E5
New Georgia (sound), Sol. 116/E5
New Glasgow, NS, Can. 131/J2
New Glasgow, Qu, Can. 131/N6
New Gretna, NJ, US 138/D4
New Guinea (isl.), Indo.,PNG 67/N10
New Hampshire (state), US 131/G3
New Hanover, SAfr. 107/E3
New Hanover, Il, US 137/G9
New Hanover (isl.), PNG 116/D4
New Haven, Ct, US 131/F3
New Haven, Mi, US 135/G6
New Hebrides (isls.), Van. 116/F6
New Holland, Pa, US 138/C3
New Hope, Pa, US 138/D3
New Hyde Park, NY, US 139/L9
New Iberia, La, US 129/K5
New Ireland (isl.),PNG 116/E5
New Jersey (state), US 138/D3
New Kensington, Pa, US 130/E3
New Kowloon, China 71/U10
New Lenox, Il, US 135/Q16
New Lisbon, NJ, US 138/D4
New Liskeard, On, Can. 130/E2
New London, Ct, US 131/G3
New Madrid, Mo, US 129/K3
New Market, Md, US 138/A5
New Meadows, Id, US 126/D4
New Mexico (state), US 128/G4
New Milford, NJ, US 139/J8
New Mills, Eng, UK 35/F5
New Norfolk, Austl. 115/C4
New Orleans, La, US 137/P17
New Orleans (Moisant Field), La, US 137/P17
New Oxford, Pa, US 138/A4
New Philadelphia, Oh, US 130/D3
New Philadelphia, Pa, US 138/B2
New Pitsligo, Sc, UK 36/D1
New Plymouth, NZ 117/S10
New Port Richey, Fl, US 133/H4
New Providence (isl.), Bahm. 141/F3
New Providence, NJ, US 139/H9
New Richmond, Qu, Can. 131/H1
New River (mts.), Az, US 137/R18
New River, Az, US 137/R18
New Rochelle, NY, US 139/K8
New Rockford, ND, US 127/J4
New Romney, Eng, UK 33/H5
New Ross, Ire. 31/Q10
New Rossington, Eng, UK 35/G5
New Sarpy, La, US 137/P17
New Schwabenland (phys. reg.), Ant. 160/Z
New Siberian (isls.), Rus. 67/N2
New Smyrna Beach, Fl, US 133/H4
New South Wales, Austl. 115/C3
New South Wales (state), Austl. 109/D4
New Stuyahok, Ak, US 134/G4
New Town, ND, US 127/H4
New Tripoli, Pa, US 138/C2
New Ulm, Mn, US 127/J4
New Waterford, NS, Can. 131/J2
New Westminster, BC, Can. 126/C3
New Windsor, Md, US 138/A4
New York (state), US 130/D3
New York, NY, US 139/K9
New Zealand (ctry.) 117/R10
Newark, Oh, US 130/D3
Newark, De, US 138/C4
Newark (int'l arpt.), NJ, US 139/J9
Newark, NJ, US 139/H9
Newark, Ca, US 135/K11
Newark (bay), NJ, US 139/J9
Newark-on-Trent, Eng, UK 35/H5
Newbern, Il, US 137/G8
Newberry, SC, US 133/H3
Newberry, Mi, US 130/C2
Newberry Nat'l Volcanic Mon., Or, US 126/C5
Newburgh, Sc, UK 36/C4
Newburn, Eng, UK 35/G2
Newbury, Eng, UK 33/E4
Newcastle, Austl. 115/D2
Newcastle, SAfr. 107/E2
Newcastle, Ire. 31/P10
Newcastle, Ire. 34/B5
Newcastle, NI, UK 34/C3
Newcastle (int'l arpt.), Eng, UK 35/G1
Newcastle, Wy, US 127/M15
Newcastle-under-Lyme, Eng, UK 35/F5
Newcastle upon Tyne, Eng, UK 35/G2
Newcastle upon Tyne (co.), Eng, UK 35/G1
Newcastleton, Sc, UK 35/F1
Newe Yam, Isr. 91/F6
Newel, Ger. 53/F4
Newell, La, US 137/M15
Newellton, La, US 129/K4
Newenham (cape), Ak, US 134/F4
Newfane, NY, US 131/S9
Newfield, NJ, US 138/C4
Newfoundland (isl.), Can. 131/L1
Newfoundland, NJ, US 139/H7
Newfoundland, Pa, US 138/C1
Newfoundland and Labrador (prov.), Can. 123/K3
Newhalen, Ak, US 134/H4
Newham (bor.), Eng, UK 30/D2
Newhaven, Eng, UK 33/F5
Newington, Eng, UK 30/F3
Newkirk, Ok, US 129/H3
Newllano, La, US 129/J5
Newmains, Sc, UK 36/C5
Newman (mt.), Austl. 112/C2
Newman, Austl. 112/C2
Newmarket, On, Can. 130/E2
Newmarket, Eng, UK 33/G2
Newmill, Sc, UK 36/D1
Newnan, Ga, US 133/G3
Newport, Eng, UK 32/D1
Newport, Wal, UK 32/C3
Newport (co.), Wal, UK 32/C3
Newport (bay), Ca, US 136/C3
Newport, De, US 138/C4
Newport, Ky, US 130/C4
Newport, NJ, US 138/C5
Newport, Or, US 126/B4
Newport, Pa, US 138/A3
Newport, RI, US 131/G3
Newport, Tn, US 130/D5
Newport, Vt, US 131/F2
Newport, Wa, US 126/D3
Newport Beach, Ca, US 136/G8
Newport Meadows (lake), NJ, US 138/C5
Newport-on-Tay, Sc, UK 36/D4
Newport Pagnell, Eng, UK 33/F2
Newquay, Eng, UK 32/A6
Newry, NI, UK 34/B3
Newry (dist.), NI, UK 34/B3
Newry (canal), NI, UK 34/B3
Newtok, Ak, US 134/F3
Newton, Tx, US 129/J5
Newton, Ma, US 131/G3
Newton, NJ, US 138/D1
Newton Abbot, Eng, UK 32/C5
Newton-le-Willows, Eng, UK 35/F5
Newton Mearns, Sc, UK 36/B5
Newton Stewart, Sc, UK 34/D2
Newton Tors (hill), Eng, UK 35/F1
Newtonmore, Sc, UK 36/B2
Newtonville, NJ, US 138/D4
Newtown, Austl. 115/B3
Newtown, Wal, UK 32/C1
Newtown, Pa, US 138/D3
Newtown Mount Kennedy, Ire. 34/B5
Newtown Saint Boswells, Sc, UK 36/D5
Newtown Square, Pa, US 138/C4
Newtownabbey, NI, UK 34/C2
Newtownards, NI, UK 34/C2
Newtownhamilton, NI, UK 34/B3
Newtownstewart, NI, UK 34/A2
Newtyle, Sc, UK 36/C3
Nextlalpan, Mex. 143/Q9
Neyagawa, Japan 77/J6
Neyrīz, Iran 89/F3
Neyshābūr, Iran 89/G1
Neyva (riv.), Rus. 61/P4
Neyveli, India 82/C5
Neyyättinkara, India 82/C6
Nezahualcóyotl, Mex. 143/Q10
Neznayka (riv.), Rus. 61/W9
Nezperce, Id, US 126/D4
Ngabang, Indo. 80/C3
Ngabordamlu (cape), Indo. 81/H5
Ngabu, Malw. 105/F4
Ngai-Ndethya Nat'l Rsv., Kenya 104/C3
Ngamring, China 85/F1
Nganda (peak), Malw. 104/B5
Ngangerabeli (plain), Kenya 104/C3
Ngaoundéré, Camr. 96/H6
Ngarkat Conservation Park, Austl. 115/D3
Ngatik (isl.), Micr. 116/E4
Ngoan Muc (pass), Viet. 78/E4
Ngoc Linh (peak), Viet. 83/J4
Ngomeni (cape), Kenya 104/D3
Ngong, Kenya 104/B3
Ngonye (falls), Zam. 105/D4
Ngorongoro Consv. Area, Tanz. 104/B3

Ngounié (riv.), Gabon 96/H8
Nguigmi, Niger 96/H5
Ngulu (isl.), Micr. 116/C4
Ngumbe Sukani (pt.), Tanz. 104/C6
Nguru (mts.), Tanz. 104/C4
Ngwenya (peak), Swaz. 107/E2
Nha Trang, Viet. 78/E3
Nhamunda (riv.), Braz. 147/D3
Nhill, Austl. 115/B3
Nhlangano, Swaz. 107/E2
Niagara (falls), Can.,US 131/R9
Niagara (riv.), Can.,US 131/R9
Niagara (co.), On, Can. 131/R9
Niagara Falls, On, Can. 131/R9
Niagara Falls, NY, US 131/R9
Niagara-on-the-Lake, On, Can. 131/R9
Niamey (dept.), Niger 103/F3
Niamey (cap.), Niger 103/F3
Niamey (int'l arpt.), Niger 103/F3
Niamtougou, Togo 103/F4
Niandan (riv.), Afr. 103/G5
Niangara, D.R. Congo 97/L7
Niangay (lake), Mali 96/F4
Niangzi (pass), China 72/C3
Nias (isl.), Indo. 67/J9
Niassa (prov.), Moz. 104/B5
Nicaragua (ctry.) 145/E3
Nicaragua (lake), Nic. 145/E4
Nicastro-Sambiase, It. 46/E3
Nice, Fr. 43/G5
Niceville, Fl, US 133/G4
Nichinan, Japan 74/B5
Nichlaul, India 84/D2
Nicholas (chan.), Bang. 145/F1
Nichols Hills, Ok, US 137/M14
Nicholson (range), Austl. 112/C3
Nickerie (dist.), Sur. 153/G3
Nickerie (riv.), Sur. 153/G3
Nickol (bay), Austl. 112/C2
Nicobar (isls.), India 67/J9
Nicolás Bravo, Mex. 144/D2
Nicolás Romero, Mex. 143/09
Nicolet, Qu, Can. 131/F2
Nicolls (pt.), NY, US 139/E2
Nicoma Park, Ok, US 137/N15
Nicosia, It. 46/D4
Nicosia (cap.), Cyp. 91/C2
Nicosia (dist.), Cyp. 91/C2
Nicotera, It. 46/D3
Nicoya (gulf), CR 140/D6
Nicoya, CR 144/E4
Nicoya, Peninsula de (pen.), CR 150/A1
Nidau, Swi. 56/D3
Nidd (riv.), Eng, UK 35/G3
Nidda, Ger. 54/B2
Nidda (riv.), Ger. 40/E3
Niddatal, Ger. 54/B2
Nidder (riv.), Ger. 54/C2
Nideggen, Ger. 53/F2
Nidge (prov.), Turk. 90/C2
Nidwalden (canton), Swi. 57/E4
Nidzica, Pol. 41/L2
Niebüll, Ger. 38/C4
Nied (riv.), Fr. 43/G2
Niedenstein, Ger. 51/G6
Nieder-Olm, Ger. 53/H4
Niederanven, Lux. 53/F4
Niederbipp, Swi. 56/D3
Niederbronn-les-Bains, Fr. 53/G6
Niedere Tauern (mts.), Aus. 43/K3
Niederfischbach, Ger. 51/G6
Niederlausitz (reg.), Ger. 41/G3
Niedernhausen, Ger. 54/B2
Niederösterreich (prov.), Aus. 48/B2
Niedersachsen (state), Ger. 38/C5
Niedersächsisches Wattenmeer NP, Ger. 51/E1
Niedersachswerfen, Ger. 51/H6
Niederstetten, Ger. 54/C4
Niederstotzingen, Ger. 54/D5
Niederurnen, Swi. 57/F3
Niederwerrn, Ger. 54/D2
Niederwinkling, Ger. 55/F5
Niederzier, Ger. 53/F2
Niederzissen, Ger. 53/G3
Niefern-Oschelbronn, Ger. 54/B5
Niegocin (lake), Pol. 39/J5
Nieheim, Ger. 51/G5
Niemodlin, Pol. 41/J3
Nienburg, Ger. 51/G3
Nienhagen, Ger. 51/H3

Niénokoué (peak), C.d'Iv. 102/D5
Nieppe, Fr. 52/B2
Niéri (riv.), Sen. 102/B3
Niers (riv.), Ger. 53/F1
Nierstein, Ger. 54/B3
Niet Ban Tinh Xa, Viet. 78/D4
Nieuw-Amsterdam, Sur. 151/G2
Nieuw-Bergen, Neth. 50/D5
Nieuw-Loosdrecht, Neth. 50/C4
Nieuw-Nickerie, Sur. 153/G3
Nieuw-Schoonebeek, Neth. 50/D3
Nieuw-Vossemeer, Neth. 50/B5
Nieuwe Pekela, Neth. 50/D2
Nieuwegein, Neth. 50/C4
Nieuwerkerk aan de IJssel, Neth. 50/B5
Nieuweschans, Neth. 51/E2
Nieuwkoop, Neth. 50/B4
Nieuwleusen, Neth. 50/D3
Nieuwouldtville, SAfr. 106/B3
Nieuwpoort, Belg. 52/B1
Nieves, Mex. 142/E3
Niğde, Turk. 90/C2
Nigel, SAfr. 106/E2
Niger (ctry.) 96/G4
Niger (delta), Nga. 103/G5
Niger (riv.), Afr. 96/F5
Nigeria (ctry.) 96/G6
Nigg (bay), Sc, UK 36/B1
Nighthawk (lake), On, Can. 130/D1
Nightmute, Ak, US 134/F3
Nigrán, Sp. 44/A1
Nigrita, Gre. 47/H2
Nihoa (isl.), Hi, US 117/J2
Nihonmatsu, Japan 75/G2
Nihtaur, India 84/B1
Nii (isl.), Viet. 75/F3
Niigata (int'l arpt.), Japan 75/F2
Niigata, Japan 75/F2
Niigata (pref.), Japan 76/A4
Niihama, Japan 74/C4
Niihari, Japan 77/E1
Niihau (isl.), Hi, US 124/R10
Niimi, Japan 74/C3
Niitsu, Japan 75/F2
Niiza, Japan 77/D2
Nijar, Sp. 44/D4
Nijkerk, Neth. 50/C4
Nijlen, Belg. 53/D1
Nijmegen, Neth. 50/C5
Nikaia, Gre. 47/H3
Nikel', Rus. 37/J1
Nikisiani, Gre. 47/J2
Nikki, Ben. 103/F4
Nikkō, Japan 75/F2
Nikkō NP, Japan 75/F2
Niklasdorf, Aus. 43/L3
Nikolai, Ak, US 134/H3
Nikolayevsk-na-Amure, Rus. 65/Q4
Nikol'sk, Rus. 63/H1
Nikolski, Ak, US 134/E5
Nikonga (riv.), Tanz. 104/A3
Nikopol', Ukr. 62/E3
Nikopol, Bul. 49/G4
Niksar, Turk. 62/F4
Nikshahr, Iran 89/H3
Nikšić, Serb. 47/F1
Nikumaroro (Gardner) (isl.), Kiri. 117/H5
Nikunau (isl.), Kiri. 116/G5
Nile (delta), Egypt 88/B2
Nile (riv.), Afr. 93/F2
Niles, Mi, US 130/C3
Niles, Oh, US 130/D3
Niles, Il, US 135/Q15
Ni'lin, Isr. 91/G8
Nilópolis, Braz. 211/K7
Nilsiä, Fin. 60/F3
Nilvange, Fr. 53/F5
Nīmāj, India 82/B2
Nimba (peak), C.d'Iv. 102/C5
Nimba (co.), Libr. 102/C5
Nîmes, Fr. 42/F5
Nimsbach (riv.), Ger. 53/F4a
Nimule NP, Sudan 104/A2
Nin, Cro. 48/B3
Nīnawá (gov.), Iraq 90/E3
Nīnawā (Nineveh) (ruin), Iraq 90/E2
Ninepin Group (isls.), China 71/V11
Ninfas (pt.), Arg. 158/D4
Ning'an, China 71/N3
Ningbo, China 72/E5
Ningde, China 79/C2
Ningdu, China 79/C2
Ningguang, China 83/K2
Ninghua, China 79/C2
Ningjin, China 72/C3
Ningjin, China 72/D3
Ninglang Yizu Zizhixian, China 83/H2
Ningming, China 72/C4
Ningming, China 83/J3
N'kongsamba, Camr. 96/G7
Ningning, China 72/D4
Ningxia Huizu (aut. reg.), China 70/J4
Ningxiang, China 79/B2
Ningyang, China 72/D4

Ningyuan, China 83/K2
Ninh Binh, Viet. 78/D1
Ninilchik, Ak, US 134/H3
Niningo (isls.), PNG 116/D5
Ninohe, Japan 76/B3
Ninomiya, Japan 77/C3
Ninove, Belg. 52/D2
Noatak (riv.), Ak, US 134/F2
Ninoy Aquino (int'l arpt.), Phil. 79/D5
Niobara (riv.), Ne, US 124/F3
Niobrara (riv.), Ne, US 127/H5
Niokolo-Koba, PN du, Sen. 102/B3
Niono, Mali 102/D3
Nioro-du-Rip, Sen. 102/B3
Nioro du Sahel, Mali 102/C3
Niort, Fr. 42/C3
Nipawin, Sk, Can. 127/H2
Nipe (bay), Cuba 145/H1
Nipigon, On, Can. 127/L3
Nipigon (lake), On, Can. 122/G3
Nipissing (lake), On, Can. 123/J4
Niquén, Chile 158/C3
Niquero, Cuba 145/G1
Nirasaki, Japan 75/F3
Nirayama, Japan 77/B3
Nirimba Army Afld., Austl. 114/G8
Nirmal, India 82/C4
Nirmāli, India 85/F2
Niš (int'l arpt.), Serb. 47/G1
Niš, Serb. 47/G1
Nišava (riv.), Serb. 47/H1
Niscemi, It. 46/D4
Nishiazai, Japan 77/K5
Nishibiwajima, Japan 77/L5
Nishiharu, Japan 77/L5
Nishikatsura, Japan 77/B2
Nishiki, Japan 74/B3
Nishiki, Japan 77/H5
Nishinomiya, Japan 77/H6
Nishino'omote, Japan 74/B5
Nishio, Japan 77/M6
Nishiwaki, Japan 77/G6
Nisko, Pol. 41/M3
Nisqually, Wa, US 135/B3
Nisqually (riv.), Wa, US 135/B3
Nisqually Ind. Res., Wa, US 135/B3
Nisqually Reach (str.), Wa, US 135/B3
Nissan (isl.), PNG 116/E5
Nisser (lake), Nor. 38/C2
Nisshin, Japan 77/M5
Nissum (bay), Den. 38/C3
Nisswa, Mn, US 127/K4
Nistru (riv.), Mol. 49/H1
Niterói, Braz. 211/K7
Nith (riv.), Sc, UK 36/C6
Nith (riv.), Sc, UK 34/E1
Nithsdale (valley), Sc, UK 34/E1
Nitra, Slvk. 48/D1
Nitra (riv.), Slvk. 41/K4
Nitriansky (pol. reg.), Slvk. 41/K4
Nitsa (riv.), Rus. 61/P4
Nitta, Japan 77/C1
Nittedal, Nor. 38/D1
Nittel, Ger. 53/F4
Nittenau, Ger. 55/F4
Niuafo'ou (isl.), Tonga 117/H6
Niuatoputapu Group (isls.), Tonga 117/H6
Niue (terr.), NZ 117/J6
Niue (isl.), Niue 117/J6
Niulakita (isl.), Tuv. 116/G6
Niulan (riv.), China 83/H2
Niut (peak), Indo. 80/C3
Niutao (isl.), Tuv. 116/G5
Nivelles, Belg. 53/D2
Nivernais, Collines de (hills), Fr. 42/E3
Niverville, Mb, Can. 127/J3
Niwot, Co, US 137/B2
Niyazov (int'l arpt.), Trkm. 87/C5
Niyodo (riv.), Japan 74/C4
Nizāmābād, India 82/C4
Nizhegorodskaya Oblast, Rus. 63/G1
Nizhnekama (res.), Rus. 61/M4
Nizhnekamsk, Rus. 61/L5
Nizhneudinsk, Rus. 65/K4
Nizhnevartovsk, Rus. 64/H3
Nizhniy Lomov, Rus. 63/G1
Nizhniy Novgorod, Rus. 61/K4
Nizhniy Tagil, Rus. 61/N4
Nizhyn, Ukr. 62/D2
Nizip, Turk. 90/D2
Nizke Tatry NP, Slvk. 41/K4
Nizza Monferrato, It. 58/B3
Nizzanim, Isr. 91/F8
Njombe (riv.), Tanz. 104/B4
Nkandla, SAfr. 107/E3
Nkayi, Congo 105/B1
Nkhata Bay, Malw. 104/B5
Nkululu (riv.), Tanz. 104/A2
Nkusi (riv.), Ugan. 104/A2
Nmai (riv.), Myan. 83/G2
Noailles, Fr. 52/B5

Noākhāli (pol. reg.), Bang. 85/H4
Noale, It. 59/F1
Noāmundi, India 85/E4
Noank, Ct, US 139/F1
Noatak, Ak, US 134/F2
Noatak (riv.), Ak, US 134/F2
Noatak Nat'l Prsv., Ak, US 134/F2
Nobeoka, Japan 74/B4
Noble, Ok, US 137/N15
Noboa, Ecu. 152/A5
Noboribetsu, Japan 76/B2
Noce (riv.), It. 57/G5
Noceto, It. 58/D3
Noci, It. 47/E2
Nockamixon State Park, Pa, US 138/C2
Noda, Japan 77/D2
Nodagawa, Japan 77/H4
Noé (cape), Alg. 100/D2
Nogales, Az, US 128/E5
Nogales, Mex. 143/M8
Nogaro, Fr. 42/C5
Nogat (riv.), Pol. 39/H4
Nogata, Japan 74/B4
Nogent, Fr. 56/B1
Nogent-l'Artaud, Fr. 52/C6
Nogent-le-Rotrou, Fr. 42/D2
Nogent-sur-Oise, Fr. 52/B5
Nogent-sur-Seine, Fr. 42/E2
Nogi, Japan 77/D1
Noginsk, Rus. 61/X9
Nogoa (riv.), Austl. 114/B4
Nogoán-san (peak), SKor. 73/D5
Nogoonnuur, Mong. 70/F2
Nogoyá, Arg. 157/E3
Nógrád (co.), Hun. 41/K5
Nogwak-san (peak), SKor. 74/A2
Nohar, India 86/C5
Noheji, Japan 76/B3
Nohfelden, Ger. 53/G4
Nohkú (pt.), Mex. 144/E2
Noi (riv.), Viet. 83/J5
Noidans-lès-Vesoul, Fr. 56/C2
Noire (riv.), Qu, Can. 130/E2
Noires, Montagnes (mts.), Fr. 42/B2
Noirmoutier, Île de (isl.), Fr. 42/B3
Noisiel, Fr. 52/B6
Noisy-le-Grand, Fr. 30/K5
Noisy-le-Mec, Fr. 30/K5
Noisy-le-Roi, Fr. 30/J5
Nojima-zaki (pt.), Japan 75/F3
Nokia, Fin. 39/K1
Nokilalaki (peak), Indo. 81/F4
Nola, CAfr. 96/J7
Nola, It. 58/B4
Noli, It. 58/B4
Noli, Capo di (cape), It. 58/B4
Nomadgi NP, Austl. 115/D2
Nombre de Dios, Mex. 142/D4
Nombre de Dios (mts.), Hon. 144/E3
Nome, Ak, US 134/E3
Nome (cape), Ak, US 134/F3
Nomény, Fr. 53/F6
Nomexy, Fr. 56/C1
Nomo-misaki (cape), Japan 74/B5
Nomo-zaki (pt.), Japan 74/A4
Nonacho (lake), NW, Can. 122/F2
Nonantola, It. 59/E3
None, It. 43/G4
Nonette (riv.), Fr. 52/B5
Nong Han (res.), Thai. 78/D2
Nong Khai, Thai. 78/C2
Nong'an, China 71/N3
Nongoma, SAfr. 107/E2
Nongstoin, India 85/H3
Nonnweiler, Ger. 53/F4
Nonoava, Mex. 142/D3
Nonouti (isl.), Kiri. 116/G5
Nonri (isl.), China 72/E5
Nonsan, SKor. 73/D4
Nontron, Fr. 42/D4
Noorama (res.), Austl. 115/C2
Noord-Brabant (prov.), Neth. 50/C5
Noord Holland (prov.), Neth. 50/B3
Noordbeveland (isl.), Neth. 50/A5
Noorderhaaks (isl.), Neth. 50/B3
Noordhollandsch Kanaal (riv.), Neth. 50/B3
Noordoostpolder (polder), Neth. 50/C3
Noordwijk aan Zee, Neth. 50/B4
Noordwijkerhout, Neth. 50/B4
Noordzeekanaal (canal), Neth. 50/B4
Noormarkku, Fin. 39/J1
Noorvik, Ak, US 134/F2
Nootka (isl.), BC, Can. 126/B3
Nora, Swe. 38/F2
Norala, Phil. 81/F2
Norberg, Swe. 38/F1
Norberto de la Riestra, Arg. 159/J11

Norchia (ruin), It. 46/B1
Norco, Ca, US 136/C3
Norco, La, US 137/P16
North (sound), Sc, UK 31/V14
North (sea), Eur. 36/D4
North (chan.), UK 34/C1
North-Kivu (pol. reg.), D.R. Congo 104/A3
Nord-Ostsee (Kiel) (canal), Ger. 51/G1
Nord-Ouest (prov.), Camr. 103/H5
Nord-Ouest (pol. reg.), Mor. 100/B2
Nord-Pas-de-Calais (pol. reg.), Fr. 42/D1
Nord-Radde (riv.), Ger. 51/E3
Nord-Sud Kanal (canal), Ger. 51/E3
Nord-Trøndelag (co.), Nor. 37/E3
Nordborg, Den. 38/C4
Nordby, Den. 38/C4
Norddeich, Ger. 51/E1
Nordela (int'l arpt.), Azor., Port. 45/T13
Norden, Ger. 51/E1
Nordenham, Ger. 51/F1
Nordenskjöld (arch.), Rus. 64/J2
Norderney, Ger. 51/E1
Norderney (isl.), Neth. 51/E1
Norderstedt, Ger. 51/G1
Nordhausen, Ger. 40/F3
Nordholz, Ger. 51/F1
Nordhorn, Ger. 51/E4
Nördlingen, Ger. 54/D5
Nordjylland (co.), Den. 38/C3
Nordkapp (cape), Nor. 37/H1
Nordkapp, Nor. 37/H1
Nordkinn (pt.), Nor. 37/H1
Nordkirchen, Ger. 51/E5
Nordland (co.), Nor. 37/E2
Nordreisa, Nor. 37/G1
Nordrhein-Westfalen (state), Ger. 40/E3
Nordwalde, Ger. 51/E4
Nore (riv.), Ire. 31/Q10
Noresund, Nor. 38/C1
Norfolk (mt.), Austl. 115/C4
Norfolk (lake), Ar,Mo, US 129/J3
Norfolk, Ne, US 127/J5
Norfolk (isl.), Austl. 116/F7
Norfolk Broads (swamp), Eng, UK 33/H1
Norg, Neth. 50/D2
Norheimsund, Nor. 38/B1
Norikura-dake (peak), Japan 75/E2
Noril'sk, Rus. 64/J3
Normal, Il, US 127/L5
Norman, Ok, US 137/N15
Norman Manley (int'l arpt.), Jam. 145/G2
Norman Wells, NW, Can. 122/D2
Normanby (isl.), PNG 116/E6
Normandie, Collines de (hills), Fr. 42/C2
Normandy (reg.), Fr. 42/C2
Normandy Beach, NJ, US 138/D4
Normandy Park, Wa, US 135/C3
Normanton, Austl. 114/A2
Normanton South, Austl. 114/A2
Norotshama (peak), Namb. 106/B3
Norquay, Sk, Can. 127/H3
Norquinco, Arg. 158/C4
Norrbotten (co.), Swe. 37/F2
Nørre Alslev, Den. 38/D4
Nørre Nebel, Den. 38/C4
Nørre Vorupør, Den. 38/C3
Norridge, Il, US 135/Q16
Norris (isl.), China 72/E5
Norris (lake), Tn, US 133/G2
Norristown, Pa, US 138/C3
Norrköping, Swe. 38/G2
Norrland (reg.), Swe. 37/F2
Norrsundet, Swe. 38/G1
Norrtälje, Swe. 39/H2
Nors, Den. 38/C3
Norseman, Austl. 112/C5
Norsjö, Swe. 37/F2
Norte (pt.), Arg. 159/F3
Norte (pt.), Arg. 158/E4
Norte, Cabo do (cape), Braz. 151/J3
Norte de Santander (dept.), Col. 145/H4
Norte Los Rodeos (int'l arpt.), Canl.,Sp. 98/A3
Norte, Serra do (mts.), Braz. 150/G6
Nortelândia, Braz. 147/G6
Nörten-Hardenberg, Ger. 51/G5
North Minch (The Minch) (str.), Sc, UK 31/V14
North (mt.), Austl. 115/C3
North (pt.), Austl. 115/C3
North (pt.), Austl. 112/B4
North (cape), Ak, US 134/D5
North (cape), NZ 117/S9

North (isl.), NZ 117/S10
North (pt.), Md, US 138/B5
North Ossetian Aut. Rep., Rus. 63/G4
North Pacific (ocean) 22/A4
North Pine (riv.), Austl. 114/E6
North Plainfield, NJ, US 139/H9
North Platte, Ne, US 127/H5
North Platte (riv.), Ne,Wy, US 129/G2
North Pole, Ak, US 134/J3
North Pole 160/G
North Potomac, Md, US 138/A5
North Prairie, Wi, US 135/P14
North Puyallup, Wa, US 135/C3
North Raccoon (riv.), Ia, US 127/K5
North Ronaldsay (isl.), Sc, UK 31/V14
North Salt Lake, Ut, US 137/K12
North Saskatchewan (riv.), Ab,Sk, Can. 122/E3
North Shields, Eng, UK 35/G2
North Siberian Lowland (plain), Rus. 64/K2
North Skunk (riv.), Ia, US 129/J2
North Somerset (co.), Eng, UK 32/D4
North Stadbroke (isl.), Austl. 109/E3
North Taranaki Bight (bay), NZ 109/H6
North Thompson (riv.), BC, Can. 126/D3
North Tolsta, Sc, UK 31/Q7
North Tonawanda, NY, US 131/S9
North Tyne (riv.), Eng, UK 35/F1
North Tyneside (co.), Eng, UK 35/G1
North Uist (isl.), Sc, UK 31/Q8
North Umpqua (riv.), Or, US 128/B2
North Valley Stream, NY, US 139/L9
North Vancouver, BC, Can. 122/D4
North Wales, Pa, US 138/C3
North Weald Bassett, Eng, UK 30/D1
North West (cape), Austl. 112/B2
North-West Frontier (co.), Pak. 86/A3
North West Highlands (uplands), Sc, UK 31/R8
North Wildwood, NJ, US 138/D6
North Wilton, Ct, US 139/E1
North York, Can. 131/D8
North York Moors NP, Eng, UK 35/G3
North Yorkshire (co.), Eng, UK 35/G3
Northallerton, Eng, UK 35/G3
Northam, Austl. 112/C4
Northampton, Austl. 112/B4
Northampton, Eng, UK 33/F2
Northampton, Ma, US 131/F3
Northampton, Pa, US 138/C2
Northampton, Pa, US 138/C2
Northampton Uplands (uplands), Eng, UK 33/E2
Northamptonshire (co.), Eng, UK 33/E2
Northbrook, Il, US 135/Q15
Northeast (cape), Ak, US 134/E3
Northeast (pt.), On, Can. 123/J4
Northeast (pt.), Jam. 145/G2
Northeast (pt.), Bahm. 145/H1
Northeast Land (isl.), Sval. 160/E
Northeast Lincolnshire (co.), Eng, UK 35/H4
Northeim, Ger. 51/G5
Northern (prov.), Ugan. 104/B2
Northern (pol. reg.), Malw. 104/B5
Northern Areas (terr.), Pak. 87/F5
Northern Cape (prov.), SAfr. 106/C3
Northern Cook (isls.), Cookls. 117/J6
Northern Dvina (riv.), Rus. 27/D2

Northern Light (lake), On, Can. 130/B1
Northern Mariana Islands (dpcy.), US 116/D3
Northern Province (prov.), SAfr. 106/E2
Northern Sporades (isls.), Gre. 47/J3
Northern Territory (terr.), Austl. 109/C2
Northern Ural (mts.), Rus. 61/N3
Northern Uvals (hills), Rus. 61/K4
Northfield, Mn, US 127/K4
Northfleet, Eng, UK 30/D2
Northglenn, Co, US 137/D3
Northport (Old Northport), NY, US 139/E2
Northumberland (str.), Can. 131/J2
Northumberland (co.), Eng, UK 35/G2
Northumberland NP, Eng, UK 36/D6
Northvale, NJ, US 139/K7
Northville, Mi, US 135/E7
Northway, Ak, US 134/K3
Northwest Gander (riv.), Nf, Can. 131/L1
Northwest Territories (terr.), Can. 122/D2
Northwich, Eng, UK 35/F5
Northwood, ND, US 127/J4
Norton (bay), Ak, US 134/F3
Norton (sound), Ak, US 134/E3
Norton Shores, Mi, US 130/C3
Nortorf, Ger. 38/C4
Norvegia (cape), Ant. 160/Y
Nörvenich, Ger. 53/F2
Norwalk, Oh, US 130/D3
Norwalk, Ca, US 136/F8
Norwalk, Ct, US 139/M7
Norwalk (riv.), Ct, US 139/M7
Norway (ctry.) 37/C3
Norwegian (bay), Nun., Can. 123/S7
Norwegian (sea), Eur. 27/D2
Norwich, NY, US 130/F3
Norwich, Eng, UK 33/H1
Norwich (int'l arpt.), Eng, UK 33/H1
Norwood, NJ, US 139/K8
Nos Emine (cape), Bul. 49/H4
Nos Kaliakra (pt.), Bul. 49/J4
Nos Maslen Nos (pt.), Bul. 49/H4
Nosappu-misaki (cape), Japan 76/D2
Nose, Japan 77/H6
Noshappu-misaki (cape), Japan 76/B1
Noshaq (peak), Afg. 89/K1
Noshiro, Japan 76/B3
Nosivka, Ukr. 62/D2
Nosong (cape), Malay. 81/E2
Noşratābād, Iran 89/G3
Noss Head (pt.), Sc, UK 31/S7
Nossa Senhora da Glória, Braz. 154/C3
Nossa Senhora das Dores, Braz. 154/C3
Nossebro, Swe. 38/E2
Nossy-Varika, Madg. 107/J8
Notch (cape), Chile 159/B6
Noto (pen.), Japan 75/E2
Noto, It. 46/D4
Noto Antica (ruin), It. 46/D4
Noto, Golfo di (gulf), It. 46/D4
Noto, Val di (valley), It. 46/D4
Notodden, Nor. 38/C2
Notogawa, Japan 77/K5
Notoro (lake), Japan 76/C1
Notre Dame (mts.), Qu, Can. 123/J4
Notre Dame (bay), Nf, Can. 123/L4
Notre-Dame, Qu, Can. 130/K5
Notre-Dame-de-l'Île-Perrot, Qu, Can. 131/N7
Notsé, Togo 103/F5
Nott (pt.), Austl. 113/G2
Nottaway (riv.), Qu, Can. 123/J3
Nøtterøy, Nor. 38/D2
Nottingham (isl.), Nun., Can. 123/H2
Nottingham, Eng, UK 35/G6
Nottingham (co.), Eng, UK 35/G6
Nottinghamshire (co.), Eng, UK 35/G5
Nottuln, Ger. 51/E5
Nouâdhibou, Mrta. 98/A5
Nouâdhibou (int'l arpt.), Mrta. 98/A5
Nouakchott (cap.), Mrta. 102/B2
Nouakchott (int'l arpt.), Mrta. 102/B2
Nouna, Burk. 102/E3
Noupoort, SAfr. 106/D3
Nouvion-sur-Meuse, Fr. 53/D4

Nœux-les-Mines, Fr. 52/B3
Nouzonville, Fr. 53/D4
Nova Andradina, Braz. 151/H8
Nova Cruz, Braz. 154/D2
Nová Dubnica, Slvk. 41/K4
Nova Friburgo, Braz. 211/L1
Nova Gorica, Slov. 59/G1
Nova Gradiška, Cro. 48/C3
Nova Iguaçu, Braz. 211/K7
Nova Kakhovka, Ukr. 49/L2
Nova Olinda, Braz. 154/C2
Nova Olinda do Norte, Braz. 150/G4
Nova Pazova, Serb. 48/E3
Nova Prata, Braz. 155/B4
Nova Russas, Braz. 154/B2
Nova Scotia (prov.), Can. 131/G2
Nova Sintra, CpV. 93/J11
Nova Soure, Braz. 154/C3
Nova Varoš, Serb. 48/D4
Nova Venécia, Braz. 155/D1
Nova Xavantina, Braz. 151/H6
Nova Zagora, Bul. 47/K1
Novafeltria, It. 59/F5
Novara, It. 58/B2
Novate Mezzola, It. 57/F5
Novaya Sibir' (isl.), Rus. 65/R2
Novaya Zemlya (isl.), Rus. 160/C
Nove, It. 59/E1
Nové Hrady, Czh. 55/H5
Nové Město nad Váhom, Slvk. 41/J4
Nové Strašecí, Czh. 55/G2
Nové Zámky, Slvk. 48/D2
Novelda, Sp. 45/E3
Novellara, It. 59/D3
Noventa, It. 59/E1
Noventa di Piave, It. 59/F2
Noventa Vicentina, It. 59/E2
Novgorod, Rus. 39/P2
Novgorodskaya Oblast, Rus. 60/G4
Novi, Mi, US 135/E7
Novi Bečej, Serb. 48/E3
Novi di Modena, It. 59/D3
Novi Iskŭr, Bul. 47/H1
Novi Ligure, It. 43/H4
Novi Pazar, Serb. 47/G1
Novi Pazar, Bul. 49/H4
Novi Sad, Serb. 48/D2
Novi Vinodolski, Cro. 48/B3
Novillars, Fr. 56/C3
Nóvita, Col. 152/B3
Novo (riv.), Braz. 211/K6
Novo Alexeyevka (int'l arpt.), Geo. 63/H4
Novo Aripuanã, Braz. 150/F5
Novo Hamburgo, Braz. 155/B4
Novo Horizonte, Braz. 155/B2
Novo Miloševo, Serb. 48/E3
Novo Oriente, Braz. 154/B2
Novoanninskiy, Rus. 63/G2
Novocheboksarsk, Rus. 61/K4
Novocherkassk, Rus. 62/G3
Novogrudok, Bela. 37/C2
Novohrad-Volyns'kyy, Ukr. 62/C2
Novohradské Hory (mts.), Czh. 55/H5
Novokuybyshevsk, Rus. 63/J1
Novokuznetsk, Rus. 64/J4
Novolazarevskaya, Rus., Ant. 160/A
Novomoskovsk, Rus. 62/F1
Novorossiysk, Rus. 62/F3
Novoshakhtinsk, Rus. 62/F3
Novosibirsk (res.), Uzb. 87/C4
Novosibirsk, Rus. 87/H1
Novosibirsk (Tolmachevo) (int'l arpt.), Rus. 87/H1
Novosibirskaya Oblast, Rus. 87/G1
Novotroitsk, Rus. 63/L2
Novoukrayinka, Ukr. 62/D2
Novovolyns'k, Ukr. 62/C2
Novovyatsk, Rus. 61/L4
Novozybkov, Rus. 62/D1
Novska, Cro. 48/C3
Nový Jičín, Czh. 41/K4
Nowa Dęba, Pol. 41/L3
Nowa Ruda, Pol. 41/J3
Nowa Sarzyna, Pol. 41/M3
Nowa Sól, Pol. 41/H3
Nowata, Ok, US 129/J3
Nowe, Pol. 41/K2
Nowe Miasto Lubawskie, Pol. 41/K2
Nowgong, India 84/B3
Nowitna (riv.), Ak, US 134/G3
Nowogard, Pol. 38/D5
Nowood (riv.), Wy, US 128/F1
Nowshāk (peak), Afg. 87/F5
Nowshera, Pak. 86/A2
Nowy Dwór Gdański, Pol. 39/H4
Nowy Sącz, Pol. 41/L4

Nowy Staw, Pol. 39/H4
Nowy Targ, Pol. 41/L4
Nowy Tomyśl, Pol. 41/J2
Nuremberg, Pa, US 138/B2
Nurhak, Turk. 90/D2
Noya, Sp. 44/A1
Noye (riv.), Fr. 52/B4
Noyon, Fr. 52/C4
Nsanje, Malw. 105/G4
Nsawam, Gha. 103/E5
Nsumbu NP, Zam. 104/A5
Nsuta, Gha. 103/E5
Ntoroko, Ugan. 104/A2
Ntungamo, Ugan. 104/A3
Ntusi, Ugan. 104/A2
Nu, Crêt du (peak), Fr. 56/B5
Nuangola, Pa, US 138/C1
Nūbah, Jibāl an (mts.), Sudan 97/M5
Nubian (des.), Sudan 93/F2
Nucet, Rom. 48/F2
Nucla, Co, US 132/A2
Nucourt, Fr. 30/H4
Nüdlingen, Ger. 54/D2
Nueces (riv.), Tx, US 140/B2
Nueltin (lake), Mb,Nun., Can. 122/G2
Nuenen, Neth. 50/C6
Nueva Alejandría, Peru 156/C2
Nueva Concepción, Guat. 144/D3
Nueva Esparta (state), Ven. 153/E2
Nueva Florida, Ven. 152/D2
Nueva Gerona, Cuba 145/F1
Nueva Helvecia, Uru. 159/E1
Nueva Imperial, Chile 158/B3
Nueva Italia de Ruiz, Mex. 142/E5
Nueva Loja, Ecu. 152/B4
Nueva Ocotepéque, Hon. 144/D3
Nueva Palmira, Uru. 159/J10
Nueva Rosita, Mex. 132/C5
Nueva Villa de Padilla, Mex. 143/F3
Nueve de Julio, Arg. 158/E2
Nuevitas, Cuba 145/G1
Nuevo, Ca, US 136/C3
Nuevo Balsas, Mex. 143/F5
Nuevo Berlín, Uru. 159/J10
Nuevo Casas Grandes, Mex. 142/D2
Nuevo Chagres, Pan. 145/F4
Nuevo Gulfo (gulf), Arg. 157/D5
Nuevo Ideal, Mex. 142/D4
Nuevo Ixcatlán, Mex. 144/C2
Nuevo Laredo, Mex. 132/D5
Nuevo Leon (state), Mex. 140/A2
Nuevo Rocafuerte, Ecu. 152/C5
Nufenen, Swi. 57/F4
Nufenenpass (pass), Swi. 57/E5
Nuguria (isls.), PNG 116/E5
Nuhne (riv.), Ger. 51/F6
Nui (isl.), Tuv. 116/G5
Nuiqsut, Ak, US 134/H1
Nuits-Saint-Georges, Fr. 56/A3
Nukata, Japan 77/M6
Nuklunek (mtn.), Ak, US 134/F4
Nuku'alofa (cap.), Tonga 117/H7
Nukufetau (isl.), Tuv. 116/G5
Nukulaelae (isl.), Tuv. 116/H5
Nukumanu (atoll), PNG 116/E5
Nukunonu (isl.), Tok. 117/H5
Nukuoro (isl.), Micr. 116/E4
Nukus (int'l arpt.), Uzb. 87/C4
Nukus, Uzb. 87/C4
Nukutavake (isl.), FrPol. 117/M6
Nulato, Ak, US 134/G3
Nules, Sp. 45/E3
Nullarbor (plain), Austl. 109/B4
Nullarbor NP, Austl. 113/F4
Numana, It. 59/G5
Numansdorp, Neth. 50/B5
Numata, Japan 75/F2
Numazu, Japan 75/F3
Nümbrecht, Ger. 53/G2
Numfoor (isl.), Indo. 81/H4
Nummi, Fin. 39/K1
Numurkah, Austl. 115/C3
Nunapitchuk, Ak, US 134/E3
Nunchia, Col. 152/C3
Nundle, Austl. 115/D1
Nuneaton, Eng, UK 33/E1
Nungarin, Austl. 112/C4
Nungatta NP, Austl. 115/D3
Nunivak (isl.), Ak, US 134/D3
Nunningen, Swi. 56/D3
Nuñoa, Peru 156/C4
Nunspeet, Neth. 50/C4
Nuon (riv.), Libr. 102/C5
Nuoro, It. 46/A2
Nuquí, Col. 152/B3
Nur (mts.), Turk. 91/E1
Nura (riv.), Kaz. 87/F2

Nürburgring, Ger. 53/F3
Nure (riv.), It. 58/C3
Nuri (ruin), Sudan 101/B5
Nuriootpa, Austl. 113/H5
Nurmijärvi, Fin. 39/L1
Nürnberg (int'l arpt.), Ger. 54/E3
Nürnberg, Ger. 54/E4
Nürnberg (hills), Ger. 54/E4
Nūrpur, Pak. 86/B3
Nurri (mt.), Austl. 115/C1
Nürtingen, Ger. 54/C5
Nushagak (riv.), Ak, US 134/G4
Nushki, Pak. 89/J3
Nutberry (hill), Sc, UK 36/C5
Nuth, Neth. 53/E2
Nuthe-Graben (riv.), Ger. 40/Q7
Nutley, NJ, US 139/J8
Nutwood, Il, US 137/F7
Nuuk (Godthåb), Grld. 119/M3
Nuvolento, It. 58/D1
Nuy (riv.), SAfr. 106/L10
Nüziders, Aus. 57/F3
Nxai Pan NP, Bots. 105/D4
Nyabisindu, Rwa. 104/A3
Nyack, NY, US 139/K7
Nyah, Austl. 115/B2
Nyah West, Austl. 115/B2
Nyainqêntanglha (peak), China 70/F5
Nyaki NP, Malw. 104/B5
Nyala, Sudan 97/K5
Nyalam, China 85/E1
Nyandoma, Rus. 60/J3
Nyanza (prov.), Kenya 104/B3
Nyasa (lake), Malw. 93/F6
Nybro, Swe. 38/F3
Nyêmo, China 85/H1
Nyeri, Kenya 104/C3
Nyima, China 70/E5
Nyíracsád, Hun. 48/F2
Nyírbátor, Hun. 48/F2
Nyíradony, Hun. 41/L5
Nyírbéltek, Hun. 41/M5
Nyíregyháza, Hun. 41/L5
Nyírmada, Hun. 41/M4
Nyiru (mt.), Kenya 104/C2
Nykøbing, Den. 38/D4
Nykøbing, Den. 38/D4
Nyköping, Swe. 38/G2
Nylstroom, SAfr. 105/E5
Nynäshamn, Swe. 38/G2
Nyngan, Austl. 115/C1
Nyoman (riv.), Bela. 62/B1
Nyon, Swi. 56/C5
Nyons, Fr. 42/F4
Nyřany, Czh. 55/G4
Nýrsko, Czh. 55/G4
Nýrsko (riv.), Czh. 55/G4
Nysa, Pol. 41/J3
Nyssa, Or, US 128/D5
Nysted, Den. 38/D4
Nyūdō-zaki (pt.), Japan 76/A4
Nyuk (isl.), Rus. 60/F2
Nyúl, Hun. 48/C2
Nyunzu, D.R. Congo 105/E2
Nyūzen, Japan 75/E2
Nzega, Tanz. 104/B4
Nzérékoré (pol. reg.), Gui. 102/C4
Nzérékoré, Gui. 102/C4
Nzi (riv.), C.d'Iv. 96/E6

O

Oaxaca (state), Mex. 140/B4
Oaxaca de Juárez, Mex. 144/B2
Ob (gulf), Rus. 67/G3
Ob' (riv.), Rus. 67/F3
Ob Luang Gorge, Thai. 78/B2
Obama, Japan 77/J5
Obama (bay), Japan 77/J4
Oban, Sc, UK 31/R8
Obanazawa, Japan 76/B4
Obara, Japan 77/M5
Obata, Japan 77/L7
Ober-Olm, Ger. 54/B3
Ober Ramstadt, Ger. 54/C3
Oberá, Arg. 157/E2
Oberalppass (pass), Swi. 57/E4
Oberalpstock (peak), Swi. 57/E4
Oberammergau, Ger. 57/H2
Oberasbach, Ger. 54/D4
Oberau, Ger. 57/H2
Oberburg, Swi. 56/D3
Oberderdingen, Ger. 54/B4
Oberdiessbach, Swi. 56/D4
Oberding, Ger. 55/E6
Oberdorf, Swi. 56/D3
Oberdorla, Ger. 51/H6
Oberelsbach, Ger. 54/D2
Oberentfelden, Swi. 56/E3
Oberglatt, Swi. 57/E3
Obergünzburg, Ger. 57/G2
Oberhaching, Ger. 55/E6
Oberhausen, Ger. 50/D5
Oberkirch, Ger. 56/E1
Oberkochen, Ger. 54/D5
Oberkotzau, Ger. 55/E2
Oberlausitz (reg.), Ger. 41/H3
Oberlin, Ks, US 129/G3
Obernai, Fr. 56/D1
Obernburg am Main, Ger. 54/C3
Oberndorf am Neckar, Ger. 57/E1
Oberndorf bei Salzburg, Aus. 55/F7
Obernkirchen, Ger. 51/G4
Oberon, Austl. 115/D2
Oberösterreich (prov.), Aus. 41/G4
Oberpfälzer Wald (for.), Ger. 55/F3
Oberrieden, Ger. 57/E3
Oberried, Swi. 57/F3
Obersaxen, Swi. 57/F4
Oberschleissheim, Ger. 55/E6
Oberschneiding, Ger. 55/F5
Obersiggenthal, Swi. 57/E3
Oberstammheim, Swi. 57/E2
Oberstaufen, Ger. 57/G2
Oberstdorf, Ger. 57/G3
Oberthal, Ger. 53/G4
Obertrum am See, Aus. 55/G7
Obertshausen, Ger. 54/B2
Oberursel, Ger. 54/B2
Oberuzwil, Swi. 57/F3
Oberviechtach, Ger. 55/F4
Oberwald, Swi. 57/E4
Oberwart, Aus. 48/C2
Oberwesel, Ger. 53/G3
Oberwil, Swi. 56/D4
Obfelden, Swi. 57/E3
Obi (str.), Indo. 81/G4
Obi (isls.), Indo. 81/G4
Óbidos, Braz. 151/G4
Óbidos, Port. 44/A3
Obihiro, Japan 76/C2
Obilić, Serb. 47/G1
Obing, Ger. 55/F6
Obira, Japan 76/B1
Obitsu (riv.), Japan 77/D3
Obluch'ye, Rus. 71/P2
Obninsk, Rus. 60/H5
Obo, CAfr. 97/L6
Oborniki, Pol. 41/J2
Oborniki Śląskie, Pol. 41/J3
Obra (riv.), Pol. 41/J3
Obrenovac, Serb. 48/E3
Obrež, Serb. 48/E4
Obrigheim, Ger. 54/C3
Obrigheim, Ger. 54/B3
Observatory, Austl. 115/G5
Obtrumer (lake), Aus. 55/F7
Obu, Japan 77/L6
Obuasi, Gha. 103/E5
Obw. (canton), Swi. 57/E4
Obzor, Bul. 49/H3
Ocala, Fl, US 133/H4
Ocampo, Mex. 142/E3
Ocaña, Sp. 44/D3
Ocaña, Col. 152/C2
Occhieppo Inferiore, It. 58/B1
Occhieppo Superiore, It. 58/A1
Occhiobello, It. 59/E3
Occidental, Cordillera (mts.), Peru 150/C3
Occidental (riv.), Austl. 115/D3
Occimiano, It. 58/B2
Ocean (cape), Ak, US 134/L3
Ocean, Co, NJ, US 138/D4
Ocean Beach, NY, US 135/M5
Ocean City, Md, US 130/F4
Ocean City, NJ, US 138/D5
Ocean Falls, BC, Can. 126/B2
Ocean Gate, NJ, US 138/D4

Ocean Grove, NJ, US 138/D3
Ocean View, NJ, US 138/D5
Oceanographic Museum, Mona. 58/J8
Oceanside, Ca, US 136/C4
Oceanside, NY, US 139/L9
Oceanville, NJ, US 138/D5
Och'amch'ire, Geo. 63/G4
Ocheltree, Ks, US 137/D6
Ochiishi-misaki (cape), Japan 76/D2
Ochil (hills), Sc, UK 36/C4
Ocho Rios, Jam. 145/G2
Ochsenfurt, Ger. 54/D3
Ochsenhausen, Ger. 57/F1
Ochsenkopf (peak), Ger. 57/F3
Ochtendung, Ger. 53/G3
Ochtrup, Ger. 50/D4
Ochtum (riv.), Ger. 51/F2
Ockelbo, Swe. 38/G1
Ockenheim, Ger. 53/G4
Ocmulgee Nat'l Mon., Ga, US 133/H3
Ocmulgee (riv.), Ga, US 133/H3
Ocna Mureş, Rom. 49/F2
Ocna Sibiului, Rom. 49/G2
Ocoña (riv.), Peru 150/D6
Ocoña, Peru 156/C5
Oconee (lake), Ga, US 133/H3
Oconee (riv.), Ga, US 133/H3
Oconto, Wi, US 127/M4
Ocosingo, Mex. 144/C2
Ocotal, Nic. 144/E3
Ocotlán, Mex. 142/E4
Ocotlán de Morelos, Mex. 144/B2
Ocoyoacac, Mex. 143/Q10
Ococozcoautla de Espinosa, Mex. 144/C2
Ocracoke, NC, US 133/K3
Ocreza (riv.), Port. 44/B3
Ocros, Peru 156/B3
Octeville, Fr. 54/C3
October Revolution (isl.), Rus. 67/H2
Ocua (peak), Sudan 101/D4
Oda, Japan 74/C3
Oda, Gha. 103/E5
Odaesan NP, SKor. 74/A2
Ōdai, Japan 77/K7
Odaigahara-san (peak), Japan 74/E3
Ōdate, Japan 76/B3
Odawara, Japan 75/F3
Odda, Nor. 38/B1
Odder, Den. 38/D4
Odeborn (riv.), Ger. 51/F6
Odelzhausen, Ger. 54/E6
Odemira, Port. 44/A4
Ödemiş, Turk. 90/A2
Odendaalsrus, SAfr. 106/D2
Odense, Den. 38/D4
Odense (int'l arpt.), Den. 38/D4
Odenthal, Ger. 53/G1
Odenton, Md, US 138/B5
Odenwald (reg.), Ger. 54/B3
Oder (Odra) (riv.), Ger.,Pol. 41/G2
Oder-Spree Kanal (canal), Ger. 40/Q7
Oderen, Fr. 56/C2
Oderhaff (lag.), Ger. 41/G1
Oderzo, It. 59/F1
Odesa, Turk. 90/B1
Odesa, Ukr. 49/K2
Odes'ka Oblasti, Ukr. 62/D3
Odessa, Wa, US 126/D4
Odessa, Tx, US 129/G5
Odessa, De, US 138/C5
Odet (riv.), Fr. 42/B2
Odienné, C.d'Iv. 102/D4
Odintsovo, Rus. 61/W9
Odiongan, Phil. 79/D5
Odivelas, Port. 45/P10
Odobeşti, Rom. 49/H3
Odón (riv.), Fr. 42/C2
Odoorn, Neth. 50/D3
Odorheiu Secuiesc, Rom. 49/H3
Odžaci, Serb. 48/D3
Odžak, PN d', Congo 96/J7
Oe, Japan 77/H5
Oe-yama (peak), Japan 77/H5
Oegstgeest, Neth. 50/B4
Oeiras, Braz. 154/B2
Oeiras, Port. 45/P10
Oelde, Ger. 51/F5
Oelsnitz, Ger. 55/F3
Oeno (isl.), Pitc. 117/M7
Oensingen, Swi. 56/D3
Oer-Erkenschwick, Ger. 50/D5
Oerel, Ger. 51/F2
Oesterdam (dam), Neth. 50/B5
Oestrich-Winkel, Ger. 54/B3
Oeta NP, Gre. 47/H3
Oebyn, Swe. 37/G2
Oey'ŏn (isl.), SKor. 73/D3
Oetz, Aus. 57/H3
Of, Turk. 90/E1
O'Fallon, Mo, US 137/F8
O'Fallon, Il, US 137/P17
Ofanto (riv.), It. 46/D2
Ofaqim, Isr. 49/D4
Ofenhorn (peak), Swi. 57/E5
Offa, Nga. 103/G4
Offaly (co.), Ire. 30/A5
Offement, Fr. 56/C2

Offenbach, Ger. 54/B2
Offenbach an der Queich, Ger. 54/B4
Offenburg, Ger. 56/D1
Offingen, Ger. 54/D6
Offstein, Ger. 54/B3
Oftersheim, Ger. 54/B3
Ofunato, Japan 76/B4
Oga (pen.), Japan 76/A4
Ogachi, Japan 76/B4
Ogadén (reg.), Eth. 97/P6
Ōgaki, Japan 77/L5
Ogano, Japan 77/C2
Ogasawara, Japan 116/D2
Ogatsu, Japan 76/B4
Ogawa, Japan 77/E1
Ogawa, Japan 77/C1
Ogawara (lake), Japan 76/B3
Ogbomosho, Nga. 103/G4
Ogden, Ut, US 137/K11
Ogden, South Fork (riv.), Ut, US 137/K11
Ogdensburg, NY, US 130/F2
Ogdensburg, NJ, US 138/D1
Ogeechee (riv.), Ga, US 133/H4
Oggiono, It. 58/C1
Ogi, Japan 75/F2
Ogidaki (mtn.), On, Can. 130/D2
Ogies, SAfr. 106/E2
Ogilvie (mts.), Yk, Can. 122/C2
Ogilvie (riv.), Yk, Can. 122/C2
Oglesby, Tx, US 143/F7
Oglio (riv.), It. 43/J4
Ognon (riv.), Fr. 40/C5
Ogoamas (peak), Indo. 81/F3
Ogoki (lake), On, Can. 127/M3
Ogoki (res.), On, Can. 127/M3
Ogoki (riv.), On, Can. 127/M3
Ogooué (riv.), Gabon 103/C5
Ogose, Japan 77/C2
Ogosta (riv.), Bul. 49/F4
Ogre, Lat. 39/L3
Oguchi, Japan 75/L5
Ōgun (riv.), Nga. 96/F6
Ogun (state), Nga. 103/G5
Oğuz, Turk. 90/D2
Oh Me Edge (hill), Eng, UK 36/D6
Ōhara, Japan 77/D3
Oharu, Japan 77/L5
Ōhata, Japan 76/B3
Ohey, Belg. 53/E3
Ōhira, Japan 77/D1
Ohlsdorf, Aus. 55/G7
Ohlstadt, Ger. 57/H2
Ōkuchi, Japan 74/B4
Ohm (riv.), Ger. 54/C1
Oho, Japan 77/E1
Ohoopee (riv.), Ga, US 133/H3
Ohře (riv.), Czh. 40/F2
Ohře (riv.), Czh. 40/H3
Ohrid, FYROM 47/G2
Ohrid (lake), Alb., Mac. 47/G2
Ohrid, FYROM 47/G2
Oi, Japan 77/D1
Oi (riv.), China 83/G2
Oi, Japan 77/D2
Oiapoque (riv.), Braz. 151/H3
Oiapoque, Braz. 151/H3
Oich (lake), Sc, UK 36/B2
Oieras, Port. 45/P10
Oignies, Fr. 52/B3
Oil City, Pa, US 130/E3
Oil Springs, On, Can. 135/L11

Oka, Nga. 103/G5
Oka (riv.), Rus. 65/L4
Oka, Qu, Can. 131/M7
Okabe, Japan 77/C1
Okahandja, Namb. 105/C5
Okak (isl.), Nf, Can. 123/K3
Okanagan (lake), BC, Can. 122/D4
Okanagan Falls, BC, Can. 126/D3
Okanda, PN de l', Gabon 105/B1
Okanogan, Wa, US 126/D3
Okanogan (riv.), Wa, US 126/D3
Okara, Pak. 86/B4
Okavango (delta), Bots. 105/D4
Okavango (riv.), 105/C4
Okawa, Japan 74/B4
Okaya, Japan 75/F2
Okayama (pref.), Japan 74/C3
Okayama, Japan 74/C3
Okazaki, Japan 77/M6
Okch'ŏn, SKor. 73/D4
Okęcie (int'l arpt.), Pol. 41/L2
Okeechobee, Fl, US 133/H5
Okeechobee (lake), Fl, US 125/K6
Okeene, Ok, US 129/H3
Okefenokee (swamp), Ga, US 133/H4
Okha, Rus. 65/Q4
Okhi Oros (peak), Gre. 47/J3
Okhotsk (sea), Rus. 67/P4
Okhotsk, Sea of (sea), Japan,Rus 71/P2
Okhta (riv.), Rus. 61/T6
Okhtyrka, Ukr. 62/E2
Oki (isls.), Japan 74/C2
Okidaitō (isl.), Japan 75/L8
Okiep, SAfr. 106/B3
Okinawa (isl.), Japan 67/M7
Okinawa (pref.), Japan 75/J8
Okino-shima (isl.), Japan 74/C4
Okinoerabu (isl.), Japan 75/K7
Okitipupa, Nga. 103/G5
Okkan, Myan. 83/G4
Okku, SKor. 73/D3
Okmulgee, Ok, US 129/J4
Oknitsa, Mol. 49/H2
Oko, Nga. 103/G5
Okobaji (lakes), Ia, US 127/J4
Okok (riv.), Ugan. 104/B2
Okolona, Ms, US 133/F3
Okoppe, Japan 76/C1
Okotoks, Ab, Can. 126/E3
Okovango (riv.), Namb. 105/C4
Oktabr'sk, Rus. 63/J1
Oktyabr'skiy, Rus. 61/M5
Oktyabr'sk, Rus. 63/J1
Okulovka, Rus. 60/G4
Okushiri (isl.), Japan 76/A2
Okutama (lake), Japan 77/C2
Okutama, Japan 77/C2
Okwa (riv.), Bots. 105/D5
Ol Doinyo Sabuk NP, Kenya 104/C3
Olafsfjördhur, Ice. 37/N6
Olafsvik, Ice. 37/M7
Olalla, Wa, US 135/B3
Olathe, Ks, US 137/D6
Olavarria, Arg. 158/E3
Olawa, Pol. 41/J3
Olbach (riv.), Ger. 51/F5
Olberg, Az, US 137/S19
Olbia, It. 46/A2
Olching, Ger. 55/E6
Olcott, NY, US 131/S9
Old (riv.), Ca, US 135/L11
Old Bahama (chan.), Cuba 145/G1
Old Bar, Austl. 115/E1
Old Bedford (canal), Eng, UK 33/G2
Old Bethpage, NY, US 139/M9
Old Bridge, NJ, US 139/H10
Old City, Isr. 91/G8
Old Crow, Yk, Can. 134/L2
Old Faithful Geyser, Wy, US 126/F4
Old Field (pt.), NY, US 139/E2
Old Fort Niagara, NY, US 131/R9
Old Harbor, Ak, US 134/H4
Old Man of Hoy, Sc, UK 31/V14
Old Mill Creek, Il, US 135/Q15
Old Nene (riv.), Eng, UK 33/G2
Old Rhine (riv.), Neth. 50/B4
Old Saybrook, Ct, US 139/F1
Old Tappan, NJ, US 139/K8
Old Town, Me, US 131/G2

Old Windsor, Eng, UK 30/B2
Old Wives (lake), Sk, Can. 127/G3
Oldeani (peak), Tanz. 104/B3
Oldebroek, Neth. 50/C3
Oldemarkt, Neth. 50/C3
Oldenburg, Ger. 51/F2
Oldenburg, Ger. 38/D4
Oldenzaal, Neth. 50/D3
Oldham, Eng, UK 35/F4
Oldham (co.), Eng, UK 35/F4
Oldman (riv.), Ab, Can. 126/E3
Oldmeldrum, Sc, UK 36/D2
Olds, Ab, Can. 126/E3
Olduvai Gorge, Tanz. 104/B3
Oldwick, NJ, US 138/D2
Olean, NY, US 130/E3
Olecko, Pol. 39/K4
Oleggio, It. 58/B1
Oleiros, Port. 44/B3
Oleiros, Sp. 44/A1
Olekma (riv.), Rus. 65/N4
Oleksandriya, Ukr. 62/E2
Olele (pt.), Wa, US 135/B2
Olema (riv.), Sur. 153/H4
Ølen, Nor. 38/A2
Olenegorsk, Rus. 60/G1
Olenëk (riv.), Rus. 65/L3
Olenëk (bay), Rus. 65/M2
Oléron, île (isl.), Fr. 42/C4
Olesa de Montserrat, Sp. 45/K6
Oleśnica, Pol. 41/J3
Olesno, Pol. 41/K3
Oley, Pa, US 138/C2
Olga (mt.), Austl. 113/F3
Olginate, It. 58/C1
Olgiy, Mong. 70/E2
Ølgod, Den. 38/C4
Olhão, Port. 44/B4
Oli Qoltyq Sory (swamp), Kaz. 87/B3
Oliena, It. 46/A2
Olifantshoek, SAfr. 106/P12
Olifantsrivier (riv.), SAfr. 105/E5
Olimarao (isl.), Micr. 116/E4
Olímbia (Olympia) (ruin), Gre. 47/G4
Ólimbos, Gre. 47/J5
Ólimbos NP (Olympos NP), Gre. 47/H2
Olímpia, Braz. 155/B2
Olimpos Beydağları NP, Turk. 91/B1
Olinalá, Mex. 144/B2
Olinda, Braz. 154/D3
Olindina, Braz. 154/C3
Oliva, Sp. 45/E3
Oliva de la Frontera, Sp. 44/B3
Olivais, Port. 44/A3
Oliveira, Braz. 155/C2
Olivenza, Sp. 44/B3
Oliver, BC, Can. 126/D3
Olivet, Fr. 42/D3
Olivone, Swi. 57/E4
Olla, La, US 129/J5
Ollachea, Peru 156/C4
Ollagüe (vol.), Bol.,Chile 150/E8
Ollainville, Fr. 30/J6
Olleria, Sp. 45/E3
Olleros, Peru 156/B3
Ollon, Swi. 56/D5
Öllür, India 82/C5
Olmaliq, Uzb. 87/F4
Olmedo, Sp. 44/C2
Olmos, Peru 156/B2
Olmos Park, Tx, US 137/U21
Olmsted, Ut, US 137/K13
Olmué, Chile 158/N8
Olney, Tx, US 129/H4
Olney, Md, US 138/A5
Olofström, Swe. 38/F3
Olomane (riv.), Qu, Can. 131/J1
Olomouc, Czh. 41/J4
Olomoucký (pol. reg.), Czh. 41/J4
Olongapo, Phil. 79/D5
Olonne-sur-Mer, Fr. 42/C3
Olorgasailie Nat'l Mon., Kenya 104/C3
Oloron-Sainte-Marie, Fr. 42/C5
Olot, Sp. 45/G1
Oloy (range), Rus. 65/S3
Olpe, Ger. 53/G1
Olsberg, Ger. 51/F6
Olst, Neth. 50/D4
Olsztyn, Pol. 39/J5
Olsztynek, Pol. 41/L2
Olt (riv.), Rom. 49/G3
Olt (prov.), Rom. 49/G3
Olte, Sierra de (hills), Arg. 158/C3
Olten, Swi. 56/D3
Olteniţa, Rom. 49/H3
Olteţ (riv.), Rom. 49/F3
Oltre il Colle, It. 58/C1
Oltu, Turk. 90/E1
Oltu (riv.), Turk. 90/E1
Olur, Turk. 90/E1
Olvera, Sp. 44/C4
Olympia (cap.), Wa, US 126/C4
Olympic (mts.), Wa, US 126/C4

Olympic Dam, Austl. 113/H4
Olympic Game Farm, Wa, US 135/A1
Olympic National Forest, Wa, US 135/A2
Olympic NP, Wa, US 126/B4
Olympic Park, SKor. 73/G6
Olympos (Mount Olympus) (peak), Gre. 47/H2
Olympus (mt.), Wa, US 126/C4
Olympus (peak), Cyp. 91/C2
Olyutorskiy (bay), Rus. 65/S3
Ōma, Japan 76/B3
Oma (riv.), Rus. 61/K2
Ōma-zaki (pt.), Japan 76/B3
Ōmachi, Japan 75/E2
Ōmae-zaki (pt.), Japan 75/F3
Ōmagari, Japan 76/B4
Omagh (dist.), NI, UK 34/A2
Omagh, NI, UK 34/A2
Omak, Wa, US 126/D3
Oman (ctry.) 89/G4
Oman (gulf), Asia 89/H4
Omar Torrijos Herrera (int'l arpt.), Pan. 152/B2
Omaruru, Namb. 105/C5
Omas, Peru 156/B4
Omatako (riv.), Namb. 105/C4
Omate, Peru 156/D5
Ombai (str.), Indo. 81/F5
Ombrone (riv.), It. 43/J5
Ombúes de Lavalle, Uru. 159/K10
Ōme, Japan 77/C2
Omeath, Ire. 34/B3
Omegna, It. 43/H4
Omeo, Austl. 115/C3
Ömerli, Turk. 90/E2
Ometepe (isl.), Nic. 144/E4
Ometepec, Mex. 144/B2
Ōmi, Japan 77/K5
Ōmihachiman, Japan 77/K5
Omiš, Cro. 46/E1
Omitlán (riv.), Mex. 144/B2
Ōmiya, Japan 75/G2
Ōmiya, Japan 77/H4
Ōmiya, Japan 77/K7
Ommaney (cape), Ak, US 134/M4
Ommen, Neth. 50/D3
Ömnögovĭ (prov.), Mong. 70/H3
Omo NP, Eth. 97/N6
Omo Wenz (riv.), Eth. 93/F4
Omodeo (lake), It. 46/A2
Omolon (riv.), Rus. 67/Q3
Omono (riv.), Japan 76/B4
Omsk, Rus. 87/F1
Omsk (int'l arpt.), Rus. 87/F2
Omskaya Oblast, Rus. 87/F1
Ōmu, Japan 76/C1
Omul (peak), Rom. 49/G3
Ōmura, Japan 74/A4
Omurtag, Bul. 49/H4
Ōmuta, Japan 74/B4
Omutninsk, Rus. 61/M4
Onagawa, Japan 76/B4
Onalaska, Tx, US 132/E4
Onaping (lake), On, Can. 130/D2
Oñate, Sp. 44/D1
Onaway, Mi, US 130/C2
Onchan, IM, UK 34/D3
Onda, Sp. 45/E3
Ondava (riv.), Slvk. 41/L4
Ondjiva, Ang. 105/C4
Ondo, Nga. 103/G5
Ondo (state), Nga. 103/G5
Öndörhaan, Mong. 71/K2
Onè, It. 59/E1
Onega, Rus. 60/H3
Onega (bay), Rus. 60/G2
Onega (lake), Rus. 160/D
Onega (pen.), Rus. 60/H2
Onega (riv.), Rus. 64/D3
Oneida, NY, US 130/F3
Oneida, Pa, US 138/B2
Oneonta, NY, US 130/F3
Onex, Swi. 56/C5
Ongjin, NKor. 73/C4
Ongole, India 82/D4
Ongtüstik Qazaqstan, Kaz. 64/G5
Onhaye, Belg. 53/D3
Onida, SD, US 127/H4
Onil, Sp. 45/E3
Onilahy (riv.), Ang. 107/G8
Onishi, Japan 77/C1
Onitsha, Nga. 103/G5
Onjuku, Japan 77/E3
Onkaparinga (riv.), Austl. 113/M8
Onnaing, Fr. 52/C3
Onny (riv.), Eng, UK 32/D2
Ōno, Japan 74/E3
Ōno, Japan 74/D3
Ōno, Japan 77/L5
Onoda, Japan 74/B4
Onomichi, Japan 74/C3
Onon, Mong. 71/K2
Onon (riv.), Rus. 71/K1
Onoto, Ven. 153/E2
Onotoa (isl.), Kiri. 116/G5
Onrusrivier, SAfr. 106/L11
Onslow, Austl. 112/B2
Ontake-san (peak), Japan 75/E3
Ontario, Or, US 126/D4
Ontario, Ca, US 136/C2
Ontario (prov.), Can. 122/H3
Ontario (lake), Can.,US 130/E3
Ontelaunee (lake), Pa, US 138/C3
Onteniente, Sp. 45/E3
Ontonagon, Mi, US 127/L4
Ontong Java (isl.), Sol. 116/E5
Onyang, SKor. 73/D4
Onzaga, Col. 152/C3
Oologah (lake), Ok, US 132/D2
Oona River, BC, Can. 134/M5
Oost-Vlaanderen (prov.), Belg. 52/C2
Oost-Vlieland, Neth. 50/C2
Oostburg, Neth. 52/C1
Oostelijk Flevoland (polder), Neth. 50/C3
Oostende (Ostend), Belg. 52/B1
Oosterhout, Neth. 50/B5
Oosterscheidedam (dam), Neth. 50/A5
Oosterschelde (riv.), Neth. 40/B3
Oosterwolde, Neth. 50/D3
Oosterzele, Belg. 52/C2
Oostkamp, Belg. 52/C1
Oostvaarderplassen (lake), Neth. 50/C4
Oostzaan, Neth. 50/B4
Ootmarsum, Neth. 50/D4
Opaka, Bul. 49/H4
Opalenica, Pol. 41/J2
Opasatika (riv.), On, Can. 130/D1
Opatija, Cro. 48/B3
Opatów, Pol. 41/L3
Opava, Czh. 41/J4
Opelika, Al, US 133/G3
Opelousas, La, US 129/J5
Opera, It. 58/C2
Opfingen, Ger. 57/F1
Opglabbeek, Belg. 53/E1
Ophir, Ak, US 134/G3
Ophir, Ut, US 137/J13
Ophthalmia (range), Austl. 112/C2
Oploo, Neth. 50/C5
Opmeer, Neth. 50/B3
Opoczno, Pol. 41/L3
Opole, Pol. 41/J3
Opole Lubelskie, Pol. 41/L3
Opolskie (prov.), Pol. 41/J3
Opovo, Serb. 48/E3
Opp, Al, US 133/G4
Oppdal, Nor. 37/D3
Oppeano, It. 59/E2
Oppenau, Ger. 56/E1
Oppenheim, Ger. 54/B3
Oppland (co.), Nor. 37/D3
Opportunity, Wa, US 126/D4
Opwijk, Belg. 53/D2
Oquirrh (mts.), Ut, US 137/J12
Or 'Aqiva, Isr. 91/F6
Or, Mont d' (peak), Fr. 56/C4
Or Yehuda, Isr. 91/F7
Ora (riv.), Mex. 142/D3
Ōra, Japan 77/C1
Oradell, NJ, US 139/J8
Oradell (res.), NJ, US 139/J8
Orahovac, Serb. 47/G1
Orahovica, Cro. 48/C3
Orai, India 84/B3
Orain (riv.), Fr. 56/B4
Oral, Kaz. 63/J2
Oran, Alg. 100/E5
Orang (riv.), NKor. 73/E2
Orange, Austl. 115/D2
Orange (cape), Braz. 151/H3
Orange, Fr. 42/F4
Orange (riv.), SAfr.,Nam 105/C6
Orange (mts.), Sur. 151/G3
Orange, Ca, US 136/G8
Orange, Ct, US 139/E1
Orange, NJ, US 139/J8
Orange (co.), NY, US 138/D1
Orange, Tx, US 129/J5
Orange, Va, US 130/E4
Orange Park, Fl, US 133/H4
Orange Walk, Belz. 144/D2
Orangeburg, SC, US 133/H3
Orangeburg, NY, US 139/K7
Orangeville, On, Can. 130/D3
Orangeville, Pa, US 138/B1
Orango (isl.), GBis. 102/A4
Oranienburg, Ger. 40/G6
Oranjekanaal (riv.), Neth. 50/D3
Oranjemund, Namb. 106/B3
Oranjestad, Aruba. 152/D1
Oranmore, Ire. 31/P10
Orapa, Bots. 105/E5
Oras, Phil. 79/E5
Orăştie, Rom. 49/F3
Oraviţa, Rom. 48/E3
Orb (riv.), Fr. 42/E5
Orba (riv.), It. 58/B3
Orbe, Swi. 56/C4
Orbe (riv.), Swi. 56/C4
Orbey, Fr. 56/D1
Órbigo (riv.), Sp. 44/C1
Orbost, Austl. 115/D3
Örbyhus, Swe. 38/G1
Orcemont, Fr. 30/H6
Orcera, Sp. 44/D3
Orchamps, Fr. 56/B3
Orchamps-Vennes, Fr. 56/C3
Orchard (lake), Mi, US 135/F6
Orchard City, Co, US 128/F3
Orchard Farm, Mo, US 137/G8
Orchard Homes, Mt, US 126/E4
Orchard Lake Village, Mi, US 135/F6
Orchid (isl.), Tai. 79/D3
Orchies, Fr. 52/C3
Orchy (riv.), Sc, UK 36/B4
Orciano di Pesaro, It. 59/F5
Orco (riv.), It. 43/G4
Orcopampa, Peru 156/C4
Orcotuna, Peru 156/C3
Ord, Ne, US 127/J5
Ordaz (int'l arpt.), Mex. 142/D4
Ordes, Sp. 44/A1
Ordesa y Monte Perdido, PN de, Sp. 45/F1
Ordos (des.), China 70/J4
Ordos (Mu Us Shamo) (des.), China 70/J4
Ordu, Turk. 90/D1
Ordu (prov.), Turk. 90/D1
Ore, Nga. 103/G5
Orealla, Guy. 153/G3
Örebro, Swe. 38/F2
Örebro (prov.), Swe. 37/E4
Orebro (int'l arpt.), Swe. 38/F2
Oregon (state), US 126/C5
Oregon Caves Nat'l Mon., Or, US 126/C5
Oregon City, Or, US 126/C4
Öregrund, Swe. 38/H1
Orekhovo-Zuyevo, Rus. 60/H5
Orël, Rus. 62/F1
Orellana, Peru 156/C2
Orellana la Vieja, Sp. 44/C3
Orem, Ut, US 137/K13
Orenberg (int'l arpt.), Rus. 63/K2
Orenburg, Rus. 63/K2
Orenburgskaya Oblast, Rus. 87/B2
Orense, Sp. 44/B1
Orestiás, Gre. 47/K2
Øresund (sound), Swe. 38/E4
Oreti (riv.), NZ 117/R12
Orford, Austl. 115/C4
Orford (pt.), Eng, UK 33/H2
Organ Pipe Cactus Nat'l Mon., Az, US 142/B1
Órgãos, Serra dos (mts.), Braz. 211/K7
Orgaz, Sp. 44/D3
Orgelet, Fr. 56/B4
Orgeurs, Fr. 30/H5
Orgeval, Fr. 30/H5
Orgosolo, It. 46/A2
Orhaneli, Turk. 62/D5
Orhangazi, Turk. 49/J5
Orhei, Mol. 49/J2
Orhon (riv.), Mong. 70/J2
Oria, Sp. 44/D4
Orient (pt.), NY, US 139/F1
Oriental, Mex. 143/M7
Oriental, Cordillera (mts.), SAm. 150/C5
Orientale (prov.), D.R. Congo 104/A2
Oriente, Arg. 158/E3
Origny-Sainte-Benoîte, Fr. 52/C4
Orihuela, Sp. 45/E3
Orillia, On, Can. 130/E2
Orimattila, Fin. 39/L1
Orinda, Ca, US 135/K11
Orinoco (delta), Ven. 147/C2
Orinoco (riv.), Col.,Ven. 147/C2
Orio al Serio (int'l arpt.), It. 58/C1
Oriolo, It. 46/E2
Orion (lake), Mi, US 135/F6
Orissa (state), India 70/D7
Orissa Coast (canal), India 85/F5
Oristano, It. 46/A3
Oristano, Golfo di (gulf), It. 46/A3
Orivesi, Fin. 39/L1
Oriximiná, Braz. 151/G4
Orizaba, Mex. 143/M8
Orizona, Braz. 154/A5
Orjen (peak), Serb. 47/F1
Orjiva, Sp. 44/D4
Orke (riv.), Ger. 51/F6
Orkelljunga, Swe. 38/E3
Orkhomenós, Gre. 47/H3
Orkney, SAfr. 106/D2
Orkney (isls.), UK 160/G
Orla, Tx, US 132/C4
Orland Park, Il, US 135/Q16
Orlândia, Braz. 155/C2
Orlando (int'l arpt.), Fl, US 133/H4
Orlando, Fl, US 133/H4
Orlando, Capo d' (cape), It. 46/D3
Orléanais (reg.), Fr. 42/D2
Orleans, Ca, US 126/C5
Orleans (parish), La, US 137/P16
Orléans, Fr. 42/D3
Orlenbach, Ger. 54/D2
Orlik (res.), Czh. 55/H3
Orlová, Czh. 41/K4
Orlovskaya Oblast, Rus. 62/F1
Orly (int'l arpt.), Fr. 30/K5
Orly, Fr. 30/K5
Ormanlı, Turk. 49/K5
Ormea, It. 58/A4
Ormília, Gre. 47/H2
Ormiston, Sc, UK 36/D5
Ormoc, Phil. 81/F1
Ormond Beach, Fl, US 133/H4
Ormskirk, Eng, UK 35/F4
Ornain (riv.), Fr. 42/F2
Ornans, Fr. 56/C3
Ornavasso, It. 57/E6
Orne (riv.), Fr. 40/C4
Ørnes, Nor. 37/E2
Orneta, Pol. 39/J4
Örnsköldsvik, Swe. 37/F3
Oro (riv.), Mex. 154/C2
Oro Grande, Ca, US 136/C1
Oro, Monte d' (peak), Fr. 46/A1
Oro Valley, Az, US 128/E4
Orocó, Braz. 154/C3
Orocué, Col. 152/D3
Orodara, Burk. 102/D4
Orofino, Id, US 126/D4
Orolo (riv.), It. 59/E1
Oroluk (isl.), Micr. 116/E4
Oromocto, NB, Can. 131/H2
Oron-la-Ville, Swi. 56/C4
Orona (Hull) (isl.), Kiri. 117/H5
Orono, Me, US 131/G2
Orontes (riv.), Syria 90/D3
Oropesa, Sp. 44/C3
Oroqen Zizhiqi, China 71/M1
Orós, Braz. 154/C2
Orosei, It. 46/A2
Orosei, Golfo di (gulf), It. 46/A2
Orosháza, Hun. 48/E2
Oroszlány, Hun. 48/D2
Orovada, Nv, US 126/D5
Oroville, Wa, US 126/D3
Oroville, Ca, US 128/B3
Orphin, Fr. 30/H6
Orpund, Swi. 56/D3
Orrefors, Swe. 38/F3
Orrell, Eng, UK 35/F4
Orrick, Mo, US 137/E5
Orrin (riv.), Sc, UK 36/B2
Orrin (res.), Sc, UK 36/B2
Orroli, It. 46/A3
Orroroo, Austl. 113/H5
Orrtanna, Pa, US 138/A4
Orry-la-Ville, Fr. 30/K4
Orsa, Swe. 38/F1
Orsago, It. 59/F1
Orsay, Fr. 30/J5
Orsett, Eng, UK 30/E2
Orsha, Bela. 39/P4
Orsk, Rus. 63/L2
Orsonnens, Swi. 56/C4
Orşova, Rom. 48/F3
Ørsta, Nor. 37/C3
Örsundsbro, Swe. 38/G2
Orta (lake), It. 43/H4
Orta, Turk. 62/E4
Orta Nova, It. 46/D2
Ortaca, Turk. 90/B2
Ortaköy, Turk. 90/C1
Ortaköy, Turk. 90/C2
Ortega, Col. 152/C4
Ortegal (cape), Sp. 44/B1
Ortenberg, Ger. 54/C2
Orth an der Donau, Aus. 49/P7
Orthez, Fr. 42/C5
Ortigara (peak), It. 57/H5
Ortigueira, Sp. 44/B1
Orting, Wa, US 135/C3
Ortiz, Mex. 142/C2
Ortles (mts.), It. 43/J3
Ortles (peak), It. 57/G4
Ortón (riv.), Bol. 150/E6
Ortona, It. 46/D1
Ortonville, Mn, US 127/J4
Ortonville, Mi, US 135/F6
Ortze (riv.), Ger. 51/H3
Orūmīyeh, Iran 90/F2
Orurillo, Peru 156/D4
Oruro, Bol. 150/E7
Orust (isl.), Swe. 38/D2
Orvieto, It. 43/K5
Orvilliers, Fr. 30/G5
Orwell (riv.), Eng, UK 33/H2
Orwigsburg, Pa, US 138/B2
Oryakhovo, Bul. 49/F4
Orzinuovi, It. 58/C2
Orzysz, Pol. 39/J5
Os, Nor. 38/A1
Osa, Rus. 61/M4
Osa, Peninsula de (pen.), CR 150/B2
Osage (riv.), Mo, US 129/J3
Osage Beach, Mo, US 129/J3
Ōsaka (pref.), Japan 74/D3
Ōsaka (int'l arpt.), Japan 77/H6
Ōsaka, Japan 77/J6
Ōsaka Castle, Japan 77/H6
Osan, SKor. 73/D4
Osasco, Braz. 211/G8
Ōsato, Japan 77/C1
Osborn (mt.), Ak, US 134/E3
Osburg, Ger. 53/F4
Osby, Swe. 38/E3
Osceola, Ar, US 130/B5
Osvaldo Cruz, Braz. 155/B2
Oschersleben, Ger. 40/F2
Oschiri, It. 46/A2
Oscura (mts.), NM, US 132/B3
Osdorf, Ger. 51/G1
Osh (obl.), Kyr. 87/F5
Osh, Kyr. 87/F4
Oshamambe, Japan 76/B2
Oshawa, On, Can. 131/S8
Oshika (pen.), Japan 76/B4
Oshino, Japan 77/B3
Oshkosh, Ne, US 127/H5
Oshnovīyeh, Iran 90/F2
Oshogbo, Nga. 103/G5
Osijek, Cro. 48/D3
Osio Sotto, It. 58/C1
Osipaonica, Serb. 48/E3
Oskarshamn, Swe. 38/G3
Oskarström, Swe. 38/E3
Oskol (riv.), Rus.,Ukr. 62/F2
Oslo (cap.), Nor. 38/D2
Osmānābād, India 89/L5
Osmancık, Turk. 90/C1
Osmaneli, Turk. 49/K5
Osmaniye, Turk. 91/E1
Osnabrück, Ger. 51/F4
Osnago, It. 58/C1
Osny, Fr. 30/J4
Oso (riv.), D.R. Congo 104/A3
Oso (mt.), Ca, US 135/M12
Osogna, Swi. 57/E5
Osório, Braz. 155/B4
Osorno, Sp. 44/C1
Osorno, Chile 158/B4
Osoyoos, BC, Can. 126/D3
Ospedaletti, It. 58/A5
Ospedaletto Euganeo, It. 59/E2
Ospitaletto, It. 58/D1
Osprey (reef), Austl. 109/D2
Oss, Neth. 50/C5
Ossa (mt.), Austl. 115/C4
Ossa, Sierra de (mts.), Port. 44/B3
Osse (riv.), Nga. 103/G5
Osséja, Fr. 42/D5
Ossett, Eng, UK 35/G4
Ossi, It. 46/A2
Ossining, NY, US 139/K7
Ostashkov, Rus. 60/G4
Ostbevern, Ger. 51/E4
Ostellato, It. 59/E3
Osten, Ger. 51/G1
Osterburg, Ger. 40/F2
Osterburken, Ger. 54/C4
Österbybruk, Swe. 38/G1
Österbymo, Swe. 38/F3
Ostercappeln, Ger. 51/F4
Österdalälven (riv.), Swe. 38/F1
Osterems (chan.), Ger. 50/D1
Östergötland (co.), Swe. 37/E4
Osterhofen, Ger. 55/G5
Osterholz-Scharmbeck, Ger. 51/F2
Osteria Grande, It. 59/E4
Ostermiething, Aus. 55/F6
Osterode am Harz, Ger. 51/H5
Östersund, Swe. 37/E3
Östervåla, Swe. 38/G1
Ostfildern, Ger. 54/C5
Østfold (co.), Nor. 37/D4
Ostfriesland (reg.), Ger. 51/E2
Östhammar, Swe. 38/H1
Ostheim vor der Rhön, Ger. 54/D2
Osthofen, Ger. 54/B3
Ostia Antica (ruin), It. 46/C2
Ostiano, It. 58/D2
Ostiglia, It. 59/E2
Ostional NWR, CR 144/E4
Ostra, It. 59/G5
Östra Silen (lake), Swe. 38/E2
Ostra Vetere, It. 59/G5
Ostrach (riv.), Ger. 54/C6
Ostrava, Czh. 41/K4
Ostravský (pol. reg.), Czh. 41/J4
Ostrhauderfehn, Ger. 51/E2
Ostri Rt (cape), Serb. 47/F1
Ostricourt, Fr. 52/C3
Ostróda, Pol. 39/H5
Ostrogozhsk, Rus. 62/F2
Ostrołęka, Pol. 41/L2
Ostrov, Czh. 55/F2
Ostrov, Rus. 39/N3
Ostrów Mazowiecka, Pol. 41/L2
Ostrów Wielkopolski, Pol. 41/J3
Ostrowiec Świętokrzyski, Pol. 41/L3
Ostrzeszów, Pol. 41/J3
Ostseebad Binz, Ger. 38/E4
Ostseebad Göhren, Ger. 38/E4
Ostseebad Prerow, Ger. 38/E4
Oststeinbek, Ger. 51/H1
Ostuni, It. 47/E2
Ostwald, Fr. 54/A5
Osŭm (riv.), Bul. 47/J1
Osum (riv.), Slvk. 48/E5
Ōsumi (pen.), Japan 74/B5
Ōsumi (isls.), Japan 116/C1
Osun (state), Nga. 103/G5
Osuna, Sp. 44/C4
Oswaldtwistle, Eng, UK 35/F4
Oswego, NY, US 130/E3
Oswego, Il, US 135/P16
Oswestry, Eng, UK 35/E6
Oświęcim (Auschwitz), Pol. 41/K3
Ōta (riv.), Japan 74/C3
Ōta, Japan 75/F2
Ōtake, Japan 74/C3
Ōtaki, Japan 75/G3
Ōtaki, Japan 77/B2
Ōtakine-yama (peak), Japan 75/G2
Otava (riv.), Czh. 43/K2
Otavalo, Ecu. 152/B4
Otavi, Namb. 105/C4
Ōtawara, Japan 75/G2
Otay, Ca, US 136/C5
Oţelu Roşu, Rom. 48/F3
Otero de Rey, Sp. 44/B1
Oteros (riv.), Mex. 142/C3
Otgon Tenger (peak), Mong. 70/G2
Othello, Wa, US 126/D4
Othis, Fr. 30/L4
Othonoí (isl.), Gre. 47/F3
Oti (riv.), Gha. 103/F4
Otjiwarongo, Namb. 105/C5
Otley, Eng, UK 35/G4
Otočac, Cro. 48/B3
Otofuke, Japan 76/C2
Otog Qi, China 70/J4
Otok, Cro. 48/D3
Ōtone, Japan 77/D1
Otopeni (int'l arpt.), Rom. 49/H3
Otoskwin (riv.), On, Can. 127/L3
Otowa, Japan 77/M6
Otra (riv.), Nor. 38/B2
Otradnyy, Rus. 63/J1
Otranto, Strait of (str.), It. 47/F2
Otrokovice, Czh. 41/J4
Otse, Bots. 106/D2
Ōtsu, Japan 77/J5
Ōtsuchi, Japan 76/B4
Ōtsuki, Japan 77/B2
Otta, Nga. 103/F5
Ottawa (cap.), On, Can. 130/F2
Ottawa, Oh, US 130/C3
Ottawa, Ks, US 129/J3
Ottawa (int'l arpt.), On, Can. 130/F2
Ottawa (isls.), Nun., Can. 123/H3
Ottawa (riv.), On, Can. 130/E2
Ottensheim, Aus. 55/H6
Otter (riv.), Eng, UK 32/C5
Otterbach, Ger. 53/G5
Otterberg, Ger. 53/G4
Otterndorf, Ger. 51/F1
Ottersberg, Ger. 51/G2
Ottershaw, Eng, UK 30/B2
Otterville, Il, US 137/G7
Ottignies-Louvain-la-Neuve, Belg. 53/D2
Öttingen im Bayern, Ger. 54/D5
Ottmarsheim, Fr. 56/D2
Ottnang am Hausruck, Aus. 55/G6
Otto, Mo, US 137/F9
Ottobeuren, Ger. 57/G2
Ottobrunn, Ger. 55/E6
Ottone, It. 58/C3
Ottosdal, SAfr. 106/D2
Ottsville, Pa, US 138/C3
Ottumwa, Ia, US 127/K5
Ottweiler, Ger. 53/G5
Otumba de Gómez Farías, Mex. 143/L7
Otuzco, Peru 156/B2
Otway (cape), Austl. 115/B3
Otway (bay), Chile 159/C7
Otway NP, Austl. 115/B3
Otwock, Pol. 41/L2
Ötztal Alps (mts.), Aus. 43/J3
Ötztaler Ache (riv.), Aus. 57/G3
Ou (mts.), Japan 76/B4
Ouachita (mts.), Ok, US 125/G5
Ouachita (riv.), Ar,La, US 125/H5
Ouadda, CAfr. 97/K6
Ouaddaï (reg.), Chad 97/J5
Ouadi Haddad (riv.), Chad 97/J4
Ouadi Rimé (riv.), Chad 96/J5
Ouagadougou (int'l arpt.), Burk. 103/E3
Ouagadougou (cap.), Burk. 103/E3
Ouahigouya, Burk. 103/E3
Ouaka (riv.), CAfr. 97/K6
Oualâta, Dhar (cliff), Mrta. 102/D2
Ouallam, Niger 103/F3
Ouanda Djallé, CAfr. 97/K6
Ouanne (riv.), Fr. 42/E3
Ouarane (pol. reg.), Mrta. 96/C3
Ouarane (reg.), Mrta. 98/C5
Ouargla (prov.), Alg. 99/G3
Ouargla, Alg. 99/G3
Ouarkziz, Jebel (mts.), Mor. 98/C3
Ouarzazate (int'l arpt.), Mor. 98/D3
Ouarzazate, Mor. 98/D3
Ouasiemsca (riv.), Qu, Can. 130/F1
Oubangui (riv.), CAfr. 96/J7
Oubritenga (prov.), Burk. 103/E3
Ouche (riv.), Fr. 56/B3
Oud-Beijerland, Neth. 50/B5
Oud-Turnhout, Belg. 50/B6
Ōuda, Japan 77/J7
Oudalan (prov.), Burk. 103/E3
Ouddorp, Neth. 50/A5
Oude IJssel (riv.), Neth. 50/D5
Oude Pekela, Neth. 50/E2
Oude Westereems (chan.), Neth. 50/D1
Oudenaarde, Belg. 52/C2
Oudenbosch, Neth. 50/B5
Oudenburg, Belg. 52/C1
Oudewater, Neth. 50/B4
Oudon (riv.), Fr. 42/C3
Oudtshoorn, SAfr. 106/C4
Oued el Hadjar (well), Mali 102/E2
Oued Moulouyadeu (riv.), Mor. 96/E1
Oued Sous (riv.), Mor. 96/D1
Oued Zem, Mor. 98/D2
Ouémé (riv.), Ben. 96/F6
Ouémé (prov.), Ben. 103/F5
Ouenza, Alg. 100/L7
Ouerrha (riv.), Mor. 100/B2
Ouessé, Ben. 103/F4
Ouesso, Congo 96/J7
Ouest (prov.), Camr. 103/H5
Ouest (pt.), Haiti 145/H1
Ouest (pt.), Haiti 145/H2
Ouezzane, Mor. 100/B2
Oughterard, Ire. 31/P10
Ouham (riv.), CAfr. 96/J6
Ouidah, Ben. 103/F5
Oujda, Mor. 100/D2
Oujda (prov.), Mor. 100/C2
Oujda (Angads) (int'l arpt.), Mor. 100/D2
Oulad Teïma, Mor. 98/C3
Oulangan NP, Fin. 60/F2
Ould Birni (well), Alg. 99/E4
Oulnina (peak), Austl. 113/H5
Oulu, Fin. 60/E2
Oulu (prov.), Fin. 37/H2
Oulujärvi (lake), Fin. 37/H2
Oum El Bouaghi, Alg. 100/K7
Oum er Rbia, Oued (riv.), Mor. 98/D2
Oum er Rhia (riv.), Mor. 96/D1
Ounasjoki (riv.), Fin. 37/H2
Oupeye, Belg. 53/E2
Our (riv.), Eur. 53/E4
Ource (riv.), Fr. 42/F3
Ourcq (riv.), Fr. 40/B4
Ourcq, Canal de l' (canal), Fr. 30/K5
Øure Anarjokka NP, Nor. 37/H1
Øure Dividal NP, Nor. 37/F1
Ouricuri, Braz. 154/B2
Ourinhos, Braz. 155/B2
Ourique, Port. 44/A4
Ouro Fino, Braz. 211/G7
Ouro, Ponta do (pt.), Moz. 107/F2
Ouro Preto, Braz. 155/D2
Ouroux-sur-Saône, Fr. 56/A4
Ourthe Occidentale (riv.), Belg. 53/E3
Ourthe Orientale (riv.), Belg. 53/E3
Ouse (riv.), Eng, UK 35/H4
Oust (riv.), Fr. 42/B3
Outaouais (riv.), Qu, Can. 130/E2
Outardes (riv.), Qu, Can. 131/G1
Outardes Quatre (lake), Qu, Can. 131/G1
Outeïd Arkas (well), Mali 102/D2
Outer Hebrides (isls.), Sc, UK 31/P8
Outes, Sp. 44/A1
Outjo, Namb. 105/C5
Outlook, Sk, Can. 126/G3
Outreau, Fr. 52/A2
Outremont, Qu, Can. 131/N6
Ouvèze (riv.), Fr. 42/F4
Ouyen, Austl. 115/B2
Ouzinkie, Ak, US 134/H4
Ovacık, Turk. 90/D2
Ovacık, Turk. 90/C1
Ovada, It. 58/B3
Ovalle, Chile 157/B3
Ovana (peak), Ven. 153/E3
Ovar, Port. 44/A2
Overath, Ger. 53/G2
Overflakkee (isl.), Neth. 50/B5
Overhalla, Nor. 37/D2
Overholser (lake), Ok, US 137/M14
Overijse, Belg. 53/D2
Overijssel (prov.), Neth. 50/D3
Overijssels (riv.), Neth. 50/D4
Överkalix, Swe. 37/G2
Overland, Mo, US 137/G8
Overland Park, Ks, US 137/D6
Overlea, Md, US 138/B5
Overo (peak), Arg. 158/C5
Overpelt, Belg. 50/C6
Overton, Nv, US 128/D3
Övertorneå, Swe. 60/D2
Överum, Swe. 38/G3
Oviedo, Sp. 44/C1
Ovoca, Ire. 34/B6
Övörhangay (prov.), Mong. 70/H2
Övre Fryken (lake), Swe. 38/E1
Øvre Pasvik NP, Nor. 37/J1
Ovriá, Gre. 47/G3
Owando, Congo 96/J8
Ōwani, Japan 76/B3
Owariasahi, Japan 77/M5
Owase, Japan 74/E3
Owassa (lake), NJ, US 138/D1
Owasso, Ok, US 129/J3
Owego, NY, US 130/E3
Owen (mt.), NZ 117/S11
Owen, Austl. 113/H5
Owen, Ger. 54/C5
Owen Falls (dam), Ugan. 104/B2
Owen Roberts (int'l arpt.), UK 145/F2
Owen Sound, On, Can. 130/D2
Owenkillew (riv.), NI, UK 34/A2
Owens (riv.), Ca, US 128/C3
Owensboro, Ky, US 130/C4
Owerri, Nga. 103/G5
Owingen, Ger. 57/F2
Owings, Md, US 138/B6
Owings Mills, Md, US 138/B5
Owl Creek (mts.), Wy, US 126/F4
Owo, Nga. 103/G5
Owosso, Mi, US 130/C3
Owyhee, Nv, US 126/D5
Owyhee (lake), Or, US 128/C2
Owyhee (mts.), Id, US 128/C2
Owyhee (riv.), Id, US 124/C3
Owyhee, South Fork (riv.), Nv, US 126/D5
Oxapampa, Peru 156/C3
Oxbow, Sk, Can. 127/H3
Oxbow (lake), Mi, US 135/F6
Oxelösund, Swe. 38/G2
Oxford (lake), Mb, Can. 127/K2
Oxford, Eng, UK 33/E3
Oxford (canal), Eng, UK 33/E3
Oxford, Mi, US 135/F6
Oxford, Ms, US 133/F3
Oxford, Pa, US 138/C4
Oxfordshire (co.), Eng, UK 33/E3
Oxie, Swe. 38/E4
Oxkutzcab, Mex. 144/D1
Oxnard, Ca, US 136/A2
Oxnard Beach, Ca, US 136/A2
Oxon Hill (farm), Md, US 138/A6
Oxon Hill-Glassmanor, Md, US 138/B6
Oxted, Eng, UK 30/D3
Oyabe, Japan 75/E2
Oyama, Japan 75/F2
Oyama, Japan 77/B3
Ōyamada, Japan 77/K6
Ōyamazaki, Japan 77/J6
Oyapock (riv.), Fr. 151/H3
Oye-Plage, Fr. 52/B2
Oyem, Gabon 96/H7
Oyen, Ab, Can. 126/F3
Øyer, Nor. 38/D1
Oykell (riv.), Sc, UK 31/R8
Oyo (state), Nga. 103/F4
Oyo, Nga. 103/F5
Ōyodo (riv.), Japan 74/B5
Ōyodo, Japan 77/J7
Oyón, Peru 156/B3
Oyonnax, Fr. 56/B5
Oyster Bay, NY, US 139/L8
Oyster Bay (har.), NY, US 139/L8
Oyster Bay Cove, NY, US 139/L8
Oyster Bay NWR, NY, US 139/L8
Oyten, Ger. 51/G2
Oyyl (riv.), Kaz. 87/B3
Ozamiz, Phil. 79/D6
Ozanne (riv.), Fr. 42/D2
Ozark (plat.), Mo, US 129/J3
Ozark, Ar, US 129/J3
Ozark, Al, US 133/G4
Ozark (mts.), Ar,Mo, US 125/H4
Ozarks (lake), Mo, US 125/H4
Ózd, Hun. 41/L4
Ozernoy (cape), Rus. 65/S4
Ozette (lake), Wa, US 126/B3
Ozhiski (lake), On, Can. 127/L3
Ozieri, It. 46/A2
Ozimek, Pol. 41/K3
Özkonak, Turk. 90/C2

Ozoir-la-Ferrière, Fr. 30/L5
Ozona, Tx, US 129/G5
Ozora, Hun. 48/D2
Ozorków, Pol. 41/K3
Ozouer-le-Voulgis, Fr. 30/L6
Ozu, Japan 74/C4
Ozuluama de Mascareñas,
Mex. 144/B1
Ozzano dell'Emilia, It. 59/E4

P

P. K. Le Rouxdam (res.),
SAfr. 106/D3
Pa-an, Myan. 78/B2
Pa Sak (riv.), Thai. 83/H4
Paar (riv.), Ger. 40/F4
Paarl, SAfr. 106/L10
Paauilo, Hi, US 124/U10
Pabbi, Pak. 86/A2
Pabellón de Arteaga,
Mex. 142/E4
Pabianice, Pol. 41/K3
Pābna, Bang. 85/G3
Pābna (pol. reg.),
Bang. 85/G3
Pacaás Novos, PN dos,
Braz. 150/F6
Pacaás Novos, Serra dos
(mts.), Braz. 150/F6
Pacajá (riv.), Braz. 151/H4
Pacajus, Braz. 154/C2
Pacaltsdorp, SAfr. 106/C4
Pacaraimã (mts.),
Braz. 150/F3
Pacaya Samiria, Reserva
Nacional, Peru 156/C2
Paccha, Peru 156/C3
Paceco, It. 46/C4
Pachacamac (ruin),
Peru 156/B4
Pachaconas, Peru 156/C4
Pachamarca (riv.),
Peru 156/B4
Pachino, It. 46/D4
Pachitea (riv.), Peru 156/C3
Pachiza, Peru 156/B2
Pachmarhī, India 84/B4
Pachuca, Mex. 143/L6
Pacific (ocean) 67/N8
Pacific (range),
BC, Can. 126/B3
Pacific, Mo, US 135/C3
Pacific Palisades,
Hi, US 124/W13
Pacifico (mtn.),
Ca, US 136/B2
Pacinan (cape), Indo. 80/D5
Pacitan, Indo. 80/D5
Paço de Arcos, Port. 45/P10
Pad Idan, Pak. 89/J3
Padampur, India 85/L2
Padang, Indo. 80/B4
Padangpanjang,
Indo. 80/B4
Padangsidempuan,
Indo. 80/A3
Paddock Lake,
Wi, US 135/P14
Paddock Wood,
Eng, UK 30/E3
Paderborn, Il, US 137/G9
Paderborn, Ger. 51/F5
Paderno, It. 59/F1
Padiham, Eng, UK 36/B2
Padilla, Bol. 150/F7
Padina, Serb. 48/E3
Padjelanta NP, Swe. 37/F2
Padova (prov.), It. 59/E2
Padova, It. 59/E2
Padrão, Ponta do (pt.),
Ang. 105/B2
Padrauna, India 85/L2
Padre (isl.), Tx, US 125/G6
Padre Island Nat'l Seashore,
Tx, US 143/F2
Padrón, Sp. 44/A1
Paducah, Tx, US 129/G4
Paducah, Ky, US 130/D4
Padul, Sp. 44/D4
Padula, It. 46/D2
Paektŏk-san (peak),
SKor. 73/E4
Paektu-san (peak),
NKor. 73/E2
Paese, It. 59/F1
Páez, Col. 152/C3
Páez, Col. 152/C4
Pafúri, Moz. 105/F5
Pag, Cro. 48/B3
Pag (isl.), Cro. 48/B3
Pagadian, Phil. 81/F2
Pagai Selatan (isl.),
Indo. 80/B4
Pagai Utara (isl.),
Indo. 80/B4
Pagan, Myan. 78/B3
Pagan (isl.), NMar. 116/E4
Paganica, It. 46/C1
Page, Az, US 128/E3
Pager (riv.), Ugan. 104/B2
Pagny-sur-Moselle, Fr. 53/F6
Pagosa Springs,
Co, US 128/F3
Pagwachuan (riv.),
On, Can. 130/C1
Pahala, Hi, US 124/U11
Pahang (riv.), Malay. 80/B3
Páhara (lag.), Nic. 145/F3
Pahārpur, Pak. 86/A3
Pahāsu, India 84/B1
Pahlgām, India 86/C2

Pahrump, Nv, US 128/D3
Pahuatlán, Mex. 143/L6
Pahute (mesa),
Nv, US 128/D3
Pai (lake), China 72/C5
Paia, Hi, US 124/T10
Paignton, Eng, UK 32/C6
Paiján, Peru 156/B2
Päijänne (lake), Fin. 37/H3
Paikü (lake), China 85/E1
Pailolo (chan.),
Hi, US 124/T10
Paimio, Fin. 39/K1
Paine (peak), Chile 159/B6
Painesville, Oh, US 130/D3
Paint (lake), Mb, Can. 127/J2
Paint Rock, Tx, US 132/D4
Painted (des.),
Az, US 128/D3
Paipa, Col. 152/C3
Paisley, Sc, UK 36/B5
Paita, Peru 156/A2
Paithan, India 82/C4
Pajala, Swe. 37/G2
Paján, Ecu. 152/A5
Pajęczno, Pol. 41/K3
Pakanbaru, Indo. 80/B3
Pakch'ŏn, NKor. 73/D3
Pakenham NP, Cro. 48/B3
Pakenham (cape),
Chile 159/B6
Pákhnes (peak), Gre. 47/J5
Pakhra (riv.), Rus. 61/W9
Pakistan (ctry.) 89/H3
Paklenica NP, Cro. 48/B3
Pakokku, Myan. 83/G3
Pakowki (lake),
Ab, Can. 126/F3
Pākpattan, Pak. 86/B4
Pakrac, Cro. 48/C3
Paks, Hun. 40/D2
Pakxe, Laos 78/D3
Pala, Chad 96/H6
Pala, Ca, US 136/C4
Pala Ind. Res., Ca, US 136/C4
Palace, Mona. 58/J8
Palafrugell, Sp. 45/L2
Palagonia, It. 46/D4
Palagruža (isls.), Cro. 46/E1
Pálairos, Gre. 47/G3
Palaiseau, Fr. 30/J5
Palakollu, India 82/D4
Palamás, Gre. 47/H3
Palamós, Sp. 45/L2
Palana, Rus. 65/R4
Palangkaraya, Indo. 80/D4
Pālanpur, India 84/B3
Palaoa (pt.), Hi, US 124/T10
Palapye, Bots. 105/E5
Palar (riv.), India 82/C5
Palásbári, India 85/G3
Palatine, Il, US 135/P15
Palatka, Fl, US 133/H4
Palau (ctry.) 116/C4
Palau (W isl.), Indo. 116/C4
Palaw, Myan. 78/B3
Palawan (isl.), Phil. 67/L9
Palawan Passage (chan.),
Phil. 81/E2
Palazzolo Acreide, It. 46/D4
Palazzolo dello
Stella, It. 59/G1
Palazzolo sull'Oglio, It. 58/C1
Palé, EgG. 96/G8
Pale, Bosn. 48/D4
Paleleh, Indo. 81/F3
Palembang, Indo. 80/B4
Palena (riv.), Chile 158/B4
Palena, Chile 158/C4
Palencia, Sp. 44/C1
Palenque, Mex. 144/D2
Palenque, PN, Mex. 144/C2
Palermo, It. 46/C3
Palermo, NJ, US 138/D5
Palese (int'l arpt.), It. 46/E2
Palestine (lake),
Tx, US 132/E3
Palestro, It. 58/B2
Pālghar, India 89/K5
Palghat, India 82/C6
Palni, India 82/C5
Palo, Phil. 79/D5
Palo Alto, Ca, US 128/C3
Palo Alto, Pa, US 138/B2
Palo Pinto, Tx, US 129/H4
Palo Verde, PN, CR 140/D5
Palomeu (riv.), Sur. 153/H4
Palon (peak), It. 59/E1
Palos (cape), Sp. 45/E4
Palos de la Frontera,
Sp. 44/B4
Palos Hills, Il, US 135/Q16
Palos Verdes (hills),
Ca, US 136/F8
Palos Verdes (pt.),
Ca, US 136/F8
Palos Verdes Estates,
Ca, US 136/F8
Palpalá, Arg. 157/C1
Paltamo, Fin. 60/C2
Palu, Indo. 81/E4
Paluan, Phil. 79/D5
Palwal, India 84/A1
Pamangkat, Indo. 80/C3
Pambula, Austl. 115/D3
Pamiers, Fr. 42/D5
Pamir (riv.), Afg.,Taj. 64/H6
Pamir (reg.),
Taj.,China 64/H6
Pamlico (riv.),
NC, US 133/J3
Pamlico (sound),
NC, US 133/J3
Pampa, Tx, US 129/G4
Pampachiri, Peru 156/C4
Pampacolca, Peru 156/C4
Pampas, Peru 156/C4
Pampas (gulf), PNG 116/D2
Pampas (plain), Arg. 147/C6
Pamphilosa da Serra,
Port. 44/A2
Pamplona, Sp. 44/E1
Pamplona, Col. 152/C2
Pamplona (int'l arpt.),
Braz. 155/D1

Palk (str.), India 82/C6
Pallamallawa, Austl. 115/D1
Pallarenda, Austl. 114/B2
Pallas-Ounastunturin NP,
Fin. 37/H1
Pallasca, Peru 156/B3
Pallastunturi (peak),
Fin. 37/H1
Palliser (cape), NZ 117/T11
Palm Bay, Fl, US 133/H4
Palm Beach (int'l arpt.),
Hi, US 124/T10
Palm City, Fl, US 133/H5
Palm Harbor, Fl, US 133/H4
Palm Island Aboriginal
Settlement, Austl. 114/B2
Palm Springs,
Ca, US 128/C4
Palma (riv.), Braz. 151/J6
Palma, Moz. 104/D5
Palma del Río, Sp. 44/C4
Palma, It. 59/G1
Palma di Montechiaro,
It. 46/C4
Palma Mallorca
(int'l arpt.), Sp. 45/G3
Palma Soriano,
Cuba 145/H1
Palmácia, Braz. 154/C2
Palmanova, It. 59/G1
Palmar (riv.), Ven. 145/H4
Palmares, Braz. 154/D3
Palmarito, Ven. 152/C2
Palmas, Braz. 155/A3
Palmas (cape), Libr. 102/D5
Palmdale, Ca, US 136/B1
Palmeira, Braz. 155/B3
Palmeira do CpV. 93/K10
Palmeira dos Indios,
Braz. 154/C3
Palmeirais, Braz. 154/B2
Palmeiras (riv.), Braz. 154/A4
Palmeiras, Braz. 154/B3
Palmeirinhas, Ponta das
(pt.), Ang. 105/B2
Pálmela, Port. 45/Q10
Palmeira (riv.), Braz. 154/C2
Palmer, Ak, US 134/J3
Palmer, US, Ant. 160/V
Palmer, Wa, US 160/V
Palmer Land (phys. reg.),
Ant. 160/V
Palmerston, NZ 117/S12
Palmerston (cape),
Austl. 114/C3
Palmerston Atoll (atoll),
Cooks. 117/J6
Palmerston North,
NZ 117/T11
Palmerston NP,
Austl. 114/B2
Palmerton, Pa, US 138/C2
Palmetto, Fl, US 133/H5
Palmi, It. 46/D3
Palmilla, Chile 158/C2
Palmillas (pt.), Cuba 145/F1
Palmira, Col. 152/B4
Palmital, Braz. 155/B2
Palmitas, Uru. 159/K10
Palmyra, Ut, US 137/K13
Palmyra (isl.) 117/J4
Palmyra, Pa, US 138/B3
Palmyra (Tadmur) (ruin),
Syria 90/D3
Palmyras (pt.), India 82/C6
Palu, Turk. 90/D2
Pama, CAfr. 96/J6
Pápa, Hun. 48/C2
Papa Westray (isl.),
Sc, UK 31/V14
Papaikou, Hi, US 124/U11
Papantla, Mex. 143/M6
Papantla, Mex. 143/M6
Papagayo (gulf), CR 140/D5
Papaikou, Hi, US 124/U11
Papantla, Mex. 143/M6
Papagayo (gulf), CR 140/D5
Papanasam, India 82/C6
Papenburg, Ger. 51/E2
Paphos, Cyp. 91/C2
Paphos (dist.), Cyp. 91/C2
Parchim, Ger. 40/F2
Parczew, Pol. 41/M3
Pardes Hanna-Karkur,
Isr. 91/F7
Pardo (riv.), Braz. 151/J8
Pardone (cape),
SAfr. 106/D4
Papudo, Chile 158/C2
Pardubický
(pol. reg.), Czh. 41/J4
Pará (riv.), Braz. 151/H4
Pará (state), Braz. 154/A1
Pará (dist.), Sur. 153/H3
Pará (falls), Ven. 153/F3

Pāmpur, India 86/C2
Pamukova, Turk. 49/K5
Pan de Azúcar, PN,
Chile 157/B2
Panaba, Mex. 144/D1
Panabo, Phil. 79/E6
Pānāgar, India 84/B4
Panagyurishte, Bul. 47/J1
Panaitan (isl.), Indo. 80/B5
Panaji, India 82/B4
Panama (ctry.) 145/F4
Panamá (bay), Pan. 145/G4
Panamá (cap.), Pan. 152/B2
Panama (canal),
Pan. 145/F4
Panama (gulf), Pan. 145/G4
Panama City,
Fl, US 133/G4
Panama, Isthmus of
(isth.), Pan. 150/C2
Panamá Viejo (ruin),
Pan. 152/B2
Panamint (range),
Ca, US 128/C3
Panao, Peru 156/B3
Panaro (riv.), It. 43/J4
Panay (isl.), Phil. 67/M8
Pancake (range),
Nv, US 128/C3
Pančevo, Serb. 48/E3
Pančicev vrh (peak),
Serb. 47/G1
Pancilet (res.), India 144/E3
Panciu, Rom. 49/H3
Pandamatenga,
Bots. 105/E4
Pandharpur, India 89/L5
Pandino, It. 58/C2
Pāndoh, India 86/D4
Pandrup, Den. 38/C3
Pandua, India 85/G4
Panevėžys, Lith. 39/L4
Panfilov, Kaz. 70/D3
Pangai, Tonga 117/H6
Pangaion (peak), Gre. 47/J2
Pangani, Tanz. 104/C4
Pangani (riv.), Tanz. 104/C3
Pangkalanberandan,
Indo. 80/A3
Pangkalaseang (cape),
Indo. 81/F4
Pangkalpinang, Indo. 80/C4
Pangnirtung,
Nun., Can. 123/K2
Panguipulli, Chile 158/B3
Panguitch, Ut, US 128/D3
Pangutaran, Phil. 81/F7
Pangutaran (isl.), Phil. 79/C6
Paniai (lake), Indo. 81/J4
Paniau (peak),
Hi, US 124/R10
Pānihāti, India 85/G4
Pānīpat, India 86/D5
Paniqui, Phil. 79/D4
Panj (riv.), Afg. 89/K1
Panjwīn, Iraq 88/E1
Panke (riv.), Ger. 40/Q6
P'anmunjŏm, NKor. 73/D4
Panna, India 84/C3
Pannawonica,
Austl. 112/C2
Pannikin (isl.),
Austl. 114/F7
Pano Lefkara, Cyp. 91/C2
Panorama, Braz. 155/B2
Pantanal (lowland),
Braz. 150/D2
Pantanal Matogrossense,
PN, Braz. 150/D2
Pantelleria, It. 46/B4
Pantelleria (isl.), It. 27/F5
Pantigliate, It. 58/C2
Pantin, Fr. 30/K5
Pantoja, Peru 152/C5
Pantón, Sp. 44/B1
Pantukan, Phil. 79/E6
Pánuco (riv.), Mex. 140/D3
Pánuco, Mex. 144/B1
Panzhihua, China 83/H2
Panzós, Guat. 144/D3
Pão de Açúcar,
Braz. 154/C3
Paola, It. 46/E3
Paola, Malta 46/M7
Paoli, Pa, US 138/C3
Paonia, Co, US 128/F3
Paonta Sahib, India 86/D4
Paoua, CAfr. 96/J6
Papá, Hun. 48/C2
Papa Westray (isl.),
Sc, UK 31/V14
Papaikou, Hi, US 124/U11
Papantla, Mex. 143/M6
Papagayo (gulf), CR 140/D5
Papanasam, India 82/C6
Papenburg, Ger. 51/E2
Paphos, Cyp. 91/C2
Paphos (dist.), Cyp. 91/C2
Parchim, Ger. 40/F2
Parczew, Pol. 41/M3
Pardes Hanna-Karkur,
Isr. 91/F7
Pardo (riv.), Braz. 151/J8
Pardone (cape),
SAfr. 106/D4
Papudo, Chile 158/C2
Pardubický
(pol. reg.), Czh. 41/J4
Pardubice, Czh. 41/H3
Pará (riv.), Braz. 151/H4
Pará (state), Braz. 154/A1
Pará (dist.), Sur. 153/H3
Pará (falls), Ven. 153/F3

Pará de Minas, Braz. 155/C1
Para, South (riv.),
Austl. 113/M8
Para Wirra NP,
Austl. 113/M8
Paraburdoo, Austl. 112/C2
Paracambi, Braz. 211/B4
Paracas (pen.) 156/B4
Paracas, Reserva Nacional,
Peru 156/B4
Paracatu, Braz. 154/C5
Paracatu (riv.),
Braz. 154/A5
Paracel (isls.),
China 83/K4
Paracho de Verduzco,
Mex. 142/E5
Paracín, Serb. 48/E4
Paracuru, Braz. 154/C1
Paradhísion (int'l arpt.),
Gre. 47/N3
Paradip, India 82/E3
Paradis, La, US 137/P17
Paradise (valley),
Az, US 137/R18
Paradise, Peru 156/B3
Paradise, Pa, US 138/B4
Paradise Valley,
Nv, US 128/C3
Az, US 137/S18
Paragominas, Braz. 154/A1
Paraguá (riv.), Bol. 150/F6
Paraguaçu, Braz. 211/H6
Paraguaçu (riv.),
Braz. 147/C4
Paraguaçu Paulista,
Braz. 155/B2
Paraguai (riv.), SAm. 147/C5
Paraguaipoa, Ven. 152/B6
Paraguaná, Península de
(pen.), Ven. 150/D1
Paraguarí, Par. 157/E2
Paraguay (ctry.) 147/C5
Paraguay (riv.), Par. 157/E1
Paraíba (state),
Braz. 154/C2
Paraíba do Sul,
Braz. 211/K7
Paraíba do Sul (riv.),
Braz. 147/E5
Paraibano, Braz. 154/B2
Paraibuna, Braz. 211/J7
Parainen (Pargas),
Fin. 39/K1
Paraíso, Mex. 144/C2
Paraíso, CR 145/F4
Paraíso do Norte de Goiás,
Braz. 151/A6
Paraisópolis, Braz. 211/H7
Parakou, Ben. 103/F4
Paramaribo (cap.),
Sur. 151/G2
Paramaribo (dist.),
Sur. 153/H3
Parambu, Braz. 154/C2
Paramillo (peak), Col. 152/C3
Paramirim, PN, Col. 150/C2
Paramirim (riv.),
Braz. 151/K6
Paramirim, Braz. 154/B4
Paramithía, Gre. 47/G3
Paramount, Ca, US 136/F8
Paramus, NJ, US 139/J8
Paramushir (isl.), Rus. 67/Q5
Paraná, Arg. 159/J8
Paraná (riv.), SAm. 147/D5
Paraná (state), Braz. 155/B3
Paraná Ibicuy (riv.),
Arg. 159/J10
Paraná Uraríá (riv.),
Braz. 150/F4
Paranaguá, Braz. 155/C3
Paranaguá, Baía de
(bay), Braz. 155/B3
Paranaíba (riv.),
Braz. 151/J7
Paranaíba, Braz. 155/B1
Paranapanema (riv.),
Braz. 157/F1
Paranapiacaba, Serra do
(mts.), Braz. 155/C2
Paranatinga, Braz. 147/D4
Paranavaí, Braz. 157/F1
Parang, Phil. 81/F2
Paraopeba, Braz. 155/C1
Parapetí (riv.), Bol. 150/F7
Parati, Braz. 211/J8
Paratico, It. 58/C1
Paratinga, Braz. 154/B4
Paratinga (riv.),
Braz. 211/H8
Paray-Vieille-Poste, Fr. 30/K5
Parazinho, Braz. 154/C2
Pārbati (riv.), India 84/C3
Parbhani, India 89/L5
Pardes Hanna-Karkur 40/F2
Parczew, Pol. 41/M3
Pardubice, Czh. 41/H3

Parece Vela (Okino-Tori-
Shima), Japan 67/N7
Pardo (riv.), Braz. 147/C4
Parede, Port. 45/P10
Paredes de Nava, Sp. 44/C1
Paredón, Mex. 144/C2
Paredones, Chile 158/C2
Parelhas, Braz. 154/D2
Parempuyre, Fr. 42/C3
Parenda, India 82/C4
Parent (lake), Qu, Can. 130/E1
Parentis-en-Born, Fr. 42/C4
Parepare, Indo. 81/E4
Parera, Arg. 158/D2
Parets del Vallès, Sp. 45/L6
Pargny-sur-Saulx, Fr. 53/D6
Paria (riv.), Ut, US 128/E3
Paria (gulf),
Trin.,Ven. 147/C1
Paria, Peninsula de
(pen.), Ven. 150/F1
Pariacoto, Peru 156/B3
Pariaguán, Ven. 153/E2
Pariaman, Indo. 80/B4
Parikkala, Fin. 37/J3
Parima (riv.), Braz. 153/F4
Parima, Serra (mts.),
Braz. 150/F3
Parinacota (peak),
Bol. 156/D5
Parinari, Peru 156/C2
Pariñas (pt.), Peru 156/A2
Paringu (riv.), Ven. 150/F2
Parintins, Braz. 151/G4
Paris, Ar, US 129/J4
Paris, Tx, US 129/J4
Paris (cap.), Fr. 30/K5
Paris (dept.), Fr. 52/B6
Parita (bay), Pan. 145/F4
Park (range), Co, US 128/F2
Park (pt.), Eng, UK 32/A5
Park City, Ut, US 137/L12
Park City, Il, US 135/Q15
Park Falls, Wi, US 127/L4
Park Rapids, Mn, US 127/K4
Park Ridge, Il, US 135/Q16
Park Ridge, NJ, US 139/J7
Park River, ND, US 127/J3
Parker, Tx, US 129/H4
Parker, Az, US 128/D4
Parker, Co, US 137/C3
Parkersburg,
WV, US 130/D4
Parkes, Austl. 115/D2
Parkesburg, Pa, US 138/C4
Parkgate, NI, UK 34/B2
Parksdale, Ca, US 137/F9
Parkside, Pa, US 138/C4
Parkstetten, Ger. 55/F5
Parkton, Md, US 138/B4
Parkville, Mo, US 137/D5
Parkville, Md, US 138/B5
Parkway-Sacramento,
Ca, US 135/L9
Parla, Sp. 45/N9
Parlakhemundi, India 82/D4
Parli, India 89/L5
Parma, Oh, US 130/D3
Parma (prov.), It. 58/D3
Parma, It. 58/D3
Parmain, Fr. 30/J4
Parnaguá, Braz. 147/E3
Parnaíba (riv.), Braz. 147/E3
Parnamirim, Braz. 154/C3
Parnamirim, Braz. 151/L5
Parnarama, Braz. 154/B2
Parnassós (peak),
Gre. 47/H3
Parnassós NP, Gre. 47/H3
Párnis (peak), Gre. 47/N8
Párnis Oros NP,
Gre. 47/N8
Párnon (mts.), Gre. 47/H4
Pärnu (bay), Est. 39/L2
Pärnu, Est. 39/L2
P'aro-ho (lake), SKor. 73/D3
Paron, Fr. 42/E2
Parona di
Valpolicella, It. 59/D2
Paroo (riv.), Austl. 109/D3
Páros (isl.), Gre. 47/J4
Páros, Gre. 47/J4
Parow, SAfr. 106/L10
Parowan, Ut, US 128/D3
Parras de la Fuente,
Mex. 142/E3
Parrett (riv.), Eng, UK 32/C4
Parrita, CR 145/E4
Parry (isls.) 123/R7
Parry, Nun., Can. 123/R7
Parry (bay),
Nun., Can. 123/K2
Parry (chan.) 123/R7
Parry, Nun., Can. 122/F1
Parry Sound, On, Can. 130/D2
Parsberg, Ger. 55/E4
Parseierspitze (peak),
Aus. 57/G3
Parshall, ND, US 127/H4
Parsippany-Troy Hills,
NJ, US 139/H9
Parsnip (riv.),
BC, Can. 126/C2
Pärtefjället (peak),
Swe. 37/F2
Partenstein, Ger. 54/C2

Parthenay, Fr. 42/C3
Partille, Swe. 38/E3
Partinico, It. 46/C3
Partinico, Braz. 155/A3
Partizansk, Rus. 71/P3
Partizánske, Slvk. 41/K4
Partridge (riv.),
On, Can. 130/D1
Partúr, India 89/L5
Paru (riv.), Braz. 151/H4
Paru de Oeste (riv.),
Braz. 147/D2
Paruro, Peru 156/D4
Pārvathipuram,
India 82/D4
Parvatsar, India 84/B3
Parys, SAfr. 106/D2
Pas-de-Calais
(dept.), Fr. 52/A3
Pas de Morgins
(pass), Fr. 56/C5
Pasadena, Tx, US 129/J5
Pasadena, Nf, Can. 131/K1
Pasadena, Md, US 138/B5
Pasadena, Ca, US 136/F7
Pasado (cape),
Ecu. 152/A5
Pasaje, Ecu. 156/B1
Pasaman (peak),
Indo. 80/B3
Pasán, India 84/D4
Pascagoula,
Ms, US 133/F4
Paşcani, Rom. 49/H2
Pasching, Aus. 55/H6
Pasco, Wa, US 126/D4
Pasco (dept.), Peru 156/C3
Pascua (riv.), Chile 159/B6
Pascua, Isla de (Easter)
(isl.), Chile 117/Q7
Pascuales, Ecu. 156/B1
Pasewalk, Ger. 38/E5
Pasian di Prato, It. 59/G1
Pasiano, It. 59/F1
Pasig, Phil. 79/D5
Pasinler, Turk. 90/E2
Pasión, Río de la (riv.),
Guat. 144/D2
Pasłęk, Pol. 39/H4
Pasłęka (riv.), Pol. 41/L2
Pasley (cape), Austl. 112/D5
Pasman (isl.), Cro. 48/B4
Pašman, Cro. 48/B4
Pasni, Pak. 89/H3
Paso de Indios, Arg. 158/C4
Paso de los Libres,
Arg. 157/E2
Paso de los Toros,
Uru. 159/K10
Paso de Ovejas,
Mex. 143/N7
Paso del Macho,
Mex. 143/N8
Paso del Planchón
(peak), Chile 158/C2
Paso Robles (El Paso de
Robles), Ca, US 128/B4
Pasrūr, Pak. 86/C3
Pass (cape), Yk, Can. 134/M3
Passa Quatro, Braz. 211/J7
Passagem Franca,
Braz. 154/B2
Passaic, Oh, US 130/D3
Passaic, NJ, US 139/J8
Passau, Ger. 55/G5
Passero (pt.), It. 46/D4
Passo Fundo, Braz. 155/A4
Passo Fundo, Barragem do
(res.), Braz. 155/A3
Passons, It. 59/G1
Passoré (prov.),
Burk. 103/E3
Passos, Braz. 155/C2
Passwang (peak),
Swi. 56/D3
Passy, Fr. 56/C5
Pastavy, Bela. 39/M4
Pastaza (riv.),
Ecu.,Peru 147/B3
Pastaza (dept.), Ecu. 152/B5
Pastek (riv.), Pol. 39/J5
Pasto, Col. 152/B4
Pastos Bons, Braz. 154/A2
Pasuruan, Indo. 80/D5
Pásztó, Hun. 41/K5
Pata, Bol. 156/D4
Patagonia (phys. reg.),
Arg. 147/B7
Patah (peak), Indo. 80/B4
Pātan, India 84/B4
Pātan, India 89/K4
Pataná (peak), Braz. 155/B3
Patapsco (riv.),
Md, US 138/B4
Patapsco, Md, US 138/B4
Pataudi, India 86/D5
Pataxó, Braz. 155/D1
Patchogue, NY, US 139/E2
Paterna, Sp. 45/E3
Paternò, It. 46/D4
Paterson, NJ, US 139/J8
Pathānkot, India 86/C3
Pathein (Bassein),
Myan. 83/F4
Pathfinder (res.),
Wy, US 126/G5
Pati, Indo. 80/D5
Patía, Col. 150/C3
Patía (riv.), Col. 152/B4
Patiāla, India 86/D4
Patikul, Phil. 81/F2
Patna, Sc, UK 36/B6

Patnongon, Phil. 81/F1
Patnos, Turk. 90/E2
Pato Branco, Braz. 155/A3
Patoka (riv.), In, US 133/G2
Patos, Braz. 154/C2
Patos, Alb. 47/F2
Patos de Minas,
Braz. 155/C1
Patos, Lagoa dos (lake),
Braz. 157/F3
Patrai (gulf), Gre. 47/G3
Patrai, Gre. 47/G3
Pātrāsaer, India 85/F4
Patrātu, India 85/E4
Patricia (mt.), Austl. 113/F2
Patricio Lynch (isl.),
Chile 159/A6
Patrocínio, Braz. 155/C1
Patscherkofel (peak),
Aus. 57/H3
Pattani, Thai. 78/C5
Pattensen, Ger. 51/G4
Patti, India 86/C4
Patti, It. 46/D3
Pattoki, Pak. 86/B4
Pattukkottai, India 82/C5
Pattullo (mt.), BC, Can. 134/N4
Patuākhāli (pol. reg.),
Bang. 85/G4
Patuākhāli, Bang. 85/H4
Patuca (riv.), Hon. 140/D5
Patuca (mts.), Hon. 144/E3
Patuca (riv.), Hon. 145/E3
Patuxent (riv.),
Md, US 138/B5
Patuxent NWR,
Md, US 138/B5
Patuxent River State Park,
Md, US 138/B5
Páty, Hun. 49/Q9
Pátzcuaro, Mex. 143/E5
Pau, Fr. 42/C5
Pau Brasil, Braz. 154/C4
Pau dos Ferros, Braz. 154/C2
Paucarbamba, Peru 156/C3
Paucartambo, Peru 156/C3
Paucartambo, Peru 156/D4
Pauillac, Fr. 42/C4
Pauini (riv.), Braz. 150/E5
Paulaya (riv.), Hon. 144/E3
Paulínia, Braz. 211/F7
Paulins Kill (riv.),
NJ, US 138/D2
Paulistana, Braz. 154/B3
Paullo, It. 58/C2
Paulo Afonso, Braz. 154/C3
Paulo Afonso, PN de,
Braz. 154/C3
Paulo Ramos, Braz. 154/A2
Paulpietersburg,
SAfr. 107/E2
Pauls Valley, Ok, US 129/H4
Paulsboro, NJ, US 138/C4
Pauma Valley, Ca, US 136/D4
Paungde, Myan. 83/G4
Pauxo, Braz. 154/B5
Pavel Banya, Bul. 47/J1
Pavia (prov.), It. 58/C2
Pavia, It. 58/C2
Pavie, Fr. 42/D5
Pavlikeni, Bul. 49/G4
Pavlodar (obl.), Kaz. 87/G2
Pavlodar, Kaz. 87/G2
Pavlof (vol.),
Ak, US 134/F4
Pavlohrad, Ukr. 62/E2
Pavlovo, Rus. 60/J5
Pavone Canavese, It. 58/A2
Pavone del Mella, It. 58/D2
Pavullo nel Frignano,
It. 59/D4
Paw Paw, Mi, US 130/C3
Pawan (riv.), Indo. 80/D4
Pawāyan, India 84/C1
Pawhuska, Ok, US 129/H3
Pawnee (riv.), Ks, US 129/G3
Pawtucket, RI, US 131/G3
Paxoí (isl.), Gre. 47/G3
Paxson, Ak, US 134/J3
Paxton, Austl. 115/D2
Pay-Khoy (mts.), Rus. 64/G3
Payakumbuh, Indo. 80/B4
Payerne, Swi. 56/C4
Payette (riv.), Id, US 126/D5
Payne (lake),
Qu, Can. 123/J3
Paynesville, Austl. 115/C3
Pays de Caux (reg.), Fr. 42/D2
Pays de France
(reg.), Fr. 30/K4
Pays de la Loire
(reg.), Fr. 42/C3
Paysandú, Uru. 159/J10
Payson, Az, US 128/E4
Payson, Ut, US 128/E2
Payún (mt.), Arg. 158/C3
Paz (riv.), Guat. 144/D3
Paz de Ariporo, Col. 152/D3
Paz de Río, Col. 152/C3
Pazar, Turk. 90/D1
Pazar, Turk. 63/G4
Pazarcık, Turk. 90/D2
Pazaryeri, Turk. 49/K5
Pazardzhik, Turk. 47/J1
Pazazik, Turk. 47/J1
Pazin, Cro. 48/A3
Peabiru, Braz. 155/A2
Peace (riv.), BC, Can. 122/D3
Peace Memorial Park,
Japan 74/C3
Peaceful Valley,
Co, US 137/B2
Peachland, BC, Can. 126/D3
Peachtree City,
Ga, US 133/G3

Peak Charles NP, Austl. 112/D5
Peak District NP, Eng, UK 35/G5
Peak Hill, Austl. 112/C3
Peapack-Gladstone, NJ, US 138/D2
Pearblossom, Ca, US 136/C1
Pearl, Ms, US 133/F3
Pearl (har.), Hi, US 124/W13
Pearl (riv.), La,Ms, US 125/J5
Pearl and Hermes (reef), Hi, US 117/H2
Pearl Beach, Mi, US 135/G6
Pearl City, Hi, US 124/W13
Pearl River (estu.), China 79/D3
Pearl River, La, US 137/Q16
Pearl River, NY, US 139/J7
Pearland, Tx, US 136/B1
Pearsall, Tx, US 129/H5
Pearson (int'l arpt.), On, Can. 131/D4
Pearston, SAfr. 106/D4
Peary (chan.), Nun., Can. 123/R7
Pease (riv.), Tx, US 129/G4
Pebane, Moz. 105/G4
Pebas, Peru 156/D1
Pebble (isl.), Mald. 159/E6
Peccia, Swi. 57/E5
Peccioli, It. 59/D5
Pécel, Hun. 49/R10
Pech de Guillaument (peak), Fr. 42/E5
Pechanga Ind. Res., Ca, US 136/C4
Pechora, Rus. 61/N2
Pechora (bay), Rus. 61/M1
Pechora (riv.), Rus. 67/C4
Peckham, Co, US 137/C2
Peconic (riv.), NY, US 139/F2
Pecos, Tx, US 132/C4
Pecos (riv.), Tx, US 132/C4
Pecq, Belg. 52/C2
Pecquencourt, Fr. 52/C3
Pécs, Hun. 48/D2
Peculiar, Mo, US 137/E6
Pecy, Fr. 30/M6
Pedasí, Pan. 152/A3
Pedder (lake), Austl. 109/G3
Pedemonte, It. 59/D2
Pedernales (riv.), Tx, US 143/F2
Pedley, Ca, US 136/C3
Pedra Azul, Braz. 154/E4
Pedra Lume, CpV 93/K10
Pedralva, Braz. 211/H7
Pedregal, Ven. 152/D2
Pedreguer, Sp. 45/E3
Pedreira, Braz. 211/L4
Pedreiras, Braz. 154/A2
Pedricktown, NJ, US 138/C4
Pedro (pt.), SrL. 82/D6
Pedro Avelino, Braz. 154/C2
Pedro Bay, Ak, US 134/H4
Pedro Betancourt, Cuba 145/F1
Pedro Carbo, Ecu. 152/A5
Pedro Cays (isl.), Jam. 141/F4
Pedro II, Braz. 154/B2
Pedro IV (isl.), Braz. 153/E4
Pedro Juan Caballero, Par. 157/E1
Pedro Leopoldo, Braz. 155/C1
Pedro Luro, Arg. 158/E3
Pedro Osório, Braz. 155/A4
Peebles, Sc, UK 36/C5
Peedamulla Abor. Land, Austl. 112/B2
Peekskill, NY, US 138/E1
Peel (inlet), Austl. 112/B5
Peel (isl.), Austl. 114/F6
Peel (sound), Nun., Can. 122/G1
Peel (co.), On, Can. 131/D4
Peel (riv.), Yk, Can. 122/C2
Peel, IM, UK 34/D3
Peel Fell (peak), Eng, UK 36/C6
Peene (riv.), Ger. 38/E5
Peer, Belg. 53/E1
Pegasus (bay), NZ 117/S11
Pegnitz, Ger. 55/E3
Pegnitz (riv.), Ger. 40/F4
Pego, Sp. 45/E3
Pego do Altar, Barragem de (res.), Port. 44/A3
Pegognaga, It. 59/D3
Pegwell (bay), Eng, UK 33/H4
Pehlivanköy, Turk. 49/H5
Pehowa, India 86/D5
Pehuajó, Arg. 158/E2
Pehuenche (pass), Chile 158/C2
Pei Xian, China 72/D4
Peine, Ger. 51/H4
Peipus (lake), Est.,Rus. 39/M2
Peiting, Ger. 57/G2
Peixe (riv.), Braz. 155/B3
Peixoto, Reprêsa de (res.), Braz. 155/C2
Pekalongan, Indo. 80/C5
Pekan, Malay. 80/B3
Pekan Nanas, Malay. 80/B3

Pekhora (riv.), Rus. 61/W9
Pekin, Il, US 127/L5
Pelada, Pampa (plain), Arg. 158/C5
Pelado (vol.), Mex. 143/Q10
Pelagie (isls.), It. 46/C5
Peleaga (peak), Rom. 48/F3
Pelee (isl.), On, Can. 130/D3
Pelee (pt.), On, Can. 123/H4
Pelée (peak), Fr. 141/N9
Pelham, Al, US 133/G3
Pelham, On, Can. 131/R9
Pelham, NY, US 139/K8
Pelham Bay Park, NY, US 139/K8
Pelham Manor, NY, US 139/K8
Pelhřimov, Czh. 41/H4
Pelican, Ab, Can. 126/E2
Pelican (lake), Sk, Can. 127/H2
Pelican, Ak, US 134/L4
Pelican Narrows, Sk, Can. 127/H2
Pelindaba, Ponta de (pt.), GBis. 102/A4
Pelister (peak), FYROM 47/G2
Pelister NP, FYROM 47/G2
Peljekaise NP, Swe. 37/G2
Pelješac (pen.), Cro. 47/E1
Pelješec (pen.), Cro. 48/C4
Pell Lake, Wi, US 135/P14
Pélla, Gre. 47/H2
Pellegrini, Arg. 158/E3
Pellestrina, It. 59/F2
Pello, Fin. 60/E2
Pelly (riv.), Yk, Can. 122/C2
Pelly (bay), Nun., Can. 122/H2
Pelly Bay, Nun., Can. 122/H2
Peloponnesus (reg.), Gre. 47/G3
Peloritani, Monti (mts.), It. 46/D4
Pelotas (riv.), Braz. 157/F2
Pelotas, Braz. 155/A4
Pelplin, Pol. 39/H5
Pemali (cape), Indo. 81/F5
Pemali (cape), Indo. 81/F4
Pematangsiantar, Indo. 80/A3
Pemba, Moz. 105/H3
Pemba (isl.), Tanz. 105/G2
Pemba North (prov.), Tanz. 104/C4
Pemba South (prov.), Tanz. 104/C4
Pemberton, Austl. 112/C5
Pemberton, BC, Can. 126/C3
Pemberton, NJ, US 138/D4
Pembina (riv.), ND, US 126/E2
Pembina, ND, US 127/J3
Pembroke, On, Can. 130/E2
Pembroke, Wal, UK 32/A3
Pembrokeshire (co.), Wal, UK 32/A3
Pembrokeshire Coast NP, Wal, UK 32/A3
Pembury, Eng, UK 33/G4
Pemuco, Chile 158/B3
Pen Argyl, Pa, US 138/C2
Pen, The (lake), Eng, UK 32/B5
Pen-y-Ghent (peak), Eng, UK 35/F3
Pen-y-Gogarth (peak), Wal, UK 34/E5
Pen y Gurnos (peak), Eng, UK 32/C2
Peña Blanca (mtn.), Pan. 145/F4
Peña de Cerredo (mtn.), Sp. 44/C1
Peñafiel, Sp. 44/C2
Peñafiel, Port. 44/A2
Peñaflor, Chile 158/N8
Penalva, Braz. 154/A1
Penamacor, Port. 44/B2
Penápolis, Braz. 155/B2
Peñaranda de Bracamonte, Sp. 44/C2
Peñarroya (peak), Sp. 44/E2
Peñarroya-Pueblonuevo, Sp. 44/C3
Penarth, Wal, UK 32/C4
Peñas (cape), Sp. 44/C1
Peñas (cape), Arg. 159/D7
Penas, Golfo de (gulf), Chile 157/A6
Peñascal (riv.), NM, US 129/F4
Pench (riv.), India 84/B5
Penchard, Fr. 30/L5
Penco, Chile 158/B3
Pend Oreille (lake), Id, US 126/D4
Pendelikón (peak), Gre. 47/N8
Pendembu, SLeo. 102/C4
Pendências, Braz. 154/C3
Pendjar (riv.), Burk. 103/F4
Pendjari, PN de la, Ben. 96/F5
Pendle (hill), Eng, UK 35/E3
Pendleton, Or, US 126/D4
Peneda-Gerês NP, Port. 44/A2
Penedo, Braz. 154/C3

Penetanguishene, On, Can. 130/E2
Perdido (mtn.), Sp. 45/F1
Penghu (Pescadores) (isls.), Tai. 79/C3
Penglai, China 72/E3
Penha, Braz. 155/B3
Penhold, Ab, Can. 126/E2
Penibético, Sistema (range), Sp. 44/C4
Penice (peak), It. 58/C3
Peniche, Port. 44/A3
Penicuik, Sc, UK 36/C5
Península de Paria, PN, Ven. 153/F2
Peñíscola, Sp. 45/F2
Penitente, Serra do (mts.), Braz. 151/J5
Penmaenmawr, Wal, UK 34/E5
Penmarch, Fr. 42/A3
Penmarc'h, Pointe de (pt.), Fr. 42/A3
Penn Forest (res.), Pa, US 138/C2
Penn Hills, Pa, US 130/E3
Penn Yan, NY, US 158/C5
Penna, Punta della (cape), It. 46/D1
Penne (pt.), It. 46/D1
Penne, It. 46/C1
Penner (riv.), India 82/C5
Pennine Alps (mts.), Swi. 43/G4
Pennine Chain (mts.), Eng, UK 35/F2
Pennington, NJ, US 138/D3
Pennino (peak), It. 43/K5
Penns Creek (mtn.), Pa, US 138/A2
Penns Grove, NJ, US 138/C4
Penns Park, Pa, US 138/D3
Pennsauken, NJ, US 138/C3
Pennsburg, Pa, US 138/C3
Pennsville, NJ, US 138/C4
Pennsylvania (state), US 130/E3
Penny (str.), Nun., Can. 123/S7
Penobscot (riv.), Me, US 131/G2
Penola, Austl. 115/B3
Peñón Blanco, Mex. 142/D3
Penon de Al Hoceima (isl.), Sp. 100/C2
Penonomé, Pan. 152/A2
Penrhyn Mawr (pt.), Wal, UK 34/D6
Penrhyn Mawr (pt.), IM, UK 34/D5
Penrith, Eng, UK 35/F2
Penrith, Eng, UK 112/K6
Penryn, Eng, UK 32/A6
Pensacola, Fl, US 133/G4
Pensacola (mts.), Ant. 160/X
Pense, Sk, Can. 127/G3
Penshurst, Austl. 137/J11
Pentagon Fed. Govt. Res., Va, US 138/A6
Pentecost (isl.), Van. 116/F6
Pentecote (riv.), Qu, Can. 154/C1
Penteleu (peak), Rom. 49/H3
Penthalaz, Swi. 56/C4
Penticton, BC, Can. 126/D3
Pentire (pt.), Eng, UK 32/B5
Pentland, Austl. 114/B3
Pentland (hills), Sc, UK 36/C5
Pentland Firth (inlet), Sc, UK 31/V14
Penuelas, PN, Chile 158/N8
Penwith (pen.), Eng, UK 32/A6
Penza, Rus. 63/H1
Penzance, Eng, UK 32/A6
Penzberg, Ger. 57/H2
Penzenskaya Oblast, Rus. 63/G1
Penzhina (riv.), Rus. 65/S3
Penzhina (bay), Rus. 65/S3
Penzing, Ger. 57/G1
Penzlin, Ger. 40/G2
Peoria, Az, US 137/R18
Peoria, Il, US 127/L5
Pepe (cape), Cuba 145/H2
Pepeekeo, Hi, US 124/U11
Pepeekeo (pt.), Hi, US 124/U11
Pepel, SLeo. 102/B4
Pepinster, Belg. 53/E2
Pequannock, NJ, US 139/H8
Pequeña Isla del Maíz (isl.), Nic. 145/F3
Pequest (riv.), NJ, US 138/D2
Perabumulih, Indo. 80/B4
Perales (riv.), Sp. 45/M9
Peralta, Sp. 44/E1
Pérama, Gre. 47/J5
Pérama, Gre. 47/N9
Percé, Qu, Can. 131/H1
Percé (peak), Fr. 56/C6
Perche, Collines du (hills), Fr. 42/D2
Percival (lakes), Austl. 109/B3
Percy (isls.), Austl. 109/E3
Percy Isles (chan.), Austl. 114/C3
Perdekop, SAfr. 107/E2
Perdida (riv.), Braz. 154/A3

Perdida (riv.), Braz. 154/A3
Peregian Beach, Austl. 114/D4
Pereira, Col. 150/C3
Pereira Barreto, Braz. 155/B2
Pereiro, Braz. 154/C2
Perelló, Sp. 45/F2
Perenjori, Austl. 112/C4
Peretola (int'l arpt.), It. 59/E5
Perg, A. 55/H6
Pergamino, Arg. 158/E2
Pergamum (ruin), Turk. 90/A2
Pergine Valsugana, It. 57/H5
Pergola, It. 43/K5
Péribonca (riv.), Qu, Can. 131/G1
Perico, Cuba 145/F1
Pericos, Mex. 142/D3
Pericos, Mex. 142/D4
Périgueux, Fr. 42/D4
Perijá, Sierra de (mts.), Col. 150/D2
Peristéra (isl.), Gre. 47/H3
Peristéri, Gre. 47/N8
Perito Moreno, Arg. 157/B6
Perito Moreno, PN, Arg. 157/B6
Perkasie, Pa, US 138/D3
Perl, Ger. 53/E4
Perlas (lag.), Nic. 140/E5
Perlas (pt.), Nic. 145/F3
Perleberg, Ger. 40/F2
Perlez, Serb. 48/E3
Perlis (state), Malay. 78/B5
Perm', Rus. 61/N4
Përmet, Alb. 47/G2
Permskaya Oblast, Rus. 61/N4
Pernambuco (state), Braz. 154/C3
Pernate, It. 58/B2
Pernes-les-Fontaines, Fr. 42/F4
Pernik, Bul. 47/H1
Perniö, Fin. 39/K1
Péronne, Fr. 52/B4
Perote, Mex. 143/M7
Pérouges, Fr. 56/B6
Perpignan, Fr. 42/E5
Perray (riv.), Fr. 30/H6
Perrigny, Fr. 56/B4
Perris (res.), Ca, US 136/C3
Perris, Ca, US 136/C3
Perris State Rec. Area, Ca, US 136/C3
Perros-Guirec, Fr. 42/B2
Perrot, Ile (isl.), Qu, Can. 131/N7
Perry, Fl, US 133/H4
Perry, Ga, US 133/H3
Perry, Ok, US 129/H3
Perry (co.), Pa, US 138/A3
Perry, Ut, US 137/J11
Perry Hall, Md, US 138/B5
Perryman, Md, US 138/B5
Perryopolis, Pa, US 130/D4
Perryville, Ak, US 134/G4
Perryville, Md, US 138/B4
Persan, Fr. 30/J4
Persian (gulf), Asia 67/D7
Perstorp, Swe. 39/H3
Perth, Austl. 115/C4
Perth, On, Can. 130/E2
Perth (int'l arpt.), Austl. 112/K6
Perth, Austl. 112/K6
Perth, Sc, UK 36/C4
Perth and Kinross (pol. reg.), Sc, UK 31/Q7
Perth Zoo, Austl. 112/K6
Pertuis, Fr. 42/F5
Pertuis Breton (inlet), Fr. 42/C3
Pertusato (cape), Fr. 46/A2
Peru (ctry.) 156/C3
Peru, In, US 127/L5
Peru, Il, US 130/C3
Perucáčko (lake), Bosn. 48/D4
Perugia, It. 43/K5
Peruíbe, Braz. 211/G9
Peruque, Mo, US 137/F8
Perushtitsa, Bul. 47/J1
Péruwelz, Belg. 52/C2
Pervari, Turk. 90/E2
Pervomays'k, Ukr. 49/K1
Pervomays'k, Rus. 61/N4
Pervoural'sk, Rus. 61/N4
Perwez, Belg. 53/D2
Péry, Swi. 56/D3
Pesa (riv.), It. 59/E5
Pesagi (peak), Indo. 80/B4
Pesaro, It. 59/F5
Pesaro e Urbino (prov.), It. 59/F5
Pescadores (Penghu) (isls.), China 79/C3
Pescantina, It. 59/D2
Pescara, It. 46/D1
Peschanyy (cape), Kaz. 63/J4
Pescia, It. 59/D5
Peseux, Swi. 56/C4
Pesha (riv.), Rus. 61/L2
Peshawar, Pak. 86/A2
Peshawar (int'l arpt.), Pak. 86/A2
Peshtera, Bul. 47/J1
Peshtigo, Wi, US 127/M4
Peshtigo (riv.), Wi, US 130/B2

Pesmes, Fr. 56/B3
Pesö da Régua, Port. 44/B2
Pesqueira, Braz. 154/C3
Pessac, Fr. 42/C4
Pest (prov.), Hun. 48/D2
Pestovkoye (lake), Rus. 61/W9
Pestovo, Rus. 60/G4
Petah Tiqwa, Isr. 91/F7
Petal, Ms, US 133/F4
Petalión (gulf), Gre. 47/J4
Petaluma (riv.), Ca, US 135/J10
Petange, Lux. 53/E4
Petare, Ven. 150/E1
Pétas, Gre. 47/G3
Petatlán (riv.), Mex. 142/D3
Petatlán, Mex. 143/E5
Petauke, Zam. 105/F3
Petawawa, On, Can. 130/E2
Petawawa, On, Can. 130/E2
Peten Itzá (lake), Guat. 144/D2
Petenwell (lake), Wi, US 127/L4
Peter (isl.), Nor. 160/U
Peterborough, Austl. 113/H5
Peterborough, On, Can. 130/E2
Peterborough, Eng, UK 33/F1
Peterborough (co.), Eng, UK 33/F1
Peterhead, Sc, UK 36/E1
Peterlee, Eng, UK 35/G2
Petermann Abor. Land, Austl. 113/F3
Pharr, Tx, US 132/D5
Petersaurach, Ger. 54/D4
Petersberg, Ger. 54/E5
Petersburg, Ak, US 134/M4
Petersfield, Eng, UK 33/F4
Petershagen, Ger. 51/F4
Petershagen, Ger. 40/G6
Petershausen, Ger. 55/E6
Peterson, Ut, US 137/K11
Pétervására, Hun. 49/Q9
Petilia Policastro, It. 46/E3
Pétionville, Haiti 145/H2
Petit Goâve, Haiti 145/H2
Petit Lac Manicouagan (lake), Qu, Can. 131/H1
Petit Loango, PN du, Gabon 105/A2
Petit-Noir, Fr. 56/B4
Petit Rosne (riv.), Fr. 30/J4
Petitcodiac, NB, Can. 131/H2
Petite Miquelon (isl.), StP.
Petite Rivière de l'Artibonite, Haiti 145/H2
Petite Rivière Noire (peak), Mrts. 107/T15
Petite-Rosselle, Fr. 53/F5
Petitt Morin (riv.), Fr. 42/E2
Petkeljärven NP, Fin. 60/Q2
Petlād, India 89/K4
Petlalcingo, Mex. 144/D1
Peto, Mex. 144/D1
Petorca, Chile 158/C2
Petoskey, Mi, US 130/C2
Petra (Batrā') (ruin), Jor. 91/F4
Petra (isl.), Rus. 65/M2
Petrel, Sp. 45/E3
Petrella (peak), It. 46/C2
Petrich, Bul. 47/H2
Petrified Forest NP, Az, US 137/R19
Petrodvorets, Rus. 63/N2
Petrokhanski Prohod (pass), Bul. 47/H1
Petrokrepost' (bay), Rus. 61/U7
Petrolândia, Braz. 154/C3
Petrolina, Braz. 154/B3
Petropavl, Kaz. 87/E2
Petropavlovsk-Kamchatskiy, Rus. 65/R4
Petrópolis, Braz. 211/K7
Petrovaradin, Serb. 48/D3
Petrovsk, Rus. 63/H1
Petrovsk-Zabaykal'skiy, Rus. 70/J1
Petrozavodsk, Rus. 60/G3
Petrus Steyn, SAfr. 106/E2
Petrusburg, SAfr. 106/D3
Petrusville, SAfr. 106/D3
Pettenbach, Aus. 55/H7
Petterril (riv.), Eng, UK 35/F2
Petzeck (peak), Aus. 43/K3
Peuerbach, Aus. 44/D3
Peulik (mt.), Ak, US 134/G4
Peumo, Chile 158/T9
Pevely, Mo, US 137/G9
Pewaukee (lake), Wi, US 135/X13
Pewaukee, Wi, US 135/P13
Peyrehorade, Fr. 42/C5
Peza (riv.), Rus. 61/K2
Pézenas, Fr. 42/E5
Pfaffenhausen, Ger. 55/D5
Pfaffenhofen an der Ilm, Ger. 55/E5
Pfaffenhofen an der Ilm, Ger. 55/E5
Pfaffenhoffen, Fr. 53/G6
Pfäffikon, Swi. 57/E3
Pfaffing, Ger. 55/F6
Pfaffnau, Swi. 56/D3

Pfahl (ridge), Ger. 55/F4
Pfälzer Wald (mts.), Port. 44/B2
Piazza, It. 53/G5
Pfälzerwald (mts.), Ger. 54/A4
Pfarrkirchen, Ger. 55/F6
Pfarrhof Esternberg, Aus. 55/H5
Pfatter, Ger. 55/F5
Pfeffenhausen, Ger. 55/E5
Pfettrach (riv.), Ger. 55/E5
Pfieffe (riv.), Ger. 51/G6
Pfinztal, Ger. 54/B5
Pforzheim, Ger. 54/B5
Pfreimd, Ger. 55/F3
Pfreimd (riv.), Ger. 55/F3
Pfronstetten, Ger. 57/F1
Pfronten, Ger. 57/G2
Pfroslkopf (peak), Aus. 57/G4
Pfullendorf, Ger. 57/F2
Pfunds, Aus. 57/G4
Pfungstadt, Ger. 54/B3
Phagwara, India 86/D5
Phalauda, India 86/D5
Phalempin, Fr. 52/C2
Phalodi, India 89/K3
Phalsbourg, Fr. 53/G6
Phan Rang, Viet. 78/E4
Phan Thiet, Viet. 78/E4
Phanat Nikhom, Thai. 78/C3
Phangnga, Thai. 78/B4
Phangnga, Thai. 78/B4
Phanom Dongrak (mts.), Thai. 83/H5
Pharr, Tx, US 132/D5
Phatthalung, Thai. 78/C5
Phaya Fo (peak), Thai. 78/C2
Phayao, Thai. 78/C2
Phelan, Ca, US 136/C2
Phelps, Ca, US 136/C2
Phenix City, Al, US 133/G3
Phet Buri, Thai. 78/B3
Phetchabun, Thai. 78/C2
Phichit, Thai. 78/C2
Philadelphia, Ms, US 133/F3
Philadelphia, Pa, US 138/C4
Philadelphia (int'l arpt.), Pa, US 138/C4
Philip, SD, US 127/H4
Philip S.W. Goldson (int'l arpt.), Belz. 144/D2
Philippeville, Belg. 52/D3
Philippi, WV, US 130/D4
Philippine (seas), Asia 79/D4
Philippines (ctry.) 79/D5
Philippsburg, Ger. 54/B4
Philipsdam (dam), Neth. 50/B3
Philipstown, SAfr. 106/D3
Phillaur, India 86/C4
Phillipsburg, NJ, US 138/C2
Phimai (ruin), Thai. 78/C3
Phitsanulok, Thai. 78/C2
Phnom Penh (Phnum Pénh) (cap.), Camb. 78/D4
Phnum Penh (int'l arpt.), Camb. 78/D4
Phoenix (cap.), Az, US 137/R19
Phoenix, La, US 137/R19
Phoenix (isls.), Kiri. 117/H5
Phoenix Park, Ire. 34/B5
Phoenix Sky Harbor (int'l arpt.), Az, US 137/S19
Phoenixville, Pa, US 138/C3
Phongsali, Laos 83/H3
Phou Bia (peak), Laos 78/C2
Phou Huatt (peak), Viet. 83/H3
Phou Loi (peak), Laos 78/C2
Phou Xai Lai Leng (peak), Laos 78/D2
Phra Nakhon Si Ayutthaya, Thai. 78/C3
Phra Thong (isl.), Thai. 78/B4
Phrae, Thai. 78/C2
Phu Hin Rong Kla NP, Thai. 78/C2
Phu Kradung NP, Thai. 78/C2
Phu Luong (peak), Viet. 83/H3
Phu Quoc NP, Viet. 78/D4
Phu Quoc (isl.), Viet. 83/H5
Phu Rua NP, Thai. 78/C2
Phu Tho, Viet. 83/J3
Phuket (isl.), Thai. 83/G6
Phuket, Thai. 78/B5
Phularwan, Pak. 84/D3
Phulpur, India 84/D3
Piaçabuçu, Braz. 154/C3
Piacenza (prov.), It. 58/C2
Piacenza, It. 58/C2
Piada, It. 58/C2
Pian di Serra (peak), It. 59/F6
Pian-Upe Game Rsv., Ugan. 104/B2
Piancastagnaio, It. 46/B1
Piancó, Braz. 154/C3
Pianella val Tidone, It. 58/C2
Pianezza, It. 59/F4
Piangipane, It. 59/F4
Pianoro, It. 59/E3
Pianosa (isl.), It. 46/A1
Piarco (int'l arpt.), Trin. 153/F2
Piasecznio, Pol. 41/L2
Piatra Neamt, Rom. 49/H2
Piauí (riv.), Braz. 154/B3

Piauí (state), Braz. 154/B2
Piave (riv.), It. 43/K3
Piazza, It. 58/D1
Piazza, It. 58/D1
Piazza al Serchio, It. 58/D4
Piazza Armerina, It. 46/D4
Piazza Brembana, It. 59/E1
Piazzola sul Brenta, It. 59/E1
Pic (riv.), On, Can. 122/G4
Pic de Nore (peak), Fr. 42/E5
Pic d'Orhy (peak), Fr. 42/C5
Pic du Canigou (peak), Fr. 42/E5
Pica, Chile 150/E8
Picacho del Centinela, Mex. 129/G5
Picachos, Cerro Dos, Mex. 142/B2
Picardie (pol. reg.), Fr. 42/E2
Picardy (reg.), Fr. 52/B4
Picatinny Arsenal, NJ, US 138/D2
Picayune, Ms, US 133/F4
Piccolo (isl.), It. 47/E2
Pichacani, Peru 156/D5
Pichanal, Arg. 157/D1
Pichidegua, Chile 158/N9
Pichilemu, Chile 158/B2
Pichincha (dept.), Ecu. 152/B3
Pichincha, Ecu. 152/B3
Pichl bei Wels, Aus. 55/G6
Pichor, India 84/B3
Pichucalco, Mex. 144/C2
Pickens, Ms, US 129/K4
Pickering, Micr. 116/D4
Pickering, On, Can. 131/R8
Pickering, Vale of (valley), Eng, UK 35/H3
Pikes Creek (res.), Pa, US 138/B1
Pikesville, Md, US 138/B5
Piketberg, SAfr. 106/L10
Pickle Lake, On, Can. 127/L3
Picnic Bay, Austl. 114/B2
Pikit, Phil. 79/D6
Pico da Neblina, PN do, Braz. 159/J12
Pila, Arg. 159/J12
Pico de Orizaba, PN, Mex. 143/M7
Pilanesberg (range), SAfr. 106/P12
Pico Rivera, Ca, US 136/F8
Pilani, India 86/C5
Pilão Arcado, Braz. 154/B3
Picos, Braz. 154/B2
Pilar, Par. 157/E2
Picota, Peru 156/B2
Pilar, Braz. 154/D3
Picsi, Peru 156/B2
Pilar, Arg. 158/E1
Picton, On, Can. 130/E3
Pilaya (riv.), Bol. 150/F8
Picton, NS, Can. 131/J2
Pilchuck (riv.), Wa, US 135/D1
Pictou, NS, Can. 131/J2
Pilcomayo (riv.), SAm. 147/C5
Pictured Rocks Nat'l Lakeshore, Mi, US 127/M4
Pictured Rocks Nat'l Lakeshore, Mi, US 130/C2
Picuí, Braz. 154/C2
Pilibhit, India 84/B1
Piddle (riv.), Eng, UK 32/D5
Pilica (riv.), Pol. 62/B2
Pidurutagala (peak), SrL. 82/D6
Pilion (peak), Gre. 47/H3
Piedade, Port. 45/P10
Pilis, Hun. 49/Q9
Piedade do Rio Grande, Braz. 211/J6
Pilis (peak), Hun. 49/Q9
Piedecuesta, Col. 152/C3
Pilis (mts.), Hun. 49/Q9
Piedimulera, It. 57/E5
Piliscsaba, Hun. 49/Q9
Piedmont (upland), US 133/J2
Pilisvörösvár, Hun. 49/Q9
Piedmont (pt.), Ca, US 135/J12
Pilkhua, India 86/D5
Piedmont, Ok, US 137/M14
Pillar (cape), Austl. 115/C4
Piedmont, Ca, US 135/K11
Pillar (pt.), Eng, UK 35/E3
Piedra Grande, Ven. 152/D2
Pilliga, Austl. 115/D1
Piedrabuena, Sp. 44/C3
Pillon, Col du (pass), Swi. 56/D5
Piedrahita, Sp. 44/C2
Pillow, Pa, US 138/B2
Piedras (pt.), Arg. 159/K11
Pilões, Serra dos (mtn.), Braz. 154/A5
Piedras Coloradas, Uru. 159/K10
Pilos, Gre. 47/G4
Piedras Negras, Mex. 132/C4
Pilot (mtn.), Tn, US 130/C4
Piedras Negras, Mex. 143/N8
Pilot Point, Ak, US 134/G4
Piedras, Rio de las (riv.), Peru 150/D6
Pilot Station, Ak, US 134/F3
Piedritas, Arg. 158/E2
Pilsting, Ger. 55/F5
Piekary Śląskie, Pol. 41/K3
Pima, Az, US 128/E4
Piekenierskloof (pass), SAfr. 106/L10
Pimpri-Chinchwad, India 89/K5
Pieksämäki, Fin. 60/E3
Piña (pt.), Pan. 152/B2
Pielavesi, Fin. 60/E3
Pináculo (peak), Arg. 159/B6
Piemonte (prov.), It. 43/G4
Pinal, Az, US 137/R19
Pieniński NP, Pol. 41/L4
Pinamar, Arg. 158/F3
Piennes, Fr. 53/E5
Pinang (cape), Malay. 80/A2
Pieńsk, Pol. 41/H3
Pinang (isl.), Malay. 78/B5
Piera, Sp. 45/K6
Pinang (isl.), Malay. 80/A2
Pierce, Id, US 127/J5
Pinar del Rio, Cuba 145/F1
Pierce, Co, US 137/C1
Pinarbaşi, Turk. 90/D2
Pierceland, Sk, Can. 126/F2
Pinarhisar, Turk. 49/H5
Pieris, It. 59/G1
Piñas, Ecu. 156/B1
Piermont, NY, US 139/K7
Pinatubo (mt.), Phil. 79/D4
Pierowall, Sc, UK 31/V14
Pinawa, Mb, Can. 127/K3
Pierre (cap.), SD, US 127/H4
Pincher Creek, Ab, Can. 126/E3
Pierre-de-Bresse, Fr. 56/B4
Pinconning, Mi, US 130/D3
Pierre-Levée, Fr. 30/M5
Pincota, Rom. 48/E2
Pierrefitte-sur-Seine, Fr. 30/K5
Pińczów, Pol. 41/L3
Pierrefonds, Qu, Can. 131/N7
Pind Dādan Khān, Pak. 86/B3
Pierrefontaine-les-Varans, Fr. 56/C3
Pindamonhangaba, Braz. 211/H7
Pierrelatte, Fr. 42/F4
Pindaré (riv.), Braz. 151/J4
Pierrelaye, Fr. 30/J4
Pindaré-Mirim, Braz. 154/A1
Pierrevert, Fr. 42/F4
Pindhos NP, Gre. 47/G3
Pierry, Fr. 52/C5
Pindi Bhattian, Pak. 86/B4
Piešťany, Slvk. 41/J4
Pindi Gheb, Pak. 86/B4
Pindobaçu, Braz. 154/B3
Piesting (riv.), Aus. 49/P7
Pindus (mts.), Gre. 47/G3
Piet Retief, SAfr. 107/E2
Pindwāra, India 89/K4
Pietermaritzburg, SAfr. 107/E3
Pine Barrens (phys. reg.), NJ, US 138/D4
Pietersburg, SAfr. 105/E5
Pietra Ligure, It. 58/B4
Pietralunga, It. 59/F6
Pietramelara, It. 46/D2
Pietravecchia (peak), It. 58/A5
Pietrosul (peak), Rom. 49/G2
Pietrosul (peak), Rom. 49/G2
Pieve del Cairo, It. 58/B2
Pieve di Cento, It. 59/E3
Pieve di Soligo, It. 59/F1
Pieve di Teco, It. 58/B4
Pieve Emanuele, It. 58/C2
Pieve Ligure, It. 58/B4
Pieve Porto Morone, It. 58/C2
Pieve Santo Stefano, It. 59/F5
Pieve Vergonte, It. 57/E6
Pigeon (lake), Ab, Can. 126/E2
Pigeon (riv.), On, Can. 122/G4
Piggott, Ar, US 129/K3
Pigs (bay), Cuba 140/E3
Pigüé, Arg. 158/E3
Pigüm (isl.), SKor. 73/C5
Pihāni, India 84/C2
Pijijiapan, Mex. 144/C3
Pijnacker, Neth. 50/B4
Pijol (peak), Hon. 144/D3
Pike (co.), Pa, US 138/C1
Pikelot (isl.), Micr. 116/D4

INDEX SECTION

212 Pine C – Port P

Pine Creek (pt.), Ct, US 139/E1
Pine Falls, Mb, Can. 127/J3
Pine Grove, Pa, US 138/B2
Pine Hill, NJ, US 138/D4
Pine Island, Mn, US 130/A2
Pine Island Bay (flat), Ant. 160/S
Pine Lawn, Mo, US 137/G8
Pine Point, NW, Can. 122/E2
Pine Ridge, SD, US 127/H5
Pine, South Branch (riv.), Mi, US 135/G6
Pine, The (hills), Mt, US 127/G4
Pinecliff (lake), NJ, US 139/H7
Pinecliffe, Co, US 137/B3
Pinedale, Wy, US 126/F5
Pinega (riv.), Rus. 64/E3
Pineimuta (riv.), On, Can. 127/L2
Pinelands, SAfr. 106/L10
Piñera, Uru. 159/K10
Pinerolo, It. 43/G4
Pinetown, SAfr. 107/E3
Pineuilh, Fr. 42/D4
Pineview (res.), Ut, US 137/K11
Pineville, La, US 129/J5
Pinewood Springs, Co, US 137/B2
Ping (riv.), Thai. 83/G4
Ping Chau (isl.), China 71/V9
Pingbian Miaozu Zizhixian, China 83/H3
Pingding, China 72/C3
Pingdingshan, China 72/C4
Pingdu, China 72/D3
Pingelap (isl.), Micr. 116/F4
Pingelly, Austl. 112/C5
Pinggu, China 72/H6
Pingguo, China 83/J3
Pinghe, China 79/C3
Pinghu, China 72/L9
Pingjiang, China 79/B2
Pingjing (pass), China 72/C5
Pingle, China 83/K3
Pinglu, China 72/B4
Pinglu, China 72/C3
Pingnan, China 79/B3
Pingquan, China 72/D2
Pingshan, China 72/C3
Pingshun, China 72/C3
Pingtan, China 79/C2
Pingtang, China 83/J2
P'ingtung, Tai. 79/D3
Pingxiang, China 83/K2
Pingxiang, China 83/J3
Pingxing Guan (pass), China 72/C3
Pingyao, China 72/C3
Pingyi, China 72/D4
Pingyin, China 72/D3
Pingyu, China 72/C4
Pingyuan, China 72/D3
Pinhal, Braz. 211/G7
Pinhal Novo, Port. 45/Q10
Pinhão, Braz. 155/B3
Pinheiro, Braz. 154/A1
Pinheiros, Braz. 154/B5
Pinhel, Port. 44/B2
Piniós (riv.), Gre. 47/G4
Pinjar (lake), Austl. 112/K6
Pinjarra, Austl. 112/B5
Pink, Ok, US 137/N15
Pinkafeld, Aus. 48/C2
Pinkawillinie Conservation Park, Austl. 113/G5
Pinkegat (chan.), Neth. 50/C2
Pinnacles Nat'l Mon., Ca, US 128/B3
Pinnaroo, Austl. 113/J5
Pinnau (riv.), Ger. 51/G1
Pinneberg, Ger. 51/G1
Pino Hachado (pass), Arg. 158/C3
Pino Torinese, It. 58/A2
Pinole, Ca, US 135/K10
Pinon Hills, Ca, US 136/C2
Pinos (mt.), Ca, US 128/C4
Pinos, Mex. 143/E4
Pinos, Isla de (Isla de la Juventud) (isl.), Cuba 140/E3
Pinos-Puente, Sp. 44/D4
Pinoso, Sp. 45/E3
Pins, Île des (isl.), NCal. 116/F7
Pinsdorf, Aus. 55/G7
Pinsk, Bela. 62/C1
Pinta, Isla (isl.), Ecu. 156/E6
Pinto, Sp. 45/N9
Pinto, Chile 158/C3
Pinzolo, It. 57/G5
Pio Ix, Braz. 154/B2
Pio Xii, Braz. 154/A1
Piobbico, It. 59/F5
Pioche, Nv, US 128/D3
Piombino, It. 43/J5
Piombino Dese, It. 59/F1
Pioneer World, Austl. 112/L7
Pioner (isl.), Rus. 64/J2
Pionki, Pol. 41/L3
Piorini (riv.), Braz. 150/F4
Piorini (lake), Braz. 153/F5
Piota (riv.), It. 58/B3
Piotrków Trybunalski, Pol. 41/K3
Piove di Sacco, It. 59/F2
Piovene-Rocchette, It. 59/E1
Piparia, India 84/B4
Pipe Spring Nat'l Mon., Az, US 128/D3
Piper, Ks, US 137/D5
Pipersville, Pa, US 138/C3
Pipestone (riv.), On, Can. 122/G3
Piplān, Pak. 86/A3
Pipmuacan (res.), Qu, Can. 123/J4
Pippingarra Abor. Land, Austl. 112/C2
Pipra, India 84/D3
Pipraich, India 84/D2
Piqua, Oh, US 130/C3
Piquet Carneiro, Braz. 154/C2
Piquete, Braz. 211/H7
Piquiri (riv.), Braz. 151/H7
Pīr Mahal, Pak. 86/B4
Pīr Panjal (range), India 86/C3
Piracanjuba, Braz. 155/B1
Piracicaba, Braz. 155/C2
Piracuruca, Braz. 154/B1
Pirae-bong (peak), NKor. 73/C2
Piraí, Braz. 211/K7
Piraí do Sul, Braz. 155/B3
Piraiévs, Gre. 47/N9
Piraju, Braz. 155/B2
Pirajuí, Braz. 155/B2
Pirámide (peak), Chile 159/B6
Piran, Slov. 59/G1
Pirané, Arg. 157/E2
Piranga (riv.), Braz. 155/D2
Piranhas (riv.), Braz. 151/L5
Piranji (riv.), Braz. 154/C2
Pirapemas, Braz. 154/A1
Pirapora, Braz. 154/A5
Pirapòzinho, Braz. 155/B2
Piraraja, Uru. 159/G2
Pirássununga, Braz. 155/C2
Pires do Rio, Braz. 155/B1
Pírgos, Gre. 47/G4
Pírgos, Gre. 47/J5
Piriápolis, Uru. 159/G2
Pirin (mts.), Bul. 47/H2
Pirin (peak), Bul. 47/H2
Pirin NP, Bul. 47/H2
Piripiri, Braz. 154/B2
Piritiba, Braz. 154/B3
Píritu, Ven. 152/D2
Pirkkala, Fin. 39/K1
Pirmasens, Ger. 53/G5
Pirna, Ger. 41/G3
Piro, India 85/E3
Pirot, Serb. 47/H1
Pirre (mtn.), Pan. 152/B3
Pirthīpur, India 84/C3
Piru (lake), Ca, US 136/B1
Piru, Ca, US 136/B2
Piryíon, Gre. 47/J3
Pisa (prov.), It. 59/D6
Pisa, It. 58/D5
Pisac, Peru 156/D4
Pisanino (peak), It. 58/D4
Pisau (cape), Malay. 81/E2
Pisba, PN, Col. 152/C3
Piscataway, Md, US 138/B6
Piscataway, NJ, US 138/D2
Pisco (riv.), Peru 150/C6
Pisco, Peru 156/B4
Piscobamba, Peru 156/B3
Písek (peak), Czh. 55/H3
Písek, Czh. 55/H4
Pishan, China 70/C4
Pishīn, Pak. 89/J2
Pīshīn, Iran 89/H3
Piskavica, Bosn. 48/C3
Pisoc (peak), Swi. 57/G4
Pisogne, It. 58/D1
Pissis (peak), Arg. 157/C2
Pistakee (lake), Il, US 135/P15
Pisticci, It. 46/E2
Pistoia (prov.), It. 59/D5
Pistoia, It. 59/D5
Pisuerga (riv.), Sp. 44/C1
Pisz, Pol. 41/L2
Pit (riv.), Ca, US 128/B2
Pitalito, Col. 152/B4
Pitanga, Braz. 155/B3
Pitcairn (isl.), Pitc. 117/N7
Pitcairn Islands (dpcy.), UK 117/N7
Piteå, Swe. 37/G2
Piteälven (riv.), Swe. 37/F2
Pitești, Rom. 49/G3
Píthion, Gre. 47/K2
Pithiviers, Fr. 42/E2
Pithoragarh, India 84/C1
Pitigliano, It. 46/B1
Pitiquito, Mex. 142/B2
Pitjantjatjara Abor. Lands, Austl. 113/F3
Pitkas Point, Ak, US 134/F3
Pitlochry, Sc, UK 36/D4
Pitman, NJ, US 138/C4
Pitmedden, Sc, UK 36/D2
Pitomača, Cro. 48/C3
Piton de la Fournaise (peak), Reun. 107/S15
Piton des Neiges (peak), Reun. 107/S15
Pitrufquén, Chile 158/B3
Pitt Water (bay), Austl. 114/H8
Pittenweem, Sc, UK 36/D4
Pittsburg, Ks, US 129/J3
Pittsburgh, Pa, US 130/E3
Pittsfield, Me, US 131/G2
Pittsfield, Ma, US 130/F3
Pittston, Pa, US 130/F3
Pittstown, NJ, US 138/D2
Pittsworth, Austl. 114/C4
Pitzbach (riv.), Aus. 57/G4
Piuí, Braz. 155/C2
Piumazzo, It. 59/E3
Piura, Peru 156/A2
Piura (dept.), Peru 156/A2
Pivdenny Buh (riv.), Ukr. 62/D2
Pivijay, Col. 152/C2
Pixoyal, Mex. 140/C4
Piz d'Err (peak), Swi. 57/F4
Pizacoma, Peru 156/D5
Pizarra, Sp. 44/C4
Pizhma (riv.), Rus. 61/K4
Pizol (peak), Swi. 57/F4
Pizzighettone, It. 58/C2
Pizzo, It. 46/E3
Pizzo dei Tre Signori (peak), It. 57/F6
Pizzo della Presolana (peak), It. 57/G6
Pizzo di Coca (peak), It. 57/G5
Pizzo di Vogorno (peak), Swi. 57/E5
Pizzuto (peak), It. 46/C1
Placentia, Nf, Can. 131/L2
Placentia (bay), Nf, Can. 131/L2
Placentia, Ca, US 136/G8
Placer, Phil. 79/E6
Placer (co.), Ca, US 135/M9
Placetas, Cuba 145/G1
Plachkovtsi, Bul. 47/J1
Plaffeien, Swi. 56/D4
Plai Mat (riv.), Thai. 78/C3
Plaidt, Ger. 53/G3
Plailly, Fr. 30/K4
Plain City, Ut, US 137/J11
Plain Dealing, La, US 129/J4
Plaine (riv.), Fr. 56/C1
Plainfield, NJ, US 139/H9
Plainfield, Il, US 135/P16
Plains, Tx, US 129/G4
Plains, Pa, US 138/C1
Plainsboro, NJ, US 138/D3
Plainview, Tx, US 129/G4
Plainview, Mn, US 130/A2
Plainview, NY, US 139/M8
Plaisir, Fr. 30/H5
Plan-les-Ouates, Swi. 56/C5
Planá, Czh. 55/F3
Plana Cays (isls.), Bahm. 145/H1
Planaltina, Braz. 154/A4
Plancher-Bas, Fr. 56/C2
Plancher-les-Mines, Fr. 56/C2
Plandište, Serb. 48/E3
Planeta Rica, Col. 152/C2
Planken, Lcht. 57/F3
Plant City, Fl, US 133/H4
Plantation, Fl, US 133/H5
Plaquemines (parish), La, US 137/Q17
Plasencia, Sp. 44/B2
Plasy, Czh. 55/G3
Plata (riv.), Arg. 147/D6
Plata (estu.), Arg.,Uru. 159/K11
Platani (riv.), It. 46/C4
Plate Taile, Barrage de la (dam), Belg. 53/D3
Plateau (state), Nga. 103/H4
Platí, Gre. 47/H2
Platinum, Ak, US 134/F4
Plato, Col. 152/C2
Platón Sánchez, Mex. 144/B1
Platte (riv.), Ne, US 129/H2
Platte City, Mo, US 137/D5
Platte, North (riv.), Ne,Wy, US 124/E3
Platte, South (riv.), Co, US 124/F3
Platteville, Co, US 137/C2
Plattling, Ger. 55/F5
Plattsburgh, NY, US 130/F2
Plauen, Ger. 55/F1
Plav, Serb. 47/F1
Plavna Dadaint (peak), Swi. 57/G4
Playa de los Muertos (ruin), Hon. 144/E3
Playa del Carmen, Mex. 144/E1
Playa Noriega (lake), Mex. 142/C2
Playa Vicente, Mex. 144/C2
Playas (lake), NM, US 128/E5
Playas, Ecu. 152/A5
Playgreen (lake), Mb, Can. 127/J2
Pleasant (lake), Az, US 137/R18
Pleasant Grove, Ut, US 137/K13
Pleasant Hill, Ca, US 135/K11
Pleasant Hill, Mo, US 137/E6
Pleasant Hills, Md, US 138/B5
Pleasant Valley, Mo, US 137/E5
Pleasant View, Ut, US 137/K11
Pleasant View, Co, US 137/B3
Pleasanton, Tx, US 129/H5
Pleasanton, Ca, US 135/L11
Pleasantville, NJ, US 138/D5
Pleasantville, NY, US 139/K7
Pleaux, Fr. 42/E4
Pleiku, Viet. 78/D3
Pleinfeld, Ger. 54/D4
Pleisse (riv.), Ger. 40/G3
Plenty (riv.), Austl. 115/G5
Plenty (bay), NZ 109/H6
Plentywood, Mt, US 127/G3
Plérin, Fr. 42/B2
Plesná (riv.), Czh. 55/F2
Pleso (int'l arpt.), Cro. 48/C3
Pleszew, Pol. 41/J3
Plétipi (lake), Qu, Can. 131/G1
Plettenberg, Ger. 51/E6
Pleurtuit (int'l arpt.), Fr. 42/B2
Pleven, Bul. 49/G4
Pliska, Bul. 49/H4
Plitvice Lakes NP, Cro. 48/B3
Pljevlja, Serb. 47/F1
Plobsheim, Fr. 56/D1
Plöcckenstein (peak), Ger. 55/G5
Ploče, Cro. 47/E1
Plochingen, Ger. 54/C5
Płock, Pol. 41/K2
Pločno (peak), Bosn. 48/C4
Plœmeur, Fr. 42/B3
Ploiești, Rom. 49/H3
Plomárion, Gre. 47/K3
Plombières, Belg. 53/E2
Plombières-lès-Dijon, Fr. 56/A3
Plön, Ger. 38/D4
Płońsk, Pol. 41/L2
Plouay, Fr. 42/B3
Ploučnice (riv.), Czh. 41/H3
Ploufragan, Fr. 42/B2
Plougastel-Daoulas, Fr. 42/A2
Plouguernével, Fr. 42/B2
Plouzané, Fr. 42/A2
Plovdiv (pol. reg.), Bul. 47/J2
Plovdiv, Bul. 47/J2
Plover Cove (res.), China 71/U10
Pluguffan (int'l arpt.), Fr. 42/A3
Plum (isl.), NY, US 139/F1
Plumridge Lakes Nature Rsv., Austl. 112/E4
Plumsteadville, Pa, US 138/C3
Plungė, Lith. 39/J4
Plymouth, Eng, UK 32/B6
Plymouth (co.), Eng, UK 32/B6
Plymouth (sound), Eng, UK 32/B6
Plymouth, NC, US 133/J3
Plymouth, NH, US 131/G3
Plymouth, In, US 130/C3
Plymouth, Wi, US 130/C3
Plymouth (cap.), Monts. 141/N8
Plymouth, Pa, US 138/C1
Plynlimon (peak), Wal, UK 32/C2
Plzeň, Czh. 55/G3
Plzeňský (pol. reg.), Czh. 55/G4
PNC Bank Arts Center, NJ, US 139/J10
Pniel, SAfr. 106/L10
Pniewy, Pol. 41/J2
Pô, Burk. 103/E4
Po (riv.), It. 27/F4
Po di Venezia (riv.), It. 59/F2
Po di Volano (riv.), It. 59/E3
Po Klong Garai Cham Towers, Viet. 78/E4
Po, Mouths of the (delta), It. 43/K4
Pô, PN de, Burk. 103/E4
Po Toi Group (isls.), China 71/V11
Po, Valle del (valley), It. 43/J4
Poá, Braz. 211/G8
Poa (riv.), Ven. 153/E2
Poag, Il, US 137/G8
Pobè, Ben. 103/F5
Pobedy (peak), Kyr. 70/D3
Pobiedziska, Pol. 41/J2
Pobla de Segur, Sp. 45/F1
Pocahontas, Ar, US 129/K3
Poção de Pedra, Braz. 154/A2
Pochep, Rus. 62/E1
P'och'ŏn, SKor. 73/G6
Pocinhos, Braz. 154/C2
Pöcking, Ger. 57/H2
Pöcking, Ger. 55/G6
Pocklington (reef), PNG 116/E6
Poço Fundo, Braz. 211/H6
Poções, Braz. 154/B4
Pocola, Ok, US 129/J4
Poconé, Braz. 151/G7
Pocono (mts.), Pa, US 138/C1
Pocono (lake), Pa, US 138/C1
Pocono Lake, Pa, US 138/C1
Pocono Pines, Pa, US 138/C1
Poços de Caldas, Braz. 211/G6
Pocrí, Pan. 152/A2
Podbořany, Czh. 55/G2
Poddębice, Pol. 41/K3
Podenzano, It. 58/C3
Podgorica, Serb. 47/F1
Podkarpackie (prov.), Pol. 41/L4
Podlasie (reg.), Bela.,Pol. 41/M3
Podlaskie (prov.), Pol. 41/M2
Podol'sk, Rus. 61/W9
Podor, Sen. 102/B2
Podporozh'ye, Rus. 60/G3
Podravska Slatina, Cro. 48/C3
Podujevo, Serb. 47/G1
Pofadder, SAfr. 106/B3
Poggibonsi, It. 59/E6
Poggio Renatico, It. 59/E3
Poggio Rusco, It. 59/E3
Poggiola, It. 59/E6
Pogromni (vol.), Ak, US 134/F5
P'ohang, SKor. 74/A2
Pohénégamook, Qu, Can. 131/G2
Pohja (Pojo), Fin. 39/K1
Pohjanmaa (reg.), Fin. 37/G3
Pohjois-Karjala (prov.), Fin. 60/F3
Pohnpei (isl.), Micr. 116/E4
Pohoiki, Hi, US 124/U11
Pohopoco Mtn. (mtn.), Pa, US 138/C2
Poigny-la-Forêt, Fr. 30/H5
Poing, Ger. 55/E6
Poinsett (cape), Ant. 160/H
Point (lake), NW, Can. 122/E2
Point au Fer (isl.), La, US 129/K5
Point Baker, Ak, US 134/M4
Point Fortin, Trin. 153/F2
Point Hope, Ak, US 134/E2
Point Lay, Ak, US 134/F2
Point Lookout (peak), Austl. 115/E1
Point Mugu Naval Air Sta., Ca, US 136/A2
Point Mugu State Park, Ca, US 136/A2
Point of Aire (pt.), Wal, UK 35/E5
Point of Ayre (pt.), IM, UK 34/D3
Point Pelee NP, On, Can. 130/D3
Point Pleasant, WV, US 130/D4
Point Pleasant, NJ, US 138/D3
Point Pleasant, Pa, US 138/C3
Point Pleasant Beach, NJ, US 138/D3
Point Salines (int'l arpt.), Gren. 153/F1
Point Salvation Abor. Rsv., Austl. 112/D4
Pointe-à-Pitre, Fr. 141/N8
Pointe à Raquette, Haiti 145/H2
Pointe-aux-Trembles, Qu, Can. 131/P6
Pointe-Calumet, Qu, Can. 131/N6
Pointe-Claire, Qu, Can. 131/N7
Pointe de Chassiron (pt.), Fr. 42/C3
Pointe de l'Arcouest (pt.), Fr. 42/B2
Pointe des Verres (peak), Fr. 56/C6
Pointe-du-Lac, Qu, Can. 131/F2
Pointe du Sablon (pt.), Fr. 42/F5
Pointe-Noire, Congo 105/B1
Poirino, It. 58/A3
Poissonier (pt.), Austl. 112/C1
Poissy, Fr. 30/J5
Poitiers, Fr. 42/D3
Poitou (reg.), Fr. 42/C3
Poitou-Charentes (reg.), Fr. 42/C3
Poix-de-Picardie, Fr. 52/A4
Poix-Terron, Fr. 53/D4
Pojuca, Braz. 154/C4
Pok Liu Chau (isl.), China 71/U11
Pokaran, India 89/K3
Pokharā, Nepal 84/D1
Pokhvistnevo, Rus. 63/K1
Pol-e Khomrī, Afg. 89/J1
Pola de Laviana, Sp. 44/C1
Pola de Lena, Sp. 44/C1
Pola de Siero, Sp. 44/C1
Polabská Nížina (phys. reg.), Czh. 43/L1
Pol'ana (peak), Slvk. 62/A2
Poland (ctry.) 41/K2
Połaniec, Pol. 41/L3
Polatlı, Turk. 90/C2
Polatsk, Bela. 39/N4
Polch, Ger. 53/G3
Połczyn-Zdrój, Pol. 38/G5
Pole of Inaccessability, Ant. 160/E
Polesella, It. 59/E3
Polesine (reg.), It. 59/E3
Poleski NP, Pol. 41/M3
Polgár, Hun. 48/E2
Pŏlgyo, SKor. 73/D5
Políaigos (isl.), Gre. 47/J4
Policastro, Golfo di (gulf), It. 46/D3
Police, Pol. 38/F5
Policoro, It. 46/E2
Poligny, Fr. 56/B4
Políkastron, Gre. 47/H2
Políkhni, Gre. 47/H2
Polikhnítos, Gre. 47/K3
Polillo (isl.), Phil. 79/D4
Polis, Cyp. 91/C2
Polistena, It. 46/E3
Políyiros, Gre. 47/H2
Polje, Slov. 43/L3
Polkowice, Pol. 41/J3
Polla, It. 46/D2
Pollença, Sp. 45/G3
Polochic (riv.), Guat. 144/D3
Polomolok, Phil. 79/E6
Polonia (cape), Uru. 159/G2
Polonnaruwa, SrL. 82/D6
Polonne, Ukr. 62/C2
Polski Trŭmbesh, Bul. 49/G4
Polson, Mt, US 126/E4
Poltava, Ukr. 62/E2
Poltavs'ka Oblasti, Ukr. 62/E2
Poluostrov Barsakel'mes (isl.), Kaz. 63/L3
Poluška (peak), Czh. 55/H5
Polvijärvi, Fin. 60/F3
Polyarnyy, Rus. 60/G1
Polynesia (reg.) 116/G6
Pomabamba, Peru 156/B3
Pomarance, It. 43/J5
Pomarico, It. 46/E2
Pomáz, Hun. 49/R9
Pomba (riv.), Som. 155/D2
Pombal, Braz. 154/C2
Pombal, Port. 44/A3
Pombas, CpV. 93/J9
Pomerania (reg.), Pol. 38/F4
Pomeranian (bay), Ger.,Pol. 38/F4
Pomerode, Braz. 155/B3
Pomeroon-Supenaam (pol. reg.), Guy. 153/G3
Pomeroy, Wa, US 126/D4
Pomeroy, NI, UK 34/B2
Pommersfelden, Ger. 54/D3
Pomona, Ca, US 136/C2
Pomona, NJ, US 138/D5
Pomona, Md, US 138/B5
Pomorie, Bul. 49/H4
Pomorskie (prov.), Pol. 41/J1
Pomos (pt.), Cyp. 91/C2
Pompano Beach, Fl, US 133/H5
Pompei (ruin), It. 46/D2
Pompeu, Braz. 155/C1
Pompey, Fr. 53/F6
Pompeys Pillar Nat'l Mon., Mt, US 126/G4
Pompiano, It. 58/C2
Pompton (riv.), NJ, US 139/H8
Pompton Lakes, NJ, US 139/H8
Poncarale, It. 58/D2
Ponce, PR 141/M8
Ponchatoula, La, US 137/P16
Poncheville (lake), Qu, Can. 130/E1
Pond, Mo, US 137/F8
Pond (inlet), Nun., Can. 123/J1
Pond (pt.), Ct, US 139/E1
Pond Inlet, Nun., Can. 123/J1
Pondicherry (terr.), India 70/D8
Pondicherry, India 82/C5
Ponente, Riviera di (coast), Fr. 58/B5
Ponferrada, Sp. 44/B1
Pongdong, SKor. 73/D5
Ponghwa, SKor. 74/A2
Pongolo (riv.), SAfr. 107/E2
Poni (prov.), Burk. 102/E4
Poniatowa, Pol. 41/M3
Ponnaiyar (riv.), India 82/C5
Ponoka, Ab, Can. 126/E2
Ponoy (riv.), Rus. 64/D3
Pons, Fr. 42/C4
Ponsacco, It. 58/D5
Pont-à-Celles, Belg. 53/D3
Pont-à-Marcq, Fr. 52/C2
Pont-D'Ain, Fr. 56/B5
Pont-de-Chéruy, Fr. 56/B6
Pont-de-Roide, Fr. 56/C3
Pont-de-Vaux, Fr. 56/A5
Pont-de-Veyle, Fr. 56/A5
Pont-du-Château, Fr. 42/E4
Pont-Remy, Fr. 52/A3
Pont-Saint-Esprit, Fr. 42/F4
Pont-Saint-Martin, It. 58/A1
Pont-Sainte-Maxence, Fr. 52/B5
Ponta Delgada, Azor., Port. 45/T13
Ponta do Pico (peak), Azor., Port. 45/S12
Ponta Grossa, Braz. 155/B3
Ponta Porã, Braz. 157/E1
Pontalina, Braz. 155/B1
Pontarlier, Fr. 56/C4
Pontarmé, Fr. 30/K4
Pontassieve, It. 59/E5
Pontault-Combault, Fr. 30/K5
Pontax (riv.), Qu, Can. 130/E1
Pontcarré, Fr. 30/L5
Pontchartrain (lake), La, US 125/H5
Pontchâteau, Fr. 42/B3
Ponte Alta do Bom Jesus, Braz. 154/A4
Ponte Alta do Tocantins, Braz. 154/A3
Ponte Buggianese, It. 59/D5
Ponte de Sor, Port. 44/A3
Ponte dell'Olio, It. 58/C3
Ponte di Legno, It. 57/G5
Ponte di Piave, It. 59/F1
Ponte do Lima, Port. 44/A2
Ponte Lambro, It. 58/C1
Ponte Nova, Braz. 155/D2
Ponte San Nicolò, It. 59/E2
Pontecagnano, It. 46/D2
Pontecorvo, It. 46/C2
Pontecurone, It. 58/B3
Pontedera, It. 58/D5
Pontefract, Eng, UK 35/G4
Ponteland, Eng, UK 35/G1
Pontelongo, It. 59/F2
Pontenure, It. 58/C3
Pontes e Lacerda, Braz. 150/G7
Pontestura, It. 58/B2
Pontevedra, Sp. 44/A1
Pontevico, It. 58/D2
Ponthévrard, Fr. 30/H6
Ponthieu (reg.), Fr. 52/A3
Pontiac, Il, US 127/L5
Pontiac, Mi, US 130/D3
Pontiac (lake), Mi, US 135/E6
Pontianak, Indo. 80/C4
Pontivy, Fr. 42/B2
Pontoise, Fr. 30/J4
Pontoon Beach, Il, US 137/G8
Pontotoc, Ms, US 133/F3
Pontpoint, Fr. 52/B5
Pontremoli, It. 58/C4
Pontresina, Swi. 57/F5
Pontypool, Wal, UK 32/C3
Ponza, It. 46/C2
Ponziane, Isole (isls.), It. 46/C2
Poole, Eng, UK 32/E5
Poole (bay), Eng, UK 33/E5
Poole (co.), Eng, UK 32/D5
Poolewe, Sc, UK 31/R8
Poona (Pune), India 89/K5
Poondarrie (peak), Austl. 112/C3
Poondinna (mt.), Austl. 113/F3
Poopó (lake), Bol. 147/C4
Poortugaal, Neth. 50/B5
Pöösapää (pt.), Est. 39/K2
Poosepatuck Ind. Res., NY, US 139/F2
Popayán, Col. 152/B4
Poperinge, Belg. 52/B2
Popigochic (riv.), Mex. 142/C2
Popilta (lake), Austl. 113/J5
Popio (lake), Austl. 115/B2
Poplar, Mt, US 127/G3
Poplar (riv.), Mb,On, Can. 122/G3
Poplar (isl.), Md, US 138/B6
Poplar Bluff, Mo, US 129/K3
Poplarville, Ms, US 133/F4
Popocatépetl (vol.), Mex. 143/L7
Popoli, It. 46/C1
Popovo, Bul. 49/H4
Poppberg (peak), Ger. 55/E4
Poppenhausen, Ger. 54/D2
Poppenhausen, Ger. 54/C2
Poppi, It. 59/E5
Poprad, Slvk. 41/L4
Poprad (riv.), Slvk. 41/L4
Poranga, Braz. 154/B2
Porangatu, Braz. 151/J6
Porbandar, India 89/J4
Porcari, It. 58/D5
Porce (riv.), Col. 152/C3
Porcheville, Fr. 30/H5
Porcia, It. 59/F1
Porcuna, Sp. 44/C4
Porcupine (riv.), Can.,US 134/K2
Porcupine Gorge NP, Austl. 114/B3
Porcupine Plain, Sk, Can. 127/H2
Pordenone (prov.), It. 59/F2
Pordenone, It. 59/F1
Pordim, Bul. 49/G4
Pore, Col. 152/D3
Poreč, Cro. 59/G2
Poretta (int'l arpt.), Fr. 46/A1
Pori (int'l arpt.), Fin. 39/J1
Pori, Fin. 39/J1
Porirua, NZ 117/S11
Porlezza, It. 57/F5
Pornic, Fr. 42/B3
Porongurup NP, Austl. 112/C5
Póros, Gre. 47/H4
Porpoise (bay), Ant. 160/J
Porrentruy, Swi. 56/D3
Porretta Terme, It. 59/D4
Porriño, Sp. 44/A1
Porsangen (inlet), Nor. 37/H1
Porsgrunn, Nor. 38/C2
Porsuk (riv.), Turk. 90/B2
Port (isl.), Japan 77/H6
Port Alberni, BC, Can. 126/B3
Port Albert, Austl. 115/C3
Port Alexander, Ak, US 134/M4
Port Alfred, SAfr. 106/D4
Port Alice, BC, Can. 126/B3
Port Angeles, Wa, US 126/C3
Port Antonio, Jam. 145/G2
Port Appin, Sc, UK 36/A3
Port Arthur, Tx, US 129/J5
Port au Choix, Nf, Can. 131/K1
Port-au-Prince (cap.), Haiti 145/H2
Port Augusta, Austl. 113/H5
Port Bannatyne, Sc, UK 36/A5
Port Blair, India 83/F5
Port Blakely, Wa, US 135/C2
Port Bolivar, Tx, US 132/E4
Port-Bouët, C.d'Iv. 102/E5
Port Bouet (Abidgan) (int'l arpt.), C.d'Iv. 102/E5
Port Broughton, Austl. 113/H5
Port Canning, India 85/G4
Port Carbon, Pa, US 138/B2
Port Charlotte, Fl, US 133/H5
Port Chester, NY, US 139/L8
Port Clements, BC, Can. 134/M5
Port Clinton, Oh, US 130/D3
Port Clinton, Pa, US 138/B2
Port Colborne, On, Can. 131/R10
Port Columbus (int'l arpt.), Oh, US 130/D4
Port Davey (har.), Austl. 115/C4
Port-de-Paix, Haiti 145/H2
Port Deposit, Md, US 138/B4
Port Dickson, Malay. 80/B3
Port Discovery (bay), Wa, US 135/B1
Port Douglas, Austl. 114/B2
Port Edward, BC, Can. 134/M4
Port Elgin, On, Can. 130/D2
Port Elizabeth, SAfr. 106/D4
Port Elizabeth, NJ, US 138/D5
Port Ellen, Sc, UK 31/Q9
Port Elliot, Austl. 113/H5
Port Erin, IM, UK 34/D3
Port-Eynon (pt.), Wal, UK 32/B3
Port Fairy, Austl. 115/B3
Port Gamble, Wa, US 135/B2
Port Gamble Ind. Res., Wa, US 135/B2
Port-Gentil, Gabon 96/G8
Port Gibson, Ms, US 129/K5
Port Glasgow, Sc, UK 36/B5
Port Graham, Ak, US 134/H4
Port Harcourt (int'l arpt.), Nga. 103/G5
Port Harcourt, Nga. 103/G5
Port Hardy, BC, Can. 126/B3
Port Hawkesbury, NS, Can. 131/J2
Port Hedland, Austl. 112/C2
Port Hedland (int'l arpt.), Austl. 112/C2
Port Heiden, Ak, US 134/G4
Port Hueneme, Ca, US 136/A2
Port Huron, Mi, US 130/D3
Port Isaac (bay), Eng, UK 32/B5
Port Jefferson, NY, US 139/E2
Port-la-Nouvelle, Fr. 42/E5
Port Lambton, On, Can. 135/H6
Port Lavaca, Tx, US 129/H5
Port Lincoln, Austl. 113/G5
Port Lions, Ak, US 134/H4
Port Loko, SLeo. 102/B4
Port-Louis, Fr. 141/N8
Port Louis (cap.), Mrts. 107/T15
Port Macdonnell, Austl. 115/B3
Port Macquarie, Austl. 115/E1
Port Madison Ind. Res., Wa, US 135/B2
Port Maria, Jam. 145/G2
Port McNeill, BC, Can. 126/B3
Port-Menier, Qu, Can. 131/H1
Port Monmouth, NJ, US 139/J10
Port Nolloth, SAfr. 106/B3
Port Norris, NJ, US 138/C5
Port of Ness, Sc, UK 31/Q7
Port-of-Spain (cap.), Trin. 153/F2
Port Orange, Fl, US 133/H4
Port Penn, De, US 138/C4
Port Phillip (bay), Austl. 115/C3

Port Pirie, Austl. 113/H5
Port Reading, NJ, US 139/J9
Port Republic, NJ, US 138/D4
Port Royal, Pa, US 138/A2
Port Saint Joe, Fl, US 133/G4
Port-Saint-Louis-du-Rhône, Fr. 42/F6
Port Saint Lucie, Fl, US 133/H6
Port Saint Mary, IM, UK 34/D3
Port Shepstone, SAfr. 107/E3
Port Stevens (bay), Austl. 109/E4
Port-sur-Saône, Fr. 56/C2
Port Townsend, Wa, US 126/C3
Port-Vendres, Fr. 42/E6
Port Victoria, Austl. 113/H5
Port-Vila (cap.), Van. 116/F6
Port Wakefield, Austl. 113/H5
Port Washington, NY, US 139/L8
Port Weld, Malay. 80/B3
Porta Westfalica (pass), Ger. 51/F4
Porta Westfalica, Ger. 51/F4
Portachuelo, Bol. 150/F7
Portadown, NI, UK 34/B3
Portaferry, NI, UK 34/C2
Portage, Mi, US 130/C3
Portage Des Sioux, Mo, US 137/G8
Portage la Prairie, Mb, Can. 127/J3
Portalegre (dist.), Port. 44/B3
Portalegre, Port. 44/B3
Portales, NM, US 129/G4
Portarlington, Ire. 31/O10
Portbou, Sp. 42/E5
Porteirinha, Braz. 154/B4
Portel, Braz. 151/H4
Porters (lake), Pa, US 138/C1
Porterville, Ca, US 128/C3
Porterville, Ut, US 137/K12
Porterville, SAfr. 106/L10
Portes-lès-Valence, Fr. 42/F4
Portet-sur-Garonne, Fr. 42/D5
Portete (bay), Col. 145/J3
Portglenone, NI, UK 34/B2
Portimão, Port. 44/A4
Portishead, Eng, UK 32/D4
Portknockie, Sc, UK 36/D1
Portland, Austl. 115/D2
Portland, Austl. 115/B3
Portland (cape), Austl. 115/C4
Portland (pt.), Jam. 145/G2
Portland, In, US 130/C4
Portland, Me, US 131/G3
Portland, Or, US 126/C4
Portland (int'l arpt.), Or, US 126/C4
Portland, Tn, US 130/C4
Portland Canal (inlet), BC, Can. 134/M4
Portland Jetport (int'l arpt.), Me, US 131/G3
Portlaoise, Ire. 31/O10
Portlaw, Ire. 31/O10
Portlethen, Sc, UK 36/D2
Portmarnock, Ire. 34/B5
Portmore, Jam. 145/G2
Portneuf (riv.), Qu, Can. 131/G1
Porto (dist.), Port. 44/A2
Porto (int'l arpt.), Port. 44/A2
Porto (gulf), Fr. 46/A1
Porto, Port. 44/A2
Porto Azzurro, It. 43/J5
Porto Belo, Braz. 155/B3
Porto Calvo, Braz. 154/D3
Porto Ceresio, It. 57/E6
Pôrto da Folha, Braz. 154/D3
Porto de Mós, Port. 44/A3
Porto Empedocle, It. 46/C4
Porto Ercole, It. 46/B1
Porto Ferreira, Braz. 155/C2
Porto Franco, Braz. 154/B2
Porto Garibaldi, It. 59/F3
Porto Inglês, CpV. 93/K10
Porto Nacional, Braz. 151/J6
Porto-Novo (cap.), Ben. 103/F5
Porto Potenza Picena, It. 59/G6
Porto Recanati, It. 59/G6
Porto Sant'Elpidio, It. 43/K5
Porto Santo (isl.), Port. 98/A3
Porto Santo Stefano, It. 46/B1
Porto Seguro, Braz. 154/D4
Porto Tolle, It. 59/F3
Porto Torres, It. 46/A2
Porto União, Braz. 155/B3
Porto Valtravaglia, It. 57/E6
Porto-Vecchio, Fr. 46/A2
Porto Velho, PN, Pan. 145/G4
Portocannone, It. 46/D2

Portocivitanova, It. 43/K5
Portoferraio, It. 43/J5
Portofino, It. 58/C4
Portogruaro, It. 59/F1
Portomaggiore, It. 59/E3
Portovenere, It. 58/C4
Portoviejo, Ecu. 152/A5
Portpatrick, Sc, UK 34/C2
Portree, Sc, UK 31/Q8
Portrush, NI, UK 34/B1
Portsea (isl.), Eng, UK 33/E6
Portslade-by-Sea, Eng, UK 33/F5
Portsmouth, Dom. 141/N9
Portsmouth, Eng, UK 33/E6
Portsmouth (co.), Eng, UK 33/E6
Portsmouth, NH, US 131/G3
Portsoy, Sc, UK 36/D1
Portstewart, NI, UK 34/B1
Portugal (ctry.) 44/A3
Portugalete, Sp. 44/D1
Portuguesa (riv.), Ven. 141/H6
Portuguesa (state), Ven. 152/D2
Portumna, Ire. 31/P10
Porvenir, Uru. 159/K10
Porvenir, Chile 159/C7
Porzuna, Sp. 44/C3
Posada, It. 46/A2
Posadas, It. 46/A2
Posadas, Arg. 157/E2
Posadas, Sp. 44/C4
Posavina (valley), Bosn. 48/C3
Poschiavo, Swi. 57/G5
Posio, Fin. 60/F2
Poso (lake), Indo. 81/F4
Posof, Turk. 90/E1
Posong, SKor. 73/D5
Posong (riv.), SKor. 73/D5
Posorja, Ecu. 152/A5
Posse, Braz. 154/A4
Possession (pt.), Wa, US 135/C2
Possession (sound), Wa, US 135/C2
Post, Tx, US 129/G4
Post Falls, Id, US 126/D4
Poste Maurice Cortier (ruin), Alg. 99/F5
Postmasburg, SAfr. 106/C3
Postojna, Slov. 43/L4
Postolprty, Czh. 55/G2
Potam, Mex. 142/C3
Potamós, Gre. 47/H5
Potaro-Siparuni (pol. reg.), Guy. 153/G3
Potchefstroom, SAfr. 106/D2
Poteau, Ok, US 129/J4
Potenza (riv.), It. 46/C1
Potenza, It. 46/D2
Potenza Picena, It. 59/G6
Potes, Sp. 44/C1
Potholes (res.), Wa, US 126/D4
Poti (riv.), Braz. 151/K4
Poti, Geo. 63/G4
P'ot'i, Geo. 63/G4
Potiraguá, Braz. 154/C4
Potomac (riv.), US 130/E4
Potomac, Md, US 138/A5
Potosi, Bol. 150/E7
Potosí, Mo, US 129/K3
Potrerillos, Chile 157/C2
Potsdam, NY, US 130/F2
Potsdam, Ger. 40/Q7
Pottawatomie (co.), Ok, US 137/N15
Pottenstein, Ger. 55/E3
Potters Bar, Eng, UK 30/C1
Pöttmes, Ger. 54/E5
Pottstown, Pa, US 138/C3
Pottsville, Pa, US 138/B2
Pottuvil, SrL. 82/D6
Poudre d'Or, Mrts. 107/T15
Poughkeepsie, NY, US 130/F3
Pouilley-les-Vignes, Fr. 56/B3
Poulaphouca (res.), Ire. 34/B5
Poulter (riv.), Eng, UK 35/G5
Poulton-le-Fylde, Eng, UK 35/G5
Poünn, SKor. 73/D4
Pourri (peak), Fr. 43/G4
Pouru-saint-Remy, Fr. 53/E4
Pouso Alegre, Braz. 211/H7
Pouthisat (riv.), Camb. 83/H5
Pouzauges, Fr. 42/C3
Považská Bystrica, Slvk. 41/K4
Povegliano Veronese, It. 59/D2
Poverty Point Nat'l Mon., La, US 129/K4
Poviglio, It. 58/D3
Póvoa de Varzim, Port. 44/A2
Povoação, Azor., Port. 45/T13
Pré-Saint-Didier, It. 56/C6
Povorino, Rus. 63/H1
Povungnituk (riv.), Qu, Can. 123/J2
Povungnituk, Qu, Can. 123/J2

Poway, Ca, US 136/C5
Powder (riv.), Mt,Wy, US 124/E2
Powell, Wy, US 126/F4
Powell (lake), Az,Ut, US 128/E3
Powell River, BC, Can. 126/B3
Power (res.), NY, US 131/R9
Powers (lake), Wi, US 135/P14
Powys (co.), Wal, UK 35/E6
Powys, Vale of (valley), Wal, UK 32/C1
Poxoreo, Braz. 151/H7
Poyang (lake), China 79/C2
Poynton, Eng, UK 35/F5
Poyo, Sp. 44/A1
Poysdorf, Aus. 41/J4
Poza Rica, Mex. 143/M6
Požarevac, Serb. 48/E3
Požega, Serb. 48/E4
Poznań, Pol. 41/J2
Pozo Alcón, Sp. 44/D3
Pozoblanco, Sp. 44/C3
Pozohondo, Sp. 44/E3
Pozuelo de Alarcón, Sp. 45/N9
Pozuelos, Ven. 153/E2
Pozuzo, Peru 156/C3
Pozza, It. 59/D3
Pozzallo, It. 46/D4
Pozzo Formigaro, It. 58/B3
Pozzonovo, It. 59/E2
Ppa. de Salamanca (plain), Arg. 158/F1
Prabuty, Pol. 39/H5
Pracham Hiang (pt.), Thai. 78/B4
Prachatice, Czh. 55/H4
Prachin Buri (riv.), Thai. 78/C3
Prachin Buri, Thai. 78/C3
Prachuap Khiri Khan, Thai. 78/B4
Praděd (peak), Czh. 41/J3
Pradera, Col. 152/B4
Prades, Fr. 42/E5
Prado, Braz. 154/C5
Prado del Rey, Sp. 44/C4
Prado Flood Control (basin), Ca, US 136/C3
Pragelpass (pass), Swi. 57/E4
Praha (Prague) (cap.), Czh. 55/H2
Praha (peak), Czh. 55/G3
Praha (pol. reg.), Czh. 55/H2
Prahova (prov.), Rom. 49/G3
Praia (cap.), CpV. 93/K11
Praia (int'l arpt.), CpV. 93/K11
Praia da Vitória, Azor., Port. 45/S12
Praia Grande, Braz. 211/G9
Prairie Dog Town Fk. (riv.), Tx, US 124/F4
Prairie du Chien, Wi, US 127/L5
Prairie Grove, Il, US 135/P15
Prairie View, Tx, US 129/J5
Prairie Village, Ks, US 137/D6
Prairies (riv.), Qu, Can. 131/N6
Pralboino, It. 58/D2
Pralungo, It. 58/B1
Pram (riv.), Aus. 55/G6
Pran Buri (riv.), Thai. 83/G5
Prangins, Swi. 56/C5
Prānhita (riv.), India 82/C4
Prapat, Indo. 80/A3
Praszka, Pol. 41/K3
Prat, Chile, Ant. 160/W
Prat (riv.), Braz. 155/B1
Prata, Braz. 155/B1
Prata di Pordenone, It. 59/F1
Prathersville, Mo, US 137/E5
Prätigau (valley), Swi. 57/F4
Prato, It. 59/E5
Prato (riv.), It. 59/E5
Prato allo Stelvio (Prad am Stilfserjoch), It. 57/G4
Prato (Leventina), Swi. 57/E5
Pratola Peligna, It. 46/C1
Pratomagno (mts.), It. 59/E5
Pratovecchio, It. 59/E5
Pratt, Ks, US 129/H3
Pratt (isl.), Chile 159/B6
Pratteln, Swi. 56/D2
Prattville, Al, US 133/G3
Prauthoy, Fr. 56/B2
Pravets, Bul. 47/H1
Pravia, Sp. 44/B1
Praxedis G. Guerrero, Mex. 129/F5
Praya, Indo. 81/E5
Preah Vihear (ruin), Camb. 78/D3
Précy-sur-Oise, Fr. 52/B5
Predappio, It. 59/E4
Predazzo, It. 43/J3

Predeal, Rom. 49/G3
Predosa, It. 58/B3
Preeceville, Sk, Can. 127/H3
Preetz, Ger. 38/D4
Preganziol, It. 59/F1
Pregarten, Aus. 55/H6
Pregolya (riv.), Pol. 39/J4
Pregolya (riv.), Rus. 41/L1
Pregonero, Ven. 152/D2
Preissac (lake), Qu, Can. 130/E1
Premana, It. 57/F5
Prémery, Fr. 42/E3
Premià de Mar, Sp. 45/L7
Prenzlau, Ger. 41/G2
Presanella (peak), It. 57/G5
Prescot, Eng, UK 35/F5
Prescott, Az, US 128/D4
Prescott, On, Can. 130/F2
Preševo, Serb. 47/G1
Presidencia Roque Sáenz Peña, Arg. 157/D2
Presidente Dutra, Braz. 154/A2
Presidente Epitácio, Braz. 155/A2
Presidente Olegário, Braz. 155/C1
Presidente Venceslau, Braz. 155/B2
Presidential Lake Estates, NJ, US 138/D4
Presidio, Tx, US 129/F5
Presidio (riv.), Mex. 142/D4
Preslav, Bul. 49/H4
Presles, Fr. 30/J4
Presles-en-Brie, Fr. 30/L5
Presnica Isabel, Braz. 154/C2
Prešov, Slvk. 41/L4
Prešovský (pol. reg.), Slvk. 41/L4
Prespa (lake), Eur. 47/G2
Presque Isle, Me, US 131/G2
Pressath, Ger. 55/E3
Pressbaum, Aus. 49/N7
Prestatyn, Wal, UK 35/E5
Prestea, Gha. 103/E5
Prestfoss, Nor. 38/C1
Preston (cape), Austl. 112/C2
Preston, Md, US 138/C6
Preston, Mn, US 135/D2
Preston, Eng, UK 35/F4
Prestonpans, Sc, UK 36/D5
Prestonsburg, Ky, US 130/D4
Prestwich, Eng, UK 35/F4
Prestwick (int'l arpt.), Sc, UK 36/B5
Prestwick, Sc, UK 36/B6
Prêto (riv.), Braz. 151/J6
Pretoria (cap.), SAfr. 106/D2
Pretty Boy (res.), Md, US 138/B4
Preussisch Oldendorf, Ger. 51/F4
Prevalje, Slov. 43/L3
Préveza, Gre. 47/G3
Prévost, Qu, Can. 131/M6
Prey Veng, Camb. 78/D5
Pribilof (isls.), Ak, US 134/D4
Priboj, Serb. 48/D4
Příbram, Czh. 55/H3
Privolzhskiy, Rus. 63/H2
Price (riv.), Ut, US 128/E3
Price, Ut, US 128/E3
Price, Md, US 138/C5
Prichard, Al, US 133/F5
Prichsenstadt, Ger. 54/D3
Priego, Sp. 44/D2
Priego de Córdoba, Sp. 44/C4
Prien am Chiemsee, Ger. 55/F7
Prieska, SAfr. 106/C3
Priest (lake), Id, US 126/D3
Priest River, Id, US 126/D3
Prieta (mtn.), Sp. 44/C1
Prievidza, Slvk. 41/K4
Prignitz (reg.), Ger. 40/F2
Prijedor, Bosn. 48/C3
Prijepolje, Serb. 48/D4
Prikaspian (plain), Kaz.,Rus. 64/C3
Prikumsk, Rus. 63/H3
Prilep, FYROM 47/G1
Prilly, Swi. 56/C4
Prima Porta, It. 46/C1
Prima Tapia, Mex. 128/C4
Prime Hook NWR, De, US 138/C6
Primeira Cruz, Braz. 154/B1
Primero (cape), Arg. 158/F1
Primero, Arg. 158/F1
Primorskiy Kray, Rus. 69/H5
Primorsko, Bul. 49/H2
Primorsko-Akhtarsk, Rus. 62/F3
Prims (riv.), Ger. 53/F4
Prince Albert, Sk, Can. 127/G2
Prince Albert (pen.), NW, Can. 122/E1
Prince Albert (sound), NW, Can. 122/E1
Prince Albert NP, Sk, Can. 122/F3
Prince Albert, SAfr. 106/C4
Prince Alfred (cape), NW, Can. 122/D1

Prince Charles (isl.), Nun., Can. 123/J2
Prince Edward (isl.), Can. 119/L5
Prince Edward Island (prov.), Can. 131/G3
Prince Edward Island NP, PE, Can. 131/J2
Prince Edward (isls.), SAfr. 23/L7
Prince George, BC, Can. 126/C2
Prince Georges (co.), Md, US 138/B6
Prince Gustav Adolf (sea), Nun., Can. 123/R7
Prince Leopold (isl.), Nun., Can. 122/G1
Prince of Wales (str.), NW, Can. 122/E1
Prince of Wales (isl.), Ak, US 122/C3
Prince Olav (coast), Ant. 160/D
Prince Patrick (isl.), NW, Can. 123/R7
Prince Regent (inlet), Nun., Can. 122/G1
Prince Rupert, BC, Can. 134/M4
Prince William (sound), Ak, US 122/B2
Princenhof (lake), Neth. 50/C2
Princes Risborough, Eng, UK 33/F3
Princes Town, Trin. 141/J5
Princesa Isabel, Braz. 154/C2
Princess Charlotte (bay), Austl. 109/D2
Princess Margaret (range), Nun., Can. 123/S6
Princess Royal (isl.), BC, Can. 122/C3
Princeton, Mn, US 127/K4
Princeton, BC, Can. 126/C3
Princeton, In, US 130/C4
Princeton, Ky, US 130/C4
Princeton, NJ, US 138/D3
Princeton Junction, NJ, US 138/D3
Princeville, Hi, US 124/S9
Príncipe (isl.), SaoT. 96/G7
Prindle (vol.), Ak, US 122/C2
Prineville, Or, US 126/C4
Pringsewu, Indo. 80/B5
Pringy, Fr. 56/C6
Prinsenbeek, Neth. 50/B5
Prinses Margriet (canal), Neth. 50/C2
Prinzapolka, Nic. 145/E3
Prinzapolka (riv.), Nic. 145/E3
Prior (cape), Sp. 44/A1
Priore (peak), It. 43/K5
Priozersk, Rus. 39/P1
Pripet Marshes (swamp), Bela.,Ukr 49/J3
Pripyat' (riv.), Ukr. 62/C2
Priština, Serb. 47/G1
Pritchard, Ger. 53/G2
Pritzwalk, Ger. 40/G2
Privas, Fr. 42/F4
Priyutovo, Rus. 63/K1
Prizren, Serb. 47/G1
Prnjavor, Bosn. 48/C3
Prnjavor, Bosn. 48/D3
Probištip, FYROM 47/H1
Probolinggo, Indo. 80/D5
Probstzella, Ger. 55/E1
Proctor (lake), Tx, US 132/D3
Proctor, Vt, US
Proddatūr, India 82/C5
Proença-a-Nova, Port. 44/B3
Profondeville, Belg. 50/C4
Progreso, Pan. 145/F4
Progreso, Mex. 144/D1
Progreso, Mex. 143/K6
Progreso, Uru. 159/K11
Progress, Rus. 71/N2
Progresso, It. 59/E3
Prokhladnyy, Rus. 63/G4
Prokuplje, Serb. 47/G1
Promised Land (lake), Pa, US 136/D8
Promissão, Braz. 155/B2
Promissão, Represa (res.), Braz. 155/B2
Propriá, Braz. 154/C3
Propriano, Fr. 46/A2
Proserpine, Austl. 114/C3
Prosna (riv.), Pol. 41/K3
Prospect Park, NJ, US 139/J8
Prosperidad, Phil. 79/E6
Prosperous, Ire. 34/C4
Prostějov, Czh. 41/J4
Proston, Austl. 114/D4
Proszowice, Pol. 41/L3
Protivín, Czh. 55/H4
Provadiya, Bul. 49/H4
Provence (reg.), Fr. 42/F5
Provence (int'l arpt.), Fr.
Provence-Alpes-Côte-d'Azur, Fr. 43/G4

Providence (cap.), RI, US 131/G3
Providencia, Isla de (isl.), Col. 140/E5
Providência, Serra de (mts.), Braz. 150/F6
Providenciales (isl.), Bahm. 145/H1
Provins, Fr. 42/E2
Provo, Ut, US 137/K13
Provo (riv.), Ut, US 137/K13
Provo (peak), Ut, US 137/K13
Provost, Ab, Can. 126/F2
Prozor, Bosn. 48/C4
Prudentópolis, Braz. 155/B3
Prudhoe (bay), Ak, US 134/J1
Prudhoe Bay, Ak, US 134/J1
Prudnik, Pol. 41/J3
Prüm (riv.), Ger. 40/D4
Prüm, Ger. 53/F3
Prunay-en-Yvelines, Fr. 30/H6
Prunelli-di-Fiumorbo, Fr. 46/A1
Pruszcz Gdański, Pol. 38/H4
Pruszków, Pol. 41/L2
Prut (riv.), Eur. 49/J2
Prutz, Aus. 57/G3
Pryluky, Ukr. 62/E2
Pryor, Ok, US 137/G5
Pryor (lake), Rus. 60/E5
Prypyats' (riv.), Bela. 62/D2
Przasnysz, Pol. 41/L2
Przemków, Pol. 41/H3
Przemyśl, Pol. 41/M4
Przeworsk, Pol. 41/M3
Przylądek Rozewie (cape), Pol. 38/H4
Przysucha, Pol. 41/L3
Psakhná, Gre. 47/H3
Psará (isl.), Gre. 47/J3
Psárion, Gre. 47/G4
Psël (riv.), Rus.,Ukr. 62/E2
Pskov (lake), Rus. 60/E5
Pskov, Rus. 39/N3
Pskovskaya Oblast, Rus. 60/F4
Psóvka (riv.), Czh. 55/H2
Pszczyna, Pol. 41/K4
Ptolemais, Gre. 47/G2
Ptuj, Slov. 43/L3
Pu Xian, China 72/B3
Puan, SKor. 73/D5
Pubei, China 79/A3
Pucacaca, Peru 156/B3
Pucallpa, Peru 156/C3
Pucará, Ecu. 156/B1
Pucará, Peru 156/B2
Pucará, Peru 156/C4
Pucarani, Bol. 156/D5
Pucauro, Peru 152/D5
Puchenau, Aus. 55/H6
Pucheng, China 79/C2
Pucheng, China 72/B4
Puchheim, Ger. 55/E6
Puch'on, SKor. 73/F7
Puchuncaví, Chile 158/N8
Puck, Pol. 38/H4
Pucking, Aus. 55/H6
Pucón, Chile 158/C3
Pucusana, Peru 156/B4
Pudasjärvi, Fin. 60/F2
Puderbach, Ger. 53/G2
Pudsey, Eng, UK 35/G4
Pudu (riv.), China 83/H2
Puebla (state), Mex. 140/B4
Puebla, Mex. 143/L7
Puebla de Alcocer, Sp. 44/C3
Puebla de Don Fadrique, Sp. 44/D4
Puebla de la Calzada, Sp. 44/B3
Puebla de Sanabria, Sp. 44/B1
Puebla de Trives, Sp. 44/B1
Puebla del Caramiñal, Sp. 44/A1
Pueblillo, Mex. 143/M6
Pueblito, Col. 152/C2
Pueblo, Co, US 129/F3
Pueblo Nuevo, Nic. 144/E3
Pueblo Nuevo, Ven. 152/D2
Pueblo Yaqui, Mex. 142/C3
Puelén, Arg. 158/C3
Puente Alto, Chile 158/N8
Puente Caldelas, Sp. 44/A1
Puente-Ceso, Sp. 44/A1
Puente del Inca, Arg. 158/C2
Puente-Genil, Sp. 44/C4
Puente Nacional, Col.
Puente Piedra, Peru 156/B3
Puenteareas, Sp. 44/A1
Puentedeume, Sp. 44/A1
Puentes de García Rodríguez, Sp. 44/A1
Pueo (pt.), Hi, US 124/R10
Puerco (riv.), NM, US 124/T8
Puerto Acosta, Bol. 156/D4
Puerto Aisén, Chile 159/B5
Puerto América, Peru 156/B2
Puerto Ángel, Mex. 144/B4
Puerto Armuelles, Pan. 145/F4
Puerto Asís, Col. 152/B4
Puerto Ayacucho, Ven. 153/E3
Puerto Ayora, Ecu. 156/E7

Puerto Baquerizo Moreno, Ecu. 156/F7
Puerto Barrios, Guat. 144/D3
Puerto Bermúdez, Peru 156/C3
Puerto Berrío, Col. 152/C3
Puerto Cabello, Ven. 152/D2
Puerto Cabezas, Nic. 145/F3
Puerto Carreño, Col. 153/E3
Puerto Cisnes, Chile 158/B5
Puerto Cortés, Col. 142/C3
Puerto Cortés, Hon. 144/E3
Puerto Cumarebo, Ven. 152/D2
Puerto de la Cruz, Canl.,Sp. 98/A3
Puerto de la Libertad, Mex. 142/B2
Puerto de Navacerrada (pass), Sp. 45/M8
Puerto del Rosario, Canl.,Sp. 98/B3
Puerto del Son, Sp. 44/A1
Puerto Deseado, Arg. 159/D5
Puerto El Carmen, Ecu. 152/C4
Puerto Escondido, Col. 152/C2
Puerto Escondido, Mex. 144/B3
Puerto Heath, Bol. 156/D4
Puerto Iguazú, Arg. 157/F2
Puerto Inca, Peru 156/C3
Puerto Ingeniero Ibáñez, Chile 159/B6
Puerto Inírida, Col. 152/E4
Puerto La Cruz, Ven. 153/E2
Puerto Leguízamo, Col. 152/C4
Puerto Lempira, Hon. 145/F3
Puerto López, Col. 152/C3
Puerto Lumbreras, Sp. 44/E4
Puerto Madero, Mex. 144/C4
Puerto Madryn, Arg. 158/D4
Puerto Magdalena, Mex. 142/B3
Puerto Maldonado, Peru 156/D4
Puerto Montt, Chile 158/B4
Puerto Morazán, Nic. 144/E3
Puerto Morelos, Mex. 140/D3
Puerto Napo, Ecu. 152/B5
Puerto Natales, Chile 159/B6
Puerto Obaldía, Pan. 152/B2
Puerto Ocopa, Peru 156/C3
Puerto Padre, Cuba 145/G1
Puerto Páez, Ven. 153/E3
Puerto Peñasco, Mex. 128/D5
Puerto Píritu, Ven. 153/E2
Puerto Portillo, Peru 156/C3
Puerto Prado, Peru 156/C3
Puerto Quellón, Chile 158/B4
Puerto Real, Sp. 44/B4
Puerto Rico, Col. 152/C4
Puerto Rico (dpcy.), US 141/M8
Puerto Rico, It. 46/C3
Puerto Rondón, Col. 152/C3
Puerto San Carlos, Mex. 142/B3
Puerto San Julián, Arg. 159/D6
Puerto Santa Cruz, Arg. 159/C6
Puerto Serrano, Sp. 44/C4
Puerto Suárez, Bol. 150/F7
Puerto Supe, Peru 156/B3
Puerto Tejada, Col. 152/B4
Puerto Vallarta, Mex. 142/D4
Puerto Varas, Chile 158/B4
Puerto Viejo, CR 145/E4
Puerto Villazón, Ecu. 156/E7
Puerto Wilches, Col. 152/C3
Puerto Williams, Chile 159/D7
Puertollano, Sp. 44/C3
Pueyrredón (lake), Arg. 158/C5
Puffin (isl.), Wal, UK 34/D5
Pugachev, Rus. 63/J1
Puget (sound), Wa, US 124/B2
Puglia (pol. reg.), It. 46/E2
Puigcerdà, Sp. 45/L6
Puiseux-en-France, Fr. 30/K4
Pujehun, SLeo. 102/C5
Pujiang, China 79/C2
Pujili, Ecu. 152/B5
Pujón (lake), NKor. 73/D2
Pujut (cape), Indo. 80/C5
Puk'an-san (peak), SKor. 73/F6
Puk'an-san NP, SKor. 73/D4
Pukapuka (isl.), Cookls. 117/J6
Pukaskwa NP, On, Can. 130/C1
Pukch'ŏng, NKor. 73/E2
Pukhan (riv.), NKor.,Rus. 73/D3
Pukhrāyān, India 84/B2
Pukovac, Serb. 47/G1
Pukp'o'ae-san (peak), NKor. 73/E2
Pula, Cro. 46/A3

Pulacayo, Bol. 150/E8
Pulandian (bay), China 73/A3
Pulandian (int'l), Phil. 81/F1
Pulap (isl.), Micr. 116/D4
Pulaski, Va, US 130/D4
Pulaski, Tn, US 133/G3
Pulau (riv.), Indo. 81/J5
Puławy, Pol. 41/L3
Pulguk-sa, SKor. 74/A3
Pulheim, Ger. 53/F2
Pulisan (cape), Indo. 81/G3
Pulkovo (int'l arpt.), Rus. 61/T7
Pullach im Isartal, Ger. 57/H1
Pullman, Wa, US 126/D4
Pully, Swi. 56/C5
Pulsnitz (riv.), Ger. 41/G3
Pułtusk, Pol. 41/L2
Pülümür, Turk. 90/D1
Puluwat (isl.), Micr. 116/D4
Pulversheim, Fr. 56/D2
Pum (riv.), China 85/F1
Puma (lake), China 83/F2
Puná, Isla (isl.), Ecu. 152/A5
Punākha, Bhu. 85/G2
Punata, Bol. 150/E7
Pünch, India 86/C3
Pünch (riv.), India 86/C3
Pündri, India 86/D5
Pune (Poona), India 89/K5
Punggai (cape), Malay. 80/B3
Punggye (falls), Zim. 89/K2
Punjab (plain), Pak. 86/C3
Punjab (state), Pak. 86/C3
Puno, Peru 156/D4
Puno (dept.), Peru 156/D4
Pünpün (riv.), India 85/E3
Punta Alta, Arg. 158/E3
Punta Arena (pt.), Mex. 142/C4
Punta Arenas, Chile 159/C7
Punta Banda (cape), Mex. 128/C5
Punta Cardón, Ven. 152/D2
Punta Celarain (pt.), Mex. 144/E1
Punta Colnett (pt.), Mex. 142/A2
Punta Colonet, Mex. 142/A2
Punta de Bombón, Peru 156/D5
Punta de Mata, Ven. 153/E2
Punta del Este, Uru. 159/G2
Punta del Este (Capitán Curbelo) (int'l arpt.), Uru. 159/G2
Punta Gorda, Fl, US 133/H5
Punta Gorda (bay), Nic. 140/E5
Punta Gorda, Belz. 144/D3
Punta Marina, It. 59/F4
Punta Raisi (int'l arpt.), It. 46/C3
Punta Umbría, Sp. 44/B4
Puntarenas, CR 145/E4
Puolo (pt.), Hi, US 124/S10
Pupiales, Col. 152/B4
Pupuya (peak), Bol. 156/D4
Puquio, Peru 156/C4
Pur (riv.), Rus. 64/H3
Puracé (vol.), Col. 152/B4
Puracé, PN, Col. 150/C3
Püranpur, India 84/C1
Purbeck (isl.), Eng, UK 32/D5
Purcell (mts.), BC, Can. 122/F3
Purcell, Ok, US 129/H4
Puré (riv.), Col. 152/D4
Purén, Chile 158/B3
Purgatoire (riv.), Co, US 129/G3
Pürgen, Ger. 57/G1
Puri, India 82/E3
Purificación, Col. 152/C4
Purkersdorf, Aus. 49/N7
Purmerend, Neth. 50/B3
Pürna, India 82/C4
Purnia, India 85/F3
Purranque, Chile 157/B5
Purué (riv.), Braz. 152/D5
Purūlia, India 85/F4
Puruni (riv.), Guy. 153/G3
Purús (riv.), Braz. 147/J23
Purushottampur, India 82/D4
Pürvomay, Bul. 47/J1
Purwa, India 84/C2
Purwokerto, Indo. 80/C5
Pusad, India 82/C4
Pusan, SKor. 71/N4
Pusan-Gwangyöksi (prov.), SKor. 74/A3
Pusat Gayo (mts.), Indo. 80/A3
Puschendorf, Ger. 54/D3
Pushkin, Rus. 61/T7
Püspökladány, Hun. 48/E2
Pusur (riv.), Bang. 85/G4
Putaendo, Chile 158/C2
Putian, China 79/C2

Redvers, Sk, Can. 127/H3   Remanso, Braz. 154/B3

Rochester, Wi, US 135/P14
Rochford, Eng, UK 30/F2
Rock (riv.), Ia,Mo, US 129/H2
Rock (riv.), Il, US 125/J3
Rock Creek, Yk, Can. 134/L3
Rock Forest, Qu, Can. 131/G2
Rock Glen, Pa, US 138/B2
Rock Hall, Md, US 138/B5
Rock Hill, SC, US 133/H3
Rock Island, Il, US 127/L5
Rock Springs,
  Wy, US 126/F5
Rockall (isl.), UK 27/C3
Rockaway (riv.),
  NJ, US 138/D2
Rockaway, NJ, US 138/D2
Rockaway (pt.),
  NY, US 139/K9
Rockaway (inlet),
  NY, US 139/K9
Rockdale, Il, US 135/P17
Rockefeller (plat.),
  Ant. 160/R
Rockenhausen, Ger. 53/G4
Rockford, Il, US 127/L5
Rockglen, Sk, Can. 126/F2
Rockhampton, Austl. 114/C3
Rockingham,
  NC, US 133/J3
Rockingham, Austl. 112/K7
Rockland, On, Can. 130/K2
Rockland, Me, US 131/G2
Rockland (co.),
  NY, US 138/D1
Rockland Lake,
  NY, US 139/K7
Rocklands (res.),
  Austl. 109/D4
Rockledge, Fl, US 133/H4
Rockledge, Pa, US 138/C3
Rockport, Tx, US 132/D4
Rocks, Md, US 138/B4
Rocksprings,
  Tx, US 129/G5
Rockstone, Guy. 153/G3
Rockville, Md, US 130/E4
Rockville Centre,
  NY, US 139/L9
Rockwall, Tx, US 129/H4
Rockwood, Tn, US 133/G3
Rocky (mtn.), Ky, US 130/D4
Rocky (pt.), NY, US 139/F1
Rocky Cape NP,
  Austl. 115/C4
Rocky Harbour,
  Nf, Can. 131/K1
Rocky Island (lake),
  On, Can. 130/D2
Rocky Mount, NC, US 133/J3
Rocky Mountain House,
  Ab, Can. 126/E2
Rocky Mountain NP,
  Co, US 126/F2
Rocroi, Fr. 53/D4
Rodach (riv.), Ger. 55/E2
Rodach bei Coburg,
  Ger. 54/D2
Rodalben, Ger. 53/G5
Rødberg, Nor. 38/C4
Rødbyhavn, Den. 38/D4
Roddickton, Nf, Can. 131/K1
Rødding, Den. 38/C4
Roden (riv.), Eng, UK 35/F6
Rodenbach, Ger. 54/C2
Rodeo, Mex. 142/D3
Rodeo, Ca, US 135/K10
Rödermark, Ger. 54/B3
Rodewisch, Ger. 55/F1
Rodez, Fr. 42/E4
Rodholivos, Gre. 47/H2
Ródhos (ruin), Gre. 90/B2
Ródhos (Rhodes),
  Gre. 90/B2
Rodigo, It. 58/D2
Roding (riv.), Eng, UK 35/H2
Roding, Ger. 55/F2
Rodinga (mt.), Austl. 113/G3
Rödinghausen, Ger. 51/F4
Rodoč, Bosn. 47/E1
Rodolfo Sánchez Toboada,
  Mex. 142/A2
Rodríguez, Uru. 159/K11
Roe (riv.), NI, UK 34/B2
Roebourne, Austl. 112/C2
Roebuck (bay), Austl. 112/D2
Roeland Park, Ks, US 137/D5
Roen (peak), It. 57/H5
Roer (riv.), Neth. 50/D6
Roermond, Neth. 50/C6
Roes Welcome Sound
  (str.), Nun., Can. 123/H2
Roeselare, Belg. 52/C2
Roesiger (lake),
  Wa, US 135/D2
Rogachev, Bela. 62/D1
Rogaland (co.), Nor. 37/C4
Rogaška Slatina, Slov. 43/L3
Rogatica, Bosn. 47/E1
Rogers (mt.), Va, US 130/D4
Rogers, Ar, US 132/J3
Rogers City,
  Mi, US 130/D3
Rogersville, Tn, US 130/D4
Roggwil, Swi. 57/F3
Rogliano, Fr. 43/H5
Roglio (riv.), It. 57/D6
Rognon (riv.), Fr. 42/F2
Rogoźno, Pol. 41/J2
Rogue (riv.), Or, US 128/B2
Rohl (riv.), Sudan 97/L6
Rohr, Ger. 55/E5
Rohrbach bei Mattersburg,
  Aus. 43/M3

Rohrbach in Oberösterreich,
  Aus. 55/G5
Rohrbach-lès-Bitche,
  Fr. 53/G5
Röhrmoos, Ger. 55/E6
Rohri, Pak. 89/J3
Rohtak, India 86/D5
Roi Et, Thai. 78/C2
Roine (lake), Fin. 39/L1
Roissy, Fr. 30/K5
Roissy-en-France, Fr. 30/K4
Rojas, Arg. 158/E2
Rojo (cape), PR 141/M8
Rojo, Cabo (cape),
  Mex. 144/B1
Roorkee, India 82/C2
Roosendaal, Neth. 50/B5
Roosevelt (canal),
  Az, US 137/S19
Roosevelt (riv.), Braz. 147/C4
Roosevelt (mt.),
  BC, Can. 122/D3
Roosevelt, NJ, US 138/D3
Roosevelt (isl.), Ant. 160/N
Roosevelt, NY, US 139/L9
Root (mt.), Ak, US 134/L4
Root (riv.), Wi, US 135/P14
Root, West Branch (riv.),
  Wi, US 135/P14
Roperton, Mb, Can. 127/J3
Roraima (peak), Braz. 153/H2
Roraima (peak), Ven. 153/F3
Roraima (state), Braz. 153/F4
Rolling Fork, Ms, US 129/K4
Rolling Hills Estates,
  Ca, US 136/F8
Rolling Meadows,
  Il, US 135/P15
Rollingbay, Wa, US 135/B2
Rollinsville, Co, US 137/D5
Rolo, It. 59/D3
Rom (peak), Ugan. 104/B2
Roma, Austl. 114/C4
Roma (Rome) (cap.),
  It. 46/C2
Romagnano Sesia,
  It. 58/B1
Romagnat, Fr. 42/E4
Romain (cape),
  SC, US 133/J3
Romaine (riv.),
  Qu, Can. 123/K3
Romano, Bul. 47/H1
Roman, Rom. 49/H2
Romang (str.), Indo. 81/G5
Romang (isl.), Indo. 81/G5
Romania (ctry.) 49/F3
Romano Canavese,
  It. 58/A2
Romano, Cayo (isl.),
  Cuba 145/G1
Romano d'Ezzelino, It. 59/E2
Romano di Lombardia,
  It. 58/C1
Romans d'Isonzo, It. 59/E2
Romans-sur-Isère, Fr. 42/F4
Romanshorn, Swi. 57/F2
Romanzof (cape),
  Ak, US 134/E3
Rombas, Fr. 53/F5
Romblon, Phil. 81/F1
Rome, NY, US 130/F3
Rome, Ga, US 133/G3
Rome, Wi, US 135/N14
Romeny, Fr. 56/B4
Romeoville, Il, US 135/P16
Römhild, Ger. 54/D2
Romilly-sur-Seine,
  Fr. 42/E2
Rommani, Mor. 76/D2
Rommerskirchen, Ger. 53/F1
Romney Marsh (phys. reg.),
  Eng, UK 33/G4
Romny, Ukr. 62/E2
Rømø (isl.), Den. 40/E1
Romoland, Ca, US 136/C3
Romont, Swi. 56/C4
Romorantin-Lanthenay,
  Fr. 42/D3
Romsey, Eng, UK 33/E5
Rømskog, Nor. 38/D2
Ronald Reagan Washington
  National (int'l arpt.),
  DC, US 138/A6
Ronan, Mt, US 126/E4
Roncade, It. 59/F1
Roncador Cay (isl.),
  Col. 141/F5
Roncador, Serra do (mts.),
  Braz. 151/H6
Ronchamp, Fr. 56/C2
Ronchi dei Legionari
  (int'l arpt.), It. 59/F1
Ronchi dei Legionari,
  It. 59/G1
Ronciglione, It. 59/F5
Ronco (riv.), It. 59/F5
Ronco All'Adige, It. 59/E2
Ronco Scrivia, It. 58/B3
Roncoferraro, It. 59/D2
Roncq, Fr. 52/C2
Rondane NP, Nor. 37/D3
Ronde, Tête (peak),
  Swi. 56/D5
Rondonópolis, Braz. 151/H7
Rong (riv.), China 83/J2
Rong Xian, China 83/K3
Rongcheng, China 73/B4
Rongcheng, China 72/G7
Ronge (lake),
  Sk, Can. 122/H2
Rongelap (isl.), Mrsh. 116/F3

Rongerik (isl.), Mrsh. 116/F3
Ronkonkoma, NY, US 139/E2
Rønne, Den. 38/F4
Ronne Ice Shelf, Ant. 160/W
Ronneby, Swe. 38/F3
Ronnenberg, Ger. 51/G4
Ronquerolles, Fr. 30/J4
Ronsard (cape), Austl. 112/B3
Ronsberg, Ger. 57/G2
Ronse, Belg. 52/C2
Ronuro (riv.), Braz. 151/H6
Roodeport, SAfr. 106/P13
Rooiberg (peak),
  Namb. 106/B2
Roorkee, India 82/C2
Roosendaal, Neth. 50/B5
Roper (riv.), Austl. 114/A1
Roque Pérez, Arg. 159/J10
Roquetas de Mar, Sp. 44/D4
Roraima (peak), Braz. 153/H2
Rorketon, Mb, Can. 127/J3
Rorschach, Swi. 57/F3
Rørvik, Nor. 37/D2
Rosa (cape), Alg. 100/L6
Rosà, It. 59/E1
Rosa (lake), Bahm. 145/H1
Rosa Punta (pt.), Mex. 142/C3
Rosa Zárate, Ecu. 152/B4
Rosablanche (peak),
  Swi. 56/D5
Rosal, Sp. 44/A2
Rosales, Mex. 132/B4
Rosamorada, Mex. 142/D4
Rosanna (riv.), Aus. 57/G3
Rosário, Braz. 154/A1
Rosario, Mex. 142/C3
Rosario, Mex. 142/D4
Rosario, Arg. 158/E2
Rosario, Uru. 159/K11
Rosario de la Frontera,
  Arg. 157/D2
Rosario del Tala,
  Arg. 159/J10
Rosário do Sul,
  Braz. 157/F3
Rosarito, Mex. 128/C4
Rosarno, It. 46/D3
Rosas, Col. 152/B4
Rosas, Golfo di (gulf),
  Sp. 45/G1
Rosate, It. 58/C2
Rosay, Fr. 30/G5
Rosbach vor der Höhe,
  Ger. 54/B2
Rosche, Ger. 51/H3
Roscoff, Fr. 42/B2
Roscommon, Ire. 31/Q10
Roscrea, Ire. 31/Q10
Rosdorf, Ger. 51/G5
Rose, It., ASam. 117/L6
Rose (pt.), BC, Can. 134/M4
Rose Belle, Mrts. 107/T15
Roseau, Mn, US 127/L4
Roseau (riv.), Mn, US 127/J3
Roseau (cap.), Dom. 141/N9
Roseaux, Haiti 145/H2
Rosebery, Austl. 115/C4
Roseburg, Or, US 126/C5
Rosedale, Ms, US 129/K4
Rosedale, Il, US 137/F7
Rosedale, Md, US 138/B5
Rosehearty, Sc, UK 36/D1
Roseland, NJ, US 139/H8
Roselette, Aiguille de
  (peak), Fr. 56/C6
Roselle, Il, US 139/H9
Roselle, Il, US 135/P16
Roselle Park, NJ, US 139/H9
Rosemead, Ca, US 136/F7
Rosemère, Qu, Can. 131/N6
Rosenberg, Tx, US 129/J5
Rosenberg, Ger. 54/D4
Rosenfeld, Ger. 57/E1
Rosenhayn, NJ, US 138/C5
Rosenheim, Ger. 43/K3
Roses, Sp. 45/G1
Roseto, Pa, US 138/C2
Roseto degli Abruzzi,
  It. 43/L5
Rosetown, Sk, Can. 126/G3
Rosetta (riv.), Egypt 91/B4
Roseville, Mi, US 135/G6
Rosewood Heights,
  Il, US 137/G8
Rosh Ha'ayin, Isr. 91/F7
Rosh Hakarmel (pt.),
  Isr. 91/F6
Rosh Haniqra (pt.),
  Isr. 91/D3
Rosheim, Fr. 56/D1
Rosières-en-Santerre,
  Fr. 52/B4
Rosignano Marittimo,
  It. 58/D6
Roşiori de Vede, Rom. 49/G3
Roskilde, Den. 38/E4

Roskilde (co.), Den. 38/D4
Roslavl', Rus. 62/E1
Roslev, Den. 38/C3
Rosmalen, Neth. 50/C5
Rosmaninhal, Port. 44/B3
Rosneath, Sc, UK 36/B4
Rosny-sous-Bois, Fr. 30/K5
Rosolina, It. 59/F2
Rosolini, It. 46/D4
Rosporden, Fr. 42/B3
Rosrath, Ger. 53/G2
Ross (isl.), Ant. 160/M
Ross (sea), Ant. 160/P
Ross, Austl. 115/C4
Ross (isl.), Mb, Can. 127/J2
Ross (pt.), On, Can. 131/S8
Ross (dist.), Sc, UK 36/C1
Ross Ice Shelf, Ant. 160/N
Rossa (peak), It. 43/K3
Rossa, Swi. 57/F5
Rossall (pt.), Eng, UK 35/E4
Rossano Stazione, It. 46/E3
Rossano Veneto, It. 59/E1
Rossbach, Ger. 55/F5
Rossberg (peak), Fr. 56/D2
Rossdorf, Ger. 54/B3
Rossel (isl.), PNG 116/E6
Rosselange, Fr. 53/F5
Rosshaupten, Ger. 57/G2
Rossiglione, It. 58/B3
Rossignol (lake),
  NS, Can. 131/H2
Rosskeeragh (pt.), Ire. 31/P9
Rossland, BC, Can. 126/D3
Rosso, Mrta. 102/B2
Rossosh', Rus. 62/F2
Rosstock (peak), Swi. 57/E4
Rosstal, Ger. 54/D4
Rossville, Ok, US 137/N14
Rostenburg an der Fulda,
  Ger. 51/G7
Roswell, NM, US 129/F4
Rot (riv.), Ger. 54/E4
Rot (riv.), Ger. 55/F5
Rota, Sp. 44/B4
Rota (isl.), NMar. 116/D3
Rote Wand (peak),
  Aus. 57/F3
Rotenburg, Ger. 51/G2
Rotenburg an der Fulda,
  Ger. 51/G7
Roter Main (riv.), Ger. 40/F3
Rötgen, Ger. 53/F2
Roth (riv.), Ger. 57/G1
Roth bei Nürnberg,
  Ger. 54/E4
Rothaargebirge (mts.),
  Ger. 51/F6
Rothau, Fr. 56/D1
Röthenbach an der Pegnitz,
  Ger. 54/E4
Rothenberg, Ger. 54/B3
Rothenburg, Ger. 55/H1
Rothenburg ob der Tauber,
  Ger. 54/D4
Rothera, UK, Ant. 160/V
Rotherham, Eng, UK 35/G5
Rotherham (co.),
  Eng, UK 35/G5
Rothes, Sc, UK 36/C1
Rothesay, Sc, UK 36/A5
Rotheux-Rimière,
  Belg. 53/E2
Rothschild, Wi, US 127/L4
Rothwell, Eng, UK 33/F2
Rothwell, Eng, UK 35/G4
Roti (isl.), Indo. 81/F6
Rotja, Serb. 47/G1
Rotorua, NZ 117/T10
Rotselaar, Belg. 52/E1
Rott am Inn, Ger. 55/F7
Rottach-Egern, Ger. 40/F5
Rotte (riv.), Swi. 57/F6
Rottenacker, Ger. 57/F1
Röttenbach, Ger. 54/E4
Rozzano, It. 58/C2
Rrëshen, Alb. 47/F2
Rt Kamenjak (cape),
  Cro. 43/L4
Rt Ploča (pt.), Cro. 48/B4
Rt Rečajna (cape),
  Cro. 48/A3
Ruacana (falls), Ang. 105/B4
Ruaha NP, Tanz. 104/B4
Ruapehu (vol.), NZ 117/T10
Rub' al Khali (des.),
  SAr. 67/D7
Rubelles, Fr. 30/L6
Rubeshibe, Japan 76/C2
Rubi, Sp. 45/L7
Rubidoux, Ca, US 137/J13
Rubiera, It. 59/D3
Rubigen, Swi. 56/D3
Rubim, Braz. 154/B5
Rubizhne, Ukr. 62/G2
Rubonda NP, Tanz. 104/A3
Rubtsovsk, Rus. 72/D1
Ruby, Ak, US 134/G3
Ruby, Laguna (lake), Fiji 116/G6
Ruby (riv.), Nv, US 128/D2
Ruby (mts.), Nv, US 128/D2
Rubyvale, Austl. 114/F7
Rucheng, China 83/H3
Rucphen, Neth. 50/B5
Ruda Woda (lake),
  Pol. 41/K2
Rudall River NP,
  Austl. 112/D2
Rudarpur, India 84/D2

Rougemont-le-Château,
  Fr. 56/C2
Rough (riv.), Ky, US 133/G2
Roullet-Saint-Estèphe,
  Fr. 42/D4
Round (hill), Pa, US 138/B3
Round Hill (pt.), Austl. 114/C4
Round Lake, Il, US 135/P15
Round Lake Beach,
  Il, US 135/P15
Round Lake Park,
  Il, US 135/P15
Round Rock, Tx, US 129/H5
Round Valley (res.),
  NJ, US 138/D2
Roundup, Mt, US 126/F4
Roundway (hill),
  Eng, UK 32/E4
Rousay (isl.), Sc, UK 31/V14
Rousies, Fr. 52/D3
Rousínov, Czh. 41/J4
Roussillon, Fr. 42/F4
Rouvres, Fr. 30/M4
Rouvroy, Belg. 53/E5
Rouxville, SAfr. 106/D3
Rouyn-Noranda,
  Qu, Can. 130/E1
Rovaniemi, Fin. 60/E2
Rovaniemi (int'l arpt.),
  Fin. 60/E2
Rovasenda, It. 58/B1
Rovato, It. 58/C1
Roverbella, It. 59/D2
Rovereto, It. 57/H6
Rovigo, It. 59/E2
Rovigo (prov.), It. 59/E2
Rovinj, Cro. 59/G2
Rovuma (riv.), Moz. 104/B5
Rowley (isl.),
  Nun., Can. 123/J2
Rowley Shoals (isl.),
  Austl. 112/C2
Roxa (isl.), GBis. 102/B4
Roxana, Il, US 137/G8
Roxas, Phil. 81/E1
Roxas, Phil. 81/F1
Roxas, Phil. 79/D4
Roxboro, NC, US 130/E4
Roxen (lake), Swe. 38/F2
Roxo (cape), Sen. 102/B3
Roy, NM, US 132/B3
Roy, Ut, US 137/J11
Roy, Wa, US 135/B3
Roya, It. 57/F3
Roya (riv.), Fr. 43/G5
Rum Cay (isl.), Bahm. 141/G3
Royal (canal), Ire. 35/B3
Royal Botanical Garden,
  On, Can. 131/Q9
Royal Chitwan NP,
  Nepal 85/E2
Royal Lakes, Il, US 137/H7
Royal Natal NP, SAfr. 106/E3
Royal NP, Austl. 115/D2
Royal NP, The, Austl. 114/H9
Royal Oak, Mi, US 135/F7
Royal Paekje Tombs,
  SKor. 73/D4
Royal Tombs, Viet. 78/D2
Royal Tunbridge Wells,
  Eng, UK 33/G4
Royale, Isle (isl.),
  Mi, US 127/L4
Royalton, Pa, US 138/B3
Royan, Fr. 42/C4
Roye, Fr. 56/C2
Roye, Fr. 52/B4
Royersford, Pa, US 138/C3
Røyken, Nor. 38/D2
Royston, Sc, UK 36/D2
Royston, Eng, UK 33/G4
Royton, Eng, UK 35/F4
Rozay-en-Brie, Fr. 30/L6
Rozenburg, Neth. 50/B5
Rozhaya (riv.), Rus. 61/W9
Rozmberk (lake),
  Czh. 55/H4
Rozmital pod Tremšínem,
  Czh. 55/G3
Rožňava, Slvk. 41/L4
Rožnjatur, India 86/D4
Rt Kamenjak (cape),
  Cro. 43/L4

Rudauli, India 84/C2
Rüdersdorf, Ger. 40/Q7
Rüdesheim, Ger. 53/G4
Rudiano, It. 58/C2
Rudkøbing, Den. 38/D4
Rudnik, Pol. 41/M3
Rudnyy, Kaz. 61/P5
Rudolf (isl.), Rus. 64/F1
Rudolstadt, Ger. 43/J1
Rudong, China 72/E4
Rüdsar, Iran 88/F1
Rudyard, Mt, US 135/P15
Rue, Fr. 52/A3
Rue (pt.), NI, UK 34/B1
Rue, Fr. 52/A3
Rueda, Sp. 44/C2
Rueil-Malmaison, Fr. 30/J5
Ruell (riv.), Ger. 53/F4
Ruelle-sur-Touvre, Fr. 42/D4
Ruen (peak), Bul. 47/H3
Ruetzbach (riv.), Aus. 57/H3
Ruffano, It. 46/F3
Ruffec, Fr. 42/D3
Rufiji (riv.), Tanz. 93/F5
Rufina, It. 59/E5
Rufirem, Won, Can. 135/G7
Rufino, Arg. 158/E2
Rufisque, Sen. 102/A3
Rugao, China 72/E4
Rugby, ND, US 127/J3
Rugby, Eng, UK 33/F2
Rugeley, Eng, UK 33/E1
Rügen (isl.), Ger. 38/E4
Ruhmannsfelden, Ger. 55/F5
Ruhnu saar (isl.), Lat. 39/K3
Ruhr (riv.), Ger. 40/D3
Ruhr (prov.), It. 59/E2
Ruhrgebiet (phys. reg.),
  Ger. 50/D6
Ruhstorf an der Rott,
  Ger. 55/F5
Rui'an, China 79/D2
Ruicheng, China 72/B4
Ruidoso, NM, US 129/F4
Ruinen, Neth. 50/D3
Ruiselede, Belg. 52/C1
Ruiz, Mex. 142/D4
Rujen (peak), FYROM 47/H1
Ruki (riv.), D.R. Congo 104/A3
Rukwa (pol. reg.),
  Tanz. 104/B4
Rules (riv.), Belg. 53/E4
Rülzheim, Ger. 54/B4
Rum, Aus. 57/H3
Rum (isl.), Sc, UK 36/A2
Ruma, Serb. 48/D3
Ruma NP, Kenya 104/B3
Rumbek, Sudan 97/L6
Rumes, Belg. 52/C2
Rumford, Me, US 131/G2
Rumia, Pol. 38/H4
Rumilly, Fr. 56/B6
Rümlang, Swi. 57/E3
Rumoi, Japan 76/B2
Rumney, Swi. 57/F4
Rumphi, Malw. 104/B5
Rumson, NJ, US 138/E3
Rumst, Belg. 53/D1
Rumuruti, Kenya 104/C2
Runabay (pt.), NI, UK 34/B1
Runcorn, Eng, UK 35/F5
Rundu, Namb. 105/B4
Rundwa (riv.), Tanz. 104/B4
Rungwa Game Rsv.,
  Tanz. 104/B4
Rungwe (peak), Tanz. 104/B4
Runkel, Ger. 54/B2
Runn (lake), Swe. 38/F1
Runnemede, NJ, US 138/C4
Running Springs,
  Ca, US 136/C2
Ruo (riv.), China 65/K5
Ruokolahti, Fin. 39/N1
Ruoqiang, China 70/E4
Rupat (isl.), Indo. 80/B3
Rupea, Rom. 49/G2
Rupel (riv.), Belg. 53/D1
Rupert (riv.), Qu, Can. 123/J3
Rupert, India 86/D4
Ruppichteroth, Ger. 53/G2
Rupt-sur-Moselle, Fr. 56/C2
Rupununi (riv.), Guy. 153/G4
Rur (riv.), Ger. 53/F2
Rur-Strasse (lake),
  Ger. 53/F2
Rurrenabaque, Bol. 150/E6
Rurutu (isl.), FrPol. 107/L7
Rusape, Zim. 105/F4
Rüschegg, Swi. 56/D4
Rüschlikon, Swi. 57/E3

Ruse (pol. reg.), Bul. 47/H1
Ruse, Bul. 49/G4
Rusera, India 85/F3
Rush, Ire. 34/B4
Rush, Laila, Ut, US 137/J13
Rushden, Eng, UK 33/F2
Rushville, In, US 130/C4
Rusk, Tx, US 129/J5
Russ Lake Nat'l Rec. Area,
  Wa, US 135/H3
Russbach (riv.), Aus. 49/N7
Russell (isls.), Austl. 114/F7
Russell, Mb, Can. 127/J3
Russell (isl.),
  Nun., Can. 123/J1
Russell (lake),
  Mb, Can. 122/G2
Russell River NP,
  Austl. 114/F6

Russell Gulch,
  Co, US 137/A3
Saanta (peak), Kenya 104/C2
Saar (riv.), Ger. 53/F5
Saarbrücken, Ger. 53/F5
Saarburg, Ger. 53/F5
Saaremaa (isl.), Est. 60/D4
Saarland (state), Ger. 43/G2
Saarlouis, Ger. 53/F5
Saas, Swi. 57/F4
Saas Fee, Swi. 56/D5
Saastal (valley), Swi. 56/D5
Sab (riv.), Camb. 78/D2
Saba (isl.), NAnt. 141/N8
Šabac, Serb. 48/D3
Sabadell, Sp. 45/L6
Sabae, Japan 74/E3
Sabah (reg.), Malay. 67/L9
Sabalgarh, India 84/A2
Sabana (arch.), Bang. 145/F1
Sabana de Uchire,
  Ven. 153/E2
Sabanalarga, Col. 152/C1
Sabanalarga, Col. 152/C2
Sabancuy, Mex. 144/D2
Sabaneta, Ven. 152/D2
Sabang, Indo. 80/A2
Sabanita, Pan. 145/G4
Sabaştiyah, WBnk. 91/G7
Sabat (riv.), Sudan 93/F4
Sabbio Chiese, It. 58/D1
Sabbioneta, It. 58/D3
Sabhã, Libya 96/H2
Sabie (riv.), Moz. 107/F2
Sabinal, Cayo (isl.),
  Cuba 145/G1
Sabiñánigo, Sp. 45/E1
Sabinas, Mex. 132/C5
Sabinas (riv.), Mex. 140/A2
Sabinas Hidalgo,
  Mex. 132/C5
Sabine (lake),
  La,Tx, US 129/J5
Sabine (riv.),
  La,Tx, US 129/J5
Sabinópolis, Braz. 155/D1
Sabkhat al Bardawïl
  (lag.), Egypt 91/C4
Sabkhat al Jabbül (lake),
  Syria 90/D3
Sabkhat al Müḥ (lake),
  Syria 90/D3
Sablayan, Phil. 81/F1
Sable (isl.), NS, Can. 131/J3
Sable (cape), NS, Can. 131/H2
Sablé-sur-Sarthe, Fr. 42/C3
Saboeiro, Braz. 154/C2
Sabor (riv.), Port. 44/B2
Sabra (cape), Indo. 81/H4
Sabrina (coast), Ant. 160/J
Sabugal, Port. 44/B2
Sabzevâr, Iran 89/G1
Sacajawea (peak),
  Or, US 126/D4
Sácama, Col. 152/D2
Sacaton, Az, US 137/S10
Saccarello (peak),
  It. 58/A4
Sacco (riv.), It. 46/C2
Sacedón, Sp. 44/D2
Săcele, Rom. 49/G3
Sachigo (lake),
  On, Can. 127/L4
Sachigo (riv.),
  On, Can. 122/G3
Sachs Harbour,
  NW, Can. 122/D1
Sachseln, Swi. 57/E4
Sachsen (state), Ger. 40/G3
Sachsen-Anhalt (state),
  Ger. 40/F3
Sachsenbrunn, Ger. 54/D2
Sachsenhagen, Ger. 51/G4
Sacile, It. 59/F1
Säckingen, Fr. 56/D3
Sackville, NB, Can. 131/H2
Saclay, Fr. 30/J5
Saco, Me, US 131/G3
Sacramento (cap.),
  Ca, US 128/B3
Sacramento, Braz. 155/C1
Sacramento (co.),
  Ca, US 135/M10
Sacramento (riv.),
  Ca, US 128/B3
Sacramento (valley),
  Ca, US 128/B3
Sacramento (mts.),
  NM, US 124/E5
Sacramento, Pampa del
  (plain), Peru 156/C2
Sacramento River
  Deep Water Ship Canal,
  Ca, US 135/L10
Sacratif (cape), Sp. 44/D4
Sacred (falls),
  Hi, US 124/W12
Sacro (peak), It. 46/E2
Sacro Monte, It. 58/B1
Sada, Braz. 106/D4
Sádaba, Sp. 44/E1
Sadabad, India 84/E1
Sa'dah, Yem. 88/D5
Saddam (int'l arpt.),
  Iraq 90/F3
Saddle (hills),
  Ab,BC, Can. 126/C2
Saddle, NJ, US 139/G8
Saddle Brook, NJ, US 139/G8
Saddle Rock, NY, US 139/K8
Saddle, The (peak),
  Sc, UK 36/A2
Saddleworth, Austl. 113/H5

Sādhaura, India 86/D4
Sādiqābād, Pak. 89/K3
Sado (isl.), Japan 71/Q4
Sado (riv.), Port. 44/A3
Sadovo, Bul. 47/J1
Sadowara, Japan 74/B4
Sādri, India 89/K3
Sadripante (mt.), Phil. 81/F1
Sadulshahar, India 86/C5
Saerbeck, Ger. 51/E4
Saeul, Lux. 53/E4
Safājah (well), Egypt 101/C3
Safāqis, Tun. 96/H1
Safāqis (gov.), Tun. 99/H2
Safed Koh (range),
Pak. 86/A3
Saffānī yah, Ra's as (pt.),
SAr. 88/E4
Saffig, Ger. 53/G3
Säffle, Swe. 38/E2
Safford, Az, US 128/E4
Saffron Walden,
Eng, UK 33/G2
Safi (cape), Mor. 98/C2
Safi, Mor. 98/C2
Safid (riv.), Afg. 89/J1
Safid Khers (mts.),
Afg. 89/K1
Safid Kūh (mts.), Afg. 89/H2
Safidon, India 86/D5
Safien, Swi. 57/F4
Safipur, India 84/C2
Säfitā, Syria 91/E2
Safonovo, Rus. 60/G5
Safranbolu, Turk. 90/C1
Sag Harbor, NY, US 139/F2
Saga (pref.), Japan 74/A4
Saga, China 85/E1
Saga, Japan 74/B4
Sagae, Japan 74/B4
Sagaing (div.), Myan. 70/F7
Sagaing, Myan. 83/F3
Sagaing (state), Myan. 83/F3
Sagami (sea), Japan 75/F3
Sagami (riv.), Japan 77/C2
Sagami (lake), Japan 77/C2
Sagami (bay), Japan 77/C3
Sagamihara, Japan 75/F3
Sagamiko, Japan 77/C2
Sagamore Hill Nat'l
Hist. Site, NY, US 139/M8
Sāgar, India 84/B4
Sagard, Ger. 38/E4
Sagarmatha (zone),
Nepal 85/E2
Sagarmatha (Everest)
(mtn.), China,Nepal 85/E2
Sagarmatha NP,
Nepal 85/E2
Sagaulī, India 85/E2
Sagavanirktok (riv.),
Ak, US 134/J2
Sagay, Phil. 81/F1
Saggart, Ire. 34/B5
Saghyz (riv.), Kaz. 63/K2
Saginaw, Mi, US 130/D3
Saginaw (bay),
Mi, US 130/D3
Saglek (bay),
Nf, Can. 123/K3
Sagone, Golfe de
(gulf), Fr. 46/A1
Sagter Ems (riv.),
Ger. 51/E2
Sagua de Tánamo,
Cuba 145/H1
Sagua la Grande,
Cuba 145/F1
Saguaro NP,
Az, US 128/E4
Saguenay (riv.),
Qu, Can. 131/G1
Saguia el Hamra
(riv.), WSah. 96/C2
Sagunto, Sp. 45/E3
Sagy, Fr. 30/H4
Sa'gya, China 85/G1
Saḥāb, Jor. 91/D4
Sahagún, Sp. 44/C1
Sahagún, Col. 152/C2
Sahagún, Mex. 143/L7
Saḥam, Jor. 91/D3
Sahand (mtn.), Iran 88/E1
Sahara (des.), Afr. 93/B2
Sahāranpur, India 86/D5
Saharsa, India 85/F3
Sahaspur, India 84/B1
Sahaswān, India 84/B1
Sahavato, Madg. 107/J8
Sahāwar, India 84/B2
Sahel, Afr. 100/H4
Sāhibganj, India 85/F3
Sāhinli, Turk. 49/H5
Sāhī wāl, Pak. 86/A4
Sahiwal, Pak. 86/B4
Saḥrā Marzūq (des.),
Libya 96/H3
Saḥrā' Rabyānah (des.),
Libya 97/K3
Sahrho, Jebel (mts.),
Mor. 98/D3
Sahuaripa, Mex. 142/C2
Sahuayo de Morelos,
Mex. 142/E4
Sahy, Slvk. 41/K4
Sai (canal), India 82/D2
Sai Yok NP, Thai. 78/B3
Saïda, Alg. 100/F5
Saidpur, India 84/D3
Saignelégier, Swi. 56/D3
Saigō, Japan 74/C2
Saigon, Viet. 78/D4
Saijō, Japan 74/C4

Saikai NP, Japan 74/A4
Saiki, Japan 74/B4
Sailly, Fr. 30/H4
Sailly-sur-la-Lys, Fr. 52/B2
Sailu, India 89/L5
Saimaa (lake), Fin. 37/J3
Sain Alto, Mex. 142/E4
Sainghin-en-Weppes,
Fr. 52/B2
Sains-du-Nord, Fr. 52/B3
Saint Abb's (pt.),
Can.,US 135/G7
Saint Agnes (pt.),
Eng, UK 32/A6
Saint Albans,
WV, US 130/D4
Saint Alban's,
Nf, Can. 131/L2
Saint Albans,
Eng, UK 30/C1
Saint Albans,
Vt, US 130/F2
Saint Albert,
Ab, Can. 126/E2
Saint-Amable,
Qu, Can. 131/P6
Saint-Amand-les-Eaux,
Fr. 52/C3
Saint-Amand-Montrond,
Fr. 42/E3
Saint-Amarin, Fr. 56/D2
Saint-Ambroise,
Qu, Can. 131/G1
Saint-Amé, Fr. 56/C1
Saint-André, Reun. 107/S15
Saint-André-de-Cubzac,
Fr. 42/C4
Saint-André-les-Vergers,
Fr. 42/F2
Saint Andrew's (bay),
Sc, UK 36/D4
Saint Andrews,
Sc, UK 36/D4
Saint Ann (cape),
SLeo. 102/B5
Saint Anns, On, Can. 131/Q9
Saint Ann's (pt.),
Wal, UK 32/A3
Saint Ann's Bay,
Jam. 141/H4
Saint Anthony, Nf, Can.131/L1
Saint-Antoine,
Qu, Can. 131/N6
Saint Arnaud, Austl. 115/B3
Saint-Arnoult-en-Yvelines,
Fr. 30/H6
Saint Aubin, Chl, UK 42/B2
Saint-Aubin, Swi. 56/C4
Saint-Aubin, Fr. 56/B3
Saint-Augustin, Fr. 30/M5
Saint Augustine,
Fl, US 133/H4
Saint Augustine Beach,
Fl, US 133/H4
Saint Austell (bay),
Eng, UK 32/B6
Saint Austell, Eng, UK 32/B6
Saint-Avé, Fr. 42/B3
Saint-Avold, Fr. 53/F5
Saint-Barthélemy (isl.),
Fr. 141/N8
Saint-Barthélemy-d'Anjou,
Fr. 42/C3
Saint-Barthélemy, Pic de
(peak), Fr. 42/D5
Saint Bees (pt.),
Eng, UK 34/E2
Saint-Benoît, Fr. 42/D3
Saint-Benoît, Reun. 107/S15
Saint-Benoît,
Qu, Can. 131/N6
Saint Bernard,
La, US 137/Q17
Saint Bernard (parish),
La, US 137/Q17
Saint-Berthevin, Fr. 42/C2
Saint-Blaise, Swi. 56/C3
Saint-Blaise, Qu, Can. 131/P7
Saint Blaize (cape),
SAfr. 106/C4
Saint Boswells,
Sc, UK 36/D5
Saint-Brice-Courcelles,
Fr. 52/C5
Saint-Brice-sous-Forêt,
Fr. 30/K5
Saint Bride's (bay),
Wal, UK 32/A3
Saint-Brieuc, Fr. 42/B2
Saint-Brieuc (bay), Fr. 42/B2
Saint-Bruno-de-Montarville,
Qu, Can. 131/P6
Saint-Calais, Fr. 42/D2
Saint-Canut, Qu, Can. 131/M6
Saint Catharines,
On, Can. 131/R9
Saint Catherine (mt.),
Gren. 153/F1
Saint Catherine's (pt.),
Eng, UK 33/E5
Saint Catherine's (hill),
Eng, UK 33/E5
Saint-Céré, Fr. 42/D4
Saint-Cergue, Swi. 56/C5
Saint-Cergues, Fr. 56/C5
Saint-Chamond, Fr. 42/F4
Saint Charles,
Ca, US 126/B5
Saint Charles,
Il, US 135/P16
Saint Charles,
La, US 137/P17
Saint Charles,
Md, US 130/E4

Saint Charles,
Mo, US 137/G8
Saint Charles (co.),
Mo, US 137/F8
Saint-Chély-d'Apcher,
Fr. 42/E4
Saint-Chéron, Fr. 30/J6
Saint Christoffel (peak),
NAnt. 152/D1
Saint Clair (lake),
Can.,US 135/G7
Saint Clair (peak),
Az, US 137/S18
Saint Clair (co.),
Il, US 137/G9
Saint Clair (co.),
Mi, US 135/G6
Saint Clair, Mi, US 135/G6
Saint Clair, Pa, US 138/B2
Saint Clair Beach,
On, Can. 135/G7
Saint Clair Shores,
Mi, US 135/G6
Saint-Claude, Fr. 56/B5
Saint Cloud, Mn, US 127/K4
Saint-Cloud, Fr. 30/J5
Saint-Constant,
Qu, Can. 131/N7
Saint Croix (riv.),
US 130/A2
Saint Croix (isl.),
USVI 141/M8
Saint Cyr (mt.),
Yk, Can. 134/M3
Saint-Cyr-l'École, Fr. 30/J5
Saint-Cyr-sous-Dourdan,
Fr. 30/J6
Saint-Cyr-sur-Morin,
Fr. 30/M5
Saint David's (pt.),
Wal, UK 32/A3
Saint David's, Wal, UK 32/A3
Saint-Denis, Reun. 30/K5
Saint-Denis, Reun. 107/S15
Saint-Denis-en-Bugey,
Fr. 56/B6
Saint-Dié, Fr. 56/C1
Saint-Dizier, Fr. 53/D6
Saint-Doulchard, Fr. 42/E3
Saint-Édouard,
Qu, Can. 131/N7
Saint Eleanors,
PE, Can. 131/J2
Saint Elias (cape),
Ak, US 134/K4
Saint Elias (mt.),
Ak, US 134/K3
Saint Elias (mts.),
Ak, US 122/B2
Saint-Éloy-les-Mines,
Fr. 42/E3
Saint-Esprit,
Qu, Can. 131/N6
Saint-Estève, Fr. 42/E5
Saint-Étienne, Fr. 42/F4
Saint-Étienne-au-Mont,
Fr. 52/A2
Saint-Étienne-de-Baïgorry,
Fr. 42/C5
Saint-Étienne-de-Tinée,
Fr. 43/G4
Saint-Étienne-du-Rouvray,
Fr. 42/D2
Saint-Étienne-lès-
Remiremont, Fr. 56/C1
Saint-Eustache,
Qu, Can. 131/N6
Saint Eustatius (isl.),
NAnt. 141/N8
Saint-Fargeau-Ponthierry,
Fr. 30/K6
Saint-Félicien,
Qu, Can. 131/F1
Saint-Félix, Fr. 56/B6
Saint-Florent-sur-Cher,
Fr. 42/E3
Saint-Florentin, Fr. 42/E2
Saint-Floris, PN de,
CAfr. 97/K6
Saint-Four, Fr. 42/E4
Saint Francis (riv.),
Ar, US 129/K4
Saint Francis (riv.),
Mo, US 133/F2
Saint Francis,
Ks, US 129/G3
Saint Francis (cape),
SAfr. 106/D4
Saint Francis,
Wi, US 135/Q14
Saint Francisville,
La, US 129/K5
Saint Francois (mts.),
US 133/F2
Saint Gallen (canton),
Swi. 57/F3
Saint-Gaudens, Fr. 42/D5
Saint-Genis-Pouilly,
Fr. 56/C5
Saint George, Austl. 114/C5
Saint George,
NB, Can. 131/H2
Saint George (cape),
Nf, Can. 131/K1
Saint George (isl.),
Ak, US 134/E4
Saint George, Ak, US 134/E4
Saint George (isl.),
Fl, US 133/H4
Saint George, SC, US 133/H3
Saint George, Ut, US 128/D3
Saint George's (bay),
Nf, Can. 131/K1

Saint George's (bay),
De, US 131/J2
Saint-Georges,
Qu, Can. 131/G2
Saint George's (cap.),
Gren. 153/F1
Saint George's (chan.),
Ire.,UK 31/Q11
Saint Georges,
De, US 138/C4
Saint-Germain, Fr. 56/D2
Saint-Germain-de-la-Grange,
Fr. 30/H5
Saint-Germain-du-Bois,
Fr. 56/B4
Saint-Germain-du-Corbéis,
Fr. 42/D2
Saint-Germain-du-Plain,
Fr. 56/A4
Saint-Germain-en-Laye,
Fr. 30/J5
Saint-Germain-lès-Corbeil,
Fr. 30/K6
Saint-Germain-sous-Doue,
Fr. 30/M5
Saint-Germain-sur-Morin,
Fr. 30/L5
Saint-Germer-de-Fly,
Fr. 30/H4
Saint-Gervais, Fr. 30/H4
Saint-Gervais-les-Bains,
Fr. 56/C6
Saint-Ghislain, Belg. 52/C3
Saint-Gilles, Fr. 42/F5
Saint-Gilles-Croix-de-Vie,
Fr. 42/C3
Saint-Gingolph, Swi. 56/C5
Saint-Girons, Fr. 42/D5
Saint-Gobain, Fr. 52/C4
Saint Govan's (pt.),
Wal, UK 32/B3
Saint-Gratien, Fr. 30/J5
Saint-Laurent-sur-Saône,
Saint Hedwig,
Tx, US 137/U21
Saint Helena (bay),
SAfr. 105/C7
Saint Helena (isl.),
Austl. 114/F6
Saint Helens, Austl. 115/D4
Saint Helens (pt.),
Austl. 115/D4
Saint Helens, Eng, UK 35/F5
Saint Helens,
(co.), Eng, UK 35/F5
Saint Helens,
Or, US 126/C4
Saint Helens (mt.),
Wa, US 126/C4
Saint Helier (cap.),
Chl, UK 42/B2
Saint-Herblain, Fr. 42/C3
Saint-Hilarion, Fr. 30/H6
Saint-Hippolyte, Fr. 56/C3
Saint-Honoré,
Qu, Can. 131/G1
Saint-Hubert,
Qu, Can. 131/P6
Saint-Hubert, Belg. 53/E3
Saint-Hyacinthe,
Qu, Can. 130/F2
Saint Ignace (isl.),
On, Can. 127/L3
Saint Ignace,
Mi, US 130/C2
Saint-Imier, Swi. 56/D3
Saint-Isidore-de-Laprairie,
Qu, Can. 131/N7
Saint Ives (bay),
Eng, UK 32/A6
Saint Ives, Eng, UK 33/F2
Saint Ives, Eng, UK 32/A6
Saint Jacques (int'l arpt.),
Fr. 30/K6
Saint-Jacques-le-Mineur,
Qu, Can. 131/P7
Saint James, NY, US 139/E2
Saint James (cape),
BC, Can. 122/C3
Saint-Jean (riv.),
Qu, Can. 131/H1
Saint-Jean (lake),
Qu, Can. 131/N7
Saint-Jean-d'Angély,
Fr. 42/C4
Saint-Jean-de-la-Ruelle,
Fr. 42/D3
Saint-Jean-de-Losne,
Fr. 56/B3
Saint-Jean-Port-Joli,
Qu, Can. 131/G2
Saint-Jean-sur-Richelieu,
Qu, Can. 130/F2
Saint-Jeoire, Fr. 56/C5
Saint-Jérôme,
Qu, Can. 130/F2
Saint Joe, La, US 137/Q16
Saint Joe (riv.),
Id,Wa, US 124/C2
Saint John, NB, Can. 131/H2
Saint John (riv.),
Me, US 123/K4
Saint John (isl.),
USVI 141/M8
Saint John The Baptist
(parish), La, US 137/P16
Saint Johns, Az, US 128/E4
Saint Johns (riv.),
Fl, US 133/H4
Saint John's (cap.),
Anti. 141/N8
Saint John's (pt.),
NI, UK 34/C3
Saint Johnsbury,
Vt, US 131/F2

Saint Jones (riv.),
De, US 138/C5
Saint Joseph (riv.), US 130/C3
Saint Joseph (isl.),
On, Can. 130/C2
Saint Joseph, La, US 129/K5
Saint Joseph,
Mo, US 129/J3
Saint Joseph (lake),
On, Can. 122/G3
Saint-Joseph,
Reun. 107/S15
Saint-Juéry, Fr. 42/E5
Saint-Julien, Fr. 56/B3
Saint-Julien-en-Genevois,
Fr. 56/C5
Saint-Julien-les-Villas,
Fr. 42/F2
Saint-Junien, Fr. 42/D4
Saint-Just-en-Chaussée,
Fr. 52/B4
Saint Kilda (isl.), UK 31/P8
Saint Kitts (isl.), StK. 141/J4
Saint Kitts and Nevis
(ctry.) 141/N8
Saint-Lambert,
Qu, Can. 131/P6
Saint Laurent,
Mb, Can. 127/J3
Saint Laurent (riv.),
Qu, Can. 131/G1
Saint-Laurent,
Ak, US 134/D3
Saint-Laurent-Blangy,
Fr. 52/B3
Saint-Laurent-de-Cerdans,
Fr. 42/E5
Saint-Laurent du Maroni,
FrG. 151/H2
Saint-Laurent-en-Grandvaux,
Fr. 30/K5
Saint-Maurice, Swi. 56/D5
Saint-Maurice (riv.),
Qu, Can. 123/J4
Saint-Max, Fr. 53/F6
Saint-Maximin-la-Sainte-
Baume, Fr. 42/F5
Saint-Memmie, Fr. 53/D6
Saint-Méry, Fr. 30/L6
Saint Michael, Ak, US 134/F3
Saint Michaels,
Md, US 138/B6
Saint-Michel (bay),
Can. 131/J1
Saint-Michel, Fr. 53/D4
Saint-Michel-sur-Meurthe,
Fr. 56/C1
Saint-Michel-sur-Orge,
Fr. 30/J6
Saint-Mihiel, Fr. 53/E6
Saint Monance,
Sc, UK 36/D4
Saint-Nabord, Fr. 56/C1
Saint-Nazaire, Fr. 42/B3
Saint Neots, Eng, UK 33/F2
Saint-Nicolas, Belg. 53/E2
Saint-Nicolas-d'Aliermont,
Fr. 42/D2
Saint Niklaus, Swi. 56/D5
Saint-Nom-la-Bretèche,
Fr. 30/H5
Saint-Omer, Fr. 52/B2
Saint-Omer-en-Chaussée,
Fr. 52/A4
Saint-Ouen, Fr. 52/B3
Saint-Ouen-en-Brie,
Fr. 30/L6
Saint-Ouen-L'Aumône,
Fr. 30/J4
Saint-Pamphile,
Qu, Can. 131/G2
Saint-Pascal,
Qu, Can. 131/G2
Saint-Pathus, Fr. 30/L4
Saint Paul, Ab, Can. 126/F2
Saint Paul (riv.), Libr. 96/C6
Saint Paul, Reun. 107/S15
Saint Paul, Ak, US 134/D4
Saint Paul (isl.),
Ak, US 134/W23
Saint Paul (cap.),
Mn, US 127/K4
Saint-Paul-lès-Dax, Fr. 42/C5
Saint Paul Rocks (isl.),
Braz. 22/H5
Saint Paul's Church Nat'l
Hist. Site, NY, US 139/K8
Saint-Pé-de-Bigorre,
Fr. 42/C5
Saint Peter, Mn, US 127/K4
Saint Peter (isl.),
Austl. 113/G5
Saint Peter Port (cap.),
Chl, UK 42/B2
Saint Peters,
Md, US 137/F6
Saint Petersburg,
Fl, US 133/H5
Saint Petersburg,
Rus. 61/T7
Saint-Philippe-de-Laprairie,
Qu, Can. 131/P7
Saint-Pierre, Mn, US 30/H6
Saint-Pierre,
StP. 30/K5
Saint-Pierre, Fr. 141/N9
Saint-Pierre, Reun. 107/S15
Saint-Pierre-du-Mont,
Fr. 42/C5

Saint-Marcel, Fr. 56/A4
Saint-Mard, Fr. 30/L4
Saint Maries, Id, US 126/D4
Saint Martin (lake),
Mb, Can. 127/J3
Saint-Martin (isl.), Fr. 141/J4
Saint-Martin, Swi. 56/D5
Saint-Martin-Boulogne,
Fr. 52/A2
Saint-Martin-d'Ablois,
Fr. 52/C6
Saint-Martin-d'Hères,
Fr. 42/F4
Saint-Martin-du-Tertre,
Fr. 30/K4
Saint-Martin-la-Garenne,
Fr. 30/H4
Saint Martinville,
La, US 129/K5
Saint Mary (cape),
Gam. 102/A3
Saint Mary (peak),
Austl. 113/H4
Saint-Raphaël, Fr. 56/B6
Saint-Rémi, Qu, Can. 131/N7
Saint-Rémy-de-Provence,
Fr. 42/F5
Saint-Rémy-lès-Chevreuse,
Fr. 30/J5
Saint-Rémy-l'Honoré,
Fr. 30/H5
Saint-Roch-de-l'Achigan,
Qu, Can. 131/N6
Sakha (Yakutiya),
Resp., 65/Q4
Sakhalin (gulf), Rus. 65/Q4
Sakhalin (isl.), Rus. 65/Q4
Sakhalinskaya Oblast,
Rus. 65/Q4
Sakhnīn, Isr. 91/G6
Sakht Sar, Iran 88/F1
Säki, Azer. 63/H4
Sakishima (isl.),
Japan 67/M7
Sakmara (riv.), Rus. 63/K2
Sakon Nakhon, Thai. 78/D2
Sakrand, Pak. 89/J3
Sakti, India 84/D4
Saku, Japan 75/F2
Saku, Japan 77/A1
Sakura, Japan 77/E1
Sakura, Japan 77/E2
Sakuragawa, Japan 77/E2
Sakurai, Japan 77/J6
Saky, Ukr. 62/E3
Sakya Monastery,
China 85/G1
Säkylä, Fin. 39/K1
Sal (isl.), CpV. 93/K10
Sal (pt.), Hon. 144/E3
Sal (riv.), Rus. 63/G3
Sal Rei, CpV. 93/K10
Sal'a, Slvk. 48/C1
Sala, Swe. 38/G2
Sala Baganza, It. 58/D3
Sala Consilina, It. 46/D2
Salada (lake), Mex. 142/B1
Saladas, Arg. 157/E2
Saladillo (riv.), Arg. 159/J11
Saladillo, Arg. 158/F2
Salado (riv.), Mex. 142/C2
Salado (riv.), Arg. 147/C6
Salado del Norte (riv.),
Arg. 147/C5
Salaga, Gha. 103/E4
Salaḥ Ad Din (gov.),
Iraq 90/E3
Sälaj (co.), Rom. 41/M5
Sälaj (prov.), Rom. 49/F2
Salālah, Oman 88/F5
Salamá, Guat. 144/D3
Salamajärven NP, Fin. 42/E3
Salamanca, Mex. 143/E4
Salamanca, Sp. 44/C2
Salamanca, NY, US 130/E3
Salamatof, Ak, US 134/H3
Salamina, Col. 150/C3
Salamis, Gre. 47/H3
Salamis (isl.), Gre. 47/N9
Salamī yah, Syria 91/E2
Salangen, Nor. 37/F1
Salas, Peru 156/B2
Salas, Sp. 44/B1
Salas de los Infantes,
Sp. 44/D1
Salavat, Rus. 63/K1
Salaverry, Peru 156/B3
Salayar (isl.), Indo. 67/F5
Salbris, Fr. 42/E3
Salcantay (peak),
Peru 156/C4
Saldaña, Sp. 44/C1
Saldanhabaai (bay),
Safr. 106/K10
Saldus, Lat. 39/K3
Sale, Austl. 115/C4
Sale, It. 58/B3
Sale, Eng, UK 35/F5
Sale Marasino, It. 58/D1
Selebaba, Burk. 81/G3
Sale, Mor. 100/A2
Salé, Mor. 100/A2
Salebabu (isl.), Indo. 67/G3
Salekhard, Rus. 64/G3
Salem, India 82/C5
Salem, In, US 130/C4
Salem, Mi, US 135/E7
Salem, NH, US 131/G3
Salem, NJ, US 138/C4
Salem (co.), NJ, US 138/C4
Salem (cap.), Or, US 126/C4
Salentina (pen.), It. 47/F2
Salerno, It. 46/D2
Salerno, Golfo di (gulf),
It. 46/D2

Sales (pt.), Eng, UK 33/G3
Saleux, Fr. 52/B4
Salfit, WBnk. 91/G7
Salford, Eng, UK 35/F5
Salford (co.), Eng, UK 35/F5
Salgado Filho (int'l arpt.), Braz. 155/B4
Salgar, Col. 152/C3
Salgesch, Swi. 56/D5
Salgótarján, Hun. 41/K4
Salgueiro, Braz. 154/C3
Salhus, Nor. 38/A1
Salies-de-Béarn, Fr. 42/C5
Salies-du-Salat, Fr. 42/D5
Şalif, Yem. 88/D5
Salihli, Turk. 90/B2
Salihorsk, Bela. 62/C1
Salima, Malw. 105/F3
Salī mah (oasis), Sudan 101/B4
Salina, Ut, US 128/E3
Salina (isl.), It. 46/D3
Salina (pt.), Bahm. 145/H1
Salina Cruz, Mex. 144/C2
Salinas (riv.), Ca, US 128/B3
Salinas, Braz. 154/B5
Salinas, Ca, US 128/B3
Salinas (cape), Sp. 45/G3
Salinas, Ecu. 152/A5
Salinas de Hidalgo, Mex. 143/E4
Salinas Pueblo Missions Nat'l Mon., NM, US 129/F4
Salinas Y Aguada Blanca, Reserva Nacional, Peru 156/D4
Saline (riv.), Ks, US 132/D2
Saline, It. 59/D6
Saline, Sc, UK 36/C4
Salinópolis, Braz. 151/J4
Salins-les-Bains, Fr. 56/B4
Salisbury, NC, US 133/H3
Salisbury (plain), Eng, UK 32/D4
Salisbury, Eng, UK 33/E4
Salisbury (isl.), Nun., Can. 123/J2
Salisbury, NY, US 139/L9
Salitre (riv.), Braz. 154/B3
Salitre, Ecu. 152/B5
Salla, Fin. 60/F2
Salladasburg, Pa, US 138/A1
Sallanches, Fr. 56/C6
Salland (phys. reg.), Neth. 50/D4
Sallatouk (pt.), Gui. 102/B4
Sallaumines, Fr. 52/B3
Sallent, Sp. 45/F2
Salliqueló, Arg. 158/E3
Sallisaw, Ok, US 129/J4
Sally (pass), Ire. 34/B5
Salm (riv.), Ger. 53/F3
Salmān Pāk, Iraq 90/F3
Salmás, Iran 90/F2
Salmon (riv.), BC, Can. 126/C2
Salmon, Id, US 126/E4
Salmon (riv.), Id, US 124/C2
Salmon Arm, BC, Can. 126/D3
Salmon Falls (riv.), Id,Nv, US 128/D2
Salmon River (mts.), Id, US 124/C2
Salmon, South Fork (riv.), US 128/C2
Salmtal, Ger. 53/F4
Salo, Fin. 39/K1
Salò, It. 58/D1
Salon, India 84/C2
Salon (riv.), Fr. 44/C5
Salon-de-Provence, Fr. 42/F5
Salonga, PN de la, D.R. Congo 97/K8
Salonta, Rom. 48/E2
Salouël, Fr. 52/B4
Salpausselkä (mts.), Fin. 39/M1
Salpo, Peru 156/B3
Salses-le-Château, Fr. 42/E5
Sal'sk, Rus. 63/G3
Salso (riv.), It. 46/C4
Salsomaggiore Terme, It. 58/C3
Salt (riv.), SAfr. 106/C4
Salt (riv.), Az, US 137/R19
Salt (range), Pak. 86/B3
Salt Cay (isl.), UK 145/J1
Salt Draw (riv.), Tx, US 142/D2
Salt Fork Arkansas (riv.), US 129/H3
Salt Fork Red (riv.), US 129/G4
Salt Lake (co.), Ut, US 137/J12
Salt Lake City (cap.), Ut, US 137/K12
Salt Meadow NWR, Ct, US 139/F1
Salt, North Fork (riv.), Mo, US 129/J2
Salt River Ind. Res., Az, US 137/S18
Salta, Arg. 157/C1
Saltaire, NY, US 139/E2
Saltash, Eng, UK 32/B6
Saltcoats, Sc, UK 36/B5
Saltdal, Nor. 37/E2
Saltee (isls.), Ire. 31/Q10
Saltfjorden (inlet), Nor. 37/E2

Saltillo, Mex. 143/E3
Salto, Uru. 157/E3
Salto, Braz. 155/C2
Salto, Arg. 158/E2
Salto da Divisa, Braz. 154/C5
Salto del Guairá, Par. 157/F1
Salto Grande (res.), Arg. 157/E3
Salto Santiago, Reprêsa de (res.), Braz. 155/A3
Salton Sea (lake), Ca, US 124/C5
Saltvik, Fin. 39/J1
Saluda (riv.), SC, US 133/H3
Salug, Phil. 79/D6
Saluggia, It. 58/B2
Salunga-Landisville, Pa, US 138/B3
Sālūr, India 82/D4
Salurn (Salorno), It. 57/H5
Salut, Îles du (isls.), FrG. 151/H2
Saluzzo, It. 43/G4
Salvación (bay), Chile 159/B6
Salvador (lake), La, US 137/P17
Salvaleón de Higüey, DRep. 141/H4
Salvaterra de Magos, Port. 44/A3
Salvatierra, Mex. 143/E4
Salvatierra de Miño, Sp. 44/A1
Salween (riv.), Asia 67/J8
Salyan, Azer. 63/J5
Salyersville, Ky, US 130/D4
Salza (riv.), Aus. 41/H5
Salzach (riv.), Ger. 40/G5
Salzano, It. 59/F1
Salzbergen, Ger. 51/E4
Salzburg, Aus. 40/K3
Salzburg (int'l arpt.), Aus. 43/H3
Salzburg (prov.), Aus. 41/G5
Salzgitter, Ger. 51/H4
Salzhausen, Ger. 51/G4
Salzkotten, Ger. 51/F5
Salzwedel, Ger. 40/F2
Sam Rayburn (res.), Tx, US 140/C1
Sam Son, Viet. 78/D2
Sama, Sp. 44/C1
Samak (cape), Indo. 80/C4
Samales Group (isls.), Phil. 81/F2
Samālkha, India 86/D5
Samalkot, India 82/D4
Samāna, India 86/D2
Samaná (cape), DRep. 141/H4
Samana (isl.), Bahm. 145/H1
Samandaği, Turk. 91/D1
Samani, Japan 76/C2
Samaniego, Col. 152/B4
Samannûd, Egypt 91/B4
Samaqua (riv.), Qu, Can. 131/F1
Samar, Jor. 91/D3
Samar (isl.), Phil. 67/M8
Samara (riv.), Rus. 87/B2
Samara (int'l arpt.), Rus. 63/J1
Samara, Rus. 63/J1
Samarskaya Oblast, Rus. 87/A2
Samarai, PNG 116/E6
Samarate, It. 58/B1
Samaria (reg.), WBnk. 91/G7
Samarinda, Indo. 81/E4
Samarqand, Uzb. 87/E5
Samarqand (pol. reg.), Uzb. 87/E5
Sāmarrā', Iraq 90/E3
Samasata, Pak. 86/A5
Samāstipur, India 85/E3
Şamaxi, Azer. 63/J4
Sāmba, India 86/C3
Sambalpur, India 82/D3
Sambao (riv.), Madg. 107/H7
Sambar (cape), Indo. 80/C3
Sambas, Indo. 80/C3
Sambava, Madg. 107/J6
Sambhal, India 84/B1
Sambir, Ukr. 41/M4
Sambor Prei Kuk (ruin), Camb. 78/D3
Samborombón (riv.), Arg. 159/K11
Samborombón (bay), Arg. 159/F2
Sambre (riv.), Fr. 40/C3
Sambre à l'Oise, Canal de (canal), Fr. 52/C4
Sambriāl, Pak. 86/C3
Sambu, Japan 77/E2
Samburu Nat'l Rsv., Kenya 104/C2
Samch'ŏk, SKor. 74/A3
Samch'ŏnp'o, SKor. 73/E5
Samedan, Swi. 57/F4
Samer, Fr. 52/A2
Samfya Mission, Zam. 104/A5
Sámi, Gre. 47/G3
Samiria (riv.), Peru 156/C2
Samit (cape), Camb. 78/C4
Samkos (peak), Camb. 78/C3
Sammamish (lake), Wa, US 135/C2

Sammeron, Fr. 30/M5
Samnangjin, SKor. 74/A3
Samnaun, Swi. 57/G4
Samoa (ctry.) 117/H6
Samobor, Cro. 48/B3
Samoëns, Fr. 56/C5
Samokov, Bul. 47/H1
Samora (riv.), Port. 45/Q10
Samora Correia, Port. 45/Q10
Sámos (isl.), Gre. 90/A2
Sámos, Gre. 90/A2
Samothráki, Gre. 47/J2
Sampacho, Arg. 158/D2
Samper de Calanda, Sp. 45/E2
Sampit (riv.), Indo. 80/D4
Sampit, Indo. 80/D4
Samsø (isl.), Den. 38/D4
Samsø Bælt (chan.), Den. 38/D4
Samson (mt.), Austl. 114/E6
Samsonvale (lake), Austl. 114/E6
Samsun, Turk. 90/D1
Samsun (prov.), Turk. 90/C1
Samthar, India 84/B3
Samugheo, It. 46/A3
Samui (isl.), Thai. 83/H6
Samukawa, Japan 77/C3
Samun (riv.), Azer.,Rus. 64/E5
Samut Prakan, Thai. 78/C3
Samut Sakhon, Thai. 78/C3
Samut Songkhram, Thai. 78/B3
Samye Monastery, China 85/H1
San, Mali 102/D3
San (riv.), Pol. 62/B2
San (riv.), Camb. 78/D3
San Adrián, Cabo de (cape), Sp. 44/A1
San Agustín (cape), Phil. 79/E6
San Agustín, Col. 152/B4
San Agustín de Guadalix, Sp. 45/N8
San Agustín, Parque Arqeológico, Col. 152/B4
San Ambrosio (isl.), Chile 147/B5
San Andreas (lake), Ca, US 135/J11
San Andres (mts.), NM, US 128/F4
San Andrés (lake), Mex. 144/B1
San Andrés, Col. 152/C3
San Andrés, Col. 145/F3
San Andrés Cuexcontitlán, Mex. 143/Q10
San Andrés de Giles, Arg. 159/J11
San Andrés de Machaca, Bol. 156/D5
San Andrés del Rabanedo, Sp. 44/C1
San Andrés, Isla de (isl.), Col. 140/E5
San Andrés Tuxtla, Mex. 144/C2
San Angelo, Tx, US 132/C4
San Anselmo, Ca, US 135/J11
San Antonio (cape), Arg. 159/F3
San Antonio, Chile 158/N8
San Antonio, Ecu. 152/B4
San Antonio, Mex. 142/B2
San Antonio, Peru 156/B4
San Antonio, Uru. 159/K11
San Antonio, Ven. 153/F2
San Antonio (mt.), Ca, US 136/C2
San Antonio (int'l arpt.), Tx, US 129/H5
San Antonio (riv.), Tx, US 140/B2
San Antonio Abad, Sp. 45/F3
San Antonio de Areco, Arg. 159/J11
San Antonio de Caparo, Ven. 152/D3
San Antonio del Golfo, Ven. 153/F2
San Antonio del Táchira, Ven. 152/C3
San Antonio Oeste, Arg. 158/D4
San Antonio, Punta (pt.), Mex. 142/B2
San Augustine, Tx, US 132/E4
San Bartolo, Peru 156/B4
San Bartolomé de Tirajana, Canl. 45/X17
San Bartolome Tlaltelulco, Mex. 143/Q10
San Bartolomeo in Bosco, It. 59/E3
San Bartolomeo in Galdo, It. 46/D2
San Bautista, Uru. 159/L11
San Benedetto (range), It. 59/E5
San Benedetto del Tronto, It. 43/K5
San Benedetto in Alpe, It. 59/E5
San Benedetto Po, It. 59/D2

San Benedicto (isl.), Mex. 142/C5
San Bernardo, Chile 158/N8
San Bernardo (pt.), Col. 152/C2
San Bernardino, Ca, US 136/C2
San Bernardino (co.), Ca, US 136/C2
San Bernardino (mts.), Ca, US 136/C2
San Bernardino Nat'l Forest, Ca, US 136/C2
San Blas, Mex. 142/D4
San Blas, Mex. 142/C3
San Blas (cape), Fl, US 133/G4
San Bonifacio, It. 59/D2
San Borja, Bol. 150/E6
San Bruno, Mex. 142/B3
San Bruno, Ca, US 135/K11
San Buenaventura, Mex. 132/C5
San Buenaventura (Ventura), Austl. 114/E6
San Candido (Innichen), It. 43/K3
San Carlos, Chile 158/C3
San Carlos, Mex. 129/G5
San Carlos, Nic. 145/E4
San Carlos, Pan. 152/B2
San Carlos, Phil. 79/D4
San Carlos, Uru. 159/G2
San Carlos, Ven. 152/D2
San Carlos (lake), Az, US 128/E4
San Carlos, Ca, US 135/K11
San Carlos de Bariloche (int'l arpt.), Arg. 158/C4
San Carlos de Bariloche, Arg. 158/C4
San Carlos de Río Negro, Ven. 153/E4
San Carlos del Zulia, Ven. 152/D2
San Casciano in Val di Pesa, It. 59/E5
San Cataldo, It. 47/J2
San Cayetano, Arg. 158/F3
San Cesario sul Panaro, It. 59/E3
San Ciro de Acosta, Mex. 143/F4
San Clemente (isl.), Ca, US 136/C4
San Clemente, Ca, US 136/C4
San Clemente, Sp. 44/D3
San Clemente, Chile 158/C2
San Clemente del Tuyú, Arg. 159/F3
San Colombano al Lambro, It. 59/D2
San Cristóbal, Arg. 157/D3
San Cristóbal (isl.), Sol. 116/F6
San Cristóbal (vol.), Nic. 144/E3
San Cristóbal, Ven. 152/C3
San Cristóbal, Cuba 145/F1
San Cristóbal (isl.), Ecu. 156/F7
San Cristóbal de las Casas, Mex. 144/C2
San Cristobal Wash (riv.), Az, US 142/B1
San Damiano d'Asti, It. 58/B3
San Diego (cape), Arg. 159/D7
San Diego, Ca, US 136/C5
San Diego (aqueduct), Ca, US 136/C4
San Diego (bay), Ca, US 136/C5
San Diego (co.), Ca, US 136/C4
San Diego, Tx, US 132/D5
San Diego International-Lindbergh Field (int'l arpt.), Ca, US 136/C5
San Diego Naval Station, Ca, US 136/C4
San Diego Wild Animal Park, Ca, US 136/C4
San Diego Zoo, Ca, US 136/C5
San Diequito (riv.), Ca, US 136/C4
San Dimas, Ca, US 136/C2
San Donà di Piave, It. 59/F1
San Donnino, It. 59/E5
San Dorligo della Valle, It. 59/G5
San Esteban de Gormaz, Sp. 44/D2
San Felice Circeo, It. 46/C2
San Felice del Benaco, It. 58/D1
San Felice sul Panaro, It. 59/E3
San Felipe, Mex. 142/B2
San Felipe, Mex. 142/D4
San Felipe, Chile 158/N8
San Felipe de Puerto Plata, DRep. 141/G4
San Felipe de Vichayal, Peru 156/A2
San Felipe Jalapa de Díaz, Mex. 143/F5
San Felipe Torres Mochas, Mex. 143/E4
San Felíx (isl.), Chile 147/A5

San Fernando (riv.), Mex. 132/D5
San Fernando, Phil. 79/D4
San Fernando, Phil. 79/D4
San Fernando (valley), Ca, US 136/B2
San Fernando, Sp. 44/B4
San Fernando, Trin. 153/F2
San Fernando, Chile 158/C2
San Fernando, Arg. 159/J11
San Fernando, Mex. 142/E3
San Fernando, Ca, US 136/F7
San Fernando de Apure, Ven. 153/E3
San Fernando de Atabapo, Ven. 153/E3
San Fernando de Henares, Sp. 45/N9
San Fernando de Presas, Mex. 143/F3
San Fior di Sopra, It. 59/F1
San Francesco al Campo, It. 58/A2
San Francisco, Arg. 157/D3
San Francisco, Col. 152/B4
San Francisco, ESal. 144/D3
San Francisco, Phil. 79/E6
San Francisco, Ven. 152/D2
San Francisco (riv.), Az,NM, US 128/E4
San Francisco (co.), Ca, US 135/K11
San Francisco (int'l arpt.), Ca, US 128/B3
San Francisco Acuautla, Mex. 143/R10
San Francisco Bay NWR, Ca, US 135/K11
San Francisco, Cabo de (cape), Ecu. 152/A4
San Francisco Chimalpa, Mex. 143/Q10
San Francisco de la Paz, Hon. 144/E3
San Francisco de Macorís, DRep. 141/H4
San Francisco de Mostazal, Chile 158/N8
San Francisco del Mezquital, Mex. 142/D4
San Francisco del Monte de Oro, Arg. 158/D2
San Francisco del Oro, Mex. 142/D3
San Francisco del Rincón, Mex. 143/E4
San Francisco Telixtlahuaca, Mex. 140/B4
San Fratello, It. 46/D3
San Gabriel (riv.), Ca, US 136/C2
San Gabriel (pt.), Mex. 142/B2
San Gabriel (res.), Mex. 143/E3
San Gabriel, Ecu. 152/C4
San Gabriel, Ca, US 136/F7
San Gavino Monreale, It. 46/A3
San Germán, Cuba 145/G1
San Germano Vercellese, It. 58/B2
San Gil, Col. 152/C4
San Gimignano, It. 59/E6
San Giorgio delle Pertiche, It. 59/E1
San Giorgio di Piano, It. 59/E3
San Giorgio Ionico, It. 47/E2
San Giorgio Piacentino, It. 58/C3
San Giovanni al Natisone, It. 59/G1
San Giovanni Bianco, It. 58/C1
San Giovanni Gemini, It. 46/C4
San Giovanni in Croce, It. 58/D2
San Giovanni in Fiore, It. 46/C4
San Giovanni in Marignano, It. 59/F5
San Giovanni in Persiceto, It. 59/E3
San Giovanni Lupatoto, It. 59/E3
San Giovanni Valdarno, It. 59/E5
San Giuliano, It. 59/G1
San Giuliano Terme, It. 58/D3
San Giustino, It. 59/F5
San Giusto Canavese, It. 58/A2
San Gorgonio (mtn.), Ca, US 128/C4
San Gottardo, Passo del (pass), Swi. 57/E4
San Gregorio, Arg. 158/E2
San Gregorio, Uru. 159/L10
San Gregorio, It. 58/C2
San Guiliano Milanese, It. 58/C2
San Hipólito Punta (pt.), Mex. 142/B3
San Ignacio, Bol. 142/B3
San Ignacio, Peru 156/B2
San Ignacio, Bol. 150/F7
San Ignacio, Mex. 142/B3

San Ignacio, Mex. 142/D4
San Ignacio, Belz. 144/D2
San Ignacio, Bol. 150/F7
San Ildefonso, Sp. 44/D2
San Isidro, Nic. 144/E3
San Isidro, CR 145/F4
San Isidro, Ca, US 152/C2
San Jacinto, Col. 152/C2
San Jacinto, Uru. 159/L11
San Javier, Chile 158/C2
San Javier, Sp. 45/E4
San Javier, Uru. 159/J10
San Jerónimo, Mex. 142/E3
San Lázaro (cape), Mex. 142/B3
San Joaquín, Bol. 150/F6
San Joaquín (riv.), Ca, US 128/C3
San Joaquín, Col. 152/C3
San Joaquín (hills), Ca, US 136/G8
San Joaquín (co.), Ca, US 135/L11
San Joaquín (peak), Ecu. 156/F7
San Jorge (cape), Arg. 158/D5
San Jorge (gulf), Arg. 147/C7
San Jorge (riv.), Col. 152/C2
San Jorge, ESal. 144/D3
San Jorge (bay), Mex. 142/B2
San Jorge, Golfo di (gulf), It. 46/A3
San José (gulf), Arg. 158/D4
San José, Col. 152/C4
San José (cap.), CR 145/E4
San José (isl.), Mex. 142/B3
San José, Peru 156/D4
San Jose, Phil. 81/F1
San Jose, Phil. 79/D4
San José, Sp. 45/F3
San Jose (hills), Ca, US 136/G7
San Jose (int'l arpt.), Ca, US 128/B3
San José de Chiquitos, Bol. 150/F7
San José de Guanipa, Ven. 153/E2
San José de Guaribe, Ven. 153/E2
San José de Jáchal, Arg. 157/C3
San José de la Esquina, Arg. 158/E2
San Jose de Los Molinos, Peru 156/C4
San José de los Remates, Nic. 144/E3
San José de Maipo, Chile 158/N8
San José de Mayo, Uru. 159/K11
San José de Raíces, Mex. 143/E3
San José de Seque, Ven. 152/D2
San José del Cabo, Mex. 142/C4
San José del Guaviare, Col. 152/C4
San José Iturbide, Mex. 143/E4
San José Viejo, Mex. 142/C4
San Juan, Arg. 157/C3
San Juan (riv.), Arg. 157/C3
San Juan, Peru 156/C4
San Juan (basin), NM, US 132/A2
San Juan (riv.), NM, US 132/B2
San Juan, Phil. 79/D5
San Juan, PR 141/M8
San Juan (riv.), 140/E5
San Juan (pt.), ESal. 144/D3
San Juan (mts.), Co, US 124/E4
San Juan Abajo, Mex. 142/D4
San Juan Bautista Coixtlahuaca, Mex. 143/F5
San Juan Bautista Tuxtepec, Mex. 144/B2
San Juan Bautista Valle Nacional, Mex. 144/B2
San Juan Capistrano, Ca, US 136/C4
San Juan de Alicante, Sp. 45/E3
San Juan de Aznalfarache, Sp. 44/B4
San Juan de la Costa, Mex. 142/C3
San Juan de Lima (pt.), Mex. 142/D5
San Juan de los Cayos, Ven. 152/E1
San Juan de los Lagos, Mex. 143/E4
San Juan de los Morros, Ven. 150/D2
San Juan del Norte, Nic. 145/F4
San Juan del Río, Mex. 143/F4
San Juan Guichicovi, Mex. 140/B4
San Juan Hot Springs, Ca, US 136/C3

San Juan Ixcaquixtla, Mex. 143/M8
San Juan Juquila Mixes, Mex. 144/C2
San Juan Nepomuceno, Col. 152/C2
San Juanico, Mex. 142/C3
San Juanico Punta (pt.), Mex. 142/B3
San Juanito, Mex. 142/D2
San Justo, Arg. 157/D3
San Lazzaro, It. 59/E4
San Leandro, Ca, US 135/K11
San Leandro (res.), Ca, US 135/K11
San Lorenzo (cape), Ecu. 150/B4
San Lorenzo, Bol. 150/E6
San Lorenzo (peak), Chile 159/B5
San Lorenzo, Ecu. 152/B4
San Lorenzo, Hon. 144/E3
San Lorenzo (cape), It. 46/A3
San Lorenzo (riv.), Mex. 142/D3
San Lorenzo, Peru 156/D3
San Lorenzo, Nic. 144/E3
San Lorenzo, Arg. 159/J11
San Lorenzo, Ca, US 135/K11
San Lorenzo al Mare, It. 58/A5
San Lorenzo de El Escorial, Sp. 45/M8
San Lorenzo in Campo, It. 59/F5
San Lucas, Nic. 144/E3
San Lucas, Cabo (cape), Mex. 142/C4
San Lucas, Bol. 150/E7
San Luis, Arg. 158/D2
San Luis, Guat. 144/D2
San Luis, Peru 156/B4
San Luis, Ven. 152/D2
San Luis (valley), Co, US 132/B2
San Luis Acatlán, Mex. 143/E3
San Luis al Medio, Uru. 159/G2
San Luis de la Paz, Mex. 143/E4
San Luis Obispo, Ca, US 128/B3
San Luis Potosí (state), Mex. 143/E4
San Luis Potosí, Mex. 143/E4
San Luis Rey (riv.), Ca, US 136/C4
San Luis Rey, Ca, US 136/C4
San Luis, Sierra de (mts.), Arg. 158/D2
San Manuel, Az, US 128/E4
San Marcello Pistoiese, It. 59/D4
San Marcos, Peru 156/B3
San Marcos, Mex. 143/E3
San Marcos, Tx, US 129/H5
San Marcos, Ca, US 136/C4
San Marcos, Mex. 140/B4
San Marcos, Guat. 144/D3
San Marcos, CR 145/E4
San Marcos, Col. 152/C2
San Mariá di Porto Novo, It. 59/G5
San Marino (ctry.) 59/F5
San Marino (cap.) 59/F5
San Marino, Ca, US 136/F7
San Martín (riv.), Bol. 150/F6
San Martín (dept.), Peru 156/B2
San Martín, Mex. 143/R9
San Martín, Col. 152/C4
San Martín (lake), Arg. 147/B7
San Martín, Arg. 158/C2
San Martín Cuautlalpan, Mex. 143/R10
San Martín de los Andes, Arg. 158/C4
San Martín de Valdeiglesias, Sp. 44/C2
San Martino Buon Albergo, It. 59/E2
San Martino-di-Lota, Fr. 46/A1
San Martino di Lupari, It. 59/E1
San Martino di Venezze, It. 59/E2
San Martino in Passiria (Sankt Martin in Passieir), It. 57/H4
San Martino in Rio, It. 59/D3
San Martino in Strada, It. 59/D3
San Martino Siccomario, It. 58/C2

San Mateo Xoloc, Mex. 143/Q9
San Matías, Bol. 150/G7
San Matías, Golfo (gulf), Arg. 147/C7
San Maurizio d'Opaglio, It. 58/B1
San Mauro Pascoli, It. 59/F4
San Mauro Torinese, It. 58/A2
San Michele al Tagliamento, It. 59/F1
San Miguel (riv.), Bol. 150/F6
San Miguel, Peru 156/B2
San Miguel, Peru 156/C4
San Miguel, Mex. 132/C4
San Miguel, ESal. 144/D3
San Miguel (gulf), Pan. 145/G4
San Miguel (riv.), Col. 152/B4
San Miguel Coatlincham, Mex. 143/R10
San Miguel de Allende, Mex. 143/E4
San Miguel de los Bancos, Ecu. 152/B4
San Miguel de Tucumán, Arg. 157/C2
San Miguel del Monte, Arg. 159/J11
San Miguel Tlaixpan, Mex. 143/R9
San Miguel Totolapan, Mex. 140/A4
San Miniato, It. 59/D5
San Nicolas (isl.), Ca, US 128/B4
San Nicolás de los Arroyos, Arg. 158/E2
San Nicolò, It. 58/C2
San Onofre (mtn.), Ca, US 136/C4
San Onofre, Ca, US 136/C4
San Onofre, Col. 152/C2
San Pablo, Chile 158/B4
San Pablo, Col. 152/B4
San Pablo, Peru 156/B2
San Pablo, Phil. 79/D5
San Pablo (int'l arpt.), Sp. 44/C4
San Pablo, Ca, US 135/K11
San Pablo (res.), Ca, US 135/K11
San Pablo Bay NWR, Ca, US 135/K10
San Pablo de las Salinas, Mex. 143/Q9
San Pablo Huixtepec, Mex. 144/B2
San Paolo, It. 58/D2
San Pawl il-Baħar, Malta 46/L7
San Pedro, Arg. 157/F1
San Pedro, Par. 157/C1
San Pedro (vol.), Chile 157/C1
San Pedro (vol.), Mex. 132/B3
San Pédro, C.d'Iv. 102/D5
San Pedro, Belz. 144/E2
San Pedro (riv.), Guat. 144/D2
San Pedro, Chile 158/N8
San Pedro, Arg. 159/J10
San Pedro Arriba, Mex. 143/Q10
San Pedro Carchá, Guat. 144/D3
San Pedro de Cajas, Peru 156/C3
San Pedro de la Cueva, Mex. 142/C2
San Pedro de las Colonias, Mex. 132/C5
San Pedro de Lloc, Peru 156/B3
San Pedro de Lóvago, Nic. 145/E3
San Pedro de Macorís, DRep. 141/H4
San Pedro del Pinatar, Sp. 45/E4
San Pedro Huamelula, Mex. 144/C2
San Pedro Pochutla, Mex. 144/B2
San Pedro, Sierra de (mts.), Sp. 44/B3
San Pedro Sula, Hon. 144/D3
San Pedro Tapanatepec, Mex. 144/C2
San Pedro Totoltepec, Mex. 143/Q10
San Pellegrino Terme, It. 58/C1
San Piero a Sieve, It. 59/E5
San Piero in Bagno, It. 59/E5
San Pietro (isl.), It. 46/A3
San Pietro in Casale, It. 59/E3
San Pietro in Gù, It. 59/E1
San Pietro in Vincoli, It. 59/F4
San Pietro in Volta, It. 59/F2
San Polo d'Enza, It. 58/D3
San Polo di Piave, It. 59/D3
San Possidonio, It. 59/D3
San Quentin, Ca, US 135/K11
San Quintín (cape), Mex. 142/B2
San Quintín, Mex. 142/B2
San Rafael (riv.), Ut, US 128/E3
San Rafael, Arg. 158/C2

San Rafael, Peru 156/B3
San Rafael, Peru 156/B2
San Rafael, Mex. 143/N6
San Rafael (hills), Ca, US 136/F7
San Rafael del Moján, Ven. 152/D2
San Ramón, Peru 156/C3
San Ramón, CR 145/E4
San Ramon, Ca, US 135/L11
San Ramón, Uru. 159/L11
San Ramón de la Nueva Orán, Arg. 157/D1
San Remo, It. 58/A5
San Rocco al Porto, It. 58/C2
San Romano, It. 59/D5
San Roque, Sp. 44/C4
San Rosendo, Chile 158/B3
San Saba (riv.), Tx, US 143/F2
San Salvador (cap.), ESal. 144/D3
San Salvador (riv.), Uru. 159/J10
San Salvador de Jujuy, Arg. 157/C1
San Salvador el Seco, Mex. 143/M7
San Salvador, Isla (isl.), Bahm. 141/G3
San Salvador (Watling) (isl.), Bahm. 141/G3
San Salvatore Monferrato, It. 58/B3
San Salvo, It. 46/D1
San Sebastián, Sp. 44/E1
San Sebastián de los Reyes, Sp. 45/N8
San Sebastián de Yalí, Nic. 144/E3
San Sebastiano, It. 58/D1
San Secondo Parmense, It. 58/D3
San Severo, It. 46/D2
San Telmo (pt.), Mex. 142/E5
San Timoteo, Ven. 152/D2
San Valentín (peak), Chile 158/B5
San Valentino, It. 59/G1
San Vicente (res.), Ca, US 136/D5
San Vicente, Mex. 142/A2
San Vicente, ESal. 144/D3
San Vicente, Chile 158/C2
San Vicente de Alcántara, Sp. 44/B3
San Vicente de Cañete, Peru 156/B4
San Vicente del Caguán, Col. 152/C4
San Vicente del Raspeig, Sp. 45/E3
San Vicino (peak), It. 43/K5
San Vincenzo, It. 43/J5
San Vito (cape), It. 46/C3
San Vito, CR 145/F4
San Vito al Tagliamento, It. 59/F1
San Ysidro, Ca, US 136/C5
Saña, Peru 156/B2
Sana (riv.), Bosn. 48/C3
Şan'ā (Sanaa) (cap.), Yem. 88/D5
Sanae IV, SAfr., Ant. 160/Z
Sanaga (riv.), Camr. 93/C4
Sanak (isl.), Ak, US 134/F5
Sanana (isl.), Indo. 81/G4
Sanandaj, Iran 88/E1
Sananduva, Braz. 155/B3
Sanaur, India 86/D4
Sānāwad, India 89/L4
Sanborn, NY, US 131/S9
Sanch'ŏng, SKor. 73/D5
Sancti Spíritu, Arg. 158/E2
Sancti Spíritus, Cuba 145/G1
Sand (riv.), Ab, Can. 126/F2
Sand (riv.), SAfr. 106/D3
Sand (pt.), Eng, UK 32/D4
Sand (hills), Ne, US 124/F3
Sand, Nor. 38/B2
Sand am Main, Ger. 54/D3
Sand Point, Ak, US 134/F4
Sanda, Japan 77/H6
Sanda (isl.), Sc, UK 34/C1
Sandakan, Malay. 81/E2
Sandane, Nor. 37/C3
Sandanski, Bul. 47/H2
Sandarne, Swe. 38/G1
Sanday (isl.), Sc, UK 31/V14
Sandbach, Eng, UK 35/F5
Sandberg, Ger. 54/C2
Sande, Ger. 51/F1
Sandefjord, Nor. 38/D2
Sandersville, Ga, US 133/H3
Sandhurst, Eng, UK 33/F4
Sandia, Peru 156/D4
Sandıklı, Turk. 90/B2
Sandīla, India 84/C2
Sandino, Cuba 140/E3
Sandnes, Nor. 38/A2
Sandomierz, Pol. 41/L3
Sandoná, Col. 152/B4
Sándorfalva, Hun. 48/E2
Sandougou (riv.), Sen. 102/B3
Sandover (riv.), Austl. 113/G2
Sandoway, Myan. 83/F4
Sandpoint, Id, US 126/D3
Sandrakatsy, Madg. 107/J7
Sandrigo, It. 59/E1
Sands (pt.), NY, US 139/L8
Sands Point, NY, US 139/L8
Sandspit, BC, Can. 134/M5
Sandstedt, Ger. 51/F2
Sandstone, Austl. 112/C3
Sandu Shuizu Zizhixian, China 83/J2
Sandusky, Mi, US 130/D3
Sandusky, Oh, US 130/D3
Sandvika, Nor. 38/D2
Sandviken, Swe. 38/G1
Sandweiler, Lux. 53/F4
Sandwell (co.), Eng, UK 32/D2
Sandwich (cape), Austl. 114/B2
Sandwich, Eng, UK 33/H4
Sandwīp (isl.), Bang. 85/H4
Sandy, Ut, US 137/K12
Sandy (cape), Austl. 114/D4
Sandy (lake), On, Can. 122/G3
Sandy (pt.), RI, US 139/G1
Sandy Bay, Sk, Can. 127/H2
Sandy Hook (bay), NJ, US 138/D3
Sandy Hook (bar), NJ, US 139/J10
Sandy Hook Lighthouse, NJ, US 139/J10
Sandy Springs, Ga, US 133/G3
Sanem, Lux. 53/E4
Sånfjällets NP, Swe. 37/E3
Sanford (mt.), Ak, US 134/K3
Sanford, Me, US 131/G3
Sanford, NC, US 133/J3
Sanford, Fl, US 133/H4
Sangamner, India 89/K5
Sangamon (riv.), Il, US 129/K3
Sangān (mtn.), Afg. 89/H2
Sangaria, India 86/C5
Sangatte, Fr. 52/A2
Sangay (vol.), Ecu. 152/B5
Sangay, PN, Ecu. 150/C4
Sangenjo, Sp. 44/A1
Sanggan (riv.), China 72/C2
Sanggau, Indo. 80/D3
Sanggou (bay), China 73/B4
Sangha (riv.), CAfr. 96/J7
Sangihe (isl.), Indo. 81/G3
Sangihe (isl.), Phil. 67/M9
Sangju, SKor. 73/E4
Sangkulirang, Indo. 81/E3
Sāngla, Pak. 86/B4
Sāngli, India 89/K5
Sangmélima, Camr. 96/H7
Sangō, Japan 77/J6
Sangre de Cristo (mts.), US 129/F3
Sangre Grande, Trin. 153/F2
Sangri, China 85/J1
Sangro (riv.), It. 46/D2
Sangrūr, India 86/C4
Sangster (int'l arpt.), Jam. 145/G2
Sangue, Rio do (riv.), Braz. 150/G6
Sangüesa, Sp. 44/E1
Sanguie (prov.), Burk. 103/E4
Sanguinetto, It. 59/E2
Sangzhi, China 79/B2
Sanhe, China 72/H7
Sani (pass), Les. 106/E3
Sāni Bheri (riv.), Nepal 84/D1
San'in Kaigin NP, Japan 74/D3
Saniquellie, Libr. 102/C5
Sanjō, Japan 75/F2
Sankanbiriwa (peak), SLeo. 102/C4
Sankh (riv.), India 85/E4
Sankoroni (riv.), Gui. 102/C4
Sankosh (riv.), India 85/G2
Sankt Aegyd am Neuwalde, Aus. 43/L3
Sankt Agatha, Aus. 55/G6
Sankt Andrä, Aus. 43/L3
Sankt Andrä-Wördern, Aus. 49/N7
Sankt Andreasberg, Ger. 51/H5
Sankt Anton am Arlberg, Aus. 57/G3
Sankt Augustin, Ger. 53/G2
Sankt Blasien, Ger. 56/E2
Sankt Florian am Inn, Aus. 55/G6
Sankt Gallen, Swi. 57/F3
Sankt Gallenkirch, Aus. 57/F3
Sankt Georgen bei Salzburg, Aus. 55/F7
Sankt Georgen im Attergau, Aus. 55/G7
Sankt Georgen im Schwarzwald, Ger. 57/E1
Sankt Goar, Ger. 53/G3
Sankt Goarshausen, Ger. 53/G3
Sankt Ingbert, Ger. 53/G5
Sankt Johann im Pongau, Aus. 43/K3
Sankt Johann in Tirol, Aus. 43/K3
Sankt Leonhard im Pitztal, Aus. 57/G3
Sankt Leonhard in Passeier (San Leonardo in Passiria), It. 57/H4
Sankt Marien, Aus. 55/H6
Sankt Martin im Mühlkreis, Aus. 55/H6
Sankt Michael in Obersteiermark, Aus. 43/L3
Sankt Moritz, Swi. 57/F5
Sankt Oswald bei Freistadt, Aus. 55/H5
Sankt Pantaleon, Aus. 55/F6
Sankt Peter am Hart, Aus. 55/G6
Sankt Peter in der Au, Aus. 55/H6
Sankt Peter-Ording, Ger. 38/C4
Sankt Pölten, Aus. 41/H4
Sankt Stephan, Swi. 56/D4
Sankt Ulrich bei Steyr, Aus. 55/H6
Sankt Valentin, Aus. 55/H6
Sankt Veit, Aus. 48/B1
Sankt Veit an der Glan, Aus. 43/L3
Sankt Wendel, Ger. 53/G5
Sankt Wolfgang, Ger. 55/F6
Sanlúcar de Barrameda, Sp. 44/B4
Sanmatenga (prov.), Burk. 103/E3
Sanmen, China 79/D2
Sanmenxia, China 72/B4
Sanming, China 79/C2
Sannan, Japan 77/H5
Sannazzaro de'Burgondi, It. 58/B2
Sannicandro Garganico, It. 46/D2
Sannikova (str.), Rus. 65/P2
San'nohe, Japan 76/B3
Sannois, Fr. 30/J5
Sano, Japan 75/F2
Sanok, Pol. 41/M4
Sanquhar, Sc, UK 36/C6
Sanquianga, PN, Col. 150/C3
Sans Bois (mts.), Ok, US 132/E3
Sansepolcro, It. 59/F5
Sanshui, China 79/B3
Sant Adrià de Besòs, Sp. 45/L7
Sant Boi de Llobregat, Sp. 45/L7
Sant Carles de la Ràpita, Sp. 45/F2
Sant Celoni, Sp. 45/L6
Sant Cugat del Vallès, Sp. 45/L7
Sant Feliu de Guíxols, Sp. 45/G2
Sant Feliu de Llobregat, Sp. 45/L7
Sant Julia, And. 42/D5
Sant Pere de Ribes, Sp. 45/K7
Sant Sadurní d'Anoia, Sp. 45/K7
Sant Vicenç de Castellet, Sp. 45/K6
Sant Vicenç dels Horts, Sp. 45/L7
Santa (riv.), Peru 156/B3
Santa, Peru 156/B3
Santa Ana, Bol. 150/E6
Santa Ana, Ecu. 152/A5
Santa Ana, ESal. 144/D3
Santa Ana, Hon. 144/E3
Santa Ana (vol.), ESal. 144/D3
Santa Ana, Mex. 142/C2
Santa Ana, Ca, US 136/G8
Santa Ana (riv.), Ca, US 136/C3
Santa Ana (mts.), Ca, US 136/C3
Santa Ana, Ven. 152/C3
Santa Ana, Ven. 152/D2
Santa Ana del Alto Beni, Bol. 150/E7
Santa Anna, Tx, US 129/H5
Santa Bárbara, Braz. 155/D1
Santa Bárbara, Chile 158/B3
Santa Bárbara, Hon. 144/D3
Santa Bárbara, Mex. 142/D3
Santa Barbara, Ca, US 136/A2
Santa Barbara (co.), Ca, US 136/A1
Santa Bárbara, Ven. 152/D3
Santa Bárbara, Ven. 152/D2
Santa Bárbara d'Oeste, Braz. 155/C2
Santa Barbara Mountains Nat'l Rec. Area, Ca, US 136/E7
Santa Catalina, Phil. 79/D6
Santa Catalina, Ven. 152/D3
Santa Catalina, Pan. 145/F4
Santa Catalina (isl.), CA, US 124/B5
Santa Catalina, Gulf of (gulf), Ca, US 128/C4
Santa Catarina (state), Braz. 155/B3
Santa Catarina, Mex. 143/E3
Santa Catarina, Ilha de (isl.), Braz. 157/G2
Santa Cecília, Braz. 155/B3
Santa Clara, Cuba 145/G1
Santa Clara, Mex. 142/E3
Santa Clara, Ven. 153/E2
Santa Clara, Ca, US 135/L12
Santa Clara (co.), Ca, US 135/L12
Santa Clara, Barragem de (res.), Port. 44/A4
Santa Clara de Olimar, Uru. 159/G2
Santa Clarita, Ca, US 136/B2
Santa Clotilde, Peru 152/C5
Santa Coloma de Farners, Sp. 45/G2
Santa Coloma de Gramanet, Sp. 45/L7
Santa Comba, Sp. 44/A1
Santa Croce di Magliano, It. 46/D2
Santa Croce sull'Arno, It. 59/D5
Santa Cruz (riv.), Az, US 129/E5
Santa Cruz, Braz. 154/C2
Santa Cruz, Peru 156/C2
Santa Cruz, Mex. 128/E5
Santa Cruz, Phil. 79/E6
Santa Cruz, Phil. 79/D5
Santa Cruz, Ca, US 128/B3
Santa Cruz, Phil. 79/D5
Santa Cruz (isls.), Sol. 116/F6
Santa Cruz (riv.), Arg. 147/B8
Santa Cruz (mts.), Guat. 144/D3
Santa Cruz, CR 144/E4
Santa Cruz, Chile 158/C2
Santa Cruz (prov.), Arg. 158/C5
Santa Cruz (isl.), Ecu. 156/E7
Santa Cruz da Graciosa, Azor., Port. 45/S12
Santa Cruz da Vitória, Braz. 154/C4
Santa Cruz das Flores, Azor., Port. 45/R12
Santa Cruz de Bucaral, Ven. 152/D2
Santa Cruz de El Seibo, DRep. 141/H4
Santa Cruz de la Palma, Canl.,Sp. 98/A3
Santa Cruz de la Sierra, Bol. 150/F7
Santa Cruz de la Zarza, Sp. 44/D3
Santa Cruz de Mudela, Sp. 44/D3
Santa Cruz de Orinoco, Ven. 153/E2
Santa Cruz de Tenerife, Canl.,Sp. 98/A3
Santa Cruz del Quiché, Guat. 144/D3
Santa Cruz del Sur, Cuba 145/G1
Santa Cruz do Capibaribe, Braz. 154/C2
Santa Cruz do Piauí, Braz. 154/B2
Santa Cruz do Rio Pardo, Braz. 155/B2
Santa Cruz do Sul, Braz. 155/A4
Santa Cruz Island (isl.), Ca, US 128/C4
Santa Elena, Peru 156/C2
Santa Elena (bay), CR 144/E4
Santa Elena, Hon. 144/E2
Santa Elena (cape), CR 144/E4
Santa Elena, Ecu. 152/A5
Santa Elena (peak), Arg. 158/D5
Santa Elena de Uairén, Ven. 153/F3
Santa Eugenia de Ribeira, Sp. 44/A1
Santa Eulalia del Río, Sp. 45/F3
Santa Fe, Arg. 157/D3
Santa Fe (cap.), NM, US 129/F4
Santa Fe (riv.), Fl, US 133/H4
Santa Fé, Sp. 44/D4
Santa Fe, Cuba 145/F1
Santa Fé do Sul, Braz. 155/B2
Santa Fe Springs, Ca, US 136/F8
Santa Felicia (dam), Ca, US 136/B2
Santa Filomena, Braz. 154/A3
Santa Giustina (lake), It. 57/H5
Santa Helena, Braz. 154/A1
Santa Helena de Goiás, Braz. 155/B1
Santa Inés (isl.), Chile 157/B7
Santa Inês, Braz. 154/C4
Santa Inês, Braz. 154/A1
Santa Isabel, Ecu. 156/B1
Santa Isabel, Braz. 211/G8
Santa Isabel (isl.), Sol. 116/E5
Santa Isabel (riv.), Guat. 144/D2
Santa Isabel, Arg. 158/D3
Santa Isabel, Arg. 158/E2
Santa Isabel de Sihuas, Peru 156/C5
Santa Isabel, Pico de (peak), EqG. 96/G7
Santa Juliana, Braz. 155/C1
Santa Lucía, Canl. 45/X17
Santa Lucía, Ecu. 152/B5
Santa Lucía, Peru 156/D4
Santa Lucía, Uru. 159/K11
Santa Lucía, Ven. 152/D2
Santa Lucia di Piave, It. 59/F1
Santa Luz, Braz. 154/C3
Santa Luzia, Braz. 154/A1
Santa Luzia, Braz. 155/D1
Santa Luzia, Braz. 154/C2
Santa Luzia (isl.), CpV. 93/J10
Santa Magdalena (isl.), Mex. 142/B3
Santa Magdalena, Arg. 158/E2
Santa Margarita (isl.), Mex. 142/B3
Santa Margarita (riv.), Ca, US 136/C4
Santa Margherita Ligure, It. 58/C4
Santa Maria, Braz. 157/F2
Santa Maria, Ca, US 128/B4
Santa Maria (riv.), Mex. 132/B4
Santa María (riv.), Mex. 142/D2
Santa Maria (bay), Mex. 142/C3
Santa María (cape), Port. 44/B4
Santa Maria (isl.), Azor., Port. 45/T13
Santa Maria (isl.), Chile 158/B3
Santa Maria, CpV. 93/K10
Santa María, Chile 158/N8
Santa María, Ecu. 156/E7
Santa María (isl.), Ecu. 156/E7
Santa Maria a Monte, It. 59/D5
Santa Maria, Cabo de (cape), Moz. 107/F2
Santa Maria Capua Vetere, It. 46/D2
Santa Maria, Chapadão de (hills), Braz. 154/A4
Santa Maria da Boa Vista, Braz. 154/C3
Santa Maria da Vitória, Braz. 154/A4
Santa María de Cayón, Sp. 44/D1
Santa María de Ipire, Ven. 153/E2
Santa María de Nanay, Peru 156/C1
Santa María del Oro, Mex. 142/D3
Santa Maria della Versa, It. 58/C3
Santa Maria di Leuca, Capo (cape), It. 47/F3
Santa Maria do Suaçui, Braz. 154/B5
Santa Maria Maddalena, It. 59/E3
Santa Maria Maggiore, It. 57/E5
Santa Maria Nuova, It. 59/G6
Santa María Xadani, Mex. 140/B4
Santa Marta, Col. 152/C2
Santa Marta Grande (cape), Braz. 155/B4
Santa Marta, Sierra Nevada de (mts.), Col. 152/C2
Santa Monica (bay), Ca, US 136/B3
Santa Monica (mts.), Ca, US 136/B2
Santa Monica, Ca, US 136/F7
Santa Monica Mountains Nat'l Rec. Area, Ca, US 136/B2
Santa Olalla del Cala, Sp. 44/B4
Santa Paula (peak), Ca, US 136/A2
Santa Paula, Ca, US 136/A2
Santa Pola, Sp. 45/E3
Santa Pola, Cabo de (cape), Sp. 45/E3
Santa Quitéria, Braz. 154/B2
Santa Quitéria do Maranhão, Braz. 154/B1
Santa Rita, Braz. 154/A1
Santa Rita, Braz. 154/D2
Santa Rita, Ven. 152/D2
Santa Rita de Cássia, Braz. 154/A3
Santa Rita do Sapucaí, Braz. 211/H7
Santa Rosa, Arg. 150/F8
Santa Rosa, Arg. 158/D3
Santa Rosa, Arg. 157/C3
Santa Rosa, Braz. 157/F2
Santa Rosa, CR 144/E4
Santa Rosa, Ecu. 156/B1
Santa Rosa, Peru 156/D4
Santa Rosa, Uru. 159/K11
Santa Rosa, Ven. 152/D2
Santa Rosa, Ca, US 128/B3
Santa Rosa, NM, US 129/F4
Santa Rosa (mts.), Nv, US 124/C3
Santa Rosa (range), Nv, US 128/C2
Santa Rosa and San Jacinto Mountains Nat'l Mon., Ca, US 128/C4
Santa Rosa, Bajo de (plain), Arg. 158/D4
Santa Rosa de Aguán, Hon. 144/E3
Santa Rosa de Copán, Hon. 144/D3
Santa Rosa de Osos, Col. 152/C3
Santa Rosa de Viterbo, Braz. 155/C2
Santa Rosa Island (isl.), Ca, US 128/B4
Santa Rosalía (pt.), Mex. 142/B2
Santa Rosalía, Mex. 142/B3
Santa Rosalía, Ven. 152/D2
Santa Rosalía, Ven. 153/E3
Santa Sofia, It. 59/E5
Santa Susana (mts.), Ca, US 136/B2
Santa Teresa (riv.), Braz. 151/J6
Santa Teresa, Austl. 113/G3
Santa Teresa Abor. Land, Austl. 113/G2
Santa Teresa, PN, Uru. 159/G2
Santa Teresinha, Braz. 151/H6
Santa Teresita, Arg. 159/F3
Santa Vitória, Braz. 155/B1
Santa Vitória do Palmar, Braz. 159/G2
Santa Ynez (mts.), Ca, US 136/A2
SantAantioco (isl.), It. 46/A3
Santaella, Sp. 44/C4
Sant'Agata Bolognese, It. 59/E3
Sant'Agata di Militello, It. 46/D3
Sant'Agata Feltria, It. 59/F5
Sant'Agostino, It. 59/E3
Sant'Alberto, It. 59/F3
Santan (canal), Az, US 137/S19
Santana, Braz. 154/A4
Santana (isl.), Braz. 154/B1
Santana do Acaraú, Braz. 154/B1
Santana do Ipanema, Braz. 154/C3
Santana do Livramento, Braz. 157/E3
Santander, Sp. 44/D1
Santander (dept.), Col. 145/H5
Santander de Quilichao, Col. 152/B4
Santander Jiménez, Mex. 143/F3
Sant'Angelo in Vado, It. 59/F5
Sant'Angelo Lodigiano, It. 58/C2
Sant'Antioco, It. 46/A3
Sant'Antonio, It. 59/D2
Santañy, Sp. 45/G3
Sant'Apollinare in Classe, It. 59/F4
Santarcángelo, It. 59/F4
Santarém, Braz. 151/H4
Santarém (dist.), Port. 44/A3
Santarém, Port. 44/A3
Sant'arsenio, It. 46/D2
Santee (riv.), SC, US 133/J3
Santee, Ca, US 136/D5
Sant'Eeufemia (gulf), It. 46/D3
Santena, It. 58/A3
Santerno (riv.), It. 43/J4
Santeuil, Fr. 30/H4
Santhia, It. 58/B2
Santiago, Braz. 157/F2
Santiago, Peru 156/C4
Santiago, Phil. 79/D4
Santiago (res.), Ca, US 136/C3
Santiago (peak), Ca, US 136/C3
Santiago (int'l arpt.), Sp. 44/A1
Santiago (riv.), Peru 152/B5
Santiago, Pan. 152/A2
Santiago (mtn.), Pan. 145/F4
Santiago (mts.), Tx, US 124/F5
Santiago (cap.), Chile 158/N8
Santiago (cape), Chile 159/B6
Santiago Cuautlalpan, Mex. 143/R10
Santiago Cuautlalpan, Mex. 143/Q9
Santiago de Cao, Peru 156/B2
Santiago de Chocorvos, Peru 156/C4
Santiago de Chuco, Peru 156/B3
Santiago de Compostela, Sp. 44/A1
Santiago de Cuba, Cuba 145/H1
Santiago de los Caballeros, DRep. 141/G4
Santiago de Machaca, Bol. 156/D5
Santiago del Estero, Arg. 157/D2
Santiago do Cacém, Port. 44/A3
Santiago Ixcuintla, Mex. 142/D4
Santiago Jamiltepec, Mex. 144/B2
Santiago Juxtlahuaca, Mex. 144/B2
Santiago Miahuatlán, Mex. 143/M8
Santiago Papasquiaro, Mex. 142/D3
Santiago Pinotepa Nacional, Mex. 144/B2
Santiago Tilapa, Mex. 143/Q10
Santiago Tolman, Mex. 143/R9
Santiago Vázquez, Uru. 159/K11
Santiago Zacatepec, Mex. 144/C2
Sant'Ilario d'Enza, It. 58/D3
Sāntipur, India 85/G4
Säntis (peak), Swi. 57/F3
Santisteban del Puerto, Sp. 44/D3
Santō, Japan 77/G5
Santō, Japan 77/K5
Santo Amaro, Braz. 154/C4
Santo Amaro, Ilha de (isl.), Braz. 211/G8
Santo Anastácio, Braz. 155/B2
Santo André, Braz. 211/G8
Santo Ângelo, Braz. 157/F2
Santo Antão (isl.), CpV. 93/J9
Santo António, SaoT. 96/G7
Santo Antônio de Jesus, Braz. 154/C4
Santo Antônio de Pádua, Braz. 155/D2
Santo Antônio do Içá, Braz. 152/E5
Santo Antônio do Jacinto, Braz. 154/B5
Santo Antônio dos Lopes, Braz. 154/A2
Santo Domingo (cap.), DRep. 141/H4
Santo Domingo, Mex. 143/E4
Santo Domingo (pt.), Mex. 142/B3
Santo Domingo, Cuba 145/F1
Santo Domingo, Chile 158/N8
Santo Domingo de la Calzada, Sp. 44/D1
Santo Domingo de los Colorados, Ecu. 152/B5
Santo Domingo Petapa, Mex. 144/C2
Santo Domingo Tehuantepec, Mex. 144/C2
Santo Domingo Zanatepec, Mex. 144/C2
Santo Estêvão, Braz. 154/C4
Santo Onofre (riv.), Braz. 154/B4
Santo Stefano Belbo, It. 58/B3
Santo Stefano d'Aveto, It. 58/C3
Santo Stefano di Magra, It. 58/C4
Santo Stino di Livenza, It. 59/F1
Santo Tomás, Peru 156/C4
Santo Tomás, Peru 156/B2
Santo Tomás, Mex. 142/A2
Santo Tomás (pt.), Mex. 142/A2
Santo Tomás (vol.), Ecu. 156/E7
Santo Tomé, Arg. 157/E2
Santo Tomé, Arg. 157/D3
Santoña, Sp. 44/D1
Santorso, It. 59/E1
Santos, Braz. 211/G8
Santos Dumont (int'l arpt.), Braz. 211/K7
Santos Dumont, Braz. 211/K6
Santos Reyes Nopala, Mex. 144/B2
Santuario di Crea, It. 58/B2
Santuario di Oropa, It. 58/A1
Şanūr, WBnk. 91/G7
Sanwa, Japan 77/D1
São Benedito, Braz. 154/B2
São Benedito do Rio Prêto, Braz. 154/B1
São Bento, Braz. 154/C2
São Bento, Braz. 154/A1
São Bento do Sapucaí, Braz. 211/H7
São Bento do Sul, Braz. 155/B3
São Bento do Una, Braz. 154/C3
São Bernardo do Campo, Braz. 211/G8
São Borja, Braz. 157/E2
São Carlos, Braz. 155/C2
São Cristóvão, Braz. 154/C3
São Desidério, Braz. 154/A4
São Domingos (riv.), Braz. 154/A4
São Domingos, Braz. 154/A4
São Domingos do Maranhão, Braz. 154/A2
São Félix do Xingu, Braz. 151/H5
São Fidélis, Braz. 155/D2
São Filipe, CpV. 93/J11
São Francisco, Braz. 154/A4
São Francisco (riv.), Braz. 147/F3
São Francisco do Sul, Braz. 155/B3
São Francisco, Ilha de (isl.), Braz. 157/G2
São Fransisco de Paula, Braz. 155/B4
São Gabriel, Braz. 157/F3
São Gabriel da Palha, Braz. 155/D1
São Gonçalo, Braz. 211/K7
São Gonçalo do Abaeté, Braz. 154/A5
São Gonçalo do Sapuçaí, Braz. 211/H6
São Gotardo, Braz. 155/C1
São Joachim da Barra, Braz. 155/C2
São João Batista, Braz. 154/A1
São João Batista, Braz. 155/B3
São João da Aliança, Braz. 154/A4
São João da Barra, Braz. 155/D2
São João da Boa Vista, Braz. 211/G6
São João da Madeira, Port. 44/A2
São João da Pesqueira, Port. 44/B2
São João da Ponte, Braz. 154/A4
São João das Lampas, Port. 45/P10
São João de Meriti, Braz. 211/K7
São João del Rei, Braz. 155/C2
São João do Paraíso, Braz. 154/B4
São João do Piauí, Braz. 154/B3
São João dos Patos, Braz. 154/B2
São João Evangelista, Braz. 155/D1
São João, Ilhas de (isl.), Braz. 151/K4
São João Nepomuceno, Braz. 211/K6
São João, Serra de (mts.), Braz. 150/F5
São Joaquim, Braz. 155/B4
São Joaquim, PN de, Braz. 155/B4
São Jorge (isl.), Azor., Port. 45/S12
São José, Braz. 155/B3
São José da Laje, Braz. 154/C3
São José de Mipibu, Braz. 154/D2
São José de Piranhas, Braz. 154/C2
São José de Ribamar, Braz. 154/A1
São José do Belmonte, Braz. 154/C2
São José do Egito, Braz. 154/C2
São José do Norte, Braz. 155/A5
São José do Peixe, Braz. 154/B2
São José do Rio Pardo, Braz. 211/G6
São José do Rio Prêto, Braz. 155/B2
São José dos Campos, Braz. 211/H8
São José dos Pinhais, Braz. 155/B3
São Julião, Braz. 154/B2
São Leopoldo, Braz. 155/B4
São Lourenço (riv.), Braz. 151/G7
São Lourenço, Braz. 211/H7
São Lourenço, Port. 45/P11
São Lourenço do Sul, Braz. 155/B4
São Luís, Braz. 154/A1
São Luís do Curu, Braz. 154/C1
São Luís do Quitunde, Braz. 154/D3
São Manoel, Braz. 155/B2
São Marcos (riv.), Braz. 154/A5
São Marcos (bay), Braz. 147/E3
São Martinho do Porto, Port. 44/A3
São Mateus, Braz. 155/E1
São Mateus (riv.), Braz. 155/D1
São Mateus do Maranhão, Braz. 154/A2
São Mateus do Sul, Braz. 155/B3
São Miguel, Braz. 154/C2
São Miguel (isl.), Azor., Port. 45/T13
São Miguel Arcanjo, Braz. 155/C2
São Miguel do Tapuio, Braz. 154/B2
São Miguel dos Campos, Braz. 154/C3
São Nicolau (isl.), CpV. 93/J10
São Paulo (state), Braz. 155/B2
São Paulo, Braz. 211/G8
São Paulo de Olivença, Braz. 150/E4
São Paulo do Potengi, Braz. 154/D2
São Pedro da Aldeia, Braz. 155/D2
São Pedro do Piauí, Braz. 154/B2
São Pedro do Sul, Port. 44/A2
São Raimundo das Mangabeiras, Braz. 154/A2
São Raimundo Nonato, Braz. 154/B3
São Romão, Braz. 154/A5

São Roque, Cabo de
(cape), Braz. 154/D2
São Roque do Pico,
Azor., Port. 45/S12
São Sebastião (pt.),
Moz. 105/G5
São Sebastião, Braz. 211/H8
São Sebastião do Paraíso,
Braz. 155/C2
São Sebastião, Ilha de
(isl.), Braz. 155/C2
São Simão, Barragem de
(res.), Braz. 155/B1
São Teotónio, Port. 44/A4
São Tiago, Braz. 155/C2
São Tiago (isl.), CpV. 93/K10
São Tomé (cap.), SaoT. 96/G7
São Tomé (isl.), SaoT. 96/G7
São Tomé and Príncipe
(ctry.) 96/F7
São Tomé, Cabo de
(cape), Braz. 155/D2
São Vicente, Braz. 211/G8
São Vicente (cape),
Port. 44/A4
São Vicente (isl.),
CpV. 93/J10
Saône (riv.), Fr. 42/D3
Saône-et-Loire (dept.),
Fr. 56/B4
Saori, Japan 77/L5
Saouru (riv.), Alg. 96/E1
Sápai, Gre. 47/J2
Sapallanga, Peru 156/C4
Sapanca, Turk. 49/K5
Sapatgrām, India 85/H2
Sapé, Braz. 154/D2
Sapele, Nga. 103/G5
Sapelo (isl.), Ga, US 133/H4
Saphane, Turk. 49/L5
Sapiéndza (isl.), Gre. 47/G4
Sapkyo, SKor. 73/D4
Sapo (mts.), Pan. 145/G5
Sapo NP, Libr. 102/C5
Saposoa, Peru 156/B2
Sappemeer, Neth. 50/D2
Sapphire, Austl. 114/B3
Sappington, Mo, US 137/G8
Sapporo, Japan 76/B2
Sapri, It. 46/D2
Sapsi (isl.), SKor. 73/D3
Sapt Kosi (riv.), Nepal 85/F2
Sapucaí (riv.), Braz. 211/H7
Sapucaia, Braz. 211/L6
Saqqez, Iran 88/E1
Saquena, Peru 156/C2
Saquisilí, Ecu. 152/B5
Šar (mts.), Serb 47/G1
Sar Dasht, Iran 90/F2
Sar-e Pol, Afg. 87/E5
Sara Buri, Thai. 78/C3
Sarāb, Iran 88/E1
Saraguro, Ecu. 156/B1
Saraí Alamgir, Pak. 86/B3
Saraí Sidhu, Pak. 86/A4
Sarajevo (cap.), Bosn. 40/D3
Saraland, Al, US 133/F4
Saramacca (dist.),
Sur. 153/H3
Saran (peak), Indo. 80/D4
Saran', Kaz. 87/F3
Saranac Lake,
NY, US 130/F2
Sarandapótamos (riv.),
Gre. 47/N8
Sarandë, Alb. 47/G3
Sarandi de Navarro,
Uru. 159/K10
Sarandí del Yi, Uru. 159/G2
Sarandí Grande, Uru. 159/K10
Sarangami
(isls.), Phil. 81/G2
Sārangpur, India 89/L4
Saransk, Rus. 63/H1
Sarapul, Rus. 61/M4
Sarare (riv.), Ven. 152/D3
Sarasota, Fl, US 133/H5
Saratoga, Wy, US 126/G5
Saratoga, Ca, US 135/K12
Saratoga Springs,
NY, US 130/F3
Saratov (res.), Rus. 63/J1
Saratov, Rus. 63/H2
Saratovskaya Oblast,
Rus. 87/A2
Saravan, Laos 78/D3
Sarawak
(reg.), Malay. 67/L9
Saray, Turk. 49/H5
Sarayacu, Ecu. 152/B5
Sarāyan (riv.), India 84/C2
Sarāyönü, Turk. 90/C2
Sárbogárd, Hun. 48/D2
Sarcelles, Fr. 30/K5
Sārda (riv.), India 84/C1
Sārda (canal), India 84/C2
Sarda (riv.), India 82/D2
Sardara, It. 46/A3
Sardārshahar, India 84/C2
Sardegna (prov.), It. 46/A2
Sardhana, India 86/D5
Sardinata, Col. 152/C2
Sardinaux, Cap des
(cape), Fr. 43/G5
Sardinia (isl.), It. 46/A2
Sardis (lake), Ms, US 129/K4
Sardis (lake),
Ok, US 129/J4
Sareks NP, Swe. 37/F2
Sarektjåkko (peak),
Swe. 37/F2
Sarempaka (peak),
Indo. 81/E4

Sarentino, It. 57/H4
Sarezzo, It. 58/D1
Sargans, Swi. 57/F3
Sargodha, Pak. 86/B3
Sarh, Chad 96/J6
Sārī, Iran 88/F1
Sari-Solenzara, Fr. 46/A2
Sariaya, Phil. 79/D5
Saribi (cape), Indo. 81/J4
Sarigan (isl.), NMar. 116/D3
Sarıgöl, Turk. 90/B2
Sarıkamış, Turk. 90/E1
Sarıkaya, Turk. 62/E5
Sarıkaya (prov.), Turk. 90/C2
Sarikei, Malay. 80/D3
Sarina, Austl. 114/C3
Sarine (riv.), Swi. 43/G3
Sariñena, Sp. 45/E2
Sarīr Kalanshiyū (des.),
Libya 96/K2
Sarīr Tibasti (des.),
Libya 96/J3
Sarita, Tx, US 132/D5
Sarju (riv.), India 84/C1
Sarkad, Hun. 48/E2
Sarkant, Kaz. 70/C2
Şarkikaraağaç, Turk. 90/B2
Şarkışla, Turk. 90/D2
Şarköy, Turk. 49/H5
Sarlat-la-Canéda, Fr. 42/D4
Sarleinsbach, Aus. 55/G5
Sarmato, It. 58/C2
Sarmeola, It. 59/E2
Sarmiento, Arg. 158/C5
Sarmiento
(peak), Chile 159/C7
Särna, Swe. 38/E1
Sarnano, It. 43/K5
Sarnen, Swi. 57/E4
Sarnia, On, Can. 130/C3
Sarnico, It. 58/C1
Sarny, Ukr. 62/C2
Saroma
(lake), Japan 76/C1
Saronic (gulf), Gre. 47/H4
Saronno, It. 58/C1
Saros (gulf), Turk. 49/H5
Sárospatak, Hun. 41/L4
Sarpsborg, Nor. 38/D2
Sarralbe, Fr. 53/G6
Sarre (riv.), Fr. 52/F6
Sarre-Union, Fr. 53/G6
Sarrebourg, Fr. 53/G6
Sarria, Sp. 44/B1
Sarroch, It. 46/A3
Sarry, Fr. 53/D6
Sarsāwa, India 86/D4
Sarsina, It. 59/F5
Savā, Hon. 144/E3
Sarstedt, Ger. 51/G4
Sarstún (riv.),
Guat. 144/D3
Sartang (riv.), Rus. 65/P3
Sarteano, It. 46/B1
Sartène, Fr. 46/A2
Sarthe (riv.), Fr. 42/C3
Sartrouville, Fr. 30/J5
Sarufutsu, Japan 76/C1
Saruhanlı, Turk. 90/A2
Sárvár, Hun. 84/M3
Sárviz (riv.), Hun. 48/D2
Saryesik Atgraü Qumy
(des.), Kaz. 70/C2
Saryshaghan, Kaz. 87/F3
Sarysu (riv.), Kaz. 64/G5
Sarzana, It. 58/C4
Sas Van Gent,
Neth. 52/C1
Sasaginnigack (lake),
Mb, Can. 127/K3
Sasarām, India 85/E3
Sasayama, Japan 77/H5
Sasayama (riv.),
Japan 77/H5
Sásd, Hun. 48/D2
Sasebo, Japan 74/A4
Sashima, Japan 77/D1
Savignano sul Panaro,
It. 59/E4
Savignano sul Rubicone,
It. 59/F4
Savigny-le-Temple,
Fr. 30/K6
Savigny-sur-Orge,
Fr. 30/K5
Savio (riv.), It. 43/K5
Sävja, Swe. 38/G2
Savognin, Swi. 57/F4
Savoie (dept.), Fr. 56/C6
Savona, BC, Can. 126/C3
Savona (prov.), It. 58/B4
Savona, It. 58/B4
Savoonga, Ak, US 134/D3
Savoy (reg.), Fr. 42/F4
Savoy Alps (mts.), Fr. 56/C6
Şavşat, Turk. 90/E1
Sävsjö, Swe. 38/F3
Savu (sea), Phil. 67/M10
Sawahlunto, Indo. 80/B4
Sawankhalok, Thai. 78/B2
Sawara, Japan 75/G3
Sawaski-bana (pt.),
Japan 75/F2
Sawatch (range),
Co, US 128/F3
Sawdā', Jabal (peak),
SAr. 88/D5
Saweba (cape), Indo. 81/H4
Sawel (mtn.), NI, UK 34/A2
Sawtell, Austl. 115/E1
Sawtooth (range),
Id, US 126/E4
Sawtooth Nat'l Rec. Area,
Id, US 126/E5
Sawu (riv.), Indo. 81/F6
Sax, Sp. 45/E3

Satipo, Peru 156/C3
Sātkhira, Bang. 85/G4
Sátoraljaújhely, Hun. 41/L4
Satpayev, Kaz. 87/E3
Satpura (range),
India 89/K4
Satte, Japan 77/D1
Satteins, Aus. 57/F3
Satteldorf, Ger. 54/D4
Sattler, Tx, US 137/U20
Satu Mare, Rom. 41/M5
Satu Mare (co.), Rom. 41/M5
Satun, Thai. 78/C5
Sauce, Peru 156/B2
Sauce Grande (riv.),
Arg. 158/D3
Saucillo, Mex. 132/B4
Sauda, Nor. 38/B2
Saúde, Braz. 154/B3
Sauðárkrókur, Ice. 37/N6
Sauer (riv.), Lux. 51/F5
Sauerlach, Ger. 57/H2
Sauerland
(reg.), Ger. 40/D3
Sauêruiná (riv.),
Braz. 150/G6
Saugatuck (riv.),
Ct, US 139/E1
Saujon, Fr. 42/C4
Sauk (riv.), Mn, US 127/K4
Sauk Centre, Mn, US 127/K4
Sauk Rapids, Mn, US 127/K4
Saül, FrG. 151/H3
Sauland, Nor. 38/C2
Sauldre (riv.), Fr. 42/E3
Saulgau, Ger. 57/F1
Saulheim, Ger. 51/H6
Saulieu, Fr. 42/F3
Sault-lès-Rethel, Fr. 53/D5
Sault Sainte Marie,
On, Can. 130/C2
Sault Ste. Marie,
Mi, US 130/C2
Saumur, Fr. 42/C3
Saunders (peak),
Austl. 112/E3
Saura (riv.), India 85/F3
Saurimo, Ang. 105/D2
Sausalito, Ca, US 135/J11
Sausseron
(riv.), Fr. 30/J4
Sauteurs, Gren. 153/F1
Sava, It. 47/E2
Sava (riv.), Slov. 43/L3
Savā, Hon. 144/E3
Schaijk, Neth. 50/C5
Schalchen, Aus. 55/G6
Schalkau, Ger. 54/E2
Schalksmühle, Ger. 51/E6
Schanck (cape),
Austl. 115/C3
Schangnau, Swi. 56/D4
Scharans, Swi. 57/F4
Schardenberg, Aus. 55/G5
Schärding, Aus. 55/G6
Scharfreiter (peak),
Aus. 57/H3
Scharhorn (isl.), Ger. 50/D2
Scharnebeck, Ger. 51/H2
Scharnitz (pass), Ger. 57/H3
Scharnstein, Ger. 55/G7
Schashagen, Ger. 40/F1
Schattdorf, Swi. 55/G5
Schauenstein, Ger. 54/E2
Schaumburg,
Il, US 135/P15
Scheemda, Neth. 50/D2
Scheer, Ger. 57/F1
Scheessel, Ger. 51/G2
Schefferville,
Qu, Can. 123/K3
Scheibbs, Aus. 41/H4
Scheidegg, Ger. 57/F3
Scheinfeld, Ger. 54/D3
Schelde (riv.), Belg. 42/E1
Schelklingen, Ger. 54/C6
Schell Creek (range),
Nv, US 128/D3
Schellerten, Ger. 51/H4
Schellville, Ca, US 135/K10
Schenectady,
NY, US 130/F3
Schenefeld, Ger. 51/G1
Schermbeck, Ger. 50/C4
Scherpenzeel, Neth. 50/C3
Schertz, Tx, US 137/U20
Schesaplana (peak),
Aus. 57/F3
Schesslitz, Ger. 54/E3
Scheyern, Ger. 57/H1
Schiedam, Neth. 50/B5
Schieder-Schwalenberg,
Ger. 51/G5
Schiehallion (peak),
Sc, UK 36/B3
Schier Monnikoog (isl.),
Neth. 40/D2
Schierling, Ger. 54/F5
Schiermonnikoog (isl.),
Neth. 50/D1
Schiermonnikoog,
Neth. 50/D1
Schiers, Swi. 57/F3
Schifferstadt, Ger. 54/B4
Schiffweiler, Ger. 53/G5
Schijndel, Neth. 50/C5
Schilde, Belg. 50/B6
Schildmeer (lake),
Neth. 50/D2
Schillighörn (cape),
Ger. 51/F1

Saxman, Ak, US 134/M4
Saxon, Swi. 56/D5
Say, Niger 103/F3
Saya, Japan 77/L5
Sayama, Japan 77/D1
Sayama, Japan 77/J6
Sayán, Peru 156/B3
Saydā, Leb. 91/D3
Sayil (ruin), Mex. 144/D1
Saynbach (riv.), Ger. 53/G2
Sayreville, NJ, US 139/H10
Sayula, Mex. 142/E5
Sayville, NY, US 139/E2
Saywün, Yem. 88/E5
Sazan (isl.), Alb. 47/F2
Sázava (riv.), Czh. 43/L2
Sbaa, Alg. 99/E3
Scafell Pikes (peak),
Eng, UK 35/E3
Scalasaig, Sc, UK 31/Q8
Scald Law (peak),
Sc, UK 36/C5
Scalea, It. 46/D3
Scalino (peak), It. 57/F5
Scalloway, Sc, UK 31/W13
Scammon Bay,
Ak, US 134/E3
Scandia, Wa, US 135/B2
Scandiano, It. 59/E3
Scandicci, It. 59/E5
Scapa Flow (chan.),
Sc, UK 31/V14
Scar Water (riv.),
Sc, UK 34/E1
Scarborough, Can. 131/R8
Scarborough,
Eng, UK 35/H3
Scarborough Shoal (isl.),
Phil. 79/C4
Scardovari, It. 59/G3
Scarpe (riv.), Fr. 40/B3
Scarperia, It. 59/E5
Scarriff, Ire. 31/P10
Scarsdale, La, US 137/Q17
Scarsdale, NY, US 139/K7
Sceaux, Fr. 30/J5
Scenic Oaks,
Tx, US 137/T20
Scey-sur-Saône-et-St-Albin,
Fr. 42/F3
Schaefferstown,
Pa, US 138/B3
Schaerbeek, Belg. 50/D2
Schaffhausen (canton),
Swi. 57/E2
Schaffhausen, Swi. 57/E2
Schagen, Neth. 50/B3
Schattdorf, Swi. 56/D4 55/F1
Schilligfürst, Ger. 54/D4
Schiltach, Ger. 57/E1
Schiltigheim, Fr. 56/D1
Schinnen, Neth. 53/E2
Schinznach-Dorf, Swi. 56/E3
Schio, It. 59/E1
Schipbeek (riv.), Neth. 50/D4
Schirmeck, Fr. 53/G6
Schkeuditz, Ger. 51/H4
Schkumbin (riv.), Alb. 47/G2
Schladen, Ger. 51/H4
Schladming, Aus. 43/K3
Schlanders (Silandro),
It. 43/J3
Schlangen, Ger. 51/F5
Schlangenbad, Ger. 54/C3
Schleiden, Ger. 53/E2
Schleitheim, Swi. 57/E2
Schleiz, Ger. 55/F1
Schlema, Ger. 55/F1
Schleswig, Ger. 38/C4
Schleswig-Holstein
(state), Ger. 38/B4
Schleswig-Holsteinisches
Wattenmeer NP, Ger. 38/C4
Schleuse (riv.), Ger. 54/D1
Schleusingen, Ger. 54/D1
Schliengen, Ger. 56/D2
Schlierbach, Aus. 55/H7
Schliersee, It. 57/E3
Schloss Herrenchiemsee,
Ger. 55/G8
Schloss Holte-Stukenbrock,
Ger. 51/F5
Schloss Sanssouci,
Ger. 40/Q7
Schloss Wilhelmstein,
Eng, UK 35/H3
Schlotheim, Ger. 51/H6
Schluchsee, Ger. 56/E2
Schlüchtern, Ger. 54/D2
Schlüsselfeld, Ger. 54/D3
Schlüsslberg, Aus. 55/G6
Schmalkalden, Ger. 43/J11
Schmallenberg, Ger. 51/F6
Schmeich (riv.),
Ger. 54/C6
Schmelz, Ger. 53/F5
Schmiech (riv.), Ger. 57/F1
Schmitten, Swi. 56/D4
Schmitten, Ger. 54/B2
Schmutter (riv.), Ger. 54/E6
Schnaitsee, Ger. 55/F6
Schnaittach, Ger. 55/E3
Schnaittenbach, Ger. 55/F3
Schnarrtanne, Ger. 55/F1
Schnecksville,
Pa, US 138/C2
Schneeberg (peak),
Ger. 54/C6
Schneeberg, It. 55/E2
Schneeberg, Ger. 55/E2
Schneeberg, Ger. 54/C3
Schneifel (upland),
Ger. 40/D7
Schneverdingen,
Ger. 51/G2
Schnuerdingen,
Ger. 51/G2
Schofield Barracks,
Hi, US 124/V12
Schollene, Ger. 40/Q2
Schöllkrippen, Ger. 54/C2
Schömberg, Ger. 57/E1
Schömberg, Ger. 54/B5
Schönaich, Ger. 54/C5
Schönau im Schwarzwald,
Ger. 56/D2
Schönberg, Ger. 38/D4
Schönberg, Ger. 55/G5
Schondorf am Ammersee,
Ger. 57/H1
Schondra (riv.),
Ger. 54/C2
Schönebeck, Ger. 40/F2
Schöneck, Ger. 54/B2
Schöneck, Ger. 54/F2
Schönecken, Ger. 53/F3
Schönefeld (int'l arpt.),
Ger. 40/Q7
Schongau, Ger. 57/H2
Schöningen, Ger. 40/F2
Schönsee, Ger. 55/F3
Schonungen, Ger. 54/D2
Schönwald im Schwarzwald,
Ger. 56/E1
Schoonebeek, Neth. 50/D3
Schoonhoven, Neth. 50/B5
Schoorl, Neth. 50/B3
Schopfheim, Ger. 56/D2
Schopfloch, Ger. 54/D4
Schöppenstedt, Ger. 51/H4
Schörfling, Aus. 55/G7
Schorndorf, Ger. 54/C5
Schorssow, It. 46/D3
Schotten, Ger. 54/C2
Schouten (isl.), Austl. 115/D4
Schouten (isl.), Indo. 116/C5
Schouwen (isl.), Neth. 50/A5
Schramberg, Ger. 56/E1
Schrankogel (peak),
Aus. 57/H3
Schreckhorn (peak),
Swi. 56/E4
Schriesheim, Ger. 54/B3
Schrobenhausen, Ger. 54/E5
Schroffenstein (peak),
Namb. 106/B2
Schrozberg, Ger. 54/D3
Schruns, Aus. 57/F3
Schübelbach, Swi. 57/F3
Schuby, Ger. 38/C4
Schulenburg, Tx, US 137/U21
Schulzendorf, Ger. 40/Q7
Schunter (riv.), Ger. 51/H4
Schüpfheim, Swi. 56/D4
Schussen (riv.), Ger. 57/F2
Schussenried, Ger. 57/F2
Schutter (riv.), Ger. 54/A6

Schutterwald, Ger. 56/D1
Schüttorf, Ger. 51/E4
Schuylkill (riv.),
Pa, US 138/C3
Schuylkill Haven,
Pa, US 138/B2
Schwabach, Ger. 54/E4
Schwabhausen bei Dachau,
Ger. 55/E6
Schwäbisch Gmünd,
Ger. 54/C5
Schwäbisch Hall, Ger. 54/D3
Schwäbische Alb
(range), Ger. 40/E4
Schwabmünchen, Ger. 57/G1
Schwaig bei Nürnberg,
Ger. 54/E4
Schwaigern, Ger. 54/C4
Schwalbach, Ger. 53/F5
Schwalbach am Taunus,
Ger. 54/B2
Schwalm (riv.), Ger. 40/E3
Schwalmtal, Ger. 50/D6
Schwanden, Swi. 57/F4
Schwandorf im Bayern,
Ger. 55/F4
Schwanebeck, Ger. 40/F2
Schwanenstadt, Aus. 55/G6
Schwanewede, Ger. 51/F2
Schwanfeld, Ger. 54/D3
Schwangau, Ger. 57/G2
Schwarmstedt, Ger. 51/G3
Schwartz Elster
(riv.), Ger. 41/G3
Schwartzenberg
(peak), Namb. 106/C4
Schwarza (riv.), Ger. 54/E1
Schwarza (riv.), Ger. 55/F5
Schwarzach im Pongau,
Aus. 43/K3
Schwarze Laber
(riv.), Ger. 54/C6
Schwarzenbach am Wald,
Ger. 55/E2
Schwarzenbek, Ger. 51/H2
Schwarzenberg, Ger. 55/F1
Schwarzenbruck, Ger. 54/D4
Schwarzenburg, Swi. 56/D4
Schwarzenfeld, Ger. 55/F4
Schwarzer Mann
(peak), Ger. 53/E3
Schwarzhorn
(peak), Swi. 57/H3
Schwarzwald (Black Forest)
(for.), Ger. 54/B6
Schwaz, Aus. 43/J3
Schwebheim, Ger. 54/D3
Schwechat, Aus. 55/M3
Schwechat
(int'l arpt.), Aus. 49/P7
Schwedt, Ger. 41/H2
Schwegenheim, Ger. 54/B4
Schweich, Ger. 53/F4
Schweighouse-sur-Moder,
Fr. 53/G6
Schweinfurt, Ger. 54/D2
Schweitenkirchen,
Ger. 55/E5
Sebring, Fl, US 133/H5
Schwelm, Ger. 51/E6
Schwendi, Ger. 57/F1
Schwenksville,
Pa, US 138/C3
Schwerin (lake), Ger. 40/F2
Schwertberg, Aus. 55/H6
Schwerte, Ger. 51/E6
Schwetzingen, Ger. 54/B4
Schwinge (riv.), Ger. 51/G1
Schwörstadt, Ger. 56/D2
Schwülme (riv.), Ger. 51/G5
Schwülper, Ger. 51/H4
Schwyz (canton), Swi. 57/E3
Schwyz, Swi. 57/E3
Sciacca, It. 46/D4
Scicli, It. 46/D4
Scilly (isls.), Eng, UK 31/Q11
Scinawa, Pol. 41/J3
Sciota, Pa, US 138/C2
Scioto (riv.), Oh, US 130/D4
Scobey, Mt, US 127/G3
Scolt (pt.), Eng, UK 33/G1
Scone, Austl. 115/D2
Scopello, It. 58/B2
Scordia, It. 46/D4
Scorzè, It. 59/F2
Scotch Corner,
Eng, UK 35/G3
Scotch Plains, NJ, US 139/H9
Scotia (sea) 160/W
Scotland, UK 36/D3
Scott (cape), BC, Can. 122/D3
Scott (cape),
NW, Can. 123/R7
Scott (lake),
NW,Sk, Can. 122/F2
Scott, NZ, Ant. 160/M
Scott NP, Austl. 112/B5
Scott (reef), Austl. 112/C2
Scottburgh, SAfr. 107/E3
Scottish Borders
(pol. reg.), Sc, UK 36/D4
Scott's Bluff Nat'l Mon.,
Ne, US 129/F2
Scottsbluff, Ne, US 129/G2
Scottsboro, Al, US 133/G3
Scottsburg, In, US 133/G3
Scottsdale, Austl. 115/C4

Scottsdale, Az, US 128/E4
Scottsville, Ky, US 133/G2
Scottville, Mi, US 130/C2
Scourie, Sc, UK 31/R7
Scranton, Pa, US 130/F3
Scunthorpe, Eng, UK 35/H4
Scrivia (riv.), It. 58/B3
Scuol, Swi. 57/G4
Scupi (mts.), Indo. 81/H4
Scuppernong
(riv.), Wi, US 135/N14
Scurdie Ness
(pt.), Sc, UK 36/D3
Scutari (lake), Serb. 47/F1
Séa Cliff, Ca, US 136/A2
Sea Cliff, NY, US 139/L8
Sea Girt, NJ, US 139/H10
Sea Isle City, NJ, US 138/D5
Sea Lake, Austl. 115/B2
Sea-Tac, Wa, US 135/C3
Seabeck, Wa, US 135/B2
Seabold, NJ, US 138/D4
Seabra, Braz. 154/B4
Seabrook, NJ, US 138/C5
Seaford, Eng, UK 33/G5
Seaford, NY, US 139/M9
Seaforde, NI, UK 34/C3
Seaforth, Austl. 114/C3
Segura (riv.), Sp. 44/D3
Seahorse
(pt.), Nun, Can. 123/J2
Seahurst, Wa, US 135/C3
Seal, Eng, UK 33/N7
Seal (riv.), MB, Can. 122/G3
Seal (pt.), Chile 158/B5
Seal (pt.), SAfr. 106/C4
Seal Beach, Ca, US 136/F8
Seale, Eng, UK 30/A3
Seamer, Eng, UK 35/H3
Seano, It. 59/E6
Searcy, Ar, US 129/K4
Seascale, Eng, UK 34/E3
Seaside, Or, US 126/B4
Seaside Heights,
NJ, US 138/D4
Seaside Park, NJ, US 138/D4
Seaton, Eng, UK 32/C5
Seaton Carew, Eng, UK 35/G2
Seattle, Wa, US 126/C4
Sébaco, Nic. 144/E3
Sebago (lake),
Me, US 130/G3
Sebastabad, India 84/C3
Sebastián, FI, US 133/H5
Sebastián Vizcaíno
(bay), Mex. 142/B2
Sebastopol, Ca, US 135/J10
Sebeş, Rom. 40/E4
Sebezh, Rus. 39/N3
Sebkhet al Kalīyah
(drylake), Mor. 100/M7
Sebnitz, Ger. 41/H3
Seboeis (riv.),
Me, US 130/S2
Sebou (riv.), Mor. 100/M4
Sebou, Oued (riv.), Mor. 98/D2
Sebree, Ky, US 133/F2
Sebring, Fl, US 133/H5
Sebuku (isl.), Indo. 81/E4
Secacucus, NJ, US 139/J8
Secchia (riv.), It. 43/J4
Sechura, Peru 156/A2
Sechura, Bay), Peru 156/A2
Sechura, Desierto de
(des.), Peru 156/A2
Seclin, Fr. 52/C2
Seco (riv.), Mex.,US 142/C2
Seco (riv.), Arg. 159/D6
Seco (riv.), Mex. 143/G5
Second Mountain
(mtn.), Pa, US 138/B2
Second Watchung
(mtn.), NJ, US 139/H9
Secunda, NY, US 139/E2
Secunda, SAfr. 106/E2
Secure (riv.), Bol. 150/E7
Seda, Lith. 39/K3
Sedalia, Mo, US 129/J3
Sedan, Fr. 53/E4
Sedano, Sp. 44/D1
Sedaung (mtn.), Myan. 78/B3
Sedbergh, Eng, UK 35/F3
Seddülbahir, Turk. 47/K2
Sedeh, Iran 89/G2
Sederot, Isr. 91/D4
Sedgefield, Eng, UK 35/G2
Sedgwick, Co, US 129/G3
Sedhiou, Sen. 102/B3
Sedílany, Czh. 55/H1
Sedlo (peak), Czh. 55/H1
Sedona, Az, US 128/E4
Sedrata, Alg. 100/K6
Sedro-Woolley, Wa, US 135/C1
See (int'l arpt.), Oman 89/G4
Seeb (int'l arpt.), Oman 89/G4
Seeboden, Aus. 57/H3
Seefeld in Tirol, Aus. 57/H3
Seeg, Ger. 57/G2
Seehausen, Ger. 40/F2
Seeheim, Namb. 106/B3
Seeheim-Jugenheim,
Ger. 54/B3
Seekirchen Markt,
Aus. 55/G7
Seekooi (riv.), SAfr. 107/E3
Seelow, Ger. 41/H2
Seeon-Seebruck, Ger. 55/F6
Seer Green, Eng, UK 30/B2
Sées, Fr. 42/C2
Seeseaupt, Ger. 57/H2
Seeve (riv.), Ger. 51/G2
Seewalchen, Aus. 55/G7

Seewies im Prättigau,
Swi. 57/F4
Sefaatlı, Turk. 90/C2
Şefrou, Mor. 100/M5
Sefton (c.), Eng, UK 35/E4
Segamat, Malay. 80/B3
Segarcea, Rom. 49/F3
Ségbana, Ben. 103/F4
Ségelo-Koro, C.d'Iv. 102/D4
Segelstad Bru, Nor. 38/D1
Seget, Indo. 81/H4
Segezha, Rus. 60/G3
Segorbe, Sp. 45/E3
Ségou, Mali 102/D3
Ségou (pol. reg.), Mali 102/D3
Segovia, Col. 152/C3
Segovia, Sp. 44/C2
Segozero (lake), Rus. 60/G3
Segrate, It. 58/C2
Segré, Fr. 42/C3
Segre (riv.), Sp. 45/F2
Seguam (isl.), Ak, US 134/D5
Séguédine, Niger 96/H3
Séguéla, C.d'Iv. 102/D5
Séguénéga, Burk. 103/E3
Seguin, Tx, US 132/D4
Segura (riv.), Sp. 44/D3
Segusino, It. 59/E2
Sehithwa, Bots. 105/D5
Sehnde, Ger. 51/G4
Sehonghong, Les. 106/E3
Sehore, India 82/C3
Sehwān, Pak. 89/J3
Seibersbach, Ger. 53/G4
Seiersberg, Aus. 48/B2
Seika, Japan 77/J6
Seiling, Ok, US 129/H3
Seille (riv.), Fr. 40/C5
Seinäjoki, Fin. 60/D3
Seine (riv.), On, Can. 127/L3
Seine (bay), Fr. 42/C2
Seine-et-Marne
(dept.), Fr. 52/B5
Seine-Maritime
(dept.), Fr. 52/A4
Seine-st-Denis
(dept.), Fr. 52/B6
Seitenstetten, Aus. 55/H6
Seiwa, Japan 77/K7
Seix, Fr. 42/D5
Seixal, Port. 45/P10
Sejaka, Indo. 81/E4
Sejera (isl.), Den. 38/D4
Sejny, Pol. 39/K4
Sekayu, Indo. 80/B4
Seke, Tanz. 104/A2
Sekenke, Tanz. 104/A3
Seki (riv.), Turk. 91/A1
Seki, Japan 77/L5
Seki, Japan 77/D1
Sekigahara, Japan 77/K5
Sekijo, Japan 77/D1
Sekiyado, Japan 77/D1
Sekondi, Gha. 103/E5
Sel, Nor. 37/D3
Selah, Wa, US 126/C4
Sélaphum, Thai. 78/C2
Selargius, It. 46/A3
Selaru (isl.), Indo. 81/H5
Selatan (cape), Indo. 80/D4
Selawik (lake),
Ak, US 134/G2
Selayar (isl.), Indo. 81/F5
Selb, Ger. 55/F2
Selbitz, Ger. 55/E2
Selbu, Nor. 37/D3
Selby, SD, US 127/H4
Selby, Eng, UK 35/G4
Selby-on-the-Bay,
Md, US 138/B4
Selci, It. 59/F6
Selçuk, Turk. 90/A2
Sele, NY, US 139/E2
Sele (riv.), It. 46/D2
Selebi-Phikwe, Bots. 105/E5
Seleli (hill), Tanz. 104/B5
Selemdzha (riv.),
Rus. 65/N4
Selenča, Serb. 48/C3
Selenge (prov.), Mong. 70/J2
Selenge (riv.), Mong. 70/J2
Selenginsk, Rus. 65/L4
Selenice, Alb. 47/F2
Sélestat, Fr. 56/D1
Selety (riv.), Kaz. 87/F2
Seleznëvo, Rus. 39/N1
Selfoss, Ice. 37/N7
Selfridge, Mrta. 102/B3
Seligenstadt, Ger. 54/B2
Seligman, Az, US 128/D4
Selimbau, Indo. 80/D3
Selimiye, Turk. 90/A2
Selinsgrove, Pa, US 138/B2
Seljord, Nor. 38/C2
Selkan (tun.), Japan 76/B3
Selkirk, Sc, UK 36/D5
Selkirk, Mb, Can. 122/G3
Selkirk (mts.),
BC, Can. 126/D3
Selleck, Wa, US 135/D3
Sellersville, Pa, US 138/C3
Sellières, Fr. 56/B4
Sells, Az, US 128/E5
Selly Oak, Eng, UK 32/E2
Sellye, Hun. 48/C3
Selm, Ger. 51/E5
Selma, Al, US 133/G3
Selma, Ca, US 135/P9
Selmer, Tn, US 133/F3
Selongey, Fr. 56/B2
Sélouma, Gui. 102/C4
Selous Game Reserve,
Tanz. 104/B4
Selsey, Eng, UK 33/F5

Selsey Bill (pt.), Eng, UK 33/F5
Selsingen, Ger. 51/G2
Sel'tso, Rus. 62/E1
Seltz, Fr. 54/B5
Sélune (riv.), Fr. 42/C2
Selvas (for.), Braz. 147/C3
Selvik, Nor. 37/R9
Selwyn, Austl. 114/A3
Selwyn (range), Austl. 114/A3
Selz (riv.), Ger. 43/H2
Semara, WSah. 96/C2
Semarang, Indo. 80/D5
Semarsot, India 86/D5
Sembehun, SLeo. 102/B5
Sembera (riv.), Czh. 55/H2
Semberong (riv.), Malay. 80/B3
Şemdinli, Turk. 90/F2
Séméac, Fr. 42/D5
Semenivka, Ukr. 62/E1
Semenivka, Ukr. 62/E2
Semenov, Rus. 61/K4
Semeru (peak), Indo. 80/D5
Semey, Kaz. 87/H2
Semikarakorsk, Rus. 63/G3
Semilovo, Rus. 63/G1
Semiluki, Rus. 62/F2
Seminole (lake), Ga, US 133/G4
Seminole, Tx, US 132/C3
Seminoe (res.), Wy, US 128/F2
Semitau, Indo. 80/D4
Semliki (riv.), D.R. Congo 104/A2
Semnān, Iran 88/F1
Semnon (riv.), Fr. 40/D4
Semois (riv.), Belg. 42/F2
Semporna, Malay. 81/E3
Semsales, Swi. 56/C4
Semskefjellet (peak), Nor. 37/E2
Sen (riv.), Camb. 83/H5
Sen-san (peak), Japan 77/G7
Sena, Thai. 83/H5
Senador Pompeu, Braz. 154/C2
Senaja, Malay. 81/E2
Senaki, Geo. 63/H4
Senanga, Zam. 105/D4
Sénas, Fr. 90/B5
Senatobia, Ms, US 133/F4
Sence (riv.), Eng, UK 33/E1
Send, Eng, UK 30/B3
Sendai (riv.), Japan 74/D3
Sendai, Japan 75/G1
Sendai, Japan 74/B5
Sendai (int'l arpt.), Japan 75/G1
Sendai (bay), Japan 76/B4
Sendai (riv.), Japan 74/B5
Senden, Ger. 54/D6
Senden, Ger. 51/E5
Sendenhorst, Ger. 51/E5
Senec, Slvk. 41/J4
Seneca Creek State Park, Md, US 138/A5
Seneffe, Belg. 53/C2
Senegal (ctry.) 102/B3
Sénégal (riv.), Afr. 102/B2
Senekal, SAfr. 106/D3
Seney NWR, Mi, US 130/C2
Senezhskoye (lake), Rus. 61/W8
Senfi, Gha. 103/E5
Senftenberg, Ger. 41/H3
Sengenthal, Ger. 55/E4
Sengilev, Rus. 63/J1
Sengor, Bhu. 85/H2
Senguer (riv.), Arg. 158/D3
Senhor do Bonfim, Braz. 154/B3
Senica, Slvk. 41/J4
Senirkent, Turk. 90/B2
Senise, It. 46/E2
Senj, Cro. 43/L4
Senja (isl.), Nor. 37/F1
Senkaku-Shotō (isl.), Japan 75/G8
Şenkaya, Turk. 90/E1
Şenköy, Turk. 91/E1
Senlis, Fr. 52/B5
Senmonoron, Camb. 78/D3
Sennan, Japan 77/H7
Sennar (dam), Sudan 97/M5
Senne (riv.), Belg. 53/D2
Sennecy-le-Grand, Fr. 52/B3
Sennfeld, Ger. 54/D2
Senno, Bela. 39/N4
Sennoy, Rus. 63/G2
Sennoy, Rus. 63/H1
Sennwald, Swi. 57/F3
Sennybridge, Wal, UK 32/C3
Séno (prov.), Burk. 103/F3
Senones, Fr. 56/C1
Senorbì, It. 46/A3
Senou (Bamako) (int'l arpt.), Mali 102/D3
Senovo, Rus. 49/H4
Sens, Fr. 42/E2
Sensuntepeque, ESal. 144/D3
Senta, Serb. 48/E3
Sentani, Indo. 81/K4
Sentery, D.R. Congo 105/E2
Senya Beraku, Gha. 103/E5
Senyavin (isls.), Micr. 116/E4
Senzig, Ger. 40/Q7
Seohāra, India 84/B1
Seon, Swi. 56/E3
Seondha, India 84/B2
Seoni, India 84/B4
Seonī Mālwā, India 84/A4
Seoul (Sŏul) (cap.), SKor. 73/D4

Seoul Grand Park, SKor. 73/G7
Seoul Jikhalsi (prov.), SKor. 73/D4
Sepetiba (bay), Braz. 155/J8
Sepik (riv.), PNG 116/D5
Sep'o, NKor. 73/D3
Sepo, Indo. 81/G3
Sępólno Krajeńskie, Pol. 41/J2
Sept-Îles, Qu, Can. 131/H2
Septemvri, Bul. 47/J1
Septeuil, Fr. 30/H5
Sepulveda (dam), Ca, US 136/F7
Sequeros, Sp. 44/B2
Sequoia NP, Ca, US 128/C3
Serafimovich, Rus. 63/G2
Seraincourt, Fr. 30/H4
Seraing, Belg. 53/E2
Serampore, India 85/G4
Sèran (riv.), Fr. 56/D3
Serasan (isl.), Indo.,Malay. 80/C3
Serasan, Indo. 80/C3
Seravezza, It. 58/D6
Serbia and Montenegro (ctry.) 48/D3
Serbia (reg.), Serb. 48/E4
Serchio (riv.), It. 58/D4
Serdobsk, Rus. 63/H1
Serdsela, It. 59/D5
Serebryansk, Kaz. 64/J5
Serednikovo, Rus. 60/H5
Seregno, It. 58/C2
Serein (riv.), Fr. 40/D4
Sérémange-Erzange, Fr. 53/F5
Seremban, Malay. 80/B3
Serengeti NP, Tanz. 97/M8
Serenje, Zam. 105/F3
Serere, Ugan. 104/A1
Sergach, Rus. 61/K5
Sergeantsville, NJ, US 138/D3
Sergen, Turk. 49/H5
Sergeya Kirova (isls.), Rus. 64/J2
Sergeyevka, Rus. 61/G5
Sergipe (state), Braz. 154/C3
Sergiyev Posad, Rus. 60/H4
Sergnano, It. 58/C3
Seria, Bru. 80/D3
Seriate, It. 58/C2
Sérifontaine, Fr. 52/A5
Sérifos, Gre. 47/J4
Sérifos (isl.), Gre. 47/J4
Sérignan, Fr. 42/E5
Serik, Turk. 90/B2
Seringa, Serra da (mts.), Braz. 151/H5
Serio (riv.), It. 58/C2
Serkout (peak), Alg. 99/G5
Sermaize-les-Bains, Fr. 53/D6
Sermide, It. 59/E4
Sermovodsk, Rus. 63/J1
Sernur, Rus. 61/K4
Serón, Sp. 44/D4
Serós, Sp. 45/F2
Serottini (peak), It. 57/G5
Serov, Rus. 64/G4
Serowe, Bots. 105/E5
Serpa, Port. 44/B4
Serpeddi (peak), It. 46/A3
Serpent's Mouth (str.), Trin.,Ven. 153/F2
Serpentine (dam), Austl. 115/C4
Serpentine Lakes, Austl. 113/F4
Serpukhov, Rus. 60/H5
Serra (peak), It. 58/D6
Serra, Braz. 155/D2
Serra Branca, Braz. 154/C2
Serra da Bocaina, PN da, Braz. 155/D2
Serra da Canastra, PN da, Braz. 155/C2
Serra da Capivara, PN da, Braz. 154/B3
Serra da Estrela (peak), Port. 44/B2
Serra da Estrela (mts.), Port. 44/A3
Serra do Cipó, PN da, Braz. 155/D1
Serra dos Órgãos, PN da, Braz. 155/K7
Serra San Bruno, It. 46/E3
Serra San Quirico, It. 59/G7
Serra Talhada, Braz. 154/C2
Serralta di San Vito (peak), It. 46/E3
Serramanna, It. 46/A3
Serramazzoni, It. 59/D5
Serrana Bank (isl.), Col. 141/F5
Serrana de la Cerbatana (mts.), Ven. 153/E3
Serrania de la Neblina, PN, Ven. 153/E4
Serranias del Burro (mts.), Mex. 142/E2
Serranilla Bank (isl.), Col. 141/F4
Serrano, Arg. 158/E2
Serranópolis, Braz. 155/B1
Serrat (cape), Tun. 100/L6
Serravalle, It. 59/F4
Serravalle, SMar. 59/F5
Serravalle Scrivia, It. 58/B4
Serravalle Sesia, It. 58/B2
Serre (riv.), Fr. 40/B4
Serrenti, It. 46/A3
Serrinha, Braz. 154/C3

Serris, Fr. 30/L5
Sersale, It. 46/E3
Sertã, Port. 44/A3
Sertânia, Braz. 154/C3
Sertãozinho, Braz. 155/H2
Sertavul (pass), Turk. 90/C2
Serteng (mts.), China 70/F4
Serui, Indo. 81/J4
Seruyan (riv.), Indo. 80/D4
Servance, Fr. 56/C2
Servi, Turk. 90/E2
Sérvia, Gre. 47/G2
Serviceton, Austl. 115/B3
Sese (isls.), Ugan. 104/A3
Sesebi (ruin), Sudan 101/B4
Sesepe, Indo. 81/G4
Sesheke, Zam. 105/D4
Sesia (riv.), It. 43/H4
Sesimbra, Port. 44/A3
Sesimbra, Port. 45/P11
Seskar (isl.), Rus. 39/N1
Sespe, Ca, US 136/B2
Sespe (cr.), Ca, US 136/A1
Sespe Condor Sanctuary, Ca, US 136/C3
Sesslach, Ger. 54/D2
Sesto Calende, It. 58/B2
Sesto Fiorentino, It. 59/E6
Sesto San Giovanni, It. 58/C2
Sesto Ulteriano, It. 58/C2
Sestola, It. 59/D5
Sestra (riv.), Rus. 60/W9
Sestri Levante, It. 58/C4
Sestroretsk, Rus. 61/S6
Sestroretskiy (lake), Rus. 61/T6
Sestu, It. 46/A3
Sesvenna (peak), It. 57/G4
Sesvete, Cro. 48/C3
Šeta, Lith. 39/L4
Setana, Japan 76/A2
Sète, Fr. 42/E5
Setermoen, Nor. 37/F2
Seti (riv.), Nepal 84/C1
Sethārja, Pak. 89/J3
Seti (riv.), Nepal 84/C1
Seti (zone), Nepal 84/C1
Sétif, Fr. 30/H4
Sétif (wilaya), Alg. 100/H4
Seto, Japan 77/M5
Seto-Naikai NP, Japan 74/C4
Setouchi, Japan 75/K6
Settat, Mor. 98/D2
Settepani (peak), It. 58/B5
Settimo Torinese, It. 58/A2
Settimo Vittone, It. 58/A1
Settle, Eng, UK 33/G3
Settsu, Japan 77/J6
Setúbal (dist.), Port. 44/A3
Setúbal (bay), Port. 44/A3
Setúbal, Port. 45/Q10
Seubersdorf, Ger. 55/E4
Seudre (riv.), Fr. 42/C4
Seugne (riv.), Fr. 42/C4
Seuil-d'Argonne, Fr. 53/D6
Seul (lake), On, Can. 122/G3
Seulimeum, Indo. 80/A2
Seurre, Fr. 56/B4
Seuzach, Swi. 57/E2
Sevan, Arm. 63/H4
Sevana (lake), Arm. 63/H4
Sevastopol', Ukr. 49/J3
Sevelen, Swi. 57/F3
Seven (riv.), Eng, UK 33/H3
Seven Heads (pt.), Ire. 31/P11
Seven Valleys, Pa, US 138/B4
Sevenoaks, Eng, UK 30/D3
Sevenoaks Weald, Eng, UK 30/D3
Sever (riv.), Wal, UK 35/F6
Severn (riv.), On, Can. 122/G3
Severn (riv.), Md, US 138/B5
Severn, Md, US 138/B5
Severn Park, Md, US 138/B5
Severnaya Osetiya-Alaniya, Resp., Rus. 63/G4
Severnaya Sos'va (riv.), Rus. 61/N3
Severnaya Zemlya (isls.), Rus. 64/J2
Severnyy, Rus. 61/P2
Severo-Kuril'sk, Rus. 65/R4
Severo-Yeniseyskiy, Rus. 64/K3
Severobaykal'sk, Rus. 65/L4
Severodvinsk, Rus. 60/H2
Severomorsk, Rus. 60/G1
Severoural'sk, Rus. 61/N3
Severskaya, Rus. 62/F3
Severukha, Rus. 47/H2
Seveso, It. 58/C2
Sevier (riv.), Ut, US 128/D3
Sevierville, Tn, US 133/H3
Sevilla, Col. 152/C3
Sevilla, Sp. 44/C4
Seville, Sp. 115/G5
Sevlievo, Bul. 49/G4
Sevnica, Slov. 48/B2
Sevojno, Serb. 48/D4
Sevran, Fr. 30/K5
Sevsk, Rus. 62/E1
Sewa (riv.), SLeo. 102/C5
Seward (pen.), Ak, US 134/E2
Seward, Ak, US 134/J3
Seward, Ne, US 129/H2
Sewaren, NJ, US 139/J9
Sewell, Chile 158/N10
Seyah Cheshmeh, Iran 63/H5
Seybaplaya, Mex. 144/D2
Seybouse, Oued (riv.), Alg. 100/K6
Seychelles (ctry.) 23/M6
Seydhisfjördhur, Ice. 37/Q6
Seydişehir, Turk. 90/B2

Seyhan (dam), Turk. 90/C2
Seyhan (riv.), Turk. 91/D1
Seyitgazi, Turk. 90/B2
Seym (riv.), Rus. 62/E1
Seymour, Austl. 115/C3
Seymour, Tx, US 129/H4
Seynod, Fr. 56/C6
Seyssel, Fr. 56/B6
Sézanne, Fr. 52/C6
Sézimovo Ústi, Czh. 55/H4
Sezze, It. 46/C2
Sfântu Gheorghe, Rom. 49/J3
Sfântu Gheorghe, Rom. 49/G3
Sfântu Gheorghe Branch (riv.), Rom. 49/J3
Sfizef, Alg. 100/E5
Sgurr na Lapaich (peak), Sc, UK 36/A2
Sha (riv.), China 72/C4
Sha Tin, China 71/U10
Shaanxi (prov.), China 70/J5
Shābāzpur (riv.), Bang. 85/H4
Shabeelle (riv.), Som. 97/P7
Shabla, Bul. 49/J4
Shabqadar, Pak. 86/A2
Shabunda, D.R. Congo 97/L8
Shache, China 87/G5
Shade (mtn.), Pa, US 138/A2
Shadrinsk, Rus. 61/P4
Shafter, Tx, US 132/B4
Shagamu, Nga. 103/F5
Shagany (lake), Ukr. 49/J3
Shageluk, Ak, US 134/G3
Shah Alam, Malay. 80/B3
Shāh Kot, Pak. 86/B4
Shāhābād, India 84/B4
Shāhābād, India 84/B1
Shāhābād, India 86/B1
Shahdād, Iran 89/G2
Shāhdādkot, Pak. 89/J3
Shahdol, India 84/C4
Shāhganj, India 84/D2
Shaḩḩāt, Libya 97/K1
Shāhjahānpur, India 84/B3
Shahpur, India 86/B3
Shāhpur Chākar, Pak. 82/A2
Shāhpura, India 84/A2
Shahr-e Kord, Iran 88/F2
Shahr Sultān, Pak. 86/A5
Shāhrūd (Emāmshahr), Iran 89/F1
Shā'ib al Banāt (peak), Egypt 101/C3
Shaikhpura, India 85/E3
Shājāpur, India 89/L4
Shakargarh, Pak. 86/C3
Shakaskraal, SAfr. 105/D4
Shakawe, Bots. 105/D4
Shakhrisabz, Uzb. 87/E5
Shakhtinsk, Kaz. 87/F2
Shakhty, Rus. 62/G3
Shakhun'ya, Rus. 61/K4
Shaki, Nga. 103/F4
Shakotan (pen.), Japan 76/B2
Shaktoolik, Ak, US 134/F3
Shalbuzdag (peak), Rus. 63/H4
Shallow Reach (inlet), Austl. 113/M8
Shalqar, Kaz. 87/D2
Shaluli (mts.), China 70/G5
Shām, Jabal ash (peak), Oman 89/G4
Shama (riv.), Tanz. 105/F2
Shamattawa (riv.), On, Can. 123/H3
Shāmgarh, India 89/L4
Shamil, Iran 89/G3
Shāmli, India 86/D5
Shammar, Jabal (mts.), SAr. 88/D3
Shamokin, Pa, US 138/B2
Shamokin Dam, Pa, US 138/B2
Shamrock (mtn.), Yk, Can. 134/L3
Shamrock, Tx, US 129/G4
Shamsābād, India 84/B2
Shamva, Zim. 105/F4
Shan (div.), Myan. 70/G7
Shan (plat.), Myan. 70/G7
Shan (state), Myan. 83/G3
Sha'nabī, Jabal ash (peak), Tun. 100/L7
Shandong (prov.), China 71/L4
Shandong (isl.), China 72/E3
Shangcai, China 72/C3
Shangcheng, China 72/C5
Shangdu, China 71/K3
Shanghai (prov.), China 71/M5
Shanghai, China 72/L8
Shanghang, China 72/D3
Shanghe, China 72/D3
Shangqiu, China 72/C3
Shangshui, China 72/C4
Shangyi, China 72/C3
Shangyou, China 79/B2
Shanshan, China 70/F3
Shantar (isls.), Rus. 67/N4
Shantar (riv.), Rus. 67/N4
Shantou, China 79/C3
Shanxi (prov.), China 71/K4
Shanyin, China 72/C3
Shaoguan, China 79/B3
Shaowu, China 79/C2
Shaoxing, China 79/D2

Shaoyang, China 79/B2
Shaoyang, China 83/K2
Shapkina (riv.), Rus. 61/M2
Shaqlāwah, Iraq 90/F2
Sharafkhāneh, Iran 90/F2
Sharbatāt, Ra's ash (pt.), Oman 89/G5
Sharga, Mong. 70/G2
Sharḩngol, Mong. 70/J2
Shari, Japan 76/D2
Sharḩngol, Mong. 70/J2
Shark (bay), Austl. 109/A3
Shark River (inlet), NJ, US 138/D3
Sharon, Pa, US 130/D3
Sharp (mtn.), Ut, US 137/K11
Sharpe (lake), SD, US 127/J4
Sharqpur, Pak. 86/C4
Shar'ya, Rus. 61/K4
Shashi, China 79/B1
Shasta (lake), Ca, US 126/C5
Shasta (mt.), Ca, US 126/C5
Shatskiy NP, Ukr. 41/M3
Shaṭṭ al Arab (riv.), Iraq 88/E2
Shaṭṭ al Jarīd (dry lake), Gabon 96/C4
Shattuck, Ok, US 129/H3
Shaunavon, Sk, Can. 126/F3
Shavano Park, Tx, US 137/T20
Shaw, Eng, UK 33/E4
Shawano, Wi, US 127/L4
Shawinigan, Qu, Can. 131/F2
Shawnee, Ok, US 129/H4
Shawnee (res.), Ok, US 137/N15
Shawnee, Ks, US 137/M4
Shay Gap, Austl. 112/B4
Shaykh, Jabal ash (peak), Iraq 90/E2
Shchara (riv.), Bela. 62/C1
Shchekino, Rus. 62/F1
Shchelkovo, Rus. 61/W9
Shchigry, Rus. 62/F2
Shchūchīnsk, Kaz. 87/F2
She Xian, China 79/C2
Shea Stadium, NY, US 139/K9
Shebelē Wenz (riv.), Eth. 97/P7
Sheberghān, Afg. 89/J1
Sheboygan, Wi, US 127/M5
Shediac, NB, Can. 131/H2
Shee (riv.), Sc, UK 36/C3
Sheelin (lake), Ire. 34/A4
Sheep (mtn.), Ak, US 134/J3
Shefar'am, Isr. 91/G6
Shefayim, Isr. 91/F7
Sheffield, Austl. 115/C4
Sheffield, Eng, UK 35/G5
Sheffield (co.), Eng, UK 35/G5
Sheffield, Al, US 133/G3
Sheffield (isl.), Ct, US 139/M7
Shehuén (riv.), Arg. 157/B6
Shek Uk (peak), HK, China 71/V10
Shekak (riv.), On, Can. 130/C1
Shekhūpura, Pak. 86/B4
Shelagskiy (cape), Rus. 65/S2
Shelburne, NS, Can. 131/H3
Shelby, Mt, US 126/F3
Shelby, Ms, US 129/K4
Shelby, Mi, US 130/C3
Shelby, NC, US 133/H4
Shelbyville (lake), Il, US 133/F2
Shelbyville, Tn, US 133/G3
Shelbyville, In, US 130/C4
Sheldon Point, Ak, US 134/F3
Shelekhov (gulf), Rus. 67/Q3
Shelikof (str.), Ak, US 134/H4
Shell (pt.), Fl, US 138/B2
Shell Lake, Wi, US 127/L4
Shell Rock (riv.), Ia, US 127/K5
Shellbrook, Sk, Can. 127/G2
Shelley (isl.), Va, US 139/F1
Shelter (isl.), NY, US 139/F1
Shelter Island (sound), NY, US 139/F1
Shelton, Wa, US 126/C3
Shelton, Ct, US 139/E1
Shen Xian, China 72/C3
Shenandoah, Pa, US 138/B2
Shenandoah NP, Va, US 130/E4
Shenchi, China 72/C3
Sheng Xian, China 79/D2
Shenge (riv.), SLeo. 102/B5
Shengena (peak), Tanz. 104/C2
Shennongjia, China 72/B5
Shenqiu, China 72/C4
Shenyang, China 73/B2
Shenzhen, China 83/K3
Shepetivka, Ukr. 62/C2
Shepherd (isls.), Van. 116/F6
Sheppey, Isle of (isl.), Eng, UK 33/G4
Shepshed, Eng, UK 33/E1
Sheqi, China 72/C4
Sherbro (isl.), SLeo. 102/B5
Sherbrooke, Qu, Can. 131/G2
Shere (hill), Nga. 103/H4
Sheremetyevo (int'l arpt.), Rus. 61/W9
Sherghāti, India 85/E3
Sheridan, Wy, US 126/G4
Sheridan, Co, US 137/B3
Sherman, Tx, US 129/H4

Sherpur, Bang. 85/H3
Sherwood (pt.), Ct, US 139/E1
Sheung Shui-Fanling, China 71/U10
Shevchenko (int'l arpt.), Kaz. 63/J4
Sheyang (riv.), China 72/D4
Sheyang, China 72/D4
Sheyenne (riv.), ND, US 127/J3
Shi (riv.), China 72/C4
Shi San Ling, China 72/H6
Shibakawa, Japan 77/T3
Shibata, Japan 75/F2
Shibayama, Japan 77/T2
Shibecha, Japan 76/D2
Shibetsu, Japan 76/D1
Shibetsu, Japan 76/D2
Shibīn al Kaum, Egypt 91/B4
Shibīn al Qanāṭir, Egypt 91/B4
Shibogama (lake), On, Can. 127/L2
Shibotsu (isl.), Rus. 76/E2
Shibushi (bay), Japan 74/B5
Shicheng, China 79/C2
Shicheng (isl.), China 73/B3
Shickshinny, Pa, US 138/B1
Shiderty (riv.), Kaz. 87/F2
Shido, Japan 74/D3
Shigaraki, Japan 77/K6
Shiga (pref.), Japan 77/K6
Shihezi, China 70/E3
Shijak, Alb. 47/F4
Shijiazhuang, China 72/C3
Shijiushan, China 79/C2
Shijōnawate, Japan 77/J6
Shikabe, Japan 76/B2
Shikarpur, India 84/B1
Shikārpur, Pak. 89/J3
Shikata, Japan 77/L5
Shikatsu, Japan 77/L5
Shikoku (isl.), Japan 67/N6
Shikoku (mts.), Japan 74/C4
Shikotsu (lake), Japan 76/B2
Shikotsu-Tōya NP, Japan 76/B2
Shildon, Eng, UK 35/G2
Shilka (riv.), Rus. 67/L4
Shilka (peak), India 89/L2
Shillington, Pa, US 138/B3
Shillong, India 83/F2
Shiloh, Il, US 137/H8
Shiloh, NJ, US 138/C5
Shilou, China 72/B3
Shimabara, Japan 74/B5
Shimagahara, Japan 77/K6
Shimamoto, Japan 77/J6
Shimane (pref.), Japan 74/C3
Shimasahi, Japan 77/K5
Shimba Hills Nat'l Rsv., Kenya 104/C4
Shimbara (bay), Japan 74/B4
Shimber Berris (peak), Som. 97/Q5
Shimizu, Japan 76/C2
Shimizu, Japan 77/B3
Shimo-Koshiki (isl.), Japan 74/A5
Shimobe, Japan 77/T3
Shimoda, Japan 75/F3
Shimodate, Japan 75/F2
Shimofusa, Japan 77/T2
Shimoichi, Japan 77/J7
Shimokita (pen.), Japan 76/B3
Shimonita, Japan 77/B1
Shimonoseki, Japan 74/B4
Shimotsuma, Japan 77/T1
Shimoyama, Japan 77/M5
Shimukappu, Japan 76/C2
Shin, Japan 77/C1
Shin (lake), Sc, UK 31/R7
Shindo, SKor. 73/F6
Shingū, Japan 74/D4
Shinhyōn, SKor. 73/F6
Shinji (lake), Japan 74/C3
Shinjō, Japan 77/J7
Shinjō, Japan 77/J7
Shinkawa, Japan 77/E2
Shinminato, Japan 75/E2
Shinnecock (bay), NY, US 139/F2
Shinnecock Ind. Res., NY, US 139/F2
Shinsei, Japan 77/K5
Shintoku, Japan 77/E2
Shintone, Japan 77/E2
Shinyanga, Tanz. 104/A3
Shinyanga (pol. reg.), Tanz. 104/A3
Shio-no-misaki (cape), Japan 74/D4
Shiogama, Japan 77/E2
Shioya-saki (pt.), Japan 75/G2
Ship Bottom, NJ, US 138/D4
Shipley, Eng, UK 33/G4
Shippan (pt.), Ct, US 139/L7
Shippegan, NB, Can. 131/H2
Shippo, Japan 77/L5
Shiprock, NM, US 128/E3
Shir (mtn.), Iran 88/F2
Shirakami-misaki (cape), Japan 76/B3
Shirakawa, Japan 75/G2
Shirakawa, Japan 77/E2
Shirakawa-tōge (pass), Japan 74/E3

Shirako, Japan 77/E3
Shirane, Japan 77/A2
Shirane-san (peak), Japan 75/F3
Shirane-san (peak), Japan 75/F2
Shiranuka, Japan 76/D2
Shiraoi, Japan 76/B2
Shiraoka, Japan 77/O1
Shīrāz, Iran 88/F3
Shirbīn, Egypt 91/B4
Shiretoko-misaki (cape), Japan 76/D1
Shiretoko NP, Japan 76/D1
Shiriya-zaki, Japan 76/B3
Shirjiu (lake), China 72/D5
Shirley, NY, US 139/F2
Shiroishi, Japan 75/G1
Shirone, Japan 75/F2
Shiroyama, Japan 77/C2
Shīrvān, Iran 89/G1
Shishaldin (vol.), Ak, US 134/F5
Shishgarh, India 84/B1
Shishi, Japan 77/E2
Shishmaref, Ak, US 134/E2
Shishou, China 79/B2
Shitara, Japan 77/F2
Shithātha, Iraq 90/E3
Shivpurī, India 84/A3
Shivpuri NP, India 84/A3
Shixing, China 83/K3
Shiyan, China 72/B4
Shizugawa, Japan 76/B4
Shizuishan, China 70/J4
Shizukuishi, Japan 76/B4
Shizunai, Japan 76/C2
Shizuoka (pref.), Japan 75/E3
Shkumbin (riv.), Alb. 48/E5
Shmidta (cape), Rus. 134/B3
Shoal (pt.), Austl. 112/B4
Shoal Lake, Mb, Can. 127/H3
Shoalhaven (riv.), Austl. 115/D2
Shōbara, Japan 74/C3
Shōbu, Japan 77/O1
Shōdo (isl.), Japan 74/D3
Shoemakersville, Pa, US 138/B3
Shokanbetsu-dake (peak), Japan 76/B2
Sholāpur, India 89/L5
Sholl (peak), Alg. 100/G5
Shomron (ruin), WBnk. 91/G7
Shōnan, Japan 77/T2
Shorāpur, India 82/C4
Shoreham-by-Sea, Eng, UK 33/F5
Shorewood, Wi, US 135/O13
Shorewood, Il, US 135/P16
Shorkot, Pak. 86/B4
Short (mtn.), Tn, US 133/G3
Shortland (isls.), Sol. 116/E5
Shoshone (riv.), Wy, US 126/F4
Shoshone (mts.), Nv, US 128/C3
Shoshoni, Wy, US 126/F5
Shostka, Ukr. 62/E2
Shotts, Sc, UK 36/C5
Shou Xian, China 72/D4
Shouguang, China 72/D3
Shouyang, China 72/C3
Show Low, Az, US 128/E4
Shōwa, Japan 77/B3
Shōwa, Japan 77/T2
Shpanberga (chan.), Rus. 76/E2
Shpola, Ukr. 62/D2
Shreveport, La, US 129/J4
Shrewsbury, Mo, US 137/G8
Shrewsbury, Eng, UK 32/D1
Shrewsbury, Pa, US 138/B3
Shriner (mtn.), Pa, US 138/A2
Shropshire (co.), Eng, UK 35/E6
Shropshire Union (canal), Eng, UK 35/E6
Shū (riv.), Kaz. 87/F2
Shū, China 87/G5
Shuangbai, China 83/H3
Shuangcheng, China 71/N2
Shuangliao, China 72/E2
Shuangyang, China 71/P2
Shuangyashan, China 71/P2
Shu'ayb, Jabal an (peak), Yem. 88/D5
Shubrā al Khaymah, Egypt 91/B4
Shubrā Khīt, Egypt 91/B4
Shuiyang (riv.), China 72/D5
Shujāābād, Pak. 86/A5
Shulan, China 71/N3
Shule, China 87/G5
Shule (riv.), China 64/K6
Shumagin (isls.), Ak, US 134/G4
Shumen, Bul. 49/H4
Shumerlya, Rus. 61/K5
Shuna (isl.), Sc, UK 36/A3
Shunak (peak), Kaz. 87/F3
Shungnak, Ak, US 134/G2
Shunyi, China 72/H6

Shuswap (lake), BC, Can. 126/D3
Shuwaykah, WBnk. 91/G7
Shuya, Rus. 60/J4
Shuyang, China 72/D4
Shwebo, Myan. 83/G3
Shwegyin, Myan. 83/G4
Shyghys Qazaqstan (obl.), Kaz. 64/J5
Shymkent, Kaz. 87/E4
Shyok (riv.), India 89/L2
Si Satchanalai (ruin), Thai. 78/B2
Si Xian, China 72/D4
Siāh Kūh (mts.), Afg. 89/H2
Siak (riv.), Indo. 80/B3
Siālkot, Pak. 86/C3
Sianów, Pol. 38/G4
Siapa (riv.), Ven. 153/E4
Siargao (isl.), Phil. 79/E6
Siasi, Phil. 81/F2
Siaton (pt.), Phil. 81/F2
Siaton, Phil. 79/D6
Siau (isl.), Indo. 81/G3
Šiauliai, Lith. 39/K4
Sibalom, Phil. 79/D5
Sibay, Rus. 63/L1
Sibbo (Sipoo), Fin. 39/L1
Šibenik, Cro. 48/B4
Siberia (reg.), Rus. 67/H3
Siberut (isl.), Indo. 67/J10
Sibi, Pak. 89/J3
Sibiloi NP, Kenya 97/N7
Sibiti, Congo 105/B1
Sibiu (prov.), Rom. 49/G2
Sibiu, Rom. 49/G3
Sibley, Mo, US 137/F5
Sibolga, Indo. 80/A3
Sibu, Malay. 80/D3
Sibuco, Phil. 81/F2
Sibut, CAfr. 97/J6
Sibuyan (sea), Phil. 81/F1
Sibuyan (isl.), Phil. 81/F1
Sicamous, BC, Can. 126/D3
Sichuan (prov.), China 70/H5
Sicilia (pol. reg.), It. 46/C4
Sicily (isl.), It. 27/F5
Sicily, Strait of (str.), It. 46/B3
Sico (riv.), Hon. 140/D2
Sicuani, Peru 156/D4
Sid, Serb. 48/D3
Siddipet, India 82/C4
Siderno Marina, It. 46/E3
Siderópolis, Braz. 155/B4
Sidewinder (mtn.), Ca, US 136/C1
Sidhaulī, India 84/C2
Sidhi, India 84/C3
Sidhirókastron, Gre. 47/H2
Sidhpur, India 89/K4
Sidi Aïssa, Alg. 100/G5
Sīdī Barrānī, Egypt 101/A2
Sidi Bel-Abbès, Alg. 100/E5
Sidi Bennour, Mor. 98/C2
Sīdī Bū Zayd, Tun. 46/A5
Sīdī Bū Zayd (gov.), Tun. 46/A5
Sidi Ifni, Mor. 98/C3
Sidi Kacem, Mor. 100/D2
Sidi Kacem (prov.), Mor. 100/D2
Sīdī Sālim, Egypt 91/B4
Sidi Slimane, Mor. 100/D2
Sidi Yahya du Rharb, Mor. 100/A2
Sidlaw (hills), Sc, UK 36/C3
Sidmouth, Eng, UK 32/C5
Sidney, BC, Can. 126/C3
Sidney, Mt, US 127/G4
Sidney, Oh, US 130/C3
Sidney Lanier (lake), Ga, US 133/H3
Sidra (gulf), Libya 93/D1
Sieci, It. 59/E5
Siedlce, Pol. 41/M2
Sieg (riv.), Ger. 43/G1
Siegburg, Ger. 53/G2
Siegen, Ger. 53/H2
Siegenburg, Ger. 55/E5
Siegendorf im Burgenland, Aus. 43/M3
Siemiatycze, Pol. 41/M2
Siemreab, Camb. 78/C3
Siena (prov.), It. 43/J5
Siena, It. 43/J5
Sienne (riv.), Fr. 42/C2
Sieradz, Pol. 41/K3
Sieraków, Pol. 41/J2
Sierpc, Pol. 41/K2
Sierra (prov.), Ca, US 136/C3
Sierra Blanca, Tx, US 132/B4
Sierra de la Macarena, PN, Col. 152/C3
Sierra de San Pedro Mártir, Mex. 142/B2
Sierra Estrella (mts.), Az, US 137/R19
Sierra Grande, Arg. 158/D4
Sierra Leone (ctry.) 102/B4
Sierra Leone (cape), SLeo. 102/B4
Sierra Madre, Ca, US 136/C3
Sierra Mojada, Mex. 132/C5
Sierra Nevada (mts.), US 128/B3
Sierra Nevada de Santa Marta, PN, Col. 152/C2
Sierra Nevada, PN, Ven. 152/D2

Sierra Vieja (mts.), Mex.,US 132/B4
Sierras Bayas, Arg. 158/E3
Sierre, Swi. 56/D5
Siete Picos (peak), Sp. 45/M8
Siete Tazas, PN, Chile 158/C2
Sieve (riv.), It. 59/E5
Sif Fatima, Alg. 99/H3
Sifnos (isl.), Gre. 47/J4
Sig, Alg. 100/E5
Siga Hills (hills), Tanz. 104/B3
Sigean, Fr. 42/E5
Siggiewi, Malta 46/L7
Sighetu Marmației, Rom. 49/F2
Sighișoara, Rom. 49/G2
Sighty Crag (hill), Eng, UK 35/F1
Sigillo, It. 59/F6
Siglı, Indo. 80/A2
Siglı (cape), Alg. 100/H4
Siglufjördhur, Ice. 37/N6
Sigmaringen, Ger. 57/F1
Sigmarszell, Ger. 57/F2
Signa, It. 59/E5
Signal de la Mère Boitier (peak), Fr. 42/F3
Signal de Toussaines (peak), Fr. 42/B2
Signal d'Écouves (peak), Fr. 42/D2
Signal Hill, Ca, US 136/F8
Signau, Swi. 56/D4
Signy-L'Abbaye, Fr. 53/D4
Signy-le-Petit, Fr. 53/E4
Signy-Signets, Fr. 30/M5
Sigriswil, Swi. 56/D4
Sigtuna, Swe. 38/G2
Siguatepeque, Hon. 144/E3
Sigüenza, Sp. 44/D2
Sihl (riv.), Swi. 57/E3
Sihlsee (lake), Swi. 57/E3
Sihochac, Mex. 144/D2
Sihong, China 72/D4
Sihorā, India 84/C4
Sihuas, Peru 156/B3
Siilinjärvi, Fin. 60/E3
Siirt (prov.), Turk. 90/E2
Siirt, Turk. 90/E2
Sikandarābād, India 84/A1
Sikandarpur, India 85/E2
Sikandra Rao, India 84/B2
Sikanni Chief (riv.), BC, Can. 122/D3
Sīkar, India 89/L3
Sikasso (pol. reg.), Mali 102/D4
Sikasso, Mali 102/D4
Sikeston, Mo, US 129/K3
Sikhote-Alin' (mts.), Rus. 65/P5
Sikinos, Gre. 47/J4
Sikinos (isl.), Gre. 47/J4
Sikkim (state), India 70/E6
Siklós, Hun. 48/D3
Sikoúrion, Gre. 47/H3
Sil (riv.), Sp. 44/B1
Silai (riv.), India 85/F4
Silandro (Schlanders), It. 57/G4
Silao, India 85/E3
Silao, Mex. 143/E4
Silat Az Zahr, WBnk. 91/G7
Silay, Phil. 81/F1
Silchar, India 83/F3
Şile, Turk. 49/J5
Silea, It. 59/F1
Silenen, Swi. 57/E4
Silesia (reg.), Pol. 41/H3
Siletitengiz (lake), Kaz. 51/H4
Silgadhī, Nepal 84/C1
Silifke, Turk. 91/C1
Silīguri, India 85/G2
Silistra, Bul. 49/H3
Silivri, Turk. 49/J5
Siljan (lake), Swe. 38/F1
Siljansnäs, Swe. 38/F1
Silkeborg, Den. 38/C3
Sill (riv.), Aus. 57/H3
Silla, Sp. 45/E3
Silla Tombs, SKor. 74/A3
Sillamäe, Est. 39/M2
Sillänwäli, Pak. 86/B4
Sillaro (riv.), It. 59/E4
Silleda, Sp. 44/A1
Sillian, Aus. 43/K3
Sillustani (ruin), Peru 156/D4
Silly-le-Long, Fr. 30/L4
Siloam Springs, Ar, US 129/J3
Silopi, Turk. 90/E2
Silsbee, Tx, US 129/J5
Silsden, Eng, UK 35/F4
Silsersee (lake), Swi. 57/F5
Siltou (well), Chad 96/J4
Šilute, Lith. 39/J4
Silvan (dam), Turk. 90/E2
Silvaplana, Swi. 57/F5
Silvassa, India 82/B3
Silver (lake), Or, US 128/B2
Silver (riv.), Or, US 128/B2
Silver (mtn.), Ca, US 136/C1
Silver Bay, Mn, US 127/L4
Silver City, NM, US 128/E4
Silver Lake, Wi, US 135/P14
Silver Lake-Fircrest, Wa, US 135/C2
Silver Meadow (lake), NJ, US 138/D5

Silver Run, Md, US 138/A4
Silver Spring, Md, US 138/A6
Silverado, Ca, US 136/C4
Silverton, Or, US 128/C3
Silverton, Co, US 128/F3
Silverton, NJ, US 138/D3
Silverwood (lake), Ca, US 136/C2
Silves, Port. 44/A4
Silvi, It. 46/D1
Silvia, Col. 152/B4
Silvies (riv.), Or, US 128/C2
Silvretta (mts.), Aus. 57/G4
Silyānah (gov.), Tun. 46/A4
Silyānah, Tun. 100/L6
Silz, Aus. 57/G3
Sim (cape), Mor. 98/C3
Simão Dias, Braz. 154/C3
Simard (lake), Qu, Can. 130/E2
Simav, Turk. 90/B2
Simbach am Inn, Ger. 55/G6
Simcoe, On, Can. 130/D3
Simcoe (lake), Qu, Can. 123/J4
Simdega, India 85/E4
Simen (mts.), Eth. 97/N5
Simeria, Rom. 48/F3
Simeulue (isl.), Indo. 67/J9
Simferopol', Ukr. 62/E3
Simi (hills), Ca, US 136/B2
Simi Valley, Ca, US 136/B2
Simiti, Col. 152/C3
Simitli, Bul. 47/H2
Simiyu (riv.), Tanz. 104/B3
Simla, India 86/D4
Simleu Silvaniei, Rom. 49/F2
Simme (riv.), Swi. 43/G3
Simmelsdorf, Ger. 55/E3
Simmerath, Ger. 53/D2
Simmerbach (riv.), Ger. 53/G4
Simmern, Ger. 53/G4
Simmertal, Ger. 53/G4
Simmszand (isl.), Neth. 50/D2
Simni (isl.), NKor. 73/C3
Simo, Fin. 60/E2
Simões, Braz. 154/D2
Simões Filho, Braz. 154/C4
Simojovel de Allende, Mex. 144/C2
Simón Bolívar (int'l arpt.), Ecu. 152/B5
Simoncello (peak), It. 59/F5
Simonstown, SAfr. 106/L11
Simpang-Kiri (riv.), Indo. 80/A3
Simpelveld, Neth. 53/E2
Simplício Mendes, Braz. 154/D2
Simplon, Swi. 56/E5
Simplonpass (pass), Swi. 56/E5
Simpson (des.), Austl. 109/C3
Simpson (pen.), Nun., Can. 122/G2
Simpson (riv.), Nun., Can. 122/G2
Simpson Desert Conservation Park, Austl. 113/H3
Simpson Desert NP, Austl. 113/H3
Simpsons Gap NP, Austl. 113/H3
Simrishamn, Swe. 38/F4
Simunul, Phil. 81/E3
Sin-le-Noble, Fr. 52/C3
Sinai (pen.), Egypt 97/M1
Sinaia, Rom. 49/G3
Sinaloa (state), Mex. 142/D3
Sinaloa de Leyva, Mex. 142/C3
Sinalunga, It. 43/J5
Sinan, China 79/K2
Sīnāwin, Libya 99/H3
Sincé, Col. 152/C2
Sincelejo, Col. 152/C2
Sinceny, Fr. 52/C4
Sinch'ön, NKor. 73/C3
Sinclair, Wy, US 126/G5
Sinclair (lake), Ga, US 133/H3
Sinclair (pt.), Austl. 113/G5
Sincorá, Serra do (range), Braz. 154/B4
Sind (riv.), India 82/C2
Sindal, Den. 38/D3
Sindangan, Phil. 79/D6
Sindangbarang, Indo. 80/C5
Sindelfingen, Ger. 54/C5
Sindh (prov.), Pak. 82/A2
Sindhulimādi, Nepal 85/F2
Sindrgı, Turk. 90/B2
Sinekçi, Turk. 49/H5
Sinendé, Ben. 103/F4
Sines (cape), Port. 44/A4
Sines, Port. 44/A4
Sinfra, C.d'Iv. 102/D5
Sing Buri, Thai. 78/C3
Singapore (ctry.) 80/B3
Singapore (cap.), Sing. 80/B3
Singen, Ger. 57/E2
Singeorz-Băi, Rom. 49/G2
Singida (pol. reg.), Tanz. 104/B4
Singida, Tanz. 104/B4
Singitic (gulf), Gre. 47/H2
Singkawang, Indo. 80/C3

Singkep (isl.), Indo. 80/B4
Singleton, Austl. 115/D2
Singleton (mt.), Austl. 112/C4
Singleton (mt.), Austl. 113/F2
Singou, Réserve Totale de Faune du, Burk. 103/F4
Sinincay, Ecu. 152/B5
Siniscola, It. 46/A2
Sinisipuk (lake), Mb,Sk, Can. 127/H2
Sinjär, Iraq 90/E2
Sinjil, WBnk. 91/G7
Sinn (riv.), Ger. 40/E3
Sinnamary, FrG. 151/H2
Sinnar, India 82/C4
Sinnard, Co, US 137/C1
Sinnicolau Mare, Rom. 48/E2
Sinnūris, Egypt 91/B5
Sinnyong, SKor. 73/E4
Sino (co.), Libr. 102/C5
Sinoe (lake), Rom. 49/J3
Sinop, Braz. 151/G6
Sinop, Turk. 90/C1
Sinop (prov.), Turk. 90/C1
Sinp'o, NKor. 73/E2
Sint-Genesius-Rode, Belg. 53/D2
Sint-Gillis-Waas, Belg. 50/B6
Sint-Katelijne-Waver, Belg. 53/D1
Sint-Laureins, Belg. 52/C1
Sint-Martens-Voeren, Belg. 53/E2
Sint-Michielsgestel, Neth. 50/C5
Sint-Niklaas, Belg. 50/B6
Sint-Oedenrode, Neth. 50/C5
Sint-Pieters-Leeuw, Belg. 53/D2
Sint-Truiden, Belg. 53/E2
Sint'aein, SKor. 73/D5
Sintang, Indo. 80/D3
Sinton, Tx, US 132/D4
Sintra, Port. 45/P10
Sintra (range), Port. 45/P10
Sinú (riv.), Col. 150/C2
Sinüiju, NKor. 73/C2
Sinzheim, Ger. 54/B5
Sió (riv.), Hun. 48/D2
Siocon, Phil. 81/F2
Siófok, Hun. 48/D2
Sioma Ngwezi NP, Zam. 105/D4
Sion, Swi. 56/D5
Sion Mills, NI, UK 31/Q9
Sioule (riv.), Fr. 42/E4
Sioux City, Ia, US 127/J5
Sioux Lookout, On, Can. 123/J1
Sipalay, Phil. 79/D6
Sipaliwini (dist.), Sur. 153/H4
Sipaliwini (riv.), Sur. 153/G4
Sipanok (chan.), Mb,Sk, Can. 127/H2
Siparia, Trin. 153/F2
Sipi, Col. 152/B3
Siping, China 72/F2
Sipiwesk (lake), Mb, Can. 122/G3
Siple (isl.), Ant. 160/R
Siponto (ruin), It. 46/D2
Sipsey (riv.), Al, US 133/G3
Sipura (isl.), Indo. 80/A4
Siqueira Campos, Braz. 155/B2
Siquia (riv.), Nic. 144/E5
Siquisique, Ven. 152/D2
Sir Alexander (mt.), BC, Can. 126/C2
Sir Edward Pellew Group (isls.), Austl. 109/C2
Sir James Macbrien (mt.), NW, Can. 122/D2
Sir James Mitchell NP, Austl. 112/C5
Sir John (cape), Ice. 37/P7
Sir Seewoosagur Ramgoolam (int'l arpt.), Mrts. 107/T15
Sir Thomas (mt.), Austl. 113/F3
Sira (riv.), Nor. 37/C4
Siracusa (Syracuse), It. 46/D4
Siran, Turk. 90/D1
Sirdaryo (pol. reg.), Uzb. 87/G4
Siret, Rom. 49/H2
Siret (riv.), Rom. 62/C1
Sirha, Nepal 85/F2
Sirhind, India 86/D4
Sirik (cape), Malay. 80/D3
Sīrīk, Iran 89/G3
Sirinhaém, Braz. 154/D2
Sīrīs, WBnk. 91/G7
Sirius (pt.), Ak, US 134/B5
Sirmilik Nat'l Park, Nun., Can. 123/J1
Sirmione, It. 58/D2
Sīrnach, Swi. 57/F3
Sīrnak, Turk. 90/E2
Sirolo, It. 59/G5
Sironj, India 84/A3
Siros (isl.), Gre. 47/J4
Siroua, Jebel (peak), Mor. 98/D3
Sirsa, India 86/C5

Sirsāganj, India 84/B2
Sirsi, India 84/B1
Sirsi, India 89/K6
Sisak, Cro. 48/C3
Sisaket, Thai. 78/D3
Sishui, China 72/D4
Sisikon, Swi. 57/E4
Sisipuk (lake), Mb,Sk, Can. 127/H2
Sisseton, SD, US 127/J4
Sissach, Swi. 56/D3
Sissonne, Fr. 52/C4
Sissonville, WV, US 130/D4
Sisterdale, Tx, US 137/T20
Sisteron, Fr. 42/B3
Siswā Bāzār, India 84/D2
Sitacocha, Peru 156/B2
Sītākunda, Bang. 83/F3
Sītāpur, India 84/D2
Sitārganj, India 84/B1
Siteki, Swaz. 107/E2
Site of World Trade Center, NY, US 139/J9
Sitges, Sp. 45/K7
Sithoniá (pen.), Gre. 62/C5
Sitía, Gre. 47/K5
Sitidgi (lake), NW, Can. 134/M1
Sítio Novo do Grajaú, Braz. 154/A2
Sitka, Ak, US 134/L4
Sittard, Neth. 53/E2
Sittensen, Ger. 51/G2
Sitter (riv.), Swi. 57/F3
Sittingbourne, Eng, UK 33/G4
Sitton (lake), Ca, US 136/C3
Sittwe (Akyab), Myan. 83/F3
Sivac, Serb. 48/D3
Sivakāsi, India 82/C6
Sīvand, Iran 88/F2
Sivas, Turk. 90/D2
Sivas (prov.), Turk. 90/D2
Siverek, Turk. 90/D2
Siviriez, Swi. 56/C4
Sivrihisar, Turk. 90/B2
Sivry-Courtry, Fr. 30/L6
Siwa Oasis (oasis), Egypt 101/A2
Siwah, Egypt 97/C2
Siwalik (range), Nepal 70/C5
Siwān, India 85/E2
Siwāni, India 86/C5
Six Flags Great Adventure, NJ, US 138/D3
Six Flags Great America, Il, US 135/Q15
Six Flags Magic Mountain, Ca, US 136/B2
Sixmilecross, NI, UK 34/A2
Sixth (falls), Sudan 97/M4
Siyabuswa, SAfr. 105/E6
Siyāna, India 84/B1
Siyang, China 72/D4
Siziano, It. 58/C2
Siziwang, China 71/K3
Sjælland (isl.), Den. 38/D4
Sjenica, Serb. 48/E3
Sjöbo, Swe. 38/E4
Sjönfridh (peak), Ice. 37/M6
Sjuntorp, Swe. 38/E2
Skaftafell NP, Ice. 37/P7
Skagen, Den. 38/D3
Skagens (The Skaw) (cape), Den. 38/D3
Skagern (lake), Swe. 38/F2
Skagerrak (str.), Nor.,Den. 27/C3
Skaget (peak), Nor. 38/C1
Skagway, Ak, US 134/L3
Skála, Gre. 47/H4
Skälderviken (bay), Swe. 38/E4
Skálfandafljót (riv.), Ice. 37/P7
Skalica, Slvk. 41/K4
Skalice (riv.), Czh. 43/K2
Skalice (res.), Czh. 55/F2
Skælskor, Den. 38/D4
Skanderborg, Den. 38/C3
Skåne (reg.), Swe. 41/J3
Skanes (int'l arpt.), Tun. 46/B5
Skånland, Nor. 37/F1
Skänninge, Swe. 38/F2
Skanör, Swe. 38/E4
Skantzoura (isl.), Gre. 47/J3
Skara, Swe. 38/E2
Skärblacka, Swe. 38/F2
Skåre, Swe. 38/E2
Skarszewy, Pol. 38/H4
Skarzysko-Kamienna, Pol. 41/L3
Skateraw, Sc, UK 36/D5
Skattkärr, Swe. 38/E2
Skawina, Pol. 41/K4
Skeena (riv.), BC, Can. 122/C3
Skeena (mts.), BC, Can. 122/D3
Skegness, Eng, UK 35/J5
Skellefteå, Swe. 37/G2
Skellefteälven (riv.), Swe. 37/F2
Skelleftehamn, Swe. 37/G2
Skelmersdale, Eng, UK 35/F4

Skelmorlie, Sc, UK 36/B5
Skerne (riv.), Eng, UK 35/G2
Skerries, Ire. 34/B4
Skhimatárion, Gre. 47/H3
Skhirat, Mor. 100/A3
Skhirat Temara (prov.), Mor. 34/A1
Skhiza (isl.), Gre. 47/G4
Skhodnya (riv.), Rus. 61/W9
Ski, Nor. 38/D2
Skiathos, Gre. 47/H3
Skiatook, Ok, US 129/H3
Skibbereen, Ire. 31/P11
Skidegate, BC, Can. 134/M5
Skidhra, Gre. 47/H2
Skien, Nor. 38/C2
Skierniewice, Pol. 41/L3
Skikda, Alg. 100/K6
Skinári (cape), Gre. 47/G4
Skinnskatteberg, Swe. 38/F2
Skipton, Eng, UK 35/F4
Skíros, Gre. 47/J3
Skíros (isl.), Gre. 47/J3
Skive, Den. 38/C3
Skjærhollen, Nor. 38/D2
Skjeberg, Nor. 38/D2
Skjelåtinden (peak), Nor. 37/E2
Skjern, Den. 38/C4
Skjern (riv.), Den. 38/C4
Škofja Loka, Slov. 40/B3
Skoghall, Swe. 38/E2
Skogstorp, Swe. 38/G2
Skokholm (isl.), Wal, UK 32/A3
Skokie (riv.), Il, US 135/Q15
Skokloster, Swe. 38/G2
Sköllersta, Swe. 38/F2
Skolniki Park, Rus. 61/W9
Skomer (isl.), Wal, UK 32/A3
Skópelos, Gre. 47/H3
Skópelos (isl.), Gre. 47/H3
Skopin, Rus. 62/F1
Skopje (cap.), FYROM 47/G1
Skopje (int'l arpt.), FYROM 47/G1
Skotterud, Nor. 38/E2
Skoútari, Gre. 47/H2
Skövde, Swe. 38/E2
Skowhegan, Me, US 131/G2
Skukum (mt.), Yk, Can. 134/L3
Skull, Ire. 31/P11
Skultorp, Swe. 38/E2
Skultuna, Swe. 38/G2
Skunk (riv.), Ia, US 130/A3
Skurup, Swe. 41/G1
Skutskär, Swe. 38/G1
Skwentna, Ak, US 134/H3
Skwierzyna, Pol. 41/H2
Skye (isl.), Sc, UK 31/Q8
Skyring (sound), Chile 159/B7
Skytop, Pa, US 138/C1
Slagelse, Den. 38/D4
Slakovský Les (for.), Czh. 55/F2
Slamannan, Sc, UK 36/C5
Slana, Ak, US 134/K3
Slaná (riv.), Slvk. 41/L4
Slane, Ire. 34/B4
Slaney (riv.), Ire. 31/Q10
Slănic, Rom. 49/H3
Slănic-Moldova, Rom. 49/H2
Slantsy, Rus. 39/N2
Slaný, Czh. 55/H2
Slapy (res.), Czh. 55/H3
Śląskie (prov.), Pol. 41/K3
Slatedale, Pa, US 138/C2
Slatina, Rom. 49/G3
Slatington, Pa, US 138/C2
Slaton, Tx, US 129/G4
Slattum, Nor. 38/V8
Slaughter Beach, De, US 138/C6
Slaughterville, Ok, US 137/N15
Slave (coast), Afr. 103/F5
Slave (riv.), NW, Can. 122/C2
Slave Lake, Ab, Can. 126/E2
Slavgorod, Rus. 87/G2
Slavkov u Brna, Czh. 43/M2
Slavonia (reg.), Cro. 48/C3
Slavonska Požega, Cro. 48/C3
Slavonski Brod, Cro. 48/D3
Slavyanovo, Bul. 49/G4
Slavyansk-na-Kubani, Rus. 62/F3
Sleen, Neth. 50/D3
Sleeper (isls.), On, Can. 123/J3
Sleeping Bear Dunes Nat'l Lakeshore, US 130/C2
Sleepy Hollow, NY, US 139/K7
Sleepy Hollow, Il, US 135/P15
Sleetmute, Ak, US 134/G3
Sliedrecht, Neth. 50/B5
Slema, Malta 46/M7
Slieve Binnian (peak), NI, UK 34/C3
Slieve Croob (peak), NI, UK 34/C3

Slieve Donard (peak), NI, UK 34/C3
Slieve Gullion (peak), NI, UK 34/B3
Slieve Snaght (peak), Ire. 34/A1
Slioch (peak), Sc, UK 36/A1
Slite, Swe. 39/H3
Sliven, Bul. 47/H1
Slivnitsa, Bul. 47/H1
Sloan, NY, US 131/S10
Sloatsburg, NY, US 139/J7
Slobodskoy, Rus. 61/L4
Slobozia, Rom. 49/H3
Slochteren, Neth. 50/D2
Slonim, Bela. 62/C1
Sloten, Neth. 50/C3
Slotermeer (lake), Neth. 50/C3
Slough, Eng, UK 30/B2
Slough (co.), Eng, UK 30/B2
Slovakia (ctry.) 41/K4
Slovenia (ctry.) 40/B3
Slovenj Gradec, Slov. 43/L3
Slovenska Bistrica, Slov. 43/L3
Slovenská Ľupča, Slvk. 41/K4
Slovenske Konjice, Slov. 43/L3
Slovenské Rudohorie (mts.), Slvk. 41/L4
Slov'yans'k, Ukr. 62/F2
Słowiński PN, Pol. 38/A4
Słubice, Pol. 41/H2
Sluch (riv.), Ukr. 62/C2
Sluderno (Schluderns), It. 57/G4
Sluis, Neth. 52/C1
Słupca, Pol. 41/J2
Słupia (riv.), Pol. 38/G4
Słupsk (prov.), Pol. 38/G4
Słupsk, Pol. 38/G4
Slutsk, Bela. 62/C1
Slyne Head (pt.), Ire. 30/F10
Smålandsstenar, Swe. 38/E3
Smallwood (res.), Nf, Can. 123/K3
Smeaton, Sk, Can. 127/G2
Smederevo, Serb. 48/E3
Smederevska Palanka, Serb. 48/E3
Smedjebacken, Swe. 38/F2
Smendou (riv.), Alg. 100/A4
Smigiel, Pol. 41/J2
Smila, Ukr. 62/D2
Smilde, Neth. 50/D3
Smith (riv.), Mt, US 126/F4
Smith (inlet), BC, Can. 126/B3
Smith (isl.), Qu, Can. 123/J2
Smith Mountain (lake), Va, US 130/E4
Smith Village, Ok, US 137/N15
Smithburg, NJ, US 138/D3
Smithers, BC, Can. 126/B2
Smithfield, Ut, US 126/F5
Smithfield, NC, US 133/J3
Smiths Creek, Mi, US 135/G6
Smiths Falls, On, Can. 130/E2
Smithton, Austl. 115/C4
Smithton, Il, US 137/H9
Smithtown (bay), NY, US 139/E2
Smithtown, NY, US 139/E2
Smithville, Ok, US 132/E3
Smithville (lake), Mo, US 137/D5
Smithville, Mo, US 137/D5
Smoky (cape), Austl. 115/E1
Smoky (hills), Ks, US 129/H3
Smoky (riv.), Ab, Can. 122/D3
Smoky Hill (riv.), Ks, US 124/F4
Smoky Lake, Ab, Can. 126/E2
Smola (isl.), Nor. 37/C3
Smolensk, Rus. 60/G5
Smolenskaya Oblast, Rus. 60/F5
Smólikas (peak), Gre. 47/G2
Smolyan, Bul. 47/H2
Smooth Rock Falls, On, Can. 130/D1
Smrčina (peak), Czh. 55/G5
Smutná (riv.), Czh. 55/H4
Smyadovo, Bul. 49/H4
Smyrna, Ga, US 133/G3
Smyrna, De, US 138/C5
Snaefell (peak), IM, UK 34/D7
Snake (riv.), US 126/E5
Snake River (plain), Id, US 126/E5
Snares (isls.), NZ 117/R12
Snåsa, Nor. 37/D2
Snedsted, Den. 38/C3
Sneek, Neth. 50/C2
Sneekermeer (lake), Neth. 50/C2
Sneeuberg (mts.), SAfr. 106/D4
Sneeuwkop (peak), SAfr. 106/L11
Snejbjerg, Den. 38/C3

Snežka (peak), Czh. 41/H3
Snežnik (peak), Slov. 43/L4
Sni Mills, Mo, US 137/E6
Śniardwy (lake), Pol. 41/L2
Snodland, Eng, UK 33/G4
Snøhetta (peak), Nor. 37/E3
Snohomish, Wa, US 135/C2
Snohomish (co.), Wa, US 135/C2
Snohomish (riv.), Wa, US 135/D2
Snoqualmie (falls), Wa, US 135/D2
Snoqualmie, Wa, US 135/D2
Snoqualmie Falls, Wa, US 135/D2
Snoqualmie, Middle Fk. (riv.), Wa, US 135/D2
Snoqualmie, North Fork (riv.), Wa, US 135/D2
Snoqualmie, South Fork (riv.), Wa, US 135/D2
Snowdon (peak), Wal, UK 34/D5
Snowdonia NP, Wal, UK 34/D6
Snowflake, Az, US 128/E4
Snowtown, Austl. 113/H5
Snowy (peak), Ak, US 134/K2
Snowy (riv.), Austl. 115/D3
Snowy River NP, Austl. 115/D3
Snyder (co.), Pa, US 138/A2
Snydertown, Pa, US 138/B2
Snyderville, Ut, US 137/K12
Soalala, Madg. 107/H7
Soanierana-Ivongo, Madg. 107/J7
Soanindrariny, Madg. 107/H7
Soar (riv.), Eng, UK 35/G6
Soavina, Madg. 107/H8
Soavina, Madg. 107/J8
Soavinandriana, Madg. 107/H7
Sobaek (mts.), SKor. 73/D5
Soběslav, Czh. 55/H4
Sobger (riv.), Indo. 81/K4
Sobhādero, Pak. 89/J3
Sobradinho, Represa (res.), Braz. 147/E3
Sobral, Braz. 154/B1
Sobretta (peak), It. 57/G5
Sobue, Japan 77/L5
Soc Trang, Viet. 78/D4
Socabaya, Peru 156/D5
Sochaczew, Pol. 41/L2
Sochi, Rus. 62/F4
Sŏch'ŏn, SKor. 73/D4
Söchtenau, Ger. 55/F7
Soci, It. 59/F5
Society (isls.), FrPol. 117/K6
Socorro, Tx, US 129/F5
Socorro, NM, US 128/F4
Socorro, Braz. 211/G7
Socorro (isl.), NM, Mex. 142/C5
Socorro, Col. 152/C3
Socota, Peru 156/B2
Socotá, Col. 152/C3
Socotra (isl.), Yem. 67/E8
Socuéllamos, Sp. 44/D3
Soda Springs, Id, US 126/F5
Sodankylä, Fin. 60/E2
Sodegaura, Japan 77/D3
Söderbärke, Swe. 38/F1
Söderfors, Swe. 38/G1
Söderhamn, Swe. 38/G1
Söderköping, Swe. 38/G2
Södermanland (co.), Swe. 38/G2
Södertälje, Swe. 38/G2
Sodo, Eth. 97/N6
Södu (riv.), NKor. 73/E2
Sodwana Bay NP, SAfr. 107/F2
Soest, Ger. 51/F5
Soest, Neth. 50/C4
Soeste (riv.), Ger. 40/D2
Sofádhes, Gre. 47/H3
Sofia (int'l arpt.), Bul. 47/H1
Sofia (riv.), Madg. 107/J6
Sofia (Sofiya) (cap.), Bul. 47/H1
Sofiya (prov.), Bul. 47/H1
Sogamoso (riv.), Col. 152/C3
Sogamoso, Col. 152/C3
Sögel, Ger. 51/E3
Sogn Og Fjordane (co.), Nor. 37/C3
Sognafjorden (inlet), Nor. 38/B1
Sogndal, Nor. 38/B1
Søgne, Nor. 38/C2
Sogollé (well), Chad 96/J4
Soğuksu NP, Turk. 90/C1
Söğüt, Turk. 90/B1
Söğütlü, Turk. 49/K5
Sogwass (peak), Ugan. 104/B2
Sohāgpur, India 84/B4
Sohren, Ger. 53/G4
Sŏhŭng, NKor. 73/D3

Sōja, Japan 74/C3
Sojat, India 89/K3
Sŏjosŏn (bay), NKor. 73/C3
Sok (riv.), Rus. 63/J1
Sok (pt.), Thai. 78/C3
Sōka, Japan 77/D2
Sokch'o, SKor. 73/E3
Sŏke, Turk. 90/A2
Sokhós, Gre. 47/H2
Sokhumi, Geo. 63/G4
Sokna, Nor. 38/C1
Soko (isls.), China 71/T11
Soko Banja, Serb. 48/E4
Sokodé, Togo 103/F4
Sokol, Rus. 60/J4
Sokol (peak), Czh. 55/G4
Sokółka, Pol. 41/M2
Sokolov, Czh. 55/F2
Sokołów Podlaski, Pol. 41/M2
Sokoto (plain), Nga. 96/F5
Sokoto (riv.), Nga. 96/F5
Sokoto, Nga. 103/G3
Sokoto (state), Nga. 103/G3
Sol, Costa del (coast), Sp. 44/C4
Sol'-Iletsk, Rus. 63/K2
Sola, Nor. 38/A2
Sola (int'l arpt.), Nor. 38/A2
Solana, Phil. 79/D4
Solana Beach, Ca, US 136/C5
Solânea, Braz. 154/D2
Solano (pt.), Col. 152/B3
Solano, Phil. 79/D4
Solano (co.), Ca, US 135/L10
Solarolo, It. 59/E4
Solca, Rom. 49/G2
Sölden, Aus. 57/H4
Soldier (riv.), Ia, US 129/J2
Soldotna, Ak, US 134/H3
Soledad, Col. 152/C2
Soledad, Ven. 153/F2
Soledad Canyon (canyon), Ca, US 136/B2
Soledad de Doblado, Mex. 143/N7
Soledad de Graciano (Sánchez), Mex. 143/E4
Soledade, Braz. 155/A4
Solent, The (chan.), Eng, UK 33/E5
Solesino, It. 59/E2
Solesmes, Fr. 52/C3
Soleuvre (peak), Lux. 53/E4
Solferino, It. 58/D2
Solhan, Turk. 90/E2
Soliera, It. 59/D3
Soligo, It. 59/F1
Solihull, Eng, UK 33/E2
Solihull (co.), Eng, UK 33/E2
Solimões (riv.), Braz. 153/E5
Solingen, Ger. 50/E6
Sollefteå, Swe. 37/F3
Sollentuna, Swe. 38/G2
Söller, Sp. 45/G3
Sollerön, Swe. 38/F1
Solling (mts.), Ger. 40/E3
Solmsbach (riv.), Ger. 54/B2
Søln (riv.), Nor. 37/D3
Solna, Swe. 38/G2
Solnan (riv.), Fr. 42/F3
Solntsevo, Rus. 61/W9
Solo (riv.), Indo. 80/D5
Solok, Indo. 80/B4
Sololá, Guat. 144/C3
Solomon, Ak, US 134/F3
Solomon (riv.), Ks, US 129/H3
Solomon (sea), PNG,Sol. 116/D5
Solomon Islands (ctry.) 116/E5
Solomon, North Fork (riv.), US 129/G3
Solonchak Goklenkui (swamp), Trkm. 87/D3
Solonópole, Braz. 154/C2
Solothurn, Swi. 56/D3
Solothurn (canton), Swi. 56/D3
Solovetskiy (isls.), Rus. 60/G2
Solre-le-Château, Fr. 53/D3
Solsona, Sp. 45/F2
Solt, Hun. 48/D2
Šolta (isl.), Cro. 46/C1
Soltau, Ger. 51/G3
Soltvadkert, Hun. 48/D2
Solunska (peak), FYROM 47/G2
Solva (riv.), Wal, UK 32/A3
Solvang, Ca, US 136/B2
Sölvesborg, Swe. 38/F3
Solway Firth (inlet), Eng.,Sc, UK 34/C6
Solwezi, Zam. 105/E3
Solymár, Hun. 49/D9
Sōma, Japan 75/G2
Soma, Turk. 90/A2
Somain, Fr. 52/C3
Somalia (ctry.) 97/Q6
Sombor, Serb. 48/D3
Sombra, On, Can. 135/H6
Sombreffe, Belg. 52/D2
Sombrerete, Mex. 142/E4
Sombrio, Braz. 155/B4
Someren, Neth. 50/C6
Somero, Fin. 39/K1
Somers, Mt, US 126/E3
Somers, Wi, US 135/Q14
Somers Point, NJ, US 138/D5

Somerset (isl.),
Nun., Can. 122/G1
Somerset (co.),
Eng, UK 32/D4
Somerset, Ky, US 130/C4
Somerset, NY, US 131/S9
Somerset, Tx, US 137/T21
Somerset East, SAfr. 106/D4
Somerset West, SAfr. 106/L11
Somersworth,
NH, US 131/G3
Somerton, Az, US 128/D4
Somerville (lake),
Tx, US 129/H5
Somerville, NJ, US 138/D2
Someş (riv.), Rom. 62/B3
Someşul Mare (riv.),
Serb. 49/G2
Someswar (range),
India 85/E2
Somis, Ca, US 136/B2
Sömjin (riv.), SKor. 73/D5
Somma Lombardo, It. 58/B1
Sommacampagna, It. 59/D2
Sommam (riv.), Alg. 100/H4
Sommariva del Bosco,
It. 58/A3
Somme (bay), Fr. 42/D1
Somme (dept.), Fr. 52/B4
Somme (riv.), Fr. 40/B3
Somme, Canal de la
(canal), Fr. 52/B4
Somme-Leuze, Belg. 53/E3
Somme-Soude (riv.), Fr. 53/D6
Sommedieue, Fr. 53/E5
Sommen (lake), Swe. 38/F2
Sommet de Finiels
(peak), Fr. 42/E4
Sommevoire, Fr. 56/A1
Somogy (prov.), Hun. 48/C2
Somoto, Nic. 144/E3
Son (riv.), India 70/D7
Son Servera, Sp. 45/G3
Sona, It. 59/D2
Sonāmukhi, India 85/E4
Sonāmura, India 85/H4
Sonār (riv.), India 84/B4
Sonchamp, Fr. 30/H6
Sŏnch'ŏn, NKor. 73/C3
Soncino, It. 58/C2
Sondalo, It. 57/G5
Sønder Nissum, Den. 38/C3
Sønderborg (int'l arpt.),
Den. 51/E6
Sønderborg, Den. 38/C4
Sonderend (riv.), SAfr. 106/L11
Sønderjylland (co.),
Den. 38/C4
Sondica (int'l arpt.),
Sp. 44/D1
Sondrio, It. 57/F5
Sondrio (dept.), It. 57/F5
Sonepur, India 82/D3
Song (peak), China 72/C4
Song Xian, China 72/C4
Songea, Tanz. 104/B5
Songeons, Fr. 52/A4
Songhua (riv.),
China 67/M5
Sŏnghwan, SKor. 73/D4
Songi (isl.), SKor. 73/C5
Songino, Mong. 70/G2
Songjiang, China 72/L8
Sŏngju, SKor. 73/E5
Songkhla, Thai. 78/C5
Songkhram (riv.),
Thai. 83/H4
Songling, China 71/M2
Songming, China 83/H2
Sŏngnam, SKor. 73/D4
Songnim, NKor. 73/C3
Songololo,
D.R. Congo 105/B2
Songt'an, SKor. 73/D4
Songtao Miaozu Zizhixian,
China 79/A2
Songxi, China 79/C2
Songxi, China 79/B1
Songzi (pass), China 72/C5
Soni, Japan 77/K6
Sonid Youqi, China 71/K3
Sonid Zuoqi, China 71/K3
Sonīpat, India 86/D5
Sonneberg, Ger. 54/E2
Sonnefeld, Ger. 54/E2
Sonnjoch (peak),
Aus. 57/H3
Sonntagshorn (peak),
Ger. 43/J3
Sonobe, Japan 77/H5
Sonoma (co.),
Ca, US 135/J10
Sonoma (mts.),
Ca, US 135/J10
Sonora, Ca, US 135/L11
Sonora, Tx, US 129/G5
Sonora (state), Mex. 128/D5
Sonoran Desert Nat'l Mon.,
Az, US 128/D4
Sonoyta, Mex. 128/D5
Sonoyta (riv.), Mex. 142/B2
Sonpur, India 85/E3
Sonqor, Iran 88/E2
Sŏnsan, SKor. 73/E4
Sonsbeck, Ger. 50/D5
Sonseca, Sp. 44/D3
Sonsonate, ESal. 144/D3
Sonsorol (isls.),
Palau 116/C4
Sonta, Serb. 40/D3
Sontheim, Ger. 57/G2
Sontheim an der Brenz,
Ger. 54/D5

Sonthofen, Ger. 57/G2
Sontra, Ger. 51/G6
Sonvico, Swi. 57/E5
Sopetrán, Col. 152/C3
Sopi (cape), Indo. 81/G3
Sopor, India 86/C2
Sopot, Bul. 61/G3
Sopot, Pol. 38/H4
Sopron, Hun. 43/M3
Sør (riv.), Wal, UK 32/D3
Sor Karatuley (salt pan),
Kaz. 87/C4
S·ør-Trøndelag (co.),
Nor. 37/D3
Sør-Varanger, Nor. 37/J1
Sora, It. 46/C2
Soragna, It. 58/D3
Sörak-san (peak),
SKor. 73/E3
Söraksan NP, SKor. 73/E3
Sorata, Bol. 150/E7
Sorbas, Sp. 44/D4
Sorbolo, It. 58/D3
Sorcy-Saint-Martin, Fr. 53/E6
Sorel, Qu, Can. 130/F2
Sorell-Midway Point,
Austl. 115/C4
Soresina, It. 58/C2
Sörforsa, Swe. 38/G1
Sorgues, Fr. 42/F5
Sorgun, Turk. 90/C2
Sori, It. 58/C4
Soria, Sp. 44/D2
Soriano (dept.), Uru. 158/G3
Soriano, Uru. 159/J10
Sorikmerapi (peak),
Indo. 80/A3
Soritor, Peru 156/B2
Sormonne (riv.), Fr. 53/D4
Sørø, Den. 38/D4
Soro, Rio do (riv.),
Braz. 151/J5
Soroca, Mol. 49/J1
Sorocaba, Braz. 155/C2
Sorochinsk, Rus. 63/K1
Sorol (isl.), Micr. 116/D4
Soron, India 84/B2
Soroti, Ugan. 104/B3
Sørøya (isl.), Nor. 37/G1
Sørøysundet (chan.),
Nor. 37/G1
Sorpetausee (lake),
Ger. 51/E6
Sorraia (riv.), Port. 44/A3
Sorrento, It. 46/D2
Sorsele, Swe. 37/F2
Sorso, It. 46/A2
Sorsogon, Phil. 79/D5
Sort, Sp. 45/F1
Sörve (pt.), Est. 39/K3
Sos del Rey Católico,
Sp. 44/E1
Sősan, SKor. 73/D4
Sösdala, Swe. 38/E3
Söse (riv.), Ger. 51/G5
Soshanguve, SAfr. 105/E6
Sosna (riv.), Rus. 62/F1
Sosneado (peak),
Arg. 158/C2
Sosnogorsk, Rus. 61/M3
Sosnovka, Rus. 61/L4
Sosnowiec, Pol. 41/K3
Sospiro, It. 58/D2
Sosúa, DRep. 141/G4
Sos'va (riv.), Rus. 64/G3
Sot (riv.), India 84/B2
Soto del Real, Sp. 45/N8
Soto la Marina, Mex. 143/F4
Sotouboua, Togo 103/F4
Sottrum, Ger. 51/G2
Sotuta, Mex. 144/D1
Soude (riv.), Fr. 53/D6
Souderton, Pa, US 138/D3
Soúdha, Gre. 47/J5
Souffelweyersheim, Fr. 53/G6
Soufflenheim, Fr. 53/G6
Soufflion, Gre. 47/K2
Soufrière (peak),
StV. 141/N9
Soufrière (peak),
Guad. 141/N8
Souillac, Fr. 42/D4
Souillac, Mrts. 107/T15
Souk Ahras, Alg. 100/K6
Souk Ahras (prov.),
Alg. 100/K6
Souk el Arba du Rharb,
Mor. 100/A2
Söul (Seoul) (cap.),
SKor. 71/N4
Soultz-Haut-Rhin, Fr. 56/D2
Soultz-sous-Forêts, Fr. 54/A5
Soum (prov.),
Burk. 103/E3
Soumagne, Belg. 53/E2
Sound, The (chan.),
Den. 37/E5
Souppes-sur-Loing, Fr. 42/E2
Sour El Ghozlane,
Alg. 100/G4
Sources, Mont aux
(peak), Les. 106/E3
Soure, Braz. 151/J4
Soure, Port. 44/A2
Souris, Mb, Can. 127/H3
Souris, PE, Can. 131/H2
Souris (riv.), Can.,US 127/H3
Sourou (prov.), Burk. 102/E3
Sous le Vent, Iles (isls.),
FrPol. 117/K6
Sousa, Braz. 154/C2

Sout (riv.), SAfr. 106/C3
South (mts.), NS, Can. 131/H2
South (bay),
Nun., Can. 123/H2
South (mtn.), Pa, US 138/A3
South (cape), NZ 117/R12
South (isl.), NZ 109/H7
South Africa (ctry.) 105/D6
South Amboy,
NJ, US 139/H10
South America (cont.) 147
South Andaman (isl.),
India 83/F5
South Anna (riv.),
Va, US 133/J2
South Augusta,
Ga, US 133/H3
South Aulatsivik (isl.),
Nf, Can. 123/K3
South Australia (state),
Austl. 109/C3
South Ayrshire (pol. reg.),
Sc, UK 36/B6
South Bend, Wa, US 126/C4
South Bend, In, US 130/C3
South Benfleet,
Eng, UK 33/G3
South Buganda (prov.),
Ugan. 104/A3
South Burlington,
Vt, US 131/F3
South Caicos (isl.), UK 145/J1
South Carolina
(state), US 133/H3
South China (sea),
Asia 67/L8
South Colby,
Wa, US 135/B2
South Dakota
(state), US 127/H4
South Dorset Downs
(uplands), Eng, UK 32/D5
South Downs (hills),
Eng, UK 33/F5
South Dum Dum,
India 85/G4
South East (pt.),
Austl. 115/C4
South East (cape),
Austl. 109/D5
South Elgin, Il, US 135/P16
South Esk (riv.), Austl. 115/C3
South Esk (riv.),
Sc, UK 36/C3
South Farmingdale,
NY, US 139/M9
South Fork,
Co, US 132/B2
South Fulton,
Tn, US 130/B4
Southampton (isl.),
Nun., Can. 123/H2
Southampton,
On, Can. 130/D2
Southampton,
Eng, UK 33/F5
Southampton (co.),
Eng, UK 33/F5
Southampton,
NY, US 139/F2
Southampton Water
(inlet), Eng, UK 33/F5
Southaven, Ms, US 129/K4
Southeast (cape),
Ak, US 134/E3
Southeast (pt.), Bahm. 145/H1
Southeast (pt.), Jam. 145/G2
Southend (int'l arpt.),
Eng, UK 33/G3
Southend-on-Sea,
Eng, UK 33/G3
Southend-on-Sea
(co.), Eng, UK 33/G3
Southern (prov.),
Ugan. 104/A3
Southern (dist.), Isr. 91/D4
Southern (mts.), NZ 109/G7
Southern (riv.),
Austl. 112/K7
Southern Cook (isls.),
CookIs. 117/J6
Southern Cross, Austl. 112/C4
Southern Indian (lake),
Mb, Can. 122/G3
Southern NP, Sudan 97/L6
Southern Pines,
NC, US 133/J3
Southern Uplands (hills),
Sc, UK 35/D1
Southesk Tablelands
(plat.), Austl. 109/C3
Southold, NY, US 139/F1
Southport, NC, US 133/J3
Southport, Eng, UK 35/E4
Southton, Tx, US 137/U21
Southport
Wa, US 126/D4
Southwark (bor.),
Eng, UK 30/A1
Southwood NP,
Austl. 114/C4
Southworth,
Wa, US 135/C3
South Para (res.),
Austl. 113/M8
Sovere, It. 58/D1
Sovetsk, Rus. 39/J4
Sowerby Bridge,
Eng, UK 35/F6
Soweto, SAfr. 106/D2
Sŏya-misaki (cape),
Japan 76/B1
Soyana (riv.), Rus. 60/J2
Soyang (riv.), SKor. 74/A2

South Prairie,
Wa, US 135/C3
South River, NJ, US 139/H10
South Rockwood,
Mi, US 135/F7
South Ronaldsay (isl.),
Sc, UK 31/V14
South Roxana, Il, US 137/G8
South Salt Lake,
Ut, US 137/K12
South San Francisco,
Ca, US 135/K11
South Sandwich
(isls.), UK 22/H8
South Saskatchewan
(riv.), Sk, Can. 122/E3
South Seaville,
NJ, US 138/D5
South Shetland
(isls.), UK 160/W
South Shields,
Eng, UK 35/G2
South Sioux City,
Ne, US 127/J5
South Skunk (riv.),
Ia, US 129/J2
South Taranaki Bight
(bay), NZ 117/S10
South Turkana Nat'l Rsv.,
Kenya 104/B2
South Tyne (riv.),
Eng, UK 35/F2
South Tyneside
(co.), Eng, UK 35/G2
South Ubian, Phil. 81/F2
South Uist (isl.),
Sc, UK 31/S8
South Umpqua (riv.),
Or, US 128/B2
South Valley Stream,
NY, US 139/L9
South Weber,
Ut, US 137/K11
South West (cape),
Austl. 115/C4
South West NP,
Austl. 115/C4
South West Rocks,
Austl. 115/E1
South Whittier,
Ca, US 136/F8
South Williamsport,
Pa, US 138/B1
South Woodham Ferrers,
Eng, UK 30/E2
South Yorkshire (co.),
Eng, UK 35/G5
Southampton (cape),
Nun., Can. 123/H2
Soyaux, Fr. 42/D4
Soyen, Ger. 55/F6
Soyhières, Swi. 56/D3
Sozh (riv.), Bela. 62/D1
Sozopol, Bul. 49/H4
Spa, Belg. 53/E3
Spada (lake), Wa, US 135/D2
Spain (ctry.) 44/C2
Spalding, Austl. 113/H5
Spalding, Eng, UK 35/H6
Spalt, Ger. 54/D4
Spanish Lake,
Mo, US 137/G8
Spanish Town, Jam. 145/G2
Spanner, It. 46/C3
Sparks, Nv, US 128/C3
Sparlingville,
Mi, US 135/G6
Sparreholm, Swe. 38/G2
Sparta, Wi, US 127/L5
Sparta, Tn, US 130/C5
Sparta, NC, US 130/D4
Sparta, NJ, US 138/D1
Spartanburg,
SC, US 133/H2
Spárti (Sparta), Gre. 47/H4
Spartivento (cape), It. 46/E4
Sparwood,
BC, Can. 126/E3
Spassk-Dal'niy, Rus. 71/P3
Spáta, Gre. 47/N9
Spátha (cape), Gre. 47/H5
Spean (riv.), Sc, UK 36/B3
Speer (peak), Swi. 57/F3
Speer Canal (canal),
Swi. 57/F3
Speicher, Swi. 57/F3
Speichersdorf, Ger. 55/E3
Speigse, It. 46/C2
Spelle, Ger. 51/E4
Spence (pt.), Ak, US 134/E2
Spencer (gulf),
Austl. 115/C4
Spencer (pt.), Ak, US 134/E2
Spencer (gulf),
Austl. 115/C4
Spencer, Ok, US 137/N14
Spencer (cape),
Austl. 113/H5
Spenge, Ger. 51/F4
Spennymoor, Eng, UK 35/G2
Spentrup, Den. 38/D3
Sperkhiós (riv.), Gre. 47/H3
Sperrin (mts.),
NI, UK 34/A2
Spessart (range), Ger. 54/C3
Spétsai, Gre. 47/H4
Spey (riv.), Sc, UK 36/B2
Spey (bay), Sc, UK 36/C1
Speyer, Ger. 54/B4
Speyerbsch (riv.),
Ger. 54/B4
Spezzano Albanese, It. 46/E3
Spičák (peak), Czh. 55/F2
Spicer (pt.),
Nun., Can. 123/H2
Spiekeroog (isl.),
Ger. 51/E1
Spiez, Swi. 56/D4
Spigno Monferrato, It. 58/B3
Spijkenisse, Neth. 50/B5
Spike (mtn.), Ak, US 134/K2
Spilion, Gre. 47/J5
Spilamberto, It. 59/E3
Spilimbergo, It. 58/D4
Spilve (int'l arpt.),
Lat. 39/L3
Spina (peak), It. 46/A2
Spinetta Marengo, It. 58/B3
Spino d'Adda, It. 58/C2
Spirano, It. 58/C1
Spirit River,
Ab, Can. 126/D2
Spiritwood,
Sk, Can. 126/G2
Spišská Nová Ves,
Slvk. 41/L4
Spiti (riv.), India 86/D3
Spitsbergen (isl.),
Sval. 160/E
Split, Cro. 40/C4
Split (int'l arpt.),
Cro. 40/C4
Split (lake),
Mb, Can. 122/G3
Splitrock (res.),
NJ, US 139/H8
Spluga, Passo dello
(pass), Swi. 57/E4
Splügen, Swi. 57/F4
Spofforth, Eng, UK 35/G5
Spokane, Wa, US 126/D4
Spokane (riv.),
Wa, US 126/D4
Spoleto, It. 46/B2
Spöl (riv.), It. 57/G5
Spooner, Wi, US 127/L4
Spoorno, It. 58/B4
Spotswood, NJ, US 139/H10
Spotsylvania, Va, US 133/J2
Sprague, Mb, Can. 127/K3
Sprang, Neth. 50/C5
Spratly (isls.), Asia 80/D2
Spree (riv.), Ger. 41/H2
Sprendlingen, Ger. 53/G4
Stalowa Wola, Pol. 41/M3
Sprimont, Belg. 53/E3
Spring, Tx, US 129/J6
Spring City, Pa, US 138/D3
Spring Grove,
Pa, US 138/B4

Spring Grove,
Il, US 135/P15
Spring Hill, Ks, US 137/D6
Spring Lake,
NJ, US 138/D3
Spring Valley,
Ca, US 136/D5
Spring Valley,
NY, US 139/J7
Springbok, SAfr. 106/B3
Springdale,
Nf, Can. 131/K1
Springdale, Ar, US 129/J3
Springe, Ger. 51/G4
Springer, NM, US 129/F3
Springerville, Az, US 128/E4
Springfield, Or, US 126/C4
Springfield, Tn, US 130/C4
Springfield, Vt, US 131/F3
Springfield, Ma, US 131/F3
Springfield, Mo, US 129/J3
Springfield, NJ, US 139/H9
Springfield, Va, US 138/A4
Springfontein,
SAfr. 106/D3
Springhill, La, US 129/J4
Springhill, NS, Can. 131/H2
Springs, SAfr. 106/E2
Springs, NY, US 139/F1
Springside,
Sk, Can. 127/H3
Springsure, Austl. 114/C4
Springville, Ut, US 137/K13
Sprockhövel, Ger. 51/E6
Spruce (peak),
WV, US 130/E4
Spruce Run (res.),
NJ, US 138/C2
Spui (riv.), Neth. 50/B5
Spurn (pt.), Eng, UK 35/J4
Squamish, BC, Can. 126/C3
Squaw Harbor,
Ak, US 134/F4
Squaxin Island Ind. Res.,
Wa, US 135/A3
Squillace, Golfo di (gulf),
It. 46/E3
Squinzano, It. 47/F2
Squires (mt.), Austl. 113/E3
Srbobran, Serb. 48/D3
Srebrenica, Bosn. 40/D3
Sredna (mts.), Bul. 49/H4
Srednogorie, Bul. 49/H4
Srem, Pol. 41/J2
Sremčica, Serb. 48/E3
Sremska Mitrovica,
Serb. 48/D3
Sreng (riv.), Camb. 78/C3
Srepok (riv.), Camb. 78/D3
Sri Dungargarh,
India 89/K3
Sri Gangānagar,
India 86/B5
Sri Jayewardenepura Kotte,
(cap.), SrL. 82/C6
Sri Lanka (ctry.) 82/D6
Srikākulam, India 82/D4
Srivardhan, India 89/K5
Środa Śląska, Pol. 41/J3
Środa Wielkopolska,
Pol. 41/J2
St. Albans, Vale of
(valley), Eng, UK 30/B1
St. John's (cap.),
Nf, Can. 131/L2
Stabbursdalen NP,
Nor. 37/H1
Staberhuk (pt.), Ger. 38/D4
Stabroek, Belg. 50/B6
Stade, Ger. 51/G1
Stadl-Paura, Aus. 55/G6
Stadskanaal, Neth. 50/D3
Stadtbergen, Ger. 54/D6
Stadthagen, Ger. 51/G4
Stadtlauringen,
Ger. 54/D2
Stadtlohn, Ger. 50/D5
Stadtoldendorf,
Ger. 51/G5
Stadtsteinach, Ger. 55/E3
Stäfa, Swi. 57/E3
Staffanstorp, Swe. 38/E4
Staffelberg (peak),
Ger. 54/E2
Staffelegg (pass),
Swi. 56/E3
Staffelsee (lake),
Swi. 56/E3
Staffhorst, Ger. 51/F3
Stafford, Eng, UK 35/E6
Stagno, It. 58/D5
Stagnone Isole Della
(isl.), It. 46/B4
Stahnsdorf, Ger. 40/Q7
Staines, Eng, UK 30/B2
Stakes (mt.),
Ca, US 135/M12
Stalden, Swi. 56/D5
Stalingrad (Volgograd),
Rus. 63/H2
Stallings, Il, US 137/G8
Stallworthy (cape),
Nun., Can. 123/S6
Stalowa Wola, Pol. 41/M3
Stalybridge,
Eng, UK 35/F6
Stamboliyski, Bul. 47/J1
Stamford,
Stamford, Tx, US 129/H4
Stamford, Eng, UK 33/F1

Stamford, Ct, US 139/L7
Stampa, Swi. 57/F5
Stamriet, Namb. 105/C5
Stamullen, Ire. 34/B4
Standerton, SAfr. 106/E2
Standish-with-Langtree,
Eng, UK 35/F4
Standley (lake),
Co, US 137/B3
Stanford-le-Hope,
Eng, UK 33/G3
Stange, Nor. 38/D1
Stanger, SAfr. 107/E3
Stanghella, It. 59/E2
Stanhope, NJ, US 138/D2
Stanišić, Serb. 48/D3
Stanislaus (co.),
Ca, US 135/M12
Stanislaus (riv.),
Ca, US 128/B3
Stanley, Austl. 115/C4
Stanley (mt.), Austl. 115/C4
Stanley (mt.), Austl. 113/F2
Stanley, NB, Can. 131/H2
Stanley (falls),
D.R. Congo 97/L3
Stanley (cap.), Falk. 159/F6
Stanley, Eng, UK 35/G2
Stanley, Sc, UK 36/C4
Stanley, ND, US 127/H3
Stanley, Ks, US 137/D6
Stanley (res.), India 82/C5
Stanley Draper (lake),
Ok, US 137/N15
Stanovo, Serb. 48/E4
Stanovoy (range),
Rus. 67/M4
Stans, Swi. 57/E4
Stansted (int'l arpt.),
Eng, UK 33/G3
Stanthorpe, Austl. 114/C5
Stanton, Ky, US 130/D4
Stanton, Tx, US 129/G4
Stanton, De, US 138/C4
Stanton, NJ, US 138/D2
Stanton, Ca, US 136/G8
Staphorst, Neth. 50/D3
Staplehurst,
Eng, UK 33/G4
Staples, On, Can. 135/G7
Stapleton, Ca, US 135/B4
Stara Pazova, Serb. 48/E3
Stara Planina (mts.),
Serb. 48/F3
Stara Zagora, Bul. 47/J1
Starachowice, Pol. 41/L3
Staranzano, It. 59/G1
Staraya Russa, Rus. 39/P3
Starbuck (isl.), Kiri. 117/K5
Starcke NP, Austl. 114/B1
Stargard Szczeciński,
Pol. 38/F5
Starke, Fl, US 133/H4
Starkville, Ms, US 133/F3
Starnbergersee (lake),
Ger. 55/E4
Starodub, Rus. 62/E1
Starogard Gdański,
Pol. 38/H5
Staroselje, It. 57/G4
Stelvio, PN Dello, It. 43/J3
Stenay, Fr. 53/E5
Stendal, Ger. 40/F2
Steneto NP, Bul. 47/J1
Stenhousemuir,
Sc, UK 36/C4
Stenungsund, Swe. 38/D2
Stephansposching,
Ger. 55/F5
Stephenville,
Nf, Can. 131/K1
Stephenville,
Tx, US 129/H4
Sterkstroom, SAfr. 106/D3
Sterling, Ak, US 134/H3
Sterling, Co, US 129/G2
Sterlitamak, Rus. 63/K1
Sternstein (peak),
Aus. 55/G5
Sterzing (Vipiteno), It. 57/H4
Steszew, Pol. 41/J2
Štěti, Czh. 55/H1
Stettler, Ab, Can. 126/E2
Steubenville, Oh, US 130/D3
Stevenage, Eng, UK 33/F3
Stevens Village,
Ak, US 134/J2
Stevenson (lake),
Mb, Can. 127/J2
Stevenson Entrance
(str.), Ak, US 134/H4
Stevenson, Sc, UK 36/B5
Stevensville,
Mt, US 126/E4
Stevensville,
Md, US 138/B6
Stevinsluizen (dam),
Neth. 50/C3
Stevzing (Vipiteno), It. 43/J3
Stewart, BC, Can. 134/N4
Stewart (riv.),
Yk, Can. 122/C2
Stewart (isl.), NZ 109/G7
Stewart Crossing,
Yk, Can. 134/L2
Stewarton, Sc, UK 36/B5
Stewartstown,
Pa, US 138/B4
Stewartstown,
NI, UK 34/B2
Stewartville,
Or, US 137/K5

Steenwijk, Neth. 50/D3
Steep (pt.), Austl. 112/B3
Steep Holm (isl.),
Eng, UK 32/C4
Steephill (lake),
Sk, Can. 127/G1
Steeping (riv.),
Eng, UK 35/J5
Steese Nat'l Conservation
Area, Ak, US 134/J2
Stefansson (isl.),
Nun., Can. 122/F1
Steffen (peak),
Chile 158/C5
Steffisburg, Swi. 56/D4
Steg, Swi. 56/D5
Stege, Den. 38/E4
Steiermark (prov.),
Aus. 41/H5
Steigerwald (for.),
Ger. 43/J2
Steilacoom, Wa, US 135/B3
Steimbke, Ger. 51/G3
Stein, Neth. 53/E2
Stein am Rhein, Swi. 57/E2
Stein bei Nünnberg,
Ger. 54/E4
Steina (riv.), Ger. 57/E2
Steinach, Ger. 55/F5
Steinach (riv.), Ger. 54/E2
Steinach am Brenner,
Aus. 57/H3
Steinbach,
Mb, Can. 127/J3
Steinbach an der Steyr,
Aus. 55/H7
Steinbourg, Fr. 53/G6
Steinen, Ger. 56/D2
Steinerkirchen an der Traun,
Aus. 55/G6
Steinfeld, Ger. 51/F3
Steinfeld, Ger. 54/B4
Steinfeld, Ger. 54/C3
Steinfort, Lux. 53/E4
Steingaden, Ger. 57/G2
Steinhagen, Ger. 51/F4
Steinhausen, Swi. 57/E3
Steinhausen an der Rottum,
Ger. 57/F1
Steinheim, Ger. 51/G5
Steinheim am Albuch,
Ger. 54/D5
Steinheim an der Murr,
Ger. 54/C5
Steinhorst, Ger. 51/H3
Steinhuder (lake),
Ger. 51/G4
Steinjker, Nor. 37/D2
Steinjker, Nor. 37/D2
Steinsland, Nor. 38/A1
Steinweiler, Ger. 54/B4
Stekene, Belg. 50/B6
Stella, SAfr. 106/D2
Stella (peak), It. 57/F5
Stellarton, NS, Can. 131/J2
Stelle, Ger. 51/H2
Stellenbosch, SAfr. 106/L10
Stello (peak), Fr. 43/H5
Stelvio, Passo dello
(pass), It. 57/G4
Stewartville,
Or, US 137/K5

Steyr (riv.), Aus. 41/H5
Steyregg, Aus. 55/H6
Steytlerville, SAfr. 106/D4
Stia, It. 59/E5
Stiava, It. 58/D5
Stickney (mt.), Wa, US 135/D2
Stiens, Neth. 50/C2
Stigler, Ok, US 129/J4
Stigtomta, Swe. 38/G2
Stikine (riv.), Can.,US 134/M4
Stilbaai, SAfr. 106/C4
Stilfontein, SAfr. 106/D2
Stilis, Gre. 47/H3
Still Creek (res.), Pa, US 138/C2
Still Pond, Md, US 138/B5
Stilling, Den. 38/D3
Stillings, Mo, US 137/D5
Stillwater (range), Nv, US 128/C3
Stillwater, Ok, US 129/H3
Stillwater, Pa, US 138/B1
Stillwater (lake), Pa, US 138/C1
Stilo (cape), It. 46/E3
Stilwell, Ok, US 129/J4
Stilwell, Ks, US 137/D6
Štimlje, Serb. 47/G1
Stimpfach, Ger. 54/D4
Stinchar (riv.), Sc, UK 34/D1
Stinnett, Tx, US 129/G4
Štip, FYROM 47/H2
Stiring-Wendel, Fr. 53/F5
Stirka (peak), Czh. 55/G4
Stirling (mt.), Austl. 112/C4
Stirling, Sc, UK 36/C4
Stirling (pol. reg.), Sc, UK 36/B4
Stirling Range NP, Austl. 112/C5
Stirone (riv.), It. 58/C3
Stjørdal, Nor. 37/D3
Stob a' Choin (peak), Sc, UK 36/B4
Stob Choire Claurigh (peak), Sc, UK 36/B3
Stochov, Czh. 55/G2
Stock, Eng, UK 30/E2
Stock (lake), Fr. 53/F6
Stockach, Ger. 57/F2
Stockerau, Aus. 49/N7
Stockertown, Pa, US 138/C2
Stockholm (cap.), Swe. 37/F4
Stockholm (co.), Swe. 38/G2
Stockhorn (peak), Swi. 56/D4
Stockport, Eng, UK 35/F5
Stockport (co.), Eng, UK 35/F5
Stocks (res.), Eng, UK 35/F4
Stocksbridge, Eng, UK 35/G5
Stockstadt am Rhein, Ger. 54/B3
Stockton (lake), Mo, US 129/J3
Stockton, Ca, US 128/B3
Stockton (plat.), Tx, US 142/E2
Stockton, Ut, US 137/K11
Stockton, NJ, US 138/D3
Stockton-on-Tees, Eng, UK 35/G2
Stockton-on-Tees (co.), Eng, UK 35/G2
Stod, Czh. 55/G2
Stoddard, Ut, US 137/K11
Stoke (pt.), Eng, UK 32/B6
Stoke-on-Trent, Eng, UK 35/F5
Stoke-on-Trent (co.), Eng, UK 35/F5
Stoke Poges, Eng, UK 30/B2
Stokenchurch, Eng, UK 30/A2
Stokes (pt.), Austl. 115/B4
Stokes NP, Austl. 112/D5
Stolac, Bosn. 47/E1
Stolberg, Ger. 53/F2
Stolbovoy (isl.), Rus. 65/P2
Stöllet, Ger. 38/E1
Stolzenau, Ger. 51/G3
Stompneuspunt (pt.), SAfr. 106/K10
Ston, Cro. 47/E1
Stone, Eng, UK 35/F6
Stone Harbor, NJ, US 138/D5
Stonehaven, Sc, UK 36/D3
Stonehenge (ruin), Eng, UK 33/E4
Stonehouse, Sc, UK 36/C5
Stonewall, Mb, Can. 127/J3
Stoney Creek, On, Can. 131/Q9
Stoney Point, On, Can. 131/G7
Stoneyburn, Sc, UK 36/C5
Stonington, Ct, US 139/G1
Stony (pt.), Mb, Can. 139/G1
Stony Brook, NY, US 139/E2
Stony Creek (lake), Mi, US 135/E7
Stony Mountain, Mb, Can. 127/J3

Stony Point, NY, US 138/E1
Stony River, Ak, US 134/G3
Stony Tunguska (riv.), Rus. 67/J3
Stonybrook-Wilshire, Pa, US 138/B4
Stooping (riv.), Co, US 130/D1
Stör (isl.) Nun., Can. 123/S7
Stör (isl.) (riv.), Ger. 51/G1
Storå, Swe. 38/F2
Stora Le (lake), Swe. 38/D2
Stora Sjöfallets NP, Swe. 37/F2
Storavan (lake), Swe. 37/F2
Stord (isl.), Nor. 38/A2
Store Bælt (chan.), Den. 38/D3
Storebø, Nor. 38/A1
Støren, Nor. 37/D3
Storfors, Swe. 38/F2
Storm (bay), Austl. 109/D5
Stormberg (mtn.), SAfr. 106/D3
Stormont, NI, UK 34/C2
Stornoway, Sc, UK 31/Q7
Storo, It. 58/D1
Storr, The (peak), Sc, UK 31/Q8
Storsjön (lake), Swe. 37/E3
Storsteinsfjellet (peak), Nor. 37/F1
Storstrøm (co.), Den. 38/D4
Storvik, Swe. 38/G1
Storvreta, Swe. 38/G2
Story, Wy, US 126/G4
Stosch (isl.), Chile 159/A6
Stötten am Auerberg, Ger. 57/G2
Stoughton, Sk, Can. 127/H3
Stoumont, Belg. 53/E3
Stour (riv.), Eng, UK 32/D5
Stourbridge, Eng, UK 32/D2
Stourport-on-Severn, Eng, UK 32/D2
Støvring, Den. 38/C3
Stowe, Pa, US 138/C3
Stowmarket, Eng, UK 33/G2
Stra, It. 59/F2
Strabane (dist.), NI 34/A2
Strabane, NI, UK 31/Q9
Stradella, It. 58/C2
Straelen, Ger. 50/D6
Strahan, Austl. 115/C4
Straldzha, Bul. 47/K1
Stralsund, Ger. 38/E4
Strambino, It. 58/A2
Strand, SAfr. 106/L11
Strangford, NI, UK 34/C3
Strangford (lake), NI, UK 34/C3
Strängnäs, Swe. 38/G2
Strangways (mt.), Austl. 113/G2
Stranocum, NI, UK 34/B1
Stranraer, Sc, UK 36/B2
Strasbourg, Fr. 56/D1
Strasbourg (Entzheim) (int'l arpt.), Fr. 56/D1
Strasburg, Mo, US 137/E6
Strasburg, Pa, US 138/B4
Strassen, Lux. 53/F4
Strasshof an der Nordbahn, Aus. 49/P7
Strasswalchen, Aus. 55/G7
Stratford, Tx, US 129/G3
Stratford, On, Can. 130/D3
Stratford, NZ 117/S10
Stratford, Ct, US 139/E1
Stratford, NJ, US 138/C4
Stratford (pt.), Ct, US 139/E1
Stratford (har.), Ct, US 139/L8
Stratford and Worcester (canal), Eng, UK 32/D2
Stratford-upon-Avon, Eng, UK 33/E2
Strathalbyn, Austl. 113/H5
Strathaven, Sc, UK 36/C5
Strathbgo (bay), Sc, UK 36/E1
Strathblane, Sc, UK 36/B5
Strathearn (valley), Sc, UK 36/C4
Strathmore, Ab, Can. 126/E3
Strathmore (valley), Sc, UK 36/C3
Strathpeffer, Sc, UK 36/B1
Strathspey (valley), Sc, UK 36/C2
Straubing, Ger. 55/F5
Straumnes Horn (pt.), Ice. 37/M6
Strausberg, Ger. 40/Q6
Strausstown, Pa, US 138/B3
Strawberry (peak), Ca, US 136/B2
Strazhitsa, Bul. 47/J4
Streaky (bay), Austl. 109/C4
Streaky Bay, Austl. 113/G5
Streamwood, Il, US 135/P15
Streator, Il, US 127/L5
Středočeská Žulová Vrchovina (mts.), Czh. 41/H4
Středočeský (pol. reg.), Czh. 43/L2
Street, Md, US 138/B4

Strehaia, Rom. 49/F3
Streich (peak), Austl. 112/D4
Strela (riv.), Czh. 41/G3
Strelley Abor. Land, Austl. 112/C2
Strel'na (riv.), Rus. 60/H2
Strengberg, Aus. 55/H6
Strengelbach, Swi. 56/D3
Strengen, Aus. 57/G3
Stresa, It. 58/B1
Stretford, Eng, UK 35/F5
Strettoia, It. 58/D5
Streu (riv.), Ger. 54/D2
Strib, Den. 38/C4
Stříbro, Czh. 55/G3
Strichen, Sc, UK 36/D1
Strigno, It. 57/H5
Strijen, Neth. 50/B5
Strimón (gulf), Gre. 62/C4
Strimónas (riv.), Gre. 47/H2
Striven (lake), Sc, UK 36/A5
Strobel (lake), Arg. 159/C6
Stroeder, Arg. 158/E4
Strofádhes (isl.), Gre. 47/G4
Strom Thurmond (lake), Ga,SC, US 133/H3
Stromberg, Ger. 54/B3
Stromboli (isl.), It. 46/D3
Stromness, Nor. 38/D2
Stromness, Sc, UK 31/V14
Strona (riv.), It. 57/E6
Strongoli, It. 47/E3
Stronie Śląskie, Pol. 41/J3
Stronsay (isl.), Sc, UK 31/V14
Stronsay Firth (inlet), Sc, UK 31/V14
Strood, Eng, UK 30/E2
Stropnice (riv.), Czh. 55/H5
Stroppiana, It. 58/B2
Stroud, Eng, UK 32/D3
Stroudsburg, Pa, US 138/C2
Struan, Sc, UK 31/Q8
Struer, Den. 38/C3
Struga, FYROM 47/G2
Struisbaai (bay), SAfr. 106/C4
Strule (riv.), NI, UK 34/A2
Struma (riv.), Bul. 62/B4
Strumble (pt.), Wal, UK 32/A2
Strumica, FYROM 47/H2
Strydenburg, SAfr. 106/C3
Stryn, Nor. 37/D3
Strzegom, Pol. 41/J3
Strzelce Krajeńskie, Pol. 41/H2
Strzelce Opolskie, Pol. 62/A2
Strzelecki (mt.), Austl. 115/D4
Strzelecki (mt.), Austl. 113/G2
Strzelin, Pol. 41/J3
Strzelno, Pol. 41/J2
Strzyżów, Pol. 41/L4
Stuart (lake), BC, Can. 126/B2
Stuart (riv.), BC, Can. 126/B2
Stuart, Fl, US 133/H5
Stuart Xian, China 72/C4
Stuarts Draft, Va, US 130/E4
Stubbekøbing, Den. 38/E4
Stubbenkammer (pt.), Ger. 38/E4
Stühlingen, Ger. 57/E2
Stupava, Slvk. 43/M2
Stupino, Rus. 60/H5
Stura di Lanzo (riv.), It. 58/A2
Sturgeon (lake), On, Can. 127/L3
Sturgeon (bay), Mb, Can. 127/J3
Sturgeon (riv.), On, Can. 130/D2
Sturgeon Falls, On, Can. 130/E2
Sturgis, Mi, US 130/C3
Sturgis, SD, US 126/F4
Šturovo, Slvk. 41/K5
Sturt (dist.), Austl. 109/D3
Sturt (mt.), Austl. 113/J4
Sturt (riv.), Austl. 113/J4
Sturt NP, Austl. 115/B1
Sturup (int'l arpt.), Swe. 38/E4
Stutterheim, SAfr. 106/D4
Stuttgart, Ger. 54/C5
Stykkishólmur, Ice. 37/M6
Styr (riv.), Ukr. 62/C2
Suaçuí Grande (riv.), Braz. 155/D1
Suakin (arch.), Sudan 97/N4
Suam (riv.), Kenya 104/D2
Suaqui Grande, Mex. 142/C2
Suār, India 84/B1
Suárez (riv.), Col. 152/C3
Subang, Indo. 80/C5
Subarnarekhā (riv.), India 85/E4
Subāṭ (riv.), Sudan 97/M6
Subaytilah, Tun. 100/L7
Subei Monggolzu Zizhixian, China 70/F4
Subi (isl.), Indo. 80/D3
Subotica, Serb. 40/D2
Succasunna-Kenvil, NJ, US 138/D2

Succiso, Alpe di (peak), It. 58/D4
Suceava, Rom. 49/H2
Suceava (prov.), Rom. 49/G2
Suceava (riv.), Rom. 49/G2
Suchedniów, Pol. 41/L3
Suches, Bol. 156/D4
Suck (riv.), Ire. 31/P10
Sucre (cap.), Bol. 150/E7
Sucre, Ecu. 152/A5
Sucre (state), Ven. 153/F2
Sucre (dept.), Col. 145/H4
Sucúa, Ecu. 152/B4
Sucumbios (prov.), Ecu. 152/B4
Sucunduri (riv.), Braz. 150/G5
Sucupira do Norte, Braz. 154/A2
Sucuriú (riv.), Braz. 151/H7
Sucy-en-Brie, Fr. 30/K5
Sud (pol. reg.), Mor. 98/C3
Sud-Ouest (prov.), Camr. 103/H5
Suda (riv.), Rus. 60/H3
Sudama, Japan 77/A2
Sudan (ctry.) 97/L5
Sudānpur, India 84/D2
Sudbury, On, Can. 130/D2
Sudbury, Eng, UK 33/G2
Suddie, Guy. 153/G3
Sude (riv.), Ger. 40/F2
Süderbrarup, Ger. 38/C4
Sudeten (mts.) 41/H3
Sudlersville, Md, US 138/C4
Südlohn, Ger. 50/D5
Sue (riv.), Sudan 93/E4
Sueca, Sp. 45/E3
Süedinenie, Phil. 67/E6
Suez (gulf), Egypt 97/M2
Suez (canal), Egypt 93/D1
Şūf, Jor. 91/D3
Sufers, Swi. 57/F4
Suffern, NY, US 139/J7
Suffolk (co.), NY, US 139/F2
Suga (isl.), Japan 77/L7
Sugar Creek, Mo, US 137/E5
Sugar Grove, Il, US 135/P16
Sugar Land, Tx, US 132/E4
Sugar Loaf (peak), Wal, UK 32/C3
Sugar Notch, Pa, US 138/C1
Sugenheim, Ger. 54/D3
Sugito, Japan 77/D1
Suğla (lake), Turk. 90/C2
Suhāj (gov.), Egypt 101/B3
Suhāj, Egypt 101/B3
Sühbaatar (prov.), Mong. 71/K2
Suhl, Ger. 54/D1
Suhlendorf, Ger. 51/H3
Suhut, Turk. 90/B2
Sui (riv.), China 79/B3
Sui (pt.), Thai. 78/B4
Sui Xian, China 72/C4
Suia-Missu (riv.), Braz. 151/H6
Suichang, China 79/C2
Suichuan, China 83/K2
Suifenhe, China 71/P3
Suihua, China 71/N2
Suijiang, China 83/H2
Suileng, China 71/N2
Suining, China 72/D4
Suipacha, Arg. 159/J11
Suiping, China 72/C4
Suippe (riv.), Fr. 40/C4
Suippes, Fr. 53/D5
Suir (riv.), Ire. 31/Q10
Suis (well), Libya 99/H4
Suisho (isl.), Rus. 76/D2
Suita, Japan 77/J6
Suitland-Silver Hill, Md, US 138/B6
Suixi, China 83/K3
Suixi, China 72/D4
Suiyang, China 79/A2
Suize (riv.), Fr. 56/B2
Suizhong, China 72/E2
Suizhou, China 71/K5
Süjāngarh, India 89/K3
Sukabumi, Indo. 80/C5
Sukadana (bay), Indo. 80/C4
Sukadana, Indo. 80/C4
Sukagawa, Japan 75/G2
Sukeke, Pak. 86/B4
Sukhindol, Bul. 47/J1
Sukhinichi, Rus. 62/E1
Sukhodol'skoye (lake), Rus. 39/N1
Sukhona (riv.), Rus. 64/G4
Sukhothai (ruin), Thai. 78/B2
Sukhothai, Thai. 78/B2
Sukkur, Pak. 89/J3
Sukkumo, Japan 74/C4
Sula (isls.), Phil. 67/M10
Sula (isl.), Rus. 61/L2
Sulaimān (range), Pak. 89/J3
Sulakyurt, Turk. 90/D1
Sulawesi (Celebes) (isl.), Indo. 81/E4
Sulb Temple (ruin), Sudan 101/B4

Sulechów, Pol. 41/H2
Sulęcin, Pol. 41/H2
Sulejów, Pol. 41/K3
Sulejówek, Pol. 41/L2
Sulina, Rom. 49/J3
Sulina Branch (riv.), Rom. 49/J3
Sulingen, Ger. 51/F3
Sulitjelma (peak), Nor. 37/F2
Sullana, Peru 156/A2
Sullivan (lake), Ab, Can. 126/E3
Sullivan, Qu, Can. 130/E1
Sullivan, Wi, US 135/N13
Sully-sur-Loire, Fr. 40/B3
Sulmona, It. 46/C1
Sulphur (riv.), Tx, US 129/J4
Sulphur, Ok, US 129/H4
Sulphur Springs, Tx, US 129/J4
Sulphur Springs, Ca, US 136/A2
Sultan, Wa, US 135/D2
Sultan (riv.), Wa, US 135/D2
Sultan Kudarat, Phil. 79/D6
Sultānpur, India 84/D2
Sulu (arch.), Phil. 67/L9
Sulu (sea), Asia 67/M9
Sülüklü, Turk. 62/E4
Suluova, Turk. 62/E4
Sulug, Libya 97/K1
Sülysáp, Hun. 49/R10
Sulz, Swi. 56/E2
Sulz (riv.), Ger. 55/E4
Sulz (riv.), Ger. 53/G2
Sulz am Neckar, Ger. 54/B6
Sulzach (riv.), Ger. 54/E3
Sulzbach, Ger. 53/G5
Sulzbach (riv.), Ger. 55/F6
Sulzbach am Main, Ger. 54/C3
Sulzbach-Rosenberg, Ger. 55/E3
Sulzberg, Ger. 57/G2
Sulzberger (bay), Ant. 160/Q
Sulzburg, Ger. 56/D2
Sulzfluh (peak), Aus. 57/F3
Sulzheim, Ger. 54/D3
Šumadija (reg.), Serb. 48/E3
Sumapaz, PN, Col. 152/C4
Sumatra (isl.), Indo. 67/J9
Sumba (str.), Indo. 81/E5
Sumba (isl.), Indo. 67/L11
Sumbar (riv.), Trkm. 86/E2
Sumbawa (isl.), Indo. 67/L10
Sumbawa Besar, Indo. 81/E5
Sumbawanga, Tanz. 104/A4
Sumbe, Ang. 105/B3
Sumburgh Head (pt.), Sc, UK 31/W14
Sumdum (mt.), Ak, US 134/M4
Sümeg, Hun. 48/C2
Sumenep, Indo. 80/D5
Sumiswald, Swi. 56/D3
Summerland, BC, Can. 126/D3
Summerland, Ca, US 136/A2
Summerside, PE, Can. 131/J2
Summerville, SC, US 133/H3
Summerville, Ga, US 133/G3
Summit, NJ, US 139/J9
Summit (co.), Ut, US 137/K12
Summit Bridge, De, US 138/C4
Summit Hill, Pa, US 138/C2
Sumner, Wa, US 135/C3
Sumoto, Japan 74/D3
Šumperk, Czh. 41/J4
Sumqayıt, Azer. 63/J4
Sums'ka Oblasti, Ukr. 62/E2
Sumter, SC, US 133/H3
Sumy, Ukr. 62/E2
Sun (riv.), Mt, US 126/E4
Sun City, Az, US 137/R18
Sun City, Ca, US 136/C3
Sun City West, Az, US 137/R18
Sun Kosi (riv.), Nepal 85/E3
Sun Lakes, Az, US 137/S19
Sunagawa, Japan 76/B2
Sunām, India 86/C4
Sunami, Japan 77/L5
Sunbury, Pa, US 138/B2
Sunbury, Austl. 115/F5
Sunbury-on-Thames, Eng, UK 30/B2
Sunch'ŏn, NKor. 73/C3
Sunch'ŏn, SKor. 73/D5
Suncook, NH, US 131/G3
Sunda (str.), Indo. 67/J10
Sunda (str.), Indo. 67/K10
Sundance, Wy, US 127/G4
Sundarbans (phys. reg.), India 85/G5
Sundargarh, India 85/E4
Sundarnagar, India 86/D4
Sundays (riv.), SAfr. 106/D4
Sunderland, Eng, UK 35/G2
Sunderland (co.), Eng, UK 35/G2
Sundern, Ger. 51/F6
Sundhouse, Fr. 56/D1
Sundown, Tx, US 129/G4

Sundown NP, Austl. 115/D1
Sundre, Ab, Can. 126/E3
Sunds, Den. 38/C3
Sungai Petani, Malay. 83/H6
Sungaipenuh, Indo. 80/B4
Süngju, SKor. 73/D5
Sungurlare, Bul. 47/K1
Sungurlu, Turk. 90/C1
Suning, China 72/C3
Sunndal, Nor. 37/D3
Sunne, Swe. 38/E2
Sunninghale, Eng, UK 33/C4
Sunnyside, Ca, US 136/C5
Sunnyside, Il, US 135/P15
Sunnyvale, Ca, US 128/B3
Sunol, Ca, US 135/L11
Sunrise (mtn.), NJ, US 138/D1
Sunrise, Or, US 126/C5
Sunset, Ut, US 137/J11
Sunset Beach, Hi, US 124/V12
Sunset Beach, Ca, US 136/F8
Sunset Country (reg.), Austl. 115/B2
Sunset Crater Volcano Nat'l Mon., Az, US 128/E4
Suntar-Khayata (mts.), Rus. 65/P3
Süntel (mts.), Ger. 51/G4
Sunwi (isl.), NKor. 73/C4
Sunwu, China 71/N2
Sunyani, Gha. 103/E5
Sunzu (peak), Zam. 104/A5
Suo (sea), Japan 74/B4
Suomenlinna, Fin. 39/L1
Suomenselkä (reg.), Fin. 39/L1
Suwanose (isl.), Japan 75/K6
Supaul, India 85/F2
Supawna Meadows NWR, NJ, US 138/C4
Supe, Peru 156/B3
Superior, Mt, US 126/E4
Superior, Az, US 128/E4
Superior (upland), Wi, US 130/B2
Superior, Co, US 137/B3
Superior (lake), Can.,US 130/B2
Suphan Buri, Thai. 78/C3
Supiori (isl.), Indo. 81/J4
Sup'ung (res.), China 73/C2
Sup'ung (dam), NKor. 73/C2
Süq ash Shuyūkh, Iraq 88/E2
Şuqaylabīyah, Syria 91/E2
Suqian, China 72/D4
Suquamish, Wa, US 135/D2
Sûr, Leb. 91/D3
Sur (riv.), Rus. 61/K5
Surabaya, Indo. 80/D5
Surada, India 82/D4
Surahammar, Swe. 38/G2
Süräjgarh, India 86/C5
Surak-san (peak), SKor. 73/G6
Surakarta, Indo. 80/D5
Surallah, Phil. 81/F2
Suran (riv.), Fr. 56/B5
Şuranı, Slvk. 48/D1
Surat, India 89/K4
Surat, Austl. 114/C4
Surat Thani, Thai. 78/B4
Suratgarh, India 86/B5
Surçin, Serb. 48/E3
Surdulica, Serb. 47/H1
Sûre (riv.), Lux. 40/C4
Surf City, NJ, US 138/D3
Surgères, Fr. 42/C3
Surgut, Rus. 64/H3
Süri, India 85/F2
Súria, Sp. 45/F2
Surigao, Phil. 79/E6
Surin, Thai. 78/C3
Suriname (ctry.) 153/G3
Surnadal, Nor. 37/D3
Surprise, Az, US 137/R18
Surrey, BC, Can. 126/D3
Surrey (co.), Eng, UK 33/F4
Surrey, Swe. 36/E3
Surt, Libya 96/J1
Surt (reefs), Ice. 37/N7
Surtsey (isl.), Ice. 37/N7
Suruçu (riv.), Braz. 155/D1
Surumu (riv.), Braz. 150/F3
Surveyor General's Corner, Guy. 153/F3
Survilliers, Fr. 30/K4
Surwakwima (falls), Guy. 153/F3
Surwold, Ger. 51/F2
Süsah, Tun. 46/B5
Süsah (gov.), Tun. 46/B5
Susaki, Japan 74/C4
Susanville, Ca, US 126/C5
Susegana, It. 59/F1
Suşehri, Turk. 90/D1
Susuki, China 73/B4
Sušice, Czh. 55/G4
Susono, Japan 75/F3
Susquehanna (riv.), Md,Pa, US 130/D3
Susquehanna NWR, Md, US 138/B5

Sussex, NB, Can. 131/H2
Sussex, De, US 138/C6
Sussex (co.), NJ, US 138/D1
Sussex, NJ, US 138/D1
Sussex Inlet, Austl. 115/D2
Sussex, Vale of (valley), Eng, UK 33/F4
Sustenhorn (peak), Swi. 57/E4
Sustenpass (pass), Swi. 57/E4
Susteren, Neth. 53/E1
Susuman, Rus. 65/Q3
Susurluk, Turk. 90/B2
Susuz, Turk. 90/B2
Sutherland, SAfr. 106/C4
Sutherland Springs, Tx, US 137/U21
Sutherlin, Or, US 126/C5
Sutjeska NP, Bosn. 47/F1
Sutlej (riv.), India 70/C5
Sutter (co.), Ca, US 135/L9
Sutton, Ak, US 134/J3
Sutton (bor.), Eng, UK 30/C2
Sutton Coldfield, Eng, UK 35/G5
Sutton in Ashfield, Eng, UK 35/G5
Suttsu, Japan 76/B2
Suur (str.), Est. 39/K2
Suurbraak, SAfr. 106/C4
Suwałki, Pol. 41/M2
Suwannee (riv.), Fl, US 140/E1
Suwanose (isl.), Japan 75/K6
Suwarrow (isl.), Cooks. 117/J6
Suwaylih, Jor. 91/D3
Suwŏn, SKor. 73/G7
Suyo, Peru 156/B2
Suze (riv.), Swi. 56/D3
Suzhou, China 72/D4
Suzhou, China 72/L8
Suzi (riv.), China 73/C2
Suzu, Japan 75/E2
Suzu-misaki (cape), Japan 77/K6
Suzuka, Japan 77/L6
Suzuka (riv.), Japan 77/L6
Suzuka (range), Japan 77/K6
Suzzara, It. 58/D2
Svalbard (isls.), Nor. 160/E
Svaneke, Den. 38/F4
Svängsta, Swe. 38/F3
Svanstein, Swe. 60/D2
Svappavaara (riv.), Czh. 55/F2
Svealand (reg.), Swe. 37/E4
Svedala, Swe. 38/E4
Sveio, Nor. 38/D2
Svelvik, Nor. 38/D2
Svendborg, Den. 38/D4
Svendsen (pen.), Nun., Can. 123/S7
Svenljunga, Swe. 38/E3
Svenstrup, Den. 38/C3
Sverdlovskaya Oblast, Rus. 64/G4
Sverdrup (chan.), Nun., Can. 123/S7
Sverdrup (isls.), Nun., Can. 123/S7
Svetlogorsk, Bela. 62/D1
Svetlograd, Rus. 63/G3
Svetlyy, Rus. 63/G3
Svetozarevo, Serb. 48/E4
Svíahnúkar (peak), Ice. 37/F7
Svilajnac, Serb. 48/E3
Svilengrad, Bul. 47/K2
Svishtov, Bul. 49/G4
Svitavy, Czh. 41/J4
Svobodnyy, Rus. 71/N1
Svoge, Bul. 47/H1
Svyatoy Nos (cape), Rus. 65/G2
Swabi, Pak. 86/B2
Swadlincote, Eng, UK 33/E1
Swain (reefs), Austl. 109/E3
Swains (isl.), ASam. 117/H6
Swakopmund, Namb. 105/B5
Swale, The (riv.), Eng, UK 35/G3
Swalmen, Neth. 50/D6
Swan (riv.), Austl. 109/B4
Swan, Mb,Sk, Can. 127/H3
Swan (isls.), Hon. 140/E4
Swan Hill, Austl. 113/H5
Swan Hills, Ab, Can. 126/E2
Swan Reach, Austl. 113/H5
Swan River, Mb, Can. 127/H3
Swanscombe, Eng, UK 30/E2
Swansea, Austl. 115/D4

Swansea (bay), Eng, UK 32/C3
Swansea, Wal, UK 32/C3
Swansea (co.), Wal, UK 32/B3
Swansea, Vale of (valley), Eng, UK 33/F4
Swansea, Il, US 137/H8
Swarthmore, Pa, US 138/C4
Swartswood (lake), NJ, US 138/D1
Swarzędz, Pol. 41/J2
Swarzenbach an der Sächsischen Saale, Ger. 55/E2
Swarzrand (mts.), Namb. 106/B2
Swät (riv.), Pak. 86/B2
Swatragh, NI, UK 34/B2
Swayambhunath, Nepal 85/E2
Swaziland (ctry.) 107/E3
Swedesboro, NJ, US 138/C4
Sweden (ctry.) 37/E3
Sweet Home, Or, US 126/C4
Sweetwater (riv.), Wy, US 126/F5
Sweetwater, Tx, US 129/G4
Sweetwater (res.), Ca, US 136/D5
Swellendam, SAfr. 106/C4
Świdnica, Pol. 41/J3
Świdnik, Pol. 41/M3
Świdwin, Pol. 38/F5
Świebodzice, Pol. 41/J3
Świebodzin, Pol. 41/H2
Świecie, Pol. 41/K2
Świętokrzyskie (prov.), Pol. 41/L3
Świętokrzyski NP, Pol. 41/L3
Swift Current, Sk, Can. 126/G3
Swifts Creek, Austl. 115/C3
Swilly, Lough (inlet), Ire. 31/Q9
Swimming River (res.), NJ, US 138/D3
Swindon, Eng, UK 33/F3
Swindon (co.), Eng, UK 33/E3
Świnoujście, Pol. 38/F5
Swinton, Eng, UK 35/G5
Swist Bach (riv.), Ger. 53/F2
Switzerland (ctry.) 56/D4
Swords, Ire. 34/B5
Swoyersville, Pa, US 138/C1
Syamozero (lake), Rus. 60/G3
Sych, Moel (peak), Wal, UK 35/E6
Syców, Pol. 41/J3
Sydney, NS, Can. 131/J2
Sydney, Austl. 114/H8
Sydney-Kingsford Smith (int'l arpt.), Austl. 114/H8
Syeverodonets'k, Ukr. 62/F2
Syke, Ger. 51/F3
Sykesville, Md, US 138/B5
Sykkylven, Nor. 37/C3
Syktyvkar, Rus. 61/L3
Sylacauga, Al, US 133/G3
Sylarna (peak), Swe. 37/E3
Sylhet (pol. reg.), Bang. 85/H3
Sylva (riv.), Rus. 61/N4
Sylvan Lake, Mi, US 135/F6
Sylvania, Oh, US 130/D3
Sylvenstein-Stausee (lake), Ger. 57/H2
Symi, Gre. 90/A2
Syntagma, Gre. 47/N8
Syosset, NY, US 139/L8
Syowa, Japan, Ant. 160/C
Syracuse, NY, US 130/E3
Syracuse, Ut, US 137/J11
Syracuse Hancock (int'l arpt.), NY, US 130/E3
Syrdarya (riv.), Kaz. 67/G5
Syria (ctry.) 90/D3
Syriam, Myan. 83/G4
Syrian (des.), Jor. 88/C2
Sysmä, Fin. 39/L1
Sysola (riv.), Rus. 61/L3
Syzran', Rus. 63/J1
Szabolcs-Szatmár-Bereg (co.), Hun. 41/L4
Szamotuły, Pol. 41/J2
Szarvas, Hun. 48/E2
Százhalombatta, Hun. 49/Q8
Szczebrzeszyn, Pol. 41/M3
Szczecin, Pol. 38/F5
Szczecinek, Pol. 38/G5
Szczytno, Pol. 41/L2
Szeged, Hun. 48/E2
Szeghalom, Hun. 48/E2
Székesfehérvár, Hun. 48/D2
Szendrő, Hun. 48/E1
Szent László-Vize (riv.), Hun. 49/Q10
Szentendre, Hun. 49/R9
Szentes, Hun. 48/E2
Szentlőrinc, Hun. 48/D2
Szerencs, Hun. 41/L4

Szeskie (peak), Pol.   39/K4
Sziget-Szentmiklós,
Hun.   49/R10
Szigetvár, Hun.   48/C2
Szirák, Hun.   41/K5
Szolnok, Hun.   48/E2
Szombathely, Hun.   43/M3
Szprotawa, Pol.   41/H3
Sztum, Pol.   39/H5
Szubin, Pol.   41/J2
Szydłowiec, Pol.   41/L3

T

Ta Khmau, Camb.   78/D4
Taabo, Barrage de
(dam), C.d'Iv.   102/D5
Tabaco, Phil.   79/D5
Tabaquite, Trin.   153/F2
Tabarqah, Tun.   100/L6
Tabas, Iran   89/G2
Tabasará (mts.), Pan.   145/F4
Tabasco (state), Mex.   140/C4
Tabatinga, Serra da
(mts.), Braz.   151/K6
Tabayama, Japan   77/E2
Tabelbala, Alg.   98/D3
Tabelbalet (well), Alg.   99/G4
Ta'benghisa, Ponta (pt.),
Malta   46/L7
Taber, Ab, Can.   126/E3
Tabernes de Valldigna,
Sp.   45/E3
Tabiang, Kiri.   116/F5
Tabira, Braz.   154/C2
Tabiteuea (isl.), Kiri.   116/F5
Tablas (isl.), Phil.   81/F1
Tablas de Daimiel NP,
Sp.   44/D3
Table (bay), SAfr.   106/B4
Table (mtn.), SAfr.   106/L10
Table Rock (lake),
Mo, US   129/K3
Tabligbo, Togo   103/F5
Tábor, Czh.   55/H4
Tabora (pol. reg.),
Tanz.   104/B4
Tabora, Tanz.   104/B4
Tabou, C.d'Iv.   102/D5
Tabuk, Phil.   79/D4
Tabūk, SAr.   88/C3
Tabuleiro do Norte,
Braz.   154/C2
Taburbah, Tun.   46/A4
Tabwemasana (peak),
Van.   116/F6
Tacabamba, Peru   156/B2
Tacámbaro de Codallos,
Mex.   143/E5
Tacaná (vol.), Mex.   144/C3
Tacarcuna (mtn.),
Pan.   152/B2
Tacheng, China   70/D2
Tachibana (bay),
Japan   74/A4
Tachikawa, Japan   75/F3
Tachinger (lake),
Ger.   55/F7
Tachira (state), Ven.   145/H5
Tachov, Czh.   55/F3
Tacloban, Phil.   79/D4
Tacna, Peru   156/D5
Tacna (dept.), Peru   156/D5
Tacoma, Wa, US   126/C4
Tacora (vol.), Chile   156/D5
Tacotalpa, Mex.   144/C2
Tacuarembó, Uru.   157/E3
Tacuarembó (dept.),
Uru.   159/G2
Tacutu (riv.), Braz.   153/F4
Tadaoka, Japan   77/H7
Ta'Delimara (pt.),
Malta   46/M7
Tademaït, Plateau du
(plat.), Alg.   96/F2
Tādepallegūdem,
India   82/D4
Tadley, Eng, UK   33/E4
Tadmur, Syria   90/D3
Tadó, Col.   152/B3
Tado, Japan   77/L5
Tadohae Hasang NP,
SKor.   73/C5
Tadotsu, Japan   74/C4
Tādpatri, India   82/C5
Tadrart (mts.),
Alg.,Libya   96/H2
Tadworth, Eng, UK   30/C3
T'aean, SKor.   73/C4
T'aebaek, SKor.   73/E4
Taebudo (isl.), SKor.   73/F7
Taech'ŏn, SKor.   73/C4
Taech'ŏng (isl.),
SKor.   73/C3
Taedŏk, SKor.   73/C5
Taedong, Inv, NKor.   73/C3
Taegang-got (pt.),
NKor.   73/B3
Taegu, SKor.   73/E5
Taegu Gwangyŏksi
(prov.), SKor.   74/A3
Taehŭksan (isl.),
SKor.   73/C5
Taehwa, SKor.   73/C3
T'aein, SKor.   73/C4
Taejŏn, SKor.   73/C4
Taejŏn Gwangyŏksi
(prov.), SKor.   73/C4
Taeryŏng (riv.), NKor.   73/C3
Tafalla, Sp.   44/E1
Tafassasset, Oued (riv.),
Alg.   99/H4

Taff (riv.), Wal, UK   32/C3
Tafí Viejo, Arg.   157/C2
Tafraout, Mor.   98/C2
Taft, La, US   137/P17
Taft, Iran   88/F2
Taftān (mtn.), Iran   89/H3
Taga, Japan   77/K5
Taganrog, Rus.   62/F3
Tagant (pol. reg.),
Trkm.   63/L5
Tagarav (peak),
Trkm.   63/L5
Tagawa, Japan   74/B4
Taggia, It.   58/A5
Taghit, Alg.   99/E3
Tagish, Yk, Can.   134/M3
Tagliamento (riv.), It.   43/K3
Taglio di Po, It.   59/F3
Tagolo (pt.), Phil.   81/F2
Tago, China   71/M1
Tagowa, Japan   77/K5
Tagum, Phil.   79/E6
Tagun (riv.), Rus.   61/P4
Tagus Rio Tejo (lake),
Port.   45/P10
Tagus (Tajo) (riv.), Sp.   44/C3
Tahan (peak), Malay.   81/F4
Tahanea (isl.), FrPol.   117/L6
Taharoz'ka Zatoka
(gulf), Rus.,Ukr.   62/F3
Tahara, Japan   77/M6
Tahat, Oued et (riv.),
Alg.   100/F5
Tahe, China   71/M1
Tahilt, Mong.   70/G2
Tahir (pass), Turk.   90/E2
Tahiti (isl.), FrPol.   117/L6
Tahkuna (pt.), Est.   39/K4
Tahlequah, Ok, US   129/J4
Tahmoor, Austl.   115/D2
Tahneta (pass),
Ak, US   134/J3
Tahoe (lake),
Ca,Nv, US   122/D5
Tahoka, Tx, US   129/G4
Tahoua (dept.),
Niger   103/G3
Tahoua, Niger   103/G3
Tahsis, BC, Can.   126/B3
Tahuamanu (riv.),
Peru   156/D3
Tahuamanú, Peru   156/D3
Tahuata (isl.), FrPol.   117/L6
Tahulandang (isl.),
Indo.   81/G3
Tahuya, Wa, US   135/A3
Tai Long Wan (bay),
China   71/V10
Tai Mo Shan (peak),
China   71/U10
Taï, PN de, C.d'Iv.   96/D6
Tai Po, China   71/U10
Tai Xian, China   72/E4
Tai'an, China   72/D3
Taiaret (well), Mor.   98/B3
Taibus, China   71/J3
Taicang, China   72/E4
T'aichung, Tai.   79/D3
Taiei, Japan   77/H7
Taieri (riv.), NZ   117/S12
Taigu, China   72/C2
Taihang (mts.), China   72/C3
Taihe, China   79/B2
Taihe, China   72/C4
Taikang, China   72/C4
Taiki, Japan   76/C2
Tailem Bend, Austl.   113/H5
Tailéng, Japan   77/L6
Taldyqorghan (obl.),
Kaz.   87/G3
Taldyqorghan, Kaz.   87/G3
Talence, Fr.   42/C4
T'ainan, Tai.   79/D3
Tainaron (cape), Gre.   47/H4
Taingainony, Madg.   107/H8
Taino, It.   58/B1
Taioběiras, Braz.   154/B4
T'aipei (cap.), Tai.   79/D2
Taiping, Malay.   80/B3
Taiping, China   79/C1
Taisha, Japan   74/C3
Taishan, China   79/B3
Taishi, Japan   77/H6
Taishun, China   79/C2
Taiskirchen im Innkreis,
Aus.   55/G6
Taissy, Fr.   53/D5
Taitao (pen.), Chile   147/B7
Taiti (peak), Kenya   104/B2
T'aitung, Tai.   79/D3
Taiwan (ctry.)   79/D3
Taiwan (str.)
China,Tai   79/C3
Taixing, China   72/E4
Taiyetos (mts.), Gre.   47/H4
Taiyuan, China   72/C2
Taizhou, China   79/D1
Taizi (riv.), China   72/F2
Ta'izz, Yem.   88/D6
Tāj Mahal, India   84/B2
Tajikistan (ctry.)   87/C2
Tajima, Japan   77/M5
Tajiri, Japan   77/H7
Tājpur, India   84/B1
Tajrīsh, Iran   88/G2
Tajumulco (vol.),
Guat.   144/D3
Tajuña (riv.), Sp.   44/D2
Tak, Thai.   78/B2
Takahagi, Japan   75/D4

Takahama, Japan   77/J5
Takahama, Japan   77/L6
Takahashi (riv.),
Japan   74/C3
Takahata, Japan   75/G1
Takaishi, Japan   77/H6
Takamatsu, Japan   74/D3
Takami-yama (peak),
Japan   77/K7
Takanabe, Japan   74/B4
Takane, Japan   77/A2
Takanosu, Japan   76/B3
Takanosu-yama (peak),
Japan   77/C2
Takaoka, Japan   77/S10
Takapuna, NZ   117/S10
Takarazuka, Japan   77/H6
Takaroa (isl.),
FrPol.   117/L6
Takasaki, Japan   75/F2
Takashima, Japan   77/K5
Takatomi, Japan   77/L5
Takatori, Japan   77/J7
Takatsuki, Japan   77/K5
Takatsuki, Japan   77/J6
Takayama, Japan   75/E2
Takefu, Japan   74/E3
Takehara, Japan   74/C3
Takeo, Japan   77/A2
Taketa, Japan   74/B4
Taketoyo, Japan   77/L6
Takhatgarh, India   82/B2
Takhatpur, India   84/C4
Takht-e Jamshid (ruin),
Iran   88/F3
Takht-i-Bhāi, Pak.   86/A2
Taki, Japan   77/L7
Takijuq (lake),
Nun., Can.   122/E2
Takikawa, Japan   76/B2
Takino, Japan   77/H6
Takla (lake), BC, Can.   126/B2
Takla Makan (des.),
China   67/K4
Tako, Japan   77/E2
Takoradi, Gha.   103/E5
Takouch (cape), Alg.   100/K6
Taksony, Hun.   49/R10
Tala, Mex.   142/E4
Talā, Egypt   49/C5
Tala, Uru.   159/L11
Talagang, Pak.   86/B3
Talagante, Chile   158/N8
Talaimannar, SrL.   89/K4
Talak (phys. reg.),
Niger   96/G4
Talamanca (mts.), CR   145/F4
Talamba, Pak.   86/B4
Talamona, It.   57/F5
Talang (peak), Indo.   80/B4
Talanga, Hon.   144/E3
Talange, Fr.   53/F5
Talant, Fr.   56/A3
Talara, Peru   156/A2
Talas, Turk.   90/C2
Talas, Kyr.   87/F4
Talas (riv.), Kaz.   87/F4
Talaud (isl.), Phil.   81/G3
Talavera de la Reina,
Sp.   44/C3
Talawakele, SrL.   82/D6
Talayuela, Sp.   44/C3
Talbingo, Austl.   115/D2
Talbot (mt.), Austl.   112/E3
Talbot (co.),
Md, US   138/B6
Talca, Chile   158/C2
Talcahuano, Chile   158/B3
Tālcher, India   82/E3
Taldyqorghan (obl.),
Kaz.   87/G3
Taldyqorghan, Kaz.   87/G3
Talence, Fr.   42/C4
Talent (riv.), Swi.   56/C4
Talfer (Talvera)
(riv.), It.   57/H4
Talgar, Kaz.   87/G4
Taliabu (isl.), Indo.   81/F4
Taliouine, Mor.   98/D3
Talkeetna, Ak, US   134/H3
Talkhā, Egypt   91/B4
Tall 'Afar, Iraq   90/E2
Tall al Muqayyar (ruin),
Iraq   88/E2
Tall 'Āsūr (peak), Isr.   91/G8
Tall Kayf, Iraq   90/E2
Talladega, Al, US   133/G3
Tallahassee (cap.),
Fl, US   133/G4
Tallahatchie (riv.),
Ms, US   129/K4
Tallangatta, Austl.   115/C3
Tallanstown, Ire.   34/B4
Tallering (peak),
Austl.   112/B4
Talleyville, De, US   138/C4
Tallinn (cap.), Est.   39/L2
Tallman Mountain State
Park, NY, US   139/K7
Talloires, Fr.   56/B5
Tallow, Ire.   31/Q10
Tallulah, La, US   129/K4
Tallulah (falls),
Ga, US   133/H3
Talmassons, It.   59/G1
Talo (peak), Eth.   97/N5
Taloda, India   89/K4
Tāloqān, Afg.   89/J1
Talpa de Allende,
Mex.   142/D4

Talsperre Pöhl (res.),
Ger.   55/F1
Taltal, Chile   157/B2
Taltson (riv.),
NW, Can.   122/E2
Talumphuk (pt.), Thai.   78/C4
Talvera (Talfer) (riv.), It. 57/H4
Talwāra, India   86/C4
Tam Ky, Viet.   78/E3
Tama, Japan   77/C2
Tama (riv.), Japan   77/D2
Tamagawa, Japan   77/A2
Tamaho, Japan   77/B2
Tamaki, Japan   77/L7
Tamalameque, Col.   152/D2
Tamale, Gha.   103/E4
Tamamura, Japan   77/C1
Taman, Indo.   80/D5
Taman-Rasset, Oued (riv.),
Alg.   99/F5
Tamaná (peak), Col.   152/B3
Tamana (isl.), Kiri.   116/G5
Tamandare, Mor.   98/C3
Tamanghasset (prov.),
Alg.   103/F1
Tamanghasset, Oued (riv.),
Alg.   99/F5
Tamanrasset, Alg.   99/G5
Tamanrasset (prov.),
Alg.   99/F4
Tamaqua, Pa, US   138/C2
Tamar (riv.),
Eng, UK   32/B5
Tamar (isl.), Japan   75/H8
Tamari, Japan   77/E1
Tamarindo NWR, CR   144/E4
Tamarite de Litera, Sp.   45/F2
Tamaro (peak), Swi.   57/E5
Tamási, Hun.   48/D2
Tamatsukuri, Japan   77/E1
Tamaulipas (state),
Mex.   140/B3
Tamazula de Gordiano,
Mex.   142/E5
Tamazunchale, Mex.   144/B1
Tamba, Japan   77/H5
Tamba (uplands),
Japan   77/H5
Tambacounda (pol. reg.),
Sen.   102/B3
Tambacounda, Sen.   102/B3
Tambaoura, Falaise de
(cliff), Mali   102/C3
Tambelan (isls.), Indo.   80/C3
Tambellup, Austl.   112/C5
Tamboli, Braz.   154/B2
Tamboritha (mt.),
Austl.   115/C3
Tambov, Rus.   63/G1
Tambovskaya Oblast,
Rus.   63/G1
Tambre (riv.), Sp.   44/A1
Tambu (uplands),
Japan   77/L4
Tambo, Peru   156/C4
Tambo (peak), Swi.   57/F5
Tambo, Austl.   114/B4
Tambo Colorado (ruin),
Peru   156/C4
Tambo de Mora, Peru   156/B4
Tambo Grande, Peru   156/A2
Tambobamba, Peru   156/C4
Tambohorano,
Madg.   107/G7
Tambopata (riv.),
Peru   156/D4
Tambora, Indo.   81/E5
Tamboril, Braz.   154/B2
Tamborine (mt.),
Austl.   115/C3
Tambov, Rus.   63/G1
Tambovskaya Oblast,
Rus.   63/G1
Tambre (riv.), Sp.   44/A1
Tame, Col.   152/D3
Tame (riv.), Eng, UK   33/E1
Támega (riv.), Port.   44/B2
Tamentit, Alg.   99/E4
Tameside (co.), Eng, UK   35/F5
Tamgak (peak),
Niger   103/H2
Tamgue (mass.), Gui.   102/B3
Tamiahua, Mex.   144/C1
Tamiahua (lag.),
Mex.   144/B1
Tamil Nādu (state),
India   82/C5
Taminango, Col.   152/B4
Tāmiyah, Egypt   91/B5
Tamlūk, India   85/F4
Tammany (mt.),
NJ, US   138/C2
Tammela, Fin.   39/K1
Tammūn, WBnk.   91/D3
Tampa, Fl, US   133/H5
Tampa (int'l arpt.),
Fl, US   133/H5
Tampere, Fin.   39/K1
Tampere-Pirkkala
(int'l arpt.), Fin.   39/K1
Tampico, Mex.   144/B1
Tampoc (riv.), FrG.   153/H4
Tampon Ambohitra
(peak), Madg.   107/J6
Tampulonanjing (peak),
Indo.   80/A3
Tamra, Isr.   91/G6
Tamsagbulag (mts.),
Mong.   71/J2
Tamshiyacu, Peru   156/C2
Tamuín (riv.), Mex.   144/B1
Tamuin, Mex.   144/B1
Tamur (riv.), Nepal   85/F2
Tamworth, Austl.   115/D1
Tamworth, Eng, UK   33/E1
Tamyang, SKor.   73/D5
Taolañaro, Madg.   107/H9
Taormina, It.   46/D4
Taōru, India   86/D5
Taos, NM, US   127/G3
Tan-Tan, Mor.   98/C3
Tana (riv.), Kenya   93/G5
Tana (riv.), Nor.   90/F3
Tana River Primate
Nat'l Rsv., Kenya   104/D3
Tanabe, Japan   74/D4

Tanabe, Japan   77/J6
Tanabi, Braz.   155/B2
Tanacross, Ak, US   134/K3
Tap Mun Chau (isl.),
China   71/V10
Taro (riv.), It.   43/J4
Tarō, Japan   76/B4
Tārom, Iran   89/G3
Tapa, Est.   39/L2
Tapachula, Mex.   144/C3
Tapajós (riv.), Braz.   147/D3
Tapah, Malay.   80/B3
Tapanahoni (riv.), Sur.   151/G3
Tapanui, NZ   117/S11
Tapani Nat'l Wild. Ref.,
CR   145/F4
Tapajós (riv.), Braz.   147/D3
Tapauá (riv.), Braz.   150/E5
Tapauá, Braz.   150/F5
Tapaz, Phil.   79/D5
Tapejara, Braz.   155/A4
Tapes, Braz.   155/B4
Tanaro (riv.), It.   43/J4
Tapia de Casariego,
Sp.   44/B1
Tapiche (riv.), Peru   156/C3
Tapilula, Mex.   144/C2
Tapis (peak), Malay.   80/B3
Tapo, Peru   156/B3
Tanda (lake), Mali   140/A4
Tanda (prov.), Burk.   102/D3
Tandā, India   84/D2
Tapolca, Hun.   48/C2
Tāndārei, Rom.   49/H3
Tandil, Arg.   158/F3
Tāndliānwāla, Pak.   86/B4
Tando Ādam, Pak.   89/J3
Tando Allāhyār, Pak.   89/J3
Tappa, Peru   156/B2
Tando Muhammad Khān,
Pak.   89/J3
Tappi-zaki (pt.), Japan   76/B3
Tandou (lake),
Austl.   109/C4
Tandragee, NI, UK   34/B3
Taneichi, Japan   76/D3
Tanezrouft (des.), Alg.   98/D2
Tanezrouft-n-Ahenet
(des), Alg.   99/F5
Tang (riv.), China   72/C4
Tanga (pol. reg.),
Tanz.   104/C4
Taquara, Braz.   155/B4
Taquari, Braz.   151/G7
Taquari (riv.), Braz.   155/B2
Taquaritinga, Braz.   155/B2
Taquarituba, Braz.   155/B2
Taquil, Ecu.   156/B1
Taquiri (riv.), Kyr.   87/F4
Tara, Rus.   87/F1
Tara (riv.), Serb.   49/D4
Tara, Austl.   114/C4
Tara (riv.), Austl.   114/C4
Taraba (state), Nga.   103/H5
Taraba (riv.), Nga.   103/H5
Tang (uplands),
Japan   77/H5
Tangail, Bang.   85/G3
Tangail (pol. reg.),
Bang.   85/G3
Tanganyika (lake),
D.R. Congo   93/F5
Tangará da Serra,
Braz.   150/G6
Tangent (pt.),
Ak, US   134/G1
Tanger, Mor.   100/A2
Tanger (prov.), Mor.   100/A2
Tangerhütte, Ger.   40/F2
Tangermünde, Ger.   40/F2
Tanggula (mts.),
China   70/E5
Tanghe, China   72/C4
Tangi, Pak.   86/A2
Tangipahoa (riv.),
La, US   137/P16
Tangipahoa (parish),
La, US   137/P16
Tangjin, SKor.   73/C4
Tanglewilde-Thompson
Place, Wa, US   135/B3
Tangshan, China   72/J7
Tangub, Phil.   79/D6
Tangyin, China   71/N2
Tangyuan, China   71/N2
Tanhaçu, Braz.   154/B4
Tanigumi, Japan   77/L4
Tanimbar (isl.), Indo.   67/N10
Taninges, Fr.   56/C5
Tanintharyi (state),
Myan.   83/G5
Tanjay, Phil.   79/D6
Tanjungbalai, Indo.   80/A3
Tanjungkarang-Telukbetung,
Indo.   80/C5
Tanjungpandan,
Indo.   80/C4
Tanjungpinang, Indo.   80/B3
Tanjungpura, Indo.   80/A3
Tänk, Pak.   86/A3
Tankwa Karoo NP,
SAfr.   106/B4
Tann, Ger.   55/F6
Tannersville,
Pa, US   138/C1
Tannu-Ola (mts.), Rus.   70/F1
Tano (riv.), Gha.   96/E6
Tānout, Niger   103/H3
Tanquián de Escobedo,
Mex.   144/B1
Tansen, Nepal   84/D2
Tanṭā, Egypt   91/B4
Tantabin, Aus.   57/G3
Tantoyuca, Mex.   144/B1
Tanunda, Austl.   115/A2
Tanuma, Japan   77/D1
Tanya Lake (basin),
Ca, US   130/D4
Tanzania (ctry.)   104/B4
Tanzawa-yama (peak),
Japan   77/C3
Taolañaro, Madg.   107/H9
Taormina, It.   46/D4

T'aoyüan, Tai.   79/D2
Taoyuan, China   83/K2
Tanabe, Japan   77/J6
Tanabi, Braz.   155/B2
Tap Mun Chau (isl.),
China   71/V10
Tapa, Est.   39/L2
Tapachula, Mex.   144/C3
Taquara, Braz.   155/B4
Taroudannt, Mor.   98/C3
Taroom, Austl.   114/C4
Taronga (riv.), Sur.   151/G3
Tarpon Springs,
Fl, US   133/H4
Tarquinia, It.   46/B1
Tarrafal, CpV.   93/K10
Tarragona, Sp.   45/F2
Tàrrega, Sp.   45/F2
Tarrenz, Aus.   37/G1
Tarrytown, NY, US   139/K7
Tarsney Lakes,
Mi, US   137/E6
Tarsus, Turk.   91/D1
Tartagal, Arg.   157/D1
Tartaro (riv.), It.   59/E2
Tartu, Est.   42/C5
Tartūs (prov.), Syria   91/C1
Tartūs, Syria   91/D2
Tarui, Japan   77/L5
Tarumizu, Japan   74/B5
Tarutao NP, Thai.   78/B5
Tarutino, Ukr.   49/J2
Tarvagatay (mts.),
Mong.   70/G2
Tarvin, Eng, UK   35/F5
Tāsch, Swi.   56/D5
Taşçı, Turk.   90/C2
Tasek (lake), Sc, UK   36/C4
Tashauz, Trkm.   87/C3
Tashkent (cap.), Uzb.   87/E4
Tashkent (int'l arpt.),
Uzb.   87/E4
Tasikmalaya, Indo.   80/C5
Tasman (sea),
Austl.,NZ   116/E8
Tasman (bay), NZ   109/H7
Tasman Head (cape),
Austl.   115/D2
Tasmania, Austl.   115/C3
Tasmania (state),
Libya   96/H1
Tasu, BC, Can.   134/M5
Tāzirbū (oasis), Libya   97/K2
Tata, Mor.   98/D3
Tata, Hun.   48/D2
Tatabánya, Hun.   48/D2
Tatakoto (isl.), FrPol.   117/L6
Tatamy, Pa, US   138/C2
Tatar (str.), Rus.   67/P5
Tatarsk, Rus.   67/G1
Tatarstan, Resp.,
Rus.   63/H1
Tatāwīn, Tun.   96/H1
Tatāwīn (gov.), Tun.   99/H2
Tate-yama (peak),
Japan   75/E2
Tatebayashi, Japan   77/D1
Tateshina, Japan   77/A1
Tateyama, Japan   75/F3
Tathra, Austl.   115/D3
Tatitlek, Ak, US   134/J3
Tatnam (cape),
Mb, Can.   122/G3
Tatranský NP, Slvk.   41/K4
Tatsuno, Japan   75/E3
Tatsuta, Japan   77/L5
Tatura, Austl.   115/C3
Tatvan, Turk.   90/E2
Tauá, Braz.   154/B2
Taubaté, Braz.   211/H8
Tauber (riv.), Ger.   40/E4
Tauberbischofsheim,
Ger.   54/C3
Tauca, Peru   156/B2
Taufers, Mor.   100/B2
Taufkirchen, Ger.   55/F6
Taufkirchen an der Pram,
Aus.   55/G6
Taufstein (peak), Ger.   54/C1
Taulihawa, Nepal   84/D2
Taung, SAfr.   106/D2
Taunggyi, Myan.   83/G3
Taungup, Pak.   86/A4
Taunsa, Pak.   86/A4
Taunton, Ma, US   139/G3
Taunton, Eng, UK   32/C4
Taunus (range), Ger.   54/B2
Taupo, NZ   117/T10
Taupo (lake), NZ   109/H6
Tauragé, Lith.   39/K4
Taurianova, It.   46/D4
Taurion (riv.), Fr.   42/D3
Tauro (riv.), Fr.   42/D3
Taurus (mts.), Turk.   90/C2
Tauste, Sp.   44/E2
Taute (riv.), Fr.   42/C2

Tauu (isls.), PNG   116/E5
Tavanbulag, Mong.   70/H2
Tavannes, Swi.   56/D3
Tavas, Turk.   90/B2
Taverne, It.   128/E3
Tavernelle, It.   59/E5
Tavernuzze, It.   59/E5
Tavas, Turk.   90/B2
Tavira, Port.   44/B4
Taviano, It.   47/F3
Tavda (riv.), Rus.   64/G4
Tavernerio, It.   58/C1
Taverny, Fr.   30/J4
Taviano, It.   47/F3
Tavira, Port.   44/B4
Tavistock, Eng, UK   32/B5
Tavoy (Dawei),
Myan.   78/B3
Tavşanlı, Turk.   90/B2
Taw (riv.), Eng, UK   32/C5
Tawau, Malay.   81/E3
Tawaramoto, Japan   77/J6
Tawas City, Mi, US   130/D2
Tawau, Malay.   81/E3
Tawe (riv.), Wal, UK   32/C3
Tawern, Ger.   53/F4
Tawi (riv.), India   86/C1
Tawi-Tawi (isl.), Phil.   79/C6
Tāwūq, Iraq   90/F3
Tawzar (gov.), Tun.   99/G2
Tawzar, Tun.   99/G2
Taxco, Mex.   143/K8
Taxila (ruin), Pak.   86/B3
Taxila, Pak.   86/B3
Taxkorgan Tajik Zizhixian,
China   89/L1
Tay (lake), Sc, UK   36/B3
Tay, Firth of (inlet),
Sc, UK   36/C4
Tay Ninh, Viet.   78/D4
Tayabamba, Peru   156/B3
Tayabas (bay), Phil.   79/C1
Taylor, Mi, US   135/F7
Taylorsville-Bennion,
Ut, US   137/K12
Taymyr (riv.), Rus.   64/K2
Taymyr (pen.), Rus.   65/L2
Taymyr (pen.), Rus.   67/H2
Taymyrskiy Aut. Okrug,
Rus.   67/H2
Tayoltita, Mex.   142/D3
Tayport, Sc, UK   36/D4
Tayshet, Rus.   65/K4
Taytay, Phil.   81/E1
Taz (riv.), Rus.   67/H3
Taza (prov.), Mor.   100/C2
Taza, Mor.   100/C2
Tazawako, Japan   76/B4
Tazekka (peak), Mor.   100/C2
Tazenakht, Mor.   98/D3
Tazewell, Tn, US   133/G3
Tazumal (ruin), ESal.   144/D3
Tazūcu, Turk.   91/D2
Tbilisi (cap.), Geo.   63/H4
T'boli, Phil.   79/D6
Tchamba, Togo   103/F4
Tchaourou, Ben.   103/F4
Tchetchikapika (riv.),
On, Can.   130/D2
Tchibanga, Gabon   96/H8
Tchollire, Camr.   103/H4
Tczew, Pol.   39/H4
Te Anau, NZ   117/R12
Te Araroa, NZ   117/T10
Te Aroha, NZ   117/T10
Te Awamutu, NZ   117/T10
Te Kao, NZ   117/S9
Te Kuiti, NZ   117/T10
Tea (riv.), It.   150/E4
Teapa, Mex.   142/D4
Teague, Tx, US   129/H5
Teaneck, NJ, US   139/J8
Teano, It.   46/D2
Teapa, Mex.   144/C2
Tearce, FYROM   48/E5
Tebak (peak), Indo.   80/B4
Tébessa (prov.), Alg.   100/L6
Tébessa (mts.), Alg.   100/L7
Tébessa, It.   100/L7
Tebesselamane (well),
Mali   103/F2
Tebicuary (riv.), Par.   157/E2
Tebingtinggi, Indo.   80/A3
Tebulos-mta (peak),
Rus.   63/H4
Tecalitlán, Mex.   142/D4
Tecamac, Mex.   143/R9
Tecamachalco,
Mex.   143/M8
Tecate, Mex.   144/C2
Tech (riv.), Fr.   42/E5
Tecirli, Turk.   91/E1
Tecka, Arg.   158/C4
Teckla, Arg.   158/C4
Tecklenberg, Ger.   51/E4
Tecoluta, Mex.   142/E5
Tecomán, Mex.   142/E5
Tecozautla, Mex.   143/K6
Tecpan de Galeana,
Mex.   142/E5
Tecuala, Mex.   142/D4
Tecuci, Rom.   49/H3
Tecumseh, Mi, US   130/D3
Tecumseh, Ne, US   129/H2
Tecumseh,
On, Can.   135/G7
Tedjert (well), Alg.   103/F2
Tedzhen (riv.), Trkm.   64/G6
Tees (riv.), Eng, UK   35/G3
Tees (bay), Eng, UK   35/G3
Teesside (int'l arpt.),
Eng, UK   35/G3

Tefé (riv.), Braz. 150/E4
Tefé, Braz. 150/F4
Teferič, Serb. 48/E4
Tega (lake), Japan 77/E2
Tegal, Indo. 80/C5
Tegel (int'l arpt.), Ger. 40/Q6
Tegelen, Neth. 50/D6
Tegeler (lake), Ger. 40/Q6
Tegheri (well), Libya 99/H4
Teghra, India 85/E3
Tegid, Llyn (lake), Wal, UK 34/E6
Teglio, It. 57/G5
Tégouma (riv.), Niger 103/H3
Tegsh, Mong. 70/G2
Tegucigalpa (cap.), Hon. 144/E3
Tehek (lake), Nun., Can. 122/G2
Tehrān (cap.), Iran 88/F1
Tehuacán, Mex. 143/M8
Tehuantepec (isth.), Mex. 143/G5
Tehuantepec (riv.), Mex. 144/C2
Tehuantepec (gulf), Mex. 144/C3
Teide, Pico de (peak), Canl.,Sp. 98/A3
Teifi (riv.), Wal, UK 32/B2
Teifiside (valley), Wal, UK 32/C2
Teiga (plat.), Sudan 97/L4
Teign (riv.), Eng, UK 32/C5
Teignmouth, Eng, UK 32/C5
Teisendorf, Ger. 55/F7
Teith (riv.), Sc, UK 36/B4
Tejen, Trkm. 89/H1
Tejn, Den. 38/F4
Tejupilco de Hidalgo, Mex. 143/E5
Tekamah, Ne, US 127/G5
Tekári, India 85/E3
Tekax de Álvaro Obregón, Mex. 144/D1
Teke, Turk. 49/J5
Tekeli, Kaz. 87/G4
Tekes (riv.), China 64/J5
Tekezē Wenz (riv.), Eth. 97/N5
Tekiliktag (peak), China 70/D4
Tekirdağ, Turk. 49/H5
Tekirdağ (prov.), Turk. 49/H5
Tekit, Mex. 144/D1
Tekkali, India 82/D4
Tekke, Turk. 90/D1
Tekkeköy, Turk. 90/D1
Tekman, Turk. 90/E2
Tel Aviv (dist.), Isr. 91/D3
Tel Aviv-Yafo, Isr. 91/F7
Tel Megiddo (ruin), Isr. 91/G6
Tela, Hon. 144/E3
Télagh, Alg. 100/D2
T'elavi, Geo. 63/H4
Telde, Canl.,Sp. 98/D3
Télé (lake), Mali 102/D2
Telêmaco Borba, Braz. 155/B3
Telemark (co.), Nor. 37/D4
Telen (riv.), Indo. 81/E3
Teleorman (prov.), Rom. 49/G4
Telertheba (peak), Alg. 99/G4
Teles Pires (riv.), Braz. 147/D3
Telford, Pa, US 138/C3
Telford Dawley, Eng, UK 32/D1
Telfs, Aus. 57/H3
Telgate, It. 58/C1
Telgte, Ger. 51/F5
Telica, Nic. 144/E3
Télig (well), Mali 102/E4
Télimélé, Gui. 102/B4
Telkwa, BC, Can. 126/B2
Tell City, In, US 130/C4
Teller, Ak, US 134/E2
Telli (riv.), Mrta. 102/D1
Tellicherry, India 82/C5
Tellin, Belg. 53/E3
Telluride, Co, US 128/F3
Telok Anson, Malay. 80/B3
Teloloapan, Mex. 143/F5
Telšiai, Lith. 39/K4
Teltow, Ger. 40/Q7
Teltow (riv.), Ger. 41/G2
Tema, Gha. 103/E5
Temagami (lake), On, Can. 130/D2
Temax, Mex. 144/D1
Tembilahan, Indo. 80/B4
Tembisa, SAfr. 106/E2
Temblador, Ven. 153/F2
Teme (riv.), Eng, UK 32/C2
Temecula, Ca, US 137/C3
Temelkovo, Bul. 47/H1
Temerin, Serb. 48/D3
Temerloh, Malay. 80/B3
Temirtaū, Kaz. 87/F2
Témiscamie (riv.), Qu, Can. 131/F1
Témiscaming, Qu, Can. 130/D2
Temoaya, Mex. 143/M7
Temoe (isl.), FrPol. 117/M7
Temora, Austl. 115/C2
Tempe, Az, US 137/S19

Tempio Pausania, It. 46/A2
Temple, Pa, US 138/C3
Temple City, Ca, US 136/F7
Temple of Lady Chua Xu, Viet. 78/D4
Templemore, Ire. 31/Q10
Templepatrick, NI, UK 34/B2
Templeuve, Fr. 52/C2
Templeville, Md, US 138/C5
Templin, Ger. 41/G2
Templiner (lake), Ger. 40/Q7
Tempoal de Sánchez, Mex. 144/B1
Temryuk, Rus. 62/F3
Temse, Belg. 53/D1
Temuco, Chile 158/B3
Temuka, NZ 117/S11
Ten Boer, Neth. 50/D2
Tena, Ecu. 152/B5
Tena Kourou (peak), Mali 96/D5
Tenabo, Mex. 144/D1
Tenafly, NJ, US 139/K8
Tenakee Springs, Ak, US 134/L4
Tenancingo, Mex. 143/K8
Tenango, Mex. 143/R10
Tenango de Arista, Mex. 143/Q10
Tenasserim (range), Myan. 78/B3
Tenasserim, Myan. 78/B3
Tenay, Fr. 56/B6
Tenby, Wal, UK 32/C5
Tende, Fr. 43/G4
Tende, Col de (pass), Fr. 58/A4
Tenderovsk (bay), Ukr. 49/K2
Tenderovsk Spit (spit), Ukr. 49/K2
Tendō, Japan 76/B4
Tendre (peak), Swi. 56/C4
Ténenkou, Mali 102/D3
Ténéré (des.), Niger 96/G4
Ténéré du Tafassasset (des.), Niger 96/G3
Tenerife, Col. 152/C2
Tenerife (isl.), Sp. 93/A2
Ténès, Alg. 100/F4
Tenes (riv.), Myan. 83/G3
Teng Xian, China 72/D4
Tenggarong, Indo. 81/E4
Tengger (des.), China 70/H4
Tengiz Köli (lake), Kaz. 64/G4
Tenguel, Ecu. 152/B5
Tenibres (peak), It. 43/G4
Teniente Enciso, PN, Par. 157/D1
Teningen, Ger. 56/D1
Tenja, Cro. 48/D3
Tenkodogo, Burk. 103/E4
Tenmile (riv.), Az, US 128/D4
Tennessee (state), US 133/G3
Tennessee (riv.), US 133/F3
Tenneville, Belg. 53/E3
Tennuaca (well), Mor. 98/B5
Tenojoki (riv.), Fin. 37/H1
Tenosique de Pino Suárez, Mex. 144/D2
Tenri, Japan 77/J6
Tenryū, Japan 75/E3
Tenryū (riv.), Japan 75/E3
Tensift (pol. reg.), Mor. 98/C3
Tensift, Oued (riv.), Mor. 98/C3
Tentena, It. 46/A3
Tenterfield, Austl. 115/E1
Tentolomatinan (peak), Indo. 81/F3
Tenus (peak), Kenya 104/C3
Teo, Sp. 44/A1
Teocaltiche, Mex. 140/A3
Teocelo, Mex. 143/N7
Teodelina, Arg. 158/E2
Teodoro Sampaio, Braz. 155/B2
Teófilo Otoni, Braz. 154/B5
Teopisca, Mex. 144/C2
Teotihuacán (ruin), Mex. 143/R9
Teotitlán del Camino, Mex. 143/R9
Tepache, Mex. 142/C2
Tepalcatepec, Mex. 142/E5
Tepalcingo, Mex. 143/L8
Tepatitlán de Morelos, Mex. 142/E4
Tepeapulco, Mex. 143/L7
Tepebaşı, Turk. 91/C1
Tepehuanes, Mex. 142/D3
Tepeji del Rio de Ocampo, Mex. 143/K7
Tepelenë, Alb. 47/G2
Tepelská Plošina (mts.), Czh. 55/H2
Tepetlaoxtoc, Mex. 143/R9
Tepexi, Mex. 143/M8
Tepexpan, Mex. 143/R9
Tepic, Mex. 142/D4
Teplá (riv.), Czh. 40/G3
Teplá Vltava (riv.), Czh. 55/G5
Teplice, Czh. 41/G3
Tepoca (cape), Mex. 142/B2

Tepoca, Cabo (cape), Mex. 142/B2
Tepoto (isl.), FrPol. 117/L6
Tepotzotlán, Mex. 143/Q9
Tepotzlán, Mex. 143/K8
Tequila, Mex. 142/E4
Tequisquiapan, Mex. 143/F4
Tequixquiac, Mex. 143/K7
Ter (riv.), Sp. 45/G1
Ter Aar, Neth. 50/B4
Téra, Niger 103/F3
Teramo, It. 46/C2
Terang, Austl. 115/B3
Tercan, Turk. 90/E2
Terceira (isl.), Azor., Port. 45/S12
Terek (riv.), Rus. 63/H4
Terepaima, PN, Ven. 152/D2
Teresina, Braz. 154/B2
Teresópolis, Braz. 211/L7
Terespol, Pol. 41/M2
Tergnier, Fr. 52/C4
Tergun Daba (mts.), China 70/F4
Terheijden, Neth. 50/B5
Teriberskiy (pt.), Rus. 60/G1
Terkaplesterpoelen (lake), Neth. 50/C2
Terlan (Terlano), It. 57/H4
Termas de Río Hondo, Arg. 157/D2
Términos (lag.), Mex. 144/D2
Termiz, Uzb. 89/J1
Termo, Ca, US 126/C5
Termoli, It. 46/D4
Termonfeckin, Ire. 34/B4
Termunten, Neth. 50/E2
Ternate, Indo. 81/G3
Ternberg, Aus. 55/H7
Terneuzen, Neth. 50/A6
Terni, It. 46/C1
Ternin (riv.), Fr. 42/F3
Ternoise (riv.), Fr. 52/B3
Ternopil', Ukr. 62/C2
Ternopil's'ka Oblasti, Ukr. 62/C2
Terpeniya (bay), Rus. 65/O5
Terpni, Gre. 47/H2
Terra Nova, Braz. 154/B4
Terra Nova, Braz. 154/C3
Terra Nova NP, Nf, Can. 131/L1
Terrace, BC, Can. 126/A2
Terrace Bay, On, Can. 127/M3
Terracina, It. 46/C2
Terralba, It. 46/A3
Terranuova Bracciolini, It. 59/E5
Terrasson-la-Villedieu, Fr. 42/D4
Terre Hill, Pa, US 138/B3
Terrebonne, Qu, Can. 131/N6
Terrell Hills, Tx, US 137/U21
Terri (peak), Swi. 57/F4
Terry, Mt, US 127/G4
Terry (lake), Co, US 137/D4
Terrytown, La, US 137/P17
Terschelling (isl.), Neth. 50/C2
Tertenia, It. 46/A3
Teruel, Sp. 45/F2
Terutao (isl.), Thai. 83/G6
Tervel, Bul. 49/H4
Terzo d'Aquileia, It. 59/G1
Tešanj, Bosn. 48/C3
Tescou (riv.), Fr. 42/D5
Teshekpuk (lake), Ak, US 134/G1
Teshikaga, Japan 76/D2
Teshio, Japan 76/C1
Teshio, Japan 76/B1
Teshio-dake (peak), Japan 76/C2
Teslić, Bosn. 48/C3
Teslin, Yk, Can. 122/C2
Teslin (lake), BC, Can. 122/C3
Tessaoua, Niger 103/G3
Tessenderlo, Belg. 53/E1
Tessenie (Teseney), Erit. 88/C5
Test (riv.), Eng, UK 33/E4
Testa del Gargano (pt.), It. 46/E2
Tét, Hun. 48/C2
Tête, Moz. 105/F4
Tête de l'Estrop (peak), Fr. 43/G4
Tetela, Mex. 143/M7
Teteringen, Ger. 50/B5
Teteven, Bul. 47/J1
Tetiaroa (isl.), FrPol. 117/L6
Tetlin, Ak, US 134/K3
Teton (riv.), Mt, US 126/F4
Tétouan, Mor. 100/B2
Tétouan (prov.), Mor. 100/B2
Tettnang, Ger. 57/F2
Tetulia (riv.), Bang. 86/F5
Teuco (riv.), Arg. 157/D1
Teufen, Swi. 57/F3

Teúl de González Ortega, Mex. 142/E4
Teulada (cape), It. 46/A3
Teulon, Mb, Can. 127/J3
Teupasenti, Hon. 144/E3
Teuri (isl.), Japan 76/B1
Teuschnitz, Ger. 55/E2
Teutoburger Wald (for.), Ger. 51/F4
Tevere (Tiber) (riv.), It. 51/F4
Teverya, Isr. 91/D3
Teviot (riv.), Sc, UK 36/D6
Teviotdale (valley), Sc, UK 36/D6
Tewantin-Noosa, Austl. 114/D4
Tewkesbury, Eng, UK 32/D3
Texarkana, Tx, US 133/E4
Texas, Austl. 115/D1
Texas (state), US 132/C4
Texas City, Tx, US 129/J5
Texcoco, Mex. 143/R9
Texel (isl.), Neth. 40/C2
Texhoma, Ok, US 132/C2
Texmelucan, Mex. 143/L7
Texoma (lake), US 125/D5
Teyateyaneng, Les. 106/D3
Teykovo, Rus. 60/G1
Tezio (peak), It. 43/K5
Teziutlán, Mex. 143/M7
Tezonapa, Mex. 143/N8
Tezontepec, Mex. 143/L7
Tezontepec de Aldama, Mex. 143/K6
Tezoyuca, Mex. 143/R9
Tezpur, India 70/F6
Tezu, India 83/G2
Tezze, It. 59/E1
Tha-Anne (riv.), Nun., Can. 122/G2
Tha Chin (riv.), Thai. 78/B3
Thabana-Ntlenyana (peak), Les. 106/E3
Thabankulu (peak), SAfr. 107/E2
Thaben (pt.), Thai. 78/B4
Thai, Gre. 47/J4
Thai Binh, Viet. 83/J3
Thai Nguyen, Viet. 83/J3
Thailand (gulf), Asia 78/C4
Thailand (ctry.) 78/C3
Thākurdwāra, India 84/B1
Thal, Pak. 86/A3
Thal (des.), Pak. 86/A4
Thaleban NP, Thai. 78/C5
Thaleischweiler-Fröschen, Ger. 53/G5
Thalerhof (int'l arpt.), Aus. 43/L3
Thalgau, Aus. 55/G7
Thalheim bei Wels, Aus. 55/H6
Thalmässing, Ger. 54/E4
Thalwil, Swi. 57/E3
Thamar, Jabal (peak), Yem. 88/E6
Thame (riv.), Eng, UK 33/F3
Thames (riv.), On, Can. 130/D3
Thames, NZ 117/T10
Thames (riv.), Eng, UK 33/G4
Thames Barrier, Eng, UK 30/D2
Thana, India 89/K5
Thana Bhawan, India 86/D5
Thanesar, India 86/D5
Thangool, Austl. 114/C4
Thanh Hoa, Viet. 83/J4
Thanjavur, India 82/C5
Thann, Fr. 56/D2
Thannhausen, Ger. 57/G1
Thaon-les-Vosges, Fr. 56/C1
Thar (des.), Pak. 86/A5
Tharād, India 89/K4
Thargomindah, Austl. 114/A5
Tharrawaddy, Myan. 83/G4
Thásos, Gre. 47/J2
Thásos (isl.), Gre. 62/C4
Thatcham, Eng, UK 33/E4
Thatcher, Az, US 128/E4
Thaton, Myan. 78/B2
Thaur, Aus. 57/H3
Thaya (riv.), Aus. 41/H4
Thayetmyo, Myan. 83/G4
Thayngen, Swi. 57/E2
Thazi, Myan. 83/G3
The Alamo, Tx, US 137/U21
The Dalles, Or, US 126/C4
The Hague ('s-Gravenhage) (cap.), Neth. 50/B4
The Oaks, Sc, UK 136/B1
The Pas, Mb, Can. 127/H2
The Rock, Austl. 126/D5
The Valley (cap.), Angu. 141/N8
The Village, Ok, US 137/M14
The Woodlands, Tx, US 129/J5
The Wrekin (co.), Eng, UK 35/F6
Thebes (ruin), Egypt 101/C3
Theil, Ger. 50/D3
Theilheim, Ger. 54/D3
Thelma, Tx, US 137/T21
Thelon (riv.), NW,Nun., Can. 122/H2
Thémericourt, Fr. 30/H4
Theo (mt.), Austl. 113/F2
Theodore, Sk, Can. 127/H3
Theodore, Austl. 114/C4
Theodore Roosevelt (lake), Az, US 128/E4

Theodore Roosevelt NP, ND, US 127/G4
Thérain (riv.), Fr. 42/D2
Thermaic (gulf), Gre. 62/B4
Thérmi, Gre. 47/H2
Thermopilai (Thermopylae) (pass), Gre. 47/H3
Thermopolis, Wy, US 126/F5
Thérouanne (riv.), Fr. 30/L4
Thesprotikón, Gre. 47/G3
Thessalon, On, Can. 130/D2
Thessaloníki, Gre. 47/H3
Thessaly (reg.), Gre. 47/H3
Thet (riv.), Eng, UK 33/G2
Thetford, Eng, UK 33/G2
Thetford Mines, Qu, Can. 131/G2
Theunissen, SAfr. 106/D3
Theux, Belg. 53/E2
Thève (riv.), Fr. 30/K4
Theydon Bois, Eng, UK 30/K5
Thiais, Fr. 30/K5
Thiamis (riv.), Gre. 47/G3
Thiant, Fr. 52/C3
Thiaucourt-Regniéville, Fr. 53/E6
Thief River Falls, Mn, US 127/J3
Thielle (riv.), Swi. 56/C4
Thielsen (mt.), Or, US 126/C5
Thiene, It. 59/E1
Thiérache (reg.), Fr. 52/C4
Thierhaupten, Ger. 54/D5
Thiers, Fr. 42/E4
Thiers-sur-Thève, Fr. 30/K4
Thierville-sur-Meuse, Fr. 53/E5
Thiès (pol. reg.), Sen. 102/A3
Thiès, Sen. 102/A3
Thika, Kenya 104/C3
Thingvellir NP, Ice. 37/N7
Thionville, Fr. 53/F5
Thíra, Gre. 47/J4
Thíra (isl.), Gre. 47/J4
Third Cataract (falls), Sudan 101/B5
Third Lake, Il, US 135/O15
Thirlmere (lake), Eng, UK 35/F3
Thirsty (mt.), Austl. 112/D5
Thirtymile (pt.), NY, US 131/V9
Thise, Fr. 56/C3
Thisted, Den. 38/C3
Thistilfjördhur (estu.), Ice. 37/P6
Thistle (isl.), Austl. 113/H5
Thistle (mtn.), Yk, Can. 134/L3
Thitu (isl.), Asia 79/B5
Thívai, Gre. 54/E4
Thiverval-Grignon, Fr. 30/H5
Thjósa (riv.), Ice. 37/N7
Thlewiaza (riv.), Nun., Can. 122/G2
Thoiry, Fr. 30/H5
Tholen, Neth. 50/B5
Tholen (isl.), Neth. 50/B5
Tholey, Ger. 53/G5
Thomaston, Ga, US 133/G3
Thomastown, Ire. 31/Q10
Thomasville, Al, US 133/G4
Thomasville, NC, US 133/H3
Thomasville, Pa, US 138/B4
Thompson, Mb, Can. 127/J2
Thompson (riv.), BC, Can. 126/C3
Thompson (lake), Austl. 112/K7
Thompson Falls, Mt, US 126/E4
Thomsen (riv.), NW, Can. 122/E1
Thomson, Ga, US 133/H3
Thomson (riv.), Austl. 109/D3
Thonburi, Myan. 78/B4
Thonnance-lès-Joinville, Fr. 56/B1
Thonon-les-Bains, Fr. 56/C5
Thoreau, NM, US 128/E4
Thorens-Glières, Fr. 56/C6
Thorø By, Den. 38/D4
Thorhild, Ab, Can. 126/E2
Thorlákshöfn, Ice. 37/N7
Thornaby-on-Tees, Eng, UK 35/G2
Thornbury, Eng, UK 32/D3
Thorndale, Pa, US 138/C4
Thorne, Eng, UK 35/H4
Thorne Bay, Ak, US 134/M4
Thornhill, Sc, UK 36/B4
Thornhill, Sc, UK 36/D5
Thornhurst, Pa, US 138/C3
Thornton, Ca, US 135/K11
Thornton, Co, US 135/M10
Thornton Cleveleys, Eng, UK 35/E4

Three Bridges, NJ, US 138/D2
Three Forks, Mt, US 126/F4
Three Guardsmen (mtn.), BC, Can. 134/L4
Three Hills, Ab, Can. 126/E3
Three Hummock (isl.), Austl. 115/C4
Three Kings (isls.), NZ 116/G8
Three Mile (isl.), Pa, US 138/B3
Three Pagodas (pass), Myan. 78/B3
Three Points (cape), On, Can. 130/D2
Three Rivers, Mi, US 130/C3
Three Rivers, Austl. 112/C3
Three Springs, Austl. 112/B4
Thriuvananthapuram, India 82/C6
Throssell (lake), Austl. 112/D4
Thrushel (riv.), Eng, UK 32/B5
Thu Dau Mot, Viet. 78/D4
Thuin, Belg. 53/D3
Thuir, Fr. 42/E5
Thulba (riv.), Ger. 54/C2
Thule Air Base, Den. 123/T7
Thun, Swi. 56/D4
Thunderbird (lake), Ok, US 137/N15
Thuner See (lake), Swi. 43/G3
Thüngersheim, Ger. 54/C3
Thur (riv.), Swi. 43/H3
Thurgau (canton), Swi. 57/E2
Thüringen (state), Ger. 43/J1
Thüringen, Aus. 57/F3
Thüringer Schiefergebirge (mts.), Ger. 54/E2
Thüringer Wald (for.), Ger. 43/J1
Thurles, Ire. 31/Q10
Thurn (riv.), Ger. 55/E2
Thurrock (co.), Eng, UK 33/G3
Thurso, Sc, UK 31/V14
Thurston (isl.), Ant. 160/T
Thurston (co.), Ak, US 134/G3
Thury-en-Valois, Fr. 30/M4
Thusis, Swi. 57/F4
Thyez, Fr. 56/C5
Thyolo, Malw. 105/G5
Ti-m-Merhsoï (riv.), Niger 103/G2
Ti-n-Jedane, Oued (riv.), Alg. 96/F4
Ti-n-Zaouâten, Alg. 96/F4
Ti-Tree Abor. Land, Austl. 113/G2
Tiahuanco (ruin), Bol. 156/D5
Tian (pt.), BC, Can. 134/M5
Tian Shan (mts.), China 67/H5
Tianchang, China 72/D3
Tianguá, Braz. 154/B1
Tianguistenco, Mex. 143/Q10
Tianjin (mun.), China 71/L4
Tianjin, China 72/H7
Tianlin, China 83/J3
Tianmen, China 79/B1
Tianmu (mts.), China 72/K9
Tianyang, China 79/A3
Tianzhen, China 72/C2
Tianzhu, China 83/J2
Tiaret, Alg. 100/F5
Tibagi, Braz. 155/B3
Tibagi (riv.), Braz. 155/B3
Tibaná, Col. 152/C3
Tibati, Camr. 96/H6
Tibba, Pak. 86/A5
Tibé, Pic de (peak), Gui. 102/C4
Tiber (Tevere) (riv.), It. 43/J5
Tiberias (lake), Isr. 91/D3
Tibesti (mts.), Chad 93/D3
Tibet (reg.), China 67/H6
Tibet (Xizang) (aut. reg.), China 70/D2
Tibro, Swe. 38/F2
Tiburon (cape), Haiti 141/G4
Tiburón, Isla (isl.), Mex. 142/B2
Ticaco, Peru 156/D5
Tichigan (lake), Wi, US 135/P14
Tichît, Dhar (cliff), Mrta. 102/C2
Ticino (canton), Swi. 57/E5
Ticleni, Rom. 48/F3
Ticonderoga, NY, US 130/D1
Ticul, Mex. 144/D1
Tidaholm, Swe. 38/E2
Tidikelt (plain), Alg. 100/G2
Tidjikdja, Mrta. 102/C2
Tidone (riv.), It. 58/C3
Tidore (isl.), Indo. 81/G3
Tidra, Île (isl.), Mrta. 102/B2
Tidsit (lake), WSah. 98/B5
Tiede, PN del, Canl.,Sp. 98/A3

Tiefencastel, Swi. 57/F4
Tiel, Neth. 50/C5
Tieling, China 72/E2
Tielt, Belg. 52/C2
Tielt-Winge, Belg. 53/D2
Tienen, Belg. 53/D2
Tieri, Austl. 114/C3
Tieroko (peak), Chad 96/H3
Tierp, Swe. 38/G1
Tierra Amarilla, NM, US 128/F3
Tierra Blanca, Mex. 143/N8
Tierra Colorada, Mex. 143/F5
Tierra del Fuego (isl.), Arg. 147/C8
Tierra del Fuego, Antártida e Islas del Atlántico Sur, Arg. 159/C7
Tierra del Fuego, PN, Arg. 157/C7
Tierradentro, Col. 152/B4
Tierranueva, Mex. 143/E4
Tiétar (riv.), Sp. 44/C2
Tietê (riv.), Braz. 147/D5
Tiffin, Oh, US 130/D3
Tiflet, Mor. 100/A3
Tifton, Ga, US 133/H4
Tigeaux, Fr. 30/L5
Tighina (Bendery), Mol. 49/J2
Tighvein (hill), Sc, UK 36/A6
Tignère, Camr. 96/H6
Tignieu-Jameyzieu, Fr. 56/B6
Tigre (riv.), Ven. 150/C4
Tigre (riv.), Peru 153/F2
Tigre, Arg. 159/J11
Tigris (riv.), Iraq 67/C6
Tigui (well), Chad 96/J4
Tiguidit, Falaise de (cliff), Niger 103/G2
Tigzirt, Alg. 100/H4
Tihosuco, Mex. 144/D1
Tihuatlán, Mex. 144/B1
Tiilikkajärven NP, Fin. 60/F3
Tijara, India 84/A2
Tijuana, Mex. 136/C5
Tijucas, Braz. 155/B3
Tijuco (riv.), Braz. 155/B1
Tikal (ruin), Guat. 144/D2
Tikamgarh, India 84/B3
Tikchik (lakes), Ak, US 134/G3
Tikehau (isl.), FrPol. 117/L6
Tikhoretsk, Rus. 62/G3
Tikhvin, Rus. 60/G4
Tikrīt, Iraq 88/E3
Tikveš (lake), FYROM 47/H2
Tila, Mex. 144/C2
Tilburg, Neth. 50/C5
Tilbury, Eng, UK 30/E2
Tilden, Tx, US 132/D4
Tilghman, Md, US 138/B6
Tilghman (isl.), Md, US 138/B6
Tilin, Myan. 83/F3
Till (riv.), Eng, UK 36/D5
Tillabéri (dept.), Niger 103/F3
Tillabéry, Niger 103/F3
Tillamook, Or, US 126/C4
Tille (riv.), Fr. 40/C5
Tillicoultry, Sc, UK 36/C4
Tilst, Den. 38/D3
Tilt (riv.), Sc, UK 36/C3
Tiltil, Chile 158/N8
Tim, Den. 38/B3
Timan (ridge), Rus. 64/F3
Timaná, Col. 152/C4
Timanfaya, PN de, Canl.,Sp. 98/B3
Timaru, NZ 117/S11
Timashevsk, Rus. 62/F3
Timbákion, Gre. 47/J5
Timbaúba, Braz. 154/D2
Timbédra, Mrta. 102/C2
Timber Lake, SD, US 127/H4
Timberlane, La, US 137/P17
Timberwood Park, Tx, US 137/U20
Timbiquí, Col. 152/B4
Timbiras, Braz. 154/B2
Timbó, Braz. 155/B3
Timboon, Austl. 115/B3
Timehri (int'l arpt.), Guy. 153/G3
Timelkam, Aus. 55/H6
Timfristós (peak), Gre. 47/G3
Timimoun, Alg. 99/F3
Timiris (cape), Mrta. 102/A2
Timiş (prov.), Rom. 48/E3
Timiş (riv.), Rom. 48/E3
Timişoara (int'l arpt.), Rom. 48/E3
Timişoara, Rom. 48/E3
Timmins, On, Can. 130/D1
Timms (riv.), Wi, US 135/O15
Timnath, Co, US 137/C1
Timon, Braz. 154/B2
Timonium, Md, US 138/B5
Timor (isl.), Asia,Austl. 67/M11
Timor (sea), ETim.,Indo. 81/H7
Timóteo, Braz. 155/D1
Timpanogos Cave Nat'l Mon., Ut, US 128/E2

Timpanogos Nat'l Mon., Ut, US 137/K13
Timpson, Tx, US 129/J5
Timpton (riv.), Rus. 65/N4
Tims Ford (lake), Tn, US 133/G3
Timurnī, India 84/A4
Tin Can Bay, Austl. 114/C4
Tin Shui Wai, China 71/T10
Tina (riv.), SAfr. 106/B1
Tinaca (pt.), Phil. 79/E6
Tinaco, Ven. 152/D2
Tindivanam, India 82/C5
Tindouf, Alg. 98/C4
Tindouf (prov.), Alg. 98/D3
Tineo, Sp. 44/B1
Tingalpa (res.), Austl. 114/F7
Tingaringy NP, Austl. 115/D3
Tingha, Austl. 115/D1
Tingi (mts.), SLeo. 102/C4
Tingmerkpuk (mtn.), Ak, US 134/F2
Tingo María, Peru 156/C3
Tingsryd, Swe. 38/F3
Tinguiririca (vol.), Chile 158/C2
Tinharé, Ilha de (isl.), Braz. 151/L6
Tinian (isl.), NMar. 116/C3
Tinicum Nat'l Consv. Area, Pa, US 138/C4
Tinkisso (riv.), Gui. 102/C4
Tinley Park, Il, US 135/Q16
Tinogasta, Arg. 157/C2
Tinos, Gre. 47/J4
Tinos (isl.), Gre. 47/J4
Tinqueux, Fr. 52/C5
Tinrhir, Mor. 98/D3
Tinta, Peru 156/D4
Tintagel (pt.), Eng, UK 32/B5
Tintern Abbey, Eng, UK 32/D3
Tintigny, Belg. 53/E4
Tintinara, Austl. 115/B2
Tinto (riv.), Sp. 44/B4
Tinto (peak), Sc, UK 36/C5
Tinton Falls (New Shrewsbury), NJ, US 138/D3
Tinyahuarco, Peru 156/B3
Tioga, ND, US 127/H3
Tioman (isl.), Malay. 80/B3
Tione di Trento, It. 57/G5
Tipasa (prov.), Alg. 100/F4
Tipasa, Alg. 100/G4
Tipperary, Ire. 31/P10
Tiptur, India 82/C5
Tir Rhiwiog (peak), Wal, UK 32/C1
Tiracambu, Serra do (mts.), Braz. 151/J4
Tiran (str.), Egypt, SA 101/C3
Tiran (isl.), Egypt 101/C3
Tīrān (isl.), Egypt 97/M2
Tirano, It. 57/G5
Tirari (des.), Austl. 113/H4
Tiraspol, Mol. 49/J2
Tire, Turk. 90/A2
Tirebolu, Turk. 62/F4
Tiree (isl.), Sc, UK 31/Q8
Tirest (well), Mali 103/F1
Tirgovişte, Rom. 49/G3
Tîrgu Bujor, Rom. 49/H3
Tirgu Cărbuneşti, Rom. 49/F3
Tirgu Frumos, Rom. 49/H2
Tirgu Jiu, Rom. 49/F2
Tirgu Lăpuş, Rom. 49/F2
Tîrgu Mureş, Rom. 49/G2
Tirgu Neamţ, Rom. 49/H2
Tirgu Ocna, Rom. 49/H2
Tirgu Secuiesc, Rom. 49/H2
Tirich Mīr (peak), Pak. 89/K1
Tiris (reg.), WSah. 98/B5
Tiris Zemmour (pol. reg.), Mrta. 98/C4
Tirnava Mare (riv.), Rom. 49/G2
Tirnava Mică (riv.), Rom. 49/G2
Tirnăveni, Rom. 49/F2
Tirnavos, Gre. 47/H3
Tiros, Braz. 155/C1
Tirschenreuth, Ger. 55/F3
Tirstrup (int'l arpt.), Den. 38/D3
Tiruchchirāppalli, India 82/C5
Tiruchendūr, India 82/C6
Tirunelveli, India 82/C6
Tiruntán, Peru 156/C2
Tirupati, India 82/C5
Tiruppattūr, India 82/C5
Tiruppūr, India 82/C5
Tiruvannāmalai, India 82/C5
Tisa (riv.), Ukr. 49/G1
Tisdale, Sk, Can. 127/H2
Tishomingo, Ok, US 129/H4
Tissemsilt (prov.), Alg. 100/F5
Tissemsilt, Alg. 100/F5
Tista (riv.), Bang. 85/G2
Tisza (riv.), Hun. 62/B3
Tiszaföldvár, Hun. 48/E2
Tiszafüred, Hun. 48/E2

Tiszakécske, Hun. 48/E2
Tiszalök, Hun. 48/E1
Tiszavasvári, Hun. 41/L5
Titano (peak),
SMar. 59/F5
Titel, Serb. 48/E3
Titicaca (lake),
Bol.,Peru 147/B4
Titisee-Neustadt, Ger. 56/E2
Titlagarh, India 82/D3
Titlis (peak), Swi. 57/E4
Tito, It. 46/D2
Titov Veles, FYROM 47/G2
Titov vrh (peak),
FYROM 47/G2
Titting, Ger. 54/E5
Tittmoning, Ger. 55/F6
Titu, Rom. 49/G3
Titusville, Fl, US 133/H4
Titusville, NJ, US 138/D3
Tiva (riv.), Kenya 104/C3
Tivaouane, Sen. 102/A3
Tivat, Serb. 47/F1
Tiverton, Eng, UK 32/C5
Tiwanaku, Bol. 156/D5
Tixán, Ecu. 156/B1
Tixtla de Guerrero,
Mex. 143/H5
Tizayuca, Mex. 143/L7
Tizi Ouzou (prov.),
Alg. 100/H4
Tizi Ouzou, Alg. 100/H4
Tizimín, Mex. 144/D1
Tiznap (riv.), China 89/L1
Tiznit, Mor. 98/C3
Tjæreborg, Den. 38/C4
Tjeldstø, Nor. 38/A1
Tjeukemeer (lake),
Neth. 50/C3
Tjøme, Nor. 38/D2
Tjorn (isl.), Den. 38/D3
Tlachichuca, Mex. 143/P7
Tlacolula de Matamoros,
Mex. 144/B2
Tlacotalpan, Mex. 143/P8
Tlacotepec, Mex. 143/F5
Tlahualilo de Zaragoza,
Mex. 132/C5
Tlalixcoyan, Mex. 143/N8
Tlalmanalco, Mex. 143/Q9
Tlalnepantla, Mex. 143/Q9
Tláloc (vol.),
Mex. 143/Q10
Tlaltenango de Sánchez
Román, Mex. 142/E4
Tlaltizapan, Mex. 143/K8
Tlapa de Comonfort,
Mex. 144/B2
Tlapacoya (ruin),
Mex. 143/Q10
Tlapacoyan, Mex. 143/M7
Tlapehuala, Mex. 143/E5
Tlaquepaque, Mex. 142/E4
Tlaquiltenango,
Mex. 143/K8
Tlatlauquitepec,
Mex. 143/M7
Tlaxcala (state),
Mex. 140/A5
Tlaxcala, Mex. 143/L7
Tlaxco, Mex. 143/L7
Tlaxcoapan, Mex. 143/K6
Tlell, BC, Can. 134/M5
Tlemcen, Alg. 100/D2
Toabré, Pan. 152/A2
Toaca (peak), Rom. 49/G2
Toachi (riv.), Ecu. 152/B4
Toamasina, Madg. 107/J7
Toamasina (prov.),
Madg. 107/J7
Toandos (pen.),
Wa, US 135/B2
Toau (isl.), FrPol. 117/L6
Toay, Arg. 158/D3
Toba (lake), Indo. 80/A3
Toba (inlet), BC, Can. 126/B3
Toba, Japan 77/L7
Toba Kākar (range),
Pak. 89/J2
Toba Tek Singh, Pak. 86/B4
Tobago (isl.), Trin. 150/F1
Tobarra, Sp. 44/E3
Tobermore, NI, UK 34/B2
Tōbetsu, Japan 76/B2
Tobias Barreto, Braz. 154/C3
Tobin (lake), Austl. 109/B3
Tobique (riv.), NB, Can. 131/H2
Tobol (riv.), Rus. 61/O5
Tobishima, Japan 77/A1
Tobyhanna (lake),
Pa, US 138/C1
Tobyhanna (riv.),
Pa, US 138/C1
Tobyhanna, Pa, US 138/C1
Tobyhanna St. Park,
Pa, US 138/C1
Tobyl, Kaz. 63/H1
Tobysh (riv.), Rus. 61/L2
Tocache, Peru 156/B3
Tocantinópolis,
Braz. 154/A2
Tocantins (state),
Braz. 154/A3
Tocantins (riv.), Braz. 147/E4
Toccoa, Ga, US 133/H4
Toce (riv.), It. 43/F5
Tochigi
(pref.), Japan 75/F2
Tochigi, Japan 75/F2
Tochimilco, Mex. 143/L8
Tochio, Japan 75/F2

Tocina, Sp. 44/C4
Töcksfors, Swe. 38/D2
Toco, Trin. 153/F2
Tocopilla, Chile 157/B1
Tocumen, Pan. 152/B2
Tocumwal, Austl. 115/C2
Tocuyito, Ven. 152/D2
Tocuyo (riv.), Ven. 150/E1
Toda, Japan 77/D2
Toda Bhim, India 82/C2
Todi, It. 46/C1
Tödi (peak), Swi. 57/E4
Todmorden, Eng, UK 35/F4
Todos os Santos, Baíaa de
(bay), Braz. 154/C4
Todos Santos, Mex. 142/C4
Todtmoos, Ger. 56/E2
Todtnau, Ger. 56/D2
Toffal (hill), Mrta. 98/C5
Toffo, Ben. 103/F5
Tofield, Ab, Can. 126/E2
Tofua (isl.), Tonga 117/H6
Tōgane, Japan 77/E2
Togba (well), Mrta. 102/C2
Toggenburg (valley),
Swi. 57/F3
Togher, Ire. 34/B5
Togiak, Ak, US 134/F4
Togo (ctry.) 103/F4
Togō, Japan 77/M5
Tōgrög, Mong. 70/F2
Togtoh, China 72/B2
Tōgyu-san NP, SKor. 73/D5
Tohana, India 86/C5
Tohatchi, NM, US 132/A3
Tōhoku (prov.),
Japan 75/F1
Toi, Japan 75/F3
Tōin, Japan 77/L5
Toiyabe (range),
Nv, US 128/C3
Tojo, Japan 74/C3
Tōjō, Japan 77/H6
Tomioka, Japan 77/N1
Tomisato, Japan 77/E2
Tomiura, Japan 77/D3
Tomiyama, Japan 75/F3
Tomizawa, Japan 77/A3
Tommot, Rus. 65/N4
Tomo (riv.), Col. 150/E2
Tompa, Hun. 48/D2
Tompkinsville, Ky, US 130/C4
Toms (riv.), NJ, US 138/D3
Toms River, NJ, US 138/D4
Tomsk, Rus. 64/J4
Tomskskaya Oblast,
Rus. 64/H4
Tōmük, Turk. 91/D1
Tonalá, Mex. 144/C2
Tonale, Passo del
(pass), It. 57/G5
Tonasket, Wa, US 126/D3
Tonawanda,
NY, US 131/S9
Tonawanda Ind. Res.,
US 131/S9
Tonbridge, Eng, UK 30/D3
Tončontin (int'l arpt.),
Hon. 144/E3
Tondabayashi, Japan 77/J7
Tondano, Indo. 81/F3
Tondou, Massif du
(plat.), CAfr.,Sud 97/K6
Tondu (peak), Fr. 56/C5
Tone (riv.), Japan 75/G3
Tone, Japan 77/E2
Tonekābon, Iran 88/F1
Tonelagee (peak),
Ire. 34/B5
Tonga (ctry.) 117/H7
Tongaat, SKor. 117/H7
Tongareva (Penrhyn)
(isl.), Cookls. 117/J5
Tongariro NP, NZ 117/T10
Tongatapu (isl.),
Tonga 117/H7
Tongbai, China 72/C4
Tongbu, SKor. 73/G6
Tongcheng, China 79/B2
Tongcheng, China 72/D5
Tongchuan, China 72/B3
T'ongch'ŏn, NKor. 73/D3
Tongde, China 72/A3
Tongduch'on, SKor. 73/G6
Tongeren, Belg. 53/E2
Tonggu
(peak), China 71/L7
Tonggu, China 73/K2
Tonghae, SKor. 73/E4
Tonghua, China 73/C2
Tonghua, China 73/C2
Tongliao, China 72/E2
Tongling, China 71/L5
Tongno (riv.), NKor. 73/D2
Tongobory, Madg. 107/H8
Tongren, China 83/J2
Tongsa, China 85/H2
Tongsa Dzong, Bhu. 85/H2
Tongshan, China 79/B2
Tongtian (riv.), China 71/U10
Tongu (chan.), China 71/U10
Tongxu, China 72/C4
Tongyu, China 71/M3
Tongzi, China 79/A2
Tonino-Anivskiy (pen.),
Rus. 76/C1
Tonk, India 89/L3
Tonkawa, Ok, US 129/H3
Tonkin (gulf),
China,Viet 67/K7

Toltén (riv.), Chile 158/B3
Tolú, Col. 152/C2
Toluca, Mex. 143/Q10
Tolúviejo, Col. 152/C2
Tol'yatti, Rus. 63/J1
Tom' (riv.), Rus. 64/J4
Tom Price, Austl. 112/C2
Tom White (mt.),
Ak, US 134/K3
Tomakomai, Japan 76/B2
Tomamae, Japan 76/B1
Tomar, Port. 44/A3
Tómaros (peak),
Gre. 47/G3
Tomarza, Turk. 90/C2
Tomás, Peru 156/C4
Tomás de Berlanga,
Ecu. 156/E7
Tomaszów Lubelski,
Pol. 41/M3
Tomaszów Mazowiecki,
Pol. 41/L3
Tomatlán, Mex. 142/D5
Tomb of Qinshihuang,
China 72/B4
Tombador, Serra do
(mts.), Braz. 150/G6
Tombigbee (riv.),
Al,Ms, US 125/J5
Tombolo, It. 59/E1
Tombouctou, Mali 102/E2
Tombouctou
(pol. reg.), Mali 98/D5
Tombstone, Az, US 128/E5
Tombua, Ang. 105/A4
Tomé, Chile 158/B3
Tomé, Ile (isl.), Fr. 42/B2
Tomelilla, Swe. 38/E4
Tomelloso, Sp. 44/D3
Tomika, Japan 77/L5
Tomini (gulf),
Indo. 67/M10
Tomiño, Sp. 44/A2
Topol'čany, Slvk. 41/K4
Topley, BC, Can. 126/B2
Topliţa, Rom. 49/G2
Topia, Mex. 142/D3
Topobelampo, Mex. 142/C3
Topoloveni, Rom. 49/G3
Topolovgrad, Bul. 47/K1
Topozero (lake), Rus. 37/J2
Toppenish, Wa, US 128/C2
Topton, Pa, US 138/C3
Tor (bay), Eng, UK 32/C6
Torahime, Japan 77/K5
Torata, Peru 156/D5
Torawitan (cape),
Indo. 81/G3
Torbat-e Ḩeydarīyeh,
Iran 89/G1
Torbat-e Jām, Iran 87/D5
Torbay, Nf, Can. 131/L2
Torbay (co.), Eng, UK 58/B3
Torbeck, Haiti 145/H2
Torbert (mt.), Ak, US 134/H3
Torcy, Fr. 30/K5
Tordera (riv.), Sp. 45/L6
Tordesillas, Sp. 44/C2
Töreboda, Swe. 38/E3
Torelló, Sp. 45/G1
Torfaen (co.),
Wal, UK 32/C3
Torgelow, Ger. 38/E5
Torghay, Kaz. 87/D3
Torghay (riv.), Kaz. 87/D3
Torghay Üstirti (plat.),
Kaz. 87/D2
Torhout, Belg. 52/C1
Tori-shima (isl.),
Japan 116/D1
Toride, Japan 77/E2
Torigni-sur-Vire, Fr. 42/C2
Torii-tōge (pass),
Japan 75/E3
Toriñana (cape), Sp. 44/A1
Torino (prov.), It. 58/A2
Torino (Turin), It. 58/A2
Torkestān (mts.),
Afg. 89/H1
Tormes (riv.), Sp. 44/C2
Torndirrup NP,
Austl. 112/C5
Torne (riv.), Eng, UK 35/H4
Torne (hill),
Eng, UK 36/E6
Torneälven (riv.),
Swe. 60/D2
Tornesch, Ger. 51/G1
Tornik (peak), Serb. 48/D4
Tornio, Fin. 37/H2
Tornionjoki (riv.), Fin. 37/G2
Toro, Sp. 44/C2
Toro, Cerro del (peak),
Arg.,Chil 157/C2
Toro Nat'l Rsv.,
Ugan. 104/A2
Toro, PN, Ven. 152/D2
Torökbálint, Hun. 49/Q10
Törökszentmiklós,
Hun. 48/E2
Toronaic (gulf),
Gre. 47/H2
Torondoy, Ven. 152/D2
Toronto (cap.),
On, Can. 131/R8
Toronto (isl.),
On, Can. 131/R8
Toropets, Rus. 39/P3
Tororo, Ugan. 104/B2
Torp (int'l arpt.),
Nor. 38/D2
Torpa, Swe. 38/E3
Torquay, Austl. 115/C3
Torquay, Eng, UK 32/C6
Torquemada, Sp. 44/C1
Torr (pt.), NI, UK 34/B1

Torrance, Ca, US 136/F8
Torraz, Tête de
(peak), Fr. 56/C6
Torre de Moncorvo,
Port. 44/B2
Torre dè Passeri, It. 46/C1
Torre del Campo,
Sp. 44/D4
Torre del Greco, It. 46/D2
Torre del Lago Puccini,
It. 58/D5
Tonoshō, Japan 74/D3
Tonosi, Pan. 152/A3
Tonota, Bots. 105/E5
Tons (riv.), India 84/C3
Tønsberg, Nor. 38/D2
Tonsina, Ak, US 134/J3
Tonstad, Nor. 38/B2
Tonto Nat'l For.,
Az, US 137/S18
Tonto Nat'l Mon.,
Az, US 128/E4
Tonya, Turk. 90/D1
Ton-y-Pandy, Wal, UK 32/C3
Toodyay, Austl. 112/C4
Tooele, Ut, US 137/J12
Tooele (co.),
Ut, US 137/J13
Tooradin, Austl. 115/C3
Toowoomba, Austl. 114/C4
Top (mt.), Austl. 113/G2
Topanga State Park,
Ca, US 136/B2
Topanga, Ca, US 136/B2
Topanga Beach,
Ca, US 136/C7
Tope de Coroa (mtn.),
CpV. 93/J10
Torridge (riv.),
Eng, UK 32/B5
Torrijos, Sp. 44/C3
Torrington,
Wy, US 127/G5
Torrington (mt.),
Wa, US 135/A2
Torrita di Siena, It. 43/J5
Torroella de Montgrí,
Sp. 45/G1
Torrone Alto (peak),
Swi. 57/F5
Torrox, Sp. 44/D4
Towson, Md, US 138/B3
Towuti (lake), Indo. 81/F4
Toya (lake), Japan 76/B2
Toyah, Tx, US 132/C4
Toyahvale, Tx, US 132/C4
Toyama, Japan 75/E2
Toyama (pref.),
Japan 75/E2
Toyang, SKor. 73/D5
Toyohashi, Japan 75/E3
Toyokawa, Japan 75/E3
Toyonaka, Japan 77/H6
Toyo'oka, Japan 74/D3
Toyosato, Japan 77/K5
Toyota, Japan 77/M5
Toyotomi, Japan 76/B1
Toyoyama, Japan 77/L5
Tozi (mt.), Ak, US 134/H2
Tra Vinh, Viet 78/D4
Trabuco Canyon,
Ca, US 136/C3
Trabzon, Turk. 90/D1
Trabzon (prov.),
Turk. 90/D1
Tracadie, NB, Can. 131/H2
Trachselwald, Swi. 57/E3
Tracy, Qu, Can. 130/F2
Tracy, Mo, US 137/D5
Tracyton, Wa, US 135/B2
Tosno, Rus. 39/P2
Tosontsengel,
Mong. 70/F2
Trafalgar (cape), Sp. 44/B4
Trafford (co.), Eng, UK 35/F5
Tragwein, Aus. 55/H6
Traiguén, Chile 158/B3
Trail, BC, Can. 126/D3
Traipu, Braz. 154/C3
Trairí, Braz. 151/G2
Traisen (riv.), Aus. 41/H5
Traiskirchen, Aus. 49/N7
Traismauer, Aus. 41/H4
Trakai NP, Lith. 39/L4
Traki, Lith. 39/L4
Tralee, Ire. 31/P10
Tralee (inlet),
Ire. 31/P10
Tottington, Eng, UK 35/F4
Tottori, Japan 74/D3
Tottori (pref.),
Japan 74/C3
Totutla, Mex. 143/N7
Touat (reg.), Alg. 99/F4
Toubkal (peak),
Mor. 98/D3
Toubkal, PN du,
Mor. 98/D3
Touchwood (hills),
Sk, Can. 127/G3
Toudao (riv.), China 73/D1
Tougan, Burk. 102/D4
Tougouuénoum,
Pa, US 138/C4
Touiel (riv.), Alg. 100/G5
Toul, Fr. 53/E6

Toulnustouc (riv.),
Qu, Can. 131/H1
Toulon, Fr. 42/F5
Toulon, Fr. 42/F5
Toumo (well), Niger 96/H3
Toumodi, C.d'Iv. 102/D5
Toungoo, Myan. 83/G4
Toura, Monts du (mts.),
C.d'Iv. 102/D5
Tourcoing, Fr. 52/C2
Tourfourine (well),
Mali 98/D2
Tourlaville, Fr. 42/C2
Tournai, Belg. 52/C2
Tournan-en-Brie, Fr. 30/L6
Tournus, Fr. 56/A4
Touros, Braz. 154/D2
Tourouvre, Fr. 42/D3
Tous, Embalse de (res.),
Sp. 45/E3
Toussidé (peak),
Chad 96/J3
Toussoro (peak),
CAfr. 97/K6
Touws (riv.), SAfr. 106/C4
Touwsrivier,
SAfr. 106/M10
Toužim, Czh. 55/G2
Tov (prov.), Mong. 70/J2
Tovar, Ven. 152/D2
Tove (riv.), Eng, UK 33/E2
Towaco, NJ, US 139/H8
Towada, Japan 75/G2
Towada (lake), Japan 76/B3
Towada-Hachimantai NP,
Japan 76/B3
Tower City, Pa, US 138/B2
Tower Hamlets (bor.),
Eng, UK 30/A1
Tower of London,
Eng, UK 30/A1
Towner, ND, US 127/H3
Townsend, Mt, US 126/F4
Townsend, De, US 138/C5
Townsend (mt.),
Wa, US 135/A2
Townsends (inlet),
NJ, US 138/D5
Townshend (cape),
Austl. 114/C3
Townsville, Austl. 114/B2
Towot, Sudan 97/N7
Traer (lake),
Sc, UK 36/B3
Treinta de Agosto,
Arg. 158/E3
Treinta y Tres (dept.),
Uru. 159/G2
Treinta y Tres, Uru. 159/G2
Trélazé, Fr. 42/C3
Trélew, Arg. 158/D4
Trélissac, Fr. 42/D4
Trelleborg, Swe. 38/E4
Trélon, Fr. 52/D3
Tremadoc (bay),
Wal, UK 34/D6
Treloudat (riv.),
Ire. 34/B4
Trembleur (lake),
BC, Can. 126/B2
Tremelo, Belg. 52/D2
Tremiti (isl.), It. 46/D1
Tremont, Pa, US 138/B2
Tiémosná (riv.), Czh. 55/G3
Tiemšín (peak),
Czh. 55/H3
Trenche (riv.),
Qu, Can. 130/F1
Trenčiansky
(pol. reg.), Slvk. 41/J4
Trenčín, Slvk. 41/J4
Trenel, Arg. 158/D2
Trenque Lauquen,
Arg. 158/E2
Trent and Mersey (canal),
Eng, UK 35/F6
Trent (riv.), Eng, UK 33/F6
Trentino-Alto Adige
(pol. reg.), It. 43/J3
Trento, It. 57/G5
Trento (prov.), It. 57/G5
Trenton, On, Can. 131/R7
Trenton, FI, US 133/H5
Trenton, Tn, US 130/B5
Trenton, Mo, US 129/J2
Trenton (cap.),
NJ, US 138/D3
Trenzano, It. 58/D2
Trepuzzi, It. 47/F2
Três Algarrobos,
Arg. 158/E2
Tres Arroyos, Arg. 158/E3
Três Corações,
Braz. 211/H6
Três Irmãos, Reprêsa
(res.), Braz. 155/B2
Tres Isletas, Arg. 157/D2
Tres Lagoas, Arg. 158/E3
Três Marias,
Braz. 154/A5
Tres Marías (isls.),
Mex. 142/D4
Tres Marías, Mex. 143/Q10
Tres Marías, Reprêsa
(res.), Braz. 151/J7
Tres Montes (cape),
Chile 159/B5

Tres Morros, Alto de
(peak), Col. 152/B3
Tres Picos, Mex. 144/C3
Tres Picos (peak),
Arg. 158/C4
Tres Picos (peak),
Arg. 158/D5
Três Pontas, Braz. 211/H6
Tres Puntas (cape),
Arg. 158/D5
Três Rios, Braz. 211/K7
Tres Valles, Mex. 144/B2
Tresa (riv.), Swi. 57/E5
Tresckow, Pa, US 138/C2
Trescore Balneario, It. 58/C1
Trescore Cremasco, It. 58/C2
Tresigallo, It. 59/E3
Tresinaro (riv.), It. 59/E3
Trestina, It. 59/F6
Trets, Fr. 42/F5
Treuchtlingen, Ger. 54/D5
Treuen, Ger. 55/F1
Treuenbrietzen, Ger. 40/G2
Treungen, Nor. 38/C2
Trevélin, Arg. 158/C4
Treviglio, It. 58/C1
Trevignano, It. 58/C1
Treviso (int'l arpt.), It. 59/F1
Treviso (prov.), It. 59/F2
Treviso, It. 59/F1
Trevorton, Pa, US 138/B2
Trevose (pt.),
Eng, UK 32/A5
Trezzano sul Naviglio,
It. 58/C2
Trezzo sull'Adda, It. 58/C2
Trhové Sviny, Czh. 55/H5
Triabunna, Austl. 115/C4
Triadelphia (res.),
Md, US 138/B5
Triángulos (reef),
Mex. 144/C1
Tré-la-Tête (peak), Fr. 56/C6
Tribbey, Ok, US 137/N15
Triberg, Ger. 57/E1
Tribugá (bay), Col. 152/B3
Tribhuvan (int'l arpt.),
Nepal 85/E2
Tribulation (cape),
Austl. 114/B2
Tribulaun (peak),
Aus. 57/H4
Tricase, It. 47/F3
Trichūr, India 82/C6
Tricora (range),
Indo. 81/J4
Tricot, Fr. 52/B4
Trie-Château, Fr. 52/B4
Trier, Ger. 53/F4
Trierweiler, Ger. 57/F3
Triesen, Lcht. 57/F3
Trieste (int'l arpt.), It. 59/G1
Trieste (prov.), It. 59/G1
Trieste, It. 43/K4
Trieux, Fr. 53/E5
Triftern, Ger. 55/G6
Trigla NP, Slov. 43/K3
Triglav (peak), Slov. 43/K3
Trigolo, It. 58/C2
Trikala, Gre. 47/G3
Trikhonis (lake), Gre. 47/G3
Trilport, Fr. 52/B6
Trim, Ire. 34/B4
Trimbach, Swi. 56/D3
Trimble, Mo, US 137/D5
Trimmis, Swi. 57/F4
Trin, Swi. 57/F4
Trincomalee, SrL. 82/D6
Trindade, Braz. 151/J7
Trindade, Ilha da (isl.),
Braz. 151/N8
Tring, Eng, UK 33/F3
Trinidad (isl.), Arg. 157/D4
Trinidad, Uru. 159/K10
Trinidad, Bol. 150/F6
Trinidad, Col. 152/D3
Trinidad (chan.),
Chile 159/B6
Trinidad, Uru. 159/K10
Trinidad (gulf),
Chile 159/A6
Trinidad and Tobago
(ctry.) 141/N10
Trinity (isls.), Ak, US 134/H4
Trinity (range),
Nv, US 128/C2
Trinity (riv.), Ca, US 126/C5
Trinity (bay), Nf, Can. 131/L2
Trinity, West Fork (riv.),
Tx, US 129/H4
Trinity, Tn, US 58/B2
Triolet, Mrts. 107/T15
Tripolis, Gre. 47/H4
Tripolitania (reg.),
Libya 96/H1
Trippstadt, Ger. 57/E5
Tripunittura, India 82/C6
Tripura (state),
India 70/F7
Trissano (riv.), Aus. 57/G4
Trissino, It. 59/E1
Tristan da Cunha (isl.),
StH. 22/J7
Triste (peak), Arg. 158/D4
Trivero (riv.), Nepal 85/E2
Trittau, Ger. 51/H1
Trivero, It. 58/B1
Trnava, Slvk. 41/J4
Trnavský
(pol. reg.), Slvk. 41/J4
Trobriand (isls.),
PNG 116/E5

Trochtelfingen, Ger. 57/F1
Troesne (riv.), Fr. 52/A5
Trofaiach, Aus. 43/L3
Trofarello, It. 58/A3
Trøgstad, Nor. 38/D2
Troia, It. 46/D2
Trois Fourches, Cap des (cape), Mor. 100/C2
Trois-Pistoles, Qu, Can. 131/G1
Trois-Ponts, Belg. 53/E3
Trois-Rivières, Qu, Can. 131/F2
Troisdorf, Ger. 53/G2
Troistorrents, Swi. 56/C5
Troisvierges, Lux. 53/F3
Troitsk, Rus. 61/P5
Trollhättan, Swe. 38/E2
Trombetas (riv.), Braz. 151/G3
Tromello, It. 58/B2
Tromie (riv.), Sc, UK 36/B3
Troms (co.), Nor. 37/F1
Tromsø, Nor. 37/F1
Tronador (peak), Arg. 158/C4
Trondheim, Nor. 37/D3
Trondheims-Fjorden (estu.), Nor. 37/D3
Tronville-en-Barrois, Fr. 53/E6
Tronzano Vercellese, It. 58/B2
Troodos (mts.), Cyp. 91/C2
Trool (lake), Sc, UK 34/D1
Troon, Sc, UK 36/B5
Trooper, Pa, US 138/C3
Tropea, It. 46/D3
Trosa, Swe. 38/G2
Trosly-Breuil, Fr. 52/B5
Trossingen, Ger. 57/E1
Trostan (peak), NI, UK 34/B1
Trostberg an der Alz, Ger. 55/F6
Trou du Nord, Haiti 145/H2
Troup (pt.), Sc, UK 36/D1
Trout (lake), NW, Can. 122/D2
Trout Lake, Ab, Can. 126/E1
Trowbridge, Eng, UK 32/D4
Troxelville, Pa, US 138/C2
Troy, Al, US 133/G4
Troy, Mi, US 130/D3
Troy, NY, US 130/F3
Troy, Oh, US 133/G1
Troy, Il, US 137/H8
Troy Center, Wi, US 135/N14
Troyan, Bul. 47/J1
Troyanski Prokhod (pass), Bul. 47/J1
Troyes, Fr. 42/F2
Trstenik, Serb. 48/E4
Trub, Swi. 56/D4
Truitt (peak), Yk, Can. 134/M3
Trujillo, Peru 156/B3
Trujillo, Sp. 44/C3
Trujillo, Ven. 152/D2
Trujillo (state), Ven. 152/D2
Trujillo, Hon. 144/E3
Truk (isls.), Micr. 116/E4
Trulben, Ger. 53/G5
Truman Library and Museum, Mo, US 137/E5
Trumauersville, Pa, US 138/C3
Trumau, Aus. 49/N8
Trumbull, Ct, US 139/E1
Trümmelbachfälle (falls), Swi. 56/D4
Trün, Bul. 47/H1
Trundle, Austl. 115/C2
Truro, NS, Can. 131/J2
Truro, Eng, UK 32/A6
Truskmore (peak), Ire. 31/P9
Trŭstenik, Bul. 49/G4
Truth or Consequences, NM, US 128/F4
Trutnov, Czh. 41/H3
Truyère (riv.), Fr. 42/E4
Trwyn Cilan (pt.), Wal, UK 34/D6
Tryavna, Bul. 49/N8
Trysil, Nor. 38/E1
Trysilelva (riv.), Nor. 38/D1
Trzcianka, Pol. 41/J2
Trzebiatów, Pol. 38/F4
Trzebnica, Pol. 41/J3
Trzemeszno, Pol. 41/J2
Tsabong, Bots. 106/C2
Tsagaan Bogd (peak), Mong. 70/G3
Tsakane, SAfr. 106/Q13
Tsalgar, Mong. 70/F2
Tsant, Mong. 70/F2
Tsao, Bots. 105/D5
Tsaratanana, Madg. 107/H7
Tsaratanana (mass.), Madg. 107/H7
Tsast (peak), Mong. 70/F2
Tsatsana (peak), Les. 106/E3

Tsavo East NP, Kenya 105/G1
Tsavo West NP, Kenya 105/G1
Tschagguns, Aus. 57/F3
Tschierv, Swi. 57/G4
Tschlin, Swi. 57/G4
Tselfat (peak), Mor. 100/B2
Tsetserleg, Mong. 70/F2
Tsetserleg, Mong. 70/H2
Tseung Kwan O, China 71/U10
Tsévié, Togo 103/F5
Tshane, Bots. 105/D5
Tshela, D.R. Congo 105/B1
Tshikapa, D.R. Congo 105/D2
Tshuapa (riv.), D.R. Congo 93/E5
Tsiafajavona (peak), Madg. 107/H7
Tsil'ma (riv.), Rus. 61/L2
Tsimlyansk (res.), Rus. 64/E5
Tsing Yi (isl.), China 71/U10
Tsiombe, Madg. 107/H9
Tsiribihina (riv.), Madg. 107/H7
Tsiroanomandidy, Madg. 107/H7
Tsitsikamma Forest and Coastal NP, SAfr. 106/C4
Tsivory, Madg. 107/H9
Ts'khinvali, Geo. 63/G4
Tsna (riv.), Rus. 60/G4
Tsomo (riv.), SAfr. 106/D3
Tsomog, Mong. 71/J2
Tsu, Japan 77/L6
Tsu (isl.), Japan 74/A3
Tsubame, Japan 75/F2
Tsubata, Japan 75/E2
Tsuchiura, Japan 75/G2
Tsuchiyama, Japan 77/K6
Tsuen Wan, China 71/U10
Tsugaru (pen.), Japan 76/B3
Tsuge, Japan 77/J6
Tsukidate, Japan 76/B4
Tsukigase, Japan 77/K6
Tsukuba, Japan 77/E1
Tsukude, Japan 77/M6
Tsukui, Japan 77/C2
Tsukumi, Japan 74/B4
Tsumeb, Namb. 105/C4
Tsuna, Japan 77/G7
Tsuruga, Japan 74/E3
Tsurugashima, Japan 77/C2
Tsurugi, Japan 74/E2
Tsurugi-san (peak), Japan 74/D4
Tsuruoka, Japan 76/A4
Tsuruta, Japan 77/L5
Tsuyama, Japan 77/L5
Tua (cape), Indo. 80/C5
Tua (riv.), Port.,Sp. 44/B2
Tuam, Ire. 31/P10
Tuamapu (chan.), Chile 158/B4
Tuamotu (arch.), FrPol. 117/L6
Tuan (pt.), Indo. 80/A3
Tuan (riv.), China 72/B2
Tuangku (isl.), Indo. 80/A3
Tuao, Phil. 79/D4
Tuapse, Rus. 63/N1
Tuba City, Az, US 128/E3
Tuban, Indo. 80/D6
Tuban (riv.), Yem. 88/D6
Tubarão, Braz. 155/B4
Tubbergen, Neth. 50/D4
Tübingen, Ger. 54/C5
Tubize, Belg. 53/D2
Tubmanburg, Libr. 102/C5
Ţubruq (Tobruk), Libya 97/K1
Tubuaï (isl.), FrPol. 117/K7
Tubualá, Pan. 152/D2
Tucacas, Ven. 152/D2
Tucano, Braz. 154/C3
Tuchola, Pol. 41/J2
Tuchów, Pol. 41/L4
Tuckahoe, NJ, US 138/D5
Tuckahoe, NY, US 139/K8
Tuckerton, NJ, US 138/D4
Tucquegnieux, Fr. 53/E5
Tucson, Az, US 128/E4
Tucson (int'l arpt.), Az, US 142/C1
Tucumcari, NM, US 129/G4
Tucupido, Ven. 153/E2
Tucupita, Ven. 153/F2
Tucuruí, Braz. 151/J4
Tucuruí (res.), Braz. 154/C1
Tudela, Sp. 44/E1
Tudela de Duero, Sp. 44/C2
Tuen Mun, China 71/T10
Tuenno, It. 57/H5
Tufanbeyli, Turk. 90/D2
Tug Fork (riv.), Ky,WV, US 133/H2
Tugela (riv.), SAfr. 107/E3
Tugela, SAfr. 107/E3
Tugela (falls), SAfr. 106/E3
Tughlakabad (ruin), India 86/D5
Tuguegarao, Phil. 79/D4
Tukangbesi (isls.), Indo. 81/F5
Ṭūkh, Egypt 91/B4

Tuktoyaktuk, NW, Can. 134/M2
Tukums, Lat. 39/K3
Tukung (peak), Indo. 80/D4
Tukuyu, Tanz. 104/B5
Tukwila, Wa, US 135/C3
Tula (riv.), Kenya 104/C3
Tula, Rus. 62/F1
Tula (riv.), Mex. 143/K6
Tula, PN, Mex. 143/K6
Tulancingo, Mex. 143/L6
Tulare, Ca, US 128/C3
Tularosa (valley), NM, US 129/F4
Tularosa, NM, US 129/F4
Tulcán, Ecu. 152/B4
Tulcea, Rom. 49/J3
Tulcea (prov.), Rom. 49/J3
Tule (canal), Ca, US 135/L9
Tüledi (isls.), Rus. 87/B3
Tulia, Tx, US 129/G4
Tulik (vol.), Ak, US 134/E5
Tulin (isls.), PNG 116/E5
Tulita, NW, Can. 134/L2
Tülkarm, WBnk. 91/G7
Tulla (lake), Sc, UK 36/B3
Tullamore, Austl. 115/C2
Tullamore, Ire. 31/Q10
Tulle, Fr. 42/D4
Tullibody, Sc, UK 36/C4
Tullnerbach, Aus. 49/N7
Tullow, Ire. 31/Q10
Tully, Austl. 114/B2
Tullytown, Pa, US 138/D3
Tuloma (riv.), Rus. 64/D3
Tulsa, Ok, US 129/J3
Tulsipur, Nepal 84/D1
Tulsipur, India 84/D2
Tul'skaya Oblast, Rus. 62/F1
Tultitlán, Mex. 143/J6
Tuluá, Col. 152/B3
Tuluksak, Ak, US 134/F3
Tulum, Mex. 144/E1
Tulum, PN, Mex. 144/E1
Tulun, Rus. 65/L4
Tumacacori Nat'l Hist. Park, Az, US 145/J1
Tumaco, Col. 152/B4
Tumatumari, Guy. 153/G3
Tumauini, Phil. 79/D4
Tumba (lake), D.R. Congo 96/J8
Tumba, Swe. 38/G2
Tumbarumba, Austl. 115/D2
Tumbes (dept.), Peru 156/A1
Tumbes, Peru 156/A1
Tumbot (peak), Camb. 78/C3
Tumby Bay, Austl. 113/H5
Tumd Youqi, China 72/B2
Tumd Zuoqi, China 72/B2
Tumen, China 71/N3
Tumen (riv.), China 73/E1
Tumeremo, Ven. 153/F3
Tumereng, Guy. 153/F3
Tumkūr, India 82/C5
Tummel (riv.), Sc, UK 36/C3
Tumpat, Malay. 83/H6
Tumpu (peak), Indo. 81/F4
Tumu, Gha. 103/E4
Tumuc-Humac (mts.), Braz. 151/G3
Tumut, Austl. 115/D2
Tunadal, Swe. 60/C3
Tunceli (prov.), Turk. 90/D2
Tunceli, Turk. 90/D2
Tunchang, China 83/K4
Tundla, India 84/B2
Tundyk (riv.), Kaz. 87/G2
Tundzha (riv.), Bul. 47/J1
Tung Chung, China 71/T10
Tung Lung (isl.), China 71/V11
Tungabhadra (res.), India 82/C4
Tungabhadra (riv.), India 82/C4
Tungamah, Austl. 115/C3
Tungsan-got (pt.), NKor. 73/C4
Tungurahua (prov.), Ecu. 152/B5
Tünhel, Mong. 70/J2
Tūnis, Tun. 46/B4
Tunis (cap.), Tun. 46/B4
Tunis, Gulf of (gulf), Tun. 46/B4
Tunisia (ctry.) 99/H2
Tunja, Col. 152/C3
Tunliu, China 72/C3
Tunnels of Vinh Moc, Viet. 78/D2
Tunnsjøen (lake), Nor. 37/H5
Tuntutuliak, Ak, US 134/F3
Tunungayualuk (isl.), Nf, Can. 123/K3
Tunuyán, Arg. 158/C2
Tunuyán (riv.), Arg. 158/C2
Tuolumne (riv.), Ca, US 128/B3
Tuoniang (riv.), China 83/J3
Tupã, Braz. 155/B2
Tupaciguara, Braz. 155/B1

Tupai (isl.), FrPol. 117/K6
Tupambaé, Uru. 159/G2
Tuparro (riv.), Col. 152/D3
Tupelo, Ms, US 133/F3
Tupi Paulista, Braz. 155/B2
Tupiza, Bol. 150/E8
Tupungato, Arg. 158/C2
Tupungato (peak), Arg. 158/P8
Tura, India 85/H3
Tura (riv.), Rus. 65/G3
Tura, Rus. 65/L3
Turaiçu (riv.), Braz. 154/A1
Turan Lowland (plain), Uzb. 64/G5
Turangi, NZ 117/T10
Turbaco, Col. 152/C2
Turbat, Pak. 89/H3
Turbenthal, Swi. 57/E3
Turbo, Col. 152/B2
Turbotville, Pa, US 138/B1
Turčiansky Svätý Martin, Slvk. 62/A2
Turckheim, Fr. 56/D1
Turda, Rom. 49/F2
Tureia (isl.), FrPol. 117/M7
Turek, Pol. 41/K2
Turgeon (riv.), Qu, Can. 130/E1
Türgovishte, Bul. 49/H4
Turgutlu, Turk. 90/A2
Turhal, Turk. 90/D1
Turia (riv.), Sp. 45/E3
Turiaçu, Braz. 151/J4
Turkana (Rudolf) (lake), Kenya 93/F4
Türkeli, Turk. 62/E4
Türkeve, Hun. 48/E2
Turkey (ctry.) 90/C2
Turkey (riv.), Ia, US 129/K2
Türkheim, Ger. 57/G1
Türkistan, Kaz. 87/E4
Turkmenbashi (Krasnovodsk), Trkm. 63/K5
Turkmenistan (ctry.) 87/C5
Türkoğlu, Turk. 90/D2
Turks and Caicos (isls.), Haiti 141/G3
Turks and Caicos (isls.), UK 141/G3
Turks Island Passage (chan.), UK 145/J1
Turku (int'l arpt.), Fin. 39/K1
Turku Ja Pori (prov.), Fin. 37/G2
Turkwel (riv.), Kenya 104/B2
Turlock, Ca, US 128/B3
Turmalina, Braz. 154/B5
Turneffe (isls.), Belz. 140/D4
Turner (mt.), Austl. 112/C2
Turnersville, NJ, US 138/C4
Turnhouse (int'l arpt.), Sc, UK 36/D5
Turnhout, Belg. 50/B6
Turnor Lake, Sk, Can. 126/F1
Turnov, Czh. 41/H3
Turnu Măgurele, Rom. 49/G4
Tuross Head, Austl. 115/D3
Tuross Head, Austl. 115/D3
Turpan, China 70/E3
Turpan (depr.), China 70/E3
Turquino (peak), Cuba 145/G2
Turriaco, It. 59/G1
Turriff, Sc, UK 36/D1
Turt, Mong. 70/F1
Turtle (isls.), SLeo. 102/B5
Turtleford, Sk, Can. 126/F2
Turugart (pass), China 87/G4
Turukhansk, Rus. 64/J3
Tuscaloosa, Al, US 133/G3
Tuscano (arch.), It. 46/B1
Tuscarora, Nv, US 126/D5
Tuscarora (mtn.), Pa, US 138/A3
Tuscarora Ind. Res., US 131/S9
Tuskegee, Al, US 133/G3
Tustin, Ca, US 136/G8
Tuszyn, Pol. 41/K3
Tutak, Turk. 90/E2
Tutayev, Rus. 60/H4
Tuticorin, India 82/C6
Tutin, Serb. 47/G1
Tutóia, Braz. 154/B1
Tutong, Bru. 80/D3
Tutrakan, Bul. 49/H3
Tuttle Creek (lake), Ks, US 129/H3
Tuttlingen, Ger. 57/E2
Tutuila (isl.), ASam. 117/H6
Tutupaca (vol.), Peru 156/D5
Tutütalak (mtn.), Ak, US 134/F2
Tutzing, Ger. 57/H2
Tuul (riv.), Mong. 70/G2
Tuusula, Fin. 39/L1
Tuvalu (ctry.) 116/G5
Tuwayq, Jabal (mts.), SAr. 88/E3
Tuxpan, Mex. 142/E5
Tuxpan, Mex. 142/D4
Tuxpan de Rodríguez Cano, Mex. 144/B1
Tuxtla Gutiérrez, Mex. 144/C2
Túy, Sp. 44/A1
Tuy Hoa, Viet. 78/E3

Tuyen Quang, Viet. 78/D1
Tuymazy, Rus. 61/M5
Tuyserkän, Iran 88/E2
Tüz Khurmätū, Iraq 90/F3
Tuz (lake), Turk. 90/C2
Tuzigoot Nat'l Mon., Az, US 128/D4
Tuzla, Bosn. 48/D3
Tuzla, Turk. 91/D1
Tuzluca, Turk. 90/E1
Tuzlukçu, Turk. 90/B2
Tvååker, Swe. 38/C2
Tvedestrand, Nor. 38/C2
Tver, Rus. 60/G4
Tver' (riv.), Rus. 60/G4
Tverskaya Oblast, Rus. 39/P3
Tvertsa (riv.), Rus. 60/G4
Tvŭrditsa, Bul. 47/J1
Twardogóra, Pol. 41/J3
Tweed (riv.), Sc, UK 36/C5
Tweed Heads, Austl. 114/D5
Tweedsmuir, Sc, UK 31/R8
Twello, Neth. 50/D4
Twente (pol. reg.), Neth. 50/D4
Twente (canal), Neth. 50/D4
Twin Buttes (res.), Tx, US 129/G5
Twin Hills, Ak, US 134/F4
Twin Lakes, Wi, US 135/P14
Twin Rivers, NJ, US 138/D3
Twiste (riv.), Ger. 51/G6
Twistringen, Ger. 51/F3
Twizel, NZ 117/S11
Two Hills, Ab, Can. 126/F2
Two Rivers, Wi, US 127/M4
Twofold (bay), Austl. 115/D3
Twyford, Eng, UK 33/F4
Twymyn (riv.), Wal, UK 32/C1
Tyatya (vol.), Rus. 76/E1
Tychy, Pol. 41/K3
Tyendinaga, On, Can. 130/E2
Tyger (riv.), SC, US 133/H3
Tyldesley, Eng, UK 35/F4
Tylersville, Pa, US 138/A2
Tŷn, Czh. 41/H4
Tyne (riv.), Sc, UK 36/D5
Tyne and Wear (co.), Eng, UK 35/G2
Tynemouth, Eng, UK 35/G1
Tynset, Nor. 37/D3
Tyonek, Ak, US 134/H3
Tyrifjorden (lake), Nor. 38/C1
Tyringe, Swe. 38/E3
Tyrnyauz, Rus. 63/G4
Tyrrell (lake), Austl. 115/B2
Tyrrhenian (sea), It. 27/F4
Tysnes, Nor. 38/A1
Tysnesøy (isl.), Nor. 38/A2
Tysons Corner, Va, US 138/A6
Tysse, Nor. 38/A1
Tystberga, Swe. 38/G2
Tyub-Karagan (pt.), Kaz. 63/J3
Tyuleniy (isl.), Rus. 63/H3
Tyumen (int'l arpt.), Rus. 61/G4
Tyumen', Rus. 61/G4
Tyumenskaya Oblast, Rus. 87/F1
Tyva, Resp., Rus. 64/K4
Tywi (riv.), Wal, UK 32/B3
Tzaneen, SAfr. 105/F5
Tzucacab, Mex. 144/D1

U

U.C.-Irvine, Ca, US 136/D8
U.K. Sovereign Base Area (gov.), Cyp. 91/C2
U.S. Naval Weapons Station, Ca, US 136/E8
U.S.S. Arizona Nat'l Mem., Hi, US 124/W13
Uad Assag (riv.), WSah. 98/B4
Uad Atui (riv.), WSah. 98/B5
Uad el Jat (riv.), WSah. 98/B4
Uad Tenuaiur (riv.), WSah. 98/A5
Uamh Bheag (peak), Sc, UK 36/B4
Uatumã (riv.), Braz. 150/G4
Uaupés (riv.), Braz. 150/E3
Uaxactún (ruin), Guat. 144/D2
Ub, Serb. 48/D3
Ubá, Braz. 155/D2
Ubach-Palenberg, Ger. 53/E2
Ubagan (riv.), Kaz. 61/G4
Ubaira, Braz. 154/C4
Ubaitaba, Braz. 154/C4
Ubajara, Braz. 154/B1
Ubajara, PN de, Braz. 154/B1
Ubangi (riv.), D.R. Congo 93/D4
Ubatã, Braz. 154/C4
Ubatuba, Braz. 211/H8
Ubay, Phil. 79/D5
Ubaye (riv.), Fr. 43/G4
Ubbergen, Neth. 50/C5
Ube, Japan 74/B4
Ubeda, Sp. 44/D3
Uberaba (lake), Braz. 150/G7
Uberaba, Braz. 155/C1
Uberherrn, Ger. 53/F5
Uberlândia, Braz. 155/B1
Überlingen, Ger. 57/F2
Überlingersee (lake), Ger. 57/E2
Ubia (peak), Indo. 81/J4
Ubinas, Peru 156/D5
Ubombo, SAfr. 107/F2
Ubon Ratchathani, Thai. 78/D3
Ubrique, Sp. 44/C4
Ubundu, D.R. Congo 97/L8
Ucayali (dept.), Peru 156/C3
Ucayali (riv.), Peru 147/B3
Uccle, Belg. 53/D2
Ucha (riv.), Rus. 61/W9
Uchaly, Rus. 61/N5
Uchāna, India 86/D5
Uchinskoye (res.), Rus. 61/W9
Uchiza, Peru 156/B2
Uchte, Ger. 51/F2
Uchte (riv.), Ger. 40/F2
Uchumarca, Peru 156/B2
Uchumayo, Peru 156/D5
Uchur (riv.), Rus. 65/P4
Ucker (riv.), Ger. 38/E5
Uckermark (reg.), Ger. 41/G2
Uckfield, Eng, UK 33/G5
Ucluelet, BC, Can. 126/B3
Udagamandalam, India 82/C5
Udaipur, India 89/K4
Udaipura, India 84/B4
Uddevalla, Swe. 38/D2
Uddingston, Sc, UK 36/B5
Uddjaure (lake), Swe. 37/F2
Udem, Ger. 50/C5
Uden, Neth. 50/C5
Udenhout, Neth. 50/C5
Udgir, India 82/C4
Udhampur, India 86/C3
Udine (prov.), It. 59/G1
Udine, It. 43/K3
Udipi, India 82/B5
Udmurtia, Resp., Rus. 61/M4
Udon Thani, Thai. 78/C2
Ueckermünde, Ger. 38/F5
Ueda, Japan 75/P2
Uele (riv.), D.R. Congo 93/E4
Uelsen, Ger. 50/D3
Uelzen, Ger. 51/H3
Ueno, Japan 77/J1
Ueno, Japan 77/K6
Uenohara, Japan 75/F3
Uetendorf, Swi. 56/D4
Uetersen, Ger. 51/G1
Uetze, Ger. 51/H4
Ufa (riv.), Rus. 61/M5
Ufa, Rus. 61/M5
Uffenheim, Ger. 54/D3
Uffing, Ger. 57/H2
Ugalla (riv.), Tanz. 104/A4
Ugalla River Game Rsv., Tanz. 104/A4
Ugento, It. 47/F3
Ugie (riv.), Sc, UK 36/E1
Ugine, Fr. 56/C6
Uglich, Rus. 60/H4
Ugod, Hun. 48/C2
Ugra (riv.), Rus. 60/G5
Ugŭrchin, Bul. 47/J1
Uherské Hradiště, Czh. 41/J4
Uhingen, Ger. 54/C5
Uhlava (riv.), Czh. 41/G4
Uhlavka (riv.), Czh. 55/J3
Uibai, Braz. 154/B3
Uíge, Ang. 105/C2
Uíge, Ang. 105/C2
Ŭijŏngbu, SKor. 73/C2
Ŭiju, NKor. 73/C2
Uilkraal (riv.), SAfr. 106/L11
Uilpata (peak), Rus. 63/G4
Uinta (mts.), Ut, US 128/E2
Uintah, Ut, US 137/K11
Uiraúna, Braz. 154/C2
Ŭiryŏng, SKor. 73/C5
Ŭisŏng, SKor. 73/D4
Uitenhage, SAfr. 106/D4
Uitgeest, Neth. 50/B4
Uithoorn, Neth. 50/B4
Uithuizen, Neth. 50/D2
Ujae (isl.), Mrsh. 116/G4
Ujelang (isl.), Mrsh. 116/F4
Újfehértó, Hun. 41/L5
Ujhāni, India 84/B1
Uji, Japan 74/D3
Uji, Japan 77/J6
Ujjain, India 89/L4
Ujitawara, Japan 77/J6
Ujung Pandang, Indo. 81/E5
Ukara (isl.), Tanz. 104/B3
Ukerewe (isl.), Tanz. 104/B3
Ukhta, Rus. 61/M3
Ukiah, Ca, US 128/B3
Uklāna, India 86/D5
Ukmergė, Lith. 39/L4
Ukraine (ctry.) 62/D2
Ulaanbaatar (cap.), Mong. 70/J2
Ulaangom, Mong. 70/D2
Ulaanjirem, Mong. 70/J2
Ulanhot, China 71/M2

Ulchin, SKor. 74/A2
Ulcumayo, Peru 156/C3
Ulefoss, Nor. 38/C2
Ulhāsnagar, India 89/K5
Uliastay, Mong. 70/G2
Ulindi (riv.), D.R. Congo 97/L8
Ulla (riv.), Sp. 44/A1
Ulla Ulla, Bol. 156/D4
Ulla Ulla, Reserva Nacional, Bol. 156/D4
Ulladulla, Austl. 115/D2
Ullapool, Sc, UK 31/R8
Ullared, Swe. 38/E3
Ulldecona, Sp. 45/F2
Ullensvang, Nor. 38/B1
Üllő, Hun. 49/R10
Ullsfjorden (estu.), Nor. 37/F1
Ullswater (lake), Eng, UK 35/F2
Ulm, Ger. 54/C6
Ulmarra, Austl. 115/E1
Ulricehamn, Swe. 38/E3
Ulrichen, Swi. 57/E5
Ulrichsberg, Aus. 55/G5
Ulrichstein, Ger. 54/C1
Ulrum, Neth. 50/D2
Ulsan, SKor. 74/A3
Ulstein, Nor. 37/C3
Ulster (reg.), Ire. 34/A3
Ulster American Folk Park, NI, UK 34/A2
Ulúa (riv.), Hon. 140/D4
Ulua (riv.), Hon. 144/E3
Uluçınar, Turk. 91/D1
Uludağ (peak), Turk. 90/B1
Uluduruk (peak), Turk. 90/D2
Uluguru (mts.), Tanz. 104/C4
Ulukışla, Turk. 90/C2
Ulundi, SAfr. 107/E3
Uluru NP, Austl. 113/F3
Ulverston, Eng, UK 35/E3
Ulverstone, Austl. 115/C4
Ulvik, Nor. 38/B1
Ulvila, Fin. 39/J1
Ulytaü (mts.), Kaz. 87/E3
Ulytau (peak), Kaz. 87/E3
Umag, Cro. 48/A3
Uman, Ukr. 62/D2
Umán, Mex. 144/D1
Umarizal, Braz. 154/C2
Umarkot, India 82/D4
Umāsi La (pass), India 86/D3
Umbertide, It. 43/K5
Umbogintwini, SAfr. 107/E3
Umboi (isl.), PNG 116/E5
Umbrail (peak), Swi. 57/G4
Umbrailpass (pass), Swi. 57/G4
Umeå, Swe. 37/G3
Umeälven (riv.), Swe. 37/F2
Umfolozi (riv.), SAfr. 107/E3
Umgeni (riv.), SAfr. 107/E3
Umhausen, Aus. 57/G3
Umiat (mtn.), Ak, US 134/H2
Umkirch, Ger. 56/D1
Umkomaas, SAfr. 107/E3
Umm Durmān, Sudan 98/D4
Umm el Fahm, Isr. 91/G6
Umm Hibal (well), Egypt 101/C4
Ummendorf, Ger. 57/F1
Umnak (isl.), Ak, US 134/E5
Umnak Pass (str.), Ak, US 134/E5
Umpqua (riv.), Or, US 124/B3
Umpulo, Ang. 105/C3
Ümraniye, Turk. 90/B2
Ŭmsŏng, SKor. 73/D4
Umtata, SAfr. 106/E3
Umuahia, Nga. 103/G5
Umuarama, Braz. 157/H2
Umurbey, Turk. 47/K2
Una, Braz. 154/D3
Una (riv.), Bosn.,Cro. 43/L4
Unaí, Braz. 155/B1
Unalakleet, Ak, US 134/F3
Unalaska, Ak, US 134/E5
Unalaska (isl.), Ak, US 134/E5
Uncastillo, Sp. 45/E1
Unchahra, India 84/C3
Uncompahgre (plat.), Co, US 128/E3
Unden (lake), Swe. 38/E2
Underberg, SAfr. 106/E3
Underbool, Austl. 115/B2

Underwood, ND, US 127/H4
Unecha, Rus. 62/E1
Unga (isl.), Ak, US 134/F4
Ungama (bay), Kenya 105/H1
Ungarie, Austl. 115/C2
Ungava (pen.), Qu, Can. 123/J2
Ungava (bay), Qu, Can. 123/K3
Ungheni, Mol. 49/H2
Unhošt, Czh. 55/H2
União, Braz. 154/B2
União da Vitória, Braz. 155/B3
União dos Palmares, Braz. 154/C3
Unimak (isl.), Ak, US 134/E4
Unimak Pass (str.), Ak, US 134/E5
Unini (riv.), Braz. 150/F4
Union, Or, US 126/D4
Union, Mo, US 129/K3
Union, SC, US 133/H3
Union (lake), NJ, US 138/C4
Union, Arg. 158/D2
Union, NJ, US 139/H9
Union (canal), Sc, UK 36/C5
Union Beach, NJ, US 139/J10
Union Bridge, Md, US 138/A4
Union City, Tn, US 130/B4
Union City, Ca, US 135/K11
Union City, NJ, US 139/J8
Unión de Reyes, Cuba 145/F1
Unión de Tula, Mex. 142/D5
Unión Hidalgo, Mex. 144/C2
Union Mills, Md, US 138/A4
Union Springs, Al, US 133/G3
Uniondale, SAfr. 106/C4
Uniondale, NY, US 139/L9
Uniontown, Pa, US 130/E4
Uniontown, Md, US 138/A4
Unionville, Mo, US 127/K5
United Arab Emirates (ctry.) 88/F4
United Kingdom (ctry.) 31/P9
United Nations, NY, US 139/K9
United Nations Mem. Cemetery, SKor. 74/A3
United States (range), Nun., Can. 123/T6
United States (ctry.) 124
United States Coast Guard Receiving Center, NJ, US 138/D6
United States Department of Energy, Md, US 138/A5
United States Naval Academy, Md, US 138/B6
United States Naval Reservation Mil. Res., PR 141/H2
Unity, Sk, Can. 126/F2
University City, Mo, US 137/G8
University Place, Wa, US 135/B3
Unja, India 89/K4
Unkel, Ger. 53/G2
Unna, Ger. 51/E5
Unnao, India 84/C2
Ünsan-ŭp, NKor. 73/D3
Unst (isl.), Sc, UK 31/W13
Unter Pleichfeld, Ger. 54/D3
Unterägeri, Swi. 57/E3
Unterargen, Fr. 57/F2
Untergriesbach, Ger. 55/G5
Unterhaching, Ger. 57/H1
Unteriberg, Swi. 57/E3
Unterkulm, Swi. 56/E3
Unterlüss, Ger. 51/H3
Unterschleissheim, Ger. 55/E6
Untersee (lake), Swi. 57/E2
Unterseen, Swi. 56/D4
Untersiggenthal, Swi. 57/G2
Unterthingau, Ger. 57/G2
Untervaz, Swi. 57/F4
Unterweissenbach, Aus. 55/H6
Ünye, Turk. 90/D1
Unzen-Amakusa NP, Japan 74/A4
Unzen-dake (peak), Japan 74/A4
Unzha (riv.), Rus. 64/F4
Upala, CR 144/E4
Upanema, Braz. 154/C2
Upata, Ven. 153/F2
Upemba, Lac (lake), D.R. Congo 105/E2
Upemba, PN de l', D.R. Congo 105/E2
Uphall, Sc, UK 36/C5
Upington, SAfr. 106/C3
Upland, Pa, US 138/C4
Upleta, India 89/K4
Upolu (pt.), Hi, US 124/U10
Upolu (isl.), Sam. 117/H6
Upper (lake), Ca, US 128/B2
Upper (bay), NY, US 138/D2
Upper (pen.), Mi, US 125/J2

Upper Arrow (lake), BC, Can. 126/D3
Upper Darby, Pa, US 138/C4
Upper Demerara-Berbice (pol. reg.), Guy. 153/G3
Upper East (pol. reg.), Gha. 103/E4
Upper Engadine (valley), Swi. 57/F5
Upper Falls, Md, US 138/B5
Upper Ganges (canal), India 84/A1
Upper Hutt, NZ 117/T11
Upper Iowa (riv.), Ia, US 129/J2
Upper Klamath (lake), Or, US 126/C5
Upper Lough Erne (lake), NI, UK 31/Q9
Upper Missouri River Breaks Nat'l Mon., Mt, US 126/F4
Upper Peoria (lake), Il, US 127/L5
Upper Red (lake), Mn, US 127/K3
Upper Rouge (riv.), Mi, US 135/F7
Upper Saddle River, NJ, US 139/J7
Upper Takutu-Upper Essequibo (pol. reg.), Guy. 153/G4
Upper Thames (valley), Eng, UK 33/E3
Upper Trajan's Wall, Mol. 62/D3
Upper West (pol. reg.), Gha. 103/E4
Upperlands, NI, UK 34/B2
Upplands-Väsby, Swe. 38/G2
Uppsala, Swe. 38/G2
Uppsala (co.), Swe. 37/F3
Upright (cape), Ak, US 134/D3
Upstart (cape), Austl. 114/B2
Upton, Wy, US 127/G4
Urabá (gulf), Col. 145/G4
Uracoa, Ven. 153/F2
Urad Qianqi, China 72/B2
Uraga (chan.), Japan 77/D3
Urahoro, Japan 76/C2
Uraim (riv.), Braz. 154/A1
Urakawa, Japan 76/C2
Ural (mts.), Rus. 27/L2
Uralla, Austl. 115/D1
Urana, Austl. 115/C2
Urandi, Braz. 154/B4
Uraricoera (riv.), Braz. 153/F2
Urasoe, Japan 75/J7
Urawa, Japan 75/F3
Uray, Rus. 64/G3
Urayasu, Japan 77/D2
Urbach, Ger. 54/C5
Urbana, Md, US 138/A5
Urbania, It. 59/F5
Urbano Santos, Braz. 154/B1
Urbenville, Austl. 114/D5
Urbino, It. 59/F5
Urcos, Peru 156/D4
Urda, Rus. 44/D3
Urdinarrain, Arg. 159/J10
Urdorf, Swi. 57/E3
Ure (riv.), Eng, UK 35/G3
Ures, Mex. 142/C2
Ureshino, Japan 77/K6
Urewera NP, NZ 117/T10
Urfa (prov.), Turk. 90/D2
Urfa, Turk. 90/D2
Urft (riv.), Ger. 51/G6
Urft (lake), Ger. 53/F2
Urganch, Uzb. 87/D4
Urgnano, It. 58/C1
Urho Kekkonen NP, Fin. 37/H1
Uri, India 86/C2
Uri-Rotstock (peak), Swi. 57/E4
Uriangato, Mex. 143/E4
Uribante (riv.), Ven. 152/D3
Uribia, Col. 152/C2
Urie (riv.), Sc, UK 36/D2
Uriménil, Fr. 56/C1
Urique (riv.), Mex. 142/D3
Urjala, Fin. 39/K1
Urk, Neth. 50/C3
Urla, Turk. 90/A2
Urlaţi, Rom. 49/H3
Urmar, India 86/C4
Urmia (lake), Iran 90/F2
Urmitz, Ger. 53/G3
Urmston, Eng, UK 35/F5
Urnäsch, Swi. 57/F3
Urnersee (lake), Swi. 57/E4
Uroševac, Serb. 47/G1
Urr Water (riv.), Sc, UK 34/E1
Ursensollen, Ger. 55/E4
Ursulo Galván, Mex. 143/N7
Uruaçu, Braz. 151/J6
Uruapan, Mex. 142/E5
Urubamba, Peru 150/D6
Urubamba, Peru 150/G4
Urubu (riv.), Braz. 150/G4
Uruburetama, Braz. 154/C1
Uruçuca, Braz. 154/A2
Uruçuí, Braz. 154/A2
Uruçuí Preto (riv.), Braz. 154/A3
Uruçuí, Serra do (mts.), Braz. 151/K5

Urucuia (riv.), Braz. 151/J7
Uruguaiana, Braz. 157/E2
Uruguay (ctry.) 157/E3
Uruguay (riv.), SAm. 157/E2
Urumaco, Ven. 152/D2
Urunga, Austl. 115/E1
Uruoca, Braz. 154/B1
Urup (isl.), Rus. 67/Q5
Ururi, Braz. 46/D2
Urussanga, Braz. 155/B4
Uryupinsk, Rus. 63/G2
Urziceni, Rom. 49/H3
Us, Fr. 30/H4
Usa, Japan 74/B4
Usa (riv.), Rus. 64/F3
Uşak, Turk. 90/B2
Uşak (prov.), Turk. 90/B2
Usakos, Namb. 105/C5
Usborne (mt.), UK 159/F6
Uscio, It. 58/C4
Usedom (isl.), Ger. 38/E4
Useldange, Lux. 53/E4
Useless Loop, Austl. 112/B3
Ushibori, Japan 77/F2
Ushibuka, Japan 74/B4
Ushiku, Japan 77/E2
Ushtobe, Kaz. 87/G3
Usibelli, Ak, US 134/J3
Usicayos, Peru 156/D4
Usilampatti, India 82/C6
Usingen, Ger. 54/B2
Üsküp, Turk. 49/H5
Uslar, Ger. 51/G5
Usman', Rus. 62/F1
Uspallata, Arg. 158/C2
Uspallata, Paso de (pass), Chile 158/N8
Usquil, Peru 156/B2
Ussel, Fr. 42/E4
Ussel (riv.), Ger. 54/D5
Usses (riv.), Fr. 56/C5
Ussuri (riv.), China,Rus. 65/P5
Ussuriysk, Rus. 71/P3
Ussy-sur-Marne, Fr. 30/M5
Ust'-Ilimsk, Rus. 65/L4
Ust'-Kamchatsk, Rus. 65/S4
Ust'-Kut, Rus. 65/L4
Ust'-Ordynskiy Buryatskiy Aut. Okrug, Rus. 65/Q7
Uštěk, Czh. 55/H1
Uster, Swi. 57/E3
Ústí nad Labem, Czh. 43/L1
Ustica (isl.), It. 46/C3
Ustica, It. 46/C3
Ustka, Pol. 38/G4
Ustrzyki Dolne, Pol. 41/M4
Ust'ya (riv.), Rus. 61/K3
Ustyurt (plat.), Kaz. 67/D5
Usu, China 70/D3
Usuda, Japan 77/A1
Usuki, Japan 74/B4
Usulután, ESal. 144/D3
Usumacinta (riv.), Mex. 140/C4
Utah (state), US 128/E3
Utah (lake), Ut, US 128/D2
Utangan (riv.), India 84/A2
Utah, Ut, US 137/K13
Utena, Lith. 39/L4
Utersky (riv.), Czh. 55/G3
Utiariti, Braz. 154/B4
Uthai Thani, Thai. 78/C4
Utica, NY, US 130/F3
Utica, Mi, US 135/F6
Utiel, Sp. 44/E3
Utik (lake), Mb, Can. 127/J2
Utila (isl.), Hon. 144/E2
Utinga, Braz. 154/B4
Utiroa, Kiri. 116/G5
Utmānzai, Pak. 86/A2
Utopia Abor. Land, Austl. 113/G2
Utraulā, India 84/D2
Utrecht, SAfr. 107/E2
Utrecht, Neth. 50/C4
Utrecht (prov.), Neth. 50/C4
Utrera, Sp. 44/C4
Utsunomiya, Japan 75/F2
Uttar Pradesh (state), India 70/C6
Uttaradit, Thai. 78/C2
Uttaranchal (state), India 84/B1
Uttenweiler, Ger. 57/F1
Uttoxeter, Eng, UK 35/G6
Utuado, PR 141/M8
Utupua (isl.), Sol. 116/F6
Uturoa, FrPol. 117/K6
Utzenstorf, Swi. 56/D3
Uusikaupunki, Fin. 39/J1
Uusimaa (prov.), Fin. 37/H3
Uva (riv.), Col. 150/E3
Uvalde, Tx, US 129/H5
Uvarovo, Rus. 63/G2
Uverito, Ven. 153/E2
Uvira, D.R. Congo 104/A3
Uvongo, SAfr. 107/E3
Uvs (prov.), Mong. 70/G2
Uwajima, Japan 74/C4
Uwimmerah (riv.), Indo. 81/K5
Uxin Qi, China 72/B3
Uxmal (ruin), Mex. 144/D1
Uydzin, Mong. 70/J3
Uyo, Nga. 103/G5
Üyönch, Mong. 70/F2
Uyuni, Bol. 150/E8

Uzbekistan (ctry.) 87/D4
Uzbekistan Nat'l Park, Uzb. 87/E3
Uzein (int'l arpt.), Fr. 42/C5
Uzerche, Fr. 42/D4
Uzès, Fr. 42/F4
Uzhhorod, Ukr. 41/M4
Uzhok (pass), Ukr. 41/M4
Uzice, Serb. 48/D4
Uzlovaya, Rus. 62/F1
Uznach, Swi. 57/E3
Üzümlü, Turk. 90/D2
Uzunköprü, Turk. 47/K2
Uzwil, Swi. 57/F3

V

V.P. Rosales, PN, Chile 158/B4
Vaal (riv.), SAfr. 93/E7
Vaala, Fin. 37/H2
Vaalbos NP, SAfr. 106/D3
Vaaldam (res.), SAfr. 106/D2
Vaals, Neth. 53/F2
Vaalserberg (hill), Neth. 53/E2
Vaasa (prov.), Fin. 37/G3
Vaasa (int'l arpt.), Fin. 37/G3
Vaasa (Vasa), Fin. 37/G3
Vaassen, Neth. 50/C4
Vác, Hun. 48/D2
Vaca (riv.), Ca, US 135/K10
Vaca (mt.), Ca, US 135/K10
Vacaria, Braz. 155/B4
Vacaville, Ca, US 128/B3
Vachon (riv.), Qu, Can. 121/J2
Vada, It. 58/D6
Vado Ligure, It. 58/B4
Vadret (peak), Swi. 57/F4
Vadsø, Nor. 37/J1
Vadstena, Swe. 38/F2
Vaduz (cap.), Lcht. 57/F3
Vaernes (int'l arpt.), Nor. 37/D3
Vaga (riv.), Rus. 60/J3
Vågå, Nor. 37/D3
Vaganski vrh (peak), Cro. 48/B3
Vagay (riv.), Rus. 61/R4
Vaggeryd, Swe. 38/F3
Vagney, Fr. 56/C1
Vagos, Port. 44/A2
Vågsøy, Nor. 37/C3
Vah (riv.), Slvk. 42/D2
Vahitahi (isl.), FrPol. 117/M6
Vaiano, It. 59/E5
Vaiano Cremasco, It. 58/C2
Vaich (lake), Sc, UK 36/B1
Vaihingen an der Enz, Ger. 54/B5
Vaijāpur, India 89/K5
Vailate, It. 58/C2
Vair (riv.), Fr. 56/B1
Vaisali (riv.), India 84/B2
Vaitupu (isl.), Tuv. 116/G5
Vaivre-et-Montoille, Fr. 56/C2
Vakfıkebir, Turk. 62/F4
Vakh (riv.), Rus. 64/J3
Vākhān (mts.), Afg. 89/K1
Vakhsh (riv.), Taj. 89/J1
Vál, Hun. 48/D2
Val-de-Marne (dept.), Fr. 52/B6
Val-d'Or, Qu, Can. 130/E1
Val Lagarina (valley), It. 59/D1
Val Marie, Sk, Can. 126/G3
Val Venosta (valley), It. 57/G4
Val Verda, Ut, US 137/K12
Val Verde, It. 136/B2
Valais (canton), Swi. 56/D5
Valbo, Swe. 38/G1
Valburg, Neth. 50/C5
Valcheta, Arg. 158/D4
Valdahon, Fr. 56/C3
Valdai (hills), Rus. 60/G4
Valdarno (valley), It. 59/E5
Valdecañas, Embalse de (res.), Sp. 44/C3
Valdemarsvik, Swe. 38/G2
Valdemorillo, Sp. 45/M8
Valdense, Uru. 159/K11
Valdepeñas, Sp. 44/D3
Valderrobres, Sp. 45/F2
Valdés (pen.), Arg. 147/C7
Valdeverdeja, Sp. 44/C3
Valdez, Ak, US 134/J3
Valdez, Ecu. 152/B4
Valdivia, Chile 158/B3
Valdobbiadene, It. 59/F1
Valdoie, Fr. 56/C2
Valdosta, Ga, US 133/H4
Valdres (valley), Nor. 37/D3
Vale, Or, US 126/D5
Vale of Glamorgan (co.), Wal, UK 32/C4
Valeggio sul Mincio, It. 59/D2
Valemount, BC, Can. 126/D2
Valença, Braz. 154/C4
Valença, Braz. 211/K7
Valença, Port. 44/A1
Valença do Piauí, Braz. 154/B2

Valence, Fr. 42/D4
Valence, Fr. 42/F4
Valence-sur-Baïse, Fr. 42/D5
Valencia, Ven. 150/E1
Valencia (int'l arpt.), Sp. 45/E3
Valencia, Sp. 45/E3
Valencia (aut. comm.), Sp. 44/E2
Valencia, Ecu. 152/B5
Valencia (isl.), Ire. 30/P11
Valencia de Alcántara, Sp. 44/B3
Valencia de Don Juan, Sp. 44/C1
Valencia, Golfo de (gulf), Sp. 45/F3
Valenciennes, Fr. 52/C3
Valendas, Swi. 57/F4
Vălenii de Munte, Rom. 49/H3
Valente, Braz. 154/C3
Valentigney, Fr. 56/C2
Valentim (range), Braz. 154/B2
Valentine, Tx, US 132/B4
Valentines, Uru. 159/G2
Valenton, Fr. 30/K5
Valera, Ven. 152/D2
Valff, Fr. 56/D1
Valga, Est. 39/M3
Valhalla, NY, US 139/K7
Valinco, Golfe de (gulf), Fr. 46/A2
Valinhos, Braz. 211/F7
Valjevo, Serb. 48/D3
Valkeakoski, Fin. 39/K1
Valkeala, Fin. 39/M1
Valkenburg, Neth. 53/E2
Valkenswaard, Neth. 50/C6
Vall de Uxó, Sp. 45/E3
Valladolid, Sp. 44/C2
Valladolid (int'l arpt.), Sp. 44/C2
Valladolid, Mex. 144/D1
Vallangoujard, Fr. 30/J4
Valle, Ecu. 152/B5
Valle, Nor. 38/D2
Valle d'Aosta (pol. reg.), It. 43/G4
Valle de Bravo, Mex. 143/E5
Valle de Cauca (dept.), Col. 152/B4
Valle de Guanape, Ven. 153/E2
Valle de La Pascua, Ven. 153/E2
Valle de Santiago, Mex. 143/E4
Valle de Zaragoza, Mex. 132/B5
Valle Hermoso, Mex. 143/F3
Valle Lomellina, It. 58/B2
Valle Mosso, It. 58/B1
Vallecitos de Zaragoza, Mex. 143/F3
Vallecrosia, It. 43/G5
Valledupar, Col. 152/C2
Vallée de l'Azaouak (riv.), Mali 103/G2
Vallée du Ferlo (riv.), Sen. 102/B3
Vallée du Mboune (riv.), Sen. 102/B3
Vallée du Saloum (riv.), Sen. 102/B3
Vallée du Serpent (riv.), Mali 102/C3
Vallegrande, Bol. 150/F7
Vallehermoso, Canl.,Sp. 98/A3
Vallejo, Ca, US 128/C3
Vallenar, Chile 157/B2
Vallendar, Ger. 53/G3
Valleroy, Fr. 30/L6
Valletta (cap.), Malta 46/M7
Valley Brook, Ok, US 137/N15
Valley Center, Ca, US 136/C4
Valley City, ND, US 127/J4
Valley Cottage, NY, US 139/K7
Valley East, On, Can. 130/F3
Valley Forge Nat'l Hist. Park, Pa, US 138/C3
Valley of Desolation, SAfr. 106/D4
Valley of the Kings, Egypt 101/C3
Valley Park, Mo, US 137/G8
Valley Spring, Tx, US 129/H5
Valley Stream, NY, US 139/L9
Vallières, Fr. 56/B4
Vallorbe, Swi. 56/C4
Valls, Sp. 45/F2
Valluga (peak), Aus. 57/G3
Valmayor (res.), Sp. 45/M8
Valme, It. 43/G5
Valmeyer, Il, US 137/G9
Valmiera, Lat. 39/L3
Valmondois, Fr. 30/J4
Valognes, Fr. 42/C2
Valois (reg.), Fr. 52/B5
Valona, Bay of (bay), Alb. 47/F2
Valpaços, Port. 44/B2
Valparai, India 82/C5
Valparaiso, Fl, US 133/G4

Valparaiso, In, US 130/C3
Valparaiso, Mex. 142/E4
Valparaíso (pol. reg.), Chile 158/C2
Valparaiso, Chile 158/N8
Valpovo, Cro. 48/D3
Valréas, Fr. 42/F4
Vals, Swi. 57/F4
Vals (riv.), SAfr. 106/D2
Vals-les-Bains, Fr. 42/F4
Valsād, India 89/K4
Valsbaai (bay), SAfr. 105/C7
Valserine (riv.), Fr. 56/B5
Valserrhein (riv.), Swi. 57/F4
Valsura (riv.), It. 57/G4
Valtellina (valley), It. 57/F5
Valtice, Czh. 43/M2
Valuyki, Rus. 62/F2
Valverde, Canl.,Sp. 98/A4
Valverde del Camino, Sp. 44/B4
Valyermo, Ca, US 136/C2
Vâmhus, Swe. 38/F1
Vammala, Fin. 39/K1
Vámos, Gre. 47/J5
Vámosmikola, Hun. 48/D2
Vámospércs, Hun. 48/E2
Van, Turk. 90/E2
Van (lake), Turk. 90/E2
Van Buren, Me, US 131/H2
Van Buren, Ar, US 129/J4
Van Cortlandt Park, NY, US 139/K8
Van Diemen (cape), Austl. 109/C2
Van Diemen (gulf), Austl. 109/C2
Van Harinxmakanaal (riv.), Neth. 50/C2
Van Horn, Tx, US 129/F5
Van Norman Lakes, Ca, US 136/B2
Van Rees (mts.), Indo. 81/J4
Van Wert, Oh, US 130/C3
Vana-Javesi (lake), Fin. 39/K1
Vanadzor, Arm. 63/H4
Vanavaro (isl.), FrPol. 117/L7
Vancouver (mt.), Yk, Can. 134/L3
Vancouver, Wa, US 126/C4
Vancouver, BC, Can. 126/C3
Vancouver (int'l arpt.), BC, Can. 126/C3
Vancouver (isl.), BC, Can. 122/D4
Vancouver (cape), Austl. 112/C5
Vandalia, Mo, US 129/K3
Vanderbijlpark, SAfr. 106/D2
Vanderbilt Museum, NY, US 139/E2
Vanderhoof, BC, Can. 126/C2
Vandoeuvre-lès-Nancy, Fr. 53/F6
Vanegas, Mex. 143/E4
Vänern (lake), Swe. 38/E2
Vänersborg, Swe. 38/E2
Vangaindrano, Madg. 107/H8
Vanier (isl.), Can. 123/R7
Vanikolo (isl.), Sol. 116/F6
Vanil Noir (peak), Swi. 56/D4
Vanimo, PNG 81/H4
Vännäs, Swe. 37/F3
Vanne (riv.), Fr. 42/E2
Vannes, Fr. 42/B3
Vanoise, PN de la, Fr. 43/G4
Vanreenenpas (pass), SAfr. 106/E3
Vanrhynsdorp, SAfr. 106/B3
Vanse, Nor. 38/B2
Vansittart (isl.), Nun., Can. 123/H2
Vantaa, Fin. 39/L1
Vanua Levu (isl.), Fiji 116/G6
Vanuatu (ctry.) 116/F6
Vanwyksvlei, SAfr. 106/C3
Var (riv.), Fr. 43/G5
Vara (riv.), It. 58/C4
Vara, Swe. 38/E2
Varadero, Cuba 145/F1
Varaita (riv.), It. 58/A3
Varallo, It. 58/B1
Varāmīn, Iran 88/F1
Varānāsi, India 84/D3
Varanger-Halvøya (pen.), Nor. 37/J1
Varangerfjorden (estu.), Nor. 37/J1
Varazdin (int'l arpt.), Swe. 38/F3
Varangéville, Fr. 53/F6
Varano (lake), It. 46/D2
Varano Borghi, It. 58/B1
Varaždin, Cro. 43/M3
Varazze, It. 58/B4
Varazze (riv.), Rus. 60/J3
Varde, Den. 38/C4
Várdha, Gre. 47/G3
Várðø, Nor. 37/J1
Varel, Ger. 51/F2

Varenne (riv.), Fr. 42/C2
Varennes, Qu, Can. 131/P6
Varennes-Jarcy, Fr. 30/K5
Varennes-Vauzelles, Fr. 42/E3
Vareš, Bosn. 48/D3
Varese, It. 58/B1
Varese (riv.), It. 57/E6
Varese Ligure, It. 58/C4
Vârgârda, Swe. 38/E2
Vargem Grande, Braz. 154/B1
Vargem Grande do Sul, Braz. 211/G6
Varginha, Braz. 211/H6
Vári, Gre. 47/H4
Varilhes, Fr. 42/D5
Värmeln (lake), Swe. 38/E2
Värmland (co.), Swe. 37/D3
Varna (pol. reg.), Bul. 49/K1
Varna, Bul. 49/K1
Värnamo, Swe. 38/F3
Varois-et-Chaignot, Fr. 56/B3
Varoška Rijeka, Bosn. 48/C3
Varzi, It. 58/C3
Varzo, It. 57/E5
Varzuga (riv.), Rus. 60/H2
Vas (prov.), Hun. 48/C2
Vasa Barris (riv.), Braz. 151/K5
Vásárosnamény, Hun. 41/M4
Vașcău, Rom. 48/F2
Vashka (riv.), Rus. 61/K2
Vashon, Wa, US 135/C3
Vashon (isl.), Wa, US 135/C3
Vasilika, Gre. 47/H2
Vasil'yevskiy (isl.), Rus. 61/S7
Vaslui (prov.), Rom. 49/H2
Vaslui, Rom. 49/H2
Vassar, Mi, US 130/D3
Vassdalsegga (peak), Nor. 38/B2
Vassouras, Braz. 211/K7
Västerås, Swe. 38/G2
Västerbotten (co.), Swe. 38/E1
Västerdalälven (riv.), Swe. 38/E1
Västernorrland (co.), Swe. 37/F3
Västervik, Swe. 38/G3
Västmanland (co.), Swe. 37/F3
Vasto, It. 46/D1
Västra Silen (lake), Swe. 38/E2
Vasvár, Hun. 48/C2
Vasyl'kiv, Ukr. 62/D2
Vaterstetten, Ger. 55/E6
Vatican City (ctry.) 46/C2
Vatnajökull (glacier), Ice. 37/P7
Vatomandry, Madg. 107/J7
Vatra Dornei, Rom. 49/G2
Vättern (lake), Swe. 37/E4
Vaucouleurs (riv.), Fr. 30/H5
Vaud (canton), Swi. 56/C4
Vaudoy-en-Brie, Fr. 30/M5
Vaudreuil-Dorion, Qu, Can. 131/N7
Vaughan, On, Can. 131/Q8
Vaughn, NM, US 129/F4
Vaughn, Wa, US 135/B3
Vaulruz, Swi. 56/C4
Vaulx-en-Velin, Fr. 56/A6
Vaupés (dept.), Col. 152/D4
Vaupés (riv.), Col. 147/B2
Vauréal, Fr. 30/J4
Vauvert, Fr. 42/F5
Vauvillers, Fr. 56/C2
Vaux (riv.), Fr. 40/C4
Vaux-sur-Seine, Fr. 30/H4
Vaux-sur-Sûre, Belg. 53/E4
Vauxhall, Ab, Can. 126/E3
Vava'u Group (isls.), Tonga 117/H6
Vavuniya, SrL. 82/D6
Vawkavysk, Bela. 41/N2
Vaxjo (int'l arpt.), Swe. 38/F3
Växjö, Swe. 38/F3
Vaygach, Rus. 64/F2
Vazante, Braz. 154/A5
Vázea Paulista, Braz. 211/G8
Vazuza (riv.), Rus. 60/G4
Vecchiano, It. 58/D5
Vechigen, Swi. 56/D3
Vecht (riv.), Neth. 50/D4
Vechta, Ger. 51/F3
Vechte (riv.), Ger. 50/D3

Vecsés, Hun. 48/D2
Vedano Olona, It. 58/B1
Veddige, Swe. 38/E3
Vedea (riv.), Rom. 49/G3
Vedelago, It. 59/F1
Vedra, Sp. 44/A1
Veendam, Neth. 50/D2
Veenendaal, Neth. 50/C4
Veere, Neth. 50/A5
Veerse Meer (res.), Neth. 50/A5
Vefsn, Nor. 37/E2
Vega, Tx, US 129/G4
Vega (pt.), Ak, US 134/B6
Vega (riv.), Nor. 37/D2
Vega de Alatorre, Mex. 143/N6
Vegafjorden (estu.), Nor. 37/D2
Veghel, Neth. 50/C5
Veglie, It. 47/G2
Véguéta, Peru 156/B3
Vehkalahti, Fin. 39/M1
Vehne (riv.), Ger. 51/F2
Veigné, Fr. 42/D3
Veinticinco de Mayo, Arg. 158/E2
Veinticinco de Mayo, Arg. 158/D3
Veintiocho de Mayo, Uru. 159/K11
Veintiocho de Noviembre, Braz. 156/B3
Veinte de Noviembre, Arg. 159/B6
Veitsch, Aus. 40/B2
Veitshöchheim, Ger. 54/C3
Vejen, Den. 38/C4
Vejer de la Frontera, Sp. 44/C4
Vejle, Den. 38/C4
Vejle (co.), Den. 38/C4
Vejprty, Czh. 55/G2
Vela, Cabo de la (pt.), Col. 152/C1
Vela Luka, Cro. 46/E1
Velaines, Fr. 53/E6
Vélan (peak), Swi. 56/D6
Velardeña, Mex. 142/E3
Velasco Ibarra, Ecu. 152/B5
Velázquez, Uru. 159/G2
Velbert, Ger. 50/E6
Velburg, Ger. 55/E4
Velddrif, SAfr. 106/L10
Velden am Wörthersee, Aus. 43/L3
Veldhoven, Neth. 50/C6
Velen, Ger. 50/D5
Velestino, Gre. 47/H3
Vélez, Col. 152/C3
Vélez-Blanco, Sp. 44/D4
Vélez-Málaga, Sp. 44/C4
Vélez-Rubio, Sp. 44/D4
Velhas, Rio das (riv.), Braz. 151/K7
Velika Gorica, Cro. 48/C3
Velika Kladuša, Bosn. 43/L4
Velika Plana, Serb. 48/E3
Velikaya (riv.), Rus. 60/F4
Veliki Ustyug, Rus. 61/K3
Velikiye Luki, Rus. 60/G4
Veliko Tŭrnovo, Bul. 47/J1
Velille, Peru 156/D4
Vel'ké Kapušany, Slvk. 41/M4
Vel'ký Krtíš, Slvk. 41/K4
Vel'ký Zvon (peak), Slvk. 48/F1
Vel'sk, Rus. 60/J3
Velletri, It. 46/C2
Vellinge, Swe. 38/E4
Vellmar, Ger. 51/G6
Vellón (res.), Sp. 45/N8
Vellore, India 82/C5
Velón, Sp. 60/J3

Veneta, Laguna (lake), It. 59/F2
Venetie, Ak, US 134/J2
Veneto (pol. reg.), It. 43/J4
Venezia (prov.), It. 59/F1
Venezia, Golfo di (gulf), Eur. 59/F2
Venezia (Venice), It. 59/F2
Venezuela (gulf), Col.,Ven. 153/D2
Venezuela (ctry.) 153/E3
Vengurla, India 89/K5
Veniaminof (vol.), Ak, US 134/G4
Venice, Fl, US 133/H5
Venice, Il, US 137/G8
Venice (Venezia), It. 43/K4
Vénissieux, Fr. 42/F4
Venjan, Swe. 38/E1
Venjansjön (lake), Swe. 38/E1
Venkatagiri, India 82/C5
Venlo, Neth. 50/D6
Vennesla, Nor. 38/B2
Veno (bay), Den. 38/C3
Venosa, It. 46/D2
Venray, Neth. 50/C5
Vent, Iles du (isls.), FrPol. 117/L6
Venta (riv.), Lat. 39/J3
Venta de Baños, Sp. 44/C2
Ventuari (riv.), Ven. 150/E3
Ventersburg, SAfr. 106/D2
Ventersdorp, SAfr. 106/D2
Venterstad, SAfr. 106/D3
Ventimiglia, It. 43/G5
Ventiseri, Fr. 46/A2
Ventnor, Eng, UK 33/E5
Ventnor City, NJ, US 138/D5
Ventspils, Lat. 39/J3
Ventuari (riv.), Ven. 153/E3
Ventura, Ca, US 136/A2
Ventura (co.), Ca, US 136/A2
Ventura (riv.), Ca, US 136/A2
Venturina, It. 43/J5
Venturosa, Braz. 154/C2
Venustiano Carranza, Mex. 140/C4
Venustiano Carranza (res.), Mex. 143/E3
Vép, Hun. 43/M3
Ver-sur-Launette, Fr. 30/L4
Vera, Arg. 157/D2
Vera Cruz, Pan. 152/B2
Veracruz, Mex. 143/N7
Veracruz-Llave (state), Mex. 140/B3
Veranópolis, Braz. 155/B4
Verāval, India 89/K4
Verbania, It. 57/E6
Verberie, Fr. 52/B5
Verbicaro, It. 46/D3
Vercelli, It. 58/B2
Vercelli (prov.), It. 57/E6
Verdal, Nor. 37/D3
Verde (riv.), Par. 157/D1
Verde (cape), Sen. 96/B5
Verde (riv.), Braz. 151/G6
Verde (coast), Sp. 44/B1
Verde (cape), It. 58/A5
Verde (bay), Arg. 158/D5
Verde Grande (riv.), Braz. 151/K7
Verden, Ger. 51/G3
Verdhikoússa, Gre. 47/G3
Verdigris (riv.), Ks, US 129/J3
Verdinho (riv.), Braz. 155/B1
Verdon (riv.), Fr. 42/F5
Verdugo (mts.), Ca, US 136/C2
Verdun, Qu, Can. 131/N7
Vereeniging, SAfr. 106/D2
Verena (peak), It. 57/H6
Vereshchagino, Rus. 61/M4
Veretskiy (pass), Ukr. 41/M4
Verga (cape), Gui. 102/B4
Vergara, Uru. 159/G2
Vergato, It. 59/E4
Vergennes, Vt, US 130/F2
Vergiate, It. 58/B1
Vergina (ruin), Gre. 47/H2
Verigenstadt, Fr. 44/B2
Verín, Sp. 44/B2
Veríssimo, Braz. 155/B1
Verkhnetulomskiy (res.), Rus. 60/F1
Verkhoyansk (range), Rus. 67/M2
Verkhoyansk, Rus. 65/P3
Vermenagna (riv.), It. 58/A4
Vermilion, Ab, Can. 126/E3
Vermilion (range), Mn, US 127/K4
Vermilion Cliffs Nat'l Mon., Az, US 128/D3
Vermillion, SD, US 127/J5
Vermont (state), US 131/F2
Vernal, Ut, US 128/E2
Vernayaz, Swi. 56/D5
Verneuil-sur-Avre, Fr. 42/D2
Verneuil-sur-Seine, Fr. 30/H5
Verneukpan (salt pan), SAfr. 106/C3

Vernier, Swi. 56/C5
Vernon, BC, Can. 126/D3
Vernon, Fr. 42/D2
Vernon Hills, Il, US 135/Q15
Vernon Valley, NJ, US 138/D1
Vernouillet, Fr. 30/H5
Vero Beach, Fl, US 133/H5
Véroia, Gre. 47/H2
Verolanuova, It. 58/D2
Verolavecchia, It. 58/D2
Verolengo, It. 58/A2
Verona (prov.), It. 59/D1
Verona (int'l arpt.), It. 59/D2
Verona, NJ, US 59/D2
Verónica, Arg. 159/K11
Verrès, It.
Verret, La, US 137/Q17
Verrières-le-Buisson, Fr. 30/J8
Versa (riv.), It. 58/B3
Versailles, Ky, US 130/C4
Versailles, Fr. 30/J5
Versigny, Fr. 30/L4
Verskla (riv.), Ukr.,Rus. 64/D4
Versmold, Ger. 51/F4
Versoix, Swi. 56/C5
Vert-le-Grand, Fr. 30/K6
Vert-le-Petit, Fr. 30/K6
Vert-Saint-Denis, Fr. 30/K6
Vertana (peak), It. 57/G4
Verte (peak), Fr. 56/C6
Vertientes, Cuba 145/G1
Vertou, Fr. 42/C3
Vertova, It. 58/C1
Vertus, Fr. 52/D6
Verviers, Belg. 53/E2
Vervins, Fr. 52/C4
Verwoerdburg, SAfr. 106/Q12
Veryan (bay), Eng, UK 32/B6
Verzasca (riv.), Swi. 57/E5
Verzasca (Gerra), Swi. 57/E5
Verzenay, Fr.
Verzuolo, It. 43/G4
Verzy, Fr.
Vescovato, Fr. 46/A1
Vescovato, It. 58/D2
Vesdre (riv.), Belg. 42/F1
Veselí nad Lužnicí, Czh. 55/H4
Veselyy (res.), Rus. 63/G3
Vesgre (riv.), Fr. 52/A6
Vesijärvi (lake), Fin. 39/L1
Vesle (riv.), Fr. 40/C4
Vesoul, Fr. 56/C2
Vespolate, It. 58/B2
Vest-Agder (co.), Nor. 37/C4
Vest-Sjælland (prov.), Den. 38/D4
Vest-Vlaanderen (prov.), Belg. 52/B2
Vestbjerg, Den. 38/C3
Vestby, Nor. 38/D2
Vesterålen (isls.), Nor. 37/E1
Vestfjorden (inlet), Nor. 37/E2
Vestfold (co.), Nor. 37/D4
Vestmannaeyjar, Ice. 37/N7
Vestone, It. 58/D1
Vestvågøy, Nor. 37/E1
Vestvågøya (isl.), Nor. 37/E1
Vesuvio (Vesuvius) (vol.), It. 46/D2
Veszprém (prov.), Hun. 48/C2
Veszprém, Hun. 48/C2
Vészto, Hun.
Vet (riv.), SAfr. 106/D3
Vétheuil, Fr. 30/H4
Vetlanda, Swe. 38/F3
Vetluga (riv.), Rus. 64/E4
Vetralla, It. 46/C1
Vétraz, Fr.
Větřni, Czh. 55/H5
Vettore (peak), It. 43/K5
Veude (riv.), Fr. 42/D3
Veurne, Belg. 52/B1
Vevey, Swi. 56/C5
Vex, Swi. 56/D5
Veyback (riv.), Ger. 53/F2
Veyle (riv.), Fr. 56/B5
Veyrier-du-Lac, Fr. 56/C6
Vézelise, Fr. 56/C1
Vézère (riv.), Fr. 42/D4
Vezirköprü, Turk. 90/C2
Vezza d'Oglio, It. 57/G5
Vezzano Ligure, It. 58/C4
Viacha, Bol. 150/D3
Viadana, It. 58/D3
Viana, Braz. 154/A1
Viana del Bollo, Sp. 44/B1
Viana do Alentejo, Port. 44/A3
Viana do Castelo, Port. 44/A2
Viana do Castelo (dist.), Port. 44/A2
Vianden, Lux. 53/F4
Vianen, Neth. 50/C4
Viangchan (Vientiane) (cap.), Laos 78/C2
Viar (riv.), Sp. 44/C4
Viareggio, It. 58/D5

Viarmes, Fr. 30/K4
Viaur (riv.), Fr. 42/E4
Vibbard, Mo, US 137/E5
Vibo Valentia, It. 46/E3
Viborg, Den. 38/C3
Viborg (co.), Den. 38/C3
Vic, Sp. 45/G2
Vic-en-Bigorre, Fr. 42/D5
Vic-Fezensac, Fr. 42/D5
Vicam, Mex. 142/C3
Vicar, Sp. 44/D4
Vicarello, It. 58/D5
Vicchio, It. 59/E6
Vice, Peru 156/A2
Vicente (pt.), Ca, US 136/F8
Vicente Guerrero, Mex. 142/E4
Vicente Guerrero, Mex. 142/A2
Vicente López, Arg. 159/J11
Vicenza, It. 59/E1
Vicenza (prov.), It. 57/H6
Vichada (riv.), Col. 150/E3
Vichada (dept.), Col. 152/D3
Vichaya, Bol. 156/B2
Vichuga, Rus. 60/J4
Vichy, Fr. 42/E3
Vickham (cape), Austl. 115/B3
Vicksburg, Ms, US 129/K4
Vicksburg Nat'l Mil. Park, Ms, US 129/K4
Vico, Fr. 46/A1
Vico (lake), It. 46/C1
Vico del Gargano, It. 48/B5
Vicopisano, It. 59/D4
Vicosa, Braz. 154/C3
Viçosa, Braz. 155/D2
Viçosa do Ceará, Braz. 154/B1
Vicosoprano, Swi. 57/F5
Vicou Gorge NP, Gre. 47/G3
Vicq, Fr. 30/H5
Victor Harbor, Austl. 113/H5
Victor Rosales, Mex. 142/E4
Victoria, Malay. 80/E2
Victoria (peak), Phil. 81/E2
Victoria, Austl. 115/B2
Victoria (falls), Zim. 105/E4
Victoria, Arg. 157/D3
Victoria (cap.), BC, Can. 126/C3
Victoria (isl.), Austl. 109/C2
Victoria (state), Austl. 109/D4
Victoria, China 83/K3
Victoria (mt.), Myan. 83/F3
Victoria, Rom. 49/G3
Victoria, Hon. 144/E3
Victoria, Chile 158/B3
Victoria (peak), Belz. 144/D2
Victoria, Gren. 153/F1
Victoria (isl.), NW,Nun., Can. 122/E1
Victoria (str.), Nun., Can. 122/F2
Victoria (lake), Ugan. 93/F5
Victoria de las Tunas, Cuba 145/G1
Victoria Land (pol. reg.), Ant. 160/M
Victoria Nile (riv.), Ugan. 97/M7
Victoria West, SAfr. 107/D3
Victorias, Phil. 79/D5
Victoriaville, Qu, Can. 131/G2
Victorica, Arg. 158/D2
Victorville, Ca, US 136/C1
Victory Junction, Ks, US 137/D5
Vicuña Mackenna, Arg. 158/D2
Vidal (cape), SAfr. 107/F3
Vidalia, It.
Vidalia, Ga, US 133/H3
Vidauban, Madg. 107/H7
Videira, Braz. 155/B2
Videle, Rom. 49/G3
Vidhošt (peak), Czh. 55/G4
Vidigueira, Port. 44/B3
Vidin, Bul. 49/F4
Vidisha, India 88/A4
Vidnoye, Rus. 61/W9
Vidor, Tx, US 129/G5
Vidor, It. 59/F1
Vidöstern (lake), Swe. 38/F3
Vidourle (riv.), Fr. 42/E5
Vie (riv.), Fr. 42/D2
Viechtach, Ger. 55/F4
Viedma, Arg. 158/E4
Viedma (lake), Arg. 159/B6
Vieira, Braz.
Viella, Sp. 45/F1
Vielha, Sp.
Vieille-Eglise-en-Yvelines, Fr. 30/H6
Viejo (peak), Peru 156/B3
Viella, Sp.
Vienenburg, Ger. 51/H5
Vienna, WV, US 130/D4
Vienna, Va, US 138/A6
Vienne, Fr. 56/A6
Vienne (riv.), Fr. 42/D3
Vientiane (int'l arpt.), Laos 78/C2
Vientiane (Viangchan) (cap.), Laos 78/C2
Vieques (isl.), PR 141/M8

Viére (riv.), Fr. 53/D6
Vierlingsbeek, Neth. 50/D5
Viernheim, Ger. 54/B3
Vierre (riv.), Belg. 53/E4
Viersen, Ger. 50/D6
Vierzon, Fr. 42/E3
Viesca, Mex. 143/E4
Vieste, It. 46/E2
Viet., Viet. 79/A5
Viet Tri, Viet. 83/J3
Vietnam (ctry.) 78/D2
Vieux-Boucau-les-Bains, Fr. 42/C5
Vieux Carré, La, US 137/P17
Vieux-Charmont, Fr. 56/C2
Vieux-Condé, Fr. 52/C3
Vieux Fort, StL. 141/N9
Vieux-Thann, Fr. 56/C2
Vieze (riv.), Swi. 56/C5
Viga, Phil. 79/D5
Vigan, Phil. 79/D4
Vigarano Mainarda, It. 59/E3
Vigasio, It. 59/D2
Vigevano, It. 58/B2
Viggiù, It. 57/E6
Vigia, Braz. 151/J4
Vigiano Biellese, It. 58/B1
Viglio (peak), It. 46/C2
Vignacourt, Fr. 52/B3
Vignanello, It. 46/C1
Vignemale (peak), Fr. 42/C5
Vigneulles-lès-Hattonchâtel, Fr.
Vigneux-sur-Seine, Fr. 30/K5
Vignola, It. 59/D4
Vignot, Fr. 53/E6
Vigo, Sp. 44/A1
Vigodarzere, It. 59/F2
Vigonovo, It. 59/F2
Vigonza, It. 59/E2
Vigrestad, Nor. 38/A2
Viguzzolo, It. 60/E2
Vihári, Pak. 86/B4
Vihti, Fin. 39/L1
Viitasaari, Fin. 39/L1
Vijayawada, India 82/D4
Vik, Nor. 37/N7
Vik, Nor. 38/B1
Vikersund, Nor. 38/C2
Vikeså, Nor. 38/B2
Vikhren (peak), Bul. 47/H2
Viking, Ab, Can. 126/F2
Vikmanshyttan, Swe. 38/F1
Vilablino, Sp. 44/B1
Vilacañas, Sp. 44/B1
Vila de Sena, Moz. 105/G4
Vila do Bispo, Port. 44/A4
Vila do Conde, Port. 44/A2
Vila do Porto, Azor., Port. 45/T13
Vila Franca de Xira, Port. 45/P10
Vila Franca do Campo, Azor., Port. 45/T13
Vila Nova de Fozcoa, Port. 44/B2
Vila Nova de Gaia, Port. 44/A2
Vila Nova de Milfontes, Port. 44/A4
Vila Pouca de Aguiar, Port. 44/B2
Vila Real, Port. 44/B2
Vila Real (dist.), Port. 44/B2
Vila Velha Argolas, Braz. 155/D2
Vila Velha de Ródão, Port. 44/B3
Vila Verde, Port. 44/A2
Viladecans, Sp. 45/K7
Vilafranca del Penedés, Sp. 45/K7
Vilaine (riv.), Fr. 42/B3
Vilanandro (cape), Madg. 107/H7
Vilanculos, Moz. 105/G5
Vilanova i la Geltrù, Sp. 45/K7
Vilar Formoso, Port. 44/B2
Vilcabamba, Peru 156/B3
Vilcea (prov.), Rom. 49/F3
Vilches, Sp. 44/C3
Vilhelmina, Swe. 37/F2
Vilhena, Braz. 150/E3
Viliya (riv.), Bela. 60/E5
Viljandi, Est. 39/L2
Viljoenskroon, SAfr. 106/D2
Vil'kitsogo (str.), 65/K2
Villa Alemana, Chile 158/N8
Villa Alhué, Chile 158/N9
Villa Ángela, Arg. 158/D2
Villa Atuel, Arg. 158/C2
Villa Bartolomea, It. 59/E2
Villa Bruzual, Ven. 152/D2
Villa Cañas, Arg. 158/D2
Villa Carcina, It. 58/D1
Villa Carlos Paz, Arg. 157/D3
Villa Chañar Ladeado, Arg. 158/D2
Villa Constitución, Arg. 158/D2
Villa Corzo, Mex. 144/C2
Villa Cuauhtemoc, Mex. 143/Q10
Villa d'Almè, It. 58/C1
Villa de Arista, Mex. 143/E4

Villa de Cos, Mex. 142/E4
Villa de Costa Rica, Mex. 142/D3
Villa de La Paz, Mex. 143/E4
Villa de Reyes, Mex. 143/E4
Villa del Carbón, Mex. 143/Q9
Villa del Carmen, Uru. 159/K10
Villa del Río, Sp. 44/C4
Villa di Serio, It. 58/C1
Villa Dolores, Arg. 157/C3
Villa Dolores, Arg. 158/D1
Villa Flores, Mex. 144/C1
Villa Gesell, Arg. 159/F3
Villa Guardia, It. 58/C2
Villa Hidalgo, Mex. 142/D4
Villa Hidalgo, Mex. 142/D2
Villa Huidobro, Arg. 158/D2
Villa Iris, Arg. 158/E3
Villa Isabela, DRep. 145/J2
Villa Jaragua, DRep. 145/J2
Villa Juárez, Mex. 142/D5
Villa Juárez, Mex. 142/D3
Villa La Angostura, Arg. 158/C4
Villa Lázaro Cárdenas, Mex. 143/M6
Villa López, Mex. 142/D3
Villa Mantero, Arg. 159/J10
Villa María, Arg. 157/D3
Villa Minozzo, It. 58/D4
Villa Montes, Bol. 150/F8
Villa Nueva, Guat. 144/E3
Villa Nueva, Nic. 144/E3
Villa Nueva, Arg. 158/C2
Villa Opicina, It. 59/G1
Villa Park, Il, US 135/Q16
Villa Park, Ca, US 136/G8
Villa Regina, Arg. 158/D3
Villa Rica, Peru 156/C3
Villa Rosario, Col. 152/C3
Villa Sandino, Nic. 145/E3
Villa Serrano, Bol. 150/F7
Villa Unión, Bol.
Villa Unión, Mex. 142/D4
Villa Valeria, Arg. 158/D2
Villa Verucchio, It. 59/F5
Villaba, Sp. 44/B1
Villablino, Sp.
Villacañas, Sp. 44/D3
Villacarrillo, Sp. 44/D3
Villada, Sp. 44/C1
Villadiego, Sp. 44/C1
Villadose, It. 59/E2
Villadossola, It. 57/E5
Villafamés, Sp. 45/E2
Villafranca, Sp. 45/P10
Villafranca d'Asti, It. 58/B3
Villafranca de los Barros, Sp. 44/B3
Villafranca del Bierzo, Sp. 44/B1
Villafranca del Cid, Sp. 45/E2
Villafranca di Verona, It. 59/D2
Villafranca in Lunigiana, It. 58/C4
Villagarcía, Sp. 44/A1
Villagrán, Mex. 143/F3
Villaguay, Arg. 157/E3
Villahermosa, Braz. 155/D2
Villahermosa, Mex. 144/C2
Villajoyosa, Sp. 45/E3
Villalba, Sp. 44/B1
Villalcampo, Embalse de (res.), Sp. 44
Villaldama, Mex. 132/C5
Villalón de Campos, Sp. 44/C1
Villalonga, Arg. 158/E3
Villalpando, Sp. 44/C2
Villamartín, Sp. 44/C4
Villandro (peak), It. 57/H4
Villanova, It. 59/F4
Villanova, It. 59/E4
Villanova d'Asti, It. 58/A3
Villanova Mondovi, It. 58/A4
Villanterio, It. 58/C2
Villanueva, Mex. 142/E4
Villanueva, Col. 152/C2
Villanueva de Arosa, Sp. 44/A1
Villanueva de Córdoba, Sp. 44/C3
Villanueva de la Serena, Sp. 44/C3
Villanueva de los Infantes, Sp. 44/D3
Villanueva de Oscos, Sp. 44/B1
Villanueva del Arzobispo, Sp. 44/D3
Villanueva sul Clisi, It. 58/C1
Villány, Hun. 48/D3
Villar del Arzobispo, Sp. 45/E2
Villarcayo, Sp. 44/D1
Villardevós, Sp. 44/B2
Villarreal de los Infantes, Sp. 45/E2
Villarrica, Par. 157/E2
Villarrica, Chile 158/B3
Villarrica (vol.), Chile 158/B3
Villarrica (lake), Chile 158/B3

Villarrica, PN, Chile 158/C3
Villarrobledo, Sp. 44/D3
Villarrubia de los Ojos, Sp. 44/D3
Villars-les-Dombes, Fr. 56/B6
Villars-sur-Glâne, Swi. 56/D4
Villas, NJ, US 138/D5
Villasana de Mena, Sp. 44/D1
Villasanta, It. 58/C1
Villastellone, It. 58/A3
Villaverde del Río, Sp. 44/C4
Villaverla, It. 59/E1
Villavicencio, Col. 152/C3
Villaviciosa, Sp. 44/C1
Villaviciosa de Odón, Sp. 44/N9
Villazón, Bol. 157/C1
Villefranche-de-Rouergue, Fr. 42/E4
Villefranche-sur-Saône, Fr. 42/F4
Villejuif, Fr. 30/K5
Villemur-sur-Tarn, Fr. 42/D5
Villena, Sp. 45/E3
Villeneuve, Swi. 56/C5
Villeneuve-d'Ascq, Fr. 52/C3
Villeneuve-le-Comte, Fr. 30/L5
Villeneuve-le-Roi, Fr. 30/K5
Villeneuve-lès-Avignon, Fr. 42/F5
Villeneuve-Saint-Denis, Fr. 30/L5
Villeneuve-Saint-Georges, Fr. 30/K5
Villeneuve-Saint-Germain, Fr.
Villeneuve-sur-Lot, Fr. 42/D4
Villeneuve-sur-Yonne, Fr. 42/E2
Villeneuve-Tolosane, Fr.
Villennes-sur-Seine, Fr. 30/J5
Villeparisis, Fr. 30/K5
Villepinte, Fr. 30/K5
Villepreux, Fr. 30/J5
Villers-Bretonneux, Fr. 52/B4
Villers-Cotterêts, Fr. 52/C5
Villers-en-Arthies, Fr. 30/H4
Villers-le-Bouillet, Belg. 53/E2
Villers-le-Lac, Fr. 56/C3
Villers-lès-Nancy, Fr. 53/F6
Villers-Saint-Genest, Fr. 30/L4
Villers-Saint-Paul, Fr. 30/K4
Villers-Semeuse, Fr. 53/D4
Villersexel, Fr. 56/C2
Villette, Fr. 30/H5
Villeurbanne, Fr. 56/A6
Villevaudé, Fr. 30/K5
Villiers, SAfr. 106/E2
Villiers-en-Lieu, Fr. 53/E2
Villiers-le-Bel, Fr. 30/K4
Villiers-Saint-Georges, Fr. 52/C6
Villiers-sur-Marne, Fr. 30/L5
Villiers-sur-Morin, Fr. 30/L5
Villiersdorp, SAfr. 106/L10
Villieu-Loyes-Mollon, Fr. 56/B6
Villingen-Schwenningen, Ger. 57/E1
Villmar, Ger. 54/B2
Villongo, It. 58/C1
Villorba, It. 59/F1
Vilnius (int'l arpt.), Lith. 39/L4
Vilnius (cap.), Lith. 39/L4
Vils, Aus. 57/G2
Vils (riv.), Ger. 40/F4
Vilsbiburg, Ger. 55/F6
Vilseck, Ger. 55/F3
Vilshofen, Ger. 55/G5
Vilters, Swi. 57/F3
Vilvoorde, Belg. 53/D2
Vit (riv.), Bul. 47/J1
Vilyuy (riv.), Rus. 67/L3
Vilyuy (range), Rus. 65/M3
Vimercate, It. 58/C1
Vimeu (reg.), Fr. 52/A3
Vimmerby, Swe. 38/F3
Vimodrone, It. 58/C1
Vimperk, Czh. 55/H4
Vina (riv.), Camr. 96/H6
Viña del Mar, Chile 158/N8
Vinalhaven, Me, US
Vinaros, Sp. 45/F2
Vincennes, In, US 130/C4
Vincennes (lake), Fr. 30/K5
Vincennes (bay), Ant. 160/H
Vincent, Ca, US 136/B1
Vincentown, NJ, US 138/D4
Vinces, Ecu. 152/B5
Vincey, Fr. 53/F6
Vinchos, Peru 156/C4
Vinci, It. 59/D5
Vindeby, Den. 38/D4
Vindeln, Swe. 37/F2
Vindhya (range), India 84/A4
Vineland, NJ, US 138/D5
Vineland Station, On, Can. 131/R9
Vineuil, Fr. 42/D3
Vingåker, Swe. 37/G2
Vinh, Viet. 78/D2
Vinh An, Viet. 79/A4
Vinh Long, Viet. 78/D4

Vinh Yen, Viet. 78/D1
Vinhais, Port. 44/B2
Vinhedo, Braz. 211/G8
Vinica, FYROM 47/H2
Vinita, Ok, US 129/J3
Vinju Mare, Rom. 48/F3
Vinkovci, Cro. 48/D3
Vinningen, Ger. 53/G5
Vinnyts'ka Oblasti, Ukr. 62/D2
Vinnytsa, Ukr. 62/D2
Vinon-sur-Verdon, Fr. 42/F5
Vinson Massif (peak), Ant. 160/U
Viola, De, US 138/C5
Viola, NY, US 139/J7
Violet, La, US 137/Q17
Violet Town, Austl. 115/C3
Viosne (riv.), Fr. 52/A5
Virac, Phil. 79/D5
Viracopos (int'l arpt.), Braz. 211/F7
Viranşehir, Turk. 90/D2
Virār, India 89/K5
Virden, Mb, Can. 127/H3
Vire, Fr. 42/C2
Vire (riv.), Fr. 42/C2
Viren (lake), Swe. 38/F2
Vireux-Wallerand, Fr. 53/D3
Virgem da Lapa, Braz. 154/B3
Virgin (riv.), US 128/D3
Virgin (isls.), UK,US 141/M8
Virgin Gorda (isl.), UK 141/M8
Virgin Islands NP, USVI 141/M8
Virginia, SAfr. 106/D3
Virginia (state), US 130/E4
Virginia City, Nv, US 128/C3
Virginia Water, Eng, UK 30/B2
Viriat, Fr. 56/B5
Virieu-le-Grand, Fr. 56/B6
Viroflay, Fr. 30/J5
Viroin (riv.), Belg. 53/D3
Viroqua, Wi, US 129/K2
Virovitica, Cro. 48/C3
Virserum, Swe. 38/F3
Virton, Belg. 53/E4
Virudunagar, India 82/C6
Virunga, D.R. Congo 104/A3
Virunga NP, D.R. Congo 104/A3
Viry-Châtillon, Fr. 30/K6
Vis (isl.), Cro. 48/C4
Visaginas, Lith. 39/M4
Visalia, Ca, US 128/C3
Visandre (riv.), Fr. 30/M5
Visayan (sea), Phil. 81/F1
Visbek, Ger. 51/F3
Visby, Swe. 38/H3
Visconde do Rio Branco, Braz. 155/D2
Viscount Melville (sound), NW,Nun., Can. 123/K7
Visé, Belg. 53/E2
Višegrad, Bosn. 48/D4
Viseu, Port. 44/B2
Viseu (dist.), Port. 44/B2
Viseu de Sus, Rom. 49/G2
Vishākhapatnam, India 82/D4
Vishoek, SAfr. 106/L11
Viskafors, Swe. 38/E3
Vislanda, Swe. 38/F3
Visnagar, India 89/K4
Višnjevac, Cro. 48/D3
Visoko, Bosn. 48/D3
Visp, Swi. 56/D5
Visperterminen, Swi. 56/D5
Visselhövede, Ger. 51/G3
Vissenbjerg, Den. 38/D4
Vissoie, Swi. 56/D5
Vista, Ca, US 136/C4
Vistonís (lake), Gre. 47/J2
Vistula (riv.), Pol. 27/K3
Vit (riv.), Bul. 47/J1
Viterbo, It. 46/C1
Vitez, Bosn. 48/C3
Viti Levu (isl.), Fiji 116/G6
Vitigudino, Sp. 44/B2
Vitim (plat.), Rus. 65/M4
Vitim (riv.), Rus. 67/L4
Vitória, Braz. 155/D2
Vitória da Conquista, Braz. 154/B2
Vitória de Santo Antão, Braz. 154/D2
Vitória do Mearim, Braz. 154/A1
Vitorino Freire, Braz. 154/A2
Vitosha NP, Bul. 47/H1
Vitré, Fr. 42/C2
Vitrey-sur-Mance, Fr. 56/B2
Vitrolles, Fr. 42/F5
Vitry-en-Artois, Fr. 52/B3
Vitry-le-François, Fr. 53/D6
Vitry-sur-Seine, Fr. 30/K5
Vitsyebsk, Bela. 39/P4
Vitsyebskaya Voblasts, Bela. 60/E5
Vittangi, Swe. 37/G2
Vittel, Fr. 56/B1
Vittoria, It. 46/D4
Vittorio Veneto, It. 43/K4

Vivarais, Monts du (mts.), Fr. 42/F4
Viveiro, Sp. 44/B1
Viverone (lake), It. 58/B2
Viverone, It. 58/B2
Vivian, La, US 129/J4
Vivonne, Fr. 42/D3
Vizcaíno, Sierra (mts.), Mex. 142/B3
Vize, Turk. 49/H5
Vizhas (riv.), Rus. 61/K2
Vizianagaram, India 82/D4
Vlaardingen, Neth. 50/B5
Vládeasa (peak), Rom. 49/F2
Vladikavkaz, Rus. 63/H4
Vladimir, Rus. 60/J4
Vladimirskaya Oblast, Rus. 60/J3
Vladivostok, Rus. 71/P3
Vlagtwedde, Neth. 51/E2
Vlăhița, Rom. 49/G2
Vlajna (peak), Serb. 47/G1
Vlasenica, Bosn. 48/D3
Vlašim, Czh. 43/L2
Vlasotince, Serb. 47/H1
Vlieland (isl.), Neth. 40/C2
Vliestroom (chan.), Neth. 50/C2
Vlijmen, Neth. 50/C5
Vlissingen, Neth. 50/A6
Vlotho, Ger. 51/F4
Vltava (riv.), Czh. 41/H4
Vnukovo (int'l arpt.), Rus. 61/W9
Vobarno, It. 58/D1
Vöcklabruck, Aus. 55/G6
Vöcklamarkt, Aus. 55/G6
Vodice, Cro. 48/B3
Vodlozero (lake), Rus. 60/H3
Vodňany, Czh. 55/H4
Vodskov, Den. 38/D3
Voerde, Ger. 50/D5
Voghera, It. 57/E6
Vogogna, It. 57/E5
Vogorno (lake), Swi. 57/E5
Vogtareuth, Ger. 55/F7
Vogtland (reg.), Ger. 40/F3
Vohenstrauss, Ger. 55/F3
Vohilava, Madg. 107/H8
Vohimena (cape), Madg. 107/H9
Vohipeno, Madg. 107/H8
Voi, Kenya 104/C3
Void-Vacon, Fr. 53/E6
Voil (lake), Sc, UK 36/B4
Voinjama, Libr. 102/C4
Voinsles, Fr. 30/M5
Voiron, Fr. 42/F4
Voise (riv.), Fr. 42/D2
Voisey (bay), Nf, Can. 123/K3
Voiteur, Fr. 56/B4
Vojens, Den. 38/C4
Vojose (riv.), Alb. 48/D5
Vojvodina (prov.), Serb. 48/D3
Volano, It. 57/H6
Volary, Czh. 55/G5
Volcán Barú, PN, Pan. 145/C4
Volcán Poás, PN, CR 145/E4
Volcano, Hi, US 124/U11
Volcano (isls.),
Volcans NP, Rwa. 104/A3
Volchiy Nos (cape), Rus. 39/Q1
Volda, Nor. 37/C3
Volendam, Neth. 50/C3
Volga (riv.), Rus. 27/J2
Volga-Baltic Waterway (canal), Rus. 60/H3
Völgelsheim, Fr. 56/D1
Volgodonsk, Rus. 63/G3
Volgograd (int'l arpt.), Rus. 63/H2
Volgograd, Rus. 63/H2
Volgograd (res.), Rus. 63/G2
Volgogradskaya Oblast, Rus. 63/G2
Volkach, Ger. 54/D3
Volkach (riv.), Ger. 54/D3
Volketswil, Swi. 57/E3
Völkermarkt, Aus. 43/L3
Völklingen, Ger. 53/F5
Volkhov, Rus. 60/F4
Volkhov (riv.), Rus. 39/Q2
Volkmarsen, Ger. 51/G6
Volksrust, SAfr. 107/E2
Volodymyr-Volyns'kyy, Ukr. 62/C2
Vologda, Rus. 60/H4
Vologodskaya Oblast, Rus. 60/J3
Vologne (riv.), Fr. 40/D4
Volos (gulf), Gre. 47/H3
Volos, Gre. 47/H3
Volpago del Montello, It. 59/F1
Volpiano, It. 57/H3
Völs, Aus. 57/H3
Vol'sk, Rus. 63/H1
Volta (riv.), Gha. 96/H6
Volta (lake), Gha. 93/B4
Volta (pol. reg.), Gha. 103/F5

Volta Redonda, Braz. 211/J7
Voltana, It. 59/E3
Volterra, It. 59/D6
Voltlage, Ger. 51/E4
Volturino (peak), It. 46/D2
Volturno (riv.), It. 46/D2
Volubilis (ruin), Mor. 100/B2
Vólvi (lake), Gre. 47/H2
Volyně, Czh. 55/G4
Volyns'ka Oblasti, Ukr. 62/C2
Volzhsk, Rus. 61/L5
Volzhskiy, Rus. 63/H2
Von Frank (mtn.), Ak, US 134/H3
Von Ormy, Tx, US 137/T21
Vondrozo, Madg. 107/H8
Vónitsa, Gre. 47/G3
Vonne (riv.), Fr. 42/D3
Voorburg, Neth. 50/B4
Voorne (isl.), Neth. 50/B5
Voorschoten, Neth. 50/B4
Voorst, Neth. 50/D4
Vopnafjördhur, Ice. 37/P6
Vorab (peak), Swi. 57/F4
Vorarlberg (prov.), Aus. 40/E5
Vorbach (riv.), Ger. 54/C4
Vorchdorf, Aus. 55/G6
Vorden, Neth. 50/D4
Vorderrhein (riv.), Swi. 43/H3
Vorderweissenbach, Aus. 55/H5
Vordingborg, Den. 38/D4
Voreppe, Fr. 42/F4
Vorkuta, Rus. 61/P2
Vorkuta (int'l arpt.), Rus. 61/Q2
Vormsi (isl.), Est. 39/K2
Vóroi, Gre. 47/H5
Vorona (riv.), Rus. 63/G1
Voronezh (int'l arpt.), Rus. 62/F2
Voronezh (riv.), Rus. 62/F1
Voronezh, Rus. 62/F1
Voronezhskaya Oblast, Rus. 63/G2
Voron'ya (riv.), Rus. 60/G1
Vorskla (riv.), Ukr. 62/E2
Vorst, Belg. 53/E1
Võrts (lake), Est. 60/E4
Võru, Est. 39/M3
Vorya (riv.), Rus. 61/X8
Vosburg, SAfr. 106/C3
Vösendorf, Aus. 49/N7
Vosges (dept.), Fr. 56/C1
Vosges (mts.), Fr. 40/D5
Voskresensk, Rus. 60/H5
Voss, Nor. 38/B1
Vostok (isl.), Kiri. 117/K6
Vostok (cape), Ant. 160/V
Vostok, Rus., Ant. 160/H
Votice, Czh. 55/H3
Votkinsk, Rus. 61/N3
Votkinsk (res.), Rus. 61/M4
Votorantim, Braz. 155/C2
Votuporanga, Braz. 155/B2
Vouga (riv.), Port. 44/A2
Vouglans (lake), Fr. 56/B5
Vouglans, Barrage de (dam), Fr. 56/B5
Voujeaucourt, Fr. 56/C3
Voula, Gre. 47/N9
Voulangis, Fr. 30/L5
Vouvry, Swi. 56/C5
Voúxa (cape), Gre. 47/H5
Vouziers, Fr. 53/D5
Voy-Vozh, Rus. 61/M3
Voyageurs NP, Mn, US 130/A1
Voyeykov Ice Shelf, Ant. 160/J2
Voytolovka (riv.), Rus. 61/T7
Vozhe (lake), Rus. 60/H3
Voznesens'k, Ukr. 49/K2
Vozrozhdeniya (isl.), Uzb. 87/C4
Vrå, Den. 38/C3
Vraine (riv.), Fr. 56/B1
Vrancea (prov.), Rom. 49/H3
Vrangelya (isl.), Rus. 65/T2
Vranjska Banja, Serb. 47/G1
Vranov nad Teplou, Slvk. 41/L4
Vrapčište, FYROM 47/G2
Vratsa, Bul. 47/H1
Vrbas, Serb. 48/D3
Vrbas (riv.), Bosn. 48/C3
Vrchy (peak), Czh. 55/H4
Vrede, SAfr. 107/E2
Vredefort, SAfr. 106/D2
Vreden, Ger. 50/D4
Vredenburg-Saldanha, SAfr. 106/K10
Vredendal, SAfr. 106/B3
Vresse-sur-Semois, Belg. 53/D4
Vrhnika, Slov. 43/L4
Vries, Neth. 50/D3
Vriezenveen, Neth. 50/D4
Vrigstad, Swe. 38/F3
Vrin (riv.), Fr. 40/B5
Vrindāban, India 84/A2
Vrnjačka Banja, Serb. 48/E4
Vrondádhos, Gre. 47/K3
Vršac, Serb. 48/E3
Vryburg, SAfr. 106/D2
Vryheid, SAfr. 107/E2

Vsetín, Czh. 41/K4
Vsevidof (mt.),
Ak, US 134/E5
Vsevolozhsk, Rus. 61/T6
Vtáčnik (peak), Slvk. 41/K4
Vught, Neth. 50/C5
Vukovar, Cro. 48/D3
Vulcan, Ab, Can. 126/E3
Vulcan, Rom. 49/F3
Vulcano (isl.), It. 46/D3
Vůlchedrům, Bul. 49/F4
Vůlchi Dol, Bul. 49/H4
Vulci (ruin), It. 46/B1
Vung Tau, Viet. 78/D4
Vuohijärvi (lake), Fin. 39/M1
Vuollerim, Swe. 37/G2
Vuoska (lake), Rus. 39/N1
Vuotso, Fin. 60/E1
Vůrbitsa, Bul. 47/K1
Vuria (peak), Kenya 104/C3
Vůrshets, Bul. 49/F4
Vyāra, India 89/K4
Vyatka (riv.), Rus. 64/E4
Vyatskiye Polyany,
Rus. 61/L4
Vyazemskiy, Rus. 71/P2
Vyaz'ma, Rus. 60/G5
Vyborg, Rus. 39/N1
Vyborg (bay), Rus. 39/N1
Vychegda (riv.), Rus. 64/F3
Vygozero (lake), Rus. 60/J5
Vyhorlat (peak), Slvk. 41/M4
Vyksa, Rus. 60/J5
Vym' (riv.), Rus. 61/L3
Vynohradiv, Ukr. 41/M4
Vyrnwy (riv.),
Wal, UK 32/C1
Vyshniy Volochek,
Rus. 60/G4
Vyškov, Czh. 41/J4

W

W du Benin, PN du,
Ben. 103/F4
W du Burkino Faso, PN du,
Burk. 103/F4
W du Niger, PN du,
Ben. 96/F3
W du Niger, PN du,
Niger 103/F3
W. J. van Blommestein
(lake), Sur. 151/G2
Wa, Gha. 103/E4
Waal, Ger. 57/G2
Waal (riv.), Neth. 50/C5
Waalre, Neth. 50/C6
Waalwijk, Neth. 50/C5
Waarschoot, Belg. 52/C1
Wabasca, Ab, Can. 126/E2
Wabasca (riv.),
Ab, Can. 122/E3
Wabash, In, US 130/C3
Wabash (riv.),
Il,In, US 125/J4
Wabē Shebelē Wenz
(riv.), Eth. 93/G4
Wabern, Ger. 51/G6
Wabigoon (lake),
On, Can. 127/K4
Wabowden,
Mb, Can. 127/J2
Wąbu (lake), China 72/D4
Wabu, SKor. 73/G6
Wachenheim an der
Weinstrasse, Ger. 54/B4
Wachi, Japan 77/H5
Wachtebeke, Belg. 52/C1
Wachtendonk, Ger. 50/D6
Wächtersbach,
Ger. 54/C2
Wackernheim, Ger. 54/B3
Wackersdorf, Ger. 55/F4
Waco, Tx, US 129/H5
Waconda (lake),
Ks, US 129/H3
Waconia, Mn, US 127/K4
Wad Medanī,
Sudan 88/B6
Wada, Japan 77/E3
Wadayama, Japan 77/G5
Wadbilliga NP,
Austl. 115/D3
Waddān, Libya 96/J2
Waddell, Az, US 137/R18
Waddell (dam),
Az, US 137/R18
Waddenzee (sound),
Neth. 40/C2
Waddington (mt.),
BC, Can. 126/B3
Waddinxveen, Neth. 50/B4
Waddy (pt.), Austl. 114/D4
Wadena, Sk, Can. 127/H3
Wadena, Mn, US 127/K4
Wädenswil, Swi. 57/E3
Wadern, Ger. 54/A3
Wadersloh, Ger. 51/F5
Wadgassen, Ger. 54/A3
Wādī al Layl,
Tun. 100/M6
Wādī As Sīr, Jor. 91/D4
Wādī Majardah (riv.),
Tun. 46/A4
Wādī Mūsá, Jor. 91/D4
Wading (riv.),
NJ, US 138/D4
Wading River,
NY, US 139/F2
Wadowice, Pol. 41/K4
Wadsworth, Il, US 135/Q15

Waegwan, SKor. 73/E5
Wafangdian, China 73/A3
Wageningen, Neth. 50/C5
Wagenfeld-Hasslingen,
Ger. 51/F3
Wager (bay),
NW, Can. 122/G2
Wagga Wagga,
Austl. 115/C2
Waggaman, La, US 137/P17
Waghäusel, Ger. 54/B4
Wagin, Austl. 112/C5
Waging am See, Ger. 55/F7
Waldron, Mo, US 137/D5
Ger. 55/F7
Wägitaler-see (lake),
Swi. 57/E3
Wagna, Aus. 43/L3
Wagrowiec, Pol. 41/J2
Wagstaff, Ks, US 137/D6
Wāh, Pak. 86/B3
Wah Wah (range),
Ut, US 128/D3
Wahiawa, Hi, US 124/V12
Wahlern, Swi. 56/D4
Wahpeton, ND, US 127/J4
Wahrenholz, Ger. 51/H3
Wai, India 82/B4
Waialee, Hi, US 124/V12
Waialeale, Hi, US 124/V12
Waialua, Hi, US 124/V12
Waianae, Hi, US 124/V12
Waiau (riv.), NZ 117/S11
Waibamiao, China 72/D2
Waiblingen, Ger. 54/C5
Waidhaus, Ger. 55/F3
Waidhofen an der Thaya,
Aus. 43/L2
Waidhofen an der Ybbs,
Aus. 55/H7
Waigeo (isl.), Indo. 81/H3
Waigolshausen,
Ger. 54/D3
Waihou (riv.), NZ 117/T10
Waikane, Hi, US 124/W12
Waikari, NZ 117/S11
Waikato (riv.), NZ 109/H6
Waikerie, Austl. 113/H5
Waikiki, Hi, US 124/W13
Waikoloa Village,
Hi, US 124/U11
Wailuku, Hi, US 124/T10
Waimanalo,
Hi, US 124/W13
Waimanalo Beach,
Hi, US 124/W13
Waimate, NZ 117/S11
Waimea, Hi, US 124/S10
Waimea (falls),
Hi, US 124/V12
Waimes, Belg. 53/F3
Wainfleet,
On, Can. 131/R10
Waingangā (riv.),
India 82/C3
Waini (riv.), Guy. 153/G2
Wainwright,
Ak, US 134/F1
Wainwright,
Ab, Can. 126/F2
Waipahu, Hi, US 124/V13
Waipio, Hi, US 124/U10
Waipio Acres,
Hi, US 124/V13
Waipukurau, NZ 117/T10
Wairau (riv.), NZ 117/S11
Wairoa, NZ 117/T10
Waischenfeld, Ger. 55/E3
Waitaki (riv.), NZ 117/S11
Waitara, NZ 117/S10
Waizenkirchen, Aus. 55/G6
Wajima, Japan 75/E2
Waka (cape), Indo. 81/G4
Wakakusa, Japan 77/D3
Wakasa, Japan 77/H4
Wakasa (bay),
Japan 77/H4
Wakaw, Sk, Can. 127/G2
Wakayama, Japan 74/D3
Wakayama (pref.),
Japan 74/D3
Wake (isl.), Pac., US 116/F3
Wakefield, Eng. UK 35/G4
Wakefield (co.),
Eng. UK 35/G4
Wakefield, Mi, US 130/B2
Wakema, Myan. 83/G4
Waki, Japan 74/D3
Wakkanai, Japan 76/B1
Wakool, Austl. 115/C2
Wakuya, Japan 76/B4
Wakwayowkastic (riv.),
On, Can. 130/D1
Wala (riv.), Tanz. 104/B4
Walachia (reg.),
Rom. 49/G3
Walagunya Abor. Land,
Austl. 112/D2
Wałbrzych, Pol. 41/J3
Walbury (hill),
Eng. UK 33/E4
Walcha, Austl. 115/H1
Walcheren (isl.), Neth. 50/A5
Wałcz, Pol. 41/J2
Wald, Swi. 57/E3
Wald, Ger. 55/H4
Waldbillig, Lux. 53/F4
Waldbröl, Ger. 53/G2
Waldbreitbach, Ger. 53/G2
Waldbrunn, Ger. 54/C3
Waldbüttelbrunn, Ger. 54/D3
Walden, Co, US 129/F2

Waldenbuch, Ger. 54/C5
Waldenburg, Swi. 56/D3
Waldenburg, Ger. 54/C4
Waldershof, Ger. 55/F3
Waldesch, Ger. 53/G3
Waldheim, Sk, Can. 126/G2
Waldighofen, Fr. 56/D2
Walding, Aus. 55/H6
Waldkirch, Ger. 56/D1
Waldmünchen, Ger. 55/F4
Waldnaab (riv.),
Ger. 55/F3
Waldrach, Ger. 53/F4
Waldron, Mo, US 137/D5
Waldsassen, Ger. 55/F3
Waldshut-Tiengen, Ger. 57/E2
Waldstetten, Ger. 54/C5
Waldviertel (reg.),
Aus. 41/H4
Waldwick, NJ, US 139/J8
Walea (str.), Indo. 81/F4
Waleabahi (isl.),
Indo. 81/F4
Walensee (lake), Swi. 57/F3
Walenstadt, Swi. 57/F3
Wales, Ak, US 134/E2
Wales, UK 32/B3
Wales (isl.), Nun., Can. 123/H2
Wales, Wi, US 135/P14
Walferdange, Lux. 53/F4
Walgett, Austl. 115/D1
Walhalla, ND, US 127/J3
Walhalla, SC, US 133/H3
Walhalla, Mi, US 55/F4
Walker (riv.),
Nv, US 128/C3
Walker (lake), Nv, US 128/C3
Walker (bay), SAfr. 106/L11
Walkerton,
On, Can. 130/D2
Walkill (riv.),
NY, US 138/D1
Walla Walla,
Austl. 115/C2
Walla Walla,
Wa, US 126/D4
Wallace, Id, US 126/E4
Wallaceburg,
On, Can. 130/D3
Wallaroo, Austl. 113/H5
Wallasey, Eng. UK 35/E5
Walldorf, Ger. 54/B4
Walldürn, Ger. 54/C3
Walled (lake),
Mi, US 135/F6
Walled City Hist. Site,
SKor. 73/G7
Walled Lake,
Mi, US 135/F6
Wallenhorst, Ger. 51/F4
Wallern im Burgenland,
Aus. 43/M3
Wallers, Fr. 52/C3
Wallersee (lake), Aus. 55/G7
Wallerstein, Ger. 54/D5
Wallington, NJ, US 139/J8
Wallis (isls.),
Wall. 117/H6
Wallis and Futuna (dpcy.),
Fr. 116/G6
Wallisellen, Swi. 57/E3
Walloon Brabant (prov.),
Belg. 53/D2
Wallowa (mts.),
Or, US 126/D4
Wallsend, Eng. UK 35/G2
Wallumbilla, Austl. 114/C4
Walney, Isle of (isl.),
Eng. UK 35/E3
Walnut, Ca, US 136/E8
Walnut Canyon Nat'l Mon.,
Az, US 128/E4
Walnut Creek,
Ca, US 135/K11
Walnut Grove,
Ca, US 135/L10
Walnut Park,
Ca, US 136/F8
Walnut Ridge,
Ar, US 129/K3
Walnutport, Pa, US 138/C2
Walpole, Austl. 112/C5
Walpole-Nornalup NP,
Austl. 112/C5
Walrus (isls.),
Ak, US 134/F4
Walsall, Eng. UK 33/E1
Walsall (co.), Eng. UK 33/E1
Walsenburg, Co, US 129/F3
Walsingham (cape),
Nun., Can. 123/K2
Walsrode, Ger. 51/G3
Waltenhofen, Ger. 57/G2
Walter F. George (res.),
US 133/G4
Walterboro,
SC, US 133/H3
Walter's Ash,
Eng. UK 30/A2
Waltham Abbey,
Eng. UK 30/D1
Waltham Forest (bor.),
Eng. UK 30/A1
Walton-on-Thames,
Eng. UK 30/B2
Waltrop, Ger. 51/E5
Walvis Bay, Namb. 105/B5
Walworth, Wi, US 135/N14
Walworth (co.),
Wi, US 135/N14
Walyahmoning (peak),
Austl. 112/C4
Walyunga NP, Austl. 112/L6

Walzenhausen, Swi. 57/F3
Wamba, Kenya 104/C2
Wamba, D.R. Congo 97/L7
Wamel, Neth. 50/D4
Wami (riv.), Tanz. 104/C4
Wampool (riv.),
Wy, US 126/G5
Wanaka, NZ 117/R11
Wanamassa,
NJ, US 138/D3
Wanaque (res.),
NJ, US 138/D1
Wanaque, NJ, US 139/H7
Wanda (mts.),
China 71/P2
Wanda, Il, US 135/G7
Wandering, Austl. 112/C5
Wanding, China 83/G3
Wando, SKor. 73/D5
Wandoan, Austl. 114/C4
Wandsworth (bor.),
Eng. UK 30/C2
Wanfried, Ger. 51/H6
Wang (riv.), Thai. 83/G4
Wang Hip (peak),
Thai. 78/B4
Wanganui, NZ 117/T10
Wangaratta, Austl. 115/C2
Wangdu, China 72/C3
Wangen, Ger. 57/F2
Wangen an der Aare,
Swi. 56/D3
Wangen bei Olten,
Swi. 56/D3
Wangerooge (isl.),
Ger. 51/E1
Wanggamet (peak),
Indo. 81/F6
Wanghai Shan (peak),
China 73/A2
Wāngi, Swi. 57/E3
Wangjing, China 79/C1
Wangpan (bay),
China 72/E5
Wani (peak), Indo. 81/F4
Wanica (dist.),
Sur. 153/H3
Wank (peak), Ger. 57/H2
Wanning, China 83/K4
Wanouchi, Japan 77/L5
Wanquan, China 72/C2
Wanrong, China 72/B4
Wansbeck (riv.),
Eng. UK 35/G1
Wantagh, NY, US 139/M9
Wanxian, China 70/J5
Wanze, Belg. 53/E2
Wapakoneta,
Oh, US 130/C3
Wapawekka (lake),
Sk, Can. 127/G2
Wapiti (riv.),
Ab,BC, Can. 126/D2
Wapoga (riv.), Indo. 81/J4
Wappapello (lake),
Mo, US 129/K3
Wappingers Falls,
NY, US 138/D1
Wappinger (riv.),
Ia, US 127/K5
Wapwallopen,
Pa, US 138/B1
Warabi, Japan 77/D2
Warangal, India 82/C4
Waratah, Austl. 115/C4
Warburg, Ger. 51/G6
Warburton, Pak. 86/B4
Warburton, Austl. 112/E3
Warburton Range Abor. Rsv.,
Austl. 112/E3
Warche (riv.), Belg. 53/F3
Ward, Co, US 137/A2
Ward, NZ 117/S11
Ward Cove, Ak, US 134/M4
Warden, SAfr. 106/E2
Warden (pt.),
Eng. UK 33/G4
Wardenburg, Ger. 51/F2
Wardha, India 82/C3
Ward's Stone (peak),
Eng. UK 35/F3
Ware, Eng. UK 33/F3
Waregem, Belg. 52/C2
Waremme, Belg. 53/E2
Waren, Ger. 38/E5
Warendorf, Ger. 51/E5
Waretown, NJ, US 138/D4
Warffum, Neth. 50/D2
Wargrave, Eng. UK 33/F4
Warialda, Austl. 115/D1
Warin Chamrap,
Thai. 78/D3
Waringstown,
NI, UK 34/B3
Warka, NZ 117/S10
Warkworth, NZ 117/S10
Warlingham,
Eng. UK 30/C3
Warmbad, Namb. 106/B3
Warme Bode (riv.),
Ger. 51/H5
Warmebach (riv.),
Ger. 51/G6
Warmenhuizen,
Neth. 50/B3
Warmeriville, Fr. 53/D5
Warmia (reg.), Pol. 41/K1
Warmińsko-Mazurskie
(prov.), Pol. 41/L2
Warminster,
Eng. UK 32/D4
Warminster, Pa, US 138/C3
Warner (mts.),
Ca, US 126/C5

Warner Robins,
Ga, US 133/H3
Warnow (riv.), Ger. 38/D5
Warnsveld, Neth. 50/D4
Waroona, Austl. 112/B5
Warr Acres,
Ok, US 137/M14
Warrabri, Austl. 113/G2
Warrandirrina (lake),
Austl. 113/H3
Warrego (range),
Austl. 109/D3
Warrego (riv.), Austl. 109/D3
Warren (pt.),
NW, Can. 134/M2
Warren, Austl. 115/C2
Warren, Mn, US 127/J3
Warren, Oh, US 133/E4
Warren, Ar, US 129/J4
Warren, Pa, US 130/E3
Warren, Mi, US 130/D3
Warren, Ut, US 137/J11
Warren (riv.),
NJ, US 112/C5
Warren, NJ, US 139/H9
Warren (co.),
NJ, US 138/C2
Warrenpoint,
NI, UK 34/B3
Warrensburg,
Mo, US 129/J3
Warrenton, SAfr. 106/D3
Warrenville,
Il, US 135/P16
Warri, Nga. 103/G5
Warrington, Fl, US 133/G4
Warrington, Eng. UK 35/F5
Warrington (riv.),
Eng. UK 35/F5
Warrnambool,
Austl. 115/B3
Warroad, Mn, US 127/K3
Warrumbungle NP,
Austl. 115/D1
Warsaw, In, US 130/C3
Warsaw (Warszawa)
(cap.), Pol. 41/L2
Warscheneck (peak),
Aus. 48/B2
Warsop, Eng. UK 35/G5
Warstein, Ger. 51/F6
Warta (riv.), Pol. 62/A1
Wartberg an der Krems,
Aus. 55/H7
Wartberg ob der Aist,
Aus. 55/H6
Wartburg, Il, US 137/G9
Watermael-Boitsfort,
Belg. 52/B2
Waterton Lakes Nat'l Pk.,
Ab, Can. 126/E3
Watertown, SD, US 127/J4
Watertown, NY, US 131/G4
Waterville, Wa, US 126/C4
Waterville, Me, US 131/G2
Waterville, Ire. 30/N11
Waterway, La, US 137/K12
Watford, Eng, UK 30/B1
Watford City, ND, US 127/H4
Wath-upon-Dearne,
Eng, UK 35/G5
Watheroo NP, Austl. 112/B4
Watkins, Co, US 137/C3
Watonwan (riv.),
Mn, US 129/J1
Watowato (peak),
Indo. 81/G3
Watrous, Sk, Can. 127/G3
Watsa,
D.R. Congo 104/A2
Washimiya, Japan 77/D1
Washington
(state), US 126/C4
Washington (cap.),
US 138/B1
Washington, Il, US 137/L5
Washington (isl.),
Wi, US 127/M4
Washington,
NC, US 133/J3
Washington,
Pa, US 130/D3
Washington (mt.),
NH, US 131/G2
Washington (lake),
Wa, US 135/C2
Washington,
Eng, UK 35/G2
Washington Dulles
(int'l arpt.), Va, US 130/E4
Washington Park,
Il, US 137/G8
Washington Terrace,
Ut, US 137/K11
Washingtonville,
Pa, US 138/B1
Washita (riv.), Ok, US 129/H4
Washtenaw (co.),
Mi, US 135/E7
Wasilków, Pol. 41/M2
Wasilla, Ak, US 134/J3
Waskaganish (Rupert
House), Qu, Can. 130/E1
Wavre, Belg. 53/D2
Waw, Sudan 97/L6
Wawa, Nic. 145/E3
Wawa (riv.), Nic. 145/E3
Wawagosic (riv.),
Qu, Can. 130/E1
Wawasang (peak),
Nic. 145/E3
Wawayanda State Park,
NJ, US 138/D1

Wasserburg am Inn,
Ger. 55/F6
Wasserkuppe (peak),
Ger. 54/C2
Wassuk (range),
Nv, US 124/C4
Wassy, Fr. 56/A1
Wast Water (lake),
Eng, UK 35/E3
Wasur-Rawa Biru NP,
Indo. 81/K5
Waswanipi (lake),
Qu, Can. 130/E1
Wat Phu, Laos 78/D3
Watampone, Indo. 81/F4
Watarai, Japan 77/L7
Watarase (riv.),
Japan 75/F2
Watari, Japan 75/G1
Watch Hill (pt.),
RI, US 139/G1
Watchung (mts.),
NJ, US 139/H9
Water of Ae (riv.),
Sc, UK 34/E1
Water of Girvan (riv.),
Sc, UK 36/B6
Water of Ken (riv.),
Sc, UK 34/E1
Waterbury, Ct, US 130/F3
Wateree (lake),
SC, US 133/H3
Wateree (riv.),
SC, US 133/H3
Waterford, Mi, US 130/D3
Waterford, Ire. 31/Q10
Waterford,
Ct, US 139/F1
Waterford Works,
NJ, US 138/D4
Watergate (bay),
Eng, UK 32/A6
Waterhen (riv.),
Mb, Can. 127/J2
Waterhen (lake),
Sk, Can. 126/F2
Waterloo, On, Can. 130/D3
Waterloo, Il, US 137/G9
Waterloo,
Belg. 53/D2
Waterloo Battlesite,
Belg. 53/D2
Waterloo Village,
NJ, US 138/D2
Weekapaug,
RI, US 139/G1
Weenen, SAfr. 107/E3
Weersel, Neth. 50/D4
Weert, Neth. 50/C6
Weesen, Swi. 57/F3
Weesp, Neth. 50/C4
Wegberg, Ger. 53/F1
Weggis, Swi. 57/E3
Węgorzewo, Pol. 39/J4
Węgrów, Pol. 41/M2
Wegscheid, Ger. 55/G5
Wehingen, Ger. 57/E1
Wehr, Ger. 56/D2
Wehra (riv.), Ger. 56/D2
Wehrheim, Ger. 54/C2
Wei Xian, China 72/C3
Weibersbrunn, Ger. 54/C3
Weichang, China 71/L3
Weida, Ger. 43/K1
Weiden, Ger. 55/F3
Weidenthal, Ger. 54/A4
Weifang, China 72/D3
Weihai, China 73/B4
Weihenzell, Ger. 54/D4
Weikersheim, Ger. 54/C4
Weil, Ger. 57/H2
Weil der Stadt, Ger. 54/B5
Weilburg, Ger. 54/C2
Weiler-Simmerberg,
Ger. 57/F2
Weilerswist, Ger. 53/F2
Weilheim, Ger. 57/H2
Weilheim an der Teck,
Ger. 54/C5
Weilmünster, Ger. 54/C2
Weimar, Ger. 40/F3
Weinan, China 72/B4
Weinfelden, Swi. 57/F2
Weingarten, Ger. 54/B4
Weingarten, Ger. 57/F2
Weinheim, Ger. 54/B3
Weinsberg, Ger. 54/C4
Weinstadt, Ger. 54/C5
Weinviertel (reg.),
Aus. 43/M2
Weirton, WV, US 133/E4
Weisendorf, Ger. 54/D3
Weisenheim am Berg,
Ger. 54/B3
Weishan, China 72/D4
Weishi, China 72/C4
Weiskirchen, Ger. 54/A3
Weismain, Ger. 54/E2
Weiss (lake), Al, US 133/G3
Weissach, Ger. 54/B5
Weisse Elster (riv.),
Ger. 40/G3
Weisse Laber (riv.),
Ger. 55/E4
Weissenbach am Lech,
Aus. 57/G3
Weissenburg im Bayern,
Ger. 54/D4
Weissenfels, Ger. 40/F3

Waxahachie,
Tx, US 129/H4
Waycross, Ga, US 133/H4
Wayne, Ne, US 127/J5
Wayne (co.), Pa, US 138/C2
Wayne, Pa, US 138/C3
Wayne, NJ, US 139/J8
Wayne, Mi, US 135/F7
Wayne, Il, US 135/P16
Waynesboro,
Pa, US 130/E4
Waynesboro,
Ms, US 133/F4
Waynesboro,
Ga, US 133/H3
Waynesville,
NC, US 133/H3
Waynesville,
Mo, US 129/J3
Wazë Xian, China 83/G3
Waziers, Fr. 52/C3
Wazirabad, Pak. 86/C3
Wazuka, Japan 77/J6
Wda (riv.), Pol. 41/K2
Welch, WV, US 130/D4
Welch (hill), Pa, US 138/A3
Weld, The (grsld.),
Eng, UK 33/H4
Weld (co.), Co, US 137/C2
Wear (riv.), Eng, UK 35/F2
Weatherby Lake,
Mo, US 137/D5
Weatherford,
Tx, US 129/H4
Weatherly, Pa, US 138/C2
Weaver (riv.),
Eng, UK 35/F5
Weaverville, Ca, US 128/B3
Weber (co.), Ut, US 137/J11
Weber (riv.), Ut, US 137/J11
Weber Hill,
Mo, US 137/F9
Webi Jubba (riv.),
Som. 93/G4
Webster, SD, US 127/J4
Webster City,
Ia, US 127/K5
Webster Groves,
Mo, US 137/G8
Weddell (isl.), Mald. 159/E6
Weddell (sea) 160/X
Wedderburn,
Austl. 115/B3
Weddin Mountains NP,
Austl. 115/C2
Wedel, Ger. 51/G1
Wedemark, Ger. 51/G3
Wee Waa, Austl. 115/D1
Weed, Ca, US 126/C5
Weehawken, NJ, US 139/J8
Weekapaug,
Weener, SAfr. 107/E3
Wells, SAfr. 106/D3
Welch, The (grsld.),
Eng, UK 33/H4
Welden, Ger. 54/D6
Weldiya, Eth. 97/N5
Weldon Spring,
Mo, US 137/F8
Welel (peak), Eth. 97/M6
Weligama, SrL. 82/D6
Welkenraedt, Belg. 53/E2
Welkom, SAfr. 106/D3
Welland (canal),
On, Can. 131/R10
Welland, On, Can. 131/R10
Welland (riv.),
Eng, UK 35/H6
Wellandport,
On, Can. 131/R9
Wellen, Belg. 53/E2
Wellesley (isls.),
Austl. 109/C2
Wellin, Belg. 53/E3
Wellingborough,
Eng, UK 33/F2
Wellington (lake),
Austl. 115/C3
Wellington, Austl. 115/D2
Wellington,
Tx, US 129/G4
Wellington (int'l arpt.),
NZ 117/S11
Wellington (cap.),
NZ 117/S11
Wellington,
NZ 32/C5
Wellington (chan.),
Nun., Can. 123/S7
Wellington (isl.),
Chile 147/B7
Wellington, SAfr. 106/L10
Wells, BC, Can. 126/C2
Wells, Nv, US 126/E5
Wells (lake),
Austl. 109/B3
Wells, Eng, UK 32/D4
Wells, Oh, US 137/N14
Wellston, Ok, US 137/N14
Wellsville, Pa, US 138/B3
Wellton, Az, US 128/D4
Welschbillig, Ger. 53/F4
Welschnofen
(Nova Levante), It. 57/H5
Welshpool, Wal, UK 32/C1
Welty, Co, US 137/B2
Welver, Ger. 51/E5
Welzheim, Ger. 54/C5
Wembere (riv.), Tanz. 105/F1
Wembley, Ab, Can. 126/D2
Wembley Stadium,
Eng, UK 30/C2
Wemding, Ger. 54/D5
Wemmel, Belg. 52/B2
Wemyss Bay, Sc, UK 36/B5
Wen Xian, China 72/C4
Wenatchee, Wa, US 126/C4
Wenchang, China 83/K4
Wenchi, Gha. 103/E5
Wendeburg, Ger. 51/H4
Wenden, Ger. 53/G2
Wendeng, China 73/B4
Wendover, Nv, US 126/E5
Wengyuan, China 83/K3
Wenling, China 79/D2
Wenlock Edge (ridge),
Eng, UK 32/D2
Wenne (riv.), Ger. 51/F6
Wennigsen, Ger. 51/G4
Wenonah, NJ, US 138/C4
Wenshan, China 83/H3
Wenshang, China 72/D4
Wenshui, China 72/C3
Wensleydale (valley),
Eng, UK 35/F3
Went (riv.), Eng, UK 35/G5
Wentworth, Austl. 115/B2
Wenxi, China 72/B4
Wenzhou, China 79/D2
Wepener, SAfr. 106/D3
Wer, India 84/A2
Werdau, Ger. 43/K1
Werdohl, Ger. 51/F6
Werkendam, Neth. 50/B5
Werl, Ger. 51/F5
Werlte, Ger. 51/E3
Wermelskirchen,
Ger. 53/G1
Wern (riv.), Ger. 54/C3
Wernberg-Köblitz,
Ger. 55/F3

Werne an der Lippe, Ger. 51/E5
Werneck, Ger. 54/D3
Wernigerode, Ger. 51/H5
Werong (mt.), Austl. 115/D2
Werra (riv.), Ger. 40/E3
Werre (riv.), Ger. 40/E2
Werrikimbe NP, Austl. 115/E1
Werris Creek, Austl. 115/D1
Werse (riv.), Ger. 51/E5
Wertach (riv.), Ger. 54/D6
Wertheim, Ger. 54/C3
Wertheim NWR, NY, US 139/F2
Werther, Ger. 51/F4
Wertingen, Ger. 54/D5
Wervershoof, Neth. 50/C3
Wervik, Belg. 52/C2
Weschnitz (riv.), Ger. 54/B3
Wesefgebirge (mts.), Ger. 51/F4
Wesel, Ger. 50/D5
Wesel-Datteln (canal), Ger. 51/E5
Weser (riv.), Ger. 40/E2
Weslaco, Tx, US 132/D5
Wesley Hills, NY, US 139/J7
Wessel (isls.), Austl. 109/C2
Wesselburen, Ger. 38/C4
Wesselsbron, SAfr. 106/D2
Wessex (reg.), Eng, UK 32/D4
Wessington Springs, SD, US 127/J4
West (pt.), Austl. 115/C4
West, Tx, US 129/H5
West (cape), NZ 117/R12
West (pt.), Wa, US 135/C2
West Allis, Wi, US 129/K2
West Alton, Mo, US 137/G8
West Babylon, NY, US 139/E2
West Bank (occ. zone), Isr. 91/D3
West Bend, Wi, US 127/L5
West Bengal (state), India 70/E7
West Berkshire (co.), Eng, UK 33/E4
West Bountiful, Ut, US 137/K12
West Branch, Mi, US 130/C2
West Bridgford, Eng, UK 35/G6
West Bromwich, Eng, UK 32/E1
West Caicos (isl.), UK 145/H1
West Calder, Sc, UK 36/C5
West Caldwell, NJ, US 139/H8
West Cap Howe NP, Austl. 112/C5
West Chester, Pa, US 138/C4
West Chicago, Il, US 135/P16
West Chyulu Game Consv. Area, Kenya 104/C3
West Coast NP, SAfr. 106/L10
West Columbia, SC, US 133/H3
West Covina, Ca, US 136/G7
West Creek, NJ, US 138/D4
West Dunbartonshire (pol. reg.), Sc, UK 36/B5
West Elk (mts.), Co, US 132/B2
West End, Eng, UK 30/B3
West Falkland (isl.), Falk. 157/D7
West Fargo, ND, US 127/J4
West Fayu (isl.), Micr. 116/D4
West Frisian (isls.), Neth. 40/C2
West Glen (riv.), Eng, UK 35/H6
West Grove, Pa, US 138/C4
West Haven, Ct, US 139/F1
West Haverstraw, NY, US 138/E1
West Helena, Ar, US 129/K4
West Hempstead, NY, US 139/L9
West Hills, NY, US 139/M8
West Hollywood, Ca, US 136/F7
West Humber (riv.), On, Can. 131/O8
West Ice Shelf, Ant. 160/F
West Indies (isls.), NAm. 145/F2
West Islet (isl.), Austl. 109/E3
West Islip, NY, US 139/E2
West Jordan, Ut, US 137/K12

West Kilbride, Sc, UK 36/B5
West Kingsdown, Eng, UK 30/D3
West Knock (peak), Sc, UK 36/D3
West Lamma (chan.), China 71/U11
West Lincoln, Ne, US 129/H2
West Lothian (pol. reg.), Sc, UK 129/H2
West Lunga NP, Zam. 105/D3
West Memphis, Ar, US 129/K4
West Midlands (co.), Eng, UK 33/E1
West Milford, NJ, US 139/H7
West Milton, Pa, US 138/B1
West Monroe, La, US 129/J4
West New York, NJ, US 139/J8
West Nyack, NY, US 139/K7
West Orange, NJ, US 139/J8
West Palm Beach, Fl, US 133/H5
West Paterson, NJ, US 139/J8
West Pensacola, Fl, US 133/G4
West Plains, Mo, US 129/K3
West Point, Ne, US 127/J5
West Point (lake), US 133/G3
West Point, NZ 117/S11
West Point, Ms, US 133/F3
West Point, Ct, US 139/E1
West Point, Ut, US 137/J11
West Reading, Pa, US 138/C3
West Redding, Ct, US 139/E1
West Road (riv.), BC, Can. 126/B2
West Sacramento, Ca, US 135/L11
West Sayville, NY, US 139/E2
West Seneca, NY, US 131/S10
West Siberian (plain), Rus. 64/H3
West Sussex (co.), Eng, UK 33/F4
West-Terschelling, Neth. 50/C2
West Valley City, Ut, US 137/K12
West Vancouver, BC, Can. 126/C3
West Virginia (state), US 125/K4
West Warren, Ut, US 137/J11
West Water (riv.), Sc, UK 36/D3
West Weber, Ut, US 137/J11
West Wyalong, Austl. 115/C2
West York, Pa, US 138/B4
Westall (pt.), Austl. 113/G5
Westbrook, Ct, US 139/F1
Westbury, NY, US 139/L9
Westchester (co.), NY, US 139/F1
Westcott, Eng, UK 30/B3
Westerbork, Neth. 50/D3
Westerburg, Ger. 53/G2
Westerham, Eng, UK 30/D3
Westerheim, Ger. 57/G1
Westerholt, Ger. 51/E1
Westerkappeln, Ger. 51/E4
Westerland, Ger. 38/C4
Westerlo, Belg. 53/D1
Western (prov.), Kenya 104/B2
Western (des.), Egypt 97/L2
Western (prov.), Ugan. 104/A2
Western (pol. reg.), Gha. 103/E5
Western (chan.), SKor. 74/A3
Western Area (prov.), SLeo. 102/B4
Western Australia (state), Austl. 109/B3
Western Cape (prov.), SAfr. 106/C4
Western Ghats (mts.), India 89/K5
Western Run (riv.), Md, US 138/B4
Western Sahara 93/A2
Western Sayans (mts.), Rus. 64/J4
Westerschelde (chan.), Belg. 50/A6
Westerstede, Ger. 51/E2
Westerville, Oh, US 130/D3
Westervoort, Neth. 50/C5
Westerwald (mts.), Ger. 40/D3

Westfield, NJ, US 139/H9
Westgat (chan.), Neth. 50/D2
Westhampton, NY, US 139/F2
Westhampton Beach, NY, US 139/F2
Westhausen, Ger. 54/D5
Westheim, Ger. 54/B4
Westhill, Sc, UK 36/D2
Westhofen, Ger. 54/B3
Westhoughton, Eng, UK 35/F4
Westkapelle, Neth. 50/A5
Westlake Village, Ca, US 136/B2
Westland, Mi, US 135/F7
Westland NP, NZ 117/R11
Westminster, Co, US 137/B3
Westminster, Md, US 138/B4
Westminster, Ca, US 136/F8
Westminster, City of (bor.), Eng, UK 30/A1
Westmont, Il, US 135/P16
Westmont (Haddon), NJ, US 138/C4
Westmorland (reg.), Eng, UK 35/F3
Westmount, Qu, Can. 131/N7
Westmount, NJ, US 139/J8
Weston, Mo, US 137/D5
Weston, Ct, US 139/E1
Weston-super-Mare, Eng, UK 32/D4
Westonaria, SAfr. 106/P13
Westport, Ire. 31/P10
Westport, NZ 117/S11
Westport, Ct, US 139/E1
Westray (isl.), Sc, UK 31/V14
Westview, Il, US 137/G8
Westwego, La, US 137/P17
Westwood, Ks, US 137/D5
Westwood, NJ, US 139/J8
Wet (mts.), Co, US 132/B2
Wetar (str.), Indo. 81/G5
Wetar (isl.), Indo. 67/M10
Wetaskiwin, Ab, Can. 126/E2
Wete, Tanz. 104/C4
Wététnagami (riv.), Qu, Can. 130/E1
Wetherell (lake), Austl. 115/B2
Wetter, Ger. 51/E6
Wetter (riv.), Ger. 54/B2
Wetterau (reg.), Ger. 54/C2
Wetteren, Belg. 52/C2
Wetterhorn (peak), Swi. 56/E4
Wettingen, Swi. 57/E3
Wettin, Swi. 51/E4
Wetzikon, Swi. 57/E3
Wetzlar, Ger. 54/B1
Wetzstein (peak), Ger. 55/E2
Wevelgem, Belg. 52/C2
Wewak, PNG 116/D5
Wewoka, Ok, US 129/H4
Wexford, Ire. 31/Q10
Wey (riv.), Eng, UK 30/A3
Weybridge, Eng, UK 30/B2
Weyburn, Sk, Can. 127/H3
Weygand (ruin), Alg. 99/F4
Weyhausen, Ger. 51/H4
Weyland (pt.), Austl. 113/G5
Weymouth, Eng, UK 32/D5
Weymouth (bay), Eng, UK 32/D5
Wha Ti, NW, Can. 122/E2
Whakatane, NZ 117/T10
Whale Cove, Nun., Can. 122/G2
Whalsey (isl.), Sc, UK 31/W13
Whangarei, NZ 117/S10
Wharfe (riv.), Eng, UK 35/G3
Wheat Ridge, Co, US 137/B3
Wheatland, Wy, US 127/G5
Wheaton, Il, US 130/B3
Wheaton-Glenmont, Md, US 138/A5
Wheaton Village, NJ, US 138/C4
Wheeler (peak), Nv, US 128/D3
Wheeler (peak), NM, US 129/F3
Wheeler (lake), Al, US 133/G3
Wheeler Springs, Ca, US 136/A1
Wheeling, WV, US 130/D3
Wheeling, Il, US 135/P15
Wheelwright, Arg. 158/E2
Whernside (peak), Eng, UK 35/F3
Whickham, Eng, UK 35/G2
Whidbey (pt.), Austl. 113/G5
Whinham (mt.), Austl. 113/F3
Whitburn, Sc, UK 36/C5
Whitby, On, Can. 131/S8

Whitby, Eng, UK 35/H3
White (lake), La, US 129/J5
White (riv.), Ar, US 129/J4
White (riv.), SD, US 127/H5
White (riv.), Tx, US 129/K2
White (lake), Austl. 109/B3
White (lake), On, Can. 130/C1
White (riv.), In, US 130/C4
White (pass), Ak, US 134/L3
White (sea), Rus. 60/H2
White (bay), Nf, Can. 123/L3
White Bear (riv.), Nf, Can. 131/K1
White City, Sk, Can. 127/G2
White Cliffs, Austl. 115/B1
White Coomb (peak), Sc, UK 36/C6
White Esk (riv.), Sc, UK 36/C6
White Fox, Sk, Can. 127/G2
White Hall, Md, US 138/B4
White Haven, Pa, US 138/C1
White Marsh, Md, US 138/B5
White Mountain, Ak, US 134/F2
White Mountains Nat'l Rec. Area, Ak, US 134/J2
White Nile (riv.), Sudan 93/F4
White Oak, Md, US 138/B5
White Otter (lake), On, Can. 127/K3
White Plains, NY, US 139/K7
White River, On, Can. 130/C1
White Rock, NM, US 132/A3
White Sands, NM, US 128/F4
White Sands Nat'l Mon., NM, US 128/F4
White Sulphur Springs, Mt, US 126/F4
White Volta (riv.), Gha. 93/B4
White, West Fork (riv.), In, US 130/C4
Whiteadder Water (riv.), Sc, UK 36/D5
Whitecourt, Ab, Can. 126/E2
Whiteface (riv.), Mn, US 127/K4
Whitefield, Eng, UK 35/F4
Whitefish, Mt, US 126/E3
Whitefish (bay), Can.,US 130/C2
Whiteford (pt.), Wal, UK 32/B3
Whiteford, Md, US 138/B4
Whitehall, Mi, US 126/E4
Whitehall, Mi, US 130/C3
Whitehaven, Eng, UK 34/E2
Whitehead, NI, UK 34/C2
Whitehills, Sc, UK 36/D1
Whitehorse (cap.), Yk, Can. 134/L3
Whitehorse (hill), Eng, UK 33/E3
Whitehouse, Tx, US 129/J4
Whitemouth (riv.), Mb, Can. 127/K3
Whiteriver, Az, US 128/E4
Whiteside (chan.), Chile 159/C7
Whitesville, NJ, US 138/D3
Whiteville, NC, US 133/J3
Whitewater (lake), On, Can. 127/L3
Whitewood, Sk, Can. 127/H3
Whithorn, Sc, UK 34/C2
Whiting, In, US 135/R16
Whitley Bay, Eng, UK 35/G1
Whitmore Village, Hi, US 124/V12
Whitney (lake), Md, US 138/B6
Whitney, Tx, US 129/H4
Whitsand (bay), Eng, UK 32/B6
Whitstable, Eng, UK 33/H4
Whitsunday (isl.), Austl. 109/D3
Whittaker, Mi, US 135/E7
Whittier, Ak, US 134/J3
Whittier, Ca, US 136/F8
Whittlesea, Austl. 115/G5
Whitton, Austl. 115/C2
Whitworth, Eng, UK 35/F4
Wholdaia (lake), NW, Can. 122/F2
Whyalla, Austl. 113/H5
Wi (isl.), SKor. 73/D5
Wiang Kosai NP, Thai. 78/B2
Wiarton, On, Can. 130/D2
Wiawso, Gha. 103/E5
Wichabai, Guy. 153/G4
Wichelen, Belg. 52/C2
Wichita (riv.), Tx, US 129/H4
Wichita (mts.), Ok, US 129/H4

Wichita Falls, Tx, US 129/H4
Wick, Sc, UK 31/S7
Wickenburg, Az, US 128/D4
Wickepin, Austl. 112/C5
Wickford, Eng, UK 30/E2
Wickham, Austl. 112/C2
Wicklow (mts.), Ire. 31/Q10
Wicklow (pass), Ire. 34/B5
Wicklow, Ire. 34/B6
Wicklow (pt.), Ire. 34/B6
Wickriede (riv.), Ger. 51/F4
Wid (riv.), Eng, UK 30/E2
Widnau, Swi. 57/F3
Widnes, Eng, UK 35/F5
Więcbork, Pol. 41/J2
Wied (riv.), Ger. 53/G2
Wiedau (riv.), Ger. 51/F2
Wiefelstede, Ger. 51/F2
Wiehengebirge (ridge), Ger. 51/F4
Wiehl, Ger. 53/G2
Wielenbach, Ger. 57/H2
Wieliczka, Pol. 41/L4
Wielkopolski NP, Pol. 41/J2
Wielkopolskie (prov.), Pol. 41/J2
Wielsbeke, Belg. 52/C2
Wieluń, Pol. 41/K3
Wien (riv.), Aus. 49/N7
Wien (prov.), Aus. 41/J4
Wien (Vienna) (cap.), Aus. 49/N7
Wiener Neudorf, Aus. 49/N7
Wiener Neustadt, Aus. 49/N7
Wienerwald (reg.), Aus. 43/M3
Wienwald (reg.), Aus. 49/N7
Wieprz (riv.), Pol. 62/B2
Wierden, Neth. 50/D4
Wieringermeerpolder (polder), Neth. 50/B3
Wieringerwerf, Neth. 50/C3
Wieruszów, Pol. 41/K3
Wiesbaden, Ger. 54/B2
Wiese (riv.), Ger. 43/G3
Wiese (isl.), Rus. 160/A
Wieseck (riv.), Ger. 54/B1
Wiesendangen, Swi. 57/E2
Wiesensteig, Ger. 54/C5
Wiesent (riv.), Ger. 54/E4
Wiesentheid, Ger. 54/D3
Wiesloch, Ger. 54/B3
Wiesmoor, Ger. 51/E2
Wietmarschen, Ger. 51/E3
Wietze, Ger. 51/G3
Wietze (riv.), Ger. 51/G3
Wietzendorf, Ger. 51/G3
Wieżyca (peak), Pol. 38/H4
Wigan, Eng, UK 35/F4
Wiggins, Ms, US 133/F4
Wight (isl.), Eng, UK 32/E5
Wigierski NP, Pol. 41/M1
Wignehies, Fr. 52/D3
Wigry (lake), Pol. 39/K5
Wigston, Eng, UK 33/E1
Wigtown, Sc, UK 34/D2
Wigtown (bay), Sc, UK 34/D2
Wijchen, Neth. 50/C5
Wijhe, Neth. 50/D4
Wijk bij Duurstede, Neth. 50/C5
Wil, Swi. 57/F3
Wilber, Ne, US 129/H2
Wilberforce, Austl. 114/G8
Wilbur, Wa, US 126/D4
Wilburton, Ok, US 129/J4
Wilcannia, Austl. 115/B1
Wilchingen, Swi. 57/E2
Wilczek (isl.), Rus. 64/G1
Wild (coast), SAfr. 106/E4
Wild Creek (res.), Pa, US 138/C2
Wild Rice (riv.), Mn, US 127/J4
Wild World, Md, US 138/B6
Wildau, Ger. 50/B3
Wildbad im Schwarzwald, Ger. 54/B5
Wildberg, Ger. 54/B5
Wilder, Ks, US 137/D5
Wilderswil, Swi. 56/D4
Wildeshausen, Ger. 51/F3
Wildflecken, Ger. 54/C2
Wildgrat (peak), Aus. 57/G3
Wildhaus, Swi. 57/F3
Wildhorn (peak), Swi. 56/D5
Wildomar, Ca, US 136/C3
Wildspitze (peak), Aus. 57/G4
Wildstrubel (peak), Swi. 56/D5
Wildwood, NJ, US 138/D6
Wildwood Crest, NJ, US 138/D6
Wilge (riv.), SAfr. 106/E2
Wilhelm II (coast), Ant. 160/F
Wilhelmina (mts.), Sur. 150/G3

Wilhelminakanaal (canal), Neth. 50/C5
Wilhelmshaven, Ger. 51/F1
Wilhering, Aus. 55/H6
Wilkes-Barre, Pa, US 138/C1
Wilkes Land (phys. reg.), Ant. 160/J
Wilkesboro, NC, US 130/D4
Wilkeson, Wa, US 135/C3
Wilkie, Sk, Can. 126/F2
Wilkins (sound), Ant. 160/U
Will (mt.), BC, Can. 134/N4
Will (co.), Il, US 135/P16
Willamette (riv.), Or, US 126/C4
Willandra NP, Austl. 115/C2
Willapa (bay), Wa, US 126/B4
Willard (bay), Ut, US 137/J11
Willard (res.), Ut, US 137/J11
Willard, Wi, US 135/P14
Willard, Ut, US 137/J11
Willaura, Austl. 115/B3
Willcox, Az, US 128/E4
Willebadessen, Ger. 51/G5
Willebroek, Belg. 53/D1
Willemstad (cap.), NAnt. 152/D1
Willemstad, Neth. 50/B5
Willesden, Eng, UK 30/B2
William (mt.), Austl. 115/B3
William B. Hartsfield Atlanta (int'l arpt.), Ga, US 133/G3
William Bay NP, Austl. 112/C5
Williams, Az, US 128/D4
Williams, Austl. 112/C5
Williams Lake, BC, Can. 126/C2
Williamsburg, Ky, US 130/C4
Williamsport, Pa, US 138/A1
Williamston, NC, US 133/J3
Williamstown, Pa, US 138/B2
Williamstown, NJ, US 138/D4
Williamsville, NY, US 131/S10
Willich, Ger. 50/D6
Willingboro, NJ, US 138/D3
Willingen, Ger. 51/F6
Willis, Tx, US 129/J5
Willis Islets (isls.), Austl. 109/E2
Willisau, Swi. 56/D3
Williston, ND, US 127/H3
Williston, Fl, US 133/H4
Williston, SAfr. 106/C3
Williston (lake), BC, Can. 122/D3
Williston Park, NY, US 139/L9
Willits, Ca, US 128/B3
Willmar, Mn, US 127/K4
Willow, Ak, US 134/H3
Willow (riv.), BC, Can. 126/C2
Willow Bunch, Sk, Can. 127/G3
Willow Grove, Pa, US 138/C3
Willow Grove, De, US 138/D4
Willow Grove Naval Air Sta., Pa, US 138/C3
Willow River, BC, Can. 126/C2
Willow Street, Pa, US 138/B4
Willow Tree, Austl. 115/D1
Willowbrook, Ca, US 136/F8
Willowbrook, Il, US 135/P16
Willowmore, SAfr. 106/C4
Willows, Ca, US 128/B3
Wills (lake), Austl. 109/B3
Wills Point, Tx, US 129/H4
Willstätt, Ger. 54/B5
Willunga, Austl. 113/H5
Wilmette, Il, US 135/Q15
Wilmington, NC, US 133/J3
Wilmington, Austl. 113/H5
Wilmington, De, US 138/C4
Wilmington Island, Ga, US 133/H4
Wilmslow, Eng, UK 35/F5
Wilnsdorf, Ger. 53/H2
Wilrijk, Belg. 50/B6
Wilseder (peak), Ger. 51/G2
Wilson, NC, US 133/J3
Wilson (co.), Tx, US 137/U21
Wilson, NY, US 131/S9
Wilson (mt.), Ca, US 136/B2
Wilson, Pa, US 138/C2
Wilson (cape), Nun., Can. 123/H2
Wilsons Promontory (pen.), Austl. 109/D4
Wilsons Promontory NP, Austl. 115/C3

Wilsonville, Il, US 137/H7
Wilstedt, Ger. 51/G2
Wilster, Ger. 51/G1
Wilsum, Ger. 50/D3
Wilton, Eng, UK 33/E4
Wilton, Ct, US 139/E1
Wiltshire (co.), Eng, UK 33/E4
Wiltz, Lux. 53/E4
Wiltz (riv.), Lux. 53/E4
Wiluna, Austl. 112/D3
Wimborne Minster, Eng, UK 32/E5
Wimereux, Fr. 52/A2
Wimmis, Swi. 56/D4
Winam (gulf), Kenya 104/B3
Winburg, SAfr. 106/D3
Winchester, Ky, US 130/C4
Winchester, Tn, US 133/G3
Winchester, Ca, US 136/C3
Winchester, Eng, UK 33/E4
Winchester Mystery House, Ca, US 135/L12
Wind (riv.), Wy, US 126/F5
Wind Cave NP, SD, US 129/G2
Wind Gap, Pa, US 138/C2
Wind Lake, Wi, US 135/P14
Wind Point, Wi, US 135/Q14
Wind River (range), Wy, US 128/E2
Windach (riv.), Ger. 57/G2
Windach, Ger. 54/E6
Windber, Ga, US 133/H3
Windermere (lake), Eng, UK 35/F3
Windermere, Eng, UK 35/F3
Windesheim, Ger. 53/G4
Windhoek (cap.), Namb. 105/C4
Windlesham, Eng, UK 30/B2
Window Rock, Az, US 128/E4
Windrush (riv.), Eng, UK 33/E3
Windsbach, Ger. 54/D4
Windsor, Nf, Can. 131/L1
Windsor, NS, Can. 131/H2
Windsor, Qu, Can. 131/G2
Windsor, On, Can. 130/D3
Windsor, Eng, UK 33/F4
Windsor, Co, US 137/C2
Windsor (res.), NJ, US 138/D3
Windsor, Md, US 138/B4
Windsor and Maidenhead (co.), Eng, UK 33/F3
Windward (isls.), StV. 141/J5
Windward Passage (passg.), Cuba,Haiti 145/H2
Winfield, BC, Can. 126/D3
Winfield, Ks, US 129/H3
Winfield, Pa, US 138/B2
Winfield, Md, US 138/A5
Wingene, Belg. 52/C1
Winger, On, Can. 131/R10
Wingham, Austl. 115/E1
Winifred (lake), Austl. 112/D2
Winifreda, Arg. 158/D3
Winisk (riv.), On, Can. 123/H3
Winkler, Mb, Can. 127/J3
Winneba, Gha. 103/E5
Winnebago (lake), Wi, US 127/L5
Winnemucca, Nv, US 128/C2
Winnenden, Ger. 54/C5
Winner, SD, US 127/J5
Winnetka, Il, US 135/Q15
Winnett, Mt, US 126/F4
Winnfield, La, US 129/J5
Winningen, Ger. 53/G3
Winnipeg (cap.), Mb, Can. 127/J3
Winnipeg (int'l arpt.), Mb, Can. 127/J3
Winnipeg (lake), Mb, Can. 127/J3
Winnipeg Beach, Mb, Can. 127/J3
Winnipegosis, Mb, Can. 127/H2
Winnipegosis (lake), Mb, Can. 127/H2
Winnsboro, La, US 129/K4
Winnsboro, SC, US 133/H3
Winschoten, Neth. 50/E2
Winsford, Eng, UK 35/F5
Winslow, Az, US 128/D4
Winslow, NJ, US 138/D4
Winston-Salem, NC, US 133/H3
Winsum, Neth. 50/D2
Winter Haven, Fl, US 133/H4
Winter Park, Fl, US 133/H4
Winterberg, Ger. 51/F6
Winterberge (mts.), SAfr. 106/D4
Winterlingen, Ger. 57/F1
Winters, Tx, US 129/H5
Winters, Ca, US 135/K9
Winters Run (riv.), Md, US 138/B4

Winterstaude (peak), Aus. 57/F3
Winterswijk, Neth. 50/D5
Winterthur, Swi. 57/E3
Winterthur Museum and Gardens, De, US 138/C4
Winthrop, Mn, US 131/G2
Winton, Austl. 114/A3
Wintzenheim, Fr. 56/D1
Wipper (riv.), Ger. 40/F3
Wipperau (riv.), Ger. 51/H2
Wipperfürth, Ger. 53/G1
Wirges, Ger. 53/G3
Wirrabara, Austl. 113/H5
Wirral (co.), Eng, UK 35/E5
Wirral (pen.), Eng, UK 35/E5
Wisbech, Eng, UK 33/G1
Wisch, Neth. 50/D5
Wischhafen, Ger. 51/G1
Wisconsin (riv.), Wi, US 127/L5
Wisconsin (state), US 127/L4
Wiseman, Ak, US 134/H2
Wisenta (riv.), Ger. 55/E1
Wishaw, Sc, UK 36/C5
Wishek, ND, US 127/J4
Wisła, Pol. 41/K4
Wiślany (lag.), Pol. 39/H4
Wisłoka (riv.), Pol. 41/L4
Wismar, Ger. 38/D5
Wisner, La, US 129/K5
Wissant, Fr. 52/A2
Wissembourg, Fr. 53/G5
Wissen, Ger. 53/G2
Wit Kei (riv.), SAfr. 106/D3
Witbank, SAfr. 106/E2
Witham, Eng, UK 33/G3
Witham (riv.), Eng, UK 35/H5
Witherspoon (mt.), Ak, US 134/J3
Withlacoochee (riv.), US 133/H4
Withnell, Eng, UK 35/F4
Witjira NP, Austl. 113/G3
Witkowo, Pol. 41/J2
Witney, Eng, UK 33/E3
Witnica, Pol. 41/H2
Witry-lès-Reims, Fr. 53/D5
Wittelsheim, Fr. 56/D2
Wittem, Neth. 53/E2
Witten, Ger. 51/E6
Wittenbach, Swi. 57/F3
Wittenberg, Ger. 40/G3
Wittenberge, Ger. 40/F2
Wittenburg, Ger. 38/D2
Wittenheim, Fr. 56/D2
Wittenoom, Austl. 112/C2
Wittingen, Ger. 51/H3
Wittislingen, Ger. 54/D5
Wittlich, Ger. 53/F4
Wittman, Md, US 138/B5
Wittmund, Ger. 51/E1
Wittmunder (riv.), Ger. 51/E1
Wittstock, Ger. 41/G1
Witu, Kenya 104/D3
Witwatersrand (reg.), SAfr. 106/P13
Witzenhausen, Ger. 51/G5
Wivenhoe (lake), Austl. 109/E3
Wixom, Mi, US 135/E6
Wkra (riv.), Pol. 60/D5
Władysławowo, Pol. 38/H4
Włocławek, Pol. 41/K2
Włocławskie (lake), Pol. 41/K2
Włodawa, Pol. 41/M3
Włoszczowa, Pol. 41/K3
Wobulenzi, Ugan. 104/B2
Wodonga, Austl. 115/C3
Wodzisław Śląski, Pol. 41/K4
Woensdrecht, Neth. 50/B6
Woerden, Neth. 50/B4
Wognum, Neth. 50/C3
Wohlen, Swi. 57/E3
Wohlen bei Bern, Swi. 56/D4
Wohlford (lake), Ca, US 136/C4
Woippy, Fr. 53/F5
Wokam (isl.), Indo. 81/H5
Woking, Eng, UK 30/B3
Wokingham, Eng, UK 33/F4
Wokingham (co.), Eng, UK 33/F4
Wŏlch'ul-san NP, SKor. 73/D5
Wolcott, Ks, US 137/D5
Wolcottsville, NY, US 131/S9
Wołczyn, Pol. 41/K3
Woleai (isl.), Micr. 116/D4
Wolf (mtn.), Ak, US 134/H2
Wolf (riv.), Wi, US 130/C2
Wolf (vol.), Ecu. 156/E7
Wolf (lake), In, US 135/Q16
Wolf Creek (mtn.), Ak, US 134/F3
Wolf Creek, Mt, US 126/E4
Wolf Point, Mt, US 127/G3
Wolfach, Ger. 57/E1
Wolfach (riv.), Ger. 54/B6
Wolfegg, Ger. 57/F2
Wolfen, Ger. 40/G3
Wolfenbüttel, Ger. 51/H4

Wolfern, Aus. 55/H6
Wölfersheim, Ger. 54/B2
Wolfhagen, Ger. 51/G6
Wolframs-Eschenbach, Ger. 54/D4
Wolfsburg, Ger. 51/H4
Wolfsegg am Hausruck, Aus. 55/G6
Wolfurt, Aus. 57/F3
Wolgast, Ger. 38/E4
Wolhusen, Swi. 56/E3
Wolin, Pol. 38/F5
Woliński PN, Pol. 41/H2
Wolkersdorf, Aus. 49/P7
Wollaston (isl.), Chile 157/C8
Wollaston (lake), Sk, Can. 122/F3
Wollaston (pen.), NW,Nun., Can. 122/E2
Wollemi NP, Austl. 115/D2
Wollerau, Swi. 57/E3
Wollongong, Austl. 115/D2
Wöllstadt, Ger. 54/B2
Wöllstein, Ger. 53/G4
Wolmaransstad, SAfr. 106/D2
Wolnzach, Ger. 55/E5
Wologizi (range), Libr. 96/C6
Wołomin, Pol. 41/L2
Wołów, Pol. 41/J3
Wolseley, SAfr. 106/L10
Wolsztyn, Pol. 41/J2
Woluwé-Saint-Lambert, Belg. 53/D2
Wolvega, Neth. 50/D3
Wolverhampton, Eng, UK 32/D1
Wolverhampton (co.), Eng, UK 32/D1
Wolverine Lake, Mi, US 135/F6
Wolziger (lake), Ger. 40/Q7
Woman (riv.), On, Can. 130/D2
Wombourne, Eng, UK 32/D1
Wombwell, Eng, UK 35/G4
Womelsdorf, Pa, US 138/B3
Wondai, Austl. 114/C4
Wonder (lake), Il, US 135/P16
Wondervu, Co, US 137/B3
Wondreb (riv.), Ger. 55/F3
Wong Chu (riv.), Bhu. 85/G2
Wongan Hills, Austl. 112/C4
Wŏnju, SKor. 73/D4
Wonnangatta-Moroka NP, Austl. 115/C3
Wŏnsan, NKor. 73/D3
Wonthaggi, Austl. 115/C3
Wonyulgunna (peak), Austl. 112/C3
Wood (mt.), Yk, Can. 134/K3
Wood (riv.), Sk, Can. 127/H2
Wood (mtn.), Sk, Can. 126/G3
Wood (riv.), Il, US 137/G8
Wood Buffalo NP, NW,Ab, Can. 122/E2
Wood Dale, Il, US 135/P16
Wood-Ridge, NJ, US 139/J8
Wood River, Il, US 137/G8
Woodbine, NJ, US 138/D5
Woodbine, Md, US 138/A5
Woodbridge, Ct, US 139/E1
Woodbridge, Ca, US 135/M10
Woodbridge, NJ, US 139/H9
Woodburn, Austl. 115/E1
Woodburn, Or, US 126/C4
Woodburn, Il, US 137/G7
Woodburn, On, Can. 131/Q9
Woodbury, NJ, US 138/C4
Woodcliff Lake, NJ, US 139/J7
Woodenbong, Austl. 115/E1
Woodenbridge, Ire. 34/B6
Woodend, Austl. 115/C3
Woodgate, Austl. 114/D4
Woodgate NP, Austl. 114/D4
Woodinville, Wa, US 135/C2
Woodland, Ca, US 128/B3
Woodlark (isl.), Sol. 116/E5
Woodlawn, Md, US 138/B5
Woodlawn Park, Ok, US 137/M14
Woodmere, NY, US 139/L9
Woodmont, Ct, US 139/F1
Woodridge, Il, US 135/P16
Woodroffe (mt.), Austl. 113/F3
Woods, Ok, US 137/N15
Woods (lake), On, Can. 122/G4
Woods Cross, Ut, US 137/K12
Woods Heights, Mo, US 137/E5
Woodsboro, Md, US 138/A4
Woodside, De, US 138/C5
Woodside, Austl. 113/M8
Woodside, Ca, US 135/K12
Woodside-Drifton, Pa, US 138/C2
Woodstock, Austl. 115/D2
Woodstock, NB, Can. 131/H2
Woodstock, Il, US 129/K2
Woodstock, Eng, UK 33/E3
Woodstock, Md, US 138/B5
Woodstown, NJ, US 138/C4
Woodville, Ms, US 129/K5
Woodway, Wa, US 135/C2
Woolgoolga, Austl. 115/E1
Wooli, Austl. 115/E1
Woolrich, Pa, US 138/A1
Woomera, Austl. 113/H4
Woomera Prohibited Area, Austl. 113/G4
Woonsocket, SD, US 129/H1
Woorabinda Aboriginal Community, Austl. 114/C4
Wooramel (riv.), Austl. 112/B3
Wooster, Oh, US 130/D3
Worb, Swi. 56/D4
Worcester, Ma, US 131/G3
Worcester, Eng, UK 32/D2
Worcester, SAfr. 106/L10
Worcestershire (co.), Eng, UK 32/D2
Worcester and Birmingham (canal), Eng, UK 32/D2
Worden, Il, US 137/H8
Wörgl, Aus. 43/K3
Workington, Eng, UK 34/E2
Worksop, Eng, UK 35/G5
Workum, Neth. 50/C3
Worland, Wy, US 126/G4
World 22
Wormer, Neth. 50/B3
Wormhoudt, Fr. 52/B2
Worms (pt.), Wal, UK 32/B3
Worms, Ger. 54/B3
Wörnitz (riv.), Ger. 43/J2
Worpswede, Ger. 51/F2
Wörrstadt, Ger. 54/B3
Wörsbach (riv.), Ger. 54/B2
Worsbrough, Eng, UK 35/G4
Worth, Il, US 135/Q16
Wörth am Rhein, Ger. 54/B4
Wörth an der Donau, Ger. 55/F4
Wörth an der Isar, Ger. 55/F5
Wortham, Tx, US 129/H5
Worthing, Eng, UK 33/F5
Wörthsee (lake), Ger. 54/E6
Worton, Md, US 138/B5
Wotho (isl.), Mrsh. 116/F3
Wotje (isl.), Mrsh. 116/G4
Woudenberg, Neth. 50/C4
Woudrichem, Neth. 50/B5
Wounta (lake), Nic. 145/F3
Wouw, Neth. 50/B5
Wowoni (isl.), Indo. 81/F4
Wrangel (isl.), Rus. 160/U
Wrangell, Ak, US 134/M4
Wrangell (mts.), Ak, US 122/B2
Wrangell-St. Elias NP and Prsv., Ak, US 134/K3
Wrath (cape), Sc, UK 31/R7
Wray, Co, US 129/G2
Wraysbury, Eng, UK 30/B2
Wraysbury (res.), Eng, UK 30/B2
Wreck (reef), Austl. 109/E3
Wreck (pt.), SAfr. 106/B3
Wrekin, The (hill), Eng, UK 32/D1
Wremen, Ger. 51/E2
Wrexham, Wal, UK 35/F5
Wrexham (co.), Wal, UK 35/E5
Wright, Wy, US 127/G5
Wrightstown, NJ, US 138/D3
Wrightwood, Ca, US 136/C2
Wrigley, NW, Can. 122/D2
Writtle, Eng, UK 33/G3
Wrocław, Pol. 41/J3
Września, Pol. 41/J2
Wschowa, Pol. 41/J3
Wu (riv.), China 79/A2
Wu'an, China 72/C3
Wuchang, China 71/N3
Wuchang (lake), China 72/D5
Wucheng, China 72/D5
Wuchuan, China 79/A2
Wuchuan, China 79/B3
Wuchuan, China 72/B2
Wudang (mtn.), China 72/B4
Wudi, China 72/D3
Wuding (riv.), China 72/B3
Wudinna, Austl. 113/G5
Wufeng, China 79/B1
Wugang, China 79/B2
Wuhai, China 70/J4
Wuhan, China 79/B1
Wuhe, China 72/D4
Wuhle (riv.), Ger. 40/Q6
Wuhu, China 72/D5
Wuhu, China 72/D5
Wuhua, China 79/C3
Wujal Wujal Aboriginal Community, Austl. 114/B1
Wujiang, China 72/L8
Wular (lake), India 86/C2
Wülfrath, Ger. 50/E6
Wulften, Ger. 51/H5
Wulian, China 72/D4
Wuling (mts.), China 79/B2
Wulong, China 83/J2
Wum, Camr. 103/H5
Wumang (isl.), China 73/B3
Wümme (riv.), Ger. 51/F2
Wūn, India 82/C3
Wungong (res.), Austl. 112/L7
Wuning, China 79/C2
Wünnenberg, Ger. 51/F5
Wünnewil, Swi. 56/D4
Wunsiedel, Ger. 55/F2
Wunstorf, Ger. 51/G4
Wupatki Nat'l Mon., Az, US 128/E4
Wuppertal, Ger. 51/E6
Wuqi, China 72/B3
Wuqia, China 87/G5
Wuqiang, China 72/C3
Wuqiao, China 72/D3
Würm (riv.), Ger. 53/H6
Würm K. (canal), Ger. 57/H1
Würselen, Ger. 53/F2
Würzburg, Ger. 54/C3
Wusheng (pass), China 72/C5
Wushi, China 70/C3
Wüstegarten (peak), Ger. 51/G6
Wüstenrot, Ger. 54/C4
Wusuli (riv.), China 71/P2
Wutach (riv.), Ger. 57/E2
Wutai (peak), China 72/C3
Wutai, China 72/C3
Wuteve (mt.), Libr. 102/C4
Wutha-Farnroda, Ger. 54/D1
Wutöschingen, Ger. 57/E2
Wuustwezel, Belg. 50/B6
Wuwei, China 70/H4
Wuwei, China 72/D5
Wuxi, China 72/L8
Wuxiang, China 72/C3
Wuyang, China 72/C4
Wuyi (mts.), China 79/C2
Wuyi, China 72/C4
Wuyuan, China 70/J3
Wuyuan, China 79/C2
Wuzhai, China 72/B3
Wuzhi (peak), China 83/J4
Wuzhi, China 72/C4
Wuzhi (peak), China 72/J6
Wuzhou, China 83/K3
Wyalkatchem, Austl. 112/C4
Wyandanch, NY, US 139/M8
Wyandotte (co.), Ks, US 137/D5
Wyandotte County (lake), Ks, US 137/D5
Wyandotte NWR, Mi, US 135/F7
Wyangala (dam), Austl. 115/D2
Wycheproof, Austl. 115/B3
Wyckoff, NJ, US 139/J8
Wye (riv.), Eng, UK 32/C2
Wye Mills, Md, US 138/B6
Wyee, Austl. 115/D2
Wyk, Ger. 38/C4
Wynigen, Swi. 56/D3
Wynne, Ar, US 129/K4
Wynyard, Austl. 115/C4
Wynyard, Sk, Can. 127/G3
Wyoming (range), Wy, US 128/E2
Wyoming, Mi, US 130/C3
Wyoming (state), US 126/F5
Wyoming, De, US 138/C5
Wyoming, Pa, US 138/C1
Wyomissing, Pa, US 138/C3
Wyperfeld NP, Austl. 115/B2
Wyralinu (peak), Austl. 112/D5
Wyre (riv.), Eng, UK 35/F4
Wyrzysk, Pol. 41/J2
Wysokie Mazowieckie, Pol. 41/M2
Wyszków, Pol. 41/L2

X

X-Can, Mex. 144/E1
Xa Binh Long, Viet. 78/D4
Xaçmaz, Azer. 63/J4
Xagħra, Malta 46/L6
Xai-Xai, Moz. 105/F6
Xainza, China 70/E5
Xaitongmoin, China 85/G1
Xaltianguis, Mex. 143/F5
Xan (riv.), Viet. 79/A5
Xankändi, Azer. 63/H5
Xanten, Ger. 50/D5
Xánthi, Gre. 47/J2
Xanxerê, Braz. 155/A3
Xar Moron (riv.), China 71/L3
Xarba (pass), China 85/E1
Xavantes, Reprêsa de (res.), Braz. 155/B2
Xavantes, Serra dos (mts.), Braz. 151/J6
Xayar, China 70/D3
Xel-há (ruin), Mex. 144/E1
Xenia, Oh, US 130/D4
Xerta, Sp. 45/F2
Xertigny, Fr. 56/C1
Xi (riv.), China 67/L7
Xi (lake), China 72/E2
Xiaguan, China 83/H2
Xiajin, China 72/C3
Xiamen, China 79/C3
Xiamen (int'l arpt.), China 79/C3
Xi'an, China 72/B4
Xiang (riv.), China 71/K6
Xiangcheng, China 83/G2
Xiangcheng, China 72/C4
Xiangcheng, China 72/C4
Xiangfan, China 72/C4
Xiangfen, China 72/B4
Xianghe, China 72/H7
Xiangkhoang, Laos 78/C2
Xiangkhoang (plat.), Laos 78/C2
Xiangning, China 72/B4
Xiangshan, China 79/D2
Xiangshui, China 72/D4
Xiangtan, China 83/K2
Xiangxiang, China 79/B2
Xiangyuan, China 72/C3
Xiangyun, China 83/H2
Xianju, China 79/D2
Xianning, China 79/B2
Xiantao, China 79/B1
Xianyang, China 70/J5
Xiao Hinggan (mts.), China 71/N2
Xiao Xian, China 72/D4
Xiaogan, China 71/K5
Xiaoqing (riv.), China 72/D3
Xiaoshan, China 72/L9
Xiaowutai (peak), China 72/C3
Xiaoyi, China 72/B3
Xiapu, China 79/C2
Xiayi, China 72/D4
Xichang, China 83/H2
Xichou, China 83/H3
Xico, Mex. 143/N7
Xicohténcatl, Mex. 143/F4
Xicotepec, Mex. 143/M6
Xifei (riv.), China 72/C4
Xifeng, China 70/J4
Xifeng, China 83/J2
Xifeng, China 72/F2
Xigazê, China 85/G1
Xihua, China 72/C4
Xilin, China 83/J3
Xilitla, Mex. 144/B1
Xilókastron, Gre. 47/H3
Ximeng Vazu Zizhixian, China 83/G3
Xin (riv.), China 79/C2
Xin Barag Zuoqi, China 71/L2
Xin'an, China 72/C4
Xin'an (riv.), China 72/D5
Xin'anjiang (res.), China 79/C2
Xin'anjiang (res.), China 72/D5
Xinbin, China 73/C2
Xincai, China 72/C4
Xinchang, China 79/D2
Xincheng, China 79/A3
Xincheng, China 72/G7
Xinfeng, China 79/B2
Xinfeng, China 83/K3
Xinfengjiang (res.), China 79/B3
Xing'an, China 79/B2
Xingcheng, China 72/E2
Xinghua, China 72/D4
Xinglong, China 72/H6
Xingshan, China 72/B5
Xingtai, China 72/C3
Xingu (riv.), Braz. 147/D3
Xingu, PN do, Braz. 151/H6
Xingyang, China 72/C4
Xingzi, China 79/C2
Xinhe, China 70/D3
Xinhe, China 72/C3
Xinhua, China 79/B2
Xinhuang Dongzu Zizhixian, China 79/A2
Xining, China 70/H4
Xinji, China 72/C3
Xinjiang, China 72/B4
Xinjiang Uygur (reg.), China 67/H5
Xinjin, China 73/A3
Xinle, China 72/C3
Xinmin, China 73/B1
Xintai, China 72/D4
Xinxiang, China 72/C4
Xinyang, China 71/K5
Xinyang, China 72/C4
Xinye, China 72/C4
Xinyi, China 83/K3
Xinyi, China 72/D4
Xinyu, China 79/B2
Xinyuan, China 70/D3
Xinzheng, China 72/C4
Xinzo de Limia, Sp. 44/B1
Xiong Xian, China 72/H7
Xiping, China 72/C4
Xiqing (mts.), China 70/H5
Xique-Xique, Braz. 154/B3
Xitang, China 72/L9
Xitiao (riv.), China 72/K9
Xiu (riv.), China 79/C2
Xiuning, China 79/C2
Xiuwen, China 83/J2
Xiuwu, China 72/C4
Xiuyan, China 73/B2
Xixabangma (peak), China 85/E1
Xixia, China 72/B4
Xiyang (riv.), China 83/J3
Xizang (Tibet) (aut. reg.), China 70/D5
Xochicalco (ruin), Mex. 143/K8
Xonacatlán, Mex. 143/Q10
Xpujil, Mex. 144/D2
Xu (riv.), China 79/C2
Xuan'en, China 79/A2
Xuanhua, China 72/G6
Xuchang, China 72/C4
Xun (riv.), China 79/B3
Xun Xian, China 72/C4
Xunke, China 71/N2
Xunwu, China 79/C3
Xunyang, China 72/B4
Xupu, China 79/B2
Xuwen, China 83/K3
Xuyi, China 72/D4
Xuzhou, China 72/D4

Y

Y Llethr (peak), Wal, UK 34/E6
Ya'an, China 70/H6
Ya'bad, Isr. 91/G7
Yabassi, Camr. 96/G7
Yablanitsa, Bul. 47/J1
Yablonovyy (range), Rus. 67/L4
Yabrūd, Isr. 91/G8
Yabucoa, PR 141/M8
Yabuki, Japan 75/G2
Yabuzukahon, Japan 77/C1
Yachi (riv.), China 70/J6
Yachiho, Japan 77/A1
Yachimata, Japan 77/E2
Yachiyo, Japan 77/D1
Yachiyo, Japan 77/G5
Yachiyo, Japan 77/E2
Yacimiento Río Turbio, Arg. 159/B6
Yacuiba, Bol. 150/F8
Yacuma (riv.), Bol. 150/E6
Yacumbu, PN, Ven. 152/D2
Yādgīr, India 82/C4
Yadkin (riv.), NC, US 133/H2
Yaeyama (isls.), Japan 75/G8
Yāfā, Isr. 91/G6
Yağcılar, Turk. 90/B2
Yagi, Japan 77/J5
Yagorlytsk (gulf), Ukr. 49/K2
Yagoua, Camr. 96/J5
Yagradagzê (peak), China 70/G4
Yaguale (riv.), Hon. 144/E3
Yaguarón (riv.), Uru. 159/G2
Yaguas (riv.), Peru 152/D5
Yague del Sur (riv.), DRep. 145/J2
Yagur, Isr. 91/G6
Yahagi (riv.), Japan 77/M6
Yahualica de Gonzalez Gallo, Mex. 142/E4
Yahyalı, Turk. 90/C2
Yáios (Paxoí), Gre. 47/G3
Yaita, Japan 75/F2
Yaizu, Japan 75/F3
Yajalón, Mex. 144/C2
Yakacık, Turk. 91/E1
Yakapınar, Turk. 91/D1
Yakima (riv.), Wa, US 126/C4
Yakima, Wa, US 126/C4
Yakishiri (isl.), Japan 76/B1
Yako, Burk. 103/E3
Yakoruda, Bul. 47/H1
Yakumo, Japan 76/B2
Yakuno, Japan 77/G5
Yakutat (bay), Ak, US 122/B3
Yakutsk, Rus. 65/N3
Yala, Thai. 78/C5
Yalahua (lag.), Mex. 144/E1
Yalangoz, Turk. 91/E1
Yalata Abor. Land, Austl. 113/F4
Yalbac (hills), Belz. 144/D2
Yalgoo, Austl. 112/C4
Yalgorup NP, Austl. 112/B5
Yalnızçam, Turk. 90/E1
Yaloké, CAfr. 96/J6
Yalong (riv.), China 67/K6
Yalova, Turk. 49/J5
Yalova, Turk. 49/H5
Yalpuh (lake), Ukr. 49/J3
Yalta, Ukr. 62/E3
Yalu (riv.), China,NKor. 73/C2
Yalutorovsk, Rus. 87/E1
Yalvaç, Turk. 90/B2
Yamada, Japan 76/B4
Yamaga, Japan 74/B4
Yamagata, Japan 71/Q4
Yamagata, Japan 75/G1
Yamagata (pref.), Japan 76/A4
Yamaguchi (pref.), Japan 74/B3
Yamaguchi, Japan 74/B3
Yamakita, Japan 77/C3
Yamal (pen.), Rus. 67/F2
Yamalo-Nenetskiy Aut. Okrug, Rus. 64/H3
Yamanaka (lake), Japan 77/B3
Yamanashi, Japan 77/B2
Yamanie (falls), Austl. 114/B2
Yamanie Falls NP, Austl. 114/B2
Yamantau (peak), Rus. 61/N5
Yamaoka, Japan 77/M5
Yamarna Abor. Rsv., Austl. 112/D4
Yamashiro, Japan 77/J6
Yamato, Japan 77/B2
Yamato, Japan 77/E1
Yamato, Japan 77/C3
Yamato (riv.), Japan 77/J6
Yamato-Kōriyama, Japan 77/J6
Yamatotakada, Japan 77/J6
Yamazoe, Japan 77/K6
Yamba, Austl. 115/E1
Yambio, Sudan 97/L7
Yambol, Bul. 47/K1
Yambrasbamba, Peru 156/B2
Yamdena (isl.), Indo. 81/H5
Yamethin, Myan. 83/G3
Yamin (peak), Indo. 81/K4
Yamma Yamma (lake), Austl. 109/D3
Yamoto, Japan 76/B4
Yamoussoukro (cap.), C.d'Iv. 102/D5
Yampa (riv.), Co, US 128/F2
Yamuna (riv.), India 70/C6
Yamunānagar, India 86/D4
Yamzho Yumco (lake), China 83/F2
Yan (riv.), SrL. 82/D6
Yan Yean (res.), Austl. 115/G5
Yana (riv.), Rus. 67/N3
Yanagawa, Japan 74/B4
Yanahuanca, Peru 156/B3
Yanai, Japan 74/C4
Yanaizu, Japan 77/L5
Yan'an, China 72/B3
Yanaoca, Peru 156/D4
Yanaul, Rus. 61/M4
Yanbian, China 83/H2
Yancheng, China 72/C4
Yancheng, China 72/E4
Yanchep NP, Austl. 112/B4
Yanco, Austl. 115/C2
Yandeearra Abor. Rsv., Austl. 112/C2
Yandoon, Myan. 83/G4
Yanfolila, Mali 102/C4
Yangambi, D.R. Congo 97/K7
Yangbi (riv.), China 83/G2
Yangcheng, China 72/C4
Yangcheng (lake), China 72/L8
Yangchun, China 79/B3
Yangdang (mts.), China 79/C2
Yangdŏk, NKor. 73/D3
Yanggang-do (prov.), NKor. 73/D2
Yanggao, China 72/C2
Yanggu, SKor. 73/D3
Yanggu, China 72/C3
Yangiyul', Uzb. 87/E4
Yangjiang, China 83/K3
Yangma (isl.), China 73/A4
Yangon (state), Myan. 83/G4
Yangp'yŏng, SKor. 73/D4
Yangqu, China 72/C3
Yangquan, China 72/C3
Yangsan, SKor. 73/E5
Yangshan, China 83/K3
Yangtze (Chang) (riv.), China 79/C1
Yangudi Rassa NP, Eth. 97/P5
Yangxin, China 79/C2
Yangxin, China 72/D3
Yangyang, SKor. 73/E3
Yangyuan, China 72/C2
Yangzhong, China 72/D4
Yangzhou, China 72/D4
Yanhe, China 79/A2
Yanji, China 71/N3
Yanjin, China 83/H2
Yanjin, China 72/C4
Yankari Game Reserve, Nga. 97/H6
Yankee Stadium, NY, US 139/K8
Yanling, China 72/C4
Yanmen (pass), China 72/C3
Yanshan, China 72/D3
Yanshan, China 83/H3
Yanshan, China 72/D3
Yanshi, China 72/C4
Yanshou, China 71/N2
Yantai, China 72/E3
Yanyuan, China 83/H2
Yanzhou, China 72/D4
Yao, Japan 77/J6
Yao'an, China 83/H2
Yaotsu, Japan 77/M5
Yaoundé (cap.), Camr. 96/H7
Yap (isls.), Micr. 116/C4
Yapacana, PN, Ven. 150/E3
Yapei, Gha. 103/E4
Yapen (isl.), Indo. 81/J4
Yapen (str.), Indo. 81/J4
Yapraklı, Turk. 90/C1
Yaqui (riv.), Mex. 142/C2
Yara, Cuba 145/G1
Yaracuy (state), Ven. 152/D2
Yaralıgöz (peak), Turk. 90/C1
Yaransk, Rus. 61/K4
Yardımcı (pt.), Turk. 91/B1
Yardley, Pa, US 138/D3
Yardville-Groveville, NJ, US 138/D3
Yare (riv.), Eng, UK 33/H1
Yarí (riv.), Col. 150/D3
Yari-ga-take (peak), Japan 75/E2
Yarımca, Turk. 49/J5
Yaritagua, Ven. 152/D2
Yarkant (riv.), China 70/C4
Yarloop, Austl. 112/B5
Yarlung Zangbo (Brahmaputra) (riv.), China 85/G1
Yarmouth, NS, Can. 131/H3
Yaroslavl', Rus. 60/H4
Yaroslavskaya Oblast, Rus. 60/H4
Yarpuz, Turk. 91/E1
Yarra (riv.), Austl. 115/G5
Yarra Glen, Austl. 115/G5
Yarram, Austl. 115/C3
Yarraman, Austl. 114/D4
Yarrawonga, Austl. 115/C3
Yarrow Point, Wa, US 135/C2
Yartsevo, Rus. 64/K3
Yarumal, Col. 152/C3
Yasato, Japan 77/E1
Yasawa Group (isls.), Fiji 116/G6
Yasel'da (riv.), Bela. 62/C1
Yashima, Japan 76/B4
Yashio, Japan 77/D2
Yashiro, Japan 77/G6
Yasnyy, Rus. 63/L2
Yasothon, Thai. 78/D3
Yass, Austl. 115/D2
Yasu (riv.), Japan 77/K6
Yasu, Japan 77/K5
Yasugi, Japan 74/C3
Yāsūj, Iran 88/F2
Yasun Burnu (pt.), Turk. 90/D1
Yasuni, PN, Ecu. 150/C4
Yatabe, Japan 75/G2
Yatağan, Turk. 90/B2
Yateley, Eng, UK 33/F4
Yatenga (prov.), Burk. 103/E3
Yathkyed (lake), Nun., Can. 122/G2
Yatomi, Japan 77/L5
Yatsu-ga-take (peak), Japan 77/A2
Yatsuo, Japan 75/E2
Yatsushiro, Japan 74/B4
Yatsushiro, Japan 77/B2
Yaṭṭah, WBnk. 91/D4
Yauca (riv.), Peru 156/C4
Yauca, Peru 156/C4
Yauco, PR 141/M8
Yauli, Peru 156/B3
Yaupi, Ecu. 152/B5
Yaután, Peru 156/B3
Yauyos, Peru 156/C4
Yauza (riv.), Rus. 61/W9
Yavarí (riv.), Braz.,Peru 147/B3
Yavarí Mirim (riv.), Peru 156/C2
Yavaros, Mex. 142/C3
Yavay (pen.), Rus. 64/H2
Yaviza, Pan. 152/B2
Yavne, Isr. 91/F8
Yavuzeli, Turk. 90/D2
Yawahara, Japan 77/E2
Yawata, Japan 77/J6
Yawatahama, Japan 74/C4
Yaxchilán (ruin), Guat. 144/D2
Yaygın, Turk. 90/E2
Yayladağı, Turk. 91/E2
Yayladere, Turk. 90/E2
Yazd, Iran 89/F2
Yazmān, Pak. 86/A5
Yazoo (riv.), Ms, US 129/K4
Yazoo City, Ms, US 129/K5
Ybbs (riv.), Aus. 41/H4
Ybbsitz, Aus. 43/L3
Yding Skovhøj (peak), Den. 38/C3
Ye, Myan. 78/B3
Ye Xian, China 72/D3
Yeay Sen (cape), Camb. 78/C4
Yecheng, China 87/G5
Yech'ŏn, SKor. 73/E4
Yecla, Sp. 45/E3
Yécora, Mex. 142/C2
Yecuatla, Mex. 143/N7
Yedigöller Nat'l Park, Turk. 49/K5
Yeditepe, Turk. 91/E2
Yefira, Gre. 47/H2
Yefremov, Rus. 62/F1
Yegizkara (peak), Kaz. 87/D3
Yegorlak (riv.), Rus. 63/G3
Yehualtepec, Mex. 143/M8
Yehud, Isr. 91/F7
Yejmiadzin, Arm. 63/H4
Yekaterinburg (Sverdlovsk), Rus. 61/P4
Yekateriny (chan.), Rus. 76/E1
Yelabuga, Rus. 61/M5
Yelan', Rus. 63/G2
Yelarbon, Austl. 114/C5
Yelets, Rus. 62/F1
Yélimané, Mali 102/C3
Yelizovo, Rus. 65/R4
Yell (isl.), Sc, UK 31/W13
Yellel, Alg. 100/F5
Yellow (riv.), Fl, US 133/G4
Yellow (sea), Asia 67/M6
Yellow Grass, Sk, Can. 127/G3
Yellowknife (riv.), NW, Can. 122/E2
Yellowknife (cap.), NW, Can. 122/E2
Yellowstone (lake), Wy, US 126/F4
Yellowstone (riv.), Mt, US 127/G4
Yellowstone NP, US 128/E1
Yellville, Ar, US 129/J3
Yemen (ctry.) 88/C5
Yenakiyeve, Ukr. 62/F2
Yenangyaung, Myan. 83/F3
Yenda, Austl. 115/C2
Yendi, Gha. 103/E4
Yengisar, China 87/G5
Yeniçağa, Turk. 49/L5
Yenice, Turk. 91/D1
Yenice, Turk. 49/L5
Yenice, Turk. 49/H6
Yenice (riv.), Turk. 62/E4
Yeniceoba, Turk. 90/C2
Yeniköy, Turk. 49/H5
Yenişehir, Turk. 49/J5
Yenisey (riv.), Rus. 67/H3
Yeniseysk, Rus. 64/K4
Yeo (lake), Austl. 109/B3
Yeo Lake Nature Rsv., Austl. 112/E3
Yeoval, Austl. 115/D2
Yeovil, Eng, UK 32/D5
Yeppoon, Austl. 114/C3
Yeraifia (well), WSah. 98/B4
Yerakovoúni (peak), Gre. 47/H3
Yères (riv.), Fr. 52/A4
Yerevan (cap.), Arm. 63/H4
Yerevan (int'l arpt.), Arm. 63/H4
Yerington, Nv, US 128/C3
Yerköy, Turk. 90/C2
Yerlisu, Turk. 47/K2
Yermak, Kaz. 87/G2
Yeroḥam, Isr. 91/D4
Yerolimín, Gre. 47/H4
Yerre (riv.), Fr. 42/D2
Yerres, Fr. 30/K5
Yerupaja (peak), Peru 156/B3
Yesagyo, Myan. 83/G3
Yesan, SKor. 73/D4
Yeşilhisar, Turk. 90/C2
Yeşilırmak (riv.), Turk. 62/F4
Yeşilkent, Turk. 91/E1
Yeşilova, Turk. 90/B2
Yesodot, Isr. 91/F8
Yesŏng (riv.), NKor. 73/D3
Yessentuki, Rus. 63/G3
Yeste, Sp. 44/D3
Yetti (reg.), Mrta. 98/D4
Yeu, Île d' (isl.), Fr. 42/B3
Yevla, India 82/B3
Yevlax, Azer. 63/H4
Yevpatoriya, Ukr. 62/E3
Yèvre (riv.), Fr. 53/D5
Yeya (riv.), Rus. 62/G3
Yeysk, Rus. 62/F3
Ygos-Saint-Saturnin, Fr. 42/C5
Yi (riv.), Uru. 159/F2
Yialousa, Cyp. 91/D2
Yiannitsá, Gre. 47/H2
Yiánnouli, Gre. 47/H3
Yíaros (isl.), Gre. 47/J4
Yibin, China 70/H6
Yichang, China 71/K5
Yicheng, China 72/C5
Yicheng, China 72/B4
Yichuan, China 72/C4
Yichun, China 71/N2
Yichun, China 83/K2
Yifeng, China 83/K2
Yığılca, Turk. 49/K5
Yihuang, China 79/C2
Yıldız (peak), Turk. 90/D1
Yıldızeli, Turk. 90/D2
Yilehuli (mts.), China 71/M1
Yiliang, China 83/H2
Yima, China 72/B4
Yimen, China 83/H3
Yin (mts.), China 70/J3
Yinan, China 72/D4
Yinchuan, China 70/J4
Yindarlgooda (lake), Austl. 109/B4
Yingcheng, China 71/K5
Yingde, China 79/B3
Yingkou, China 73/B2
Yingshan, China 72/C5
Yingshang, China 72/D4
Yingtan, China 79/C2
Yining, China 70/D3
Yishan, China 79/A3
Yishui, China 72/D4
Yíthion, Gre. 47/H4
Yitong (riv.), SKor. 72/C5
Yiwu, China 70/F3
Yixing, China 72/K8
Yiyang, China 83/K2
Yiyang, China 72/C4
Yiyuan, China 72/D3
Yizhang, China 83/K2
Yizheng, China 72/D4
Ylöjärvi, Fin. 39/K1

Ÿnder (lake), Kaz. 63/K2
Yngaren (lake), Swe. 38/G2
Yobe (state), Nga. 103/H3
Yŏch'ŏn, SKor. 73/D5
Yodo (riv.), Japan 77/J6
Yoduma (riv.), Rus. 65/P4
Yoff (Dakar)
(int'l arpt.), Sen. 102/A3
Yogo, Japan 77/K4
Yogoum (well), Chad 97/J4
Yoğuntaş, Turk. 49/H5
Yogyakarta, Indo. 80/D5
Yoho NP, BC, Can. 126/D3
Yoichi, Japan 76/B2
Yojoa (lake), Hon. 144/D3
Yōju, SKor. 73/D4
Yokadouma, Camr. 96/J7
Yōkaichi, Japan 77/K5
Yokawa, Japan 77/H6
Yokkaichi, Japan 77/L6
Yokohama, Japan 75/F3
Yokoshiba, Japan 77/E2
Yokosuka, Japan 75/F3
Yokote, Japan 76/B4
Yokoze, Japan 77/C2
Yola, Nga. 96/H6
Yolaina (mts.), Nic. 145/E4
Yolboyu, Turk. 90/D2
Yolo, Ca, US 135/L9
Yolo (co.), Ca, US 135/L9
Yom (riv.), Thai. 83/H4
Yon (riv.), Fr. 42/C3
Yonago, Japan 74/C3
Yonaguni (isl.),
Japan 75/G8
Yonaha-dake (peak),
Japan 75/K7
Yoneshiro (riv.),
Japan 76/B3
Yonezawa, Japan 75/G2
Yŏng-yang, SKor. 73/E4
Yongam'o, NKor. 73/C3
Yong'an, China 79/C2
Yongchang, China 70/H4
Yongcheng, China 72/D4
Yŏngch'ŏn, SKor. 74/A3
Yongchun, China 79/C2
Yongding, China 79/C3
Yongde, China 83/G3
Yongding (riv.), China 72/G6
Yŏngdŏk, SKor. 74/A2
Yŏngdong, SKor. 73/D4
Yŏnggwang, SKor. 73/D5
Yŏnghae, SKor. 73/E4
Yonghe, China 72/B3
Yŏnghŭng (riv.), NKor. 73/D3
Yŏnghŭng, NKor. 73/D3
Yongji, China 72/B4
Yŏngjong (isl.), SKor. 73/F6
Yŏngju, SKor. 74/A2
Yongkang, China 79/D2
Yongmun-san
(peak), SKor. 73/D4
Yŏngnian, China 72/C3
Yongqing, China 72/H7
Yongren, China 83/H2
Yongsheng, China 83/H2
Yongshun, China 83/J2
Yongtai, China 79/C2
Yŏngwŏl, SKor. 74/A2
Yongxing, China 79/B2
Yongxiu, China 79/D2
Yonkers, NY, US 139/K8
Yonne (riv.), Fr. 40/B5
Yono, Japan 77/D2
Yopal, Col. 152/D3
Yopurga, China 87/G5
Yoqne'am 'Illit, Isr. 91/G6
Yorba Linda, Ca, US 136/E8
Yorii, Japan 77/C1
York, Austl. 112/C4
York (cape), Austl. 109/D2
York (sound), Austl. 109/B2
York, Eng, UK 35/G4
York (co.), Eng, UK 35/G4
York, Al, US 133/F3
York, Ne, US 127/J5
York, Pa, US 138/B4
York, SC, US 133/H3
York, Va, US 130/E4
York Haven, Pa, US 138/B3
York Landing,
Mb, Can. 127/J1
York Minster, Eng, UK 35/G4
York Springs, Pa, US 138/A4
York, Vale of (valley),
Eng, UK 35/G3
Yorke, Austl. 109/C4
Yorketown, Austl. 109/H5
Yorkshire Dales NP,
Eng, UK 35/F3
Yorkshire Wolds (hills),
Eng, UK 35/H3
Yorkton, Sk, Can. 127/H3
Yorktown, Tx, US 129/H5
Yorktown Heights,
NY, US 139/E1

Yoro, Hon. 144/E3
Yōrō (riv.), Japan 77/E3
Yōrō, Japan 77/L5
Yoroi-zaki (pt.),
Japan 77/L7
Yorosso, Mali 102/D3
Yorubaland (plat.),
Nga. 96/F6
Yos Sudarso (isl.),
Indo. 81/J5
Yosemite NP,
Ca, US 128/C3
Yoshida, Japan 74/C4
Yoshida, Japan 77/C1
Yoshii (riv.), Japan 74/D3
Yoshii, Japan 77/B1
Yoshikawa, Japan 77/D2
Yoshima (riv.),
Japan 74/D3
Yoshimi, Japan 77/C1
Yoshino (riv.), Japan 74/C4
Yoshino-Kumano NP,
Japan 77/J7
Yoshkar-Ola, Rus. 61/L4
Yōsu, SKor. 73/D5
Yōtei-san (peak),
Japan 76/B2
Yotsukaidō, Japan 77/E2
You (riv.), China 79/A3
Young, Austl. 115/D4
Young, Uru. 159/K10
Youngs (lake), Wa, US 135/C3
Youngstown, Oh, US 130/D3
Youngstown, NY, US 131/R9
Youngtown, Az, US 137/R18
Yountville, Ca, US 135/K10
Youssoufia, Mor. 98/C2
Youyang, China 83/J2
Yovi (peak), Ven. 153/E3
Yozgat, Turk. 90/C2
Ypsilanti, Mi, US 135/E7
Yr Eifl (peak),
Wal, UK 34/D6
Yreka, Ca, US 128/B2
Yser (riv.), Fr. 40/B3
Ysieux (riv.), Fr. 30/K4
Ystad, Swe. 38/E4
Ysyk-Köl (lake), Kyr. 70/C3
Ysyk-Köl (obl.), Kyr. 87/G4
Ythan (riv.), Sc, UK 36/D2
Ytrac, Fr. 42/E4
Ytre Sula (isl.), Nor. 38/A1
Ytterby, Swe. 38/D3
Ytterbyn, Swe. 37/G2
Yü (peak), Tai. 79/D3
Yu (riv.), China 83/J3
Yu Xian, China 72/C3
Yu Xian, China 72/C3
Yu (riv.), China 71/K6
Yuan (lake), China 83/J3
Yuan'an, China 72/B5
Yüanlin, Tai. 79/D3
Yuanping, China 72/C3
Yuanqu, China 72/C4
Yuanshi, China 72/C3
Yuanyang, China 72/C4
Yuba City, Ca, US 128/B3
Yūbari, Japan 76/B2
Yūbetsu, Japan 76/C1
Yūbetsu (riv.),
Japan 76/C2
Yucaipa, Ca, US 136/C2
Yucatán (state), Mex. 144/D1
Yucatán (pen.), Mex. 144/D2
Yucatan (chan.),
NAm. 144/E1
Yucca House Nat'l Mon.,
Co, US 128/E3
Yucheng, China 72/D3
Yucheng, China 72/C4
Yuci, China 72/C3
Yuen Long, China 71/U10
Yuendumu, Austl. 109/B2
Yuendumu Abor. Land,
Austl. 113/F2
Yueqing, China 79/D2
Yueyang, China 79/B2
Yug (riv.), Rus. 64/E4
Yugan, China 79/C2
Yugawara, Japan 77/C3
Yugorskiy (pen.), Rus. 61/P1
Yuhang, China 79/D2
Yuhuan, China 79/D2
Yui, Japan 77/C3
Yujiang, China 79/C2
Yūki, Japan 77/D2
Yukon, Ok, US 137/M14
Yukon (riv.), Can.,US 134/L3
Yukon-Charley Rivers
Nat'l Prsv., Ak, US 134/K2
Yukon Territory
(terr.), Can. 134/L3
Yüksekova, Turk. 90/F2
Yukuhashi, Japan 74/B4
Yulara, Austl. 113/F3
Yuleba, Austl. 114/C4
Yulin, China 83/K3
Yulin, China 83/J4
Yulin, China 72/B3

Yuma, Az, US 128/D4
Yuma, Co, US 129/G2
Yuma (riv.), Dom.Rep. 124/D5
Yumbarra Consv. Park,
Austl. 113/G4
Yumbel, Chile 158/B3
Yumbo, Col. 152/B3
Yumen, China 70/G4
Yumin, China 70/D2
Yumurtalık, Turk. 91/D1
Yun (riv.), China 72/C5
Yun Xian, China 83/H3
Yun Xian, China 72/B4
Yunak, Turk. 90/B2
Yuncheng, China 72/C4
Yuncheng, China 72/B4
Yundum (Banjul)
(int'l arpt.), Gam. 102/A3
Yungang Caves,
China 72/C2
Yungas (phys. reg.),
Bol. 150/E7
Yungay, Chile 158/B3
Yungk'ang, Tai. 79/D3
Yunguyo, Peru 156/D5
Yunkanjini Abor. Land,
Austl. 113/F2
Yunlong, China 83/G2
Yunnan (prov.),
China 70/H7
Yuntai (peak), China 72/D4
Yunxi, China 72/B4
Yunxiao, China 79/C3
Yunyang (riv.), China 72/C3
Yunzhong (mtn.),
China 72/C3
Yuping, China 83/J2
Yupukarri, Guy. 153/G4
Yuqiao (res.), China 72/H7
Yuracyacu, Peru 156/B2
Yurga, Rus. 64/J4
Yuri (riv.), Rus. 76/E2
Yurimaguas, Peru 156/B2
Yuruari (riv.), Ven. 153/F3
Yürük, Turk. 49/H5
Yur'yevets, Rus. 60/J4
Yuryuzan' (riv.), Rus. 61/N5
Yuscarán, Hon. 144/E3
Yushan, China 79/C3
Yushe, China 72/C3
Yushu, China 71/N3
Yusŏng, SKor. 73/D4
Yusufeli, Turk. 90/E1
Yutai, China 72/D4
Yutian, China 70/D4
Yutian, China 72/H7
Yutz, Fr. 53/F5
Yuza, Japan 76/A4
Yuzawa, Japan 76/B4
Yuzhno-Sakhalinsk,
Rus. 71/R2
Yverdon, Swi. 56/C4
Yvette (riv.), Fr. 52/B6
Yvoir, Belg. 53/D3
Yvonand, Swi. 56/C4
Yvre, Fr. 30/L6
Yzeure, Fr. 42/E3

Z

Za (riv.), Mor. 100/C2
Zaachila, Mex. 144/B2
Zaandam, Neth. 40/C2
Zaanstad, Neth. 50/B4
Zabbar, Malta 46/M7
Zaber (riv.), Ger. 54/C4
Ząbki, Pol. 41/L2
Ząbkowice Śląskie,
Pol. 41/J3
Žabljak, Serb. 47/F1
Zábřeh, Czh. 41/J4
Zabrze, Pol. 41/K3
Zacapa, Guat. 144/D3
Zacapoaxtla, Mex. 143/M7
Zacapu, Mex. 143/E5
Zacatecas (state),
Mex. 140/A3
Zacatecas, Mex. 142/E4
Zacatecoluca,
ESal. 144/D3
Zacatelco, Mex. 143/L7
Zacatepec, Mex. 143/K8
Zacatlán, Mex. 143/M7
Zachary, La, US 133/F4
Zachodniopomorskie
(prov.), Pol. 41/H2
Zacoalco de Torres,
Mex. 142/E4
Zacualtipán, Mex. 143/L4
Zadar, Cro. 43/L4
Zadetkyi (isl.), Myan. 80/A2
Zafarwāl, Pak. 86/C3
Zafra, Sp. 44/B3
Zagań, Pol. 41/H3
Zaghwān (gov.), Tun. 46/A4
Zaghwān, Tun. 100/M6
Zagora, Mor. 98/D3
Zagorje ob Savi, Slov. 43/L3
Zagreb (cap.), Cro. 48/B3

Zagros (mts.), Iran 88/E1
Zāhedān, Iran 89/H3
Zahirābād, India 82/C4
Zahlah, Leb. 91/D3
Záhony, Hun. 41/M4
Zaïdin, Sp. 45/F2
Zaidpur, India 84/C2
Zaïo, Mor. 100/C2
Zaire (see Congo,
Democratic Republic of the)
Zakamensk, Rus. 70/H1
Zakarpats'ka Oblasti,
Ukr. 62/B2
Zakháro, Gre. 47/G4
Zakhodnyaya Dzvina (riv.),
Bela. 60/E5
Zākhū, Iraq 90/E2
Zakopane, Pol. 41/K4
Zákinthos (isl.), Gre. 47/G4
Zákinthos, Gre. 47/G4
Zakouma, PN de,
Chad 97/J5
Zala (riv.), Hun. 48/C2
Zala (prov.), Hun. 48/C2
Zalaegerszeg, Hun. 48/C2
Zalamea de la Serena,
Sp. 44/C3
Zalamea la Real, Sp. 44/B4
Zalaszentgrót, Hun. 48/C2
Zalău, Rom. 49/F2
Žalec, Slov. 43/L3
Zaltan (well), Libya 96/J2
Zaltbommel, Neth. 50/C5
Zalun, Myan. 83/G4
Zama, Japan 77/C3
Zamania, India 84/D3
Zambezi, Zam. 105/D3
Zambezi (riv.), Moz. 93/E6
Zambia (ctry.), 105/E3
Zamboanga, Phil. 81/F2
Zambrów, Pol. 41/L2
Zamfara (riv.), Nga. 103/G3
Zami (riv.), Myan. 78/B3
Zamora, Ecu. 156/B2
Zamora (riv.), Ecu. 156/C4
Zamora, Sp. 44/C2
Zamora-Chinchipe
(prov.), Ecu. 156/B2
Zamora de Hidalgo,
Mex. 142/E5
Zamość, Pol. 41/M3
Zancara (riv.), Sp. 44/D3
Zanda, China 70/C5
Zandkreekdam (dam),
Neth. 50/A5
Zandvoort, Neth. 50/B4
Zané, It. 59/E1
Zanhuang, China 72/C3
Zanjān, Iran 88/E1
Zanjón (riv.), Mex. 128/E5
Zánka, Hun. 48/C2
Zanzibar (isl.), Tanz. 93/F5
Zanzibar (Kisauni)
(int'l arpt.), Tanz. 104/C4
Zanzibar Central/South
(pol. reg.), Tanz. 104/C4
Zanzibar North (prov.),
Tanz. 104/C4
Zanzibar Urban/West
(pol. reg.), Tanz. 104/C4
Zanzuzi (hill), Tanz. 104/B3
Zaō-san (peak),
Japan 75/G1
Zaoqiang, China 72/C3
Zaouiet Kounta, Alg. 99/E4
Zaoyang, China 72/C4
Zaozhuang, China 72/D4
Zapala, Arg. 158/C3
Zapaleri (peak), SA 157/C1
Zapallar, Chile 158/C2
Zapata (pen.), Cuba 145/F1
Zapata, Tx, US 132/D5
Zapatosa (swamp),
Col. 145/H4
Zapatosa (lake), Col. 152/C2
Zapopan, Mex. 142/E4
Zaporizhzhya, Ukr. 62/E3
Zaporizhzhya (int'l arpt.),
Ukr. 62/E3
Zaporiz'ka Oblasti,
Ukr. 62/E3
Zapotal, Ecu. 152/B5
Zapotillo, Ecu. 156/A2
Zapponeta, It. 46/D2
Zaprešić, Cro. 48/B3
Zara, Turk. 90/D2
Zaragoza, Mex. 143/M7
Zaragoza, Col. 152/C3
Zaragoza (int'l arpt.),
Sp. 45/E2
Zaragoza (Saragossa),
Sp. 45/E2

Zarah, Ks, US 137/D6
Zarand, Iran 89/G2
Zaranda (hill), Nga. 103/H4
Zaranj, Afg. 87/J2
Zárate, Arg. 159/J11
Zaraza, Ven. 153/E2
Zarauz, Sp. 44/D1
Zard (mtn.), Iran 88/F2
Zareh Sharan, Afg. 89/J2
Zargān, Iran 88/F3
Zaria, Nga. 103/G4
Zarmast (pass), Afg. 89/H2
Zărnești, Rom. 49/G3
Žarnovica, Slvk. 48/D1
Zaroś, Gre. 47/J5
Záruby (peak), Slvk. 48/C1
Zaruma, Ecu. 156/B3
Zarumilla, Peru 156/A1
Zary, Pol. 41/H3
Zarza la Mayor, Sp. 44/B3
Zarzal, Col. 152/B3
Zāskār (range), India 70/C5
Zāskār (riv.), India 86/D3
Zastron, SAfr. 106/D3
Zauche (reg.), Ger. 40/P7
Zavalla, Arg. 158/E2
Zavdi'el, Isr. 91/F8
Zaventem, Belg. 53/D2
Zavet, Bul. 49/H4
Zavidovići, Bosn. 48/D3
Zavitinsk, Rus. 71/M1
Zavolzh'ye, Rus. 60/J4
Zawadzkie, Pol. 41/K3
Zawiercie, Pol. 41/K3
Zaysan, Kaz. 70/D2
Zaysan (lake), Kaz. 67/H5
Zayü (riv.), China 83/G2
Zaza (riv.), Cuba 145/G1
Zazárida, Ven. 152/D2
Zbąszyń, Pol. 41/H2
Zd'ár nad Sázavou,
Czh. 41/H4
Zdice, Czh. 41/H4
Zduńska Wola, Pol. 41/K3
Zeballos (peak),
Arg. 159/C5
Zebbuġ, Malta 46/L7
Zeddine (riv.), Alg. 100/F5
Zedelgem, Belg. 52/C1
Zeehan, Austl. 115/C4
Zeeland, Mi, US 130/C3
Zeeland (prov.),
Neth. 50/A5
Zeerust, SAfr. 105/E6
Zeewolde, Neth. 50/C4
Zefat, Isr. 91/D3
Zegrzyńskie
(res.), Pol. 41/L2
Zehdenick, Ger. 41/G2
Zeil (mt.), Austl. 113/G2
Zeil, Ger. 54/D2
Zeiselmauer, Aus. 49/N7
Zeist, Neth. 50/C4
Zeitz, Ger. 40/G3
Zejtun, Malta 46/M7
Zekharya, Isr. 91/F8
Zele, Belg. 52/D1
Zelenodol'sk, Rus. 61/L5
Zelenogorsk, Rus. 63/N3
Zelenokumsk, Rus. 63/H4
Zelhem, Neth. 50/D4
Zell, Swi. 56/D3
Zell, Swi. 56/D3
Zell, Ger. 53/G3
Zell am Harmersbach,
Ger. 56/E1
Zell am Main, Ger. 54/D2
Zell am Moos, Aus. 55/G2
Zell am See, Aus. 55/G6
Zell an der Pram,
Aus. 55/G6
Zell in Wiesental,
Ger. 56/E1
Zellersee (lake), Aus. 54/G2
Zellingen, Ger. 54/D2
Zelów, Pol. 41/K3
Zeltingen-Rachtig,
Ger. 53/G4
Zeltweg, Aus. 43/J3
Zelzate, Belg. 52/C1
Zemaitija NP, Lith. 39/J3
Zembra (isls.), Tun. 46/A4
Zemen, Bul. 47/H1
Zemio, CAfr. 97/L6
Zemmer, Ger. 53/F4
Zemmora, Alg. 100/F5
Zempoala, Mex. 143/N7
Zempoala (peak),
Mex. 143/Q10
Zempoaltepec, Cerro
(peak), Mex. 144/C2
Zemst, Belg. 53/D2
Zenica, Bosn. 48/D3
Zenith, Wa, US 135/C3
Zenn (riv.), Ger. 54/D2
Zenne (riv.), Belg. 53/D1
Zenon Park,
Sk, Can. 127/H2
Zepče, Bosn. 48/D3
Zepu, China 87/G5
Zeralda, Alg. 100/G4

Zeravshan (riv.),
Taj.,Uzb. 87/E5
Zermatt, Swi. 56/D5
Zernez, Swi. 57/G4
Zernien, Ger. 51/H2
Zernograd, Rus. 62/G3
Zero Branco, It. 59/F1
Zeta (lake), Nun., Can. 122/F1
Zetel, Ger. 51/E2
Zeuthen, Ger. 40/Q7
Zeven, Ger. 51/G2
Zevenaar, Neth. 50/D5
Zevenbergen, Neth. 50/B5
Zevgolation, Gre. 47/H4
Zevio, It. 59/E2
Zeya (res.), Rus. 65/M4
Zeya (riv.), Rus. 65/N4
Zeya-Bureya (plain),
Rus. 65/N4
Zeytindağ, Turk. 90/A2
Zêzere (riv.), Port. 44/A3
Zghartā, Leb. 91/D2
Zgorzelec, Pol. 41/H3
Zgierz, Pol. 41/K3
Zhambyl (obl.), Kaz. 87/H4
Zhambyl, Kaz. 87/H4
Zhangaözen, Kaz. 63/K4
Zhangaqazaly, Kaz. 87/D3
Zhangatas, Kaz. 87/E4
Zhanghei, China 72/C3
Zhangjiakou, China 72/C2
Zhangping, China 79/C2
Zhangpu, China 79/C3
Zhangqiu, China 72/D3
Zhangshu, China 79/C2
Zhangwei (riv.),
China 72/D3
Zhangye, China 70/H4
Zhangzhou, China 79/C3
Zhangzi, China 72/C3
Zhanhua, China 72/D3
Zhanjiang, China 83/K3
Zhao Xian, China 79/C3
Zhaojue, China 83/H2
Zhaoqing, China 83/K3
Zhaotong, China 83/H2
Zhaoyuan, China 72/D3
Zhaozhou, China 71/N2
Zhayya (Ural) (riv.),
Kaz.,Rus. 64/F5
Zhayyq (riv.), Kaz. 67/E5
Zhecheng, China 72/C4
Zhejiang (prov.),
China 79/D2
Zhelaniya (cape), Rus. 64/G2
Zheleznodorozhnyy,
Rus. 61/L3
Zheleznogorsk, Rus. 62/E1
Zheleznogorsk-Ilimskiy,
Rus. 65/L4
Zhenfeng Bouyeizu Miaozu
Zizhixian, China 83/J2
Zhengding, China 72/C3
Zhenglan, China 71/L3
Zhenning, China 83/H2
Zhenyang, China 83/H3
Zhengzhou, China 72/C4
Zhenhai, China 79/D2
Zhenjiang, China 79/D2
Zhenkang, China 83/G3
Zhenning Bouyeizu Miaozu
Zizhixian, China 83/J2
Zhenping, China 72/C4
Zhentou (riv.),
China 72/B3
Zhenwu (mtn.),
China 72/B3
Zhenxiong, China 83/H2
Zhenyuan, China 83/H3
Zhenyuan, China 83/H3
Zhetiqara, Kaz. 63/M1
Zhezqazghan, Kaz. 87/F3
Zhezqazghan (obl.),
Kaz. 87/E3
Zhicheng, China 79/B1
Zhigulevsk, Rus. 63/J1
Zhijiang, China 79/B1
Zhijin, China 83/H2
Zhiloy (isl.), Azer. 63/J4
Zhlobin, Bela. 62/D1
Zhmerynka, Ukr. 62/D2
Zhob, Pak. 89/J2
Zhob (riv.), Pak. 89/J2
Zhodino, Bela. 39/N4
Zhokhov (isl.), Rus. 65/R2
Zhongba, China 83/D3
Zhongshan, China 72/C5
Zhongxiang, China 72/C5
Zhoukou, China 72/C4
Zhoushan, China 79/D2
Zhoushan (isls.),
China 79/D2
Zhouzhou, China 72/C4
Zhovtneve, Ukr. 49/J1
Zhovtneve, Ukr. 62/E3
Zhuanghe, China 72/E2
Zhucheng, China 72/D4
Zhugqu, China 72/A4
Zhuhai, China 79/C4
Zhuji, China 79/D2
Zhujiang Kou (bay),
China 71/T10
Zhukovka, Rus. 62/E1
Zhukovskiy, Rus. 61/X9

Zhumadian, China 72/C4
Zhuolu, China 72/G6
Zhuozi, China 72/C2
Zhushan, China 72/B4
Zhuxi, China 72/B4
Zhuzhou, China 83/K2
Zhuzhou, China 83/K2
Zhytomyr, Ukr. 62/D2
Zhytomyrs'ka Oblasti,
Ukr. 62/C2
Zi (riv.), China 79/B2
Zia (int'l arpt.), Bang. 85/H4
Zibo, China 72/D3
Zielona Góra, Pol. 41/H3
Zierenberg, Ger. 51/G6
Zierikzee, Neth. 50/A5
Ziftá, Egypt 91/B4
Zigong, China 83/H2
Zigui, China 72/B5
Ziguinchor
(int'l arpt.), Sen. 102/A3
Ziguinchor (pol. reg.),
Sen. 102/A3
Zihuatanejo, Mex. 143/E5
Zijing (mtn.), China 72/C6
Zikhron Ya'aqov, Isr. 91/F6
Zile, Turk. 90/C1
Žilina, Slvk. 41/K4
Žilina
(pol. reg.), Slvk. 41/K4
Zillah, Libya 96/J2
Ziller (riv.), Aus. 43/J3
Zillisheim, Fr. 56/D2
Zilupe, Lat. 39/N4
Zimapán, Mex. 143/F4
Zimatlán de Alvarez,
Mex. 144/B2
Zimba, Zam. 105/E4
Zimbabwe (ctry.) 105/E4
Zimla (well), Alg. 98/E4
Zimnicea, Rom. 49/G4
Zinapécuaro de Figueroa,
Mex. 143/E5
Zinave, PN de, Moz. 105/F4
Zinder, Niger 103/H3
Zinder (dept.), Niger 103/H3
Ziniaré, Burk. 103/E3
Zinjin, China 79/C3
Zion, Md, US 138/C4
Zion NP, Ut, US 128/D3
Zippori, Isr. 91/G6
Zirc, Hun. 48/C2
Žirje (isl.), Cro. 48/B4
Zirl, Aus. 57/H3
Ziro, India 83/F2
Zitácuaro, Mex. 143/E5
Zittau, Ger. 41/H3
Živinice, Bosn. 48/D3
Ziwa Magharibi
(pol. reg.), Tanz. 104/A3
Zixi, China 79/C2
Zixing, China 83/K2
Ziya (riv.), China 72/D3
Ziyyon, Isr. 91/G8
Ziz, Oued (riv.), Mor. 98/D2
Zlatna, Rom. 49/F2
Zlatograd, Bul. 47/J2
Zlatorsko (lake), Serb. 47/E1
Zlatoust, Rus. 61/N5
Zlin, Czh. 41/J4
Zliv, Czh. 55/H4
Zlín (pol. reg.), Czh. 41/J4
Zliv, Czh. 55/H4
Złocieniec, Pol. 41/J2
Złot, Serb. 48/E3
Złotoryja, Pol. 41/H3
Złotów, Pol. 41/J2
Žlutice, Czh. 55/G2
Żmigród, Pol. 41/J3
Znam'yanka, Ukr. 62/E2
Žnin, Pol. 41/J2
Znojmo, Czh. 41/J4
Zocca, It. 59/D4

Zou (prov.), Ben. 103/F5
Zou Xian, China 72/D4
Zouérat, Mrta. 98/B5
Zound-Wéogo (prov.),
Burk. 103/E4
Zouping, China 72/D3
Zousfana, Oued (riv.),
Alg. 99/E3
Zrenjanin, Serb. 48/E3
Zschopau
(riv.), Ger. 55/F1
Zuata, Ven. 153/E2
Zubia, Sp. 44/D4
Zucchero (peak),
Swi. 57/E5
Zuckerhütl (peak),
Aus. 57/H4
Zuehl, Tx, US 137/U21
Zug, Swi. 57/E3
Zug (canton), Swi. 57/E3
Zugdidi, Geo. 63/G4
Zugersee (lake), Swi. 43/H3
Zughrār (well), Libya 99/H3
Zugspitze (peak),
Ger. 57/G3
Zuid Holland (prov.),
Neth. 50/A5
Zuid-Willemsvaart
(canal), Belg.,Neth 50/C6
Zuidbeveland (isl.),
Neth. 50/A6
Zuidelijk Flevoland
(polder), Neth. 50/C4
Zuidhorn, Neth. 50/D2
Zuidlaardermeer
(lake), Neth. 50/D2
Zuidlaren, Neth. 50/D2
Zuidwolde, Neth. 50/D3
Zuienkerke, Belg. 52/C1
Zújar (riv.), Sp. 44/C3
Zújar, Sp. 44/D4
Zújar, Embalse
(res.), Sp. 44/C3
Zulia (riv.), Ven. 150/D2
Zulia (state), Ven. 145/H4
Zülpich, Ger. 53/F2
Zulte, Belg. 52/C2
Zululand (reg.), SAfr. 107/E2
Zumárraga, Sp. 44/D1
Zumba, Ecu. 156/B2
Zumbo, Moz. 105/E3
Zumpango de Ocampo,
Mex. 143/K7
Zumpango del Río,
Mex. 143/F5
Zundert, Neth. 50/B5
Zunhua, China 72/H6
Zuni (riv.), Az,NM, US 128/E4
Zuni, NM, US 128/E4
Zuni (res.), NM, US 132/A3
Zunyi, China 83/J2
Zuo (riv.), China 79/A3
Zuo Jiang (riv.),
China 78/D1
Zuoquan, China 72/C3
Zuoyun, China 72/C3
Zuoz, Swi. 57/F4
Županja, Cro. 48/D3
Žur, Serb. 47/G1
Zurbāţīyah, Iraq 88/E2
Zürich (canton), Swi. 57/E2
Zürich, Swi. 57/E3
Zürich (int'l arpt.), Swi. 57/E3
Zürich, Swi. 57/E3
Zürichsee (lake), Swi. 43/H3
Zuromin, Pol. 41/K2
Zurrieq, Malta 46/L7
Zurzach, Swi. 57/E2
Zusam (riv.), Ger. 43/J2
Zushi, Japan 77/D3
Zusmarshausen, Ger. 54/D6
Zutiua (riv.), Braz. 154/A2
Zutphen, Neth. 50/D4
Zuurberg NP, SAfr. 106/D4
Zuwārah, Libya 96/H1
Zuyevka, Rus. 61/L4
Zvijesda NP, Bosn. 48/D4
Zvishavane, Zim. 105/F5
Zvolen, Slvk. 62/A2
Zvornik, Bosn. 48/D3
Zwarte Meer
(lake), Neth. 50/D3
Zwartsluis, Neth. 50/D3
Zwedru, Libr. 102/C5
Zweibrücken, Ger. 53/G5
Zweisimmen, Swi. 56/D4
Zwesten, Ger. 51/G6
Zwevegem, Belg. 52/C2
Zwickau, Ger. 43/K1
Zwickauer Mulde
(riv.), Ger. 40/G3
Zwijndrecht, Belg. 53/D1
Zwischenahner Meer
(lake), Ger. 51/F2
Zwischenwasser,
Aus. 57/F3
Zwoleń, Pol. 41/L3
Żywiec, Pol. 41/K4

THE WORLD ALMANAC®
WORLD ATLAS

World Almanac Section

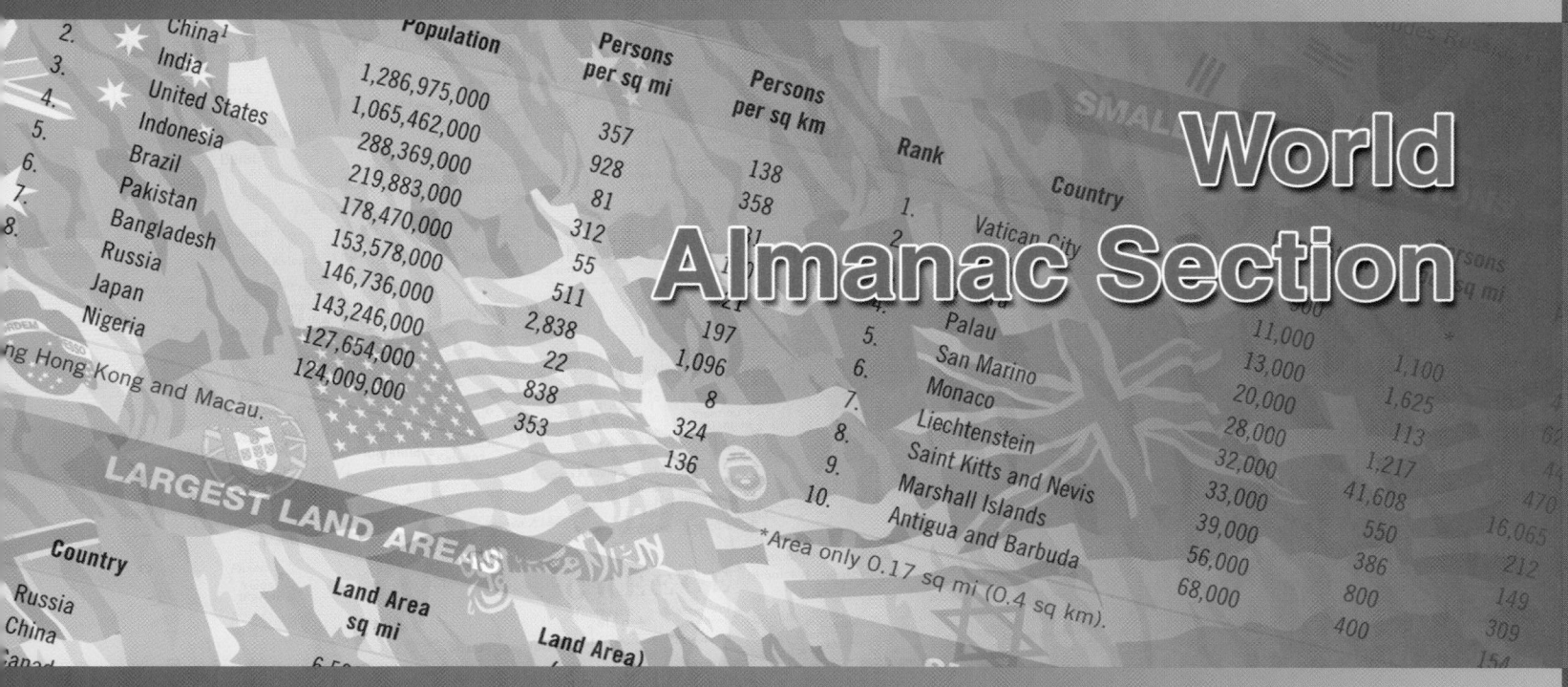

	Country	Population	Persons per sq mi	Persons per sq km
2.	China[1]	1,286,975,000	357	138
3.	India	1,065,462,000	928	358
4.	United States	288,369,000	81	
5.	Indonesia	219,883,000	312	
6.	Brazil	178,470,000	55	
7.	Pakistan	153,578,000	511	197
8.	Bangladesh	146,736,000	2,838	1,096
	Russia	143,246,000	22	8
	Japan	127,654,000	838	324
	Nigeria	124,009,000	353	136

Hong Kong and Macau.

LARGEST LAND AREAS

Country	Land Area sq mi	Land Area (
Russia		
China	6,59	
Canada		

SMALL

Rank	Country		
1.	Vatican City	11,000	
2.		13,000	1,100
4.		20,000	1,625
5.	Palau	28,000	113
6.	San Marino	32,000	1,217
7.	Monaco	33,000	41,608
8.	Liechtenstein	39,000	550
9.	Saint Kitts and Nevis	56,000	386
10.	Marshall Islands	68,000	800
	Antigua and Barbuda		400

*Area only 0.17 sq mi (0.4 sq km).

Nation Facts and Figures
from The World Almanac®

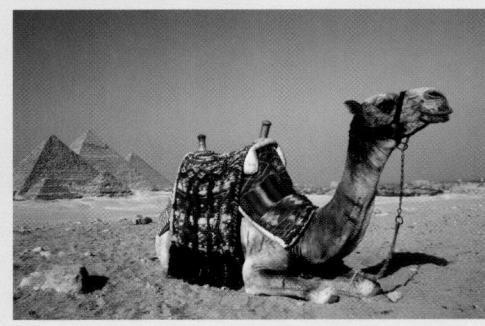

AFRICA

Among African nations, Sudan occupies the largest total area, but Nigeria has the largest population, ranking tenth in the world as of 2003.

ALGERIA

FOR MAP, SEE PAGE 96

Population: 31,800,000
Ethnic groups: Arab-Berber 99%
Principal languages: Arabic (official), French, Berber dialects
Chief religion: Sunni Muslim (official) 99%
Area: 919,600 sq mi (2,381,741 sq km)
Topography: The Tell, located on the coast, comprises fertile plains 50-100 mi (80-160 km) wide. Two major chains of the Atlas Mountains, running roughly east to west and reaching 7,000 ft (2,100 m), enclose a dry plateau region. Below lies the Sahara, mostly desert with major mineral resources.
Capital: Algiers (pop., 2,861,000)
Independence date: July 5, 1962   **Government type:** republic
Head of state: Pres. Abdelaziz Bouteflika
Head of government: Prime Min. Ahmed Ouyahia
Monetary unit: dinar
GDP: $177 billion (2001 est.)   **Per capita GDP:** $5,600
Industries: petroleum, natural gas, light industries, mining, electrical, petrochemical, food processing
Chief crops: wheat, barley, oats, grapes, olives, citrus, fruits
Minerals: petroleum, natural gas, iron ore, phosphates, uranium, lead, zinc
Life expectancy at birth (years): male, 69.1; female, 72.0
Literacy rate: 61.6%
Website: www.algeria-us.org

ANGOLA

FOR MAP, SEE PAGE 105

Population: 13,625,000
Ethnic groups: Ovimbundu 37%, Kimbundu 25%, Bakongo 13%
Principal languages: Portuguese (official), Bantu and other African languages
Chief religions: indigenous beliefs 47%, Roman Catholic 38%, Protestant 15%
Area: 481,400 sq mi (1,246,700 sq km)`
Topography: Most of Angola consists of a plateau elevated 3,000 to 5,000 ft (900 to 1,500 m) above sea level, rising from a narrow coastal strip. There is also a temperate highland area in the west-central region, a desert in the south, and a tropical rain forest covering Cabinda.
Capital: Luanda (pop., 2,819,000)
Independence date: November 11, 1975   **Government type:** republic
Head of state: Pres. José Eduardo dos Santos
Head of government: Prime Min. Fernando da Piedade Dias dos Santos
Monetary unit: kwanza
GDP: $13.3 billion (2001 est.)   **Per capita GDP:** $1,330
Industries: petroleum, mining, cement, basic metal products, fish processing, food processing
Chief crops: bananas, sugarcane, coffee, sisal, corn, cotton, manioc, tobacco, vegetables, plantains
Minerals: petroleum, diamonds, iron ore, phosphates, copper, feldspar, gold, bauxite, uranium
Life expectancy at birth (years): male, 36.1; female, 37.8
Literacy rate: 42%
Website: www.angola.org

ABOUT THE WORLD ALMANAC DATA: Population figures for cities generally pertain to the entire metropolitan area. GDP (gross domestic product) estimates are based on so-called purchasing power parity calculations, which make use of weighted prices in order to take into account differences in price levels between countries. Please note that the addresses and content of websites are subject to change.

CHIEF ABBREVIATIONS USED IN THE WORLD ALMANAC SECTION

| est. | estimate(d) | ft | foot, feet | Gov.-Gen. | Governor-General | in | inch(es) | km | kilometer(s) | m | meter(s) |
| mi | mile(s) | NA | not available | pop. | population | Pres. | President | Prime Min. | Prime Minister | sq | square |

BENIN

FOR MAP, SEE PAGE 103

Population: 6,736,000

Ethnic groups: 42 groups, including Fon, Adja, Yoruba, and Bariba

Principal languages: French (official), Fon, Yoruba, various tribal languages

Chief religions: indigenous beliefs 50%, Christian 30%, Muslim 20%

Area: 43,480 sq mi (112,620 sq km)

Capital: Porto-Novo (pop., 225,000)

Topography: Most of Benin is flat and covered with dense vegetation. The coast is hot, humid, and rainy.

Independence date: August 1, 1960

Government type: republic

Head of state and government: Pres. Mathieu Kerekou

Monetary unit: CFA franc

GDP: $6.8 billion (2001 est.)

Per capita GDP: $1,040

Industries: textiles, food processing, chemical production, construction materials

Chief crops: cotton, corn, cassava, yams, beans, palm oil, peanuts

Minerals: offshore oil, limestone, marble

Life expectancy at birth (years): male, 50.4; female, 51.8

Literacy rate: 37.5%

Website: www.embassy.org/embassies/bj.html

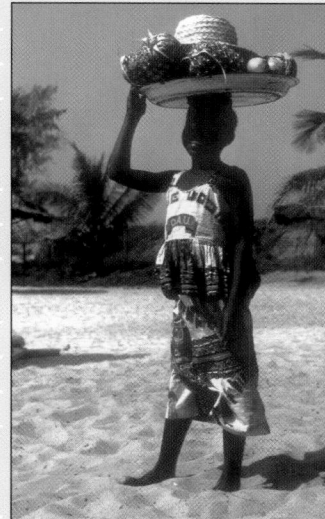

West African fruit seller

BOTSWANA

FOR MAP, SEE PAGE 105

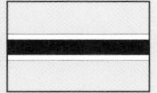

Population: 1,785,000

Ethnic groups: Tswana 79%, Kalanga 11%, Basarwa 3%

Principal languages: English (official), Setswana

Chief religions: indigenous beliefs 85%, Christian 15%

Area: 231,800 sq mi (600,370 sq km)

Topography: The Kalahari Desert, supporting nomadic Bushmen and wildlife, spreads over the southwest; there are swamplands and farming areas in the north, and rolling plains in the east where livestock are grazed.

Capital: Gaborone (pop., 225,000)

Independence date: September 30, 1966

Government type: parliamentary republic

Head of state and government: Pres. Festus Mogae

Monetary unit: pula

GDP: $12.4 billion (2001 est.)   **Per capita GDP:** $7,800

Industries: mining, livestock processing, textiles

Chief crops: sorghum, maize, millet, beans, sunflowers, groundnuts

Minerals: diamonds, copper, nickel, salt, soda ash, potash, coal, iron ore, silver

Life expectancy at birth (years): male, 32.2; female, 32.3

Literacy rate: 69.8%   **Website:** www.gov.bw

BURKINA FASO

FOR MAP, SEE PAGE 103

Population: 13,002,000

Ethnic groups: Mossi (approximately 40%), Gurunsi, Senufo, Lobi, Bobo, Mande, Fulani

Principal languages: French (official), Sudanic languages

Chief religions: Muslim 50%, indigenous beliefs 40%, Christian (mainly Roman Catholic) 10%

Area: 105,900 sq mi (274,200 sq km)

Topography: Landlocked Burkina Faso is in the savanna region of West Africa. The north is arid, hot, and thinly populated.

Capital: Ouagadougou (pop., 862,000)

Independence date: August 5, 1960 **Government type:** republic

Head of state: Pres. Blaise Compaoré

Head of government: Prime Min. Paramanga Ernest Yonli

Monetary unit: CFA franc

GDP: $12.8 billion (2001 est.)   **Per capita GDP:** $1,040

Industries: cotton lint, beverages, agricultural processing, soap, cigarettes, textiles, gold

Chief crops: peanuts, shea nuts, sesame, cotton, sorghum, millet, corn, rice

Minerals: manganese, limestone, marble, gold, antimony, copper, nickel, bauxite, lead, phosphates, zinc, silver

Life expectancy at birth (years): male, 43.0; female, 45.9

Literacy rate: 36%

Website: www.burkinaembassy–usa.org

BURUNDI

FOR MAP, SEE PAGE 104

Population: 6,825,000

Ethnic groups: Hutu 85%, Tutsi 14%, Twa (Pygmy) 1%

Principal languages: Kirundi, French (both official); Swahili

Chief religions: Roman Catholic 62%, indigenous beliefs 23%, Muslim 10%, Protestant 5%

Area: 10,750 sq mi (27,830 sq km)

Topography: Much of the country is grassy highland, with mountains reaching 8,900 ft (2,700 m). The southernmost source of the White Nile is located in Burundi. Lake Tanganyika is the second deepest lake in the world.

Capital: Bujumbura (pop., 346,000)

Independence date: July 1, 1962

Government type: in transition

Head of state and government: Pres. Domitien Ndayizeye

Monetary unit: franc

GDP: $3.7 billion (2001 est.)

Per capita GDP: $600

Industries: light consumer goods, assembly of imported components, public works construction, food processing

Chief crops: coffee, cotton, tea, corn, sorghum, sweet potatoes, bananas, manioc

Minerals: nickel, uranium, rare earth oxides, peat, cobalt, copper, platinum (not yet exploited), vanadium

Life expectancy at birth (years): male, 42.5; female, 43.9

Literacy rate: 35.3%

Website: www.burundi.gov.bi

CAMEROON

FOR MAP, SEE PAGE 96

Population: 16,018,000

Ethnic groups: Highlanders 31%, Equatorial Bantu 19%, Kirdi 11%, Fulani 10%, northwest Bantu 8%, east Nigritic 7%

Principal languages: English, French (both official); 24 African language groups

Chief religions: indigenous beliefs 40%, Christian 40%, Muslim 20%

Nation Facts and Figures

Cameroon (continued)

Area: 183,570 sq mi (475,440 sq km)

Topography: A low coastal plain with rain forests is in the south; plateaus in the center lead to forested mountains in the west, including Mt. Cameroon, 13,350 ft (4,070 m); grasslands in the north lead to marshes around Lake Chad.

Capital: Yaoundé (pop., 1,481,000)

Independence date: January 1, 1960 **Government type:** republic

Head of state: Pres. Paul Biya

Head of government: Prime Min. Peter Mafani Musonge

Monetary unit: CFA franc **GDP:** $26.4 billion (2001 est.)

Per capita GDP: $1,700

Industries: petroleum production and refining, food processing, light consumer goods, textiles, lumber

Chief crops: coffee, cocoa, cotton, rubber, bananas, oilseed, grains, root starches

Minerals: petroleum, bauxite, iron ore

Life expectancy at birth (years): male, 47.2; female, 49.0

Literacy rate: 63.4%

Website: www.cameroon.gov.cm

CAPE VERDE

FOR MAP, SEE PAGE 93

Population: 463,000

Ethnic groups: Creole 71%, African 28%, European 1%

Principal languages: Portuguese (official), Crioulo

Chief religions: Roman Catholic (infused with indigenous beliefs), Protestant (mostly Church of the Nazarene)

Area: 1,560 sq mi (4,030 sq km)

Topography: Cape Verde Islands are 15 in number, volcanic in origin (active crater on Fogo). The landscape is eroded and stark, with vegetation mostly in interior valleys.

Ripe papayas

Capital: Praia (pop., 82,000)

Independence date: July 5, 1975

Government type: republic

Head of state: Pres. Pedro Pires

Head of government: Prime Min. José Maria Neves

Monetary unit: escudo

GDP: $600 million (2001 est.) **Per capita GDP:** $1,500

Industries: food and beverages, fish processing, shoes and garments, salt mining, ship repair

Chief crops: bananas, corn, beans, sweet potatoes, sugarcane, coffee, peanuts

Minerals: salt, basalt rock, limestone, kaolin

Life expectancy at birth (years): male, 66.5; female, 73.2

Literacy rate: 71.6%

Website: capeverdeusaembassy.org

CENTRAL AFRICAN REPUBLIC

FOR MAP, SEE PAGE 97

Population: 3,865,000

Ethnic groups: Baya 33%, Banda 27%, Mandjia 13%, Sara 10%, Mboum 7%, M'Baka 4%, Yakoma 4%

Principal languages: French (official), Sangho (national), tribal languages

Chief religions: indigenous beliefs 35%, Protestant 25%, Roman Catholic 25%, Muslim 15%

Area: 240,530 sq mi (622,984 sq km)

Topography: Mostly rolling plateau, average altitude 2,000 ft (600 m), with rivers draining south to the Congo and north to Lake Chad. Open, well-watered savanna covers most of the area, with an arid area in the northeast and tropical rain forest in the southwest.

Capital: Bangui (pop., 666,000)

Independence date: August 13, 1960

Government type: in transition

Head of state: Pres. François Bozizé

Head of government: Prime Min. Abel Goumba

Monetary unit: CFA franc

GDP: $4.6 billion (2001 est.) **Per capita GDP:** $1,300

Industries: diamond mining, sawmills, breweries, textiles, footwear, assembly of bicycles and motorcycles

Chief crops: cotton, coffee, tobacco, manioc, yams, millet, corn, bananas

Minerals: diamonds, uranium, gold, oil

Life expectancy at birth (years): male, 40.2; female, 43.3

Literacy rate: 60% **Website:** embassy.org/embassies/cf.html

CHAD

FOR MAP, SEE PAGE 97

Population: 8,598,000

Ethnic groups: about 200 groups; largest are Arabs in north and Sara in south

Principal languages: French, Arabic (both official); Sara; more than 120 different languages and dialects

Chief religions: Muslim 51%, Christian 35%, animist 7%, other 7%

Area: 496,000 sq mi (1,284,000 sq km)

Topography: Wooded savanna, steppe, and desert in the south; part of the Sahara in the north. Southern rivers flow north to Lake Chad, surrounded by marshland.

Capital: N'Djamena (pop., 735,000)

Independence date: August 11, 1960

Government type: republic

Head of state: Pres. Idriss Déby

Head of government: Prime Min. Moussa Faki

Monetary unit: CFA franc

GDP: $8.9 billion (2001 est.) **Per capita GDP:** $1,030

Industries: cotton textiles, meatpacking, beer brewing, natron, soap, cigarettes, construction materials

Chief crops: cotton, sorghum, millet, peanuts, rice, potatoes, manioc

Minerals: petroleum (unexploited but exploration under way), uranium, natron, kaolin

Life expectancy at birth (years): male, 47.0; female, 50.1

Literacy rate: 40%

Website: chadembassy.org

COMOROS

FOR MAP, SEE PAGE 107

Population: 768,000

Ethnic groups: Antalote, Cafre, Makoa, Oimatsaha, Sakalava (all are mostly an African-Arab mix)

Principal languages: Arabic, French (both official); Shikomoro (a blend of Swahili and Arabic)

Chief religion: Muslim (official) 98%

Area: 840 sq mi (2,170 sq km)

Topography: The islands are of volcanic origin, with an active volcano on Grande Comore.

Capital: Moroni (pop., 49,000)

Independence date: July 6, 1975   **Government type:** in transition

Head of state and government: Pres. Azali Assoumanis

Monetary unit: franc

GDP: $424 million (2001 est.)   **Per capita GDP:** $710

Industries: tourism, perfume distillation

Chief crops: vanilla, cloves, perfume essences, copra, coconuts, bananas, cassava

Life expectancy at birth (years): male, 58.9; female, 63.5

Literacy rate: 57.3%

Website: www.presidence-uniondescomores.com/v2/Pages/anglais/index_a.html

CONGO, DEMOCRATIC REPUBLIC OF THE

Population: 52,771,000   FOR MAP, SEE PAGE 93

Ethnic groups: Over 200 groups; the four largest, the Mongo, Luba, Kongo (all Bantu), and Mangbetu-Azande (Hamitic), make up 45% of the population

Principal languages: French (official), Lingala, Kingwana (a Swahili dialect), Kikongo, Tshiluba

Chief religions: Roman Catholic 50%, Protestant 20%, Kimbanguist 10%, Muslim 10%

Area: 905,570 sq mi (2,345,410 sq km)

Topography: Congo includes the bulk of the Congo River basin. The vast central region is a low-lying plateau covered by rain forest. Mountainous terraces in the west, savannas in the south and southeast, grasslands toward the north, and the high Ruwenzori Mountains in the east surround the central region. A short strip of territory borders the Atlantic Ocean. The Congo River is 2,718 mi (4,374 km) long.

Capital: Kinshasa (pop., 5,064,000)

Independence date: June 30, 1960

Government type: republic with strong presidential authority (in transition)

Head of state and government: Pres. Joseph Kabila

Monetary unit: Congolese franc

GDP: $32 billion (2001 est.)   **Per capita GDP:** $590

Industries: mining, mineral processing, consumer products, cement

Chief crops: coffee, sugar, palm oil, rubber, tea, quinine, cassava, palm oil, bananas, root crops, corn, fruits

Minerals: cobalt, copper, cadmium, petroleum, industrial and gem diamonds, gold, silver, zinc, manganese, tin, germanium, uranium, radium, bauxite, iron ore, coal

Life expectancy at birth (years): male, 46.8; female, 51.1

Literacy rate: 77.3%

Website: www.embassy.org/embassies/ZR.html

CONGO REPUBLIC

FOR MAP, SEE PAGE 93

Population: 3,724,000

Ethnic groups: Kongo 48%, Sangha 20%, M'Bochi 12%, Teke 17%

Principal languages: French (official), Lingala, Monokutuba, Kikongo, many local languages and dialects

Chief religions: Christian 50%, animist 48%, Muslim 2%

Area: 132,000 sq mi (342,000 sq km)

Topography: Much of the Congo is covered by thick forests. A coastal plain leads to the fertile Niari Valley. The center is a plateau; the Congo River basin consists of flood plains in the lower portion and savanna in the upper.

Capital: Brazzaville (pop., 1,360,000)

Independence date: August 15, 1960   **Government type:** republic

Head of state and government: Pres. Denis Sassou-Nguesso

Monetary unit: CFA franc

GDP: $2.5 billion (2001 est.)   **Per capita GDP:** $900

Industries: petroleum extraction, cement, lumber, brewing, sugar, palm oil, soap, flour, cigarettes

Chief crops: cassava, sugar, rice, corn, peanuts, vegetables, coffee, cocoa

Minerals: petroleum, potash, lead, zinc, uranium, copper, phosphates, natural gas

Life expectancy at birth (years): male, 49.0; female, 51.0

Literacy rate: 74.9%   **Website:** www.embassyofcongo.org

CÔTE D'IVOIRE (IVORY COAST)

FOR MAP, SEE PAGE 102

Population: 16,631,000

Ethnic groups: Akan 42%, Voltaiques (Gur) 18%, north Mandes 17%, Krous 11%, south Mandes 10%

Principal languages: French (official), Dioula, many native dialects

Chief religions: Muslim 35-40%, Christian 20-30%, indigenous beliefs 25-40%

Area: 124,500 sq mi (322,460 sq km)

Familiar wildlife of sub-Saharan Africa: zebras (right) rank among the favorite prey of lions (left)

Côte d'Ivoire (Ivory Coast) *(continued)*

Topography: Forests cover the western half of the country, and range from a coastal strip to halfway to the north in the east. A sparse inland plain leads to low mountains in the northwest.

Official capital: Yamoussoukro (pop., 120,000); de facto capital, Abidjan (pop., 3,956,000)

Independence date: August 7, 1960   **Government type:** in transition

Head of state: Pres. Laurent Gbagbo

Head of government: Prime Min. Seydou Diarra

Monetary unit: CFA franc

GDP: $25.5 billion (2001 est.)   **Per capita GDP:** $1,550

Industries: foodstuffs, beverages, wood products, oil refining, truck and bus assembly, textiles, fertilizer, building materials, electricity

Chief crops: coffee, cocoa beans, bananas, palm kernels, corn, rice, manioc, sweet potatoes, sugar, cotton, rubber

Minerals: petroleum, natural gas, diamonds, manganese, iron ore, cobalt, bauxite, copper

Life expectancy at birth (years): male, 40.3; female, 45.0

Literacy rate: 48.5%

Website: www.embassies.org/embassies/ci.html

DJIBOUTI

FOR MAP, SEE PAGE 97

Population: 703,000

Ethnic groups: Somali 60%, Afar 35%

Principal languages: French, Arabic (both official); Afar, Somali

Chief religions: Muslim 94%, Christian 6%

Area: 8,500 sq mi (22,000 sq km)

Topography: The territory—divided into a low coastal plain, mountains behind, and an interior plateau—is arid, sandy, and desolate.

Capital: Djibouti (pop., 542,000)

Independence date: June 27, 1977   **Government type:** republic

Head of state: Pres. Ismail Omar Guelleh

Head of government: Prime Min. Dileita Mohamed Dileita

Monetary unit: Djibouti franc

GDP: $586 million (2001 est.)   **Per capita GDP:** $1,400

Industries: construction, agricultural processing

Chief crops: fruits, vegetables

Life expectancy at birth (years): male, 41.8; female, 44.5

Literacy rate: 46.2%

Website: embassy.org/embassies/dj.html

EGYPT

FOR MAP, SEE PAGE 97

Population: 71,931,000

Ethnic groups: Egyptian Arab 99%

Principal languages: Arabic (official), English, French

Chief religions: Muslim (official; mostly Sunni) 94%, Coptic Christian and other 6%

Area: 386,660 sq mi (1,001,450 sq km)

Topography: Almost entirely desolate and barren, with hills and mountains in the east and along the Nile. The Nile Valley, where most of the people live, stretches 550 mi (885 km).

Capital: Cairo (pop., 9,586,000)

Independence date: February 28, 1922   **Government type:** republic

Head of state: Pres. Hosni Mubarak

The Great Sphinx and pyramids at Giza (Al Jizah), Egypt

Head of government: Prime Min. Atef Obeid

Monetary unit: pound

GDP: $258 billion (2001 est.)   **Per capita GDP:** $3,700

Industries: textiles, food processing, tourism, chemicals, hydrocarbons, construction, cement, metals

Chief crops: cotton, rice, corn, wheat, beans, fruits, vegetables

Minerals: petroleum, natural gas, iron ore, phosphates, manganese, limestone, gypsum, talc, asbestos, lead, zinc

Life expectancy at birth (years): male, 67.9; female, 73.0

Literacy rate: 51.4%

Website: www.sis.gov.eg

EQUATORIAL GUINEA

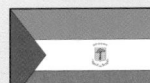

FOR MAP, SEE PAGE 96

Population: 494,000

Ethnic groups: Fang 83%, Bubi 10%

Principal languages: Spanish, French (both official); Fang, Bubi, pidgin English, Portuguese Creole, Ibo

Chief religions: nominally Christian and predominantly Roman Catholic, traditional practices

Area: 10,830 sq mi (28,050 sq km)

Topography: Bioko Island consists of two volcanic mountains and a connecting valley. Rio Muni, with over 90% of the area, has a coastal plain and low hills beyond.

Capital: Malabo (pop., 33,000)

Independence date: October 12, 1968   **Government type:** republic

Head of state: Pres. Teodoro Obiang Nguema Mbasogo

Head of government: Prime Min. Cándido Muatetema Rivas

Monetary unit: CFA franc

GDP: $1.04 billion (2001 est.)   **Per capita GDP:** $2,100

Industries: petroleum, fishing, sawmilling, natural gas

Chief crops: coffee, cocoa, rice, yams, cassava, bananas, palm oil, nuts

Minerals: oil, petroleum, gold, manganese, uranium

Life expectancy at birth (years): male, 52.6; female, 56.9

Literacy rate: 78.5%

Website: www.embassy.org/embassies/gq.html

ERITREA

FOR MAP, SEE PAGE 97

Population: 4,141,000

Ethnic groups: Tigrinya 50%, Tigre and Kunama 40%, Afar 4%, Saho 3%

Principal languages: Arabic, Tigrinya (both official); Afar, Amharic, Tigre, Kunama, other Cushitic languages

Chief religions: Muslim, Coptic Christian, Roman Catholic, Protestant

Area: 46,840 sq mi (121,320 sq km)

Topography: Eritrea includes many islands of the Dahlak Archipelago. It has low coastal plains in the south and a mountain range with peaks to 9,000 ft (2,700 m) in the north.

Capital: Asmara (pop., 503,000)   Independence date: May 24, 1993

Government type: in transition

Head of state and government: Pres. Isaias Afwerki

Monetary unit: nakfa

GDP: $3.2 billion (2001 est.)   Per capita GDP: $740

Industries: food processing, beverages, clothing and textiles

Chief crops: sorghum, lentils, vegetables, corn, cotton, tobacco, coffee, sisal

Minerals: gold, potash, zinc, copper, salt, possibly oil and natural gas

Life expectancy at birth (years): male, 51.5; female, 54.9

Literacy rate: 25%

Website: www.embassy.org/embassies/er.html

ETHIOPIA

FOR MAP, SEE PAGE 97

Population: 70,678,000

Ethnic groups: Oromo 40%, Amhara and Tigre 32%, Sidamo 9%, Shankella 6%, Somali 6%, Afar 4%, Gurage 2%

Principal languages: Amharic, Tigrinya, Oromigna, Guaragigna, Somali, Arabic, over 200 other languages

Chief religions: Muslim 45-50%, Ethiopian Orthodox 35-40%, animist 12%

Area: 435,190 sq mi (1,127,130 sq km)

Topography: A high central plateau, between 6,000 and 10,000 ft (1,800 and 3,000 m) high, rises to higher mountains near the Great Rift Valley, cutting in from the southwest. The Blue Nile and other rivers cross the plateau, which descends to plains on both the west and southeast.

Capital: Addis Ababa (pop., 2,753,000)

Independence date: more than 2,000 years ago (ancient kingdom of Aksum)

Government type: federal republic

Head of state: Pres. Girma Wolde Giorgis

Head of government: Prime Min. Meles Zenawi

Monetary unit: birr

GDP: $46 billion (2001 est.)   Per capita GDP: $700

Industries: food processing, beverages, textiles, chemicals, metals processing, cement

Chief crops: cereals, pulses, coffee, oilseed, sugarcane, potatoes, qat

Minerals: small reserves of gold, platinum, copper, potash, natural gas

Life expectancy at birth (years): male, 40.4; female, 42.1

Literacy rate: 35.5%

Websites: ethiospokes.net
www.ethiiopianembassy.org

GABON

FOR MAP, SEE PAGE 96

Population: 1,329,000

Ethnic groups: Fang, Bapounou, Nzebi, Obamba, European

Principal languages: French (official), Fang, Myene, Nzebi, Bapounou/Eschira, Bandjabi

Chief religion: Christian 55-75%

Area: 103,350 sq mi (267,670 sq km)

Topography: Heavily forested, the country consists of coastal lowlands; plateaus in the north, east, and south; and mountains in the north, southeast, and center. The Ogooue River system covers most of Gabon.

Capital: Libreville (pop., 573,000)

Independence date: August 17, 1960   Government type: republic

Head of state: Pres. Omar Bongo

Head of government: Prime Min. Jean-François Ntoutoume-Emane

Monetary unit: CFA franc

GDP: $6.7 billion (2001 est.)   Per capita GDP: $5,500

Industries: food and beverages, textile, lumber, cement, petroleum extraction and refining, mining, chemicals, ship repair

Chief crops: cocoa, coffee, sugar, palm oil, rubber

Minerals: petroleum, manganese, uranium, gold, iron ore

Life expectancy at birth (years): male, 55.5; female, 58.8

Literacy rate: 63.2%

Website: www.embassy.org/embassies/ga.html

THE GAMBIA

FOR MAP, SEE PAGE 102

Population: 1,426,000

Ethnic groups: Mandinka 42%, Fula 18%, Wolof 16%, Jola 10%, Serahuli 9%

Principal languages: English (official), Mandinka, Wolof, Fula, other native dialects

Chief religions: Muslim 90%, Christian 9%

Area: 4,400 sq mi (11,300 sq km)

Topography: The country consists of a narrow strip of land on each side of the lower Gambia River.

Capital: Banjul (pop., 418,000)

Independence date: February 18, 1965

Government type: republic

Head of state and government: Pres. Yahya Jammeh

Monetary unit: dalasi

GDP: $2.5 billion (2001 est.)   Per capita GDP: $1,770

Industries: processing of peanuts, fish, and hides; tourism; beverages; agricultural machinery assembly; woodworking; metalworking; clothing

Chief crops: peanuts, millet, sorghum, rice, corn, sesame, cassava, palm kernels

Life expectancy at birth (years): male, 52.4; female, 56.4

Literacy rate: 47.5%

Website: www.Gambia.com

West African craftswoman

Nation Facts and Figures

GHANA – LESOTHO

GHANA

FOR MAP, SEE PAGE 103

Population: 20,922,000

Ethnic groups: Akan 44%, Moshi-Dagomba 16%, Ewe 13%, Ga 8%, Gurma 3%, Yoruba 1%

Principal languages: English (official); about 75 African languages, including Akan, Moshi-Dagomba, Ewe, and Ga

Chief religions: Christian 63%, indigenous beliefs 21%, Muslim 16%

Area: 92,100 sq mi (238,540 sq km)

Topography: Most of Ghana consists of low fertile plains and scrubland, cut by rivers and by the artificial Lake Volta.

Capital: Accra (pop., 1,925,000)

Independence date: March 6, 1957   **Government type:** republic

Head of state and government: Pres. John Agyekum Kufuor

Monetary unit: cedi

GDP: $39.4 billion (2001 est.)   **Per capita GDP:** $1,980

Industries: mining, lumbering, light manufacturing, aluminum smelting, food processing

Chief crops: cocoa, rice, coffee, cassava, peanuts, corn, shea nuts, bananas

Minerals: gold, diamonds, bauxite, manganese

Life expectancy at birth (years): male, 55.7; female, 57.4

Literacy rate: 64.5%

Website: www.ghana.gov.gh

GUINEA

FOR MAP, SEE PAGE 102

Population: 8,480,000

Ethnic groups: Peuhl 40%, Malinke 30%, Soussou 20%

Principal languages: French (official), many African languages

Chief religions: Muslim 85%, Christian 8%, indigenous beliefs 7%

Area: 94,930 sq mi (245,860 sq km)

Topography: A narrow coastal belt leads to the mountainous middle region, the source of the Gambia, Senegal, and Niger rivers. Upper Guinea, farther inland, is a cooler upland. The southeast is forested.

Capital: Conakry (pop., 1,272,000)   **Independence date:** October 2, 1958

Government type: republic

Head of state: Pres. Gen. Lansana Conté

Head of government: Prime Min. Lamine Sidimé

Monetary unit: franc

GDP: $15 billion (2001 est.)   **Per capita GDP:** $1,970

Industries: mining, alumina refining, light manufacturing, agricultural processing

Chief crops: rice, coffee, pineapples, palm kernels, cassava, bananas, sweet potatoes

Minerals: bauxite, iron ore, diamonds, gold, uranium

Life expectancy at birth (years): male, 48.3; female, 50.8

Literacy rate: 35.9%

Website: www.embassy.org/gn.html

GUINEA-BISSAU

FOR MAP, SEE PAGE 102

Population: 1,493,000

Ethnic groups: Balanta 30%, Fula 20%, Manjaca 14%, Mandinga 13%, Papel 7%

Principal languages: Portuguese (official), Crioulo, tribal languages

Chief religions: indigenous beliefs 50%, Muslim 45%, Christian 5%

Area: 13,950 sq mi (36,120 sq km)

Topography: A swampy coastal plain covers most of the country; to the east is a low savanna region.

Capital: Bissau (pop., 292,000)   **Independence date:** September 24, 1973

Head of state: Pres. Kumba Yala

Head of government: Prime Min. Mario Pires

Monetary unit: CFA franc

GDP: $1.2 billion (2001 est.)   **Per capita GDP:** $900

Industries: agricultural processing, beer, soft drinks

Chief crops: rice, corn, beans, cassava, cashew nuts, peanuts, palm kernels, cotton

Minerals: phosphates, bauxite, petroleum

Life expectancy at birth (years): male, 45.1; female, 48.9

Literacy rate: 34%

Website: embassy.org/embassies/gw.html

KENYA

FOR MAP, SEE PAGE 104

Population: 31,987,000

Ethnic groups: Kikuyu 22%, Luhya 14%, Luo 13%, Kalenjin 12%, Kamba 11%, Kisii 6%, Meru 6%

Principal languages: English, Swahili (both official); numerous indigenous languages

Chief religions: Protestant 45%, Roman Catholic 33%, indigenous beliefs 10%, Muslim 10%

Area: 224,960 sq mi (582,650 sq km)

Topography: The northern three-fifths of Kenya is arid. To the south, there are a low coastal area and a plateau varying from 3,000 to 10,000 ft (900 to 3,000 m). The Great Rift Valley enters the country north to south, flanked by high mountains.

Capital: Nairobi (pop., 2,343,000)

Independence date: December 12, 1963   **Government type:** republic

Head of state and government: Pres. Mwai Kibaki

Monetary unit: shilling

GDP: $31 billion (2001 est.)   **Per capita GDP:** $1,000

Industries: small-scale consumer goods, agricultural processing, oil refining, cement, tourism

Chief crops: coffee, tea, corn, wheat, sugarcane, fruit, vegetables

Minerals: gold, limestone, soda ash, salt barites, rubies, fluorspar, garnets

Life expectancy at birth (years): male, 45.0; female, 45.4

Literacy rate: 78.1%

Websites: www.kenyaembassy.com
www.kenya.go.ke

Typical door of a residence on the island of Lamu, Kenya

LESOTHO

FOR MAP, SEE PAGE 106

Population: 1,802,000

Ethnic groups: Sotho 99%

Principal languages: Sesotho, English (both official); Zulu, Xhosa

Chief religions: Christian 80%, indigenous beliefs 20%

Area: 11,720 sq mi (30,350 sq km)

Topography: Lesotho is landlocked and mountainous, with altitudes from 5,000 to 11,000 ft (1,500 to 3,300 m).

Capital: Maseru (pop., 271,000)   Independence date: October 4, 1966

Government type: modified constitutional monarchy

Head of state: King Letsie III

Head of government: Prime Min. Pakalitha Mosisili

Monetary unit: maloti

GDP: $5.3 billion (2001 est.)   Per capita GDP: $2,450

Industries: food, beverages, textiles, apparel assembly, handicrafts, construction, tourism

Chief crops: corn, wheat, pulses, sorghum, barley

Minerals: diamonds

Life expectancy at birth (years): male, 36.8; female, 37.1

Literacy rate: 83%

Website: www.lesotho.gov.ls

LIBERIA

FOR MAP, SEE PAGE 102

Population: 3,367,000

Ethnic groups: Kpelle, Bassa, Dey, and other tribes 95%; Americo-Liberians 2.5%, Caribbean 2.5%

Principal languages: English (official), Mande, West Atlantic, and Kwa languages

Chief religions: indigenous beliefs 40%, Christian 40%, Muslim 20%

Area: 43,000 sq mi (111,370 sq km)

Topography: Marshy Atlantic coastline rises to low mountains and plateaus in the forested interior; six major rivers flow in parallel courses to the ocean.

Capital: Monrovia (pop., 491,000)

Independence date: July 26, 1847   Government type: republic

Head of state and government: in transition

Monetary unit: U.S. dollar

GDP: $3.6 billion (2001 est.)   Per capita GDP: $1,100

Industries: rubber processing, palm oil processing, timber, diamonds

Chief crops: rubber, coffee, cocoa, rice, cassava, palm oil, sugarcane, bananas

Minerals: iron ore, diamonds, gold

Life expectancy at birth (years): male, 47.0; female, 49.3

Literacy rate: 38.3%

Website: www.liberiaemb.org

LIBYA

FOR MAP, SEE PAGE 97

Population: 5,551,000

Ethnic groups: Arab-Berber 97%

Principal languages: Arabic (official), Italian, English

Chief religion: Muslim (official; mostly Sunni) 97%

Area: 679,360 sq mi (1,759,540 sq km)

Topography: Desert and semidesert regions cover 92% of the land, with low mountains in the north, higher mountains in the south, and a narrow coastal zone.

Capital: Tripoli (pop., 1,776,000)

Independence date: December 24, 1951

Government type: Islamic Arabic Socialist "Mass-State"

Head of state and government: Col. Muammar al-Qaddafi

Monetary unit: dinar

GDP: $40 billion (2001 est.)   Per capita GDP: $7,600

Industries: petroleum, food processing, textiles, handicrafts, cement

Chief crops: wheat, barley, olives, dates, citrus, vegetables, peanuts, soybeans

Minerals: petroleum, natural gas, gypsum

Life expectancy at birth (years): male, 73.9; female, 78.3

Literacy rate: 76.2%

Website: www.libya–un.org

MADAGASCAR

FOR MAP, SEE PAGE 107

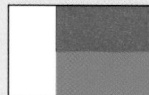

Population: 17,404,000

Ethnic groups: Mainly Malagasy (Indonesian-African); also Cotiers, French, Indian, Chinese

Principal languages: Malagasy, French (both official)

Chief religions: indigenous beliefs 52%, Christian 41%, Muslim 7%

Area: 226,660 sq mi (587,040 sq km)

Topography: Madagascar has a humid coastal strip in the east, fertile valleys in the mountainous center plateau region, and a wider coastal strip in the west.

Capital: Antananarivo (pop., 1,689,000)

Independence date: June 26, 1960   Government type: republic

Head of state: Pres. Marc Ravalomanana

Head of government: Prime Min. Jacques Sylla

Monetary unit: Malagasy franc

GDP: $14 billion (2001 est.)   Per capita GDP: $870

Industries: meat processing, soap, breweries, tanneries, sugar, textiles, glassware, cement, automobile assembly, paper, petroleum, tourism

Chief crops: coffee, vanilla, sugarcane, cloves, cocoa, rice, cassava, beans, bananas, peanuts

Minerals: graphite, chromite, coal, bauxite, salt, quartz, tar sands, semiprecious stones, mica

Life expectancy at birth (years): male, 53.8; female, 58.5

Literacy rate: 80%

Website: madagascar–gov.net

MALAWI

FOR MAP, SEE PAGE 105

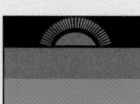

Population: 12,105,000

Ethnic groups: Chewa, Nyanja, Tumbuka, Yao, Lomwe, Sena, Tonga, Ngoni, Ngonde

Principal languages: Chichewa, English (both official); several African languages

Chief religions: Protestant 55%, Roman Catholic 20%, Muslim 20%

Area: 45,750 sq mi (118,480 sq km)

Topography: Malawi stretches 560 mi (900 m) north to south along Lake Malawi (Lake Nyasa), most of which belongs to Malawi. High plateaus and mountains line the Rift Valley the length of the nation.

Capital: Lilongwe (pop., 523,000)   Independence date: July 6, 1964

Government type: republic

Head of state and government: Pres. Bakili Muluzi

Monetary unit: kwacha

GDP: $7 billion (2001 est.)   Per capita GDP: $660

Industries: tobacco, tea, sugar, sawmill products, cement, consumer goods

Chief crops: tobacco, sugarcane, cotton, tea, corn, potatoes, cassava, sorghum, pulses

Minerals: limestone, uranium, coal, and bauxite

Life expectancy at birth (years): male, 37.6; female, 38.4

Literacy rate: 58%

Website: www.maform.malawi.net/MAIN.htm

Nation Facts and Figures

MALI

FOR MAP, SEE PAGE 96

Population: 13,007,000

Ethnic groups: Mande 50% (Bambara, Malinke, Soninke), Peul 17%, Voltaic 12%, Tuareg and Moor 10%, Songhai 6%

Principal languages: French (official), Bambara and other African languages

Chief religions: Muslim 90%, indigenous beliefs 9%

Area: 480,000 sq mi (1,240,000 sq km)

Topography: A landlocked grassy plain in the upper basins of the Senegal and Niger rivers, extending north into the Sahara.

Capital: Bamako (pop., 1,161,000)

Independence date: September 22, 1960   **Government type:** republic

Head of state: Pres. Amadou Toumani Touré

Head of government: Prime Min. Ahmed Mohamed Ag Hamani

Monetary unit: CFA franc

GDP: $9.2 billion (2001 est.)   **Per capita GDP:** $840

Industries: food processing, construction, gold mining

Chief crops: cotton, millet, rice, corn, vegetables, peanuts

Minerals: gold, phosphates, kaolin, salt, limestone, uranium

Life expectancy at birth (years): male, 44.7; female, 46.2

Literacy rate: 38%

Website: www.maliembassy–usa.org

MAURITANIA

FOR MAP, SEE PAGE 96

Population: 2,893,000

Ethnic groups: mixed Maur/black 40%, Maur 30%, black 30%

Principal languages: Hassaniya Arabic, Wolof (both official); Fulani, Pulaar, Soninke (all national); French

Chief religion: predominantly Muslim (official)

Area: 398,000 sq mi (1,030,700 sq km)

Topography: The fertile Senegal River valley in the south gives way to a wide central region of sandy plains and scrub trees. The north is arid and extends into the Sahara.

Capital: Nouakchott (pop., 626,000)

Independence date: November 28, 1960 **Government type:** Islamic republic

Head of state: Pres. Maaouya Ould Sidi Ahmed Taya

Head of government: Prime Min. Cheikh El Afia Ould Mohamed Khouna

Monetary unit: ouguiya

GDP: $5 billion (2001 est.)   **Per capita GDP:** $1,800

Industries: fish processing, mining

Chief crops: dates, millet, sorghum, rice, corn, dates

Minerals: iron ore, gypsum, copper, phosphate, diamonds, gold, oil

Life expectancy at birth (years): male, 49.8; female, 54.1

Literacy rate: 41.2%

Website: www.embassy.org/mauritania

MAURITIUS

FOR MAP, SEE PAGE 107

Population: 1,221,000

Ethnic groups: Indo-Mauritian 68%, Creole 27%, Sino-Mauritian 3%, Franco-Mauritian 2%

Principal languages: English (official), Creole, French, Hindi, Urdu, Hakka, Bhojpuri

Chief religions: Hindu 52%, Christian 28%, Muslim 17%

Area: 720 sq mi (1,860 sq km)

Topography: Mauritius is a volcanic island nearly surrounded by coral reefs. A central plateau is encircled by mountain peaks.

Capital: Port Louis (pop., 176,000)

Independence date: March 12, 1968   **Government type:** republic

Head of state: Pres. Karl Auguste Offmann

Head of government: Prime Min. Anerood Jugnauth

Monetary unit: Mauritian rupee

GDP: $12.9 billion (2001 est.)   **Per capita GDP:** $10,800

Industries: food processing, textiles, clothing, chemicals, metal products, transport equipment, nonelectrical machinery, tourism

Chief crops: sugarcane, tea, corn, potatoes, bananas, pulses

Life expectancy at birth (years): male, 67.8; female, 75.9

Literacy rate: 82.9%

Website: www.ncb.intnet.mu/govt

MOROCCO

FOR MAP, SEE PAGE 98

Population: 30,566,000

Ethnic groups: Arab-Berber 99%

Principal languages: Arabic (official), Berber dialects, French, Spanish, English

Chief religion: Muslim (official) 99%

Area: 172,410 sq mi (446,550 sq km)

Topography: Morocco consists of five natural regions: mountain ranges (Riff in the north, Middle Atlas, Upper Atlas, and Anti-Atlas); rich plains in the west; alluvial plains in the southwest; well-cultivated plateaus in the center; and a pre-Sahara arid zone extending from the southeast.

Capital: Rabat (pop., 1,668,000)   **Independence date:** March 2, 1956

Government type: constitutional monarchy

Head of state: King Mohammed VI

Head of government: Prime Min. Driss Jettou

Monetary unit: dirham

GDP: $112 billion (2001 est.)   **Per capita GDP:** $3,700

Industries: mining, food processing, leather goods, textiles, construction, tourism

Chief crops: barley, wheat, citrus, wine, vegetables, olives

Minerals: phosphates, iron ore, manganese, lead, zinc

Life expectancy at birth (years): male, 67.8; female, 72.4

Literacy rate: 43.7%

Website: www.mincom.gov.ma

Casbah, Ait Ben Haddou, Morocco

MOZAMBIQUE

FOR MAP, SEE PAGE 105

Population: 18,863,000

Ethnic groups: Shangaan, Chokwe, Manyika, Sena, Makua

Principal languages: Portuguese (official) and dialects, English

Chief religions: indigenous beliefs 50%, Christian 30%, Muslim 20%

Area: 309,500 sq mi (801,590 sq km)

Topography: Coastal lowlands make up nearly half the country, with plateaus rising in steps to the mountains along the western border.

Capital: Maputo (pop., 1,134,000)

Independence date: June 25, 1975   **Government type:** republic

Head of state: Pres. Joaquim Chissano

Head of government: Prime Min. Pascoal Mocumbi

Monetary unit: metical

GDP: $17.5 billion (2001 est.)   **Per capita GDP:** $900

Industries: food, beverages, chemicals, petroleum products, textiles, cement, glass, asbestos, tobacco

Chief crops: cotton, cashew nuts, sugarcane, tea, cassava, corn, coconuts, sisal, citrus and tropical fruits

Minerals: coal, titanium, natural gas, tantalum, graphite

Life expectancy at birth (years): male, 31.0; female, 31.6

Literacy rate: 42.3%

Website: www.mozambique.mz/eindex.htm

NAMIBIA

FOR MAP, SEE PAGE 105

Population: 1,987,000

Ethnic groups: Ovambo 50%, Kavangos 9%, Herero 7%, Damara 7%, white 6%, mixed 7%

Principal languages: English (official), Afrikaans, German, Oshivambo, Herero, Nama

Chief religions: Lutheran 50%, other Christian 30%, indigenous beliefs 10-20%

Area: 318,700 sq mi (825,420 sq km)

Topography: Three distinct regions include the Namib Desert along the Atlantic coast, a mountainous central plateau with woodland savanna, and the Kalahari Desert in the east. True forests are found in the northeast. There are four rivers, but little other surface water.

Capital: Windhoek (pop., 216,000)

Independence date: March 21, 1990

Government type: republic

Head of state: Pres. Sam Nujoma

Head of government: Prime Min. Theo-Ben Gurirab

Monetary unit: dollar

GDP: $8.1 billion (2001 est.)

Per capita GDP: $4,500

Elephants on the savanna at dawn

Industries: meatpacking, fish processing, dairy products, mining

Chief crops: millet, sorghum, peanuts

Minerals: diamonds, copper, uranium, gold, lead, tin, lithium, cadmium, zinc, salt, vanadium, natural gas

Life expectancy at birth (years): male, 44.3; female, 41.2

Literacy rate: 38%

Website: www.grnnet.gov.ng/intro.htm

NIGER

FOR MAP, SEE PAGE 96

Population: 11,972,000

Ethnic groups: Hausa 56%, Djerma 22%, Fula 9%, Tuareg 8%, Beri Beri (Kanouri) 4%

Principal languages: French (official); Hausa, Djerma, Fulani (all national)

Chief religion: Muslim 80%

Area: 489,000 sq mi (1,267,000 sq km)

Topography: Mostly arid desert and mountains. A narrow savanna in the south and the Niger River basin in the southwest contain most of the population.

Capital: Niamey (pop., 821,000)

Independence date: August 3, 1960   **Government type:** republic

Head of state: Pres. Tandja Mamadou

Head of government: Prime Min. Hama Amadou

Monetary unit: CFA franc

GDP: $8.4 billion (2001 est.)   **Per capita GDP:** $820

Industries: mining, cement, brick, textiles, food processing, chemicals

Chief crops: cowpeas, cotton, peanuts, millet, sorghum, cassava, rice

Minerals: uranium, coal, iron ore, tin, phosphates, gold, petroleum

Life expectancy at birth (years): male, 42.3; female, 42.1

Literacy rate: 15.3%

Website: www.nigerembassyusa.org

NIGERIA

FOR MAP, SEE PAGE 96

Population: 124,009,000

Ethnic groups: more than 250; Hausa and Fulani 29%, Yoruba 21%, Igbo (Ibo) 18%, Ijaw 10%

Principal languages: English (official), Hausa, Yoruba, Igbo (Ibo), Fulani

Chief religions: Muslim 50%, Christian 40%, indigenous beliefs 10%

Area: 356,670 sq mi (923,770 sq km)

Topography: Four east-to-west regions divide Nigeria: a coastal mangrove swamp 10 to 60 mi (16 to 100 km) wide, a tropical rain forest 50 to 100 mi (80 to 160 km) wide, a plateau of savanna and open woodland, and semidesert in the north.

Capital: Abuja (pop., 420,000)

Independence date: October 1, 1960   **Government type:** republic

Head of state and government: Pres. Olusegun Obasanjo

Monetary unit: naira

GDP: $105.9 billion (2001 est.)   **Per capita GDP:** $840

Industries: petroleum extraction, mining, agricultural processing, cotton, rubber, wood, hides and skins, textiles, cement and other construction materials, footwear, chemicals, fertilizer, printing, ceramics, steel

Chief crops: cocoa, peanuts, palm oil, corn, rice, sorghum, millet, cassava, yams

Minerals: natural gas, petroleum, tin, columbite, iron ore, coal, limestone, lead, zinc

Life expectancy at birth (years): male, 50.9; female, 51.1

Literacy rate: 57.1%

Website: www.nigeriaembassyusa.org

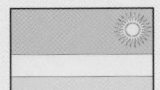

Nation Facts and Figures

RWANDA

FOR MAP, SEE PAGE 104

Population: 8,387,000

Ethnic groups: Hutu 84%, Tutsi 15%, Twa (Pygmy) 1%

Principal languages: Kinyarwanda, French, English (all official); Swahili

Chief religions: Roman Catholic 57%, Protestant 26%, Adventist 11%, Muslim 5%

Area: 10,170 sq mi (26,340 sq km)

Topography: Grassy uplands and hills cover most of the country, with a chain of volcanoes in the northwest. The source of the Nile River has been located in the headwaters of the Kagera (Akagera) River, southwest of Kigali.

Capital: Kigali (pop., 412,000)

Independence date: July 1, 1962　　**Government type:** republic

Head of state: Pres. Paul Kagame

Head of government: Prime Min. Bernard Makuza

Monetary unit: franc

GDP: $7.2 billion (2001 est.)　　**Per capita GDP:** $1,000

Industries: cement, agricultural products, small-scale beverages, soap, furniture, shoes, plastic goods, textiles, cigarettes

Chief crops: coffee, tea, pyrethrum, bananas, beans, sorghum, potatoes

Minerals: gold, tin ore, tungsten ore, methane

Life expectancy at birth (years): male, 38.5; female, 40.2

Literacy rate: 48%

Website: www.rwanda1.com

SÃO TOMÉ AND PRÍNCIPE

FOR MAP, SEE PAGE 96

Population: 161,000

Ethnic groups: mestizo, black, Portuguese

Principal languages: Portuguese (official), Creole, Fang

Chief religions: predominantly Roman Catholic

Area: 390 sq mi (1,000 sq km)

Topography: São Tomé and Príncipe islands, part of an extinct volcano chain, are both covered by lush forests and croplands.

Capital: São Tomé (pop., 67,000)　　**Independence date:** July 12, 1975

Government type: republic

Head of state: Pres. Fradique Melo de Menezes

Head of government: Prime Min. Maria das Neves

Monetary unit: dobra

GDP: $189 million (2001 est.)　　**Per capita GDP:** $1,200

Industries: light construction, textiles, soap, beer, fish processing, timber

Chief crops: cocoa, coconuts, palm kernels, copra, cinnamon, pepper, coffee, bananas, papayas, beans

Life expectancy at birth (years): male, 64.8; female, 67.8

Literacy rate: 79.3%

SENEGAL

FOR MAP, SEE PAGE 102

Population: 10,095,000

Ethnic groups: Wolof 43%, Pular 24%, Serer 15%, Jola 4%, Mandinka 3%, Soninke 1%

Principal languages: French (official), Wolof, Pulaar, Jola, Mandinka

Chief religions: Muslim 94%, Christian 5%

Area: 75,750 sq mi (196,190 sq km)

Water-loving hippopotamuses

Topography: Low rolling plains cover most of Senegal, rising somewhat in the southeast. Swamp and jungles are in the southwest.

Capital: Dakar (pop., 2,160,000)

Independence date: April 4, 1960　　**Government type:** republic

Head of state: Pres. Abdoulaye Wade

Head of government: Prime Min. Idrissa Seck

Monetary unit: CFA franc

GDP: $16.2 billion (2001 est.)　　**Per capita GDP:** $1,580

Industries: agricultural and fish processing, mining, fertilizer production, petroleum refining, construction materials

Chief crops: peanuts, millet, corn, sorghum, rice, cotton, tomatoes, green vegetables

Minerals: phosphates, iron ore

Life expectancy at birth (years): male, 54.8; female, 58.0

Literacy rate: 39.1%

SEYCHELLES

FOR MAP, SEE PAGE 23

Population: 80,000

Ethnic groups: mainly Seychellois (mix of French, African, and Asian)

Principal languages: English, French, Creole (all official)

Chief religions: Roman Catholic 87%, Anglican 7%

Area: 180 sq mi (460 sq km)

Topography: A group of 86 islands, about half of them composed of coral, the other half granite, the latter predominantly mountainous.

Capital: Victoria (pop., 30,000)

Independence date: June 29, 1976

Government type: republic

Head of state and government: Pres. France-Albert René

Monetary unit: rupee

GDP: $605 million (2001 est.)

Per capita GDP: $7,600

A Seychelles beach

Industries: fishing, tourism, coconut and vanilla processing, rope, boat building, printing, furniture, beverages

Chief crops: coconuts, cinnamon, vanilla, sweet potatoes, cassava, bananas

Life expectancy at birth (years): male, 65.8; female, 76.9

Literacy rate: 58%

Website: www.seychelles-online.com.sc/governement.htm

SIERRA LEONE

For map, see page 102

Population: 4,971,000

Ethnic groups: Temne 30%, Mende 30%, other tribes 30%; Creole 10%

Principal languages: English (official), Mende in the south, Temne in the north, Krio (English Creole)

Chief religions: Muslim 60%, indigenous beliefs 30%, Christian 10%

Area: 27,700 sq mi (71,740 sq km)

Topography: The heavily indented, 210-mi (340-km) coastline has mangrove swamps. Behind are wooded hills, rising to a plateau and mountains in the east.

Capital: Freetown (pop., 837,000)

Independence date: April 27, 1961   **Government type:** republic

Head of state and government: Pres. Ahmad Tejan Kabbah

Monetary unit: leone

GDP: $2.7 billion (2001 est.)   **Per capita GDP:** $500

Industries: mining, small-scale manufacturing, petroleum refining

Chief crops: rice, coffee, cocoa, palm kernels, palm oil, peanuts

Minerals: diamonds, titanium ore, bauxite, iron ore, gold, chromite

Life expectancy at birth (years): male, 40.3; female, 45.4

Literacy rate: 31.4%

Website: www.Sierra-Leone.org

Rural life in Sierra Leone

SOMALIA

For map, see page 97

Population: 9,890,000

Ethnic groups: Somali 85%, Bantu and other 15%

Principal languages: Somali, Arabic (both official); Italian, English

Chief religion: Sunni Muslim (official)

Area: 246,200 sq mi (637,660 sq km)

Topography: The coastline extends for 1,700 mi (2,700 km). Hills cover the north; the center and south are flat.

Capital: Mogadishu (pop., 1,212,000)

Independence date: July 1, 1960   **Government type:** in transition

Head of state: Abdiqassim Salad Hassan

Head of government: Prime Min. Hassan Abshir Farah

Monetary unit: shilling

GDP: $4.1 billion (2001 est.)   **Per capita GDP:** $550

Industries: sugar refining, textiles, wireless communication

Chief crops: bananas, sorghum, corn, coconuts, rice, sugarcane, mangoes, sesame seeds, beans

Minerals: uranium and largely unexploited reserves of iron ore, tin, gypsum, bauxite, copper, salt, natural gas, likely oil reserves

Life expectancy at birth (years): male, 45.7; female, 49.1

Literacy rate: 37.8%

SOUTH AFRICA

For map, see page 105

Population: 45,026,000

Ethnic groups: black 75%, white 14%, mixed 8%, Indian 3%

Principal languages: Afrikaans, English, Ndebele, Pedi, Sotho, Swazi, Tsonga, Tswana, Venda, Xhosa, Zulu (all official)

Chief religions: Christian 68%, indigenous beliefs and animist 29%

Area: 471,010 sq mi (1,219,910 sq km)

Topography: The large interior plateau reaches close to the country's 2,700-mi (4,300-km) coastline. There are few major rivers or lakes; rainfall is sparse in the west, more plentiful in the east.

Capitals: Pretoria (administrative) (pop., 1,590,000), Cape Town (legislative) (pop., 2,993,000), Bloemfontein (judicial) (pop., 1,590,000)

Independence date: May 31, 1910

Government type: republic

Head of state and government: Pres. Thabo Mvuyelwa Mbeki

Monetary unit: rand

GDP: $412 billion (2001 est.)   **Per capita GDP:** $9,400

Industries: mining, automobile assembly, metalworking, machinery, textile, iron and steel, chemicals, fertilizer, foodstuffs

Chief crops: corn, wheat, sugarcane, fruits, vegetables

Minerals: gold, chromium, antimony, coal, iron ore, manganese, nickel, phosphates, tin, uranium, gem diamonds, platinum, copper, vanadium, salt, natural gas

Diamond mining— a key source of South Africa's wealth

Life expectancy at birth (years): male, 46.6; female, 46.5

Literacy rate: 85%

Website: www.gov.za

Cape Town, South Africa

SUDAN

FOR MAP, SEE PAGE 97

Population: 33,610,000

Ethnic groups: black 52%, Arab 39%, Beja 6%

Principal languages: Arabic (official), Nubian, Ta Bedawie; Nilotic, Sudanic dialects; English

Chief religions: Sunni Muslim 70%, indigenous beliefs 25%, Christian 5%

Area: 967,500 sq mi (2,505,810 sq km)

Topography: The north consists of the Libyan Desert in the west and the mountainous Nubia Desert in the east, with the narrow Nile valley between. The center contains large, fertile, rainy areas with fields, pasture, and forest. The south has rich soil and heavy rain.

Capital: Khartoum (pop., 2,853,000)

Independence date: January 1, 1956

Government type: republic with strong military influence

Head of state and government: Pres. Gen. Omar Hassan Ahmad Al-Bashir

Monetary unit: dinar

GDP: $49.3 billion (2001 est.)

Per capita GDP: $1,360

Industries: oil, cotton ginning, textiles, cement, edible oils, sugar, soap distilling, shoes, petroleum refining, pharmaceuticals, armaments, automobile/light truck assembly

Chief crops: cotton, groundnuts, sorghum, millet, wheat, gum arabic, sugarcane, cassava, mangos, papaya, bananas, sweet potatoes, sesame

Minerals: petroleum, iron ore, copper, chromium ore, zinc, tungsten, mica, silver, gold

Life expectancy at birth (years): male, 56.6; female, 58.9

Literacy rate: 46.1%

Website: www.sudanembassy.org

SWAZILAND

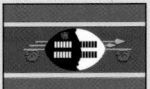

FOR MAP, SEE PAGE 107

Population: 1,077,000

Ethnic groups: African 97%, European 3%

Principal languages: English, siSwati (both official)

Chief religions: Christian 60%, Muslim 10%, indigenous and other 30%

Area: 6,700 sq mi (17,360 sq km)

Topography: The country descends from W to E in broad belts, becoming more arid in the low veld region, then rising to a plateau in the E.

Capitals: Mbabane (administrative) (pop., 80,000), Lobamba (legislative) (pop., 5,000)

Independence date: September 6, 1968

Government type: constitutional monarchy

Head of state: King Mswati III

Head of government: Prime Min. Barnabas Sibusiso Dlamini

Monetary unit: lilangeni

GDP: $4.6 billion (2001 est.)

Per capita GDP: $4,200

Industries: mining, wood pulp, sugar, soft drink concentrates, textile and apparel

Chief crops: sugarcane, cotton, corn, tobacco, rice, citrus, pineapples, sorghum, peanuts

Minerals: asbestos, coal, clay, cassiterite, gold, diamonds, quarry stone, talc

Life expectancy at birth (years): male, 41.0; female, 37.9

Literacy rate: 78.3%

Website: www.swazi.com/government

TANZANIA

FOR MAP, SEE PAGE 104

Population: 36,977,000

Ethnic groups: mainland: Bantu 95%; Zanzibar: Arab, African, mixed

Principal languages: Swahili, English (both official); Arabic, many local languages

Chief religions: Christian 30%, Muslim 35%, indigenous beliefs 35%; Zanzibar is 99% Muslim

Area: 364,900 sq mi (945,090 sq km)

Topography: Hot, arid central plateau, surrounded by the lake region in the west, temperate highlands in the north and south, and the coastal plains. Mt. Kilimanjaro, 19,340 ft (5,895 m), is the highest peak in Africa.

Capital: Dodoma (pop., 180,000), in transition from Dar-es-Salaam (pop., 2,347,000)

Independence date: April 26, 1964   Government type: republic

Head of state: Pres. Benjamin William Mkapa

Head of government: Prime Min. Frederick Tluway Sumaye

Monetary unit: shilling

GDP: $22.1 billion (2001 est.)   Per capita GDP: $610

Industries: agricultural processing, mining, oil refining, shoes, cement, textiles, wood products, fertilizer, salt

Chief crops: coffee, sisal, tea, cotton, pyrethrum, cashew nuts, tobacco, cloves, corn, wheat, cassava, bananas, fruits, vegetables

Minerals: tin, phosphates, iron ore, coal, diamonds, gemstones, gold, natural gas, nickel

Life expectancy at birth (years): male, 43.3; female, 45.8

Literacy rate: 67.8%

Website: www.tanzania.go.tz/index2E.html

Masai giraffe calf, Serengeti National Park, Tanzania

TOGO

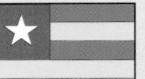

FOR MAP, SEE PAGE 103

Population: 4,909,000

Ethnic groups: 37 African tribes; largest are Ewe, Mina, and Kabre

Principal languages: French (official), Ewe, Mina in the south; Kabye, Dagomba in the north

Chief religions: indigenous beliefs 51%, Christian 29%, Muslim 20%

Area: 21,930 sq mi (56,790 sq km)

Topography: A range of hills running southwest to northeast splits Togo into two savanna plains regions.

Capital: Lomé (pop., 732,000)   Independence date: April 27, 1960

Government type: republic

Head of state: Pres. Gnassingbé Eyadéma

Head of government: Prime Min. Koffi Sama

Monetary unit: CFA franc

GDP: $7.6 billion (2001 est.) **Per capita GDP:** $1,500

Industries: mining, agricultural processing, cement, handicrafts, textiles, beverages

Chief crops: coffee, cocoa, cotton, yams, cassava, corn, beans, rice, millet, sorghum

Minerals: phosphates, limestone, marble

Life expectancy at birth (years): male, 51.5; female, 55.5

Literacy rate: 51.7%

Website: www.republicoftogo.com/english/index.htm

TUNISIA

FOR MAP, SEE PAGE 99

Population: 9,832,000

Ethnic groups: Arab 98%, European 1%, Jewish and other 1%

Principal languages: Arabic (official), French prevalent

Chief religion: Muslim (official; mostly Sunni) 98%

Area: 63,170 sq mi (163,610 sq km)

Topography: The north is wooded and fertile. The central coastal plains are given to grazing and orchards. The south is arid, merging into the Sahara Desert.

Capital: Tunis (pop., 1,927,000)

Independence date: March 20, 1956 **Government type:** republic

Head of state: Pres. Gen. Zine al-Abidine Ben Ali

Head of government: Prime Min. Mohamed Ghannouchi

Monetary unit: dinar

GDP: $64.5 billion (2001 est.) **Per capita GDP:** $6,600

Industries: petroleum, mining, tourism, textiles, footwear, agribusiness, beverages

Chief crops: olives, olive oil, grain, tomatoes, citrus fruit, sugar beets, dates, almonds

Minerals: petroleum, phosphates, iron ore, lead, zinc, salt

Life expectancy at birth (years): male, 72.8; female, 76.2

Literacy rate: 66.7% **Website:** www.ministeres.tn/index.html

UGANDA

FOR MAP, SEE PAGE 104

Population: 25,827,000

Ethnic groups: Baganda 17%, Ankole 8%, Basoga 8%, Iteso 8%, Bakiga 7%; many other groups

Principal languages: English (official), Swahili, Ganda, many Bantu and Nilotic languages, Arabic

Chief religions: Protestant 33%, Roman Catholic 33%, indigenous beliefs 18%, Muslim 16%

Area: 91,140 sq mi (236,040 sq km)

Topography: Most of Uganda is a high plateau 3,000 to 6,000 ft (900 to 1,800 m) high, with the high Ruwenzori range in the west (Mt. Margherita 16,750 ft [5,105 m]) and volcanoes in the southwest; the northeast is arid, and the west and southwest rainy. Lakes Victoria, Edward, and Albert form much of the borders.

Capital: Kampala (pop., 1,274,000) **Independence date:** October 9, 1962

Government type: republic **Head of state:** Pres. Yoweri Kaguta Museveni

Head of government: Prime Min. Apollo Nsibambi

Monetary unit: shilling **GDP:** $29 billion (2001 est.)

Per capita GDP: $1,200

Industries: sugar, brewing, tobacco, cotton textiles, cement

Chief crops: coffee, tea, cotton, tobacco, cassava, potatoes, corn, millet, pulses

Minerals: copper, cobalt, limestone, salt

Life expectancy at birth (years): male, 43.4; female, 46.4

Literacy rate: 62.7% **Website:** www.government.go.ug

ZAMBIA

FOR MAP, SEE PAGE 105

Population: 10,812,000

Ethnic groups: more than 70 groups; largest are Bemba, Tonga, Ngoni, and Lozi

Principal languages: English (official), Bemba, Kaonda, Lozi, Lunda, Luvale, Nyanja, Tonga, 70 others

Chief religions: Christian 50-75%, Hindu and Muslim 24-49%

Area: 290,580 sq mi (752,610 sq km)

Topography: Zambia is mostly high plateau country covered with thick forests and drained by several important rivers, including the Zambezi.

Capital: Lusaka (pop., 1,718,000)

Independence date: October 24, 1964 **Government type:** republic

Head of state and government: Pres. Levy Patrick Mwanawasa

Monetary unit: kwacha

GDP: $8.5 billion (2001 est.) **Per capita GDP:** $870

Industries: mining, construction, foodstuffs, beverages, chemicals, textiles, fertilizer

Chief crops: corn, sorghum, rice, peanuts, sunflower seed, vegetables, flowers, tobacco, cotton, sugarcane, cassava

Minerals: copper, cobalt, zinc, lead, coal, emeralds, gold, silver, uranium

Life expectancy at birth (years): male, 35.3; female, 35.3

Literacy rate: 78.9%

ZIMBABWE

FOR MAP, SEE PAGE 105

Population: 12,891,000

Ethnic groups: Shona 82%, Ndebele 14%

Principal languages: English (official), Shona, Sindebele, numerous dialects

Chief religions: syncretic (Christian-indigenous mix) 50%, Christian 25%, indigenous beliefs 24%

Area: 150,800 sq mi (390,580 sq km)

Topography: Zimbabwe is high plateau country, rising to mountains on the eastern border, sloping down on the other borders.

Capital: Harare (pop., 1,868,000)

Independence date: April 18, 1980

Government type: republic

Head of state and government: Pres. Robert Mugabe

Monetary unit: Zimbabwe dollar

GDP: $28 billion (2001 est.)

Per capita GDP: $2,450

Industries: mining, steel, wood products, cement, chemicals, fertilizer, clothing and footwear, foodstuffs, beverages

Chief crops: corn, cotton, tobacco, wheat, coffee, sugarcane, peanuts

Minerals: coal, chromium ore, asbestos, gold, nickel, copper, iron ore, vanadium, lithium, tin, platinum group metals

Life expectancy at birth (years): male, 40.1; female, 37.9

Literacy rate: 85%

Website: www.gta.gov.zw

Devil's Cataract, Victoria Falls, on the Zambezi River between Zambia and Zimbabwe

ASIA

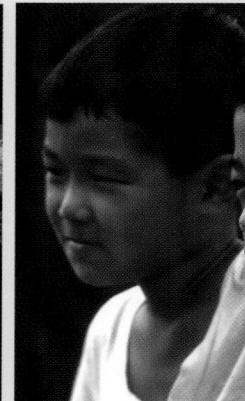

Asia has three of the five most populous countries in the world. China and India, each with more than 1 billion people, rank number 1 and number 2, respectively. Indonesia, with well over 200 million, is number 4.

AFGHANISTAN

FOR MAP, SEE PAGE 89

Population: 23,897,000

Ethnic groups: Pashtun 44%, Tajik 25%, Hazara 10%, Uzbek 8%

Principal languages: Dari (Afghan Persian), Pashtu (both official); Turkic (including Uzbek, Turkmen); Balochi, Pashai, many others

Chief religions: Muslim (official; Sunni 85%, Shi'a 15%)

Area: 250,000 sq mi (647,500 sq km)

Topography: The country is landlocked and mountainous, much of it over 4,000 ft (1,200 m) above sea level. The Hindu Kush Mountains tower 16,000 ft (4,800 m) above Kabul and reach a height of 25,000 ft (7,600 m) to the east. Trade with Pakistan flows through the 35-mi (56-km) Khyber Pass. There are large desert regions, though mountain rivers produce intermittent fertile valleys.

Capital: Kabul (pop., 2,734,000)

Independence date: August 19, 1919

Government type: transitional administration

Head of state and government: Pres. Hamid Karzai

Monetary unit: afghani

GDP: $21 billion (2000 est.)   **Per capita GDP:** $800

Industries: textiles, soap, furniture, shoes, fertilizer, cement, handwoven carpets

Chief crops: wheat, fruits, nuts

Minerals: natural gas, petroleum, coal, copper, chromite, talc, barites, sulfur, lead, zinc, iron ore, salt, precious and semiprecious stones

Life expectancy at birth (years): male, 47.7; female, 46.2

Literacy rate: 36%

Website: www.afghanistanembassy.org

ARMENIA

FOR MAP, SEE PAGE 63

Population: 3,061,000

Ethnic groups: Armenian 93%, Russian 2%

Principal languages: Armenian (official), Russian

Chief religions: Armenian Apostolic 94%, other Christian 4%, Yezidi 2%

Area: 11,500 sq mi (29,800 sq km)

Topography: Mountainous, with many peaks above 10,000 ft (3,000 m).

Capital: Yerevan (pop., 1,420,000)

Independence date: September 21, 1991

Government type: republic

Head of state: Pres. Robert Kocharian

Head of government: Prime Min. Andranik Markarian

Monetary unit: dram

GDP: $11.2 billion (2001 est.)

Per capita GDP: $3,350

Industries: machine tools, forging-pressing machines, electric motors, tires, knitted wear, footwear, silk fabric, chemicals, trucks, instruments, microelectronics, jewelry, software development, food processing

Chief crops: grapes, vegetables

Minerals: gold, copper, molybdenum, zinc, alumina

Life expectancy at birth (years): male, 62.4; female, 71.2

Literacy rate: 99%

Website: www.gov.am/en

AZERBAIJAN

FOR MAP, SEE PAGE 63

Population: 8,370,000

Ethnic groups: Azeri 90%, Dagestani 3%, Russian 3%, Armenian 2%

Principal languages: Azeri (official), Russian, Armenian

Chief religions: Muslim 93%, Russian Orthodox 3%, Armenian Orthodox 2%

Area: 33,440 sq mi (86,600 sq km)

Topography: The Great Caucasus Mountains in the north and the Karabakh Upland in the west border the Kur-Abas Lowland; climate is arid except in the subtropical southeast.

Capital: Baku (pop., 1,964,000)

Independence date: August 30, 1991   **Government type:** republic

Head of state: Pres. Haydar A. Aliyev

Head of government: Prime Min. Artur Rasizade

Monetary unit: manat

GDP: $24.3 billion (2001 est.)   **Per capita GDP:** $3,100

Industries: petroleum products, oilfield equipment, steel, iron ore, cement, chemicals, textiles

Chief crops: cotton, grain, rice, grapes, fruit, vegetables, tea, tobacco

Minerals: petroleum, natural gas, iron ore, nonferrous metals, alumina

Life expectancy at birth (years): male, 59.0; female, 67.6

Literacy rate: 97%

Website: www.president.az

BAHRAIN

FOR MAP, SEE PAGE 88

Population: 724,000

Ethnic groups: Arab 73%, Asian 19%, Iranian 8%

Principal languages: Arabic (official), English, Farsi, Urdu

Chief religions: Muslim (official; Shi'a 70%, Sunni 30%)

Area: 240 sq mi (620 sq km)

Topography: Bahrain Island, and several adjacent, smaller islands, are flat, hot, and humid, with little rain.

Capital: Manama (pop., 150,000)   **Independence date:** August 15, 1971

Government type: constitutional monarchy

Head of state: King Hamad bin Isa al-Khalifa

Head of government: Prime Min. Khalifa bin Sulman al-Khalifa

Monetary unit: dinar

GDP: $24.3 billion (2001 est.)   **Per capita GDP:** $13,000

Industries: petroleum processing and refining, aluminum smelting, offshore banking, ship repairing, tourism

Chief crops: fruit, vegetables

Minerals: oil, natural gas

Life expectancy at birth (years): male, 71.3; female, 76.2

Literacy rate: 88.5%

Website: www.bahrain.gov.bh/english/index.asp

BANGLADESH

FOR MAP, SEE PAGE 82

Population: 146,736,000

Ethnic groups: Bengali 98%

Principal languages: Bangla (official, also known as Bengali), English

Chief religions: Muslim (official) 83%, Hindu 16%

Area: 56,000 sq mi (144,000 sq km)

Topography: The country is mostly a low plain cut by the Ganges and Brahmaputra rivers and their delta. The land is alluvial and marshy along the coast, with hills only in the extreme southeast and northeast.

Capital: Dhaka (pop., 13,181,000)

Independence date: December 16, 1971

Government type: parliamentary democracy

Head of state: Pres. Iajuddin Ahmed

Head of government: Prime Min. Khaleda Zia

Monetary unit: taka

GDP: $230 billion (2001 est.)   **Per capita GDP:** $1,750

Industries: cotton textiles, jute, garments, tea processing, paper newsprint, cement, chemical fertilizer, light engineering

Chief crops: rice, jute, tea, wheat, sugarcane, potatoes, tobacco, pulses, oilseeds, spices, fruit

Minerals: natural gas, coal

Life expectancy at birth (years): male, 61.5; female, 61.2

Literacy rate: 56%

Website: www.bangladeshgov.com

BHUTAN

FOR MAP, SEE PAGE 85

Population: 2,257,000

Ethnic groups: Bhote 50%, Nepalese 35%, indigenous tribes 15%

Principal languages: Dzongkha (official), Tibetan, Nepalese dialects

Chief religions: Lamaistic Buddhist (official) 75%, Hindu 25%

Area: 18,000 sq mi (47,000 sq km)

Topography: Bhutan is comprised of very high mountains in the north, fertile valleys in the center, and thick forests in the Duar Plain in the south.

Capital: Thimphu (pop., 32,000)

Independence date: August 8, 1949

Government type: monarchy

Head of state and government: King Jigme Singye Wangchuk

Head of government: Prime Min. Lyonpo Kinzang Dorji

Monetary unit: ngultrum

GDP: $2.5 billion (2001 est.)   **Per capita GDP:** $1,200

Industries: cement, wood products, processed fruits, alcoholic beverages

Chief crops: rice, corn, root crops, citrus, foodgrains

Minerals: gypsum, calcium carbide

Life expectancy at birth (years): male, 53.9; female, 53.3

Literacy rate: 42.2%

Website: www.kingdomofbhutan.com

BRUNEI

FOR MAP, SEE PAGE 80

Population: 358,000

Ethnic groups: Malay 67%, Chinese 15%, indigenous 6%

Principal languages: Malay (official), English, Chinese

Chief religions: Muslim (official) 67%; Buddhist 13%; Christian 10%; indigenous beliefs, other 10%

Area: 2,230 sq mi (5,770 sq km)

Topography: Brunei has a narrow coastal plain, with mountains in the east, hilly lowlands in the west. There are swamps in the west and northeast.

Nation Facts and Figures

252

Brunei *(continued)*

Capital: Bandar Seri Begawan (pop., 46,000)

Independence date: January 1, 1984

Government type: independent sultanate

Head of state and government: Sultan Sir Muda Hassanal Bolkiah Mu'izzadin Waddaulah

Monetary unit: Brunei dollar

GDP: $6.2 billion (2001 est.)   **Per capita GDP:** $18,000

Industries: petroleum, petroleum refining, liquefied natural gas, construction

Chief crops: rice, vegetables, fruits

Minerals: petroleum, natural gas

Life expectancy at birth (years): male, 71.9; female, 76.8

Literacy rate: 88.2%   **Website:** www.gov.bn

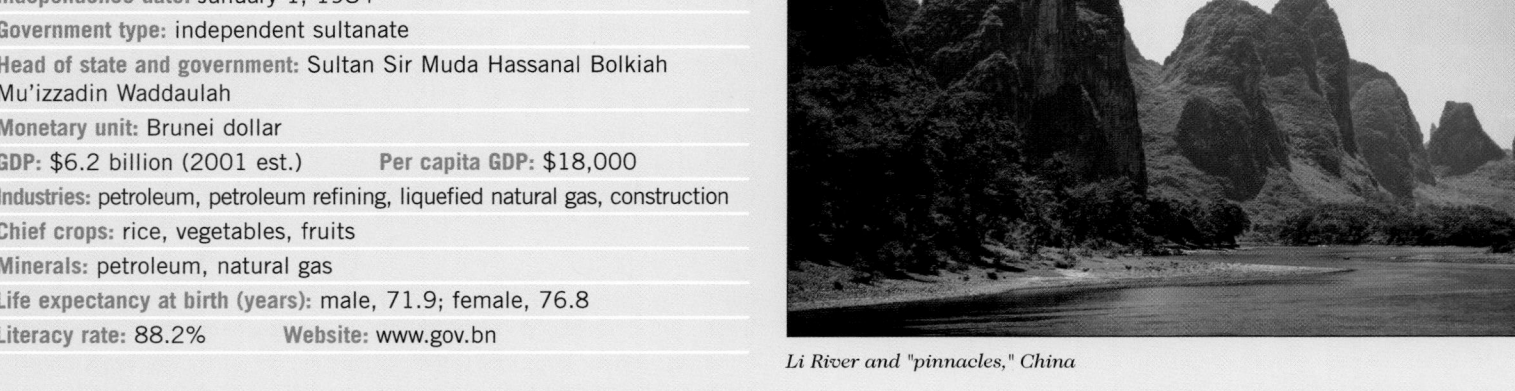

Li River and "pinnacles," China

CAMBODIA

For map, see page 78

Population: 14,144,000

Ethnic groups: Khmer 90%, Vietnamese 5%, Chinese 1%

Principal languages: Khmer (official), French, English

Chief religion: Theravada Buddhist (official) 95%

Area: 69,900 sq mi (181,040 sq km)

Topography: The central area, formed by the Mekong River basin and Tonle Sap lake, is level. Hills and mountains are in the southeast, a long escarpment separates the country from Thailand in the northwest. 76% of the area is forested.

Capital: Phnom Penh (pop., 1,109,000)

Independence date: November 9, 1953

Government type: constitutional monarchy

Head of state: King Norodom Sihanouk

Head of government: Prime Min. Hun Sen

Monetary unit: riel

GDP: $18.7 billion (2001 est.)   **Per capita GDP:** $1,500

Industries: tourism, garments, rice milling, fishing, wood and wood products, rubber, cement, gem mining, textiles

Chief crops: rice, rubber, corn, vegetables

Minerals: gemstones, iron ore, manganese, phosphates

Life expectancy at birth (years): male, 55.5; female, 60.5

Literacy rate: 35%

Website: www.cambodia.gov.kh

Angkor Wat ruins, Cambodia

CHINA

For map, see page 70

(Statistical data do not include Hong Kong or Macau.)

Population: 1,286,975,000

Ethnic groups: 56 groups; Han 92%; also Zhuang, Manchu, Hui, Miao, Uygur, Yi, Tujia, Tong, Tibetan, Mongol, et al.

Principal languages: Mandarin (official), Yue (Cantonese), Wu (Shanghaiese), Minbei (Fuzhou), Minnan (Hokkien-Taiwanese), Xiang, Gan, Hakka, minority languages

Chief religions: officially atheist; Buddhism, Taoism; some Muslims, Christians

Area: 3,705,410 sq mi (9,596,960 sq km)

Topography: Two-thirds of China's vast territory is mountainous or desert; only one-tenth is cultivated. Rolling topography rises to high elevations in the Daxinganlingshanmai separating Manchuria and Mongolia in the north; the Tien Shan in Xinjiang; and the Himalayan range and Kunlunshanmai in the southwest and in Tibet. Length is 1,860 mi (3,000 km) from north to south, width east to west is more than 2,000 mi (3,200 km). The eastern half of China is one of the world's best-watered lands. Three great river systems, the Chang (Yangtze), Huang (Yellow), and Xi, provide water for vast farmlands.

Capital: Beijing (pop., 10,836,000)

Independence date: 221 BC

Government type: Communist Party-led state

Head of state: Pres. Hu Jintao

Head of government: Premier Wen Jiabao   **Monetary unit:** renminbi

GDP: $5.56 trillion (2001 est.)   **Per capita GDP:** $4,300

Industries: iron and steel, coal, machine building, armaments, textiles and apparel, petroleum, cement, chemical fertilizers, footwear, toys, food processing, automobiles, consumer electronics, telecommunications

Chief crops: rice, wheat, potatoes, sorghum, peanuts, tea, millet, barley, cotton, oilseed

Minerals: coal, iron ore, petroleum, natural gas, mercury, tin, tungsten, antimony, manganese, molybdenum, vanadium, magnetite, aluminum, lead, zinc, uranium

The Forbidden City (former imperial residence), Beijing, China

Life expectancy at birth (years): male, 70.3; female, 74.3

Literacy rate: 81.5%

Website: www.china-embassy.org

HONG KONG, formerly a British dependency, in 1997 became a special admin-istrative region of China, which agreed to allow the territory to keep its capitalist system for 50 years. Hong Kong is a major center for trade and banking and has a per capita GDP of $25,400 (2000 est.), among the highest in the world. Population, 7,394,170, including fewer than 20,000 British; area, 422 sq mi (1,090 sq km); chief executive, Tung Chee-hwa.

MACAU, formerly under Portuguese control, reverted to China in 1999, again with a guarantee of noninterference in its way of life and capitalist system for 50 years. Population, 469,903; area, 6 sq mi; chief executive, Ho Hau-wah (Edmund).

CYPRUS

FOR MAP, SEE PAGE 91

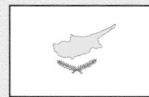

Population: 802,000

Ethnic groups: Greek 85%, Turkish 12%

Principal languages: Greek, Turkish (both official); English

Chief religions: Greek Orthodox 78%, Muslim 18%

Area: 3,570 sq mi (9,250 sq km)

Topography: Two mountain ranges run east to west, separated by a wide, fertile plain.

Capital: Nicosia (pop., 199,000)

Independence date: August 16, 1960

Government type: republic

Head of state and government: Pres. Tassos Papadopolous

Monetary unit: pound

GDP: Greek Cypriot area, $9.1 billion (2001 est.); Turkish Cypriot area, $1.1 billion (2000 est.)

Per capita GDP: Greek Cypriot area, $15,000; Turkish Cypriot area, $7,000

Industries: food, beverages, textiles, chemicals, metal products, tourism, wood products

Chief crops: potatoes, citrus, vegetables, barley, grapes, olives, vegetables

Minerals: copper, pyrites, asbestos, gypsum, salt, marble, clay earth pigment

Life expectancy at birth (years): male, 74.9; female, 79.7

Literacy rate: 97%

Website: www.pio.gov.cy

The TURKISH REPUBLIC OF NORTHERN CYPRUS declared independence in 1983 but failed to gain international recognition. Area, 1,295 sq mi (3,354 sq km); population, 134,000; capital, Lefkosa (Nicosia); president, Rauf Denktash.

EAST TIMOR

FOR MAP, SEE PAGE 81

Population: 778,000

Ethnic groups: Austronesian; Papuan

Principal languages: Tetum, Portuguese (both official); Indonesian, English, other native languages

Chief religions: Roman Catholic 90%, Muslim 4%, Protestant 3%

Area: 5,740 sq mi (14,880 sq km)

Topography: Terrain is rugged, rising to 9,721 ft (2,963 m) at Mt. Ramelau.

Capital: Dili (pop., 140,000)

Independence date: May 20, 2002

Government type: republic

Head of state: Pres. Xanana Gusmão

Head of government: Prime Min. Mari Alkatiri

Monetary unit: U.S. dollar

GDP: $415 million (2001 est.)   Per capita GDP: $500

Industries: printing, soap manufacturing, handicrafts, woven cloth

Chief crops: coffee, rice, maize, cassava, sweet potatoes, soybeans, cabbage, mangoes, bananas, vanilla

Minerals: gold, petroleum, natural gas, manganese, marble

Life expectancy at birth (years): male, 63.0; female, 67.6

Literacy rate: 48%

Website: www.un.org/peace/etimor/etimor.htm

GEORGIA

FOR MAP, SEE PAGE 63

Population: 5,126,000

Ethnic groups: Georgian 70%, Armenian 8%, Russian 6%, Azeri 6%

Principal languages: Georgian (official), Russian, Armenian, Azeri, Abkhaz (official in Abkhazia)

Chief religions: Georgian Orthodox 65%, Muslim 11%, Russian Orthodox 10%, Armenian Apostolic 8%

Area: 26,900 sq mi (69,700 sq km)

Topography: Georgia is separated from Russia in the northeast by the main range of the Caucasus Mountains.

Capital: Tbilisi (pop., 1,406,000)

Independence date: April 9, 1991   Government type: republic

Head of state and government: Pres. Eduard A. Shevardnadze

Monetary unit: lari

GDP: $15.5 billion (2001 est.)   Per capita GDP: $3,100

Industries: steel, aircraft, machine tools, electrical appliances, mining, chemicals, wood products, wine

Chief crops: citrus, grapes, tea, vegetables

Minerals: manganese, iron ore, copper, coal, oil

Life expectancy at birth (years): male, 61.3; female, 68.4

Literacy rate: 99%

Website: www.parliament.ge

INDIA

FOR MAP, SEE PAGE 67

Population: 1,065,462,000

Ethnic groups: Indo-Aryan 72%, Dravidian 25%

Principal languages: Hindi, English, Bengali, Telugu, Marathi, Tamil, Urdu, Gujarati, Malayalam, Kannada, Oriya, Punjabi, Assamese, Kashmiri, Sindhi, and Sanskrit (all official); Hindustani, a mix of Hindi and Urdu spoken in the north, is popular but not official

Chief religions: Hindu 82%, Muslim 12%, Christian 2%, Sikh 2%

Columned architectural treasures of India: Agra Fort (left); the Qutb Minar complex, near Delhi (right)

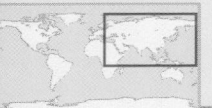

India *(continued)*

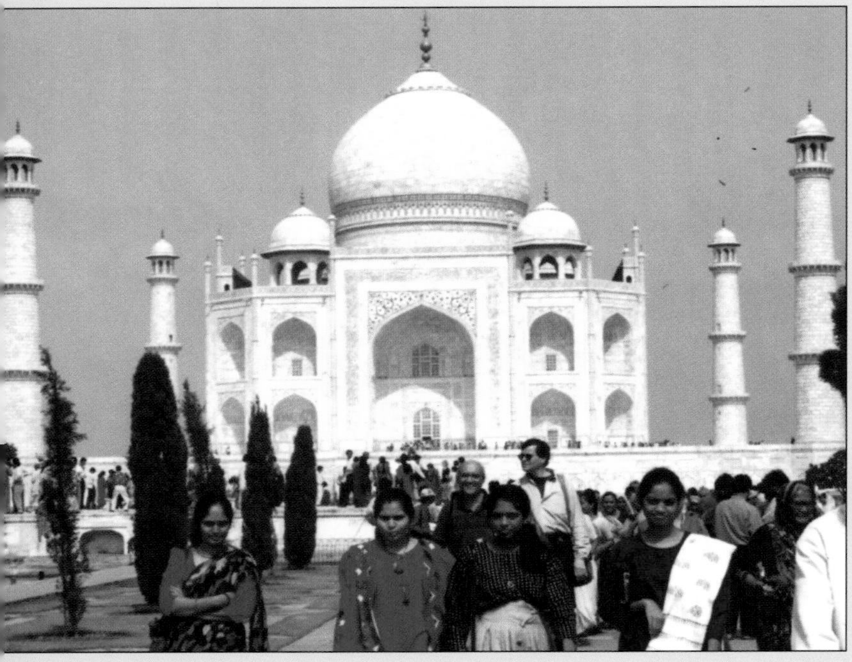

Taj Mahal, Agra, India

Area: 1,269,350 sq mi (3,287,590 sq km)

Topography: The Himalaya Mountains, highest in world, stretch across India's northern borders. Below, the Ganges Plain is wide, fertile, and among the most densely populated regions of the world. The area below includes the Deccan Peninsula. Close to one-quarter of the area is forested.

Capital: New Delhi (pop. of city proper, 300,000)

Independence date: August 15, 1947

Government type: federal republic

Head of state: Pres. A. P. J. Abdul Kalam

Head of government: Prime Min. Atal Bihari Vajpayee

Monetary unit: rupee

GDP: $2.5 trillion (2001 est.) **Per capita GDP:** $2,500

Industries: textiles, chemicals, food processing, steel, transport equipment, cement, mining, petroleum, machinery, software

Chief crops: rice, wheat, oilseed, cotton, jute, tea, sugarcane, potatoes

Minerals: coal, iron ore, manganese, mica, bauxite, titanium ore, chromite, natural gas, diamonds, petroleum, limestone

Life expectancy at birth (years): male, 62.9; female, 64.4

Literacy rate: 52% **Website:** www.indianembassy.org

INDONESIA

For map, see page 80

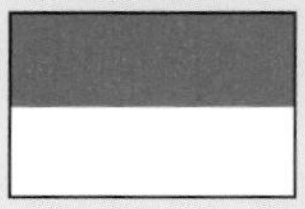

Population: 219,883,000

Ethnic groups: Javanese 45%, Sundanese 14%, Madurese 8%, Malay 8%

Principal languages: Bahasa Indonesia (official, modified form of Malay), English, Dutch, Javanese, other dialects

Chief religions: Muslim 88%, Protestant 5%, Roman Catholic 3%, Hindu 2%, Buddhist 1%

Area: 705,190 sq mi (1,826,440 sq km)

Topography: Indonesia comprises over 13,500 islands (6,000 inhabited), including Java (one of the most densely populated areas in the world with over 2,000 persons per sq mi [770 per sq km]), Sumatra, Kalimantan (most of Borneo), Sulawesi (Celebes), and West Irian (Irian Jaya, the western half of New Guinea). Also: Bangka, Billiton, Madura, Bali, Timor. The mountains and plateaus on the major islands have a cooler climate than the tropical lowlands.

Capital: Jakarta (pop., 11,429,000) **Independence date:** August 17, 1945

Government type: republic

Head of state and government: Pres. Megawati Sukarnoputri

Monetary unit: rupiah

GDP: $687 billion (2001 est.) **Per capita GDP:** $3,000

Industries: petroleum and natural gas, textiles, apparel, footwear, mining, cement, chemical fertilizers, plywood, rubber, food, tourism

Chief crops: rice, cassava, peanuts, rubber, cocoa, coffee, palm oil, copra

Minerals: petroleum, tin, natural gas, nickel, bauxite, copper, coal, gold, silver

Life expectancy at birth (years): male, 66.5; female, 71.5

Literacy rate: 83.8%

Websites: www.indonesiamission–ny.org
www.embassy.org/embassy.org/embassies/id.html

IRAN

For map, see page 67

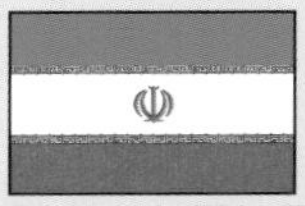

Population: 68,920,000

Ethnic groups: Persian 51%, Azeri 24%, Gilaki/Mazandarani 8%, Kurd 7%, Arab 3%, Lur 2%, Balochi 2%, Turkmen 2%

Principal languages: Farsi (Persian; official), Kurdish, Pashto, Luri, Balochi, Gilaki, Mazandarami, Turkic languages (including Azeri and Turkish), Arabic

Chief religions: Muslim (official; Shi'a 89%, Sunni 10%)

Area: 636,000 sq mi (1,648,000 sq km)

Topography: Interior highlands and plains surrounded by high mountains, up to 18,000 ft (5,500 m). Large salt deserts cover much of area, but there are many oases and forest areas. Most of the population inhabits the north and northwest.

Capital: Tehran (pop., 7,038,000) **Independence date:** April 1, 1979

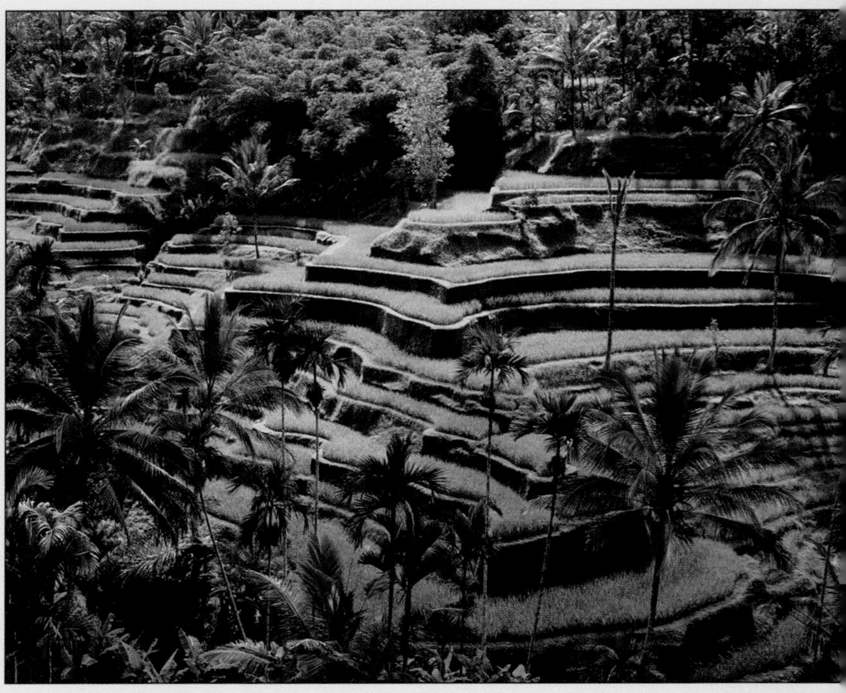

Rice terraces, Bali, Indonesia

Government type: Islamic republic

Religious head: Ayatollah Sayyed Ali Khamenei

Head of state and government: Pres. Mohammad Khatami

Monetary unit: rial

GDP: $426 billion (2001 est.)   Per capita GDP: $6,400

Industries: petroleum, petrochemicals, textiles, construction materials, food processing, metal fabricating, armaments

Chief crops: wheat, rice, other grains, sugar beets, fruits, nuts, cotton

Minerals: petroleum, natural gas, coal, chromium, copper, iron ore, lead, manganese, zinc, sulfur

Life expectancy at birth (years): male, 68.0; female, 70.7

Literacy rate: 72.1%

Websites: www.daftar.org
www.un.int/iran

IRAQ

FOR MAP, SEE PAGE 88

Population: 25,175,000

Ethnic groups: Arab 75%-80%, Kurdish 15%-20%

Principal languages: Arabic (official), Kurdish (official in Kurdish regions), Assyrian, Armenian

Chief religions: Muslim (official; Shi'a 60-65%, Sunni 32-37%)

Area: 168,750 sq mi (437,070 sq km)

Topography: Mostly an alluvial plain, including the Tigris and Euphrates rivers, descending from mountains in the north to desert in the southwest. The Persian Gulf region is marshland.

Capital: Baghdad (pop., 4,958,000)

Independence date: October 3, 1932   Government type: in transition

Head of state and government: in transition

Monetary unit: dinar

GDP: $59 billion (2001 est.)   Per capita GDP: $2,500

Industries: petroleum, chemicals, textiles, construction materials, food processing

Chief crops: wheat, barley, rice, vegetables, dates, cotton

Minerals: petroleum, natural gas, phosphates, sulfur

Life expectancy at birth (years): male, 66.7; female, 69.0

Literacy rate: 58%

Websites: www.Iraqi-mission.org
www.uruklinkinet/iraq/epage1.htm

ISRAEL

FOR MAP, SEE PAGE 91

Population: 6,433,000

Ethnic groups: Jewish 80%, Arab and other 20%

Principal languages: Hebrew, Arabic (both official); English

Chief religions: Jewish 80%, Muslim (mostly Sunni) 15%, Christian 2%

Area: 8,020 sq mi (20,770 sq km)

Topography: The Mediterranean coastal plain is fertile and well-watered. In the center is the Judean Plateau. A triangular-shaped semidesert region, the Negev, extends from south of Beersheba to an apex at the head of the Gulf of Aqaba. The eastern border drops sharply into the Jordan Rift Valley, including Lake Tiberias (Sea of Galilee) and the Dead Sea, which is 1,312 ft (400 m) below sea level, the lowest point on the earth's surface.

Capital: Jerusalem (pop., 661,000)

Independence date: May 14, 1948   Government type: republic

Head of state: Pres. Moshe Katsav

Head of government: Prime Min. Ariel Sharon

Temple Mount, with the Dome of the Rock shrine, Jerusalem, Israel

Monetary unit: new shekel

GDP: $119 billion (2001 est.)   Per capita GDP: $20,000

Industries: high-tech design and manufactures, wood and paper products, food, beverages, tobacco, caustic soda, cement, diamond cutting

Chief crops: citrus, vegetables, cotton

Minerals: potash, copper ore, natural gas, phosphate rock, magnesium bromide, clays, sand

Life expectancy at birth (years): male, 77.0; female, 81.2

Literacy rate: 95%

Websites: www.israel.org
www.israelemb.org

The PALESTINIAN AUTHORITY is responsible for civil government in the Gaza Strip and portions of the West Bank. Gaza: population, 1,275,000; area, 140 sq mi (360 sq km). West Bank: total population, 2,237,000; area, 2,200 sq mi (5,700 sq km).

JAPAN

FOR MAP, SEE PAGE 71

Population: 127,654,000

Ethnic groups: Japanese 99%; Korean, Chinese, and other 1%

Principal languages: Japanese (official), Ainu, Korean

Chief religions: Shinto and Buddhist observed together by 84%

Area: 145,880 sq mi (377,840 sq km)

Topography: Japan consists of four main islands: Honshu ("mainland"), 87,805 sq mi; Hokkaido, 30,144 sq mi (227,415 sq km); Kyushu, 14,114 sq mi (36,555 sq km); and Shikoku, 7,049 sq mi (18,257 sq km). The coast, deeply indented, measures 16,654 mi (26,802 km). The northern islands are a continuation of the Sakhalin Mountains. The Kunlun range of China continues into the southern islands, the ranges meeting in the Japanese Alps. In a vast transverse fissure crossing Honshu east to west rises a group of volcanoes, mostly extinct or inactive, including 12,388-ft (3,776-m) Mt. Fuji (Fujiyama) near Tokyo.

Capital: Tokyo (pop., 26,546,000)   Independence date: 660 BC

Government type: parliamentary democracy

Head of state: Emperor Akihito

Head of government: Prime Min. Junichiro Koizumi

Monetary unit: yen

GDP: $3.45 trillion (2001 est.)

Per capita GDP: $27,200

Industries: motor vehicles, electronic equipment, machine tools, steel and nonferrous metals, ships, chemicals, textiles, processed foods

Three aspects of Japan: Mt. Fuji (top), a lake temple (above left), and Tokyo (above right)

Japan *(continued)*

Chief crops: rice, sugar beets, vegetables, fruit

Life expectancy at birth (years): male, 77.6; female, 84.4

Literacy rate: 99%

Websites: www.us.emb-japan.go.jp
www.mofa.go.jp

JORDAN

FOR MAP, SEE PAGE 88

Population: 5,473,000

Ethnic groups: Arab 98%, Armenian 1%, Circassian 1%

Principal languages: Arabic (official), English

Chief religions: Muslim (official; mostly Sunni) 92%, Christian 6%

Area: 35,300 sq mi (91,540 sq km)

Topography: About 88% of Jordan is arid. Fertile areas are in the west. The only port is on the short Aqaba Gulf coast. The country shares the Dead Sea (1,312 ft [400 m] below sea level) with Israel.

Capital: Amman (pop., 1,181,000)

Independence date: May 25, 1946

Government type: constitutional monarchy

Head of state: King Abdullah II

Head of government: Prime Min. Ali Abu al-Ragheb

Monetary unit: dinar

GDP: $21.6 billion (2001 est.)

Per capita GDP: $4,200

Industries: mining, petroleum refining, cement, light manufacturing, tourism

Chief crops: wheat, barley, citrus, tomatoes, melons, olives

Minerals: phosphates, potash, shale oil

Life expectancy at birth (years): male, 75.4; female, 80.5

Literacy rate: 86.6%

Websites: www.nic.gov.jo
www.jordanembassyus.org/new/index.shtml

KAZAKHSTAN

FOR MAP, SEE PAGE 64

Population: 15,433,000

Ethnic groups: Kazakh 53%, Russian 30%, Ukrainian 4%, Uzbek 3%, German 2%, Uighur 1%

Principal languages: Kazakh, Russian (both official); Ukranian, German, Uzbek

Chief religions: Muslim 47%, Russian Orthodox 44%

Area: 1,049,200 sq mi (2,717,300 sq km)

Topography: Kazakhstan extends from the lower reaches of the Volga River in Europe to the Altay Mountains on the Chinese border.

Capital: Astana (pop., 328,000)

Independence date: December 16, 1991

Government type: republic

Head of state: Pres. Nursultan A. Nazarbayev

Head of government: Prime Min. Daniyal Akhmetov

Monetary unit: tenge

GDP: $98.1 billion (2001 est.)   Per capita GDP: $5,900

Industries: oil, mining, iron and steel, tractors and other agricultural machinery, electric motors, construction materials

Chief crops: spring wheat, cotton

Minerals: petroleum, natural gas, coal, iron ore, manganese, chrome ore, nickel, cobalt, copper, molybdenum, lead, zinc, bauxite, gold, uranium

Life expectancy at birth (years): male, 58.2; female, 69.1

Literacy rate: 98.4%

Websites: www.un.int/kazakhstan
www.president.kz

KOREA, NORTH

FOR MAP, SEE PAGE 73

Population: 22,664,000

Ethnic group: Korean

Principal language: Korean (official)

Chief religions: activities almost nonexistent; traditionally Buddhist, Confucianist, Chondogyo

Area: 46,540 sq mi (120,540 sq km)

Topography: Mountains and hills cover nearly all the country, with narrow valleys and small plains in between. The northern and the eastern coasts are the most rugged areas.

Capital: Pyongyang (pop., 3,197,000)

Independence date: September 9, 1948

Government type: Communist state

Leader: Kim Jong Il

Monetary unit: won

GDP: $21.8 billion (2001 est.)   Per capita GDP: $1,000

Industries: military products, machine building, electric power, chemicals, mining, metallurgy, textiles, food processing

Chief crops: rice, corn, potatoes, soybeans, pulses

Minerals: coal, lead, tungsten, zinc, graphite, magnesite, iron ore, copper, gold, pyrites, salt, fluorspar

Life expectancy at birth (years): male, 68.1; female, 73.6

Literacy rate: 99%

KOREA, SOUTH

FOR MAP, SEE PAGE 73

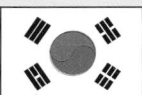

Population: 47,700,000

Ethnic group: Korean

Principal language: Korean (official)

Chief religions: Christian 49%, Buddhist 47%, Confucianist 3%

Area: 38,020 sq mi (98,480 sq km)

Topography: The country is mountainous, with a rugged eastern coast. The western and southern coasts are deeply indented, with many islands and harbors.

Capital: Seoul (pop., 9,862,000)

Independence date: August 15, 1948

Government type: republic

Head of state: Pres. Roh Moo Hyun

Head of government: Prime Min. Goh Kun

Monetary unit: won

GDP: $865 billion (2001 est.)

Per capita GDP: $18,000

A painting from a Seoul museum

Industries: electronics, automobile production, chemicals, shipbuilding, steel, textiles, clothing, footwear, food processing

Chief crops: rice, root crops, barley, vegetables, fruit

Minerals: coal, tungsten, graphite, molybdenum, lead

Life expectancy at birth (years): male, 71.7; female, 79.3

Literacy rate: 98%

Website: www.korea.net

Seoul, South Korea

KUWAIT

FOR MAP, SEE PAGE 88

Population: 2,521,000

Ethnic groups: Arab 80%, South Asian 9%, Iranian 4%

Principal languages: Arabic (official), English

Chief religion: Muslim 85% (official; Sunni 70%, Shi'a 30%)

Area: 6,880 sq mi (17,820 sq km)

Topography: The country is flat, very dry, and extremely hot.

Capital: Kuwait City (pop., 888,000)

Independence date: June 19, 1961

Government type: constitutional monarchy

Head of state: Emir Sheikh Jabir al-Ahmad al-Jabir as-Sabah

Head of government: Prime Min. Sheikh Saad Abdulla as-Salim as-Sabah

Monetary unit: dinar

GDP: $30.9 billion (2001 est.)   **Per capita GDP:** $15,100

Industries: petroleum, petrochemicals, desalination, food processing, construction materials

Minerals: petroleum, natural gas

Life expectancy at birth (years): male, 75.7; female, 77.6

Literacy rate: 78.6%   **Website:** www.moinfo.gov.kw

KYRGYZSTAN

FOR MAP, SEE PAGE 87

Population: 5,138,000

Ethnic groups: Kyrgyz 52%, Russian 18%, Uzbek 13%, Ukrainian 3%, German 2%

Principal languages: Kyrgyz, Russian (both official); Uzbek

Chief religions: Muslim 75%, Russian Orthodox 20%

Area: 76,600 sq mi (198,500 sq km)

Topography: Kyrgystan is a landlocked country nearly covered by the Tien Shan and Pamir Mountains; the average elevation is 9,020 ft (2,750 m). A large lake, Issyk-Kul, in the northeast is 1 mi (1.6 km) above sea level.

Capital: Bishkek (pop., 736,000)   **Independence date:** August 31, 1991

Government type: republic

Head of state: Pres. Askar Akayev

Head of government: Prime Min. Nikolay Tanayev

Monetary unit: som

GDP: $13.5 billion (2001 est.)   **Per capita GDP:** $2,800

Industries: small machinery, textiles, food processing, cement, shoes, sawn logs, refrigerators, furniture, electric motors

Chief crops: tobacco, cotton, potatoes, vegetables, grapes, fruits and berries

Minerals: gold and rare earth metals, coal, oil, natural gas, nepheline, mercury, bismuth, lead, zinc

Life expectancy at birth (years): male, 59.5; female, 68.0

Literacy rate: 97%

Website: www.kyrgyzstan.org

LAOS

FOR MAP, SEE PAGE 78

Population: 5,657,000

Ethnic groups: Lao Loum 68%, Lao Theung 22%, Lao Soung (includes Hmong and Yao) 9%

Principal languages: Lao (official), French, English, and various ethnic languages

258

Nation Facts and Figures

LEBANON – MALDIVES

Laos (continued)

Chief religions: Buddhism 60%, animist and other 40%

Area: 91,400 sq mi (236,800 sq km)

Topography: Laos is landlocked, dominated by jungle. High mountains along the eastern border are the source of the east to west rivers slicing across the country to the Mekong River, which defines most of the western border.

Capital: Vientiane (pop., 663,000)   **Independence date:** July 19, 1949

Government type: Communist

Head of state: Pres. Khamtai Siphandon

Head of government: Prime Min. Boungnang Vorachith

Monetary unit: kip

GDP: $9.2 billion (2001 est.)   **Per capita GDP:** $1,630

Industries: mining, timber, electric power, agricultural processing, construction, garments, tourism

Chief crops: sweet potatoes, vegetables, corn, coffee, sugarcane, tobacco, cotton, tea, peanuts, rice

Minerals: gypsum, tin, gold, gemstones

Life expectancy at birth (years): male, 52.3; female, 56.3

Literacy rate: 57%

Website: www.laoembassy.com/discover/index.htm

Thean Hou Temple, Kuala Lumpur, Malaysia

LEBANON

FOR MAP, SEE PAGE 91

Population: 3,653,000

Ethnic groups: Arab 95%, Armenian 4%

Principal languages: Arabic (official), French, English, Armenian

Chief religions: Muslim 70%, Christian 30%

Topography: There is a narrow coastal strip, and two mountain ranges running north to south enclosing the fertile Beqaa Valley. The Litani River runs south through the valley, turning west to empty into the Mediterranean.

Area: 4,000 sq mi (10,400 sq km)

Capital: Beirut (pop., 2,115,000)   **Independence date:** November 22, 1943

Government type: republic

Head of state: Pres. Emile Lahoud

Head of government: Prime Min. Rafiq al-Hariri

Monetary unit: pound

GDP: $18.8 billion (2001 est.)   **Per capita GDP:** $5,200

Industries: banking, food processing, jewelry, cement, textiles, mineral and chemical products, wood and furniture products, oil refining, metal fabricating

Chief crops: citrus, grapes, tomatoes, apples, vegetables, potatoes, olives, tobacco

Minerals: limestone, iron ore, salt

Life expectancy at birth (years): male, 69.6; female, 74.6

Literacy rate: 86.4%

Website: http://www.presidency.gov.lb

MALAYSIA

FOR MAP, SEE PAGE 80

Population: 24,425,000

Ethnic groups: Malay and other indigenous 58%, Chinese 24%, Indian 8%

Principal languages: Malay (official), English, Chinese dialects, Tamil, Telugu, Malayalam, Panjabi, Thai; Iban and Kadazan in the east

Chief religions: Muslim (official) 60%, Buddhist 19%, Christian 9%, Hindu 6%, Confucianist/Taoist 3%

Area: 127,320 sq mi (329,750 sq km)

Topography: Most of western Malaysia is covered by tropical jungle, including the central mountain range that runs north to south through the peninsula. The western coast is marshy, the eastern coast, sandy. Eastern Malaysia has a wide, swampy coastal plain, with interior jungles and mountains.

Capital: Kuala Lumpur (pop., 1,410,000)

Independence date: August 31, 1957

Government type: federal parliamentary democracy with a constitutional monarch

Head of state: Paramount Ruler Syed Sirajuddin Syed Putra Jamalullail

Head of government: Prime Min. Datuk Seri Mahathir bin Mohamad

Monetary unit: ringgit

GDP: $200 billion (2001 est.)   **Per capita GDP:** $9,000

Industries: rubber/oil-palm goods, light manufacturing, electronics, mining, logging

Chief crops: rubber, palm oil, cocoa, rice, coconuts, pepper

Minerals: tin, petroleum, copper, iron ore, natural gas, bauxite

Life expectancy at birth (years): male, 69.0; female, 74.5

Literacy rate: 83.5%

Websites: www.embassy.org/embassies/my.html
www.tourism.gov.my

MALDIVES

FOR MAP, SEE PAGE 67

Population: 318,000

Ethnic groups: Dravidian, Sinhalese, Arab

Principal languages: Divehi (Sinhala dialect, Arabic script; official), English

Chief religion: Muslim (official; mostly Sunni)

Area: 116 sq mi (300 sq km)

Topography: The Maldives consists of 19 atolls with 1,190 islands, 198 inhabited. None of the islands are over 5 sq mi (13 sq km) in area, and all are nearly flat.

Capital: Male (pop., 84,000)   **Independence date:** July 26, 1965

Government type: republic

Head of state and government: Pres. Maumoon Abdul Gayoom

Monetary unit: rufiyaa

GDP: $1.2 billion (2001 est.)   Per capita GDP: $3,870

Industries: fish processing, tourism, shipping, boatbuilding, coconut processing, garments, woven mats, rope, handicrafts, coral and sand mining

Chief crops: coconuts, corn, sweet potatoes

Life expectancy at birth (years): male, 62.1; female, 64.6

Literacy rate: 93.2%   Website: www.un.int/maldives

MONGOLIA

FOR MAP, SEE PAGE 70

Population: 2,594,000

Ethnic groups: Mongol 85%, Turkic 7%, Tungusic 5%

Principal languages: Khalkha Mongol, Turkic, Russian

Chief religion: Tibetan Buddhist Lamaism 96%

Area: 604,000 sq mi (1,565,000 sq km)

Topography: Mongolia is mostly a high plateau with mountains, salt lakes, and vast grasslands. Arid lands in the southern are part of the Gobi Desert.

Capital: Ulaanbaatar (pop., 781,000)

Independence date: July 11, 1921

Government type: republic

Head of state: Pres. Natsagiyn Bagabandi

Head of government: Prime Min. Nambaryn Enkhbayar

Monetary unit: tugrik

GDP: $4.7 billion (2001 est.)   Per capita GDP: $1,770

Industries: construction materials, mining, food and beverages, processing of animal products

Chief crops: wheat, barley, potatoes, forage crops

Minerals: oil, coal, copper, molybdenum, tungsten, phosphates, tin, nickel, zinc, wolfram, fluorspar, gold, silver, iron, phosphate

Life expectancy at birth (years): male, 61.6; female, 66.1

Literacy rate: 97.8%

Website: www.pmls.gov.mn/engmain.htm

MYANMAR (FORMERLY BURMA)

FOR MAP, SEE PAGE 83

Population: 49,485,000

Ethnic groups: Burman 68%, Shan 9%, Karen 7%, Rakhine 4%, Chinese 3%, Indian 2%, Mon 2%

Principal languages: Burmese (official); many ethnic minority languages

Chief religions: Buddhist 89%, Christian 4%, Muslim 4%, animist 1%

Area: 262,000 sq mi (678,500 sq km)

Topography: Mountains surround Myanmar on the west, north, and east, and dense forests cover much of the nation. North to south rivers provide habitable valleys and communications, especially the Irrawaddy, navigable for 900 mi (1,400 km).

Capital: Yangon (Rangoon) (pop., 4,504,000)

Independence date: January 4, 1948

Government type: military

Hsinbyume Pagoda, Mingun, Myanmar

Head of state and government: Gen. Than Shwe

Monetary unit: kyat

GDP: $63 billion (2001 est.)   Per capita GDP: $1,500

Industries: agricultural processing, knit and woven apparel, wood and wood products, mining, construction materials, pharmaceuticals, fertilizer

Chief crops: rice, pulses, beans, sesame, groundnuts, sugarcane

Minerals: petroleum, tin, antimony, zinc, copper, tungsten, lead, coal, marble, limestone, precious stones, natural gas

Life expectancy at birth (years): male, 54.1; female, 57.6

Literacy rate: 83.1%

Website: www.myanmar.com/eng

NEPAL

FOR MAP, SEE PAGE 84

Population: 25,164,000

Ethnic groups: Newar, Indian, Gurung, Magar, Tamang, Rai, Limbu, Sherpa, Tharu

Principal languages: Nepali (official); about 30 dialects and 12 other languages

Chief religions: Hindu (official) 86%, Buddhist 8%, Muslim 4%

Area: 54,400 sq mi (140,800 sq km)

Topography: The Himalayas stretch across the north, the hill country with its fertile valleys extends across the center, while the southern border region is part of the flat, subtropical Ganges Plain.

Capital: Kathmandu (pop., 755,000)

Independence date: 1768

Government type: constitutional monarchy

Head of state: King Gyanendra Bir Bikram Shah Dev

Head of government: Prime Min. Surya Bahadur Thapa

Monetary unit: rupee

GDP: $35.6 billion (2001 est.)   Per capita GDP: $1,400

Industries: tourism, carpet, textile, rice, jute, sugar, oilseed mills, cigarettes, cement and brick production

Chief crops: rice, corn, wheat, sugarcane, root crops

Minerals: quartz, lignite, copper, cobalt, iron ore

Life expectancy at birth (years): male, 59.4; female, 58.6

Literacy rate: 27.5%   Website: www.nepalembassy/usa.org

Machapuchare peak, Nepal

OMAN

FOR MAP, SEE PAGE 89

Population: 2,851,000

Ethnic groups: Arab, Baluchi, South Asian, African

Principal languages: Arabic (official), English, Baluchi, Urdu, Indian dialects

Chief religion: Muslim 75% (official; mostly Ibadhi)

Area: 82,030 sq mi (212,460 sq km)

Topography: Oman has a narrow coastal plain up to 10 mi (16 km) wide, a range of barren mountains reaching 9,900 ft (3,000 m), and a wide, stony, mostly waterless plateau, with an average altitude of 1,000 ft (300 m). Also, an exclave at the tip of the Musandam peninsula controls access to the Persian Gulf.

Capital: Muscat (pop., 540,000)

Independence date: 1650   **Government type:** absolute monarchy

Head of state and government: Sultan Qabus bin Said

Monetary unit: rial Omani

GDP: $21.5 billion (2001 est.)   **Per capita GDP:** $8,200

Industries: oil and gas, construction, cement, copper

Chief crops: dates, limes, bananas, alfalfa, vegetables

Minerals: petroleum, copper, asbestos, marble, limestone, chromium, gypsum, natural gas

Life expectancy at birth (years): male, 70.4; female, 74.9

Literacy rate: approaching 80%   **Website:** www.omanet.com

PAKISTAN

FOR MAP, SEE PAGE 89

Population: 153,578,000

Ethnic groups: Punjabi, Sindhi, Pashtun, Balochi

Principal languages: English, Urdu (both official); Punjabi, Sindhi, Siraiki, Pashtu, Balochi, Hindko, Brahui, Burushaski

Chief religions: Muslim 97% (official; Sunni 77%, Shi'a 20%)

Area: 310,400 sq mi (803,940 sq km)

Topography: The Indus River rises in the Hindu Kush and Himalaya mountains in the north (highest is K2, or Godwin Austen, 28,250 ft [8,610 m], second highest in the world), then flows over 1,000 mi (1,600 km) through fertile valley and empties into Arabian Sea. The Thar Desert and Eastern Plains flank the Indus Valley.

Capital: Islamabad (pop., 636,000)

Independence date: August 14, 1947

Government type: republic with strong military influence

Head of state and government: Pres. Pervez Musharraf

Monetary unit: rupee

GDP: $299 billion (2001 est.)   **Per capita GDP:** $2,100

Industries: textiles, food processing, beverages, construction materials, clothing, paper products

Chief crops: cotton, wheat, rice, sugarcane, fruits, vegetables

Minerals: natural gas, limited petroleum, poor quality coal, iron ore, copper, salt, limestone

Life expectancy at birth (years): male, 61.3; female, 63.1

Literacy rate: 42.7%

Website: www.pakistan-embassy.com/index.asp

PAPUA NEW GUINEA

FOR MAP, SEE PAGE 116

Population: 5,711,000

Ethnic groups: Melanesian, Papuan, Negrito, Micronesian, Polynesian

Principal languages: English (official), pidgin English, Motu; 715 indigenous languages

Chief religions: indigenous beliefs 34%, Roman Catholic 22%, Protestant 44%

Area: 178,700 sq mi (462,840 sq km)

Topography: Thickly forested mountains cover much of the center of the country, with lowlands along the coasts. Included are some islands of the Bismarck and Solomon groups, such as the Admiralty Islands, New Ireland, New Britain, and Bougainville.

Capital: Port Moresby (pop., 259,000)

Independence date: September 16, 1975

Government type: parliamentary democracy

Head of state: Queen Elizabeth II, represented by Gov-Gen. Silas Atopare

Head of government: Prime Min. Sir Michael Somare

Monetary unit: kina

GDP: $12.2 billion (2001 est.)   **Per capita GDP:** $2,400

Industries: copra and palm oil processing, wood products, mining, construction, tourism

Chief crops: coffee, cocoa, coconuts, palm kernels, tea, rubber, sweet potatoes, fruit, vegetables

Minerals: gold, copper, silver, natural gas, oil

Life expectancy at birth (years): male, 62.1; female, 66.4

Literacy rate: 64.5%

Websites: www.pngonline.gov.pg www.pngembassy.org

PHILIPPINES

FOR MAP, SEE PAGE 79

Population: 79,999,000

Ethnic groups: Christian Malay 91.5%, Muslim Malay 4%, Chinese 1.5%

Principal languages: Filipino, English (both official); many dialects

Chief religions: Roman Catholic 83%, Protestant 9%, Muslim 5%

Area: 115,830 sq mi (300,000 sq km)

Topography: The country consists of some 7,100 islands stretching 1,100 mi (1,770 km) north to south. About 95% of the area and population are on the 11 largest islands, which are mountainous, except for the heavily indented coastlines and the central plain on Luzon.

Capital: Manila (pop., 10,069,000)

Independence date: July 4, 1946   **Government type:** republic

Head of state and government: Pres. Gloria Macapagal Arroyo

Monetary unit: peso

Fishing boat, Boracay, Philippines

GDP: $335 billion (2001 est.)   Per capita GDP: $4,000

Industries: textiles, pharmaceuticals, chemicals, wood products, food processing, electronics assembly

Chief crops: rice, coconuts, corn, sugarcane, bananas, pineapples, mangoes

Minerals: petroleum, nickel, cobalt, silver, gold, salt, copper

Life expectancy at birth (years): male, 66.4; female, 72.3

Literacy rate: 94.6%

Websites: www.philippineembassy-usa.org www.gov.ph

QATAR

For map, see page 88

Population: 610,000

Ethnic groups: Arab 40%, Pakistani 18%, Indian 18%, Iranian 10%

Principal languages: Arabic (official), English

Chief religion: Muslim (official) 95%

Area: 4,420 sq mi (11,440 sq km)

Topography: Qatar is mostly a flat desert, with some limestone ridges; vegetation of any kind is scarce.

Capital: Doha (pop., 285,000)

Independence date: September 3, 1971

Government type: traditional monarchy

Head of state: Emir Hamad bin Khalifa ath-Thani

Head of government: Prime Min. Abdullah bin Khalifa ath-Thani

Monetary unit: riyal

GDP: $16.3 billion (2001 est.)   Per capita GDP: $21,200

Industries: oil production and refining, fertilizers, petrochemicals, steel reinforcing bars, cement

Chief crops: fruits, vegetables

Minerals: petroleum, natural gas

Life expectancy at birth (years): male, 70.7; female, 75.8

Literacy rate: 79%   Website: www.english.mofa.gov.qa

SAUDI ARABIA

For map, see page 88

Population: 24,217,000

Ethnic groups: Arab 90%, Afro-Asian 10%

Principal language: Arabic (official)

Chief religion: Muslim (official)

Area: 756,990 sq mi (1,960,580 sq km)

Topography: Saudi Arabia is bordered by the Red Sea in the west. The highlands in the west, up to 9,000 ft (2,700 m), slope as an arid, barren desert to the Persian Gulf in the east.

Capital: Riyadh (pop., 4,761,000)

Independence date: September 23, 1932

Government type: constitutional monarchy with strong Islamic influence

Head of state and government: King Fahd ibn Abdul Aziz

Monetary unit: riyal

GDP: $241 billion (2001 est.)   Per capita GDP: $10,600

Industries: oil production and refining, basic petrochemicals, cement, construction, fertilizer, plastics

Chief crops: wheat, barley, tomatoes, melons, dates, citrus

Minerals: petroleum, natural gas, iron ore, gold, copper

Life expectancy at birth (years): male, 67.0; female, 70.6

Literacy rate: 78%   Website: www.saudiembassy.net

SINGAPORE

For map, see page 80

Population: 4,253,000

Ethnic groups: Chinese 77%, Malay 14%, Indian 8%

Principal languages: Chinese, Malay, Tamil, English (all official)

Chief religions: Buddhist, Muslim, Christian, Taoist, Hindu

Area: 250 sq mi (650 sq km)

Topography: Singapore is a flat, formerly swampy island. The nation includes 40 nearby islets.

Capital: Singapore (pop., 4,108,000)

Independence date: August 9, 1965

Government type: republic   Head of state: Pres. S. R. Nathan

Head of government: Prime Min. Goh Chok Tong

Monetary unit: Singapore dollar

GDP: $106.3 billion (2001 est.)   Per capita GDP: $24,700

Industries: electronics, chemicals, financial services, oil-drilling equipment, petroleum refining, rubber products, processed food and beverages, ship repair, entrepot trade, biotechnology

Chief crops: rubber, copra, fruit, orchids, vegetables

Life expectancy at birth (years): male, 77.5; female, 83.6

Literacy rate: 93.5%   Website: www.gov.sg

Singapore

SRI LANKA

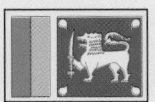

For map, see page 82

Population: 19,065,000

Ethnic groups: Sinhalese 74%, Tamil 18%, Moor 7%

Principal languages: Sinhala, Tamil (both official); English

Chief religions: Buddhist 70%, Hindu 15%, Christian 8%, Muslim 7%

Area: 25,330 sq mi (65,610 sq km)

Topography: The coastal area and the northern half are flat; the south-central area is hilly and mountainous.

Capitals: Colombo (administrative) (pop., 681,000), Sri Jayawardenepura Kotte (legislative) (pop., 109,000)

Independence date: February 4, 1948

Government type: republic

Head of state: Pres. Chandrika Bandaranaike Kumaratunga

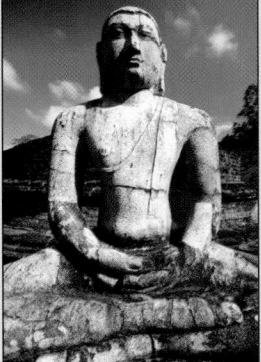

Buddha statue, Polonnaruwa, Sri Lanka

Sri Lanka (continued)

Tea plantation, Sri Lanka

Head of government: Prime Min. Ranil Wickremesinghe

Monetary unit: rupee

GDP: $62.7 billion (2001 est.)   Per capita GDP: $3,250

Industries: rubber processing, agricultural commodities, clothing, cement, petroleum refining, textiles, tobacco

Chief crops: rice, sugarcane, grains, pulses, oilseed, spices, tea, rubber, coconuts

Minerals: limestone, graphite, mineral sands, gems, phosphates, clay

Life expectancy at birth (years): male, 70.1; female, 75.3

Literacy rate: 90.2%   Website: www.priv.gov.lk

Government type: republic (under military regime)

Head of state: Pres. Bashar al-Assad

Head of government: Prime Min. Muhammad Mustafa Meros

Monetary unit: pound

GDP: $54.2 billion (2001 est.)

Per capita GDP: $3,200

Industries: petroleum, textiles, food processing, beverages, tobacco

Chief crops: wheat, barley, cotton, lentils, chickpeas, olives, sugar beets

Minerals: petroleum, phosphates, chrome and manganese ores, asphalt, iron ore, rock salt, marble, gypsum

Life expectancy at birth (years): male, 68.2; female, 70.7

Literacy rate: 70.8%

TAIWAN
FOR MAP, SEE PAGE 79

Population: 22,603,000

Ethnic groups: Taiwanese 84%, mainland Chinese 14%, aborigine 2%

Principal languages: Mandarin Chinese (official), Taiwanese (Min), Hakka dialects

Chief religions: Buddhist, Confucian, and Taoist 93%; Christian 5%

Area: 13,890 sq mi (35,980 sq km)

Topography: A mountain range forms the backbone of the island; the eastern half is very steep and craggy, and the western slope is flat, fertile, and well cultivated.

Capital: Taipei (pop., 2,595,699)

Independence date: 1949

Government type: democracy

Head of state: Pres. Chen Shui-bian

Head of government: Prime Min. Yu Shyi-kun

Monetary unit: new Taiwan dollar

GDP: $386 billion (2001 est.)

Per capita GDP: $17,200

Industries: electronics, petroleum refining, chemicals, textiles, iron and steel, machinery, cement, food processing

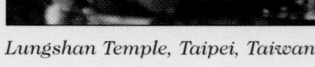

Lungshan Temple, Taipei, Taiwan

Chief crops: rice, corn, vegetables, fruit, tea

Minerals: coal, natural gas, limestone, marble, asbestos

Life expectancy at birth (years): male, 74.1; female, 79.9

Literacy rate: 86%

Website: www.taiwan.gov.tw/ENGLISH/

SYRIA
FOR MAP, SEE PAGE 90

Population: 17,800,000

Ethnic groups: Arab 90%, Kurds, Armenians, and other 10%

Principal languages: Arabic (official), Kurdish, Armenian

Chief religions: Sunni Muslim 74%, other Muslims 16%, Christian 10%

Area: 71,500 sq mi (185,180 sq km)

Topography: Syria has a short Mediterranean coastline, then stretches east and south with fertile lowlands and plains, alternating with mountains and large desert areas.

Capital: Damascus (pop., 2,195,000)

Independence date: April 17, 1946

TAJIKISTAN
FOR MAP, SEE PAGE 87

Population: 6,245,000

Ethnic groups: Tajik 65%, Uzbek 25%, Russian 4%

Principal languages: Tajik (official), Russian

Chief religion: Muslim (Sunni 85%, Shi'a 5%)

Area: 55,300 sq mi (143,100 sq km)

Topography: Mountainous region that contains the Pamirs and the Trans-Alai mountain system.

Capital: Dushanbe (pop., 522,000)

Independence date: September 9, 1991

Government type: republic   Head of state: Pres. Imomali Rakhmonov

Head of government: Prime Min. Akil Akilov

Monetary unit: Tajik ruble

GDP: $7.5 billion (2001 est.)   Per capita GDP: $1,140

Industries: aluminum, zinc, lead, chemicals and fertilizers, cement, vegetable oil, metal-cutting machine tools, refrigerators and freezers

Chief crops: cotton, grain, fruits, grapes, vegetables

Minerals: petroleum, uranium, mercury, brown coal, lead, zinc, antimony, tungsten, silver, gold

Life expectancy at birth (years): male, 61.4; female, 67.5

Literacy rate: 98%

THAILAND
FOR MAP, SEE PAGE 78

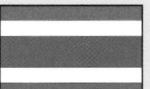

Population: 62,833,000

Ethnic groups: Thai 75%, Chinese 14%

Principal languages: Thai, Chinese, Malay, Khmer

Chief religions: Buddhism (official) 95%, Muslim 4%

Area: 198,000 sq mi (514,000 sq km)

Topography: A plateau dominates the northeast third of Thailand, dropping to the fertile alluvial valley of the Chao Phraya River in the center. Forested mountains are in the north, with narrow fertile valleys. The southern peninsula region is covered by rain forests.

Capital: Bangkok (pop., 7,527,000)   Independence date: 1238

Government type: constitutional monarchy

Head of state: King Bhumibol Adulyadej

Head of government: Prime Min. Thaksin Shinawatra

Monetary unit: baht

GDP: $410 billion (2001 est.)   Per capita GDP: $6,600

Industries: tourism, textiles and garments, agricultural processing, beverages, tobacco, cement, light manufacturing, electric appliances and components, computers and parts, integrated circuits, furniture, plastics

Chief crops: rice, cassava, rubber, corn, sugarcane, coconuts, soybeans

Minerals: tin, rubber, natural gas, tungsten, tantalum, lead, gypsum, lignite, fluorite

Life expectancy at birth (years): male, 69.1; female, 73.5

Literacy rate: 93.8%

Website: www.thaigov.go.th/index-eng.htm

River market, Thailand

Hagia Sophia, Istanbul, Turkey

TURKEY
FOR MAP, SEE PAGE 90

Population: 71,325,000

Ethnic groups: Turk 80%, Kurd 20%

Principal languages: Turkish (official), Kurdish, Arabic, Armenian, Greek

Chief religion: Muslim 99.8% (mostly Sunni)

Area: 301,380 sq mi (780,580 sq km)

Topography: Central Turkey has wide plateaus, with hot, dry summers and cold winters. High mountains ring the interior in all but the west, with more than 20 peaks over 10,000 ft (3,000 m). Rolling plains are in the west; mild, fertile coastal plains are in the south and west.

Capital: Ankara (pop., 3,208,000)

Independence date: October 29, 1923

Government type: republic

Head of state: Pres. Ahmet Necdet Sezer

Head of government: Prime Min. Recep Tayyip Erdogan

Monetary unit: Turkish lira

GDP: $443 billion (2001 est.)   Per capita GDP: $6,700

Industries: textiles, food processing, autos, mining, steel, petroleum, construction, lumber, paper

Chief crops: tobacco, cotton, grain, olives, sugar beets, pulse, citrus

Minerals: antimony, coal, chromium, mercury, copper, borate, sulfur, iron ore

Life expectancy at birth (years): male, 69.4; female, 74.3

Literacy rate: 85%   Website: www.turkey.org

TURKMENISTAN
FOR MAP, SEE PAGE 87

Population: 4,867,000

Ethnic groups: Turkmen 77%, Uzbek 9%, Russian 7%, Kazakh 2%

Principal languages: Turkmen, Russian, Uzbek

Chief religions: Muslim 89%, Eastern Orthodox 9%

Area: 188,500 sq mi (488,100 sq km)

Topography: The Kara Kum Desert occupies 80% of the area. The country is bordered on the west by the Caspian Sea.

Capital: Ashgabat (pop., 558,000)

Nation Facts and Figures

Turkmenistan (continued)

Independence date: October 27, 1991

Government type: republic with authoritarian rule

Head of state and government: Pres. Saparmurad Niyazov ("Turkmenbashi")

Monetary unit: manat

GDP: $21.5 billion (2001 est.)   Per capita GDP: $4,700

Industries: petroleum products, textiles, food processing

Chief crops: cotton, grain

Minerals: petroleum, natural gas, coal, sulfur, salt

Life expectancy at birth (years): male, 57.7; female, 64.8

Literacy rate: 98%   Website: www.turkmenistanembassy.org

UNITED ARAB EMIRATES

FOR MAP, SEE PAGE 88

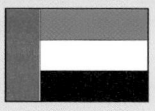

Population: 2,995,000

Ethnic groups: Arab and Iranian 42%, Indian 50%

Principal languages: Arabic (official), Persian, English, Hindi, Urdu

Chief religion: Muslim 96% (official; Shi'a 16%)

Area: 32,000 sq mi (82,880 sq km)

Topography: A barren, flat coastal plain gives way to uninhabited sand dunes on the south. The Hajar Mountains are in the east.

Capital: Abu Dhabi (pop., 471,000)

Independence date: December 2, 1971

Government type: federation of emirates

Head of state: Pres. Zaid ibn Sultan an-Nahayan

Head of government: Prime Min. Sheik Maktum ibn Rashid al-Maktum

Monetary unit: dirham

GDP: $51 billion (2001 est.)   Per capita GDP: $21,100

Industries: petroleum, fishing, petrochemicals, construction materials, boatbuilding, handicrafts, pearling

Chief crops: dates, vegetables, watermelons

Minerals: petroleum, natural gas

Life expectancy at birth (years): male, 72.3; female, 77.4

Literacy rate: 79.2%

Websites: www.uae.org.ae
ww.emirates.org

UZBEKISTAN

FOR MAP, SEE PAGE 87

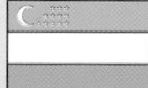

Population: 26,093,000

Ethnic groups: Uzbek 80%, Russian 6%, Tajik 5%, Kazakh 3%, Karakalpak 3%, Tatar 2%

Principal languages: Uzbek (official), Russian, Tajik

Chief religions: Muslim 88% (mostly Sunni), Eastern Orthodox 9%

Area: 172,740 sq mi (447,400 sq km)

Topography: Uzbekistan consists mostly of plains and desert.

Capital: Tashkent (pop., 2,157,000)

Independence date: August 31, 1991

Government type: republic with authoritarian rule

Head of state: Pres. Islam A. Karimov

Head of government: Prime Min. Utkir Sultanov

Monetary unit: som

GDP: $62 billion (2001 est.)   Per capita GDP: $2,500

Industries: textiles, food processing, machine building, metallurgy, natural gas, chemicals

Chief crops: cotton, vegetables, fruits, grain

Minerals: natural gas, petroleum, coal, gold, uranium, silver, copper, lead and zinc, tungsten, molybdenum

Life expectancy at birth (years): male, 60.5; female, 67.6

Literacy rate: 97.3%

VIETNAM

FOR MAP, SEE PAGE 78

Population: 81,377,000

Ethnic groups: Vietnamese 85%-90%, Chinese, Hmong, Thai, Khmer, Cham

Principal languages: Vietnamese (official), English, French, Chinese, Khmer

Chief religions: Buddhist, Roman Catholic

Area: 127,240 sq mi (329,560 sq km)

Topography: Vietnam is long and narrow, with a 1,400-mi (2,300-km) coast. About 22% of the country is readily arable, including the densely settled Red River valley in the north, narrow coastal plains in the center, and the wide, often marshy Mekong River Delta in the south. The rest consists of semiarid plateaus and barren mountains, with some stretches of tropical rain forest.

Capital: Hanoi (pop., 3,822,000)   Independence date: September 2, 1945

Government type: Communist

Head of state: Pres. Tran Duc Luong

Head of government: Prime Min. Phan Van Khai

Monetary unit: dong

GDP: $168.1 billion (2001 est.)   Per capita GDP: $2,100

Industries: food processing, garments, shoes, machine building, mining, cement, chemical fertilizer, glass, tires, oil, coal, steel, paper

Chief crops: paddy rice, corn, potatoes, rubber, soybeans, coffee, tea, bananas

Minerals: phosphates, coal, manganese, bauxite, chromate, offshore oil and gas

Life expectancy at birth (years): male, 67.6; female, 72.7

Literacy rate: 93.7%

Website: www.vietnamembassy-usa.org

YEMEN

FOR MAP, SEE PAGE 88

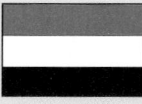

Population: 20,010,000

Ethnic groups: Mainly Arab; Afro-Arab, South Asian, European

Principal language: Arabic (official)

Chief religions: Muslim (official; Sunni 60%, Shi'a 40%)

Area: 203,850 sq mi (527,970 sq km)

Topography: A sandy coastal strip leads to well-watered fertile mountains in the interior.

Capital: Sanaa (pop., 1,410,000)   Independence date: May 22, 1990

Government type: republic

Head of state: Pres. Ali Abdullah Saleh

Head of government: Prime Min. Abd-al-Qadir Bajamal

Monetary unit: rial

GDP: $14.8 billion (2001 est.)   Per capita GDP: $820

Industries: oil, cotton textiles, leather goods, food processing, handicrafts, aluminum products, cement

Chief crops: grain, fruits, vegetables, pulses, qat, coffee, cotton

Minerals: petroleum, rock salt, marble, coal, gold, lead, nickel, copper

Life expectancy at birth (years): male, 59.2; female, 62.9

Literacy rate: 38%   Website: www.yemenembassy.org

AUSTRALIA, NEW ZEALAND, AND THE PACIFIC

The nation of Australia, which spans the entire continent of Australia, has the sixth biggest land area among the countries of the world. The Pacific island nations of Nauru and Tuvalu fall among the world's five smallest countries in terms of land area; as of 2003, Tuvalu and Nauru, along with Palau, ranked among the five smallest countries in terms of population.

AUSTRALIA

FOR MAP, SEE PAGE 109

Population: 19,731,000
Ethnic groups: white 92%, Asian 7%, Aborigine and other 1%
Principal languages: English (official), aboriginal languages
Chief religions: Anglican 26%, Roman Catholic 26%, other Christian 24%
Area: 2,967,910 sq mi (7,686,850 sq km)
Topography: An island continent. The Great Dividing Range along the eastern coast has Mt. Kosciusko, 7,310 ft (2,230 m). The western plateau rises to 2,000 ft (600 m), with arid areas in the Great Sandy and Great Victoria deserts. The northwestern part of Western Australia and the Northern Territory are arid and hot. The northeast has heavy rainfall, and Cape York Peninsula has jungles.
Capital: Canberra (pop., 387,000)

Independence date: January 1, 1901
Government type: democratic, federal state system
Head of state: Queen Elizabeth II, represented by Gov.-Gen. Michael Jeffery
Head of government: Prime Min. John Howard
Monetary unit: Australian dollar
GDP: $465.9 billion (2001 est.)   **Per capita GDP:** $24,000
Industries: mining, industrial and transport equipment, food processing, chemicals, steel
Chief crops: wheat, barley, sugarcane, fruits
Minerals: bauxite, coal, iron ore, copper, tin, silver, uranium, nickel, tungsten, mineral sands, lead, zinc, diamonds, natural gas, petroleum
Life expectancy at birth (years): male, 77.3; female, 83.1
Literacy rate: 100%   **Website:** www.gov.au

Ayers Rock (Uluru), Northern Territory, Australia

Perth, Australia

Nation Facts and Figures

FIJI – NAURU

FIJI

FOR MAP, SEE PAGE 116

Population: 839,000

Ethnic groups: Fijian 51%, Indian 44%

Principal languages: English (official), Fijian, Hindustani

Chief religions: Christian 52%, Hindu 38%, Muslim 8%

Area: 7,050 sq mi (18,270 sq km)

Topography: Fiji consists of 322 islands (106 inhabited), many mountainous, with tropical forests and large fertile areas. Viti Levu, the largest island, has over half the total land area.

Capital: Suva (pop., 203,000)

Independence date: October 19, 1970

Government type: republic

Head of state: Pres. Ratu Josefa Iloilo

Head of government: Prime Min. Laisenia Qarase

Monetary unit: Fiji dollar

GDP $4.4 billion (2001 est.)   **Per capita GDP:** $5,200

Industries: tourism, sugar, clothing, copra, small cottage industries

Chief crops: sugarcane, coconuts, cassava, rice, sweet potatoes, bananas

Minerals: gold, copper, offshore oil potential

Life expectancy at birth (years): male, 66.4; female, 71.4

Literacy rate: 92.5%

Websites: www.embassy.org/embassies/fj.html
www.fiji.org.fj

KIRIBATI

FOR MAP, SEE PAGE 116

Population: 99,000

Ethnic groups: Micronesian

Principal languages: English (official), I-Kiribati

Chief religions: Roman Catholic 52%, Protestant 40%

Area: 280 sq mi (720 sq km)

Topography: Kiribati comprises 33 coral islands, all of which, except Banaba (Ocean) Island, are low-lying, with soil of coral sand and rock fragments, subject to erratic rainfall.

Capital: Tarawa (pop., 32,000)

Independence date: July 12, 1979

Government type: republic

Head of state and government: Tion Otang (acting)

Monetary unit: Australian dollar

GDP: $79 million (2001 est.)   **Per capita GDP:** $840

Industries: fishing, handicrafts

Chief crops: copra, taro, breadfruit, sweet potatoes, vegetables

Life expectancy at birth (years): male, 58.0; female, 64.0

Literacy rate: NA

MARSHALL ISLANDS

FOR MAP, SEE PAGE 116

Population: 56,000

Ethnic groups: Micronesian

Principal languages: English, Marshallese (both official); Malay-Polynesian dialects, Japanese

Chief religion: mostly Protestant

Area: 70 sq mi (181 sq km)

Topography: The Marshalls are low coral limestone and sand islands.

Capital: Majuro (pop., 25,000)

Independence date: October 21, 1986   **Government type:** republic

Traditional hut, Lifou Island, New Caledonia (French overseas territory)

Head of state and government: Pres. Kessai Note

Monetary unit: U.S. dollar

GDP: $115 million (2001 est.)   **Per capita GDP:** $1,600

Industries: copra, fish, tourism, craft items from shell, wood, and pearls

Chief crops: coconuts, tomatoes, melons, taro, breadfruit, fruits

Minerals: deep seabed minerals

Life expectancy at birth (years): male, 67.5; female, 71.4

Literacy rate: 93.7%   **Website:** www.miembassyus.org

MICRONESIA

FOR MAP, SEE PAGE 116

Population: 109,000

Ethnic groups: 9 distinct Micronesian and Polynesian groups

Principal languages: English (official), Trukese, Pohnpeian, Yapese, Kosrean, Ulithian, Woleaian, Nukuoro, Kapingamarangi

Chief religions: Roman Catholic 50%, Protestant 47%

Area: 270 sq mi (700 sq km)

Topography: The country includes both high mountainous islands and low coral atolls; volcanic outcroppings on Pohnpei, Kosrae, and Truk.

Capital: Palikir, on Pohnpei (island pop., 33,372)

Independence date: November 3, 1986

Government type: republic

Head of state and government: Pres. Joseph J. Urusemal

Monetary unit: U.S. dollar

GDP: $269 million (2001 est.)   **Per capita GDP:** $2,000

Industries: tourism, construction, fish processing, craft items from shell, wood, and pearls

Chief crops: black pepper, tropical fruits and vegetables, coconuts, cassava, sweet potatoes

Minerals: deep-seabed minerals

Life expectancy at birth (years): male, 66.7; female, 70.6

Literacy rate: 89%   **Website:** www.fsmgov.org

NAURU

FOR MAP, SEE PAGE 116

Population: 13,000

Ethnic groups: Nauruan 58%, other Pacific Islander 26%, Chinese 8%, European 8%

Principal languages: Nauruan (official), English

Chief religions: Protestant 66%, Roman Catholic 33%

Area: 8 sq mi (21 sq km)

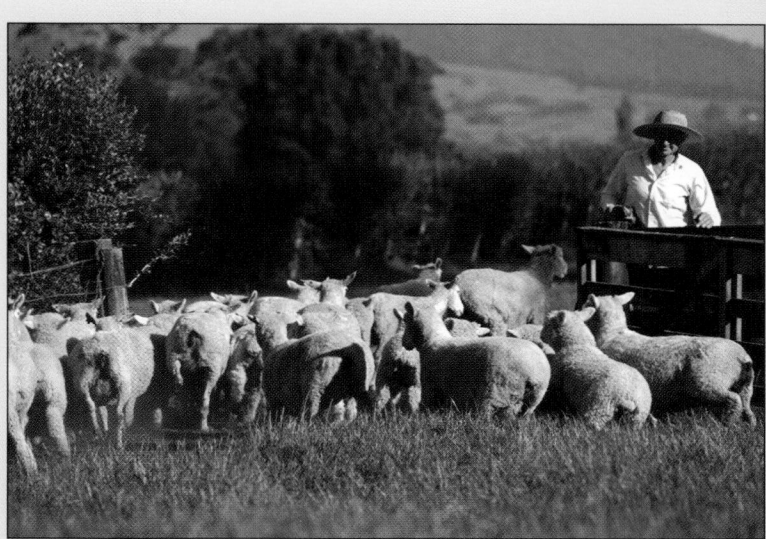
Topography: Mostly a plateau bearing high-grade phosphate deposits, surrounded by a sandy shore and coral reef in concentric rings.

Capital: offices in Yaren District

Independence date: January 31, 1968

Government type: republic

Head of state and government: Pres. Ludwig Scotty

Monetary unit: Australian dollar

GDP: $60 million (2001 est.)   **Per capita GDP:** $5,000

Industries: mining, offshore banking, coconut products

Chief crops: rice, corn, wheat, sugarcane, root crops

Minerals: phosphates

Life expectancy at birth (years): male, 58.4; female, 65.7

Literacy rate: NA

A New Zealand shepherd with his sheep

NEW ZEALAND

FOR MAP, SEE PAGE 117

Population: 3,875,000

Ethnic groups: New Zealand European 75%, Maori 10%, other European 5%, Pacific Islander 4%

Principal languages: English, Maori (both official)

Chief religions: Protestant 52%, Roman Catholic 15%

Area: 103,740 sq mi (268,680 sq km)

Topography: Each of the two main islands (North and South Islands) is mainly hilly and mountainous. The eastern coasts consist of fertile plains, especially the broad Canterbury Plains on South Island. A volcanic plateau is in the center of North Island. South Island has glaciers and 15 peaks over 10,000 ft (3,000 m).

Capital: Wellington (pop., 345,000)

Independence date: September 26, 1907

Government type: parliamentary democracy

Head of state: Queen Elizabeth II, represented by Gov.-Gen. Dame Silvia Cartwright

Head of government: Prime Min. Helen Clark

Monetary unit: New Zealand dollar

GDP: $75.4 billion (2001 est.)

Per capita GDP: $19,500

Industries: food processing, wood and paper products, textiles, machinery, transport equipment, banking and insurance, tourism, mining

Chief crops: wheat, barley, potatoes, pulses, fruits, vegetables

Minerals: natural gas, iron ore, sand, coal, gold, limestone

Life expectancy at birth (years): male, 75.3; female, 81.47

Literacy rate: 99%

Websites: www.govt.nz
www.stats.govt.nz/statsweb.nsf

Shotover River, New Zealand

PALAU

FOR MAP, SEE PAGE 116

Population: 20,000

Ethnic groups: Palauan (Micronesian/Malayan/Melanesian mix) 70%, Asian 28%, white 2%

Principal languages: English (official); Palauan, Sonsorolese, Tobi, Angaur, Japanese (all official in certain states)

Chief religions: Roman Catholic 49%, Modekngei 30%

Area: 180 sq mi (460 sq km)

Topography: Palau is made up of a mountainous main island and low coral atolls, usually fringed with large barrier reefs.

Capital: Koror (pop., 14,000)

Independence date: October 1, 1994

Government type: republic

Head of state and government: Pres. Tommy Remengesaus

Monetary unit: U.S. dollar

GDP: $174 million (2001 est.)   **Per capita GDP:** $9,000

Industries: tourism, craft items, construction, garment making

Chief crops: coconuts, copra, cassava, sweet potatoes

Minerals: gold, deep-seabed minerals

Life expectancy at birth (years): male, 66.4; female, 72.8

Literacy rate: 92%

SAMOA (FORMERLY WESTERN SAMOA)

FOR MAP, SEE PAGE 117

Population: 178,000

Ethnic groups: Samoan 92.5%, Euronesians 7%

Principal languages: Samoan, English (both official)

Chief religion: Christian 99.7%

Area: 1,100 sq mi (2,860 sq km)

Topography: Samoa consists of two main islands, Savaii (659 sq mi [1,710 sq km]) and Upolu (432 sq mi [1,120 sq km]), both ruggedly mountainous, and several small islands, of which Manono and Apolima are inhabited.

Capital: Apia (pop., 35,000)   **Independence date:** January 1, 1962

Government type: constitutional monarchy

Head of state: Malietoa Tanumafili II

Head of government: Prime Min. Tuilaepa Sailele Malielegaoi

Samoa *(continued)*

Monetary unit: tala

GDP: $618 million (2001 est.)   Per capita GDP: $3,500

Industries: food processing, building materials, auto parts

Chief crops: coconuts, bananas, taro, yams

Life expectancy at birth (years): male, 67.4; female, 73.0

Literacy rate: 80%

Website: www.samoa.ws/govtsamoapress

SOLOMON ISLANDS

For map, see page 116

Population: 477,000

Ethnic groups: Melanesian 93%, Polynesian 4%, Micronesian, European, and others 3%

Principal languages: English (official), Melanesian pidgin, and 120 indigenous languages

Chief religions: Anglican 45%, Roman Catholic 18%, other Christian 35%

Area: 10,980 sq mi (28,450 sq km)

Topography: 10 large volcanic and rugged islands and 4 groups of smaller ones.

Capital: Honiara (pop., 78,000)

Independence date: July 7, 1978

Government type: in transition

Head of state: Queen Elizabeth II, represented by Gov.-Gen. Sir John Lapli

Head of government: Prime Min. Sir Allan Kemakeza

Monetary unit: Solomon Islands dollar

GDP: $800 million (2001 est.)   Per capita GDP: $1,700

Industries: fish, mining, timber

Chief crops: cocoa, beans, coconuts, palm kernels, rice, potatoes, vegetables, fruit

Minerals: gold, bauxite, phosphates, lead, zinc, nickel

Life expectancy at birth (years): male, 69.6; female, 74.7

Literacy rate: NA

Website: www.commerce.gov.sb

TONGA

For map, see page 117

Population: 104,000

Ethnic groups: Polynesian

Principal languages: Tongan, English (both official)

Chief religions: Wesleyan 41%, Roman Catholic 16%, Mormon 14%

Area: 290 sq mi (750 sq km)

Topography: Tonga comprises 170 volcanic and coral islands, 36 inhabited.

Capital: Nuku'alofa (pop., 33,000)

Independence date: June 4, 1970

Government type: constitutional monarchy

Head of state: King Taufa'ahau Tupou IV

Head of government: Prime Min. Prince Ulukalala Lavaka Ata

Monetary unit: pa'anga

GDP: $225 million (2000 est.)

Per capita GDP: $2,200

Industries: tourism, fishing

Chief crops: squash, coconuts, copra, bananas, vanilla beans, cocoa, coffee, ginger, black pepper

Life expectancy at birth (years): male, 66.4; female, 71.4

Literacy rate: 98.5%

Website: www.pmo.gov.to

TUVALU

For map, see page 116

Population: 11,000

Ethnic group: Polynesian 96%, Micronesian 4%

Principal languages: Tuvaluan, English, Samoan, Kiribati (on the island of Nui)

Chief religion: Church of Tuvalu (Congregationalist) 97%

Area: 10 sq mi (26 sq km)

Topography: Tuvalu's nine islands are all low-lying coral atolls, nowhere rising more than 15 ft (4.6 m) above sea level.

Capital: Funafuti (pop., 5,000)   Independence date: October 1, 1978

Government type: parliamentary democracy

Head of state: Queen Elizabeth II, represented by Gov.-Gen. Tomasi Puapua

Head of government: Prime Min. Saufatu Sopoaga

Monetary unit: Australian dollar

GDP: $12.2 million (2000 est.)   Per capita GDP: $1,100

Industries: fishing, tourism, copra

Chief crops: coconuts

Life expectancy at birth (years): male, 65.2; female, 69.6

Literacy rate: 55%

VANUATU

For map, see page 116

Population: 212,000

Ethnic groups: Melanesian 98%, French, Vietnamese, Chinese, other Pacific Islanders

Principal languages: Bislama, English, French (all official); more than 100 local languages

Chief religions: Presbyterian 37%, Anglican 15%, Roman Catholic 15%, other Christian 10%, indigenous beliefs 8%

Area: 5,700 sq mi (14,760 sq km)

Topography: Dense forest with narrow coastal strips of cultivated land.

Capital: Port-Vila (pop., 31,000)   Independence date: July 30, 1980

Government type: republic

Head of state: Pres. John Bani

Head of government: Prime Min. Edward Natapei

Monetary unit: vatu

GDP: $257 million (2000 est.)   Per capita GDP: $1,300

Industries: food and fish freezing, wood processing, meat canning

Chief crops: copra, coconuts, cocoa, coffee, taro, yams, coconuts, fruits, vegetables

Minerals: manganese

Life expectancy at birth (years): male, 60.3; female, 63.2

Literacy rate: 53%

Website: www.vanuatugovernment.gov.vu

EUROPE

Fifteen nations were members of the European Union as of 2003: Austria, Belgium, Denmark, Finland, France, Germany, Greece, Ireland, Italy, Luxembourg, the Netherlands, Portugal, Spain, Sweden, and the United Kingdom. Ten additional countries were expected to officially join the Union in 2004: Cyprus, the Czech Republic, Estonia, Hungary, Latvia, Lithuania, Malta, Poland, Slovakia, and Slovenia.

ALBANIA

FOR MAP, SEE PAGE 47

Population: 3,166,000
Ethnic groups: Albanian 95%, Greek 3%
Principal languages: Albanian (Tosk is the official dialect), Greek
Chief religions: Muslim 70%, Albanian Orthodox 20%, Roman Catholic 10%
Area: 11,100 sq mi (28,750 sq km)
Topography: Apart from a narrow coastal plain, Albania consists of hills and mountains covered with scrub forest, cut by small east to west rivers.
Capital: Tiranë (pop., 299,000)
Independence date: November 28, 1912   **Government type:** republic
Head of state: Pres. Alfred Moisiu
Head of government: Prime Min. Fatos Nano   **Monetary unit:** lek
GDP: $13.2 billion (2001 est.)   **Per capita GDP:** $3,800
Industries: food processing, textiles and clothing, lumber, oil, cement, chemicals, mining, basic metals, hydropower
Chief crops: wheat, corn, potatoes, vegetables, fruits, sugar beets, grapes
Minerals: petroleum, natural gas, coal, chromium, copper, timber, nickel
Life expectancy at birth (years): male, 69.5; female, 75.4
Literacy rate: 93%
Website: depinf.governmental/english/default1.html

ANDORRA

FOR MAP, SEE PAGE 45

Population: 69,000
Ethnic groups: Spanish 43%, Andorran 33%, Portuguese 11%, French 7%
Principal languages: Catalan (official), Castilian Spanish, French
Chief religion: predominantly Roman Catholic
Area: 174 sq mi (450 sq km)
Topography: High mountains and narrow valleys cover the country.
Capital: Andorra la Vella (pop., 21,000)
Independence date: 1278
Government type: parliamentary co-principality
Heads of state: president of France & bishop of Urgel (Spain), as co-princes
Head of government: Pres. Marc Forné Molné
Monetary unit: euro
GDP: $1.3 billion (2000 est.)   **Per capita GDP:** $19,000
Industries: tourism, cattle raising, timber, tobacco, banking
Chief crops: tobacco, rye, wheat, barley, oats, vegetables
Minerals: iron ore, lead
Life expectancy at birth (years): male, 80.6; female, 86.6
Literacy rate: 100%
Website: www.andorra.ad/govern/governuk.html

AUSTRIA*

FOR MAP, SEE PAGE 43

Population: 8,116,000
Ethnic groups: German 88%
Principal languages: German (official), Serbo-Croatian, Slovenian
Chief religions: Roman Catholic 78%, Protestant 5%

*Member of the European Union

Austria (continued)

Area: 32,380 sq mi (83,860 sq km)

Topography: Austria is primarily mountainous, with the Alps and foothills covering the western and southern provinces. The eastern provinces and Vienna are located in the Danube River Basin.

Capital: Vienna (pop., 2,066,000)

Independence date: 1156

Government type: federal republic

Head of state: Pres. Thomas Klestil

Head of government: Chancellor Wolfgang Schüssel

Monetary unit: euro

GDP: $220 billion (2001 est.)   **Per capita GDP:** $27,000

Industries: construction, machinery, vehicles and parts, food, chemicals, lumber and wood processing, paper and paperboard, commercial equipment, tourism

Chief crops: grains, potatoes, sugar beets, fruit

Minerals: iron ore, oil, timber, magnesite, lead, coal, copper

Life expectancy at birth (years): male, 75.0; female, 81.5

Literacy rate: 98%   **Website:** www.austria.gv.at/e

Innsbruck, Austria

BELARUS

FOR MAP, SEE PAGE 27

Population: 9,895,000

Ethnic groups: Belarusian 81%, Russian 11%

Principal languages: Belarusian, Russian

Chief religions: Eastern Orthodox 80%, other 20%

Area: 80,200 sq mi (207,600 sq km)

Topography: Belarus is a landlocked country consisting mostly of hilly lowland with significant marsh areas in the south.

Capital: Minsk (pop., 1,664,000)   **Independence date:** August 25, 1991

Government type: republic

Head of state: Pres. Aleksandr Lukashenko

Head of government: Prime Min. Henadz Navitski

Monetary unit: ruble

GDP: $84.8 billion (2001 est.)   **Per capita GDP:** $8,200

Industries: machine tools, tractors, trucks, earthmovers, motorcycles, domestic appliances, chemical fibers, fertilizer, textiles

Chief crops: grain, potatoes, vegetables, sugar beets, flax

Minerals: oil and natural gas, granite, dolomitic limestone, marl, chalk, sand, gravel, clay

Life expectancy at birth (years): male, 62.5; female, 74.6

Literacy rate: 98%

Website: www.belarusembassy.org

BELGIUM*

FOR MAP, SEE PAGE 40

Population: 10,318,000

Ethnic groups: Fleming 58%, Walloon 31%

Principal languages: Dutch, French, German (all official); Flemish, Luxembourgish

*Member of the European Union

Chief religions: Roman Catholic 75%; Protestant, other 25%

Area: 11,780 sq mi (30,510 sq km)

Topography: Mostly flat, the country is trisected by the Scheldt and Meuse, major commercial rivers. The land becomes hilly and forested in the southeast (Ardennes) region.

Capital: Brussels (pop., 1,134,000)

Independence date: October 4, 1830

Government type: parliamentary democracy under a constitutional monarch

Head of state: King Albert II

Head of government: Premier Guy Verhofstadt

Monetary unit: euro

GDP: $267.7 billion (2001 est.)   **Per capita GDP:** $26,100

Industries: engineering and metal products, motor vehicle assembly, processed food and beverages, chemicals, basic metals, textiles, glass, petroleum, coal

Chief crops: sugar beets, fresh vegetables, fruits, grain, tobacco

Minerals: coal, natural gas

Life expectancy at birth (years): male, 75.0; female, 81.8

Literacy rate: 98%

Website: www.belgium.fgov.be

BOSNIA AND HERZEGOVINA FOR MAP, SEE PAGE 48

Population: 4,161,000

Ethnic groups: Bosniak 48%, Serbian 37%, Croatian 14%

Principal languages: Bosnian (official), Croatian, Serbian

Chief religions: Muslim 40%, Orthodox 31%, Roman Catholic 15%, Protestant 4%

Area: 19,740 sq mi (51,130 sq km)

Topography: Hilly with some mountains. About 36% of the land is forested.

Capital: Sarajevo (pop., 552,000)

Independence date: March 1, 1992

Government type: federal republic

Heads of state: collective presidency with rotating leadership

Head of government: Prime Min. Adnan Terzic

Monetary unit: mark

GDP: $7 billion (2001 est.)   **Per capita GDP:** $1,800

Industries: steel, mining, vehicle assembly, textiles, tobacco products, wooden furniture, tank and aircraft assembly, domestic appliances, oil refining

Chief crops: wheat, corn, fruits, vegetables

Minerals: coal, iron, bauxite, manganese, copper, chromium, lead, zinc

Life expectancy at birth (years): male, 69.6; female, 75.2

Literacy rate: NA

Websites: www.bosnianembassy.org
www.fbihvlada.gov.ba

BULGARIA

FOR MAP, SEE PAGE 49

Population: 7,897,000

Ethnic groups: Bulgarian 84%, Turk 10%, Roma 5%

Principal languages: Bulgarian (official), Turkish

Chief religions: Bulgarian Orthodox 84%, Muslim 12%

Area: 42,820 sq mi (110,910 sq km)

Topography: The Stara Planina (Balkan) Mountains stretch east to west across the center of the country, with the Danubian plain in the north, the

Rhodope Mountains in the southwest, and the Thracian Plain in the southeast.

Capital: Sofia (pop., 1,187,000)

Independence date: March 3, 1878

Government type: republic

Head of state: Pres. Georgi Parvanov

Head of government: Prime Min. Simeon Sakskoburggotski (Simeon II)

Monetary unit: lev

GDP: $48 billion (2001 est.)

Per capita GDP: $6,200

Industries: electricity, gas and water, food, beverages and tobacco, machinery and equipment, base metals, chemical products, coke, refined petroleum, nuclear fuel

Chief crops: vegetables, fruits, tobacco, wheat, barley, sunflowers, sugar beets

Minerals: bauxite, copper, lead, zinc, coal

Life expectancy at birth (years): male, 68.3; female, 75.6

Literacy rate: 98%

Website: www.government.bg/English

A Bulgarian cathedral

CROATIA

FOR MAP, SEE PAGE 48

Population: 4,428,000

Ethnic groups: Croat 78%, Serb 12%, Bosniak 1%

Principal languages Croatian (official), Serbian

Chief religions: Roman Catholic 88%, Orthodox 5%

Area: 21,830 sq mi (56,540 sq km)

Topography: Flat plains in the northeast; highlands, low mountains along the Adriatic coast.

Capital: Zagreb (pop., 1,081,000)   **Independence date:** June 25, 1991

Government type: parliamentary democracy

Head of state: Pres. Stipe Mesic

Head of government: Prime Min. Ivica Racan

Monetary unit: kuna

GDP: $36.1 billion (2001 est.)   **Per capita GDP:** $8,300

Industries: chemicals and plastics, machine tools, fabricated metal, electronics, pig iron and rolled steel products, aluminum, paper, wood products, construction materials, textiles, shipbuilding, tourism

Chief crops: wheat, corn, sugar beets, sunflower seed, barley, alfalfa, clover, olives, citrus, grapes, soybeans, potatoes

Minerals: oil, coal, bauxite, iron ore, calcium, natural asphalt, silica, mica, clays, salt

Life expectancy at birth (years): male, 70.8; female, 78.2

Literacy rate: 97%

Website: www.vlada.hr/english/contents.html

CZECH REPUBLIC

FOR MAP, SEE PAGE 41

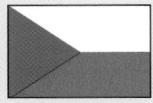

Population: 10,236,000

Ethnic groups: Czech 81%, Moravian 13%, Slovak 3%

Principal languages: Czech (official), German, Polish, Romani

Chief religions: atheist 40%, Roman Catholic 39%, Protestant 5%, Orthodox 3%

Area: 30,350 sq mi (78,870 sq km)

Topography: Bohemia, in the west, is a plateau surrounded by mountains; Moravia is hilly.

Capital: Prague (pop., 1,202,000)

Independence date: January 1, 1993   **Government type:** republic

Head of state: Pres. Václav Klaus

Head of government: Prime Min. Vladimir Spidla

Monetary unit: koruna

GDP: $147.9 billion (2001 est.)   **Per capita GDP:** $14,400

Industries: metallurgy, machinery and equipment, motor vehicles, glass, armaments

Chief crops: wheat, potatoes, sugar beets, hops, fruit

Minerals: coal, kaolin, clay, graphite

Life expectancy at birth (years): male, 71.7; female, 78.9

Literacy rate: 99.9%   **Website:** www.czech.cz

Prague, Czech Republic

DENMARK*

FOR MAP, SEE PAGE 38

Population: 5,364,000

Ethnic groups: Mainly Danish; German minority in south

Principal languages: Danish (official), Faroese, Greenlandic (an Inuit dialect), German

Chief religions: Evangelical Lutheran (official) 95%, other Christian 3%, Muslim 2%

Area: 16,640 sq mi (43,090 sq km)

Topography: Denmark consists of the Jutland Peninsula and about 500 islands, 100 inhabited. The land is flat or gently rolling and is almost all in productive use.

Capital: Copenhagen (pop., 1,332,000)

Independence date: 10th century

Government type: constitutional monarchy

Head of state: Queen Margrethe II

Head of government: Prime Min. Anders Fogh Rasmussen

Monetary unit: krone

GDP: $149.8 billion (2001 est.)   **Per capita GDP:** $28,000

Industries: food processing, machinery and equipment, textiles and clothing, chemical products, electronics, construction, furniture, shipbuilding

Chief crops: barley, wheat, potatoes, sugar beets

Minerals: petroleum, natural gas, salt, limestone, stone, gravel and sand

Life expectancy at birth (years): male, 74.5; female, 79.9

Literacy rate: 100%

Websites: www.denmarkemb.org
www.umidk/english/

GREENLAND (Kalaallit Nunaat), a huge island situated between the North Atlantic and the Polar Sea and separated from the North American continent by the Davis Strait and Baffin Bay, is part of the Danish realm but possesses home rule. Population, 56,000; area, 840,000 sq mi (2,180,000 sq km), 84% of which is ice-capped; capital, Nuuk (Godthab).

*Member of the European Union

Nation Facts and Figures

ESTONIA – GERMANY

ESTONIA

FOR MAP, SEE PAGE 39

Population: 1,323,000

Ethnic groups: Estonian 65%, Russian 28%

Principal languages: Estonian (official), Russian, Ukrainian, Finnish

Chief religions: Evangelical Lutheran, Russian Orthodox, Estonian Orthodox

Area: 17,460 sq mi (45,230 sq km)

Topography: Estonia is a marshy lowland with numerous lakes and swamps; about 40% forested. Elongated hills show evidence of former glaciation. There are more than 800 islands on the Baltic coast.

Capital: Tallinn (pop., 401,000)

Independence date: August 20, 1991   Government type: republic

Head of state: Pres. Arnold Rüütel

Head of government: Prime Min. Juhan Parts

Monetary unit: kroon

GDP: $14.3 billion (2001 est.)   Per capita GDP: $10,000

Industries: engineering, electronics, wood and wood products, textile, information technology, telecommunications

Chief crops: potatoes, vegetables

Minerals: oil shale, peat, phosphorite, clay, limestone, sand, dolomite, sea mud

Life expectancy at birth (years): male, 64.4; female, 76.6

Literacy rate: 100%   Website: www.riik.ee/en/valitsus/

FINLAND*

FOR MAP, SEE PAGE 37

Population: 5,207,000

Ethnic groups: Finnish 93%, Swedish 6%

Principal languages: Finnish, Swedish (both official); Russian, Sami

Chief religion: Evangelical Lutheran 89%

Area: 130,130 sq mi (337,030 sq km)

Topography: South and central Finland are generally flat areas with low hills and many lakes. The north has mountainous areas, 3,000 to 4,000 ft (900 to 1,200 m) above sea level.

Capital: Helsinki (pop., 936,000)

Independence date: December 6, 1917

Government type: republic   Head of state: Pres. Tarja Halonen

Head of government: Prime Min. Matti Vanhanen

Monetary unit: euro

GDP: $133.5 billion (2001 est.)   Per capita GDP: $25,800

Industries: metal products, electronics, shipbuilding, pulp and paper, copper refining, foodstuffs, chemicals, textiles, clothing

Chief crops: barley, wheat, sugar beets, potatoes

Minerals: copper, zinc, iron ore, silver

Life expectancy at birth (years): male, 74.3; female, 81.7

Literacy rate: 100%

Website: www.president.fi/netcomm/

The ÅLAND ISLANDS (Ahvenanmaa), constituting an autonomous province, are a group of small islands in the Gulf of Bothnia. Population 25,766; area, 590 sq mi (1,500 sq km); capital, Mariehamn.

FRANCE*

FOR MAP, SEE PAGE 42

Population: 60,144,000

Ethnic groups: French, with Slavic, North African, Indochinese, Basque minorities

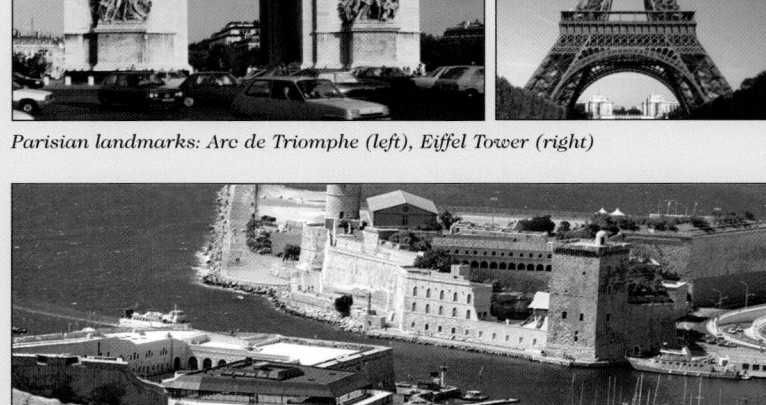

Parisian landmarks: Arc de Triomphe (left), Eiffel Tower (right)

Marseille, France

Principal languages: French (official), Italian, Breton, Alsatian (German), Corsican, Gascon, Portuguese, Provençal, Dutch, Flemish, Catalan, Basque, Romani

Chief religions: Roman Catholic 83-88%, Muslim 5-10%

Area: 211,210 sq mi (547,030 sq km)

Topography: A wide plain covers more than half of the country, in the north and west, drained to the west by the Seine, Loire, and Garonne rivers. The Massif Central is a mountainous plateau in the center. In the east are the Alps (Mt. Blanc is the tallest peak in Western Europe, 15,771 ft [4,807 m]), the lower Jura range, and the forested Vosges. The Rhone flows from Lake Geneva to the Mediterranean. The Pyrenees are in the southwest, on the border with Spain.

Capital: Paris (pop., 9,658,000)   Independence date: 486

Government type: republic   Head of state: Pres. Jacques Chirac

Head of government: Prime Min. Jean-Pierre Raffarin

Monetary unit: euro

GDP: $1.51 trillion (2001 est.)   Per capita GDP: $25,400

Industries: machinery, chemicals, automobiles, metallurgy, aircraft, electronics, textiles, food processing, tourism

Chief crops: wheat, cereals, sugar beets, potatoes, wine grapes

Minerals: coal, iron ore, bauxite, zinc, potash

Life expectancy at birth (years): male, 75.6; female, 83.1

Literacy rate: 99%   Website: www.ambafrance–us.org

GERMANY*

FOR MAP, SEE PAGE 40

Population: 82,476,000

Ethnic groups: German 92%, Turkish 2%

Principal languages: German (official), Turkish, Italian, Greek, English, Danish, Dutch, Slavic languages

*Member of the European Union

Looking down a German street

Chief religions: Protestant 34%, Roman Catholic 34%, Muslim 4%

Area: 137,890 sq mi (357,070 sq km)

Topography: Germany is flat in the north, hilly in the center and west, and mountainous in Bavaria in the south. The chief rivers are the Elbe, Weser, Ems, Rhine, and Main, all flowing toward the North Sea, and the Danube, flowing toward the Black Sea.

Capital: Berlin (pop., 3,310,000)

Independence date: January 18, 1871

Government type: federal republic

Head of state: Pres. Johannes Rau

Head of government: Chancellor Gerhard Schröder

Monetary unit: euro

GDP: $2.174 trillion (2001 est.)   **Per capita GDP:** $26,200

Industries: mining, steel, cement, chemicals, machinery, vehicles, machine tools, electronics, food and beverages, shipbuilding, textiles

Chief crops: potatoes, wheat, barley, sugar beets, fruit, cabbages

Minerals: iron ore, coal, potash, lignite, uranium, copper, natural gas, salt, nickel

Life expectancy at birth (years): male, 75.5; female, 81.6

Literacy rate: 99%   **Website:** www.germany–info.org

Bavarian village church, Germany

GREECE*

FOR MAP, SEE PAGE 47

Population: 10,976,000

Ethnic groups: Greek 98%

Principal languages: Greek (official), English, French

Chief religions: Greek Orthodox (official) 98%, Muslim 1%

Parthenon, Athens, Greece

*Member of the European Union

Area: 50,940 sq mi (131,940 sq km)

Topography: About three-quarters of Greece is nonarable, with mountains in all areas. Pindus Mountains run through the country north to south. The heavily indented coastline is 9,385 mi (15,100 km) long. Of over 2,000 islands, only 169 are inhabited, among them Crete, Rhodes, Milos, Kerkira (Corfu), Chios, Lesbos, Samos, Euboea, Delos, and Mykonos.

Capital: Athens (pop., 3,120,000)   **Independence date:** 1829

Government type: parliamentary republic

Head of state: Pres. Konstantinos Stephanopoulos

Head of government: Prime Min. Costas Simitis

Monetary unit: euro

GDP: $189.7 billion (2001 est.)   **Per capita GDP:** $17,900

Industries: tourism, food and tobacco processing, textiles, chemicals, metal products, mining, petroleum

Chief crops: wheat, corn, barley, sugar beets, olives, tomatoes, tobacco, potatoes

Minerals: bauxite, lignite, magnesite, petroleum, marble

Life expectancy at birth (years): male, 76.3; female, 81.7

Literacy rate: 97%   **Website:** www.greekembassy.org

HUNGARY

FOR MAP, SEE PAGE 48

Population: 9,877,000

Ethnic groups: Hungarian 90%, Roma 4%, German 3%, Serb 2%

Principal languages: Hungarian (official), Romani, German, Slavic languages, Romanian

Chief religions: Roman Catholic 68%, Protestant 25%

Area: 35,920 sq mi (93,030 sq km)

Topography: The Danube River forms the Slovak border in the northwest, then swings south to bisect the country. The eastern half of Hungary is mainly a great fertile plain, the Alfold; the west and north are hilly.

Capital: Budapest (pop., 1,812,000)

Independence date: 1001

Government type: parliamentary democracy

Head of state: Pres. Ferenc Mádl

Head of government: Prime Min. Péter Medgyessy

Monetary unit: forint

GDP: $120.9 billion (2001 est.)
Per capita GDP: $12,000

Industries: mining, metallurgy, construction materials, processed foods, textiles, pharmaceuticals, motor vehicles

Chief crops: wheat, corn, sunflower seed, potatoes, sugar beets

Minerals: bauxite, coal, natural gas

Life expectancy at birth (years): male, 67.8; female, 76.8

Literacy rate: 99%   **Website:** www.eKormanyzat.hu/english

A Budapest market, Hungary

ICELAND

FOR MAP, SEE PAGE 37

Population: 290,000

Ethnic groups: Icelandic 94%

Principal language: Icelandic (official)

Chief religion: Evangelical Lutheran 93%

Nation Facts and Figures

IRELAND – LATVIA

Iceland *(continued)*

Area: 40,000 sq mi (103,000 sq km)

Topography: Iceland is of recent volcanic origin. Three-quarters of the surface is wasteland: glaciers, lakes, a lava desert. There are geysers and hot springs.

Capital: Reykjavík (pop., 175,000)   **Independence date:** June 17, 1944

Government type: constitutional republic

Head of state: Pres. Olafur Ragnar Grímsson

Head of government: Prime Min. David Oddsson

Monetary unit: krona

GDP: $6.85 billion (2000 est.)   **Per capita GDP:** $24,800

Industries: fish processing, aluminum smelting, ferrosilicon production, geothermal power, tourism

Chief crops: potatoes, turnips   **Minerals:** diatomite

Life expectancy at birth (years): male, 77.5; female, 82.2

Literacy rate: 99.9%

Website: www.brunnur.stjr.is/interpro/stjr/stjr.nsf/pages/ english–index

IRELAND*

FOR MAP, SEE PAGE 31

Population: 3,956,000

Ethnic groups: Celtic; English minority

Principal languages: English, Irish Gaelic (both official); Irish Gaelic spoken by small number in western areas

Chief religions: Roman Catholic 92%, Anglican 3%

Area: 27,140 sq mi (70,280 sq km)

Topography: Ireland consists of a central plateau surrounded by isolated groups of hills and mountains. The coastline is heavily indented by the Atlantic Ocean.

Capital: Dublin (pop., 993,000)   **Independence date:** December 6, 1921

Government type: parliamentary republic

Head of state: Pres. Mary McAleese

Head of government: Prime Min. Bertie Ahern

Monetary unit: euro

GDP: $104.7 billion (2001 est.)   **Per capita GDP:** $27,300

Industries: food products, brewing, textiles, clothing, chemicals, pharmaceuticals, machinery, transport equipment, glass and crystal, software

Chief crops: turnips, barley, potatoes, sugar beets, wheat

Minerals: zinc, lead, natural gas, barite, copper, gypsum, limestone, dolomite, peat, silver

Life expectancy at birth (years): male, 74.6; female, 80.3

Literacy rate: 98%

Websites: www.irlgov.ie
www.irelandemb.org

ITALY*

FOR MAP, SEE PAGE 27

Population: 57,423,000

Ethnic groups: mostly Italian; small minorities of German, Slovene, Albanian

Principal languages: Italian (official), German, French, Slovenian, Albanian

Chief religion: predominantly Roman Catholic

Area: 116,310 sq mi (301,230 sq km)

Topography: Italy occupies a long boot-shaped peninsula, extending southeast from the Alps into the Mediterranean, with the islands of

Colosseum, Rome, Italy

Sicily and Sardinia offshore. The alluvial Po Valley drains most of the north. The rest of the country is rugged and mountainous, except for intermittent coastal plains, like the Campania, south of Rome. The Apennine Mountains run down through the center of the peninsula.

Capital: Rome (pop., 2,651,000)

Independence date: March 17, 1861

Government type: republic

Head of state: Pres. Carlo Azeglio Ciampi

Head of government: Prime Min. Silvio Berlusconi

Monetary unit: euro

GDP: $1.402 trillion (2001 est.)

Per capita GDP: $24,300

Industries: tourism, machinery, iron and steel, chemicals, food processing, textiles, motor vehicles, clothing, footwear, ceramics

Leaning Tower of Pisa, Italy

Chief crops: fruits, vegetables, grapes, potatoes, sugar beets, soybeans, grain, olives

Minerals: mercury, potash, marble, sulfur, natural gas, oil, coal

Life expectancy at birth (years): male, 76.5; female, 82.5

Literacy rate: 98%

Websites: www.italyemb.org
istat.it/homeing.html

LATVIA

FOR MAP, SEE PAGE 39

Population: 2,307,000

Ethnic groups: Latvian 58%, Russian 30%, Belarusian 4%, Ukrainian 3%, Polish 2%, Lithuanian 1%

Principal languages: Latvian (official), Russian, Belarusian, Ukrainian, Polish

Chief religions: Lutheran, Roman Catholic, Russian Orthodox

Area: 24,900 sq mi (64,590 sq km)

Topography: Latvia is a lowland with numerous lakes, marshes and peat bogs. The principal river, the Western Dvina (Daugava), rises in Russia. There are glacial hills in the east.

Capital: Riga (pop., 756,000)

Independence date: August 21, 1991

Government type: republic

Head of state: Pres. Vaira Vike-Freiberga

Head of government: Prime Min. Einars Repse

Monetary unit: lat

GDP: $18.6 billion (2001 est.)   Per capita GDP: $7,800

Industries: motor vehicles, railroad cars, synthetic fibers, agricultural machinery, fertilizers, household appliances, pharmaceuticals, processed foods, textiles

Chief crops: grain, sugar beets, potatoes, vegetables

Minerals: peat, limestone, dolomite, amber

Life expectancy at birth (years): male, 63.5; female, 75.5

Literacy rate: 99.8%

Websites: www.latvia-usa.org
www.csb.lvavidus.cfm

LIECHTENSTEIN For map, see page 57

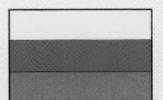

Population: 33,000

Ethnic groups: Alemannic 86%; Italian, Turkish, and other 14%

Principal languages: German (official), Alemannic dialect

Chief religions: Roman Catholic 80%, Protestant 7%

Area: 62 sq mi (161 sq km)

Topography: The Rhine Valley occupies one-third of the country; the Alps cover the rest.

Capital: Vaduz (pop., 5,000)   Independence date: January 23, 1719

Government type: hereditary constitutional monarchy

Head of state: Prince Hans-Adam II   Head of government: Otmar Hasler

Monetary unit: Swiss franc

GDP: $730 million (1998 est.)   Per capita GDP: $23,000

Industries: electronics, metal manufacturing, textiles, ceramics, pharmaceuticals, food products, precision instruments, tourism

Chief crops: wheat, barley, corn, potatoes

Life expectancy at birth (years): male, 75.6; female, 82.9

Literacy rate: 100%   Website: www.news.li

LITHUANIA For map, see page 39

Population: 3,444,000

Ethnic groups: Lithuanian 81%, Russian 9%, Polish 7%, Belarusian 2%

Principal languages: Lithuanian (official), Belarusian, Russian, Polish

Chief religion: predominantly Roman Catholic

Area: 25,200 sq mi (65,200 sq km)

Topography: Lithuania is a lowland with hills in the west and south; fertile soil; many small lakes and rivers, with marshes especially in the north and west.

Capital: Vilnius (pop., 579,000)   Independence date: March 11, 1990

Government type: republic   Head of state: Pres. Rolandas Paksas

Head of government: Prime Min. Algirdas Brazauskas

Monetary unit: litas

GDP: $27.4 billion (2001 est.)   Per capita GDP: $7,600

Industries: machine tools, electric motors, household appliances, petroleum refining, shipbuilding, furniture making, textiles, food processing, fertilizers, agricultural machinery, optical equipment, electronic components, computers, amber

Chief crops: grain, potatoes, sugar beets, flax, vegetables

Minerals: peat

Life expectancy at birth (years): male, 63.8; female, 75.7

Literacy rate: 98%

Websites: www.lruk.lt/anglu/home_anglo.htm
www.ltembassyus.org

LUXEMBOURG* For map, see page 53

Population: 453,000

Ethnic groups: Mixture of French and German

Principal languages: Luxembourgish (national), German, French (official)

Chief religion: majority is Roman Catholic; 1979 law forbids collection of such statistics

Area: 1,000 sq mi (2,590 sq km)

Topography: Heavy forests (Ardennes) cover the north; the south is a low, open plateau.

Capital: Luxembourg (pop., 82,000)   Independence date: 1839

Government type: constitutional monarchy

Head of state: Grand Duke Henri

Head of government: Prime Min. Jean-Claude Juncker

Monetary unit: euro

GDP: $19.2 billion (2001 est.)   Per capita GDP: $43,400

Industries: banking, iron and steel, food processing, chemicals, metal products, tires, glass, aluminum

Chief crops: barley, oats, potatoes, wheat, fruits, wine grapes

Life expectancy at birth (years): male, 74.4; female, 81.2

Literacy rate: 100%   Website: www.gouvernement.lu

MACEDONIA (FORMER YUGOSLAV REPUBLIC OF MACEDONIA) For map, see page 47

Population: 2,056,000

Ethnic groups: Macedonian 67%, Albanian 23%, Turkish 4%, Roma 2%, Serb 2%

Principal languages: Macedonian (official), Albanian, Turkish, Romani, Serbo-Croatian

Chief religions: Macedonian Orthodox 67%, Muslim 30%

Area: 9,780 sq mi (25,330 sq km)

Topography: Macedonia is a landlocked, mostly mountainous country, with deep river valleys and three large lakes; the country is bisected by the Vardar River.

Capital: Skopje (pop., 437,000)   Independence date: September 17, 1991

Government type: republic   Head of state: Pres. Boris Trajkovski

Head of government: Prime Min. Branko Crvenkovski

Monetary unit: denar

GDP: $9 billion (2001 est.)   Per capita GDP: $4,400

Industries: mining, textiles, wood products, tobacco, food processing, buses

Chief crops: rice, tobacco, wheat, corn, millet, cotton, sesame, mulberry leaves, citrus, vegetables

Minerals: chromium, lead, zinc, manganese, tungsten, nickel, iron ore, asbestos, sulfur

Life expectancy at birth (years): male, 72.2; female, 76.9

Literacy rate: NA   Website: www.gov.mk

MALTA For map, see page 46

Population: 394,000

Ethnic group: Maltese, other Mediterranean

Principal languages: Maltese (a Semitic dialect), English (both official)

*Member of the European Union

Malta *(continued)*

Chief religion: Roman Catholic (official) 91%

Area: 124 sq mi (321 sq km)

Topography: The island of Malta is 95 sq mi (246 sq km); other islands in the group: Gozo, 26 sq mi (67 sq km); Comino, 1 sq mi (2.6 sq km). The coastline is heavily indented. Low hills cover the interior.

Capital: Valletta (pop., 82,000)

Independence date: September 21, 1964

Government type: parliamentary democracy

Head of state: Pres. Guido de Marco

Head of government: Prime Min. Edward Fenech-Adami

Monetary unit: Maltese lira

GDP: $5.95 billion (2001 est.)   **Per capita GDP:** $15,000

Industries: tourism, electronics, shipbuilding, construction, food and beverages, textiles, footwear, clothing, tobacco

Chief crops: potatoes, cauliflower, grapes, wheat, barley, tomatoes, citrus, cut flowers, green peppers

Minerals: limestone, salt

Life expectancy at birth (years): male, 75.9; female, 81.1

Literacy rate: 88.76%

Website: www.gov.mt/index.asp?l=2

MOLDOVA

FOR MAP, SEE PAGE 49

Population: 4,267,000

Ethnic groups: Moldovan/Romanian 65%, Ukrainian 14%, Russian 13%

Principal languages: Moldovan (official), Russian, Gagauz (a Turkish dialect)

Chief religion: Eastern Orthodox 99%

Area: 13,000 sq mi (33,700 sq km)

Topography: The country is landlocked; mainly hilly plains, with steppelands in the south near the Black Sea.

Capital: Chisinau (pop., 662,000)   **Independence date:** August 27, 1991

Government type: republic

Head of state: Pres. Vladimir Voronin

Head of government: Prime Min. Vasile Tarlev

Monetary unit: leu

GDP: $11.3 billion (2001 est.)   **Per capita GDP:** $2,550

Industries: food processing, agricultural machinery, foundry equipment, household appliances, hosiery, sugar, vegetable oil, shoes, textiles

Chief crops: vegetables, fruits, wine, grain, sugar beets, sunflower seed, tobacco

Minerals: lignite, phosphorites, gypsum, limestone

Life expectancy at birth (years): male, 60.6; female, 69.4

Literacy rate: 96%   **Website:** www.moldova.md

MONACO

FOR MAP, SEE PAGE 58

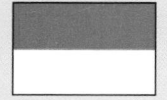

Population: 32,000

Ethnic groups: French 47%, Monegasque 16%, Italian 16%

Principal languages: French (official), English, Italian, Monegasque

Chief religion: Roman Catholic (official) 90%

Area: 0.75 sq mi (1.9 sq km)

Topography: Monaco-Ville sits atop a high promontory; the rest of the principality rises from the port up the hillside.

Capital: Monaco (pop., 34,000)   **Independence date:** 1419

Government type: constitutional monarchy

Head of state: Prince Rainier III

Head of government: Min. of State Patrick Leclercq

Monetary unit: euro

GDP: $870 million (1999 est.)   **Per capita GDP:** $27,000

Industries: tourism, construction, small-scale industrial and consumer products

Life expectancy at birth (years): male, 75.4; female, 83.4

Literacy rate: 99%   **Website:** www.gouv.mc/PortGb

NETHERLANDS*

FOR MAP, SEE PAGE 50

Population: 16,149,000

Ethnic groups: Dutch 83%

Principal languages: Dutch (official), Frisian, Flemish

Chief religions: Roman Catholic 31%, Protestant 21%, Muslim 4%

Area: 16,030 sq mi (41,530 sq km)

Topography: The land is flat, with an average altitude of 37 ft (11 m) above sea level. Much land is below sea level, reclaimed and protected by some 1,500 mi (2,400 km) of dikes. Since 1920 the government has been draining the IJsselmeer, formerly the Zuider Zee.

Capital: Amsterdam (pop., 1,105,151); seat of government, The Hague (pop., 442,799)

Independence date: 1579

Government type: parliamentary democracy under a constitutional monarch

Head of state: Queen Beatrix

Head of government: Prime Min. Jan Peter Balkenende

Monetary unit: euro

GDP: $413 billion (2001 est.)

Per capita GDP: $25,800

Industries: agroindustries, metal and engineering products, electrical machinery and equipment, chemicals, petroleum,construction, microelectronics, fishing

Chief crops: grains, potatoes, sugar beets, fruits, vegetables

Minerals: natural gas, petroleum

Life expectancy at birth (years): male, 75.9; female, 81.8

Literacy rate: 99%

Website: www.cbs.nl/enindex.htm

Traditional attributes of the Netherlands: tulips (top, with windmill in background) and wooden shoes (bottom)

NETHERLANDS DEPENDENCIES, constitutionally on a level of equality with the Netherlands homeland within the kingdom, are Aruba and the Netherlands Antilles.
ARUBA: population, 70,000; area, 75 sq mi (194 sq km); capital, Oranjestad.
NETHERLANDS ANTILLES (CURAÇAO, BONAIRE, SAINT EUSTATIUS, SABA, southern part of SAINT MAARTEN): population, 221,000; area, 309 sq mi (800 sq km), capital, Willemstad, on Curaçao.

NORWAY

FOR MAP, SEE PAGE 37

Population: 4,533,000

Ethnic groups: Norwegian, Sami

Principal languages: Norwegian (official), Sami, Finnish

*Member of the European Union

Chief religion: Evangelical Lutheran (official) 86%

Area: 125,180 sq mi (324,220 sq km)

Topography: A highly indented coast is lined with tens of thousands of islands. Mountains and plateaus cover most of the country, which is only 25% forested.

Capital: Oslo (pop., 787,000)

Independence date: June 7, 1905

Government type: hereditary constitutional monarchy

Head of state: King Harald V

Head of government: Prime Min. Kjell Magne Bondevik

Monetary unit: krone

GDP: $138.7 billion (2001 est.)   Per capita GDP: $30,800

Industries: petroleum and gas, food processing, shipbuilding, pulp and paper products, metals, chemicals, timber, mining, textiles, fishing

Chief crops: barley, wheat, potatoes

Minerals: petroleum, copper, natural gas, pyrites, nickel, iron ore, zinc, lead

Life expectancy at birth (years): male, 76.2; female, 82.2

Literacy rate: 100%

Websites: www.norway.org
odin.dep.no/smk/engelsk

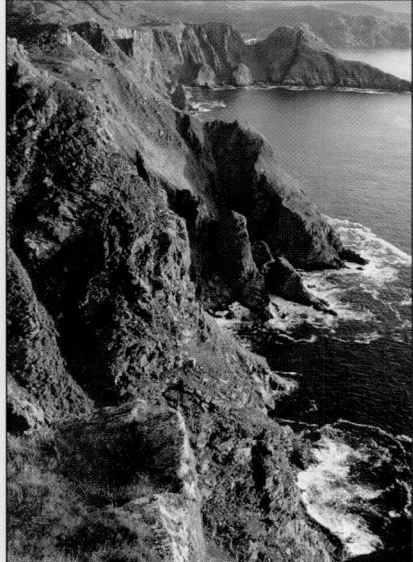

Norwegian coast

POLAND

FOR MAP, SEE PAGE 41

Population: 38,587,000

Ethnic groups: Polish 98%, German 1%

Principal languages: Polish (official), Ukrainian, German

Chief religion: Roman Catholic 95%

Area: 120,730 sq mi (312,680 sq km)

Topography: Poland consists mostly of lowlands forming part of the Northern European Plain. The Carpathian Mountains along the southern border rise to 8,200 ft (2,500 m).

Capital: Warsaw (pop., 2,282,000)

Independence date: November 11, 1918   Government type: republic

Head of state: Pres. Aleksander Kwasniewski

Head of government: Prime Min. Leszek Miller

Monetary unit: zloty

GDP: $339.6 billion (2001 est.)   Per capita GDP: $8,800

Industries: machine building, iron and steel, mining, chemicals, shipbuilding, food processing, glass, beverages, textiles

Chief crops: potatoes, fruits, vegetables, wheat

Minerals: coal, sulfur, copper, natural gas, silver, lead, salt

Life expectancy at birth (years): male, 69.8; female, 78.3

Literacy rate: 99%

Websites: www.polandembassy.org
www.poland.pl

PORTUGAL*

FOR MAP, SEE PAGE 44

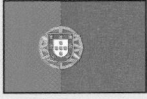

Population: 10,062,000

Ethnic groups: mainly Portuguese

Principal language: Portuguese (official)

*Member of the European Union

Chief religion: Roman Catholic 94%

Area: 35,670 sq mi (92,390 sq km)

Topography: Portugal north of the Tajus River, which bisects the country northeast to southwest, is mountainous, cool, and rainy. To the south there are drier, rolling plains and a warm climate.

Capital: Lisbon (pop., 3,942,000)

Independence date: 1143   Government type: republic

Head of state: Pres. Jorge Sampaio

Head of government: Prime Min. José Manuel Durão Barroso

Monetary unit: euro

GDP: $174.1 billion (2001 est.)   Per capita GDP: $17,300

Industries: textiles, footwear, pulp and paper, cork, metalworking, oil refining, chemicals, fish canning, wine, tourism

Chief crops: grain, potatoes, olives, grapes

Minerals: tungsten, iron ore, uranium ore, marble

Life expectancy at birth (years): male, 72.9; female, 80.1

Literacy rate: 87.4%

Website: www.presidenciarepublica.pt/en/main.html

ROMANIA

FOR MAP, SEE PAGE 49

Population: 22,334,000

Ethnic groups: Romanian 90%, Hungarian, Roma, and others 10%

Principal languages: Romanian (official), Hungarian, German, Romani

Chief religions: Romanian Orthodox 70%, Roman Catholic 6%, Protestant 6%

Area: 91,700 sq mi (237,500 sq km)

Topography: The Carpathian Mountains encase the north-central Transylvanian plateau. There are wide plains south and east of the mountains, through which flow the lower reaches of the rivers of the Danube system.

Capital: Bucharest (pop., 1,998,000)

Independence date: May 9, 1877   Government type: republic

Head of state: Pres. Ion Iliescu

Head of government: Prime Min. Adrian Nastase

Monetary unit: leu

GDP: $152.7 billion (2001 est.)   Per capita GDP: $6,800

Industries: textiles, footwear, light machinery, auto assembly, mining, timber, construction materials, metallurgy, chemicals, food processing, petroleum refining

Chief crops: wheat, corn, sugar beets, sunflower seed, potatoes, grapes

Minerals: petroleum, natural gas, coal, iron ore, salt

Life expectancy at birth (years): male, 66.9; female, 74.6

Literacy rate: 97%

Websites: www.gov.ro/engleza/index.html
www.roembus.org

RUSSIA

FOR MAP, SEE PAGE 64

Population: 143,246,000

Ethnic groups: Russian 82%, Tatar 4%, Ukrainian 3%, Chuvash 1%, Bashkir 1%, Belarusian 1%, Moldavian 1%

Principal languages: Russian (official), many others

Chief religions: Russian Orthodox, Muslim

Area: 6,592,800 sq mi (17,075,400 sq km)

Topography: Russia contains every type of climate except the distinctly tropical and has a varied topography. The European portion is a low

Nation Facts and Figures

Russia *(continued)*

plain, grassy in the south, wooded in the north, with the Ural Mountains in the east and the Caucasus Mountains in the south. The Urals stretch north to south for 2,500 mi (4,000 km). The Asiatic portion is also a vast plain, with mountains in the south and in the east; tundra covers the extreme north, with forest belt below; plains, marshes are in the west, desert in the southwest.

Capital: Moscow (pop., 8,316,000)

Independence date: August 24, 1991

Government type: federal republic

Head of state: Pres. Vladimir Putin

Head of government: Prime Min. Mikhail Kasyanov

Monetary unit: ruble

GDP: $1.2 trillion (2001 est.)

Per capita GDP: $8,300

Industries: mining, extractive industries, machine building, shipbuilding, vehicles, commercial equipment, agricultural machinery, construction equipment, instruments, consumer durables, textiles, foodstuffs, handicrafts

Chief crops: grain, sugar beets, sunflower seed, vegetables, fruits

Minerals: large variety, including oil, natural gas, coal, strategic minerals

Life expectancy at birth (years): male, 62.5; female, 73.1

Literacy rate: 98%

Website: www.un.int/russia

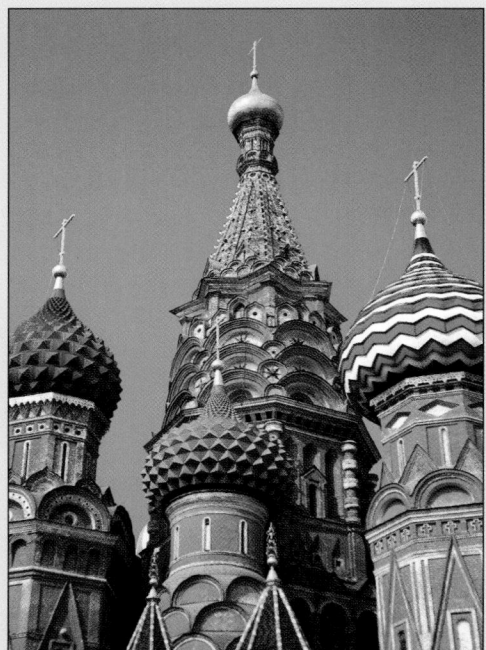

St. Basil's Cathedral, Moscow, Russia

SAN MARINO

FOR MAP, SEE PAGE 59

Population: 28,000

Ethnic groups: Sammarinese, Italian

Principal language: Italian (official)

Chief religion: predominantly Roman Catholic

Area: 23 sq mi (60 sq km)

Topography: The country lies on the slopes of Mt. Titano.

Capital: San Marino (pop., 5,000)

Independence date: September 3, 301

Government type: republic

Heads of state and government: two co-regents appointed every 6 months

Monetary unit: euro

GDP: $940 million (2001 est.)

Per capita GDP: $34,600

Industries: tourism, banking, textiles, electronics, ceramics, cement, wine

Chief crops: wheat, grapes, corn, olives

Minerals: building stone

Life expectancy at birth (years): male, 77.9; female, 85.3

Literacy rate: 96%

SERBIA AND MONTENEGRO (FORMERLY YUGOSLAVIA)

FOR MAP, SEE PAGE 48

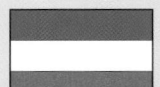

Population: 10,527,000

Ethnic groups: Serb 63%, Albanian 17%, Montenegrin 5%, Hungarian 3%

Principal languages: Serbian (official), Albanian

Chief religions: Orthodox 65%, Muslim 19%, Roman Catholic 4%

Area: 39,520 sq mi (102,350 sq km)

Topography: Terrain varies widely, with fertile plains drained by the Danube and other rivers in the north, limestone basins in the east, ancient mountains and hills in the southeast, and very high coastline in Montenegro along the southwest.

Capital: Belgrade (pop., 1,687,000)

Independence date: February 4, 2003

Government type: federal republic

Head of state and government: Pres. Svetozar Marovic

Monetary unit: new dinar

GDP: $24 billion (2001 est.) **Per capita GDP:** $2,250

Industries: machine building, metallurgy, mining, consumer goods, electronics, petroleum products, chemicals, pharmaceuticals

Chief crops: cereals, fruits, vegetables, tobacco, olives

Minerals: oil, gas, coal, antimony, copper, lead, zinc, nickel, gold, pyrite, chrome

Life expectancy at birth (years): male, 71.0; female, 77.2

Literacy rate: 93% **Website:** www.gov.yu

SLOVAKIA

FOR MAP, SEE PAGE 41

Population: 5,402,000

Ethnic groups: Slovak 86%, Hungarian 11%, Roma 2%

Principal languages: Slovak (official), Hungarian

Chief religions: Roman Catholic 60%, Protestant 8%, Orthodox 4%

Area: 18,860 sq mi (48,850 sq km)

Topography: Mountains (Carpathians) in the north, and the fertile Danube plane in the south.

Capital: Bratislava (pop., 464,000)

Independence date: January 1, 1993 **Government type:** republic

Head of state: Pres. Rudolf Schuster

Head of government: Prime Min. Mikulás Dzurinda

Monetary unit: koruna

GDP: $62 billion (2001 est.) **Per capita GDP:** $11,500

Industries: metal and metal products, food and beverages, electricity, chemicals and manmade fibers, machinery, paper and printing, earthenware and ceramics, transport vehicles, textiles, electrical and optical apparatus, rubber products

Chief crops: grains, potatoes, sugar beets, hops, fruit

Minerals: coal, iron ore, copper, manganese, salt

Life expectancy at birth (years): male, 70.4; female, 78.6

Literacy rate: NA

Website: www.government.gov.sk/english/

SLOVENIA

FOR MAP, SEE PAGE 48

Population: 1,984,000

Ethnic groups: Slovene 88%, Croat 3%, Serb 2%, Bosniak 1%

Principal languages: Slovenian (official), Serbo-Croatian

Chief religion: Roman Catholic 71%

Area: 7,820 sq mi (20,250 sq km)

Topography: Mostly hilly; 42% of the land is forested.

Capital: Ljubljana (pop., 250,000)

Independence date: June 25, 1991   Government type: republic

Head of state: Pres. Janez Drnovsek

Head of government: Prime Min. Anton Rop

Monetary unit: tolar

GDP: $31 billion (2001 est.)   Per capita GDP: $16,000

Industries: metallurgy and metal products, electronics, trucks, electric power equipment, wood products, textiles, chemicals, machine tools

Chief crops: potatoes, hops, wheat, sugar beets, corn, grapes

Minerals: coal, lead, zinc, mercury, uranium, silver

Life expectancy at birth (years): male, 71.7; female, 79.6

Literacy rate: 99%   Website: www.sigov.si

SPAIN*

FOR MAP, SEE PAGE 44

Population: 41,060,000

Ethnic groups: Castilian, Catalan, Basque, Galician

Principal languages: Castilian Spanish (official), Catalan, Galician, Basque

Chief religion: Roman Catholic 94%

Area: 194,890 sq mi (504,780 sq km)

Topography: The interior is a high, arid plateau broken by mountain ranges and river valleys. The northwest is heavily watered; the south has lowlands and a Mediterranean climate.

Capital: Madrid (pop., 3,969,000)   Independence date: 1492

Government type: constitutional monarchy

Head of state: King Juan Carlos I de Borbon y Borbon

Head of government: Prime Min. José María Aznar

Monetary unit: euro

GDP: $757 billion (2001 est.)   Per capita GDP: $18,900

Industries: textiles and apparel, food and beverages, metals and metal manufactures, chemicals, shipbuilding, automobiles, machine tools, tourism

Chief crops: grain, vegetables, olives, wine grapes, sugar beets, citrus

Minerals: coal, iron ore, uranium, mercury, pyrites, fluorspar, gypsum, zinc, lead, tungsten, copper, kaolin, potash

Life expectancy at birth (years): male, 75.9; female, 82.8

Literacy rate: 97%

Website: www.spainemb.org/ingles/indexing.htm

Spanish olive groves

*Member of the European Union

SWEDEN*

FOR MAP, SEE PAGE 37

Population: 8,876,000

Ethnic groups: Swedish 89%, Finnish 2%; Sami and others 9%

Principal languages: Swedish (official), Sami, Finnish

Chief religion: Lutheran 87%

Area: 173,730 sq mi (449,960 sq km)

Topography: Mountains along the northwestern border cover 25% of Sweden; flat or rolling terrain covers the central and southern areas, which include several large lakes.

Capital: Stockholm (pop., 1,626,000)

Independence date: June 6, 1523

Government type: constitutional monarchy

Head of state: King Carl XVI Gustaf

Head of government: Prime Min. Goran Persson

Monetary unit: krona

GDP: $219 billion (2001 est.)   Per capita GDP: $24,700

Industries: iron and steel, precision equipment, pulp and paper products, processed foods, motor vehicles

Chief crops: barley, wheat, sugar beets

Minerals: zinc, iron ore, lead, copper, silver, uranium

Life expectancy at birth (years): male, 77.3; female, 82.8

Literacy rate: 99%

Website: www.swedish-embassy.org

SWITZERLAND

FOR MAP, SEE PAGE 56

Population: 7,169,000

Ethnic groups: German 65%, French 18%, Italian 10%, Romansch 1%

Principal languages: German, French, Italian (all official); Romansch (semi-official)

Chief religions: Roman Catholic 46%, Protestant 40%

Area: 15,940 sq mi (41,290 sq km)

Topography: The Alps cover 60% of the land area; the Jura, near France, 10%. Running between, from northeast to southwest, are midlands, 30%.

Capitals: Bern (administrative) (pop., 316,000), Lausanne (judicial) (pop., 285,000)

Independence date: August 1, 1291

Government type: federal republic

Head of state and government: president elected by the Federal Assembly to a nonrenewable one-year term

Matterhorn, Switzerland

Switzerland *(continued)*

Monetary unit: franc

GDP: $226 billion (2001 est.) **Per capita GDP:** $31,100

Industries: machinery, chemicals, watches, textiles, precision instruments

Chief crops: grains, fruits, vegetables **Minerals:** salt

Life expectancy at birth (years): male, 77.1; female, 83.0

Literacy rate: 99% **Website:** www.admin.ch/index.en.html

UKRAINE

FOR MAP, SEE PAGE 62

Population: 48,523,000

Ethnic groups: Ukrainian 78%, Russian 17%

Principal languages: Ukrainian (official), Russian, Romanian, Polish, Hungarian

Chief religions: Ukrainian Orthodox (Kiev patriarchate and Russian patriarchate), Autocephalous Orthodox, Ukrainian Greek Catholic

Area: 233,100 sq mi (603,700 sq km)

Topography: Ukraine is part of the East European plain. Mountainous areas include the Carpathians in the southwest and the Crimean chain in the south. Arable black soil constitutes a large part of the country.

Capital: Kiev (pop., 2,488,000) **Independence date:** August 24, 1991

Government type: constitutional republic

Head of state: Pres. Leonid Danylovich Kuchma

Head of government: Prime Min. Viktor Yanukovych

Monetary unit: hryvnia

GDP: $205 billion (2001 est.) **Per capita GDP:** $4,200

Industries: mining, electric power, ferrous and nonferrous metals, machinery and transport equipment, chemicals, food processing

Chief crops: grain, sugar beets, sunflower seeds, vegetables

Minerals: iron ore, coal, manganese, natural gas, oil, salt, sulfur, graphite, titanium, magnesium, kaolin, nickel, mercury

Life expectancy at birth (years): male, 61.1; female, 72.2

Literacy rate: 98%

Websites: www.ukremb.com
www.kmu.gov.ua

UNITED KINGDOM*

FOR MAP, SEE PAGE 31

Population: 59,251,000

Ethnic groups: English 81.5%, Scottish 9.6%, Irish 2.4%, Welsh 1.9%, Ulster 1.9%; West Indian, Indo-Pakistani, and other 2.8%

Principal languages: English (official), Welsh and Scottish Gaelic

Chief religions: Christian 72%, Muslim 3%, many others

Area: 94,530 sq mi (244,820 sq km)

Topography: England is mostly rolling land, rising to the Uplands of southern Scotland; the Lowlands are in the center of Scotland, and the granite Highlands are in the north. The coast is heavily indented, especially on the west. The Severn, 220 mi (354 km), and the Thames, 215 mi (346 km), are the longest rivers.

Houses of Parliament with Big Ben, London, United Kingdom

*Member of the European Union

Stonehenge, England

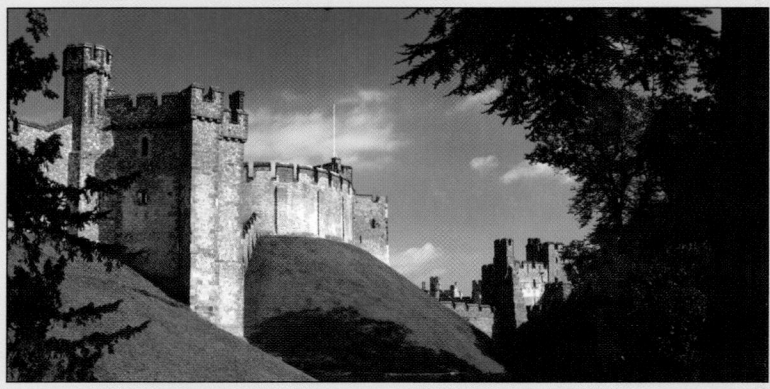
Arundel Castle, England

Capital: London (pop., 7,640,000)

Independence date: 1801 **Government type:** constitutional monarchy

Head of state: Queen Elizabeth II

Head of government: Prime Min. Tony Blair

Monetary unit: pound

GDP: $1.47 trillion (2001 est.) **Per capita GDP:** $24,700

Industries: machine tools, electric power and automation equipment, rail, shipbuilding, aircraft, motor vehicles and parts, electronics and communication equipment, mining, chemicals, paper and paper products, food processing, textiles, clothing and other consumer goods

Chief crops: cereals, oilseed, potatoes, vegetables

Minerals: coal, petroleum, natural gas, tin, limestone, iron ore, salt, clay, chalk, gypsum, lead, silica

Life expectancy at birth (years): male, 75.7; female, 80.7

Literacy rate: 99% **Website:** www.britainusa.com

The CHANNEL ISLANDS—Jersey, Guernsey, and the dependencies of Guernsey (Alderney, Brechou, Great Sark, Little Sark, Herm, Jethou, and Lihou)—are situated off the northwest coast of France. Jersey and Guernsey have separate legal existences and lieutenant governors named by the Crown. Population, 145,000; area, 75 sq mi (194 sq km).

The ISLE OF MAN, in the Irish Sea, has its own laws and a lieutenant governor appointed by the Crown. Population, 74,000; area 227 sq mi (588 sq km).

VATICAN CITY (THE HOLY SEE)

FOR MAP, SEE PAGE 46

Population: 900

Ethnic groups: Italian, Swiss, other

Principal languages: Latin (official), Italian, French, Monastic Sign Language, various others

Chief religion: Roman Catholic

Area: 0.17 sq mi (0.4 sq km)

Independence date: February 11, 1929

Government type: ecclesiastical state

Sovereign: Pope John Paul II

Monetary unit: euro **Website:** www.vatican.va

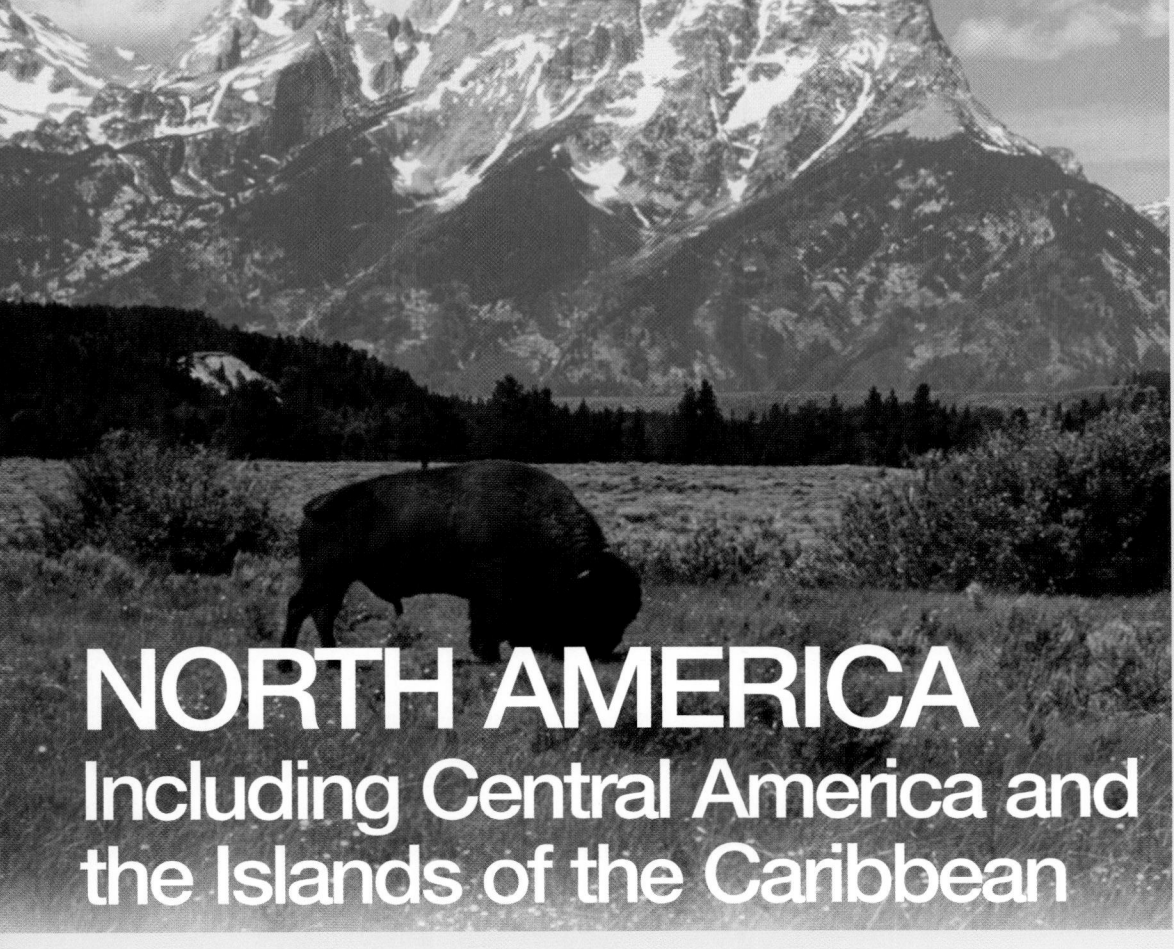

NORTH AMERICA
Including Central America and the Islands of the Caribbean

Two of the world's five biggest countries, in terms of land area, are in North America: Canada, which ranks Number 3, and the United States, Number 4. The United States, as of 2003, had the third largest population in the world, while Canada was the world's ninth most sparsely populated country.

ANTIGUA AND BARBUDA

FOR MAP, SEE PAGE 141

Population: 68,000
Ethnic groups: black, British, Portuguese, Lebanese, Syrian
Principal languages: English (official), local dialects
Chief religions: predominantly Protestant, some Roman Catholic
Area: 174 sq mi (440 sq km)
Topography: These are mostly low-lying and limestone coral islands. Antigua is mostly hilly with an indented coast; Barbuda is a flat island with a large lagoon on the west.
Capital: Saint John's (pop., 24,000)
Independence date: November 1, 1981
Government type: constitutional monarchy with British-style parliament
Head of state: Queen Elizabeth II, represented by Gov.-Gen. James Carlisle
Head of government: Prime Min. Lester Bird
Monetary unit: East Caribbean dollar
GDP: $674 million (2000 est.)   **Per capita GDP:** $10,000
Industries: tourism, construction, light manufacturing
Chief crops: cotton, fruits, vegetables, bananas, coconuts, cucumbers, mangoes, sugarcane
Life expectancy at birth (years): male, 69.0; female, 73.8
Literacy rate: 89%   **Website:** www.antigua-barbuda.com

THE BAHAMAS

FOR MAP, SEE PAGE 141

Population: 314,000
Ethnic groups: black 85%, white 12%
Principal languages: English, Creole (among Haitian immigrants)

Chief religions: Baptist 32%, Anglican 20%, Roman Catholic 19%, other Christian 24%
Area: 5,380 sq mi (13,940 sq km)
Topography: Nearly 700 islands (29 inhabited) and over 2,000 islets in the western Atlantic Ocean extend 760 mi (1,220 km) northwest to southeast.
Capital: Nassau (pop.,220,000)
Independence date: July 10, 1973
Government type: independent commonwealth
Head of state: Queen Elizabeth II, represented by Gov.-Gen. Dame Ivy Dumont
Head of government: Prime Min. Perry Christie
Monetary unit: Bahamas dollar
GDP: $5 billion (2001 est.)
Per capita GDP: $16,800
Industries: tourism, banking, cement, oil refining and transshipment, pharmaceuticals, steel pipe
Chief crops: citrus, vegetables
Minerals: salt, aragonite
Life expectancy at birth (years): male, 62.3; female, 69.2
Literacy rate: 98.2%
Website: www.bahamas.net

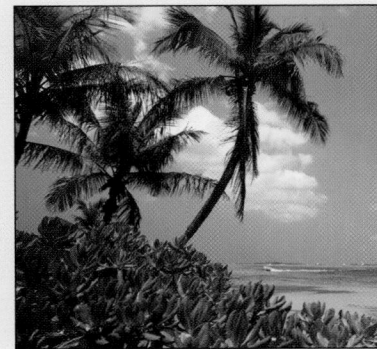

Nassau, the Bahamas

BARBADOS

FOR MAP, SEE PAGE 141

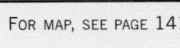

Population: 270,000
Ethnic groups: black 90%, white 4%
Principal language: English

Barbados *(continued)*

Chief religions: Protestant 67%, Roman Catholic 4%

Area: 165 sq mi (430 sq km)

Topography: The island lies alone in the Atlantic almost completely surrounded by coral reefs. The highest point is Mt. Hillaby, 1,115 ft (340 m).

Capital: Bridgetown (pop., 136,000)

Independence date: November 30, 1966

Government type: parliamentary democracy

Head of state: Queen Elizabeth II, represented by Gov.-Gen. Sir Clifford Husbands

Head of government: Prime Min. Owen Arthur

Monetary unit: Barbados dollar

GDP: $4 billion (2001 est.)   **Per capita GDP:** $14,500

Industries: tourism, sugar, light manufacturing, component assembly for export

Chief crops: sugarcane, vegetables, cotton

Minerals: petroleum, natural gas

Life expectancy at birth (years): 69.6; female, 74.1

Literacy rate: 97.4%

Website: www.barbados.gov.bb

BELIZE

FOR MAP, SEE PAGE 144

Population: 256,000

Ethnic groups: mestizo 49%, Creole 25%, Maya 11%, Garifuna 6%

Principal languages: English (official), Spanish, Mayan, Garifuna (Carib), Creole

Chief religions: Roman Catholic 50%, Protestant 27%

Area: 8,860 sq mi (22,960 sq km)

Topography: Belize has swampy lowlands in the north, Maya Mountains in the south, coral reefs and cays near the coast.

Capital: Belmopan (pop., 9,000)

Independence date: September 21, 1981

Government type: parliamentary democracy

Head of state: Queen Elizabeth II, represented by Gov.-Gen. Sir Colville Young

Head of government: Prime Min. Said Musa

Monetary unit: Belize dollar

GDP: $830 million (2001 est.)   **Per capita GDP:** $3,250

Industries: garment production, food processing, tourism, construction

Chief crops: bananas, coca, citrus, sugarcane

Life expectancy at birth (years): male, 65.2; female, 69.6

Literacy rate: 70.3%   **Website:** www.belize.gov.bz

CANADA

FOR MAP, SEE PAGE 122

Population: 31,510,000

Ethnic groups: British 28%, French 23%, other European 15%, Amerindian 2%

Principal languages: English, French (both official)

Chief religions: Roman Catholic 46%, Protestant 36%, other 18%

Area: 3,851,810 sq mi (9,976,140 sq km)

Topography: Canada stretches 3,426 mi (5,514 km) from east to west and extends south from the North Pole to the U.S. border. Its seacoast includes 36,356 mi (58,509 km) of mainland and 115,133 mi (185,289 km) of islands, including the Arctic islands almost from Greenland to near the Alaskan border.

Capital: Ottawa (pop., 1,094,000)

Images of Canada: Vancouver, British Columbia (top); Manitoba farmland (middle); lobster traps in Nova Scotia (above left); Welland Canal, Ontario (above right)

Independence date: July 1, 1867

Government type: confederation with parliamentary democracy

Head of state: Queen Elizabeth II, represented by Gov.-Gen. Adrienne Clarkson

Head of government: Prime Min. Jean Chrétien

Monetary unit: Canadian dollar

GDP: $875 billion (2001 est.)   **Per capita GDP:** $27,700

Industries: transport equipment, chemicals, mining, food products, wood and paper products, fish products, petroleum and natural gas

Chief crops: wheat, barley, oilseed, tobacco, fruits, vegetables

Minerals: iron ore, nickel, zinc, copper, gold, lead, molybdenum, potash, silver, coal, petroleum, natural gas

Life expectancy at birth (years): male, 76.4; female, 83.4

Literacy rate: 97%

Websites: www.statcan.ca
canada.gc.ca

COSTA RICA

FOR MAP, SEE PAGE 145

Population: 4,173,000

Ethnic groups: European and mestizo 94%, black 3%, Amerindian 1%, Chinese 1%

Principal languages: Spanish (official), English spoken around Puerto Limon

Chief religions: Roman Catholic (official) 76%, Protestant 14%

Area: 19,700 sq mi (51,100 sq km)

Topography: Lowlands by the Caribbean are tropical. The interior plateau, with an altitude of about 4,000 ft (1,200 m), is temperate.

Capital: San José (pop., 983,000)

Independence date: September 15, 1821　Government type: republic

Head of state and government: Pres. Abel Pacheco

Monetary unit: colon

GDP: $31.9 billion (2001 est.)　Per capita GDP: $8,500

Industries: microprocessors, food processing, textiles and clothing, construction materials, fertilizer, plastic products

Chief crops: coffee, pineapples, bananas, sugar, corn, rice, beans, potatoes

Life expectancy at birth (years): male, 73.9; female, 79.1

Literacy rate: 95.5%

Websites: www.tourism–costarica.com embassy.org/embassies/cr.html

CUBA
FOR MAP, SEE PAGE 145

Population: 11,300,000

Ethnic groups: Creole 51%, white 37%, black 11%, Chinese 1%

Principal language: Spanish (official)

Chief religions: Roman Catholic, Santeria

Area: 42,800 sq mi (110,860 sq km)

Topography: The coastline is about 2,500 mi (4,000 km). The northern coast is steep and rocky, and the southern coast low and marshy. Low hills and fertile valleys cover more than half the country. The Sierra Maestra, in the east, is the highest of three mountain ranges.

Capital: Havana (pop., 2,268,000)

Independence date: May 20, 1902　Government type: Communist state

Head of state and government: Pres. Fidel Castro Ruz

Monetary unit: peso

GDP: $25.5 billion (2001 est.)　Per capita GDP: $2,300

Industries: sugar, petroleum, tobacco, chemicals, construction, mining, cement, agricultural machinery, biotechnology

Chief crops: sugar, tobacco, citrus, coffee, rice, potatoes, beans

Minerals: cobalt, nickel, iron ore, copper, manganese, salt, silica, petroleum

Life expectancy at birth (years): male, 74.4; female, 79.4

Literacy rate: 95.7%

Website: cubagob.cu

Scuba diving in the Caribbean

DOMINICA
FOR MAP, SEE PAGE 141

Population: 70,000

Ethnic groups: black, Carib Amerindian

Principal languages: English (official), French patois

Chief religions: Roman Catholic 77%, Protestant 15%

Area: 290 sq mi (750 sq km)

Topography: Mountainous, with a central ridge running from north to south, terminating in cliffs. Dominica is volcanic in origin, with numerous thermal springs; there is rich deep topsoil on the leeward side, red tropical clay on the windward coast.

Capital: Roseau (pop., 26,000)

Independence date: November 3, 1978

Government type: parliamentary democracy

Head of state: Pres. Vernon Lorden Shaw

Head of government: Prime Min. Pierre Charles

Monetary unit: East Caribbean dollar

GDP: $262 million (2001 est.)　Per capita GDP: $3,700

Industries: soap, coconut oil, tourism, copra, furniture, cement blocks, shoes

Chief crops: bananas, citrus, mangoes, root crops, coconuts, cocoa

Life expectancy at birth (years): male, 71.2; female, 77.2

Literacy rate: 94%

Website: www.ndcdominica.dm/index.htm

DOMINICAN REPUBLIC
FOR MAP, SEE PAGE 141

Population: 8,745,000

Ethnic groups: Creole 73%, white 16%, black 11%

Principal language: Spanish (official)

Chief religion: Roman Catholic 95%

Area: 18,810 sq mi (48,730 sq km)

Topography: The Cordillera Central range crosses the center of the country, rising to over 10,000 ft (3,000 m), the highest mountains in the Caribbean. The Cibao Valley to the north is a major agricultural area.

Capital: Santo Domingo (pop., 2,629,000)

Independence date: February 27, 1844

Government type: republic

Head of state and government: Pres. Hipólito Mejía

Monetary unit: peso

GDP: $50 billion (2001 est.)

Per capita GDP: $5,800

Industries: tourism, sugar processing, mining, textiles, cement, tobacco

Chief crops: sugarcane, coffee, cotton, cocoa, tobacco, rice, beans, potatoes, corn, bananas

Minerals: nickel, bauxite, gold, silver

Life expectancy at birth (years): male, 66.4; female, 69.6

Literacy rate: 82.1%

Website: www.presidencia.gov.do/Ingles/welcome.htm

EL SALVADOR
FOR MAP, SEE PAGE 144

Population: 6,515,000

Ethnic groups: mestizo 90%, white 9%, Amerindian 1%

Principal languages: Spanish (official), Nahua

Chief religions: Roman Catholic 83%, many Protestant groups

Area: 8,120 sq mi (21,040 sq km)

El Salvador *(continued)*

Topography: A hot Pacific coastal plain in the south rises to a cooler plateau and valley region, densely populated. The north is mountainous, including many volcanoes.

Capital: San Salvador (pop., 1,381,000)

Independence date: September 15, 1821   **Government type:** republic

Head of state and government: Pres. Francisco Flores

Monetary unit: colon

GDP: $28.4 billion (2001 est.)   **Per capita GDP:** $4,600

Industries: food processing, beverages, petroleum, chemicals, fertilizer, textiles, furniture, light metals

Chief crops: coffee, sugar, corn, rice, beans, oilseed, cotton, sorghum

Minerals: petroleum

Life expectancy at birth (years): male, 67.0; female, 74.4

Literacy rate: 71.5%

Website: www.elsalvador.org

GRENADA
FOR MAP, SEE PAGE 141

Population: 89,000

Ethnic groups: black 82%, Creole 13%

Principal languages: English (official), French patois

Chief religions: Roman Catholic 53%, Anglican 14%, other Protestant 33%

Area: 131 sq mi (339 sq km)

Topography: The main island is mountainous; the country includes Carriacou and Petit Martinique islands.

Capital: Saint George's (pop., 36,000)

Independence date: February 7, 1974

Government type: parliamentary democracy

Head of state: Queen Elizabeth II, represented by Gov.-Gen. Daniel Williams

Head of government: Prime Min. Keith Mitchell

Monetary unit: East Caribbean dollar

GDP: $424 million (2001 est.)   **Per capita GDP:** $4,750

Industries: food and beverages, textiles, light assembly operations, tourism, construction

Chief crops: bananas, cocoa, nutmeg, mace, citrus, avocados, root crops, sugarcane, corn, vegetables

Life expectancy at birth (years): male, 62.7; female, 66.3

Literacy rate: 98%

Website: www.embassy.org/embassies/gd.html

GUATEMALA
FOR MAP, SEE PAGE 144

Population: 12,347,000

Ethnic groups: mestizo 55%, Amerindian 43%

Principal languages: Spanish (official); more than 20 Amerindian languages, including Quiche, Cakchiquel, Kekchi, Mam, Garifuna, and Xinca

Chief religions: mostly Roman Catholic; some Protestant, indigenous Mayan beliefs

Area: 42,040 sq mi (108,890 sq km)

Topography: The central highland and mountain areas are bordered by the narrow Pacific coast and the lowlands and fertile river valleys on the Caribbean. There are numerous volcanoes in the south, more than half a dozen over 11,000 ft (3,350 m).

Capital: Guatemala City (pop., 3,366,000)

Independence date:
September 15, 1821

Government type: republic

Head of state and government: Pres. Alfonso Portillo Cabrera

Monetary unit: quetzal

GDP: $48.3 billion (2001 est.)

Per capita GDP: $3,700

Industries: sugar, textiles and clothing, furniture, chemicals, petroleum, metals, rubber, tourism

Chief crops: sugarcane, corn, bananas, coffee, beans, cardamom

Minerals: petroleum, nickel

Life expectancy at birth (years): male, 64.3; female, 66.2

Literacy rate: 63.6%

Website: www.guatemala-embassy.org

Nutmeg factory, Grenada

HAITI
FOR MAP, SEE PAGE 145

Population: 8,326,000

Ethnic groups: black 95%, Creole and other 5%

Principal languages: French, Creole (both official)

Chief religions: Roman Catholic 80%, Protestant 16%; voodoo widely practiced

Area: 10,710 sq mi (27,750 sq km)

Topography: About two-thirds of Haiti is mountainous. Much of the rest is semiarid. Coastal areas are warm and moist.

Capital: Port-au-Prince (pop., 1,838,000)

Independence date: January 1, 1804

Government type: republic

Head of state: Pres. Jean-Baptiste Aristide

Head of government: Prime Min. Yvon Neptune

Monetary unit: gourde

GDP: $12 billion (2001 est.)   **Per capita GDP:** $1,700

Industries: sugar refining, flour milling, textiles, cement, light assembly industries

Chief crops: coffee, mangoes, sugarcane, rice, corn, sorghum

Minerals: bauxite, copper, calcium carbonate, gold, marble

Life expectancy at birth (years): male, 50.4; female, 52.9

Literacy rate: 45%

Website: www.haitifocus.com/haitie/gov.html

HONDURAS
FOR MAP, SEE PAGE 144

Population: 6,941,000

Ethnic groups: mestizo 90%, Amerindian 7%, black 2%, white 1%

Principal languages: Spanish (official), Garífuna, Amerindian dialects

Chief religion: Roman Catholic 97%

Area: 43,280 sq mi (112,090 sq km)

Topography: The Caribbean coast is 500 mi (800 km) long. The Pacific coast, on the Gulf of Fonseca, is 40 mi (65 km) long. Honduras is mountainous, with wide fertile valleys and rich forests.

Capital: Tegucigalpa (pop., 980,000)

Independence date: September 15, 1821

Government type: republic

Head of state and government: Pres. Ricardo Maduro

Monetary unit: lempira

GDP: $17 billion (2001 est.)   Per capita GDP: $2,600

Industries: sugar, coffee, textiles, clothing, wood products

Chief crops: bananas, coffee, citrus

Minerals: gold, silver, copper, lead, zinc, iron ore, antimony, coal

Life expectancy at birth (years): male, 65.3; female, 68.1

Literacy rate: 74%

Website: www.hondurasemb.org

JAMAICA

FOR MAP, SEE PAGE 145

Population: 2,651,000

Ethnic groups: black 91%, mixed 7%, East Indian and other 2%

Principal languages: English, patois English

Chief religions: Protestant 61%, Roman Catholic 4%, spiritual cults and other 35%

Area: 4,240 sq mi (10,990 sq km)

Topography: Four-fifths of Jamaica is covered by mountains.

Capital: Kingston (pop., 672,000)   Independence date: August 6, 1962

Government type: parliamentary democracy

Head of state: Queen Elizabeth II, represented by Gov.-Gen. Sir Howard Cooke

Head of government: Prime Min. Percival J. Patterson

Monetary unit: Jamaican dollar

GDP: $9.8 billion (2001 est.)   Per capita GDP: $3,700

Industries: tourism, bauxite, textiles, food processing, light manufactures, rum, cement, metal, paper, chemical products

Chief crops: sugarcane, bananas, coffee, citrus, potatoes, vegetables

Minerals: bauxite, gypsum, limestone

Life expectancy at birth (years): male, 73.8; female, 78.0

Literacy rate: 85%

Websites: www.cabinet.gov.jm
www.emjamusa.org

MEXICO

FOR MAP, SEE PAGE 119

Population: 103,457,000

Ethnic groups: mestizo 60%, Amerindian 30%, white 9%

Principal languages: Spanish (official), Náhuatl, Maya, Zaptec, Otomi, Miztec, other indigenous

Mayan ruins, Chichen Itza, Mexico

Cathedral on the Zocalo (main square), Mexico City, Mexico

Chief religions: Roman Catholic 89%, Protestant 6%

Area: 761,610 sq mi (1,972,550 sq km)

Topography: The Sierra Madre Occidental Mountains run northwest to southeast near the west coast; the Sierra Madre Oriental Mountains run near the Gulf of Mexico. They join south of Mexico City. Between the two ranges lies the dry central plateau, 5,000 to 8,000 ft (1,500 to 2,400 m) in altitude, rising toward the south, with temperate vegetation. Coastal lowlands are tropical. About 45% of the land is arid.

Capital: Mexico City (pop., 18,268,000)

Independence date: September 16, 1810

Government type: federal republic

Head of state and government: Pres. Vicente Fox Quesada

Monetary unit: new peso

GDP: $920 billion (2001 est.)   Per capita GDP: $9,000

Industries: food and beverages, tobacco, chemicals, iron and steel, petroleum, mining, textiles, clothing, motor vehicles, consumer durables, tourism

Chief crops: corn, wheat, soybeans, rice, beans, cotton, coffee, fruit, tomatoes

Minerals: petroleum, silver, copper, gold, lead, zinc, natural gas

Life expectancy at birth (years): male, 69.3; female, 75.5

Literacy rate: 89.6%

Website: www.presidencia.gob.mx/?NLang=en

NICARAGUA

FOR MAP, SEE PAGE 145

Population: 5,466,000

Ethnic groups: mestizo 69%, white 17%, black 9%, Amerindian 5%

Principal languages: Spanish (official), indigenous languages, English on Atlantic coast

Chief religion: Roman Catholic 85%

Area: 50,000 sq mi (129,490 sq km)

Topography: Both the Caribbean and the Pacific coasts are over 200 mi (320 m) long. The Cordillera Mountains, with many volcanic peaks, run northwest to southeast through the middle of the country. Between this and a volcanic range to the east lie Lakes Managua and Nicaragua.

Capital: Managua (pop., 1,039,000)

Independence date: September 15, 1821

Nicaragua *(continued)*

Government type: republic

Head of state and government: Pres. Enrique Bolaños Geyer

Monetary unit: gold cordoba

GDP: $12.3 billion (2001 est.)   **Per capita GDP:** $2,500

Industries: food processing, chemicals, machinery and metal products, textiles, clothing, petroleum refining and distribution, beverages, footwear, wood

Chief crops: coffee, bananas, sugarcane, cotton, rice, corn, tobacco, sesame, soya, beans

Minerals: gold, silver, copper, tungsten, lead, zinc

Life expectancy at birth (years): male, 67.7; female, 71.8

Literacy rate: 68.2%

Website: www.embassy.org/embassies/ni.html

PANAMA

FOR MAP, SEE PAGE 145

Population: 3,120,000

Ethnic groups: mestizo 70%, Amerindian-West Indian 14%, white 10%, Amerindian 6%

Principal languages: Spanish (official), English

Chief religions: Roman Catholic 85%, Protestant 15%

Area: 30,200 sq mi (78,200 sq km)

Topography: 2 mountain ranges run the length of the isthmus. Tropical rain forests cover the Caribbean coast and E Panama.

Capital: Panamá (pop., 1,202,000)

Independence date: November 3, 1903   **Government type:** republic

Head of state and government: Pres. Mireya Elisa Moscoso

Monetary unit: balboa

GDP: $16.9 billion (2001 est.)   **Per capita GDP:** $5,900

Industries: construction, petroleum refining, brewing, cement, sugar milling

Chief crops: bananas, rice, corn, coffee, sugarcane, vegetables

Minerals: copper

Life expectancy at birth (years): male, 70.0; female, 74.8

Literacy rate: 90.8%

Panama Canal

SAINT KITTS AND NEVIS

FOR MAP, SEE PAGE 141

Population: 39,000

Ethnic group: black, British, Portuguese, Lebanese

Principal language: English (official)

Chief religions: Anglican, other Protestant, Roman Catholic

Area: 101 sq mi (261 sq km)

Topography: Saint Kitts has forested volcanic slopes; Nevis rises from beaches to a central peak.

Capital: Basseterre (pop., 12,000)

Independence date: September 19, 1983

Government type: constitutional monarchy

Head of state: Queen Elizabeth II, represented by Gov.-Gen. Sir Cuthbert Montraville Sebastian

Head of government: Prime Min. Denzil Llewellyn Douglas

Monetary unit: East Caribbean dollar

GDP: $339 million (2001 est.)   **Per capita GDP:** $8,700

Industries: sugar processing, tourism, cotton, salt, copra, clothing, footwear, beverages

Chief crops: sugarcane, rice, yams, vegetables, bananas

Life expectancy at birth (years): male, 68.8; female, 74.6

Literacy rate: 97%

Website: www.stkittsnevis.net

SAINT LUCIA

FOR MAP, SEE PAGE 141

Population: 149,000

Ethnic groups: black 90%, mixed 6%, East Indian 3%, white 1%

Principal languages: English (official), French patois

Chief religions: Roman Catholic 90%, Protestant 10%

Area: 240 sq mi (620 sq km)

Topography: Saint Lucia is mountainous, volcanic in origin; Soufriere, a volcanic crater, is in the south. Wooded mountains run north to south to Mt. Gimie, 3,145 ft (960 m), with streams through fertile valleys.

Capital: Castries (pop., 57,000)

Independence date: February 22, 1979

Government type: parliamentary democracy

Head of state: Queen Elizabeth II, represented by Gov.-Gen. Calliopa Pearlette Louisy

Head of government: Prime Min. Kenny Anthony

Monetary unit: East Caribbean dollar

GDP: $700 million (2000 est.)   **Per capita GDP:** $4,400

Industries: clothing, assembly of electronic components, beverages, corrugated cardboard boxes, tourism

Chief crops: bananas, coconuts, vegetables, citrus, root crops, cocoa

Minerals: pumice

Life expectancy at birth (years): male, 69.5; female, 76.9

Literacy rate: 67%

Website: www.stlucia.gov.lc

SAINT VINCENT AND THE GRENADINES

FOR MAP, SEE PAGE 141

Population: 120,000

Ethnic groups: black 66%, mixed 19%, East Indian 6%, Carib Amerindian 2%

Principal languages: English (official), French patois

Chief religions: Anglican 47%, Methodist 28%, Roman Catholic 13%

Area: 131 sq mi (339 sq km)

Topography: St. Vincent is volcanic, with a ridge of thickly wooded mountains running its length.

Capital: Kingstown (pop., 28,000)

Independence date: October 27, 1979

Government type: constitutional monarchy

Head of state: Queen Elizabeth II, represented by Gov.-Gen. Charles James Antrobus

Head of government: Prime Min. Ralph Gonsalves

Monetary unit: East Caribbean dollar

GDP: $339 million (2001 est.)   Per capita GDP: $2,900

Industries: food processing, cement, furniture, clothing

Chief crops: bananas, coconuts, sweet potatoes, spices

Life expectancy at birth (years): male, 71.3; female, 74.9

Literacy rate: 96%

TRINIDAD AND TOBAGO

FOR MAP, SEE PAGE 141

Population: 1,303,000

Ethnic groups: black 40%, East Indian 40%, mixed 18%

Principal languages: English (official), Hindi, French, Spanish, Chinese

Chief religions: Roman Catholic 29%, Hindu 24%, Protestant 14%, Muslim 6%

Area: 1,980 sq mi (5,130 sq km)

Topography: Three low mountain ranges cross Trinidad east to west, with a well-watered plain between the north and central ranges. Parts of the east and west coasts are swamps. Tobago, 116 sq mi (300 sq km), lies 20 mi (30 km) northeast.

Capital: Port-of-Spain (pop., 54,000)

Independence date: August 31, 1962

Government type: parliamentary democracy

Head of state: Pres. Maxwell Richards

Head of government: Prime Min. Patrick Augustus Mervyn Manning

Monetary unit: Trinidad and Tobago dollar

GDP: $10.6 billion (2001 est.)   Per capita GDP: $9,000

Industries: petroleum products, chemicals, tourism, food processing, cement, beverage, cotton textiles

Chief crops: cocoa, sugarcane, rice, citrus, coffee, vegetables

Minerals: petroleum, natural gas, asphalt

Life expectancy at birth (years): male, 67.1; female, 72.2

Literacy rate: 94%   Website: www.gov.tt

UNITED STATES

For map, see page 124

Population: 288,369,000 (50 states and District of Columbia)

Ethnic groups: white 75.1%, black 12.3%, Asian 3.6%, Amerindian and Alaska native 0.9% (Hispanics of any race or group 12.5%)

Principal languages: English, Spanish

Chief religions: Protestant 56%, Roman Catholic 28%, Jewish 2%

Area: 3,794,085 sq mi (9,826,635 sq km)

Topography: The area comprising the contiguous 48 states has a vast central plain, mountains in the west, and hills and low mountains in the east. Rugged mountains and broad river valleys are found in Alaska, and rugged, volcanic topography in Hawaii.

Capital: Washington, D.C. (pop., 3,997,000)

Independence date: July 4, 1776

Government type: federal republic

Head of state and government: Pres. George W. Bush

Monetary unit: U.S. dollar

GDP: $10.082 trillion (2001 est.)   Per capita GDP: $36,300

Industries: petroleum, steel, motor vehicles, aerospace, telecommunications, chemicals, electronics, food processing, consumer goods, lumber, mining

Chief crops: wheat, other grains, corn, fruits, vegetables, cotton

Minerals: coal, copper, lead, molybdenum, phosphates, uranium, bauxite, gold, iron, mercury, nickel, potash, silver, tungsten, zinc, petroleum, natural gas

Life expectancy at birth (years): male, 74.4; female, 80.1

Literacy rate: 97%

Websites: www.census.gov
www.whitehouse.gov
www.firstgov.gov

MAJOR OUTLYING U.S. AREAS include two commonwealths—the Northern Mariana Islands in the Pacific Ocean and Puerto Rico in the West Indies—as well as the unincorporated territories American Samoa and Guam in the Pacific and the Virgin Islands in the West Indies.

AMERICAN SAMOA: population, 70,000; area, 90 sq mi; capital, Pago Pago on island of Tutuila

GUAM: population, 163,000; area, 217 sq mi; capital, Hagåtña

NORTHERN MARIANA ISLANDS: population, 80,000; area, 189 sq mi; seat of government, Saipan

PUERTO RICO: population, 3,879,000; area: 5,324 sq mi; capital: San Juan

VIRGIN ISLANDS (ST. JOHN, ST. CROIX, ST. THOMAS): population, 111,000; area, 171 sq mi; capital: Charlotte Amalie on St. Thomas

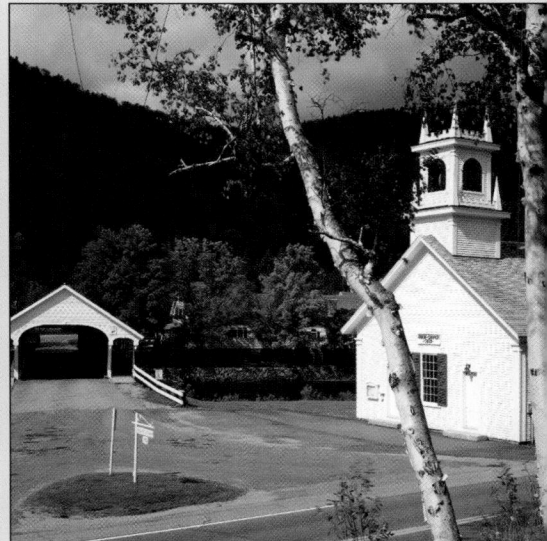

Three U.S. hallmarks: Statue of Liberty, New York (left); cable car, San Francisco (middle); New England church, New Hampshire (right)

SOUTH AMERICA

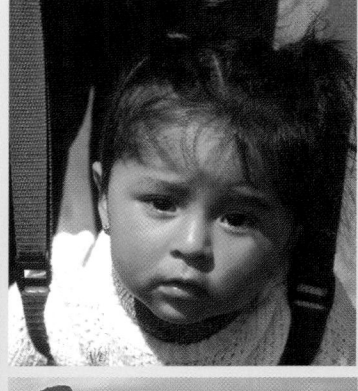

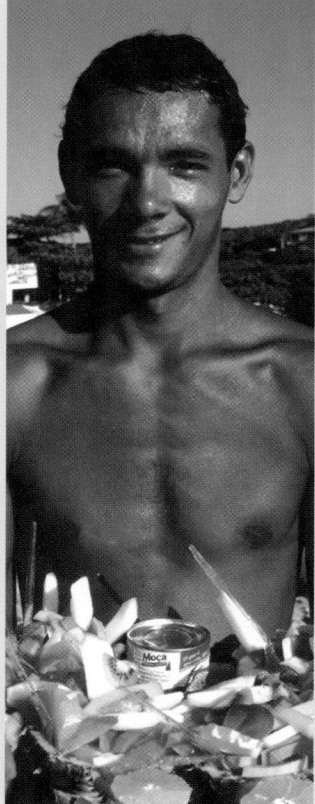

Brazil is the biggest nation in South America, and the fifth biggest in the world, in terms of both land area and population. It also has the continent's largest economy.

ARGENTINA

FOR MAP, SEE PAGE 157

Population: 38,428,000

Ethnic groups: European 97%, Amerindian 3%

Principal languages: Spanish (official), English, Italian, German, French

Chief religion: Roman Catholic 92% (official)

Area: 1,068,300 sq mi (2,766,890 sq km)

Topography: Mountains in the west are the Andean, Central, Misiones, and Southern ranges. Aconcagua is the highest peak in the western hemisphere, altitude 22,834 ft (6,060 m). East of the Andes are heavily wooded plains, called the Gran Chaco in the north, and the fertile, treeless Pampas in the central region. Patagonia, in the south, is bleak and arid. Rio de la Plata, an estuary in the northeast, 170 by 140 mi (270 by 225 km), is mostly fresh water, from the 2,485-mi (4,000-km) Parana and 1,000-mi (1,600-km) Uruguay rivers.

Capital: Buenos Aires (pop., 12,106,000)

Iguaçú Falls, Argentine-Brazilian border

Independence date: July 9, 1816   **Government type:** republic

Head of state and government: Pres. Néstor Kirchner

Monetary unit: peso

GDP: $453 billion (2001 est.)   **Per capita GDP:** $12,000

Industries: food processing, motor vehicles, consumer durables, textiles, chemicals and petrochemicals, printing, metallurgy, steel

Chief crops: sunflower seeds, lemons, soybeans, grapes, corn, tobacco, peanuts, tea, wheat

Minerals: lead, zinc, tin, copper, iron ore, manganese, petroleum, uranium

Life expectancy at birth (years): male, 71.71; female, 79.4

Literacy rate: 96.2%

Websites: www.un.int/argentina   www.congenargentinany.com

BOLIVIA

FOR MAP, SEE PAGE 150

Population: 8,808,000

Ethnic groups: Quechua 30%, mestizo 30%, Aymara 25%, white 15%

Principal languages: Spanish, Quechua, Aymara (all official)

Chief religion: Roman Catholic (official) 95%

Area: 424,160 sq mi (1,098,580 sq km)

Topography: The great central plateau, at an altitude of 12,000 ft (3,600 m), over 500 mi (800 km) long, lies between two great cordilleras having three of the highest peaks in South America. Lake Titicaca, on the Peruvian border, is the highest lake in the world on which steamboats ply (12,506 ft [3,812 m]). The east-central region has semitropical forests; the llanos, or Amazon-Chaco lowlands, are in the east.

Capitals: La Paz (adminstrative) (pop., 1,499,000), Sucre (judicial) (pop., 183,000)

Independence date: August 6, 1825

Government type: republic

Head of state and government: Pres. Gonzalo Sánchez de Lozada

Monetary unit: boliviano

GDP: $21.4 billion (2001 est.)   Per capita GDP: $2,600

Industries: mining, smelting, petroleum, food and beverages, tobacco, handicrafts, clothing

Chief crops: soybeans, coffee, coca, cotton, corn, sugarcane, rice, potatoes

Minerals: tin, natural gas, petroleum, zinc, tungsten, antimony, silver, iron, lead, gold

Life expectancy at birth (years): male, 62.2; female, 67.5

Literacy rate: 83.1%

Websites: www.embassy.org/embassies/bo.html
www.boliviaweb.com/embassies.html

BRAZIL

FOR MAP, SEE PAGE 147

Population: 178,470,000

Ethnic groups: European 55%, Creole 38%, African 6%

Principal languages: Portuguese (official), Spanish, English, French

Chief religion: Roman Catholic (nominal) 80%

Area: 3,286,490 sq mi (8,511,970 sq km)

Topography: Brazil's Atlantic coastline stretches 4,603 mi (7,408 km). In the north is the heavily wooded Amazon basin covering half the country. Its network of rivers is navigable for 15,814 mi (25,450 km). The Amazon itself flows 2,093 mi (3,368 km) in Brazil, all navigable. The northeast region is semiarid scrubland, heavily settled and poor. The south-central region, favored by climate and resources, has almost half of the population and produces 75% of farm goods and 80% of industrial output. The narrow coastal belt includes most of the major cities.

Capital: Brasília (pop., 2,073,000)

Independence date: September 7, 1822

Government type: federal republic

Head of state and government: Pres. Luis Inacio Lula da Silva

Monetary unit: real

GDP: $1.34 trillion (2001 est.)   Per capita GDP: $7,400

Ipanema Beach and Rio de Janeiro, Brazil

Industries: textiles, shoes, chemicals, cement, lumber, aircraft, motor vehicles and parts, other machinery and equipment

Chief crops: coffee, soybeans, wheat, rice, corn, sugarcane, cocoa, citrus

Minerals: bauxite, gold, iron ore, manganese, nickel, phosphates, platinum, tin, uranium, petroleum

Life expectancy at birth (years): male, 67.2; female, 75.3

Literacy rate: 83.3%

Website: www.brasilemb.org

CHILE

FOR MAP, SEE PAGE 157

Population: 15,805,000

Ethnic groups: European and mestizo 95%, Amerindian 3%

Principal languages: Spanish (official), Araucanian

Chief religions: Roman Catholic 89%, Protestant 11%

Area: 292,260 sq mi (756,950 sq km)

Topography: The Andes Mountains on the eastern border include some of the world's highest peaks; in the west is the 2,650 mi (4,265 km) Pacific coast. The country's width varies between 100 and 250 mi (160 and 400 km). In the north is the Atacama Desert, in the center are agricultural regions, in the south, forests and grazing lands.

Capital: Santiago (pop., 5,551,000)

Independence date: September 18, 1810

Government type: republic

Head of state and government: Pres. Ricardo Lagos Escobar

Monetary unit: peso

GDP: $153 billion (2001 est.)

Per capita GDP: $10,000

Industries: mining, foodstuffs, fish processing, iron and steel, wood and wood products, transport equipment, cement, textiles

Chief crops: wheat, corn, grapes, beans, sugar beets, potatoes, fruit

Minerals: copper, timber, iron ore, nitrates, precious metals, molybdenum

Life expectancy at birth (years): male, 73.0; female, 79.8

Literacy rate: 95.2%

Website: www.chile-usa.org

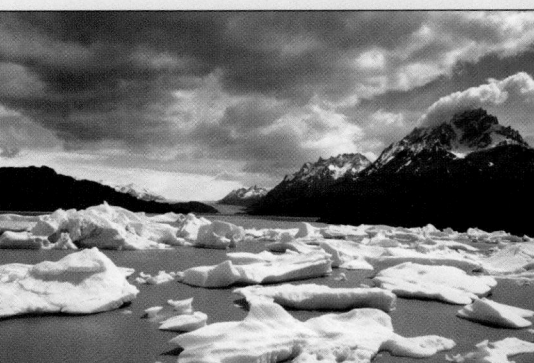

Torres del Paine National Park, Chile

TIERRA DEL FUEGO is the largest (18,800 sq mi [48,700 sq km]) island in the archipelago of the same name at the southern tip of South America, an area of majestic mountains, tortuous channels, and high winds. Part of the island is in Chile, part in Argentina. Punta Arenas, on a mainland peninsula, is the world's southernmost city (population about 70,000); Puerto Williams is the southernmost settlement.

COLOMBIA

FOR MAP, SEE PAGE 152

Population: 44,222,000

Ethnic groups: mestizo 58%, European 20%, Creole 14%, black 4%, black-Amerindian 1%, Amerindian 3%

Principal language: Spanish (official)

Chief religion: Roman Catholic 90%

Acknowledgements

292

Publisher	Hammond World Atlas Corporation
President	Stuart Dolgins
Director of Cartography	Vera Benson
Director of Sales Administration	Charles L. Koch
Director of Database Resources	Theophrastos E. Giovanous
Production Manager	Susan Miskewitz

Map Section

Cartography	John Benitez
	Janice Hulik
	Walter H. Jones Jr.
	Sharon Lightner
	Harry E. Morin
	Andrew J. Murphy
	James Padykula
	Thomas J. Scheffer
	John DiGiorgio
Technology	Barry A. Moraller

World Almanac Section

Editorial and Art Direction	Vera Benson
Content Development Consultant	Richard W. Eiger
Editor	Richard Hantula
Design and Page Layout	Lee Goldstein
Graphic Design Concept and Development; Cover Design	Yang Zhao

Photo Credits

Portraits on pages 10, 236, 250, 265, 269, 288
– APA Publication GMBH & Co. Verlag KG

Photos on pages 237, 241, 242, 247 (L), 253, 254 – Vera Benson

Portraits on page 281 – Yang Zhao

Other photos, PhotoDisc™

Satellite images: NASA – Greece, Peloponnesus Peninsula – p.26;
Pakistan, Indus River Delta – p.66; Egypt, Sinai Peninsula – p.92;
Australia, Lake Eyre – p.108; United States, Grand Canyon – p.118;
Argentina/Chile, Andes Mountains – p.146.

World Time Zones

165° W	150° W	135° W	120° W	105° W	90° W	75° W	60° W	45° W	30° W	15° W	0°
1 A.M.	2 A.M.	3 A.M.	4 A.M.	5 A.M.	6 A.M.	7 A.M.	8 A.M.	9 A.M.	10 A.M.	11 A.M.	NOON

NOON

GREENLAND

11 A.M.

3 A.M.
ALASKA

ICELAND

Anchorage

Nuuk

Reykjavík

Whitehorse

NO

CANADA

UNITED
KINGDOM

Edmonton

IRELAND

NF

Winnipeg

London

BEL

1 A.M.

Seattle

Montréal

NEWFOUNDLAND
8:30 A.M.

Paris

FRANC

Boise

Chicago

Detroit

Halifax

ST. PIERRE
& MIQUELON
9 A.M.

UNITED   STATES

PORTUGAL

Madrid

SPAIN

San Francisco

Denver

New York
Washington

AZORES

Al

Los Angeles

Phoenix

Atlanta

MOROCCO

Houston

BERMUDA

CANARY IS.

ALGER

Honolulu

Miami

W. SAHARA

HAWAII

MEXICO

BAHAMAS

MAURITANIA

CUBA

CAPE
VERDE

Dakar

MALI

Mexico

HAITI DOM.
REP.

PUERTO
RICO

GAMBIA

SENEGAL

BELIZE

JAMAICA

ANTIGUA & BARBUDA

GUINEA-BISSAU

BURKINA
FASO

1 A.M.

GUATEMALA

HONDURAS

DOMINICA

GUINEA

BEN

EL SALVADOR

NICARAGUA

GRENADA

BARBADOS

SIERRA LEONE

CÔTE
D'IVOIRE

GHANA

COSTA RICA

PANAMA

TRINIDAD & TOBAGO

LIBERIA

TOGO

INT'L DATE LINE

VENEZUELA

GUYANA

SÃO TOM
PRINC

KIRIBATI

COLOMBIA

SUR. FR. GUIANA

MIDNIGHT

Bogotá

ECUADOR

GALÁPAGOS IS.

Manaus

Recife

MARQUESAS IS.
2:30 A.M.

ASCENSION

Lima

PERU

B R A Z I L

La Paz

FRENCH   POLYNESIA

BOLIVIA

PARAGUAY

Rio de
Janeiro

PITCAIRN IS.

EASTER I.

CHILE

TRISTAN DA CUNHA

Santiago

Buenos
Aires

URUGUAY

ARGENTINA

FALKLAND IS.

S. GEORGIA

TIME ZONES OF THE WORLD

STANDARD TIME ZONES	3 A.M.	4 A.M.	5 A.M.	6 A.M.
AREAS USING HALF HOUR DEVIATIONS	5:30 P.M.			

1 A.M.	2 A.M.	3 A.M.	4 A.M.	5 A.M.	6 A.M.	7 A.M.	8 A.M.	9 A.M.	10 A.M.	11 A.M.	NOON